# ENCYCLOPEDIA OF DISTRIBUTED LEARNING

# ENCYCLOPEDIA OF DISTRIBUTED LEARNING

*EDITORS*

## ANNA DISTEFANO • KJELL ERIK RUDESTAM
## ROBERT J. SILVERMAN

*Fielding Graduate Institute*

A SAGE Reference Publication

**SAGE Publications**
*International Educational and Professional Publisher*
Thousand Oaks ▪ London ▪ New Delhi

*For information:*

Sage Publications, Inc.
2455 Teller Road
Thousand Oaks, California 91320
E-mail: order@sagepub.com

Sage Publications Ltd.
6 Bonhill Street
London EC2A 4PU
United Kingdom

Sage Publications India Pvt. Ltd.
B-42 Panchsheel Enclave
New Delhi 110017   India

Printed in the United States of America

*Library of Congress Cataloging-in-Publication Data*

Encyclopedia of distributed learning / Anna DiStefano, Kjell Erik Rudestam, Robert J. Silverman, editors.
        p. cm.
"A Sage reference publication."
Includes bibliographical references and index.
ISBN 0-7619-2451-5 (cloth)
    1.  Continuing education—Encyclopedias. 2.  Distance education—Encyclopedias.
3. Adult learning—Encyclopedias. I.  DiStefano, Anna. II.  Rudestam, Kjell Erik.
III.  Silverman, Robert J.
(Robert Jay), 1940-
LC5211.E52 2004
374′.003—dc22                                2003015573

This book is printed on acid-free paper.

03   04   05   06   10   9   8   7   6   5   4   3   2   1

| | |
|---|---|
| *Acquisitions Editor:* | Jim Brace-Thompson |
| *Editorial Assistant:* | Karen Ehrmann |
| *Developmental Editor:* | Vince Burns |
| *Production Editor:* | Diane S. Foster |
| *Copy Editor:* | Toni Zuccarini Ackley |
| *Typesetter:* | C&M Digitals (P) Ltd. |
| *Proofreader:* | Andrea Martin |
| *Indexer:* | Molly Hall |
| *Cover Designer:* | Ravi Balasuriya |

# Contents

# Advisory Board

# List of Entries

# Reader's Guide

## ADMINISTRATIVE PROCESSES

Academic Calendar
Administrative Leadership
Administrative Planning and Support of Information
   Technology
Admission Criteria and Processes
Career Planning and Development
Course Credit/Credit Transfer
Enrollment Status
Knowledge Management
Library Services
Markets/Marketing
Online Orientation
   and Navigation Tools
Operations and Management
Orientation
Outsourcing
Program Evaluation
Staffing
Telecommuting/Teleworking
Transcripts

## POLICY, FINANCE, AND GOVERNANCE

Accreditation
Alliances
Degrees/Degree Programs
Disability Law
Federal Laws
Finance
Financial Aid
For-Profit Institutions
Free Speech
Governance
Grants
Intellectual Property
Legal Issues
Licensing
Policies

Strategic Planning
Unbundling of Higher Education

## SOCIAL AND CULTURAL PERSPECTIVES

Adult Education Learning Model
Cognitive Skills/Cognitive Development
Corporate Training
Cultural Access/Digital Divide
Cultural Diversity
Demographics
Gender
Globalization
Intranet
Knowledge Building/Knowledge Work
Knowledge Economy
Learning Communities
Netiquette
Online Universities
Relationships
Social Constructionism
Social Issues
Sociocultural Perspectives
Sociotechnical Issues
Virtual Communities
World Wide Web

## STUDENT AND FACULTY ISSUES

Academic Advising
Adjunct Faculty
Alumni
Cohorts
Ethics
Faculty Development, Selection, and Training
Faculty Evaluation
Faculty Policies
Plagiarism
Retention

# Contributors

Agger-Gupta, Dorothy E.
Fielding Graduate Institute

Agger-Gupta, Niels
Share Works Associates

Aldridge, John W.
aboutChange Solutions, Inc.

Barrett, Frank
Fielding Graduate Institute

Bélanger, Marc
International Labour Organization, Turin, Italy

Beneker, Phil
Fielding Graduate Institute

Berg, Gary A.
Chapman University

Bertrand, Nicolas
HEC-Montreal and University of Montreal

Bishop, Karen
Bishop-Futures High School

Blimling, Gregory S.
Appalachian State University

Bock, Janice Safian
Fielding Graduate Institute

Brady, Bridget Lee
Fielding Graduate Institute

Brookfield, Stephen D.
University of St. Thomas

Brown, Barbara Mahone
Elbow Room Consulting

Bryant, Janet
Old Dominion University

Collins, Lynn H.
LaSalle University

Coombs, Norman
Rochester Institute of Technology and CEO of Equal
    Access to Software and Information (EASI)

Coulter, Xenia
SUNY, Empire State College

Cox, Geoffrey M.
Cardean University

Crafts, Linda F.
Cumulus Resources LLC

Dagavarian, Debra A.
The Richard Stockton College of New Jersey

Davis, Donald D.
Old Dominion University

Deegan, Marilyn
University of Oxford

Dennen, Vanessa
San Diego State University

DeWeese, Debra J.
Fielding Graduate Institute

DiGregorio, Gaye Golter
Colorado State University

DiStefano, Anna
Fielding Graduate Institute

Dominguez, Paula Szulc
Hezel Associates

Duguid, Paul
University of California, Berkeley

Duin, Ann Hill
University of Minnesota

Dussert, Alain
Fielding Graduate Institute

Edwards, Jenny
Fielding Graduate Institute

Farmer, Alain
University of Quebec at Montreal

Feenberg, Andrew
San Diego State University

Fels, Deborah
Ryerson Polytechnic University

Forsyth, Rachel
Manchester Metropolitan University, UK

Frayer, Dorothy A.
Duquesne University

Gergen, Kenneth J.
Swarthmore College

Gibbons, Tracy C.
CoastWise Consulting, Inc.

Goldstein, Jinny
Goldstein Education Group

Goldstein, Michael B.
Dow, Lohnes & Albertson

Goodwin, Shelley L.
Fielding Graduate Institute

Gourley, Don
Washington Research Library Consortium

Griffiths, José-Marie
University of Pittsburgh

Gullahorn, Jeanne
SUNY, Albany

Gurse, Cheri
Fielding Graduate Institute

Gyllenpalm, Bo
Fielding Graduate Institute

Hall, Brandon
brandon-hall.com

Hanna, Donald E.
University of Wisconsin-Extension

Hara, Noriko
Indiana University-Bloomington

Harasim, Linda
Simon Fraser University

Harvey, Pierre-Léonard
University of Quebec at Montreal

Hezel, Richard T.
Hezel Associates

Hiltz, Starr Roxanne
New Jersey Institute of Technology

Hitt, John C.
University of Central Florida

Hodgins, H. Wayne
Autodesk. Inc.

Hudson, Barclay
Fielding Graduate Institute

Hudson, Frederic M.
The Hudson Institute of Santa Barbara

Hughes, Shelley K.
Fielding Graduate Institute

Janoff, Dean S.
Fielding Graduate Institute

Johnstone, Sally M.
WCET

Katz, Richard
EDUCAUSE

Keeton, Morris T.
University of Maryland

Kirkwood, Adrian
The Open University

Klein, Julie Thompson
Wayne State University

Kling, Rob [1945–2003]
Indiana University-Bloomington

Kramarae, Cheris
University of Oregon

Kramer, Stefan
Fielding Graduate Institute

Krebs, Arlene
California State University-Monterey Bay

Kroc, Rick
University of Arizona

Kuhne, Gary William
The Pennsylvania State University

Landon, Bruce
Douglas College

Lankes, R. David
ERIC Clearinghouse on Information & Technology

Lejeune, Albert
University of Quebec at Montreal

Levy, Suzanne
Allan Hancock College

Lindstrom, Phyllis Hendry
San Jose State University

Long, Phillip D.
Massachusetts Institute of Technology

Luskin, Bernard J.
Fielding Graduate Institute

Maehl, William H.
Fielding Graduate Institute

Magolda, Marcia B. Baxter
Miami University at Ohio

Mandell, Alan
SUNY, Empire State College

Marcum, James
Farleigh Dickinson University

Mason, Jeff J.
Register.com

Mason, Robin
The Open University

Mayadas, A. Frank
Alfred P. Sloan Foundation

McClean, Pamela D.
The Hudson Institute of Santa Barbara

McClintock, Charles
Fielding Graduate Institute

McDermott, Richard
McDermott Consulting

McFerran Virginia, A.
W Technologies

McGreal, Rory
Athabasca University

McRobbie, Michael
Indiana University

Meacham, Martha
Austin Community College

Metros, Susan E.
The Ohio State University

Mihalescz, Michael
Old Dominion University

Murphy, James C.
Fielding Graduate Institute

Nakasone, Kerry
Colorado State University

Olson, Christi A.
Fielding Graduate Institute

O'Neal, Mary L.
University of North Florida

Palloff, Rena M.
Crossroads Consulting Group

Paulson, Karen
(NCHEMS) National Center for Higher Education
    Management Systems

Peek, Robin
Simmons College

Perrin, Donald
United States Distance Learning Association

Pittman, Von
University of Missouri-Columbia

Poley, Janet
American Distance Education Consortium (ADEC)

Pratt, Keith
Crossroads Consulting Group

Ragan, Lawrence C.
Penn State University

Riel, Margaret
Pepperdine University

Robbins, David B.
University of Pittsburgh

Rosenblum, Don
Nova Southeastern University

Rudestam, Kjell Erik
Fielding Graduate Institute

Rudestam, Rolf C.
The Rudestam Group

Rupp, Rebecca
Shaftsbury, Vermont

Saba, Lynne
Fielding Graduate Institute

Salomon, Kenneth D.
Dow, Lohnes & Albertson, PLLC

Say, Rebecca
Old Dominion University

Scardamalia, Marlene
Ontario Institute for the Study of Education, University
    of Toronto

Scheid, Gibson
Gibson Scheid Works

Schoenholtz-Read, Judith
Fielding Graduate Institute

Schwartz, Larissa
Fielding Graduate Institute

Schwitzer, Alan M.
Old Dominion University

Sedlacek, William E.
University of Maryland-College Park

Seidman, Alan
Collegeways

Shang, Paul
Colorado State University

Shapiro, Jeremy J.
Fielding Graduate Institute

Shaw, Margie Hodges
University of Rochester

Sheu, Hung-Bin
University of Maryland-College Park

Silverman, Charles
Ryerson Polytechnic University

Silverman, Robert J.
Fielding Graduate Institute

Snyder, Deborah
The University of Michigan-Flint

Sonwalker, Nishikant
Massachusetts Institute of Technology

Stamm, B. Hudnall
Idaho State University

Stevens-Long, Judith
Fielding Graduate Institute

Taylor, Richard E.
University of Leeds

Treichler, Shari Lamkin
Hezel Associates

Trujillo, Candido
Fielding Graduate Institute

Turner, Phillip
University of North Texas

Turoff, Murray
New Jersey Institute of Technology

Ubell, Robert
Stevens Institute of Technology

Vallee, Jason C.
DeVry University

Vigneault, Karine
McGill University

Volger, Barbara J.
Fielding Graduate Institute

von Lubtiz, Dag K. J. E.
MedSMART, Inc.

Wallis, Nancy C.
Chapman University

Wijekumar, Kay J.
Pennsylvania State University-Beaver

Wildflower, Leni
Fielding Graduate Institute

Williams, Mark S.
The University of North Carolina at Wilmington

Wolff, Ralph A.
Western Association of Schools and Colleges

Xin, Cindy
San Diego State University

Zemsky, Robert
University of Pennsylvania

Ziegler, Gene
American Graduate School of Management

# Preface

With the increasing acceptance of distributed education in both the public and private sectors, it seems timely to publish an *Encyclopedia of Distributed Learning* to capture the concepts and methods that reflect this phenomenon. We came to this project with great passion and many years of experience working within a distributed model of higher education. We have spent several years of our professional careers with Fielding Graduate Institute, which, since 1974, has offered graduate degrees in clinical psychology, human and organizational development, and educational leadership. Fielding's mission has been to provide high-quality educational experiences for mid-life, mid-career professionals who, because of work, family, and financial commitments, are unable to move to a campus-based school for the duration of their educational preparations. Fielding's response to meet the needs of its students has been to create a distributed learning model that integrates face-to-face teaching with independent and interactive learning at a distance and a competency-based approach to assessing learning outcomes. During the early years of our programs there was no computer network connecting students and faculty and we relied on telephone and mail systems for communication. Today, as might be expected, our training model is facilitated by the presence of an active Internet-based electronic network.

The same satisfactions and challenges that we experience in our academic world have played out in completing this encyclopedia. For the most part we have communicated with the administrative staff of Sage Publications, our board of editorial advisors, and our writers through our computer terminals. We enjoyed collaborating with people all over the world, some of whom we know well and others with whom we are working for the first time and have never met face-to-face. We have appreciated the benefits of technology-mediated collaboration, consisting of numerous e-mails and a Web site where editors and writers could post, organize, and review our tasks and our entries. At the same time we drew upon periodic face-to-face meetings as an Editorial Board to develop a vibrant, shared sense of purpose and direction. Throughout this endeavor we have appreciated being on the leading edge of an important societal and educational phenomenon while straining to keep up with the latest developments.

A project of this magnitude relies on the participation, skills, and goodwill of many contributors. We are thankful to Sara Miller McCune, Chairman and Publisher of Sage Publications, who convened the conversation that led to the encyclopedia. Several colleagues at Sage, including Rolf Janke, Jim Brace-Thompson, Denise Simon, Vince Burns, Karen Ehrmann, Diane Foster, and Toni Zuccarini Ackley, worked side-by-side with us for all or part of the way. Susan Taira was an enthusiastic member of the Editorial Board until illness made her participation impossible. Our Advisory Board consists of many special people, with great talent and experience in the field of distributed learning. They helped generate the list of headwords and helped locate just the right contributors to write the entries. Our colleagues at Fielding, represented by faculty, staff, students, administration, and Board members, have served in the capacity of contributors, supporters, and cheerleaders. In particular, we owe a debt of gratitude to Susan Street Sanchez, Fielding project manager for the encyclopedia, for keeping us organized and helping us maintain our momentum.

As in any project of this scope, we apologize for our omissions and hope that we have produced a resource that accurately reflects the current scope of understanding in this rapidly changing field that has moved from the margins to the mainstream.

*—Anna DiStefano*
*—Kjell Erik Rudestam*
*—Robert J. Silverman*

# About the Editors

**Anna DiStefano** has served as Provost for Fielding Graduate Institute since 1996. She has been a part of the Fielding community since 1983, serving in several senior executive capacities including Vice President of Academic Planning & Program Development, and Dean, Human and Organization Development (HOD).

Dr. DiStefano received her Ed.D. (1977) and her M.Ed. (1972), both in Counseling, from Boston University. Her undergraduate degree, A.B. (1969), was received from Trinity College, DC. She was also selected as an American Council of Education Fellow (1987–1988).

Dr. DiStefano's specialized areas of interest are planning and leadership in higher education, especially distributed education; feminism; public schooling; moral development; and conflict resolution. Her most recent publications include co-editing with Jody Veroff a special issue of *The American Behavioral Scientist* titled, "Researching Across Difference."

**Kjell Erik Rudestam** is Associate Dean in the School of Psychology at Fielding Graduate Institute, where he has been a faculty member and administrator for almost 20 years. Prior to that, he was Professor of Psychology at York University in Toronto.

Dr. Rudestam holds a Ph.D. in psychology (clinical) from the University of Oregon and an honorary doctorate from the Professional School of Psychology. He is the author of six books, including two Sage publications (*Surviving Your Dissertation,* 2nd ed., and *Your Statistical Consultant,* both with Rae Newton), and numerous published articles in the areas of clinical psychology (psychotherapy and change processes and suicide), research methodology, and online pedagogy. In addition, he is the co-editor of the recent *Handbook of Online Learning,* also published by Sage.

Dr. Rudestam is a fellow of the American Psychological Association (Division 12) and a diplomate of the American Board of Examiners in Professional Psychology (clinical) and the American Academy of Experts in Traumatic Stress.

**Robert J. Silverman** joined the faculty of the Human and Organization Program of the Fielding Graduate Institute in 1995, after becoming Professor Emeritus at Ohio State University, where he had taught since 1969 and where he had edited the *Journal of Higher Education* from 1970 to 1994. He works with adult learners, as scholar-practitioners, in developing an understanding of organizational theory and management, with a particular focus on organizational learning and change. He also works with students in the sociology of science and technology and in studies in the philosophy of knowledge.

Dr. Silverman received an A.B. in English from Rutgers University in 1961; an M.A. in Higher Education and Student Affairs from Teachers College, Columbia University in 1963; and a Ph.D. focusing on organizational studies from Cornell University in 1969. His publications include two professionally oriented books, *Getting Published in Education Journals* and *Organizational DNA: Diagnosing Your Organization for Increased Effectiveness,* and numerous academically oriented articles on epistemological foundations of research integrity practices and other knowledge-production activities, such as peer review and editors' roles in a postmodern academic society.

# Introduction

In the not-so-distant past, distributed education was a topic of limited interest to a relatively small number of educators. That is no longer the case. The tentacles of distributed education have spread to mainstream public and private education, from elementary school to graduate study and adult continuing education. It has become big business in the corporate world and an indispensable resource in the public sector. As such, this encyclopedia should be of interest to a large constituency of educators, students, managers, consultants, and policymakers.

The notion of "place" is a primary but poorly understood dimension of educational practice. Most of us have vivid memories of our educational experiences and recall the settings in which they occurred—where other students sat, the scratching of a chalkboard, the aromas of a cafeteria, the crowded halls and walkways of a school building. For some, neo-Gothic architecture and oiled floors reflect the prestige of an old private university; for others, an open enrollment and entrepreneurial society are represented by residence halls and newly minted business colleges.

The virtual world changes this scenario in a number of ways. The relationships among learners, teachers, resources, and places are put into new configurations in ways that challenge our notions of time and place. There are patterns of engagement that are not measurable by the traditional calendar and clock divisions. This new freedom forces us to rethink the relationship between learning and physical setting. It also requires recalibrations by other social institutions, whose policies are based on such divisions, such as banks for their loans and firms for their tuition reimbursement practices, as well as individuals whose life patterns regarding schooling are often regulated by the age of the learner. All this needs to be rethought and redefined. In the end, the practice of distributed education requires the revision of many traditionally held understandings and routines, with their associated emotional histories and commitments.

This encyclopedia is a resource that provides descriptions, explanations, and institutional and social challenges related to distributed education. We have deliberately chosen the terms *distributed education* and *distributed learning,* because they are somewhat broader in scope than related terms such as *distance education* and *online learning.* This is a distinction that is clarified in the encyclopedia entry on "Distributed Learning/Distributed Education," which might serve as a suitable entry point for the typical reader. The encyclopedia has been designed to describe the parameters and activities associated with distributed learning, recognizing that both the educational environment and the practices discussed in this work are experiencing continuous and sometimes nonincremental change. Given the social and cultural turbulence that extends to the field of education, the challenge for the editors and authors of this encyclopedia has been to shape a resource of enduring relevance. We trust that this encyclopedia has achieved this goal.

We have had the additional challenge of delimiting the focus of this encyclopedia in light of the ubiquitous nature and impact of distributed learning at all educational levels and in so many venues.

The encyclopedia consists of 174 entries of various lengths and 3 appendices. The scope of the topics is broad, ranging from historical predecessors of distributed education as we know it today to projections into the future, from classroom modifications to sophisticated technological devices, from infrastructure to ethics, from teaching skills to theories of pedagogy. At the same time we appreciate that our readers will engage this resource for particular and focused purposes and with an interest in efficient if not comprehensive "answers." As editors, we wanted to ensure that a full range of information would be made available, but we also recognize that for practices that redefine virtually everything in traditional education, certain limits had to be imposed.

At the beginning of this project, we assembled an advisory board of accomplished scholars and distinguished practitioners who helped us develop a list of relevant topics and identify knowledgeable authors for the entries. The authors themselves reflect the scope of the field of distributed education. It was important that the entries include practices associated with distributed learning, the experiences of those who engage in it, research that evokes deeper understanding of it, and challenges for the future. We invite our readers to serve as educational partners who can have a hand in shaping that future in distributed education.

We have included a Reader's Guide, which organizes the entries around six primary themes, although each reader will undoubtedly approach the encyclopedia from the vantage point of his or her personal questions and interests. The themes are: Administrative Processes; Technical Tools and Supports; Policy, Finance, and Governance; Social and Cultural Perspectives; Student and Faculty Issues; and Teaching and Learning Processes and Technologies. Administrative Processes refers to the institutional resources and procedures that play a foundational role in implementing and administering successful distributed education programs. Technical Tools and Supports includes a host of technical terms, many of which refer to the software, hardware, and allied processes that link the learner to the world of the computer. These entries may be more easily negotiated by readers with a technical background, but, although challenging for the computer novice, they provide one of the most comprehensive and up-to-date categorizations of the machinery that fuels the distributed learning experience. Policy, Finance, and Governance refers to the regulations and standards that serve as legal and moral guidance for conducting learning programs at a distance. Social and Cultural Perspectives includes terms that address the social and philosophical context out of which the field of distributed education germinated and continues to grow. Student and Faculty Issues refers to needs and services that apply to faculty and/or students as they work to enhance the teaching and learning experience at a distance. Finally, Teaching and Learning Processes and Technologies includes a broad range of topics that generally focus on how distributed learning takes place and the pedagogical vehicles that are available to make it happen.

The entries themselves differ significantly in terms of detail and sophistication. This is largely a function of the topics. In an effort to be comprehensive we have included entries that can easily be appreciated by the average young adult or high school student who is seeking to become more familiar with the field, as well as entries that are very relevant to the professional work of current scholars and practitioners. Faculty and instructors who are already active in teaching and facilitating courses online, or who envision doing so, may appreciate entries that focus on pedagogy and skill development. Administrators and information technology specialists may be drawn to entries that deal with infrastructure and computer topics. Policymakers may be most interested in issues of governance and educational philosophy.

It should be said that the boundaries between individual entries are not always precise. Thus, some topics are approached from multiple perspectives, because different entries may overlap or make reference to other entries. We trust that there is sufficient guidance in the table of contents and index to provide direction, but we have supplemented these tools with cross-referencing so that the connections among the entries can be more fully appreciated. These cross-references come at the end of each entry in the form of a short list of other entries that relate to some key aspect of the topic or to the topic as a whole. Finally, a limited number of references and additional readings follow most entries for those who wish to pursue an area in greater depth.

It has been a challenge to develop an encyclopedia around the dynamic and rapidly changing practice of distributed education. We believe that this volume will provide a foundation for the present and that its vision for the future will help shape the field for years to come.

## ACADEMIC ADVISING

The goal of academic advising is to promote student growth by assisting students with the development of their academic and career goals. Academic advisers encourage student development by promoting effective decision-making skills, working with each student as an individual, implementing a holistic approach to advising, and providing each student with a balance of challenge and support during advising interactions. Academic advising can be one of the most influential collegiate experiences. Each student is provided with the opportunity to have a quality one-on-one interaction with a representative of the institution that, in the case of distance advising, can take place in a variety of venues. Additionally, the advising session is an appropriate opportunity for a comprehensive discussion of the student's experiences. Therefore, effective academic advising can positively influence retention.

Advisers help students to actively learn effective decision-making skills while choosing an academic major, selecting general education courses, and determining the number of courses and course combinations. These experiences provide skills that can apply to any other life decision. Rather than telling a student what to do, it is important that advisers emphasize individual responsibility in making choices. Young adults often think in very black and white terms, and want to hear the "right answer" from an authority figure such as an academic adviser. Advisers need to encourage students to move from concrete thinking to a mindset that allows consideration of a variety of

perspectives. For instance, when advisers are approached with questions such as, "What is the best major in order to go into banking?" they need to describe a wide range of options to encourage a broader worldview.

Each student should be advised as an individual with unique characteristics and background. Academic advisers need to go beyond simply suggesting courses based on the requirements of a major program of study and also take into consideration the personal characteristics of students when assisting with course selection. Nowadays, such external factors as student work schedules and personal responsibilities should also be considered during advising. More specifically, when advising first year students, advisers should take into account each student's unique high school experiences, college entrance exam scores, commitment to major(s), other commitments, and interest in various subject areas. Through the use of technology, advisers can easily access information about each student, which can enhance this individualized approach.

Additionally, academic advising should be approached in a holistic manner. Instead of dealing solely with academic coursework, advisers should explore other aspects of each student, such as future aspirations, extracurricular experiences, and connectedness to the college or university. This is not to say that an academic adviser is a personal or career counselor, but an ability to integrate academic, career, and personal issues when advising is essential in encouraging students to become successful learners. Updates in technology can reduce the amount of time required to do such mundane tasks as completing academic check sheets that previously had to be done manually, allowing more time for substantive academic advising sessions.

Finally, when advising students, a balance of challenge and support is necessary to promote student growth. If this balance does not exist, then no personal growth will occur. For instance, a sophomore student who sees his or her adviser without any preparation and knows that the adviser will figure out the entire schedule is receiving too much support without enough challenge. This situation could be changed if the adviser gave the student some basic information and then let the student develop some course possibilities before coming back for a follow-up appointment.

In order for advising to be effective, certain components need to be in place. Students must know who their adviser is, how and when to access their adviser, and what to expect from an academic adviser. They must also realize that the advising process is a shared responsibility.

Now that more information regarding advising resources and processes is available online for students, they are encouraged and often required to review materials before talking with an academic adviser. This ensures that a student is fully aware of the advising process, and reinforces that students should take responsibility for understanding the advising information. This will hopefully enhance the quality of the advising process.

Academic advisers need to be dependable, accessible, caring, appreciative of diversity, accurate, and committed to the learning process. In fulfilling their academic advising responsibilities, they should encourage frequent contact with students, maintain appropriate confidentiality, and be accountable for information disseminated. Technology has definitely increased the accuracy of information in areas such as calculating estimated grades, provided venues for accountability such as electronic advising comment systems, and maintained confidentiality in the advising process. Technology can enhance the frequency of contact with advisees through e-mail, but it also can decrease the amount of face-to-face interaction with academic advisers, so it may take a longer period of time for the student and adviser to get to know each other. It remains a constant challenge to utilize the most effective aspects of technology without undermining the personalized interaction that is a cornerstone to effective academic advising.

Because of the changing responsibilities of faculty and the increasing complexity of curricula and academic options, more advising is being assigned to staff whose sole function at many institutions is to advise students. Professional academic advisers may serve students in the process of choosing academic majors, in an academic department, and even in graduate and professional programs. Many campuses have a combination of faculty, professional, and, at times, student peer advisers.

Because academic advisers have a broad vision of the institution, they can assist campus personnel in gaining a better understanding of students' developmental needs. Additionally, advisers should advocate for changes in policies that are barriers to students. This can include simplifying the curriculum or explaining the curriculum in a user-friendly way to benefit students that are being advised at a distance. Academic advisers are also responsible for explaining the reasons for institutional policies and procedures as well as the culture of higher education.

Promoting a comprehensive approach to academic advising along with a quality relationship between the adviser and student will impact student academic success, satisfaction, and retention. Likewise, the value of the educational experiences offered at colleges and universities will also be enhanced.

—*Gaye Golter DiGregorio*
—*Paul Shang*

*See also* CAREER PLANNING AND DEVELOPMENT; FINANCIAL AID

## Bibliography

Gordon, V., and W. Habley. (2000). *Academic advising: A comprehensive handbook.* San Francisco, CA: Jossey-Bass.

National Academic Advising Association (NACADA). (2002, May). *NACADA statement of core values of academic advising.* Retrieved from http://www.nacada.ksu.edu/Clearinghouse/Research_Related/corevalues.htm.

Perry, W. G., Jr. (1970). *Forms of intellectual and ethical development in the college years.* New York: Holt, Rinehart, and Winston.

Sanford, N. (1966). *Self & society: Social change and individual development.* New York: Atherton.

# ACADEMIC CALENDAR

An academic calendar refers to an institution's campus-wide schedule of events. Minimally, this includes when instruction/classes will begin and end each term, scheduled breaks from classes, mid-term and final exam days, and holidays observed by the institution. Special events and deadlines that students or faculty may need to meet may be included in the academic calendar to facilitate planning. *Schedule* is a term used more frequently in regards to a specific portion of the academic calendar, usually in reference to the schedule of classes offered during a term. The full academic calendar for the year is typically printed in the hard-copy version of the institution's catalog, and versions of the calendar will be found in the hard-copy schedule of classes produced for each term. Additionally, or alternatively, the academic calendar and schedule of classes for a term will be made available on the institution's Web site.

## STANDARDS OF THE ACADEMIC CALENDAR

There are two major types of academic calendars: semester and quarter. The semester calendars consist of two major types. The first is known as the traditional semester calendar. It divides the academic year into two roughly equal periods of about 15 weeks, with the first term beginning usually in September and ending in January. The second term begins in February or March and ends in the summer.

The second type of semester calendar, and the one most commonly used today, is referred to as the early semester calendar. In an early semester calendar, the year is again divided into two parts. The first term usually begins in late August or early September and ends prior to Christmas. The second term may be slightly longer than the first by a few days and can begin anytime in the late winter or early spring (January, February). The second term in an early semester calendar typically ends in late spring or early summer, which could be May or June. Many schools incorporate a third semester that takes place during the summer months, in which case the terms are referred to as trimesters. Less frequently, the school may have an accelerated interim term that takes place in full during just one calendar month (usually January), inserted between the fall and spring semesters.

An academic calendar that uses a quarter system is divided into four terms, each approximately 10 weeks long, usually called fall, winter, spring, and summer quarters. The bulk of student attendance occurs in the fall, winter, and spring quarters.

## CLASS SCHEDULES

Class schedules will vary depending largely on the primary mode of instruction or delivery of the course. For courses that utilize the traditional method of face-to-face discussion, laboratory, or lecture, the daily class schedule is usually arranged in a combination of Monday-Wednesday-Friday and Tuesday-Thursday arrangements. Saturday classes that meet once a week are also common. Courses conducted via teleconferencing also typically follow this scheduling model.

The class schedules for courses conducted entirely online may vary dramatically, however. Instead of attending at a set time, students may be required to show participation by posting messages to asynchronous message boards or by completing other assignments. Real-time or synchronous attendance may also be required through the use of chat room technologies. It is becoming rather common for online or traditional face-to-face programs to be on a monthly or bi-monthly schedule where the students take one course at a time at an accelerated pace over the course of 1 or 2 months. After the cycle of that course is completed, another cycle begins with a new course.

Courses that are delivered via an independent study model are the least likely to have daily class schedules. There may be a set day the independent study courses begin and end for all students, or the course start and end dates may be based on a more flexible arrangement determined by each student and their faculty and tracked by the institution's records office.

## DETERMINING THE ACADEMIC CALENDAR

The institution's registrar usually sets and maintains the academic calendar. This may be done annually or bi-annually. Many schools will have tentative academic calendars in place for several years at a time. Several factors need to be considered in determining the dates of the academic calendar; for example, most public schools are required by their state to have a certain number of instructional days, when classes must be in session. Federal, state, and religious holidays must also be taken into account when setting the academic calendar. Faculty unions may place stipulations on the institution as to how early or late in the year classes may begin or end.

It is not uncommon for institutions with distributed learning models, where the vast majority of courses are offered mainly via independent study methods, to use an academic calendar that is continuous (i.e., one term ends and another begins on consecutive days), so that the end result for the student is an enrollment period of 365 days. In such distributed learning models, students have considerable freedom in determining at what time of the year they will begin and end their coursework, as long as satisfactory academic progress is maintained over the course of the year. In such a model, administrative methods must be created to account for the independent nature of each student's plan of study.

—*Bridget Lee Brady*

*See also* COURSE CREDIT/CREDIT TRANSFER; ENROLLMENT STATUS

### Bibliography

Munsen, Glenn W. (1989, April). *Variations on a theme: The semester calendar.* Retrieved from http://www.registrar.rhodes.edu/semester_cal.HTML.

Quann, C. James, and Associates. (1979). *Admissions, academic records, and registrar services.* Washington, DC: Jossey-Bass.

# ACCREDITATION

The increase in distance education programs and institutions, and questions about extending financial aid to them, has given rise to questions of whether accreditation is an adequate means to ensure the quality and integrity of this new medium of delivery. This entry offers a frame for understanding and responding to the emerging forces of change in distance education and accreditation. The history and multiple forms of accreditation will be briefly described. The unfolding policy issues in the federal arena and the different approaches used by the regional accrediting commissions to review and accredit distance education will be discussed along with special issues facing the accreditation of distance education and how accreditation has responded.

## HISTORY AND TYPES OF ACCREDITATION REVIEWING DISTANCE EDUCATION

Accreditation in the United States has been taking place for more than 100 years. It is conducted by nongovernmental organizations emphasizing peer review processes supported by formal standards and processes and is organized into three major types of accrediting agencies: regional, national, and specialized/professional. Each is involved with distance education, though in different ways.

Regional accreditation is the most commonly held accreditation and is institutional in form. Created first in the North Central region to ensure quality in high schools, it quickly moved to colleges who wanted to verify the quality of courses and degrees earned at other institutions. A process of peer review was established, whereby evaluators would visit an institution and review its resources, policies, and structures. On the basis of such reviews, credits and degrees earned at one institution became accepted by others. The success of this process led, in the early twentieth century, to the creation of several regional accrediting associations for both schools and colleges. There are now six regional associations[1] and eight regional commissions,[2] with the Western Association of Schools and Colleges formed the most recently in 1964. Regional commissions accredit the most commonly known academic institutions, nearly 3,000 in number, and require institutions to be degree-granting to be eligible.

National accrediting agencies are also institutional in scope but accredit similar institutional types across the United States, such as technical and vocational institutions, as well as many that offer degrees in business, computer science, technology, and other fields. Several of these agencies accredit institutions that award certificates, and others are moving into the accreditation of distance education programs, including one that focuses exclusively on distance education, the Distance Education Training Council.

Specialized/programmatic accreditation is limited to specialized fields of study, such as medicine, law, business, or education. Specialized accrediting agencies focus on programs, and do not accredit institutions. Many, though not all, specialized accrediting agencies require regional or institutional accreditation as a foundation for programmatic accreditation.

Regardless of the type of accrediting agency, a similar process is used. The institution prepares a self-study against agency standards or uses other frameworks offered by the agency, and is then reviewed on site by an external team of evaluators. The evaluation team prepares a written report, which is acted upon by an accrediting commission. Accreditation is periodic, usually for a maximum of 5–7 year periods for specialized accredition agencies, and up to 10 years for the regional accrediting commissions.

This entry focuses on regional accreditation because it is the most commonly referenced for standards in evaluating distance education, and because the regional commissions accredit the majority of academically oriented distance education institutions and programs.

## FEDERAL POLICIES ON ACCREDITATION OF DISTANCE EDUCATION

In order to oversee the allocation of student financial aid to institutions, Congress established a process of "recognition" for those accrediting agencies able to demonstrate they are "a reliable authority as to the quality of education or training offered" (20 U.S.C. 1099b(a)). Congress uses the Higher Education Act, first enacted in 1965 and periodically reauthorized thereafter, to define criteria for student financial aid, to recognize accrediting agencies, and more recently, to address issues related to distance education programs. Under authority from the Reauthorization Acts, three different issues arise from the U.S. Department of Education's (USDE) treatment of distance education and accreditation: 1) recognition of accrediting agencies to evaluate distance education programs and institutions; 2) regulations addressing financial aid eligibility for programs offered through distance education; and 3) substantive change procedures for institutions instituting distance education programs.

*Recognition.* Formally included in the review of accrediting agencies in the 1992 Reauthorization Act, a distance education program must now demonstrate it

> consistently applies and enforces standards that ensure that the courses or program of instruction, training or study offered by the institution of higher education, including distance education courses and programs, are of sufficient quality to achieve, for the duration of the accreditation period, the stated objective for which the courses or programs are offered.

Recognition involves an extensive review process of the agency's standards, policies, procedures, and records, and is granted for a maximum period of 5 years.[3]

Over the years, and prior to the development of the Internet, regional accrediting commissions dealt with a number of external degree programs and institutions. Some were offered at multiple sites, others were offered through television, radio, microwave, or satellite transmissions; videotape distribution; or a mixture of these approaches. The development of the Internet made the offering of distance education more feasible and accessible. In response, accrediting agencies extended existing standards to evaluate those programs and institutions that functioned exclusively through these early forms of distance education. These early experiences led to the development of the approaches used by regional accrediting commissions. From the standpoint of regional accreditation, the existing process has worked effectively and is not in need of major change.

With the inclusion of distance education in the Reauthorization Act and the increase in the number of programs and institutions using distance education, the USDE determined that unless an agency had a prior history of accrediting distance education programs, it must establish its capacity to evaluate distance education programs and institutions. To date, all of the regional accrediting commissions have been grandfathered due to their prior history of evaluating distance education, and the authority to accredit distance education institutions and programs has been included within the scope of their authority.

In 2002, however, both the Inspector General's Office of the Department of Education and the General Accounting Office have reviewed how effectively accrediting associations evaluate distance education programs and student learning outcomes. In their reports, concerns were raised about the perceived lack of "specific standards," which could be a prelude to new legislative proposals. Some believe that revisions will be made in the 2004 Reauthorization Act that will define specific standards for reviewing distance education.

*Financial Aid Eligibility.* Under current federal regulations, three rules prohibit distance education programs from being eligible for student financial aid: The 50% rule, the 12-hour rule, and the Satisfactory Academic Progress rule. It is these rules that currently pose the greatest challenge to traditional definitions of academic quality. The 50% rule denies institutional eligibility if more than 50% of the program is conducted by distance education. The 12-hour rule requires 12 hours of instruction a week during the academic calendar, with the expectation that at least 30 weeks of academic instruction are offered per year. The third rule requires students to demonstrate "satisfactory academic progress" through their program. Distance education students are not engaged in the formal instruction that site-based programs provide, and academic progress is often different for distance education students who may take only one or two courses at a time and be on a different timetable of completion than the traditional academic calendar.

These rules, although obsolete in their rigidity, address the genuine concern that significant relaxation of these rules could lead to fraud and abuse. In July 2002, the Department of Education made the 12-hour rule more flexible, creating regulations for "nonstandard terms." It has also worked out arrangements with several institutions, including the University of Phoenix and Western Governors University, to resolve issues concerning the satisfactory academic progress rule for students enrolled in their programs.

In response to the direct and intense pressure from institutions to extend financial aid eligibility to the growing number of distance education students, the 1998 Reauthorization Act called for a "distance education demonstration program," in which the USDE made eligible for financial aid a limited number of programs or institutions that offered more than 50% of credit through distance education, in an effort to learn how to ensure quality and integrity in such programs. The purpose of the project was to test the quality and viability of expanded distance education programs, determine the most effective means of delivering quality education via distance education, and determine the "appropriate level of federal assistance to students enrolled in distance education programs" (Wellman, 2002). The law permitted the USDE to work with up to 15 institutions or programs offering distance education not otherwise eligible for federal aid. For the first time students earning more than 50% of their credits through distance education became eligible for financial aid.

The demonstration program is now well underway and the USDE is monitoring it to learn more about the application, and waiver, of some of its rules. The program expires in 2004, and it is expected that the USDE will recommend changes to the law in the 2004

Reauthorization Act based on the experience with the demonstration program. All of the programs or institutions included in this demonstration program now have some form of status with a recognized accrediting association, so the demonstration programs are also reviewed within the scope of each institution's accreditation (or candidacy).

*Substantive Change.* Legislation requires accrediting agencies to review a number of institutional changes, characterized as substantive changes, in advance of their implementation. Under the 1992 Reauthorization Act, the definition of substantive change was amended to include "[t]he addition of courses or programs that represent a significant departure, in either content or method of delivery, from those that were offered when the agency last evaluated the institution" (USDE regulations, Section 602.22(2)(iii)). This has been interpreted by the USDE to include the initiation of distance education programs when it is a new method of delivery.

USDE regulations identify a number of areas that must be reviewed in the substantive change process through the institutional presentation of a feasibility study. As a result, all accrediting associations have established procedures for the review of distance education programs as a substantive change. With some regional commissions, the first distance education program triggers an institutional review and action; if the institution is determined to have the capacity to mount and maintain distance education programs, it may be permitted to open additional programs from that point forward without prior review. Where warranted, however, conditions may be set or additional reviews may be requested. These three options make up the policy and practice of, for example, the Higher Learning Commission of the North Central Association.

Other commissions require prior review and approval of all distance education programs even after the first program has been approved; exemptions are granted only after the institution has had a number of distance education programs operating and reviewed. This is the policy of the Senior College Commission of the Western Association and the Southern Association, for example. At some regional agencies, the decision is made by the accrediting commission, whereas in others, a substantive change committee is delegated authority to act on behalf of the commission. In all cases, accrediting associations are responsible for evaluating distance education programs as part of the comprehensive review of the institution.

## DEVELOPMENT OF INTER-REGIONAL GOOD PRACTICES FOR DISTANCE EDUCATION REVIEW

Distance education programs, by their very nature, can move well beyond state, regional, and national boundaries, and many have done so. As more institutions initiated distance education programs, the need arose to assist these institutions by articulating the areas, issues, and good practices necessary for implementing quality programs. The Council of Regional Accrediting Commissions (C-RAC), which is composed of the chairs and executive directors of the regional accrediting commissions, worked with the Western Cooperative for Educational Telecommunications in 2000–2001 to develop two statements—one on core values for reviewing distance education programs and institutions (Statement of Commitment) and the other a set of good practices for institutions and evaluators (Statement of Good Practices). The regional commissions felt a strong and unified statement would demonstrate the importance of distance education in the accreditation process. They formally adopted the two statements in June 2001, and they now apply within the framework of each region's own accreditation standards and support the development of improved quality in distance education. They are as relevant to distance education programs within a traditional institution as they are for virtual institutions.

The Statement of Commitment identifies three basic commitments that guide the regional accreditation of distance education: commitment to tradition, values, and principles; commitment to cooperation, consistency, and collaboration; and commitment to supporting good practice. The first commitment places distance education within, rather than outside, the traditions and values of higher education. By so doing, it emphasizes the need for an educational community to support learning, for institutions to provide effective services to support the needs of students enrolled in such programs, and to ensure that programs have coherence and integrity. In this regard, expectations of distance education programs are no different from other programs offered by accredited institutions, which counters the belief held by some that separate accreditation standards are needed for distance education programs.

The second commitment (cooperation, consistency, and collaboration) addresses the perceived differences among regional accreditation agencies in their standards and review processes for distance education. These differences could lead to an institution "region shopping" to incorporate in a region seen as more hospitable to distance education. Therefore, in order to achieve fairness and a "level playing field" for established institutions that have moved their offerings across regional boundaries using new distance education programs, as well as for new virtual institutions, cooperation, consistency, and collaboration are important.

The third commitment (to support good practices) grew out of the reviews by regional accreditors of both established institutions launching distance education programs and new institutions intending to operate completely by distance education. Common problems were being identified across regions and institutions and it became clear that accreditation had a sense of the emerging challenges and processes and thus needed to guide and develop institutional good practice, not just evaluate them after the fact. Each of the commissions now makes the *Good Practice Guide* available to institutions and evaluation teams. It addresses five significant issues that arise when developing, operating, and evaluating distance education: institutional context and commitment, curriculum and instruction, faculty support, student support, and evaluation and assessment.

*Institutional Context and Commitment.* All too often institutions move into distance education without considering how such programs fit within the institution's mission or understanding the nature of the commitment of resources and services needed to support even one or two programs. Although many of the students served by distance education are simultaneously enrolled in the institution's own campus-based courses, institutions are not always prepared to serve geographically dispersed students. Similarly, it is often assumed that a small group of distance education students can be handled incrementally by institutional offices, without considering the special services, and costs, of supporting such students.

*Curriculum and Instruction.* The use of the Internet to support distance education has led to the need to rethink course and curricular design, because traditional pedagogical strategies do not transfer effectively to a Web-based medium. Thus, whereas television or satellite-broadcast courses could (and often did) replicate whatever was happening in the classroom, good or bad, the Internet requires approaching course design differently. Careful attention has to be given to how to create student–faculty and student–student interaction. Decisions need to be made as to which parts of the course should be conducted synchronously and which can be done asynchronously. On-campus programs provide for great flexibility, whereas most distance education programs offer a limited choice of courses, and many now use a cohort-based approach, where a group or "cohort" of students go through the program together. All of these decisions require a substantial level of planning and curricular development. Too often institutions begin offering distance education courses by intending to transfer pre-existing syllabi to a Web format. One of the most positive effects of distance education is the creativity being generated to transform courses and whole curricula, developing clearer outcomes and aligning course activities with intended learning goals.

*Faculty Support.* Nearly all institutions now provide media support to faculty who want to incorporate technology into their teaching. Even so, there is a great need for faculty to work with technology and instructional design experts to create learning experiences that parallel or improve upon the dynamics of a classroom. This can impose an additional workload on faculty, and experience shows that students in distance education have more contact with faculty than traditional students, thanks to e-mail, chat rooms, and other devices. Institutions need to consider the heavier workload of program start-up and the increased interactions with students when making faculty assignments, as well as the costs and time involved in providing ongoing technology and pedagogical support.

*Student Support.* Early accreditation reviews of distance education programs found that student support services often lagged behind other areas. Too often it was assumed that, beyond technical support, little student support or information would be needed. Many institutions now provide exemplary library, financial aid, and advising support online, although doing so requires considerable planning and investment.

*Evaluation and Assessment.* Many institutions have found that distance education programs caused the faculty to develop clearer learning outcomes and assessment tools for determining both student and program success. In this way, distance education is beginning to powerfully influence faculty behavior in traditional courses as well. It is important for institutions to tailor the evaluation of distance education programs to address the special attributes and needs of these programs and their students, rather than only subsuming evaluation within the larger institutional process. Many institutions carefully assess grading practices and review the archive of online interactions to ensure comparability with classroom courses. To date, much of the research has found no significant difference between classroom and distance education performance. In terms of accreditation review, evaluation of distance education programs requires a focus on outcomes assessment because traditional indicators of quality are not as relevant.

## CURRENT ISSUES FACING ACCREDITATION OF DISTANCE EDUCATION

Although possible legislative changes are the most visible issue, additional issues are of importance to the accreditation of distance education:

*Virtual Institutions.* Years ago, predictions claimed that virtual education would lead to the end of traditional classroom education. Although enrollments in distance education are growing, they are not sufficient to supplant traditional institutions; technology-mediated instruction is, however, significantly supplementing traditional offerings. Nonetheless, in the last decade, the number of institutions operating only through distance education are increasing, and include such institutions as Western Governors University, the University of Phoenix Online Division, Jones International University, and Cappella University. Regional accrediting commissions have been able to address the needs and different characteristics of these institutions by using and adapting existing standards and processes. Already, several have been accredited. Initially there was concern that regional accreditation could not adapt to these new institutional forms; however, the current processes appear effective in reviewing exclusively distance education institutions.

*Certificate Programs.* Regional accreditation focuses almost exclusively on degree granting programs, but a significant proportion of distance education enrollments are in certificate programs. Often these programs fall outside of the specific review of accreditation. As enrollments increase, new approaches may need to include review of these programs, either as a separate process or as part of the regular accreditation review of the institution.

*IRAC and Western Governors University.* When the Western Governors University (WGU) was formed in 1996, 13 states, within the jurisdictions of four accrediting commissions, participated—the Northwest, North Central, and two Western Associations. Questions arose as to whether regional accreditation could adapt to the proposed innovative design and multiregional scope of WGU. In response, the four commissions created a unique accrediting commission to address such a multiregional institution. Each of the four commissions appointed three commissioners who, along with the executive directors of the commissions, constituted an Inter-Regional Accrediting Commission (IRAC), with fully delegated authority to develop standards and act on the accreditation of WGU. The resulting composite standards drew upon the standards of the four commissions, with adaptations for the special format of WGU, especially its lack of a traditional faculty. IRAC granted WGU the status of a candidate for accreditation in 2000, and granted accreditation to WGU in 2003. Always considered a pilot project, now that IRAC has finished its review of WGU for initial accreditation, it is expected to dissolve, and WGU, incorporated in Utah, will eventually become a member of the Northwest Association. This special commission demonstrated how effectively these four regional commissions could work together.

*Maintaining Proportionality.* One of the greatest challenges facing accreditation is maintaining proportionality in the review of distance education. Regional accreditation emphasizes *institutional* systems of quality and capacity. Current and proposed legislation dealing with distance education moves regional accreditation into the active review of individual programs. Thus, a new program offered on campus would not be reviewed, but the same program offered through distance education would be reviewed. Moreover, the requirement that all comprehensive institutional reviews include distance education gives a level of prominence to these programs, even though only a small fraction of students may be enrolled.

## SUMMARY

The growth of distance education and the extension of federal financial aid to students enrolled in such programs have given rise to intense scrutiny of the quality and integrity of these programs. Regional accrediting agencies have attempted to respond to these concerns with the development of statements, good practices, and revisions to their standards and review procedures. These agencies believe they have adapted the accreditation process to become an effective review system for distance education programs and institutions. Yet questions remain among those in Congress and the Department of Education as to whether the current system adequately reviews distance education.

However the next Reauthorization Act changes the role of accreditation, it is likely that technology-mediated courses and programs will continue to grow in the form of revisions to on-campus courses with technology, formal distance education programs, and new institutions operating entirely through distance education. Accreditation will remain a primary source of quality assurance for such activities. As faculty become more involved with distance education and Web-based instruction, there is likely to be greater attention given to pedagogical design, learning outcomes, and the assessment of learning outcomes. This attention should help to improve more traditional classroom-based courses and programs as well.

*—Ralph A. Wolff*

***See also*** Federal Laws; Financial Aid; Legal Issues

### Bibliography

TeleEducation NB. (1999). The "no significant difference phenomenon." Retrieved from http://teleeducation.nb.ca/nosignificantdifference/.

TeleEducation NB. (n.d.). The "significant difference phenomenon." Retrieved from http://teleeducation.nb.ca/significantdifference/.

U.S. Department of Education. Part 602—Secretary's recognition of accrediting agencies. Retrieved from http://www.ed.gov/offices/OPE/accreditation/part602.html.

Wellman, Jane. (2002). Of time and the feds: The federal role in student credit hour enforcement. Unpublished manuscript.

Western Association of Schools and Colleges. (n.d.). Good practices for electronically offered degree and certificate programs. Retrieved from http://www.wascweb.org/senior/Good_Practices_in_DEd1.pdf.

Western Association of Schools and Colleges. (n.d.). Statement of commitment by the regional accrediting commissions for the evaluation of electronically offered degree and certificate programs. Retrieved from http://www.wascweb.org/senior/Statement_of_Commitment.htm.

## Notes

1. The six regional associations are the New England Association of Schools and Colleges, the Middle States Association of Schools and Colleges, the Southern Association of Colleges and Schools, the North Central Association (now separately incorporated at the college level as the Higher Learning Commission), the Western Association of Schools and Colleges, and the Northwest Association of Schools and Colleges.

2. The Western Association has two college commissions, one for community and junior colleges and the other for senior college (4 year and graduate) institutions. The New England Association has a commission for colleges and a second commission for occupational and technical schools and colleges. The remaining six regional accrediting commissions have a single commission for schools and a single commission for colleges and universities.

3. The law specifies 10 areas that accrediting agencies standards must address: 1) success with respect to student achievement in relation to the institution's mission; 2) curricula; 3) faculty; 4) facilities, equipment, and supplies; 5) fiscal and administrative capacity; 6) student support services; 7) recruiting and admissions practices; 8) measures of program length in relation to the objectives of the degree or credentials offered; 9) record of student complaints received by or available to the agency; and 10) a record of compliance with Title IV responsibilities (20 U.S.C. 1099b (a)(4) and (5). The law and USDE regulations also define a series of additional reporting and other requirements for recognition.

# ADAPTIVE TECHNOLOGY

The terms *adaptive technology* and *assistive technology* are used interchangeably, although *assistive* is the more formalized term, because it is incorporated into a number of legislative acts in both the United States and Canada. The acronym *AT* is also used frequently.

Two common concepts describe adaptive technologies. The first concept is that adaptive technologies involve a device, service, strategy, practice, or protocol that is uniquely designed, modified, or customized. The second concept is that adaptive technologies are intended to meet or improve the functional, social, daily living, or psychological needs of people with disabilities. The Americans with Disabilities Act of 1988, sec. 3.1, provides a comprehensive treatment of this definition.

Adaptive technology is an interdisciplinary field. The rehabilitation and biomedical engineering fields have been working with adaptive technology issues for many decades. Over the last 15 years, special education, speech therapy, occupational therapy, physical therapy, and other allied health professions have all incorporated adaptive technology training into their degree and accreditation programs. A number of undergraduate accreditation and degree programs that focus on adaptive technology have also sprung up. The rise of the personal computer and its obvious advantage as a highly malleable tool for people with disabilities has been a core reason for the recent interdisciplinary focus on adaptive technology. As technology becomes faster, smaller, cheaper, and more pervasive in our lives, it brings with it a wealth of solutions for people with disabilities.

There are two theoretical approaches to designing or using AT. With the specialized approach, the individual receives a mix of commercial, commercially modified, and specialized adaptive technology solutions, along with any required training. An example of this might be the creation of an accessible apartment for an individual. The major emphasis with the specialized approach is on "fixing" the individual's problem—much of the responsibility is placed on the individual and his or her rehabilitation professionals. Modifying bathrooms, kitchens, phones, and doorways, and adding lifts are usually fairly expensive. *Retrofitting* is when the environment must be fixed or altered after the fact, to accommodate a user with a disability.

On the other end of the spectrum is the Universal Design (UD) approach. The concept of UD is that mainstream technologies should be designed to work for everyone, which includes people with disabilities. If the initial design of an apartment building takes into account accessibility, fewer (and often less costly) modifications are required.

By taking a UD approach, a feature that was initially created to meet a disability need can become useful to many users. The sidewalk curb cut is the classic example. A curb cut enables people in wheelchairs to gain access to sidewalks, but many other people, including children on bicycles and roller blades, delivery people with hand trucks, and people pushing baby carriages, also use the cuts.

The phrases *electronic curb cuts* and *curb cut metaphor* have both been used to describe the principles of UD. Closed captioning is a good example of an electronic curb cut. Closed caption chips have been required by law since June 1993 in all televisions 13 inches or larger in the United States. This adds approximately $1 to the cost of the television, compared with the few hundred dollars required to purchase the special setup box previously required to receive closed captions. As captioning has become "universally" available, hearing people have discovered many uses for it, such as teaching English as a second language and "hearing" in noisy public places. An excellent example is a "hearing" teenager using the closed caption feature on her TV to do her homework and watch her favorite show simultaneously. She can divide her time between the work and the show, and evade the dreaded "parental detection."

One other important aspect of UD is the inclusion of customization features in the original design of the product or software. Customization features allow users to select display types, user interface settings, and presentation styles that suit their particular display needs. For example, a customizable online learning environment would allow an individual to select information to be displayed visually with graphics, text, or simplified text; audibly; using tactile systems such as Braille; or in a different language. Students could access learning content and communication facilities such as chat and bulletin boards using their preferred settings without the risk of missing content, information, or opportunities for participation. Users can indicate their preferred settings by selecting them directly or by accessing a pre-established profile through a centralized database or a specialized device such as a smart card.

In summary, adaptive technology represents a broad range of solutions and strategies, from expensive modifications to pre-existing inflexible commercial systems, to designing systems that support many different abilities and needs from the beginning. Regardless of the strategy, the goal is to ensure that people with disabilities are able to function effectively and efficiently and thus achieve equality and participation.

*—Deborah Fels*
*—Charles Silverman*

*See also* DISABILITY LAW; SPECIAL NEEDS POPULATION; VOICE ACTIVATION PROGRAMS

## Bibliography

Jakob Nielsen's Alertbox. (2001, November 11). *Beyond accessibility: Treating users with disabilities as people.* Retrieved from www.useit.com/alertbox/20011111.html.

Cook, A., and Hussey, S. (1995). *Assistive technologies: Principles and practice.* St. Louis: Mosby.

ICDRI. (n.d.). *The international center for disability resources on the Internet.* Retrieved from www.icdri.org.

Leventhal, J., Scherer, M., and Galvin, J. (Eds.). (1996). *Evaluating, selecting, and using appropriate assistive technology.* Gaithersburg, MD: Aspen.

CPB/WGBH. (n.d.). *National center for accessible media.* Retrieved from http://ncam.wgbh.org.

RESNA. (n.d.). *Rehabilitation engineering and assistive technology society of North America.* Retrieved from www.resna.org.

Scherer, M. J. (2001). *Living in the state of stuck*, 4th Edition. Cambridge, MA: Brookline Books.

Trace Center, College of Engineering, University of Wisconsin, Madison. (n.d.). *Designing a more usable world—for all.* Retrieved from http://trace.wisc.edu.

U.S. Department of Justice. (n.d.). *Information and Technical Assistance on the Americans with Disabilities Act.* Retrieved from http://www.usdoj.gov/crt/ada/adahom1.htm.

# ADJUNCT FACULTY

The use of adjunct or part-time faculty members to teach distance learning courses is an important issue because distance learning may accelerate the trend in higher education toward the greater use of adjunct faculty. Adjunct or part-time faculty may affect the quality of instruction, and use of non–full time faculty may be connected to a general move in higher education toward market models driven by economic necessity to lower the cost of higher education. Key issues regarding adjunct faculty are: What percentage of distance learning courses are taught by adjunct faculty? What are the current policies and trends in higher education for compensating faculty who create and teach distributed learning format courses? What is the effect of the use or nonuse of adjunct faculty on the quality of distance learning format courses? Is the use of adjunct faculty to teach distance learning courses bound tightly with market models in higher education?

The majority of distance learning courses are developed by faculty, not commercial publishers or providers. According to the National Center For Education Statistics, three-quarters of the higher education institutions that offered distance education courses in fall 1995 used distance education course curricula developed by the institution's faculty. This represents a new form of employment likely to impact traditional faculty roles. How are faculty paid or provided compensatory time for course development? Who owns course materials and other intellectual property?

The use of adjunct faculty is strongly connected to the overall economics of distance learning. There are two basic economic models for distance learning: replace variable costs with fixed costs, or replace expensive labor with cheap labor. John Daniel, former vice-chancellor of the British Open University, claims that the basic economic approach of distance learning is to replace labor with capital. He proposes that the per unit cost of teaching can be cut either by adding more students to existing courses or by making instruction more efficient. The British Open University has used this model to reduce faculty labor costs from 66% to 20% of the total budget. In the United States, economic models for distance learning in higher education at the degree level are still being developed. Finkelstein, Frances, Jewett, and Scholz offer the most complete description to date of the economics of distance learning in the United States. In this collection, Jewett follows Daniel in arguing that distance learning offers economies of scale after an up-front capital investment. Jewett sees the solution to finding a positive economic model for distance learning in discovering ways to "unbundle" faculty tasks and reduce labor costs.

The second basic approach, a labor for labor model, divides the faculty role into segments and reduces the total labor cost by replacing higher priced faculty with less expensive labor. Jewett identifies three basic functions of faculty in a cost analysis: preparation, presentation, and assessment. To the extent that these functions can be performed individually by less expensive labor, the overall cost will be reduced. The British Open University divides up these functions with course design teams and 7,000 part-time tutors (associate lecturers) whose task is to provide academic support to local groups of students. Adjunct faculty play a role in this second economic model by simply supplanting more expensive labor, or by taking over some of the unbundled activities. In this way, full-time faculty might develop distance learning courses, and then adjuncts might take over some of the interaction and assessment responsibilities. Overall, this might lead to lower expenses.

What does current research show about the use of adjunct faculty to teach distance learning courses? First, Berg found that the majority (76.6%) of institutions responded that only 0–25% of those teaching distance learning courses are classified as adjunct faculty. In trying to understand these surprising data it is useful to consider the results from the Primary Research Group study, which found an increased use of part-time faculty from 1998 to 1999. In that study, the authors surmised that full-time faculty had been used to develop and teach new distance learning courses at first, but then later on had been replaced by part-time faculty. Therefore, it is possible that the low use of adjunct faculty thus far is a result of the early stage of development of distance learning programs. Given the controversial nature of distance learning, it makes sense that administrators would turn to full-time faculty rather than adjunct to develop and teach courses at the beginning when they are under the most scrutiny.

Overall, the current data indicate that in the United States, thus far the two basic strategies for achieving increased productivity (capital for labor, and labor for labor) are in early stages of implementation. In terms of direct compensation, one source has found a decrease in the percentage of faculty pay in the overall distance learning budget, at 31.72% for 1998, down from 37.21% in 1997. In terms of indirect compensation, a systematic restructuring of the work of faculty into discrete tasks, such as is done at the British Open University, is thus far only occurring at nontraditional institutions such as the University of Phoenix. Although it is unlikely that this kind of division of faculty labor will occur in the immediate future at traditional institutions, replacement of expensive faculty may instead occur through the general increased use of part-time or adjunct faculty, as documented in Finkelstein, Seal, and Schuster. Although information is limited thus far, research indicates that faculty work in both developing and teaching distance learning courses tends, thus far in this early stage, to be seen as work-for-hire under regular load with little additional indirect compensation or royalty arrangements. When broken down by institutional type, it was found that community colleges have a stronger tendency to pay faculty through a load arrangement. On the very sensitive issue of ownership of intellectual property, 2-year institutions also were clearly more likely to claim ownership of distance learning courses.

Finally, there are indications that market approaches are influencing the use of distance learning, causing faculty roles to change. One study finds that distance learning is often connected to revenue-seeking activity by those who initiated the use and where the activity is administratively housed within universities. Nevertheless, although a revenue-seeking administrative structure was found, evidence of lower academic standards was not apparent in standard course approval and assessment methods. It is reasonable to conclude that the high use of regular faculty has contributed to stronger academic quality and pedagogical practices. Nevertheless, one needs to question whether this level of quality will continue if the use of adjunct faculty is increased greatly in the future.

—*Gary A. Berg*

*See also* FACULTY POLICIES; POLICIES; UNBUNDLING OF HIGHER EDUCATION

## Bibliography

Bates, A. W. (1995). *Technology, open learning and distance education.* London: Routledge.

Berg, G. A. (2002). *Why distance learning?* Arizona: Greenwood Press (American Council on Education, Higher Education Series).

Daniel, J. S. (1998). *Mega-universities and knowledge media: Technology strategies for higher education.* London: Kogan Page.

Edwards, R., & Minich, E. (1998). *Faculty compensation and support issues in distance education.* Washington, DC: The Instructional Telecommunication Council.

Finkelstein, M. J., Frances, C., Jewett, F. I., & Scholz, B. W. (2000). *Dollars, distance, and online education: The new economics of college teaching and learning.* Phoenix, AZ: ACE/Oryx.

Finkelstein, M. J., Seal, R. K., & Schuster, J. H. (1998). *The new academic generation: A profession in transformation.* Baltimore, MD: Johns Hopkins University Press.

Jewett, F. (1999, April 16). *A framework for the comparative analysis of the costs of classroom instruction vis-à-vis distributed instruction.* Paper presented at Executive Forum on Managing the Cost of Information Technology in Higher Education sponsored by the New Jersey Institute for Collegiate Teaching and Learning (NJICTL). Retrieved February 19, 2001, from http://academic.shu.edu/itcosts/papers.html.

Massy, W. F., & Zemsky, R. (1995, June). *Using information technology to enhance academic productivity.* A report from an Educom Roundtable. EDUCAUSE. Retrieved February 19, 2001, from http://www.educause.edu/nlii/keydocs/massy.html.

Metlitzky, L. (1999). *Bridging the gap for the mainstream faculty: Understanding the use of technology in instruction.* Unpublished doctoral dissertation. Claremont, CA: Claremont Graduate University.

National Center for Education Statistics. (1997). *Distance education in higher education institutions.* NCES 97–062. Washington, DC: National Center for Education Statistics.

Primary Research Group, Inc. (1999). *The survey of distance learning programs in higher education.* New York: Primary Research Group, Inc.

# ADMINISTRATIVE LEADERSHIP

Although the terms *leadership* and *administration* may seem to be redundant, there is a subtle difference between them that is very important when used in discussing distributed learning. An administrator carries out or implements policies, whereas a leader influences behavior, often well beyond the boundaries where his or her behavior ceases. Given the potential human and fiscal costs of implementing distributed learning and the often highly emotive responses involved, it is critical that those who are charged with administering distributed learning exert effective leadership.

## PLANNING FOR DISTRIBUTED LEARNING

Many prognosticators predict the demise or downsizing of institutions of higher education as the result of distributed learning. Although these predictions may be overstated, institutions that do not engage in timely and effective planning to adapt to the changes engendered by emerging technologies are at risk. Leadership in the distributed learning planning process is crucial. The institutional leadership must agree upon a set of assumptions that will guide the planning process, and these assumptions should be clearly evident in vision and mission statements of the institution. These assumptions can vary, but they should include an institutional reaction to the following statements:

- Distributed learning is not traditional classroom instruction delivered "at the speed of light."
- Forcing a choice between distance education and traditional classroom instruction is not the issue. Current sixth grade students 6 years from now will have low tolerance for lecture-based instruction and will expect an electronically rich and peer-oriented learning experience (distributed learning).
- The costs of creating and maintaining high-quality Web-based courses will result in the licensing and importing of the vast majority of courseware in the form of reusable learning objects.
- Faculty roles will diversify dramatically with entirely new classes of faculty emerging, including designer/developer of courseware and instructional team leader.

With distributed learning as a formal or informal part of the institutional vision and mission, the distributed learning leader must ensure that the infrastructure to support distributed learning is in place. This infrastructure consists of several components including technology, faculty support, policy, and student services. If any of these components is not in place, there is a high likelihood that the resources spent on the others will be wasted.

## Technology

A significant challenge is to inculcate in institutional decision makers the realization that if the server is down or the connectivity is broken, the institution is "gone" for those students who are obtaining their instruction virtually. For an institution with many millions of dollars invested in classrooms, dormitories, libraries, and other forms of

physical plant, this realization may be counterintuitive. The distributed learning leader needs to help the institutional leadership realize that both the physical and virtual institutions need to be supported. This leader needs to have enough understanding of the technological functioning of the network to be conversant with both internal information technologists and vendors.

## Faculty Support

The immediate challenge that most distributed learning leaders face is to bring together existing faculty support functions throughout the university. Often, there will be several entities that list as one of their services assisting faculty to migrate courses to the Web. These might include a faculty development laboratory, instructional television services, the library, and academic computing. Coordinating these services to provide seamless cradle-to-grave assistance for faculty is a formidable but necessary challenge.

Often, one of the first tasks in the area of technology is to provide leadership in the selection of a Web platform or platforms. Although the level of acrimony that results from this selection will not usually reach that of the selection of a campus-wide word processing program, emotions can run high. In order to provide campus-wide support for both faculty and students, the selection of Web platforms is best done sooner rather than later.

Migrating a course to the Web requires a significant up-front commitment, so an effective distributed learning leader will work with the institutional leadership to provide grants and release time for faculty. This can be done at both the institutional level, through a grant process, and at the college, school, or department level through course release.

Leadership in the area of quality is also an important area of faculty support. Probably one of the most effective means of providing this is through peer modeling. The effective leader can facilitate the liberation of faculty imaginations in a risk-free environment through the sharing of courses and modules and successful examples of building learning communities. Another successful technique is to provide instructional consultants who hold extended visits in an online course and issue a private report to the faculty member to assist them in quality enhancement.

Most institutions require or encourage visits by the department chair to view and evaluate classroom teaching. The distributed learning leader can assist both the evaluators and the faculty to develop virtual classroom observation techniques. These might include criteria for syllabi, "start here" pages, faculty-to-student and student-to-student communication, organizational and navigational attributes, and instructional strategy.

## Policy

One of the most important infrastructure components, and one that is often overlooked, is the policy that underpins the successful operation of a distributed learning program. Although an institution may begin creating and offering electronically based courses with few policies in place, failure to move forward in developing policies in this area can have significant negative consequences and put a halt to progress. The following are some areas in which the institution needs to develop distributed learning policies:

*Intellectual Property.* Ownership of electronically developed course materials is often a very emotional issue on campus, with faculty and administrators often holding opposite and extreme views on this issue. One extreme purports that creating electronically developed course materials should be regarded as analogous to authoring a textbook, whereby the faculty member retains copyright and commercial rights. The other extreme maintains that these materials should fall under the work-for-hire rubric with the institution retaining all rights.

Some institutions have developed intellectual property policies that recognize that the relative contribution of the faculty author and the institution may vary and that the rights involved should also vary depending upon the relative weights of these contributions. As an example, if the university contributed substantially to the creation of the courseware, it might be entitled to utilize the course materials within its own educational programs (nonexclusive educational license) with payment of a royalty to the faculty author. The university and the faculty might both have the right to market the course materials to other institutions (nonexclusive commercial license) with royalties shared between them.

The distributed learning leader can play an important role in the creation of an effective intellectual property policy. He or she might stress the importance of the policy; bring in consultants; or work with the faculty governance body, the institutional counsel, and the administration to consider possible approaches and adopt an approach that matches the institutional culture.

*Tenure and Promotion.* If the faculty reward system does not take into account the substantial amount of time and energy involved in developing and maintaining quality courseware, the involvement by faculty may be limited to tenured full professors. Tenure and promotion decisions, although often guided by institution-wide policies, are ultimately influenced most strongly at the departmental level. The distributed learning leader, by working with the top management at the institution, may have influence on the institutional vision and mission and, ultimately, on institutional tenure and promotion policy. The leader's influence on college and departmental practices will probably be much more tangential. Ultimately, it is the realization of the enhanced learning that is possible with distributed learning, combined with financial policies that enable departments to benefit directly from increased enrollments, that will motivate change at the departmental level. The distributed learning leader can promulgate this realization and can also have an impact on the creation of financial policies that spur distributed learning.

*Compensation.* Because enrollments in electronically delivered programs will likely fluctuate more than for on-campus programs, it is important that a program's response time in addressing these fluctuations be shortened. A flexible and nimble program is more likely to succeed than one with little or no financial flexibility. A department chair needs to have the ability to compensate existing faculty for expanded enrollment in a class as well as to quickly acquire additional teaching support for program-wide increases. Participation in the creation of models that provide for compensation to both individual faculty and departments is an important role for the distributed learning leader. Faculty compensation can be based on a formula that recognizes the increase in enrollment over the "standard," nondistributed class. Departments may receive a portion of the tuition of students who are "net" enrollment (i.e., would not have attended the institution if the program were not online).

### Student Services

Unless the institution is being created *de novo,* the distributed learning enterprise will likely be added onto an existing student services area. Even a small number of distance students can have a profound impact on almost every student service. One of the most important roles for the distributed learning leader is to bring together, in advance of the implementation of a distance program, all of the key players in student services. Lead time is important because existing services are often not designed for students who do not come to campus. As an example, many financial aid offices require recipients to sign in person for financial aid. State-supported institutions often require careful tracking and reporting of students that reside out of state, and separate sections of a course may have to be created for these students. The issue of fees must be addressed (e.g., which fees should distance students pay? Should there be additional fees for these students?).

Billing of and payment by students, as well as counseling and career services, must be considered and expanded to serve the distant student. Access to the institution's library services is a paramount issue, and addressing this will include the development of cooperative arrangements with other institutions and a rapid expansion of licenses to electronic journals and books.

The distributed learning leader often must facilitate the provision of this array of student services with little or no additional resources being provided to the support areas. Endorsement by the upper administration is important, but continued communication between the distributed learning leader and those in charge of student services is crucial.

### FINANCIAL ISSUES

The provision of an information-rich electronic environment is a valuable goal in itself. However, unless the costs associated with this provision can be controlled, distributed learning efforts will not be sustainable.

*Distributed Learning Costs, Income, and Savings.* The distributed learning leader can promote methods by which information on costs, income, and savings can be gathered and analyzed. Cost categories include production (personnel, increased space, equipment,

and licensing), delivery (increased bandwidth, servers, delivery platform, and personnel), faculty (release time, grants, and student support), and increased student services. Income is often difficult to track but is often interpreted as tuition and fees paid by students who would not have attended the institution if the course or program were not distributed. Although this concept is easy to operationalize for students who reside at a distance, determining which local students chose to attend the institution as a residential student because of the sophistication of the instructional delivery is much more difficult. Tracking savings that can be attributed to distributed learning is difficult. It is obvious that if 30% of the student contact hours occurred in an electronic environment, this would have a substantial impact on the physical plant, especially in the long term. Attributing dollar savings to this impact is problematic, especially because a drop in students living on campus might have an immediate negative impact on the institution's ability to meet fiscal obligations such as dormitory bonds.

*Licensing and Consortia.* In the next decade, many programs will recognize that creating and maintaining high-quality electronically delivered programs will be prohibitively expensive. Programs will form consortia to share courseware and a lucrative, but highly competitive, market will emerge for licensing both full courses and course components.

A challenge for the distributed learning leader will be to identify and gather the financial information critical to informed decision making. An equally important task will be to assist administrators in making decisions when all of the financial data are not available.

### CHARACTERISTICS OF AN EFFECTIVE DISTRIBUTED LEARNING LEADER

The role of distributed learning leader is very complex and requires an individual with a variety of skills and abilities. The effective distributed learning leader will be placed high enough in the organizational chart to have access to the vice presidents and to have credibility among the deans. The successful leader needs to have a grasp of the technical aspects of distributed learning so that he or she can conduct an informed discussion with those that will design, implement, and maintain the physical infrastructure necessary. This leader must also have a firm understanding of pedagogy and personal experience in the design and delivery of distributed learning. He or she should have a clear understanding of the various aspects of an institution of higher education.

At its essence, this role involves serving as a change agent within the institution, and the successful leader will be able to understand and relate to a variety of often conflicting parties. He or she must have an informed vision of the impact of distributed learning on higher education and the ability to articulate this vision so that it resonates with each segment of the institution. This person will need to be enthusiastic, persistent, and patient.

Institutions of higher education face a formidable challenge in identifying an individual that can successfully perform as a leader in distributed learning. The right blend of technical and pedagogical skills, knowledge of higher education issues, and personality traits is rare. Unless these leaders are identified, recruited, and retained, the promise of distributed learning will not be realized.

*—Philip Turner*

*See also* FACULTY POLICIES; FINANCE; STRATEGIC PLANNING; STUDENT SERVICES

## Bibliography

Bates, T. (2000). *Managing technological change.* San Francisco: Jossey-Bass.

Belanger, F. (2000). *Evaluation and implementation of distance learning.* Hershey, PA: Idea Group Publishing.

Claeys, C. (1999). Assessing cost-effectiveness for virtual learning and instruction: Why and how? In C. Feyten & J. Nutta (Eds.), *Virtual instruction: Issues and insights from an international perspective.* Englewood, CO: Libraries Unlimited.

Collis, D. (2001, Fall). When industries change: The future of higher education. *Continuing Higher Education Review, 65,* 7–24.

King, B. (2001). Managing the changing nature of distance and open education at the institutional level. *Open Learning, 16,* 47–60.

Lau, L. (2000). *Distance learning technologies: Issues, trends, and opportunities.* Hershey, PA: Idea Group Publishing.

Weigel, V. (2000, Sept/Oct). E-Learning and the tradeoff between richness and reach in higher education. *Change, 33*(5), 10–15.

# ADMINISTRATIVE PLANNING AND SUPPORT OF INFORMATION TECHNOLOGY

During the last 30 years, the emergence of new communications technologies, including the Internet and the World Wide Web, has provided the impetus for many higher education institutions to examine how they deliver instruction and to whom. During this time period, the personal computer, the Internet, and the World Wide Web have been the technologies and tools that have fundamentally changed many aspects of higher education in America and throughout the world. Neilsen//NetRatings and Fortt report that today, more than 60% of U.S. homes have at least one personal computer and Internet access. The rate of diffusion of Internet use since the development of the World Wide Web is greater than for any previous communications technology.

The National Center for Education Statistics reports that nearly 44% of all higher education institutions had offered distance learning courses by 1997–1998, an increase of one-third over the previous 3 years. Over the same reporting period, higher education institutions more than doubled their distance learning course offerings. As of 1999, approximately 10% of all U.S. higher education students (1.4 million of a total 14 million) were enrolled in online courses delivered via Web technology.

According to the 2001 Campus Computing Survey, more than two-thirds of U.S. institutions of higher education deliver instruction via the Web; however, few institutions have yet taken a comprehensive, institutional approach to online learning.

On many college and university campuses across the country, questions are being raised about how best to employ various technologies to support teaching and learning. One of the most significant questions is whether to take a centralized or a distributed approach to distributed learning and the use of technology in instruction.

Some institutions use a completely decentralized approach to instructional activities, allowing individual faculty members to choose and implement instructional technologies and decide whether or not to teach online. Generally, this approach is accomplished by providing faculty with direct access to hardware and software. Some high quality instructional materials may result from this approach, but it is difficult to scale the successful projects, and it is unlikely that systemic institutional change will result.

In other institutions, decisions have been made to institutionalize distributed learning through activities that involve the entire university. In these institutions, efforts are being made to provide systematic support for and confront issues related to:

- Increasing student access to instruction and services across the institution
- Using instructional and information technologies
- Providing faculty development and course development support
- Assessing the impact and results of what is being done for continuous improvement

The provision of increased student access to high quality instruction and services across an institution is definitely part of the planning discussions at campuses where student enrollments are growing. In institutions experiencing or anticipating enrollment growth, providing increased access to instruction can be accomplished by strategically offering programs and select courses fully online or through an instructional approach that blends face-to-face and online instruction. These instructional modalities provide help to growing institutions to accommodate increasing enrollments while relieving some of the demands for new buildings. They are not expected to eliminate the need for more brick and mortar, but rather to help as part of a larger campus growth plan.

Likewise, these same strategies and discussions are taking place in institutions with declining enrollments in order to provide access to programs and courses to populations not usually served by the institution, especially those at some geographic distance from the campus. The plan here is to increase enrollments with these previously untapped populations.

The use of instructional and information technologies must be part of an institutional strategic or long-range planning process. The tools and software options in the areas of instructional and information technologies offer increased capabilities and efficiencies. What efficiencies would be lost without access to e-mail and the Internet at our institutions? Issues related to selection of the *best* tools, usability, training, ongoing support, and scalability are critical to what have become some of the largest purchases made at higher education institutions today.

Higher education institutions have two very important groups at the heart of their capabilities and strength: faculty and staff; and students. Therefore, providing faculty development and course development support will help faculty and their students to be successful in the online teaching and learning environment. Improvement of teaching and learning through planned faculty development programs and centers is a goal on many campuses. Expanding those efforts to include preparing faculty to teach and support online instruction will enable online teaching and learning to become part of the fabric of the institution rather than a randomly occurring phenomenon.

Quality improvement assessments are part of our lives in higher education, whether done to satisfy external accreditation requirements, governing boards, or state agencies. Focusing special attention on assessing the impact and results of an institutional initiative in online teaching and learning will yield valuable data. Those data can help to identify best practices and serve as a vehicle for continuous improvement. Existing assessment units can serve this function, or, as is done in some institutions, a special unit can focus on assessing the impact of online teaching and learning on students, faculty, and the institution.

The answers to questions of whether to engage in distributed or distance learning and how to implement it should be guided by the institution's mission and strategic plan. An institutional strategic plan can help answer questions related to the institution's rationale for using distributed learning and the programs that should be delivered fully or partially online. Will distributed learning be used in an effort to grow enrollment, ease campus overcrowding, provide greater access to students, improve student learning, or a combination of these and other reasons? Will distributed learning be of benefit to the whole institution and all students or only to selected segments of the student population?

Adopting a technology generally comes with costs. Because significant up-front costs often are followed by regular planned upgrades to the technology, institutional administrators must find answers to questions such as:

- Does the technical infrastructure already exist for the type of delivery system chosen to reach institutional goals?
- Are the financial resources available to accomplish stated goals?

- How will the institution keep up with changing technologies?
- Does the institution have the capability to do everything itself or will any infrastructure or development activities have to be outsourced?

The technical infrastructure in higher education institutions is ever-changing. Cutting-edge technology users are constantly pushing the institution to purchase and employ new technologies to support research and teaching. Although it may be impossible or even inappropriate to provide all that they would like to have at their disposal, cutting-edge users might make up the best usability testers prior to making purchases and scaling for institution-wide use. The key here is to follow the institution's goals and vision for its future rather than individual desires. Tying technology purchases and infrastructure build-out to institutional goals is critical. If an institutional goal is to provide greater access to a wider range of potential students, decisions must be made about the role technology might play in reaching that goal. Keep your eyes on the goal and look at the options, the costs, the funds, and the personnel resources available, and make decisions accordingly.

Key to any institution's success in teaching and research is its faculty. What must they know and what skills must they have to successfully teach in the online environment? Many institutions are providing specialized faculty development programs to prepare faculty to teach in the new environment.

The ubiquitous nature of the Web makes it the medium of choice for many institutions. Three common types of online courses are:

- World Wide Web courses delivered entirely over the Internet
- Hybrid courses delivered partially in classrooms and partially over the Web
- Face-to-face courses that are enhanced with the Web

These distributed learning modalities may help fulfill an institution's goals, such as support of high quality instruction, operational excellence, and innovative uses of technology. To achieve these and other institutional goals, one institution has created a unit charged with providing specialized faculty development to help faculty to design courses for and to teach in these online environments. The faculty development program is in the form of a hybrid noncredit course that models how to teach online using a combination of class meetings, labs, and Web-based instruction. The purpose of this professional development program is to help faculty succeed as they plan, design, develop, and teach online or media-enhanced courses and programs. The support unit provides instructional designers, programmers, software engineers, and digital media specialists to support the faculty development and course development processes.

Policy issues related to the new teaching environment(s) must also be addressed at institutional and department levels. At institutional and program levels, accreditation may be affected. Special efforts to review and adjust institutional policies and practices to meet accreditation requirements should be undertaken. Other institutional, college, or departmental practices that should be reviewed include intellectual property, faculty load, faculty compensation, and the effects of involvement in online course delivery on the tenure and promotion process.

Assessment is critical to the long-term success of any project or institutional initiative such as distributed learning. Institutions should plan a continuous assessment strategy for program improvement purposes that includes both quantitative data collection and analysis and qualitative assessments involving students and faculty.

Institutions should collect data on the impact of their distributed learning initiatives. Such evaluation activities can result in coordinated approaches to collecting data about student and faculty demographics, growth in online enrollment and sections, student and faculty perceptions about teaching and learning online, and problems encountered while teaching and learning in the online environment. These evaluation data can be used to target improvements in faculty development, learner support, and technical support needed by faculty and students. Learning styles of students in the online courses can be studied with the intention of helping faculty to address the needs of these different learning styles and to enable students to determine their own learning styles and make informed choices about the types of courses they select as part of their college education.

The growth of online teaching and learning at many other colleges and universities across the nation shows its acceptance by faculty and students. The convergence of the two ITs, information technology and instructional technology, has made this possible. A concerted effort will be required to involve the many units on a college campus that provide and support these technologies and the faculty and students who will use and benefit from them.

*—John C. Hitt*

*See also* INFORMATION TECHNOLOGY (IT);
    OPERATIONS AND MANAGEMENT

### Bibliography

Fortt, J. (2002, March). The truth behind PC sales figures: Is the market saturated? *The Mercury News.* Retrieved March 23, 2002, from http://www.siliconvalley.com/mld/siliconvalley/2901515.htm

Greene, K. C. (2001). *Campus computing 2001.* Encino, CA: The Campus Computing Project.

Howard, P., Rainie, L. & Jones, S. (2001). Days and nights on the Internet: The impact of a diffusing technology. *American Behavioral Scientist, 45,* 383–404.

National Center for Education Statistics (NCES). (1999). *Distance education at postsecondary education institutions: 1997–1998.* Washington, DC: U.S. Department of Education, Office of Educational Research and Improvement.

Nielsen//NetRatings. (2001, November 13). *Internet usage climbs to record high in October, with 115 million Americans online, according to Nielsen//Netratings.* Retrieved March 31, 2002, from http://www.nielsen-netratings.com

Sorg, S. (2001). Thinking about distributed learning? Issues and questions to ponder. *Metropolitan Universities, 12,* 1.

# ADMISSION CRITERIA AND PROCESSES

Admission criteria are the requirements established by colleges and universities to ensure the adequate preparation of students for postsecondary education and to manage the demand for enrollment. Applicants who meet the criteria are admitted; those who do not are rejected. These criteria (known also as admission standards) define gateways into postsecondary academic programs at the baccalaureate, master's, doctoral, and professional levels. Generally, however, community colleges maintain open enrollment policies, with very liberal, access-oriented admission criteria for their courses and academic programs, including associate degree programs.

Public colleges and universities tend to be more explicit and formula-driven with their requirements, whereas private institutions are more likely to be less specific and to weigh a wider array of factors in their decisions. Nearly all colleges and universities permit students to enroll in a few credit-bearing courses as nondegree or "special" students without meeting the admission standards required of degree-seeking students.

Admission requirements vary greatly among institutions, and may vary from year to year for a particular college. Three fundamental issues affect how standards are established:

- The college curriculum dictates what students need to know prior to college enrollment, so that students can successfully achieve their degree aspirations. As a result, admission standards put pressure on secondary institutions to provide adequate course offerings and on students to achieve adequate mastery.
- Market forces affect standards. Colleges and universities need to maintain an enrollment equilibrium where enrollment is sufficient to maintain financial solvency, but not so high as to badly damage the educational experience. Because these market forces change over time (as a result, for example, of more high school graduates, economic recession, or increased competition from other institutions), colleges and universities may adjust their admission standards each year to maintain a steady enrollment of students.
- The institutional mission affects standards. A highly selective college, for example, may have a mission and tradition of serving only the best-prepared students. Another college, however, may have a mission that requires it to maintain access to a wide array of students.

The interplay of these three factors creates considerable variation in higher education admission criteria.

At the undergraduate level, admission is commonly based on some combination of four criteria: the number of high school preparatory courses, high school grade point average, class rank, and standardized test scores (SAT or ACT). A substantial body of research has shown these variables to be moderately correlated with college achievement, as measured by students' first-year grade point averages. Generally, high school grades and class rank are most strongly related to college success. Although standardized test scores are less predictive of college success, they can be used effectively in combination with high school grades to improve predictions of academic success. Standardized tests, however, have generated considerable controversy over the years. First, they are sometimes viewed as having little relationship to the high school curriculum or to student achievement. Second, they are sometimes perceived as contributing toward bias against minority students. This second concern stems from the fact that underrepresented minority students tend to have results that, on average, are somewhat lower than those of other students. These issues (and others, including the effects of test preparation) continue to be debated, and the testing companies continue to consider revisions to their tests. Most recently, the Educational Testing Service (ETS) decided to add a writing sample and to change the content of some multiple choice sections of the SAT in response to national concerns. In addition to the four primary criteria, many institutions consider additional factors for undergraduate admission, including personal essays and recommendations.

At the graduate and professional levels, similar admission criteria are often used: review of undergraduate course work, undergraduate grade point average, and standardized test scores. These criteria are also often supplemented with recommendations and essays.

It is important to note that college success depends on a wide range of factors, many of which are not measured by traditional admission criteria. Some promising efforts have been made to find better measures that might be used for college admission. Clifford Adelman makes a case for linking college admission more tightly to specific aspects of the high school curriculum, such as the number of advanced placement courses taken and the highest level math course taken. Even if such efforts result in improved criteria, critical issues like motivation and commitment are not easily assessed. Many students who are predicted to succeed in college will not—and many who are not expected to succeed will excel.

Maintaining a balance between academic preparation and access to higher education is a crucial concern in any consideration of admission criteria. Setting very high standards helps ensure that most enrolled students will successfully earn degrees, but denies direct access to many students. Moreover, because traditional admission standards are correlated with family income and socioeconomic status, economically disadvantaged students, including many minority students, are more likely to be denied admission. Setting low standards opens access to a greater diversity of students, but makes it difficult to achieve higher levels of curricular excellence, which can reduce the level of skills and knowledge attained by college graduates.

For undergraduates seeking baccalaureate degrees, admissions processes often separate prospective students into two groups: early admission applicants and regular admission applicants. Early admission, which usually occurs about a year before actual enrollment, benefits colleges and students by providing a much longer time to prepare for enrollment. In particular, college admission offices get an earlier picture of their progress toward achieving enrollment targets. Because acceptance of the early admission offer is often binding, however, students lose the flexibility to change their decision during their senior high school year. Because of this restrictive effect on students, some colleges are working to revise or eliminate early admission policies. Deadlines for regular admission are generally in the spring prior to fall matriculation. Most colleges now support online applications for admission.

Students seeking distributed learning options may be looking to enroll in either particular courses, certificate programs, or degree programs. As described above, criteria for admission to degree programs are unique to the institution and program, usually having little to do with how the program or the associated courses are delivered. Students interested in particular courses or certificates can usually apply as nondegree students, which is much less restrictive than admission into degree programs. Few, if any, admission standards must be met for nondegree status.

Often, students seeking distributed learning courses or programs are older, working students looking for the flexibility that such courses provide. For older students, colleges often modify their admission criteria to accommodate prospective students whose high school performance may not be predictive of their potential for college success. Such students are generally afforded much more flexibility regarding what they must submit to demonstrate their readiness for college-level study.

—*Rick Kroc*

***See also*** Online Orientation and Navigation Tools; Orientation; Student Preparation

## Bibliography

Adelman, C. (1999). *Answers in the toolbox: Academic intensity, attendance patterns, and bachelor's degree attainment.* Jessup, MD: U.S. Department of Education.

Loeb, J.W. (1992). *Academic standards in higher education.* New York: College Entrance Examination Board.

Swann, C., & Henderson, S. E. (1998). *Handbook for the college admissions profession.* Westport, CT: Greenwood.

# ADULT EDUCATION LEARNING MODEL

The learning model of adult education assumes that the practice of adult education should start with, and focus consistently on, the distinctive ways adult learners experience participation in education. In this learner-centered model, all curricular, pedagogic, and evaluative decisions are shaped by what we know about adults' experiences of learning. The learning model assumes that adults display a distinctive motivation toward their learning; that they prize the incorporation of their experiences, and the critical analysis of these, into the curriculum; that they possess a methodological preference for self-directed modes of learning; that they exhibit distinctively adult modes of cognition; and that they experience certain predictable emotional reactions when returning to learning. From this understanding of learning, certain modes of practice emerge as central to the learning model of adult education. Specifically, the model advocates the integration of adult learners' experiences into the curriculum, an emphasis on the adult's self-directed control over the process of learning, the development of adult curricula as a negotiated process, and the importance of continually researching how adults are experiencing learning and adjusting practice to take account of what this research uncovers.

## ADULTS' EXPERIENCES OF LEARNING

Much research on adults as learners contends that they bring a distinctive motivational orientation to learning and a clear sense of why they initiate particular learning efforts. The highly influential andragogical model of adult education developed by Malcolm Knowles holds that adults desire to see the immediate application of their learning to their circumstances or problems, a motivation he describes as "performance centered." More recently Wlodkowski has argued that we must move away from a unidimensional understanding of motivation to one in which interrelated components of motivation are emphasized—establishing an inclusive learning atmosphere in which learners feel respected and connected to each other, developing a favorable attitude to learning by allowing adults to create personally relevant learning programs, enhancing the meaning of learning by finding ways to include the analysis of learners' experiences, and engendering competence by demonstrating to learners their effectiveness as learners.

The importance of recognizing learners' experiences has long been a prized tenet of adult education. The idea that adult educators should honor adults' experiences, while simultaneously helping them to view them critically, is what makes the field distinctive in the eyes of many of its practitioners. One of the earliest expressions of this view was Eduard Lindeman's definition of adult education as a cooperative venture in nonauthoritarian, informal learning, the chief purpose of which is to discover the meaning of experience. Founder Myles Horton's highly regarded work at Highlander Folk School in Tennessee, believed by many to represent what's best in the adult education tradition, focused on helping activists learn from their experiences by working in groups to analyze the experiences collaboratively and critically. In Australia, David Boud and a series of collaborators have carefully explored the place of experience in adult learning.

Adults' instinctive preference for learning in a self-directed manner was first highlighted by Canadian researcher Allen Tough in the 1960s. Tough contended that more than 80% of adult learning efforts were planned, conducted, and evaluated by adults without any external instructional help from adult educators. His work inspired numerous replicatory studies, an annual international research conference devoted solely to research and conceptual analysis in self-directed learning, and the generation of scales designed to measure adults' readiness for self-directed learning. Over time, the concept of self-directed learning has been broadened to emphasize its situational, contextual nature. Critics have argued that self-directed learning projects framed by dominant ideology uncritically serve to perpetuate existing structures and contend that self-directed learning, far from representing a liberating exercise of learner autonomy, has now been co-opted by formal education through the use of learning contracts.

The existence of distinctively adult modes of cognition has been proposed by a number of developmental and cognitive psychologists interested in moving beyond Piaget's model of formal intellectual operations. These researchers posit a model of adult cognition that focuses on adults' increasing capacity to think reflectively and contextually. Dialectical thinking is one form of adult reasoning in which universalistic and relativistic modes of thought are claimed to co-exist. Its essence is the continuous exploration of the interrelationships between general rules and contextual necessities with the realization that no fixed patterns of thought or conduct, and no permanent resolutions to intractable problems, are possible. Embedded logic is the capacity to think logically in terms of judging the imperatives and contextual cues to be observed in a situation, but to adapt this logic to the situation's contextual necessities. Epistemic cognition is the development by adults of a self-conscious awareness of how they come to know what they know, and of how they come to determine the grounds for validity. Transformative learning focuses on how adults come to reframe meaning schemes and meaning perspectives so as to be ever more inclusive and discriminating; that is, to be able to account for a wider and wider range of experiences. Critical reflection explores how adults learn to make evident power dynamics in their relationships and practices, and how they become aware of hegemony (the process by which they enthusiastically embrace ideas and practices that work against their own best interests).

Finally, adults are thought to exhibit particular emotional responses to finding themselves in learning situations. They experience feelings of impostorship—the sense that others (particularly younger learners) are smarter than they are and that sooner or later their own unsuitability for learning will be publicly revealed by their making an egregious error that cannot be ignored. They acknowledge a disturbing loss of innocence as their educational activities demonstrate to them that the further they explore an area the more that area is revealed as increasingly complex. There is also the common perception that if adult learners talk to their peers and family members about the significance learning has for them they risk committing cultural suicide, of being thought "stuck up" and excluded from the culture or reference group that has defined and sustained their identity. These tales from the dark side of adult learning are counterbalanced by a recognition of the significance that membership in an emotionally sustaining learning community has for adult learners.

## LEARNING MODEL PRACTICES

The learning model of adult education comprises a number of practice orientations that flow from the experience of adult learning outlined above. The first is the attempt to integrate adults' experiences into the curriculum. In the learning model, any needs assessment that happens is grounded in an attempt to encourage adults to explore the educative dimensions of their previous experiences. The model does not assume that adults enter an educational program as empty vessels or blank canvases. Instead they are viewed as active constructers and construers of their own experience. The learning model puts a premium on working with adults to help them document the skills, knowledge, insights, and wisdom that they have acquired as part of their life experience. Many models of accreditation of prior learning or portfolio assessment have been developed around the world to assist this process.

Once engaged in learning, adults are encouraged to explore how their previous experiences frame how they engage in new learning, how they draw meaning from new knowledge, and how they respond to learning's inevitable problems and plateaus. The model's practices also focus on helping adults to realize the value of their own experiences in helping them deal with whatever problems they face. Instead of assuming that learners need outside experts to help them deal with their problems, the learning model assumes that adults often are the experts on their own problems, but that they need some assistance in analyzing their experiences critically to learn from them. "Helping people learn what they do" is how Myles Horton, the founder of the Highlander Folk School in Tennessee, summarized this process. The concept of critically reflective practice, so much a part of contemporary adult education, is in many ways focused on helping people take a critical look at their experience, while also realizing its contribution to the formation of the adult learner's identity.

The learning model also emphasizes the importance of adults retaining and exercising as much control as possible over the course of their own learning efforts. Ideas of self-directed learning, autonomous learning, self-organized learning, and learner-managed learning become central to the model. Adult learners are assumed to possess a level of mature self-awareness that allows them to conceive appropriate learning objectives, plan a course of self-managed learning, choose the most conducive learning methodologies, conduct the learning, and evaluate its success. Some models assume these abilities to be more or less innate; others place more emphasis on administering diagnostic scales, such as the self-directed learning readiness scale, to assess the likely success of a self-directed learning effort.

Both of these positions have been criticized. Assuming that learners can conduct, without assistance, learning projects that are in their own best interests assumes that they can stand outside dominant ideology and see how ideology defines what they need to know. This assumption is unwarranted. This position also assumes that adults have unfettered access to whatever sources of knowledge or information they need to conduct learning. In an increasingly professionalized world in which access to knowledge is restricted to those licensed by accrediting bodies, information necessary to learning is often politically controlled. Furthermore, scales to measure self-directedness have been judged by some to be too reductionist and to favor learners drawn from a restricted segment of the population. The role of the adult educator as a catalyst and assister of self-directed learning has also been neglected.

The learning model also emphasizes that adult education should be a negotiated process between learners and educators, and that this negotiation should be as democratic as possible. Much writing in adult education over the past 75 years has concerned the ways in which adult education has a role in helping people learn to participate in the democratic process of negotiating their own learning. This was the central concern of Eduard Lindeman, and it is echoed in the work of Paulo Freire and Myles Horton, all of whom saw living democratically as an adult learning process. The learning model does not assume that learners or teachers have any innate knowledge of how to engage in a democratic negotiation of learning efforts. Instead, it requires its participants to study, and become increasingly adept at practicing, what Lindeman called the democratic disciplines. These include learning to honor a diversity of perspectives

and desires, learning to live with the partial functioning of the democratic ideal, learning to avoid the trap of false antithesis (where we are forced to choose between mutually exclusive options), learning to accept the compatibility of ends and means (where we avoid the temptation to bypass the democratic process in the interests of reaching speedily a decision regarded as obviously right and necessary), learning to live with contrary decisions, and learning to appreciate the comedy inherent in democracy's contradictions.

Finally, the learning model urges that adult educators consistently research how learners experience participating in learning. In recent years, the literature on classroom assessment and classroom research has explored this process and provided numerous suggestions for techniques (such as "the muddiest point" and the "one-minute paper") that have become popular with many instructors. At the heart of classroom research is the belief that informed decision making depends on educators having accurate information regarding how and what students are learning. Often teachers are profoundly surprised by the diversity of meanings adults read into their words and actions or by the spread of abilities and levels of learner comprehension revealed. One example of an attempt to turn the constant research of adult learners' experiences into adult educators' practice is the weekly critical incident questionnaire (CIQ) developed by Brookfield. In this questionnaire, learners anonymously answer five questions concerning engaging, distancing, or surprising moments and affirming or puzzling actions in their learning. These responses are then summarized, reported back to learners, and used as the basis of a conversation on how the learning process can best be negotiated. Learners can use the CIQ to give an anonymous critique of the learning program, and practitioners can use it to check the validity and accuracy of their educational assumptions. This instrument has also been used online.

The learning model of adult education is often viewed as emancipatory because it stresses the learner's role in creating and conducting her own learning and the educator's role in supporting these activities. Humanistically inclined adult educators are drawn to its stress on self-actualization and the realization of individual potential, individually determined. Radically inclined adult educators appreciate its conception of learning as a participatory process in which adults learn habits of genuinely democratic practice. One area that has been undertheorized in this model is the exercise of power on the part of the educator. There is a need for more study of how power flows reciprocally between learners and educators, and the way that learner-centered practices sometimes function as what Foucault calls "disciplinary power"; that is, as a way of ensuring that adult learners keep themselves in line. Another area for further scrutiny is the way that learner-centered practices uncritically support dominant ideology. If critical theory's supposition that dominant ideology frames our identities, shapes our world view, and determines our structures of feeling is correct, then allowing learners to decide what and how they wish to learn only serves to keep the status quo intact. From this viewpoint, true learner autonomy is realized only when adults can stand outside the dominant ideological framework and discern how their choices and forms of reasoning have been shaped by it. A critically inclined learning model of adult education would focus on helping adults engage in ideology critique. Such a practice would explore how adults learn to recognize the predominance of ideology in their everyday thoughts and actions and in the institutions of civil society. It would also illuminate how adults learn to challenge ideology that serves the interests of the few against the well-being of the many.

—*Stephen D. Brookfield*

*See also* PEDAGOGY/ANDRAGOGY; SELF-DIRECTED LEARNING

## Bibliography

Boud, D. (Ed.). (1988). *Developing student autonomy in learning.* 2nd ed. East Brunswick, NJ: Nichols.

Brookfield, S. D. (Ed.). (1988). *Learning democracy: Eduard Lindeman on adult education and social change.* New York/London: Routledge.

Brookfield, S. D. (1995). *Becoming a critically reflective teacher.* San Francisco: Jossey-Bass.

Brookhart, S. M. (2000). The art and science of classroom assessment: The missing part of pedagogy. *ASHE-ERIC Higher Education Report Series 27* (1). San Francisco: Jossey-Bass.

Freire, P. (1994). *Pedagogy of hope.* New York: Continuum.

Horton, M. (1990). *The long haul: An autobiography.* New York: Doubleday.

Knowles, M. S. (1984). *Andragogy in action: Applying modern principles of adult learning.* San Francisco: Jossey-Bass.

Tough, A. M. (1979). *The adult's learning projects: A fresh approach to theory and practice in adult learning.* Toronto: Ontario Institute for Studies in Education.

Wlodkowski, R. J. (1999). *Enhancing adult motivation to learn: A comprehensive guide for teaching all adults.* 2nd ed. San Francisco: Jossey-Bass.

# ALLIANCES

Alliances among higher education institutions have been around for a long time. The use of information and communication technologies has promoted the development of new types of alliances in recent years. Traditional on-campus students seem to be shopping for distance learning courses. In 2002, many campuses estimated that the vast majority of their online students were also on campus. As Web-savvy students click their way through course offerings by their local institution, they are expecting more and more courses to be available in multiple formats to fit their schedules and learning preferences. The leaders of higher education institutions recognize the growing need to develop some level of coordination to ensure curricular continuity, enrich the breadth of distance learning options, and keep their students' affiliation.

In the field of distance learning, alliances take on a multitude of forms. Traditionally, alliances defined relationships among similarly situated institutions to allow for the expansion of educational programs beyond the capacity of any one school. In the 1990s, a new form of alliance began to appear: one between "traditional" institutions and other types of enterprises, both within and outside of the postsecondary education community. Alliances are driven by several factors:

- Economies of scale derived from aggregating services and resources (e.g., marketing)
- The ability to participate in programs beyond existing institutional scope (e.g., end-to-end programs among community colleges and upper-division institutions or combining online and clinical programs)
- The ability to award course credits for industry-specific training programs (e.g., project management)
- The ability to "rent" capital that cannot readily be secured by the institution (e.g., capital cost of courseware development)

## ALLIANCES AMONG INSTITUTIONS OF HIGHER EDUCATION

"Conventional" alliances assume several discrete forms. The principal characteristic is that these alliances are among institutions that are each authorized and accredited to offer at least some portion of the academic program. The types of alliances include the following:

*Vertical Online Alliances.* Typically entered into between 2-year and 4-year institutions or between undergraduate and graduate institutions, to allow for seamless articulation across institutional boundaries. So, for example, a student may start with enrollment in the online program of a community college and on completion of that program automatically become enrolled in an upper division program, the outcome of which is a baccalaureate degree.

*Cross-Sector Online Alliances.* Usually involving training materials from a company in the information technology industry paired with student support and guidance from an accredited college or university. It is typical for a student to receive the industry certification as he or she studies a wider set of curriculum materials offered by the institution that awards the course credit.

*Horizontal Online Alliances.* Often described as consortia or competitor alliances, these consist of similar institutions banding together to jointly market their online courses and programs. One form of horizontal alliance simply provides for joint marketing and services, with each institution providing its courses, programs, and degrees independently. Although a common name may be used for marketing purposes, each institution remains separately identifiable: Students enroll in one of the participating schools and receive their credential from that school. However, under the consortium/alliance agreement, the student can seamlessly take courses from any participating institution.

Another form submerges the individual institutional identities into a single "virtual university," with the participating schools becoming transparent to the student. The student enrolls in the virtual institution, taking courses that are actually administered by the participating institutions. The virtual institution creates transcripts of the student's performance and grants the credential.

Horizontal alliances are also useful in enabling institutions to operate across jurisdictional lines, whether interstate or international, by providing access to an already authorized institution within the jurisdiction. In these cases a student within a state or country is able to enroll in an institution authorized to operate within that jurisdiction, and yet take advantage of courses and programs developed by the other participants in the alliance. Each institution adopts the courses offered by the others, so that the students within each jurisdiction are seen as enrolled in local institutions.

*Hybrid Alliances.* These are typically, but not necessarily, entered into between different levels of institutions, but this time the pedagogy changes from one institution to the other. In nursing, for example, a student may enroll in the clinical program offered through a community college and at the same time enroll in the online general education program offered by a 4-year institution.

Another form of hybrid alliance involves the separation of the instructional function from the process of certifying learning (otherwise known as competencies). In this structure, one institution assumes the responsibility of certifying competencies that may have been secured through enrollment in distance learning or other courses offered through a number of cooperating institutions. The student is technically enrolled in the former institution, which provides transcripts for credits arising from competencies earned and ultimately awards an academic credential. This model is different from that of the traditional competency-based institution, which does not involve itself in the prior learning activities of its students.

*Multi-Brand Alliances.* This relatively rare model involves an alliance among a group of institutions that permits one of the group to use the names of the other participants in conjunction with a single brand that denominates the program (and the degree offered). Typically, the participating schools assist in the development of the courseware with the named degree marketed as being offered "in conjunction with" or "in cooperation with" the other participating institutions, or with the participation, advice, or guidance of their faculty.

All these types of alliances are found among the different statewide consortia. In a 2002 survey, Epper and Garn revealed there was a precipitous growth in the number of states forming virtual universities/colleges in

**Table 1**

| Core Academic Function | Function That May Be Contracted Out |
|---|---|
| Establish curriculum | Develop curriculum (courseware) |
| Establish qualifications for, appoint, and generally oversee faculty | Hire and directly supervise faculty |
| Set tuition and fees | Administer collection of tuition and fees and manage financial operations |
| Establish standards for physical facilities | Provide physical facilities |
| Establish standards for learning resources | Provide online or other remote learning resources |
| Establish standards for and admit students | Market and promote the educational program, recruit students, and process their applications for admission |
| Establish standards for academic performance | Administer courses; provide for evaluation of performance (e.g., secure testing) |
| Establish standards for student services | Administer student services |
| Establish standards for and monitor regulatory compliance for student financial assistance | Administer student financial assistance |
| Establish standards for award of credentials and award credentials | Certify satisfactory completion of coursework |

the 2 years following the announcement of the Western Governors University. Although most of these were formed to increase access to underserved populations, regardless of the model, they are now focusing on different goals. The most popular new goals include reducing costs/centralizing resources, increasing communication/collaboration, and developing a better-educated workforce for the organizing state.

## ALLIANCES BETWEEN INSTITUTIONS OF HIGHER EDUCATION AND OTHER ENTITIES

Nontraditional alliances come in even more flavors (see Table 1). The principal characteristic is that one (or more) of the parties is not an *institution* in the sense of being authorized to offer an academic program or grant an academic credential. The key here is the concept of "contracting out" and its converse, "core academic functions." Very simply put, an institution may (with proper supervision) contract out *all* of its activities *other than* its core academic functions.

It should be apparent that each of the functions in the right column, with very limited exception, has individually long been performed by outside entities. What makes the new alliances different is the extent to which these functions are bundled, so that the institution's functions, in their purest form, are exclusively those on the left side of the table. Various forms of nontraditional alliances exist:

*Contractor.* The simplest form of alliance involves the contracting out of certain institutional roles to another, noninstitutional entity. Although institutions have

been doing this for decades, distance learning has opened entirely new markets for contractual services. Very simply put, the institution pays a fee to the contractor to provide services that the contractor has developed through the use of its capital. The contractor benefits from the difference between the cost of providing the service and the price paid by the institution; the contractor has no ownership interest in the educational activity. A contractor usually enters into an agreement directly with the institution.

*Strategic Partner/Contractual.* The contractual strategic partner is not simply providing services to the institution; it is a participant in the service and benefits from the value created by it. In short, there is a common business interest. Typically the contractual strategic partner shares in some of the risk involved in developing the distance learning service and in return receives a portion of the benefit, typically through the sharing of tuition revenues.

*Strategic Partner/Ownership.* This variation creates a joint venture relationship between the institution and the strategic partner. Typically the institution creates, either on its own or in conjunction with the strategic partner, a new entity in which both the institution and the strategic partner have an ownership interest. The institution receives equity in the new entity in return for its contribution of intellectual property; the strategic partner typically provides the cash capitalization. All or some of the activities in the right column may be transferred to the new entity, which in turn contracts with the institution and with the strategic partner for the actual provision of the services. The agreement with the institution is particularly important, because it is intended to protect academic integrity through control over the use of the institution's name and marks.

*Financial Partner.* The partner need not be directly involved in the delivery of services. The development of distance learning programs, including creating courseware and promoting the program, is capital intensive. Institutions tend to be limited in their ability to create capital for short-duration uses; the traditional method of bonded debt is not particularly applicable to courseware, for which the useful life may be a very few years, or for working capital to promote new services. An investor, on the other hand, sees such uses as very appropriate. The common model is much like that of the strategic partner/ownership, except that although the investor capitalizes the new entity created by the institution, it is not involved in the delivery of services.

*—Michael B. Goldstein*
*—Sally M. Johnstone*

*See also* FINANCE; GOVERNANCE

## Bibliography

Epper, R. & Garn, M. (2003, May). *Survey of Statewide Virtual Colleges and Universities.* Retrieved May 2003, from www.wcet.info and www.sheeo.org.

# ALTERNATIVE SECONDARY EDUCATION

Alternative education requires more than a change in the structure of the school. To be considered an alternative school, there must be a difference in the learning process. Alternative educational programs are student centered, and instruction is modified for the student's interests and needs. A distance education school could be very traditional.

## HISTORY

Historically, parents have sought schools in which they could be involved in governance and their children could be self-expressive. In some areas, alternative schools are equated with students lacking achievement or behaving poorly. However, alternative education is appropriate for a wide range of learner abilities and needs, and is not limited to at-risk students with behavioral and academic problems. The empowerment students feel leads to success regardless of ability. Gifted students having difficulty conforming to mass education, special education students in need of personalized attention, and athletes who need to travel during the traditional school year are all candidates for alternative education programs.

In the mid-twentieth century, American alternative schools were created in response to the unhappiness of parents with traditional comprehensive secondary school programs. Schools were often modeled after Maria Montessori's schools and Alexander S. Neill's work, as described in the book *Summerhill.* Families and students participated in self-governing within the learning situation, and self-motivation was encouraged. Accepting learning environments valued both the intellect and the creativity of students. Students had the freedom to learn through exploration, and student opinion was respected and considered. The uniqueness of the child was more important than conformity of behavior and academics.

At the end of the twentieth century, the term *alternative education* was also linked to solutions for at-risk and learning disabled students who did not perform well in traditional high schools. Personalized learning environments could respond to the social and behavioral issues by being student centered.

Currently, alternative secondary education is found in many settings. The education may be provided by a school offering a diploma or in a program within a larger school. A traditional high school may provide online courses, and a school may award credit for community learning. Alternative schools and programs may be public, district supported, state adopted, private, or charter. The structure of publicly supported programs must adhere to state mandates.

## CHALLENGES

Attempts at offering alternative programs at the secondary level run into difficulty when schools are pressured to report credit that may be transferred to traditional schools and accepted by colleges. Some alternative education programs have been highly creative in curriculum and assessment. Assessment is more difficult when students complete project-based assignments or work on thematic units. Schools may report progress in a narrative format rather than using the widely adopted Carnegie unit.

There are also difficulties in offering alternative models when attempting to receive accreditation. The six regional accrediting agencies in the United States have varied ways of evaluating the quality of nontraditional programs. The accrediting agencies that truly evaluate a program based on student learning are not concerned about the structure of the school or the delivery model.

## DISTRIBUTED LEARNING

Distributed learning has been conducted for years through correspondence schools. In a correspondence school, teachers mail assignments to students. Students then complete the course assignments at their own rate and mail them back. Students may complete assignments at different rates. With the advent of computers and the Internet, students may study through electronic correspondence schools. Instead of the mail, coursework is delivered through e-mail or is available on a Web site accessible 24 hours a day. Instruction is conducted using computer programs, video, mail, e-mail, and/or telephone. Teachers e-mail feedback to the students, or the computer grades the work.

Distributed education programs at the secondary level are sometimes referred to as alternative when their structure is compared to traditional high schools: teachers and students are not in the same location, students can complete assignments anytime during the week, and students may complete courses at different rates.

Many distributed learning programs require students to complete a traditional secondary curriculum. All students are required to complete the same assignments regardless of ability and/or interests. Some schools rely on programmed computer applications that may alter assignments based on a pretest, but require students to complete identical lessons. Many distributed education programs have teachers who grade student work but do not provide direct instruction.

Except for the flexibility of study time and the location of the teacher and student, the distance education program may maintain many of the attributes of a traditional brick and mortar school. But the alternative education differs in many more ways than just the location of the teacher and student.

## ALTERNATIVE LEARNING ENVIRONMENT

Alternative secondary education programs are student centered. Instruction is interactive and adjusted to the needs and interests of students in grades 7–12. Although learning expectations may be identical to traditional schools, the process can vary widely. The distributed education model allows for learning to occur in a wide range of environments (see Table 1).

Alternative schools using the distributed education model can apply a variety of the following attributes:

- The school may be committed to a particular teaching philosophy such as mastery learning, where the emphasis is on academic achievement.
- Students are involved in the learning process.
- Teachers modify instructional strategies to meet the student's rate of learning, interests, strengths, and areas needing improvement.
- The staff and teachers are committed to creating an environment that addresses the whole child.
- The student–teacher relationship plays an important part in the development of the student's self-esteem.
- The school may emphasize a particular content area or area of interest.

## ATTRIBUTES

To be considered an alternative school in distributive education, a program must differ from traditional secondary programs in more ways than locality. The attributes of an alternative secondary education program offered distributively may include personalized instruction, modified school attendance, involvement of students and parents in the decision making, emphasis on self-esteem and behavior programs, and open admissions standards.

### Assessment

Assessment in alternative education programs may expand beyond the limits of preprinted tests from textbooks and computer scored tests. Generally, a smaller class size allows teachers to modify the testing format to include oral exams, untimed tests, comfortable settings, immediate feedback, and the like. If students do not understand a concept, it is taught again. The students are reassessed and grades may be improved.

Programs with special emphasis may assess admissions requirements. For example, a school of

**Table 1**

| ATTRIBUTES | Traditional Brick & Mortar | Traditional Distance Education | Alternative Distance Education |
|---|---|---|---|
| Assessment | Standardized | Preprinted | Varied, oral |
| Assignments | Standard for all | Preprinted | Personalized |
| Communication | Teacher to student | Mail or e-mail | Interactive |
| Community | Used sparingly | Used sparingly | Widely used |
| Completion Rate | Semester | Varies | Based on mastery |
| Computer Instruction | Computer lab | Programmed | Computer resources |
| Direct Instruction | Group | None or group | Individual |
| Emphasis | Curriculum | Curriculum | Student |
| Faculty and Staff | Content oriented | Content oriented | Student oriented |
| Location | On site | Distance | Distance |
| Philosophy | General | General | Specific |

performing arts may require students to demonstrate talent. Schools may conduct a prequalification assessment to determine if the student can benefit from the instruction.

## Assignments

Curriculum is often presented in a contractual way to students. They receive credit for assignments when the objectives are achieved. Students may be involved in the development of a learning contract. Assignments may be personalized to a student's interests and needs. No credit is awarded for seat time.

## Communication

In many alternative programs, staff, parents, and students have a role in the governance of the school and the development of the curriculum. Students are empowered when they are involved in this way. Online schools may allow parents to observe instruction and read online grade books. E-mail is used for daily communication and newsletters.

## Community

Alternative schools expand the learning environment by incorporating community activities into the curriculum. Vocational skills are developed through internships and work experience. Credits may be awarded for participation in community programs such as junior theater, private tutoring in music, and sports training. Credits earned in adult school or community colleges may count toward graduation

requirements. Volunteer work is often used to build good citizenship and respect for others.

## Completion Rate

Many alternative schools use mastery learning theory as described by Dr. Benjamin Bloom from the University of Chicago. Students must have a solid knowledge foundation before new learning can occur. Teachers demand demonstration of a minimum level of mastery of each assignment's objectives before allowing students to continue to subsequent lessons. Teachers teach concepts until they are learned.

## Computer Instruction

Alternative education programs may use computer programs to supplement instruction. Computer applications can provide flexibility and creativity in completing assignments and projects. This is different from schools that rely on computer-managed programs in which the student completes a pretest and the computer assigns lessons. Many of these programs' assigned learning activities are identical regardless of the student's interests.

## Direct Instruction

Direct instruction occurs when one student interacts with one teacher. This differs from independent study in which students complete assignments without assistance. Some state education laws set the minimum of teacher interaction to as little as 1 hour per week.

## Emphasis

Students at risk of failing in a traditional school may be referred to alternative education programs. At-risk behaviors may be addressed through specific programs designed to improve self-concept and decision making. In specialized alternative education programs, standards may be adapted to meet the needs of a particular focus such as performing arts. Programs may personalize the program to the student's ability and goals. Districts may require these students to complete the same graduation requirements, but they may receive modified instructional strategies and materials.

## Faculty and Staff

Staff members of alternative schools are empathic to student needs. A major positive attribute of alternative schools is a manageable student–teacher ratio. Teachers can develop personalized relationships with students. There is more direct instruction, faster teacher feedback, and frequent interaction between the student and the teacher.

Students receive the respect of their teachers. Teachers strive to identify ways to motivate the individual student. Ongoing advisement is usually provided to monitor student progress and encourage student motivation. Career and college counseling may be provided from online sources. With distributed learning, students may receive instruction from experts in their fields or via interactive video. Lessons can be archived for replay at a later date.

## Philosophy

Alternative programs offering distributed learning must assist students in developing good study techniques. Successful students have self-motivating behaviors to accomplish assignments. Most alternative education programs stress positive reinforcement that builds self-esteem.

## DISTRIBUTED LEARNING PROGRAMS THAT MAY PROVIDE ALTERNATIVE EDUCATION

Alternative secondary programs can be public or private; currently, the charter school movement is increasing the number of alternatives at the secondary school level. An analysis of each school's attributes must be made to determine whether the program is traditional or alternative. Three major delivery models of distributed education can be considered alternative, depending on the particular program's attributes.

*Correspondence Schools.* Correspondence schools have provided distributed education for decades, but may not provide an alternative learning environment. Lessons and assessments are mailed (or e-mailed) from teacher to student and returned when they are completed. Many of these schools are very structured in their requirements, with little student involvement in the learning process.

*Independent Study.* Students receive work that they complete with no direct instruction. Students may be required to meet with a school staff member for one or more hours each week. Students complete assignments independently. Students may be allowed to enroll in only one subject at a time. In an alternative education program, assignments are adjusted to the student's performance and/or interests.

*Online and Virtual Schools.* The amount of instruction provided by an online or virtual school can vary greatly. Students may receive a lot of direct instruction via two-way video with the teacher or interaction with the teacher in a small group. The student may receive instruction by watching a teacher video and participating in a chat with other students. Or, the student can receive no direct instruction while completing computer programs or assignments posted on a Web site.

## SUPPORT ORGANIZATIONS

Numerous organizations support alternative education. The following descriptions of the organizations are taken from their Web sites:

- The Alternative Education Resource Organization (AERO) was founded to advance learner-centered approaches to education. AERO is a primary hub of communications for educational alternatives around the world. Established 1989. http://www.education-revolution.org
- The *Alternative Network Journal* is dedicated to providing practical information for teachers, counselors, and administrators working with troubled youth. Published by At-Risk Programs Network, Inc. http://www.altnetjnl.org

- The National Coalition of Alternative Community Schools supports the work of students, parents, teachers, and others in the field of alternative education. Established 1978. http://www.ncacs.org
- The National Dropout Prevention Center/Network provides publications, networking, professional development, technical assistance, and an online clearinghouse. Established 1986. http://www.dropoutprevention.org
- San José State University's Alternative Education efforts include a Web site containing activities, instructional strategies, interventions, and field-tested educational materials appropriate for teachers of youth in alternative educational settings. http://alternativeed.sjsu.edu

*—Phyllis Hendry Lindstrom*
*—Karen Bishop*

*See also* HOME SCHOOLING; ONLINE LEARNING

## Bibliography

Barr, R. D. & Parrett, W. H. (1997). *How to create alternative, magnet & charter schools that work.* Bloomington, IN: National Educational Service.

Bloom, Benjamin. (1987). Association of California School Administrators lecture.

Gardner, H. (1991). *The unschooled mind: How children think & how schools should teach.* New York: Basic Books.

Koetzsch, R. E. (1997). *The parents' guide to alternatives in education.* Boston: Shambhala.

McLaughlin, M. W., Irby, M. A., & Langman, J. (1994). *Urban sanctuaries: Neighborhood organizations in the lives and futures of inner-city youth.* San Francisco: Jossey-Bass.

Mintz, Jerry. (Ed.). (1995). *The almanac of education choices.* Roslyn Heights, NY: Macmillan Library Reference.

Neill, Alexander S. (1960). *Summerhill.* New York: Hart.

NCACS. (2002). *The national directory of alternative schools.* Ann Arbor, MI: NCACS.

# ALUMNI

Alumni/ae are the graduates or former students of a university, college, or school. Each school may define its alumni/ae membership differently. Most will include all students who received a degree from the university, but some institutions will also include people who were enrolled for different amounts of time but did not graduate, or those who completed a certificate program. For example, the following is a description of six different ways that campuses define *alumni,* from a survey conducted by the Council for Advancement and Support of Education (CASE), 2001:

1. Former students who have completed at least one year; other former students can apply for alumni/ae status.
2. Graduates of the university, excluding those who graduated only from its continuing education program.
3. Graduates of the university and all former students who have completed some credit.
4. Former students who have completed at least one semester full time.
5. Graduates of a for-profit university's physical campuses and its online programs.
6. Varies according to study-related alumni groups that make up the alumni association.

An institution that makes learning possible online and through other distributed modalities has *de facto* expanded its parameters for defining *student* and *graduate* by not confining the definitions to those who study "on campus."

Coeducational institutions usually use the word *alumni* for graduates of both sexes. Institutions whose student and graduate bodies comprise either a large percentage of women and/or students attuned to the use of nongender-specific language, or those who object to masculine forms in such cases may wish to consider usage that linguistically reflects both masculine and feminine gender (i.e., *alumni/ae* or *alumnae/i*). Or they may prefer the phrase *alumni and alumnae.* We will use the term *alumni/ae.*

Alumni/ae relations professionals focus on making connections with and between graduates that will advance their institutions. The primary purpose of an alumni/ae relations program is to create opportunities for alumni/ae to contribute to the university, college, or school—for example, by helping to develop ambassadors and advocates, recruit prospective students, mentor current students, assist new graduates with the transition, help alumni/ae stay connected with each other, obtain worldly feedback for the institute, and cultivate donors and philanthropic support. Most institutions now understand that the most enduring and successful connections are those made at the beginning—that is, when students commence their relationship and studies with the school. Alumni/ae relations programs routinely reach out to brand-new students and even to prospective students—with alum-student "buddy" offers, or question-and-answer meetings with alumni/ae for new students, for example—in order to set the stage for lifetime involvement early on: "You will be a member of this school for the rest of your life. In partnership together, we will create a meaningful relationship that benefits you the graduate *and* the institution."

## CHARACTERISTICS OF A DISTRIBUTED LEARNING ALUMNI/AE PROGRAM

Why should an institute dedicate resources to develop and maintain a relationship with alumni/ae who live far away and/or connect only through distributed modalities? There are a number of reasons, but these are most fundamental: to involve alumni/ae in spreading the word about the institution, which will attract new students and diversified funding; because the institution thinks it has something worthwhile and special to offer; and because the institution promised its students *a lifelong learning community for lifelong learning.*

The distributed learning institution can maintain traditional contact with its alumni/ae even though the alumni/ae are used to a nontraditional relationship that probably included a significant percentage of its contact online, by e-mail, and possibly in periodic face-to-face exchanges. Hard copy newsletters, magazines, and letters, as well as telephone contact, from the president, provost, deans, advancement team, and faculty remain a vital part of the alumni/ae relations communication strategy. The institute should also ensure that alumni/ae are informed about and invited to all opportunities for learning and for community, both online and face-to-face. To reach a dispersed community, if possible, the institute should organize learning and social events in various regions where students, faculty, and alumni/ae live, and assist alumni/ae in coordination of ongoing periodic meetings for networking, socializing, learning, support, or outreach. Activities and strategies that bring alumni/ae into contact with faculty, with each other, and with students will contribute to fulfillment of the promise for lifelong learning.

Certain basic provisions of an alumni/ae relations program in a distributed learning environment will benefit the alumna or alumnus *and* the program. The institute will need to meet the following objectives:

- *Know where their graduates are.* A data maintenance function must keep up-to-date basic profile information, such as street address, phone numbers, and e-mail addresses.
- *Know more about their graduates.* The Alumni/ae Relations office will want to survey annually or bi-annually for interests, activities, affiliations, research, accomplishments, and competencies of its graduates.
- *Make it easy for graduates to connect; volunteer; locate events; make financial contributions; and locate one another by interests, geography, and year.* All of this can be accomplished by a low-technology, well-maintained Web site with search capabilities, a secure server for making donations, calendars, surveys, and a directory.

Beyond the basics, the distributed learning institution that wants a rich relationship with its alumni/ae will provide:

- *Online learning opportunities* Alumni education programs range from free to expensive registration; from low-tech e-mail contact to high-tech video-streamed conversations. The alumni/ae gain the opportunity to learn from and contribute to other participants online, and the institute reaches alumni/ae who may be too far away to take advantage of face-to-face opportunities.
- *Online Web communities*—These are password-protected places on the Internet where alumni/ae may talk to one another, exchange information ranging from book reviews to networking referrals to personal data, update their profiles, enroll in credit card and other incentive programs, and contribute to the school by shopping at certain stores online. The range of possibilities seems unlimited.
- *Real-time chats and discussion groups*—These can be part of the online seminar or online Web community.
- *Lifetime e-mail address*—This address links the alumna or alumnus with the school (e.g., graduate@ college.edu) and acts as a marketing tool for the institute.

## WILL DISTRIBUTED LEARNING ENVIRONMENTS AFFECT ALUMNI/AE GIVING?

The integrated alumni/ae relations program makes important contributions to the overall advancement program of the institute through such activities as fund raising, development, and communications. By providing multiple opportunities for alumni/ae to feel valued and contribute to the institution, alumni/ae relations programs pave the way for the advancement team to turn students and alumni/ae into donors.

With the growth of distributed learning environments, advancement professionals wonder whether distributed learning alumni/ae will become donors. Research into alumni/ae giving indicates that the most powerful discriminating variables between high and low donors are family income; perceived need for financial support; involvement within the university as alumni, in the Greek system, or in departmental clubs or organizations; and religious preference. This sort of participation is associated with taking courses on campus, not online.

However, research on alumni/ae giving habits for distance education students points to some positive directions for distributed learning institutions to take in their advancement approach. The researchers—David Schejbal, associate provost and director of continuing education at the University of Illinois at Champaign-Urbana, and Faye Lesht, head of academic outreach of the office of continuing education at the same school—report that a "donor-sensibility" seems to arise from *nonacademic activities and relationships*. This suggests that personalizing the relationships between faculty, students, and student services in distributed learning education programs may be vitally important for the creation and maintenance of a long-term healthy fiscal environment for the institution.

For the distributed learning university, college, or school committed to creating and maintaining positive and enriching connections with its alumni/ae, the best results will come from programs and activities that are high-touch, accessible, consistent, relationship-oriented, current, and responsive. Graduates of a distributed learning program will expect to stay connected when the school has provided a relationship-oriented and responsive student experience that seamlessly transitions to one that provides multiple opportunities to contribute as alumni/ae.

*—Cheri Gurse*

*See also* TRANSFORMATIONAL LEARNING

### Bibliography

Brant, Keith. (2002, February). An antidote to the alumni-giving trap. *Currents XXVIII* (2), CASE (Council for Advancement and Support of Education, 202-328-5900).

Shaindlin, Andrew. (2001, February). What's holding us back? *Currents XXVII* (2), CASE (Council for Advancement and Support of Education, 202-328-5900).

Stone, William. (2001, July/August). Rethinking our craft, *Currents XXVII* (6), CASE (Council for Advancement and Support of Education, 202-328-5900).

What's in a Name? (2001, March). *Currents XXVII* (3), CASE (Council for Advancement and Support of Education, 202-328-5900)

Schejbal, D., & Lesht, F. (2002, July). *Distance Education Report*.

# ASSESSMENT OF PRIOR LEARNING

Prior learning assessment usually refers to the evaluation of knowledge acquired through life's experiences by the examination of documentation and/or other evidence. It may also refer to the evaluation of such knowledge by other methods, including testing, interview, demonstration, or performance. A successful assessment of prior learning typically results in earning academic credit, usually toward a college degree. It is essential for the assessment to be conducted by one or more content experts in the subject area under consideration, most often college faculty. In most cases, it is not necessary for the student and the evaluator(s) to be located in the same place.

The most common method used to evaluate prior learning is portfolio assessment; another method is known as credit-by-evaluation or individualized assessment. Prior learning assessment is most commonly conducted at the undergraduate level, but is also done at the graduate level, and even at the secondary level.

Prior learning is acquired "outside the classroom," through a variety of experiences including employment, on-the-job training, volunteer work, reading, hobbies, military or religious training, travel, or through special talents and skills. To earn college credit for prior learning, students must prove to faculty that they possess knowledge of the subject. Evidence of knowledge varies according to the subject under review, but can include certificates, transcripts, licenses, reports, computer programs, creative writing, photographs, artwork, audio and videotapes, job descriptions, resumes, performance evaluations, employment records, annotated bibliographies, letters of recommendation or of verification, or an oral interview.

## THE HISTORY OF THE PRIOR LEARNING ASSESSMENT MOVEMENT

The face of higher education changed considerably after World War II, with larger than ever numbers of adults over the traditional age of 18 entering colleges and universities. In response to this increase in older students, some colleges and universities began devising ways in which to better serve this growing contingent. One of the innovations developed was the assessment of prior learning through methods other than testing. There were no general standards for prior learning assessment at that time, and the institutions that offered it did so with strong faculty support.

In the late 1960s and early 1970s the adult population in higher education soared. This precipitated the creation of collegiate institutions designed solely to serve adults. These institutions offered alternative methods of learning, often independently or under guided mentorship as opposed to traditional instruction, as well as different ways to assess prior experiential learning. Prior learning assessment sent the message to adult students that colleges valued the knowledge they had gained throughout their lives, and that such knowledge could be creditworthy. It was a way of showing acknowledgment of the more mature student, as well as a way to make attainment of a college degree more attractive.

Throughout the country, faculty who respected and were committed to serving adult students participated in what was essentially a grass roots movement to evaluate experiential learning acquired outside the classroom. The Commission on Nontraditional Study, the Carnegie Commission, suggested that methods be devised to assess prior experiential learning. The Cooperative Assessment of Experiential Learning in the mid-1970s, a project of the Educational Testing Service that eventually became the Council for Adult and Experiential Learning (CAEL), endeavored to develop guidelines for this relatively new assessment methodology. The founding leaders in the field of prior learning assessment include Morris Keeton, Urban Whitaker, Warren Willingham, and Harriet Cabell. Innovative faculty and administrative leaders in a scattering of colleges and universities set about to discuss the logistics of implementing prior learning assessment, as well as the method's validity as a means of earning college credit.

Resistance to prior learning assessment within institutions was often vociferous and widespread, with those opposed asserting that the knowledge was not valid or worthy of college credit because it was not acquired in the classroom. Opponents claimed that colleges would be giving away credits, and cheapening the value of a college degree. Proponents, however, eventually convinced many of the recalcitrant that prior learning assessment was a worthy endeavor. The most convincing evidence of the value of knowledge acquired outside the classroom was the adult students themselves. Whether demonstrated in writing or orally, prior learning assessment eventually became more widely accepted as a way for adult students to earn college credit.

## METHODS OF ASSESSING PRIOR LEARNING

The two main ways to assess prior learning are portfolio assessment and credit-by-evaluation or individualized assessment. Different institutions have variations on these basic methods, and some may even use a combination of the two. By far, however, the most common method is portfolio assessment.

Portfolio assessment is the evaluation of a notebook, or portfolio, of evidence of knowledge about a particular subject area, supported by an essay. This method is usually course-driven in that a single portfolio usually represents one college course. (One portfolio may also represent a cluster of closely related courses, such as Beginning, Intermediate, and Advanced Spanish, or Calculus I and II.) The portfolio process typically assumes no discussion or interaction between the student and the faculty evaluator(s), except what is included in the portfolio itself. The student and evaluator(s) may be located at a distance from one another. Therefore, in portfolio assessment, it is paramount that the student clearly express his or her knowledge of the subject matter in an essay designed to elaborate on the enclosed documentation. It is also critical for the documentation or other evidence to be strong and compelling. The evidence, coupled with the essay, needs to present an irrefutable case to the evaluator or evaluation committee that the student truly possesses knowledge of the subject.

Students prepare portfolios by identifying areas of their learning and seeking college course descriptions or syllabi that most closely match their knowledge. The course description or syllabus contains the criteria upon which the student's challenge will be considered. It is most important for the student to select a course that truly reflects his or her knowledge. It is also critical that the student be able to articulate this knowledge in writing. The essay in a portfolio is the student's opportunity to make a case for knowledge acquisition, as well as to explain any deficiencies in the evidence. It is a written request for credit for a particular college course, and must present a persuasive argument to the faculty expert(s) conducting the assessment.

It is also incumbent upon the student to convince the evaluator(s), through the essay, that the evidence contained in the portfolio is authentically the student's. One way to accomplish this is for the student to describe in detail how, when, where, and even why the knowledge was acquired. The portfolio should show both a depth of knowledge in the subject and a breadth of knowledge. Also important is to show that the knowledge possessed by the student is college level, and of a high enough quality to warrant the granting of credit.

For portfolios to be successful, they must show, incontrovertibly, direct evidence of the student's possession of the knowledge. Direct evidence of knowledge, for example, goes beyond a letter from an employer testifying to the student's having held particular duties or accomplished certain achievements. Direct evidence is provided by the student alone, and offers proof of the knowledge or ability in question.

Typically, if there is any doubt as to the student's knowledge of the subject matter, portfolio assessment programs allow for some sort of follow-up challenge. In other words, an evaluator may send back the portfolio asking for additional, specific documentation, or for verification or elaboration of certain statements in the essay. If the evaluator believes the student does not, in fact, have knowledge of the subject matter, he or she will recommend that credit not be awarded.

In contrast to portfolio assessment is credit-by-evaluation or individualized assessment. In this method of prior learning assessment, the parameters of knowledge are usually defined not by a course description or syllabus, but by the student and/or the faculty evaluator(s). Therefore, the criteria by which the student's learning is evaluated need to be explicated in writing. In essence, the faculty evaluator(s), or the student, writes a detailed course description or syllabus, based on the particular knowledge of the student. The knowledge parameters do not need to mirror that which would be covered in an existing course.

The most critical aspect of credit-by-evaluation or individualized assessment is the student's ability to articulate his or her knowledge, either orally or in writing. This type of assessment may very well be conducted in person, with the student and evaluator(s) sitting face-to-face. Or it may be conducted over the telephone, or even online. Documentation is often important, but it may be overlooked or even considered superfluous, depending on the quality of the student's articulation of the learning. As in portfolio assessment, there needs to be no doubt that knowledge of the subject is truly and authentically possessed by the student.

## THE PROCESS OF ASSESSING PRIOR LEARNING

In institutions that conduct prior learning assessment, faculty, or those whose credentials attest to their expertise in the subject matter, are selected for assessments. Faculty evaluators also need to be trained in how to conduct assessments of prior learning to ensure that they apply the appropriate criteria, as well as validate the areas of knowledge. In addition to being subject-matter experts, evaluators should be sensitive to the way in which adult students learn through experience, and open to the value of independent learning. Evaluators should also provide appropriate and adequate feedback to students; any student who becomes engaged in the assessment process has invested time and effort, and deserves to receive a thorough and thoughtful evaluation. Detailed feedback is especially crucial when some sort of follow-up response is sought from the student before the assessment can be completed.

The credit value of each learning component or subject area being assessed may vary. If, as in portfolio assessment, the student is challenging a specific course, the number of credits challenged is usually the same as those of the course. If, as in credit-by-evaluation or individualized assessment, the student or evaluator is defining the parameters of the learning component, the number of credits is often assigned by the evaluator(s), and validated by a faculty committee (or some other individual or group that provides oversight of the assessment process).

The total number of credits earned through prior learning assessment that may be used toward a college degree varies from one institution to the next. Some institutions place arbitrary limits, some have limits based on their residency requirements, and very few have no limits. (Most institutions have residency requirements that cannot be fulfilled by credit earned through prior learning assessment.)

## Quality Assurance in Assessing Prior Learning for Credit

The "bible" of prior learning assessment is Dr. Urban Whitaker's book, *Assessing Learning: Standards, Principles, and Procedures.* In it he discusses the "10 standards" for quality assurance in assessing learning, in general, for credit. For prior learning assessment programs to be valid, it is essential that they espouse and exhibit these 10 academic and administrative standards.

### Academic Standards

1. *Credit should be awarded only for learning, and not for experience.* Experience may be easier to measure than learning, but there is no guarantee that any given experience will result in learning, or that the same experience will yield the same breadth and depth of learning for two different individuals. Knowledge, or the *outcome* of one's life experiences, should be what is assessed.

2. *College credit should be awarded only for college-level learning.* If undergraduate credit is being sought, the learning should be at a level similar to what is taught in an undergraduate college course. Likewise, if secondary level or graduate level credit is sought, the learning should be at that level. The level of knowledge is not always clear cut (e.g., the difference between high school foreign language studies or beginning college-level foreign language studies). Informed judgment is necessary to make a valid assessment.

3. *Credit should be awarded only for learning that has a balance, appropriate to the subject, between theory and practical application.* Stereotypically, classroom learners comprehend the theoretical aspects of a subject, and experiential learners grasp the practical aspects. Appropriate mastery of theoretical or practical aspects depends on the subject matter; however, experiential learning may be deemed college level and appropriately theoretical if it is transferable to contexts other than the one specific to the individual's experience.

4. *The determination of competence levels and of credit awards must be made by appropriate subject matter and academic experts.* Both content expertise and an understanding of academic contexts are necessary to make a valid assessment; therefore, faculty are usually most qualified to conduct this work.

5. *Credit should be appropriate to the academic context in which it is accepted.* A student's prior learning may fit into the degree program's major, general education requirement, or electives; credit should be granted as appropriate.

### Administrative Standards

6. *Credit awards and their transcript entries should be monitored to avoid giving credit twice for the same learning.* Errors of this kind can be avoided by well-classified transfer credit in the degree program, and clear and elaborated assessments of prior experiential learning.

7. *Policies and procedures applied to assessment, including provision for appeal, should be fully disclosed and prominently available.* Students should be made aware of the exact policies governing the assessment process, preferably through print materials, before beginning.

8. *Fees charged for assessment should be based on the services performed in the process and not determined by the amount of credit awarded.* As in the traditional classroom, whether or not credit is earned, a fee (or tuition) is charged. To ensure fairness and quality, fees may be contingent on the number of credits *attempted* or *assessed,* but never on the number of credits *awarded.*

9. *All personnel involved in the assessment of learning should receive adequate training for the functions*

*they perform, and there should be provision for their continued professional development.* It is critical that faculty assessing learning, as well as advisers and other staff working with students in prior learning assessment, be well trained and receive continued development.

10. *Assessment programs should be regularly monitored, reviewed, evaluated, and revised as needed to reflect changes in the needs being served and in the state of the assessment arts.* Prior learning assessment programs may be reviewed internally, or through external professional development of staff, advisory committees, external evaluations, and adherence to the guidelines set forth by various professional organizations.

## THE VALUE OF PRIOR LEARNING ASSESSMENT FOR STUDENTS, FACULTY, AND INSTITUTIONS

Faculty and administrative practitioners familiar with prior learning assessment are well aware of the benefits it may hold for students beyond the acquisition of college credit. Prior learning assessment also may have value for the faculty who conduct assessments, as well as the institutions that house such programs. This was discussed in "Outcomes Assessment of Prior Learning Assessment Programs," by Debra A. Dagavarian and William M. Walters in a 1993 monograph.

In addition to earning credit toward a college degree, students may profit from prior learning assessment in other ways. Prior learning assessment provides students with a context for understanding the nature and structure of college-level learning; it is in itself a learning experience and helps students to begin setting educational objectives; it gives students enhanced self-esteem and a sense of "self"; it validates the student's readiness to continue on for further education; and, very simply, it expedites the student's achievement of a college degree.

Faculty and institutions may derive benefits, as well. Prior learning assessment broadens a faculty's usual way of interacting with, and changes their perspective on, the subject matter; it enhances their understanding in other disciplines; it raises their sense of self-esteem within the institution; and it enables them to interact with students in a qualitatively different way than is traditional. The value of prior learning assessment to institutions is in an enhanced institutional image. Prior learning assessment demonstrates the institution's flexibility and responsiveness to adult students; it creates a culture of self-examination with the institution; and it attracts greater numbers and diversity of adult students and faculty.

*—Debra A. Dagavarian*

*See also* EXPERIENTIAL LEARNING

### Bibliography

Dagavarian, D. A. (2000). The coming of age of prior learning assessment. *The Journal of Continuing Higher Education, 48*(1).

Dagavarian, D. A., & Walters, W. M. (1993). Outcomes assessment of prior learning assessment programs. In *Support of prior learning assessment and outcomes assessment of prior learning assessment programs: The proceedings of the National Institute on the Assessment of Experiential Learning.* Trenton: Thomas Edison State College.

Flint, T. A. (1999). *Best practices in adult learning: A CAEL/APQC benchmarking study.* New York: Forbes Custom Publishing.

Lamdin, L. (1997). *Earn college credit for what you know,* 3rd edition. Dubuque: Kendall/Hunt.

Mandell, A., & Michelson, E. (1990). *Portfolio development and adult learning: Purposes and strategies.* Chicago: Council for Adult and Experiential Learning.

Simosko, S., and Associates. (1988). *Assessing learning: A CAEL handbook for faculty.* Columbia, MD: Council for Adult and Experiential Learning.

Whitaker, U. (1989). *Assessing learning: Standards, principles, and procedures.* Philadelphia: Council for Adult and Experiential Learning.

Zucker, B. J., Johnson, C. C., & Flint, T. A. (1999). *Prior learning assessment: A guidebook to American institutional practices.* Chicago: Council for Adult and Experiential Learning.

# ASSESSMENT OF STUDENT COMPETENCE

Assessment in higher education historically refers to the evaluation of student learning. Although assessment has recently come to encompass the evaluation of teaching, programs of study, and even whole institutions of learning, these other arenas of assessment are still significant only with respect to student learning. Currently, in what has become a vast and contested area of study, the field of assessment is in flux. Much that has been taken for granted is now under critical review, and many new concepts and theories are being developed and rigorously tested as scholarly research. Nonetheless, assessment activities are mostly conceptualized as occurring within the context of individual classrooms and single institutions. Thus, the potential impact of distributed learning environments on our understanding and practice of assessment has yet to be fully appreciated.

A distributed learning environment recognizes, even legitimizes, learning that takes place in a variety of settings, in a variety of ways, and for a variety of purposes. When students acquire knowledge on their own, at work, in the community, from locally accredited private institutions, as well as from conventional institutions of higher learning, assessment procedures developed only in the conventional institutions become problematic. Moreover, the diversity, not only of the settings for learning, but also of the learners themselves, significantly increases the number of reasons students pursue new knowledge. The range of purposes is further extended by goals vigorously promoted by new, nonacademic stakeholders. As learners seek new sources of relevant knowledge, not only term by term, but course by course; as online learning becomes more prevalent; and as life-long learning becomes so important that nonacademic institutions compete in developing new courses and whole curricula, new concerns, not yet fully recognized, come to increasingly dominate the field of assessment. What is learned, how its quality should be judged, and how its outcome should be evaluated are questions that can no longer rest upon the tacit understandings of the past. Thus, distributed learning environments bring into focus new complexities of assessment that will undoubtedly alter the current terrain. Just as it redefines what it means to learn, so too does distributed learning redefine how that learning is assessed.

The best way to illustrate the range of issues associated with the assessment of learning not controlled by a single academic entity is to identify and describe the questions that the world of distributed learning has provoked. Indeed, the exploration of these questions may well become integral to the process of creating the specific evaluative procedures that the answers demand. In other words, asking questions is not only

useful, but it also may become a defining, possibly transformative, feature in the field of assessment as it confronts an environment consisting of multiple and diverse opportunities for learning.

## WHAT IS THE GOAL OF THE LEARNING TO BE ASSESSED?

In a world of diverse learning opportunities, learner demands for relevance, fairness, and accountability require that the assessment process begin by determining what each student expects to acquire. Is the goal of their learning?

- To gain new information?
- To legitimize previous learning?
- To develop specific technical skills?
- To become broadly literate in certain scholarly disciplines?
- To prepare for professional training?
- To learn new and better ways of acquiring knowledge?
- To become more emotionally and/or cognitively mature?
- To see the world from a new and more critical perspective?

Moreover, what outcome do the learners expect? Are they seeking a credential, such as a certificate or a degree? Do they intend to acquire a marketable professional or vocational skill? Or are they expecting to become broadly (or liberally) educated in preparation for an as yet unspecified future? To assess whether learners' purposes have been met, it almost goes without saying that those purposes must first be clearly specified.

In the past, particularly in relatively structured or formal educational settings, students rarely have been seriously asked such questions. In assessing the success of the learning process, it has been the teacher (or teachers) that represents an academic institution or learning organization who has been expected to know, or decide, what the learner's purposes should be, and then later whether they have been met. And for many teachers, it seemed self-evident that whatever they were interested in teaching would be, by definition, what the students should want to learn. However, with an increasingly diverse student body and many new constituents interested in educational outcomes, such as employers, state legislators, and policy-makers, the authority and power of the teacher have greatly lessened. Particularly in today's world, where the learning process is increasingly conceptualized and operationalized as a highly politicized and market-driven industry, these multiple interests must be explicitly acknowledged and weighed in the development of any new effective system of assessment.

## WHY IS THIS LEARNING BEING ASSESSED?

Another set of questions that in the past was rarely considered relates to the purposes of the assessments themselves. Why is it important to know, and indeed, who wants to know, how well the students have acquired whatever they intended, or expected, to learn? Is the evaluation primarily for the learner? Or is it also for the teacher? What about the institution that controls the learning process? Or the learner's employer or the organizations that might hire the student now or in the future? Or even the learner's community or the government? Obviously, different stakeholders will have different reasons for wanting assessments to take place, and thus assessment processes will necessarily differ considerably depending on what they are designed to achieve. Are they expected to provide motivational or informational feedback to the learner? Or are they helping to improve the pedagogy of the teacher? Should they be designed to evaluate the effectiveness of the organization in which the learning occurs? Or should the assessments primarily determine whether the learner has met the criteria required for all students with similar learning interests? Should assessments take into account the needs and expectations of present or potential employers? Or, should they be designed to help the community or government better understand the talents and skills of the population? As learning increasingly becomes a valued commodity in today's "information society," even more groups will become interested in determining the nature and quality of any new learning. Thus, the evaluative situation promises to become even more complex, underscoring the importance of identifying the reasons for engaging in assessment as explicitly as possible.

The involvement of more and diverse audiences makes clear that the concept of successful learning is not singular or simple. Moreover, the distributed learning environment itself adds another complicating factor to this process. In this new environment, the learner will be acquiring knowledge from many sources, so each different source expects to design and implement its own "local" assessments. So far, it has fallen largely upon the academic community to coordinate and judge these different evaluations, and then to convert them into a common language. However, as learning becomes less uniquely concentrated on college campuses, and as the effectiveness of learning becomes an important issue to many people who are not directly connected to the academic world, institutions of higher learning will be less able to monopolize the role of final assessment authority.

## WHEN SHOULD ASSESSMENT TAKE PLACE?

The purposes of assessment also affect questions of when and how often these assessments ought to take place. For example, should the learners be assessed prior to beginning some specified learning engagement? If so, for what purpose? To evaluate and accredit their previously acquired knowledge? To assess their "readiness" or capability or motivation to acquire new knowledge? To determine what the individual or group of students actually needs to learn? To help the teacher develop appropriate learning materials? To establish a benchmark against which to evaluate what value may be added by the planned learning engagement?

Assuming some decision can be made about the purpose of examining the learner's existing knowledge, other questions follow: Should assessment be continued as an ongoing process throughout the learning engagement, or should it be confined to some agreed upon endpoint? If it is to be a formative process, what does the assessor hope to achieve? To improve the efficiency or effectiveness of the ongoing learning? To assist the teacher in the development of activities and appropriate resources? To serve as a learning opportunity for the student? If, on the other hand, it is to be a summative process, again, what is the purpose? To allow the learner to be compared to other learners by sorting them into some kind of hierarchy of achievement? To satisfy an external audience that the learning engagement was successful or useful? To determine whether a student can earn a formal statement of achievement that she can use in other settings? Or to meet some particular, often parochial, need of the institution, of the community, or of the government?

How often assessments should occur is also related to the question of particularity. Should learners be evaluated task by task, topic area by topic area, skill by skill? Or should they be assessed at, for example, the beginning and then again at the end of a larger educational journey? Or should they be tested throughout their lifetimes with respect to the acquisition, or maintenance, of any number of different conceptualizations of new knowledge?

## WHO SHOULD DO THE ASSESSMENTS?

Prior to the recognition of distributed learning opportunities, the agents of assessment were almost always the teachers, unless they themselves were to be evaluated. Conflicts of interest were rarely considered systematically. In an environment where learning may occur in a variety of settings (for example, if students study on their own, if workers train each other, if private or public institutions offer their own courses taught by their own employees), it becomes evident that the student, the worker, or the institution is not the most appropriate agent to conduct objective assessments. Logic would suggest that a similar situation occurs in those more formal learning situations that involve professional teachers. In other words, if the role of instructor-as-assessor can be called into question in one setting, that dual role becomes questionable in any setting. Of course, teachers are as yet very reluctant, indeed hostile, to any suggestion that their students be evaluated by someone other than themselves, They argue, rightly so, that only they know what it is that they intended. However, in a world of distributed learning, their intentions are no longer the only key determinant of learning outcomes.

Thus, it becomes a question of some import to ask who should perform, indeed control, these assessments. To what degree, for example, should they be developed so as to satisfy the teacher, and to what degree should they be expected to also satisfy the individual learner and address his or her particular, perhaps even idiosyncratic, goals? How much control over the assessment process should be exerted by the other stakeholders in a given learning situation, such as the academic institution, other similar institutions, the community, the workplace, other organizations, and/or the government? No matter what response these questions elicit, the answers will still fall short if they do not also address one of the most important expectations of assessment in a distributed learning environment: namely, that whoever controls the assessment process can no longer be answerable to only one or two constituencies. Assessment in one setting now has to be acceptable and useable in any of the many other settings that define this new and complex learning environment. Failure to meet this criterion will clearly call into question the academic legitimacy, if not the viability, of distributed learning.

## HOW SHOULD THE LEARNING BE ASSESSED?

The last step in developing a program of assessment in any environment is to create or locate the appropriate means of evaluating what the learner has acquired. In the past, this aspect of assessment has been subject to intense scrutiny and considerable research. Indeed, it has often been considered the primary question in the field. A very large body of knowledge has accumulated related to testing instruments, theories of measurement, statistical methods, issues of reliability, validity, and standardization. The advent of distributed learning does not seriously challenge that literature, because most assessment questions concerned with the method or instrument to use in a distributed environment are the same as those raised in more conventional settings. Many of these questions are familiar ones: Should the assessment tools use existing models or be customized? Should tests be exclusively scorable by machine or should they include "short answers" or essays that must be scored by hand? Less familiar questions are equally relevant: What value is added by alternative methods such as oral examinations, portfolios, checklists or rubrics, performance evaluations, and other types of "authentic" assessments, and for what kinds of learning are they best suited? Should learning be defined primarily as the acquisition of new information and cognitive skills, or should the definition also include the expectation of change in affective aspects and such seemingly "ineffable" attributes of the learner as citizenship, moral character, or spirituality? Distributed learning environments offer a new opportunity for considering these important questions in yet another way.

Certainly, technology and distance have already added some interesting challenges to the testing field. These center around such concerns as preventing or detecting new ways of performing academically dishonest acts; effectively assessing learning and performance when the student is physically distant from the teacher; evaluating the usefulness of assessment techniques that have become only recently available, such as computerized discourse analyses; and finding ways of assessing virtual classrooms that may now include learners from different cultures with different learning styles and different levels of skill in the English language. The field of testing, however, has been built around the process of asking such questions, and for that reason alone, the development of actual evaluation instruments is probably the area of assessment that is least affected by the introduction of distributed learning.

On the other hand, the field of tests and measurements has also served as a platform for the development of a large and powerful testing industry. What role will this industry play as a mechanism of "quality control" in a world of distributed learning? One possibility is that the industry could itself become the primary agent of control in assessment, a third party outside the complexity of multiple learning environments. Another possibility is that the testing industry might successfully ignore these issues by embracing the learning methods and goals of only one dominant interest group. Yet a third, rather different, possibility is that the industry, because of its long association with research, could address the challenges raised by distributed learning environments by exploring new and creative methods of assessment. For example, by capitalizing on current and emerging technologies, testing companies could take the lead in investigating other approaches to assessment besides those that are standardized, which, although seemingly practical, are nonetheless problematic in a world that encourages and supports diversity. As with all other questions about assessment in a distributed learning environment, issues related to the tools of assessment will also deserve thoughtful and critical attention.

## CONCLUDING COMMENT

The major challenge in assessing distributed learning is to recognize that open-endedness, rather than closure, will define this field. Certainty will become a casualty in the practice of assessment. Assessment theory, too, will need to attend to current conceptualizations of knowledge and research in a postmodern world. The kinds of questions introduced above reflect these new directions in inquiry. They also have the potential to stimulate new ways of thinking about and evaluating learning that have

not yet been imagined. That is the very heart of the promise of assessment in the world of distributed learning.

—*Xenia Coulter*
—*Alan Mandell*

*See also* Cognitive Skills/Cognitive Development; Outcomes; Plagiarism

## Bibliography

American Council on Education. Center for Adult Learning Educational Credentials. (n.d.). *Guiding principles: Learning outcomes.* Retrieved from http://www.acenet.edu/calec/dist_learning/dl_outcomes.cfm.

American Council on Education. Center for Adult Learning Educational Credentials. (n.d.). *Joint statement on the transfer and award of credit.* Retrieved from http://www.acenet.edu/calec/pdfs/Credit_Transfer.pdf.

Banta, Trudy. (Ed.). (2002). *Building a scholarship of assessment.* San Francisco: Jossey-Bass.

Heywood, John. (2000). *Assessment in higher education: Student learning, teaching, programmes and institutions.* Philadelphia: Jessica Kingsley.

Higher Learning Commission. (2002, March). *Assessment of student academic achievement: Levels of implementation.* Retrieved from: http://www.ncacihe.org/resources/assessment/ 02-Adndm-Levels.pdf.

Higher Learning Commission (n.d.). *Assessing prior learning for credit.* Retrieved from http://www.ncacihe.org/resources/adctf/assessing.pdf.

Mandell, Alan, & Michelson, Elana. (in press). *Portfolio development and adult learning: Purposes and strategies,* 2nd Edition. Dubuque, IA: Kendall/Hunt.

Palomba, Catherine, & Banta, Trudy. (1999). *Assessment essentials: Planning, implementing, and improving assessment in higher education.* San Francisco: Jossey-Bass.

Zucker, B. J., Joynson, C. C., & Flint, T. A. (1999). *Prior learning assessment: A guidebook to American institutional practices.* Dubuque, IA: Kendall/Hunt.

## Relevant Periodicals

*Assessment and Accountability Forum* (formerly *Adult Assessment Forum*). For information, see http://www.Phoenix-institute.org

*Assessment Update.* For information, see http://www.interscience.wiley.com/cgi-bin/jtoci?ID=86511121

# ASYNCHRONOUS FORMATS

*Synchronous* formats (for example, in-person conversations) require specific, on-time exchanges. *Asynchronous* formats are used for communication and information exchanges that are intermittent and do not have specific timing requirements. In online conversations, where the dialogue occurs through Internet-based exchanges of ideas and information, asynchronous formats allow the conversations to be extended over time. Freed from the constraints of real-time interaction, asynchronous online dialogue allows time for reflection and thoughtful responses.

E-mail and newsgroups use asynchronous formats to exchange information directly among people, via the Internet. In other asynchronous formats, people send information, via the Internet, to Web site–based newsgroups, mailing lists, discussions, or bulletin boards. When information is posted onto a Web site, it becomes available for others to read and will remain available until it is removed.

Asynchronous formats are ideal for distributed learning communities in which people live in different time zones and have varying levels and forms of hardware, software, and Internet access capacity. With more time to consider and respond to ideas, online learning opportunities are equalized among people with different learning styles, work schedules, languages, cultures, online competencies, and physical needs. As flexibility in response time supports reflective inquiry and critical thinking, learning is associated with the thoughtfulness and quality of ideas, rather than the quickness of response.

Although material that is posted online is immediately available, participants have time to retrieve, read, and respond to messages. Similar to written correspondence in which a note is delivered to a colleague's mailbox, an asynchronous online message may remain unopened and unread for a period of time. The pace of communication depends on the time it takes the recipient to respond to a message. As the time between the sending of a message and its response shortens, asynchronous dialogue becomes similar to synchronous dialogue.

Although asynchronous formats support in-depth learning, they often require competent facilitation and careful organization to achieve their intended learning outcomes. Unattended asynchronous communication can fade into inactivity and increase the sense of isolation among distributed learners. When people send messages and no one responds, it is easy to feel alone and to interpret the lack of response as meaning that others do not care.

## VARIETIES OF ASYNCHRONOUS FORMATS

Specialized server computers employ the specific software and hardware needed to support each asynchronous format. Server computers are maintained by Internet service providers (ISPs) and online services that specialize in Internet access, as well as some organizations, universities, and distributed learning institutions. Each of the following asynchronous formats uses a unique set of guidelines, referred to as *protocols,* that guide and direct the transmission of its messages across the Internet.

- *Linear asynchronous formats* display messages in the order in which they were posted. Although linear formats are useful for brainstorming, socializing, and keeping current on news, they are often problematic for tracking specific topics or themes, especially when there is a jumble of posted messages concerning multiple topics.
- *Hierarchical asynchronous formats* organize messages by topics and themes, while retaining information on the author and the time of posting. Conversations need to be on topic, because shifting and intermingled themes can reduce the value of topic-focused dialogues.
- *Threaded conversations* within hierarchical models retain linkages among postings for a single topic and all of its associated subtopics. Just as a single thread can be traced through a complex tapestry, so may topics be traced from the most recent messages back to their original postings, revealing the development of threads of ideas.
- *Directed hierarchical formats* use facilitators to create and post the topics, and other participants post replies. In *nondirected hierarchical formats,* all participants can create and reply to topics. Nondirected formats may have poor responses if participants have low expectations for interaction. By rotating facilitation, participants can develop a greater sense of cohesion and shared ownership for the liveliness and depth of online conversation.

Some models of asynchronous communication require all participants to post messages at prespecified intervals. Although these models can maintain high levels of participation, they require careful planning and preagreements to adhere to the rules of the dialogue.

## E-MAIL

The most common asynchronous format is electronic mail, widely known as e-mail. To use e-mail services, people need to have e-mail accounts with unique e-mail addresses, use e-mail software to send and receive e-mails, and have access to an e-mail service. When an e-mail message is sent over the Internet to a recipient's e-mail address, it is stored in an electronic mailbox, located on an e-mail server computer. Using e-mail software, recipients access their mailboxes via the Internet and retrieve messages into their own computers.

Although e-mail has been available since the early 1970s, and remains the primary form of Internet-based communication, its effectiveness for online learning is impacted by an increase in e-mail volume, often creating *e-mail overload,* in which people receive more e-mails than they can manage. Each day's e-mail may include messages from family and friends, business communications, educational notices, commercial messages, and unwanted junk e-mail. Strategies to manage this increasing volume of messages include software-based prescreening of messages, automatic deletion of junk e-mail, and organizing messages into predefined folders, according to the topic or the e-mail address of the sender.

E-mail viruses are mini software programs that disrupt, damage, or destroy computer data. They are pervasive, deceptive, and increasingly sophisticated. Once released into the online environment, these viruses are designed to invade a computer's programs and data, and then to proliferate, infiltrating e-mail address books and attaching duplicates of themselves onto outgoing e-mail messages. As virus-detection systems are revised, the developers of illicit viruses create more cunning and powerful generations of viruses that bypass existing detection systems.

## NEWSGROUPS

Newsgroups are asynchronous e-mail discussion groups that focus on a special topic. People access newsgroups through ISPs and online services that manage and maintain the newsgroups on specialized news server computers.

A newsgroup message is similar to a notice on a bulletin board—it can be read by anyone who has access to the newsgroup. Newsgroup messages are physically posted on each news server computer that offers access to the particular newsgroup. Although anyone can create a newsgroup, the ISP or online service is not obligated to post any particular newsgroup on its news server; it can screen out or censor messages it does not want posted.

People add messages to the newsgroup by e-mailing messages to their own news server. The news server distributes the messages, via the Internet, to all other news servers that offer the newsgroup. Because the postings on newsgroups are physically located on multiple news servers, if a newsgroup disbands, its messages may continue to exist on news servers around the world.

Newsgroups may be open to the public for reading and posting, or may be restricted to registered users. The groups are often moderated to ensure that the postings are relevant and otherwise acceptable. With moderated newsgroups, the newsgroup software intercepts submissions and e-mails them to a moderator who serves as a gatekeeper, reviewing and approving them before they are posted. The moderator may be an individual, a group, or customized moderator software.

The name of a newsgroup describes the conversation topic of the group, and locates it within an existing hierarchy of topics. There is a specific naming schema that flows from the most general to the most specific (e.g., alt.soc.college.financial-aid).

*Usenet* refers to the set of all Internet newsgroups. The Big Eight newsgroups are large, highly respected newsgroup topics: computing, humanities, miscellaneous topics, news, recreation, science, society, and talk. Specific rules and requirements regulate the establishment and management of all Big Eight newsgroups, helping to ensure consistently high quality.

## MAILING LISTS

Mailing lists support the asynchronous exchange of e-mail messages among groups of people who share interests on a specific topic. Thousands of mailing lists are dispersed across the Internet, distributing documents, electronic journals, news bulletins, advertisements, pictures, audio, and video material on an ever-increasing variety of topics.

To subscribe to a list, a person sends a request to a designated e-mail address linked to a list's server computer. Any subscriber to the list can post a message by sending it to the list's e-mail address. The file server then distributes a copy of the e-mail message to all members of the mailing list.

Once a subscriber joins a mailing list, it is easy to stay connected and to use the service. The management of mailing lists normally involves only maintaining accurate member information. Subscribers are able to remove their names from the list through an *unsubscribe* message. When mailing lists are disbanded, access to messages (if they have been archived) is dependent on the willingness of the list sponsor to store the messages and/or to make them available through various means such as search engines.

## WEB-BASED DISCUSSIONS: BULLETIN BOARDS AND ONLINE FORUMS

Web-based discussions take many forms, from simple bulletin boards to complex online forums. To access Web-based discussions, people have to be online and connected to the Web site that holds the discussion. Simple *bulletin board* forums contain posted messages and replies to the messages. More complex online forums have several layers of hierarchical topics, including archived files of prior discussions.

Some Web-based discussions are public, open to anyone who accesses the associated Web site. Access to a private Web-based discussion requires preregistration, which can be either open to anyone who self-registers or restricted to members of a specific group. Some forums require registration fees or active subscriptions to sponsoring newspapers, publications, or associations. If registration is required, members must use a unique username and password to access the dialogue. There may be different levels of member access, with members at some access levels allowed to read only, and members at other levels able to add and modify topics, documents, pictures, audio, and video.

Bulletin board Web forums are sequential postings of messages related to specific topics. Web forums often have thousands of members worldwide, who share interests on a single bulletin board. Academic institutions often support multiple levels of bulletin boards. Top-level bulletin boards contain institutional information. The curriculum level contains specific material for each course. A help level may contain frequently asked questions (FAQs) regarding the technology and e-mail service. Special interest groups (SIGs) focus on topics related to specific interests. News groups contain current information from Internet news services and other news organizations. There is also often a free-for-all board where people are free to post anything of interest to the community.

Web-based forums range from complex, multi-faceted conversations sponsored by institutions and large organizations to small forums built on an individual's personal Web site. Each forum has rules for posting, reading, and organizing messages.

*Unmoderated forums* are self-organized and uncensored, encouraging the free exchange of ideas and information by all participants. In *moderated forums,* postings are initially screened by a person or by specialized software. The moderator is responsible for the entire site and makes decisions about editing, archiving, and removing postings.

In *threaded discussions,* comments and postings are organized in a relational manner, based on the topic of the discussion. Other designs are based on chronology, usually with the most recent postings appearing first, regardless of topic. The remaining postings follow, in linear fashion.

Web-based discussions often include direct links to other Web sites, encouraging participants to access additional Web-based information, databases, and discussion groups.

If participants have access to compatible software tools, they can create and modify documents asynchronously. With collaborative document sharing software, participants can identify and track changes made to an existing document. When other users retrieve the modified document, they are able to identify the changes that were made by previous authors. Revisions are often tracked by software that may use different colors for the text, highlight changed text, and use a strike-through format—as in ~~strike through~~ for the letters of deleted text. Modified documents can be viewed and printed in a final format that includes (but does not indicate) changes, or in a format that identifies all of the modifications, including designating which author created each modification.

Because the information posted on a Web-based forum physically exists only on the server that holds the Web site, if the forum is deleted from its Web server, it no longer exists.

## STAY TUNED . . .

As new generations of innovative technologies are created and refined, there will be even more powerful ways for members of distributed learning communities to collaborate and engage in meaningful asynchronous dialogue. Language translation software, voice recognition systems, virtual realities, and robotics are just a few of the emerging technologies that will extend the scope and power of asynchronous online learning opportunities.

*—Dorothy E. Agger-Gupta*

*See also* Synchronous Formats

### Bibliography

Adams, T., & Clark, N. (2001). *Effective online communication.* Fort Worth: Harcourt College.

Bonk, C. J., & King, K. S. (1998). *Electronic collaborators: Learner-centered technologies for literacy, apprenticeship, and discourse.* Mahwah, NJ: Lawrence Erlbaum.

Davis, B. H., & Brewer, J. P. (1997). *Electronic discourse: Linguistic individuals in virtual space.* Albany: State University of New York Press.

Hoefling, T. (2001). *Working virtually: Managing people for successful virtual teams and organizations.* Sterling, VA: Stylus Publishing, LLC.

Jonassen, D. H. & Peck, K. L. (1999). *Learning with technology: A constructivist perspective.* Upper Saddle River, NJ: Merrill.

McLaughlin, M., & Rafaeli, S. (Eds.). *Journal of Computer Mediated Communication.* Available at http://www.ascusc.org/jcmc/index.html.

Mehrotra, C., Hollister, C. D., & McGahey, L. (2001). *Distance learning: Principles for effective design, delivery, and evaluation.* Thousand Oaks, CA: Sage.

# AUTHORING TOOLS

Authoring tools are often described as software programs that let developers or instructional designers create content without needing to write programming code. For a large number of authoring tools, this is true. Many of the most popular tools, however, include their own sophisticated scripting languages or use programming languages such as JavaScript to allow developers to create powerful e-learning content by writing functions line by line.

As little as 10 or 15 years ago, it was easy to identify authoring tools. The instructional development process was straightforward and well-established. Computer-based training (CBT) courses, delivered via CD-ROM or over a network server, were designed and authored using turnkey authoring packages—and there were many. By 1993, there were over 165 authoring tools; however, many of these no longer exist. Some of these tools have survived and been adapted for use on the Internet; others have simply disappeared without a trace.

Back then, developers would go through a process of careful analysis, create high-level design documents, and then create script storyboards with extensive detail describing how the courses would be authored. The next step in development was called "authoring." Authoring specialists and/or programmers would use authoring tools to convert the paper-based design into actual learning programs. This allowed authors to assemble text, graphics, media, and animations, and to thread them into interactive, programmed instruction.

Remnants of this process still exist in current instructional development models. However, they have been dramatically altered to accommodate rapidly changing content and rapid content creation needs. Beyond that, content authoring really has not changed much.

What has changed is the spectrum of products that provide different styles of content authoring. There is no longer just a simple list of popular authoring products to choose from. Now, one can choose from many different methods of authoring content. Authoring functionality can even be found embedded inside other products, such as a learning management system (LMS). Many organizations simply choose to author in the same LMS product that manages learner access and keeps track of learner progress. Others will use off-the-shelf, general-purpose Web page creation tools to create learning content.

Web page developers have quickly adopted the term *authoring* to describe the process of creating a home page, although this term was clearly borrowed from early instructional developers. The broad use of the term *authoring* makes defining authoring tools specifically for creating learning applications difficult. Applications provide exceptions to almost every criterion. Attempting to compare two different authoring tools to find what they have in common can be much more difficult than listing their differences.

## AUTHORING TOOL DIFFERENCES

Authoring tools are often imagined to be in the realm of WYSIWYG (What You See Is What You Get) environments, where objects such as graphics, audio, and video clips are simply imported and dropped into position on a page. In reality, many authoring tools lack a WYSIWYG environment. Instead, they use a form-based interface. To create content, the user enters content into fields, making selections using checkboxes and drop-down lists, and then previews or publishes the work.

Other authoring tools use a timeline metaphor, allowing the user to drag objects and actions onto the timeline, so that they appear or disappear at a specific point in time in the lesson, as if one were editing a movie. Or, the tool might use a flow chart metaphor, with icons representing images, sounds, decisions, and the like placed on the flow line of a flow chart.

Still other authoring tools (in particular products used to create software simulations) use a recorder metaphor. The developer turns the recorder on and clicks through a procedure that is to be simulated for learners. The developer stops recording and edits the result, adding text, audio, and interactions.

Very rarely, a new product appears that uses an entirely different authoring metaphor, for example working within a spreadsheet interface and synchronizing events using the time stamp of a video clip.

A factor contributing to the difficulty in defining authoring tools is that these applications are quickly evolving. For example, a growing number of tools have appeared that are designed for content sharing and reusability. These use a database to store components of a course, and the individual "learning objects" are broken down to the smallest size possible for easier reusability. This allows a developer to update the source content in the database and have all courses automatically updated. Although many agree that working with content in this way is logical and efficient, creating an infrastructure that can manage content in this way (especially media that consume a lot of bandwidth) can become expensive.

## AUTHORING TOOLS AND CONTENT

When one looks at the richness and variety of available e-learning content, it shouldn't be surprising that authoring tools are so different from each other. E-learning content includes courses, assessments, simulations, demos, Web pages, and presentations. Also, e-learning content often comprises Adobe Acrobat and Microsoft Office files, further blurring the lines between authoring tools and other software applications such as conversion software and business application suites.

Authoring tools produce e-learning content that is as varied in format as in function and appearance. E-learning authoring tools publish content in HTML, DHTML, XML, and Java applets as well as in a large number of proprietary file formats that require a browser plug-in. In addition, individual authoring tools can publish content in different formats for specific situations. This allows developers to author content for an environment that uses browser plug-ins, or create generic HTML and JavaScript using the same tool.

Not only can modern authoring tools often publish content to many different formats, but they also are increasingly able to publish to entirely new platforms. As wireless information devices such as Palm and Windows CE handhelds, pagers, and smart phones (among others) continue to find their way into our daily lives, so too is training content. More and more authoring tool vendors are either including the ability to publish to these devices in their existing authoring tools or producing authoring tools specifically aimed at this fast-growing sector of learning that deals with PDA-type devices. Although these applications are often aimed at corporate markets (e.g., field training in the construction industry), they hold much promise for academic use (e.g., teaching and training doctors).

## AUTHORING TOOLS AND STANDARDS

As e-learning becomes an increasingly popular training and learning solution, LMSs are being installed and implemented in growing numbers. An LMS automates the administration of training events, registers users, tracks courses in a catalog, manages online assessments, records data from learners, and provides reports to instructors.

Although many learning management systems contain built-in authoring capabilities, none offer the ability to create such a wide range of content as is possible with a suite of third-party tools. No single LMS, for instance, can provide the ability to create Flash animations, Java applets, animated GIF files, and instructional games. Authoring tools built into an LMS are often aimed at importing media elements such as images, audio and video clips, animations, and simulations, and assembling the pages using this content. So, although an LMS may contain authoring capabilities, many developers still turn to third-party authoring tools for the development of specific components.

Integration of authoring tool content with learning management systems raises the issue of interoperability. For an LMS to be able to track a course or assessment created with a third-party authoring tool, the LMS and authoring tool must be able to communicate. The course, for instance, may contain assessment questions. The LMS must be able to track whether the student successfully answers these questions, as well as whether the course was completed or abandoned. For the LMS to be able to track the course, communication standards need to be in place.

The e-learning world contains a number of standards, including Aviation Industry CBT Committee (AICC), Sharable Courseware Object Reference Model (SCORM), IMS (IMS Global Learning Consortium Inc.), and Dublin Core Metadata Initiative (DCMI). By far the most popular standards are AICC and SCORM. SCORM is currently receiving more attention, even though its specification is still evolving and no SCORM certification is presently available.

If a tool is AICC-certified, it means the Aviation Industry CBT Committee has tested the product and attests that it conforms to their specifications. Other authoring tools may state that they conform to SCORM or are compliant with AICC. Some authoring tool companies have made standards compliance a priority. It's important to remember, however, that terms such as "compliance" and "conformance" mean that the authoring tool vendor feels the product adheres to these standards. No objective third-party testing and certification has taken place.

Also, some authoring tool vendors claim that their product is AICC-compliant if they feel that they comply with *any* of the nine AICC Guidelines and Recommendations (AGRs). This can be quite confusing and requires diligence on the part of developers when choosing an authoring tool.

This may paint a poor picture of the state of authoring tool compliance to standards, but in reality, standards compliance holds great promise for the future. Using compliant authoring tools assures developers that they can create and publish e-learning content to their learning management system and also assures them of the interoperability of content and presentation.

## AUTHORING TOOL CHOICES

E-learning content developers now have a greater choice of authoring tools than ever before. Not only are many specialized tools available to create specific types of content, but also many products are presently available to create traditional online courses. That means content developers now can select a tool that best suits their preferred method of authoring or their level of technical ability.

Ease of use has become an important criterion for many content developers. Some authoring tools on the market allow developers to publish e-learning content to the Web after only minutes spent learning the tool. Many of these tools come with attractive graphical templates. With these tools, there's no need to design an interface, make the interface elements such as buttons operational, manually manage hyperlinks, and so on. The authoring tool does all of that. Developers simply select their preferred graphical template, type in content, and publish.

Whereas ease of use may be an important requirement for some content developers, others may prefer a tool that provides powerful extensibility and flexibility. These authoring tools may take much longer to learn but provide complete control over the functionality and presentation of content. Some of these products are so powerful they even provide programmers and developers with functions needed to write complex, database-driven Web applications.

Products exist to fit all levels of technical expertise and just about any budget, and they can deliver e-learning content to a wide range of platforms in many different formats. More and more product vendors provide fully functional trial versions of their authoring tools, allowing developers the luxury of working with an application before buying. Although most authoring tools have been used to create interactive learning for corporate training (i.e., the efficient delivery of content and courses), there is every reason to believe that the same types of authoring tools (be they Web-based, open-standards tools, or proprietary tools) will continue to be used by all proponents of distributed learning, and will simply follow the technology and delivery needs of instructors.

—*Brandon Hall*

*See also* LEARNING MANAGEMENT SYSTEMS (LMS)

## Bibliography

Beckschi, Peter, Hall, Brandon, & Piskurich, George M. (1999). *The ASTD handbook of training design and delivery.* New York: McGraw-Hill Professional.

Hall, Brandon (1997). *The Web-based training cookbook.* New York: John Wiley & Sons.

Horton, William K. (2000). *Designing Web-based training.* New York: John Wiley & Sons.

Khan, Badrul H. (1997). *Web-based learning.* Englewood Cliffs, NJ: Educational Technology.

Khan, Badrul H. (2001). *Web-based training.* Englewood Cliffs, NJ: Educational Technology.

Kruse, Keving, & Keil, Jason. (1999). *Technology-based training.* San Francisco: Jossey-Bass.

Lee, William W., & Owens, Diana L. (2000). *Multimedia-based instructional design.* San Francisco: Jossey-Bass.

# B

## BROWSER

A browser is a software program that, once loaded onto a computer, helps the user to navigate the Web. Popular browsers include Microsoft Internet Explorer and Netscape Navigator. Most computers come with Internet Explorer or Netscape Navigator already loaded. Some Internet service providers (ISPs) such as AOL and Earthlink offer their own browsers as part of the software package. In most cases users can exit their software and use other browsers once they are connected to their ISP.

When loaded, browsers act like attractive, colorful universal remote controls for the Web. Whereas a universal remote for television controls what and how the viewer watches, a Web browser influences the user's Web surfing experience. Any time a user visits a site, she views it through a template on her monitor's screen that is created by the browser software. The browser "controls" consist of clickable buttons at the top of the screen. The Web pages themselves are viewed through a window within the browser's boundaries, in the bottom of the screen.

As time goes by and Web programming languages evolve, browsers are periodically updated to be able to interpret new types of programs. Creators of different browsers compete by coming out with new versions of their browsers that incorporate new links, code, technology, scripts, and functions. Users should update their browser software periodically to take advantage of these improvements.

Like a universal remote, a browser contains a variety of common functions, in addition to some special functions that may or may not work with all Web sites and Internet service providers. Common features include buttons that, when clicked by a mouse, allow the user to search for a topic, review previously viewed pages, and then return to the page they started with. Another button can stop a Web page from loading. Browsers also include access to search engines, such as Google, Yahoo, Lycos, Netscape Search, and LookSmart. Search engines help the user find Web pages about particular topics. To use a search engine, the user types words related to a topic into a space on the screen and clicks on the "search" button.

The top of the browser contains options that allow the user to set "preferences" (e.g., set the size of the type on the page, show or hide hints and toolbars, access e-mail accounts, or use security features), set up "bookmarks" or "favorites" (these save information about favorite pages and offer quicker access to them), and/or set up e-mail address books. There is also a "help" button to help the user acquire additional information about browsers, programs, computers, and the Web.

Browsers often have a Web site associated with them called a *home page*. Netscape's home page is http://www.netscape.com, and Internet Explorer's page is http://www.msn.com. These pages are similar to magazines and newspapers in content. They include links to sections about sports, news, business, weather, entertainment, and the like. They also include advertisements and a classified section. In addition, these home pages offer resources such as phone and e-mail directories, free software, maps, stock market reports, headlines, tools, and other useful information. To return to a browser's home page, the user just clicks on a button marked "home" or on the icon (picture) of a house.

—*Lynn H. Collins*

*See also* INFORMATION RETRIEVAL; INTERNET; INTRANET; INTERNET SERVICE PROVIDER

# CAFÉ

A virtual learning café is built on principles developed by Juanita Brown and a global network of dialogue practitioners in their work on world café conversations. World cafés are a way to create a living network of conversations around questions that matter. A face-to-face café conversation is a creative process for leading collaborative dialogue, sharing knowledge, and creating possibilities for action in groups of all sizes. A virtual learning café uses these same principles, but for asynchronous online learning and collaboration. The seven basic principles are:

- Create hospitable space.
- Clarify the context.
- Explore questions that matter.
- Encourage everyone's contribution.
- Connect diverse perspectives.
- Listen together for insights, patterns, and deeper questions.
- Share collective discoveries.

To create a "hospitable virtual space" where the participants feel safe and comfortable, participants are asked to introduce themselves and describe their backgrounds and interests, as well as their goals and expectations for the time they will be participating together. The participants then suggest and agree on some basic norms for how to use the space and how to carry on a respectful dialogue. They are encouraged to speak from their hearts and use a first-person voice in their online postings. This initial check-in helps establish mutual trust and a willingness to be open.

As a facilitator/teacher, it is important to set the stage by creating a structure and a common understanding of the learning topic. This is done by letting the participants choose different texts to read and post short reviews focused on what caught their interest. This helps establish a common conceptual context and vocabulary that will be used in the cafés. The first real learning dialogue consists of commenting on each other's reviews with a focus on what new insights they have learned. This activity is designed to help the participants feel comfortable giving positive feedback and to show that there is no right or wrong way, but rather many different ways, to view a topic. The role of the facilitator is to create an atmosphere that is welcoming and inclusive, and at the same time to establish clear expectations of what is acceptable and what is not.

After the first two weeks of "check-in" and getting comfortable, virtual learning cafés are set up. Every participant serves as a café "table host" for at least one topic. The café question/topic might be connected to a project the hosts are involved in at work or a concept they want to learn more about. The individual hosts post a "think paper" with information about the topic, their own reflections, and why this topic matters to them. They include references to a variety of additional resources, including books, articles, and Web sites where the participants or visitors to their café conversation can find more information. The hosts also frame a question or questions that will serve as the "attractor" for the café dialogue. At the end of each café period the hosts post a summary of what they learned in their café.

The cafés contain ongoing dialogues and suggestions posted by the visitors. The facilitator's role is to make sure the focus is on the topic, participate in the dialogue, and make new connections or encourage a direction of inquiry that might not have occurred to the participants. The facilitator also gives tips regarding where to find more information in order to gain new insights and learning. The virtual café uses threaded discussion software that helps the user follow a thread, or postings that are interconnected.

Virtual cafés function best with between six and nine participants. If there are fewer than six participants, the dialogue becomes less dynamic; if there are more than nine participants, exchange of ideas is extremely hard to follow because the threads can be incredibly long and complicated, and it is easy to get lost. Larger groups can be divided into two or more subgroups, each consisting of six to nine participants.

By having the participants move from café to café, carrying seed ideas from one café conversation to another, they are continually exchanging thoughts, experiences, ideas, and questions. Participants are weaving ideas between the café conversations and bringing additional references into the evolving online café conversations. Each café round spans a period of 2–3 weeks, and two or three cafés usually take place simultaneously, so there are opportunities for concepts to combine and recombine, forming a rich web of interconnections and interactions between the participants. This moving around and cross-fertilizing of ideas and experiences between cafés creates a highly collaborative learning experience. The facilitator then hosts a special café, a social space, where people can drop in at any time for a chat with the facilitator or others regarding non–topic-related interests and concerns. This is one of the cafés where the most authentic personal dialogue occurs around key issues in peoples' lives and work.

The virtual learning café emphasizes the role of contribution. The individual café hosts post their think papers as a "gift" to others in the learning community. The purpose of the café is not to criticize, but to give and contribute something. The visitors are asked to contribute their own experiences, thoughts, ideas, or references to different resources by checking in at least twice a week. By doing this they experience how knowledge is alive and growing as different themes, threads, and patterns begin to emerge.

The participants realize that the quality of their learning can actually be much higher than in a normal face-to-face classroom setting where the instructors put themselves in the role of experts. In the virtual café, everyone is the expert. Knowledge shared in a café is "egalitarian"—everyone's ideas are thoughtfully considered as contributions to the whole. The participants have more time to reflect before making contributions than in a face-to-face classroom setting. Everybody's voice is heard. Another advantage is that people can see everyone's contribution in writing. They can see the patterns and weave ideas more easily when they can read through what everyone has said. They also have time to find interesting resources and make a deeper contribution into each café topic, including testing assumptions and mental models.

At the end of a virtual learning café, all participants post a reflection paper about what they have learned from the overall café process and discuss how they can use this shared knowledge in their lives and work. This enables all participants to get a sense of the whole by seeing the patterns made by everyone's diverse contributions.

*—Bo Gyllenpalm*

*See also* CRITICAL DIALOGUES; FACILITATION; GROUP PROCESS; INSTRUCTIONAL TECHNIQUES

### Bibliography

Brown, J. (2002). *The world café. A resource guide for hosting conversations that matter.* Mill Valley, CA: Whole Systems Associates.

Brown, J. (2001). *The world café. Living knowledge through conversations that matter.* Mill Valley, CA: Whole Systems Associates.

Gyllenpalm, B. (2002). Virtual knowledge cafés. In K. E. Rudestam and J. Schoenholtz-Read (Eds.). *Handbook of online learning: Innovations in higher education and corporate training* (pp. 419–436). Thousand Oaks, CA: Sage.

For more information see http://www.theworldcafe.com

# CAREER PLANNING AND DEVELOPMENT

Career planning and development refers to the process of attempting to find a successful match between the learner and the world of work. Through the career planning and development process, learners attempt to gain a clear understanding of self, research occupational choices, establish career and professional goals, and design and implement an academic plan for achieving these career goals. To gain a clear understanding of self, learners clarify their own career or professional interests, preferences, and values; realistically appraise their academic- and career-related abilities, skills, and aptitudes; gather information about occupations and the working world; sometimes gain some exposure to occupational fields they are exploring through volunteer work, internships, and field placements; and develop an academic and career plan for achieving the goals they set. In this way, career development and planning emphasizes effective decision making. Career planning also involves learning job search and placement skills such as successful application and resume writing, interviewing, and managing the job search experience. Finally, career planning and development usually is closely linked with academic planning and advising, because academic choices usually are influenced by career goals—especially for nontraditionally aged distance learners who pursue distributed learning.

Community colleges, colleges, and universities usually offer comprehensive services to assist the learner in the career planning and placement process. Most commonly, institutions offer a stand-alone career development center, staffed by career counselors as well as college student personnel generalists. Comprehensive career counseling centers offer a wide range of services, including the following:

- Individual or small group career counseling and standardized assessments (paper and pencil or computerized measures) of career interests and preferences to assist learners' self-exploration
- Individualized instruction, consultation, and workshops regarding nuts-and-bolts job search skills such as resume writing and interviewing
- Placement services, including job information, internship or field placement programs, job fairs, and bridges between job-searchers and employers.

Many career centers bring employers to the institution to conduct interviews right on campus. Career counseling services also may be found outside the career development center, in college counseling and mental health centers, or in individual academic colleges. Career development may also be a part of academic planning and advising services at the institutional or departmental level.

## CAREER INTERESTS, VALUES, NEEDS, AND PREFERENCES

Many of the traditional career development services are aimed at helping learners analyze data about their own interests, values, needs, and abilities, so they can search for career choices that are a good match with their own intrapersonal and interpersonal characteristics and qualities. Career decision-making considerations also include the practical, such as financial goals, academic ambitions, the relative prominence career will have in the person's life, and geography. Most career centers use occupational inventories to provide learners with feedback about their personality characteristics, preferences, and interests. Some of the most widely used inventories are the Self-Directed Search (SDS), the Myers-Briggs Type Indicator (MBTI), the Strong Interest Inventory (SII), and the Kuder Occupational Interest Survey (KOIS).

The best-known system for organizing and interpreting career preference information is Holland's basic personality typology. SDS and SII both are based on "Holland codes." According to Holland's typology, a person's career interests may be divided into six categories or themes:

- *Realistic theme*—Tends to center around active work with one's hands, using tools, and building and repairing. Learners with strong "realistic" preferences like to work with material things rather than people or ideas. They may be less skilled when expressing themselves verbally or communicating feelings. Often they prefer working outdoors. Some ideal career matches for those with strong realistic preferences include technology, agriculture, some engineering specialties, military work, agriculture and farming, and construction or skilled trades.
- *Investigative theme*—Tends to center around science and scientific activities. Learners with strong "investigative" preferences enjoy solving abstract problems and are motivated to understand the physical world around them. They prefer thinking through problems to acting them out. Such people enjoy ambiguous challenges and do not prefer structured situations

with many rules. Some ideal career matches for those with strong investigative preferences include engineer, biologist, social scientist, research laboratory work, physicist, and technical writer.

- *Artistic theme*—Tends to center around self-expression. Learners with strong "artistic" preferences are aesthetically oriented and motivated by problems and challenges that require originality and individualistic expression. They prefer work settings emphasizing independence. They do not prefer highly structured problems. People with high artistic scores are interested in artistic creation, such as through writing, music, art, or theater. Some ideal career matches for those with strong artistic preferences include author, artist, composer, interior designer, or drama coach.

- *Social theme*—Tends to center around social, humanistic interests and concerns about the welfare of others. Learners with strong "social" preferences usually express themselves well and have good interpersonal skills. They prefer being involved in interpersonal situations and group dynamics, and having an effect on the interpersonal arrangements and relationships of others. They do not prefer physical work or an emphasis on working with equipment. Some ideal career matches for those with strong social preferences include clinical psychologist, counselor, teacher, school administrator, therapist, and leisure and recreation professional.

- *Enterprising theme*—Tends to center around the use of communication to sell, lead, and persuade other people. Learners with strong "enterprising" preferences tend to pursue higher-than-average incomes, are energetic and self-confident, and often pursue work in sales. They prefer involvement in power, status, persuasion, and the pursuit of material wealth. Some ideal career matches for those with strong enterprising preferences include sales work, business executive, political campaigner, realtor, marketing or sales manager, lawyer, or insurance agent.

- *Conventional theme*—Tends to center around highly ordered activities, both verbal and numerical, that characterize office activities. Learners with strong "conventional" preferences seek structure, order, and predictability. They prefer structured job settings where they know exactly what is expected and what is required of them. They work effectively within a chain of command or in an organizational structure, and may be somewhat uncomfortable in leadership roles. Like enterprising types, they often value

material possessions and status. Some ideal career matches for those with strong conventional themes include tax expert, financial analyst, accountant, computer technologist, bank teller, and examiner.

Correspondingly, workplaces and career settings also may be characterized according to Holland's system. Realistic work environments require manipulation of tools, machines, and objects. Investigative work environments require research and study of the physical, biological, social, or cultural world. Artistic work environments require artistic, literary, musical, or dramatic creation. Social work environments require interaction with others to teach, train, educate, facilitate, or improve adjustment or functioning. Enterprising work environments require persuasion of others to achieve personal and organizational goals. Conventional work environments require organization and manipulation of data, information, materials, and the work space.

Career development and planning centers help learners gain a better understanding of self and different work environments by using Holland's typology as well as other measures, systems, methods, and educational or counseling formats. These methods help learners identify the best potential fit between their own characteristics, interests, and needs, on the one hand, and the characteristics of different workplaces, jobs, and career settings on the other hand.

## JOB SEARCH SKILLS

Comprehensive career planning and development centers also teach learners the job search strategies and skills required to pursue and land the jobs that will begin, advance, or change their lifelong career path. These services include individual consultations, workshops, role-plays and mock interviews, and resume editing services.

Covered in these formats are job-searching skills such as establishing goals and a plan; sources of job leads and job opening information, such as newspapers, Internet, professional journals, and government listings; and use of field placements to gain exposure and experience. Also covered are career writing skills for completing job applications, traditional resumes, electronic resumes and personal Web pages, cover letters, and other forms of communication. Similarly, interview skills and other forms of communication are reviewed and practiced.

## CAREER PLACEMENT

The institution's career planning and development center often has primary responsibility for helping learners successfully gain employment. Job search information usually is provided in both hard copy and electronic databases that list openings in industry, business, teaching and education, government, social services, and nonprofit sectors and fields of most interest to the institution's learner population. Many institutions hold general or specialized job fairs, which offer learners and potential employers an opportunity for brief, preliminary application reviews and first interviews. Many institutions, or individual colleges within the institution, provide space, scheduling services, and other resources that allow employers to conduct full searches and interviews "on location." Career center staff may be assigned to particular colleges or academic programs in order to provide more specialized job search assistance to learners in particular fields.

## CAREER PLANNING AND DEVELOPMENT, ACADEMIC PLANNING AND ADVISING, AND DISTANCE LEARNERS

Traditional career planning and development focuses on increasing learners' understanding of self (one's career-related interests, values, needs, ambitions, and abilities), improving the learners' knowledge of the working world (types of work environments best suited to their own characteristics, different jobs and fields, working conditions and expectations, as well as academic and other qualifications for entry employment and advancement in different fields), and facilitating good decision making (making effective lifelong career decisions that combine an understanding of self, the working world, and academic preparation). Career planning and development also is closely linked to academic planning and academic advising. Choices about academic program or course of study, degree, major, and classes are influenced in part—often in large part—by career plans.

All institutions provide academic advising for their learners, and many find ways to link career planning and development services with academic advising and planning services. Methods include offering career assistance and academic advising together in a single office at the institutional, academic college, or academic department level; offering career development courses (either credit or noncredit) that combine career and academic decision making; and integrating career information into the regular academic advising process.

Some research has begun to show that the combination of academic advising, counseling on course work, and career development services is of special importance when providing support for the retention and success of learners at a distance. Although the distance learning population continues to change, today's distance learner typically is a nontraditionally aged adult student who already has work experience, often has had limited or unsuccessful prior college academic experiences, is balancing work and family with school, and is pursuing distributed learning mainly to achieve career-related goals such as career advancement, certification or licensure, or change of occupational fields. Therefore, they often have different career planning needs than traditional campus learners.

Along with career decision-making and job placement issues, nontraditional learners in distributed settings who are less familiar with academic planning and college life management skills often require new skills for academic decision making and academic life management. In turn, career planning and development for the distance population often is more closely and explicitly linked with academic planning. For example, combined career and academic planning services for nontraditional learners at a distance also may be designed to teach course scheduling skills and advise learners about curriculum and course selection as a decision-making process related to eventual career goals; show relationships among different degree programs, majors, and specific courses and the related career decisions, job placement, career advancement, professional certification, or salary increases; help learners explore different educational alternatives, choices, and formats; and provide resources and support. Nontraditional career planning may focus on how specific components of an overall degree program are interrelated, short-term and long-term benefits of academic selections, meaningfulness of the educational experience to real-life outcomes, and the practical relevance of academic choices to career development goals.

At some institutions, career planning and development services and academic planning and advising are provided to distributed learners in part by college student services generalists, who combine career and academic issues and have a special focus on distance learners. At other institutions, traditional career planning and development services, as well as combined career and academic planning, are provided to learners at a distance via telephone tie-ins, toll-free phone lines, and e-mail to main campus career specialists and academic planners. Some institutions adapt nearly all of the main campus career planning and development center's job search and job placement services and other functions for interactive use via the Web. For example, many of the most common career self-exploration inventories, such as the SII and MBTI, are available at institutional or other Web sites in formats designed for Internet use. Computerized career development packages also are used; two of the most well-known are the System of Interactive Guidance and Information (SIGI Plus) and Discover. Similarly, instructional components regarding resume design and interviewing, as well as electronic databases of job openings, are offered.

Faculty may augment career planning services during virtual office hours. Alternatively, some institutions rely on student services personnel, faculty, teaching assistants, or others at special, geographically remote sites to provide career assistance in person. In addition, learners at a distance sometimes make periodic visits to an institution's main campus for services.

*—Alan M. Schwitzer*

**See also** ACADEMIC ADVISING

## Bibliography

Holland, J. L. (1997). *Making vocational choices: A theory of vocational personalities and work environments,* 3rd ed. Odessa, FL: Psychological Assessment Resources.

Lock, R. D. (2000a). *Taking charge of your career direction: Career planning guide, Book 1*, 4th ed. Belmont, CA: Wadsworth.

Lock, R. D. (2000b). *Job search: Career planning guide, Book 2*, 4th ed. Belmont, CA: Wadsworth.

Meyers, I. B. (1993). *Introduction to type.* Palo Alto, CA: Consulting Psychologists Press.

Schwitzer, A. M., Ancis, J. R., & Brown, N. (2001). *Promoting student learning and student development at a distance: Student affairs concepts and practices for televised instruction and other forms of distance learning.* Washington, DC: American College Personnel Association.

Walsh, W. B., & Osipow, S. H. (1994). *Career counseling for women.* Hillsdale, NJ: Lawrence Erlbaum.

# CASE STUDIES

Case studies are descriptive texts of human experience that include real-life details of environmental conditions surrounding particular events. The narratives may vary in length from a few paragraphs to book chapters or longer, often including exhibits and endnotes. The case study is both a research design for empirical investigations and a pedagogical method for teaching problem solving. As research designs, case studies are often employed to describe, analyze, and evaluate material of contextual richness and complexity. Research questions dealing with issues of *how* and *why* phenomena occur, such as group-, organizational-, and system-level events, are suited to this method of investigation. These studies may include both quantitative and qualitative data collected from a variety of sources with inputs reflecting multiple perspectives. When intended for teaching purposes, case studies are developed and used to illustrate concepts and principles of an academic field or discipline, with discussion questions, suggested readings, and case teaching notes.

A scholar wishing to use case studies for teaching or research should first look for resources and support within that scholar's own discipline. Business management, public administration, social work, political science, environmental sciences, and neuropsychology are among a growing number of fields utilizing case studies for both research and teaching. Long a favorite teaching method of sociologists and business professors, case study adoptions have grown to include new disciplines and a wide variety of study topics. Traditional sources of published cases include academic journals, casebooks, textbooks, educational publishers' lists, and libraries. Newer or less well known sources include professional organizations, such as case writers associations, which offer advice and assistance to those wishing to develop their own cases for publication in a supportive atmosphere. Other sources include corporate and public sector training programs, online publishers, online libraries, and course Web sites.

Unlike traditional educational settings where case studies are used, distributed learning environments offer special opportunities for materials integration and collaborative experiences. Typically, class discussion is a critical part of teaching and learning from case studies. Online discussion sessions can be structured in several ways. Case study questions may be addressed thoughtfully in threaded group conversations (asynchronous), moderated by either the instructor or a designated group leader; alternately, questions may arise in chat rooms (synchronous) during impromptu conversations, or as features of special events online. Sensitive student questions can be submitted and responded to individually via e-mail. For computer-mediated courses, Web sites can be designed to include rich text with embedded hyperlinks to additional learning resources. Other useful teaching materials include archival video or audio interviews; texts of official documents, memos, letters, and e-mail addresses; and diagrams, drawings, charts, and graphs. Possibilities for collaborative exercises include project teamwork to manipulate spreadsheet data, for example, provided the learning software permits this type of data sharing. Another activity might be editing text documents in small groups. Appeals to multiple sensory experiences, flexible formats, and computer-mediated interactivity may increase student involvement with the learning materials.

Interest in using case studies in teaching has increased dramatically during recent years, in part as a reaction to education's traditional dependence on lecturing. Case discussion classes help to achieve core educational objectives, including developing curiosity, sensitivity, judgment, discernment, and the ability to apply specific knowledge and general concepts to particular situations. The case method has proven highly effective pedagogically in accomplishing these objectives. Learning theorists also agree that developing critical thinking skills fits well with the case method of teaching. A classic taxonomy of critical thinking skills describes critical thinking as a hierarchical progression, developing from relatively low levels of comprehension to higher levels of application,

analysis, and synthesis, to the highest level of evaluation. However, learners tend to move back and forth among these various levels—often intuitively—in the critical thinking process. The case method challenges students to consciously and formally (1) describe what they have understood and absorbed from the case; (2) apply whatever decision rules seem relevant; (3) analyze the facts; (4) synthesize what has been learned; and (5) evaluate the data for qualitative and quantitative implications with recommendations for action and implementation. This is the general approach to critical thinking using case study materials.

To assist the instructor, published teaching cases usually include an instructor's manual or case teaching notes. A successful teaching note includes a brief abstract highlighting the key issues in the case, a description of the intended audience for which the case has been developed, suggested teaching and learning objectives, discussion questions and answers, and a bibliography. A case teaching note may also contain additional teaching ideas and an epilogue to bring the case up to date. Supplementary materials available for use with the case may include videos, audiotapes, CD-ROMs, games or simulations, and URLs for recommended Web sites.

For research purposes, designs involving multiple case studies or embedded cases can allow for more rigorous data collection methods and systems approaches. The use of a case study for formal program evaluation is another special type of case methodology. With very complex problems, such as crisis management or environmental safety, the analysis may involve inputs from interdisciplinary teams (e.g., integrated risk assessment, multi-attribute utility theory, and scenario analysis). Key issues and problem areas are often nontransparent, and multiple stakeholder interests are involved. All phases of the research process require systematic care, including study design and methodology, data collection, data analysis, and report writing/editing phases to enhance validity and reliability of results.

As noted earlier, case writing associations are excellent resources for scholars wishing to develop expertise in case research, case-based instruction, or case writing skills. Organizations such as the North American Case Research Association (http://nacra.net) and the World Association for Case Method Research and Application (http://www.wacra.org) provide leading edge support for professional development, including opportunities to attend conferences, to publish, and to develop professional relationships with other case writers and teachers.

—*Barbara Mahone Brown*

*See also* INSTRUCTIONAL TECHNIQUES; MBA ONLINE

### Bibliography

Brown, Barbara Mahone. (2002). Teaching virtual leadership: Using the case method online. In K. E. Rudestam and J. Schoenholtz-Read (Eds.), *Handbook of online learning: Innovations in higher education and corporate training* (pp. 375–387). Thousand Oaks, CA: Sage.

Christensen, C. R. (1987). *Teaching and the case method.* Boston: Harvard Business School Press.

Horton, William. (2000). *Designing Web-based training.* New York: John Wiley & Sons.

Scholz, Roland W., & Olaf Tietje. (2002). *Embedded case study methods.* Thousand Oaks, CA: Sage.

Yin, Robert K. (1994). *Case study research: Design and methods,* 2nd ed. Thousand Oaks, CA: Sage.

# CLINICAL TRAINING

Clinical training is an organized sequence of learning activities that provides therapeutic skills to trainees for the purpose of evaluation and treatment of individuals with health and/or mental health problems. Standards of clinical practice are developed by professional licensing boards and associations and represent disciplines, such as clinical or counseling psychology, social work, nursing, medicine, or psychiatry. Academic and practice standards guide the trainee toward the development of a professional identity and competency. Each discipline's core values, theories, and principles are taught through course work and applied through supervised experiences with clients/patients in clinical settings. Training outcomes include the trainee's ability to create a therapeutic relationship and provide interventions that will facilitate improved health and/or mental health. Learning activities are formalized into graduate degree programs, professional training programs, or continuing education courses or workshops. Qualified faculty who teach clinical skills are expected to be experienced professionals with appropriate credentials. Clinical competence is evaluated by training institutions and state professional licensure boards.

The online clinical training environment offers a wide range of activities based on the trainee's need and stage of professional development. A graduate degree is the first step in the preparation for licensure to practice. Because graduate programs must meet accreditation requirements that were developed prior to the new technological advances, the shift to the online environment moves degree programs into relatively uncharted territory. In each of the clinical disciplines, graduate degree programs have begun to provide at least part of their academic course work online. In the area of clinical psychology, examples of individual courses that can be found online include theories of personality, theories of psychological assessment, and ethics and professional practice. Movement from the classroom to Web-based courses is highly dependent on the faculty's and student's competence and comfort with an online teaching and learning environment, as well as the school's development and support for the online environment. Clinical training programs also provide online resources in the form of Web-based study groups and bibliographic references.

Graduate degree programs require that students have specific training in clinical settings (e.g., hospitals and outpatient clinics). Clinical supervision requires that faculty or clinical supervisors meet with students to discuss clinical cases or directly observe clinical activities with clients/patients. The clinical supervisory relationship between the supervisor and student is a significant one that needs regular contact. Clinical supervisors are responsible for the student's clients/patients, and therefore, must be on-site in the clinical setting at least part of the time. Online supervision of a student's practicum or internship and direct contact with clients/patients is constrained by the need for confidentiality and ethical practices. With the improvement in video conferencing, it will be possible for students at remote sites to have face-to-face video interactions with supervisors. Consultation e-mail is more common, but as yet does not replace face-to-face contact. With the growth in telehealth capacities (where mental health services are provided online), online supervision and consultation is expected to expand. Graduate programs will need to offer training in online service delivery.

Postdoctoral training programs and professional training institutes have begun to move their activities online. Similar to graduate training programs, the clinical training activities are based on a combination of didactic coursework, direct service, and supervision.

Licensed professionals who have completed their graduate training are required to continue their education to maintain their clinical skills and professional licensure. For practicing clinicians, a broad array of online clinical training activities are offered in a variety of Web-based contexts. Continuing education (CE) courses are available online in synchronous and asynchronous formats and will continue to develop as many state licensing boards accept credit for a limited number of online training hours. In addition, professional organizations' Web sites for each discipline offer a variety of online resources that support the clinical training of professionals in their specific field. For example, the American Psychological Association Web site (www.apa.org) provides services for data-based searching and up-to-date information about important changes in legislation and related standards that affect clinical psychologists' practice.

Web sites related to specific health and mental health disorders developed by professional organizations and clinicians are a resource for training information and consultation. Online newsletters deliver health and mental research and information directly to clinicians through e-mail lists. Chat rooms have proliferated for clinicians who need collegial consultation and clinical information. For example, clinicians who have had traumatic stress or vicarious traumatization can find a variety of Web sites that offer chat rooms, assessment tools, and bibliographic information. Many of these sites connect clinicians worldwide and provide a level of peer contact unique to the Web environment. Practicing clinicians can seek and find an increasingly rich variety of both structured and informal online training activities to support their ongoing clinical development and learning needs.

—*Judith Schoenholtz-Read*

*See also* GRADUATE STUDY; TELEHEALTH AND TELEMEDICINE

## Bibliography

American Psychological Association. (1992). Ethical principles of psychologists and code of conduct. *American Psychologist, 47,* 1597–1611.

American Psychological Association. (2000). *Book 1: Guidelines and principles for accreditation of programs in professional psychology.* Washington, DC: Author.

Buchanan, T. (2002). Online assessment. Desirable or dangerous? *Professional psychology: Research and practice, 33*(2), 148–154.

Janoff, D. S. (2002). Healthcare meets technology: Web-based professional training. In K. E. Rudestam & J. Schoenholtz-Read (Eds.), *Handbook of online learning: Innovations in graduate education and corporate training.* Thousand Oaks, CA: Sage.

Vodanovich, S. J. (2001). Internet based instruction: National survey of psychology faculty. *Journal of Instructional Psychology, 28*(4), 253–255.

# COGNITIVE SKILLS/ COGNITIVE DEVELOPMENT

American higher education prepares adults for productive citizenship in a democratic society. Successful adults in 21st century America must gather and process rapidly evolving information, cope with ambiguity and complexity, manage diverse perspectives in a global society, and make informed judgments in the face of competing arguments. These advanced cognitive abilities and skills, often called critical or reflective thinking, are essential outcomes of higher education. In addition to acquiring knowledge, successful learners discover how to continue learning beyond formal educational settings. The role of distributed learning environments in promoting cognitive skill and ability raises questions about the role of human interaction, the role of educator and learner, and learners' self-directedness.

## COGNITIVE DEVELOPMENT AND LEARNING

Learning is the process of acquiring basic knowledge, the ability to apply it in new situations, and the ability to develop new knowledge. In most academic disciplines, learning initially focuses on basic cognitive skills such as familiarity with key concepts, gathering data, and understanding and developing arguments. Advanced learning focuses on the ability to think critically, discover new insights, and construct new perspectives. Advanced cognitive skills include the ability to analyze arguments, perspectives, or data to determine their quality and the ability to make informed judgments about them based on analysis of relevant evidence. These analytical skills lead to the ability to develop new insights and knowledge.

*Critical thinking* and *reflective thinking* are terms commonly associated with advanced cognitive skills. Proponents of critical thinking argue that it is more complex than a set of analytic skills. Critical thinking requires particular sets of assumptions about the nature of knowledge that underlie reasoning and analytical skills. These sets of assumptions evolve in early adulthood, and are influenced by one's educational experiences. Early educational experiences yield the assumption that knowledge is absolute, one truth exists, and authorities hold that truth. Learners holding these assumptions view learning as acquiring the right answers from expert authorities. Typical college educational experiences lead learners to the realization that there are multiple perspectives, that knowledge is still under construction, and that authorities do not know all the answers. These learners focus on the process of finding the answers, making them amenable to learning reasoning and analytical skills. Further encounters with ambiguity and uncertainty yield the assumption that all knowledge is uncertain and people are free to believe whatever they wish. These learners focus on exploring multiple perspectives but are hesitant to make judgments because they assume that truth is impossible. Critical thinking requires making judgments using appropriate evidence and thus requires the more complex assumption that people choose what to believe by analyzing the relevant evidence and hold these choices as true. Cognitive development is the evolution of these assumptions.

Educators help learners develop cognitive skills by teaching basic reasoning and analytical processes and by providing opportunities for students to practice these skills. Although these processes have traditionally been taught through interactive seminars in which educators and learners discuss how to make decisions, proponents of distributed learning argue that computers can simulate these processes and offer multiple virtual scenarios for learners to sharpen their cognitive skills. Online chats, discussion boards, and electronic communication among educators and learners offer opportunities for dialogue about these skills.

Helping learners achieve complex assumptions about knowledge is more complicated. Educators help learners arrive at more complex assumptions about knowledge by introducing them to experiences that challenge their current assumptions and supporting them in resolving the challenge by adopting new assumptions. For example, tracing the evolution of a scientific argument would challenge a learner who assumes that scientists know the truth. Yet promoting cognitive development requires more than refuting the original set of assumptions; it necessitates collaborating with the learner to make sense of the situation and construct a new, more workable set of assumptions that account for the situation. Because relinquishing assumptions of how knowledge is created is difficult, collaboration between educator and learner is an important component of supporting this transformation. Such collaboration in distributed learning environments could occur through real-time chats or videoconferencing. Additional dimensions of human development that are intertwined with cognitive development help to support learners' cognitive transformations.

## COGNITIVE DEVELOPMENT REQUIRES AFFECTIVE DEVELOPMENT

Inherent in complex cognitive development is the awareness that people actively interpret their experience, analyze information, consciously choose what to believe, and use those beliefs to guide action. Personal responsibility increases as assumptions about the nature of knowledge evolve. Accepting this personal responsibility requires complexity in two additional affective areas—identity and relationship development. First, self-confidence or trust in one's own ability to express an opinion and make informed judgments is necessary. Assumptions about how people see themselves evolve similarly to assumptions about knowledge. Adolescents generally use external sources to define their identity. Traditional college-age adults continue to rely heavily on their peers for defining their view of themselves. During their twenties or beyond, depending on the nature of life experiences, adults begin to de-emphasize external influence and take up personal responsibility for their definition of themselves. Second, the confidence to share perspectives with others, not fearing their disapproval, is crucial to making informed judgments. When external influence is a central force in defining oneself, taking a stance contrary to external others is difficult. Personal responsibility for self-definition is accompanied by a revision of relationships with others from seeking their approval to mutual respect. Without progress in self-definition and mature relationships with others, the full potential of cognitive development cannot be realized.

Meaningful involvement with peers and educators enriches identity and relationship development. Transforming one's sense of self and developing mutual relationships with others requires intensive reflection, risk taking in interactions, experimenting with new behaviors and roles, acquiring feedback, developing increased comfort with personal responsibility and self-directedness, and a supportive learning community. On traditional campuses, educators strive to incorporate these dynamics via seminar instruction, independent work with educators, and interactions outside of the classroom among educators and learners— all formats that rely heavily on face-to-face interaction. In distributed learning environments, these components occur in televised, electronic, or virtual environments. A fundamental question for educators is to what extent face-to-face and virtual interactions contribute to the effectiveness of these components of learning and how communities of support can be developed in either context.

## EFFECTIVE EDUCATIONAL ENVIRONMENTS

Contemporary educational approaches to promoting cognitive, identity, and relationship development share three common characteristics: complexity of knowledge construction, personal responsibility in learning, and shared authority in learning. First, knowledge is portrayed as complex and constructed via the processes of expert analysis, reflection, and informed judgment. Learning activities focus on problems, tasks, and situations in which there is no clear answer or solution. Learners are engaged in interpreting the situation, searching for relevant information, sharing perspectives and resources, constructing reasonable arguments using the information they find, judging the quality of various perspectives, developing a plan for responding, and sometimes implementing or reporting on the plan.

Second, learning is framed as an active process in which personal responsibility is central. Throughout the learning activities learners are encouraged to experiment with ideas, take risks, broaden their perspectives,

and apply what they are learning to their own thinking. The learner's thinking, values, and identity are actively engaged in the learning process.

Third, learning is the mutual responsibility of educator and learner. Authority, responsibility, and control are shared as the educator continually strives to engage the learner in taking more personal responsibility for learning and deciding what to believe. The educator structures and guides the learning process, yet invites the learner to collaborate in developing mutual plans to enhance learning and cognitive development. Collaboration among learners, referred to as a learning community approach, promotes mature relationships, identity development, and appreciation of multiple perspectives required for complex knowledge construction. These three characteristics are central to promoting cognitive development for learners of diverse ages, experiences, and cultures. Because learners' experience and thinking are incorporated into learning, the learning environment becomes inclusive and welcomes difference.

Distributed learning environments pose a formidable challenge to creating these three characteristics. The complexity of knowledge can be conveyed in online tasks, materials, and discussions. In some cases, complex scenarios can be more easily constructed in online formats than in a traditional classroom. The challenge for this characteristic is structuring the reflection and decision-making processes necessary for learners to interpret and make sense of these complex activities. Distributed learning can be structured to actively engage learners, and in many forms it necessitates self-directedness and personal responsibility. The challenge here is in soliciting the learners' values, thinking, and identity through virtual modes of interaction. Mutual responsibility is also possible and desirable in distributed learning environments. Challenges here include gauging the learners' progress to revise structure and guidance and promoting meaningful collaboration among learners with diverse perspectives.

When learners and educators are located in the same physical space, many educators are able to judge the readiness of learners for particular tasks and to provide the degree of guidance necessary for less complex learners to participate meaningfully. Distributed learning environments depend on learners exercising some degree of self-directness and personal responsibility, characteristics that are uncommon among those with early cognitive assumptions and externally focused identity and relationship conceptualizations. Older adults are more likely to accept personal responsibility, but they still need support to develop belief systems and mature relations with diverse others. Three principles are commonly viewed as helpful for educators to coach or mentor these learners. These principles are based on the notion that development results from an appropriate combination of challenge and support. Challenge is necessary to initiate growth and reconsideration of one's views and assumptions; support is necessary to engage the issue rather than avoid it and to consciously rebuild one's perspectives. Because the three common characteristics of educational environments to promote cognitive development pose a substantial challenge to less complex or less confident learners, additional support is required to maintain their engagement in the learning process.

The first principle affirms the learners' ability to participate in the thinking process. Educators help learners build self-confidence by teaching basic cognitive skills, giving feedback, and affirming potential. The second principle also helps learners gain confidence by framing learning in ways that connect to experiences familiar to the learner. Learning starts on familiar ground before moving to the unknown. If learners lack relevant experiences, they are created in the educational context. The good news for distributed learning environments is that college-age adults today have been raised with advanced technology such as Internet access and instant messaging; thus, they are familiar with electronic forms of interaction even if they lack some other experience base relevant to the learning context. The third principle supports the mutual responsibility of educator and learning by constantly drawing the learner into decisions about learning and about what to believe, providing the necessary structure for learners to engage in this responsibility.

Using these principles to coach or mentor students is complex in face-to-face interaction in which educators can use nonverbal cues and observations to understand their interactions with learners. Their use in distributed learning environments is more complex because educators are less accustomed to understanding interactions in a virtual environment. It may be more difficult to gauge learners' readiness to face challenges or their response to mentoring activities until new modes of interaction (such as videoconferencing) blend technology and human interaction.

These principles also rely heavily on collaboration among peers in the learning community. Educators in distributed learning environments are crafting new ways to intentionally build collaborative learning communities.

## FUNDAMENTAL ISSUES

Learning for the 21st century requires cognitive complexity to make informed judgments in complex contexts where diverse perspectives abound. Confidence in one's own perspectives and mature relationships are crucial to working and living effectively with diverse others. College environments characterized by face-to-face interaction struggle to promote the level of cognitive development necessary for success in adult life. Alternate forms of interaction in distributed learning environments hold promise for promoting cognitive development. Educators have yet to determine the effectiveness of various forms of interaction between educator and learner and among a community of learners. The challenge for educators is to identify new opportunities inherent in distributed learning to promote cognitive development and use those in combination with face-to-face interaction to ensure that college graduates are adequately prepared for the complexity that awaits them.

*—Marcia B. Baxter Magolda*

***See also*** Assessment of Student Competence

## Bibliography

Baxter Magolda, M. B. (2001). *Making their own way: Narratives for transforming higher education to promote self-development.* Sterling, VA: Stylus.

King, P. M., & Kitchener, K. S. (1994). *Developing reflective judgment: Understanding and promoting intellectual growth and critical thinking in adolescents and adults.* San Francisco: Jossey-Bass.

Mentkowski, M., & Associates (2000). *Learning that lasts: Integrating learning, development, and performance in college and beyond.* San Francisco: Jossey-Bass.

Mezirow, J. (Ed.). (1990). *Fostering critical reflection in adulthood: A guide to transformative and emancipatory learning.* San Francisco: Jossey-Bass.

Palloff, R. M., & Pratt, K. (1999). *Building learning communities in cyberspace: Effective strategies for the online classroom.* San Francisco: Jossey-Bass.

Schwitzer, A. M., Ancis, J. R., & Brown, N. (2001). *Promoting student learning and student development at a distance: Student affairs concepts and practices for televised instruction and other forms of distance learning.* Lanham, MD: American College Personnel Association.

# COHORTS

A cohort is a group of people who all experience a set of influences together. Historically, this term has been used to designate a birth cohort. In educational settings, it means a group that is admitted and begins a program at the same time. In online learning, orientation and face-to-face meetings are often designed around particular cohort groups. All the members of this group are expected to move through the program and graduate at the same time. Policies and procedures may be developed to encourage members of the group to stay together, and members may be expected to take core courses at the same time, to enter advanced studies together.

In online learning, the formation of cohort groups is encouraged so that members of geographically dispersed learning groups will have increased feelings of belonging. For example, a group of 50 students might be admitted to an online program with the expectation that they will all start classes in the Fall term. At the orientation, these 50 students are introduced to one another and divided into working groups of 10. Each set of 10 students will attend the first few courses together. All 50 students will be expected to attend face-to-face sessions together or to join in community discussions together. Photographs of these students may be posted together as "the class of 2004." Relationships among members of this group are encouraged and supported by the scheduling of events and classes.

In developing online cohort groups, educational designers should take care to introduce members to one another (whether at face-to-face orientations or online), to encourage moderate levels of self-disclosure, to develop course structures in which members of particular cohorts are present together online, and to create community events in which members are identified by cohort and participate in various activities based on these designations. Achievements of various cohort groups might be published and the achievements of individual members of cohort groups should be publicized by cohort. All activities and events that increase feelings of belonging to a cohort and of the cohort being valued by the institution will lead to increased group cohesion and its related benefits, from lower withdrawal to greater productiveness.

—*Judith Stevens-Long*

*See also* NORMS

## Bibliography

Stevens-Long, J., & Crowell, C. (2002). The design and delivery of interactive online graduate education. In K. E. Rudestam & J. Schoenholtz-Read (Eds.), *Handbook of online learning: Innovations in higher education and corporate training.* Thousand Oaks, CA: Sage.

# COLLABORATION

From the earliest explorations in online education theory and practice, collaborative learning (CL) has proven to be a powerful principle of e-learning design and delivery. E-learning has been shaped by, and is also shaping, learning theory, especially that of collaborative learning.

Collaborative learning is an interactive group knowledge-building process. The term *collaboration* derives from the concept of co-laboring, whereby people work jointly (especially to create physical, social, cultural, or intellectual artifacts). In educational usage, collaborative learning refers to the process whereby learners work together to build knowledge by formulating their ideas into words and then developing these ideas/concepts as they react to other students' responses (positive, negative, questioning, elaborating, etc.) to their formulations. There is ultimately a level of convergence, either of agreement (intellectual or co-production, as in an artistic output, a treatise, or a scientific report or theory) or in agreeing to disagree. Bruffee describes the process of the collaborative learning classroom: "(1) group work toward local consensus, (2) reports and plenary discussion toward plenary consensus, and (3) comparison of the class's plenary consensus with the consensus of a larger relevant knowledge community." As Bruffee states, class discussions focus on open-ended learning tasks:

One purpose is . . . to help students work collaboratively, without further help from the teacher, toward membership in the discourse community that the teacher represents. A second purpose is to lead students to do that not by "assimilating" "correct answers" but by constructing collaboratively some knowledge that is basic to the knowledge community in question. The criterion for success is whether or not students themselves have discovered or constructed—and appropriately applied—the tools they need to solve the eccentric puzzle that the task presents them with.

Collaborative learning and knowledge building gained significant acceptance and power as educational principles in the late 20th and early 21st centuries, in part the result of the phenomenal rate of educational adoption of e-learning and networked communications and the high rates of user satisfaction and completion rates in online educational courses and programs using CL. But the roots of the modern concept of collaborative learning began in the early 20th century.

Vygotsky was an early major force in advancing the theory of collaborative learning for knowledge construction, revising educational theory by moving the unit of analysis from the individual per se to the individual in relationship to the environment and in interaction with others. Research today defines learning as a social process and increasingly as the meaningful construction and creative use of cognitive resources and tools, and active participation, collaboration, and dialogue in communities of practice. The general outlines of a "postindustrial" approach to teaching and learning have been taking shape for decades. In process terms, the new approach is characterized by a greatly increased emphasis on inquiry, dialogue, collaboration, and community. This is especially true in public schools; it is also true in graduate school and adult education. Adult education has long held collaborative learning to be a central tenet. Constructivist definitions of learning parallel the changing definition of workplace learning in which, through active participation and collaboration, employees create their firm's future. Senge defined new economy work organizations as "learning organizations." More recently, the importance of collaboration for learning and entry to the knowledge community in postsecondary learning has been articulated by Bruffee. Knowledge (science, learning, invention) is viewed as a construct of the community's

form of discourse, negotiated and maintained by local consensus and subject to endless conversation.

Arguably, the introduction of computer networking and the rise of e-learning have dramatically illuminated the power of collaborative learning. Educational applications of computer networking have led to major insights and advances in collaborative learning, knowledge communities, and knowledge construction.

A brief history of the use of networking for collaborative learning demonstrates that since its very beginnings, a major thrust of e-learning has been solidly based in collaborative learning and knowledge building.

- *Mid-1970s*—The first use of computer conferencing for nonformal education and communities of practice. Online communities of scientists are organized through computer conferencing for online discussion and workgroups.
- *1981*—The first totally online mini courses, based on group discussions.
- *1982*—The first totally Online Executive Education Program, ultimately based on collaborative learning.
- *1983*—Networked classroom model for primary and secondary education—approaches such as learning circles and knowledge-building communities influence networking applications in schools.
- *1984*—The first totally online undergraduate university courses, based on collaborative learning.
- *1985*—The first totally online graduate university courses, based on collaborative learning.
- *1986*—The first totally online professional development courses.

These early experiments in online learning were based on collaborative learning, an educational process reformulated for the very new online environment (based on asynchronous, place-independent, many-to-many, text-based, computer mediation). Designing for this new online environment, characterized by such a unique set of attributes, was (and continues to be) a significant challenge. Nonetheless, these experiences have created the basis for powerful models that today characterize much of e-learning, even as new models and options continue to emerge.

Related fields emerged, such as computer-supported cooperative work and collaborative learning, and virtual classrooms. Roschelle, working with school children in computer labs, observed that collaboration was a key process in conceptual change, arguing that the "crux of learning by collaboration is convergence," a process of mutual construction of knowledge.

Networked interaction and collaboration provide the opportunity for increasingly seamless access to different forms of learning, even as part of face-to-face (F2F) education. E-learning is becoming part of all learning as we know it, enhancing education in remarkable, unprecedented directions.

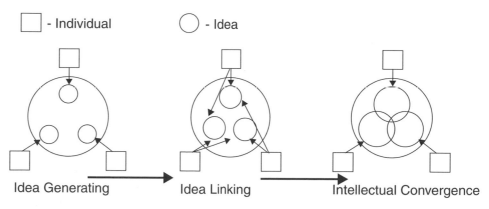

**Figure 1**

Collaborative learning online also suggests ways to forge new linkages and interaction between formal, nonformal, and informal educational settings and approaches. Indeed, in order to understand and employ all of a society's institutions as educational resources, it is essential to recognize these three types of education and to view them as interactive.

## THEORETICAL FRAMEWORKS FOR ONLINE COLLABORATIVE LEARNING

Harasim's model of conceptual change focuses on collaborative learning in the online (Web-based) discourse environment, identifying three processes/ phases describing the path from divergent to convergent thinking: idea generating, idea linking, and intellectual convergence. This conceptualization resonates with Bruffee's theoretical position that intellectual convergence through collaborative discourse is key. It also suggests a framework for understanding discourse in e-learning discussions and online seminars.

Figure 1 illustrates the three stages of collaborative discourse, from idea generation to intellectual convergence. At the idea generating stage, individual participants, represented by squares, contribute their ideas and opinions, represented by circles, on the topics to the shared space, represented by an oval. Through the process of brainstorming, the participants begin to relate with each other's ideas. This leads to the second stage of the discourse—idea linking. At this stage, the participants begin to agree or to disagree, clarify and elaborate, and reflect and organize their own and others' ideas and positions. As a result, discrete ideas start to come together; many smaller ideas become a few big ones; and individual understandings grow into

group shared understanding. At this point, the discourse is ready to advance to the next higher level—intellectual convergence. At this third stage, the group actively engages in the co-construction of the knowledge based on shared understanding. The group members synthesize their ideas and knowledge into explicit points of view or products (such as theories, positions, works of art, manifestos, scientific theories/hypotheses). They may also extend their ideas and understanding to new territories. The outcomes of this stage are consolidated shared understanding and group convergence, as evidenced by co-production.

*—Linda Harasim*

*See also* ADULT EDUCATION LEARNING MODEL; KNOWLEDGE BUILDING/KNOWLEDGE WORK; LEARNING COMMUNITIES; LEARNING ENVIRONMENTS; ONLINE LEARNING ENVIRONMENTS; SOCIAL CONSTRUCTIONISM

### Bibliography

Brookfield, S. D. (1986). *Understanding and facilitating adult learning.* San Francisco: Jossey-Bass.

Brown, John Seely, Collins, A., & Duguid, P. (1989). Situated cognition and the culture of learning. *Educational Researcher, 18,* 32–42.

Bruffee, K. A. (1999). *Collaborative learning: Higher education, interdependence, and the authority of knowledge,* 2nd edition. Baltimore, MD: John Hopkins University Press.

Harasim, L. (1990). Online education: An environment for collaboration and intellectual amplification. In L. Harasim (Ed.), *Online education: Perspectives on a new environment* (pp. 39–66). New York: Praeger.

Harasim, L. (1999). A Framework for Online Learning: The Virtual-U. *IEEE Computer Society Journal "Computer,"* *32*(3): 44–49.

Harasim, L. (2000). *Shift happens: Online education as a new paradigm in learning. Internet and higher education. Special issue.* U.K.: Elsevier Science, 41–61.

Harasim, L., Calvert, T., & Groeneboer, C. (1997). Virtual-U: A Web-based system to support collaborative learning. In B. Khan (Ed.), *Web-based instruction.* Englewood Cliffs, NJ: Educational Technology.

Harasim, L., Hiltz, R., Teles, L., & Turoff, M. (1995). *Learning networks: A field guide to teaching & learning online.* Cambridge: MIT Press.

Hiltz, S. R. (1994). *The virtual classroom: Learning without limits via computer networks.* Norwood, NJ: Ablex.

Knowles, M. S. (1980). *The modern practice of adult education: From pedagogy to andragogy,* 2nd edition. New York: Cambridge Books.

Koschmann, T. (1996). *CSCL: Theory and practice of an emerging paradigm.* Mahwah, NJ: Lawrence Erlbaum.

Lave, J. (1988). *Cognition in practice.* Cambridge, England: Cambridge University Press.

Resnick, L. B. (1987). Learning in school and out: The 1986 presidential address. *Educational Researcher, 16*(9), 13–19.

Riel, M. (1996). Cross-classroom collaboration: Communication and education. In T. Koschmann (Ed.), *CSCL: Theory and practices of an emerging paradigm* (pp. 187–207). Mahwah, NJ: Lawrence Erlbaum.

Roschelle, J. (1996). Learning by collaborating: Convergent conceptual change. In T. Koschmann (Ed.), *CSCL: Theory and practice of an emerging paradigm.* Mahwah, NJ: Lawrence Erlbaum.

Scardamalia, M., & Bereiter, C. (1993). Technologies for knowledge-building discourse. *Communications of the ACM, 36*(5), 37–41.

Senge, P. (1990). *The fifth discipline: The art and practice of the learning organization.* New York: Doubleday.

Vygotsky, L. S. (1934). *Mind in society: The development of higher psychological processes.* Cambridge, MA: Harvard University Press.

# COMPUTER

Currently, almost every aspect of distributed learning takes place either partly or wholly through, on, or in computers. Students write papers, take exams, and perform experiments by means of computers; students and faculty send one another messages, participate in discussions, create diagrams, search for and retrieve information, read articles and books, and engage in research with the aid of computers; student records and institutional policies are kept on computers; video lectures and voice conversations are communicated through computer networks; and personal and institutional finance are managed via computers. All of this occurs in a wider context in which computers are increasingly embedded in the objects and activities of human life, to the point where computer scientists speak of and study "pervasive computing" and "ubiquitous computing."

That so many aspects of distributed learning are undergirded by computers points directly to the most outstanding feature of this technology: that the computer is what Alan Turing, the founder of computer science, conceptualized as a "universal machine." That is, a digital computer is neither primarily something that "computes" in the usual sense of calculation nor primarily a machine in the usual sense of an instrument that transmits or modifies force or motion, even though it can calculate and can operate as a conventional machine or as a controller of conventional machines. Rather, it has two fundamental properties that differentiate it from all prior machines and from mere calculators. First, the computer is an abstract, general-purpose, symbol-processing machine that can become or simulate any number of other machines or real-world or mental processes as long as they can be represented as clearly defined data or symbols and structured as clearly defined sequences of operations. The terms that have been applied to the computer in this sense—universal machine, abstract machine, mathematical machine, symbolic machine, theoretical machine, algorithmic machine—are indicators of this property. Second, it is an intelligent, or at least quasi-intelligent, machine (it has even been labeled a "spiritual machine") in that it can identify different conditions in the world, draw inferences from them, alter its own sequence of operations in consequence of these inferences, and thereby undertake different actions in response. Taken together, the universality and quasi-intelligence of the computer define its special nature and place in the history of technology.

Before entering into discussion of the universal machine and computer intelligence, it is useful to review the computer's structural characteristics.

A modern electronic general-purpose digital computer consists of a central processing unit (CPU) containing an arithmetic-logic unit (ALU) and a control unit that do the computational work. Every CPU comes with a built-in "instruction set" consisting of the commands it can execute, such as adding two numbers or comparing two numbers to see if they are equal. Working memory (RAM or random access memory) holds both the computer program whose instructions it follows (hence the phrase *stored-program computer*) as well as data used, produced, or altered by the program. It consists of sequentially numbered memory locations or addresses. The computer has input/output (I/O) points (ports) that connect it to the outside world, often via peripherals (such devices as a keyboard, monitor, modem, or printer); to longer-term storage such as disk drives, tape drives, and the like; and to other computers via computer networks. The internal parts of the computer are connected via electronic circuits called *buses.* Programs and data inside computers and on digital media are represented in the binary number system, that is, as sequences of electronic representations of the digits 0 and 1. Inside a working computer they are represented as different electrical voltages. The first general purpose stored-program computer went into operation at Manchester University in 1948, followed shortly thereafter by the American EDVAC.

A computer program—software—is executed sequentially unless or until its own operation leads it to alter the sequence in consequence of data input and/or the results of its processing. This sequence alteration is known as *conditional branching.* In its practical use, a modern computer executes a program (usually called an *application program*), such as a word-processing program, mathematical program, or database program. To give the application program access to the computer's resources, such as its file system, memory, and peripherals, the computer runs in the background a meta-program called an *operating system* (such as Windows, Linux, or Unix). In networked environments, the operating system is integrated with networking software that links the computer to other computers and networks, such as the Internet, and it is this connection that serves as the infrastructure of much of distributed learning. In online distributed learning environments, individuals and groups communicate and collaborate via a system that integrates application programs, operating systems, and networking software across multiple remote computers and the networks that connect them.

## THE UNIVERSAL MACHINE AND THE PROCESS OF RATIONALIZATION

The abstractness and universality of the computer are due to the logical simplicity of the limited set of operations it can perform: moving data from one location to another, such as from RAM to the CPU or from the CPU to an output port; applying a few arithmetic and logical processes to data, such as addition and negation; testing the condition of data, such as whether a certain number equals zero or not; and altering the sequence of its operations, especially based on the conditions it has tested. All digital computers can perform only these operations, and in this sense all computers are identical, differing only in the way that they are physically implemented and the speed at which they operate. The vast power of the computer, which enables it to control airplanes and space satellites, compose music, enable online discussions, assist surgeons, produce financial statements of corporations and governments, draw maps, locate stars through analyzing data from radio telescopes, and myriad other complex activities, does not reside in the computer, which in all of these domains and activities is only performing the same small number of operations. Rather, it resides in the human accomplishment of creating machine-like models of these domains and activities, conceiving, constructing, and representing them as though they consisted of the kinds of processes and data on which computers can operate, namely algorithms and data structures.

An algorithm is a precisely defined, unambiguous sequence of operations undertaken to attain a result, one that includes instructions as to what to do about anything that can be expected to happen along the way and how to tell when the result has been obtained. For example, most people learn in school the algorithm for adding a column of numbers: write them on paper right under one another, so that the rightmost digits of the numbers are lined up and then all digits to the left are lined up, column by column, until there are no more digits; draw a line under the last number and have the total accumulate under the line; then carry out the following procedure on each column, starting on the right and moving leftwards, until there are no more columns to add: 1) add the digits in the column; 2) place the sum's rightmost digit in that column's place in the total; 3) if the column's sum is greater than 9, carry its other digits to the next column to the left and add them to the sum of that next column.

The core of modern computer science, first clearly formulated by Turing in 1936 in his paper "On Computable Numbers, With an Application to the *Entscheidungsproblem* [decision problem]," are the twin notions that any such algorithm or set of instructions is already a mathematical, theoretical, or abstract machine—in other words, it is a mental representation or model of a machine-like process—and therefore can be implemented on a computer. Conversely, a computer is a universal machine that can become the particular machine that is represented by that algorithm.

A data structure is a precisely organized way of representing information that facilitates efficient and unambiguous processing by a computer; for example, a mailing list database that is an alphabetically sorted sequence of records, one for each individual, consisting of the same fields (e.g., first name, last name, street address, city, state or province, country, and postal code), with the same number of characters allotted to each field. So, for example, if 20 characters were allotted for the first name, then the computer would always "know" or treat the 21st character as the first character of the last name. A computer program translates the algorithm and data structure used to represent part of the world or the mind into the instructions that have been built into a particular computer.

Computers are part of a long-term social process, called purposive, instrumental, or strategic rationalization by sociologists, that puts a premium on efficiency, calculability, predictability, and control in the attainment of goals and that sacrifices everything else to this pursuit. Because algorithms embody this orientation, one aspect of the rationalization process is the increasing construction or interpretation of social and natural processes as algorithms and the increasing capture and organization into data structures and databases of representations of the world and society. That is why computers and purposive rationalization are mutually reinforcing. The more powerful the computers, the more incentive there is to improve the data and the algorithms; the more extensive the data and the more advanced the algorithms, the more incentive there is to make the computers faster, provide them with more memory, and increase the amount of data storage.

## THE QUASI-INTELLIGENT MACHINE

Whether computers are or could ever become "really" intelligent and think like human beings, and whether human thinking is computation or algorithmic processing have been controversial questions in philosophy, computer science, psychology, and cognitive science since Alan Turing first wrote about them in 1950 in his paper "Computing Machinery and Intelligence." Putting aside these perhaps irresolvable questions, nevertheless there can be no doubt that computers are intelligent in a pragmatic everyday sense, in that, if they are programmed to do so, they can respond differently and "appropriately" (as defined by their programs) to conditions in the world. It is this characteristic that has made them impact so significantly on many areas of human endeavor.

The quasi-intelligence of the computer lies in the combination of five of its features. First, a state of affairs in the world can be represented in the computer's memory by devoting a memory location to it, such as by having input from a certain input port (e.g., to which a keyboard is attached) be represented by giving that location a particular numeric value (e.g., 1). Thus, when the program inspects that memory location, it "knows" that if its value is 0, a key on the keyboard has not been pressed; if its value is 1, a key has been pressed.

Second, a computer can test not only a condition (e.g., whether a key on the keyboard has been pressed), but also any complex combination of conditions for which it has relevant data. For example, assuming that the computer's input ports are attached to the appropriate sensors, is it true that a) the traffic light is red; b) more than 30 cars have gone through the intersection in the past 4 minutes; c) it is during rush hour; and d) the temperature is more than 90° Fahrenheit? Computers can analyze such complex conditions using Boolean algebra, a method of assessing the truth of complex statements by performing simple mathematical operations on the truth of their components. In Boolean algebra, a true statement is represented by the digit 1, and a false one by the digit 0. A conjunction of statements is true (1) if all of its component statements are true (1); otherwise it is false (0). Thus, if four memory locations were devoted to the four conditions above, and each of them contained a 1, then the conjunction of all of them (i.e., a AND b AND c AND d), would be true and yield a 1. If one of them contained a 0, then the conjunction of all of them (i.e., the assertion that all of them, a AND b AND c AND d, are true) would be false and yield a 0.

Third, perhaps the most significant and defining feature of a computer is its ability to perform conditional branching; that is, it can execute different parts of the program it is running based on the state of certain conditions. This is what enables the computer to react differently to different situations—programmers have devoted different sections of the computer program to correspondingly different actions or behaviors. Thus, if condition X is true or present, it will branch (or "jump") to the section of the program for responding to condition X; if condition Y is present, it will branch to the section for condition Y, and so on. So, in the previous example, a computer dedicated to monitoring automotive traffic and controlling traffic lights and signs could evaluate a Boolean expression representing the conjunction of the conditions listed and reroute traffic if the conjunction resulted in a 1 (if all conditions were true); otherwise, if the result is 0 (false), it could let the traffic continue as is.

Fourth, as is clear from this example, through its connection to the world, either through output devices (e.g., computer-controlled traffic lights or airplane navigational equipment) or through human intermediaries (e.g., doctors and nurses interpreting the results of computer-controlled medical monitoring devices), the computer's testing of conditions or states of affairs and Boolean inferences from them can have a direct impact on the world. Thus, if it is so programmed, the computer can respond "intelligently" to the state of the world.

Fifth, all of the prior features appear intelligent to human beings because of the essential final feature, which is an accident of nature: the speed of electricity. Because a modern electronic computer can execute more than a million instructions per second it can carry out in what appears a useful or even instantaneous amount of time the large number of steps that are normally part of any substantial computer program. For example, in the situation of a person typing in a word-processing program, when the typist approaches the end of a line the program moves the next word to the beginning of the next line. That is because it has been recording and updating, after every typed letter, a running count of the number of characters on the line and moves a new word down to the next line when the number gets to the appropriate line length. If the typist is using justified text, then, at the moment of doing so, the program will also move the most recently typed word to the right margin and even out all of the spaces between the words, which involves counting all of the spaces in the line and then reformatting the line to make them approximately equal. If the typist is also

using automatic hyphenation, then the program also will break the last word, insert a hyphen, and then move the second half of the word to the next line, which may involve consulting a dictionary to see where that particular word should be hyphenated. Yet, from the typist's point of view, the hundreds or thousands of operations involved in doing these things occur instantaneously and invisibly, simply as a consequence of the literally "lightning" speed of the electricity that is executing them. If the typist had to wait 10 seconds for the program to do these things before being able to continue typing on the next line, the computer would seem idiotic rather than intelligent, and the typist would replace the computer with a typewriter. Thus, the computer's ability to take in information, test its status, perform logical operations on it, and branch to different parts of the program in consequence of those operations is of value to human beings only because of the speed at which all of this occurs, which normally exceeds by a vast amount the speed at which human beings could carry out the same operations.

## A VERY SHORT HISTORY OF COMPUTING

The major intellectual innovations that led to the computer are associated with the individuals who either first enunciated them or had the most important influence in their development and propagation. In the 17th century the German philosopher Gottfried Wilhelm von Leibniz, one of the first people to create a calculating machine, proposed a universal language or code for concepts and argued that new knowledge could be derived from it through logical calculation. The French philosopher René Descartes and the British philosopher John Locke, also in the 17th century, differentiated between *primary qualities,* the objective features of nature that could be studied mathematically and scientifically, and *secondary qualities,* the subjective impact of the former on individuals perceiving them. This distinction underlies the mathematical algorithms that, when run on a computer, will simulate certain kinds of subjective experience for the user (e.g., video games, flight simulators, virtual reality).

In the 19th century, the British mathematician Charles Babbage put forward the idea of an "analytical engine" featuring most of the characteristics of modern digital computers, including a CPU and working memory, as well as programming with conditional branching. It was never implemented, partly because of lack of financial support and partly because of the difficulty of implementing such an idea with purely mechanical, as opposed to electronic, means. Although Babbage's engine was conceptualized as a general purpose symbol processor, Babbage was focused more on mathematical calculation than other computing tasks. In 1854 the British mathematician and logician George Boole published a method, fundamental to modern logic, mathematics, and computing, for performing logical operations through mathematical calculation. Shortly thereafter the American philosopher Charles Sanders Peirce realized that logical calculation of the kind developed by Boole could be performed by electrical circuits. This idea was finally fully elaborated by the American engineer Claude Shannon in 1938.

There has been a direct link between the development of modern symbolic logic, with its mathematical orientation, and the reducibility of computational processes to a small number of simple logical operations. In 1936 the British mathematician Alan Turing worked out the underlying ideas of modern computer science as the theory of abstract, universal, symbol-processing, algorithmic machines. In 1945 the Hungarian-born, American mathematician and scientist John von Neumann, influenced by Turing as well as by the ENIAC proto-computer developed by J. Presper Eckert and John Mauchly for the U.S. Army during World War II (which required the machine to be reconfigured with plugs and switches for each program to be run), worked out a clear statement of the fundamental idea of the electronic stored-program computer, essentially an electronic version of Babbage's idea structured in accordance with Turing's model of the universal machine. Meanwhile Turing, who became a major figure in the British intelligence project of breaking German codes during World War II, used his experience with cryptography machines to pursue the development of computers in Great Britain and wrote the programming manual for the first working computer at Manchester University.

In the decade after the first general-purpose, stored-program computers were produced in the late 1940s and early 1950s, two major innovations occurred. The first was the American mathematician and early computer programmer Grace Hopper's creation of a high-level programming language that was translated ("compiled") automatically into electronic machine language. High-level languages such as Fortran, COBOL, BASIC, Pascal, and C enabled programmers to work at the level of linguistically formulated concepts and constructs. The second was the use of virtual memory in computer operating systems, enabling computer programs to function with more apparent memory than was physically available. Taken together, these innovations introduced the notion and principles of virtuality: virtual machines (i.e., the algorithmic machine corresponding to a high-level computer language), virtual memory, virtual files, virtual devices, and so on. Virtuality split the logical structures with which humans operated from the physical structures through which they were implemented, so that programmers and users no longer had to be concerned with the physical structures. This also meant that one and the same virtual entity could be implemented in alternative physical structures and that computer programmers and the computer industry could create a world of simulation distinguishable from its implementation. In the early 1980s, John Gage and Bill Joy, American co-founders of Sun Microsystems, introduced the principle that "the computer is the network." According to this concept, a computer network and the computers connected to it all become extensions of the individual computer, which can use their resources, so that there is no absolute separation between a computer, other computers, and the network. This principle underlies Internet developments of the late 20th and early 21st centuries. The combination of networks and virtuality makes possible the virtual spaces and cyberspace in which much distributed learning occurs.

—*Jeremy J. Shapiro*

*See also* INFORMATION TECHNOLOGY (IT)

## Bibliography

Berlinski, D. (2000). *The advent of the algorithm: The idea that rules the world.* New York: Harcourt, Inc.

Blank, G., & Barnes, R. (1998). *The universal machine: A multimedia introduction to computing.* Boston: McGraw-Hill.

Brookshear, J. G. (1997). *Computer science: An overview,* 5th ed. Redwood City: Benjamin/Cummings.

Bolter, J. D. (1984). *Turing's man: Western culture in the computer age.* Chapel Hill: University of North Carolina Press.

Hillis, W. D. (1998). *The pattern on the stone: The simple ideas that make computers work.* New York: Basic Books.

Mowshowitz, A. (2002). *Virtual organization: Toward a theory of societal transformation stimulated by information technology.* Westport: Quorum Books.

# COMPUTER-BASED TRAINING (CBT)

CBT is an acronym for computer-based training; however, there has been a profusion of acronyms that refer to educational software. Many of them are or have become synonymous with CBT, including:

- Computer-assisted audiovisual instruction (CAAI)
- Computer-assisted instruction (CAI)
- Computer-assisted learning (CAL)
- Computer-assisted language learning (CALL)
- Computer-assisted training (CAT)
- Computer-assisted teaching (CAT)
- Computer-assisted teachers training systems (CATTS)
- Computer-assisted video (CAV)
- Computer-based education (CBE)
- Computer-based instruction (CBI)
- Computer-based instructional management (CBIM)
- Computer-based learning (CBL)
- Computer-illustrated teaching (CIT)
- Computer-managed instruction (CMI)
- Computer-managed learning (CML)
- Computer and video assisted teaching (CVAT)
- Intelligent computer-aided instruction (ICAI)

CBT amounts to using a computer for training and instruction. Specifically, the student learns by executing a training program, referred to as *courseware,* on a computer, which typically provides interactive training for specific disciplines. When it targets adult or continuing education, it is referred to as CAT. Regardless of the student's age, when the discipline being taught is a language, it is CALL. When the discipline is teacher training, then the method is CATTS. CBIM is also aimed at teachers, but in this case it is focused on their class management and evaluation practices instead of the students' learning.

CBT courseware is typically developed with authoring tools that are designed to create interactive question/answer sessions. When it uses a tutorial approach, it is known as CAI. When the results of these sessions are tracked and students' progress is monitored, then it's

CMI. If this tracking or monitoring of the learner feeds into a model of the learner, in the form of an expert system or other artificial intelligence technology, then it is ICAI. CBT has benefited from the relatively recent advent and popularization of the Internet. Nowadays, most CBT solutions either are on the Web, are Web-enabled, or will be so shortly. This online form of CBT via the Web is often referred to as Web-based training (WBT).

## PEDAGOGICAL USES OF CBT

With traditional CBT systems, an individual learner is exposed to the material of the courseware. The student is subsequently tested on his or her proper assimilation and retention of the material, with some questions and/or exercises that are automatically corrected by the courseware. When relevant, the system detects and interactively corrects the learner's mistakes. It performs this auto-evaluation either throughout the learner's training or after an entire program has been completed. The more primitive systems have a bounded set of questions that can sometimes be exhausted rather quickly; more evolved systems can generate new questions based on the perceived needs of the learner. The latter is achieved by tracking the progress of the learner within and throughout the disciplines that the courseware endeavors to teach. The degree of sophistication of this tracking, and the analyses/reports inferred from these logs, vary a lot, ranging from nil to "intelligent," with varying degrees of automation, user-friendliness, and sophistication in between these two extremes.

The most often cited advantages of computer-based training versus traditional teaching practices are:

- The learner can study when it's convenient.
- The student can learn at his or her own pace.
- The learner can repeat the material as often as he or she deems necessary.
- The learner can repeat without any feelings of embarrassment due to a slower pace.
- The CBT system will never become impatient with the student.
- The content and/or interactivity of the CBT can be customized to match the learner's abilities and preferences, as well as the teacher's pedagogical strategy for a particular learner or, more commonly, a particular profile of learners.

Teachers use CBT for a number of reasons, including:

- A complete unit of learning
- A complementary learning unit
- A unit to introduce learners to new material and/or to trigger reflection and/or action
- An instrument to diagnose and/or evaluate the learner's knowledge and abilities before beginning a course
- An instrument to diagnose the learner's learning during the course
- An instrument to evaluate the learner's learning upon completion of the course
- An instrument to reinforce the learner's assimilation and retention of the material
- Remedial work for slower learners that need more attention than the teacher can reasonably provide.

Socioconstructivist teachers use CBT for the same knowledge-transfer activities expected of any teacher, and dedicate their class time to socioconstructivist activities that engage the students in higher-order cognitive and social processes (a group form of situated learning).

One of the earliest forms of computer-based training was PLATO, a proprietary mainframe-based system that was invented more than 35 years ago at the University of Illinois. It became a dominant CBT platform in those pioneering years because its software was innovative for the time. By today's standards, however, these early systems were quite primitive. The best they could muster was a rigid text-based drill and practice type of programmed learning, which is too reductive. Although teaching inevitably transfers formalized knowledge from the teacher to the learner(s), there is more to teaching and learning than the communication of formalized knowledge.

Although most CBT programs have traditionally tended to be of the drill and practice variety, this overly simplistic instructional strategy is not the only type of learning that can be supported by CBT. Courseware can also be designed for learning activities such as problem solving, case-based learning, inductive learning, simulations, and educational games. The most interesting educational activities are those that present a challenge for the learner and/or involve elements of fantasy that stimulate the imagination as well as those that engender and partially satisfy the learner's curiosity. Multimedia is instrumental in these enriched cases because without it,

CBT cannot adequately communicate the meta, nonverbal, and situated aspects of learning a discipline. The focus of multimedia has shifted from stand-alone audiovisual materials in various formats to seamless integration in interactive computer-based systems. At first this interactive multimedia was only mildly interactive, but it has become increasingly interactive as technology has advanced.

Although interactive multimedia enhances a text-based modality, it still leaves the individual learner to fare for himself. To compensate for this lack of human input, these closed coursewares are often combined with one or more means of communication, ranging from traditional mentoring in person or by phone, to the very rich set of synchronous and asynchronous means of communication provided by the Web: e-mail, newsgroups, ICQ, chats, conferencing, and the like.

## HISTORY OF CBT

The history of using technology for learning is replete with promises and disappointments. Film was the first modern learning technology. It was used extensively by the United States military as it prepared for the second World War. They were concerned that the consistency and thoroughness of U.S.-based training would be lost overseas, so they decided to train their millions of recruits with film. This approach was so successful for them that, after the war, they continued research on the use of film, and later television, for learning.

Eventually the military partnered with leading universities to bring the benefits of both behavioral and cognitive psychology to learning. Instructional films became more creative and covered more topics appropriate for schools, thus becoming a central part of public schools' curricula in the social and physical sciences in the 1950s and 1960s. But it was television that really excited educators. It could purportedly bring almost any form of learning into the classroom. In spite of a few successes, however, educational television was disappointing overall. The technology and its content were so expensive that many schools had no money left for the programs or for the staff to create and manage them. From a pedagogical point of view, instructors didn't know how to make television instructional. The poorly designed programs were too boring, and the teachers didn't know how to integrate them into their classroom. But the main reason why television was not successful was that it lacked an essential quality of teaching: the ability to interact with the learner, provide feedback, and customize the presentation to meet the learner's needs.

It was this necessity for interactivity that renewed efforts in the area of CBT. The early teaching machines and programmed texts of the 1960s paved the way for an embryonic form of CBT, but CBT really blossomed in the 1970s and 1980s when a tremendous amount of effort was invested in this field. The advent of the PC was a turning point. As more PCs were deployed in offices, homes, and schools, they provided a growing base of PC hardware on which to run courseware; however, the differences in hardware, software, and other technical barriers wreaked havoc on their accessibility. A chronic lack of authoring standards and affordable tools that were easy enough for teachers to use for developing CBT further aggravated the problems associated with CBT, to the point where many questioned its viability as an educational technology.

Another problem with CBT was caused by the rapidly changing knowledge base. CBT programs were barely released when some of their content was rendered obsolete by a technological change, product update, or the like. Content stability thus became a criterion for determining if a CBT solution should be built; this stability was an elusive goal. Eventually planners grew more conservative, refusing to invest in CBT for fear of premature obsolescence and the high cost of updating. Add to this the large up-front investment needed to build a CBT solution, along with the questionable likelihood of achieving the large-scale use needed to justify that investment, and it's easy to see why people became so hesitant about it. Teachers used CBT only when there were either a lot of people to train over a short period of time or a large number of people to train over a long period of time and the content was not going to change.

Another problem with CBT was that many of the programs were very dull. One of the reasons was the technical limitations of these pioneering attempts at CBT: small hard drives, lack of a CD-ROM drive, slow computer speeds, poor graphics, and no multimedia. The content and interactivity of courseware were thus severely constrained by technical limitations, but also because of a generalized disregard of what constitutes quality learning by the developers, due mainly to the lack of teachers' participation in CBT development and a natural tendency to reproduce in the new media what had already been done in previous medias. As a result, most CBT were text-based and textbook-like, and predominantly used a drill-and-practice instructional strategy. Although some interesting efforts broke away from this mold, most were never used, and CBT fell out of favor.

While all of this was going on, tremendous advances were being made in understanding how people learn. New principles of learning were incorporated into the emerging field of instructional design. But this increasing awareness of what worked often ran into the limitations of the computing technologies of the time, which severely limited the instructional strategies that could be used in CBT solutions. The solution was to combine these state-of-the-art instructional design approaches with flexible technologies.

## PROGRESS OF CBT

Media-rich CBT was originally introduced on laserdiscs, but the high-cost of the hardware and the exorbitant costs of developing these discs, along with the concomitant lack of content in this format, resulted in this early laserdisc technology not taking hold. The exponential increase in PC computing power, the growing prevalence of computers with CD-ROM drives, and the dramatic decrease in the development and replication costs of the discs clearly established CD-ROM as a more viable option for CBT than its laserdisc counterpart. Although adequate for large amounts of data, CD-ROMs are not the ideal support for video, however, leaving the door open for a reintroduction of laserdisc technology in a smaller denser format: DVD discs.

CBT has also benefited from the widespread popularization of the Internet. When combined with the communication and collaboration allowed by the Web, online CBT systems become very effective teaching and learning tools—far more effective than their non-networked counterparts, because studying online adds a social component to the learner's educational experience. It increases learners' motivation by decreasing their isolation. It allows them and their teacher to employ communicative pedagogical strategies that go well beyond what can be achieved by the isolated users of stand-alone CBT courseware. The use of communication and collaboration as an adjunct to a more traditional CBT program is one of several strategies that augments the learning efficacy of these computer-mediated approaches. Other pedagogical strategies, such as socioconstructivism, focus even more on communication and collaboration as key building blocks of learners' successful completion of a course. The Internet has been a boon here, but it has also created some problems of its own: The limited bandwidth of current networks, for instance, still limits the quantity and the quality of the content that can reasonably be delivered in this manner. The architecture of the Internet was not designed with interactivity in mind, and consequently does not adequately support all types of teaching models and learning strategies. The ideal scenario, a synergetic approach that takes into account the limitations of each medium, is to provide the media-rich and/or highly interactive portions of a course locally on a CD-ROM, and integrate this disc seamlessly with the Internet, such that the latter provides any timely content that expires, as well as the communication, collaboration, and other low-bandwidth pedagogical services that a learning community needs for optimal learning to take place.

Despite the stigma attached to using CBT, and learning technologies in general, many traditional teachers still perceive CBT as a threat to their profession because CBT positions itself as a computer-mediated teacher substitute, and because its economies of scale may prompt some budget-conscious administrators to increase the number of students managed by a dwindling number of teachers and/or to increasingly hire cheaper, less-qualified teaching assistants that can manage the technology as well as teachers can. These fears are grounded in some cases, but, from a broader perspective, casting CBT in a supportive role is a fresh opportunity to improve on the traditional model of instruction, and to allow teachers to redefine their role, tasks, and instructional strategies. The infamous cycle of failure of CBT can therefore be broken, as long as we are careful about how we view and use it.

—*Pierre-Léonard Harvey*
—*Alain Farmer*

*See also* Instructional Course Design; Learning Management Systems (LMS); Social Constructionism; Web-Based Course Management Systems (WBCMS)

### Bibliography

Lee, W. W., & Owens, D. L. (2000). *Multimedia-based instructional design: Computer-based training, Web-based training and distance learning.* San Francisco: Jossey-Bass.

Kruse, K., & Keil, J. (1999). *Technology-based training: The art and science of design, development, and delivery.* San Francisco: Jossey-Bass.

# COMPUTER LITERACY

A scan of newspaper and journal articles reveals that a number of "literacies" are emerging as the Information Age unfolds, including computer literacy, information literacy, media literacy, and visual literacy. Computer literacy was one of the first of the new literacies to be identified when computers became readily available for individual and home use, and it can be considered a component of information literacy, a broader term. As computers have replaced typewriters, people of all ages who had mastered that convenient means of writing have been obliged to learn to use a computer that resembles a typewriter in that it has a keyboard, but that has the potential to perform many other seemingly miraculous tasks. Typing documents is only one of many tasks that a person with a computer can do, but for many adults this has been their initial introduction to computer use.

Computer literacy, to be educated about computers, is a deceptively simple phrase in that it implies that there is a known and manageable set of skills that one can learn that would make one knowledgeable about computers. Because a computer is a virtual machine and can become many different machines, such as a calculating machine, a payroll machine, a communicating machine, a game, or a publishing device, depending on which software program is being run, it is not clear that there really is a single set of skills that will hold across all the domains in which computers are used.

When the focus is on distributed or distance learning, a proposed skill set could be narrowed to those skills needed to operate one's own computer, such as creating, finding, deleting, managing, formatting, and transferring files for online reading, writing, and communication with others who are also online, along with those skills needed to navigate network spaces. A minimal skill set may need to include additional functions and software competence depending on the discipline or course content. For example, computer literacy for humanities students who deal primarily with text would be different than literacy for science students who need to be able to design models.

One of the things computers excel at is the ability to automatically perform repetitive tasks, but it takes a certain amount of literacy for a person to be able to take advantage of this. Too often more primitive computer users will spend time manually adjusting text formatting while using a word processor, when a knowledge of styles would enable them to make global formatting changes to a document with one or two moves. Or if there is a series of tasks one routinely performs, such as loading or backing up certain files every time the computer is started or regularly copying particular files, a computer literate person could write a small computer program or configure the computer to perform these tasks automatically.

People can learn computing skills through organized training or classes, but often learn from trial and error or by talking to or watching others. In fact, one of the goals of software and interface designers has been to make computer use more intuitively obvious so that a person can easily navigate through computer software, locate icons (small graphic images of functions), and click on them to perform various functions. Also typical is learning just enough to accomplish a task at hand, which means that there may be easier or more efficient ways of using the computer to get the same job done. Furthermore, people may learn to do certain tasks and feel competent using computers, but when faced with a new task, using different software, they may suddenly feel confused and at sea. The result of learning by observation and trial and error may be an uneven or shallow understanding of computer use, and a person who works alone and is remote from other computer users often misses the opportunity to learn by looking over another person's shoulder. He or she misses out by not being part of an embodied, computer-literate culture where tips and concepts are transmitted as a part of normal, daily interaction.

Computer literacy, composed of an understanding of physical devices and software as well as a multiplicity of practical and social functions, is complex to define in any universal way. Some will say that computer literacy, or a minimum set of computer skills that is universally useful, does not exist. Regardless, an educator is wise to attend to the computer literacy of enrolling and continuing students by making clear what functional levels are required and what skills will be relevant for success in the context of the academic program, and to describe them in enough detail so that a person can evaluate or be evaluated as to where she is with respect to them. Specifically, what must a student know about computers and computer use in order to participate effectively in the educational program being offered? This usually means that specific skills are needed and the user must be able to use certain software programs. But there are also

higher levels of integration and comprehension in order to move from one software program to another and from one's local computer to a remote server—all of which are mediated by or accessed through the same computer monitor or screen.

Having a mental map of the computer space one operates in is immensely helpful in troubleshooting problems. This space is composed of the different layers of the operating system and software applications (which can interact in both intended and unintended ways), as well as the connections to remote servers from one's own computer through the Internet by means of a modem, a cable modem, a DSL line or other broadband connection, and an Internet service provider. Computer users without such a mental model have trouble getting help from technical support personnel because they cannot adequately describe a problem they are experiencing. A computer-literate person will know that a support person will need to know the context in which a problem occurred in order to diagnose and suggest remedies. The context may include the computer type, the operating system, the software applications that were running, the task the person was engaged in, and even the specific mouse clicks made or keys struck.

Providers of distributed education find that they need to provide help to users even if they have the prerequisite computer skills. A help desk is a remote location for users to telephone or e-mail when they have problems. A review of help desk calls can yield useful information about literacy needs among the callers, which can then be addressed by modifying the prerequisite skills, changing online training or education, or making referrals to local resources.

What does computer literacy look like? It certainly includes being able to use computer hardware and software for specific tasks, but it goes beyond having the skills needed for a particular online course. Here are some components:

- Having an appreciation for what computers can and cannot do
- Having realistic expectations about what one can and cannot accomplish with a computer and software
- Being able to shop for computer hardware and software and to distinguish a sales pitch from personal needs
- Being aware of the hazards of computer use, including ergonomic aspects for the user and the vulnerability of the computer to virus or unauthorized entry

- Being able to update software as it ages with patches and version upgrades
- Being able to use appropriate software applications for tasks as needed
- Knowing how to create documents or other files as well as how to save, move, find, copy, retrieve, back up, and delete them
- Being able to start the process of troubleshooting a problem and knowing where to go for help if needed
- Understanding ethical use with respect to copyright and fair use but, just as important, understanding how one's use of computer technology affects others

Specific skills as well as higher levels of computer and information literacy are needed in order to be a citizen and participate in a world that, in education and in general, is increasingly made available and interacted with via digitized, computerized text, sound, and images. As the number of human-made tools and systems increases, new literacies are needed (e.g., visual and multimedia literacy, because much of current life is mediated through a computer or television screen, via sound and image). These literacies are important not just to individuals, but also to the social and economic networks in which individuals participate.

*—Shelley K. Hughes*

*See also* Computer; Information Literacy

### Bibliography

McKenzie, J. (2003). *From now on: The educational technology journal.* Retrieved March 17, 2003, from http://www.fno.org/index.html.

Shapiro, J. J., & Hughes, S. K. (1996). Information literacy as a liberal art. Enlightenment proposals for a new curriculum. *EDUCOM Review, 31*(2), 31–35. Retrieved from http://www.educause.edu/pub/er/review/reviewArticles/31231.html.

Smith, J. (2003, February 15). *Jan's illustrated computer literacy 101.* Retrieved March 17, 2003, from http://www.jegsworks.com/Lessons/index.html.

# COMPUTER-MEDIATED COMMUNICATION (CMC)

Computer conferencing is based on the premise that the introduction of a computer as the host for asynchronous group communications allows the tailoring of both the protocols of communication and the structure of the underlying group process, in order to improve the ability of humans to communicate.

It is mathematically clear that groups of more than five to nine people who have basic keyboarding skills can exchange more information in writing than in verbal communication, given equal investments in time for the individuals involved. With today's technology, the added introduction of graphical and multimedia-based digital information further increases the efficiency of group communications conducted through the computer. However, the ultimate goal of this form of group communications is not efficiency of communication, but rather the development of computer-mediated communications systems that would allow human groups to consistently exhibit "collective intelligence." This means that group activity produces a higher quality result than what would have been created by the best member of the group acting alone. Typically, many face-to-face groups produce results that are an average of the inputs by the individual members and a less intelligent result than the best member would have produced. Surprisingly, much of the experimentation in group decision support systems has not addressed this fundamental issue.

## CLARIFYING THE TERMINOLOGY

Unfortunately, many different terms are used to mean "group communications via computer systems and networks." This is due to the high degree of commercialization within the field of computer applications, where vendors seek to make their products sound like they are new. We can gain some understanding by looking at a few of the current labels and what they seem, in general, to imply.

*Computer-mediated communications* is the preferred name for all forms of group communication including both synchronous and asynchronous message systems. The oldest computer conferencing systems, from the 1970s, such as Party-Line in the original EMISARI system and the Talk system in the Plato CAI system, had the ability to provide instant chat and instant messaging. Group message systems today typically have a stored archive, which is a central file of all messages sent to everyone in the group. This is an attempt to provide a feature already found in a computer conferencing system: a common shared transcript. This transcript helps remind members of what has been discussed and when, and allows new members to catch up on what they have missed in the past. Perhaps the name that comes the closest to the meaning of computer conferencing is *groupware* (originally proposed by Peter and Trudy Johnson Lenz), meaning the equal contribution of the group and the software to create a unique combination of group characteristics and software characteristics suited to the given application.

*Computer-supported cooperative work* focuses on the use of communications in the typical work environment, including such areas as work flow, project management, and calendars. Its philosophy appeals to industry—build it and get it into the hands of users quickly with very weak evaluation. The result is a lot of rediscovery of the wheel. However, the magnitude of the effort has resulted in a small but significant number of major successes, along with the many failures. A lot of interesting work regarding tailoring protocols and structures to fit the nature of the group and the task does occur in this school of design; this follows the spirit of computer conferencing, if not the objectives. A lot more attention is paid to selling or marketing to the user instead of trying to understand the long-term impacts and outcomes.

*Knowledge systems* are one of the more interesting recent trends. This work grows out of the idea of capturing the lore of the organization (organizational memory) into wisdom-oriented databases that make the organization more effective. Most knowledge systems focus on using domain-oriented knowledge structures (ontologies) as the basis for artificial intelligence methods to capture and organize this information and turn it into knowledge or wisdom. Standards such as Extensible Markup Language (XML) are seen as the mechanism for building a universal language that somehow avoids the fundamental problem of ambiguity in language. This computer science approach strives to have the computer do it all and attempts to remove humans from having effective input and control of such systems.

A more interesting line of research and development is in *collaborative knowledge systems*, and the associated area of *online communities*. In both of these areas, a primary premise is the importance of the information provided by knowledgeable individuals and the requirements to:

- Structure information to allow ease of retrieval
- Allow feedback and change over time

- Support voting and other summarization processes
- Recognize the need for updating and change as a dynamic process
- Recognize that those creating knowledge in the given domain need to guide the evolving structure of such systems, as well as contribute to the content

For example, knowledgeable members of an online community for people with a particular disease might include those having to cope with the disease, and who have acquired knowledge about the disease's associated living problems, as well as medical experts. In this sense these collaborative knowledge systems begin to sound very much like the concepts underlying the *Delphi method*. Most such systems are integrations of communications and database structures for capturing and organization of knowledge, similar to the concept of using semantic models of group-oriented conceptual maps to focus the discussions around the nodes and relationships in the conceptual maps. The need for semantic (i.e., hypertext) models to capture knowledge appropriate to a given application domain is common to all knowledge system approaches. The key difference in the collaborative orientation is to recognize that the core group creating knowledge must have a meta-process to evolve and tailor the underlying model or structure of the knowledge to accommodate change over time.

One can use a combination of some of the commercial computer conferencing systems and some of the survey design systems to execute *online Delphi exercises*. The results of a recent thesis by Cho and associates comparing a Delphi structure to a pure computerized conferencing mode shows that the number of ideas generated by groups is more productive in the Delphi approach as well as for larger groups. Furthermore, the number of ideas per person is also higher in the same conditions. This is contrary to the findings of many of the idea-generation experiments in the *group decision support system* studies.

It is becoming considerably easier to build a completely self-contained Delphi structure using tools like ColdFusion. This system is designed specifically for capturing a list of items, and then allowing a continuous voting process while further discussion is taking place about the list. The vote is organized in terms of pro, con, and neutral comments about each item. The system provides a wide range of voting tools and allows participants to change their vote as often as they wish because of the ongoing discussion. In the experiments that have been conducted, researchers have been surprised that some subjects find it a novel concept to be able to change their vote at any time. Many people have the impression that a vote is a final concluding action, and not a guide to either the discovery or a focusing process, which has always been a part of the Delphi process. It follows very closely the *social decision support systems* concept and should allow hundreds of participants to create a collaborative list of items (objectives, tasks, criteria, problems, solutions, etc.) and to meaningfully discuss and evaluate the resulting list.

One of the major growth areas in the application of computer conferencing has been *learning networks* and the resulting delivery of college courses at a distance. Today this application has begun to penetrate public elementary and secondary schools. The rapid growth in this area has been accompanied by the creation of many simple conference systems that focus more on course management support software and show little recognition of the importance of structuring discussions. A very simple and effective structuring tool in early systems such as the EIES Virtual Classroom, which forced every student to answer a discussion question before they could see the answers of the other students, exists in only one commercial product out of the hundreds available. Most educators utilizing the more popular products are unaware of what they are missing and how it can improve the learning process.

## KEY COMPUTER CONFERENCING SYSTEM FEATURES

The necessary and/or desirable properties of a computer conferencing system are:

- All inputs identify who authored them, who last modified them, and when these operations were performed.
- Sequential protocols such as "Roberts's rules of order," where certain actions must be accomplished before others, should be allowed on an individual or group basis.
- The opposite extreme of individuals being free to deal with any part of the discussion at any time should also be allowed.
- Semantic structures capture and organize incoming material. These structures represent nonlinear graphs on which both the links and the nodes may be labeled.

- Software-supported roles include monitor, moderator, facilitator, indexer, observer, contributor, voter, linker, organizer, editor, reviewer, briefer.
- Various voting and scaling methods apply to distinct entries or lists of entries.
- Vote changes are allowed based on the associated discussion, and "no judgment" votes should be included for those not ready to exercise this option.
- Input collection for quantitative data includes functions such as probability estimates or budget estimates
- Two-way linkages are semantically typed among comments, between anchors in comments, and between comments and entries in external databases.
- Contextual menus can be created dynamically from the content of added contributions.
- Membership lists indicate the status of the participants.
- Directories of conferences and topic descriptions are provided.
- Notifications alert members to occurrences they need to know about (e.g., an item needs their vote or the votes are viewable because the threshold of voters needed for this has been reached).
- Notifications reduce the information overload problem (e.g., "I agree" automatically attached to an original entry as an appendage doesn't require a whole new reply).
- Pen names allow users to establish personas and/or to organize role-playing games.

The specific benefits that computer conferencing systems provide groups are the ability to:

- Eliminate many group process losses (e.g., production blocking), thus allowing more ideas to be exposed and considered
- Eliminate some human biases by allowing anonymous or pen name inputs
- Use voting and scaling techniques to allow groups to understand what they agree and disagree about and to aid in focusing the discussion
- Allow very large groups, up to many hundreds, to engage in meaningful discussions
- Reflect as long as is needed on a person's input or responses to the inputs of others, rather than replying immediately "off the top of one's head"
- Provide the individual the flexibility of when to exercise personal problem-solving processes and when to engage in group problem-solving process (i.e., eliminating group dominance of the problem-solving process)

- Offer self-organizing structures for the collection of the content
- Allow any individual to focus at a given moment on whatever aspect of the problem he or she wishes to deal with
- Use meta-processes to control both the structuring and the protocols of the process, as well as to support individual unique roles in the process
- Vary the degree of computer vs. human facilitation that exists in a given application

## THE FUTURE OF COMPUTER-MEDIATED COMMUNICATION

Future directions include the development of toolkits for the components of a group communication system, which allow a single discussion and associated scaling, voting, and structuring tools that can be pasted anywhere on a computer screen to become an integral part of the object at that point on the screen. A particular electronic report from a database or an entry in a calendar could be the node for a groupware process linked to the actual data object. This will be the ultimate maturation of the observation that computer-based communications differ from all prior forms of communications, in that the content can be the address. This is particularly critical in such areas as crisis response management, and was one of the factors that made the early EMISARI systems a dramatic success.

Designing group communication systems is, in effect, the designing of social systems. As a result, the technology offers the possibility of new social structures for organizations and for society. Clearly, those building online communities (which are combinations of messaging, bulletin boards, and databases, integrated into a common interface) are an excellent example of people designing conferencing systems without knowing that this is what they are doing.

Perhaps the most impressive examples of modern groupware or structured computer conferencing systems are multiplayer games and virtual stock markets. Clearly, a structured game is a large group communication system with very specific protocols that must be followed. A stock market for predicting the winners of elections or the profit-making potential for a new movie is a new method of using scaling to improve the group judgment or social judgment function. In 1978, the book *Network Nation* included information about playing bridge and other games online. Today there is an international network for bridge players that allows a group of four to play together at any hour of the day and from anywhere in the world where they can reach the Web.

## CHALLENGES FOR THE FUTURE

A significant number of research and development challenges still face those in the field. Perhaps the most significant is efforts to allow large groups to build collaborative models of complex situations. This area requires medium to large multidisciplinary teams that may not be able to commit enough face-to-face time to accomplish a truly collaborative effort. Increasingly, many development projects in the software industry employ geographically dispersed professionals and teams.

A key part of any software development effort is the underlying structure for the software components that will make up the final product and the relationships among these components. This conceptual design is critical to the ultimate success of the effort and the ability of the system to adapt to changing requirements.

Many other planning areas in industry have the same fundamental tasks for any large project of this structural type. Now that most professional users have the computer power to deal with graphics and more complex modeling software, the next obvious challenge is how to make this a truly collaborative group effort with the tools to aid in the process of exploring and resolving differences of viewpoint in the components to be used in the model. A typical development plan for a new technical product may involve a hundred or more people spread out laterally across an organization. Reducing this problem to independent small face-to-face teams is a very real cause of poor estimates and poor plans for accomplishing the finished product without major overruns and miscalculations.

—*Murray Turoff*

*See also* Virtual Communities

## Bibliography

Bieber, Michael, Goldman, Ricki, Hiltz, Starr Roxanne, Im, Il, Paul, Ravi, Preece, Jennifer, Rice, Ron, Stohr, Edward, & Turoff, Murray. (2002, January). *Towards knowledge-sharing and learning in virtual professional communities.* Proceedings of the 35th HICSS, IEEE Computer Society Press.

Cho, H. K., Turoff, M., & Hiltz, S. R. (2003, January). *The impacts of Delphi communication structures on small and medium sized asynchronous groups.* Proceedings of the 36th HICSS, IEEE Computer Society Press.

Fjermestad, Jerry, & Hiltz, Roxanne. (Winter 1998–99). An assessment of group support systems experimental research: Methodology and results. *Journal of Management Information Systems, 13*(1), 7–150.

Harasim, L., Hiltz, S. R., Teles, L., & Turoff, M. (1995). *Learning networks.* Cambridge: MIT Press.

Hiltz, S. R., & Turoff, M. (1993, 1978). *The network nation,* Revised Edition. Cambridge: MIT Press.

Hiltz, S. R., & Turoff, Murray. (2002, April). What makes learning networks effective? *CACM, 45*(4), 56–59.

Linstone, Harold, & Turoff, Murray. (Eds.). (1975). *The Delphi method: Techniques and applications.* Retrieved from http://is.njit.edu/turoff.

Preece, J. (2000). *Online communities.* Hoboken, NJ: John Wiley & Sons.

Turoff, Murray. (2002, April). Past and future emergency response information systems. *CACM, 45*(4), 29–33.

Turoff, M., & Hiltz, S. R. (1995). Computer based Delphi processes. In Michael Adler and Erio Ziglio (Eds.), *Gazing into the oracle: The Delphi method and its application to social policy and public health* (pp. 56–88). London: Kingsley.

Turoff, Murray, Hiltz, Starr Roxanne, Fjermestad, Jerry, Bieber, Michael, & Whitworth, Brian. (2002). Computer mediated communications for group support: Past and future. In John M. Carroll (Ed.), *Human computer interaction in the new millennium.* New York: ACM Press and Addison-Wesley.

Turoff, M., Hiltz, R., Bieber, M., Rana, A., & Fjermestad, J. (1999). Collaborative discourse structures in computer mediated group communications, *HICSS, 32.*

Turoff, Murray, Hiltz, Starr Roxanne, Hee-Kyung, Cho, Li, Zheng, & Wang Yuanqiong. (2002, January). *Social decision support systems (SDSS).* Proceedings of the 35th HICSS, IEEE Computer Society Press.

Turoff, Murray, Rao, Usha, & Hiltz, S. R. (1991). Collaborative hypertext in computer mediated communications. *Proceeding of the Hawaii International Conference on Systems Science, 4*, IEEE Computer Society, 357–366.

Wang, Y., Li, Z., Turoff, M., & Hiltz, S. R. (2003). Using a SDSS toolkit to evaluate achieved course objectives. Presented at *America's Conference on Information Systems (AMCIS),* Boston, MA.

# CONNECTIVITY

When you connect a computer to the Internet, it becomes part of a global *mega-network* of millions of other computers that are able to quickly and accurately transmit information to each other. The Internet's early development, in the 1960s and early 1970s, laid the foundation for a decentralized network of connections among an ever-increasing number of computers. Data is transmitted from computer to computer across these connections, guided by *protocols,* specialized format languages that direct Internet-based systems such as e-mail, news lists, and the World Wide Web.

The Internet depends on the seamless transmission of data among digital computers through analog forms of connections. Analog systems, such as electricity and the telephone, represent and transmit data using a system that allows an infinite variety of values, as in electric voltages or radio frequencies. Digital computers, however, specify data with a discrete numbering system, much like counting the fingers (or digits) on one's hand. Calculations using digitized data are accurate, unambiguous, and precise. The hands of a clock represent analog values. As the hands move around the face of the clock, the time is never quite precise—an infinite number of values can be represented. In a digital watch, as in a digital computer, the numbers are specific and unambiguous.

## BITS, BYTES, BANDWIDTH, AND HERTZ

Digital computers convert all information—including text, video, graphics, sound, and multimedia—into digitized data, which is encoded into *bits.* Bits represent electronic switches that are either "on," represented by "1," or "off," represented by "0." Using digital terminology, 8 bits become a *byte,* and 1,000 bytes become a *kilobyte.* Subsequent increments are megabytes, gigabytes, terabytes, and beyond.

*Bandwidth* refers to the capacity of a connection to carry encoded bits of data from one point to another, as measured by the number of bits that can be carried within a specified time period. The basic unit of bandwidth is the number of bits per second (bps) that the connection can transport. These units can be represented as Kbps (thousands of bits per second), Mbps (millions of bits per second), and beyond.

*Hertz* are the number of cycles per second being transported, and can be considered equivalent to bps. Thousands of cycles per second are referred to as KHz (kilohertz), and millions of cycles per second are called MHz (megahertz).

## NETWORKED CONNECTIONS

Networked connections transmit information among computers. These connections may be through a variety of wired and wireless connections, including cables, wires, infrared frequencies, microwaves, and satellites. Through remote access connections, it is possible to connect additional computers to any of these networks from remote locations.

In *peer-to-peer networks,* up to 15 computers exchange information on an equal basis—each computer makes its information available to all other computers on the network. These networks can be built and maintained with readily available software and general computer expertise.

In *client-server networks,* one or more *server* computers provide all of the networked information and services to the other computers—the *clients* or *workstations.* Client-server networks require complex hardware and software as well as specialized expertise. They often have high levels of security, reliability, and speed.

*Local area networks (LANs)* are normally located within a single building and consist of direct connections between server and client computers. In organizations with large numbers of computers that are dispersed over wide areas, LANs are linked together to form *wide area networks (WANs),* creating potentially global networks of shared information exchanges through very secure and rapid connections.

*Campus area networks (CANs)* provide connections within multiple buildings on a campus or community. *Home area networks (HANs)* connect computers, printers, and other devices within the home.

Individual computers, as well as those linked together in a network configuration, connect to the Internet through Internet service providers (ISPs), online services, or specialized gateway server computers that have direct, hard-wired connections.

All forms of computer-based information can be shared among networked computers, including those connected via the Internet. Documents, programs, text, pictures, and video and audio information can be *downloaded,* or copied, from a source computer to a receiving computer. Similarly, you can *upload,* or copy, information from one computer to other computers, as when you send e-mails or post documents onto a Web-based forum.

E-mail is one form of sending and accessing information over the Internet. E-mail services are accessed through online services, ISPs, or an organization's direct e-mail server computers.

The *World Wide Web* (WWW or Web) is another way of locating, retrieving, and sharing information over the Internet. It uses a unique addressing schema to identify and precisely locate each Web site that is connected to the Internet, and the specific *Internet server* computer on which the Web site physically resides. Since its inception in 1990, the Web has become the primary vehicle for information sharing over the Internet.

Videoconferences are temporary, multimedia networks that use the Internet to connect people at different locations, so that they can work together in *real time,* sharing sound, video, text, data files, whiteboards, and other information and processes. Desktop videoconferencing systems use personal computers with small cameras, which are connected to each other via Internet connections. *Roll out* systems may have several screens, cameras, and speakers, providing a greater capacity to include many people in a single conference. *Studio systems* include all of the equipment of the roll out system, but are permanently located in a studio.

## PROTOCOLS

Protocols are specialized computer languages that provide formats and standards that allow networks to "speak" to each other, guiding the transmission of data across networks that may have different forms of connections, hardware, and software that would otherwise be incompatible. The *Transmission Control Protocol/Internet Protocol (TCP/IP)* suite of standards was designed by the U.S. Department of Defense. It includes four layers of protocols for network access, host-to-host (computer-to-computer) communication, Internet connections, and network access.

The first layer of the TCP/IP suite guides the delivery of data to the appropriate host computer. *File Transfer Protocol (FTP)* supports the transfer of data sets created by different types of computer systems. *Simple Mail Transfer Protocol (SMTP)* supports the transfer of e-mail messages. The *Terminal Emulation Standard (TELNET)* allows users to connect with a remote host computer as though it were locally connected.

The second layer, *Transmission Control Protocol (TCP),* supports computer-to-computer connections. It numbers outgoing packets of data bits and acknowledges the arrival of the packets, again by number. It reports on transmission errors, allows for security and priority levels, and optimizes network resources.

The third layer, *Internet Protocol (IP),* directs the reliable transfer of data over the Internet. Every computer that is connected to the Internet has a unique address that contains a network number and a number for the host computer that is running the application. Large organizations often subdivide their computers into subnets.

The final layer of the TCP/IP suite manages the exchange of data within a host computer, among the hosts attached to a network, and between the network and the hosts.

## PHYSICAL CONNECTIONS

Connectivity among computers and networks occurs through copper wires, cabling, fiber optics, microwave frequencies, infrared signals, and visible light lasers. These connections vary in cost, capacity, reliability, security, and accessibility.

Basic connections are still made through *plain old telephone service (POTS)* lines that carry varying voltage over one or two sets of *unshielded twisted pairs (UTP)* of copper wires that are connected to a telephone company. These basic telephone lines use analog (continuous wave) signals to transmit 33.6Kbps of data, which can be enhanced to reach 56Kbps of data. Analog signals are converted into digital format through a *modem,* a *modulator/demodulator* that manages the two-way conversion between the analog and digital transmissions.

*Ethernet* connections provided the initial standards for network connections, known as 10Base5, to reflect a 10Mbps transmission rate. These connections used coaxial cable, which has a center core of copper wire, wrapped by plastic, a metal shield, and an outer plastic coating.

*Cable modem* systems provide high-speed connections that can carry voice and video as well as data. Users may experience a slowdown during periods of heavy usage, however.

*Fiber optics cabling* offers greater bandwidth capacity than wire cables. SONET, the Synchronous Optical Network, provides standards for high-speed communications over fiber optic cable and protocols for converting electrical signals into optical light pulses, and also supports the synchronization of different forms of transmissions.

*Digital subscriber lines (DSL)* carry both voice and data transmissions. The DS1 line, referred to as a T-1 connection, uses a four-wire, twisted-pair connection, and can carry 1.544Mbps (million bits per second). The higher capacity DS3 connection (T-3 lines) can carry 44.736Mbps of data. Different forms of DSL include asymmetric DSL (ADSL), high speed DSL (HDSL), and very-high speed DSL (VDSL).

*ISDN (Integrated Services Digital Network)* lines were developed to carry voice, data, and video communications in a single system. They are intended to integrate into one service the types of communication that previously needed dial-up analog lines (voice), digital data lines, and coaxial cable lines for video.

## WIRELESS CONNECTIONS

Wireless technologies are being developed to enable faster and more reliable transmission of data without the need for physical links of wire or cable. *Infrared connections* use light waves that are invisible to humans to transport data at speeds of 1,000GHz and higher, but require unobscured pathways. Infrared is most suitable for local devices, such as beaming data between personal data devices and laptops.

*Radio frequency (RF)* transmissions have been used for wireless connections for more than a hundred years, with a wide band of electromagnetic frequencies that range from AM radio at 1MHz to the cellular phone band at 2GHz. Radio frequency transmissions are subject to a variety of transmissions problems such as rain and other impediments.

The *microwave* RF band ranges from 1GHz to 300GHz. The microwave system can be quickly installed, at minimal cost compared to landline connections that require wires or cable lines. It is used for cellular phone and data connections, and can link to geographic regions where landlines are difficult to install.

Although wireless connections were originally designed for peer-to-peer transmission of data, they are increasingly being used for connecting mobile technologies (such as laptops) and host computer services through wide area networks.

*Satellite* transmission for voice and data is nearly universal in coverage and is adequate for most e-mail communication. It supports Internet communications in all areas of the world that are covered by the satellites' span.

*Asynchronous transfer mode (ATM)* supports the high-speed transmission of data between computers and locations in a network. It is *multiplexing*—combining multiple streams of data into a single connection. Most data transmission within computers is synchronous—data is transmitted at timed intervals with no peak or valley levels of activity. However, most communications within networks are asynchronous, transmitted at varying times and quantities. There are times of the day when there are large volumes of data being transmitted, and other times when there is very little data transmission. By breaking up data into discrete packets, each of which includes the path of the data and other information such as the beginning and ending of the packet and data stream, the ATM approach delivers needed bandwidth on an as-needed basis. Voice, data, and video can be transmitted rapidly and accurately, with wide variations in volume, yet at a reasonable cost.

## RESILIENCE AND SECURITY

As a global, interconnected society we have become dependent on connectivity for nearly all aspects of our lives. Because failures in data transmission have far-reaching consequences, today's networks are designed to withstand hardware failures. Through a variety of backup schemas and operational procedures, networks can recover quickly from most connectivity breakdowns.

In our uncertain world, continuous improvements in the resiliency and security of vital connectivity systems, including those in our homes and institutions, is essential for learning, working, and living in the information age.

—*Dorothy E. Agger-Gupta*

*See also* LEARNING COMMUNITIES; RELATIONSHIPS; SOCIAL CONSTRUCTIONISM

### Bibliography

Hallberg, B. (2001). *Networking: A beginner's guide.* New York: McGraw-Hill.

Hobart, M. E., & Schiffman, Z. S. (1998). *Information ages: Literacy, numeracy, and the computer revolution.* Baltimore, MD: Johns Hopkins University Press.

International Engineering Consortium. (n.d.). *Online tutorials.* Retrieved from http://www.iec.org/online/tutorials/.

Jonassen, D. H., & Peck, K. L. (1999). *Learning with technology: A constructivist perspective.* Upper Saddle River, NJ: Merrill.

Sexton, M., & Reid, A. (1997). *Broadband networking: ATM, SDH, and SONET.* Norwood, MA: Artech House.

Steinke, S., & Editors of Network Magazine. (2000). *Network tutorial: A complete introduction to networks.* San Francisco: CMP Books.

Webopedia. (2002). Retrieved from http://www.webopedia.com.

# CONTINUING EDUCATION

Continuing education (CE) refers at the most general level to all education and learning in formal or informal settings that takes place after the conclusion of mandatory education (school-based), and following a significant amount of time out of formal education. CE thus covers a very broad range of activity, virtually all of it undertaken by part-time rather than full-time study.

Terminology is significant. In Britain, adult education and adult learning are longstanding terms, associated predominantly with nonvocational and leisure education, provided by agencies across a wide range of levels and types. Historically, much of this provision in Britain and elsewhere in Western Europe has been undertaken through or on behalf of religious organizations and, in some societies, also through political parties and industrial, trade union bodies. Most commonly, though, certainly in Britain, adult education has been provided by the "local state," that is, in this context, by Local Education Authorities (LEAs). The large majority of such work has been either in areas such as basic skills (literacy and numeracy), community education and neighborhood renewal, various leisure interest pursuits, or in certificate work at various levels in either vocational or academic subjects.

Adult education has also always had strong associations with social purpose and social movement cultures and aspirations (discussed below). In Britain these have largely been delivered through bodies such as the Workers' Educational Association (WEA) and university extramural or continuing education departments, and in many parts of Western Europe through folk high schools and the like.

In the 1970s, continuing education became the more modern term for this whole area of work, at least in Britain. This change in terminology, however, didn't simply denote modernity and fashion; it also signified an increased concentration on the more vocational, professional, and work-related aspects of provision. One example of the way in which the term *continuing education* came into common usage was the distinction made, arcane in some ways though it may have been, in many British universities between "extension" and "joint tutorial classes"; that is, between provision made for the personal and particularly the professional interests of the relatively well-qualified and educationally engaged sectors of the community, who would benefit from the "extension" of the university's mainstream provision, and provision made jointly by the university and the WEA for those who had not had the (assumed) benefits of tertiary education. Continuing education was thus seen as a means of bringing together organizationally as well as conceptually two distinct types of provision *and* two different cultures. Similarly, in other areas of adult learning, continuing education became a relatively widespread term—an acknowledgement of the increasing emphases of government and funding bodies on the importance of vocational and labor-market–oriented provision. Increasingly, governments saw the justification for continuing education provision as based on the needs of the economy for a more skilled and educated workforce.

This conception of continuing education co-existed uneasily with more liberal perceptions of the rationale for continuing education. From this latter perspective, the main purposes of continuing education were twofold: personal development—the opening up through learning opportunity of an enhanced appreciation of the arts, sciences, and social sciences—and the more collectively oriented objective of contributing to the analysis, understanding, and amelioration of social inequality.

Continuing education had greater currency, terminologically, in Britain than elsewhere. In North America, for example, "extension studies" has been and remains a huge area of service, usually self-financed at full cost and provided largely for a public

willing to pay a relatively high fee for provision (both certificated or accredited, and noncertificated) for either personal development or professional reasons. There have also been many examples of cross-subsidy of budgets in such programs to provide public service—community education for disadvantaged groups at greatly reduced cost. However, all this work has normally been very separate from the concerns of university departments or centers of adult education, which have concentrated on providing programs of postgraduate study for those interested in a professional qualification in aspects of adult learning, and have undertaken research and scholarly publication in adult learning as a specialist field within education.

Looking at the development in the field in the 1990s, many analysts, whatever their ideological views, saw this shift in emphasis as underpinned by the recognition of the necessity for greater interaction between the world of continuing education, broadly defined, and what was perceived as a significantly changed socioeconomic system. Whether this represented an unwarranted incorporation of the academy into a global capitalist culture, or merely a necessary readjustment of higher education's focuses and provision to a rapidly changing environment, were issues of contention.

By the later 1990s, however, continuing education as an organizing concept had been largely superceded, in Britain as elsewhere, by lifelong learning. The "rise of Lifelong Learning up the policy agenda has been a remarkable one," as John Field and Mal Leicester have noted. As the term implies, lifelong learning has a much wider scope and purpose than continuing education, and its prevalence is explicable at least in part by the common acceptance of the advent of the "knowledge society." Once this characterization is accepted, then the importance of learning throughout life becomes almost axiomatic.

Lifelong learning, in most policy formulations, emphasizes vocational and skills-enhancing education even more than was the case with continuing education. Globalization, the rapid rise of information and communication technologies (ICT), the remarkable volatility of the labor market, and, generally, the accelerating pace of change are all held by the advocates of lifelong learning to require a "step change" in governmental and societal perspectives on structures and practices of learning. Governments, as well as bodies like the Organization for Economic Cooperation and Development (OECD), have placed a strong emphasis on "human capital" arguments in relation to lifelong learning. Education, training, and learning are looked at as "capital goods," necessary elements in achieving a competitive economic basis for modern societies. This perspective has not been without its critics, mainly from the left, but it has also been complemented by those who acknowledge and, indeed, celebrate the knowledge society as part of the Third Way philosophy of the New Labour movement in Britain, and see learning as a key element in effective contemporary living.

Adult education and the broader concept of lifelong learning are thus both important elements in modern social policy in virtually all developed societies, but differ greatly in their concept, level, and type of provision. Adult education in the developing world, however, has somewhat different dimensions—which is hardly surprising, given the context of poverty and deprivation. Here, adult education is concerned primarily with basic skills, such as literacy and numeracy; related areas of social policy, such as health care and education; and agriculture.

In summary, this field of education is so varied and sprawling that it defies any neat definition or boundary. It is, however, clear that its importance, indeed centrality, to the well-being of contemporary societies and their citizens is recognized and acknowledged. The twenty-first century is likely to see a growth in the profile and importance of continuing education/lifelong learning given the volatility of the labor market, the increasingly complex and sophisticated patterns of social organization and social life, and the rapid pace of change.

—*Richard E. Taylor*

*See also* CORPORATE TRAINING; WORK-BASED DISTRIBUTED LEARNING

## Bibliography

Coffield, F. (1998). *Why the beer's always stronger up north? Studies in lifelong learning in Europe.* London: Policy Press/ESRC.

Coffield, F. (1999). Breaking the consensus: Lifelong learning as a form of social control. *British Education Research Journal, 25*(4), 479–499.

Delanty, G. (2001). *Challenging knowledge: The university in the knowledge society.* Buckingham: SRHE and Open University Press.

Field, J. (2000). *Lifelong learning and the new educational order.* Stoke-on-Trent: Trentham Books.

Field, J., & Leicester, M. (Eds.). (2000). *Lifelong learning: Education across the lifespan.* London: Routledge Falmer.

Fieldhouse, R., & Associates. (1998). *A history of modern British adult education.* Leicester: NIACE.

Giddens, A. (1998). *The third way: The renewal of social democracy.* Cambridge: Polity.

Holford, J., Jarvis, P., & Griffin, C. (Eds.). (1998). *International perspectives in lifelong learning.* London: Kogan Page.

Schuetze, H., & Slowey, M. (Eds.). (2000). *Higher education and lifelong learners: International perspectives on change.* London: Routledge Falmer.

Taylor, R., Rockhill, K., & Fieldhouse, R. (1985). *University adult education in England and the USA: A reappraisal of the liberal tradition.* Beckenham: Croom Helm.

Wallis, J. E. (Ed.). (1996). *Liberal adult education: The end of an era?* Nottingham: Nottingham University Press.

Watson, D., & Taylor, R. (1998). *Lifelong learning and the university: A post-Dearing agenda.* Brighton: Falmer.

# CORPORATE TRAINING

Corporate training in distributed learning refers to the development, design, and delivery of training and education programs for employees who are dispersed geographically. Corporate training programs can be delivered in both in-person and online learning formats. Training and education programs range from technical courses to executive-level leadership development programs, depending upon the business needs, size, employee skills, and available resources in corporate organizations. Corporate training programs are generally part of the Human Resources department in a small or medium sized corporation, and can be departments or units of their own in larger national and global corporations. The primary components of corporate training and education include 1) corporate universities, 2) e-learning and blended learning, 3) Web learning platform technologies, and 4) return on investment and learning metrics.

## CORPORATE UNIVERSITIES

The emergence of corporate universities within the workplace signaled a new trend in employee training over the last decade. As the economy expanded, corporations began to hire more workers, especially in the technology and industry sectors. As a result of high growth, companies hired rapidly to meet expansion needs. They also had to quickly figure out ways to improve employee productivity and training internally in order to keep pace with new technologies, market growth, and customer demand. At the same time, some corporations felt that higher education had not kept up with the pace of change, lagged behind the curve in terms of offering the latest technology, and was focused on educational outcomes that were not necessarily in line with what corporations needed to remain competitive. In response to this market growth and perceived lack of business-based outcomes, corporations began to form university-like programs internally in order to gain control over the training and learning needs of the business and, by extension, their employees. In times of economic downturn, corporate universities focus more on developing existing employees, preparing them to gain skills and knowledge that enable the business to move through difficult times and prepare for future growth and new market challenges. The larger learning challenge now for corporate universities is to expand by offering more courses and programs in a distributed and electronic learning format.

Corporate universities offer a full range of courses, certification, training workshops, and even academic degree programs to employees, in subjects that include both technical (hard skills) and management (soft skills) development. The curriculum includes a general understanding of theory with an emphasis on practical application and a focus on skills development that meets the specific needs and business goals of the corporation. Programs include technical training on specific hardware platforms, software platforms, and other applications technologies; orientations to specific work functions, such as accounting, policies (especially in the area of human resources), manufacturing, and quality programs; program or project management; selected management values and issues, such as workplace diversity, negotiation and conflict resolution, supervisory training, and strategic business planning; and leadership and management development programs designed especially for executives and employees with "high potential" or identified as next generation leaders within the corporation.

Corporate training programs often link course or training outcomes to employee development and core competencies that include 360-degree feedback performance. This type of feedback refers to an assessment or employee performance evaluation program that incorporates feedback from an employee's peers, manager, customers or clients, and direct reports (employees who work directly for the employee). Core competencies are generally composed of three key components: management, technical, and business objectives. Examples of core competencies include client relationship management, interpersonal communications, team building and team development, technical fluency, customer satisfaction measurements, and revenue and expense management. Together, the employee and her or his manager determine the core competencies required for the job.

Corporate training programs are typically designed and developed internally by in-house trainers or course developers or contracted and outsourced using a formal bid process to external consulting firms and/or educational partners. Educational partners are often local or national educational institutions and universities that specialize in one or many of the core competencies identified by the corporate university as critical to business success. The trend in program development and delivery is toward outsourcing and partnering with these third-party developers. This trend benefits corporations because they can 1) hire consultants or partner with educational institutions who have a core expertise in a given subject, thus delivering a higher quality program to employees; 2) maintain costs and manage the budget by not hiring a large cadre of training and development personnel; 3) offer the most up-to-date curriculum, generally at a lower cost than what can be developed internally; 4) offer academic and for-credit courses that employees can leverage into certificate and degree programs to meet career development goals; 5) influence course outcomes to meet specific training goals; and 6) impose their own evaluation and technology integration criteria.

## E-LEARNING AND BLENDED LEARNING

Distributed corporate training programs range from network-based delivery to in-person courses and workshops to degree learning programs that include both e-learning and blended learning solutions. E-learning is defined as skills and/or knowledge transfer that occurs over the Internet or an electronic network. The mix of in-person and online program delivery is called *blended learning*. The e-learning and blended learning terminology is somewhat interchangeable and reflects an industry trend toward Internet-based or networked learning technologies and processes. Typical learning components include self-paced training modules, such as CBTs (computer-based training), CD-ROMs, and DVD technology; assessment and diagnostic tools that are redesigned for online access and use; lab facilities with some traditional classroom learning that is instructor led; collaboration software and programs that allow employees working at a distance or across geographical boundaries to dialogue and do work as one team; and a learning management system that manages course or training resources, including automatic testing and grading, course evaluations, attendance and employee tracking, and setting priorities and goals for achieving these performance objectives.

E-learning programs are becoming essential to meeting employee learning outcomes and goals because they solve real business problems. E-learning has proven its value in five key areas: 1) improving skill- or knowledge-related job performance issues, 2) enhancing employee productivity, 3) meeting customer satisfaction goals and metrics, 4) attaining revenue goals, and 5) reducing the time it takes for new employees to ramp up. E-learning also reduces training costs by reducing travel expenses and offering a convenient method for employees to do training on their own time, when it fits their schedule. Training centers are rapidly incorporating online-based components into their curriculum in order to maximize these perceived employee and workplace benefits.

The other important factor in developing an effective blended or e-learning solution is the learning method. Making this shift from expert and in-person training to adult-based, collaborative learning within an e-learning or blended learning environment is a challenge for corporate trainers and educators. Because most of the corporate workforce consists of adults, it is important to design and offer courses or programs that are built on the foundational principles of adult learning, or what is called the androgogical model. These principles include using real-world problems and issues as the starting point for engaging the adult learner, experiential learning opportunities such as case studies and role playing, and partnering with employees to assist in developing learning objectives and outcomes, content modules, and performance evaluation indicators that are meaningful to both the employee and the business. Blending or e-learning programs that rely on the traditional expert or lecture-based model are typically less effective in their outcomes and do more harm than good in terms of promoting e-learning as a viable learning model for employees.

## WEB LEARNING PLATFORM TECHNOLOGIES

Web-based hardware and software platforms used in corporate training environments consist of six primary components: real-time and asynchronous collaboration, Web conferencing, content management, third-party content development, authoring tools, and course management. Real-time or chat (learners using the system and communicating online at the same time) and asynchronous (learners using the system one at a time and communicating online within a defined time period) collaboration software are designed to foster team projects and group learning. As such, the technology design is team-based and makes heavy use of key features such as team folders, discussion topic areas, team membership lists and e-mail addresses (making it easy to communicate with other team members), and security to form and maintain ad hoc teams. Web conferencing includes e-mail, phone, audio, and video capabilities that can be applied as part of a multi-modal learning experience. Web conferencing is also heavily utilized in other business functions such as project management, sales, marketing, and customer service centers.

Content management refers to technology platforms that incorporate specific content from vendors, such as integrated ordering and manufacturing modules from SAP and Oracle, that employees can use for technical training and access to reference data and materials. Third-party content development allows third-party contractors or content developers to import their content modules directly into the system and integrate between systems. Authoring tools refer to the features course developers and trainers use to develop the courses. Authoring tools typically include the ability to create and modify course design; incorporate Web articles and references for an online course; bring in added functionality, such as PowerPoint presentations and spreadsheets; perform calculations; and design custom features. Course management consists of the overall management of a course or training module. Typical functionality includes tracking of student or employee progress, grading, automatic testing and scoring, attendance, tracking the number of times an employee logs on and off, and integration with other human resource applications such as training records or performance evaluations.

In addition, it is important to keep in mind the learning methodology—adult learning or expert learning—when considering Web technology options. Vendors or suppliers of Web learning platform technologies tend to offer technologies that maximize expert and course-centric features on one end and collaborative, discussion, or dialogue-based features at the other end of the spectrum. Determining an organization's learning model ahead of time is important because it will assist in focusing on the right mix of technologies to meet employee learning needs, and will save time and resources downstream during the implementation process. Lastly, in a multi-language environment, it is important that vendors can provide language translation to support key areas of functionality.

## RETURN ON INVESTMENT AND LEARNING METRICS

One of the primary goals of any corporate training program is to align corporate training with the business. From a corporate training perspective, it is critical to measure the effectiveness of employee training in order to prove the value of learning to the business. Measuring effectiveness is often referred to as the learning return on investment or learning ROI. Measuring the e-learning ROI includes qualitative and quantitative metrics that can be directly and/or indirectly linked to business objectives and results. Quantitative metrics include the major categories of learner satisfaction, penetration and usage (tracking the employee's use or level of engagement in an e-learning course), effectiveness (the time it takes to absorb the learning and apply it on the job), relevance and cost of development, and delivery and maintenance of hardware, software, and support systems. Examples of quantitative metrics include percentage of employees enrolling in courses, percentage of employees completing courses, employee scores on technical or functional training, the time it takes for an employee to become proficient at a new task, the time to completion, reduction in errors, turnover, and so forth. Examples of qualitative metrics include impact on customer satisfaction, increased confidence working with customers or clients, and perceived improvements in communication or interpersonal relationships.

It is important to consider and include business-driven metrics in the design stage of a course or program. There are four levels of evaluation to consider in developing learning metrics: Level one evaluation measures learner satisfaction; level two tests for learner competence; level three examines changes in behavior on the job; and level four measures the impact on business results. These evaluation tools can range from a simple, end-of-course evaluation that includes a quantitative component (scale that measures satisfaction) and open-ended (qualitative) questions to follow-up evaluations and testing 30, 60, or 120 days after an employee has completed a course or program. The use of 360-degree feedback is also a way to assess results for level three evaluation.

For level four evaluation, it is recommended that the learning ROI be linked to key business performance indicators, such as percent of customers satisfied with products and services, revenue and expense targets, reductions in error rates, or percent of on time delivery. Key business performance indicators will vary according to a corporation's business strategy. Metrics need to be relevant, measurable (or measurable at not too high a cost), and understandable by all levels of employees and customers (if applicable). It is possible that in multinational corporations, metrics may vary between cultures or geographic regions, so it is important to consider local benchmarks as well as national standards when developing key metrics.

Measuring the cost and effectiveness of e-learning remains one of the key challenges in corporate training. Data systems and processes historically have focused on cost measurements, with the explicit goal of cost reduction. New business models focus on investment and attempt to measure the investment of dollars on learning to achieve or maximize results. Many corporate training departments are now focused on partnering with business units in order to mutually agree upon outcomes and key benchmarks.

*—Christi A. Olson*

***See also*** CONTINUING EDUCATION;
    WORK-BASED DISTRIBUTED LEARNING

## Bibliography

American Society for Training and Development (ASTD). (n.d.). Retrieved from www.astd.org.

Bassi, Laurie J. (2000). *Measuring the economic value of learning.* Retrieved from www.saba.com.

Bersin, Josh. (2002, June). Measure the metrics. *E-learning Magazine, 3*(6), 26–28.

Cisco Systems. (2000, June 26). *Global e-learning evaluation systems overview and requirements.* Retrieved from www. cisco.com.

Corporate University Xchange. (n.d.). Retrieved from www.corpu.com.

Schacht, Nick. (2002, May). Blended learning: Turning the training center into a learning center. *E-learning Magazine, 3*(5), 34–36.

# CORRESPONDENCE COURSES

The correspondence course is the ancestor of all forms of distributed learning. It is also one of today's most frequently used distance teaching formats. Essentially, correspondence courses (the terms *independent study, home study,* and *correspondence study* are generally used interchangeably) provide a form of asynchronous (not in "real time") instruction, in which teachers and students do not encounter each other in person. In most cases, the student can enroll at any time, and he or she sets the pace and timing of the course, within a stipulated number of months. Interaction between student and teacher takes place primarily in writing, communicated through the mail or the Internet.

Educational institutions of all sorts have employed correspondence courses to teach students around the world. Primary and secondary schools have reached children in rural and otherwise isolated areas. Commercial or "proprietary" schools have sought— and sometimes found—profit through home study courses. The military, professional associations, and churches have used them to provide specialized training to widely dispersed populations. Colleges and universities have extended their reach and conducted the public service part of their stated missions by targeting such courses primarily to working adults. In addition, postsecondary independent study departments provided the structure, organizational home, and basic methodology used in early distributed learning experiments with radio and television. At the same time, its radical departure from nineteenth-century teaching practices, its overtly egalitarian appeal, and its vulnerability to abuse have made correspondence study highly controversial throughout the course of its history.

Teaching via the mail originated in England and Western Europe, and then became popular around the globe. In the 1840s, Isaac Pitman introduced a new shorthand method by critiquing the work of customers, which they submitted on penny postcards. The Toussaint-Langenschiedt Correspondence School began to teach languages in 1856, using a method that would serve as a prototype for other educators. Students received monthly letters directing their efforts and demanding a "written recitation" for the instructors to correct. In England, proprietary correspondence schools sprang up to support students throughout the Commonwealth as they prepared for examinations leading to the University of London's external degree.

In spite of several early experiments, correspondence study truly began to emerge as an important and permanent factor in American education only in 1892, a year that saw three important developments. First, William Rainey Harper included an extensive correspondence course program in his design for the founding of the University of Chicago. Harper's personal credibility and the new university's prestige proved critical in establishing correspondence study as a credible means of college teaching. The same year, the Pennsylvania State College (now Pennsylvania State University) began to conduct correspondence courses in agriculture in furtherance of the Land Grant mission. Finally, Thomas J. Foster began teaching formal courses in mining safety via correspondence study in 1892. His school would eventually become the International Correspondence Schools (ICS), still the largest and most successful of all proprietary schools.

Both the higher education and proprietary sectors flourished. Large universities, most often public, and teachers colleges used correspondence courses to extend their reach and to serve working adults, particularly schoolteachers. During the Progressive Era in American history (roughly 1900–1915), this orientation proved politically wise, as well as educationally effective. The University of Wisconsin's correspondence program, for example, was an integral part of the progressive movement in that state. Although programs came and went in the first half of the twentieth century, by the 1970s more than 70 major colleges and universities offered correspondence courses as a part of their continuing education missions.

Proprietary programs also grew quickly during the Progressive Era, and even more so during the 1920s.

On the positive side, such programs offered education or vocational training, and thus hope, to hundreds of thousands of people public higher education had always ignored. In 1924, more than four times as many people were enrolled in proprietary correspondence schools than were attending all American colleges, universities, and resident technical schools combined. On the negative side, however, many proprietary schools were small and short-lived; the worst were fraudulent. These schools without doubt contributed to the ongoing skepticism on the part of the public and many academics about the utility and integrity of the correspondence method. This problem of academic credibility has persisted, not only for correspondence courses, but also for other forms of distributed learning as they emerged.

Written language has always been the essential component of correspondence study, both in the transmission of content and in student–teacher interaction. However, university independent study programs, more than proprietary schools, have frequently attempted to use telecommunications media to bolster their programs. In the 1920s and 1930s, a dozen American colleges and universities experimented with instructional radio, combining broadcast lectures with correspondence methodology. The University of Iowa's correspondence bureau participated in the first educational television experiments in 1933. Other university correspondence programs invested great amounts of time and money in the development of courses incorporating television in the 1950s and 1960s.

More recently, the use of the Internet has proven very effective in independent study programs. Online courses are well suited to their asynchronous, student-paced nature. Online independent study courses also speed up student–teacher interaction. Further, the Internet has brought immediate access to sophisticated reference materials and databases to independent study students. Previously, the restricted use of library materials had been one of the chief drawbacks of the correspondence method.

The pedagogy of correspondence study varies according to the nature of the agency providing it. There is no dominant model for developing and offering courses. Some take an approach reminiscent of industry: Teams of professors or other content experts, editors, instructional designers, and others create highly sophisticated courses—often using several media—for mass delivery to thousands of students. Courses of this type are not identified with particular instructors, and most often employ objective testing. Proprietary schools, the military, and some college programs, most notably Britain's Open University, favor this model. Most university programs use a smaller scale developmental model. Correspondence study specialists assist faculty in converting a given course from a face-to-face classroom format into a course designed for asynchronous distance delivery. Generally, the faculty member who writes the course also teaches it. Therefore, these courses reflect the individual personalities and teaching styles of the faculty. Some use objective testing, as they do in the classroom; others avoid it and demand the kind of frequent, copious written interaction they demand in their traditional format courses.

Most correspondence courses employ a written manual or "study guide"—presented either in a paper version or on a Web page—textbooks, and ancillary materials as needed (rock kits in geology courses, for example). Courses are divided into units, each with specific assigned readings, instructor commentary—intended as a substitute for the physical presence of a teacher—and self-testing exercises. Most courses, especially those for which academic credit is awarded, also include frequent exercises or quizzes that students mail, e-mail, or otherwise deliver to the independent study office, which forwards them to the instructor, who marks or critiques and then returns them. In a well-designed course, these exchanges should lead to one-to-one interaction that can become more extensive and intense than typical conversations in conventional classrooms.

Correspondence courses for which college or high school credit is awarded require students to take their examinations in the presence of a proctor approved in advance by the sponsoring school. For this part of the course, the Internet has not yet replaced the mail. Because the exams are the only course component for which the originating schools can be certain of the identity of the person doing the work, most independent study programs require students to receive passing marks on the proctored exams—regardless of their scores on the unit assignments—in order to receive credit for the course.

Because of the varied nature of the schools and institutions that offer correspondence courses, and due to nomenclature problems in distributed learning, enrollment figures are elusive and—at best—inexact. However, the Distance Education and Training Council (DETC), a national accrediting agency for distance education programs, estimates that each year about 8 million people enroll in correspondence courses offered by schools located in the United States, exclusive of in-house corporate programs and unaccredited schools. About 250,000 of them take college and university courses. Roughly 2.5 million each enroll in courses offered through religious programs, the military, and other DETC members, including proprietary schools.

—*Von Pittman*

*See also* Degrees/Degree Programs

## Bibliography

Bittner, W. S., & Mallory, H. F. (1933). *University teaching by mail: A survey of correspondence instruction conducted by American universities.* New York: Macmillan.

MacKenzie, O., Christensen, E. L., & Rigby, P. H. (1968). *Correspondence instruction in the United States.* New York: McGraw-Hill.

Noffsinger, J. S. (1926). *Correspondence schools, lyceums, chautauquas.* New York: Macmillan.

Watkins, B. L., & Wright, S. J. (Eds.). (1991). *The foundations of American distance education: A century of collegiate correspondence study.* Dubuque, IA: Kendall/Hunt.

Wedemeyer, C. A., & Childs, G. B. (1961). *New perspectives in university correspondence study.* Chicago: Center for the Study of Liberal Education for Adults.

# COURSE CREDIT/CREDIT TRANSFER

Academic course credit, credit hour, and unit of credit are all terms that refer to a unit of measure used by higher education institutions to place a value on the amount of time or learning a course's content encompasses. Each course offered by an institution is assigned a value of how many credits or units it is worth. When students have completed the course content satisfactorily, they are awarded the appropriate number of units or credits on their transcript. Courses are the basis on which an academic transcript is built. Other degree requirements, such as practica, internships, comprehensive examinations, theses, or dissertations, may also be represented as courses on the transcript and assigned credit hour values.

## STANDARDS OF THE ACADEMIC CREDIT HOUR

There is no nationally mandated definition of the academic credit hour, although there are some nationwide commonalities. The traditional form of the credit hour is one credit assigned to a class that meets one hour a week over a period of a semester, quarter, or term. Although there is no set standard for the length of a term, a length of anywhere from 12 to 18 weeks is fairly common for schools that use an early semester calendar. Common practice has created what many schools refer to as the Carnegie unit, which is defined as 15 class contact hours (a 50-minute meeting once a week during a 15-week semester, or 750 minutes) equals one credit.

In distributed learning programs that are delivered asynchronously or through independent study models, course credit might not be defined by class contact hours, but rather as the amount of learning the student is expected to demonstrate in regards to the course content. In such a program, the amount of time spent in actual class meetings, or on study time, research, or writing is unimportant. What is important is the breadth and depth of the specified knowledge base that is achieved by the student, and not the means or length of time required for the student to master that particular knowledge base.

In a degree program that offers coursework via both traditional instructional methods and distributed or distance learning methods, a limit may be placed on the number of distance learning credit hours the student may apply to the degree program. In others, the number of credit hours used for the degree and delivered via distance learning methods is unimportant.

## CREDIT BY EXAMINATION

If a student is familiar with a particular subject or is able to master content readily without teaching assistance, he or she may be able to obtain course credit through examination. The student must prepare for examination without any assistance, although a syllabus, texts, or sample exams to help the student study may be made available as part of the exam fee or for separate purchase. The grade on the examination becomes the grade on the course, although the amount of course credit received is determined by the receiving institution. Institutions usually have a limit on how many courses by examination a student may use toward the degree. An institution may also offer its own proctored exams throughout the year, or it may accept test results from some or all of the more prominent nationwide testing services, including The College Board, which administers CLEP and AP exams; American College Testing (ACT), formerly known as American Testing Service; Educational Testing Service (ETS), which administers the Graduate Record Exam (GRE); and The Thomas Edison College Examination Program (TECEP), which was originally offered only to students of Thomas Edison College, but is now administered nationwide.

## CREDIT TRANSFER

Schools that accept transfer credit evaluate the student's previous coursework completed at other institutions. If the receiving or accepting school is accredited, usually it will only accept transfer credit from other regionally accredited schools. The student provides information on the courses completed, usually including a transcript displaying course number and title, and the number of credit hours the course is worth. The evaluator may also require the course description from the university's catalog, and possibly the course syllabus in order to make the determination of transfer credit. This information is compared to the course offering at the current institution for equivalency. Transfer credit is normally determined either prior to admission or during the student's first semester after admission, but no later. When students receive transfer credit at their new school, that credit is applied to their degree program, thus relieving them of having to complete coursework in the same subject matter as the work they had previously completed at the other school. A limit is usually placed on the number of credit hours that can be accepted and applied to a student's degree program.

No school can guarantee that credits from courses are transferable to another school, unless two schools have a consortium agreement in place. Such a consortium agreement is often referred to as a course articulation, or more frequently, an articulation agreement. Transfer of credits is always at the discretion of the receiving school and depends on the comparability of curricula.

Some schools limit the number of distributed or distance-learning credit hours that they will accept for transfer credit.

## CONTINUING EDUCATION UNITS

The continuing education unit (CEU) is different from the academic credit hour, in that it does have a standardized ratio of contact hours to units. The CEU is 10 contact hours to 1 unit, and is representative of participation in an organized educational experience. CEUs are not academic credits and are not applicable toward an academic degree. Sponsors of continuing education experiences are not limited to accredited institutions of higher education, but can include corporations and other learning organizations.

—*Bridget Lee Brady*

*See also* Academic Calendar

### Bibliography

American Council on Education. (1996). *Guide to educational credit by examination,* 4th edition. Washington, DC: American Council on Education and Macmillan.

Christensen, James. (Ed.). (1994). *Transfer credit practices of designated educational institutions, 1994–96.* Washington, DC: American Association of Collegiate Registrars and Admissions Officers.

# CRITICAL DIALOGUES

Critical dialogues are the means by which an online course is conducted. Most online courses contain a discussion board on which weekly discussion questions are posted, either by the instructor or by one of the students, as assigned. Students are then expected to respond to the discussion question and to one another, providing the means by which an online discussion occurs. In so doing, students are expected to demonstrate higher level thinking or critical thinking ability. Given that the online course is generally conducted in a text-based environment, one means of stimulating critical dialogue is through the provision of open-ended questions that allow for the contribution of multiple opinions and viewpoints, moving students away from textbook-based boundaries into collaboratively constructed areas of knowledge and meaning regarding the topic under study. Simply summarizing the reading for the week or responding with an "I agree" answer would not contribute to the development of a critical dialogue on the topic for the week.

In online learning, the instructor acts as a facilitator of the learning process and is considered to be a "guide on the side" rather than the fount of knowledge through which all information is transmitted to learners. In order to maximize the online learning experience, students need to take charge of that process themselves. Engaging in online discussion with other students, conducting Internet research, or following the trail that another student has suggested for supplementing the material in the course helps the student to see that knowledge creation occurs mutually and collaboratively online, leading to increasing levels of critical thinking ability.

The instructor can assist in the development of critical thinking skills and stimulate critical dialogues through the use of various instructional techniques, such as case studies, debates, and simulations. But it is the students who recognize, through reflection on the learning that emerges from those activities, that their knowledge base and ability to critically reflect is increasing. The ability to reflect is a critical quality for the successful online student to possess. Consequently, the inclusion of activities and questions in an online course that promote reflection is important. Additionally, the instructor may want to consider rotating the facilitation role among the learners in order to foster the ability to create critical dialogue and reflection.

Reflection often takes the form of not only processing the information presented, but also exploring the meaning that the material has in the student's life, reviewing the changes that may need to be made in order to accommodate this new learning, and questioning where the ideas come from and how they were constructed. Often this is the element that helps to transform him or her from a student to a reflective practitioner. In the online classroom, the sharing of reflections transforms not only the individual learner, but also the group and instructor. Consequently, engaging in a process of reflection on the content, the process of online learning, and the communication process in which students are engaged (or meta-communication) helps to develop students into reflective practitioners.

There are several means by which an instructor can promote reflection and the consequent development of critical thinking skills. The first is the ability to ask good discussion questions that promote expansive, higher-order thinking. Good discussion questions

avoid simple repetition or regurgitation of facts and encourage students to reflect and think. Questions that are helpful in this regard ask students to draw upon not only the literature available on a topic, but also their own experience. Other types of questions that promote critical dialogue include evaluative questions, controversial or provocative questions, analyses of scenarios or cases, questions that ask students to critique a theory or idea, questions that ask for more evidence or clarification, the presentation of hypothetical situations, synthesis questions, and questions that link to and then expand on ideas presented.

Coupled with the presentation of good questions is an expectation that, as part of course requirements, students will respond to the contributions of their colleagues. Without an expectation of active participation, some students may not engage with one another and the course material, reducing the possibility for critical dialogue. An instructor can develop guidelines by asking students to contribute to the discussion a minimum number of times per week. Instructors can also integrate what is termed a 2+2 model, wherein students are expected to either respond twice to the initial discussion question and to two of their peers or with the additional expectation that one post, in response to a peer, needs to be supportive and one evaluative, both of which would contribute to critical evaluation and reflection. Regardless of how the participants' expectations are structured, it is important to prepare students to engage in discussion and provide feedback to one another in a course. This is a skill that must be taught and cannot be assumed. Consequently, providing information to students about how to give and receive feedback, as well as what constitutes a substantive post to a discussion, can be helpful.

The inclusion of collaborative activity in an online course can also assist in promoting critical dialogue. Collaboration helps to promote the development of critical thinking skills because this form of activity does not allow students to leave things to assumption. Assumptions must be supported as well as checked out with peers through dialogue. Working in a small group thereby helps to deepen the thinking process. Collaboration also assists students in the co-creation of knowledge and meaning by broadening their thinking on a topic through sharing and working with all viewpoints in the group; thus, they are engaging in a process wherein a new sense of knowledge and meaning about the topic being studied is created. Collaborative activity allows students to take their time to discuss and think about the project they are working on together. Through collaborative practice and reflection, the group is able to produce a more meaningful product. Collaborative activity promotes reflection, allowing students to think about and experience learning in a new way. For many, this is transformative.

Finally, an instructor needs to know when to join an online discussion to keep it moving. If things are going well, students are actively interacting with one another, and critical dialogue is taking place, an instructor's best action is likely to be no action. By jumping in, the instructor risks interfering with the process and becoming the focus of the discussion. Students often view the instructor as the "final word" in an online discussion. Consequently, when the instructor posts, the discussion is generally viewed as closed. If the instructor waits, however, until the discussion wanes and then posts some summary comments and a new question, the likelihood is that the discussion will be recharged and the potential exists for deeper learning to occur.

In conclusion, critical dialogue can be seen as an essential feature of an online course. Instructors can prepare students to engage in critical dialogue through course expectations and information regarding giving and receiving good feedback. Instructors, by practicing good online questioning and facilitation techniques, can maximize the potential for deep learning through dialogue in the online course.

—*Rena M. Palloff*
—*Keith Pratt*

*See also* COLLABORATION; METACOMMUNICATION

## Bibliography

Brookfield, Stephen D. (1987). *Developing critical thinkers: Challenging adults to explore alternative ways of thinking and acting.* San Francisco: Jossey-Bass.

Brookfield, Stephen D., & Preskill, Stephen. (1999). *Discussion as a way of teaching.* San Francisco: Jossey-Bass.

Hudson, Barclay. (2002). The jungle syndrome: Some perils and pleasure of learning without walls, in K. E. Rudestam and J. Schoenholtz-Read (Eds.), *Handbook of online learning.* Thousand Oaks, CA: Sage.

Muilenburg, Lin, & Berge, Zane L. (2000). A framework for designing questions for online learning. *DEOSNEWS, 10*(2). Retrieved from http://www.emoderators.com/moderators/muilenburg.html.

Palloff, Rena M., & Pratt, Keith. (1999). *Building learning communities in cyberspace.* San Francisco: Jossey-Bass.

Palloff, Rena M., & Pratt, Keith. (2003). *The virtual student: A profile and guide.* San Francisco: Jossey-Bass.

# CULTURAL ACCESS/DIGITAL DIVIDE

The digital divide is the separation of those with information and telecommunication technology (ITC) access from those without. Population, income, culture, and race are predictors of access. Higher density areas, wealthier people, more Westernized countries, and whites are more likely to have access, and of higher quality, than others. Although ITC itself does not discriminate across culture lines, the availability and the applications of ITC are culturally linked. ITC was originally seen as the great equalizer with regard to having one's voice heard. To some extent, this is true. Many people have found that the Internet and other technology venues are successful tools with which make their case heard. However, not dissimilar to other distributions of power, ITC tends to be concentrated in the hands of those who already have resources, further marginalizing those who do not have access.

The World Wide Web Consortium (W3C) (www.w3.org), founded in 1994 when more people began to use the World Wide Web, seeks to support equal access to the Web. Its three goals include universal access, a semantic Web that optimizes resource use, and a Web of trust that takes into account the novel legal, commercial, and social issues raised by the technology. The first goal, universal access, addresses the issues that underlie cultural access and the digital divide: "promoting technologies that take into account the vast differences in culture, languages, education, ability, material resources, and physical limitations of users on all continents." Access to health care technology also has been seen as driven by existing resources, which can be affected by sociocultural and geopolitical status.

## INTERNATIONAL DISTRIBUTION OF ITC

Forty percent of the world's population—2.5 billion people—live in rural areas in emerging nations. Only a miniscule fraction of these people has access to telecommunications, which are usually voice telephony with little capacity for even modest Internet or videoconference access for health care and educational activities.

Access to ITC had increased dramatically for all countries over the past decade; however, the increase has not been equal. In 1991, the telephone penetration (total fixed and mobile lines per 100 people) was 49 in developed countries, 3.3 in emerging nations, and .3 in the least developed nations. In 2001, the figures were 121, 18, and 1.1, respectively. The gap between developed and emerging countries shifted from a ratio of 15:1 to 6:1 over the period, a significant gain by emerging countries. However, the gap between emerging and the least developed countries widened substantially.

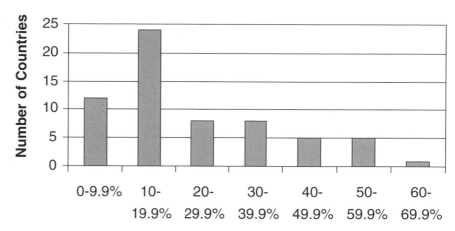

**Figure 1**

Based on analysis of data gathered by the U.S. Central Intelligence Agency *World Fact Book* and the *CyberAtlas* (http://cyberatlas.internet.com), Iceland is the most "connected" country in the world, with 60% of its citizens online. Five countries have more than 50% of their citizenry online: Sweden (50.56%), the United States (53.60%), Hong Kong (54.17%), the United Kingdom (55.37%), and Iceland (60.07%). Seventy-two of the world's 227 countries account for 72.8% of the world's population (4,566,053,061 people out of 6,262,471,109 people). Of these 4.5 billion people, an estimated 9.4%—or 429,422,100—are online. In summary, of the world's 6 billion people, an estimated 7% have Internet access. The graph above illustrates the percent of citizens with access. The most common access range is 10–20% for the countries with documented census reports of Internet access. Africa is the least connected continent, with only four countries included in the global Internet census.

## CROSS-CULTURAL ISSUES

There is a paucity of literature on the interaction of culture and technology. Viewed in the extreme, some see the infusion of technology as offering individuals opportunities to participate on equal footing in a global economy, whereas others see it as an encroachment of Western imperialism. Regardless of the perspective, it is important to understand cultural literacy and apply its ideas to the global infusion of technology. For example, cultures that are based on an oral tradition may find it difficult to adapt to a written culture, which is common on the Web. Language may also be a barrier. Some technology is available with built-in translation but the translations often do not convey the richness of the original ideas. In some cases they are actually inaccurate. Because the majority of users of the Internet are residents of countries where English is commonly used (e.g., United States, Canada, England, Australia, New Zealand), much of the content on the Internet is in English. Thus, those in non-English speaking areas must use the resources in a language that is not indigenous to their country. Language conveys culture, and in many ways, the culture of the Web is an English-speaking, consumer-driven culture. Most online educational access originates from Westernized countries, yet may be consumed by people in non-Western countries, providing another opportunity for cultural transmission.

In addition to racial or country-based cultural differences, important differences exist in the use of technology, which relate to the culture of disabilities. The Internet is a place of both increased and decreased access for people with disabilities. Although physical barriers such as staircases may be missing, many sites are graphically rich and may prohibit people (for example, those who use text readers) from accessing the full information on the site. According to the U.S. Department of Commerce National Telecommunications and Information Administration's (NITA) 2002 report, people with disabilities (physical and/or mental) are less likely than those without such disabilities to use computers or the Internet.

## DIGITAL DIVIDE

The development of ITC, particularly the Internet, has been likened to the development of the printing press by Johann Gutenberg in the mid-1400s. Books shifted from hand printed, one copy at a time, to mass production in printing businesses. As a result, more people had access to the printed word. The development of the digital age mirrors the change brought about by shifting from individual craft to mass production. Moreover, the Internet has opened heretofore unknown avenues for marketing ideas. Only 50 years following the introduction of modern computers, 320 million people worldwide will access the Internet. Digital technology is estimated to comprise 8.2% of the gross domestic product of the United States.

The diffusion of ITC has been concentrated in the largest cities in the United States. According to the report 'Net Equity, in 1998, 86% of the world's Internet capacity was contained in the 20 largest cities in the United States. Within these cities, Internet access was concentrated in the richer financial and scientific districts, bypassing many inner city areas. By 2002, NITA reported that strides have been made in increasing access for people in the United States, but differences that can be explained by race, income, and location continue to exist in the quality of the access, especially when considering the infrastructure for dial-up vs. broadband.

In the United States, where more than half the nation is online, income and education affect who has access. When someone uses a computer at work, it increases the probability that he or she will have access at home: 77% compared to 35% for those who do not use computers at work. The digital divide separating the highest and lowest incomes widened 29% between 1997 and 1999, a trend that has slowed in the United States but continues in other parts of the world. When it comes to the digital divide, whether in the United States or around the globe, already having access to resources is a major predictor of accessing the Internet.

—*B. Hudnall Stamm*

*See also* COMPUTER LITERACY; CULTURAL DIVERSITY; GLOBALIZATION; SOCIOCULTURAL PERSPECTIVES; WORLD WIDE WEB

## Bibliography

International Telecommunication Union. (2001). *Final report of ITU-D focus group 7: New technologies for rural applications.* Retrieved December 15, 2002, from http://www.itu.int/publications/docs/group7.html.

International Telecommunication Union. (2002). *World telecommunication development report: Reinventing telecoms 2002.* Retrieved December 12, 2002, from http://www.itu.int/ITU-D/ict/publications/wtdr_02/.

Kenney, G. I., & Eng, P. (1990). Cutting the costs of telecommunications links for telemedicine in the Third World. In R. M. Rangayyan (Ed.), *Proceedings of SPIE: Telecommunications for health care: Telemetry, teleradiology and telemedicine.* Volume 1355. 90–4. Bellingham, WA: SPIE Press.

Moss, M. L., & Mitra, S. (1998). *'Net equity.* Robert F. Wagner School of Public Service, New York University. Retrieved December 12, 2002, from http://urban.nyu.edu/research/net-equity/net-equity.pdf.

Nader, K., Dubrow, N., & Stamm, B. H. (Eds.). (1999). *Cultural issues and the treatment of trauma and loss.* Philadelphia: Taylor & Francis.

National Telecommunications and Information Administration (NITA). (1999). *Falling through the net: Defining the digital divide.* Retrieved March 11, 2001, from http://www.ntia.doc.gov/ntiahome/fttn99/contents.html.

National Telecommunications and Information Administration (NITA). (2002). *A nation online: How Americans are expanding their use of the Internet.* Retrieved December 15, 2001, from http://www.ntia.doc.gov/ntiahome/dn/index.html.

Stamm, B. H. (2002). Bridging the rural-urban divide with telehealth and telemedicine. In B. H. Stamm (Ed.), *Rural behavioral healthcare: An interdisciplinary guide* (pp. 145–155). Washington, DC: APA Books.

World Wide Web Consortium. (2002, September 5). *Internationalization activity proposal.* Retrieved from http://www.w3.org/2002/05/i18n-recharter/activity.html.

# CULTURAL DIVERSITY

## CULTURE

*Culture* is not neatly defined in the minds of social scientists. Instead of a term with a consistent definition across different disciplines, it is a construct that has variations in meaning depending on the branch of social science from which the definition is offered. Two definitions are provided here.

> Culture consists of patterns, explicit and implicit, of and for behavior acquired and transmitted by symbols, constituting the distinctive achievement of human groups, including their embodiments in artifacts; the essential core of culture consists of traditional (i.e., historically derived and selected) ideas and especially their attached values; cultural systems may, on the one hand, be considered as products of action, on the other as conditioning influences upon further action. (Kluckhohn, 1962: 73)

> Culture consists of shared elements . . . that provide the standards for perceiving, believing, evaluating, communicating, and acting among those who share a language, a historic period, and a geographic location. The shared elements are transmitted from generation to generation with modifications. They include unexamined assumptions and standard operating procedures that reflect "what has worked" at one point in the history of a cultural group. (Triandis, 1996: 408)

## CULTURAL DIVERSITY

*Cultural diversity* refers to the array of differences that exist among groups of people with definable and unique cultural backgrounds. This term implies that the two or more interacting groups have different cultural experiences. By this definition of cultural diversity, no value judgment is suggested as to the superiority of one culture over the other, only that people from the two have been socialized in different ways, and may have various worldviews and cultural beliefs that may make communication problematic.

One of the issues related to the definition of cultural diversity is that there are always at least two perspectives on every phenomenon: the *emic*, which is the insider's understanding of a situation, and the *etic*, which is the outsider's point of view. Thus, the operational definition of a "minority group" consists not only of the cultural perceptions and demographic backgrounds of people in this group, but also the perceptions of them by other cultural groups, especially the majority one that has control and influence on their lives.

Another concern regarding cultural diversity is the potential problem with the practice of using the concept. Social scientists have argued that the concept of cultural diversity might encourage educators and psychological professionals to treat all of the so-called minority cultures as a single culture, or as a separate cultural group, contrasted against a standard White or mainstream "American" culture. Such comparisons may perpetuate the idea that the culture with the most power (White) is normative, and only minority cultures must be explained. In other words, the usage of cultural diversity may imply White culture as universal, and contribute to maintaining the social status quo in relation to power differentials.

An example of this concern is how helping professionals conceptualize help-seeking patterns of people of color. Researchers in the area of multicultural counseling have long used terminologies, such as *over-utilization* and *under-utilization,* to describe how often minority racial groups take advantage of mental health services. Although widely accepted, the practice of using the terms of *over-* and *under-utilization* may encourage mental health professionals to treat White culture as the norm. It perpetuates the orientation that Whites' utilization pattern of psychological resources is a normative criterion, which can be implemented to evaluate help-seeking attitudes and behaviors of other racial groups. Finally, it is important to note that diversity exists both across and within culture groups. In this culturally diverse society, people within one group have different levels of acculturation depending on their education and work experiences, their interactions with other groups, and their racial identities. Therefore, often one can observe diversity on various dimensions within cultural groups, which may be categorized solely on the basis of demographic variables.

## MINORITY GROUPS

Although various terms (e.g., acculturation, disadvantaged, diversity) have been used to describe groups with nonmainstream cultural experiences at different periods of time in history, those terms may portray the same people. Specifically, "minority" status refers to a social position that is less than that ascribed to members of another group or groups. People who share certain distinctive physical or cultural characteristics, and are subjected to prejudice and discrimination, constitute a minority group. In other words, people with minority status are those with cultural experiences different from those of White, middle-class, heterosexual men of European descent, those having fewer resources to access, those with less control of their lives, and those experiencing discrimination in the United States.

Minority groups with limited power, status, and wealth often are composed of those who are older, children, and women; those who have disabilities; and those who are lesbian, gay, bisexual, or transgendered (LGBT). Minority groups differ in terms of religion, cultural beliefs and worldviews, and ability to function in daily life. Various minority groups have received differential attention from researchers and practitioners. Most research has focused on four major racial groups: African Americans, Hispanics/Latinos, Asian Americans, and American Indians.

## HOW TO IDENTIFY MINORITY (NONTRADITIONAL) GROUPS

An ongoing debate exists regarding how diversity and minority groups should be defined. It may not be optimal to use only demographic variables, such as sex, race, or age, to describe various aspects of cultural experience. W. E. Sedlacek developed two criteria with empirical methods to add to the demographic variables in defining minority or nontraditional groups. These two criteria are whether a minority is a target of prejudicial attitudes by others, and whether the success of members of a given group (e.g., African Americans, people with disabilities) systematically correlates more with noncognitive variables than it does for traditional White men.

The first criterion can be assessed by the Situational Attitude Scale (SAS). The SAS is based on an experimental-control methodology. An experimental form or forms of a questionnaire are developed that contain situations depicting a certain reference group (e.g., Arab) in a variety of situations that might generate prejudice toward them among others (e.g., you are boarding a plane for a vacation in Florida, and two young Arab men are boarding immediately behind you). The control form of the SAS contains the same situations with no reference to Arabs or any other group. If respondents are randomly assigned to forms, and then mean responses are compared on a series of responses to each situation, any significant difference in response would be the result of the only difference between the forms—the term *Arab*.

In other words, the SAS uses experimental and control forms, and provides a situational context to measure prejudicial attitudes toward a certain group

designated as the experimental group. Scores from the SAS methodology have been demonstrated to have reliability and validity in assessing attitudes toward racial and religious groups such as African Americans, Latino/as, Asian Americans, Jews, and Arabs. Researchers have also shown the SAS to be useful in measuring prejudicial attitudes toward women; gays, lesbians, and bisexuals; the elderly; and athletes. In short, one can use the SAS to determine whether a group is a minority based on its being a target of prejudicial attitudes by others.

The second criterion is measured by the Noncognitive Questionnaire (NCQ). The NCQ is designed to assess attributes that are not typically measured by other instruments, and which may be common ways for persons with nontraditional experiences to show their abilities. Consisting of eight subscales, the NCQ yields scores on positive self-concept or confidence, realistic self-appraisal, understanding and dealing with racism, preference for long-range goals, availability of strong support person to turn to in crises, successful leadership experiences, demonstrated community service, and knowledge acquired in a field relevant to their cultural experiences.

The noncognitive variable system seems to measure experiential and systemic ability, which members of minority groups need more in order to survive and negotiate their environments than do people with White cultural experiences. Research has documented the reliability and validity of NCQ scores in assessing the performance of a variety of nontraditional groups including Asian Americans, African Americans, Latino/as, international students, and athletes. These studies have demonstrated that scores from the NCQ scales successfully predict grades, retention, and graduation for college students from various cultural groups.

The use of the SAS and the NCQ adds significantly to the practice of solely relying on demographic variables, such as gender and race, in understanding the experiences of people with various cultural backgrounds. By incorporating the SAS and the NCQ in deciding whether a group is nontraditional, one not only determines to what extent members of a specific group receive prejudice from other groups, but also one comes to appreciate how nontraditional abilities relate to success and survival in the society.

In summary, if a group receives prejudice and demonstrates abilities in ways different from those with traditional experiences, it is operationally defined as nontraditional. Even though groups as different as athletes and older people may show their diversity in different ways, the variables underlying their problems in dealing with their development and in coping with a traditional system that was not designed for them may have some similarities.

## CULTURAL DIVERSITY AND MULTICULTURAL COMPETENCY

As minority populations have increased significantly in the United States, issues regarding cultural diversity have received more attention. One of the implications of cultural diversity is the multicultural competency of educators and service providers. A decade ago, the 3 (characteristics) by 3 (dimensions) model of multicultural counseling competency was proposed by D. W. Sue, P. Arredondo, and R. J. McDavis for training culturally competent helping professionals. Specifically, these three characteristics depict a culturally skilled counselor as one who: (1) actively becomes aware of his or her own assumptions about human behavior, values, biases, preconceived notions, personal limitations, and so forth; (2) actively attempts to understand the worldview of his or her culturally different clients without negative judgments; and (3) actively develops and practices appropriate, relevant, and sensitive intervention strategies and skills in working with his or her culturally different clients. On the other hand, these three dimensions include beliefs and attitudes, knowledge, and skills. Based on this model, Sue et al. suggested a set of criteria for helping professionals to be judged as culturally competent. Recently, this model was expanded to specifically cover five racial groups (African Americans, Asian Americans, Latino Americans, Native Americans, and European Americans) and different levels of cultural competency (individual, professional, organizational, and societal).

## PROMOTING CULTURAL DIVERSITY

K. H. Kavanagh and P. H. Kennedy indicated that cultural diversity should be advocated for the following reasons:

- Cultural diversity increases freedom of choice and expands the available range of options.
- Cultural diversity creates an aesthetically rich, pleasing, and stimulating world.
- Cultural diversity encourages a healthy competition between different systems of ideas and worldviews.
- Cultural diversity facilitates the appearance of new truths.

For promoting cultural diversity in education systems, strategies at the administrative level include:

- Integrating minority-related content into the curriculum
- Incorporating religion into established diversity programs
- Distributing an annual calendar of religious holidays
- Changing the use of standardized test scores
- Finding ways of involving minority students' parents in school affairs
- Achieving central administration support for positions that are taken to improve cultural diversity
- Finding culturally appropriate standards for judging and developing programs for minority groups in a positive way
- Requiring all student affairs professionals to experience and understand cultural diversity.

## IMPLICATIONS OF DISTRIBUTED LEARNING FOR CULTURAL DIVERSITY

Beyond the limits of the traditional classroom, distributed learning refers to using a wide range of information technologies to offer learning opportunities. Information technologies include, but are not limited to, the World Wide Web, e-mail, chat rooms, instructional software, video conferencing, distribution lists, and simulations. Without doubt, the advance in and the use of information technologies have changed our lives and the ways we learn. Also, they have facilitating and hindering effects on cultural diversity.

Distributed learning can improve cultural diversity in several ways. First of all, people in the distributed learning environment have more means to surround themselves with information from different cultures. For example, learners in two different countries now can easily communicate with each other through the Internet or video conferencing. Compared with the traditional classroom, a distributed learning environment breaks through the physical limits and brings learners instant information from different parts of the country and the world. Second, distributed learning supports a model of education in which a person engages in learning activities at his or her own pace and at a self-selected time. This advantage allows learners to take initiatives to improve their knowledge and experiences regarding various cultures.

However, the advantages of information technologies are coupled with some problems. Because distributed learning relies heavily on computers or audio/video equipment as communication media, learners lose the face-to-face context and first-hand opportunities to interact with people from different cultural backgrounds. Moreover, the context of interactions may disappear in a distributed learning environment. This lack of context may increase the probability of cross-cultural misunderstandings. Finally, utilizing technologies may create barriers for people who prefer to learn in the traditional way and who have no access to the equipment required in the distributed learning environment. This weakness may have larger negative effects on improving cultural diversity in rural areas than in urban areas. Also, people who did not grow up in the computer age may find it difficult to increase their knowledge and skills regarding various cultures through the distributed learning environment.

—*Hung-Bin Sheu*
—*William E. Sedlacek*

*See also* CULTURAL ACCESS/DIGITAL DIVIDE; DEMOGRAPHICS

## Bibliography

Diller, J. V. (1999). *Cultural diversity: A primer for the human services.* Belmont, CA: Wadsworth.

Helms, J. E., & Cook, D. A. (1999). *Using race and culture in counseling and psychotherapy: Therapy and process.* Needham Heights, MA: Allyn & Bacon.

Kavanagh, K. H., & Kennedy, P. H. (1992). *Promoting cultural diversity: Strategies for health care professionals.* Newbury Park, CA: Sage.

Kluckhohn, C. (1962). The concept of culture. In R. Kluckhohn (Ed.), *Culture and behavior* (pp. 19–73). New York: Free Press.

Matsumoto, D. (2001). *The handbook of culture and psychology.* New York: Oxford University Press.

Parekh, B. (2000). *Rethinking multiculturalism: Cultural diversity and political theory.* Cambridge, MA: Harvard University Press.

Sedlacek, W. E. (1994). Issues in advancing diversity through assessment. *Journal of Counseling and Development, 72,* 549–553.

Sedlacek, W. E. (1996). An empirical method of determining nontraditional group status. *Measurement and Evaluation in Counseling and Development, 28,* 200–209.

Sedlacek, W. E. (2003). *Beyond the big test: Noncognitive assessment in higher education.* San Francisco: Jossey-Bass.

Sedlacek, W. E., & Brooks, G. C., Jr. (1970). Measuring racial attitudes in a situational context. *Psychological Reports, 27,* 971–980.

Sue, D. W., Arredondo, P., & McDavis, R. J. (1992). Multicultural counseling competencies and standards: A call to the profession. *Journal of Counseling and Development, 70,* 477–486.

Sue, D. W., & Sue, D. (2003). *Counseling the culturally diverse: Theory and practice,* 4th ed. New York: John Wiley & Sons.

Triandis, H. C. (1996). The psychological measurement of cultural syndromes. *American Psychologist, 51*(4), 407–415.

# CURRICULUM MODELS

The typology of inter/trans/multi/pluri-disciplinary derives from the first international conference on interdisciplinarity in higher education, held in Europe in 1970. The term *pluri,* which is used less frequently than the other three prefixes, means the juxtaposition of disciplines that are more or less related, such as mathematics and physics. *Multidisciplinary* models juxtapose separate disciplinary or professional perspectives, adding breadth but aligning them in encyclopedic fashion. *Interdisciplinary* models integrate separate perspectives, data, methods, tools, concepts, or theories in order to create a holistic view or to answer a question or solve a problem that is too complex for a mono-disciplinary approach. *Transdisciplinary* models are comprehensive frameworks that transcend the narrow scope of disciplinary worldviews. The term is also used for collaborative research among multiple sectors of society. In common parlance, *integrative* and *interdisciplinary* are used as generic adjectives for any crossing of disciplinary boundaries.

### THE GROWING IMPETUS

Integrative approaches have become prominent for several reasons. To begin with, the "knowledge explosion" makes it impossible to teach everything, heightening the need for more integrated and coherent curricula across the K–16 spectrum of primary, secondary, and postsecondary education. The emergence of interdisciplinary fields is another factor. During the 1930s and 1940s, American and area studies began and, during the 1960s and 1970s, women's, ethnic, urban, and environmental studies, along with studies of science, technology, and society, began to be common. By the 1980s and 1990s, the new field of cultural studies was expanding, along with cognitive and information sciences, neuroscience, molecular biology, international and policy studies, gerontology, and criminology. The knowledge produced in such fields enters the curriculum in three ways: as the intellectual foundation for interdisciplinary programs, as topics in general education, and as new foci in traditional subjects. Across K–16, environmental themes such as ecology and pollution are popular foci in general education. They also have a growing presence in science education; college students can major, minor, or take electives in environmental studies. Cultural diversity is another common theme. Interdisciplinary programs are offered in women's, African American, ethnic, and international studies. Theory and content from these fields have been incorporated into the disciplines; general education is a major site for the teaching of domestic and global diversity.

In K–12, the term *integrated curriculum* has appeared in many contexts: the project approach and the Progressivists' vision of integrating students' personal and social concerns in the 1920s; the core curriculum movement in the 1930s; and problem-centered core curricula in the 1940s and 1950s. The word *integration* also appeared in conjunction with the psychological process of holistic learning, moral education, experience-based curricula and merging learning and work, child-centered curricula and teacher–student planning, and a broad-fields approach. During the 1980s and 1990s, *curriculum integration* reappeared in K–12 as a generic label for varied approaches, including thematic studies, multidisciplinary and multisubject designs, integrated units, skills across the curriculum, a social-problems approach to science, and social studies and whole language. The concept of "teacher as generalist" and project approach also appear in the Coalition of Essential Schools and Theodore Sizer's work, and the term *interdisciplinary* appears often in discussions of

school reform. In high school, traditionally more resistant to interdisciplinarity, constructivist and project learning, problem-solving, integrations of subject-matter knowledge, and new approaches to teaching and learning are promoting integration.

General education reform is an added factor. In K–12, block-time core classes and team teaching have been features of middle schools since their inception. Across K–16, integrative models promote multidisciplinary breadth and the integrative skills needed to understand complex themes and problems. In college, the most common practices are creating interdisciplinary alternatives to traditional distribution models, providing multidisciplinary breadth, clustering and linking courses, building learning communities, incorporating diversity, drawing on interdisciplinary fields, and using innovative pedagogies. Heightened demand for problem solving is an added impetus. Inter-institutional partnerships link academic and private sectors in research on technological and economic problems. In K–12, the school-to-work movement prepares students for high-skill careers in project- and service-based learning, youth apprenticeship and community programs, and career academies that emphasize themes, collaboration, connection making, problem solving, and critical thinking. The workplace is not the only context. In K–12, state mandates call for studying problems of drug use, sex education, and family life. In college, problems of crime, juvenile violence, infant mortality, AIDS, ethnic tensions, and pollution require interdisciplinary study.

As this list suggests, all problems are not the same. Courses on equality and crime stem from a different motivation than improving economic competition. Disagreements about interdisciplinarity often center on which problems should be the focus. In a number of new fields, critique takes center stage. Women's studies and cultural studies, for example, are changing the ways that gender and culture are understood and taught. During the late 1980s and 1990s, multiculturalism and postmodernism further challenged the dominance of traditional subjects and disciplines. The cumulative effect of these developments is to call into question all forms of knowledge, while generating new categories and structures. Critique also raises the most fundamental question of all: What is the purpose of education? Interdisciplinarity is not simply a new technique or an adjustment in the schedule.

## INTEGRATIVE MODELS

The conventional picture of the curriculum is a set of boxes containing credits in specific subjects or disciplines. Integrative models redraw the boundaries of the boxes. The major distinction is degree of integration. In K–12, the lowest degree is "parallel disciplines," also called "correlated" design. Rebecca Burns's keywords are helpful, beginning with *sequencing.* When disciplines have a "parallel" relationship, content does not change, only the order of presentation. Class schedules are reconfigured to explore similar themes, topics, or problems simultaneously. However, students must uncover connections by themselves, the content and procedures of disciplines remain intact, and team teaching is absent. In K–12, an English teacher might present a historical novel while a history teacher works with the same era in another class. A unit on hurricanes might be taught simultaneously in separate English, geography, and science classes. In college, students take separate courses in twentieth-century literature and history during the same semester, or separate courses on women, environment, or urban affairs. This model is common, because it is easy, inexpensive, and does not disrupt the status quo.

A "multidisciplinary" approach intentionally aligns courses by *coordinating* a theme, problem, or question through multiple disciplines and subjects. In K–12, historical periods such as the Renaissance and events such as the Civil War are typical coordinating themes. So are problems of the environment and concepts such as change. In a college American studies program, courses from separate departments are aligned, although students do not necessarily experience integrative seminars or projects. If team teaching occurs, individuals present their perspectives separately in "tag" teaching.

Integrated designs go further, restructuring the curriculum through focusing and blending. Content is revised, a deeper connection is created, and team teaching may occur. In K–12, *curriculum integration, unified studies,* and *fusion model* are common terms; across K–16, *interdisciplinary* is used in a technical sense at this level of integration. Formats vary, from one unit or course to a year-long program or a student's entire experience in an "academy," "whole school," "school-within-a-school," or autonomous program or college. In high school, English and history are combined in a fusion model that facilitates broad study of American history centered on themes such as culture, identity, ethnicity, and regionalism. In college, an American studies program offers introductory and/or capstone core seminars. At the highest level of integration, the keyword is *transcending.* A student's world, not a school or a state syllabus, becomes the center of learning or a new intellectual paradigm or comprehensive model.

The most common organizing centers for courses are a problem, question, idea, or theme. *Thematic studies* is the generic term. Themes vary in length from one class period or a week to a semester or entire program. Actual themes also vary, from personal issues of identity and the body to social problems and abstract questions. In K–12, annual events are popular, as are seasons, special events, and themes related to the environment and animals, the planetary system, and space exploration. The most common structures of fused courses in high school are cultural perspective and historical change. Students across K–16 also explore topics in history (e.g., immigration, genealogy, exploration, and war), social problems (violence, hunger, poverty, and racism), institutions (family, community, and government), systems (transportation, the economy, and ecology), and abstract concepts (conflict, change, democracy, and responsibility).

In college, typical themes in general education include the individual and community, authority, values, and democracy; cultural diversity and globalism; the environment; and topics in science and technology. "Great" books and ideas still anchor many courses, and theme-based surveys of humanities, social sciences, and science provide multidisciplinary breadth. In interdisciplinary fields, relevant disciplines and interdisciplinary concepts are major rubrics. In American studies, culture and society are prominent foci, along with the topics of diversity and the American dream. In women's studies, gender and sexuality are defining concepts, with the topics of family, ethnicity, and feminist theory and methodologies. In peace and justice studies, peace and justice are core concepts, with the topics of nonviolence, power, conflict resolution, and international relations also being discussed.

## CHALLENGES IN DISTRIBUTED LEARNING SETTINGS

Like interdisciplinarity, distributed learning is defined in many ways. The most common association is an environment removed from a traditional campus. Teacher and student interactions may occur face-to-face or through technologies such as interactive video or the Internet. These interactions may be asynchronous or occur in real time and may be based in one or more institutions. Regardless, one rule applies universally: Integration is never automatic. Without professional development, teachers will not necessarily know how to engage in integrative teaching. The challenge is exacerbated by the number of part-time faculty in distributive settings. Advance orientation is mandatory, and instructional listservs provide ongoing forums for peer coaching.

For the benefit of faculty and students alike, curriculum designers and administrators should ensure that course materials, including syllabi and study guides, include definitions of interdisciplinary study. Readings should represent a range of disciplinary/professional perspectives and models of integrative thinking. Technology is not a panacea, but online communities can be powerful catalysts for collaboration and connections. Hot links to relevant Web sites can broaden the network of resources. Formal coursework should include assignments that foster connection making. Course portfolios, in print or electronic, can be vital tools. For teachers, they are instructional archives containing all assignments, materials, and teaching tools. For students, they are the place where personal integration occurs. Off-the-shelf products for laboratory work and video resources in any area need added commentary on how they may be used in integrative contexts. Likewise, all assessment activities and instruments providing feedback on student learning and program review must include interdisciplinary variables.

Distributive learning and interdisciplinary approaches share a common characteristic: The traditional teaching functions of telling, delivering, directing, and being a "sage on the stage" are replaced by the role models of mentor, mediator, facilitator, coach, and guide. Correspondingly, integrative pedagogy is active, dynamic, and process-oriented. Application of knowledge takes precedence over acquisition alone. Teachers use innovative approaches that promote exploration, problem-posing and problem-solving, comparing and contrasting different perspectives, critical thinking and synthesis, and holistic thinking. For that reason, projects and case studies are common. Integrative learning also overlaps with other approaches, including inquiry and discovery-based learning, collaborative learning and learning communities, feminist and multicultural pedagogy, team teaching, writing-intensive teaching, and performance-based learning.

Distributed learning often involves adult learners. In one sense, adults are already integrators, earning a living in workplaces where collaborative work and peer interaction are becoming increasingly common while juggling family responsibilities and the demands of school. They are also problem solvers who work with multiple forms of knowledge and information, grappling with conflicting expertise and weighing alternatives to produce answers to complex questions in dynamic settings. At the same time, they often have fears about returning to school. The disequilibrium they experience can be a powerful source of both personal and academic learning. However, in all settings and formats attention to the integrative process in any curriculum model must be proactive, explicit, and sustained throughout the entire course.

*—Julie Thompson Klein*

*See also* Experiential Learning; Learning Circles

## Bibliography

Beane, J. (1997). *Curriculum integration: Designing the core of democratic education.* New York: Teachers College Press.

Clarke, J., & Russell A. (Eds.). (1997). *Interdisciplinary high school teaching: Strategies for integrated learning.* Boston, MA: Allyn and Bacon.

Fiscella, J., & Kimmel, S. (1998). *Interdisciplinary education: A guide to resources.* New York: The College Board.

Haynes, C. (Ed.). (2001). *Innovations in interdisciplinary teaching.* Westport, CT: Greenwood. Includes R. Schindler, "Interdisciplinarity and the Adult/Lifelong Learning Connection."

Klein, J. T. (1999). *Mapping interdisciplinary studies.* Washington, DC: Association of American Colleges and Universities.

Klein, J. T. (Ed.). (2001). *Interdisciplinary education in K-12 and college: A foundation for K-16 dialogue.* New York: The College Board. Includes R. Burns, "Interdisciplinary Teamed Instruction."

Newell, W. (Ed.). (1998). *Interdisciplinarity: Essays from the literature.* New York: The College Board.

# CYBERSPACE

Cyberspace is the mental representation of the nonphysical world created by the communications between people using digital media and computer networks like the Internet. When people use e-mail or chat, or when they surf the Web, they perceive it as another world, where they virtually reach other minds. Cyberspace is an intermediate zone, without any particular space or time constraints, between and within the mind of individuals, communities, and groups communicating digitally.

Cyberspace could not exist without the infrastructure that allows the transmission of data. Interconnected networks of computers that make the Internet, as well as common standards, the hypertext system, graphical interfaces, and the World Wide Web, have greatly facilitated these digital interactions. In addition, tools like e-mail protocols and software, chat room technologies, and virtual reality development environments allow people to re-create their physical world virtually, giving cyberspace its metaphoric connotations.

## ORIGINS OF THE WORD

As defined by William Gibson, in his 1983 novel *Neuromancer,* the word *cyberspace* connotes space (as in a location), and cyber, which is derived from three different origins: the Ancient Greek word *kubernetike,* meaning to pilot, to govern; the 19th century French word *cybernétique,* which means study of government ways; and from the 1940s American word *cybernetics,* meaning the study of process and communications between machines and human beings.

Cyberspace is a consensual hallucination experienced daily by billions of legitimate operators, in every nation—a graphic representation of data abstracted from the memory banks of every computer in the human system. Unthinkable complexity, lines of light in the nonspace of the mind, clusters and constellations of data. Like city lights, receding.

## GOING BACK TO THE ORIGINAL IDEOLOGY

As early as the 1960s, computer networks became powerful digital communication tools, but were used by only a few specialists: scientists, computer engineers, and U.S. Department of Defense technicians. However, the appearance of the Internet in 1982 and the World Wide Web in 1991 were the main driving forces behind the development, democratization, and popularity of the cyberspace concept. Forty years ago, only a few thousand specialists were using computer networks; the number of network users has now swelled to more than 700 million Internet users.

Cyberspace has recently reverted back to its original ideology. From 1996 to 2000, it was believed that the Internet and cyberspace would change the economic system as we know it. Investors and business people perceived it to be and promoted it as a gold rush. The exponential growth of the Web, for example, prompted them to believe that if you put a store online, customers would inevitably buy from it and, consequently, that e-commerce (doing business over computer networks like the Internet) was necessarily *the* future of the economy. Many fortunes were made in Internet enterprises, but this activity was mostly speculation, and many of the "dot-com" entrepreneurs that became overnight successes in the pioneering days of the World Wide Web have since filed for bankruptcy.

But e-business is still business, and business is about people. So investors and business people are now paying more and more attention to the fact that it's not the technologies or the possible return on investment that is the primary driver of successful cyberspace projects, but rather the way people behave in cyberspace. The way humans integrate information technologies is more important than the functionalities provided by the technologies. In sum, it is cyberspace's psychological dimension, the fundamental social needs that explain human behaviors, and these behaviors and psychological aspects have to be taken into account when studying human interaction in cyberspace.

## THE PSYCHOSOCIOLOGICAL ASPECT OF CYBERSPACE

According to John Suler, several psychological effects occur due to the communication between individuals in cyberspace:

- Reduced sensations
- Texting
- Identity flexibility
- Altered perceptions
- Equalized status
- Transcended space
- Temporal flexibility

- Social multiplicity
- Recordability
- Media disruption

We now see why cyberspace is so popular; most people, to some degree, would like to experience these psychological impacts in their real life. But besides these special psychological aspects, we also have to keep in mind that it is humans who are in cyberspace, and that humans have their very own intrinsic patterns of social behaviors. For centuries, social groups have been a major element in the life of people. Humans are social animals, and that fact will not disappear in cyberspace. Instead, to cope with the special psychological aspects of cyberspace, we create metaphors, like chat rooms, lounges, and smileys :). Studies have shown that even if friendship in cyberspace tends to exhibit less emotional signalling, social networks and communities nonetheless have similar characteristics as in the physical world.

Mutual interest versus self-interest is an important distinction in cyberspace. Friends socialize and help each other in traditional social networks, as well as in cyberspace. People give and share, digitally or otherwise, knowing that their mutual interests ultimately serve their own long-term self-interest. This is particularly true in "gift cultures" like the Web where the prevailing abundance of what is being exchanged makes generosity a key factor in gaining status and recognition in one's community. This is in stark contrast, of course, to the scarcity economics that prevail in our current market economies, which are focused on the exchange of scarce physical resources. These economic models premised on scarcity are often perceived as unavoidable but, if we take at face value the "fact" that we are inexorably moving toward an information-based society, as well as the fact that information is anything but scarce, the logical conclusion is that cyberspace may have a profound impact on the sociopolitical aspects of the real world.

Socioconstructivism—the way we see ourselves and the way social networks, relationships, and interaction with others shape our definition of reality—is also a very important concept in cyberspace. Cyberspace is a mental representation—people shape their own representation of cyberspace when they interact digitally with communicative technologies and with each other. Socioconstructivism is a particularly powerful strategy of appropriation or adaptation of cyberspace by people, and it also explains why behavior in cyberspace is so close to human behavior in the physical world.

## CYBERSPACE AND DISTRIBUTED LEARNING

Cyberspace has a lot of pedagogical potential. Imagine the possibility of studying anything, from anywhere, anytime. Cyberspace is free from time and place, so organizations, especially those already dispensing distance learning, have begun using it as an education communication tool. Good examples are TELUQ (the distance learning division of the Quebec public system of education in Canada) and the Fielding Graduate Institute in California, which developed virtual campuses. According to Forum Telecom, a virtual campus is a Web site that provides pedagogical resources for a community of learners, as well as various means of communication and collaboration that allow the campus's participants to interact with their teacher and with each other. Most of the first virtual campuses were only learning tools—they were delivering only information. As people began to better understand the psychosociological aspects of cyberspace, they began to re-create online the entire environment of students in traditional education. It is now common to see learning centers that virtually re-create classes, study groups, student interaction, real-time teacher support, and the like.

## CONTROL OF CYBERSPACE

At the beginning of the Internet era, it was believed that cyberspace was an example of direct democracy, by the people for the people. It was also perceived by many as "the Wild West"—a world with little or no regulations or authorities to enforce them. There was even a declaration of independence of cyberspace, reflecting the thinking of the users at that time:

Governments of the Industrial World, you weary giants of flesh and steel, I come from Cyberspace, the new home of Mind. On behalf of the future, I ask you of the past to leave us alone. You are not welcome among us. You have no sovereignty where we gather. . . .

—John Perry Barlow, 1996

But the real-time online democracy and ideal world promoted by the pioneers of cyberspace have recently been challenged by the need for regulation, the need for further capitalization, the Internet dot-com frenzy, and many other issues. As cyberspace began to be a market in the mind of capitalists, regulation began to be needed to facilitate business. The debate as to whether or not to regulate cyberspace has increasingly centered on preventing fraud, pornography, and other ethical abuses. Although laudable, the specifics of how to regulate the abuses and who will do the regulating are still unresolved issues.

Because it is a mental representation of the people, cyberspace cannot truly be regulated; only its underlying infrastructure can be partially regulated. It is very difficult, for instance, to keep someone from putting prohibited material on a Web server (thus making it available to download on the Internet), but you can get a court order to keep an Internet service provider from selling bandwidth (and thus access to the Internet network) to the owner of that rogue Web server.

Adding to the intangibility of cyberspace, the lack of being rooted in a specific place has brought more than its share of conflicts. Which country is responsible for conflicts in cyberspace? Who has jurisdiction over international networks? International organizations like UNESCO and the World Trade Organization have devised ways of dealing with this problem by providing legal guidelines to countries. If countries adopt and adhere to these guidelines and/or pass laws to enforce them, they will all be regulated in about the same way.

All the problems mentioned so far, compounded by the fact that technology is evolving very rapidly, have made the application of these laws very difficult, because they deal with our real concrete world, whereas cyberspace is a world of dynamic mental representations made of time-sensitive digital interactions.

*—Pierre-Léonard Harvey*
*—Nicolas Bertrand*

***See also*** Virtual Campus; World Wide Web

## Bibliography

Barlow, J. P. (1996, February 8). *A declaration of the independence of cyberspace.* Davos, Switzerland. Retrieved from http://www.eff.org/~barlow.

Harvey, P. L. (1995). *Cyberespace et communautique: Appropriation-réseaux-groupes virtuels.* Québec, Canada: Les Presse de l'Université Laval.

Harvey, P. L., & Lemire, G. (2001). *La nouvelle éducation: NTIC, transdisciplinarité et communautique.* Québec, Canada: Les Presse de l'Université Laval.

Lessig, L. (1999). The law of the horse— What cyberlaw might teach. *Stanford Technology Law Review, 113,* 501–546.

Levy, P. (1994). *L'Intelligence collective-pour une antropologie du cyberespace.* Paris, France: Éditions La Découverte.

Rheingold, H. (1993). *Virtual communities—Homesteading on the electronic frontier reality.* Canada: Addison-Wesley.

Suler, J. (2002, January). The basic psychological features of cyberspace. In *The Psychology of Cyberspace* (orig. pub. 1996). Retrieved from www.rider.edu/users/suler/psycyber.

# DEGREES/DEGREE PROGRAMS

Degrees are titles conferred on individuals, usually by colleges or universities, in recognition of the completion of courses of study or other extensive academic achievement. Degrees vary in level and title, as well as the content they signify. Consequently, they differ among nations, and sometimes within countries. Occasionally, academic institutions also confer degrees *honoris causa,* or honorary degrees, on distinguished persons for nonacademic achievements, such as public service and contributions to general welfare. Usually, a document called a diploma, containing the institution's seal and the signatures of officers of the awarding institution, attests to the conferral of the degree.

Degrees based on academic achievement, or earned degrees, historically have required that candidates reside for extended periods at the site of instruction and comply with formal degree program regulations. By the mid-nineteenth century, these obligations became serious barriers to the development of competent personnel for complex nations. The problem led to authorization of the University of London External Degree in 1858. Over the next century, other experiments with degree awards occurred. By the early 1970s, the popular desire for access as well as the knowledge requirements of societies triggered a wave of innovative programs that facilitated degree study, especially for adult learners. Because the new degree participants often studied away from the main institutional site and outside the context of its traditional rules, these programs became known as external degrees. External degrees now play a fundamental role in providing distributed learning.

## EARNED DEGREE PROGRAMS

Degrees based on study originated in mid-twelfth century Europe. Powerful religious or political figures granted some of the relatively new universities authority to award master's or doctoral degrees as licenses to teach. At this time the baccalaureate was an admission requirement for master's or doctoral study, not a degree in itself. Subsequently, degrees and the activities required for them evolved in different ways. In the United States, the United Kingdom (except for Scotland), and other countries strongly influenced by them, three levels of degree emerged: baccalaureate, master's, and doctorate, each with its own requirements for fulfillment. A fourth level, the 2-year associate degree, also became prevalent in the United States following World War II. European and Latin American countries and parts of Africa and Asia shared the same medieval origins but their degree programs took different forms.

American colleges and universities adopted generally similar requirements for the four degree levels they offered, although the institutional requirements often varied in specific detail:

*Associate Degree.* Students normally take the equivalent of 2 years of full-time enrollment to complete the degree. They either prepare to continue toward a baccalaureate degree by taking courses in general education and fields that will apply in a 4-year institution, or they follow an occupational or vocational course leading to employment.

*Baccalaureate Degree.* These programs require 4 years of full-time study or its equivalent. Normally content includes general education; approximately 1 year in a specific discipline or concentration, including work at an advanced level; and other concentration or elective courses to complete the degree.

*Master's Degree.* Typical degree plans require 1–2 years of full-time study, mainly focused on advanced course work in a discipline or a planned concentration that may be interdisciplinary. Students may need to demonstrate competence in a research skill, and often they complete a capstone project followed by an oral or written degree examination. Thesis requirements have diminished in recent years. The master's serves as a preliminary to doctoral research study and also as a vehicle to serve the knowledge needs of an information-based society. American universities award approximately 90% of their master's degrees in professional fields.

*Doctoral Degree.* The American doctorate has developed three separate tracks: first professional degrees in selected fields, the research-based doctor of philosophy, and professional doctorates emphasizing both research and application. The first professional degrees attest to completion of requirements for beginning practice in a given profession. The degrees normally require several years of course work and practical experience beyond the bachelor's level. The degrees fall in areas related to health, law, and theology such as doctorates in medicine, jurisprudence, and divinity. The fields may require further examinations by public agencies or professional associations for licenses to practice.

The modern research doctorate, or doctor of philosophy (Ph.D.), developed from nineteenth-century German practice, emphasizing mastery of a discipline, intensive research, and an original contribution to knowledge. Yale University awarded the first American doctorate in 1861, and other universities followed in the late nineteenth century. In the twentieth century, the need for advanced qualifications in the professions led to doctorates in professional fields, beginning with the Doctor of Education (Ed.D.) at Harvard in 1920. Doctorates followed in engineering,

music, business administration, and other fields, each with its own designation. These degrees adhered to the model of the Ph.D. by requiring research and a dissertation, but they also emphasized preparation for practice.

Admission to either research or professional doctoral study normally requires at least a bachelor's degree in a related field. Institutions typically state that attaining a doctoral degree will take a minimum of 3 years' study beyond the baccalaureate degree, but often students take longer. They usually must demonstrate mastery of related research skills such as a foreign language or quantitative analysis, and sometimes practice skills in the doctoral field. Study covers main subdivisions of the field, and leads to major written and/or oral general or preliminary examinations covering this content. In some instances, alternatives to the examinations are possible. Successful completion of the examinations or alternatives and presentation of an acceptable dissertation proposal admits students to degree candidacy, after which they undertake a year or more of research on a selected topic under the guidance of a faculty committee. The research culminates in a dissertation presenting the research conclusions, which the candidate defends in an oral interview.

## EXTERNAL DEGREES

Contemporary use of the term *external degree* arose around 1970. It described a number of new degree programs at all levels that challenged traditional degree characteristics; especially the requirements that students reside for extended periods at the site of instruction and comply with rules designed for younger people. External degrees mainly seek to serve adult learners, but some started with or became open to students of all ages.

The key to the development of the external degree has been the disaggregation or, to use an anti-trust term, the "unbundling" of various services and functions that colleges and universities have performed as integrated systems. External degrees depart from these encompassing systems by adopting more flexible approaches to issues such as demands of time and place, or by providing only one or more, but not all, of the traditional university services. This enables students to accommodate degree activities within other demands of their lives and to apply experiences from many sources to degree requirements.

## ANTECEDENTS OF
## THE EXTERNAL DEGREE

Several efforts to provide degrees for adults preceded the external degree movement. The first was the University of London External Degree, mentioned earlier. The university did not offer instruction or other usual services, but it matriculated and examined persons for degrees regardless of where or how they had studied. The system provided an opportunity for thousands who could not attend residential courses to earn a degree. This system continued until the late twentieth century when a new body, the Council for National Academic Awards, superseded London's external examining and crediting function.

Late in the nineteenth century, universities in both the United Kingdom and the United States began providing extramural or extension instruction at sites away from the universities and at times convenient for adults, such as evenings and weekends. Gradually some American universities awarded credit and entire degrees based on extension enrollment. The difficulty with these degrees was that they made few concessions to adult experience and circumstances, and they took many years to complete on a part-time basis.

Recognition grew that adults needed a more learner-friendly model. In the 1960s, a group of new baccalaureate programs appeared that focused on adult circumstances and radically changed many undergraduate practices. The University of Oklahoma, which offered the first such program in 1961, addressed three issues for adult learners: to progress in areas that have meaning for adults, to build on what they already know, and to study at convenient times and places. Oklahoma and others created curricula that were broadly based in liberal education. The organization of content, learning modes, and crediting processes, however, departed from the typical academic pattern. The degrees' main difficulties were the limitation to liberal education and the lack of student input into the design.

In 1971 the United Kingdom took leadership in adult degree education when it launched the Open University. Initially it applied an age requirement of 21 years old, although later it lowered the entry age to 18. Its founders originally planned it to be a "university of the air," delivering instruction by open television broadcasts. It retained that mode, but in practice it became a complex system of independent study courses and innovative learning kits designed by core faculty and consisting of learning assessment procedures, television presentations, local and regional centers for support and meetings, and annual week-long seminars. The university attracted many applicants, and it has grown to over 200,000 students, the largest enrollment of any university in Britain. Numerous countries in Europe, Latin America, Asia, and Africa followed its example with similar universities.

## UNITED STATES EXTERNAL
## DEGREE INNOVATIONS

Several American universities experimented with the British Open University model, but it never gained the prominence that it did in other countries. From 1970 on, however, many new degree programs appeared in response to fresh motivations, such as the impatience among younger people for change, the hope of adults with no or some college experience to improve their life chances through education, the increasing numbers of associate degree graduates who wished to continue their educations, and the recognition by many persons at mid-life that learning could continue throughout their lives. Women were more interested than men in enrolling in these alternative forms of higher education, a trend that continues today.

The innovative patterns differed from earlier changes in that they broke sharply from the rigidity of institutionally oriented internal degree programs. They recognized the maturity of adults and the complexity of their lives by placing the interest of the learner ahead of institutional conformity.

The individual programs differed in how they addressed various issues, but they drew on one or more of several elements that came to be associated with external degrees. The first was open or more flexible admissions policies that allowed broader access. Second, they reduced or even eliminated the requirement of attendance at a fixed site, so that learners could progress at their own location and pace and adapt study to their personal schedules. Various modes of distance learning facilitated this. Third was the use of improved methods to assess learning that occurred prior to as well as after enrollment. These included advanced placement examinations for college course credit, guides to credit for military- or employer-provided courses, and procedures to assess individual portfolios of learning from experience for credit. This credit, along with transfer of credit earned at accredited institutions, could shorten considerably the time to degree completion. Fourth, contract learning enabled learners and their teachers or counselors to work out agreements on individual learning goals, the activities and resources needed to reach them, and the means and date by which the learning would be evaluated. This mode altered the teacher/student relationship to one of facilitation or partnership in which both had active roles. Fifth, competency-based degree curricula defined learning goals in terms of ability to perform in specific roles. Competence could incorporate learning from previous or current experience, such as employment, a civic role, or voluntary activity. Learners completed competency requirements whenever they could demonstrate the necessary knowledge and capability. Finally, and closely related to competence, was the explicit statement of the outcomes sought in a learning activity. Understanding of these expectations benefits adult learners. They can see clearly what they have to do, whether they already have a background that applies to the expected outcome, and whether the activity contributes to their overall goals for learning and application. Often outcomes-oriented programs include capstone or concluding projects that integrate learners' total degree experiences.

## PROGRAM EXAMPLES

The new external degree programs emphasized one or another of these elements, or they combined several of the elements into more complex systems. Some offered curriculum guidance but no instruction. They focused instead on assembly of evidence of previous learning and validation of new learning through examinations they developed. Several described degree plans in terms of competences, partly set by the institution and partly by the students. Students then negotiated with faculty counselors a plan of activities to fulfill the competences, some of which did not require attendance. Still others used the learning contract to individualize the degree plans. The institution might provide guidelines or an organizing shell within which a faculty facilitator and a student would create a plan that reflected the learner's initiative and the facilitator's suggestions.

An interesting development alongside the mainly associate and baccalaureate external degree programs was the appearance of a number of external graduate institutions offering both master's and doctoral degrees on a national basis. They employed many similar processes to the undergraduate programs, such as mentoring or co-learner relationships with faculty, study in large blocks of content, individualization of learning goals within a broad context, alternation of short-term seminar meetings with independent study at a distance, and use of cluster groups of students led by faculty in local areas. At the same time, the rigor demanded by the degree level, the complexity of the fields, and special skills and clinical or practicum experience that were necessary all placed extra burdens on the external graduate institutions that offer these programs.

At first these unfamiliar procedures raised doubts about external degrees, but by the end of the 1970s they had established their credibility. A preponderant majority of programs surveyed reported that employers recognized graduates for job advancement, and higher-level academic programs accepted these graduates for admission. More discriminating standards in state legislation, regional and professional accreditation, and guides to external degree programs allayed some initial concern about the unfamiliar models. The American Council on Education and the Adult Higher Education Association jointly published a set of principles of good practice that was also helpful.

Over the next two decades additional programs appeared, some experimenting with new modalities or responding to emerging needs. One example was a degree completion model to serve persons with associate degrees or 2 years of previous credit. Typically they enrolled students in cohorts that followed highly prescribed curricula and maintained an accelerated, year-round calendar, often at convenient sites near their homes. In contrast to the earlier individualized contract programs, they imposed considerable control on participants, in return for which students gained security in the definition of their responsibilities, the time to completion, and the cost of the degree. In other cases, institutions worked with employers to upgrade the content of in-house training programs to credit level and to supplement it with additional credit courses presented at the work site to qualify for a degree. Increasingly, programs adopted mediated delivery of courses or whole certificate and degree programs. These methods included delivery of videotapes or satellite broadcasts to participating sites, cable television distribution, and with the growth of the Internet, presentation of whole degrees online anywhere in the world.

## CONCLUSION

The external degree model, with its many variations, has become a well-established option within higher education offerings worldwide. As some of the early commentators on external degrees had predicted, the terms used to describe new approaches, such as *degree completion programs, distance learning,* and *online programs,* began to supersede *external degree.* Yet they continued to pursue the original external degree goals of greater convenience and accessibility to an even larger audience.

*—William H. Maehl*

*See also* ACCREDITATION; ASSESSMENT OF PRIOR LEARNING; ASSESSMENT OF STUDENT COMPETENCE; DISTRIBUTED LEARNING/DISTRIBUTED EDUCATION; EXPERIENTIAL LEARNING

## Bibliography

American Council of Education, Center for Adult Learning and Educational Credentials, & The Adult Higher Education Alliance. (1990, 2000). *Principles of good practice for alternative and external degree programs for adults.* Washington, DC: American Council on Education.

Council of Graduate Schools. (1990). *The doctor of philosophy degree.* Washington, DC: Author.

Council of Graduate Schools. (1994). *Master's education. A guide for faculty and administrators.* Washington, DC: Author.

Dolence, M. G., & Norris, D. M. (1995). *Transforming higher education: A vision for learning in the 21st century.* Ann Arbor, MI: Society for College and University Planning.

Houle, C. O. (1973). *The external degree.* San Francisco: Jossey-Bass.

Maehl, W. H. (2000). *Lifelong learning at its best: Innovative practices in adult credit programs.* San Francisco: Jossey-Bass.

Medsker, L., Edelstein, S., Kreplin, H., Ruyle, J., & Shea, J. (1975). *Extending opportunities for a college degree: Practices, problems, and potentials.* Berkeley, CA: Center for Research and Development in Higher Education, University of California, Berkeley.

Rowley, D. J., Lujan, H. D., & Dolence, M. D. (1998). *Strategic choices for the academy: How demand for lifelong learning will re-create higher education.* San Francisco: Jossey-Bass.

Sharp, L. M., & Sosdian, C. P. (1979). External degrees: How well do they serve their holders? *Journal of Higher Education, 50*(5), 615–649.

Spille, H. A., Stewart, D. A., & Sullivan, E. (1997). *External degrees in the information age: Legitimate choices.* Phoenix, AZ: Oryx.

Spurr, S. H. (1970). *Academic degree structures: Innovative approaches; principles of reform in degree structures in the United States.* New York: McGraw-Hill.

Stewart, D. W., & Spille, H. A. (1988). *Diploma mills: Degrees of fraud.* New York: American Council on Education/Macmillan.

Valley, J. R. (1972). External degree programs. In S. B. Gould & K. P. Cross (Eds.), *Explorations in nontraditional study* (pp. 95–128). San Francisco: Jossey-Bass.

Wang, W. K. S. (1975). The unbundling of higher education. *Duke Law Journal, 1975*(53), 53–89.

# DELIVERY SYSTEMS

A delivery system is a way of getting learning materials to learners and assessment and other information back to teachers. A familiar example is the traditional university course consisting of seminars, lectures, essays, and examinations. In distributed learning, the learners are separated from the instructors, so the delivery system ensures that the learners receive the learning materials that they need at the right time. Examples of delivery systems for distributed learning include printed materials sent through the mail, radio and television broadcasts, and the World Wide Web.

The design of a delivery system for distributed learning needs to reflect learner profiles, the subject matter, and the course structure. Learning materials are typically prepared some time in advance and then distributed to learners either according to a predefined schedule or in a single package that contains everything they need.

For most of the twentieth century, the principal delivery system for noncampus learners involved the use of the postal system. Books, journals, videotapes, and CD-ROMs can be delivered in batches to learners' home addresses, together with instructions for using the materials. These packages may be supplemented with radio and TV broadcasts, weekend campus classes, and summer courses as appropriate. This "one-to-many" approach to the distribution of materials is often supplemented by fax and telephone support from instructors, as well as tutorial groups that might occasionally meet face-to-face. As well as having personal contact with their instructors and peers, learners also send in assignments for assessment and feedback, also usually via the postal system. Such delivery systems are still in widespread use across the world, and continue to be a very effective way of supporting distributed learning. The infrastructure needed to run such delivery systems means that they may be practical only for large numbers of learners, or in situations where learners are so geographically dispersed that this is a more economic option than campus teaching.

The availability of the Internet as a medium for managing distributed learning has brought with it more opportunities. Online course delivery systems can be an extremely effective way of managing campus-based as well as distance learning. Course management software such as Blackboard and WebCT provides tutors with tools to make the learning environment more interactive, responsive, and personalized. The use of electronic discussion areas, or bulletin boards, enables learners to communicate with all other participants, rather than being restricted to the one-to-one dialogue with their instructor that they would get in the postal system described earlier. Tutors can choose to release learning materials according to the performance, learning style, or individual needs of a learner, so that each person can receive a personalized set of materials online.

Synchronous communication tools allow participants who are online at the same time to exchange typed messages (chat or instant messaging) or to look at and work on graphical images together (whiteboard). These can create a real sense of community, as well as offering the opportunity to solve problems quickly. Tutors can offer online assessment tools that allow learners to have instant feedback on their progress. In addition, materials can be presented with interactive links to glossary definitions, text references, and relevant Web sites. The use of animations and interactive diagrams can also help explain complex or visual concepts in a way that print cannot.

The one thing that online courses are not good for is the delivery of large quantities of text. If learners need to read pages of text at the same time, then this is best presented in a printed format, or offered in a form that can be downloaded and printed. Online text needs to be short, to the point, and linked to interactions such as self-tests, glossaries, and other Web sites.

## ORGANIZATION AND MANAGEMENT

As part of the delivery system, someone needs to be responsible for ensuring that materials have been sent to learners, or that materials have been made available on the Web. Learners will need to know what should be available at what times, and who to contact if they don't have what they need. With the online system, it is usually possible to check whether learners have looked at materials, and it can be useful to check this regularly and to contact learners who seem to be finding it difficult to log on. This is the online equivalent of monitoring attendance at lectures.

The use of an online delivery system can give instructors much more control over the ways in which they interact with learners when compared with a traditional system for distributed learning. This can make distributed learning an attractive proposition for use with all learners, not just those who are off campus. However, instructors need to design their courses with care once the familiar constraints of timetables and room bookings have been removed. The organization and management of the online delivery system is critical to making the course work and to making the instructor's workload manageable.

As part of the delivery system, it is important to build in maintenance. All forms of learning materials need to be checked regularly for currency. Although it may be easier to update online materials than books or videotapes, it is still a chore to troll through dozens of pages of online text. It is useful to keep material that will be changed from one semester to another in separate files. For instance, the main body of the materials might refer to "Assignment 1" without giving any dates. In the calendar section, the date for Assignment 1 would be altered with each administration of the course.

Any type of delivery system will require clear and simple arrangements for solving routine learner problems such as missing materials, forgotten passwords, or assignment submission rules. Some large institutions are able to offer 24 hour, 7 day a week service because they have so many learners using a similar system. Smaller institutions are unlikely to be able to do this, but the important thing is to make sure that learners know what to do when they have a problem, and at what times help is available. Many problems will be solvable by a centralized technical or administrative support service, but these staff need to know when and how to refer issues to faculty members.

Faculty or academic support also needs to be structured sensibly. Learners need to know how to contact instructors, and how long to expect to wait for a reply. Response times should be realistic to avoid disappointment, and instructors who will be unavailable at certain periods should make sure that learners know about it. If the service is available, using chat or instant messaging to hold "virtual office hours" at specific times can be a very useful way of handling routine, non-urgent queries. By logging onto the chat room, learners can type in their questions and get a quick answer from an instructor, and instructors should be less disturbed with e-mail or telephone queries at other times of the week. It is also a good idea to compile questions and answers into a Frequently Asked Questions (FAQ) section on an online site, to which learners are encouraged to refer before approaching the instructor.

## ASSESSMENT

The management of learner assessment is a key part of the design of the delivery system. Learners will appreciate opportunities for formative assessment. In an online delivery system, this can be done using computer-marked quizzes. With other systems, more ingenuity is required to give feedback without requiring an exchange of materials between learner and instructor that may take too long to be useful to the learner, as well as creating a lot of work for the instructor.

Summative, or final, assessment also needs careful planning. Validation panels are rightly concerned about the integrity of academic awards, and they are often concerned with the management of assessment for distributed learning. The delivery system needs to be able to get information about final assessment to learners in a timely way and to get assignments back from learners securely. It needs to acknowledge receipt of work submitted by learners and give them an idea of when it will be graded and returned. Institutions need to be confident that the work to be assessed was indeed produced by the learner. This may mean organizing formal examination sessions or interviews where the learners defend their work.

## FACULTY TRAINING AND DEVELOPMENT

Faculty members involved in teaching students need to have a thorough induction into the organization and management of the delivery system. Even if they will not be involved in sending out materials or logging the receipt of assignments, they need to know how the system works so that they can handle learner queries appropriately. Instructors need to know what is expected of them and to be made aware of the differences between learners who are on campus and those who are undertaking coursework at a distance.

## LEARNING STYLES

Delivery systems for distributed learning can be designed to cope better with different learning styles than traditional forms of teaching. Well-designed systems can allow learners to take different paths through materials depending on their interests and needs. Learners could select from a range of activities to reinforce learning, such as choosing to complete "drill and practice" quizzes to check knowledge acquisition, being asked to apply information to a work or personal situation, or finding related case studies in the library or via a structured Web search. Learners will need general study skills advice on how to select activities that suit their personal learning style and on how to consolidate the outcomes.

*—Rachel Forsyth*

***See also*** Learning Management Systems (LMS); Teaching in an Electronic Classroom; Web-Based Course Management Systems (WBCMS)

### Bibliography

Lockwood, F., & Gooley, A. (Eds.). (2001). *Innovation in open and distance learning.* London: Kogan Page.

Morgan, C., & O'Reilly, M. (1999). *Assessing open and distance learners.* London: Kogan Page.

Simpson, O. (2000). *Supporting students in open and distance learning.* London: Kogan Page.

# DEMOGRAPHICS

A consumer revolution in learning has been underway throughout the world over the past 30 years. The resulting changes are global in scope, but they are local in the types of structural and demographic changes that are occurring in specific countries. In a great many countries the demand for higher education has outstripped the capacity of governments and institutions to provide access to residential face-to-face universities for young people, and a range of new government-sponsored flexible learning programs and open universities have been created. In economically advantaged countries that are well along in the transition from an industrial economy to one based on information and knowledge, more adults with increasing levels of education are entering the workforce. Women make up a greater percentage of the workforce in many countries, including the United States, and are increasingly "at home" in an online environment. Changing demographics and improved communications are also creating demand for learning about the diversity of languages and cultures throughout the world. Language ability and facility is becoming essential to citizenship and to commerce, and this change demands both learning and practice.

A fast-paced economy has also forced people to change careers more than ever before. Americans can now be expected, on average, to change careers at least six times during their lifetime. With each career change, the individual must meet the requirement to gain new knowledge in order to be productive, and at the same time, the change in perspective and environment opens up new opportunities for learning. Changing careers frequently, or simply keeping current within a rapidly changing profession, industry, or skilled area of work, requires updating of knowledge, and has dramatically increased demand for distributed learning programs.

Especially in the area of technology, changes are happening so quickly that, for example, the knowledge acquired by engineers who graduate from universities is quickly obsolete. A university degree in any field of study is no longer the end point of learning, but simply a stepping-stone to learning that must continue throughout a career. And technology affects everyone's careers, not just those who are technically trained. The U.S. Bureau of Labor Statistics projects that most new jobs in the U.S. economy in the first decade of the 21st century will require managerial and professional skills. As recently as the 1950s, 20% of the workforce was professional, 20% was *skilled,* and 60% was *unskilled.* In dramatic contrast, by 1997, although professionals continued to be about 20% of the workforce, *unskilled* workers comprised less than 20%, whereas the proportion of *skilled* workers grew to more than 60%. These trends are expected to continue well into the 21st century, reinforcing the fact

that to be competitive in the job market, an individual must be conversant with the most recent tools, which are increasingly technology and computer-based.

People are also better educated, and research consistently shows that better educated individuals pursue continuing education more frequently and aggressively. As the age of retirement begins to increase again, and as life expectancies increase for most countries, greater demand for flexible, convenient, and readily accessible education is projected.

Two-career families are now the norm in America, and are increasingly the norm throughout the world. As a result, the trend toward workplace learning affects many more people than was the case only 30 years ago. Sixty-five percent of all U.S. households are now two-income or single-parent families. Along with the emergence of two-career families comes a reduction in the amount of available time for learning, with increasing pressure to learn in the most effective manner possible. People are also better educated than ever before, and their education has resulted in better outcomes in the workplace. In 1980, a college-educated worker was paid only 28% more than an employee with only a high school diploma; in contrast, in 1996, the average college-educated worker was paid 77% more. This trend of income differentiation according to educational attainment is likely to accelerate, as more and more jobs require the ability to learn a changing set of skills.

Education is rapidly becoming "big business," and a major force in the world economy. Businesses are investing heavily in new information technologies to bolster productivity. An analysis by the Bureau of Economic Analysis and the Bureau of Labor Statistics shows that average investment in technology per employee doubled from May 1991 to September 1996. Globally, estimates of total annual expenditures on all forms of education range from $1 trillion to more than $2 trillion. In all countries, learning through formal schooling, which has been the dominant feature of educational systems throughout most of the past century, is increasingly just the beginning of a continuous lifetime education.

Technology and especially the recent development of the World Wide Web have been important drivers of change in distributed learning patterns, with a dramatic increase in learning through personal computers and, more recently, the Web. As recently as 1990, personal computers were found in less than 10% of U.S. homes. By 1995 they were in 36% of all homes; by

1997 this figure had increased to 46%, and by 2001 to 65.6%. Saturation is expected sometime in the early part of the 21st century.

Yet, despite this rapid overall growth in computer accessibility, the concept of a digital divide between those with access to technology and learning and those without access remains a fundamental concern within the United States and globally. For example, throughout the last decade of the 20th century, family income was a primary indicator of an individual having access to a computer and to the Internet. Although the gap in access between low- and high-income families is narrowing rapidly, it is still the case that people with lower incomes, and countries with lower per capita incomes, have far lower individual computer and Internet access. Education is also a factor that influences the level of computer and Internet access, and this factor is highly related to levels of income. Being in the workforce, especially in fields where computers are prevalent, also positively influences levels of access, and as the workforce ages, people leaving the workforce through retirement can be expected to continue to use both computers and the Internet, resulting in higher usage patterns among the elderly. Significantly, children are much more likely to have access to and to use computers than they were just a few years ago, and at the beginning of the 21st century, gender has become a much less important factor defining the digital divide as both computer and Internet usage among adult males and females in the United States has equalized. The geographic divide between urban and rural citizens has also been significantly reduced, with major exceptions being fewer users within both the central cities and within Native American communities.

Language is also a significant barrier affecting participation. For example, most Internet pages in the United States, and a significant percentage globally, provide links only in English, making the language capabilities of the user a significant barrier to using the Internet. In the United States, one result of the language barrier is a significantly lower level of Internet use among Hispanics who speak only Spanish in the home. And globally, the domination of English as the language of technology has had a comparable dilatory effect upon Internet use.

Finally, race and ethnic backgrounds generally continue to be important elements defining the digital divide in the United States, with Blacks, Hispanics, and Native Americans all generally lagging behind national averages. However, once again, the gap in access among these groups, although still significant, is narrowing rapidly.

According to the *Computer Industry Almanac,* the number of Internet users in the United States will grow from approximately 149 million in 2001 to 189 million in 2004, and is projected to reach almost 240 million by the year 2007. Worldwide, growth is expected to almost triple from approximately 500 million to almost 1 1/2 billion users by 2007, with the greatest percentage growth occurring in the Asian-Pacific area. Growth in demand, and in the power of learning technologies, is expected to provide the foundation for rapid expansion of distributed learning opportunities provided by educational organizations at all levels.

Educational organizations are responding to global trends and demands for increased access to and flexibility of education. A 1995 study by the National Center for Education Statistics found that one-third of higher education institutions offered distance education courses in the fall of 1995, another quarter planned to offer such courses in the next 3 years, and 42% did not offer and did not plan to offer distance education courses in the next 3 years. By the year 2000, almost 100% of U.S. universities were either using or were planning to expand distributed learning. Educational organizations across the globe are recognizing that education is increasingly competitive and full of opportunity, and that the marketplace is growing. New technologies offer the potential of linking learners and teachers in completely new ways, and new for-profit organizations, especially in the United States, have developed to explore technology delivery of programs and degrees.

The forces of globalization have brought the world together, but they have also elevated awareness and exacerbated conditions of inequity, and nowhere is this more evident than in education and telecommunications. Across the globe, serious gaps exist among countries and regions of the world regarding access to all levels of education.

In the United States, expenditures on K–12, postsecondary, and workplace education in 2000 accounted for almost $700 billion, or more than 7% of the U.S. Gross National Product and an estimated one-third of global educational expenditures. More than $400 billion was spent on K–12 education alone, placing the United States in the upper tier worldwide just behind Switzerland, Denmark, and Austria. The

**Table 1**    Percentage of students enrolled in tertiary or post-secondary education per 100,000 of population

| *Countries with greater than 4,000 students per 100,000 population (1996)* | *Countries with fewer than 400 students per 100,000 population (1996)* |
| --- | --- |
| **Europe**: Finland, Norway, Spain<br>**Asia**: Australia, Korea, New Zealand<br>**North America**: Canada, United States | **Asia**: Afghanistan, Cambodia, Laos, Papua New Guinea<br><br>**Africa**: Angola, Chad, Congo, Eritrea, Ethiopia, Gambia, Ghana Guinea, Kenya, Lesotho, Madagascar, Malawi, Mali, Mauritania, Mozambique, Senegal, Tanzania, Togo, Uganda, Zambia |

Source: UNESCO, 2000.

United States also led the world in expenditures for each university student, and again the divide is substantial between developed industrial nations and developing countries. With respect to participation in tertiary or postsecondary education, Table 1 shows some of the disparities of participation.

Participation in all forms of adult education in the United States increased dramatically in the 1990s. A recent study by the National Center for Educational Statistics found that the percentage of adults participating in adult education increased from 33% in 1991 to 46% in 1999, and from approximately 60 million adults participating in 1995 to 89 million in 1999. Clearly these trends are significant in their general form, and even more so when distance education and distributed learning are considered. More than 50% of adults who participated were engaged in work-related training, and almost 25% of those who participated were enrolled in degree programs. Of those enrolled in degree programs, less than one-third were enrolled in full-time programs, with the remaining two-thirds enrolled in career-oriented or part-time programs.

All of these changes are driven by an economy that is based on knowledge and its application, and not on agricultural or industrial output per se, and they have been fueled by globalization of the economy and by advancing technologies such as the Internet and the World Wide Web. Distributed learning has become a critical strategy for societies, communities, businesses, governments, and individuals to cope with the demand for continuous learning.

—*Donald E. Hanna*

*See also* Cultural Access/Digital Divide; Cultural Diversity; Gender; Globalization

## Bibliography

Bureau of Labor Statistics. (1998). *Employment and total job openings, 1996–2006, and 1996 median weekly earnings by education and training category.* Washington, DC: Bureau of Labor Statistics.

Computer Industry Almanac. (2002). *Computer Industry Almanac.* Press Release.

Murane, Richard J., & Levy, Frank. (1997). *Teaching the new basic skills principles for educating children to thrive in a changing economy.* New York: Free Press.

National Center for Educational Statistics. (2001). *Digest of educational statistics.* Washington, DC: National Center for Educational Statistics.

Stuart, Lisa. (1998). *21st century skills for 21st century jobs.* Washington, DC: U.S. Department of Labor.

U.S. Department of Commerce, Economics and Statistics Administration, and the National Telecommunications and Information Administration. (2002). *A nation online: How Americans are expanding their use of the Internet.* Washington, DC: U.S. Department of Commerce.

U.S. Department of Education, National Center for Educational Statistics. (2002). *Participation trends and patterns in adult education: 1991 to 1999.* Washington, DC: National Center for Educational Statistics.

UNESCO. (2000). *World education report, 2000: The right to education: Towards education for all throughout life.* Paris: UNESCO.

# DESIGN STRATEGIES

Educators began to adopt computer networking in the mid-1970s, soon after the invention of packet-switched networks in 1969 and of e-mail and computer conferencing in 1971. Many of the researchers involved in early networking experiments were also academics and educators. They introduced e-mail and computer conferencing as topics into their courses, and through class use and experimentation with these tools, discovered expanded opportunities for student communication, interaction, and collaboration. By the mid-1970s and then into the 1980s, the use of e-mail to participate in question and answer activities with the professor and one's peers, to submit assignments, and to engage in extended class discussions increasingly became part of academic life, and by the 1980s filtered into all levels of educational activities, including primary and secondary schooling, and nonformal education and training. These activities launched the social and educational shaping and design of online environments to advance effective teaching and learning.

As access to computer networks grew in the late 1970s and 1980s, the new field of online education emerged, contributing significantly to socializing cyberspace into human space. It signaled an unprecedented event in human history: the ability of people in widely distributed geographics to communicate and collaborate asynchronously. Computer networks were originally developed by researchers working for the U.S. Department of Defense, but for many of these researchers, the dream was to design communication technologies to enable "meetings of minds" across time and space. With e-mail and conferencing, the dream became possible. The field of online learning environments was thus born, as educators and learners grappled with the opportunity and challenge of designing the new network technologies into spaces and determining means to enhance and expand human community, communication, and collaboration. Educators were among the first user groups to grasp the potential of network communications technologies for collaborative learning. Although e-mail (called electronic mail until the late 1980s and early 1990s) and newsgroups were used to augment the traditional classroom activities, computer conferencing[1] was adopted for many if not most of the early online or mixed-mode (blended) courses.

Research demonstrated the potential of networked technologies such as e-mail and computer conferencing to support active collaborative learning and interaction, but it also revealed important problems with generic tools as online learning environments.

## EDUCATIONAL WEAKNESSES OF GENERIC TOOLS

The use of generic networking tools, such as e-mail, computer conferencing, and newsgroups, imposes significant overhead on the user because these tools were not specifically designed to support educational activities. They are tools for general human communication, not customized for specific purposes or disciplines. Although these generic tools were the original environments used for online learning, they require significant effort by both instructors and learners to shape, access, and organize the educational activities and interactions. Instructors had to expend great effort to rethink and reformulate their traditional classroom activities for a totally new environment, with new attributes, potentialities, and limits. Doing so without models or tools to "shape" the "virtual" learning environment involved substantial administrative, organizational, and pedagogical challenges and costs. These challenges and costs were borne, for the most part, by individual faculty who were exploring these educational innovations. Many experiments failed and many early enthusiasts were discouraged.

Educators from the traditional face-to-face classroom found that the adoption of networking technologies for totally online or mixed-mode educational applications might be tantalizing in terms of new opportunities, but daunting due to the lack of support. Online environments offered no tools for designing the curriculum, uploading files or class resources, or organizing the class into distinct discussion or work groups, over time and by topic. Nor were there mental or representational models to guide early adopters or widely available exemplars of best practice in how to effectively teach online, thus exacerbating the lack of online environments customized to support effective learning and teaching. Design of the learning environments and curriculum were in their infancy; there was no practice and hence no research or evidence to inform best practice.

Classroom educators typically had the experience and expectation of some level of class discourse, in terms of both instructional presentations and class discussions or questions. The adoption of the asynchronous online text-based environment required significant shaping of the system into an environment to support learning. For example, in adopting computer conferencing for course activity, educators had to engage in both metaphorical and organizational shaping of virtual space, such as representing different conferences as formal educational "rooms" (i.e., distinguishing each new topic, seminar, or workgroup with a new named conference), designating other computer conferences as a "café" for socializing, or naming another conference as a space for administrative activities. Instructors also needed to set out temporal organization, in order to have a beginning and end time for each seminar (to provide a shared object whereby students could collaborate on the same topic and coordinate their work). Computer conferencing provided some very important benefits over e-mail because the conferencing system *did* organize messages into topical groupings that were shared by all members of that topic (i.e., all members of the group saw the same organization of messages, typically based on when they were sent and the name of the topic/conference). This organizational capability also facilitated multiple and yet distinct discussions/conferences. In contrast, e-mail and newsgroups allowed messages to be sent, but organization had to be done by each individual recipient. These networking technologies enable group communication and, especially in the case of computer conferencing, group collaboration, but success involved significant effort on the part of the instructor in "constructing" the collaborative learning environment, and on the part of the students in understanding and navigating that environment.

Traditional distance education or correspondence courses have in many cases used e-mail; nonetheless, each learner still typically works alone on the same course package and set of assignments with some level of access to the course instructor for clarification or further direction. Over the years, some distance education programs have added such elements as teleconferencing or e-mail groups, which allow a degree of real-time discussion or unsupervised opportunities to connect with other students. Even online variations of distance education remain by and large based on an individualized rather than a collaborative learning experience. Nonetheless, distance education programs are increasingly adding opportunities for collaborative discussion and work into their courses, and hence

seeking new environments that can support these innovations.

Overall, during the 1980s and early 1990s, many of the online education efforts were based on trial and error and were shaped by design principles brought to the projects by the educators and researchers. Researchers coming from the traditional classroom or seminar experience emphasized the design of learning environments and processes that supported collaborative learning and knowledge building. Those coming from the distance education and training areas by and large emphasized individualized learning programs and scenarios. The success of certain models—and there were many major successes, especially those based on collaborative learning—influenced subsequent design of learning environments.

## EVIDENCE

A paradigmatic breakthrough of the 1980s was the concept of online collaborative learning, an educational breakthrough in shaping an environment characterized by five main attributes: asynchronous, place-independent, many-to-many, text-based/multimedia, computer-mediated communication (CMC). This unique collaborative approach underwent numerous name changes to describe the educational environment and the process: educational CMC, educational computer conferencing, online education, educational networking, networked learning, computer-supported cooperative learning, telelearning, asynchronous learning networks, and most recently e-learning.

This approach is set apart and distinguished from the knowledge transmission mode of the lecture hall or traditional correspondence education model (one-to-many) in two main ways. First, courses are designed so that the instructor acts as a facilitator and moderator; students collaborate in gathering, organizing, and analyzing information to collectively produce a scientific, artistic, or other product such as a paper, a project, a report, a hypothesis, or a work of art. Second, students work asynchronously—that is, they do not have to be online at a specified time to take part in the class. The class will have scheduled times by which messages or assignments must be received, but students can prepare and send their work at whatever time of the day or night is convenient to them.

By the early 1990s, the concept of principled design began to influence technology design and curriculum design of online educational applications.

KnowledgeForum (formerly CSILE), the Virtual Classroom, and the Virtual-U were early examples of designing and customizing online learning environments to support educational principles such as multiple perspectives, active collaborative learning, and knowledge building. They introduced tools to support basic instructional activities such as course design, organization of group spaces and personal space, grading, and easy integration of multiple media files. They also offered tools and models to support and scaffold learning strategies that involve collaborative learning, knowledge building, and multiple representations of ideas and knowledge structures.

System-generated data showed that students wrote a high volume of conference messages. They regularly contributed large amounts of original text, generating a rich database of information. Not only was the overall volume of messaging high, but it was also fairly evenly distributed among the students. Students attributed the increased participation to the increased access opportunities that the asynchronous, place-independent environment offers.

Group interaction was also motivating to students. Student interviews and feedback comments emphasized that it was intellectually stimulating and fun and that they worked harder and produced higher quality work online. Some online courses developed strong communities of friendship.

Students also benefited from the exposure to a diverse range of perspectives in the group learning design: They read input from all other students, rather than hearing only the ideas of the instructor. Student interaction also produced a high quality of intellectual content. Analysis indicates that learners formulated positions and responded to their peers with active questioning, elaboration, and/or debate. Transcript analysis and message map analysis of interaction patterns showed that students used the online seminars and small group activities to add and build on one another's ideas and that they referred to one another's messages.

In the early weeks of online discussions, students often reported communication anxiety and feeling "lost in space." Most, however, soon learned how to direct their comments to the appropriate conference space. Having conferences for different topics and types of activities helped to orient them to the course curriculum and facilitated their navigation through the conferencing system.

These early field studies on networked learning environments suggest that if participants form mental models of the "spaces" where they are working—the virtual seminar, the virtual discussion group, the virtual laboratory, the café for social interactions, and so forth—they will learn to apply appropriate "social factors" to their interactions.

## NEW DIRECTIONS

Ironically, two basic models of learning have emerged: one based on collaborative learning, knowledge building, and interaction, and the second based on individualized learning, publishing of information, course materials, lecture notes, multimedia presentations and interactions, and individual assignments based on these forms of transmitted knowledge.

The first model is the most successful in terms of completion rates, faculty and student satisfaction, and quality of learning. It is, however, the newcomer on the block, and represents not only a new learning environment, but also a paradigmatic shift in education based on knowledge building for a knowledge society. It thus challenges the traditional model—but creating environments for these new approaches has not been easy. The traditional approaches, based on the transmission model of lectures, correspondence education, and increasingly, new high bandwidth environments such as the Web (publishing), videoconferencing, and gaming are still powerful in the R&D and commercial marketplace. The second model does not promote active and interactive construction of knowledge.

Despite their advanced technical capabilities, most state-of-the-art communication systems have not significantly supported effective learning environments. The invention of the Web in 1993 unleashed an unprecedented wave of publication (one-to-many, rather than collaborative education [based on many-to-many]). Video-conferencing and streaming, as well as high-bandwidth games and simulations, are based on the old lecture modalities or individualized CAI (computer-assisted instruction) or training (knowledge transmission) approaches. They represent more efficient forms of correspondence/distance education models, but they fall far short of realizing the education potential for collaborative learning and knowledge construction.

The marketplace is being flooded with products and services offering Web-based learning, but they are characterized more by proliferation than by excellence or distinctive advances.

The educational quality of online courses thus remains a major issue and challenge. The design of learning environments should arguably be based on educational principles and evidence.

—*Linda Harasim*

***See also*** Distributed Learning/Distributed Education; Learning Environments; Online Learning; Virtual Classroom

## Bibliography

Communications of the ACM. (April 1996). *Special section: Learner centred education, 39*(4). Retrieved from http://www.acm.org/cacm/.

Feenberg, A. (1990). Social factor research in computer-mediated communications. In L. Harasim (Ed.), *Online education: Perspectives on a new environment* (pp. 67–97). New York: Praeger.

Harasim, L. (1990). Online education: An environment for collaboration and intellectual amplification. In L. Harasim (Ed.), *Online education: Perspectives on a new environment* (pp. 39–66). New York: Praeger.

Harasim, L. (1993). Collaborating in cyberspace: Using computer conferences as a group learning environment. *Interactive Learning Environments, 3*(2), 119–130.

Harasim, L., Hiltz, R., Teles, L., & Turoff, M. (1995). *Learning networks: A field guide to teaching & learning online.* Cambridge: MIT Press.

Hiltz, S. R. (1993). *The virtual classroom: A new option for learning via computer networking.* Norwood, NJ: Ablex.

Koshmann, T., Myers, A., Feltovich, P., & Barrows, H. (1994). Using technology to assist in realizing effective learning and instruction: A principled approach to the use of computers in collaborative learning. *Journal of the Learning Sciences, 3*(3), 227–264.

Scardamalia, M., & Bereiter, C. (1993). Technologies for knowledge-building discourse. *Communications of the ACM, 36*(5), 37–41.

Sharan, S. (1980). Cooperative learning in small groups: Recent methods and effects on achievement, attitudes, and ethnic relations. *Review of Educational Research, 50*(2), 241–271.

Slavin, R. E. (1980). Cooperative learning. *Review of Educational Research, 50*(2), 315–342.

Stodolsky, S. S. (1984). Frameworks for studying instructional processes in peer work-groups. In P. L. Peterson, L. C. Wilkinson, & M. Hallinan (Eds.), *The social context of education* (pp. 107–124). New York: Academic.

Turoff, M. (1972). Delphi conferencing: Computer-based conferencing with anonymity. *Technological Forecasting and Social Change, 3*(2), 159–204.

Webb, N. (1989). Peer interaction and learning in small groups. *International Journal of Educational Research, 13*(1), 21–29.

## Note

1. Bulletin board systems, invented in 1978, were also used for educational discussions during the 1980s, but their use diminished and disappeared in the 1990s as more sophisticated forms of conferencing systems became widely available.

# DESIGNING LEARNING ENVIRONMENTS

Design is the first of five interrelated didactical disciplines: design, development, implementation, maintenance, and evaluation of pedagogical strategies. Design involves only the prescription of pedagogical strategies. It is a harmonious ensemble of strategies for organizing the message, communicating this message to a specific target audience, and managing these pedagogical situations optimally.

Design also involves the development of our knowledge about the pedagogical strategies and methodologies used in the teaching profession. It is focused on the uses and environmental conditions that optimally facilitate effective learning outcomes and a lasting impact on the learners. Design is a science that involves the crafting of educational material and procedures aimed at helping learning, with respect to the results expected and the goals of the targeted learners. This educational discipline therefore generates prescriptions for the development, evaluation, and maintenance of pedagogical situations. These didactic plans and their instructional strategies are adapted to the particular conditions of each learning situation in order to achieve the training's goals.

## DESIGN PROCESS

### Needs Analysis

The process of needs analysis precedes any training. Its goal is to make sure that the subsequent training is really needed and that it will genuinely solve the learner's problem(s). Trainers are apt to recommend a program of instruction, but instruction is not necessarily the best solution in many cases.

Instead of training, a designer can recommend a job aid (tool) that will help the target audience to accomplish the task they are not accomplishing now, or to accomplish it better than they are now. A job aid can be as simple as a checklist or as complex and sophisticated as a full-blown management information system (MIS).

Needs analysis evaluates the activity and prospects of an enterprise and the corresponding needs of its human resources, in order to determine what is required by the target audience to overcome the current discrepancy between where they are now and where they want to be in the future. Groups of learners are commonly involved, but it can also be applied to individuals that need to qualify for an existing or future position in the enterprise.

This, in turn, requires an analysis of the job and its context (the enterprise), otherwise known as an occupational analysis. This analysis typically includes a description of the tasks expected of the employee, along with the qualifications that the employee needs to accomplish them. In some cases, it may allow the planners to identify shared tasks that affect many of the employees of an enterprise, in which case a training program or job aid can be devised that will suit many employees at once.

## Tasks Analysis

Tasks analysis is a systemic planning process that has the following steps:

1. Determine the current state of the learners' knowledge and skills with respect to the identified goal(s) of the training.
2. Establish the results that are expected from the training.
3. List the prerequisites that the learners must have in order to successfully complete the training.
4. Identify the desirable conditions and the necessary resources.
5. Specify the intermediary objectives that will ease the accomplishment of the training's terminal objectives.

Tasks analysis is often preceded by a skills analysis, whereby the skills, aptitudes, and attitudes of experienced workers are studied systematically, in order to establish the goals and standards of a training program.

## Analysis of the Target Audience

In the two preceding sections, the trainer/designer has already implicitly judged who the learners are, what they are doing now, how they are doing it, and what their needs are. The analysis of the target audience takes this a step further. Beyond the learners' knowledge, experience, skills, and mastery, the trainer/designer must take into account such aspects as: (1) language usage, which includes their vocabulary, their level of discourse, and their reading proficiency; (2) their age, autonomy, and level of maturity; (3) if applicable, their physical and/or cognitive handicaps; (4) psychological and/or social behavioral adaptation problems, if any; and (5) their positive or negative attitudes toward learning, toward the means and approaches used by the trainer, and so on.

## Analysis of the Context

In this analysis, the trainer/designer must take into account aspects such as: (1) the political landscape; (2) the administration's rules, regulations, policies, habits, and so on for both locations; (3) the educational facilities and resources of the learning location and, in some cases, of the workplace; and (4) classroom management issues. The specifics of this analysis are dependent on the context as well.

For some trainers, this section is rolled into one of the previous steps—either with the analysis of the target audience or as part of the needs analysis. The analysis of the context of the target audience (workplace) and the context of the learning situation (learning environment) can be analyzed separately, particularly when the workplace and the learning environment are not at the same location.

## Specifying the Objectives

An objective is a precise statement that specifies a well-circumscribed, tangible result that can reasonably be expected from a learner, or a group of learners, during or at the end of a specific training sequence. The result must be verifiable, and thus it must be tangible enough to be measurable; otherwise, one cannot ascertain whether the objective is genuinely accomplished.

An objective also specifies the relevant actions that must be taken by the learners, as well as the circumstances and the constraints that characterize the attainment of these actions. This stage also specifies the time frame for the accomplishment of the objective (when it begins and when it ends, or expressed as a duration).

### Specifying the Means of Evaluation

The focus of the objectives is on measurable results that genuinely evaluate learning. The evaluation should therefore be quite straightforward. It should verify whether the expected actions have indeed taken place and, thus, that the objectives have in fact been accomplished by the learner or group of learners and, hence, that genuine learning has taken place. Evaluation therefore implies measuring the learners' performance of the expected actions, which may require evaluation of the resulting products in the specified time frame, criterion-based tests, observation of their new skills in action, and other methods too numerous to mention here. In all cases, these measurements of evaluation can be quantitative and/or qualitative, and some are more subjective than others. The selection of the appropriate means of evaluation depends on the skill being measured, the pedagogical strategy and means selected by the teacher, and the temperament of the learners.

The means of evaluation should be selected or crafted immediately after specifying the objectives; this ensures a close coupling between the objectives and the measurement of their attainment. Evaluating any skills, abilities, or knowledge that arc not specified as objectives and/or that were not taught during the training is unfair to the learners, of course; in practice, however, it frequently occurs. Designers must be vigilant about avoiding this mistake.

### Selecting the Pedagogical Strategy and Means

A pedagogical strategy is selected by a teacher according to the kind of results that he or she expects to elicit from his or her learners. It refers to the manner in which the teaching will take place, how it will be taught or animated by the teacher, and so on. Some teachers still favor, for example, an interactive presentation in a classroom. Others may prefer socio-constructivist strategies whereby the learners themselves have more control over their learning process. There is a whole range of other strategies that exist between these two extremes.

## CHARACTERISTICS OF THE PROCESS

The attentive reader may have noticed that selecting the appropriate means of evaluation depends in part on the teacher's pedagogical strategy while, at the same time, the selection of the pedagogical strategy is seemingly performed after the choice of evaluation. This apparent contradiction is due to the sequential nature of this medium. Although the design process is systemic and iterative, it is also systematic.

J. De Rosnay defines a systemic approach as a method of organizing knowledge into a human augmentation system that empowers effective action. This approach is also referred to as the systems approach or cybernetics, which in turn involves the feedback and control of open systems that automatically adapt to their environment. This approach views each system as a dynamic whole with interrelated components that affect each other in many ways and at many different levels. It has been used to study or design systems ranging from binary computers to natural ecosystems, including the design of learning environments. In essence, the systemic approach takes into account the fact that the components of a learning system cannot be designed linearly because changes in one component will impact upon the other components. One has to "juggle" several components at once, but overall it amounts to making the process highly iterative. The design process becomes cyclical. The more cycles in the process the better, because the impacts of the other components can be more often discerned and adapted to the benefit of the entire system.

Evaluation of the design itself is performed throughout the design process. This design can also be evaluated as a whole after the design process has ended (summatively); however, given the fact that societal and learning contexts and learners change over time, an effective educational resource will have to adapt accordingly in order to remain effective and relevant. Every group of learners is different so, in principle, a teacher should revise the design every time it is reused. Ideally, the design of the learning system would be a continuous process, automatically adapting to the users as they progress in their learning. This degree of adaptation is available in some recent computer-based training (CBT) programs and in some Web-based training (WBT).

Whether it is evaluated once per group, in the traditional manner, or whether it is partially automated by a computer-based cybernetic approach, the learners themselves should be involved in the iterative evaluation of their learning environment. This is sometimes referred to as *learner verification and revision (LVR)*. Rapid application development (RAD) is an increasingly popular and highly iterative systemic development process that involves the eventual users of a system as early as possible in the process, and continuously adapts to their needs thereafter.

## THE FUTURE OF DESIGN

Systemic approaches to design are the norm these days, but most of the focus has been on the systemic design of an object, such as a course plan, by one individual teacher communicating informally with her surroundings. Imagine instead a groupware solution that includes databases, or a general knowledge base (including people). Consulting these sources would be very simple, thus streamlining the design process. The data will also be more accurate because it can be obtained and updated at will. That is, it will be a "just-in-time" approach, where the teachers get the information when they need it (traditional process lag does not usually allow this) instead of using the best information that they had at the time they designed the course. The teacher does not necessarily have to fetch the information herself—it can be provided automatically by an MIS system and/or by proactive human and software agents in the community of practice.

Designing learning environments in general, or more specifically designing CBT courseware, is a complex project that is also a very costly undertaking. Professional-quality interactive multimedia, whether Web-based or disc-based (CD-ROM or DVD), requires a large number of specialists. Interactive multimedia, to say the least, is multi-disciplinary to say the least. Like any computer-based solution, it requires programmers and user-interface specialists. Multimedia in particular requires many types of media specialists, for sound, music, video, animation, multimedia integration, and so on, not to mention all of the disciplines that are common to all projects: project managers, information and database managers, and documentation-related specialties. If, in addition, the interactive multimedia is Web-based, as most increasingly are, then you need Web designers, Webmasters, and other server-side professionals. Even the traditional design processes require the designer to consult with various agents in order to accomplish his or her work. So why not include them in a groupware? In other words, why not form a community of practice (CoP)? Why not use this augmentation system to tackle the complexities of the design process in general, and of learning environments and educational wares in particular.

From a pedagogical point of view, educational quality and efficacy have often been neglected by these specialists because they were not networked. Quality courseware that is well adapted to a specific group of learners, in terms of content, interactivity, and so on, requires practicing teachers (the teacher who is training the learners at the very least), the course designer(s), the educational technology experts, and other pedagogical researchers and experts. This potential synergy between R&D and practice, despite its obvious benefits, has always been a very difficult goal to attain. Many astute theoretical and technical developments are never used by teachers because they are not aware of these developments and/or cannot implement them in their teaching practice or classrooms.

The CoP approach will change all of this. By bringing together researchers and practitioners, CoP will ground researchers in the real preoccupations of the practicing teachers. Informed by didactic researchers, the practicing teachers will be better informed and will thus benefit from research results, some of which will be honed to the specific teacher's real needs. The teachers will be able to communicate their findings to the CoP which, of course, also includes other teachers, and thus build a rich body of implicit knowledge that they can draw upon to improve their practices. They would get low- and high-level support on a continuous basis, perhaps even during the use of the technologies in their classroom, which will in turn undoubtedly facilitate the integration of these technologies in teaching practices. This could possibly encourage practitioners to implement new research findings more regularly. To complete the cycle, the results in the field could be fed back into the research and development processes.

And why not include the learners? Communities of learners are, after all, the target audience, and therefore the *raison-d'être* of the training. So why not include them in the design of their learning environment as soon as possible? Involving the learners would lighten some of the design burden. Instead of the teacher's analysis of this target group (a best guess), the target group could provide its input first-hand. Involving learners in the design of their learning, such as by selecting the content or the medium, would have a very positive impact on their motivation to learn with it. The solution would be well adapted to their needs and relevant because the content was selected by them according to their cultural specificities. The learners' involvement in the design of their learning process need not be limited; instead, they could be encouraged to be autonomous and to embrace lifelong learning as a personal and public pursuit to discover themselves and to enrich their communities. This pedagogical strategy/approach is also known as socioconstructivism.

With a CoP instructors could apply a systemic approach to the research, design, development, and practice of a large-scale system that could be open-ended, if and when communities of learners are included. It then becomes a social system that is computer-assisted, but which goes well beyond the groupware technologies that compose it.

—*Pierre-Léonard Harvey*
—*Alain Farmer*

*See also* LEARNING CIRCLES; LEARNING COMMUNITIES

## Bibliography

Horton, W. (2000). *Designing Web-based training: How to teach anyone anything anywhere anytime.* New York: John Wiley & Sons.

Kruse, K., & Keil, J. (1999). *Technology-based training: The art and science of design, development, and delivery.* San Francisco: Jossey-Bass.

Lee, W. W., & Owens, D. L. (2000). *Multimedia-based instructional design: Computer-based training, Web-based training and distance learning.* San Francisco: Jossey-Bass.

Scheizer, H. (1999). *Designing and teaching an online course: Spinning your Web classroom.* Needham Heights, MA: Allyn & Bacon.

# DESKTOP PUBLISHING

Desktop publishing involves the use of a computer to create high quality documents that are intended to be either printed by the user on a personal printer or sent to a commercial printing house. However, a user may elect to view files on a screen using page-viewing software such as Adobe Acrobat Reader or Microsoft E-Book Reader.

One key feature in most definitions of desktop publishing is the software that is used to produce the files. Traditionally this has meant the use of specific high-end page layout programs such as QuarkXPress or Adobe PageMaker. However, many of the features that differentiated these programs from word processing have become incorporated into programs such as Microsoft Word of Corel WordPerfect.

The definition of desktop publishing extends beyond page layout programs to include design, images, photography, and the selection of appropriate printing technologies. Thus, desktop publishing includes additional software packages like Adobe Photoshop for working with bitmap images such as photographs or CorelDraw for creating vector-based drawings such as logos, although these programs can be used for other functions beyond desktop publishing.

Key elements of desktop publishing include image control, font management, and the ability to manage the layout of the file. A word processor could be used to create a simple brochure or newsletter. A high-end desktop publishing package can be used to create a magazine, including outputting PostScript files for a commercial printing service bureau. These service bureaus then convert PostScript files to film, which is used for offset printing.

In distributed learning systems, the most common file type for desktop publishing is the Portable Document Format, usually known simply as PDF. Created by Adobe, PDF has become an open standard file format that preserves the fonts, graphics, and formatting of the source document. The advantage of PDF is that the files can be shared, viewed, and printed without the user being able to alter the document (if he or she, like the majority of users, has only Acrobat Reader). The files are typically created from the source program using Adobe Acrobat, although other programs also can create PDF files. The file can then be viewed using the freely available Adobe Acrobat Reader. According to the Adobe Web site more than 300 million copies of the Reader have been distributed worldwide.

—*Robin Peek*

*See also* ELECTRONIC JOURNALS AND PUBLICATIONS

# DISABILITY LAW

## THE ARCHITECTURAL BARRIERS ACT

The first significant piece of legislation for persons with disabilities was the 1968 Architectural Barriers Act. Although this act is irrelevant to distributed learning, it marks a historic paradigm shift in society's relationship to this population. Previously, people with disabilities were either confined to poor houses with the indigent or were the object of a paternalistic humanitarianism. It is no coincidence that this transformation happened at the height of the 1960s civil rights movement. Other minorities were demanding their full rights to participate in society rather than being pacified with charity. Many veterans from World War II and the Korean and Vietnam conflicts were not content to receive charity either. They had fought for America, and they demanded the right to be able to participate fully as Americans. They wanted access to society rather than its pity. The Architectural Barriers Act said that it was society that needed to be fixed to permit people with mobility disabilities into schools, government buildings, libraries, and commercial establishments. People with disabilities were demanding that social attitudes and structures be altered to let them compete and participate rather than be kept outside as helpless wards of society.

## THE VOCATIONAL REHABILITATION ACT

In 1973, the Vocational Rehabilitation Act was passed. It focused on opening education and employment and forbade discrimination on the basis of disability. Many returning war veterans received government help to attend college and to purchase a home. Some of these veterans had war-related disabilities. They were disillusioned when they faced discrimination after their sacrifice. This legislation was a partial attempt to address this injustice. Although computers were used in business and education by this date, they played only a limited role, and the act did not impact distributed learning issues until more recently. Section 503 spoke to discrimination in employment but was not enforced vigorously. Section 504 barred discrimination in education and played a significant part in opening higher education to students with disabilities. Presently, courts and the Office for Civil Rights are using this section to require schools to make their computer and information technology systems accessible to these students.

The Department of Education Office for Civil Rights has compared providing access to information through adaptive computer technology with the need to provide ramps on buildings for physical access to students with mobility impairments. This was spelled out clearly in Case Docket No. 09–97–2002:

> The magnitude of the task public entities now face in developing systems for becoming accessible to individuals with disabilities . . . is comparable to the task previously undertaken in developing a process by which buildings were to be brought up to specific architectural standards for access.

## THE AMERICANS WITH DISABILITIES ACT

In 1990 Congress passed and the President signed the Americans with Disabilities Act (ADA), the best known of all the disability-related legislation. Although it is a far-reaching law, its major achievement is to extend the equal protection of the law to include persons with disabilities.

Title II of the ADA requires that communications be made accessible to people with disabilities. Increasingly, the courts are making it clear that communications include electronic communications and digital information. Title II of the ADA requires that communications with persons with disabilities "are as effective as communications with others." In this context, communication means "the transfer of information, including (but not limited to) the verbal presentation of a lecture, the printed text of a book, and the resources of the Internet."

The Office of Civil Rights (OCR) has held that "the three basic components of effectiveness are timeliness of delivery, accuracy of the translation, and provision in a manner and medium appropriate to the significance of the message and the abilities of the individual with the disability."

Timeliness is particularly relevant to discussions of accessibility to electronic information. One of the features of distributed learning is its immediacy. Even when the information is located on a computer halfway around the world, it appears on a person's computer with almost no noticeable wait. It is also usually on demand at any time of the day or night. When that information is available in a suitable format for a user with a disability, that user receives it as quickly as anyone else. However, if the person has to wait for someone to be available to read the monitor or to wait for a copy of the information to be put in Braille and mailed, the time lag is very significant. This means that the only way to provide communication in a timely manner is to provide access to that same electronic information. It means adapting the interface to meet the person's needs and creating a more level playing field.

Providing an accurate translation of information is obviously important. In many cases, providing an interface that permits the user with a disability to access the same information ensures accuracy. Where a translation is necessary, such as providing a text transcription of Internet audio for a person who is deaf, the court requires the provider to strive for an accurate translation. This is extremely important in a situation like an online learning class, where the student will be graded on comprehension.

Finally, the court's third requirement for making communications accessible is the "provision in a manner and medium appropriate to the significance of the message and the abilities of the individual." In some situations, the material could be provided in more than one medium. A user who is blind could receive text as audio or in text that a screen reader could output with synthesized speech. The audio would be the best medium for something like a poem. Electronic text would be better if it were a composition course where the student had to analyze the grammar. Remember, however, that students with disabilities have varying ability levels. A format that is suited to students in graduate school studying computer science may well not work for a student in first grade.

One of the clauses in the ADA that institutions frequently point to as limiting their responsibilities says that institutions have to provide "reasonable accommodations." Congress did not want to create legislation that would impose an undue burden on institutions. The clause implies that, when providing accommodations is too costly or inconvenient and disruptive to the institution, then it might be exempt from the requirement to provide accommodations. Clearly, there is great room for disagreement about which accommodations are reasonable and which are unreasonable. The law, itself, does not give much help. "Reasonable" has become gradually defined and redefined by the courts and by the actions of the

Office of Civil Rights. Increasingly, the law is being interpreted in a way that sets the standard very high. In a case involving a university library, Case Docket No. 09–97–2002, OCR states,

> The larger and more financially endowed the library, the higher the expectation that a greater volume of information will be made available within a shorter amount of time, particularly when reasonably priced adaptive technology is available to replace tasks that previously required personnel.

It held that the more an institution used technology in its activities, the more it would be expected to provide accessible information technology for persons with disabilities.

## THE INDIVIDUALS WITH DISABILITIES EDUCATION ACT

This act relates primarily to education in grade school and high school. The recent amendments to it added regulations related to access to computers and electronic information. Schools are required to develop an individualized education plan for special needs students in conjunction with the student and parents. Now, the law specifically adds the right for a student to have access to assistive computer technology when it is appropriate to that student's needs. As schools are rapidly moving into the use of computers in these grades, this addition is important.

## SECTION 508

The 1998 revision of Section 508 of the Vocational Rehabilitation Act addresses accessibility of distributed learning in considerable detail. The law "requires access to electronic and information technology provided by the federal government" and specifies that federal agencies must ensure that this technology is accessible to both government employees and members of the public with disabilities. Section 508 is primarily a federal government procurement requirement setting standards for electronic equipment accessibility and for Web page accessibility. The legislation designated the Federal Access Board as the agency responsible for setting the actual standards. Both people with disabilities and the institutions that have to meet the requirements appreciate having specific standards, removing much of the confusion about what was really mandated. Uncertainty still exists, however, as to what agencies and organizations are covered by Section 508. There is language in the Technology Assistance Act that many believe binds states receiving federal funds to conform to Section 508. Then, the further question is to know just what state agencies are covered. However, many states and a number of colleges and universities believe it may include them. Others are not certain but want to provide accessibility to people with disabilities, and Section 508 provides a convenient set of standards to adopt.

The largest impact of Section 508 appears to be on the producers of electronic equipment and computer software. Although it does not specifically cover them, they are aware that if they do not conform to the standards they will lose all their government business. The federal government makes up a large segment of the market.

At the same time as people with disabilities have campaigned for legislation that opens up opportunities for their full participation in society, education, work, and entertainment, the rapid development of the information age and of computers and computer-like devices provides new tools that empower many persons with disabilities to participate more fully in these areas. Digitized information is display-independent and can be produced in formats that greatly reduce the impact of many disabilities.

*—Norman Coombs*

***See also*** ADAPTIVE TECHNOLOGY; SPECIAL NEEDS POPULATIONS

## Bibliography

The Americans with Disabilities Act can be found at http://www.usdoj.gov/crt/ada/adahom1.htm

The Individuals with Disabilities Education Act (IDEA) can be found at http://www.ed.gov/offices/OSERS/Policy/IDEA/

Information on the Architectural Barriers Act can be found at http://www.access-board.gov/about/ABA.htm

Information regarding Section 508 can be found at http://www.access-board.gov

The Vocational Rehabilitation Act Section 504 can be found at http://www.dol.gov/oasam/regs/statutes/sec504.htm

# DISTRIBUTED LEARNING/ DISTRIBUTED EDUCATION

Distributed learning (or distributed education) refers to the delivery of educational resources over a distance, allowing instruction and learning to occur independent of time and place. Originally, the term was applied to instruction that was "distributed" to students in off-campus locations, and included not only correspondence courses by mail, but also face-to-face instruction at noncampus sites. Currently, distributed learning refers to educational activities that integrate information technology into the learning and teaching enterprise.

The mandate of some educational institutions is to train students who are geographically dispersed from one another and from the institutions themselves. They represent what has historically been known as "distance education." These institutions used to rely on individually directed study, mail, the telephone, and/or infrequent residential sessions for contact between students and instructors. More recently, many distance learning institutions, committed to the delivery of course materials or instruction over a distance, have adopted a strong online presence. They generally employ the Internet as an alternative means of service delivery to learners, although they may also include other technologies such as videoconferencing, audioconferencing, CD-ROMs, audiotapes, and videotapes.

At a pedagogical level, those who support a model of education that emphasizes student-initiated access to learning resources have recommended the use of the term *distributed learning* to refer to new forms of online learning. The face of the field has changed dramatically over the past several decades. First there was correspondence study, using the postal service to provide education to learners at a distance. In the early part of the 20th century, educational institutions used radio, and then television, to deliver courses from a central location to other areas. Several decades later enhancements in media and technology led to the introduction of the open university and the virtual classroom. Now, distributed education has entered the digital world. With the abundance of personal computers and Web technologies, diverse models of distributed education are expanding rapidly.

Distributed learning can be viewed as learning that takes place in any technologically mediated, non–face-to-face setting. Such settings range from online courses delivered to students who are living in different parts of the world and have never met to students who are enrolled in a traditional campus-based course that contains a supplemental discussion group that students can access by video from their campus residences. Models of distributed education include the following: nonprofit traditional distance learning universities, new for-profit (virtual) universities, corporate online universities, extensions of residential classrooms in traditional universities, partnerships between traditional universities and online learning companies to deliver courses on the World Wide Web, and nonprofit or for-profit subsidiaries of traditional universities.

Distributed learning portends to become the dominant paradigm of higher education. There are a number of reasons for its burgeoning popularity:

- The physical classroom no longer defines the learning environment. Therefore, the model not only helps solve the problem of the crowded classroom, but also avoids the need for expensive capital investment in buildings and physical plants. This factor is particularly important in resource-limited developing countries. More resources can be devoted to designing educational materials and supporting faculty and students.

- Education can be "anytime" and "anyplace." Students living at a distance from educational institutions, as well as adult learners who cannot easily attend regularly scheduled classes on campus because of work and family commitments, are able to pursue degree programs and continuing education and training on a par with more traditional students. New groups of learners are able to access formal education, including members of traditionally underrepresented groups. The "anytime, anyplace" nature of distributed learning allows both students and faculty the flexibility of participating at any convenient time from any location that has a suitable computer connection.

- Online classes level the instructional playing field, in the sense that everyone's voice can be equally loud in cyberspace. Learners who are normally quiet and reserved in the classroom setting have an equal opportunity to participate actively in the virtual setting without interruption. Stereotyping and discrimination based on gender, ethnicity, and other visual cues are generally not a factor in the online learning environment. Participation tends to be more thoughtful, especially in asynchronous formats, because learners have the opportunity to reflect on their comments and contributions before posting them on a Web site.

A number of important ingredients go into establishing a viable distributed learning program. The first task is to determine the goals and purpose of the program. Some contemporary academic institutions rely exclusively on online courses and offer bachelor's, master's, and/or doctoral degrees at a distance. In contrast, an increasing number of institutions of higher learning offer alternative online courses within a standard curriculum. Another possible objective is to provide computer conferencing or access to online course materials or databases as part of a face-to-face course. In addition to online degree programs, continuing education and professional training may be prominent distributed learning goals within both academic institutions and the corporate sector. Finally, distributed education can take place within informal learning networks.

Distributed learning environments can connect learners with each other and with teachers, consultants, and supervisors, and provide them ready access to knowledge and information provided by new technologies. An example is research scientists from different parts of the world who create online communities to share data and exchange opinions without waiting for the publication of their studies in research journals. This kind of knowledge networking takes advantage of recruiting participants with different perspectives and types of experience and expertise to participate in collaborative inquiry about complex research or social problems. Another determinant in networking is consistency with the goals of the sponsoring institution in terms of values—regard for the residential experience, access to education, and commitment to technology.

A second issue in planning a distributed learning program is the selection of an appropriate learning platform to support the content and method of the program. One decision concerns the choice between a synchronous and an asynchronous format. Synchronous formats operate in "real time" at scheduled times, whereas asynchronous formats operate at the learner's convenience. Another decision concerns the relative need for discussion among the participants as opposed to working one-on-one with the instructor or the computer. Yet another issue involves inclusion of multimedia resources, such as streaming audio or video, as opposed to pure text.

Another issue to consider in designing and implementing a distributed learning program is the need for an infrastructure consisting of reliable, up-to-date information technology equipment and the staff to support it on an ongoing basis. The availability of good instructional support personnel seems to be critical for the success of the program. Effort should be taken to minimize the impact of change on students and faculty by stabilizing and routinizing the technology platform and delivery system as much as possible. Moreover, electronic security measures should be installed to address concerns about confidentiality, reliability, and integrity of student records.

Choice of instructors is another concern. They need to be adept at using the technology and dedicated to the concept and pedagogy of distributed learning. There is reason to believe that teaching online takes more time than anticipated and calls for different skill sets and temperaments than classroom teaching. Programs need to assess and provide the knowledge and skills necessary to succeed in the distributed environment.

Distributed learning is conceptually different from classroom learning. Because the boundaries of the classroom do not exist in cyberspace, it is possible for students and faculty to interact throughout the week at their convenience. Increasingly, the form of interaction is collaborative. On the one hand, the collaboration is a result of the technology itself: Students can share their work and give each other feedback, and they can participate in group projects and simulations. Distributed learning environments support regular contact and cooperation, active learning, and outcomes that profit from the collective wisdom of the participants. The medium encourages attention to differences in learning styles and levels of experience. It suggests a pedagogy that is quite different from the traditional classroom. Rather than a hierarchically organized lecture hall with an instructor disseminating information to relatively passive students, the online classroom becomes a decentralized, distributed, threaded dialogue constructed as a process of self-organized discovery.

The trend in distributed education is to take advantage of the flexibility of networking technology to combine campus-based instruction with online delivery systems. Instruction can take place either synchronously or asynchronously. The most likely scenario for the future is distributed learning programs that customize learning to take advantage of individual needs and learning styles and combine the best elements of classroom education and technology. On-campus, face-to-face learning is not the solution for all students, and consideration needs to be given to what method of teaching is best for what type of student under what circumstances. The types of integration may include the use of small networked groups operating from workstations, large groups attending to a video screen, and individual students working alone using electronic library resources. The modality depends, to some extent, on the information to be learned. The dissemination of highly structured basic content might not require much discussion and may be suitable for a teacher-focused approach. Content that is heavily value laden may be more appropriate for peer discussion. It is up to educators to blend teaching modalities and methods in ways that match student needs and capacities to create optimal learning outcomes.

A challenge for the future of distributed education is to meet the needs and values of individual institutions while serving the high market demand for life-long learning worldwide. Technology is becoming increasingly sophisticated and responsive to learning applications outside the classroom. This allows educational institutions to revisit a traditional pedagogy or curriculum and adopt information technology to become more competitive in the educational marketplace. For instance, students on campuses will shortly be able to carry wireless notepad computers that will allow them to access instructors, classmates, and databases to complete their academic work online. Yet almost all advocates of distributed learning agree that technology should never drive educational needs; educational needs should determine the appropriate use of technology. It is not unlikely that the distinctions between campus-based learning and distributed learning, between classroom-based education and Internet-based education, will continue to erode and that teaching methods will be increasingly tailored to the particular subject matter, group of students, and learning objectives.

—*Kjell Erik Rudestam*

*See also* Degrees/Degree Programs; Online Learning Environments; Online Universities

## Bibliography

Carr-Chellman, A. A., & Duchastel, P. (2000). The ideal online course. *British Journal of Educational Technology, 31,* 229–241.

Dede, C. (2000). Advanced technologies and distributed learning in higher education. In D. E. Hanna & Associates, *Higher education in an age of digital competition.* Madison, WI: Atwood.

Lau, L. (2000). *Distance learning technologies: Issues, trends and opportunities.* Hershey, PA: Idea Group Publishing.

Oblinger, D. G., Barone, C. A., & Hawkins, B. L. (2001). *Distributed education and its challenges: An overview.* American Council on Education/EDUCAUSE.

# DOCUMENT MANAGEMENT SYSTEMS

A document management system (DMS) provides a secure electronic environment for management, control, and distribution of electronic documents. The fundamental purpose of DMS, digital library technology, or the World Wide Web is to organize, keep track of, and efficiently retrieve documents produced by individuals, workgroups, or enterprises. DMS offers a single application for both local and global organizations that is accessible 24/7. It also allows for the storage and flow of documents using any format, including images, spreadsheets, PDFs, and PowerPoint presentations. DMS is a collaborative tool with full permission capability, so access can be granted as Edit, Read Only, or No Access.

In the last 2 or 3 years, personal computers have become much more powerful and accessible. As a result, the Internet and worldwide network computing have gained a strong foothold in both individual and multiple user environments.

The distributed learning environment integrates a number of technologies to provide opportunities for activities and interaction in both asynchronous and real-time modes. Distributed learning is based on a model that incorporates a blending approach of technologies. It borrows aspects from campus-based delivery, open learning systems, and distance education to provide a rich learning experience that is learner-centered. Instructors are able to customize their environments to meet the needs of diverse student populations. This allows for flexibility with high-quality and cost-effective learning.

## FUNCTIONS OF A DOCUMENT MANAGEMENT SYSTEM

Because the term *document management system* signifies a broad collection of related systems that perform one or more of several functions, it is useful in describing the distributed learning environment, which needs space for growth and flexibility. DMS does not describe any one single type of software package or technology; instead, it more accurately describes a multi-functional system that can manage documents.

Typical functions that document management systems perform, although no one system can perform them all, include:

- *Descriptive file naming*—Descriptive file naming makes files easier to retrieve. This feature also allows for longer and more descriptive file names.
- *Indexing*—This function generates lists of keywords.
- *Multi-file document control*—This key feature of document management systems treats various files and data associated with one document as a single object during archival and retrieval transactions.
- *Storage and retrieval*—This function assists in managing storage and retrieval functions.
- *Library services*—Library services use the check in, check out audit trail; protection/security; and audit control to refer to document control mechanisms.

## PRESENTATION AND DISTRIBUTION SERVICES

Document management systems are "multi-purposing." This allows information to be distributed in different formats, such as viewed on a network (e.g., the Web), distributed on a CD-ROM, or printed on paper. This feature is outstanding for the distributed learning environment, because it offers ease of use and flexibility worldwide.

## ADVANTAGES OF DOCUMENT MANAGEMENT SYSTEMS

Document management systems enable large amounts of information to be stored electronically, which requires much less physical space than the equivalent paper storage. These systems, unlike other storage systems, allow documents to be viewed in their native formats and by multiple users simultaneously. This adaptability provides access to a large audience. DMS also makes available password protection of sensitive documents and restricts access to documents, which increase security.

Another feature of a document management system is that it improves the speed of retrieving documents.

A well-organized system that utilizes good indexing makes it possible to categorize documents using key words, phrases, or particular categories, which enhance the speed even more. Document management systems make it possible for someone to look up correspondences with a person, or to search all documents for a particular name or phrase, thus widening the area of knowledge available in educational technology or distributed learning. Increased speed of retrieval is beneficial to individuals and also allows efficient assistance to be provided to groups anytime, anywhere.

## COMPATIBILITY WITH OTHER ELECTRONIC INFORMATION SYSTEMS

DMS documents are compatible with systems such as groupware, e-mail, intranets, and the Internet. It is possible for a document stored via DMS to be viewed remotely via the Internet, or even to make documents available via groupware as well as over the Internet, thereby reaching a much larger number of people. DMS also permits integration of documents within an intranet or Internet site.

## IMPROVEMENT OF WORKFLOW

With improved document handling and increased speed of information retrieval, DMS has a significant impact on workflow. In a business or educational setting, rapid and improved retrieval of information allows for more flexibility, regardless of the distance between users.

*—Barbara J. Volger*

*See also* INFORMATION SYSTEMS; LIBRARY TECHNOLOGIES

## Bibliography

Allessi, S. M., & Trollip, S. R. (1991). *Computer-based instruction: Methods and development.* Englewood Cliffs, NJ: Prentice Hall.

Bielawski, L. (1997). *Electronic document management systems: A user centered approach for creating, distributing and managing online publications.* Upper Saddle River, NJ: Prentice Hall PTR.

Koulopoulos, T. M., & Frappaolo, C. (1994). *Electronic document management systems: A portable consultant.* New York: McGraw-Hill.

Robek, M. F., Brown, G. F., & Stephens, D. O. (1995). *Information and records management: Document-based information systems.* New York: Glencoe/McGraw-Hill.

# DOMAIN NAME

Domain names are tools to help individuals find their way around the Internet. Domain names are mnemonic devices that make it simpler and easier to remember Internet Protocol (IP) addresses. Every computer, including personal computers (PCs), has an IP address. An IP address identifies the computer. It can be compared to an address or a telephone number. While utilizing the World Wide Web, a set of numbers identifies the computer from which you are working, but also allows you to contact other computer bases. For example 192.232.125.61 is the IP address for Kodak. Remembering these numbers is difficult, so domain names are used to help access the sites. Instead of remembering and then typing in these numbers, a person can type in the domain name www.kodak.com, which then directly accesses the desired Web site. This facilitates the connection by making it easier and faster to access the site.

With the expanding global economy, primarily as a result of the Internet, the increased use of the World Wide Web has resulted in further need to expand the options available when using domain names. Initially, top level domains (TLDs) included *.com* and *.org,* which were used on the end of each domain name to help users identify whether the organization they were contacting was a commercial business or an organization. The *.net* domain was also used, and indicated a computer-related site, and *.edu* referred to an educational institution. Currently, domain names also can be delineated by country. These are called country code TLDs, or CCTLDs. For example, *.ca* indicates Canada, *.us* indicates the United States, and *.uk* indicates a United Kingdom location. Several of the other TLDs include *.biz* for businesses; *.info* for promoting special products or events; *.name* to indicate that it is a personalized domain name (e.g., www.shelley. name; *.museum* for museums; *.coop* for cooperatives; *.pro* for professionals such as lawyers, accountants, and physicians; and finally *.aero* for the air transport industry.

Initially, TLDs were meant to identify the specific type of business (i.e., *.com* was for commercial businesses only); however, with the increased demand for certain names, domain name registrars have resorted to using other endings in order to get the name they want. For example if a business by the name of Smith & Jones, wanted its Web site to bear its name it would want www.smith&jones.com. However, if that was taken it might then use *.org* or *.ca* instead, even though the appropriate ending should be *.com.* The other alternative would be to attempt to buy the domain name from the person or company who owned the www.smith&jones.com domain name.

Large Web sites may contain numerous servers, all with different IP addresses. So when users attempt to access a specific Web site that is part of a bigger server, domain names can be used to direct them. In this case, domain aliases are frequently used to direct users to a specific page on the Web site or server. Financial institutions such as banks, for example, may have aliases such as accounts.theirdomainname or loans.theirdomainname to point their customers to a certain location. Internet service providers use aliases to direct their customers to a specific server they use for certain services (e.g., a customer's home page).

Domain names also play a role in e-mail addresses. A mail server is set up for a particular domain name, such as *aol.com,* which resolves to, or ends up at, a particular IP address. Thus, any e-mail address that includes *@aol.com,* such as samplename@aol.com, would be directed to the mail server first and then into the e-mail account of samplename.

Several companies are specifically set up and authorized to register domain names. These companies, called registrars, have been approved by the Internet Corporation for Assigned Names and Numbers (ICANN), which can be found at www.icann.org.

—*Shelley L. Goodwin*
—*Jeff J. Mason*

*See also* INTERNET; WEB SITES

## Bibliography

The Internet Corporation for Assigned Names and Numbers: www.icann.org.

Levine, J., & Baroudi, C. (1997). *Internet for dummies.* New York: IDG Books Worldwide.

# E

## E-LEARNING STRATEGIES

The basic purpose of research is to "observe" and to make sense of these "observations." Research, the asking of questions and the seeking of understanding, is one of the most fundamental features of human activity throughout history. Scientific research is a more rigorous form of this basic activity: It involves posing questions, seeking understanding through evidence, and exploring new opportunities to resolve existing challenges. Scientific research asks questions and seeks answers (data collection, measurement, and observation) that contribute to scientific and social understanding (data analysis, interpretation, and results). Research is the basis of knowledge seeking, creation, and testing and is key to innovation.

Social science research is the systematic observation of social life for the purpose of finding and understanding patterns among what is observed. Social scientists measure aspects of social reality and then analyze and draw conclusions about the meaning of what they have measured.

All researchers, whether physical scientists or social scientists, have their tools, instruments, and methodologies for collecting and measuring data. Research methods and tools are ways of gathering evidence about a topic or problem. Traditionally, social science researchers have employed a number of tools or instruments, including surveys, interviews, focus groups, field records, documentation, and observation. Many, if not most of these tools are significantly enhanced and empowered online, enabling effective storage, retrieval, analysis, and various integrations and visualizations of results. In particular, the power of observation expands online and becomes far more objective, rigorous, and accessible to multiple forms of scrutiny. Perhaps equally important, new tools/technologies are emerging that expand what is possible and enable entirely new approaches to observing and analyzing our world, especially the world of e-learning.

This entry provides a capsule of how e-learning research has been approached and what it tells us.

## ROLE OF COMPUTERS IN E-LEARNING RESEARCH

Social science research, and in fact all science, has long been viewed as organized around two major activities: data collection and data analysis. Computers have become an integral force in the study of social sciences, including e-learning research, both as tools for collecting data and as tools for the analysis of data. Moreover, computers have introduced a new category: computer environments as *a source of data*. Computer networks today are also learning environments and as such are sources of data. Individually—as tools for collecting data, analyzing data, or providing data—or in combination, computers and computer networking tools enable extraordinarily powerful illuminations of learning online.

From the earliest applications, e-learning has been distinguished by the incorporation of an active research component. Even as the field was first launched, there was a base of empirical evidence to accompany it. This research component provided an important source of empirical information, first to assist researchers and educators interested in the new media, but also—eventually—to establish the credibility of the field. The strength of this research distinguished e-learning from distance education, and even from traditional approaches such as the lecture hall.

It was realized and largely accepted by e-learning's early adopters that new media both demand and facilitate new research methodologies that can take into account the unique characteristics of e-learning applications. Research into new educational media typically benefited from traditional approaches, which were reformulated into e-learning tools, hence the use of online surveys, questionnaires, and interviews. Researchers eventually realized, however, that traditional research methods and tools were by themselves inadequate and inappropriate—the new e-learning environments required new tools and approaches that could utilize the educational innovations, processes, and outcomes, and illuminate important issues related to the general study of learning and understanding. Computers have introduced entirely new forms of educational applications and have afforded opportunities for research that have expanded traditional insights and enabled research into learning and understanding that has hitherto been extremely difficult if not impossible.

The following sections explore three categories related to computers and e-learning:

1. Computers as research tools to collect data
2. Computers as research tools to analyze data
3. Computers as learning environments providing a source of data

## Data Collection

Data collection is a form of observation. Although people are always observing the life around them, the collection and measurement of data refers to something more deliberate and rigorous. Computers support data collection in a variety of ways, particularly in collecting and recording data (observations) systematically. Sometimes the measurements are numerical or *quantitative* (e.g., each student logged on to the site 10 times per week during the semester). Quantitative research studies include experimental (or, in the case of e-learning, usually quasi-experimental) studies, and use approaches such as surveys, usage statistics, completion rates, and grades. Measurement can also be

*qualitative,* that is, using words to describe the qualities of an event (e.g., the subject reported anxiety about access). Qualitative research studies include ethnographies, case studies, and, typically, descriptive studies. Qualitative research methods typically include interviews, historical and document analysis, and observations.

Qualitative research does not mean that numbers or quantification are not used, and quantitative research does not necessarily exclude textual description. The two methods should not be viewed as diametrically opposed. Historically, research has benefited from the integration of multiple methods.

### Surveys, Questionnaires, and Polls

Surveys, polls, and questionnaires are among the oldest research techniques in human history (the Old Testament refers to the use of census surveys), and remain the most frequently used form of observation and data collection in the social sciences. These three approaches have become the most prevalent computer-based research tool. Whereas traditional forms of surveys (postal mailings, telephone surveys, etc.) are still predominant in general applications such as census data (gathering and measuring original data from large populations) or public opinion polls, e-learning applications typically use an online version of a survey or poll to collect data on topics such as user satisfaction (faculty and/or student satisfaction). Online surveys can be created using a word processing program, but most are created with commercial packages or freeware available online. Packages tend to support a variety of types of items such as multiple choice, ranking, short answer, and essay. Online surveys can be sent as an e-mail to a designated set of addressees, or they can be posted on a particular Web site populated by a specific group (e.g., students studying a particular online course or program).

Most of the studies published on e-learning employ quantitative methods to study student outcomes, particularly postcourse surveys that measure subjective satisfaction. In e-learning contexts, computer-based surveys and questionnaires are powerful tools to gather large-scale levels of data from key stakeholders.

For a fairly complete collection of empirical research papers on asynchronous learning networks (ALN), go to http://www.ALNResearch.org.

## Interviews

Interviews have traditionally been distinguished from surveys by the nature of the questions (open-ended) and by the approach (an interview researcher asks the questions and records the responses, typically face-to-face or sometimes by phone). The online interview (typically using e-mail) is similarly open-ended, but offers additional opportunities and constraints. One major advantage of the online interview is that the respondent inputs the responses (and hence provides a verbatim transcript). An online transcript also can be imported into a data analysis software. Yet there are also important constraints: The researcher cannot observe the respondent, and the lack of direct connection between the researcher and the respondent can result in a low response rate. Moreover, the importance of clear, well-organized, and well-presented questions is at least as important as in a survey, because the opportunities for probing or subsequent clarification are few.

## Documents and Field Notes

Data in the form of online documents (newspaper clippings, articles, online readings, course notes, field notes, and even audio or video clips) can be collected and stored online, for subsequent analysis, as discussed in the next section.

# Data Analysis

The second pillar of social research is data analysis. Logic and sometimes mathematics are brought to bear on a body of observations in order to discover meaningful patterns. Computers are especially valuable for helping researchers to explore multiple perspectives for making sense of the data and/or to analyze large bodies of data (data sets). Since the 1990s, new software tools have been developed to assist in the analysis of qualitative data.

## Content Analysis, Pattern Analysis, and Document Analysis

The use of computer tools for qualitative analysis is a relatively new but welcome phenomenon. These tools assist researchers in organizing and analyzing social science data, which are frequently based not on numbers but on text (interviews, open-ended questionnaires, online documents, and the like). Qualitative software can facilitate the analyses of textual or even multimedia (video clips, audio clips) artifacts through coding, identifying categories, and organizing the patterns or themes that emerge from the data to discern relationships.

These software allow researchers to code data by dragging and dropping highlighted text selections onto various frameworks such as a networked format, a hierarchical coding tree, or an unstructured coding list. Researchers import the artifacts as rich text files into a project database for analysis. The researcher then selects a meaningful section of text for coding and codes it using either a researcher-created code or the software's default coding system to uncover relationships between codes and categories, mappings, or themes that can then generate theory. Content analysis can also include quantitative data (statistical) analysis.

## Statistical Analysis

Some survey packages provide data analysis tools that can calculate and display the results of the surveys, using simple descriptive statistics. For more complex analyses, researchers import the survey results into widely available commercial statistical packages.

# Computer Networks as Learning Environments

The use of computer networks as learning environments has introduced an unprecedented source of educational activity and research opportunities. Computer networking has enabled a new set of educational environments and models such as totally online course and program delivery and distributed learning/mixed mode classrooms. These new learning environments are also an important source of educational data, inviting new forms of data collection and analyses. Among the most significant opportunities associated with new e-learning environments is the unprecedented potential for research into learning processes, depth of understanding, conceptual change over time, level and quality of participation and engagement, and access. Not only does e-learning represent a paradigmatic shift in how learning occurs, but also in how learning can be studied and understood. The basic reason for this profound shift that affects both learning applications and research lies in the nature of the online medium. For example, e-learning media that are text-based, asynchronous, many-to-many, or computer mediated afford unprecedented opportunities for retrospective and objective collection of discourse data, in terms of quality, volumes/patterns, and flows of discourse over time in learner–learner and learner–instructor interactions.

## Usage Statistics

Computer mediation provides a unique capability to capture and analyze individual and group usage statistics, volume, patterns, and times, as well as message headers and message threads. Computers automatically generate a log of user participation and related statistics, and can collect data on the number of messages read, messages written, volume of messages written, amount of user time online, and usage over specific periods of time, such as per day, per week, or per course. Computer-generated usage statistics represent an objective count, which is a tremendous advance in observation and measurement of the quantity of interaction and participation. Unlike the face-to-face context, in which it is impossible for a researcher to accurately note all the interactions in the room, even using audio or video recording, the online environment provides an unobtrusive and objective record. Moreover, usage statistics, although in some ways a crude measure, have provided valuable insights into the profile of online learning activities, which are quite different from those in the traditional classroom.

In the online classroom (depending on the nature and quality of the design of the curriculum), learners can log on 24 hours of the day, 7 days per week (hence, taking full advantage of asynchronicity). Students can be very active, typically logging on 10 or even more times per week to read messages and writing several messages each week to one another on the topic. Students may interact on a topic for a week or longer, hence increasing the depth of understanding and processing of the topic. Most participants send messages, and this participation is distributed more or less equitably (unlike in the face-to-face classroom, in which the instructor dominates and only a few students are active). Analysis of usage statistics can also provide insights into other variables such as the role of the instructor and instructional design, the nature of the discipline, and cultural factors regarding the nature of learner participation and interaction.

## Transcript Analysis

Transcript analysis provides an unprecedented opportunity to study learning and understanding. The presence of a verbatim, automatically generated transcript of the discourse online lets researchers study learning across time. This transcript also offers insights into the nature of understanding, because in order to actively participate in the course students must not only read the messages of their colleagues, but also actively write replies, engage in debate or elaboration, or input new ideas and perspectives. Writing is a form of frozen thought, which in the form of a transcript can then be studied. Transcripts of online discussions provide a complete, objective, verbatim, and archived text-based record. The challenge is then for the researcher to make sense of and analyze these data.

## Content Analysis and Discourse Analysis

*Content analysis* is a commonly used term, although it is sometimes mistakenly used to describe what is actually *discourse analysis*. Some researchers distinguish between the two by defining content analysis as categorization of text (focusing on the subject matter of the discourse) and discourse analysis as studying communication processes (social and cognitive) and change over time. For this entry, because the data analysis tools serve both purposes, the two terms are viewed as complementary.

Although research methods such as surveys, questionnaires, polls, and interviews can inform us about the outcomes of online learning, especially regarding user response, they do not provide insight into the process of what goes on inside the virtual classrooms, how this may differ from traditional classrooms, and most importantly, which pedagogical processes are especially effective for online learning. To answer such questions, we must turn to qualitative data such as direct observation of online interactions (e.g., recorded transcripts of online courses) and to methods for making sense of such "in depth" data.

The nature of the discourse between peers and with the instructor is typically text-based, stored as a transcript that enables analyses of the discourse patterns, volumes, distributions, types, and progress. E-learning environments provide a verbatim transcript of the interaction that can enable a unique view of the educational exchange and discourse. This archive of the transcripts or proceedings can be studied from multiple perspectives to assess the nature of the learning processes, especially over time; to determine the nature of the interaction between the instructional and learning processes and outcomes; and to potentially generate new theories of learning and understanding. At their most basic, qualitative software tools enable the importation and conceptual organization of the text, to be coded by the researcher. Coding and categorization may be theory-based (deduced a priori from a theory; see *Collaboration*) or induced, as in grounded theory.

### Large-Scale, Integrated Studies

The field of e-learning research is characterized by field studies rather than experimental clinical research approaches. E-learning increasingly uses large-scale studies that collect data from the learning environments and user populations and integrates various quantitative (surveys, polls) and qualitative (interviews, content analysis, discourse analysis) data in which the usage and discourse data are generated and stored online, enabling a variety of tools and methods to provide data analysis, interpretation, and conclusions that inform evidence-based practice, theory, or policy.

Large-scale studies using multiple methods began in the mid-1970s studying scientific online communities; in the 1980s they studied networked classrooms and virtual classrooms, and by the 1990s they studied online courses and programs delivered around the world. More recently, the Virtual-U field trials (studying over 15,000 students engaged in 500 courses in various sites internationally) and the ALN Research Network (studying large-scale e-learning applications in the United States) exemplified the use of multiple tools and methods to generate a composite of e-learning processes and outcomes.

### New Directions

The field of e-learning research is still very new. E-learning applications enable and invite new research tools and approaches, but the very newness of the field remains a challenge. One of the greatest challenges being addressed is the need for research tools that can study large data sets, either qualitative (text) or quantitative (usage statistics).

## LATENT SEMANTIC ANALYSIS

Latent semantic analysis (LSA) is an advanced approach that provides both a computer-based and a scientifically tested analysis of semantics. Landauer and Dumais introduced LSA as a statistical, corpus-based text comparison mechanism originally developed for text retrieval. However, unlike simple techniques, which rely on weighted matches of keywords in texts and queries, LSA created a high dimensional, spatial representation of a corpus and allowed texts to be compared geometrically. In recent years LSA has been applied by researchers to a variety of educational tests, including the Test of English as a Foreign Language, general lexical acquisition from text, selected texts for students to read, judging student essays, and evaluating student contributions in intelligent tutoring environments. Researchers concluded that in all of these tasks the reliability of LSA's "judgments" was found to be very similar to that of humans. The application of LSA to online educational transcripts is of particular interest in the search to identify conceptual/analytical change and progress in student discourse.

## DATA MINING

Data mining, like LSA, is an advanced research methodology first developed in computer science, which shows promise for educational study. Data mining attempts to extract knowledge from data, analyzing large data sets involving computer logs, usage data, and conferencing transcripts.

What distinguishes the resulting data—from Web-based activities in general and e-learning activities in particular—is the vast size of the data (log files) available. Data mining has the potential to make sense of these large and important collections of data.

Quantitative measure through data mining can process vast quantities of usage data and coded text databases and provide semi-automatic identification and illumination of change over time, patterns, and relationships, to help build a solid foundation for understanding collaborative knowledge work. Data mining also progresses from exploratory analysis to developing models and enabling "what if" questions and rigorous statistical analysis and testing. The combination of exploration, model building, and statistical verification is extremely important in the new field of e-learning sciences.

*—Linda Harasim*

*See also* OPERATIONS AND MANAGEMENT; SOCIOTECHNICAL ISSUES; STRATEGIC PLANNING

## Bibliography

Anderson, T., & Kanuka, A. (2003). *E-Research: Methods, strategies, and issues.* Lebanon, IN: Pearson Education/ Allyn and Bacon.

Babbie, E. (1992). *The practice of social research,* 6th Edition. Belmont, CA: Wadsworth.

Harasim, L. (Ed.). (1990). *Online education: Perspectives on a new environment.* New York: Praeger/Greenwood.

Landauer, T. K., & Dumais, S. T. (1997). A solution to Plato's problem: The latent semantic analysis theory of acquisition, induction, and representation of knowledge. *Psychological Review, 104,* 211–240.

# ELECTRONIC JOURNALS AND PUBLICATIONS

This entry spells out parallels and differences between print and Web publications. Successful publications depend on appeal, uniqueness, significant content, excellent organization, lucid writing, and immaculate presentation. The initial stages—research, planning, writing, and editing—are essentially the same for print and Web. Layout, production, distribution, and presentation for electronic delivery, whether it is viewed on a computer or on a television screen or printer, involve technologies and design considerations that are very different from a commercially printed journal or magazine.

## WORKING DEFINITIONS

*Journals* are the repository of significant content with high editorial standards and professional layout and presentation. Compared to a magazine, articles are longer and more substantive with more than temporal value. A professional journal offers exemplary research and writing for a specialized audience or discipline such as medicine, education, or engineering. A literary journal publishes the best writing of leading authors. An academic journal focuses on a specific discipline such as science, mathematics, philosophy, or arts and humanities. Journals are published monthly, quarterly, or on an annual basis. Refereed journals use qualified leaders to select articles for publication.

*Magazines* are upscale weekly newspapers with pictures and short articles organized in sections or departments. They include a broad range of topics—feature stories and news highlights designed to attract a large readership. Many "journals" are quality magazines designed for a select or elite readership (e.g., *Ladies Home Journal*).

*Newsletters* are the domain of special interest groups that include professional, business, government, and community organizations. They are short, rich in summary information and notes, and often social and informal. They come out at regular intervals and do not aspire to high journalistic standards. Their purpose is to inform, promote networking, and combine news of special interest to members with information about coming events.

*Electronic communications* are replacing printed media because of their low cost, instant availability, and global reach. Almost any computer can be used to prepare a publication and any computer attached to a network can be used to distribute or access what is published. Computer networks eliminate the need for expensive production and distribution technologies and potentially, any person or organization can be a publisher. The following are some of the features of electronic communications:

- Publications are accessible to a global audience via links in e-mails, indexes, search engines, portals, and reference sources.
- Anyone can distribute publications from their unique Internet address (Universal Resource Locator or URL).
- Copy is prepared using word processing software. Layout is achieved by adding Hypertext Markup Language (HTML). This is accomplished by saving files in HTML format, or using authoring programs such as Dreamweaver or FrontPage.
- There is no printing and binding cost. Storage and distribution from a professionally maintained "host" server costs as little as $10 per month.
- Publications can be accessed by up to 500 million computers worldwide.

## ECONOMICS OF WEB PUBLICATION

Web publication changes the dynamics and cost of promotion, production, distribution, and storage. Many organizations have discontinued publication in print because of the compelling advantages of the Web—low-cost production and distribution, instant publication, ease of updating, and global access. Organizations that use volunteers for editing and publication can do very significant publications for very low budgets. Large Web sites are supported by teams that include a Webmaster, graphic artists, editors, copy writers, and a programmer or program analyst.

Web users are accustomed to accessing a broad spectrum of information resources without charge. Funding models for Web publications may include one or more of the following:

- *Membership* or *subscription* is a source of revenue for special interest groups. Membership implies a package of services, whereas subscription may be for the publication only. Membership is a primary source of income for professional associations. Sometimes it is secondary to income from conventions, workshops, and sales.
- *Sponsored advertising* in the form of banners, medallions, and links is used for revenue enhancement. Information providers such as CNN use banners to promote the company image and sell products and services. For portals such as Yahoo, it is the primary source of income.
- *Collaborative marketing* includes sites such as eBay, a reputable and well-managed auction for every imaginable product and service. Indexes and search engines provide extensive lists that buyers can review for the wares of individual vendors.
- *Direct sales* work best for very large organizations such as amazon.com, or businesses with a unique product or associations with large memberships.

*Hybrid* business models combine storefront and Web-based operations (e.g., Barnes & Noble) or relegate specific functions to the Web (e.g., JCPenney catalog). Manufacturers and publishers use their Web sites to reduce time-to-market and to introduce new products to the global marketplace.

Some journals make judicious use of sponsored advertising; magazines integrate advertising into the page layout; and newsletters often provide summaries and links for new products and services. All Web-based publications use links to primary references where these resources are available on the Internet.

## PRODUCTION

The computer plays a key role in every aspect of acquisition, design, production, storage, distribution,

management, record keeping, and accounting. The ability to automate functions and make them available on a $24 \times 7 \times 365$ basis facilitates a new level of efficiency for global business. Publication is simplified by the elimination of printing, storage, and maintenance of costly inventories.

Acquisition, design, editing, and layout rely heavily on electronic communications and computers. E-mail simplifies communication between editors, committees, and "referees." E-mail is used to transmit drafts and final documents, and to negotiate rights for publication. Prior to electronic communications, these tasks required weeks or months; now they can be accomplished in days or even hours. "Snail mail" continues to be used by some organizations for legal documents and signatures.

Editing is accomplished using word processing. Layout requires desktop publishing software if both print and Web versions are required. Acrobat files ensure exact layout when publications are either viewed on the computer screen or sent to the computer's printer. Authoring software is designed specifically for producing Web pages.

## Print Publications

If the publication is designed as a printed document, there is no restriction in format. Pages can be of any size and proportion to meet the needs or desires of the publisher. Print resolutions may be 2400 pixels per inch or higher. Graphics and photographs can be in multiples of megabytes to maximize image quality.

## Web Version of a Print Publication

If the same publication is available on the Web, an Adobe Acrobat file enables exact replication of the printed page on a computer screen or a computer printer. Because of the inferior resolution of the computer screen, it is often necessary to magnify and scroll the Acrobat image. Also, the height of print publications' pages is greater than their width (portrait mode), whereas computer screens' width is greater than their height (landscape mode), another reason for magnification and scrolling.

When Acrobat files are printed, they replicate the layout, fonts, images, and colors of the original document, within the limits of the printing device.

## Publication on CD-ROM

If offline publication is preferred, CD-ROMs provide a low cost option for publication and replication. CD-ROMs are widely used for legal documents, catalogs, complete sets of journals, and archival materials. They can utilize Acrobat, HTML, or database formats, depending on the need to protect data in their original form as well as the level of indexing or searching required by the user. When the CD needs to be updated, it is replaced by a new CD.

## Web Publication

With Web publication, one central copy is kept up-to-date. Print publications have a fixed page size with a predetermined ratio of height and width. Portrait format is preferred, meaning that height is greater than width. Computer screens use landscape mode—width is greater than height. There are three options to accommodate this difference:

1. Lay out pages in landscape mode.
2. Scroll down to see the bottom of the page.
3. Publish the entire article as one long page. The reader uses the scroll bar to advance one "screen" at a time, or to scroll in single line increments.

Regardless of the method chosen, the appearance of the article should meet acceptable aesthetic and communication standards.

## TECHNICAL ISSUES

### Bandwidth

Under favorable circumstances, a modem attached to a regular telephone line can transmit up to 56 kilobits (thousand bits) of data each second. A page of text comes up almost instantly. This same page with a few small graphics may take seconds to load. Large graphics may take a minute or more. High bandwidth connections are available for home and small businesses using a digital service line (DSL), cable modem, or satellite. Organizations might have T1 or higher bandwidth connections to simultaneously support a large number of users.

Bandwidth is conserved by handling text, compression of graphic files, and HTML efficiently. Digital coding of text enables any character, number, or symbol to be communicated as one byte (eight bits)

of information. Graphics are compressed by reducing resolution (number of pixels), gradation (number of steps in gray scale or hue), and number of colors (from millions to 256 colors), and by using compressed storage (e.g., JPEG or GIF file formats). This provides acceptable screen quality. Note that printed graphics are optimized for quality; Web graphics are optimized for performance.

### HTML

HTML tags are interpreted by the browser to lay out text and graphics on the screen; for example, **Bold**, <i>*Italic*</i>. Tags designate font type, size, and color; headings; centering; paragraphs; placement of graphic images; and almost everything else having to do with layout. Different browsers and different screen resolutions may alter the appearance of the Web page. Most Web pages are designed for $800 \times 600$ pixels (SVGA). Higher resolutions provide space on both sides of the page so that the original layout is retained.

*Hyperlinks* enable the user to link seamlessly to another location within a page or site or to a page at a different site. Electronic messages travel at the speed of light, so it is possible to link to a Web site anywhere round the globe in a tiny fraction of a second.

## WHAT MAKES A SUCCESSFUL WEB PUBLICATION

When you publish a printed book or journal, there are several ways to measure success:

- Critical reviews
- Number of sales or sales revenues
- Number of references in other publications
- Persistence in the marketplace

Typically, sales begin slowly, experience accelerated growth, and eventually level off. Effective marketing accelerates growth and increases sales. Traditional book sales are influenced by promotion, cost of publication, and distribution network.

Web publications are instantly available to networked computers anywhere in the world. The link is easily bookmarked and shared by e-mail, listservs, or other Web publications. As a result, successful publications are promoted rapidly by users who copy the URL—the hyperlink that requires one click to take you instantly to the publication. As a result, publications with a circulation of 500 or 5,000 may expand readership by many orders of magnitude (50,000, 500,000, or 5 million) depending on the size of the target audience and their interest in the topic. Web statistics provide demographics on readers.

## Statistics: Hits, Visitors, and Viewing Time

For a sports event, the turnstiles count the number of people. On the Web, we measure hits (the number of people who access a page) and visitors (the number of people who spend time to view each page). Programs such as WebTrends or WebStat are used to gather data.

In an electronic journal or magazine, it is possible to measure hits and average viewing time hour by hour over a period of months. It is also possible to gather demographics on the users—IP address, category of user (whether their domain is .com, .org, .edu, etc.), country of origin, entry page, exit page, search engine, referrer, duration of visit, number of views, length of visit, and whether this is their first time or they're a returning visitor. If a referrer site provides a link to a specific article, the visitor bypasses the home page and enters the site on the first page of the article.

Analysis of the statistical data provides significant information for managing a Web site. Here are some examples from the author's experience with an academic journal:

- Lead articles (1, 2, and 3) receive a much greater number of hits compared to later articles (4, 5, and 6). *Interpretation: The editor's choice of lead articles gets the largest readership.*
- There was one notable exception where article #5 eclipsed all monthly data in the history of the site. *Interpretation: This should have been the lead article.*
- For this journal, lead articles accumulate 100,000 hits in the first 3–4 months and decrease in number over a 2–3 year period. *Interpretation: The content continues to be of value, but is most valuable when first published.*
- Average viewing time exceeds 2 minutes for each hit. *Interpretation: Many users read or scan articles from the screen even though they can be printed.*
- The number of returning visitors is about 25,000 each month. *Interpretation: Approximately half of the readers are regular visitors to the site.*

- Users are predominantly from North America, with a much smaller number from Europe and Asia. *Interpretation: The dominance of North America suggests that the journal is not known in other countries. A review of sites of comparable organizations confirmed this.*

If the reader must pass through a page to get to another page, that counts as a hit. Thus, the number of hits does not always accurately reflect the number of visitors. However, the average reading time (total time divided by number of hits) is useful as a measure of reader interest.

## Ways to Increase Readership

A high percentage of hits result from searches. For this reason, it is important for journals and specific articles to find their way quickly into search engines and indexes. Adding keywords to the header of each HTML file is an important step. It is also important to submit links to indexes such as Yahoo. There are hundreds of different search engines used worldwide. An aware Webmaster who properly presents data to search engines and indexes can greatly expand readership.

## Reliable Web Hosting

In addition to excellence in selection, design, and presentation of a world class Web site, the journal editor must be concerned with the quality of technical support for the host server and networks. The site must be easily accessed on a $24 \times 7 \times 365$ basis. He or she must ensure that the server and Internet connection are adequate to meet peak demands and should employ an external monitor site to detect and report errors and broken links before the user—or sponsor—is aware of the problem.

## ECONOMICS OF WEB PUBLICATION

Web publications can be used to do the following:

- Promote other member services and recruit membership (loss leader).
- Attract advertisers and sponsors to defray publication cost. This requires assigned spaces for banners and sponsored articles and an index of advertisers.

- Provide a "members only" service; for example, the journal may be accessible to members for 3 months before being open to the public (incentive to join).

A name brand is significant in attracting readership, but small organizations and individuals can create Web pages of very high quality without sponsorship. Stephen Downes's Web page at http://www.downes.ca is an excellent example of a small site done well.

## REGULAR READERSHIP

A vital Web site offers new information on an almost daily basis. It takes into account the broad spectrum of defined needs of its target audience. In addition to its own unique offerings, it may be a portal to other relevant sites via links that are constantly monitored and updated. A site that changes infrequently or does not offer pertinent information is like a graveyard. It attracts fewer visitors over time and falls into disrepair.

For a Web site to attract large numbers of visitors, editors should reinvest the proceeds to stay ahead of competitors—it should be an innovator, not a follower. Editors need to insist on relevant selection and high editorial quality, monitor statistics, and establish mechanisms for continuous quality improvement. Responses from readers should be forwarded to those people in the organization who need to read them. Records need to be kept of all events and communications that can be used to assess return on investment (ROI) for the electronic journal or magazine.

Newsletters complement journals and Web pages. They can be sent as e-mail to funnel readers back to the Web site. A dynamic Web site with a large readership can promote an organization as a leading source of information, products, and services.

*—Donald Perrin*

*See also* DESKTOP PUBLISHING; WORLD WIDE WEB

# E-MAIL

The term *e-mail* (occasionally *email*)—originally an abbreviation of *electronic mail* but now a word in its own right—denotes the vehicle or method for sending relatively instantaneously a message, letter, or other information object (a computer file of almost any sort containing a document, image, sound, video, spreadsheet, computer program, book, etc.) to someone by means of a computer network or computer connection.

Although e-mail is one of the more simple and straightforward computer applications currently in use over the Internet, it is also the most popular and universal and can be regarded in some measure as the interpersonal bond that holds together the global information infrastructure. E-mail enables instant personal communication between any two individuals, or between any individual and any aggregate of individuals, and between any two (or multiple) points on the globe (and, in principle, in the universe) that are connected via the Internet. About 1 billion people worldwide have e-mail accounts (electronic mailboxes) on home or workplace computers or on mail servers accessible through Web browsers in public places; these people send about 10 billion e-mail messages a day. Families, work teams, businesses and customers, teachers and students, friends, lovers, and special interest groups stay connected across distances through the use of e-mail.

In educational environments, e-mail is used both to facilitate general communication among individuals, whether residing on a campus or geographically distant from one another, and to enable specifically educational activities such as courses, discussions, tests, and exams; submission and evaluation of student work; tutorial, mentoring, and advising relationships; information queries and responses; and the distribution of educational materials. This is already the case in traditional, campus-based educational institutions. In distributed environments, e-mail has moved from being not only an auxiliary to face-to-face interaction but, in some cases, the primary way in which individuals communicate. In institutional contexts that involve communication among and the coordination of individuals across multiple locations, time zones, and schedule patterns, e-mail has shown itself to be effective in exchanging information and establishing and maintaining relationships. The e-mail medium has been observed to encourage expression through writing as well as a more reflective relationship regarding one's own thoughts and feelings than often occurs in conversation. Both of these effects can be valuable in educational context.

## E-MAIL ARCHITECTURE

E-mail accounts and addresses are provided to individuals either by organizations of which they are a part or by Internet service providers (ISPs) of one flavor or another. Some ISPs primarily provide Internet access for both e-mail and the World Wide Web, whereas others (such as AOL) provide information services of their own in addition to basic Internet access.

The basic structure of e-mail messages, which was defined in an Internet document called RFC822, includes a "header" that contains the following fields: Date, To, From, Cc (carbon copy), Subject, and Bcc (Blind carbon copy—recipients cannot see those listed in the To and Cc fields). Other kinds of files can be "attached" to the e-mail, making the message a delivery vehicle for more complexly formatted material such as spreadsheets, images, computer programs, or sound or video files. A number of methods are used for encoding such binary data so that it can be attached to or incorporated in e-mail messages. The most popular method is the Multi-purpose Internet Mail Extensions (MIME) standard. MIME extends the format of Internet mail to allow non-U.S. ASCII textual messages, nontextual messages, and multi-part message bodies to be included in message headers. BinHex and Uuencode are other methods of encoding attachments.

Behind the individual message and its structure are the mail protocols or recipes for information exchange, as well as the network of computer servers that carry out these exchanges in conjunction with each individual's own computer software, which acts as a "client" to the server software (the client-server relationship is basic to network environments). Internet e-mail is transferred from mail server to mail server according to a protocol (standard set of rules) known as Simple Mail Transfer Protocol (SMTP), and from the server to the individual's e-mail account, software, and computer via mail retrieval protocols such as Post Office Protocol 3 (POP3) and Internet Message Access Protocol (IMAP). The individual is usually unaware of these except when setting up a personal e-mail software client such as Eudora or Outlook (Standard or Express) to mention only two of the more popular e-mail software programs. Some Web browsers also handle e-mail, and some e-mail services are Web-based. People retrieve Web-based email by using their Internet browser to go to the site of their e-mail server, log in, and receive and send mail, thus enabling access from anywhere that a Web browser is available.

E-mail transfer may in some cases be almost instantaneous, but it is in principle asynchronous; that is, it does not require the senders and the recipients to be online at the same time. It is a "store and forward" technology: Messages from senders travel to the e-mail server of the recipient's service provider and are stored there until the receiver's software client contacts the server and the messages are forwarded, transferred, or downloaded to her computer, with or without the recipient's attention. E-mail is referred to as a "push" technology. That is, one person pushes a message to one or more others. The recipient does not have to go anywhere to find the information, unlike most Web use. Newsgroups or other groupware are termed "pull" technology because prospective readers must intentionally retrieve the information. This distinction is not as clear in the case of Web-based e-mail, in which the individual uses her browser to visit the site of the e-mail server.

Functionally as important as e-mail between two individuals are e-mail mailing lists, which transmit a message to a number of individuals, the analogue of a postal mass mailing. A list may range in size from a few individuals to several million. From the Internet perspective, all Internet users are equidistant from one another, so once a mailing list is compiled there is no functional difference or cost, from the sender's point of view, between a message sent to one person and one sent to a million. Mailing lists can be maintained on the individual's own computer, on a mail server, or on special mailing-list management servers usually referred to as *listservs*.

Over and above the private mailing lists that an individual or organization may maintain, listservs are generally used for publicly available lists of people with common interests. In addition to automating the process of subscribing to and unsubscribing from such lists, they provide other functions to members, such as access to archived messages, stopping mail delivery while traveling or on vacation, arranging for messages to arrive one by one or in a digest form, and so on. Rules of etiquette have developed around the use of lists. When one subscribes, these rules and the context for the list are often communicated in a "welcome" message. Responsibility for appropriate communications falls to the individual list users, and observing list dynamics can be enlightening to new participants. Most listserv software enables the list "owner" or moderator to remove individuals from the list, and this occasionally happens in the case of individuals who refuse to follow the list-specific rules or understandings about appropriate communication.

Text e-mail messages, even very long ones, take up very little space compared with image or sound files, which means that e-mail can be done successfully even over slow, dial-up Internet connections of low bandwidth. E-mail can, therefore, be a very reliable means of communication in rural or remote geographic regions, which may be important for distance education providers and participants. Very fine seminars have been organized around and taken place via text e-mail. But all e-mail messages are not equal. When e-mail is used as a carrier of large attachments or is itself styled (i.e., with formatting) or includes images, message size may be increased significantly and transfer from personal computer to server or vice versa may take much more time, especially over low-speed dial-up connections.

A valuable capability provided by e-mail software on the individual's computer or in her personal e-mail account is an address book. This tool allows individuals to create easily remembered nicknames or aliases for frequently used or hard-to-remember e-mail addresses or for groups of addresses (thus enabling individuals to create their own mailing lists).

## HISTORY OF ELECTRONIC MAIL

Transmission of electronic messages from one individual to another has accompanied the use of mainframe and mini computers since the 1960s. The first e-mail program that permitted the transmission of a message from one computer system to another was written by Ray Tomlinson in 1971. Tomlinson used the @ symbol to differentiate mail generated on a remote server (computer) from local e-mail generated on the same server. This symbol is still used today to identify the computer on which an individual has an e-mail account. In 1972 Lawrence Roberts made e-mail easier to use by adding the functions of replying to, forwarding, filing, and deleting messages. Thus e-mail, along with FTP (File Transfer Protocol) and Telnet (remote access to time-sharing supercomputers), was one of the first services available on the ARPANET, the predecessor of the Internet. The ARPANET had 2,000 users in 1973; three-quarters of its traffic consisted of e-mail. The first ARPANET mailing list was created in 1975. Because computer

networks were originally developed within university and research environments, it was only natural for higher education to be one of the first sectors in which e-mail was widely diffused, through both the Internet and BITNET, a network that played an important role in higher-education networking and e-mail use.

By 1980, there were about 430,000 users of e-mail systems sending 95 million messages a year, and, by the mid-1980s, e-mail had become widely available within corporations and organizations on their own internal computer systems as well as, via modem/telephone dial-up, to individual subscribers to commercial e-mail services such as CompuServe, MCI Mail, and Sprintmail. Initially an individual could communicate via e-mail only to others who subscribed to the same service. Eventually some of the commercial services became interconnected. By the late 1980s commercial and corporate e-mail connections to the Internet became available through these same services, and in the early 1990s the major online services not only connected to the Internet, but also adopted Internet e-mail protocols, thus making Internet e-mail a global standard. Only at this point was seemingly universal e-mail communication possible—any individual with an e-mail account could reach any other individual in the world with an e-mail account.

From humble text-based beginnings, e-mail has changed how we communicate with others, do business, and learn. A critical mass has been reached in substantial portions of the world where one can expect that others will have e-mail addresses and can be communicated with in that way.

## SOCIAL AND EDUCATIONAL IMPACT

The simplicity and relative cheapness of e-mail make it relatively easy and affordable for large numbers of individuals to communicate with one another instantly regardless of the geographical distance between them. In turn, the possibility and reality of such immediate connection, overcoming the barriers of space and time, has changed the fabric of human relationships and many sectors of social life, including education and learning. Because ease or difficulty of interpersonal contact and of access to information are determining factors for education and learning, the tremendous leap over spatial and temporal distance provided by e-mail as well as by other network applications generally has had a radical impact. Although organized learning at a distance is not a new phenomenon (witness correspondence courses via postal mail), the connectivity provided by e-mail (as well as the World Wide Web) represents a qualitative and quantitative transformation. Thus, it is only since the emergence of e-mail that we can speak of "distance learning," "distributed learning," or "networked learning," although e-mail is only one of a number of educationally relevant network applications that include Web-based courses, groupware, video, and online libraries.

The spatial and temporal barriers created by physical mail (via rail, ship, or plane) tend to confine much important communication and information within an individual's or group's local area; everything else is "long distance," "abroad," or "overseas." This changed to a significant degree with the invention of electronic media such as the telegraph, telephone, and radio in the late 19th and early 20th centuries. People could talk to someone in another country or on another continent, or listen to a radio announcer from around the world, as though they were "next door," and there were no spatial or temporal barriers. Nevertheless, prior to e-mail, that is, prior to the last two decades, it was impractical for individual citizens to send large amounts of information (e.g., a term paper, book chapter, or diagram) via electronic means. On a global scale, access to these media was limited—even now two-thirds of the world's population do not have a telephone and those who have them use them primarily for voice conversations.

When it becomes as normal to engage in instantaneous electronic communication that can transmit a term paper, book chapter, or chart across the globe as it is to send them down the hall, the distinctions between local and long-distance will be significantly transformed if not eliminated.

Because e-mail is the most universal, accessible, and easy-to-use network application, it has been a major vehicle for transforming distance, relationships, and education. The ability to send to groups as easily and quickly as to individuals is particularly relevant to education. The fact that all members of an e-mail list can receive the same information at the same time means that those further away geographically are in this respect not disadvantaged by their distance. This is particularly important in distributed learning, because it can make all participants in an online group experience themselves as equally central to the educational context. This is also true of groupware.

## THE CONTEXT

One issue for users of most current electronic communication tools including e-mail is that the media, on their own, provide little sense of context, and it is often context that determines whether message content or construction is appropriate. Some dichotomies that are worth considering that affect message construction include: Are the relationships personal or professional? Should the tone be informal or formal? Are the organizations educational or corporate or something else? Are the individuals novices or experts in the use of technology? Are participants members of the same or different national or ethnic cultures? Are participants using computers or hand-held devices that may affect their ability to create or receive text or attachments? The individual must decide if a given e-mail message is closer to a mini-report or an informal conversation. Participants will create a more or less coherent context through their communications, and educational facilitators will do well to provide information and guidelines to potential participants to help create an educational environment where relationships support learning. Educational institutions have found that they need to have in place policies regarding e-mail so that users will know both their responsibilities and their rights within the system.

## E-MAIL CHALLENGES

In the 20 to 30 years of e-mail's relatively short existence, the uses and challenges of this medium have shifted and will no doubt continue to shift as it evolves. Now that e-mail usage is so common, getting too much e-mail is a problem for professionals in many sectors, some of whom routinely receive hundreds of messages a day, more than they have time to read or answer. And now that the Internet has become a marketplace that provides a cheap and easy way to send large quantities of e-mail, every e-mail address is a candidate for receiving unwanted advertisements. *Spam* is the term used for the broadcast of unwanted mail, of which marketing material is only one of many kinds. One person's important message may be junk mail to many others, which is one of the problems for large e-mail groups. Another problem with e-mail is naïve users forwarding chain letters, pyramid schemes, and virus warnings/alerts that are in fact hoaxes or urban legends.

Technical solutions to these social issues have been sought. One solution is e-mail software that allows "filtering" or sorting of messages into different inboxes or even the trash, thus giving users some control over the electronic inflow. In the future we can expect to have this filtering and sorting service take place on the e-mail servers before the messages even get to our own accounts, which will help eliminate much personal effort. Another way that individuals manage the volume and variety of their e-mail is through using multiple e-mail accounts and addresses corresponding to their different social roles and identities, such as one as an employee, another as a family member, a third as a participant in discussions in online mailings lists, and a fourth for their role as hobbyist or Internet adventurer. Many Internet access providers enable individuals to have multiple addresses, and at the time of writing free Web-based accounts are available on various Web servers. Having multiple addresses is especially practical because, as roles change, the associated e-mail addresses are likely to change (for example, changing jobs will usually necessitate a change in one's professional e-mail address).

Excessive emotional content in messages is often referred to as "flaming," and "flame wars" among members of lists are one of the downsides of this medium. They can lead to other members' escalating exchanges of requests to be removed from the list instead of going through the appropriate procedure for unsubscribing from the list.

Excessive or inappropriate personal content is another potentially problematic situation because the e-mail can easily be forwarded beyond the intended recipient or circle. Composing e-mail messages often feels quite intimate, and love affairs and courtships are now conducted via e-mail. But the nature of the medium is both to persist and to be more public and less private than users of e-mail may be conscious of when they are composing their messages. Messages may feel transitory and private, but e-mails often remain on recipients' computers, in backups of both servers and individual computers, and in public archives that are searchable on the Internet. From a technical point of view, e-mail is not a secure medium and is easy to monitor. In the United States, a majority of employers read or monitor their employees' e-mail, and some maintain that they, in effect, "own" the e-mail written by their employees at work. Government agencies monitor e-mail for purposes of

criminal investigation or national security. Indeed, e-mail messages are now routinely subpoenaed in criminal investigations and legal proceedings. Thus, from the individual's point of view it would be accurate to think of an e-mail message as one would think of a postcard—as something that might be read by the mail delivery person, by anyone else who finds it lying around, or, as was pointed out in an Internet netiquette document, by a future employer (or family member). Further, it is so easy to forward, as well as to "blind copy" to unknown others, that it behooves a person to consider the wider system in which one is participating. The most effective method for guaranteeing the privacy and security of e-mail is encryption—coding the message in a way that only the recipient can decode. The most widely available encryption scheme available to the average user is the PGP (Pretty Good Privacy) system. The software to implement it can be found on and downloaded from the Internet.

*—Shelley K. Hughe*
*—Jeremy J. Shapiro*

*See also* Asynchronous Formats; Computer-Mediated Communication (CMC); Internet; Internet Service Provider

## Bibliography

Crocker, David H. (n.d.). *RFC822: Standard for ARPA Internet text messages.* Retrieved August 27, 2002, from http://www.w3.org/Protocols/rfc822/.

Flynn, Nancy L. (2000). *The e-policy handbook: Designing and implementing effective e-mail, Internet, and software policies.* New York: AMACOM Books.

Huang, Albert. (2001). Innovative use of e-mail for teaching. *Communications of the ACM, 44*(11), 29–32.

Lamb, Linda, & Peek, Jerry. (1995). *Using email effectively: What you need to know.* Sebastopol, CA: O'Reilly.

Palloff, Rena M., & Pratt, Keith. (1999). *Building learning communities in cyberspace: Effective strategies for the online classroom.* San Francisco, CA: Jossey-Bass.

Rose, Marshall T. (1993). *The Internet message: Closing the book with electronic mail.* Englewood Cliffs: Prentice Hall.

Shapiro, Jeremy J., & Hughes, Shelley K. (2002). The case of the inflammatory e-mail: Building culture and community in online academic environments. In Kjell E. Rudestam & Judith Schoenholtz-Read (Eds.), *Handbook of online learning: Innovations in higher education and corporate training* (pp. 91–124). Thousand Oaks, CA: Sage.

# ENROLLMENT STATUS

Enrollment status has varying meanings. It can refer to the student's basic association with the institution (as in whether or not he or she is an actively enrolled student), a graduate or alumnus of a degree or certificate program, or a student who has ceased attendance (not enrolled). It may refer to the student's admission status in a degree program: whether he or she is non–degree seeking (admitted for general study not leading to a degree), or conditionally or provisionally admitted to a degree program. A conditionally or provisionally admitted student is required to complete one or more terms of attendance at a specific level of academic performance, at which point the institution will formally admit the student to the degree program. Some schools also refer to students who need to complete admissions paperwork in their first term (such as submitting official transcripts), due to being admitted late in the admissions cycle, as provisionally admitted. Those provisional or conditionally admitted students who do not meet the specified criteria during their time limit are usually not allowed to register for the subsequent academic term.

The most frequent use of the term *enrollment status* refers to the amount of coursework (or course load) a student is registered for during a given term, semester, or quarter. Enrollment status is also used, although less frequently, to classify students' academic performance over time in their degree program, and whether or not they are eligible to continue with their studies.

Enrollment status can also refer to the availability of a course. Each course an institution offers usually has an assigned number of students the course can accommodate. Small seminar type courses may only allow 8–10 students to register, as opposed to large lecture type classes, which may be able to accommodate hundreds of students. An open course is one in which "seats" or openings are available for students to register, whereas a closed course means the course has reached its allotted limit, and there are no more openings for other students to register for the course.

## STUDENT STATUS

Actively enrolled students are students who are considered currently enrolled by the institution, are receiving instructional services, and are paying tuition. A graduate of a degree or certificate program is a student who has completed all the course requirements for his or her program, with the degree having been administratively awarded by the records office. Other institutions refer to any student who attended for any length of time as alumni, even through a degree may not have been earned. Some institutions offer what is called *incidental degrees,* which are degrees that are earned along the way to the terminal degree the student is seeking. For example, a student who is enrolled in a Ph.D. program might earn enough credits for a master's degree in the same subject, and then withdraw before receiving the Ph.D. That student would likely be considered an alumnus by the institution for having earned that master's degree, although the terminal degree was not earned.

A student who has withdrawn is one who has notified the records office that he or she will not be able to complete the academic term or program and needs to cease attendance. A dismissed student indicates one who has been involuntarily dismissed from the institution, usually for a failure to maintain academic standards.

## COURSE LOAD

*Full time, half time,* and *less than half time* are the most common definitions of enrollment status when referring to the course load of a student. In undergraduate programs, a student who is carrying 12 to 15 credit hours during a given academic term is generally considered to be full time. For students enrolled in graduate programs, a 9-hour credit load is considered full time. The distinctions between half time and less than half time are not as clearly standardized nationally; however, half time is approximately 6 to 11 credit hours at the undergraduate level and 5 to 8 credit hours at the graduate level. The distinction of full time, half time, or less than half time is determined by the policy of the institution, although the institution may be strongly guided by agencies with which they interact, such as the federal student loan programs administered by the Department of Education or the Immigration and Naturalization Service. Half time and less than half time are sometimes referred to as attending part time. Another phrase used is *three-quarter status,* which is when a student is enrolled in total credit hours during the term of study between the half time and full time demarcations.

Distributed learning programs tend to offer more opportunities for students to complete their coursework at a part-time pace, which is often easier for them to accomplish when they are already very busy with other roles and responsibilities, such as employment or family.

In the independent study model, or in a model with a continuous academic calendar, the student who is designated as full time or part time will have to satisfactorily complete an appropriate course load over the given year.

## ACADEMIC PROBATION, DISMISSAL, OR SUSPENSION

Academic probation or academic warning indicates that the student's academic performance has not met the standards of satisfactory academic performance as defined by the institution. Usually those standards include completing a certain number of credit hours with passing grades within a specified number of terms, or within a given term. A student placed on academic probation is usually required to complete credit hours with passing grades within subsequent academic term(s) before the probation status can be removed. An academic dismissal of a student indicates that the institution dismissed the student for a failure to maintain academic standards. This may mean that the student was unable to remove him- or herself from academic probation status for several terms, or that the student committed plagiarism or some other form of academic misconduct. Academic dismissal usually means the student will not be allowed to return to the institution. Suspension implies that the student's status is not permanent, and there may be other conditions under which the student would be allowed to be readmitted.

## REGISTRATION

Registration is the process by which students select and sign up for those classes that they wish to take during an academic term. In these modern times, the process by which a student registers tends to utilize technology, the most common methods being registration via the Internet or touch-tone phone registration. In those systems, the student is interacting with the institution's database of offered courses. This technology has the distinct advantage of automating certain tasks, such as compiling wait-lists for courses that are full, enforcing required prerequisites or petitions, suggesting alternate courses to students if their first choice is unavailable, and many other tasks.

Registration can also be done without benefit of such technologies, but only on a residential campus, where students can wait in lines and pass their registration choices to campus administrators who will then check the course records for availability.

In distance learning models of any type, registration is much more likely to be via the Internet. In courses with independent study models, the registration may be more complex than a simple selection of courses. Students will generally have to write a contract of study with the professor, to indicate what they plan to study and how they plan to demonstrate mastery of the subject. In effect, the student and the professor write the syllabus together, before the course registration can be approved.

In many institutions, a student's proposed schedule must be approved by his or her assigned academic adviser or mentor before registration is allowed to proceed. Although the technology or methods in place at the institution may not obstruct students from making changes to their schedule later on, the intent of the advising approval step is to confirm that the students are making wise course selections that will allow them to be academically successful in the course, and that will contribute to their overall academic success and progress towards degree completion.

—*Bridget Lee Brady*

*See also* ACADEMIC CALENDAR; COURSE CREDIT/CREDIT TRANSFER

### Bibliography

American Council on Education. (1987). *1986–87 fact book on higher education.* New York: American Council on Education and Macmillan.

Aucoin, Paul, Bolli, Gerhard J., Bradely, Elva E., Brown, William O., Mack, Greta S., Posey, Columbus H., Robertson, Michael N., & Stewart, John T. (1996). *AACRAO academic record and transcript guide.* Washington, DC: American Association of Collegiate Registrars and Admissions Officers.

# ERIC: THE EDUCATION RESOURCE INFORMATION CENTER

ERIC, located at http://www.eric.ed.gov, is one of the premier education information systems in the world. The primary mission of ERIC, a part of the U.S. Department of Education's National Library of Education, is to meet the education information needs of teachers, administrators, librarians, counselors, preservice teachers, parents, decision makers, education researchers, and practitioners in related fields. ERIC serves its constituents by providing an array of products, services, and systems for dissemination. These services and products are provided by:

- Sixteen subject-specific clearinghouses that collect, abstract, and index education materials for the ERIC database; respond to requests for information in their subject-specific areas; and produce special publications on current research, programs, and practices.
- Eleven adjunct clearinghouses that are affiliated with one of the 16 subject-specific clearinghouses, but are more specialized and funded by non-ERIC resources.
- A central processing facility that merges all the inputs of the clearinghouses into the ERIC database, redistributes the ERIC database to other organizations to provide to their users, and manages the ERIC Thesaurus.
- The Education Document Reproduction Service (EDRS), which archives ERIC materials electronically and on microfiche, and provides document delivery services to customers.
- AskERIC, a unified Internet service of the ERIC system that provides electronic resources to frontline educators and answers education-related questions online.
- ACCESS ERIC, which acts as the central distribution point for ERIC system-wide information and publications.

Each of these components contributes to the ERIC database, which is the world's largest source of education information, containing more than 1 million abstracts of education-related documents and journal articles. The database is organized into CIJE (Current Index to Journals in Education) and RIE (Resources in Education). Although few users will see this division (virtually every interface to the ERIC database on the Web or through online vendors combines these datasets into a unified search), it is important to note that ERIC only archives and provides access to fulltext RIE items.

Although many people associate ERIC with a database of journals and other documents in education, ERIC also provides a wide range of other resources.

From publications of detailed monographs on topics in education to simple two-page digests that quickly introduce a "hot topic" and associated resources, ERIC clearinghouses seek to synthesize current thinking in a particular field. Each ERIC component provides a range of user services that includes toll-free numbers for telephone support, Web sites with fulltext articles, bibliographies, and Web guides. ERIC also produces the ERIC Thesaurus of education terms, which is used to find information in the ERIC database, as well as an index of education materials from a variety of other organizations. ERIC has also been a research and development center contributing to advances in digital libraries and dissemination of education information.

When ERIC first began in 1965, its database and activities were on the cutting edge of service provision through information technology. For many years, the ERIC system flourished, reaching new audiences and offering new products. However, in the late 1970s and early 1980s, various constraints (financial and otherwise) limited ERIC's growth and its ability to take advantage of emerging technologies. In those years, the ERIC system focused primarily on maintaining the ERIC database and maintaining existing levels of service.

The 1986–87 ERIC Redesign Study marked a turning point in the development of ERIC. This intense examination of ERIC provided the impetus for the ERIC system to re-assert itself as the leader in providing needed information to the full range of education users. This was the challenge for ERIC—to once again be a leader in meeting the education information needs of all education users through all possible means of information services, resources, and dissemination.

By all possible measures, ERIC has met this challenge. In the past 10 years, the ERIC system has done the following:

- Made ERIC products and services more widely available
- Integrated ERIC activities with those of other Office of Educational Research and Improvement (OERI) and U.S. Department of Education programs, including the educational labs, centers, regional technology information centers, and now the National Library of Education (NLE)
- Served a wide, diverse audience by recognizing that practitioners comprised approximately 60% of ERIC users

Building on this work, ERIC is now known globally for highly successful, technology-based information services and resources, including:

- The award-winning AskERIC e-mail question-answering service
- The National Parent Information Network (NPIN)
- The ETS/ERIC Test Locator and related systems
- Full-text digitization of ERIC documents (begun in January 1996)

Today, ERIC is positioned to respond as a system to changing user needs and national initiatives. In many ways, ERIC is unique among NLE and OERI programs. It is decentralized for subject expertise, services, and product creation and delivery, but unified and coordinated in responding to user needs and new initiatives. Each ERIC component has unique expertise in relation to audience, subject area, and scope, but in contacts with individuals or organizations, every ERIC component assumes system-wide responsibilities.

—*R. David Lankes*

*See also* ELECTRONIC JOURNALS AND PUBLICATIONS; LIBRARY SERVICES; LIBRARY TECHNOLOGIES

### Bibliography

AskERIC: http://www.askeric.org
EDRS: http://www.edrs.com
ERIC Home page: http://www.eric.ed.gov
Eric Ready Reference #7, 1996
The National Library of Education:
    http://www.ed.gov/NLE
The U.S. Department of Education: http://www.ed.gov

# ETHICS

The term *ethics* is commonly used in different ways, including to describe a way of being, synonymous with *morals* (e.g., "The President is an ethical leader."); to identify rules or a moral code, often affiliated with a professional organization (e.g., legal ethics and the American Bar Association's Code of Professional Responsibility); to denote the philosophical study of morality; and to identify a particular philosopher's moral theory (e.g., Kantian ethics). All of these uses are relevant to educational institutions and to the professionals who work there. Some ethical problems in educational settings, such as academic integrity issues, are relevant to both institutional ethics and professional ethics. Because technology influences the pattern of ethical issues, distributed learning environments face special ethical challenges. A general understanding of academic ethics and professional ethics provides a foundation for considering ethical issues in distributed learning environments. The nature of the institution and the educational technology used influence ethical decisions and methods of teaching.

## INSTITUTIONAL ETHICS AND ACADEMIC ADMINISTRATION

As corporate entities, educational institutions have obligations of general business ethics. Corporate or business ethics broadly includes stakeholder relations (e.g., employment agreements and workplace environment issues), legal and regulatory compliance (e.g., environmental and nondiscrimination regulations), and external relations (e.g., philanthropic activities and neighbor relationships). Academic institutions have additional commitments to core academic values, which changes the ethical considerations and raises the ethical bar.

Educational institutions are corporate entities created for a variety of stated purposes. For example, the mission of an independent secondary school may include character formation enhanced by a boarding component or open access through entirely online classes offered to students unable to attend a traditional school for fiscal, physical, or social reasons. The mission of a public K–12 school may be to serve all members of the district equally or to serve all students in a state through charter Internet schooling. The mission of a private college may be to develop students of faith, to further the education of women, to facilitate the study of any field by any person, or to serve the educational needs of working professionals entirely through online delivery. Many public colleges and universities have extended their mission to include service to those beyond state boundaries, or at least to those residents unable to travel to the campus. These educational institutions have obligations to fulfill their varied educational missions and uphold core academic values in addition to the common corporate obligations and responsibilities. These combined obligations make up academic ethics.

One significant difference between the corporate setting and the educational setting is in the area of conflicts of interest. Distributed learning further complicates this issue. Many businesses require employees to sign conflict of interest agreements limiting employees from engaging in work-related activities outside of the supervision of the employer. In contrast, educational institutions have historically allowed faculty to consult, teach, and conduct research outside of the institution as long as the faculty member limits that work to a predetermined percentage of time. In making this decision, educational institutions value the benefits of these activities over the potential harms. Distributed learning technology changes the nature of the educational business environment, causing some institutions to rewrite conflict of interest policies to include regulations for previously unfettered freelance work. Those institutions view distributed courses, unlike previous face-to-face instruction, as direct competition because the distributed course can occur simultaneously with face-to-face instruction. Academic ethics requires educational institutions to conscientiously decide how to reconcile these kinds of potentially competing institutional values. This presupposes a fundamental understanding and articulation of the mission and values of the particular institution.

Under traditional educational business practices, many institutional intellectual property policies allow faculty members who create course material and literary works to retain all copyrights in the work. The complexity of distributed learning environments often changes work distribution and requires institutional administration of courses when that work was traditionally done by the faculty member or teacher. This raises the question of whether distributed learning material is covered by an existing intellectual property policy or requires new policy creation (e.g., course syllabus, lecture notes, articles written by the professor/teacher, or multimedia productions jointly created by the professor/teacher and technology staff). A related question is whether institutions offering distributed learning consider the use of educational technology in employment decisions such as promotions, pay increases, or the granting of tenure. The variety in terms of employment and increased use of part-time employees exacerbates the potential for unfairness in employment practices. Commitments to fair and equitable treatment demand that institutions requiring faculty/teacher participation in distributed learning

review terms of employment and compensation agreements, especially if those obligations are not equally assigned.

Due to the variety of institutional missions and extent of technology use, there is a wide range of potential answers to the ethical questions raised by the use of educational technology. Academic ethics requires thoughtful decision-making practices. The institutional policy creation and review processes provide opportunities to practice good academic ethics by ensuring full consideration of the issues, including the role of educational technology, and participation of all affected parties. Policy creation and education practices influence the institutional ethic and relationships among community members.

## PROFESSIONAL ETHICS: RESEARCH, TEACHING, AND LEARNING

Professional ethics is usually defined by a code of ethics specific to a particular profession. This code sets forth the rules of behavior, typically above or more specific than normal societal expectations, that are agreed upon by members of a professional community. Consequences for failing to abide by such a code are sanctioned by the professional community or affiliated organizations and can include expulsion from the profession. The American Association of University Professors adopted such a code in 1966 and revised it in 1987. The National Education Association adopted such a code in 1975. National organizations for academic administrators, such as the National Association of Student Personnel Administrators and the Association for Student Judicial Affairs, often promulgate statements of ethical principles and standards of conduct. Statements or codes usually begin with the moral purpose of the profession before outlining the ideal relationship of the professional member with others both inside and outside the professional community. Professional ethics in academic institutions vary depending on the professional association, but most associations expect members to support core academic values.

Codes for teachers and professors tend to require individuals to have a commitment to intellectual honesty, academic integrity, appropriate assessment and grading practices, positive educational environments for all, and confidentiality of personal records. Codes for academic administrators are similar and tend to require individuals to have a commitment to ethical business practices, confidentiality, accuracy of information, and respect for others. Some ethical issues specific to teaching, learning, and research include power, friendship, and consensual sexual relationships; loyalty, friendship, and community; privacy, tolerance, diversity, open discussion, and academic freedom; academic integrity, grading practices, and cheating; honesty and informed consent in human research; private and corporate donations and educational influence; and the role of the institution in teaching ethics.

The extent of the use of educational technology does not alter the requirements of a profession, but distributed learning technology may change the exact nature of the obligations. For example, a commitment to privacy of student information may have different consequences depending on whether the record is in paper or electronic form. Psychological and physical distance associated with asynchronous distributed learning raise different concerns about identity and authentication of authorship from face-to-face instruction. The concerns are also different in synchronous distributed learning programs. Students' educational motivation and reason for participation may differ in distributed learning settings. Moreover, many technology users approach ethical issues online differently from how they do offline: Technology use changes behavior. These factors suggest the need to reassess teaching styles when using technology-enhanced delivery and the related ethical issues of inclusion, participation, and assessment. Academic professionals engaged in distributed learning should consider how the technology affects the way they uphold the standards of their profession.

## ACADEMIC INTEGRITY

Academic integrity is an ethical issue that plays a role in both academic ethics and, generally, professional ethics. Educational institutions and educators have long believed in the importance of academic integrity, which, as defined by the Center for Academic Integrity, requires a commitment to five fundamental values: honesty, trust, fairness, respect, and responsibility. Academic integrity violations include misrepresenting another's ideas or work as one's own; falsifying research data; misappropriation of institutional resources; fraudulently advancing one's own academic standing; and disrupting the academic environment of others, such as through hoarding or

damaging educational materials. Although these issues have always concerned educational institutions and educators, distributed learning technologies have changed the patterns of academic dishonesty. The most common form of academic dishonesty, plagiarism, is facilitated by the access to virtually unlimited data, the difficulty faculty have in knowing all of that data, and the ease of cut and paste commands. Moreover, the technology culture supports the belief that "information is free" regardless of regulations that apply to material. The early Internet notion that technically possible behavior is permitted behavior persists. As a result, many individuals who would never steal a CD from a music store not only freely copy that same CD from an online site, but also insist the behavior is ethical and not equivalent to stealing or, more specifically, copyright infringement. In the same problematic way, it may feel different to a student to execute the cut and paste commands than to copy another's work by long hand or to retype it. Technology removes the physical labor that serves as a reminder of authorship and ownership. The ease of technology-facilitated academic dishonesty may require institutions and faculty to take a different approach to academic integrity issues, particularly in the educational efforts designed to address these issues.

## TEACHING ETHICS

The earliest American schools, including colleges, were primarily concerned about molding the character of the student and approached the teaching of ethics through a variety of means, including curriculum decisions, faculty/teacher participation in students' lives, campus rules and regulations, required chapel attendance for residential campuses, and, in colleges, a required course on moral philosophy that was intended to be both academic and practical. The goals of these institutions included the creation of a common ethic and positively influencing the character of the students, as well as teaching meta-ethics and moral theories to more advanced students. The missions of the early schools included teaching ethics (in every sense of the current meaning). Today, the approaches to teaching ethics in educational institutions are as varied as the educational institutions themselves, and often the ethical goals are unclearly defined. Many institutions teach meta-ethics and moral theories. The real variations occur in decisions about the creation of a common campus ethic and the role of the institution in teaching ethics for character development as part of the general education of the student. Ideally, the approach taken is conscientiously determined and consistent with the institutional mission.

Tools used to create a common ethic today are the same as in the early schools and include curriculum decisions; requirements that faculty participate in campus life or extracurricular activities; rules, regulations, and codes of conduct; honor codes and modified honor codes; and required courses in ethics. Even institutions that do not view character development as part of the mission use codes of conduct to encourage and enforce a common ethic and appropriate educational environment among community members. Codes of conduct tend to prohibit criminal-like behavior and give institutions the ability to discipline violators, up to and including removal from the community. Institutions that adopt honor codes usually hope to further influence the character development of community members. Institutions most concerned with teaching ethics incorporate ethics in curriculum decisions and course development.

Distributed learning environments can adopt codes of conduct, honor codes, and modified honor codes to influence the learning environment, create a common ethic, and encourage character development. Distributed learning environments can also incorporate ethics in curriculum decisions and course development. Institutions with a strong academic ethic consider all these teaching tools in light of each other to ensure consistency of supported ethical values. Professionals with strong professional ethics also encourage institutions to consider a unified ethical approach to decisions.

## CONCLUDING COMMENT

The use of educational technology influences the ethical issues faced by academic institutions and the professionals who work in them. Most ethical issues in distributed learning environments are variations of ethical issues in traditional delivery environments, and are influenced by the nature of the institution and the technology used. Strong institutional and professional ethics requires an understanding of, and commitment to, the core organizational values and an understanding of how the technology changes the teaching and learning environment.

*—Margie Hodges Shaw*

*See also* INTELLECTUAL PROPERTY; PLAGIARISM

## Bibliography

American Association of University Professors. (1987). *Policy documents and reports: Statement on professional ethics of the American Association of University Professors.* Washington, DC: AAUP, 105–106.

Cahn, S. M. (Ed.). (1990). *Morality, responsibility, and the university.* Philadelphia: Temple University Press.

Callahan, D., & Bok, S. (Eds.). (1980). *Ethics teaching in higher education.* New York: The Hastings Center.

Davis, M. (1999). *Ethics and the university.* London: Routledge.

Eaton, J. S. (2000). *Core academic values, quality, and regional accreditation: The challenge of distance learning.* Washington, DC: CHEA Monograph Series. Retrieved from http://www.chea.org/Research/corevalues.cfm.

National Education Association. (1975). *Code of ethics of the educational profession.* Washington, DC: NEA. Retrieved from http://www.nea.org/aboutnea/code.html.

Roworth, W. W. (January/February 2002). Professional ethics, day by day. *Academe Online, 88*(1). Retrieved from http://www.aaup.org/publications/Academe/02JF/02jfrow.htm

Weingartner, R. H. (1999). *The moral dimensions of academic administration.* Lanham, MD: Rowman & Littlefield.

# EVOLVING TECHNOLOGIES

Technologies evolve through refinements in new versions and upgrades to products. Usually the enhancements are minor, but eventually older systems or hardware are no longer compatible or supported and soon become unusable. Leading edge software often contains bugs or is not robust when used outside the laboratory. Later releases become increasingly stable and appropriate for novice users. From the first telephone call to the mobile phone, telephony has evolved in imperceptible steps punctuated by a few grand leaps. So it is with the technologies for distributed learning.

One of the acknowledged truisms of educational technology is that technology evolves much more rapidly than the willingness of teachers, learners, and educational institutions to exploit those technologies for learning. In short, there is usually a long lag time between the appearance of a new technology and its eventual widespread adoption for educational purposes. Educational authorities are often reluctant to invest in buying hardware and software that will be out of date before the teachers have really begun to make good use of them. A vicious cycle can develop whereby educators wait for the next evolution of the software or hardware to become available, but the next version is rapidly followed by another that may be incompatible with the previous version. This is particularly true with respect to the technologies underpinning distributed education, where over the last 20 years, information and communication technologies have evolved very rapidly. However on the whole, the early adopters among educators at the postcompulsory level have been quick to apply each new refinement to improve the quality of distributed learning and to increase access and enhance the online learning environment for the benefit of distributed learners.

The evolution of technologies for distributed learning is characterized by convergence: stand-alone systems have converged onto the Web; the distinct technologies for synchronous and asynchronous communication have blurred into each other; and the separate teaching modes of face-to-face and distance education have converged with the evolution of the technology such that the most common mode is now "blended learning."

## FOUR TECHNOLOGIES FOR DISTRIBUTED LEARNING

Asynchronous threaded discussion software—often called *computer-mediated communication*—allows distributed learners to discuss course issues with a tutor or instructor and with each other over the whole period of the course. Since about the mid-1980s, these systems have been used for various kinds of distributed education: K–12 students networking across different schools, remote and housebound students, tertiary education students wanting more flexible learning than campus education allows, and adults wanting continuing professional development and many kinds of training that fit around full time employment.

The first software to support this form of asynchronous discussion was called "command line" software, and required skill and patience from even the dedicated user, let alone the novice. A perusal of early literature on computer conferencing produces a litany

of concerns about training materials, help desk queries, and front-end programs, as well as discussions about how best to help new users become active participants. The difficulties encountered by home-based students in logging on, and the training needed to navigate around the system, remember the correct terms, and get a message into the right conference, all amounted to a steep learning curve for students before they started learning the course material. Newer conferencing systems that became available in the early 1990s provided a graphical interface to messaging. Training in the technicalities of using such systems gradually became less and less problematic and now occupies a negligible amount of the course time. With the advent of the Web, discussion has been integrated with the content of the course. For example, comment functions can be linked to course material, and whole documents can have comment functions built around them. Instant messaging is a near-synchronous form of online interaction that has developed from the quest for "presence" in the online environment—the sense that other users are present and available for communication. So we can trace an evolution in online educational interaction from separate systems, such as for delivering course content and resources and for participant interaction (which used to require a separate login and separate password), to current systems that offer a user-driven, single sign-on learning environment providing seamless access to resources and other learners.

*Audiographics* technology used to provide multiway audio and a shared screen, and was used to conduct real-time tutorials with remote students (usually connected from a study center to the host institution). The first systems required two telephone lines: one for the sound and one for the audio. Few home-based learners had two lines, so this technology was confined to inter-institutional applications. With the growth of the Internet, audiographics migrated onto the Web and has become a viable way of introducing small-group, synchronous events into distributed learning. It is particularly useful for problem-solving sessions in mathematics, language practice in second language classes, syndicate work in business courses, and collaborative project work among students in many subject areas. Current software supports a shared screen for real-time annotation, as well as document sharing and even application sharing. The integration of the personal computer with the telephone and particularly with the mobile telephone is already the focus of research and trials in a number of distributed learning centers. A very early application involves access to library databases for finding and reserving books.

*Videoconferencing,* like audiographics, used to be carried out on dedicated hardware, but has similarly converged onto the Web. Distributed lectures can now be Webcast and students can respond with questions and discussion through a chat board. In addition, the real-time lecture can be "canned" and stored on the Web for students to access at their convenience. Two-way video communication on the Web also has many applications for distributed learning; for example, for student–instructor communications and for student–student work on joint projects. Multi-way video communication on the Web has not yet evolved sufficiently to be robust for home-based learners, but the spread of broadband may soon make a difference. Research studies have questioned the value of video when it is used merely to see the remote lecturer talking. Audio is critical, and seeing the slides or other illustrative material is also important. However, even a small window showing the lecturer and views of the remote students do add to the vital sense of "presence" that helps to motivate students and enliven the subject.

The delivery of course content in distributed learning has been carried out through video lectures, but also through print sent through the mail. With the development of the personal computer, multimedia learning materials and particularly training materials could be produced on CD-ROM. This led to an explosion of computer-based learning courses in which students could interact with the materials, practice various techniques and skills, and work through lessons at their convenience and as many times as they needed. However, the cost of developing stimulating, interactive multimedia materials was very great (in fact, it still is), and much of the material produced was not very stimulating and interactive beyond learners pressing the "Next" button at the bottom of the screen. Furthermore, once the CD-ROMs had been produced they were difficult to change or update. Consequently, the Web soon became the preferred option for content delivery, because it offered the possibility of interaction with other students as well as with the materials, and the content was easy for the developers to update. Furthermore, learners could supplement the course content with any of the resources of the Web.

## ISSUES ARISING FROM EVOLVING TECHNOLOGIES

The speed with which technology has evolved raises a number of pedagogical, human, and institutional issues for distributed learning. New opportunities regarding the process of assessing students have been provided by the Web. Multiple choice testing has become more challenging with matching, sequencing, and identification questions available in multimedia. Collaborative assignments for students at a distance, joint projects and presentations, and student-produced Web pages have all expanded the range and quality of assessments. However, the vast resources of the Web and the ease of access to them have created a major problem regarding plagiarism, ranging from unacknowledged use of material to wholesale buying of complete assignments. Concern over this kind of cheating has led to the development of plagiarism detection software and processes to help markers identify work not authored by the student.

A related issue is the ownership of Web-based material in general and the copyright protection of teaching material in particular. Academics have begun to assert their rights over course material that they author for Web-based courses. This creates difficulties for institutions wanting to reuse, update, or re-version materials for other markets and adds considerable cost to the development of high quality Web-based courses. From the learner's perspective, there is increasing evidence that students are becoming more demanding and have higher expectations about the content and the processes of learning. For example, in the areas of postgraduate education, continuing professional development, and lifelong learning, there are demands for just-in-time learning that fits the learner's immediate needs and has direct application to the workplace. Influenced by other technologies such as television, games, and mobile phones, students expect to be able to personalize their learning environment, choosing the colors, fonts, navigation routes, and presentation of the Web materials. This has led to the development of course material that can be customized to different learning styles and different learning materials tailored to the background and existing knowledge of the learner.

Another set of issues relates to the globalization of education that has evolved with the Web. Satellite-based videoconferencing was used to connect several sites to the host institution, and in some cases to make international connections, for delivering lectures. Many of these programs have evolved to Web-based courses, using Webcast lectures and supporting resources and interaction. Similarly, print-based distance education has also moved onto the Web and exploits the possibility of peer-to-peer discussion, access to resource materials, and online submission of assignments. Institutions are now grappling with the implications of a global student body, as first expatriate students living abroad began registering for distributed courses, and then virtual universities were set up to accept students from around the world. A parallel development is seen in campus education where various elements of distributed learning have been introduced to add flexibility, interaction, and extra resources to traditional lecture courses. Emerging from the many combinations of face-to-face and distributed modes of course delivery that have been tried for various levels, markets, and situations, it is increasingly clear that this "blended learning" meets the needs of the majority of learners. Combining synchronous and asynchronous forms of communication is one aspect of the blend. Asynchronous interaction has the advantage of allowing time for reflection, of being more flexible, and of preserving a written record of discussions. Synchronous interaction provides immediate feedback, motivates students, and helps them pace their work. Working out the best use of these two modes of learning is part of good course design and will inevitably vary with different contexts, levels, and types of learners. Synchronous tools are obviously more difficult to employ when students span many time zones and are less appropriate when students can meet on campus.

However distributed courses provide for interaction and communication, the development of online community—the learner's sense of being part of a learning group—is seen as contributing invaluably to the success of the course, to the retention of students, and to their learning outcomes. The sense of presence in an online community can be developed partly through effective group learning activities and partly through effective use of technology. Examples of both of these include voting systems, instant messaging, socializing conferences, ice-breaking exercises, small group activities, debates and role plays, photographs, learning logs, problem-solving tutorials, and student moderating opportunities.

## LEARNING MANAGEMENT SYSTEMS

The convergence of separate systems for developing, delivering, and administering distributed courses into one easy-to-use system has undoubtedly contributed to the growth of distributed learning. Most products provide a content management system to allow academics to develop course materials without having to master HTML or XML. Most also provide online assessment support for sending, storing, and even marking assignments. The major component, however, is both synchronous and asynchronous support for student and instructor interaction. With single sign-on, the same navigation and presentation across all courses, and integration of content and interaction, these environments certainly make distributed learning a much less difficult process than it was 15 years ago.

—*Robin Mason*

*See also* ASYNCHRONOUS FORMATS; COMPUTER-MEDIATED COMMUNICATION (CMC); DESIGNING LEARNING ENVIRONMENTS; LEARNING MANAGEMENT SYSTEMS (LMS); ONLINE LEARNING ENVIRONMENTS; SYNCHRONOUS FORMATS

## Bibliography

Adelsberger, H., Collis, B., & Pawlowski, J. (Eds.). (2002). *Handbook on information technologies for education and training.* Berlin: Springer-Verlag.

Baumgardner, G. (2000). *Strategies for effective online education.* New York: Forbes Custom Publishing.

Burge, E. (Ed.). (2000). *The strategic use of learning technologies.* San Francisco: Jossey-Bass.

Dede, C. (1996). The evolution of distance education: Emerging technologies and distributed learning. *American Journal of Distance Education, 10*(2), 4–36.

Farrell, G. (Ed.). (2001). *The changing faces of virtual education.* The Commonwealth of Learning. Retrieved from http://www.col.org/virtualed/virtual2pdfs/v2%5-Fprelims.pdf.

Laurillard, D. (2002). *Rethinking university teaching: A conversational framework for the effective use of learning technologies,* 2nd edition. London: Routledge Falmer.

Mason, R. (1998). *Globalising education. Trends and applications.* London: Routledge.

McConnell, D. (2000). *Implementing computer supported co-operative learning,* 2nd edition. London: Kogan Page.

# EXPERIENTIAL LEARNING

Experiential learning is defined as learning in which the learner is in direct contact with the reality being studied, as opposed to learning in which the learner is reading or hearing about or discussing the reality. Experiential learning is often referred to as involving "hands-on experience."

If a distributed learning site is engaging students in an experience of learning, as in practicing a foreign language (hearing, speaking, and being understood), the activity combines experiential learning and distributed learning.

Being in direct touch with something may involve directly observing it without further intervention, or it may involve interaction of some kind. For example, in a science laboratory the inquirer may want to control the conditions to measure precisely how the object of study reacts when treated differently. In a chemistry experiment, different substances may be introduced to see whether new compounds are formed, explosive reactions occur, or no change is observed.

We learn implicitly (gaining an unarticulated grasp) as well as explicitly (gaining narrative knowledge) through hands-on experience. As one drives a car, the driver develops a "feel for" increasingly skillful performance, but may be unable to explain how to another person. Learning to be an effective leader is more a matter of tacit understanding derived from practice than of book knowledge derived from lectures and discussion. Can tacit understanding be gleaned from distributed experiential learning? It would seem that very little development of tacit understanding would result from merely receiving instruction from afar; but if the receiving students then practice using the knowledge and get feedback from the distant instructor, such implicit learning may indeed occur.

Classes in school or college do not usually provide opportunities for experiential learning. It is not possible to bring ancient Greece into a twenty-first-century classroom nor to transfer an Afghan village into an American campus for hands-on study, although movies of life in the village can be used.

Some learning goals can be pursued experientially in classes. For example, a native speaker of a foreign language can come to class and engage students in practicing the language. Writing proficiency can be developed by performance in class, or by combining in-class work with out-of-class drafting, with the instructor analyzing the composition and evaluating it in or out of class or by having students exchange papers.

## OBSTACLES TO EXPERIENTIAL AND DISTRIBUTED LEARNING

Empirical knowledge must ultimately be obtained by way of direct encounter with the phenomena being studied, but teaching students in this way does not necessarily require that the students engage in such an encounter themselves. One reason that the human community can accumulate and use so much knowledge is that we can benefit from, and build upon, what others have first discovered. Learning from learners of the past can be done distributively, and often more efficiently than if done only in face-to-face activities.

There are very good reasons for not engaging in experiential learning on some matters. One such reason is the dangers that may be involved. For example, learning to fly a supersonic airplane is more safely done by starting with a simulator. Investigating the causes of the bubonic plague is a highly risky endeavor. Experimentation with chemicals can be dangerous in the hands of inexperienced persons. Such dangers would seem to be heightened when using distributed learning.

Some learning tasks are also highly expensive. The study of atomic fission and fusion is a matter of high risk, high expense, sophisticated equipment, and great expertise on the part of the investigators. In such cases the use of distributed learning can save time and money. Again, how can distributed learning be used for this purpose?

Normally, courses or classes are too short in duration to permit students to see the full course of the process being studied. For example, studies of family deterioration under conditions of poverty and discrimination or studies of the origin of an international conflict or of the liberation of a people from oppression continue long past the schedule of college classes. Hands-on experience can be too time consuming for timely completion of a learning task for which the alternative of distributed learning (piggy-backing on others' work) is available.

## IMPROVING SKILLS IN LEARNING

Hands-on investigation is essential to the growth of original knowledge; and distributed learning is essential to the distribution of learning at affordable costs, risks, and other conditions of its feasibility.

The scope of what is unknown is so great that there is a continuing need to develop competent investigators. The need for the improvement of medicine calls for a steady supply of newly trained scientists, who must engage in hands-on inquiry under the supervision of expert instructors. The amateur anthropologist needs help in recognizing what he is experiencing, and the novice at an archeological dig can destroy evidence without knowing it unless properly supervised and supported.

The skills of critical thinking are also not a given for most learners, who need the assistance of teachers in recognizing questionable assumptions, identifying mistaken inferences, and developing awareness of alternative explanations of what has been directly observed. These skills can generally be acquired in the classroom. Interaction with a teacher or co-learner is essential to such learning, and can be arranged in a context of either face-to-face or distributed learning.

## RECOGNITION OF EXPERIENTIAL LEARNING

Historically, colleges have tended to think that advanced learning occurs only under their own auspices or those of other similar institutions. During the twentieth century this idea was replaced by the development of tests of knowledge gained outside of schools and colleges: standardized examinations, essay examinations, performance assessments, product evaluations, and learning portfolios. Assessors expert in both their fields of knowledge and in the processes of assessment have been trained to use these means for arriving at a clear identification of learning that is worthy of postsecondary credit. Hundreds of colleges now employ faculty with these competences. Students with sufficient experiential learning have received credit and advanced standing and have saved years in furthering their education while also saving the costs of unneeded formal instruction. In a sense, learning outside of school or college that can later be recognized as equivalent to that achieved in classrooms is a case of distributed learning.

## INSTITUTIONS THAT EMPHASIZE EXPERIENTIAL AND DISTRIBUTED LEARNING

More than 1,100 institutions of postsecondary education employ alternating work and study as a strategy combining earning and learning. Park College did so as early as 1876. Berea College adopted the practice of requiring able but low-income students to work for the college to help it run its operations. The University of Cincinnati applied cooperative education to studies in management and engineering as early as 1913. The first liberal arts college to require all students to alternate work and study was Antioch College (1920). Concurrent work and study has been a growing feature of postsecondary institutions serving working adults.

Also available in more than 1,000 colleges and universities are internship programs and service learning opportunities. Skill development, including leadership skills, is the focus of a more limited array of offerings. Three associations have played a leading role in the fostering of experiential learning and its recognition: The Council for Adult and Experiential Learning, the National Society for Experiential Education, and the Association for Experiential Education. Prominent among the practitioner colleges are Antioch University, Excelsior College (formerly Regents College of New York), Thomas Edison State College, Empire State College, The School for New Learning of DePaul University, The School of Adult Learning of University of New Hampshire, Fielding Graduate Institute, and the Union Institute.

Distributed learning facilitated by institutions as a matter of policy is a recent development. The Sloan Foundation's Web site (http://www.sloan.org/main.shtml) provides a list of such institutions with a record of the degree and certificate programs they offer. However, the difference between the number of institutions listed there and the published estimates of the number actually offering online programs is so great that the registry gives a far from adequate picture of the reality.

—*Morris T. Keeton*

*See also* CLINICAL TRAINING; CURRICULUM MODELS; INSTRUCTIONAL TECHNIQUES; SCHOLAR PRACTITIONER MODEL

## Bibliography

Berry, D. C. (1991). The role of action in implicit learning. *The Quarterly Journal of Experimental Psychology, 43A*(4), 881–906.

Dewey, J. (1902). *The school and society*. Chicago: The University of Chicago Press.

Houle, C. (1976). The deep traditions of experiential learning. In Keeton & Associates (Eds.), *Experiential learning: Rationale, characteristics and assessment.* San Francisco: Jossey-Bass.

Kolb, David. (1984). *Experiential learning: Experience as the source of learning and development.* Englewood Cliffs, NJ: Prentice Hall.

Reber, A. S. (1993). *Implicit learning and tacit knowledge: An essay on the cognitive unconscious.* Volume 19. New York: Oxford University Press.

Sheckley, B. G. & Keeton, M. T. (1997). Service learning: A theoretical model. In J. Schine (Ed.), *Service Learning, 96th Yearbook of the National Society for the Study of Education, Part I.* Chicago: The University of Chicago Press.

The Sloan Foundation. (November 2002). *Five pillars of quality online education.* Eighth Sloan-C International Conference on Asynchronous Learning Networks (ALN).

# FACILITATION

*Facilitation* is the art of leadership in group communication. A *facilitator* is one who fulfills this leadership role. In online settings, these terms are often employed interchangeably with *moderating* and *moderator*.

Facilitation in both online and face-to-face settings aims to promote a congenial social atmosphere and a lively exchange of views. The online facilitator resembles his or her face-to-face equivalent in important respects. Here is how facilitation is described in a classic account by Hiltz and Turoff:

> In order for a computerized conference to be successful the moderator has to work very hard at both the "social host" and the "meeting chairperson" roles. As social host she/he has to issue warm invitations to people; send encouraging private messages to people complimenting them or at least commenting on their entries, or suggesting what they may be uniquely qualified to contribute. As meeting chairperson, she/he must prepare an enticing-sounding initial agenda; frequently summarize or clarify what has been going on; try to express the emerging consensus or call for a formal vote; sense and announce when it is time to move on to a new topic. Without this kind of active moderator role, a conference is not apt to get off the ground.

## CLASSIFICATIONS OF FACILITATING ACTIVITIES

One popular approach to classifying facilitation activities is to separate them into four categories: pedagogical, social, managerial, and technical. The pedagogical role concerns the teacher's contribution of specialized knowledge and insights to the discussion, using questions and probes to encourage student responses, and to focus discussion on critical concepts. In addition, by modeling such behavior, the teacher prepares the students to lead the pedagogical activities themselves.

Successful online teaching requires a friendly social environment. The social role of the teacher includes promoting human relationships, affirming and recognizing students' inputs, providing opportunities for students to develop a sense of group cohesiveness, maintaining the group as a unit, and helping students to work together in a mutual cause.

The managerial role concerns organizational, procedural, and administrative activities. This role involves providing objectives, setting timetables, and setting procedural rules and decision-making norms. The technical role concerns responsibility for ensuring participants' comfort and ease in using the network system and the conferencing software. It requires the facilitator to be proficient with the technology.

An issue of some importance in discussions of online pedagogy concerns what has been called "teaching presence." Teaching presence is defined as the extent to which the participants, especially the teacher, are able to design educational experiences, provide direct instruction, and facilitate discourse. In this context, facilitation involves identifying areas of agreement and disagreement, seeking consensus, acknowledging student contributions and posing questions, prompting and summarizing discussions, establishing netiquette, and diagnosing and dealing with misconceptions.

Like most of the large literature on the subject, these approaches describe online facilitation in terms of corresponding face-to-face activities. However, the correspondences are not exact. The subtle differences between online and face-to-face facilitation are due to the differences in the means of communication in the two settings.

A communication-theoretic approach to facilitation emphasizes the differences between online and face-to-face activities. This approach highlights the specific communicative activities belonging to the online facilitating role. These can be distinguished for analytic purposes from other activities of facilitators such as the social management of personal relationships in the group, technical support for participants with difficulties, and pedagogical practices such as asking questions and explaining concepts. Focusing on these communicative differences is helpful in gaining a fuller understanding of the online setting and the special demands it makes on facilitators. (For a full list of communicative functions, see Facilitation Form 1.)

## ESTABLISHING A COMMUNICATION MODEL

In face-to-face settings the facilitator's most difficult challenge is to manage turn taking skillfully to ensure that everyone has a chance to speak. Turn-taking is not a problem in asynchronous online forums. Instead, the online facilitator is mainly engaged in compensating for the absence of the usual tacit cues that enable communication partners to understand and recognize each other when face-to-face. The online facilitator's first and most basic task is to construct the social reality of the electronic encounter by choosing a communication model for the group. As soon as we enter a room, we orient ourselves more or less consciously in response to tacit cues we notice in the context of the communication process we are about to join. These contextual cues establish a shared communication model from which flows roles, norms, and expectations.

Because no tacit signs visible in the environment establish a communication model online, facilitators typically must make an explicit choice for the group they lead, reducing the strangeness of the medium by defining a familiar context with a system of roles and rules imitated from everyday life. The facilitator must outline the norms of online behavior early in the life

of the group. These contextualizing functions are all-important in relieving some of the anxiety participants experience in a communication setting that is not defined in advance by tacit cues. Once a communication model has been established, the facilitator must play the specific leadership role it implies, such as chairperson, host, teacher, or entertainer. In part, this role will consist of monitoring conformity with the communication model and reassuring participants that their contributions to the discussion are appropriate, or where they are not, gently guiding them toward a better understanding of the model. To keep the conversation on track the facilitator must also occasionally offer explicit "meta-comments," which broach communication problems encountered by the group as a whole.

## SUSTAINING MOTIVATION TO PARTICIPATE

Members of an online forum often have extrinsic motivations to participate, such as job requirements or grades. But the social cohesion of an online forum depends not only on the extrinsic motives participants bring from their offline lives, but also on the intrinsic motives that emerge in the course of the interaction. In this respect, too, online forums resemble the face-to-face meetings and classes they imitate. Without skillful facilitation, concern for grades is usually insufficient to sustain an interesting classroom discussion. Similarly, facilitation is necessary to maintain participation in online classes.

Students bring some measure of curiosity and a desire to shine to the classroom. Facilitation works with these motivations. The teacher awakens the students' curiosity and the suspense keeps the students attentive till it is satisfied. Surprising facts or concepts excite interest and provoke comments. Recognition for contributing stimulates the desire to contribute again. Every teacher is aware of these dynamics and plays on them in facilitating classroom discussion. Students online respond to the same stimuli; only the environment is different.

This difference, however, is considerable. Misunderstandings can be rapidly corrected in the classroom, leaving a far larger margin for ambiguity and error than in an online forum where confusion may take days to straighten out. Clarity of expression is thus required of everyone, and of the facilitator above all. Sometimes this means writing far longer topic raisers and summary comments than would seem

**Facilitation Form 1** Communicative Functions

## Contextualizing functions:

1. *Opening discussions.* The moderator must provide an opening comment that states the theme of the discussion and establishes a communication model. The moderator may periodically contribute "topic raisers" or "prompts" that open further discussions within the framework of the forum's general theme.
2. *Setting the norms:* suggesting rules of procedure for the discussion. Some norms are modeled by the form and style of the moderator's opening comments. Others are explicitly formulated in comments that set the stage for the discussion.
3. *Setting the agenda:* managing the forum over time, selecting an order and flow of themes and topics of discussion. The moderator generally shares part or all of the agenda with participants at the outset.
4. *Referring.* The conference may be contextualized by referring to materials available on the Internet, for example, by hyperlinking, or offline materials such as textbooks.

## Monitoring functions:

5. *Recognition:* referring explicitly to participants' comments to assure them that their contribution is valued and welcome, or to correct misapprehensions about the context of the discussion.
6. *Prompting:* addressing requests for comments to individuals or the group. Prompting includes asking questions and may be formalized as "assignments" or tasks. Prompting may be carried out through public requests in the forum or by private messages.
7. *Assessing.* Participant accomplishment may be assessed by tests, review sessions, or other formal procedures.

## Meta functions:

8. *Meta-commenting:* remarks directed at such things as the context, norms, or agenda of the forum; or at solving problems such as lack of clarity, irrelevance, and information overload. Meta-comments play an important role in maintaining the conditions of successful communication.
9. *Weaving:* summarizing the state of the discussion and finding threads of unity in the comments of participants. It recognizes the authors of the comments it weaves together, and often implicitly prompts them to continue along lines that advance the conference agenda.
10. *Delegating.* Certain moderating functions such as weaving can be assigned to individual participants to perform for a shorter or longer period.

appropriate spoken in front of a class. Similarly, recognizing student contributions is a heavier burden online, where students do not see the tacit response of their comrades and so need more frequent reassurance from the teacher.

Despite these problems, students enjoy well-facilitated online discussions and learn a great deal from the practice of writing about the concepts of their field of study. There is something exciting about the daily rhythm of signing on and looking for the next batch of messages, which may include responses to one's own comments and new perspectives introduced by the teacher. Participation in an online discussion forum can acquire an "addictive" quality that keeps the students coming back for more day after day throughout the term.

## FACILITATION AND TEACHING

The 10 communicative functions outlined in Form 1 maintain the flow of the online conversation regardless of its purpose and content. They will be performed one way or another in any successful online group. Sometimes responsibility for maintaining the flow is widely distributed among members of the group, each of whom occasionally performs one or another function; sometimes it is concentrated primarily in a single facilitator. There are strong reasons to prefer the latter pattern in the online class.

In online education, skillful facilitation is skillful teaching. There is no alternative pedagogy available, due to inherent limitations of the medium. Online lecturing, either in print or on video, lacks the interactive qualities essential to good teaching. The problem is not with lecturing as such. In a small classroom the teacher can encourage interaction by remaining open to comments and questions, but this flexibility is lost when lectures are reproduced online. Online lectures thus differ little from ordinary reading assignments, which by themselves hardly constitute a classroom experience. Technically sophisticated solutions employing interactive video are still too complicated for most classroom instruction. In response to this limitation, most online educators employ discussion in asynchronous forums as the nearest practical equivalent to a familiar face-to-face classroom experience.

As in a face-to-face class, online facilitation of discussion offers the teacher many opportunities to advance students' understanding. In this context, the communicative functions of facilitation are not purely social, distinct from the delivery of educational content. Many social and pedagogical activities are best carried out in the course of performing the communicative functions. For example, maintaining a friendly environment requires recognizing individual contributions promptly so that no one feels left out. Similarly, concepts are often explained in the context of opening discussions with topic raisers.

Weaving comments are of particular importance in the online pedagogy practiced by many teachers. As a communicative function, weaving enables the group to take stock of agreements and disagreements and to mark its place on its agenda. This is accomplished by grasping in one text the pattern found in a number of previous comments. To write weaving comments, it is necessary to review the discussion archive carefully, refreshing students' memories regarding earlier contributions, clarifying confused expressions, identifying the themes, and making connections.

In the context of an online course, these activities create pedagogical opportunities. The weaving comment can do more than just summarize the previous discussion in the language of that discussion. It can connect student contributions to the themes of the forum and apply higher level concepts from the teacher's discipline to the students' ideas and experiences. This is a particularly effective way of enhancing teaching presence in the online class.

## CONCLUSION

Online education is scarcely more than 20 years old. In that short period, there have been many

discussions of facilitation in the literature (see Bibliography), but the same themes reappear over and over. For the most part this literature is not based on elaborate research but on practical experience. Nevertheless, there is a well-grounded consensus on the essential aspects of online facilitation. The different emphases of different commentators help to build a full picture of the art. No doubt further research on facilitation will contribute new elements to our understanding of this important activity, but enough is already known to inform the practice of teachers new to the field.

*—Andrew Feenberg*
*—Cindy Xin*

***See also*** CLINICAL TRAINING; CURRICULUM MODELS; INSTRUCTIONAL TECHNIQUES; SCHOLAR PRACTITIONER MODEL

## Bibliography

Anderson, T., Rourke, L., Garrison, D. R., & Archer, W. (2001). Assessing teaching presence in a computer conferencing environment. *Journal of Asynchronous Learning Networks, 5*(2).

Berge, Z. L. (1995). Facilitating computer conferencing: Recommendations from the field. *Educational Technology, 15*(1), 22–30.

Feenberg, A. (1989). The written world. In R. Mason and A. Kaye (Eds.), *Mindweave: Communication, computers, and distance education* (pp. 22–39). Oxford: Pergamon.

Hiltz, S. R., & Turoff, M. (1978, 1993). *The network nation: Human communication via computer.* Cambridge: MIT Press.

Paulsen, M. F. (1995). Moderating educational computer conferences. In Z. L. Berge & M. P. Collins (Eds.), *Computer-mediated communication and the on-line classroom in distance education.* Cresskill, NJ: Hampton Press.

# FACULTY DEVELOPMENT, SELECTION, AND TRAINING

Faculty development and training is critical to the success of any distributed learning program. The pedagogy of effective distributed learning is significantly different from that of the traditional face-to-face class.

Without guidance, many faculty who are planning their first online course try to emulate their standard course, perhaps by scheduling a synchronous chat during a specific class time. This approach, however, fails to leverage the potential of technology for online teaching, while losing the benefits of oral communication and the ability to read body language inherent in the face-to-face class. Therefore, a critical aspect of faculty development is knowledge of how students learn and how an online course can be structured to maximize learning. More obvious, perhaps, is the need for faculty to develop a suite of basic computer skills, a comfort level in using the specific technologies that will be employed to teach the course, and information literacy skills. In identifying faculty to teach online courses, it is preferable to select those who volunteer. Willingness to explore new ways of teaching, to collaborate with others in designing and developing the course, and tolerance of risk are characteristic of successful online teachers. Incentives such as released time and recognition in promotion and tenure are helpful in recruiting and retaining faculty to teach online.

## FACULTY TRAINING AND DEVELOPMENT

The greatest challenge that confronts faculty who will begin *teaching* in the online environment is that few have had any experience in being a *learner* in the online environment. Even early career faculty who have highly developed technology skills typically have learned their subject matter discipline in a traditional face-to-face environment. They have learned from hundreds of teachers during their many years as a student and have formed ideas about effective teaching strategies from those firsthand experiences. More senior faculty may have extensive teaching experience in the face-to-face classroom, but have no models for effective teaching in the online environment. Given the lack of experience in the online environment, most faculty begin to transition their course by emulating the face-to-face teaching environment. This emulation loses crucial factors in the translation (e.g., facial expressions, body language) and rarely takes full advantage of the potential advantages of the technology. However, making significant changes in teaching strategies may move even seasoned teachers out of their "comfort zones."

A faculty development program to prepare for effective online teaching will provide experience as an online learner, guidance in rethinking teaching strategies to leverage the power of technology, and direct instruction in the needed technology skills. If at all possible, faculty new to online teaching should begin this training and development process several months in advance of actually offering the course. This will allow time for them to develop a comfort level in using the technology, to redesign the course for optimal learning in the online environment, and to develop course materials and upload them to the Web-based tools to be used in delivering the course. These materials can be self-developed if the faculty member has the requisite technological/graphic design skills or they can be created in partnership with instructional technology staff.

## EXPERIENCE AS AN ONLINE LEARNER

Offering at least part of the faculty development program online provides the prospective instructor with important insights into the way an online student may perceive a course and the challenges often encountered by students. This experience can be used to model a wide range of effective pedagogical strategies and instructional resources. For example, an online workshop for faculty might provide an overview of principles of learning in a text document. Faculty could then be presented with a case that portrayed some of these principles being applied in the design of an online course. Subsequently, the faculty might analyze the case, evaluating the quality of the application of learning principles and making suggestions for improvement, then post their thoughts to an asynchronous discussion board. The workshop might also incorporate the use of surveys, online self-scoring quizzes, PowerPoint presentations, and streaming media. By taking part in such an online workshop, faculty can gain experience in using various features of the technology that could be deployed in their own course, as well as become aware of possible strategies and resources.

Instructional strategies that have been shown to be especially effective in the online learning environment are interaction with the content, interaction among students, and interaction between the instructor and the student. Interaction with the content might, for example, entail manipulating molecular models of various types of drugs in pharmacology or analyzing the structure of an argument in English. Interaction among students can take place in synchronous or asynchronous discussion and helps students clarify their understanding of a concept, see it from multiple perspectives, identify examples, and try to describe the idea in their own words. E-mail, threaded discussion, or synchronous chat can enable rich interaction between the instructor and each member of the class. These strategies may be characterized as learner-centered, constructivist (making meaning by personal interaction or social interaction with content), and collaborative. Although many faculty use such strategies in their classroom classes, others may use more teacher-centered models. The online workshop can introduce all faculty to the potential of learner-centered approaches in online teaching.

## GUIDANCE IN RETHINKING TEACHING STRATEGIES

Following the experience as an online learner, faculty members can begin to plan the particular online course they will offer. This planning may take place in a workshop setting or in one-to-one consultation with an instructional designer. There are many formal models of instructional design that might be drawn upon as a framework for planning, but experience has shown that it is usually best to work with the faculty member in an informal way, posing questions about the course and generating ideas for its development. Perhaps the most important question to be answered is "What are the learning objectives of the course?" Few faculty articulate the learning objectives of a course in ways that are helpful to them in planning instructional strategies, assignments, and assessments. This lack of clarity also compromises students' ability to work toward the objectives in a purposeful way. It is worthwhile to spend time at the beginning of a course planning to carefully craft learning objectives, a process that is facilitated by using the stem "Students will be able to. . . ." The *wording* of the objectives should also be reviewed to ensure that their meaning will be clear to students.

After objectives are formalized, the faculty member and the instructional design consultant can review what instructional resources and strategies would be most appropriate in assisting students to attain the objectives. Faculty often are constrained in their thinking about these possibilities, envisioning the posting of their lectures on a Web site, facilitating student discussion, and administering an objective or essay test. In fact, long pages of text are difficult to read on screen and usually are less engaging than face-to-face lectures. If more than 10–12 students are enrolled in a class, large group discussion may impose a very heavy reading load on both students and faculty. Finally, faculty are often skeptical about whether they can be sure that students are who they claim to be when taking an objective or essay test online. To make the course more engaging, faculty should consider a wide array of resources when selecting those to be used in their course. These resources might include textbooks, CD-ROMs, streaming video, Web sites (either those that already exist or ones created specifically for the course), simulations, and databases that enable the student to *formulate* a question as well as analyze information to *answer* the question. Teaching strategies might include role playing, problem-based learning in simulated real-life contexts, case studies, and debates. Note that these resources and strategies may invite the learner to interact with the content and with other students. This leads to the next step in planning the course, which is to develop activities and assignments that will foster this kind of interaction and assist the learner in reaching the objectives of the course. Finally, faculty need to consider how they will determine whether the students have mastered course objectives. If they wish to give an objective or essay test, one option is to arrange for this to be administered in a proctored environment. Proctoring is a long-established practice in distance learning, and appropriate sites are available both nationally and internationally. Another option is to grade based on students' performance on assignments throughout the course. These assignments should align with the course objectives and require familiarity with the interactions during the flow of the course to mitigate the possibility of cheating.

Prompt, helpful, and continuous feedback helps to maximize students' learning. One way of providing this kind of feedback without undue time demands on the instructor is to create online, self-scoring quizzes. These will enable students to check their understanding of the course content on a regular basis. Quiz scores might count for a small percentage of the course grade, but are primarily intended to give feedback and increase motivation.

In addition to designing their own course, faculty new to online teaching should be given examples of "best practices" and suggestions of how to implement these practices in teaching their courses. A few of these practices are:

- Craft clear directions for assignments, providing model examples of completed assignments where possible.
- Create a grading rubric for assignments to inform students of the criteria on which they will be evaluated.
- Learn to structure and moderate online discussion in ways that promote the attainment of course objectives.
- Develop approaches that will create a sense of community among students enrolled in the course.
- Learn ways to manage time effectively by setting expectations concerning response to student e-mail messages and creating a FAQ (list of frequently asked questions).

## DIRECT INSTRUCTION IN TECHNOLOGY SKILLS AND RESOURCES

Faculty who plan to teach online should have a strong foundation of basic computer and information literacy skills. Some examples of such skills are creating, saving, manipulating, finding, and opening files; working simultaneously with more than one window open; using various kinds of files such as .wav, .pdf, and PowerPoint; and knowing how to assess the validity of Web-based resources. In addition to these basic skills, the instructor should develop a mastery of the specific technologies to be used in the delivery of the course being designed. Within higher education, many faculty use institutionally supported, Web-based course management systems (CMSs) such as Blackboard or WebCT, which integrate many tools for teaching online courses. If a CMS is to be used, the faculty member should become familiar with most or all of the tools provided by the software. In some cases, faculty may have already used a CMS to enhance a face-to-face course, and this will ease the transition to online teaching.

In addition to developing basic computer skills and attaining a comfort level with the technologies to be used in the course, it is important that faculty know all of the resources that will be available to them and any policies that have been promulgated by the institution. Examples of resources are the library (especially electronic databases and document delivery services) and technical support (instructional design, video/graphics production, help desk, and access to software tools). Examples of policies are the Family Educational Rights and Privacy Act (FERPA), which limits the information that can be divulged about a student; intellectual property agreements; and copyright law.

Many sources are available for professional development related to online learning. These include university instructional development staff, vendor-provided training, online tutorials created in-house or by other universities or consulting firms, online programs in online teaching that lead to a certificate or degree, and virtual universities that now exist in 40 states.

Faculty development should continue during the course offering and beyond. An excellent way of providing this is to have an experienced mentor observe the course during its first offering and offer support and advice. Instructional development staff can assist the instructor in developing forms to garner both formative and summative feedback about the course and the effectiveness of teaching. Also, an online community can be established for those who are teaching online so that they can request assistance with teaching concerns; share innovative ideas that have proven successful; and share knowledge about tools, resources, teaching strategies, or assessment of learning.

## RECRUITMENT AND SELECTION OF ONLINE FACULTY

Faculty who volunteer to teach online are usually more successful and express greater satisfaction than those who are required to do so. Current online faculty who are successful and enthusiastic about the experience are often helpful in recruiting other faculty. Allowing prospective faculty to observe live online courses that have been selected to demonstrate high quality and a range of instructional approaches may demystify the process of online teaching and help them envision the possibilities for their own courses.

## INCENTIVES FOR ONLINE TEACHING

Most faculty who teach online indicate that it is more time consuming than teaching face-to-face classes. Nontenured faculty may hesitate to become involved in distributed learning because the time required might divert them from research and scholarship. In many colleges and universities, scholarship is more highly valued than teaching. Several approaches may mitigate these obstacles. The institution should consider giving release time to the faculty member, at least during the planning and development stage.

A sound instructional design is crucial to the success of an online course, and it is important to allow the faculty member sufficient time to rethink pedagogical options and to consult with instructional technology staff. Also, development of course materials requires a significant amount of time, whether self-developed or in partnership with a graphics designer and other relevant staff. Promotion and tenure criteria may be modified to explicitly recognize teaching, especially teaching that requires creativity and new approaches. Staff with expertise in classroom research may assist the faculty member in designing research related to pedagogical techniques used in online learning, characteristics of successful learners, or outcomes. If published, this research might support the faculty member's case for promotion and tenure.

## FACULTY SATISFACTION

Many studies have confirmed the importance of faculty satisfaction to the success of an online learning program. Excellent preparation for online teaching via faculty training and development is an important step toward ensuring faculty satisfaction as well as ensuring the quality of online courses.

—*Dorothy A. Frayer*

*See also* COMPUTER-MEDIATED COMMUNICATION (CMC); DESIGNING LEARNING ENVIRONMENTS; INSTRUCTIONAL COURSE DESIGN; INSTRUCTIONAL TECHNIQUES; WEB-BASED COURSE MANAGEMENT SYSTEMS (WBCMS)

### Bibliography

American Federation of Teachers, Higher Education Program and Policy Council. (2000). *Distance education: Guidelines for good practice.* Washington, DC: American Federation of Teachers. Available online at http://www.aft.org/higher_ed/downloadable/distance.pdf.

Bates, A. W. (2000). *Managing technological change: Strategies for college and university leaders.* San Francisco: Jossey-Bass.

Bonk, C. J. (2001). *Online teaching in an online world.* Bloomington, IN: CourseShare.com. Retrieved from http://www.publicationshare.com/docs/faculty_survey_report.pdf.

Epper, R. M., & Bates, A. W. (Eds.). (2001). *Teaching faculty how to use technology: Best practices from leading institutions.* Westport, CT: American Council on Education/Oryx.

Fredericksen, E., Pickett, A., Shea, P., Pelz, W., & Swan, K. (2000). Factors influencing faculty satisfaction with asynchronous teaching and learning in the SUNY Learning Network. *Journal of Asynchronous Learning Networks, 4*(3). Available online at http://www.aln.org/publications/jaln/v4n3/v4n3_fredericksen.asp.

Hiltz, S. R., Coppola, N., Rotter, N., Turoff, M., & Benbunan-Fich, R. (2000). Measuring the importance of collaborative learning for the effectiveness of ALN: A multi-measure, multi-method approach. *Journal of Asynchronous Learning Networks, 4*(2). Available online at http://www.aln.org/publications/jaln/v4n2/v4n2_hiltz.asp.

## FACULTY EVALUATION

The purpose of evaluating faculty is to improve their practice and to assist administrators in making decisions about further contractual obligations. Faculty evaluation in distributed learning communities is different from faculty evaluation in traditional institutions. First of all, faculty in distributed learning communities are not interacting face-to-face on a daily basis. In addition, methods for serving students and determining competence are generally different. Faculty are likely to be interacting with students during nontraditional hours on the phone and by e-mail. Furthermore, their method of instructional delivery is different from that of the professor giving lectures. Because many faculty involved with distance learning work at home, supervisors and peers cannot directly observe them as they do their work.

### DEVELOPMENT OF A FACULTY EVALUATION SYSTEM

When formulating a faculty evaluation system, it is helpful to get input from all faculty about the process. When people are able to contribute their ideas to developing a system, they are generally more accepting of the system. This tends to lessen faculty resistance to being evaluated.

Formative evaluation is conducted to help faculty members assess themselves and set new goals for growing professionally. Summative evaluation is conducted by leaders in colleges and universities to determine whether to retain faculty members. Increasingly, the two are being combined.

All policies and procedures for conducting evaluations must be in writing and agreed upon by all parties. The evaluation system should also be tied to a faculty development system so that faculty members have the opportunity to learn the skills on which they will be evaluated, particularly if they are making the transition from on-campus teaching to teaching at a distance. Forms must be developed to gather feedback from students, peers, staff, and others, and criteria for determining competence must be agreed upon.

## NOTIFICATION OF EVALUATION

Faculty need to be notified at least a year prior to being evaluated, and they should know the criteria upon which they will be evaluated. Frequently, faculty are evaluated based on the year they were hired. In some institutions, faculty are evaluated on a rotating basis so that all faculty are not evaluated in the same year; in other institutions, every faculty member is evaluated every year.

## CRITERIA FOR DETERMINING COMPETENCE

Most institutions have their own guidelines for determining competence, and these are to be followed in evaluating faculty members. The standards should be clearly articulated, and they should be applied consistently with all faculty. Faculty should be evaluated based on their job descriptions and on whether they attained the specified levels of competence.

Faculty workload is also a consideration in the evaluation process. Percentage of importance can be assigned to the various activities in which faculty participate. For example, faculty who are teaching in distributed programs may be spending more time putting their courses online than faculty who teach in traditional institutions spend preparing to teach a class. This should be taken into consideration when assessing faculty workload. In addition, the time that faculty members spend learning the technology to put their courses online should be noted.

Adjunct faculty members are generally evaluated on criteria that are different from the criteria by which full-time faculty members are judged. They also usually have different evaluation processes from full-time faculty. For example, in some institutions, adjunct faculty are evaluated by a dean, rather than by a committee.

## INTERACTIONS WITH STUDENTS

Because faculty who are associated with distributed learning communities cannot be judged by their teaching abilities in the classrooms, other criteria may apply, such as their relationship with students, their ability to communicate effectively, and their ability to encourage students at all levels. As a result, student evaluations will not focus on the faculty's classroom presentations, but rather on the personal relationships that the faculty has formed with them.

## SCHOLARLY OUTPUT

In distributed learning organizations, the emphasis on scholarly output—"publish or perish"—often does not hold quite the importance that it does in traditional institutions. Typically, other forms of output are honored, such as service to the community, consulting work with organizations, presentations at national conferences, training, certifications, and engaging in social change projects. Service to students is generally weighted as being more important than scholarly output, although some scholarly output is expected. It is important for faculty teaching in distributed institutions to find out just what is expected in the way of publishing.

## SERVICE

Faculty can also be evaluated based on their service to the institution. Ways of serving the institution include serving on committees and task forces, revising learning guides, serving on or chairing governance committees, volunteering for special tasks, and performing other duties within the institution. Being willing to take notes and do other less desirable things can gain favor in the eyes of other faculty members. Rather than meeting face-to-face, meetings are generally held in conference calls.

Service to the larger community is also important and takes various forms, including serving on boards, making speeches, and volunteering. It can also involve serving professional organizations locally, regionally, nationally, and internationally.

## UNWRITTEN EXPECTATIONS

In addition to the written expectations, faculty members would be wise to inquire about the unwritten expectations by which they will be judged. They can do so by talking with more experienced faculty members, the department chairperson, and the dean. Reading the portfolios or dossiers of other faculty members who have either received satisfactory evaluations or been denied them can also be helpful, if they are available.

In addition, an often unspoken criterion for evaluation involves being compatible with other faculty members. Faculty tend not to want to work with people who continually raise objections and cause conflicts.

## OBTAINING FEEDBACK

### Peer Feedback

An important part of faculty evaluation in distributed learning communities is obtaining feedback from colleagues about the faculty members who are being evaluated. Faculty being evaluated can be asked for the names of peers from whom they would like to receive feedback. In some institutions, all faculty are asked to give feedback.

The feedback should be focused on the faculty member's job description and can be requested in narrative form, in the form of a checklist, or a combination of both. In distributed learning communities, peer feedback might be more difficult to give than when faculty are located in adjacent offices and interact with each other daily. Still, many faculty in distributed learning communities are in daily contact with each other via phone and e-mail, and they often work closely with each other on student work. They are also aware of what the students with whom they are in contact say about other faculty members.

### Student Feedback

Student feedback is critical in contributing to faculty evaluations. By putting their names on the forms, students will be more responsible for their comments. Names can be removed before the faculty member reads them, if desired.

A narrative form is preferred over a checklist to encourage students to engage in reflective thought. The result is far richer than if students are merely asked to use a Likert-type scale to check off their impressions of a faculty member. On the other hand, checklists require less time to complete, so a higher rate of return may be obtained.

Numerous reasons exist as to why students may give positive or negative evaluations of faculty, including amount of homework, sense of humor, ease of tests, relationship with faculty, responsiveness of faculty, effectiveness of teaching, grade leniency, level of the course, and faculty enthusiasm, among other variables. Student evaluations should not be the only source of evaluation for faculty members.

Perhaps the most efficient way to gather student feedback on faculty members is for the evaluation forms to be sent out electronically, accompanied by a letter from the dean. By giving students a deadline, along with adequate time to complete the evaluations and a follow-up e-mail, higher response rates are ensured.

The timing for asking for student input is important. It must be after the student has received a grade from the faculty member to eliminate the possibility of retaliation on the part of the faculty member. If students are asked to provide input immediately after they have completed the course, their input might be skewed. Some time should be allowed to elapse between the time that students complete the course and when they are asked to provide input. Still, if too much time elapses, students might move away or forget about what the faculty did.

Sensitivity to times of the year is also important when asking for student input. Holiday seasons can be especially hectic, and many people are on vacation during the summer. It is a good idea to check with the population being served in order to determine the times of the year that will result in the best response rate.

### Staff Feedback

It is also advisable to obtain input from staff members with whom the faculty member works. Staff are in a position to evaluate timeliness, interaction skills, and other aspects of a faculty member's performance that may not be as evident to students and peers.

### External Feedback

Evaluation from peers outside of the institution can also be sought to determine evidence of scholarly output and contributions to the field. Faculty can request input from co-authors, publishers, colleagues in organizations, and others who are in a position to assess their professional competence.

## CREATING A PORTFOLIO

The portfolio can include a variety of artifacts that provide the faculty member being evaluated with information upon which to engage in substantive self-evaluation. The portfolio can include items such as feedback from other faculty members, feedback from students, feedback from professional colleagues outside the institution, feedback from staff, papers that the faculty member has written, and presentations that the faculty member has made. Unless a specific order of materials has been specified, it is beneficial to put the most positive comments in the beginning.

The faculty member being evaluated can then write a summary of the contents of the portfolio, including a discussion of scholarly work and service, both to the institution and outside of the institution; a discussion of how he or she meets (or does not meet) the criteria; a summary of the feedback given by faculty peers, staff, external evaluators, and students; and an in-depth reflection on the feedback received, along with identification of strengths and areas for growth. Goals for professional growth should also be included.

## THE EVALUATION MEETING

It is generally advisable to have the evaluation meeting at a time when the evaluation committee can meet face-to-face. Distributed learning institutions often have yearly meetings during which time they can schedule the evaluation sessions. If meetings are not possible, then technology can be used.

Institutions have different configurations of people who attend the meeting. One option is to have the faculty member being evaluated choose several colleagues and staff members to attend the meeting, along with one or more students. Other options are for the dean to choose the evaluation team, or for the dean to choose the team in consultation with the faculty member being evaluated. Still other institutions have a team that conducts all faculty evaluations. Smaller groups of people tend to be more intimate than large groups with implications for the meaning of the conversations.

The presence of students can add a great deal to the meeting or detract from it, depending on the faculty's level of trust. The students must attend with positive intentions and with the attitude of contributing to the process. Still, the faculty members may feel inhibited in addressing important issues because of the presence of the students.

The faculty being evaluated should first have the opportunity to present the portfolio and discuss it. After that, the participants can engage in dialogue and ask questions of the faculty, as appropriate. The faculty member can talk about strengths, possible areas for growth, and professional growth goals. The meeting can end with the faculty member summarizing the meeting and determining next steps.

## AFTER THE EVALUATION MEETING

Regardless of who attends the evaluation meeting and the input from students and colleagues, the final decision as to whether a faculty member is offered a continuing contract rests with the dean of the institution. Either the dean can write the narrative evaluation summary or the committee that evaluated the faculty can write it collaboratively.

As a result of the evaluation process, the faculty member either will receive a contract, will be given a provisional contract while being asked to correct certain deficiencies, or will be terminated. Faculty can receive ratings of "Outstanding," "Satisfactory," "Acceptable (changes are needed)," or "Unsatisfactory." Some institutions may wish to have only two categories: "Satisfactory" and "Unsatisfactory." If the faculty needs to make certain improvements before being offered a long-term contract, a 1-year provisional contract can be issued. At the end of that period of time, the dean, in consultation with the committee, can make the decision as to whether to offer a continuing contract or to terminate the faculty member. The faculty member being terminated should be treated with respect, compassion, and professionalism. Assistance in making the transition to another position should be offered.

A faculty appeals procedure needs to be in place for faculty who do not agree with the outcome of their evaluations. Typically, timelines are set, and a certain order of appeal is put in place. For example, the faculty can first appeal to the provost, and then to the president. In all cases, the appeal needs to be in writing, with the faculty member stating the reasons for the appeal.

## OUTCOMES FOR FACULTY

Numerous benefits to faculty can result from the evaluation process. The whole process provides faculty members with the opportunity to obtain feedback about their work, reflect on it, and set goals for growing professionally. This should result in their becoming rejuvenated and even more excited about their careers. On the other hand, the evaluation process can evoke strong emotions in faculty members, resulting in their being discouraged. Evaluations should be substantive, honest, and done with compassion.

## EVALUATION OF THE PROCESS

After each round of evaluations, it is helpful to have the faculty who went through the evaluation process evaluate the process, dialoguing with each other about what was helpful to them and what changes should be made. By inviting faculty members to provide feedback about the process, institutions can ensure continuous improvement in the evaluation process from year to year. Evaluation by the faculty a year after they have been evaluated can also prove to be helpful. They can discuss how the process affected their morale, their performance, and the larger community culture.

## CONCLUSION

The faculty evaluation process in distributed learning institutions can differ from evaluation in traditional institutions. Fortunately, faculty can be involved in creating a process that results in positive outcomes for them, their students, and their institutions.

—*Jenny Edwards*

***See also*** FACULTY DEVELOPMENT, SELECTION, AND TRAINING: FACULTY POLICIES; FEEDBACK; TEACHING IN AN ELECTRONIC CLASSROOM

### Bibliography

American Council on Education, The American Association of University Professors, & United Educators Insurance. (2000). *Good practice in tenure evaluation: Advice for tenured faculty, department chairs, and academic administrators.* Washington, DC: American Council on Education.

Arreola, R. A. (2000). *Developing a comprehensive faculty evaluation system: A handbook for college faculty and administrators on designing and operating a comprehensive faculty evaluation system* (2nd ed.). Bolton, MA: Anker.

Braskamp, L. A., & Ory, J. C. (1994). *Assessing faculty work: Enhancing individual and institutional performance.* San Francisco: Jossey-Bass.

Centra, J. A. (1993). *Reflective faculty evaluation: Enhancing teaching and determining faculty effectiveness.* San Francisco: Jossey-Bass.

Murray, J. P. (1997). *Successful faculty development and evaluation: The complete teaching portfolio. ASHE-ERIC Higher Education Report No. 8.* New York: John Wiley & Sons.

Redmon, K. D. (1999). ERIC review faculty evaluation: A response to competing values. *Community College Review, 27*(1), 57–71.

# FACULTY POLICIES

Faculty policies serve as guides to appropriate teaching and administrative policies and procedures practiced at learning institutions. These policies provide important information and boundaries for appropriate instructor behaviors and actions in the classroom. Policies may differ greatly from institution to institution. Although many of an institution's faculty policies may accommodate differences in traditional and distributed learning environments, education delivered via modes of distributed learning warrant additional policies to encompass the differences in distance-delivered education.

Faculty policies answer commonly asked questions often posed by new faculty members regarding compensation, grading, issue resolution, and other important facts and information. Often written policies are provided as a part of a faculty handbook distributed to new instructors to provide answers to questions an instructor may have. Thorough faculty policy handbooks provide instructors with a reference that clearly defines the boundaries within which the instructor will be expected to perform. Faculty policies that are a condition of employment may be included in the instructor's teaching contract. Institutions may request that a new faculty member sign an agreement of understanding prior to hire.

## INSTITUTIONAL POLICIES AND PROCEDURES

Institutions providing traditional classroom education generally provide a faculty policy handbook that covers all of the issues that might normally arise as the instructors perform their duties as a part of that particular institution. These policies cover workplace issues that are a normal part of the traditional mode of delivery. Some of the common topics in the handbook are classroom instruction policies, library support, administrative support, grading policies, compensation procedures, definitions of faculty status, forms and notifications, merit salary, promotion, and tenure, if offered.

Faculty policy handbooks offer guidance for a number of important informational items. Many institutions publish a mission statement or guiding principles that set expectations for all employees as a part of a larger community. The mission statement may also have implications for faculty performance and can provide guidelines for appropriate behavior. Other general information such as an administrative organizational chart, contact information, and a school calendar detailing standard holidays, length of semester or term, and religious occasion observation are necessary for faculty planning.

Faculty policies may also encompass less common and unforeseen personnel issues in addition to policies that are mandated by governmental regulations and law. Leaves of absence, definitions and reporting of sexual harassment, removal of a faculty member, or change of title or status are all important to document in a faculty policy handbook. Review processes and contact information are also often covered under faculty policies.

Institutions whose faculty members are organized by a union typically have strict guidelines for institution action and faculty member activity. Clearly stated and published faculty policies and procedures that have been agreed upon through the bargaining process are often a part of the faculty member's contract. Institutions whose faculty members are not a part of a union may or may not solicit a faculty governance group to assist in the creation of faculty policies. Accreditation organizations look favorably on institutions that utilize faculty governance and participation in such efforts.

## FACULTY STATUS AND PERSONNEL INFORMATION

Appointment of new faculty requires adherence to strict federal and often state regulatory guidelines. Forms for compliance, such as employment applications, governmental tax and identification, benefits, and other necessary paperwork are explained and included. Minimum qualifications for faculty status are often published, including definitions and general institutional and regulatory guidelines.

Some of the regulatory information commonly found in faculty handbooks relates to equal opportunity, diversity, sexual harassment, and associated policies. These provisions are mandated by the U.S. government for all employees. Institutions may have a stated diversity policy that reflects adherence to federal law. Institutions must publish their procedure for reporting sexual harassment as a part of the Title VII code. Additionally, grievances against the institution or its employees typically follow a process for reporting. Other personnel policies may also be published, including appropriate faculty–student relationships and appropriate behavior inside and outside of the classroom.

Faculty meetings/administrative function attendance, the nature of committee participation, and additional administrative functions are other areas of concern for institutions and faculty.

Evaluation, with resulting compensation, is perhaps one of the most important concerns for new faculty. The method for determining compensation for teaching salaries, additional stipends, and merit increases should be stated. Publishing payment schedules and discrepancy reporting reduces misunderstandings. The evaluation process may involve a range of activities including formal student classroom evaluations, surveys, peer evaluations, and manager evaluations. This process needs to be clearly communicated.

Length of service, and how the institution calculates it, can be complex, especially for adjunct faculty. Formulas for calculation need to be communicated. Normal teaching and administrative load information is critical to accurate pay considerations. Overload teaching and administration schedules should be published.

A sabbatical leave of absence is time granted to a faculty member, usually with pay, to pursue educational research activities. Sabbaticals usually excuse the instructor from teaching and administrative responsibilities for the time period allowed for the sabbatical. It is important to publish the rules governing sabbaticals.

Explanation for the process for receiving merit increases, or pay raises based on achievement and performance, is commonly published. The policy on an institution's renewal of faculty contracts should be available and publicly stated prior to performance reviews. The schedule for receiving tenure and the criteria for tenure and promotion should also be provided. Other monetary considerations include reimbursement for expenses. Two major areas that faculty encounter are expenses related to travel and supplies. Each institution must consider which expenses it will be responsible for and communicate that policy in advance.

Mileage rates are often dictated by the amount the state government will allow. When mileage will be compensated, the qualifying criteria for need to be clarified in advance. How to order supplies and what will be subject to compensation, as well as the process for reimbursement, and the receipt policy, should also be stated.

Many institutions publish policies on outside employment, consulting, and on-campus extra compensation. If the institution allows these types of activities, it is good to identify circumstances under which they are allowable, as well as the relevant limitations. Conflict of interest is becoming increasingly important as higher education has become more competitive. A policy describing what constitutes conflict of interest in outside employment and consulting needs to be communicated. Rules regarding grant application and funding are also appropriately published in a faculty policy handbook to ensure compliance with institutional policy and government guidelines.

Faculty are typically granted regular, visiting, lecturer, or adjunct status. Regular instructors often have privileges and responsibilities associated with that status. Rules governing regular status should be defined in order to be in compliance with employment law and to provide appropriate expectations for newly hired faculty members. There may also be two regular faculty tracks, tenure and nontenure. Tenure is a status granted to regular tenure-track faculty who have met institutional requirements for such status. It usually involves a combination of research, publishing, service, and teaching excellence within a specified time period.

Institutions may offer regular faculty members the option of performing on a non–tenure-track basis. This status often lacks the prestige of the tenure-track faculty positions. Visiting professor and lecturer status are usually assigned to full-time instructors with a limited contract period. Tenure is typically not associated with

this arrangement. Part-time or adjunct faculty status may provide fewer benefits and job security than regular status. Service, research, publishing, and other institutional requirements for these positions may not be as strict as those for regular faculty positions.

## INSTRUCTIONAL DELIVERY POLICIES AND PROCEDURES

Many policies need to be communicated to guide the faculty member in creating instructional materials and conducting the class appropriately. The requirements for spending time on campus may differ greatly from institution to institution. Some simply require the instructor to show up for classes and office hours. Others require faculty to be on campus a minimum number of hours per week and to participate in activities outside the classroom.

Each credit hour typically translates into time in the classroom. This information needs to be communicated to the faculty member and to students. Office hours are usually additional to classroom teaching requirements. Each institution has a formula or policy for assignment of faculty availability for students in the form of office hours.

Grading system policies, including grade reporting, grade posting and appeals, record maintenance, auditing, and the method of alerting students of grades earned, are typically described in the policy handbook. Student classroom attendance record keeping may be controlled by the institution because financial aid recipients may need their presence in the class documented. The Drop/Add policy and the related forms may appear in a student handbook or catalog; however, faculty need guidance regarding process, dates, and forms.

Student privacy policies are becoming more commonplace. Maintaining student privacy is an important part of an institution's charge. The government enforces privacy laws, so these laws need to be communicated to faculty. Release of student information is typically decided at the institutional level in conjunction with governmental requirements. In some cases, student notification may be required when information is requested by outside parties.

Guidelines for syllabus construction may or may not be included in a faculty handbook. Often, if a template is used, or if mandatory institutional policy information is required as a part of the syllabus, it is noted in the handbook. Timetables and guidelines for submitting and posting the syllabus for a course can be communicated. Institutions may have a policy regarding instructor changes to a syllabus once the students have received it for a class. For some institutions, it is considered a contract and may not be changed easily once the semester is underway. For others, the faculty member has full authority over any and all changes made. In either case, the policy must be made clear.

Legal issues involving use of copyrighted materials in the classroom should be outlined as policy. Institutions may want to publish the legal requirements and enforcement policies regarding photocopying. As publishers change editions of textbooks, the institution should publish the procedure for ordering new editions. The availability and process for obtaining desk copies of textbooks may be described.

Policy on testing, including the types of tests, the timing of tests, proctoring, automated grading, test banks, and the like are covered in this area of the handbook. Academic misconduct (plagiarism/cheating) is an important topic to clarify for faculty and students.

Other classroom-related policies are final exam regulations and information concerning mandatory or optional testing periods; field study and the appropriateness of outside classroom experiences; and guest speakers, criteria, and stipends for speaking.

Faculty should be familiar with services that the institution provides students. Academic counseling, special needs assistance, tutoring, career counseling, and the referral process should be communicated to faculty, and the policies for their use described.

## INSTRUCTIONAL SUPPORT SERVICES

Faculty members may receive administrative support from the institution's staff. The more commonly offered support areas are described in this section of a handbook. Equipment and supplies ordering and use, including such things as overhead projectors, video projectors, computers, and other audio-visual support equipment policies, should be covered. The process for ordering such equipment, contact information for delivery, assistance in usage, and other important information should be readily available to faculty members.

The lead time and personnel, necessary for reproducing materials for faculty are an often overlooked area of importance to the instructor. Assignment of classroom space may be subject to policices regarding

size of room or nature of the course. Proctoring services may be subject to a policy governing the use of proctors to administer exams. If the institution has a policy for giving out faculty contact information, it nccds to bc communicated.

## FACULTY WORK-RELATED REGULATIONS AND GUIDELINES

Several areas need to be considered as policies are developed covering a variety of faculty involvement issues. Research institutions typically have strict guidelines for engaging in research. The process, committee contact information, and rules governing research, especially involving human subjects, should be covered.

Copyrightable materials and intellectual property rights are very critical issues today. Inventions and innovations that the faculty member and/or the institution may hold claim to are typically outlined by institutional guidelines.

Storing and retrieving data on institutional equipment is becoming an important issue for faculty and institutions. If faculty increasingly use institutional computers for such purpose, policies regarding the nature of information that may be stored need to be clearly communicated.

## ADDITIONAL CONSIDERATIONS FOR DISTANCE LEARNING

Communication of written faculty policies is critical, in situations where an instructor is not physically teaching on campus. In addition to many of the faculty policies already described, institutions engaging in distributed learning must consider policies specific to distance learning. An institution must make several major considerations, especially when instructors and students are not meeting face-to-face in the traditional classroom.

One of the major considerations, particularly for Internet-delivered education, is policy involving course development and ownership. This issue continues to be debated across the country as instructors are asked to develop an online version of their classroom course. Often the instructor develops the course based on lecture notes and materials he or she considers proprietary. Institutions increasingly are forming and communicating policies that designate the rules for ownership of distributed learning course materials.

Some institutions have the instructor sign an agreement designating ownership of the course to the institution. Others grant ownership to the developer. In the absence of a policy, institutions and instructors are settling disagreements in the courts.

Another consideration is fair use of copyrighted materials. This may warrant separate discussion for distance learning instructors. One area of concern is using Internet links in the online course. Often links may not be used without prior approval. The process for gaining this approval must be stated. Information published at Web sites may or may not be copied and used in the online classroom. This is another area that institutions need to monitor and for which they need to provide guidance.

An important policy area that is specific to distributed learning is faculty–student communication. Without "seat-time"—the gauge of appropriate time the instructor and the students spend together in order to sanction that learning requirements are met—alternative structures must be established that guide the instructor's lectures, assignments, and communication with students. This may be in the form of a minimum number of contacts per week or per semester, actual time spent on the course, or number of contacts per course per semester. Related to this is the faculty-to-student ratio in the online virtual classroom. The number of students allowed in an online class, for example, is related to many of the other faculty policies like pay and involvement in other institutional activities. It may also be a reflection on the quality of the institution's distributed learning program.

Technology requirements must also be a consideration for most distributed learning models. Courses taught using the Internet as a mode of delivery require basic computer skills and knowledge. They also require possession of minimum computer hardware and software at the location where the course will be taught. What electronic resources the institution will provide needs to be communicated, and instructions for access must be offered. All of the rules and regulations warranted by the institution and its accrediting organization(s) in order to teach at a distance also need to be disseminated.

Many of the traditional means for providing student services and instructor referral procedures are less appropriate for students who may never see their instructor or visit the campus. Additional faculty policy considerations need to be identified and addressed, especially if the services are not the same as those offered on-campus for instructors teaching in the traditional classroom.

Distributed learning is not new, but more contemporary forms of distributed learning like Internet-based courses may warrant policy revisions and additions to reflect the changing nature of course delivery in higher education. Forward-thinking institutions are revising many faculty policies to reflect the changing nature of educational delivery and trends in learning. The increased use of technology-driven education heightens the importance of creating faculty policies for distance learning to ensure accurate communication and application of institutional policies and procedures.

—*Deborah Snyder*

**See also** FACULTY DEVELOPMENT, SELECTION, AND TRAINING; FACULTY EVALUATION

## Bibliography

American Council on Education: http://www.acenet.edu/washington/distance_ed/2000/03march/distance_ed.html

DePaul University: https://dlweb.cti.depaul.edu/info/login/dlPolicy.htm

Indiana Higher Education Telecommunication System: http://www.ihets.org/learntech/facprinc.html

NCA Guidelines for Distance Education: http://www.ncahigherlearningcommission.org/resources/guidelines/gdistance.html

Oregon Network for Education. Distance Learning: http://oregonone.org/DEpolicy.htm

Southern Region Education Board: http://www.electronic-campus.org/policylab/docs/Issues/faculty.asp

The University of North Alabama: http://distance.una.edu/policies/

Western Interstate Commission for Higher Education: http://www.wiche.edu/Resources/links.htm

# FEDERAL LAWS

Federal laws are those rules and principles governing the affairs of the country and enforced by the legal system. In regards to distributed education, the federal government has passed limited legislation. The government prefers to defer this responsibility to the states and accrediting bodies. Exceptions lie in specific subjects for which the federal government has passed or is currently considering legislation that affects distributed education: accessibility for the disabled, copyright law, financial aid, intellectual property, and Web site protection.

## AMERICANS WITH DISABILITIES ACT (ADA)

The Americans with Disabilities Act (1990) is a section of civil-rights law that forbids discrimination of various sorts against persons with physical or mental handicaps. Section 508 (1998) requires that federal agencies' electronic and information technology be accessible to people with disabilities. Public education institutions are subject to this law, requiring that online courses are accessible to those with visual and other disabilities.

Accessible Web sites should meet the following guidelines:

- A text equivalent should be included for every nontext element (i.e., pictures, graphs, charts, diagrams).
- Equivalent alternatives for any multimedia presentation should be synchronized with the presentation.
- All information available in color should also be available without color.
- Documents should be organized so that they are readable without requiring an associated style sheet.
- Redundant text links should be provided for each active region (e.g., Mailbox icon vs. Click here to send mail).
- Row and column headers should be identified for data tables.
- Cells should be identified by row and column headers.
- Frames should be titled with text that facilitates frame identification and navigation.
- Pages should be designed to avoid screen flickering with a frequency greater than 2 Hz and lower than 55 Hz.
- A text-only page with equivalent information or functionality should be provided if compliance cannot be accomplished in another way.
- If scripting languages are used to display content (e.g., rolling banners, flashing messages), descriptive text should be included.
- When a Web page requires another application to be present to interpret page content (e.g., video or music software), a link to that software should be provided.

- When electronic forms are designed to be completed online, the form should include written directions and cues.
- A method should be provided that permits users to skip repetitive navigation links.
- If a timed response is required, the user should be alerted and given sufficient time to indicate that more time is required.

## COPYRIGHT LAW

A copyright gives the holder the sole right to reproduce or grant permission to others to reproduce the copyrighted works. It is the expression of the idea that is copyrighted, not the idea itself.

The Copyright Law of 1976 allows the copyright holder to reproduce the copyrighted work in any format and to prepare derivative works; to distribute copies of the copyrighted work to the public by sale, rent, lease, or gift; to perform the copyrighted work publicly; and to display the copyrighted work publicly.

The privilege of fair use allows copyrighted materials to be used without the express permission of the copyright holder under specific conditions. If the purpose and character of the use is educational or nonprofit; if an excerpt or a noncritical portion of the original work is being used; if the marketability of the work is not impaired; if the work is a performance; and if the work is being used within a class, then it is a regular part of systematic instructional activity related to the teaching content.

A noncritical portion of the work is defined as a complete article or story that contains less than 2,500 words; 1,000 words or 10% (whichever is shorter) of excerpted articles or stories; and one illustration, chart, diagram, or picture per work. The material can be used only for one course, with no more than two works from one author. Copied material must show the original copyright notice from the work.

Marketability of a work on a Web site can be affected if a site provides advertising or if the Web site holder can gain profit from the visit to the Web page. In this case, the content of the Web page, under the guiding principle of fair use, may be used only once in a classroom situation.

The Technology, Education, and Copyright Harmonization (TEACH) Act (2002) rectified the problem of using online video clips. TEACH allows Web sites to host video clips and other copyrighted items that are used in classroom, provided access is limited to students within the course.

## FINANCIAL AID

Financial aid is used by the federal government to assist students in obtaining higher education via grants, loans, and scholarships. Historically, financial aid was only for full-time students, which was defined by the federal government as those students taking 12 or more class credits at an institution of higher education. The government had also limited federal aid to those institutions where students were present in the classroom for more than 50% of the time.

The purpose of the Internet Equity and Education Act (2001, H.R. 1992, S. 1445) was to exempt courses offered through telecommunications from certain limitations on student financial assistance relevant to correspondence courses. These exemptions are allowed if the institution already offers the course through telecommunications and participates in the student loan program, and the student loan default rate for the institution is less than 10% for the past 3 years. The act also eliminates the requirement, for financial aid purposes, that students be registered for at least 12 hours of instruction a week to be considered full-time.

Another issue concerning federal financial aid is that such funds include a reasonable allowance in the student's cost of attendance. The documented rental or purchase of a personal computer is not allowed as a reasonable cost of student attendance according to Title IV of Federal Code, Section 471.

## INTELLECTUAL PROPERTY

According to copyright law, when someone is employed to do a specific task and/or receives compensation (such as reassigned time or a stipend), institutional support is provided (such as an office or computer), and when work is done in an office or lab owned by the school, then the work is owned by the school. Based on cases under the 1909 Copyright Act, faculty own their own intellectual property. This is a tradition or practice, and not a legal requirement. In regard to course materials, faculty can change them, distribute them, and use them at another institution without the expressed written consent of their employer. Associate faculty, who under copyright law are considered employees under contract, own their own work

and can legally change it, distribute it, and use it at another institution.

In distributed education, many higher education administrators are realizing that material used for online courses can be easily distributed and reused at other institutions. Institutions may consider these courses "marketable" and look at the work done by the instructor as a way of providing income to the institution. Because the institution legally owns this material according to current copyright legislation, faculty may no longer be able to change, distribute, and use their own professional work at another institution. The institution, by default, has rights to the work, so faculty should be sure that they have established, in writing, an arrangement with their employer as to who owns the work being used in an online course.

## WEB SITE PROTECTION

The School Website Protection Act (2001, S. 1252), proposes to amend Title 18, U.S. Code, to make it unlawful to tamper with computers of schools and institutions of higher education. This includes software such as programs, as well as Web site code.

## CONCLUSION

Those laws cited in this entry with bill numbers were well on their way to being made into federal law, until September 11, 2001. Unfortunately, the events of that day forced the legislators to make these bills a lower priority, and the legislative bodies are slowly reconsidering them. Passage of these bills will take students who learn via distributed learning a long way toward receiving an education equivalent to on-campus students.

*—Suzanne Levy*

***See also*** ACCREDITATION; DISABILITY LAW; FINANCIAL AID; INTELLECTUAL PROPERTY; LEGAL ISSUES

### Bibliography

Gasaway, L. N. (2002). Drafting a faculty copyright ownership policy. *The Technology Source, 2.* Retrieved March 11, 2002, from http://ts.mivu.org/default.asp?show=article&id = 982.

Janes, S. S. (1988). Administrative practice: A day-to-day guide to legal requirements. In M. J. Barr (Ed.), *Student services and the law: A handbook for practitioners* (pp. 129–151). San Francisco: Jossey-Bass.

Primo, L. H., & Lesage, T. (2001). Survey of intellectual property issues for distance learning and online educators. *Education at a Distance, 15*(20). Retrieved June 9, 2001, from http://www.usdla.org/ED_magazine/illuminactive/FEB01_Issue/article03.html.

Simpson, C. (2001). Copyright 101. *Educational Leadership, 59*(4), 36–38.

Young, J. R. (2001). Law student warns that professors' quest for rights to lectures could backfire. *The Chronicle of Higher Education.* Retrieved November 6, 2001, from http://www.chronicle.com/cgi2-bin/printable.cgi.

# FEEDBACK

Feedback in the sense of a written or spoken response postdates the electrical meaning of the word by about 20 years. Like the sound created when a microphone is accidentally carried in front of a speaker, academic feedback can loop back and forth. It can also grow, as an observation broadens into dialogue.

The optimal aim of effective feedback is to enhance the capacity for self-reflection and self-correction on the part of the recipient. Whether given by the facilitator or the learner, the primary goal is the same: to help the recipient to focus honestly and positively on the opportunities for improvement and development in his or her own work. Sensitively delivered, feedback also offers reassurance and encouragement, and is an essential element in the building of an academic relationship.

## WHO GIVES IT

As in more traditional educational forums, the most common type of feedback in a distance learning environment is initiated by the facilitator. The learner acquires a sense of his or her progress through the course from the facilitator's comments. In most adult learning environments, learners also are expected to comment on the effectiveness of the facilitator and on the qualities of the courses and programs. A third type of feedback, less often required or encouraged, involves learners assessing each other's work. This process is highly motivating, tends to engage the learners more fully in the educational process, and is a valuable learning experience in itself.

## QUANTITY AND TIMING

The efficacy of feedback depends not only on content, but also on quantity and timing. Too much feedback from the facilitator tends to dampen the learner's creative energy and intellectual enthusiasm. Too little leaves the learner feeling isolated and insecure about his or her performance. Judging the right amount depends on the nature of the assignment, the styles of both the learner and the facilitator, and an intuitive sense on the part of the facilitator of what will motivate, challenge, and inspire an individual.

The casual day-to-day exchanges that characterize the traditional face-to-face learning environment are not possible in a distance learning environment. In such a context, feedback becomes, by necessity, the primary mode of communication between facilitator and learner. In circumstances in which silence is experienced as absence, timeliness of feedback is crucial. Furthermore, thoughtful feedback skilfully delivered can turn what would otherwise be a drawback into an advantage. The following are some tips for giving effective feedback:

- Begin with a positive message and use motivating language. Good feedback often sounds like a cross between a critical assessment and a pep talk.
- Deliver clear and specific messages. Simply praising a piece of work ("This is excellent") without identifying its specific qualities may provide an emotional high, but will leave the learner feeling intellectually hungry.
- Make the feedback personal. Whenever possible, begin by addressing the recipient directly. Put remarks in a broader context by referring to previous work, or to the recipient's other skills.
- Relate comments to the criteria for good academic work established for the course or the program.
- Relate the learner's work to theoretical assumptions, case studies, outside references, or other sources of information.

## MEANS OF DELIVERY

Of the various media through which feedback might be delivered, three can be briefly assessed. Snail mail is arguably the most private, but undoubtedly the slowest. A fax can be delivered quickly, but only to a house or office with a fax machine, and then anyone can read it. The advantages of e-mail for transmitting messages and additional text, which can then be manipulated, stored, and printed, are widely understood. For good or ill, an e-mail address is rapidly becoming an essential qualification for full membership in modern society, and has already become a requirement of contemporary academic life.

A fourth medium, the face-to-face conference, remains an optional element in the context of distance learning, but its occasional nature gives it a more intense significance. The participants at such a meeting, whether they are expecting to deliver or receive feedback, will be more conscious of the necessity to prepare their comments and questions and to take thorough notes.

The most exciting contemporary development, a new fifth medium, is the Web-based online dialogue, which offers opportunities for ongoing feedback among a group of co-learners, between the facilitator and an individual, or between the facilitator and the group. The opportunities for modeling effective styles of feedback within the private space of the virtual classroom and for enriching multiple relationships of learning are unprecedented.

## LEARNER-TO-LEARNER FEEDBACK

Depending on the aim of a particular course, learner-to-learner feedback can be encouraged or required. It can involve one-to-one communication or, in its more sophisticated forms, collective dialogue. Learner-to-learner feedback can achieve several significant outcomes associated with adult learning and collaborative work. Such feedback

- Sharpens the learner's ability to think critically
- Increases the capacity to assess and contain multiple viewpoints
- Encourages the learner to reflect on his or her own assumptions in light of conflicting points of view
- Provides a specific kind of intellectual support that can be surprisingly intimate
- Develops the learner's capacity to deliver thoughtful feedback to colleagues in professional and other working environments

## FEEDBACK IN DIALOGUE-BASED ONLINE LEARNING

Where online learning is dialogue-based and collaborative, it is likely that learners will be required to provide feedback on each other's work, and that their feedback and the feedback of the facilitator will be available to the group. The individuals engaged in online learning may not know each other well, or at all. They might never have met outside the virtual classroom. In this situation, the quality of the feedback and the thoughtfulness and sensitivity with which it is delivered will have a major impact on the progress of the course.

While being answerable as always for the quality of their own work, the online learners carry an additional responsibility for the progress of the group and the other individuals within it. The online facilitator, in addition to challenging and motivating the learners individually and collectively, needs to hold the boundaries of the online environment, so that learners feel safe exploring intellectual ideas and sharing personal responses. A specific piece of feedback by the facilitator might serve three purposes in this context. In addition to its explicit purpose, it will serve as a model of appropriate feedback to the whole group. It might also be required to complement the comments of other learners, counterbalancing feedback less skilfully expressed.

*—Leni Wildflower*

***See also*** CRITICAL DIALOGUES; GROUP PROCESS; TEACHING IN AN ELECTRONIC CLASSROOM

## Bibliography

Brinko, K. T. (1993). The practice of giving feedback to improve teaching. *Journal of Higher Education, 64*(5), 575–594.

Hudson, B. (2002). Critical dialogue online: Personas, covenants, and candlepower. In K. Rudestam & J. Schoenholtz-Read (Eds.), *Handbook of online learning.* Thousand Oaks, CA: Sage.

Palmer, P. (1998). *The courage to teach: Exploring the inner landscape of a teacher's life.* San Francisco: Jossey-Bass.

# FINANCE

Those who would calculate the cost of distributive learning begin with two strikes against them. First, very little is actually known about the costs of delivering *nondistributive* learning. Historically, postsecondary education has shied away from identifying the specific costs attributable to the delivery of a single course or curriculum. Faculty do much more than teach, facilities have multiple purposes, and there are no clear rules for factoring in the costs of the co-curriculum (e.g., student services and athletics). Furthermore, institutional overhead remains a mystery best left to federal auditors and institutional accountants. The result is that no one can say with any certainty just what teaching and learning cost, other than to acknowledge that such activities are becoming more expensive.

Second, distributed learning is turning out to be a much different kind of economic enterprise than was first imagined. Initially, it was viewed as an educational business that would be characterized by rapid growth, robust revenue streams, and a customer base largely outside the confines of traditional higher education. What most institutions and providers who invested in distributive learning enterprises ultimately discovered, however, was just how difficult it was for programs to generate either additional revenues or new enrollments.

Two models have dominated early discussions of the financing of distributed learning. The first model assumed that distributed learning enterprises would be separate businesses—separately financed and independently chartered as stand-alone for-profit entities, as self-contained units within established institutions, or as joint ventures linking distributed learning programs that combine offerings from several institutions. The funds needed to launch these businesses would be supplied as venture capital, often by the sponsoring institution or institutions. In its most developed form, this model became something of a hybrid, with a for-profit aggregator drawing on courses and programs designed and delivered by a limited number of selective institutions. Cardean University, UNEXT's principal educational outlet, was the best known of these ventures, if for no other reason than that it combined educational programs leading to the MBA supplied by Columbia, Stanford, the University of Chicago, Carnegie Mellon, and the London School of Economics.

By 2002, however, the educational landscape was littered with the remains of independent distributed learning enterprises that could not sustain themselves financially. The for-profit ventures, despite being remarkably well funded, never developed a viable market. Projects either mounted by or drawing together some of the world's most prestigious universities fared no better, having failed to generate

sufficient demand to justify their pricey tuitions. What all these enterprises quickly discovered was that online education, the dominant form of distributed learning, was economically tough territory. In almost every case the problem was the same: high start-up costs, modest revenues at best, and repeated infusions of fresh capital in order to continue operations. Columbia University invested more than $40 million in Fathom.com without generating a sustainable revenue stream. New York University shut down its NYU On-line, Inc. for exactly that reason, and netLibrary watched as its principal assets were sold off by a federal bankruptcy judge. Even UNEXT, the most visible of the distributed learning aggregators, has twice remade itself, each time downsizing both its expectations and its staff.

Distributed learning's second financial model closely resembles that of educational extension programs operating as separate units within a traditional college or university. Historically, extension programs have hired their own faculty, enrolled their own students, and maintained distinct facilities, usually off campus. At the same time, extension programs have been expected to be "tubs-on-their-own-bottoms," drawing new students to the enterprise whose separate tuitions would cover all costs, including a modest share of the institution's central overhead.

Most institutions that pursued distributed learning programs to tap what was expected to be a growing market in distance education organized them as if they were extension programs, assuming that the new revenues generated would cover all of the costs associated with developing content, acquiring the necessary technologies (both hardware and software), and marketing the enterprise. Many of these programs were initiated by public institutions and funded through special state appropriations to cover the start-up costs plus an initial period of operation.

Unlike their for-profit counterparts, most of these distributed learning enterprises survived, even prospered, but not as tubs-on-their-own-bottoms. Rather, most viable programs evolved as complementary, even supplementary educational activities economically dependent on the colleges and universities that first launched and now host them. Why? Because most collegiate distributed learning programs quickly discovered that there was not a growing market of new students for distance education. Having invested substantial start-up funds in the launching of innovative online educational programs, sponsoring colleges and universities found that most of their online customers were in fact their own regular students. In some of the best documented cases, upwards of 80% of the undergraduates enrolled in online courses were the sponsoring institution's resident students, who were taking the course because it was more convenient. In such cases, the institutions found themselves incurring substantial additional expenses without realizing much additional revenue, either in the form of new tuitions or through increased state appropriations based on additional head-count.

The experience of these, the most sustainable distributed programs, provides a framework for understanding the current finances of distributed learning in general. First there is a need to enlist—though entice is perhaps the better term—faculty to design and deliver distributed learning programs. Most such faculty will expect substantial assistance, including release time from regular teaching, funding for acquiring special materials and equipment, and access to technical specialists skilled in the use of information technologies for educational purposes. This latter need has led most campuses making substantial investments in distributed learning to establish special technical centers, staffed with e-learning specialists and state-of-the-art equipment, whose principal task is to support the faculty developing distributed learning materials. These technical centers often have the added responsibility of managing the institution's course management software (e.g., Blackboard, eCollege, and WebCT) and of designing and operating electronically smart classrooms, distance education servers, and associated hardware.

On most campuses, each of these expenses adds to the overall costs associated with distributed learning programs without yielding substantial new revenue to the sponsoring institution. The cost of acquiring, maintaining, and training faculty to use course management software is a sunk cost—one that students increasingly insist their institutions bear as part of the price of being student centered and market responsive. Indeed, the justification for the growing investments that institutions find they must make in electronically smart classrooms sounds suspiciously like that used to rationalize new investments in athletic and recreational facilities: "It's what the market demands."

Mature distributed learning programs are also learning a second tough lesson about the underlying cost structure of their enterprise—most expenditures are recurring rather than one-time. The financial half-life of most equipment is less than 3 years; most software becomes outdated in about the same time; and the funds spent on faculty to design and implement distributed learning courses have to be constantly reinvested. Few faculty want to adopt or adapt a distributed learning course developed by a colleague or purchased off-the-shelf. The enticement for a faculty member to invest his or her own time and energy in the development of a distributed learning course lies in the invitation to teach as they please—specifically, to teach either their specialty or a more generalized course exactly as they have always wanted, including having access to sufficient funds to "do it right."

The financial specter facing most institutions is a growing demand for a kind of teaching that is inherently more expensive, that faculty are likely to find liberating, and that students will demand in increasing numbers. The success of course management software is a case in point. By making the basic materials of the course readily available electronically, the software yields substantial gains in learning efficiency (often expressed in terms of the power and convenience of 24–7 access), not at reduced but at increased costs. Smart classrooms and the interactive media they make readily available hold out the same promise.

Are there no efficiencies? Most faculty engaged in the delivery of distributed learning programs discount the likelihood that their institution or program will realize financial efficiencies from investments in distributed learning. They also doubt that, in the end, the electronic technologies that make distributed learning possible will expand their institutions' student markets. Rather, these faculty see distributed learning as an exciting augment, a new way to get and keep students involved in their own learning experience. Where distributed learning has thrived, it has done so because the institution itself has made substantial investments that, with very few exceptions, have represented new rather than replacement funds.

If and when distributed learning is forced to pay its own way by achieving substantial savings in the delivery of traditional educational programs, the result is likely to be a hybrid model that combines both distributed and traditional learning. The most likely spur for the development of such programs will be a shortage of space, specifically traditional classrooms and laboratories. Already a few campuses that have run out of space are experimenting with courses that combine two sessions of in-class instruction with two sessions of online instruction, thus increasing by nearly 50% the capacity of the programs to enroll additional students. The savings inherent in such hybrids—the forgone costs of building and maintaining new classrooms—more than exceed the additional costs associated with developing the online components themselves.

To repeat the caveat stated at the beginning of this entry, none of these observations is the product of precise analysis, largely because little is actually known about either the incidence or the actual cost of distributed learning. What is clear, however, is just how often past discussions have combined missing data with hopeful assumptions to yield hopelessly optimistic projections about the costs and revenues of distributed learning. The most obvious fact is that there have been no facts: no tracking of students, revenues, or expenses (either direct or indirect). No one knows how many students have taken a distributed learning course in any given year; nor how much either businesses or colleges and universities have spent in pursuit of distributed learning initiatives; nor what dollars students or employees themselves have expended. The cost associated with the conversion to smart classrooms is similarly shrouded in uncertainty, largely because the expenses are incurred piecemeal, and hence are not separately reported. And almost no one has tackled the arduous task of assigning a portion of overhead to distributed learning programs—a task made all the more difficult because distributed learning has proven to be much more of a program supplement than a separate program.

The irony, however, is that despite the industry's inability to document either the costs or the savings associated with distributed learning, the enterprise itself is alive and well. Money is being spent, smart classrooms are being built everywhere, and collegiate faculty and corporate trainers are successfully integrating electronically mediated learning into literally thousands of courses focusing on both traditional and nontraditional subjects. That said, it is also the case that distributed learning is evolving in ways few predicted, and with economic consequences that even its most ardent supporters are struggling to understand.

—*Robert Zemsky*

*See also* ADMINISTRATIVE LEADERSHIP; ALLIANCES; STRATEGIC PLANNING

# FINANCIAL AID

Financial aid provides money, including grants, scholarships, employment, and loans to assist students in paying for college costs. Allowed costs include tuition, fees, books and supplies, living expenses, and other educationally related costs to attend college. Funding sources for financial aid include the U.S. government, state governments, private foundations, and the colleges themselves. Approximately $65 billion in federal funds were used for student financial aid last year. Until the 1992 Higher Education Amendments (HEA), federal law addressed traditional term-based academic programs. High-profile fraud and abuse by some colleges—especially correspondence schools—caused the U.S. government to heavily restrict financial aid for students studying through nontraditional academic programs. In an effort to prevent fraud and ensure quality educational programs, the 1992 HEA restricted federal funds for nontraditional education including distributed education programs such as distance learning and correspondence courses. The law limits distributed education programs and the amount of federal financial aid available to students enrolled in them. Institutions have also faced problems administering federal financial aid for students enrolled in distributed education programs. These problems have mainly been with using information systems designed for traditional term-based curriculums and managing the complexity of federal requirements specific to distributed education, often without computer support.

## FEDERAL LIMITATIONS

Postsecondary educational institutions jeopardize their eligibility to participate in federal financial aid programs when the majority of course offerings are through distance education and/or correspondence courses. If eligibility is lost, institutions face financial liabilities for noncompliance, and students become ineligible for all federal financial assistance including grants, loans, and employment programs.

Educational institutions offering distance education, as well as other distributed education programs deemed eligible for federal student aid, are subject to additional restrictions on the length of the academic program and the student's eligibility. Congress forced colleges to comply with a minimum 30-week academic year in which programs of study taught in nonstandard academic terms must include at least 12 hours of instruction per week. Such workload limitations are very difficult to apply in programs that are self-paced or offered in timeframes that deviate from standard semesters or quarters, such as weekend programs.

The law also limits the amount of financial aid available to students studying through distributed education programs. A full-time student, studying solely through correspondence courses, may not receive the same level of financial aid that a full-time student enrolled in a traditional curriculum receives. Financial aid for a student enrolled through correspondence courses is generally limited to tuition, fees, books, and supplies. A student enrolled in telecommunications courses, however, is eligible for the same level of financial aid as a student enrolled in a traditional curriculum. Financial aid for students enrolled in telecommunications courses may not only include tuition, fees, books, and supplies, but also living expenses, transportation costs, child care, and the cost of equipment such as a computer.

The complexity of financial aid regulations, the limited eligibility for students enrolled in distributed education programs, and the potential financial risk of noncompliance all act as a disincentive for educational institutions to expand distributed education programs.

In recognition of the growing number of distance education and nontraditional academic programs offered by postsecondary educational institutions, the U.S. Congress authorized the Distance Education Demonstration Program as part of the 1998 HEA. The program was created to test the quality and viability of distance education programs currently limited by the Higher Education Act. The program is expected to help determine changes needed in current law and regulations, to provide greater access to distance education programs, and determine appropriate levels of federal student aid for students enrolled in such programs. The program started on July 1, 1999, with 15 higher education participants. The first report to Congress was published in January 2001, and raises several issues that Congress must address in its next reauthorization of the Higher Education Act.

## INSTITUTIONAL ISSUES

Postsecondary educational institutions faced new administrative and operational challenges with nontraditional education. Similar to processing issues experienced in admissions, registration, and academic advising, colleges administered financial aid in the early 1960s with index cards or IBM-style keypunch cards. In 1954, a group of 95 private colleges established the College Scholarship Service (CSS). CSS developed a common financial aid application form and standardized the determination of student eligibility. Colleges generally adopted the CSS standard nationwide.

With the passage of the Higher Education Act of 1965, new federal requirements were placed on schools participating in the federal student aid programs. These requirements increased the amount of paperwork and documentation required, but colleges still maintained a great deal of autonomy with respect to student eligibility determinations.

The 1992 HEA mandated the use of a single Free Application for Federal Student Aid (FAFSA). All colleges are required to use the FAFSA for federal aid but may establish their own application process for other aid. As a result of this mandate, many colleges discontinued the use of the CSS application form for administering nonfederal aid, which required students to pay a fee, and began using the no-cost FAFSA. In 1994, the U.S. Department of Education (USDE) freely distributed financial aid software (EDExpress) to colleges. The software allowed institutions to electronically submit a FAFSA on behalf of a financial aid applicant and submit required reports to the USDE.

In 1996, the USDE published regulations that require colleges to participate in USDE electronic processes and meet minimum computer standards. Since that time, the USDE has implemented FAFSA on the Web, a Web-based version of the paper FAFSA; electronic signatures; the National Student Loan Database System, which stores financial aid transcript and enrollment information on every federal student aid recipient; and other electronic processes. Although these processes have eased the administrative burden for students studying at a distance, colleges have struggled with their own computer systems.

As the number of students receiving financial aid and the complexity of administering federal aid grew, colleges turned to integrated mainframe student information systems or nonintegrated client-server systems to administer student aid. The problem with these systems is they are structured for standard terms and are not designed to accommodate nontraditional education. These systems are not flexible or easily reconfigured to accommodate new nontraditional education formats.

Some of the problems colleges have faced include maintaining separate eligibility and disbursement rules, and reporting information for students enrolled in traditional curriculum programs versus nontraditional programs. Schools must also maintain information necessary to monitor whether the institution is close to the federal threshold on distance education, so that it would not lose eligibility when the majority of courses and/or the majority of students are enrolled through distance education.

Due to these problems, some institutions continued to use their legacy computer systems for students in the traditional curriculum and implemented new systems for students enrolled in nontraditional education. This approach has not fully solved the problems because some students enroll in courses taught through both traditional and nontraditional formats. The USDE requires that colleges review all information on student financial aid recipients and resolve any conflicting information. The USDE also requires an annual Fiscal Operations Report (FISAP) with unduplicated student statistical information. As a result, some level of integration and reconciliation between the two systems must occur.

Another problem faced by schools administering financial aid to students studying through distributed education is the requirement that financial aid can be awarded only to degree-seeking students. Several institutions have entered into consortium agreements that allow students to enroll in distance education courses toward their academic program of study offered by any school that is a member of the consortium. In order for the student to receive financial aid for coursework taken through such consortium arrangements, the "home" school must enter into a written agreement with the other schools so that the student can receive federal financial aid for the combined enrollment at all schools. These written agreements may be blanket agreements covering all students studying through the consortia or they may be specific to each student. Either approach requires that the institutions in the consortia share a great deal of information and establish systems to do so. If any of the institutions in the consortia are not eligible to participate in the federal financial aid programs, additional limitations apply. Institutions that are not eligible to participate in the federal financial aid programs may not generally provide more than 25% of the academic program of study.

—*Mark S. Williams*

***See also*** ACADEMIC ADVISING; ADMISSION CRITERIA AND PROCESSES; FEDERAL LAWS

### Bibliography

U.S. Department of Education. (2001). *Delivering student financial aid in nontraditional programs.* Retrieved from http://ifap.ed.gov/presentations/attachments/nontraditional.pdf.

U.S. Department of Education. (2001). *Student financial aid handbook: 2001–2002.* Retrieved from http://www.ifap.ed.gov/IFAPWebApp/currentSFAHandbooksPag.jsp.

U.S. Department of Education, Office of Postsecondary Education, Policy Planning and Innovation. (2001). *Report to Congress on the distance education demonstration programs.* Retrieved from http://www.ed.gov/offices/OPE/PPI/DistEd/DistanceDemoReport.pdf.

# FOR-PROFIT INSTITUTIONS

The technical difference between for-profit and not-for-profit educational institutions rests primarily on the treatment of net income, or surplus revenue. In the case of a not-for-profit institution, all net income must be retained by the institution and used to support its educational or charitable mission. Such income is not subject to taxation by the government provided that it is derived from and used to support the institution's central educational purposes. In the case of for-profit institutions, net income is available for distribution to owners or shareholders, or can be used for other business investments. Income from such for-profit institutions is taxed in the same manner as other corporate earnings. This technical difference, however, does not fully explain the substantial historical and cultural differences between for-profit and not-for-profit institutions.

## SEPARATE HISTORIES

Education, from primary levels through higher education, has traditionally been seen as a social good and therefore a responsibility of either the state or of social or religious organizations. Many of the earliest colleges and universities in the United States were founded by religious groups that included education as part of their mission to improve social welfare. Organizations and wealthy individuals often created endowments for private colleges and universities that were perpetually dedicated to a founding educational mission. These endowments subsidized ongoing operations and provided a buffer against short-term economic forces. By the mid-19th century, with the passage of the Morrill Land Grant Act of 1862, state governments also began setting up colleges and universities as public institutions dedicated to education, training, and the general welfare of the citizenry. Because of the broad benefits they provided, the operations of public institutions were heavily subsidized. Thus, the state-supported university and the privately endowed, not-for-profit college or university became the two standard models of institutional organization for higher education. These models were gradually taken as the norm and therefore came to be reinforced by tax laws, accrediting standards, and other regulations over time. This pattern of development can be found in many countries outside of the United States as well, though in most countries the reliance on state-sponsored institutions is much greater than in the United States.

Although not-for-profit institutions have always been the most visible institutions on the landscape of higher education, there is also a long, parallel history of proprietary schools that meet the definition of for-profit institutions. In many small towns in colonial America it was common to find a headmaster making a living by tutoring students for fees. By the mid-19th century a number of proprietary institutions had been established, sometimes with multiple locations serving relatively large numbers of students. Some of these multi-campus institutions still survive (e.g., the Bryant and Stratton chain, founded in 1854, or Sanford-Brown College founded in 1866). The most pervasive model of for-profit higher education, however, was the local, single site business or technical college that provided career-oriented education to people who otherwise would not be likely to pursue postsecondary education. These colleges typically served women, working adults, minorities, and others who generally did not have access to traditional private colleges or state universities. Although aggregate statistics do not exist, these small-scale for-profit institutions served significant numbers of students and provided an alternative career development path for much of the population.

## THE NEW FOR-PROFITS

Although for-profit education has a complementary, if somewhat overshadowed, history alongside of not-for-profit education, the relationship between the two sectors began to change in the 1990s as a result of several factors. First, the perceived demand for postsecondary education led many business analysts to conclude that a very large market existed that could not be serviced by traditional not-for-profit institutions. The financial growth and success of such early for-profit entrants as the University of Phoenix and DeVry, Inc. fueled interest in higher education as an industry ripe for investment. As a result, private investment in higher education grew at an unprecedented rate. Richard Ruch, in his book *Higher Ed, Inc.,* reports that between 1994 and 1999 more than $4.8 billion in private investment capital was raised for for-profit ventures in postsecondary education. Roughly 40 for-profit higher education businesses became listed on public stock exchanges during the 1990s. Data from the U.S. Department of Education's National Center for Education Statistics show that between 1989 and 1999, the number of 2-year for-profit institutions increased by 78% and the number of 4-year for-profit institutions grew by 266%. This period of dramatic growth seemed to signal the arrival of for-profit institutions as a much more visible and prevalent form of organization for higher education. Not only were entirely new institutions created (e.g., Cardean University, Jones International University, and Capella University), but investment capital was also used to purchase existing schools in order to assemble large multi-campus chains. This latter strategy is exemplified by Corinthian Colleges, Inc., the Quest Education Corporation, and ITT Technical Institutes.

A second factor in the rise of for-profit education has been the development of the Internet. By the mid-1990s, many educators and entrepreneurs saw a new potential to deliver quality education on a large scale through the use of Internet-based tools and methods. The economics of distributed education appeared to change substantially because an institution could mount a single course or degree program that could reach potentially large numbers of students without expenditures for facilities or specialized communication networks such as for the broadcast of television. Many for-profit concerns began to assemble courses, text, and other content through associations with individual faculty members working at traditional colleges and universities; through partnerships with colleges, universities, and publishers; or by building in-house expertise.

A third factor leading to an increase in the number of for-profit institutions was a change in the regulatory environment in the 1990s. Both the U.S. Department of Education and regional accrediting authorities began to adopt policies that were more inclusive of for-profit institutions, providing access to traditional accreditation, federal loan support, and other benefits. For-profit institutions such as the University of Phoenix and Jones International University began applying for and receiving regional accreditation during the 1990s, a controversial development that suggested for-profit universities could be considered full members of the higher education establishment.

Statistics on the growth of student enrollment in the for-profit sector of higher education are difficult to come by, because most for-profit data were not systematically collected and separated from other sectors by the U.S. Department of Education until 1996. That first year of data (for academic year 1995–96) reveals that 6% of all students in postsecondary education attended a private, for-profit institution, the majority of whom were enrolled in 2-year institutions. The data further show that minorities, especially African Americans and Hispanics, account for a larger share of for-profit enrollments than in not-for-profit or public institutions; women are especially concentrated among the 2-year for-profit institutions; and most students at for-profit institutions attend full time. These data will provide a benchmark against which future growth and enrollment trends will be measured.

## DISTRIBUTED EDUCATION

The idea of formal distributed or distance education dates back at least to the mid 19th century in Great Britain and to the university extension movement in late 19th century U.S. institutions. Many universities offered instruction by correspondence as well as various forms of off-site educational outreach. To cite one example, the University of Chicago was established in 1892 with a large continuing education department as a centerpiece of its founding vision. University-based distributed education however, has, with a few exceptions, been limited in scope because of the heavy demands it places on faculty and student support services.

Profit-making concerns have been particularly attracted to distributed education models because of their potential for growth. When educational services can be organized in such a way as to be easily replicated in many locations, or through a pervasive medium such as the Internet, the potential for profit increases dramatically.

The most obvious example of large-scale for-profit education in the United States is the University of Phoenix (UoP), founded in 1976 and now operating at more than 100 locations across the U.S. The UoP model relies on a standard curriculum that can be taught by adjunct faculty, most of whom are local practitioners rather than professional academics. Admission is restricted to working adults, with courses offered in the evening and usually at sites near major business centers. This model can be replicated efficiently at new sites and in new curricular areas. With the addition of Internet-based courses to supplement or replace site-based instruction, UoP has grown rapidly and now calls itself the largest private university in the United States, offering degrees ranging from associates through doctorates in a broad number of disciplines. UoP competes aggressively for students by marketing itself as an institution specifically tailored to the needs of working adults. Other for-profit educational institutions with similar business models exist, but they tend to focus on technical and vocational education.

The idea of a very large, distributed university is not limited to the for-profit sector. The British Open University, which is supported by the British government, is the largest single university in Great Britain. Large state-sponsored open universities exist in several other countries also, giving rise to what Sir John Daniel, former British Open University vice chancellor, has called the mega-university. These are educational institutions that serve 100,000 students or more through a combination of distributed sites and communications technology.

In both the for-profit and not-for-profit models, large-scale distributed education depends on a different distribution of functions than in a traditional university setting. In all large-scale operations, curriculum and academic requirements are established by a centralized academic group. If the Internet or other media are part of the course design, the preparation of such tools is usually done by technology experts and course designers. Instruction is carried out by another group, usually made up of part-time teachers. Yet another group may design and carry out evaluation and monitor quality. Still others may be involved in student counseling and academic advising. This "unbundling" of traditional faculty roles causes some academics to be concerned about the educational quality of these services. However, the growth of the model, elements of which are now also found on many traditional campuses, suggests that it is increasingly accepted by both students and academic professionals.

## CONTROVERSIES

The surge in for-profit education has not been without controversy. Some observers contend that the profit motive must necessarily distort or compete with the traditional mission of higher education. For-profit institutions, they argue, will offer only the most lucrative programs and do so in a way that minimizes cost at the expense of quality. Furthermore, some aspects of traditional higher education, such as faculty governance and a strong mission orientation, are lacking in for-profit institutions. Finally, some not-for-profit institutions are threatened by competition from for-profit schools that, with their access to capital, can attract students with large investments in services, technology, and aggressive advertising. Thus, their critics contend, for-profit institutions will tend to weaken the overall system of higher education by driving out smaller institutions and by homogenizing programs through a franchise approach to building institutions.

These arguments are countered by defenders of for-profit education who contend that traditional higher education institutions have been too insulated from market forces and are increasingly out of step with the needs of students. For-profit institutions, they argue, have strong incentives to provide excellent services and support to students, to offer programs that have practical value to students, and to develop innovative and flexible ways to deliver effective training and education.

As might be expected, neither of these extreme positions represents the situation with complete accuracy. For-profit institutions clearly select academic programs based on market demand and the potential career opportunities they offer to students. Furthermore, little if any attention is paid to the classical ideals of higher education such as those formulated by Cardinal Newman or von Humboldt. The role of faculty members in for-profit institutions tends to be more regimented and more focused on teaching as opposed to research or service. Administrators of for-profit institutions may be heavily influenced by the opportunity for personal gain through stock options or other financial incentives. On the other hand, many for-profit institutions point to their substantial investments in learning technology and in studies of student learning outcomes and student service as evidence of a genuine commitment to quality education. Furthermore, as for-profit institutions apply for accreditation they are compelled to adopt more traditional forms of academic governance and commitment to an educational mission.

At the same time, leaders of not-for-profit institutions are much more inclined to talk about "markets" for their programs and services, and have steadily adapted to the changing demographics and interests of students. Institutions that do not have large endowments or research budgets are particularly sensitive to enrollment shifts and must compete annually for tuition dollars. Many colleges and universities have added professional and career-oriented programs (such as business) in order to draw more students. More not-for-profit universities are offering distance education, night and weekend courses, or other programs specifically designed for the convenience of students. Finally, several prominent institutions have formed for-profit subsidiaries, or partnerships with for-profit firms, through which they plan to compete directly with for-profit institutions in distance education and professional education markets.

These developments suggest that the boundaries between for-profit and not-for-profit institutions are likely to become blurred. Although the prototypical research university or liberal arts college will continue to represent higher education in its most traditional guise, it is likely that not-for-profit and for-profit institutions will increasingly borrow from each other as they compete for many of the same students, and both types of institutions align themselves with regulatory and market forces.

—*Geoffrey M. Cox*

***See also*** ALLIANCES; GOVERNANCE; UNBUNDLING OF HIGHER EDUCATION

## Bibliography

Bailey, Thomas, Badway, Norena, & Gumport, Patricia. (2001). *For profit higher education and community college.* Stanford, CA: Stanford University, National Center for PostSecondary Improvement.

Daniel, John S. (1996). *Mega-universities and knowledge media: Technology strategies for higher education.* London: Kogan Page.

Phipps, Ronald A., Harrison, Katheryn V., & Merisotis, Jamie P. (1999). *Students at private for-profit institutions.* Washington, DC: The National Center for Education Statistics, Office of Educational Research and Improvement.

Ruch, Richard S. (2001). *Higher ed., Inc.* Baltimore: Johns Hopkins University Press.

Sperling, John G. (1999). *Rebel with a cause: The entrepreneur who created the University of Phoenix and the for profit revolution in higher education.* New York: John Wiley and Sons.

Tucker, Robert W., & Sperling, John G. (1997). *For-profit higher education: Developing a world class workforce.* New Brunswick, NJ: Transaction.

# FREE SPEECH

Congress shall make no law respecting an establishment of religion, or prohibiting the free exercise thereof; or abridging the freedom of speech, or of the press; or the right of the people peaceably to assemble, and to petition the Government for a redress of grievances. (United States Constitution, Amendment 1, December 15, 1791, First Congress of the United States)

Freedom of opinion and expression is a fundamental right in most countries of the world, but each country interprets these rights differently. As these rights—and differences—extend into academic and Internet-based environments, they are especially relevant for online distributed learning, raising new questions about institutional and governmental control of online expressions by students or faculty. Individual rights of free speech and institutional rights of academic freedom are both guaranteed by the First Amendment to the United States Constitution, creating tensions and an uncertain legal environment for teachers, students, and administrators concerned about these freedoms in online distributed learning.

In 1791, the First Amendment to the Constitution of the United States established the right to freedom of opinion and expression, even when that expression is offensive to others. Subsequent court decisions granted special privileges to colleges and universities.

The U.S. courts have consistently found that an individual's right to free speech cannot be regulated except when there is a compelling government reason to do so—and any restriction must be narrowly tailored to the specifics of the situation.

In 1957, the United States Supreme Court confirmed that academic freedom is inherent in the First Amendment, and state governments could not question professors about the content of their courses. In a concurring opinion, Justice Felix Frankfurter confirmed that the First Amendment protected the academic institution's freedom for autonomous decision making concerning "who may teach, what may be taught, how it shall be taught, and who may be admitted to study" (Sweezy v. New Hampshire 354 U.S. 234, 1957).

These rights were extended when the U.S. Supreme Court upheld the constitutionally protected right under the First Amendment for universities to legitimately consider race in decisions about admissions (California v. Bakke, 438 U.S. 265, 1978).

New technologies raise additional free speech issues. When the invention of the printing press raised new fears of the spread of "evil" ideas, governments and institutions used censorship, including the banning and burning books, to protect themselves from offensive speech. The Internet adds to these unresolved tensions because it provides full access to unlimited varieties of expressions and content from ever-increasing millions of people from around the world.

Even speech that is offensive to people of good will is protected. Although educational institutions may try to create cultures of tolerance for others, the courts have consistently held that the individual's right to free speech cannot be curtailed through university speech codes, even when that speech opposes deeply held values such as social justice.

Courts have extended their jurisdiction into electronic media and the Internet, holding that, even in online environments, there are few justifications for censorship—and these justify only "time, place, and manner" restrictions to free speech. Most "hate speech" regulations created by academic institutions have been found to be unconstitutional.

U.S. courts have supported the rights of universities to block access to specific Internet sites, to limit expressions on private online forums, to support the rights of students to block offensive e-mails from reaching them, and to limit the use of university networks for personal financial gain. Harassment can be controlled in the online environments when unwanted and repeated words consistently target and annoy specific individuals.

Universities that restrict Internet access through usernames and passwords contend that, because access to the Internet is restricted, the institution can limit freedoms of what is accessed as well as expressed. In a sharply divided court decision on the rights of a university to limit access to online pornography (Urofsky v. Gilmore No. 98–1481, 4th Cir. 2000, en banc), the majority found that First Amendment rights to academic freedom reside within the university, not individual professors. The university could not withhold the right of Internet access, but could restrict the content of what professors and students were allowed to access.

As distributed education spreads around the world, some students and teachers will live in countries with laws on free expression that are radically different from those in the "home" country of their distributed learning institution. There is no simple resolution to this situation. Some learners in an online course may live in a country that has no restrictions on their online expression or Internet access. Other learners, in the same online course, may live in a country that censors e-mails and forbids access to Web sites that reside on servers in specific censored countries.

Many issues of free speech may ultimately be resolved by technologies and the people who use them, rather than by the courts. When educational institutions and governments impose restrictions on free expression, individuals and groups will devise alternate ways to use the Internet to exercise their rights to freedom of expression and opinion.

Everyone has the right to freedom of opinion and expression; this right includes freedom to hold opinions without interference and to seek, receive, and impart information and ideas through any media and regardless of frontiers (Article 19 of the Universal Declaration of Human Rights, adopted by the General Assembly of the United Nations, December 10, 1948).

—*Dorothy E. Agger-Gupta*

*See also* ETHICS; FEDERAL LAWS; LEGAL ISSUES

## Bibliography

Findlaw: Cases and codes of the U.S. court system. Retrieved from http://www.findlaw.com/casecode/.

Godwin, M. (1998). *Cyber rights: Defending free speech in the digital age.* New York: Times Books.

Golding, M. P. (2000). *Free speech on campus.* Lanham, MD: Rowman & Littlefield.

Hawke, C. S. (2001). *Computer and Internet use on campus: A legal guide to issues of intellectual property, free speech and privacy.* San Francisco: Jossey-Bass.

Lipschultz, J. H. (2000). *Free expression in the age of the Internet: Social and legal boundaries.* Boulder, CO: Westview.

Rabban, D. M. (2001). Academic freedom, individual or institutional? *Academe, 87*(6), 16–20.

# FUNDING SOURCES

Computers, servers, routers, and telecommunications connectivity form part of the technology platform for distributed learning. Hand in hand with the infrastructure "hardware" is all the "software"—software needed to roll out a multimedia curriculum, and the software that is the educators, technicians, administrators, and student assistants who make $24 \times 7$ teaching and learning viable. How to fund all of these pieces and write a winning grant proposal are challenges that can be met head-on with preparation and teamwork.

Successful fundraising requires careful planning. A campus should have: 1) a mission statement that reflects the school's academic goals and its commitment to infuse technology into teaching and learning; 2) a strategic distributed learning and technology plan; and 3) a strategic funding plan. Having these in hand will allow the school to organize educational technology goals and objectives, plan a time frame for implementation, select a project team to spearhead the campus's initiatives, and strategize appropriate private and public funding agencies for the grant request.

Faculty, administrators, IT staff, and the development office must work hand-in-hand. Each contributes expertise to strategic planning and can facilitate the coordination necessary for sound fundraising. Too often, one academic department on campus undertakes an initiative without consulting with the IT staff (to be sure that the appropriate technology is consistent) or winds up actually competing with another academic program for a grant from the same funding agency. Therefore, it is crucial that critical planning be undertaken.

How many distributed learning courses will be rolled out, over what time frame, and involving which academic programs and what constituency? Is the campus implementing a wireless infrastructure, and therefore needing to consider wireless laptops, cards, and personal digital assistants (PDAs) as part of its technology plan? What are the hardware, software, and personnel requirements and costs? What is the return on investment (ROI)? How will the campus realize cost-savings so that it may continue to launch new projects—which will be justified by the success of earlier ones?

The team approach means that specific tasks for the grant proposal need to be assigned (i.e., someone takes care of the hardware list and budget; another person is responsible for lining up the partnerships and supporting letters; another works on the narrative and timeline, and so on). Internal deadlines must be established for tasks to be completed, for small and full group meetings, and for aggregating all the grant components into a coherent whole. Careful planning is a good reflection of how the grant will be managed, and a sound fundraising strategy will help the grant proposal receive more serious consideration.

## GRANT WRITING—MATCHING GOALS TO FUNDING AGENCIES

Funding relates primarily to the content and context of a project. A school's major objectives are teaching and learning, *not* computing. The hardware and infrastructure are means to an end—to help meet the project's goals.

Listing goals also helps to match the funding request to the most appropriate foundations, corporate giving programs, and state and federal government agencies. Each agency's programs and grant priorities should be carefully researched, in order to write a grant proposal that aligns with the funding agency's main concerns and criteria.

For example, consider the priorities of the United States in business, science, and technology within the context of a competitive global economy. Curriculum areas such as business, management, engineering, information technology, mathematics, and the sciences are essential to corporate success. In addition, companies seek minority (women and people of color) applicants

to hire, particularly in the engineering and science fields. These objectives—a skilled and diverse workforce trained for the 21st century—thus become key goals in their giving programs.

Also, the $24 \times 7$ e-learning environment requires technical support, course support, and student services (such as advising, tutorials, and access to library resources). These may translate into budgeting for additional personnel, including IT staff as well as student assistants. The yearly costs for additional technical, library (including library assistants and help desks), graduate teaching, and student assistant staff should be included in the personnel section of the budget and explained in the budget narrative.

The campus's hardware and software vendors should be at the top of the list as a funding source. Sales representatives should be consulted to find out what funding programs the company supports. Hardware budgets should be well documented, in both the narrative and budget sections of a grant application. With the hardware and software industries changing products and services so rapidly, it is also essential that technical staff receive ongoing professional development—to attend industry conferences, to upgrade their own skills through course certifications, and to learn new areas, such as management and business communications skills. Therefore, professional development for both technical staff and faculty should be included.

As more and more educators migrate to the e-learning environment, they too are gaining skills in course design and delivery. Instead of planning professional development with a "one-shot serves all" approach, it is recommended that the narrative, and hence budget, delineate among teachers who are new to e-learning versus those who are prepared to acquire intermediate and advanced levels of multimedia design and curriculum development. Assisting educators to gain skills in creating Web content and courseware often requires training that may be offered either throughout the academic year or during summer months, which may mean additional staff stipends.

Additional staff hires and professional development activities for technical personnel, faculty, and student assistants translate into often larger annual operating budgets for support services and continuing access to technology and information. The operating budget is an area where a funding agency would like to see project sustainability. The grant proposal should demonstrate that within approximately 2 years, the project's income (from tuition and school budget allocations from state education agencies) will cover the ongoing operating costs, including personnel salaries and fringe benefits, equipment maintenance, and telecommunications fees.

In state and federal grant applications, which are usually scored on a 100-point rating system, the budget generally rates 10–15 points. Obviously, a grant seeker should try to gain the highest possible points. Grant application reviewers are often experienced practitioners who are familiar with hardware, software, personnel, and operating costs. The costs of salaries or equipment should not be overstated. The budget should accurately reflect the project's design as well. The budget needs to match the implementation plan to be certain that the money requested realistically matches the work to be undertaken. Analysis of the budget should show:

- The budget is adequate to support the project.
- Costs are reasonable in relation to the objectives of the project.
- Costs accurately reflect the work undertaken in each stage of the implementation process.
- Administrative overhead is attuned to the authorizing guidelines.

Organizing a grant application in a clear, structured, well-conceived format produces a well-defined document that reviewers can follow easily. Reviewers often do "judge a book by its cover," so the application needs to reflect the best of an organization's capabilities to successfully manage and fulfill a project's goals.

Finally, the grant request must be well written, with a strong and appealing project overview. A written request demonstrates the school's ability to manage and successfully complete a project; in other words, it is a reflection of the school.

Over the past few years, many funding agencies have begun accepting the new Common Grant Application form. This is a relatively straightforward document with a cover page, a maximum five-page narrative, a one-page budget sheet, plus supporting materials. This Common Grant Application can be used as a stepping-stone for other grant applications, and can be expanded on for more detailed requirements of state and federal funding submissions.

Having a carefully conceived project that represents initiatives that can be replicated and that includes an evaluation component to demonstrate student and teaching learning outcomes will help a school succeed. In hard fiscal times, it takes twice as much effort to raise money as it did when the economy was booming. So what's a school or university to do to support its distributed learning initiatives? It must be prepared to work harder than ever to reap monetary and equipment rewards. That is the bottom line for all funding.

*—Arlene Krebs*

**See also** ADMINISTRATIVE PLANNING AND SUPPORT OF INFORMATION TECHNOLOGY; FINANCE; GRANTS

## Bibliography

Browning, Beverly A. (2001). *Grant writing for dummies.* New York: IDG Books.

The Foundation Center: http://fdncenter.org.

Krebs, Arlene. (1998). *The distance learning funding $ourcebook: A guide to foundation, corporate and government support for telecommunications and the new media.* Dubuque, IA: Kendall-Hunt.

Technology Grant News: http://www.technology-grantnews.com.

U.S. Department of Education: http://www.ed.gov.

## GENDER

For the past 100 years, women have constituted the majority of students in distributed learning, initially through correspondence courses. During those years, most administrators and faculty did not consider them an important student body. Their individual and collective political and ideological struggles in higher education were seldom considered important educational issues.

Currently, women are the majority not only of the distributed learning (DL) population, but also of the nontraditional-age campus college students. So it is particularly important to focus on why women pursue online education, the constraints they may face in doing so, and the impact that gender has on classes that are not face-to-face.

Many of the women returning to college classes (whether for career advancement, higher wages, or personal satisfaction) face significant barriers not experienced by as many men, or at least not experienced to the same degree. Many women must balance job, community, and heavy family responsibilities against their academic work. They often have serious financial burdens. Traditionally they have often experienced these difficulties while also facing inflexible class schedules and academic policies, inadequate childcare, lack of appropriate housing, and lack of reliable transportation. Distance learning programs would seem to alleviate some of these difficulties. Certainly many people suggest that online education seems particularly valuable for women.

Indeed, online education is the choice of many women when asked if they prefer online or on-campus classes. However, for many women "preference" in the abstract has little meaning. Many of them state that, although they might prefer traditional education, their employment and families dictate that they have a chance to take courses only if they are online. Other themes given as a primary reason for the preference for online courses have been pacing (being able to work at own speed), lack of needed courses at nearby campuses, enjoyment of online courses, need to avoid childcare expenses, and disabilities that make attending campus classes difficult.

## TIME

Women enrolled in online courses have even less time to call their own than do most traditional students in face-to-face environments; in addition to their work on courses, many serve as primary caretakers of family members and also work at jobs outside the home. Women, especially those with children, have less "free" time away from their family responsibilities and other work. DL can allow them to both stay at home *and* study, at least in the evenings or when off work, while still taking care of home duties. Men are more likely to have more time that they can use more or less as they wish, in or out of the home.

## FAMILY SUPPORT

For online students, the lack of family support may come in the form of increased demands for attention and help, destruction of course materials, "guilt-tripping," denying childcare assistance, refusing to set aside time or space in the home for study, and refusing to spend "family" finances on women's education. Spousal support is often limited to affective help, which sometimes diminishes as women's study demands increase.

## COSTS

Many people remain convinced that eventually, at least, distance learning will be a relatively inexpensive mode of education. However, certainly for new programs, the costs for universities and students (in faculty development, implementation, delivery, and equipment) may be substantially higher. Many women with difficult economic situations are expressing keen interest in taking courses; however, at the moment, distance learning opportunities are disproportionately taken by the already relatively well-resourced.

Understanding the varying meanings of the costs of education also requires understanding structural inequalities of power in families. For example, for married students the cost of childcare is often added to the women's list of expenses, but not the men's. Successful students report that they have obtained the support of other family members. Many adult education students are single parents, with very heavy work and family responsibilities. However, many of those single parents report that they feel that they have more freedom of action (e.g., in terms of making financial decisions and of deciding on what meals to make and when) than do many married women with children.

## ACCESS

We know that "family resources" are often not evenly divided among males and females in a household. "Access" to computers can mean getting one's hands on a computer once in a while (perhaps in a library or an office) or can mean having everyday opportunities to use a computer and to find and download content-rich resources whenever they are needed. The fact that there is a computer in the home does not mean that everyone in the home has equal access. Studies that treat the family as one unit do not give us adequate information about what is going on inside a home.

## COMPUTER-MEDIATED COMMUNICATION (CMC)

Once enrolled and online, women students may experience somewhat different interactions with teachers and other students. Even when interaction patterns are similar, they may be evaluated differently because of the stereotypes of gender differences in conversations. Research on computer-mediated communication is providing information that, if heeded, could make distributed learning classes much more equitable. Recent research indicates that gender asymmetry exists in both synchronous and asynchronous interaction.

Some administrators and teachers have talked about the advantages of online (asynchronous) discussions for marginalized students who are "marked" by such status cues as gender, race, or physical disability. Online, such students no longer have to wait for a teacher to call upon them, and students who have trouble presenting their thoughts orally can take their time to think and compose. However, although such participants *could* write at length without interruptions, in actuality women whose comments are not noticed by others often decrease their amount of participation. In online discussions, women's topics tend to receive fewer responses from others, both females and males. Women do not usually control the topics of discussion except in groups where women are a clear majority.

Although CMC is increasingly seen as at the heart of learning online, not everyone enjoys electronic talk, and some are finding the experience threatening, time-consuming, and frustrating. Women in computer-mediated discussions have been shown just as likely as men to initiate disagreements, but the women tend to use more agreement terms (which can encourage and promote the participation of others), and they tend to drop out of the conversations rather than to continue to defend their ideas when they are repetitively challenged.

Studies of online classroom interaction have found women participating more, sometimes even more than men, when the teacher moderates the interaction, even when the teacher is male. It would seem that the presence of an acknowledged leader taking the responsibility of ensuring an environment free of incivility and harassment actually creates a freer atmosphere for the women. Teachers might think that setting up self-regulating online class discussions is the more democratic policy in encouraging students to take part in interactive learning. However, such a laissez-faire approach allows the most aggressive individuals to have the most "freedom."

Although single-sex groups might not be feasible or even permitted in many online courses, just the knowledge that women on their own are considered more supportive of each other and more understanding of the kinds of difficulties many women experience—especially when they have heavy family responsibilities—may help teachers and students find ways to encourage supportive behavior even in mixed-sex groups.

Gender never exists separate from other life factors such as age, ethnicity, and race. The conversational factors that silence white women are often different from those that silence students of color. In fact, the cultural conversational traits of some marginalized cultures may conflict with the particular conversational styles that electronic conversations encourage. For example, Hispanic students are often described as using more physical gestures in their conversations, as being more reluctant to disagree with others, and as less competitive. The textual-based electronic conversations may present a particular barrier for the participation of Hispanics, men as well as women.

Online courses in particular are likely to include students from very diverse populations. If contributions from everyone are to be encouraged, then teachers and students will need to know more about people from different age, ethnic, racial, cultural, language, and gender backgrounds, and about how discrimination operates. It will not be enough to just try to ignore the stereotypes.

## FACULTY AND COURSE CONTENT

Many online teachers are adjuncts; many of them teach full-time for other colleges, whereas others take part-time teaching jobs with several online institutions. Given that teaching online often takes more time than teaching campus courses, the issues about "who" is teaching "what" for "how" many students and courses complicate any comparisons of on-site and online courses. Although many on-campus faculty have worked hard during the past 30 years to increase the number of women teaching courses and to increase the amount of course material related to women's history and concerns, many of the established guidelines, standards, and checks may be lost in the move to distributed learning.

## DROPOUT FIGURES

Information on the numbers and gender of students who do not complete courses is very difficult to locate, for several reasons. Institutions do not keep comparable figures (some counting those students who officially unenroll before the end of the "trial time" of the course, some only counting those who fail to take the final exam). Also, institutions have not been eager to make public their dropout rates. The terminology can also be a problem. Many women report feeling that the term *dropout* is not appropriate in their situations. They want a distinction made between failing in their studies and having to leave classes because of circumstances they feel are beyond their control.

## THE FUTURE

Worldwide, girls and women, often denied schooling when income is low and when they assume or are required to take on large household and childcare duties, are the majority of the illiterate; they are less likely than are boys and men to learn to read and write. If current trends continue, girls and women will also be less likely to have information literacy. This has everyday implications: Problems are more difficult to solve when people do not have access to meaningful information vital to good decision making. Some educators suggest that women's needs should become more central in all educational programs, and that the overall goal should be to provide an educational environment that is inclusive of gender as well as ethnicity.

In addition to more attention to time, family support, costs, access, and CMC, additional research is needed to discover the type and extent of women's access to information via informal channels. One study of women in business and political leadership positions in 27 countries, including the United States, found a higher level of access to informal information channels and more satisfaction with their degree of access to informal channels than the men reported. More information about women's existing information networks is needed, along with analyses of how online programs can utilize the various types of knowledge held by students.

Many educators suggest that online education seems particularly valuable for women. And certainly over the years many women have made good use of distributed learning courses. However, simply to say that distributed learning (in whatever form) is a good (or only) option for women with heavy family responsibilities is a misleading assumption.

—*Cheris Kramarae*

*See also* CULTURAL DIVERSITY; DEMOGRAPHICS; GLOBALIZATION

### Bibliography

Hawisher, Gail E., & Selfe, Cynthia L. (1999). *Passions, pedagogies, and 21st century technologies.* Logan and Urbana: Utah State University Press and NCTE.

Herring, Susan C. (Ed.). (2003). *Computer-mediated conversation.* Greenskill, NJ: Hampton Press.

Kirkup, Gill. (1999, April 23–25). A computer of one's own (with an Internet connection!). *Adults Learning, 10,* 8.

Kramarae, C. (2001). *The third shift: Women learning online.* Washington, DC: American Association of University Women.

# GLOBALIZATION

*Globalization* in and of itself is neither good nor evil. It was a popular buzzword of the 20th century and it continues into the 21st. Although not a new issue, the complexities of globalization make it a difficult topic with which to grapple.

Ethics, governance structures, and world legal and regulatory systems, including trade and intellectual property, are all important components of the international fishbowl. New learning possibilities, including distance education and distributed learning, are increasingly becoming possible; however, historically, education through secondary school has been considered to be under state and local governance, including public and/or private bodies. Tremendous differences exist around the planet as to the purpose of education and what constitutes appropriate educational content, methods, and language. In addition, questions as to who can participate in educational programs, to what levels, for what purposes, and who pays continue to be issues. Concerns have long existed with respect to curriculum control, homogenization versus heterogeneity, local versus global, and use of Internet space for education.

Globalization of education began prior to the development of today's technologies, and included correspondence courses, paper-based open universities, audio tapes, radio, and television. Many governments and international organizations sponsored international training programs for citizens of developing countries, and demand for U.S. higher education became particularly strong during the 1980s and 1990s. In addition to concerns about cultural retention, the problem of "brain drain" became apparent as new immigrants took leading positions in the development of economic and political structures in their newly adopted countries and international corporations.

The global facts haven't changed much in the last 20 years—the "haves" in all countries have access to all types of educational opportunity. The world's "have nots" increased by almost 100 million in the past decade, and many in the Third World still live on less than a dollar a day, even though world income actually increased by an average of 2.5% annually.

September 11 in the United States placed on the table questions related to security and international education. In his *New York Times* article of September 22, 2002, Thomas Friedman noted that "globalization fatigue" is very much in evidence in Europe and America, but in countries such as China and India, the desire is great to participate in economic expansion processes. Bangalore is India's Silicon Valley, and information technology has made millionaires out of ordinary people because brainpower trumps caste, land, and heredity. China is actively participating in building an advanced Internet, rapidly connecting schools, businesses, and digitizing learning resources at a phenomenal pace.

## DISTANCE EDUCATION AND DISTRIBUTED LEARNING

Whether education is delivered in traditional face-to-face mode or via technology, it is viewed by many around the world as one of the few true "win-win" development strategies. It is fundamental to both economic growth and greater equality. Asking people in developing countries to pay school fees is now considered to be very shortsighted. Even the world banking community is beginning to agree that governments must mitigate market failures and ensure social justice. Education is one of the few agreed-upon ways to do this.

## STUDENTS IN MOST NEED OF EDUCATION

Beginning in the 1960s, a women's equality movement took root and grew into a force for global change. Two interrelated factors were critical—education and the ability to control money. Due in part to the fact that it could be done, it was done—not only were more women from developed countries educated more highly than ever before, so were women in all cultures and countries throughout the world. The job is far from complete, however, and the historic gender bias remains in development banks, international organizations and agencies, educational institutions, and governments. Although female enrollment in primary and secondary schools has increased, as has literacy, women still lag substantially behind men in the Middle East, North Africa, Sub-Saharan Africa, and South Asia. A sustainable and stable world society requires the education of women.

The reach to and involvement of women must be central when considering technology applications for distance education, distributed learning, and open universities. In the developed world, women empowered with technology have been among the most avid users of distance education. But as global classrooms and distributed learning environments become more possible, the classrooms and environments will not overcome in and of themselves the historic barriers of inequity, leaving women in many societies less literate, less educated, and poorer than men.

## THE KNOWLEDGE BASE AND THE FACULTY

Content is not neutral, and as knowledge is increasingly digitized and shared, questions are debated as to whose knowledge is being transmitted. Although the true knowledge base is the aggregation of human learning and repositories, including living people and all artifacts, many fear that English and westernization will overrun other languages and cultures. For this reason, global distributed learning environments are coming into vogue at many levels, particularly in higher education.

An example of global distributed learning is the Cornell Global Seminar conducted by H. Dean Sutphin and an international faculty from Australian and European institutions. It is focused on environmental sustainability as a global issue and includes case studies in areas such as population, food safety, water management, distribution of wealth, and global learning. The course uses a variety of technologies including the Internet and video conferencing, both synchronous and asynchronous. Donated funds have supported the effort to date. Many high schools, community colleges, and higher education institutions around the world are participating. Interesting preliminary findings may be helpful in scaling the model and decreasing costs so that it can be self-sustaining.

At all levels of education, the faculty who choose to teach globally and use technology is growing. However, the initiatives are not yet large and mainstream. Faculty teams that include learning facilitators from multiple countries are one promising way to overcome some of the difficulties and arguments encountered with respect to exporting only one language and one culture. Someday this way of learning will be commonplace—the "death of distance" touted in Frances Cairncross's book of the same name. Someday people from all over the globe will be able to interact in real time and at the same time. Prior to September 11, the U.S. business ethics crisis, and the "Dot.Bomb," most people believed the marketing hype that said broadband access by the global village was just around the corner. It was not then and is not yet, if digital inclusion means more than simply rich and already well-educated users participating via some type of Internet/interactive television system.

Faculty experienced in multicultural education know that it isn't simply about the technology, but rather developing access systems that guarantee learning success. Useful technology systems are far from in place and at the fingertips of most faculty, let alone students (the global digital divide). Barriers such as language, price, accreditation differences, poor learner support systems, lack of learning resources, and a host of other issues remain to be solved.

## GLOBAL NETWORKS

Despite all the problems and issues, a distributed global learning network is emerging. Today's Internet is the framework for it, and assuming that it is not stopped or co-opted for commercial or security reasons, it will provide the best hope for international peace and prosperity in the future. Networks, like globalization, are neutral, not forces for good or evil, and the promises and perils of global networks have already been demonstrated. Just because someone can use a vehicle to commit a crime does not mean we should ban vehicles (nor by implication, the Internet).

However, networks are far more than just fibers, wires, satellites, and radio signals—networks are first and foremost the human connections that make certain types of cooperative and concerted action possible.

Critical issues being debated with respect to global networks include who gets access, what is the business model, who controls the networks, how to handle privacy, how to preserve security, what types of devices should be used, who makes the devices, what type of network should carry the signals, how can the various types of networks interoperate, what is open and what is proprietary, who can own intellectual property, how are the networks governed, how will global digital libraries develop, what metadata standards should be adopted, and most importantly, what difference will any of this ultimately make in learning and people's daily lives?

## LEARNING PLACES

The concept of distance education implies that teacher and learner are separated by space and, by implication, the learner may be in a rural or remote location where connectivity to a high-speed broadband network does not exist and where it is too costly to install. Around the globe, distant learners have included rural women using audiotapes, soldiers in the bush doing "freedom fighting," place-bound individuals with physical disabilities, people located in war-torn places, adults employed in communities not offering the continuing education required, and a variety of other people in circumstances that make it difficult for them to learn in their area. Debates also continue about whether to establish physical learning centers or to make the home the primary center for distant and distributed learning activities. The most probable answer is that increasingly, many will primarily learn from home in the developed world where people can afford computers; in areas where the technology is too expensive or unavailable, many will learn in some type of community technology learning center. Determining the characteristics of quality distance learning centers is an important area of research; a better understanding is emerging in various countries regarding how best to establish these learning places. Increasingly, learning opportunities will travel to communities via mobile Internet, and the possibilities for satellite and radio networks are yet in their infancy.

## LEARNING COMMUNITIES

The most important long-term question with respect to globalization of education and distributed learning is whether the political will exists to establish real learning communities that include and span boundaries of many types. As with globalization and global networks, learning communities are neither good nor evil; they are, however, already emerging and will continue to emerge in many shapes and forms.

—*Janet Poley*

***See also*** Cultural Access/Digital Divide; Demographics; Gender

### Bibliography

Cairncross, Frances. (1997). *The death of distance.* London: Orion Publishing Group Limited.
Friedman, Thomas. (2002, September 22). Globalization, alive and well. *New York Times.* Retrieved from http://www.nytimes.com/2002/09/22/opinion/22FRIE.html?ex=033691426&ei=1&en=0de1375af5aa96e5.
Lechner, Frank J., & Boli, John. (2002). *The globalization reader.* Malden, MA: Blackwell.
Stiglitz, Joseph. (2002). *Globalization and its discontents.* New York: W. W. Norton.

# GOVERNANCE

Governance is how educational institutions, especially not-for-profit colleges and universities, describe the way decisions are made about major organizational matters. Governance arrangements tell people both inside and outside the institution who has been given the responsibility and authority for determining specific things. *Shared governance* is the term used to emphasize the significant role that faculty traditionally have played in the decision making of educational organizations. Although the governing board, along with the chief executive officer, has ultimate authority for establishing the mission of the organization and maintaining its financial welfare, decision-making responsibility in educational institutions has been more widely delegated than in other organizational structures, particularly for-profit corporations. In distributed learning environments, shared governance often takes place through nontraditional structures or processes (e.g., issue-specific task forces and online discussion groups). Also, given the various interest groups involved in distributed learning, there are often special challenges in making complex decisions in timely ways.

## GOVERNING BOARDS

Lay citizens are elected to serve on college and university boards as volunteers (or stewards) serving the public good. They typically are not compensated for their work, which, if taken seriously, can often be quite demanding in its scope and importance. In addition to establishing the mission or purpose of the organization and making sure its activities are in keeping with that mission, boards have the duty of overseeing the college or university's funds. Boards also must see to it that the institution is planning for the future, both financially and otherwise. A primary method that boards use in doing their work is the creation of policies that guide the work of others.

Boards are responsible for the hiring of the chief executive officer, for determining that person's compensation, and for conducting regular performance reviews with that person. The board and the CEO work as partners leading the institution, although with very different roles. Most effective boards work very hard to stay out of the daily management of the organization and to support the CEO and senior administration in carrying out their responsibilities.

Distributed learning environments exist within both organizations that are wholly designed for such an approach to education and institutions whose primary mission may not be the support of distributed learning. In the first instance, the governing board has an obligation to understand and respect the distinctive character and culture of such institutions. In the latter situation, boards that have responsibility for distributed learning components of traditionally constructed learning environments may have an even greater challenge. The mission of traditional institutions may have led to policies and procedures that are not responsive to the particular demands of distributed learning. This mismatch can lead to conflicts or to gaps in needed policies. For example, boards that govern distributed learning environments need to pay attention to technology issues and to the use of part-time faculty in ways that may differ from institutions that are exclusively campus-based.

In distributed learning environments where shared governance is valued, boards need to be especially clear about their decision-making processes. They cannot rely on informal face-to-face opportunities to supplement the formal structures. They must be explicit in their communications with various constituencies, making it clear when they are informing them of certain matters, when they are consulting with them before making decisions, and when they are involving them in some specific way in making final decisions.

## THE ROLE OF FACULTY

Many organizations involve their members in decision making. Colleges and university faculty, however, see their role in decision making as unique. In 1996, the American Association of University Professors (AAUP) published a landmark statement regarding this role. AAUP outlined the relationship between the faculty's role in governance and issues of academic freedom and academic quality. Because the purpose and "business" of colleges and universities is teaching and learning, the AAUP endorsed the idea that the responsibility for these activities belongs in the hands of faculty. Furthermore, there should be no administrative policies or procedures that infringe on the faculty's right and responsibility to carry out their duties. Clearly, this point of view makes the faculty a more powerful constituency within organizations than their organizational counterparts. It is a view that has led to their being likened to "managers" in corporate environments (although the success of unionization of faculty in many colleges and universities has called that distinction into question).

The management of educational institutions—often referred to as "internal governance"—has been criticized as cumbersome, factionalized, and producing low-quality outcomes, and taking an excessively long time to do so. There is too often confusion about who has the authority to make a decision. Responsibility is shared, as is accountability. A great deal of information is demanded and is reviewed carefully and slowly.

Faculty see these negative aspects as part of the price to be paid for the inclusion of all those necessary in the decision-making process. Even faculty, however, often complain about the difficulty of getting things done in colleges and universities. Those educational environments that have achieved an effective balance between inclusion and rapidity in decision making are seen as models for the best of what higher education aspires to.

Distributed learning has created challenges for faculty involvement in governance. First of all, some faculty have objected to models of learning that seem to de-emphasize or significantly alter the role of faculty in supporting student learning. Other institutions have struggled with how to include faculty who are part-time or off-site in faculty governance. Colleges and universities cannot assume that policies and practices that have worked in the governance of on-campus faculty will work in distributed settings.

Some distributed learning institutions have created new ways of making decisions involving faculty. For example, they have created online environments that provide opportunities for both discussion and debate, as well as polling or voting among faculty. Another format brings the faculty together physically periodically (e.g., two to four times per year) to discuss and decide upon important matters. Some institutions do both (e.g., providing for online committee work, but face-to-face decision making by the whole faculty). What is striking to some observers is the extent to which a distributed faculty can create its own enduring culture. At the same time, other distributed learning organizations have largely excluded faculty from governance as they strive to adopt more business-like models of making decisions. For these, the emphasis is on speeding up the process and making choices more strategically than democratically.

## EXTERNAL STAKEHOLDERS

Part of the obligation of boards of not-for-profit corporations like colleges and universities is to represent the public interest, so in that sense, the influence of interests external to the organization are built into the governance structure. In addition to this general influence, other specialized groups have an impact on decisions that need to be made. For instance, state and federal government and accrediting bodies often dictate policies that institutions must follow in areas such as contact hours between faculty and students or the substance of the bachelor's degree. These policies can be challenging for distributed learning programs that have been designed without the assumptions or constraints of traditional campus-based programs. However, both government and accrediting bodies have begun developing new guidelines or "principles of good practice" for distributed and distance learning activities in an attempt to balance their concern for protecting the public and ensuring quality while supporting educational innovation and flexibility.

A more problematic set of relationships for many colleges and universities is that with for-profit corporations. Historically, business has had significant influence on educational institutions through the service of their leaders on boards and through their financial support of a wide range of curricular and extracurricular activities. More recently, colleges and universities have begun to partner with the for-profit sector in new and creative ways so as to benefit from the expertise and resources found there. These relationships have concerned some faculty who worry that the mission of their institutions will be compromised in pursuit of the bottom line. Other faculty and administrators see these alliances as a way for colleges and universities to participate in and benefit from the market economy.

Distributed learning programs, in particular, have led to some interesting partnerships between colleges and universities and the private sector. The willingness of those involved with distributed learning to take learning opportunities into the workplace and community, to use technology, and to create curricula that are responsive to the needs of external organizations has made them especially attractive as partners. Some of these partnerships have taken the form of joint, for-profit ventures that are connected to but independent from the primary organizational structure of the college or university. These educational institutions are breaking new ground as they seek to remain true to the mission and culture of education while taking advantage of new societal arrangements.

## WHAT ABOUT STUDENTS?

The role of students in governance remains unclear. Since the early 1970s, students have advocated for greater involvement in the decision making of educational institutions. Most colleges and universities include students on governance committees with a range of involvement from consultation to full decision-making authority. Some colleges and universities include students on their governing boards (although the Association of Governing Boards discourages this, as well as frowning on the membership of faculty, seeing these as conflicts of interest).

In environments that serve adult students primarily, as many distributed learning programs do, the role of students can be quite significant. These students are often quite mature and bring a good deal of useful life experience and professional expertise to bear on decisions that need to be made. Of course, the challenge is to make sure that matters of academic integrity and quality are not sacrificed to satisfy unreasonable needs or demands posed by the "consumer"—a very problematic term for many in traditional environments. This potential conflict may be addressed by those efforts at creating "learning communities" where all members share rights and responsibilities appropriate to their roles and goals.

It should also be noted that some distributed learning environments do not include students in governance at all, and students find that quite acceptable. For them, such involvement is at best a distraction from their primary purpose of study or akin to high school "student government" (which is often viewed as developing skills in students rather than capitalizing on established expertise).

## FUNDAMENTAL ISSUES

In the end, much of governance boils down to matters of control and money. The control of most not-for-profit organizations and educational institutions, in particular, is not held in the hands of a few. It is shared by the board with a chief executive officer, with the faculty, with some students, and with specific external bodies, including the government, accreditors, and for-profit corporations. Financial stewardship is ultimately the responsibility of the board, but there, too, financial performance can and will be influenced significantly by all the players previously mentioned. Governance of colleges and universities, including distributed learning environments, is an exercise in collaboration that demands excellent communication skills, patience, sensitivity, and courage.

—*Anna DiStefano*

*See also* ACCREDITATION; ADMINISTRATIVE LEADERSHIP; ALLIANCES

### Bibliography

American Association of University Professors, American Council on Education, & Association of Governing Boards of Colleges and Universities. (October 1966). *Statement on government of colleges and universities.* Retrieved from http://www.aaup.org/statements/Redbook/Govern.htm.

Board of Directors of the Association of Governing Boards of Universities and Colleges. (1999). *AGB statement on institutional governance.* Washington, DC: Association of Governing Boards of Universities and Colleges.

Hawkins, Brian. (July-August 1999). Distributed learning and institutional restructuring. *Educom Review, 34*(4), 12–15, 42–44.

Hickman, Clark J. (Spring 1999). Public policy: Implications associated with technology assisted distance learning. *Adult Learning, 10*(3), 17–20.

Miller, Margaret A. (September 4, 1998). Speed up the pace of campus governance, or lose the authority to make decisions. *Chronicle of Higher Education,* B6.

Van Dusen, Gerald C. (1997). The virtual campus: Technology and reform in higher education. *ASHE-ERIC Higher Education Report, 25*(5).

# GRADUATE STUDY

U.S. graduate education has evolved over the past century into a unique blend of elements that were adapted initially from European advanced degrees. The master's degree originated from the French equivalent, and the Doctor of Philosophy (Ph.D.), which is the highest degree conferred by American universities, combines the German amalgam of seminars, specialist lectures, and the research dissertation with intensive research apprenticeship.

During the past decades, the portfolio of American graduate degrees has increased significantly to incorporate and generate new knowledge bases and to meet changing societal needs. Doctoral degrees now include the Doctor of Education (Ed.D.), Doctor of Business Administration (D.B.A.), Doctor of Public Administration (D.P.A.), and Doctor of Psychology (Psy.D.).

The real growth in graduate degrees, however, has been at the master's level with the development of some 1,000 distinct titles for master's degrees besides the generic Master of Arts (M.A.) and Master of Science (M.S.). Master's programs now not only involve advanced scholarship as an end in itself or as a step toward a doctorate, but also provide advanced professional training in a vast array of fields, many of which did not exist a generation ago. These new professional master's programs are the most prevalent among distributed graduate degrees whose delivery allows faculty, students, and educational resources to be in different locations.

## ATTRIBUTES OF GRADUATE EDUCATION

Although all U.S. graduate degree programs build on the broad-based baccalaureate, they are not a simple extension of coursework beyond the bachelor's degree. Designed by faculty experts in their fields, graduate programs integrate advanced and in-depth, focused study in a scholarly experience that goes beyond the transmission of knowledge to, as noted by LaPidus, "actual involvement in the processes by which knowledge is attained." Students' active involvement in the learning and discovery process is promoted by faculty mentoring and frequent interaction between faculty and students as well as among students in structured and informal settings. Together, the faculty and students form a graduate community of scholars that enhances learning and discovery as well as personal growth and professional socialization.

Typically students demonstrate their mastery of a graduate program's advanced, specialized subject matter and of its methodology of discovery in their performance on qualifying and comprehensive examinations and in their completion of a capstone scholarly/research experience such as a thesis, artistic presentation, or dissertation. In particular, Ph.D. candidates must demonstrate their capacity to make independent contributions to knowledge through original dissertation research and scholarship. Even in master's programs that do not require a thesis, the methodology of discovery is imparted so that degree recipients can be informed and critical consumers of the research and scholarship in their fields.

This model of graduate education has been a resounding success. U.S. educational institutions now annually enroll over 1.8 million graduate students and confer over 450,000 master's and over 40,000 doctoral degrees. Many of these graduate programs are acknowledged internationally as world leaders, and students from around the globe seek American graduate degrees. U.S. graduate education prepares future college and university faculty; scientists who conduct cutting-edge research; scholars who augment our understanding of human thought, creative expression, and social conditions; and advanced practitioners who contribute to professions, clients, and the overall economy.

## DISTRIBUTED GRADUATE EDUCATION

The traditional campus-based model has been the gold standard of U.S. graduate education. Particularly for Ph.D. preparation, face-to-face interactive delivery, intensive research apprenticeship, and dynamic faculty–student partnership in the enriched campus environment provide a model without peer. By its very nature, however, the campus-based model cannot accommodate the increasing demand for graduate education in the U.S. information economy, where an undergraduate degree no longer imparts a sufficient knowledge base to support a lifetime career. To be competitive in remaining abreast in their fields or in preparing to enter new and emerging fields, increasing numbers of employed adults are seeking postbaccalaureate education. Many of these individuals, however, are unable or unwilling to take time out for full-time, on-campus graduate study. Reflecting these trends, part-time students have increased to the point where they now are the majority of graduate enrollees.

In their commitment to serve society as they preserve, disseminate, and create knowledge, graduate educators have sought to respond to the compelling need for advanced education and to the time and place constraints of the new student majority. In extending graduate programming by connecting students with distributed learning resources, educators have been seeking to maintain standards of excellence and to preserve essential elements of the on-campus graduate experience.

Developments in distance education and other graduate concerns are monitored by the Council of Graduate Schools (CGS), which includes over 700 institutions that annually grant most U.S. graduate degrees. During the past three decades, CGS has issued policy statements on distance education as nonresidential graduate programs expanded from off-campus delivery by peripatetic professors to include delivery via evolving telecommunications technologies and delivery online. The major concern in all the relevant policy documents is the assurance that all graduate degrees, which bear the imprimatur of the institution awarding them, represent the same level of excellence, regardless of their delivery mode. The documents delineate means to maintain constancy in such critical programmatic areas as the qualifications and quality of faculty and students; the degree programs' academic objectives, content, requirements, evaluation standards, and learning outcomes; and institutional academic review processes and student support services.

Regardless of how a graduate degree program has been distributed, achieving and measuring such tangible learning outcomes as domain knowledge, critical reasoning, and mastery of the methodology of discovery in the field is relatively straightforward. The graduate degree experience, however, encompasses some less tangible but significant learning experiences. Many of these experiences are unplanned and generally are a byproduct of on-campus residency, which facilitates frequent and varied faculty–student and student–student interaction as well as easy access to student support services and to learning resources such as libraries, labs, colloquia, and visiting scholars.

To realize some of the benefits associated with a campus residential experience, many distributed programs incorporate technologies for participant communication such as e-mail, chat rooms, and threaded discussions, which involve a series of messages on a specific topic posted in a discussion forum. Learning resources also are enhanced by simulations, online labs, and streaming video; and online library services are now widely available to all users. While acknowledging the utility of these enhancements, distributed program designers are continuing research and development efforts to increase and enrich interaction opportunities and also provide "face time" for faculty and students. At this time, many distributed degree programs involve a hybrid model, requiring on-campus residency experience(s) along with online components.

## DISTANCE EDUCATION EXPANSION

As documented by statistics from the U.S. Department of Education, distance education has expanded rapidly in the past decade. By 1995, 34% of higher education institutions were offering graduate distance education courses, primarily via two-way interactive and one-way prerecorded video. In 1997, over 280,000 students were enrolled in distance graduate education courses. In 1999–2000, almost two-fifths of graduate distance education participants were pursuing degree programs taught entirely through distance education and predominantly via the Internet. In comparison with their counterparts, graduate distance program enrollees were more likely to be married and to have dependent children, and they were more likely to be employed, with over two-fifths working

full-time. The majority of these participants indicated that they were at least "equally satisfied" with distance as compared with nondistance education courses.

Most distance graduate offerings are professional master's degree programs, reflecting student and employer demand and possibly also the relative ease, in comparison to some arts and sciences degrees, of achieving these programs' learning objectives in a distributed mode. The increase in online graduate programs in business, education, engineering, library science, and public health is documented in the Web-based compendium maintained by *U.S. News and World Report.* In 2002, the list of such master's programs offered by regionally accredited institutions had grown to 240, compared to 130 in 2001.

Highly selective universities have only recently begun to launch online graduate programs, often in a hybrid model. As a step toward such offerings, Harvard has just modified its 1-year campus residency requirement, allowing residency modifications on a case-by-case basis for master's programs that are not research-intensive. A newly designed Harvard Master of Public Health program combines online coursework with 2 months of on-campus residency over two summers.

## GRADUATE PROGRAM DISTRIBUTORS

Given the market demand, distributed graduate education is becoming big business, attracting many for-profit providers. Among these is the regionally accredited University of Phoenix, which is the largest U.S. virtual university (having no central physical campus), enrolling more students than any other private institution. In addition to delivering graduate programs at classroom locations nationwide, the university offers several degree programs entirely online, and enrollment in its online offerings has increased more than tenfold since 1997. Recently the university introduced "Flexnet" graduate programs in which two-thirds of the coursework is online and one-third is at classroom sites with an instructor and other students.

In addition to distribution by single not-for-profit or for-profit educational institutions, some graduate programs are distributed by a partnership or consortium. Some of these alliances are composed of academic institutions; others are formed between universities and commercial enterprises. As noted by Katz, all members in such partnerships share risks and pool their resources and talents in leveraging each other's expertise.

Many partnerships among academic institutions involve linkages of colleges and universities within a particular state. Multi-state alliances include the 10-state Great Plains Interactive Distance Education Alliance; the Southern Regional Electronic University, with over 325 member institutions; and the virtual Western Governors University, which utilizes 45 education providers from across the United States and Canada. Partnership benefits for university participants include augmented enrollments, broadened course offerings, participation in graduate programs that an institution could not mount independently, and eventual cost savings in technological and administrative support.

For graduate students, these alliances facilitate access to a plethora of courses and degree programs. In addition, the graduate experience of students in on-campus as well as in online degree programs can be enhanced significantly when academic partnerships distribute scarce instructional resources, such as infrequently taught foreign language courses and advanced data analysis seminars that might not otherwise be available. The Committee on Institution Cooperation (CIC), which is an academic consortium of 12 major research universities in the Midwest, is developing CIC CourseShare to facilitate and administratively support inter-institutional sharing of specialized online graduate courses.

Cooperative ventures between universities and other organizations, such as Internet start-ups, involve a different model of sharing complementary capabilities and resources. Generally, university faculty members provide the academic content, and the partner manages the logistics, business affairs, and marketing. For example, an academic consortium consisting of Carnegie Mellon University, the University of Chicago, Columbia, Stanford, and the London School of Economics has developed online business education (including a Master of Business Administration program) in collaboration with UNext.com. UNext.com has founded a virtual university, known as Cardean University, to supply these consortium-developed online offerings to corporate clients.

## CONCLUSION

Distributed graduate education is designed to facilitate and broaden students' access to advanced study irrespective of place and time constraints. As student and employer demand for distributed graduate education has increased, so have the number and variety of distributors, including more and more public and private universities, for-profit educational companies, and partnerships involving various combinations of these providers. All of these developments are spurring further innovations and synergistic collaborations that can enhance learning in campus-based as well as in distance degree programs. As in all educational pursuits, however, quality outcomes require steadfast maintenance of standards of excellence. Quality outcomes in distributed graduate programming are dependent also on the provision of meaningful interaction experiences for participants and on creative incorporation of technological and other resources for learning and for student support.

Pragmatism has always been a hallmark of U.S. graduate education as educators have adopted, adapted, and invented educational practices, implementing those that work and modifying or discarding those that do not. The pace of pragmatic adaptation and change has been accelerating, however, with distributed graduate education. At this time, therefore, it is very much a work in progress.

—*Jeanne Gullahorn*

**See also** CLINICAL TRAINING; DEGREES/DEGREE PROGRAMS; MBA ONLINE; MEDICAL EDUCATION; SCHOLAR PRACTITIONER MODEL

## Bibliography

Council of Graduate Schools. (1977). *Non-residential graduate degree programs.* Washington, DC: Author.

Council of Graduate Schools. (1989). *Off-campus graduate education.* Washington, DC: Author.

Council of Graduate Schools. (1998). *Distance graduate education: Opportunities and challenges for the 21st century.* Washington, DC: Author.

Council of Graduate Schools. (2000). *Graduate enrollment and degrees: 1986 to 2000.* Washington, DC: Author.

Katz, R., Napier, I., & Ferrara, E. (2002). *Distance learning partnerships.* Washington, DC: American Council on Education.

LaPidus, J. B. (1989). Graduate education—the next twenty-five years. Paper presented at the 25th anniversary event, faculty of graduate studies, University of Guelph, Ontario, Canada.

U.S. Department of Education, National Center for Education Statistics. (1998). *Distance education in higher education institutions.* Washington, DC: Author. NCES 98-062.

U.S. Department of Education, National Center for Education Statistics, Postsecondary Education Quick Information System. (1999). *Survey on distance education at postsecondary education institutions, 1997–1998.* Washington, DC: Author.

U.S. Department of Education, National Center for Education Statistics. (2000). *1999–2000 national postsecondary student aid study.* Washington, DC: Author.

# GRANTS

Grants have played a key role in the growth of the educational sector in the United States and abroad, and in supporting research within educational institutions. Grants have not as yet, however, been a large or integral part of the proliferation and growth of distributed education. This may be due partly to the organic nature of distributed education's emergence within the educational sector, growing, for the most part, out of traditional educational institutions as an extension of the classroom delivery of educational matter. This entry focuses on grants and grant making in higher education, with reference to distributed education, and on the relationship between foundations and institutions of higher education.

## DEFINITIONS

*Grants* are a distinct form of philanthropy. A grant may be defined as a legally sanctioned transfer of funds from one organization to another, or from an organization to an individual to support a specific purpose or achieve a given end. Grants thus have legal and economic status within society, as well as social context, as do the organizations engaged in grant making. *Grant making* is the process of awarding funds, including the submission of an application from a grant seeker, grantor decision making, and funds disbursement. The activity and process of grant making is thus a necessary component of the awarding of grants.

Grants are based on an exchange relationship requiring a donor and a recipient. Grants serve the interests of foundations, hospitals, charities, cultural institutions, corporations, educational institutions, and a number of other social, economic, and political actors. As nonprofits seek grants, they are required to interact with groups that control resources. Grants therefore may influence or define power relationships between groups and organizations, serve to replicate elite structures and channels of influence, or perpetuate or alter sociopolitical and economic relationships, the variations within which depend on the ideological or philosophical aims and beliefs of elites within the organizations making grants.

Grant seeking is a fact of life for nonprofit organizations, including higher education. As a measure of the importance placed on grants, institutions of higher education have developed formal administrative structures and processes to seek grants from foundations, corporations, and government. Grant-making organizations have proliferated, and have likewise developed formal administrative structures and processes. Grant makers have sought to define specific areas of interest to guide their grant making, reducing the roles of discretion and flexibility while simultaneously making an implicit—if not always explicit—judgment about the relative merits of educational issues and related social trends.

## GRANTS FOR HIGHER EDUCATION

Grant makers view education as a priority area for funding because of the perceived range of social influence and training that are possible within educational settings. Higher education, in particular, has been greatly influenced by grants made by elite foundations with vast resources. Guided by the norms and values of leading foundations such as the Carnegie Corporation and the Ford Foundation, major foundations have formed close and enduring relationships with institutions of higher education that have shaped the character, direction, values, growth, and research agendas of universities and colleges.

## TYPES OF GRANTS

Grants may be given to support a broad range of activities. Grants are made for academic research, to provide "seed" funding for innovative projects, to support communities or individuals in times of need or who are undergoing rapid changes in circumstance, to provide operating support, or to fund endowments. There are also challenge grants, which require a matching component. The common thread of all grants is that funds are distributed on a nonrepayable basis with no expectation of commercial return.

## SOURCES OF GRANTS: THE FEDERAL GOVERNMENT

Grant making has become an important activity of government, particularly in the immediate post-Sputnik era, as federally encouraged and funded research came to be seen as critical to U.S. scientific and technological leadership. Additionally, the vast range of social and educational programs stemming from Great Society legislation during the 1960s has given rise to a set of nongovernmental organizations administering social welfare and educational programs funded with federal government grants. These programs and initiatives have helped shape the course of higher education in a variety of ways, from scholarship programs to research awards, as institutions respond to myriad federal regulations that accompany funding. Institutions have devoted substantial resources to managerial structures designed to secure extramural funding, thereby increasing bureaucratization and professionalization stimulated by grant seeking activities.

Government is by far the largest source of grants. Through agencies such as the National Science Foundation (NSF), the National Institutes of Health (NIH), the National Endowment for the Humanities (NEH), and the National Endowment for the Arts (NEA), the federal government makes available grant funds that can be obtained through a competitive, often peer-review process that is theoretically not subject to political influence. The federal government may also make agency grants in a variety of other ways, including Congressional appropriation. State, county, and local governments may act as recipients of federal grants and/or as regranting agencies to support a range of services and activities, education prominent among them.

Grants for educational activities—teaching, research, support technologies, conferences, and the like—may come from the above-named agencies or from the Department of Education or other cabinet-level departments. The Fund for the Improvement of Post-Secondary Education (FIPSE) has been the Department of Education's most prominent and long-lived program to support higher education. The FIPSE program is beginning to award grants related to distributed education.

## SOURCES OF GRANTS: FOUNDATIONS

The foundation sector, through its grant-making activity, has played a prominent role in the growth of higher education. After the federal government, foundations are the largest source of grants in the United States. It is estimated that foundations were responsible for giving grants in 2001 totaling approximately $26 billion, or 12% of total privately contributed funds to organizations. Of an estimated total of $212 billion in private contributions, education received $32 billion, or 15% of total charitable contributions. The top 50 recipient universities received $1,726,447,848 in foundation grants in 2000.

Foundations in the United States owe their growth largely to the development of favorable tax rules during the early 20th century. Beginning with legislation in the 1930s and through subsequent legislation modifying and extending the favorable treatment of charitable gifts, foundations became important vehicles for the conscientious disbursement in the public interest of some of the proceeds from great industrial fortunes. Industrialists such as Rockefeller, Ford, Carnegie, Dodge, Irvine, Sloan, and more recently Packard, Hewlett, and Gates and their families all established foundations whose assets have grown exponentially over the decades with a corresponding increase in the number and value of grants made.

## THE GRANT APPLICATION PROCESS

Researchers and others in higher education typically follow a well-defined process involving elaborate rituals to obtain grants. Although personal relationships used on behalf of an institution may be valuable in gaining the attention of funding agencies, most foundations and agencies rely on an ostensibly objective process that, although its specifics may vary from organization to organization, generally hews to type whether the organization is a government agency or a private foundation.

With a defined project in mind, a researcher, project director, or principal investigator (PI) may perform a search using resources such as The Foundation Center to identify possible sources of funding for the project. Typically, foundations and government agencies provide detailed guidelines on the types of projects supported, or develop special programs and initiatives designed to attract specific types of proposals for funding. Additionally, foundations may issue special calls for proposals based on predetermined programs, or initiate grants to fund areas deemed important within the purview of the foundation's mission and funding priorities.

Because competition for funds is keen, foundations and agencies must attempt to define priorities to guide funding decisions and make those guidelines transparent to grant seekers. From the perspective of the PI, finding the right "match" or congruence between the project and the funding source is the key first step in applying for and obtaining a grant. PIs may be aided in their search by university offices of research or by the development office, both of which provide in-house resources and specialists, including grant writers, to facilitate the grant application process and to support faculty or administrators in the process of securing funding.

Once a potential source of funding has been identified, the next step is to develop a grant proposal that provides a narrative rationale for the funding requested as well as a detailed project budget. Successful grant writing is a highly developed skill. Often, a professional grant writer will be employed to construct the grant proposal. In academic disciplines where extramural funding is a major component of research activity, such as in the sciences, the skills of a competent grant writer are indispensable to success. Backgrounds of grant writers may vary widely because grant writing is a craft learned via informal apprenticeship and practice, although there are a number of training courses now available.

When the proposal has been completed and received administrative approvals, it is submitted to the funding agency or foundation for review. The review process and response time may be well-established, as with government agencies, or more flexible in the case of foundations where grant decision making is subject to internal review by program officers and administrative leadership, and commonly by the board of trustees of the foundation in the case of larger grants. During the process the PI may be contacted by a program officer to provide further information or clarification, particularly if there is a predisposition to make the grant because of the prestige of the researcher or of the institution with which the researcher is associated.

If the grant request is declined, the researcher must attempt to secure funding from another foundation source and navigate a similar course. In the event of a grant award, the researcher works with the office of research to establish an internal account from which to draw the funds. The awarding agency may require detailed progress reports or a final evaluative report on the use of the funds and their impact on the project.

Government grants may be audited to ensure proper use of the funds. The research office of an educational institution, as well as the PI, is responsible for following established guidelines and preparing reports. Although foundations may also require an audit of a grant, in practice this is rarely done. Usually, a simple written report is accepted to account for the use of funds.

## DEVELOPING FUNDING OPPORTUNITIES FOR DISTRIBUTED EDUCATION

Some observers hypothesize a trend in foundation funding that appears to favor more prestigious academic institutions over those perceived to have less prestige. The Chronicle of Philanthropy's list of top educational grant recipients shows a strong correlation between competitive admissions, faculty prestige, size of endowment—in short the key measures of educational quality—and extramural funding levels from the top 100 foundations. Thus, a researcher or PI would do well to affiliate with a perceived high-status institution to increase the chances of a successful grant proposal. This hypothesis, however, does not account for the important role of smaller foundations, often community- or state-based, that support a variety of institutions of higher education. The Foundation Center's database shows over 56,000 foundations in the United States, many of which support higher education.

A fertile area of investigation might be to analyze the grant-making relationship between the 100 academic institutions ranking highest in perceived quality and the 100 largest foundations giving to higher education to determine whether, in fact, high-quality, well-endowed institutions receive a disproportionate share of grant funds.

The concept and practice of distributed education may require further definition and elaboration in theory if not in practice before it begins to attract the levels of grant support enjoyed by traditional educational delivery methods. One may distinguish between the educational outcomes of distributed education and the method of delivering education, of which distributed education is one variant. Foundations and grant makers will need to be educated on the salient variables distinguishing distributed education from other types of education, and therefore understand the types of funding opportunities presented by distributed education. Of the top 100 recipients of foundation funding for higher education, none are institutions of distributed learning. Foundation funding appears to go largely to established institutions of higher education, many of which now have online educational offerings that could be defined as distributed education. Further research may establish whether there is a perceived quality issue between traditional institutions of higher education and distributed learning institutions, many of which were established only in recent decades, and the extent to which this issue influences foundation and government grants to distributed education. Research is also needed to understand the factors that would influence grant makers to make available funding for distributed education.

The Alfred P. Sloan Foundation has pioneered grants for asynchronous learning networks (ALNs), and continues its innovative funding initiatives to promote "anytime, anywhere" online learning. As stated by the Sloan Foundation, "there is a great need for careful empirical studies that can identify the educational, economic, and social consequences of online learning and distance education."

—*James C. Murphy*

*See also* FINANCE; FUNDING SOURCES

## Bibliography

Alfred P. Sloan Foundation: www.sloan.org.

American Association of Fundraising Counsel. (2002). *Giving USA*. Retrieved from http://www.aafrc.org/giving/index.html.

Andrew W. Mellon Foundation: http://www.mellon.org.

*The Chronicle of Philanthropy:* http://www.philanthropy.com.

Distance Education Clearinghouse, University of Wisconsin-Extension: http://www.uwex.edu/disted/funding.html.

The Foundation Center: http://www.fdncenter.org.

Froelich, Karen A. (1999). Diversification of revenue strategies: Evolving resource dependence in nonprofit organizations. *Nonprofit and Voluntary Sector Quarterly, 28*(3), 246–268.

Indiana University Center on Philanthropy: http://www.philanthropy.iupui.edu.

Krebs, Arlene. (1998). *The distance learning funding sourcebook: A guide to foundation, corporate and government support for telecommunications and the new media,* 4th edition. Dubuque, IA: Kendall/Hunt Publishing Company.

Orosz, Joel J. (2000). *The insider's guide to grantmaking: How foundations find, fund, and manage effective programs.* San Francisco: Jossey-Bass.

Prewitt, Kenneth. (1996). *American foundations and the funding of science.* Indianapolis: Indiana University Center on Philanthropy.

The U.S. Department of Education's NonProfit Gateway: http://www.ed.gov/NPAdvisor/index.html.

The Web of Asynchronous Learning Networks: www.aln.org.

# GRAPHICS

Graphics consist of depictive techniques that utilize both words and images as tools of communication. Examples of graphics include charts and tables, pictures, and illustrations. In the context of distance learning, another dimension of the definition of graphics can be added: Graphics are words and images that can be shared *electronically.*

Because distance learning involves the separation of learner and educator—in both space and time—the methods of communication between the two are of paramount importance. With the continuation of technological advancements, these communications can occur in multiple ways. Methods for computer-based interactions include the ubiquitous electronic mail (e-mail) for sharing conversations, information, and files; electronic discussion forums (newsgroups) for having conversations about topics of interests; audio, video, and desktop multimedia conferencing for sharing both sound and visual information; and the Internet, which links computer networks, thus enabling all of these computer interactions to take place. Because of the availability of these tools, the communication and collaboration *between* educator and learner, as well as *among* learners have been greatly enhanced.

Adding graphics to convey information often results in a more engaged learner who has an improved understanding of the material being communicated. Graphics can be a powerful addition to an educator's "presentation toolkit." By including graphics in a distance learning presentation, educators have the ability to increase both the type and the quantity of information they can share electronically; however, graphics must be carefully chosen and used.

Graphics can both aid and hinder the learning process, so it is necessary for the educator to learn the techniques of using graphics in presentations, as well as the drawbacks and limitations of doing so. Often, as educators are beginning to utilize graphics tools for instruction, they focus on the graphics software and techniques, rather than on their content. When using graphics in presentations it is important that the educator stay focused on the instructional design and content. Graphics should be seen as a way to enhance the understanding of the material, not as a replacement for meaningful content. Edward Tufte, an authority on the visual communication of information, cautions educators, "In the first place, don't begin with the question 'What presentation software should one use?' but rather with 'What are the thinking-learning-understanding tasks that my displays and presentations are supposed to help with?' Answering this second question will then suggest technologies of information transmission."

Don Norman, the author of *The Design of Everyday Things* and the writer of numerous works on computer usability, considers the following advantages and disadvantages of using graphics to disseminate information.

The advantages are:

- "They are fun."
- "They are lightweight, so they don't detract from the experience by significantly impacting load times."
- "They are written in JavaScript and Dynamic HTML so they should work on most systems."

The disadvantages are:

- "They get in the way. After the first few minutes of delight, the next few minutes are spent trying to figure out how to get rid of them."
- "Not everyone can see them . . ." (Norman, 2003).

In spite of the positive reasons for using graphics to enhance distance learning, why aren't more educators using graphics in their communications with learners? One possible explanation is because of the many challenges facing them. Both educators and learners wanting to use graphics are forced to grapple with unfamiliar technology and to face multiple challenges to the effective use of graphics, such as the following:

- To use graphics effectively in electronically delivered presentations requires that both the educator and learner acquire new skills. Often the learning curve is steep, requiring a significant commitment of time, energy, and patience.
- Although improvements continue to be made to hardware, software, and communication networks, technological limitations and compatibility issues still exist. Many computer monitors are small and have relatively low resolution, resulting in a significant hindrance to using graphics. In addition, all computer monitors are oriented horizontally, sometimes making the effective display of images challenging.
- The differences in the types of systems (both hardware and software) used by both educators and learners can also be problematic. Different monitors mean differences in the size and resolution of images. The amount of system memory available will likewise create differences in the quality of graphic images. Different systems have different graphics capabilities, and some will have minimal, if any, graphics capabilities. The way in which the Internet is accessed (i.e., dial-up, DSL, cable) impacts both the speed and the reliability of the transmission of graphics. In addition, most graphics files must be compressed (i.e., made smaller) prior to transmitting them. There are various file formats to contend with, such as GIF (Graphic Interchange Format), JPEG (Joint Photographic Experts Group), and PNG (Portable Network Graphic). All of these variations provide creative challenges for employing graphics in distance learning.
- It is a certainty that technical problems will occur when creating, transmitting, and using graphics. Learners may experience difficulty in downloading and viewing the graphics. Educators may have problems converting files to a format that allows them to be transmitting electronically. How and by whom will these problems be addressed?

In spite of the challenges facing both educators and learners in the use of graphics to convey information in distance learning, graphics can be a powerful tool for facilitating the communication between educator and learner. Graphics will remain a critical component to the way in which information is shared in distance learning programs.

Graphics "done properly" enhance the communication of information and facilitate the understanding of content. Learning to use (i.e., create, manipulate, transmit, and download) graphics is quickly becoming a required skill for both distance learning educators and learners.

*—Gibson Scheid*

*See also* HYPERTEXT; WEB SITES

### Bibliography

Norman, Donald A. (2002). *The design of everyday things.* New York: Basic Books.

Norman, D. A. (n.d.). *Gratuitous graphics and human-centered Website design.* Retrieved January 2003 from http://www.jnd.org/dn.mss/hcd_website_design.html.

Tufte, Edward. (May 28, 2001). *E.T. on technologies for making presentations.* Retrieved January 2003 from http://www.edwardtufte.com/1535689023/bboard/q-and-a-fetch-msg?msg_id=00001B&topic_id=1.

# GROUP PROCESS

Group process describes the comprehensive and integrated package of a group's experiences throughout its lifespan. Group process refers to all of the interactions, events, stages, methods, and processes experienced and used by a group and its members in the completion of their task or the meeting of their purpose. In other words, group process is how the group goes about doing what it does. The terms *group process* and *group dynamics* are often used interchangeably; however, a commonly accepted distinction is that "dynamics" refers to individual elements of influence (e.g., norms as a dynamic) and "process" refers to how the elements are interwoven over time.

Commonly known and accepted elements, or dynamics, of group process that affect a group's performance include shared vision, values, purpose, and norms; leadership structure and style; role structure and responsibilities; composition; size; identity; boundaries; decision-making processes; evaluation methods; feedback loops; and conflict management practices. A complete analysis of group process also considers the reasons and underlying assumptions, including beliefs and feelings, that have an effect on a group's behavior.

The purpose of paying attention to group process, through monitoring and analysis, is to ensure that the group is doing what it should be doing at any point in time, moving in the right direction toward the accomplishment of its goals, making adequate progress, adhering to its values and agreements, and behaving in an acceptable manner. Analysis of group process takes into consideration the vast array of elements and influences that affect how the members work together and is used to assist in developing new strategies and successful interventions to keep a group on track and optimally successful. The ultimate quality of a group's performance can be linked directly to the quality of its process. Group process may be examined from the perspective of different theories and models across disciplines that provide frameworks for understanding, predicting, and assessing how a group functions and that guide the development of interventions.

## DIFFERENCES WITH ONLINE GROUPS

Group process in a distributed learning system is usually considered in the context of asynchronous or synchronous, online, interactive classes, but also comes into play with administrative or faculty groups that meet online. Group process issues in distributed learning groups are similar in most ways to those in face-to-face groups, with the major exceptions being that online groups generally rely on text-based interactions between geographically dispersed members to conduct their business, and the interactions are computer mediated. Although group process is always an important consideration when working with any group, and although the issues are similar, the different dynamics involved in the online environment add a requirement for heightened awareness of the group's process.

Communication in a virtual, or computer-mediated, learning system is typically engaged through the exchange of posted or electronic mail (e-mail) messages between members and the class, committee, team, or community at large using an asynchronous forum (e.g., electronic bulletin board, newsgroup). It also occurs by using the synchronous, real-time, "chat" type technology that enables instant exchange and simultaneous composing, reading, and replying. In the online environment, traditional environmental and social conditions and cues are different or missing and, especially in the case of online classes, members often do not know or see each other. Physical meeting rooms are changed to virtual spaces. Specific, regular, start-and-stop meeting times may be traded for extended, around-the-clock sessions. Facial expressions, body language, physical gestures, verbal inflections, pace, rhythm, and volume are either absent or conveyed with textual formatting. Personal characteristics such as gender, race, age, ethnicity, and handicapping conditions are not visibly discernable. The different dynamics that emerge in online groups can be loosely grouped into text-oriented considerations, anonymity effects, data and time management concerns, and boundary issues.

One process support method often used to address the different dynamics is an orientation. Face-to-face or online orientation sessions are conducted to bring the group together as a whole, create an identity, begin its development, and generate initial cohesion. Orientations allow for acculturation into the specific learning institution and system, provide an opportunity to collectively establish norms and boundaries, and help to reduce the effects of anonymity. Including education about online communication concepts and etiquette (netiquette), as well as instruction, familiarization, and practice with the technology the group will be using, can help minimize text and technology-related problems.

## TEXT-ORIENTED CONSIDERATIONS

Although communication and facilitation methods in an online learning environment may be similar to those used in face-to-face groups (e.g., agendas, charters, clarifying questions, probing questions, paraphrasing, inclusion seeking, consensus, summarizing, and feedback), a number of additional considerations exist. Because most of the interactions are text-based, the degree of facility with the written word can enhance or inhibit how any communication is conveyed and interpreted. It is important to recognize that typing skills and other word processing proficiency can affect how well messages are constructed, how long it takes to do the task, and how well messages are understood. Referring members to various tutorial programs is an effective method of addressing proficiency issues.

Different forms of word-processing netiquette are generally followed to facilitate communication and avoid misunderstandings. For instance, it is common to denote emphasis on a word or phrase by using a different *font,* **bolding**, underlining or placing an *asterisk* on both sides of the word or phrase. Conversely, words or phrases that are completely capitalized are difficult to read and often interpreted as an emotional expression (e.g., SHOUTING, ANGER) that may elicit an unintended reaction. Overuse of punctuation (e.g., Please Reply!!!) can also signify strong emotional expression or an emphatic directive. Learning, agreeing upon, and consistently practicing a form of netiquette can make the difference between inhibiting communication or inciting conflict, and being understood and effective.

## DATA AND TIME MANAGEMENT CONCERNS

The number of responses that group members post, the frequency of posts, the content volume in the responses, and the quality of the content are largely unpredictable in the computer-mediated learning environment. They vary in manageability with each group, with the subject matter around which the group is gathered, and with the task on which the group is working; however, the combination of response frequency, volume, and content quality greatly contributes to the effectiveness of the group's process. For example, when the frequency of posted messages exceeds group members' ability to track, read, and respond meaningfully, then confusion, loss of focus, and giving up may occur. The timing of postings may be delayed and messages may be received out of sequence, or confused with other unrelated messages, further exacerbating any process management problems.

Messages that are too long to read and digest within a reasonable amount of time will cause some members to fall behind while they attempt to read everything, or to respond in kind. Others often elect to ignore the long messages altogether. Messages with content quality that doesn't meet expected standards can generate a loss of energy, enthusiasm, and interest that results in the subsequent lessening of overall group quality, productivity, and learning opportunities. Similarly, any particular member who consistently posts too many messages within a short period of time, or contributes messages that are too long-winded or lack substantive quality, may incur direct or indirect negative responses from other group members.

Syllabi, assignment instructions, and charters that clearly outline posting requirements and expectations are most helpful in preventing data and time management issues. For example, a formal written assignment for a week may be limited to 1 page, or 500 words, with responses not to exceed 2 paragraphs, and the number of postings to which a member is required to respond can be limited to a select group or number of members (e.g., only reply to 2 members). Spelling out requirements about the quality of the content expected, and giving examples, provides a common, observable standard for everyone to match.

## ANONYMITY EFFECTS

Relative anonymity is another characteristic that can greatly affect a group's communication and facilitation processes. Anonymity can come in the form of group members not knowing each other at all, or knowing each other but not being physically and visibly present with each other. Members communicating via computer at a distance may feel isolated or depersonalized and can experience feelings of uncertainty, depression, and anxiety. They may withdraw from active participation and follow a vicious cycle that keeps them from becoming more participatory.

Group members who feel that they don't know each other well enough may hold back from participating in processes such as authentic dialogue, appropriate disclosure and feedback, and information sharing that facilitates trust, cohesion, and development. Conversely, it is not unusual for members who experience themselves as relatively anonymous to communicate reactively with others in inappropriate ways commonly labeled as "flaming." Flaming can consist of any type of communication that is experienced as scolding, disrespectful, uncivil, angry, sarcastic, hurtful, or degrading and is generally aimed at a particular person rather than any specific issue. Flaming behaviors can quickly destroy the integrity of the group.

Members who are slower to respond, or respond less often than expected, may be experienced by the rest of the group as absent, aloof, or distressed when in fact they may be thinking, writing, or experiencing technical difficulties. They may also have simply missed or misinterpreted instructions, expectations, or significant messages. In response to the real or perceived absence of participation of any members, the other members may become worried or obsessed with the absence, or they may exclude or discount the missing members and their contributions. These reactions cause group members to be distracted from the group's primary purpose and negatively affect their collective process.

Participation and attendance issues are linked to the combination of anonymity and boundary permeability. Making participation and attendance expectations explicit at the beginning of the course through orientations, course requirements, team or committee charters, and established norms encourages consistent interaction and reduces boundary-related anonymity effects. For example, a course requirement to make two substantive postings a week can keep members present and engaged and minimizes member loss and isolation. It can simultaneously alert the facilitator or leader to potential problems before they get out of hand.

Anonymity issues can also be mitigated by including and integrating structural and social aspects. Creating places to post personal profiles and pictures, and initiating introductions that include personal and subject matter details, help to establish relationships, identify common areas of interest, and highlight different qualities that each member brings to the group. Setting up a common area in which to socialize and share different experiences, thoughts, and general conversation that is not course or project specific is another effective way to build and maintain cohesion.

## BOUNDARY ISSUES

Groups in a distributed learning environment must contend with three major boundary considerations that can substantially affect their process: time and space, information processing, and course environment structure and use. Groups that meet online, particularly asynchronous groups, often experience process losses, containment issues, and weak cohesion because they lack a common, physical meeting space and time. It is easier for members to disappear, get lost, and become unnoticed in the online shuffle than if they walked out of a room, didn't show up at the allotted time, or were inordinately quiet and nonparticipatory during a meeting in a closed room. Alternatively, subgroups may form outside of the main group, depriving it of vital information and support and contributing to a feeling of mistrust among other members.

Information processing issues relate to confidentiality, use, access, and security of all the interactions, ideas, proprietary information, assignments, and products that the group members share with each other. Group process concerns about information are primarily associated with conditions of trust (e.g., maintenance and breaches) and regulate the quality and quantity of shared information. Coming to a common understanding about what comprises individual intellectual capital, privileged information, and community knowledge, and then developing guidelines about what can be used, shared, copied, and forwarded are useful ways of addressing information processing boundaries.

The design of the meeting environment, group operating procedures, and the features and constraints of existing technology affect the internal order and manageability of the group's interactions and contributions by controlling where and when specific information is posted. If there are not clearly identifiable and easily accessible places to post information and replies, or if members don't understand how to use the technology appropriately, the postings can easily become lost or difficult to track. Related information can get fragmented into different areas, or unrelated information can collect in one area, causing distractions and confusion. Setting up special areas for schedules, instructions, directions, resources, member lists, and any other pertinent subjects maintains structural boundaries. Course structure outlines, systems training, and instruction in common posting and interaction practices further contribute to organization and manageability.

## FACILITATION

Effective online group process begins with designing environmentally specific structures and procedures and continues with ongoing facilitation that integrates the group's dynamics and promotes smooth operation. Positive facilitation practices consist of monitoring participation and quality levels, assisting struggling members, offering encouragement, providing alternate methods of communication (e.g., e-mail, telephone, third party), answering questions, and supporting appropriate communication practices and norms.

—*Candido Trujillo*

*See also* FACILITATION; GROUP SIZE; NETIQUETTE; TEACHING IN AN ELECTRONIC CLASSROOM

### Bibliography

Harasim, L., Hiltz, S. R., Teles, L., & Turoff, M. (1996). *Learning networks.* Cambridge: MIT Press.

Hiltz, S. R., & Turoff, M. (1993). *The network nation: Human communication via computer.* Cambridge: MIT Press.

Jessup, L. M., Connolly, T., & Tansik, D. A. (1990). Toward a theory of automated group work: The deindividuating effects of anonymity. *Small Group Research, 21,* 333–348.

Palloff, R. M., & Pratt, K. (2001). *Lessons from the cyberspace classroom: The realities of online teaching.* San Francisco, CA: Jossey-Bass.

Rudestam, K. E., & Schoenholtz-Read, J. (Eds.). (2002). *Handbook of online learning: Innovations in higher education and corporate training.* Thousand Oaks, CA: Sage.

Schopler, J. H., Abell, M. D., & Galinsky, M. J. (1998). Technology-based groups: A review and conceptual framework for practice. *Social Work, 43*(3), 254–268.

Valacich, J. S., Dennis, A. R., & Connolly, T. (1994). Idea generation in computer-based groups: A new ending to an old story. *Organizational Behavior and Human Decision Processes, 57,* 448–467.

Walther, J. B., & Burgoon, J. K. (1992). Relational communication in computer-mediated interaction. *Human Communication Research, 19*(1), 5088.

## GROUP SIZE

Group size refers to the number of students participating in an online, computer-mediated class. It is an element of group composition and structure that should be considered when designing an online course. It derives its significance from its effects on group process and subsequent measures of class success. Size is important in any group; however, it becomes a critical factor when setting up a virtual classroom because of the limited channels of communication, loss or changing of traditional social cues, changes to characteristic boundaries of structure, time, and space, and technology constraints that differentiate this group from a face-to-face group.

Group size is an essential consideration when creating classes using either asynchronous, bulletin board, forum, or newsgroup types of technology, or synchronous, real-time, "chat" types of technology. Effective group process is directly related to the combination of size and type of class being conducted. Different sizes of groups produce their own unique dynamics, whether they are well known and readily observable dynamics commonly seen in many groups, such as the two against one pairing in a triad or the formation of subgroups with competing agendas in larger groups, or whether they are more obscure dynamics that affect the quality of interaction.

Asynchronous content delivery courses using the expert-instructor model often found in colleges and universities are primarily affected by course management issues. The instructor in these courses usually provides the same assignments, resources, references, and prepared content to all students, and the students are typically responsible for turning in assignments to the instructor. Dialogue or feedback may be conducted in public or private, and usually occurs directly between the student and the instructor. The process that occurs is usually limited to a dyadic, information exchanging, teaching relationship that is different than those of a more interactive, collaborative group.

Group size in an asynchronous content delivery class is determined by general course management considerations such as how much information the students are expected to read and understand within a particular time frame, how much volume the instructor can process, and the volume of data exchange and storage that the technology can support. Considerations also include the desired depth of thinking and analysis, the breadth of study and scope of understanding expected from the students, the methods of demonstrating learning and knowledge, and the quality and type of feedback, grading, or responses expected from the instructor. This type of class can often accommodate 20 or more students, depending on design and objectives.

Asynchronous classes that employ facilitative instruction techniques, collaborative processes, and synergistic learning methods add a significant group process component to consider. The quality of student–student interaction and instructor–student interaction, as well as the content provided by both instructor and students, combine to determine the quality of these classes. The instructor in this type of class usually provides the same assignments, resources, references, and prepared content to all the students; however, students are often expected to provide instructor-evaluated feedback and critiques to each others' assignments and to engage in dialogue about the work. Collaborative group projects are often assigned that rely on optimal group process. Understanding the effects of group size on the process can greatly contribute to the successful design and facilitation of an online, interactive course.

The course management considerations previously noted still apply; however, the dynamics of interacting students and faculty are greatly expanded. Experience with online, experiential, and interactive educational groups demonstrates that there are three basic class sizes that affect optimal learning processes and outcomes within the areas of course management and quality of interaction: 5 or fewer, 6 to 9, and 10 and above. For example, although five students in a group may be manageable in terms of time and volume, that number often falls short of the critical mass required to generate continued energy, interest, and synergistic learning. On the other hand, groups of 10 may suffer both course management and group process losses. Depending on how the assignments are constructed and scheduled, the effects of trying to do too much work in too little time and space can dilute learning and increase confusion and anxiety due to information overload. The most readily observable size effects on large groups are the formation of subgroups and inclusion/exclusion issues among the participants that restrict the sharing of information and reduce learning opportunities.

Asynchronous interactive groups having between six and nine members offer an optimal configuration in terms of course management and group process considerations. The members in this size group oscillate between content exchange processing and creative knowledge generation, and avoid the previously noted issues experienced in smaller and larger groups. In any window of time (e.g., weekly creation and discussion of assignments), there is opportunity for substantive reading, analysis, reflection, and writing without becoming too overwhelmed or confused. There is enough variety and interaction to stimulate continued thought, interest, and additional learning.

Synchronous real-time groups are commonly used in conjunction with other methods to conduct brainstorming, discussion, presentation, demonstration, and question and answer sessions. Although many of the same considerations previously noted apply (e.g., too many participants create an information processing overload), the nature of these groups adds a different layer of complexity and requires active facilitation. As the number of participants rises, so do issues concerning turn-taking, interruptions, topic changes, strict time boundaries, tracking subjects, relating points, typing proficiency, and message exchange delays. Synchronous groups having between six and nine members can work well depending on the facilitation and technical proficiency of the instructor. Collaborative groups generally should have fewer members, whereas less interactive groups may be manageable even with more participants.

Although determining group size ultimately depends on learning outcome goals, course design, capabilities of technology, group process considerations, and the expertise of the instructor, it should also be noted that time and capacity issues can vary from one course, instructor, and set of students to another, and that each group will experience its dynamics somewhat differently.

*—Candido Trujillo*

*See also* GROUP PROCESS; NORMS; TEACHING IN AN ELECTRONIC CLASSROOM

## Bibliography

Harasim, L., Hiltz, S. R., Teles, L., & Turoff, M. (1996). *Learning networks.* Cambridge: MIT Press.

Hiltz, S. R., & Turoff, M. (1993). *The network nation: Human communication via computer.* Cambridge: MIT Press.

Palloff, R. M., & Pratt, K. (1999). *Building learning communities in cyberspace.* San Francisco, CA: Jossey-Bass.

# GROUPWARE

Groupware is an ensemble of computer-mediated technologies, know-how, and methods that allows networked workgroups to communicate, collaborate, and cooperate by sharing information and other digital resources. Pierre Lévy defines groupware as a decision support model for distributed groups that uses the hypertextual and iconographic potential of contemporary computer-mediated networking solutions. Groupware can also be defined by enumerating the functionalities that we expect from the technologies that support it. Given the numerous and diverse nature of the functionalities, as well as the underlying technologies of groupware, the functionalities can be classified into five categories: 1) interpersonal communication, 2) coordination, 3) collaboration, 4) access to the information and collective memory of the group, and 5) automation of the administrative processes.

## INTERPERSONAL COMMUNICATION

At a minimum, groupware allows its users to communicate amongst themselves in a digital format. The most common form of interpersonal communication in groupware involves the exchange of messages between two users, akin to the person-to-person communication we are accustomed to in nonmediated contexts. This fundamental form of communication is commonly instantiated asynchronously via electronic mail (e-mail); this is sometimes complemented by a synchronous communication tool to make exchanges more spontaneous (e.g., chats). These synchronous tools are never used exclusively, whereas e-mail is invariably present. E-mail is deemed essential in any groupware because its absence would grievously handicap all of the functionalities that it supports and complements. In some cases, e-mail alone can constitute a complete, albeit limited, form of groupware containing all of the functionalities normally expected of more elaborate types of groupware—communication, sharing, and collaboration—especially if the e-mail client supports more than just plain text.

Interpersonal communication is greatly facilitated by several features typically found in e-mail software. E-mail not only allows person-to-person exchanges, but also one-to-many postings, thus forming a shared space of computer-mediated communication and community. The same software can also be used to participate in newsgroups, many of which are descendants of Usenet, a very popular network that predates the World Wide Web. Most e-mail clients also support attachments, which enables the sharing of digital resources with one or more colleagues. With a few methodological rules, a group can implement a basic workflow system in which the collective work is automatically circulated among its contributors. E-mail clients typically allow users to conserve, classify, and search (either manually or automatically) the messages they have received, thus creating a collective knowledge base that can be accessed and searched by any of the members of the group. Some e-mail programs further facilitate interpersonal communication by making it secure through authentification and cryptography.

E-mail is not a panacea, however. It allows for the informal exchange of messages among individuals, but when several individuals want to establish a discussion on a specific topic, more elaborate means of structuring these exchanges become necessary. Typically this is accomplished with threaded conferences in which the thread of the discussion can be followed easily and a message/reply can be appended to the thread of the running discussion.

## COORDINATION

Working in a group necessarily involves negotiations and accommodations among the group's participants so that they can accomplish their work cooperatively. The singular efforts of each participant must contribute to the goals and planning of the group as a dynamic whole, and thus take into account what the others are doing and when they are doing it. To ensure this synchronization of the group's activities and tasks, coordination mechanisms need to be established and then enforced. A typical method of implementation is a shared agenda that tracks the activities and schedules of each participant, and shares this sensitive information securely with participants who are authorized to browse it and have been properly authenticated.

Many computer-mediated groups also meet in person on occasion. Consequently, negotiating the time and the place of such meetings is an important groupware feature. Dates and times can be set using the shared agenda, but given the informal nature and broad scope of e-mail, it is still the decision-support technology of choice for negotiating the logistics of a face-to-face meeting.

In a group's most modular form, participants perform their work separately and synchronize with other group members only when their portion of the whole is ready to be integrated. This rudimentary type of coordination does not require much effort to implement; e-mail is often sufficient for coordination. If and when the tasks become less modular, the increased coordination needs make e-mail a less-than-ideal solution. A more formal coordination solution is then needed, ranging from a free-form wiki (similar to a Web site except that any authorized visitor can edit the site's pages with an ordinary browser) to a highly structured software solution specializing in networked project management. Between these extremes are a Web site, a shared agenda, and an increasing number of free groupware solutions based on open source technologies.

Regardless of how sophisticated the coordination solution is, it will undoubtedly track who is in the group, their abilities, their roles, their tasks, their commitments, and their progress. In some cases, notably in larger organizations where accountability is a key factor, the partially completed work of the participants is submitted to their supervisor(s) for approval.

## COLLABORATION

As mentioned in the previous section, one mode of cooperation has all participants working separately on a project, and then coming together to combine their work. In some slightly more complex cases, a "workflow" architecture can be implemented with e-mail so that participants circulate their work according to an agreed-upon chain of execution, allowing each user to contribute in turn to the shared resource. The versioning of the shared resource is handled implicitly because only one person has control of the resource at any given time.

Both of these scenarios presume that the tasks of each participant will be performed by one individual at a time because the tasks are modular enough to make this approach feasible. This is often not the case. The execution of a task often depends on the results obtained during the simultaneous execution of the associated tasks of the other participants. Some design and implementation steps in one task, particularly if they are transversal ones, often have a huge impact on the design and implementation of the other tasks. These unplanned changes, due to unanticipated problems and unforetold opportunities, arise during the process, making it necessary for some or all of the participants to interact with each other on an ongoing basis, in order to negotiate how the group should react to the changes and adapt their plans.

Numerous groupware systems can provide this degree of collaboration:

- Electronic meeting tools allow a networked group to host virtual meetings, group brainstorming sessions, group categorization and prioritization of ideas and plans, polling of opinions to discern whether a consensus is being reached, and voting if a consensus is hard to reach.
- Audioconferencing allows two or more participants to converse with each other (instead of typing). Videoconferencing takes this a step further by allowing participants to hold a virtual meeting in which they can talk to and see the other participants. The

key feature that makes these tools genuine groupware is the ability of many of them to make available a shared workspace that all of the participants can simultaneously access and edit in real time.

- More sophisticated forms of the group editing feature allow participants to collaboratively elaborate on a shared document or resource, synchronously and/or asynchronously, with the added benefit of an automatic tracking and versioning solution that ensures the integrity and the reversibility of the various versions of the document/resource at every step of the collaborative development process. Various open source wikis provide a simple form of this feature but, for a more robust open source versioning solution, developers tend to favor CVS (Concurrent Versioning System).

## ACCESS TO THE INFORMATION AND COLLECTIVE MEMORY OF THE GROUP

Working in a group presumes that the participants are sharing information. Communication, coordination, and collaboration involve access and contributions to this shared knowledge, which in turn involves 1) data entry and validation of new data, 2) automatic processing and encoding of some of the data, 3) storage and backup of this stored data, 4) organizing of this data for its ulterior uses, and 5) browsing and searching this knowledge for specific information.

These functionalities are commonly found in database management systems (DBMS), but with DBMS, the knowledge management process is focused on providing detailed, accurate, reliable reports that synthesize the key parameters that managers need to efficiently manage their enterprise. With DBMS, data end up being very rigorously structured, unambiguous, and delivered efficiently. On the other hand, DBMS leave little room for flexible handling of the heterogeneous unstructured and semi-structured information that is commonly exchanged in groupware circumstances. So, although the groupware may use DBMS for some of its data, the group as a whole may not rely solely on DBMS to manage the integrity of its entire knowledge base.

A group also specifies what is shared by the participants: requests, agreements, commitments, negotiations, and so on. Many of these items are textual in nature, but not necessarily so—some may be multimedia documents. The collective memory of the group also contains some methodological information (rules, procedures, guidelines, etc.) and some logs (which record every change made so that these changes can be reversed if needed). Ultimately the content of the "database" resides in the minds of the participants.

## AUTOMATION OF THE ADMINISTRATIVE PROCESSES (WORKFLOW)

The circulation of documents, commonly called "workflow," is often a key feature of groupware. It's a form of structured collaboration. Each participant is integrated into a workflow architecture, centralized or decentralized, where the circulation of the group's work follows a predetermined path. In general, the successive and/or iterative phases of the development process (and the approval of them) are rigorously enforced and adhered to. A workflow can allow for more freedom than this, but more formal is better than less, because formal procedures can be easily automated. This in turn makes the rigor and discipline of using a workflow less tedious and less error prone. This method is not for every group though. It is aimed at larger organizations that have a well-established chain of command and that do not have quality-control methods that require successive approvals during the development process. Medium-sized groups with well-defined roles may also find workflow to be an asset, but smaller informal ones will justifiably shun it.

## THE FUTURE OF GROUPWARE IN EDUCATION

A Web-based e-learning environment, sometimes employing a virtual campus metaphor, typically is implemented as a Web site or an educational portal. With an ordinary Web browser, learners can browse the learning environment and the educational resources that it shares with the learning community. With a secured connection, learners can even register for courses, view their progress, work in their personal space, and so on. These Web sites can thus be an important component in a learning environment, but they lack some characteristics that make them genuinely pedagogical. Most Web sites are only mildly interactive, even when taking into account Web forms, CGI programs, dynamic HTML, PHP, and other "interactive" Web technologies.

The presence of a rich set of communication tools provided by the Internet satisfies many of the needs that Web sites alone cannot. Learners can communicate with their teachers, as well as their peers, thus forming a genuine learning community, as opposed to disparate individuals consuming broadcasted educational media. Communication adds a very enriching social dimension, which bolsters motivation and strengthens students' resolve to continue their learning. It allows for pedagogical strategies that focus on communication as a learning activity, including activities such as exchanges with students abroad, unmoderated discussions, moderated debates, forums, asynchronous exchanges via e-mail, synchronous chatting, and interactive games. Communication also provides opportunities for collaboration in a relatively unstructured manner; however, this lack of structure eventually inhibits the group's progress as it expands. Groupware was designed to aid this problem. It is a worthy solution that scales nicely (thus accommodating many people). Moreover, given groupware's potential to satisfy more of the needs of learners than the other means discussed in this entry, its implementation becomes the best tactic to use to achieve the virtual campus metaphor's goal of approximating a real campus.

Another option is to employ "communityware" to achieve the virtual campus. Communityware is frequently confused with groupware. Technically, they are roughly the same. What distinguishes them is their philosophy and their organization principles. Groupware is modeled on project management, where the tasks and responsibilities are formally determined and frequently hierarchical. Communityware, on the other hand, is focused on facilitating exchanges and resource sharing in informal groups where participation is voluntary and guided by communitarian principles.

Selecting which of these two concepts (and corresponding technologies) is the best choice to use to implement a virtual campus depends on the principles that guide the university. If it's a hierarchical organization with well-defined roles and responsibilities, then groupware is the best choice. If, on the other hand, the university is more akin to a democratic community of coordinated free agents, to a community of practice, or to a learning community, then communityware is the best choice. Either way, it's hard to go wrong because, technically, they are approximately the same technologies. As always, it is not the technologies that determine what we will do, but rather our values and goals that will determine what uses will be made of the technologies at our disposal.

—*Pierre-Léonard Harvey*
—*Alain Farmer*

***See also*** Document Management Systems; E-mail; Knowledge Management; Learning Management Systems (LMS); Virtual Campus

## Bibliography

Coovert, M. D., & Thompson, L. F. (2001). *Computer supported cooperative work: Issues and implications for workers, organizations, and human resource management.* Thousand Oaks, CA: Sage.

Courbon, J. C., & Tajan, S. (1997). *Groupware et intranet.* Masson, Paris: InterEditions.

Lloyd, P., & Whitehead, R. (Ed.). (1996). *Transforming organisations through groupware: Lotus Notes in action.* Berlin: Springer Verlag.

Udell, J. (2002). *Practical Internet groupware.* Sebastopol, CA: O'Reilly.

# H

## HOME SCHOOLING

Home schooling is a form of education in which children learn at home rather than in a conventional classroom, with their parents as their primary teachers. Approximately 1.5 to 2 million American children are home schooled today, and home schooling is a rapidly growing subset of the educational community, increasing by 10–30% each year. According to educational researcher Patricia Lines, home schooling "is one of the most significant social trends of the past half century."

Home schooling is not a new practice: For much of human history, children routinely have been educated at home. Institutionalized education is a more recent phenomenon, becoming near-universal in the United States with the enactment of compulsory school attendance laws in the 19th and early 20th centuries. Although home schooling has been continually practiced to a limited degree, most notably among isolated rural families, its popular resurgence as an alternative to traditional schooling began in the 1960s and 1970s. During this period, home schooling was promulgated by educational reformers and social nonconformists dissatisfied with compulsory mass schooling, notably Ivan Illich, Paul Goodman, Raymond and Dorothy Moore, and John Holt. Holt, sometimes nicknamed the "Father of Home Schooling," wrote several influential books on the subject and founded the first national magazine about home schooling—*Growing Without Schooling*—in 1977.

In the early days of the modern home school movement, hopeful home schoolers encountered considerable opposition from the educational establishment. The basic right of parents to control their children's education had been previously established by the Supreme Court in the cases of *Pierce v. Society of Sisters* (1925) and *Farrington v. Tokushige* (1927), in which the Court ruled, respectively, that the state could neither compel all children to attend public schools nor follow a uniform educational curriculum. Rulings specific to home schoolers followed: In *Yoder v. Wisconsin* (1972) and *Perchemlides v. Frizzle* (1978), the Court affirmed the constitutional right of parents to teach their children at home. Ultimately, however, the practice of home schooling is regulated by the individual states.

Today home schooling is legal in all 50 states, although regulations vary widely, ranging from the permissive to the restrictive. For example, states may require home schooled children to study the same subjects that are taught at their appropriate grade levels in the public schools, to attend home school for the same number of hours that the public school is in session, or to take annual standardized tests. Home schooling parents may have to submit an annual curriculum for local or state approval; they may also be required to possess a high-school or college diploma, or to be supervised by a state-certified educational professional.

Home schoolers are a diverse group; and their reasons for home schooling reflect their varied lifestyles and philosophies. According to recent studies, at least half of all families home school primarily for academic reasons, often citing enhanced opportunities for flexibility and creativity, and the advantages of one-on-one tutorials and individualized learning programs, tailored to their children's interests, learning styles, and skill levels. About 33% of home schoolers do so for religious reasons; others home school in order to promote family solidarity and self-reliance. Some home schoolers object to the negative social environment of the public schools; for example, in a 1995–96 survey sponsored by the Florida Department of Education, 42% of respondents attributed their home school decision to worries about school violence, adverse peer pressure, teen sex, and drug and alcohol abuse.

Home schooling methods also vary widely, ranging from highly structured "school at home" programs to largely unstructured "unschooling" or "natural learning" approaches, featuring active child-directed investigation and emphasizing real-world experience. Some families design their own programs, often using a multidisciplinary "unit study" approach, in which all academic subjects are centered around common unifying themes. Others purchase commercial curricula, participate in learning cooperatives, or enroll in online or correspondence programs, supplementary classes, or tutorials. A large and varied number of K–12 programs are available to home-educated students. Among the providers are Clonlara School (Ann Arbor, MI), Calvert School (Baltimore, MD), Laurel Springs School (Ojai, CA), and Oak Meadow School (Putney, VT); online sources include Beyond Books (www.beyond-books.com), William Bennett's K12 (www.k12.com), and E. D. Hirsch's Core Knowledge Foundation (www.coreknowledge.org). Home schoolers also take high school and college-level classes through the distance-learning programs now offered by many colleges and universities.

As assessed by standardized tests, home schooling is markedly successful: Home schoolers, by and large, score at or above the national average. A 1998 survey by Lawrence Rudner of the University of Maryland, for example, found that home schooled students scored in the 62nd to the 91st percentile of national norms. Many home schoolers, however, feel that standardized test scores are poor indications of educational quality and attainment, and emphasize instead their children's creativity, motivation, and general and in-depth knowledge. Home school graduates seem as well equipped as or better equipped than their conventionally schooled peers for work or college: Studies show that home schoolers have successfully matriculated at over 900 colleges and universities,

among them such prestigious institutions as Harvard, Stanford, Cornell, Brown, Dartmouth, and Princeton.

Critics, among them the National Education Association, argue that home schools cannot provide children with a comprehensive educational experience. Opponents claim that without the opportunities for group interaction provided by the school system, children cannot acquire essential social skills. Furthermore, because they are not exposed to the broad range of socioeconomic and ethnic groups found in conventional classrooms, home schooled children may become bigoted and intolerant. Finally, if taught by parents lacking proper academic credentials, they may be poorly informed, biased, or intellectually stunted.

Studies to date, however, indicate that such is not the case. Home schooled children appear to be academically proficient, well-socialized, self-confident, and notably free from behavioral problems. Most home schoolers, far from suffering social isolation, participate in a wide range of organizations and activities, including sports teams, 4-H clubs, scout troops, music and dance lessons, art and drama workshops, and play groups. A survey of over 10,000 home schooled students by the National Home Education Research Institute (NHERI) found that 98% participated in two or more regular activities outside the home, and 30% worked as community volunteers, as opposed to 6–12% of public-school students.

There are now numerous national and regional organizations for home schoolers, among them the Alliance for Parental Involvement in Education (AllPIE), the National Home Education Network (NHEN), and the Home School Legal Defense Association (HSLDA), as well as many community-based support groups. There is also an active home school Internet community providing online chat and discussion groups and educational resource exchange, and a substantial body of home school literature, including magazines, journals, newsletters, resource manuals, and books.

Famous home schoolers include architect Frank Lloyd Wright, artist Andrew Wyeth, inventor Thomas Edison, photographer Ansel Adams, writers Pearl Buck and Agatha Christie, and anthropologist Margaret Mead.

*—Rebecca Rupp*

***See also*** ALTERNATIVE SECONDARY EDUCATION

## Bibliography

Bauman, Kurt J. (2002). Home schooling in the United States: Trends and characteristics. *Education Policy Analysis Archives, 10.*

Cohen, Cafi.. (2000). *And what about college?: How homeschooling leads to admissions to the best colleges and universities.* Wakefield, MA: Holt Associates.

Dobson, Linda. (Ed.). (1998). *The homeschooling book of answers.* Roseville, CA: Prima.

Dobson, Linda. (2001). *Homeschoolers' success stories.* Roseville, CA: Prima.

Farenga, Patrick. (1999). John Holt and the origins of contemporary homeschooling. *Paths of Learning, 1.*

Griffith, Mary. (1997). *The homeschooling handbook.* Roseville, CA: Prima.

Holt, John. (1981). *Teach your own: A hopeful path for education.* New York: Delta/Seymour Lawrence.

Lines, Patricia. (1991). Home instruction: Characteristics, size and growth. In Jane Van Galen & Mary Anne Pittman (Eds.), *Home schooling: Political, historical, and pedagogical perspectives.* Westport, CT: Ablex.

Lines, Patricia. (2000, Summer). Homeschooling comes of age. *The Public Interest,* 74–85.

Ray, Brian. (1997). *Strengths of their own.* Salem, OR: NHERI Publications.

Rudner, Lawrence M. (1999). Scholastic achievement and demographic characteristics of home school students in 1998. *Education Policy Analysis Archives, 7.*

Rupp, Rebecca. (1986, December). Home schooling. *Country Journal,* 67–74.

Rupp, Rebecca. (1993, September/October). Teach your children well. *Harrowsmith Country Life,* 26–35.

Rupp, Rebecca. (1999). *Getting started on home learning: How and why to teach your kids at home.* New York: Three Rivers Press.

## HYPERMEDIA

The concepts of *hypertext* and *hypermedia* were conceived in a visionary paper by Vannevar Bush in 1945. Hypermedia is a collection of multimedia objects such as text, graphics, audio, video, animations, and simulations connected through associative links based on context. Hypermedia provides a paradigm for accessing information in nonlinear fashion.

Over the last several decades, the development of hypermedia was focused on creating links between media objects based on their relationships. In the early 1980s, Apple Computer introduced HyperCard software, which created cards that were linked nonlinearly to explore a subject matter. These cards contained various media elements such as audio and graphics. The linking was primarily done using a scripting language called HyperScript. Standard Generalized Markup Language (SGML), a standardized method of connecting documents, was then created, followed by the development of markup tags for linking chunks of text and media elements.

While working at a European particle physics lab (CERN), Tim Berners-Lee developed the Hypertext Transfer Protocol (HTTP), thus creating a networked hypermedia that today is known as the World Wide Web. HTTP provides a means to connect multimedia elements (text, graphics, audio, video, animation, and simulation) over Internet servers. The explosive growth of the Web is a clear indication of the pervasive, global impact of hypermedia in everyday life.

—*Nishikant Sunwalker*

*See also* HYPERTEXT; WORLD WIDE WEB

## Bibliography

Bush, Vannevar. (1945, July). As we may think. *Atlantic Monthly,* 101–108.

## HYPERTEXT

Hypertext is a collection of text segments that can be connected via links to other segments. It allows the presentation of information in a complex manner compared to the traditional printed medium. Hypertext is the fundamental unit of the World Wide Web, but can also be used without the Web. Hypertext has also been touted as a great learning tool, having the flexibility to provide information to students and showcase the complexity of real-life information.

Hypertext is an innovation from the early 1980s that allows text and information to be organized in a nonlinear fashion. Text that traditionally was presented in a linear printed medium is transformed into hypertext by the computer and organized as nodes with connecting links; for example, a paragraph containing information about the Olympics (the node) can have links to information about individual games, countries represented, the athletes, and any other related information.

The nodes and related links allow readers to traverse the information in a nonlinear style. Instead of reading a book from cover to cover, page by page, readers can jump around and be connected to other related information easily.

Hypertext Markup Language (HTML) describes how a Web page should look. Browsers (like Netscape Navigator or Internet Explorer) use the Hypertext Transfer Protocol (HTTP) to translate information transmitted from the source site (a server) so that it can be viewed by the user.

Web-based courses use the World Wide Web and hypertext as the media for delivering instructional content, getting responses from the user, and communicating. Hypertext allows designers to create a Web page from which students can link to a glossary, references, and sample problems. HTML allows the integration of multimedia into the course, and has expanded the capabilities of the Web as a medium for distributed courses.

To connect pieces of text, computer programs and architectures must be able to create nodes and links. This requires an addressing mechanism. Just as a letter needs an address so that it can be delivered, a link within a hypertext environment is programmed to retrieve text based on its address. Moving from link to link requires a system that keeps track of all the links the user has traversed so that he or she can backtrack, if necessary.

At its invention, hypertext was promoted as a great tool for presenting information to learners, showcasing the complexity of information, and providing learners more control over their learning environment. Hypertext can be used to show multiple perspectives of a complex problem, allow learners to criss-cross the problem landscape, and introduce complexity to learners.

However, the expectations of the designers and researchers were never fully achieved because of many intervening factors, including learner variables (such as prior knowledge, working memory capacity, and metacognition) that affected how the hypertext presentation was received, processed, and synthesized. Research findings have shown that learners have difficulty in determining the best links to follow, how much information should be reviewed, and what information is necessary, and they get easily distracted while following links in hypertext. Students in hypertext conditions also generally perform poorly in tests compared to their counterparts who are forced to review the identical materials in a linear format.

Some theoretical concepts are beginning to emerge suggesting that learners create shallow knowledge structures when they bounce around from site to site in a hypertext environment. The multiple levels of text and organization of hypertext can affect how the human mind processes information and increase the mind's cognitive load. For example, instead of simply reading a linear text passage, hypertext confronts readers with many options, such as whether to follow links, when to follow links, and when to come back to the original passage. These choices may overwhelm some readers. Those not overwhelmed may only see the multimedia animations or colors and not read the content deeply.

Traditional text passages use the first sentence of each paragraph as a key to the content and also use signals within text that focus attention to important content. For example, bold or italicized typeface, ordering the text, and starting each element with a number allow the reader to synthesize information. In contrast, hypertext links may highlight unimportant concepts, simply because the link's color can change; this can affect how this information is processed.

In summary, hypertext is a powerful invention allowing the creation of complex learning materials. The applications that use hypertext should focus on learners' interactions with hypertext to effectively use its power.

*—Kay J. Wijekumar*

***See also*** Virtual Learning Tools; World Wide Web

# I

## INFORMATICS

The term *informatics* has been used in a number of ways since the 1960s. In Northern Europe, academic departments of informatics cover a range of topics that are similar to those covered in the academic departments of computer science and information systems in the United States. In the United States, informatics has come to include a wider array of connotations because it is usually coupled with some adjective, such as medical informatics, bio-informatics, chemical informatics, or educational informatics. These "X-informatics fields" are often defined as the application of information and communication technologies (IT) and information management (IM) techniques to "topic X." These applications-focused definitions are much too narrow. Although X-informatics often include these IT and IM applications, it is also important to include 1) the study of (and ways to understand) the appropriate application of IT and IM to X, as well as 2) how to evaluate the human consequences of IT and IM application approaches upon the participants in X.

In this broader view of informatics, the role of educational informatics in distributed learning involves more than just providing knowledge about the design of relevant IT and IM strategies. Educational informatics should also include the awareness, development, and synthesis of appropriate pedagogies for these IT-enabled "learning environments," and also the consequences of different approaches for teachers, students, and relevant other participants. In short, educational informatics should not be limited to topics such as how to design an online multimedia conferencing system. It should also examine topics such as how to stimulate high quality human conferences in online environments to compensate for the known limitations of non–face-to-face media/interactions, when an online conference may not be as effective as a face-to-face meeting of the participants, and ways to evaluate the educational quality of IT-enabled distributed learning courses.

Educational informatics is not the only informatics specialty that is important for distributed learning. The fields of legal informatics, organizational informatics, and social informatics are defined somewhat differently than the X-informatics specialties already described. Legal informatics includes the legal analysis of IT issues and IM practices, including copyright in electronic environments. Social informatics has been defined as "the interdisciplinary study of the design, uses and consequences of IT that takes into account their interaction with institutional and cultural contexts" (Kling, 2000). Organizational informatics is a subfield of social informatics that focuses on "the design, uses and consequences of IT that takes into account their interaction with organizations." Because distributed learning is a service of specific organizations, such as schools, organizational informatics research is also an important source of insight. For example, organizational informatics contributes important understandings about the role of IT infrastructure in distributed workplaces, the complexities of developing high-performance IT-supported teams in distributed workplaces, and the cultural construction of IT-based communication systems. Although the field of informatics can be viewed as the sum of all of the specialty X-informatics topics, only a few of these specialties directly apply to distributed learning.

## PEDAGOGIES

One complexity of the discussions of educational informatics and distributed learning is the differing beliefs about education and technology held by various participants, including students, teachers, technical staff, administrators, and politicians. One dimension of this difference is the extent to which learning is viewed as relatively active or passive. In a passive conception, teaching is largely a matter of directly instructing students (i.e., via lectures) and students watching a lecture or reading selected materials. In an active conception, students learn through vigorous inquiry about "authentic issues," either alone or in groups. Currently, many educational researchers favor active modes of learning; however, teaching practices in many colleges and universities still emphasize lectures, especially in large introductory courses.

For those who adhere to a relatively passive model of education, a major problem of the educational system is students' limited access to appropriate information. Online distributed learning environments enable participants to have instructional resources available 24 hours a day, 7 days a week, almost anywhere that they can have Internet access. The simplest of these environments includes instructional materials such as syllabi, instructional texts, lecture notes, and homework. Students could download instructional materials and upload their homework, and use e-mail and perhaps discussion lists to communicate with instructors and other students.

In the mid-1990s, a number of U.S. politicians and higher education administrators hoped that some kind of IT-enabled distributed learning environment would reduce the costs of public higher education (by reducing the demand for new buildings) and also enable instruction to be more readily provided to people at their workplaces. In addition, some academic administrators hoped that these environments could help them reach students (and their tuitions) who could not visit their campuses. This type of relatively simple online instructional environment is most similar to a large lecture course, with its associated economies of scale and limitations for intensive learning. If such a learning environment is appropriately structured, it could be more flexible than a face-to-face lecture course because it would enable students to pace themselves and to select customized subsets of the instructional materials.

For those who prefer a more active model of education, this conception of "Upload/Download University" is very unappealing. They believe that the various IT-enabled learning environments can and should support richer ways for students to interact with each other, including debates, small group discussions, and shared projects. Some online environments may also enable students to more readily share their course materials for comment by their classmates. Courses designed around activities like these require much more careful structuring by their instructors. They are more complicated and labor intensive to teach well because the instructors have to pay much closer attention to students' communications, as well as to be able to rapidly respond to possible communications. In contrast, an instructor can more readily set boundaries on the time that she spends interacting in a face-to-face seminar or workshop. Educators who take this more active interaction-intensive approach are particularly concerned with improving the quality of education, rather than reducing its cost or increasing its availability.

Today, instructors use a wide variety of practices with IT-enabled distributed learning environments. They range from those that rely on more passive models of learning to others that emphasize more active approaches to learning. As with face-to-face instruction, courses can display a wide variety of quality because of variations in instructors' quality, instructors' attention, course design, materials selected, and students' expectations. The IT-enabled environments can also add three new issues: students' abilities to be more effectively self-motivated than in face-to-face courses; students' abilities to effectively work with the IT environment from their homes, workplaces, or school sites; and students' abilities to communicate in highly nuanced ways through writing. The seeming ease and convenience of distributed learning also comes with offsetting complexities.

Educational informatics research has found that high-quality instruction with IT-enabled environments usually requires a course to be redesigned (and sometimes reconceptualized) rather than simply "uploaded to a Web site." Some distributed courses mix face-to-face activities with activities within the IT-enabled learning environment. Some distance education degree programs require that their students visit a campus for a "boot camp" at the beginning of their study, in order to more readily develop durable personal relationships with their instructors and classmates, as well as occasional wrap-up sessions.

## NO SIGNIFICANT DIFFERENCE PHENOMENA

In the fields of education and technology, there is a classic discussion regarding the comparison of different media and instruction. The majority of studies claim that there is no significant difference between classroom, stand-up instruction, and instruction using certain media, such as radio, film, TV, computer-based tutorials, or Web-based materials, in terms of their learning outcomes and students' satisfaction. This set of findings advocates IT-enabled distributed learning environments, despite some cautions that the quality of education in such environments might be lower than that in face-to-face learning environments. We have to interpret these media comparison studies carefully because most of them are flawed. The more vital issue is to investigate the appropriate pedagogies for different media/learning environments and educational contexts. The best quality courses in IT-enabled distributed learning environments may sometimes be of much higher quality than many of their traditional face-to-face alternatives.

## INSTITUTIONAL INTEGRATION

Although much of the research in educational informatics tends to focus on technology, some research views technology within the context of an educational institution with local resources, routines, and norms. For example, introducing IT to school settings can be perceived as a part of broader instructional reform efforts. Further, there are important issues about how well IT-enabled courses are integrated into institutions' operations. Is the IT environment for distributed learning incorporated with other local IT applications? How well are IT-enabled courses and the distributed instructional faculty integrated into overall curricula and the school's instructional staff? Low levels of institutional integration may reduce the quality of distributed learning courses. There is some tension between the possibility of educational innovation through new IT-enabled instruction and the more conservative influences of several kinds of institutional integration, such as using uniform criteria to evaluate all courses.

## CLOSING

The mid-1990s expectations of some politicians and academic administrators that IT-enabled distance education could be a relatively inexpensive way to reduce the public costs of high-quality higher education or that it could easily scale up enrollments inexpensively have not proven to be valid. The research frontier for educational informatics is to understand more effectively how the interplay of different kinds of IT-enabled learning environments and specific pedagogical approaches can improve the quality of education and increase access, with reasonable costs for all participants. However, understanding the overall character of IT-enabled distributed learning programs also requires drawing on insights about topics such as institutional integration and pedagogies in online environments from organizational informatics and social informatics.

—*Rob Kling*
—*Noriko Hara*

*See also* DISTRIBUTED LEARNING/DISTRIBUTED EDUCATION; INFORMATION TECHNOLOGY (IT); LEARNING ENVIRONMENTS

### Bibliography

Barab, S., Kling, R., & Gray, J. (Eds.). (in press). *Designing virtual communities in the service of learning.* Cambridge: Cambridge University Press.

Dutton, W. H., & Loader, B. D. (Eds.). (2002). *Digital academe: New media and institutions in higher education and learning.* London: Taylor & Francis/Routledge.

Kling, R. (2000). Learning about information technologies and social change: The contribution of social informatics. *The Information Society, 16*(3), 217–232.

Schofield, J. W., & Davidson, A. L. (2002). *Bringing the Internet to school: Lessons from an urban district.* San Francisco: Jossey-Bass.

# INFORMATION LITERACY

Information literacy is today's "4th R" of basic literacy, complementing the "readin', 'ritin', and 'rithmetic" of the early days of American education with "retrieval"—it is a survival skill for the Age of Information. The ability to access, manage, and utilize information to make decisions and solve problems is a necessary competence for effective participation in the 21st century. Ensuring that educated people have this competence is precisely the goal of the information literacy initiative.

Some measure of learner self-reliance is a fundamental assumption of distributed learning. In a world of infinite information, self-reliance in accessing and managing appropriate information is a daunting challenge. Competence in navigating the complex universe of information for both learning and work requires information literacy. Supporting the lifelong learning process and "learning how to learn" has been a central goal of information literacy from the early stages of the movement. This challenge is rendered urgent by the accelerating preeminence of knowledge work, which can be described as using information to make decisions and carry out tasks. It is not the expansion of knowledge workers that is important here so much as the penetration of the role of knowledge into all work, be it in the research lab or the factory floor.

To the extent that the knowledge required for a given course, task, or skill can be contained in a closed selection of lectures, presentations, and readings, information literacy (IL) is superfluous. In a "transmission" or information transfer and processing paradigm—which long prevailed in education—managing diverse sources of information was not considered critical. That explains why the early literature of distance, or distributed, education rarely mentioned libraries and ignored the importance of alternative sources of information and explanation. But such closed learning is of limited utility in today's fast-changing world. Enduring assumptions about "right" and "objective" information frequently do not withstand the tests of currency, diversity, and relativity, just as assumptions about the singular way people learn are inadequate now that we better understand multiple "intelligences" and learning styles. Diverse—and sometimes inconsistent—definitions and explanations are often required for comprehensive understanding. All this makes information literacy a necessity, not a luxury.

## DEFINITION

The most familiar definition of information literacy is that promoted by the American Library Association, namely:

- Realizing when information is needed
- Identifying the information needed

- Accessing the needed information
- Evaluating the information
- Organizing the information
- Using the information effectively to complete the task or solve the problem

Adopted in 1989, this definition guided a decade of work by large segments of the library profession. Institutes trained, and libraries hired, professionals to lead the adoption of IL courses and competencies across the spectrum of higher education, particularly in the United States. Accrediting agencies began to require colleges and universities to implement IL standards in their curricula. Public schools and libraries began implementing IL in their goals and programs. The working definition of IL expanded well beyond earlier standards for computer literacy, which seemed less critical considering the widespread adoption of user-friendly, graphics-based operating systems requiring less technical competence. Critics, however, pointed out that working assumptions about IL were oriented toward print media and did not address the growing role of visual and multiple media in education and social communication. Only slowly did mainstream library-led IL initiatives address this criticism.

## FROM SKILLS TO OUTCOMES

In their early stages, library-led IL initiatives stressed information content and certain required skills, such as basic computer operation, database searching, and Internet research. Accessing, capturing, and manipulating information to support an argument or solve a problem were central to the process. Many books, articles, and conferences covered the successes and inadequacies of various IL programs, training, exercises, and research. Considerable discussion and debate focused on whether IL should be a "stand alone" course or whether the skills should be incorporated into regular academic disciplines. In time, however, skills training came to be considered inadequate. What was the purpose? Unused skills quickly deteriorate. Skills in accessing information for academic purposes do not necessarily transfer easily to the more specific problems of the professions and workplace. Mastery of online searching techniques does not automatically ensure that an individual understands "how to learn" and adapt to the fast-changing universe of telecommunications, computers, and the Internet. Individual skills likewise do not guarantee the ability to work in groups, teams, and situations requiring effective collaboration. Successful resolution of these matters required a different perspective.

To address these concerns the IL "community" shifted its emphasis from teaching skills to ensuring outcomes. Assessment became a central issue. The Association of College and Research Libraries, the academic arm of the American Library Association, adopted a new set of standards and outcomes. These standards stressed competencies that an "information literate" person possessed, such as critically evaluating information, incorporating it into his or her "knowledge base," and using the information legally and ethically. About the same time, various IL programs expanded their purview to deal with video and other continuous media, as well as graphics and the presentation of information in different media. Working with information interactively in groups and promoting greater awareness of the importance of learning became other criteria for many IL programs.

By the turn of the century, IL was a diverse movement extending well beyond the library profession to scholars, teachers, and researchers in information science, learning theory, instruction design, and other disciplines. Academic librarians remained at the center of activity in disseminating IL skills, but much of the important research and analysis work passed to others. Studies of student–faculty relationships, the learning assumptions of the student, and variations in how IL is addressed in different cultures broadened the understanding of attentive professionals. Human–computer (or human–information) interaction, action research, knowledge construction and extension, constructivist learning, and the social context of learning are matters of inquiry for and experimentation by IL researchers and practitioners. The basic issue of whether libraries are necessary for effective distributed learning is another topic of intense discussion. Popular assumptions that "everything is on the Internet" do not address the growing commercialization, privatization, and ephemeral nature of much of the information on the Internet. Hopes for an inexpensive "virtual library" to support distributed learning startups have not been realized.

## DEFINITIONS RECONSIDERED

As the early years of the new millennium unfold, there is general agreement that information literacy is important, but a lack of consensus exists about which literacies are absolutely essential, how they best can be learned, and how they best can be assessed. Important guidelines currently under review include visual literacy (for mediating a visual culture), media literacy (to cope with the variety of information formats), multiple literacies (a meta-perspective), technological competence or fitness, and workplace competence. Further explanations are in order.

Too much attention has been paid to information literacy as a skill, and more recently as a demonstrable competence. Such views fail to acknowledge its potential. IL should be considered a gateway to broader, essential competencies. Just as math and languages are never totally mastered but rather serve as conduits for exploring quantitative matters or communicating with others, so IL should be viewed as a fundamental literacy-competency-expertise journey required for broader effectiveness in an age of information, knowledge, and continual learning. Explaining this process fully requires more space than is available here, but the following matrix suggests the extent of the issue. This figure should be seen as a range of skills, some of which are critical and others superfluous to a given profession or community of learning. The three levels of the matrix (literacy, competence, and expertise) are treated as the levels of "know what," which typically is acquired in school; the "know how" required on the job; and the expertise and understanding (or "know why") demanded of a professional. A given type of work may not require competence or expertise in every category, but it will require literacy in each. And genuine literacy can quickly be expanded into competency when the occasion demands.

Distributed learning theory provides a larger role for individual motivation, engagement, and self-determination than required by traditional, instruction-based learning theory. Distributed learning also has greater expectations of technological competence, communication skills, and multimedia competence. Information literacy must mature and expand its scope if it is to secure its place in the educational lexicon of the future. The literacy-competency-expertise continuum outlined here offers guidelines for that development.

—*James Marcum*

***See also*** ASSESSMENT OF STUDENT COMPETENCE

Information literacy—knowledge fluency matrix

| LEVELS (Depth) | Literacy (academic, school) | Competence (workplace) | Expertise (professional) |
|---|---|---|---|
| **Critical/Higher Level Skills** | | | |
| C __ Intellectual ability | Propose projects | Lead projects | "Global" perspective |
| A __ Problem solving | Analyze data | Solve problems | Intellectual agility |
| T __ Presentation | Present ideas | Utilize new ideas | Create new ideas |
| E __ Social/civic responsibility | Influence others | Persuade others | Strategic engagement |
| G | | | |
| O  **Meta-Learning** | | | |
| R __ Individual learning | Know when need | Cooperation | Collaboration |
| I __ Interactive communication | information | Interactive learning | Monitor group |
| E __ Group learning | Self knowledge | Adapt "instruction" | HCI improvement |
| S __ Human-computer interaction | Use new knowledge | Self-direction | Self motivation |
| /  **Research** | | | |
| __ Processes | Formulate questions | Research strategies | Critical review |
| B __ Methods | Discipline familiarity | Cross-disciplinary | Discovery |
| r __ Language | Research process | methods | Instruction |
| e __ Tools (i.e., SPSS) | Report findings | Evaluate findings | Interpret findings |
| a | | | |
| d  **Resources** | | | |
| t __ Print | Gather information | Visual literacy | Use information |
| h __ Visual Media | Categorize media | Translate between | legally and ethically |
| __ Web | Basic databases | media | Multiple literacies |
| __ Multiple media | Reference, books, | Evaluate databases | Manipulate databases |
| __ Publishing alternatives | journals | | Utilize meta-data |
| **Technology (Tools)** | | | |
| __ Networks | Communication | Design, maintain | Write programs |
| __ Interfaces | Productivity (word | Web pages | Innovate |
| __ Web (search engines) | processing, spread- | Troubleshooting | Select and adapt |
| __ Portals | sheets, database) | Manage system | systems |
| __ Emerging Technologies | Computer literacy | | |
| __ Productivity | Internet searching | | |

## Bibliography

ACRL Task Force on Information Literacy Competency Standards. (March 2000). Information literacy competency standards for higher education. *C&RL News, 61*(3), 207–215. Retrieved from http://www.ala.org/acrl/ilcomstan.html.

Breivik, Patricia Senn. (1998). *Student learning in the information age.* Phoenix, AZ: Oryx.

Bruce, Christine Susan. (1997). *The seven faces of information literacy.* Adelaide, Australia: Auslib Press.

Marcum, James W. (January 2002). Rethinking information literacy. *Library Quarterly, 72*(1), 1–26.

Shapiro, Jeremy, & Hughes, Shelly K. (March/April 1996). Information literacy as a liberal art. *Educom Review, 31*(2).

Tyner, Kathleen. (1998). *Literacy in a digital world: Teaching and learning in an age of information.* Matawah, NJ: Lawrence Erlbaum.

# INFORMATION RETRIEVAL

The term *information retrieval* is attributed to Calvin Mooers around 1950, and its use is associated with the explosion of scientific documentation produced during and following World War II. Information retrieval refers to the set of processes by which information can be extracted from a larger accumulation. Most typically, the term refers to the identification of documents from a collection or database of documents, or of specific information (e.g., facts, paragraphs, phrases, etc.) within a set of documents. As computer-based systems have evolved to support storage and retrieval of information in a variety of forms, some have broadened the definition of information retrieval to include retrieval of data elements and values from numeric and statistical databases, image retrieval from image databases, and audio retrieval from databases of sound recordings.

Information retrieval focuses on four basic functions in a broader communications context:

- Analysis of information content including description of elements such as author/creator, title, volume, and date; abstracting; indexing; and other representational processing
- Identification and location of information through browsing and searching through databases and other information collections
- Evaluation and assessment of information identified and retrieved through browsing and searching
- Provision of physical access to the information identified and retrieved in appropriate form such as paper, microfilm, file transfer, visual display, and soundtracks

Early information retrieval systems were simple manual systems, consisting of fairly rudimentary subject indexing. As technology evolved, the capabilities of information retrieval systems were extended and led to a considerable amount of experimentation and evaluation applied to each of the four basic functions. Early efforts were aimed at information retrieval systems' inherent weaknesses: slow response time, need for expensive human intervention, and limited scalability. Furthermore, two kinds of information retrieval errors were apparent: relevant information or documents were missed, and irrelevant ones were retrieved. Efforts to reduce these two errors began to drive information retrieval developments, along with technological progress and capabilities, and continue to do so today. Information retrieval systems have evolved significantly since the early 1950s when crude mechanical devices, such as punched cards, were used to implement simple Boolean logic (combining search terms using the operators "and," "or," and "not") for retrieval. Other early developments focused on the structure and quality of indexing (or document description) languages.

In a second development phase, information retrieval systems were automated and bibliographic databases developed. The ability to manipulate bibliographic databases (which contained information about documents and other databases, but did not contain the documents or datasets themselves) gave rise to significant improvements in retrieval system performance. Thought of by many researchers as the "golden age of information retrieval," this phase produced innovations in automated indexing, right- and left-hand truncation of search terms, term weighting (associated with both documents and search queries), statistical word association methods, ranking of search outputs, citation searching, use of vocabulary links and roles (the designation of term relationships and specific syntactical roles), the beginning of full-text input, natural language queries, and current awareness services. During this phase and continuing into the early past of the third phase, information system evaluation emerged as a significant concern.

Considerable attention was paid to definitions of relevance and related concepts. Several information retrieval system performance measures were developed to determine the existence and extent of the two main error types. Two measures, in particular, are still used today—recall (the proportion of relevant items in the collection that are retrieved) and precision (the proportion of items retrieved that are relevant). The focus on evaluation led to recognition that the two kinds of retrieval errors result from input errors and weakness of subject indexes and natural language as search tools, as well as errors in search query formulation and in screening search output. Two major experimental environments were established during the 1960s: the Cranfield tests by Cyril Cleverdon and the SMART system by Gerry Salton at Cornell.

The third major development phase was based on online and interactive technological capabilities, but developmental emphases changed. Input errors were de-emphasized as the ability to perform efficiently iterative searches grew. Information retrieval research focused more on full-text input and natural language searching, relevance feedback, human–computer interaction, and the relative merits of end-user searching versus search intermediaries (such as reference librarians and information specialists). This third phase also saw tremendous growth in commercially available databases and search services. As commercial sector involvement in information retrieval grew, experimentation and evaluation slowed down as performance improvements took a "back seat" to market share. As a result, research shifted from system improvements to the user community. Numerous studies were performed on the extent of online searching, the proportion of information used that had been found through online searching, and the usefulness and value of information retrieval systems.

The latest phase of information retrieval developments results from the extraordinary capacity and penetration of the Internet and World Wide Web, which have had profound effects on electronic/digital publishing, libraries, repositories, and archives. Opportunities for full-text and multimedia searching are tremendous. However, the penalties of de-emphasizing information and vocabulary structures have been apparent, and the Web search engines of the past decade have resurrected ghostly images of early, mechanized information retrieval. Major efforts are once again underway to create semantic and other structures to improve retrieval performance on the

Web. The TREC (Text Retrieval Conference) group has designed an evaluation laboratory environment to encourage further information retrieval research, establish relevant evaluation methods, and facilitate the development and sharing of research ideas and results. It remains to be seen the extent to which current experimentation and evaluation, versus market demand, will drive future developments.

—*José-Marie Griffiths*

*See also* Browser; Document Management Systems; Library Technologies; Literature Searching

## Bibliography

Bourne, C. P., & Bellardo Hahn, T. (2003). *A history of online information services, 1963–1976.* Cambridge: MIT Press.

Griffiths, J. M., & King, D. W. (2002, July–September). U.S. information retrieval system evolution and evaluation (1945–1975). *IEEE Annals of the History of Computing,* 35–55.

Lancaster, F. W., & Fayen, E. G. (1973). *Information retrieval on-line.* Los Angeles, CA: Melville.

Rasmussen, E. (2003). Indexing and retrieval for the WWW. In B. Cronin (Ed.), *Annual review of information science and technology.* Medford, NJ: Information Today.

Salton, G. (Ed.). (1971). *The SMART retrieval system: Experiments in automatic document processing.* Englewood Cliffs, NJ: Prentice Hall.

Spark Jones, K. (Ed.). (1981). *Information retrieval experiment.* London: Butterworths.

## INFORMATION SYSTEMS

An *information system*—as opposed to concepts such as *information technology (IT)* or *information and communication technology (ICT)*—is a fairly old concept that appeared as the first commercial applications of the computer were developed at the dawn of the general systems theory era. According to Davis and Olson, a *management information system,* as the term is generally understood, is "an integrated, user-machine system for providing information to support operations, management, and decision-making functions in an organization. The system utilizes computer hardware and software; manual procedures; models for analysis planning, control, and decision-making; and a database." The U.K. Academy of Information Systems (UKAIS) defines information systems as "the means by which people and organizations, utilizing technology, gather, process, store, use and disseminate information."

There is no clear consensus on the definition of the term *IS*. This confusing situation is rooted in the rapid growth of the MIS field (from the data-processing era, powered by early mainframes, to the strategic information system era powered by the Internet and the Web), and in the multiple points of view adopted by researchers and writers in management, communications, decision making, political science, sociology, economics, and strategy. As a result, there is an alternative terminology for information systems and management information systems, which includes expressions such as "information and communication system," "information and decision system," "organizational information system," and "strategic information system" to refer to a computer-based information processing system.

By definition, the term *IS* is not an alternative name for IT. The use of the word *system* indicates that the users are a part of the information system. At a more abstract level, an IS can be imagined, designed, or proposed without any technological reference. The IS is a part of a larger social system composed of individuals and groups. In their social lives, individuals, groups, or business units experience information needs whose satisfaction would enable them to solve organizational problems. These organizational problems may be located at the level of the task, process, organization, or industry. Information needs pertaining to a problem can be formalized into a requirements analysis. In this sense, an IS is an answer to information requirements for a particular problem; the IS, combined with new procedures, processes, competencies, and resources will lead to new capabilities that will solve the identified problem with the help of information technology.

In order for a problem to be solved, an IS must be developed or adapted in accordance with the requirements analysis. Approaches and methods for developing an IS have changed with the appearance of new IT capabilities. Each IS development project requires the explicit and formal expression of a stated problem. That formalization expressed through various approaches and formal languages leads to design and implementation phases.

Figure 1 shows the inextricable hard and soft links between the IS in use and its organizational and technological contexts. This figure can be read as a succession of four layers: the IT infrastructure, the IS, information management (IM), and the value generated by applying IT, IS, and IM to tasks, activities, and processes. The figure can also be read from right to left as a continuum between hard and soft dimensions. At the bottom of Figure 1, at the IT infrastructure level, the model displays mostly hard technological dimensions. The soft aspect of the layer is the quality of management of the hard dimensions.

The IS layer is just above the IT layer, benefiting from its services. The soft dimensions are very important in the IS layer. IS participants are numerous (users, analysts, programmers, interface designers, project managers, etc.), and bring a human and organizational dimension to the success or failure of any IS implementation. The hard dimensions are the machine domain of the system where data architecture, storage, processes, inputs, and outputs have to be designed, programmed, and implemented by using IT application packages or by developing a new application. Both the hard and soft dimensions of the IS layer are closely intertwined with the organization's tasks, activities, and processes. In some cases (e.g., Web-based order processing at Dell), the IS has completely permeated work processes by fully automating a task, activity, or process.

At the information management level, hard dimensions are related to information as a means to control organizational performance (efficiency and effectiveness) through the continuous monitoring of people, tasks, activities, and processes. Soft dimensions are mostly culture-based (within the society, organization, and group culture), providing for information exchange and knowledge creation.

The value-added layer displays information technology, system, and management intangible benefits as the soft dimension and IT-IS-IM tangible, financial benefits as the hard dimension.

## EVOLUTION AND CATEGORIES OF INFORMATION SYSTEMS

In North America, IT has evolved through three eras, each era leading to new IS definitions and uses. During the first era, approximately 1965–1975, large corporations and government agencies developed large-scale transactional applications running on centralized mainframes. This was the data processing

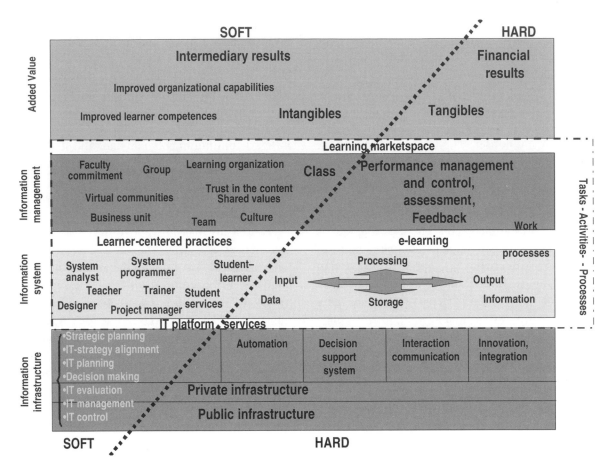

**Figure 1**

era. Automation, and the substitution of machines for human work, were the catchwords of the day. Information systems were deployed at the operational level using detailed historical data. The evolution of hardware led to the invention of the mini- and later the micro-computer.

The next era extended from 1975 to 1985, as the business unit (with the mini-computer) and soon middle management (with the micro-computer) became the new participants, developers, and users in the world of management information systems (MIS). This was truly a new era for managers as they acquired a range of radically new information systems based on spreadsheet packages and the new relational databases. These applications led to new interactive information systems using simulation models and sophisticated query languages. New applications were built around the rules-based approach to application development, bringing the notion of expert systems to life. Expert systems, decision support systems, executive information systems, and exploitation of massive databases were

the new products of the MIS era. The growth of local and wide area networks built bridges between the islands of automated information systems.

The most recent era, beginning around 1985, can be described as the strategic network era. Its characteristics are the integration and networking of all informational applications—which are more and more frequently Web-based—through new data warehouses and intelligent applications: data-mining and text-mining software, online analytical processing (OLAP) applications, decision support systems, and reporting capabilities. New information development techniques are object- or hypertext-based. The multimedia capabilities of new personal computers offer more intuitive interfaces and better person–machine interaction. During this period, top managers have come to realize the competitive or strategic benefits of IS. The quest for competitive advantage through a well-designed and well-deployed IS began to be acknowledged in American head offices in the 1980s, at a time when their Japanese counterparts were still committed to more of a social process of sharing and managing information and knowledge. With the exponential success of Internet and the Web, this most recent era is a period of IS-IT networked architecture enabling the implementation of e-commerce, e-business, e-government, e-learning, e-health, and the like as new collaborative ways of doing business. The new applications are not the office automation applications of the MIS era (the Big Four personal applications: word processor, spreadsheet, database, and graphics presentation support), but industrial, corporate, or organizational IS-IT concepts connecting employees, customers, suppliers, stakeholders, and managers: CRM (customer relationship management), ERP (enterprise resources planning), BI (business intelligence), SCM (supply chain management), and LMS (learning management system).

## THE INFORMATION SYSTEM AS A SET OF COMPONENTS IN THE DISTRIBUTED LEARNING APPROACH

The strategic network era can handle heterogeneous, distributed, and decentralized systems as long as a set of standards is respected. Distributed learning standards—such as Sharable Content Object Reference Model (SCORM)—are emerging around the work done at the Aviation Industry CBT Committee (AICC), Institute of Electrical and Electronics Engineers (IEEE), and IMS. These standards are paving the way for better content portability between learning management systems (LMS) and learning content management systems (LCMS) through a better definition of learning objects.

Each IS has a hard aspect—the machine domain in which an application has to be designed or set up using parameters—and a soft aspect—the problem domain in which the IS will display the results of its functionality. The area of overlap between the learning problem domain and the machine domain is the interface domain.

### The Hard Dimension: The Machine Domain

From data-processing systems to learning and knowledge management information systems, there is a data continuum. Between atomic data representing an event in a transactional system and data for learning and knowledge development, however, there is a gap, indicating that old development concepts and practices may no longer apply to the distributed learning approach. LMS is a learner-centered approach

based on the use of learning objects and e-portfolios. An object is a small and coherent piece or chunk of knowledge that can be stored in the form of text, animation, simulation, image, sound, or video. Because they are reusable, learning objects are becoming the building blocks of course content. Unlike data-processing systems, learning management systems offer dynamic and interactive multimedia sequences through specific frameworks that make process, data, and explicit knowledge work together.

### The Soft Dimension: The Learning Problem Domain

The goal of distributed learning is to change people's behavior and performance level by transferring and converting specific knowledge—for a specific audience—into mental models leading to new actions. This is the learning problem domain where cognitive scientists, psychologists, educators, and other soft experts have to cooperate to discover how to help an organization successfully disseminate explicit knowledge to people. The most sensitive issue in the problem domain is the precise definition and analysis of learning needs for the eventual purpose of implementing LMS functionalities.

## THE INTERFACE DOMAIN

There is an overlap between the machine domain and the learning problem domain. This shared domain is the interface domain, where the learner has to interact with the machine and machines have to work together for peer-to-peer content sharing.

### Person–Machine

The person–machine interface is not just a question of simple graphical interfaces (scrolling menus, multiple windows, hypertext links, buttons, etc.). Simulations are used often in LMS, and these require multimedia animation relying on audio and video streaming, plug-ins, and languages such as Java. This is clearly a domain requiring the professional expertise of experienced designers.

### Machine–Machine

In the old days of computer-based learning, the learner sat in front of a PC using a CD-ROM. In the distributed learning approach, although the learner still has access to a PC or a mobile equivalent, content, animations, and trainers may be connected to different PCs or servers. The link, for example, with human resources management applications leads to another machine–machine interface design as peer-to-peer (P2P) solutions are deployed.

## THE IS–IT DYNAMICS: DEMAND AND SUPPLY

Another difference between an IS and its IT layers is evident in the balance between demand (the IS) and supply (the IT or ICT) within a firm or an organization. The classic steps leading from business needs to IS deployment through genuine development or package acquisition imply the use of organizational resources—time, money, and competences. In that sense, an IS project is tied to an individual, group, or business unit demand looking for an IT solution. Conversely, the technology domain—located either inside organizational boundaries (the data processing department) or outside (consulting firms and suppliers of hardware, software, or networks)—may be viewed as the supplier of technology and expertise. An IS will be implemented or deployed when it finds its technology supply through organizational resources (internal billing or real money).

## BENEFITS OF THE STRATEGIC LEARNING MANAGEMENT SYSTEM

An IS, and particularly an LMS, can be identified through its impacts on the individual, the group, or the organization, whereas IT—however radical its potential power—simply provides services for IS deployment and use. For example, the Dell online order processing system is a strategic IS creating competitive advantages for the company. The technological components of that system are available on the market to all industry players. In that sense, the IS is strategic and very specific to the firm (supporting genuine processes), whereas the IT platform is strategic but generic from a competitive point of view.

Within the IS, the soft (human and social) dimension can be the most strategic differentiator. As an example, the first online reservation system—the Sabre system developed by American Airlines to connect customers to its reservation system through terminals located inside travel agencies—had a strategic design. The system gave American Airlines a greater market share because it provided data-browsing capability and made it possible to book flights and later cars and hotel rooms from the travel agency. In the 1990s, a new IS at American Airlines, the Yield Management System (YMS), was developed as an additional layer for the online transactional reservation system. The new system allowed the company to maximize the revenue generated by each flight through modeling and optimization techniques. In this case, the capability to explore data and use the models to optimize the revenue from each flight remained in the professional's head. From the point of view of the manager in charge of the system, no risk was involved in selling the YMS software to every competitor. American Airline's key strategic advantage was its ability to leverage YMS's potential through its employees' knowledge and competencies. As companies move from decision-support systems to communications, cooperation, coordination, knowledge, and learning systems, the key strategic factors or complementary assets become, in addition to skills, knowledge, and competencies, the group and organizational cultures that will foster innovation and enact new capabilities.

—*Albert Lejeune*

*See also* DISTRIBUTED LEARNING/DISTRIBUTED EDUCATION; INFORMATION TECHNOLOGY (IT); KNOWLEDGE MANAGEMENT; LEARNING MANAGEMENT SYSTEMS (LMS); LEARNING OBJECTS

## Bibliography

Anthony, R. N. (1965). *Planning and control: A framework for analysis.* Cambridge, MA: Harvard University Press.

Ciborra, C., & Jelessi, T. (Eds.). (1994). *Strategic information systems: An European perspective.* Chichester, UK: John Wiley & Sons.

Earl, M. J. (1989). *Management strategies for information technology.* Englewood Cliffs, NJ: Prentice Hall.

Earl, M. J. (Ed.). (1996). *Information management: The organizational dimension.* Oxford, UK: Oxford University Press.

Hartman, A., & Sifonis, J. (2000). *Net ready—strategies for success in the e-economy.* New York: McGraw-Hill.

Sloman, M. (2002). *The e-learning revolution. How technology is driving a new training paradigm.* New York: AMACOM.

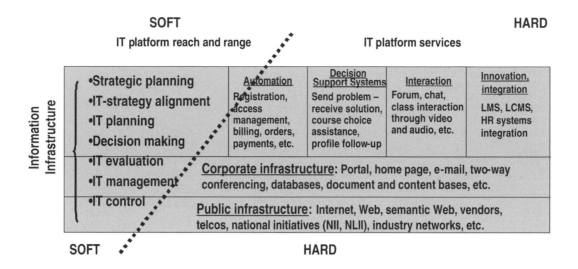

**Figure 1**

Ward, J., & Peppard, J. (2002). *Strategic planning for information systems*. New York: John Wiley & Sons.

Wiseman, C. (1985). *Strategy and computers*. Homewood, IL: Dow-Jones Irwin.

Zackman, J. A. (1987). A framework for information systems architecture. *IBM Systems Journal, 26*(3), 276–292.

# INFORMATION TECHNOLOGY (IT)

In the 1980s, the expression *information technology (IT)* appeared in the MIS field in competition with two previous terms, *management information system (MIS)* and *information system (IS)*. The success of the new IT concept is related to spectacular progress realized in the networks, machines, and person–machine interface domains—progress that redefined the new potential of information systems of any kind. With the dramatic development of communications networks since the 1980s (local and wide area networks, digitalization of old telephone company networks, digital cellular phone networks and deployment of the Internet, networks of networks), which was accompanied by massive deployment of optical fiber, new wireless capabilities, and the availability of a shared network protocol (TCP/IP, the Internet protocol), it has become apparent that information technology is really the fusion of communication, processing, storage, and multimedia interface capabilities. The key role played by communication networks explains the European expression ICT, which stands for *information and communication technology*.

The technological improvements that created an integrated IT platform among companies, customers, and suppliers paved the way for new organizational forms (electronic markets, virtual firms, modular companies, industry networks) through horizontal or vertical company and inter-company integration. Since the early 1990s, the new potential of IT (or ICT in Europe) has triggered a movement to reengineer or redesign business processes, identifying the firm's performance as a direct consequence of the mix of IT investments and redefinition of business processes. Thus, the quest for organizational performance through IT integration has redefined the boundaries of training and learning tasks, activities, and processes.

The concepts of IT, MIS, and information management (IM) can be thought of as a continuum of practices, from IT infrastructure management to the development and implementation of information systems and the production of value through information management. The first and fundamental layer remains information technology. This infrastructure layer can be represented as a public infrastructure supporting a corporate infrastructure that supports business units and corporate applications.

At the IT infrastructure level, IT services are produced by a mix of *soft* dimensions, illustrating the quality of IT management and the IT–strategy partnership and alignment, and the *hard* dimensions of computers and networks. The production of IT quality services requires a high level of IT capital expenditures

**Table 1**    Public Organizations Working Toward a Common IT Infrastructure for Distributed Learning

| | |
|---|---|
| United States | IEEE Learning Technology Standards Committee |
| | Advanced Distributed Learning Initiative (ADL) |
| | The Instructional Management Systems (IMS) |
| | The Web-Based Education Commission |
| | Aviation Industry CBT Committee (AICC) |
| | International Society for Technology in Education (ISTE) |
| | The United States Distance Learning Association (USDLA) |
| OECD | Education, Employment, Labour and Social Affairs Education |
| | CERI Centre for Educational Research and Innovation |
| | IMHE Institutional Management in Higher Education |
| Europe | Education, Training and Youth |
| | CSCL Competence Centre |
| | European Commission Education and Culture DG |
| | CEN/ISSS Learning Technologies Workshop |
| | PROmoting Multimedia Access to Education and Training in EUropean Society (PROMETEUS) |

generating recurring operating costs. The soft dimensions are of an organizational (application development process) and human (programming skills) nature. Hard dimensions include hardware, the network, standards, storage, and the software used to operate computers and run applications. At the beginning of the 21st century, IT investments represent the largest portion of North American firms' investments. These investments can be broken down into public IT infrastructure, corporate IT infrastructure, and corporate and business unit applications. The following figure (see Figure 1) shows details of public and corporate infrastructures and identifies applications supported by the distributed learning approach.

## COMPONENTS OF PUBLIC INFRASTRUCTURE

Generally speaking, the basic elements of public infrastructure are the Internet, value-added bandwidth vendors, telephone companies' (telcos') channel capacity, and the other industry networks. All of these (except for the Internet protocol, TCP/IP) may involve different standards and levels of performance depending on country or continent. Companies such as e-Bay and Amazon.com use the public infrastructure extensively in their business models. In the case of distributed learning, the continuous transmission of high-bandwidth video and multimedia information

without errors and delays is difficult in public networks under ordinary protocols.

In a distributed learning approach, new standards must be shared to support effective applications such as the learning management system (LMS) for students and the learning content management system (LCMS) for developers. Existing standards have been created by the Aviation Industry Computer-Based Training Committee (AICC) and Advanced Distributed Learning/Sharable Content Object Reference Model (ADL/SCORM). The latest standard is dedicated to Extensible Markup Language (XML)-based learning objects.

This is not the first attempt to define IT standards for an IT infrastructure. In the United States, the key principle of the National Information Infrastructure (NII) initiative was the delivery of universal access to all Americans, avoiding the so-called digital divide. Following the Clinton-Gore initiative of a National Information Infrastructure, the National Learning Information Infrastructure (NLII) is defined on the EDUCAUSE Web site (www.educause.edu). Similar initiatives exist in Europe, such as the Minerva Action.

The Web sites of public organizations that are working toward a common infrastructure and compatible applications for distributed learning are listed in Table 1.

## COMPONENTS OF CORPORATE INFRASTRUCTURE

IT infrastructure investments account for more than 50% of large firms' investments in IT. Beyond intranets, extranets, and portals, this private IT infrastructure has a storage dimension (customer databases, document and content databases, corporate data warehouses, etc.), a processing dimension (large-scale or server computing capacities), a communications dimension (electronic mail, videoconferences, etc.), and a personal computer and LAN services dimension.

## IT APPLICATIONS

An IT application can be described as the use of IT hardware, software, and networks to carry out particular tasks at a personal level (word-processing) or business activities and processes at a group or organizational level (an accounting package). Applications deployed on corporate and public infrastructures will support users engaged as participants in an information system.

In a distributed learning context, applications will support learners or students, teachers, trainers, HR professionals, and the like. Major applications fall into the categories of automation, decision support systems, interaction/communication, and innovation/ integration.

### Automation

Some aspects of the distributed learning approach are transactional: They generate repetitive data, as does the scanner used by a cashier at a supermarket. Registering, setting up, invoicing, making payments, ordering CD-ROMs and other learning materials, shipping and tracking, using automated test correction, and so on are basic examples of these applications that can be integrated into an e-learning package. This package is usually called the learning management system.

### Decision Support Systems

Some aspects of the distributed learning approach are of an informational and decisional nature. Applications bring information to the trainer or teacher about the student's performance and whether the learning material is being used effectively. A learner may need an evaluation of his or her skills and competencies before choosing a course. An expert system may support analysis of learning requirements and needs. An HR professional may use an application to monitor the gap between competencies that should be available and those that really exist at a given point in time.

### Interaction and Communication

In the distributed learning approach, many applications are dedicated to communications support; communications can be synchronous (occurring at the same time) or asynchronous (occurring at different times). Applications such as chat, forums, two-way video and audio, and whiteboards support student interactions with the trainer, teacher, and class. These applications can be used as distribution channels for specialized learning materials such as audio and video streaming.

### Innovation and Integration

IT-based innovation can produce new informational products, better information for users and managers on organizational performance, tighter integration of internal processes, and closer interconnection with external stakeholders such as suppliers and consumers. The lessons learned from research on strategic information systems can be used as a framework for distributed learning software—the systems are becoming more and more integrated. A simple Web-based static application used to publish written content has become an integrated package connecting human resource managers, information brokers, multimedia developers, trainers, teachers, designers, and students or learners. More than 1,000 applications are available on the market as more or less integrated packages of learning management systems and/or learning content management systems.

## IT ARCHITECTURE

An application's architecture can be strategic if that architecture enables the building and deployment of new applications at a low marginal cost. This is the case once an organization installs a new LMS or LCMS, installs a new corporate database management system or a modular package such as the Supply Chain Management system, and then chooses to add a module from the package to the existing configuration. The danger is that the IT capacity will reach a limit (in storage, processing, or bandwidth and speed) as the IT platform is impacted by deployment of new IS and applications.

## SOFT DIMENSIONS OF THE IT INFRASTRUCTURE

### IT Planning, Strategic Alignment, Evaluation, Management, and Control

The quality of management is important. In a faculty, public department, or firm, IT services—resulting from the installed IT platform—are on the supply side of the IS–IT internal market. The demand comes from managers and directors experiencing performance problems linked with training and learning weaknesses. Different strategies can be implemented to make supply meet demand, including utilizing the free market; outsourcing; achieving a technological edge, which can be an obsession in high-tech firms; maintaining a bureaucratic monopoly; or focusing on central planning involving both the IT and business sides of the organization. The IS–IT literature shows that the central planning approach is the best way for information systems to generate lasting competitive advantages. The quality of the IT–business partnership is the key to a responsive IS delivery for better performance on the business side, where there is always a need to improve customer service.

## IT SERVICES

Key technical performance measures for the IT platform are the bandwidth for transmission channels, microchip power, memory and processing speed, the storage capacity of disks and other media, and speed of access to storage. The better the performance of individual components, the better the architecture and level of integration and the greater degree of liberty that is given to human beings connected to the IT platform, freeing them from constraints of time, space, and speed. The better the IT platform, the better the organizational and human capabilities with regard to mobility, cooperative work, openness, innovation, transformation, partnerships, contracts, and globalization.

Services can be extremely varied and specialized, from setting up a new employee's machine to implementing computer security, encryption, and firewalls.

IT services usually fall within the following categories: networking, telecommunications, Web services, multimedia, help desk, training, resources management, internal consulting, workstation administration, Webcasting, video-teleconferencing, and corporate computing. To some extent the quality of transmission and the rate of error can be defined in a business–IT contract, and hence measured, controlled, and sometimes guaranteed in advance.

### The Power of the IT Platform: Reach and Range

In the information age, anything that can be digitized is information. Even telco networks, like the newer cellular networks, are becoming digitized, offering new services such as computer-based voice mail and messaging services. On the Internet, voice over IP services turn the computer into simply an interface between two or more people. The IP (Internet Protocol) takes charge of the entire communication process through its various dimensions: syntactic (the signal level), semantic (the meaning level), and pragmatic (the action level). The combination of information processing, database management, networks, channels, operating systems, software, and user interfaces has led to new levels of IT services that are impacting the power of the IT platform (i.e., its reach and range).

When IT components (hardware, operating system, applications software, and networks) are fully connected and integrated according to shared standards (see, for example, the e-learning standards developed by IEEE, ADL, IMS, and AICC in the United States), they constitute an IT platform. For example, powerful integrated packages such as enterprise resource planning (ERP), customer relationship management (CRM), and business intelligence (BI), coupled with a three-tier server architecture and networks using the TCP/IP protocol are the integrated components of an IT platform.

An IT platform—such as a large integrated LMS operating on a powerful corporate and public infrastructure—exhibits two key dimensions: reach and range. The reach dimension starts with a local area network (LAN) connecting workstations inside a business unit, and ends with the capability to connect or interface a firm or an organization with anybody, anywhere, anytime through a Web browser. The range dimension, from message exchange to complex transactions processing, describes a state of integration of the different ISs operating on an IT platform. In a distributed learning environment where resources are located in different places, the reach dimension is essential to the learner-centered approach. The range dimension enables the user or student to participate in forums, to be evaluated and followed by a trainer, to attend synchronized video sessions, and to update his or her profile on the HR database after a course is finished. By contrast, the very basic range option in the distributed learning approach allows only the downloading of raw text files.

—*Albert Lejeune*

*See also* Administrative Planning and Support of Information Technology; Computer; Information Systems; Internet; Learning Management Systems (LMS); Learning Objects; World Wide Web

### Bibliography

Galliers, R. D., & Baets, W. R. J. (1998). *Information technology and organizational transformation.* New York: John Wiley & Sons.

Marchand, D. A., Davenport, T. H., & Dickson, T. (Eds.). (2000). *Mastering information management.* London, UK: Financial Times–Prentice Hall.

O'Brien, J. A. (2002). *Management information systems. Managing information technology in the e-business enterprise.* San Francisco: McGraw-Hill/Irwin.

Parker, M. M. (1996). *Strategic transformation and information technology.* Upper Saddle River, NJ: Prentice Hall.

Remenyi, D., Money, A., & Twite, A. (1998). *Effective measurement & management of IT costs & benefits.* Boston: Butterworth-Heinemann.

Ward, J., & Peppard, J. (2002). *Strategic planning for information systems.* New York: John Wiley & Sons.

Weill, P., & Broadbent, M. (1998). Leveraging the new infrastructure. *How market leaders capitalize on information technology.* Boston: Harvard Business School Press.

# INSTRUCTIONAL COURSE DESIGN

Instructional course design is a critical process in much human learning. Human learning occurs from a combination of planned and unplanned educational experiences. Unplanned learning, also called incidental learning, occurs when the learner is focused on objective other than learning and in the process gains unsought insight. For example, a learner's goal might be to watch a play for entertainment and in the midst of the play unexpectedly gain an insight into relationships. Despite the value of such unplanned learning experiences, most human learning occurs within the context of planned, organized educational experiences in which the learner's primary goal is learning. Although formal instructional course design has little or no role in the many incidental learning experiences in life, the value of planned educational experiences is very much related to the quality of the instructional design effort underlying the educational program.

## THE PROCESS OF INSTRUCTIONAL DESIGN

The term *instructional design* refers to the systematic procedures utilized by educators when developing educational programs. Usually these procedures form an integrated process incorporating several distinct elements or steps. Although often presented in a sequential fashion, most models suggest that the steps should not be followed in a strictly linear manner. Many models of instructional design have been proposed in the literature, but despite the nuances of distinction within a specific model, most include a number of similar foundational elements. These common elements of instructional course design include: 1) assessing the learning needs in the targeted learners for the program, 2) establishing learning goals and objectives based on uncovered learner needs, 3) determining the curriculum and content to fulfill the established objectives for the program, 4) choosing the appropriate mix of teaching and learning methods and strategies, 5) coordinating the support systems for delivery of the program, and 6) evaluating the various learning outcomes for the program. These primary elements in the instructional design process will be evident whether the courses are designed for traditional, face-to-face settings or are delivered via distance education.

Identifying needs is the critical root of all effective instructional design because learner motivation is very related to the learner's perception of whether an educational program addresses a perceived need. A variety of tools are used for needs assessment, including interviews, surveys, focus groups, expert opinion, and observation. Once the needs have been determined, the instructional designer develops specific learning objectives. Such objectives guide the development of content as well as create a basis for program evaluation. Learning objectives are usually organized according to the knowledge, skill, and attitudinal components of uncovered needs. Knowledge components refer to the facts, information, and thought processes essential to meeting a need. Skill components refer to the psycho-motor, relational, and professional skills that must be connected to thinking to successfully address the need. Many uncovered needs will also have attitude components, which refer to the perceptions and perspectives developed in the learner to meet the uncovered need, such as being willing to adopt new value systems and beliefs.

Designing content for courses occurs as instructional designers take each of the identified knowledge, skill, and attitudinal components and determines the specific content needing to be learned to achieve each objective. Such content is often developed with the aid of content experts. After developing the specific content, instructional designers are better able to determine the appropriate prerequisites for the course. The established content is then organized and sequenced by instructional designers, usually by starting with the familiar, in order to create a link to the existing schema and experiences of the learner and then building up to the new and more complex information. Instructional designers organize content by using classifying strategies like taxonomies to help "chunk" information; spatial learning strategies such as visual displays, frames or matrices, and concept mapping; bridging strategies to help learners apply prior knowledge to new information, such as advanced organizers or creating metaphors and analogies; and rehearsal strategies to review material, ask questions, and summarize.

Having developed and organized the content, instructional designers must then choose the proper formats for the learning, basing format decisions on the background and experience of the participants, the expertise of the instructional staff, the available facilities and equipment, and the program content's "fit" to a particular format. Designers in distance education use a number of formats, including correspondence study, audio/videoconferencing, broadcast and cable television, satellite communication, and Web-based delivery. A critical final step is to design evaluation tools to better uncover the learning outcomes in the course. Such evaluation helps to identify changes in

knowledge and skills arising from the educational offering, as well as the degree to which such learning transfers to the practice setting. In addition to pretests and posttests, the tools for such evaluation are often the same tools used for needs assessment.

## DISTANCE EDUCATION AS A SETTING FOR INSTRUCTIONAL DESIGN

Four key differences distinguish distance education (particularly the online forms of distance education) from traditional, face-to-face education. First, there is a separation in space between the teacher and learner during the majority of the educational process, which removes the normal visual clues that are often relied upon in face-to-face settings by instructors and learners to better understand both the teaching content and student questions. Second, there is the need to use some form of educational media to carry course content. The human voice (in the sense of lecture) can no longer be the main method of content transfer between the instructor and the learner. Third, the instructional designer must provide some form of two-way communication to facilitate interaction between the teacher and learner, as well as among learners. The most common technology tools for two-way interaction in contemporary distance education are audio/videoconferencing and computers for connecting participants online through e-mail, bulletin boards, and chat rooms. Fourth, the volitional control of the learning process is in the hands of the learners more than the instructors because the learner, not the instructor, makes the choice about when to study, when to read assignments, when to interact with the instructor or fellow learners through the chosen media of the course, and which learning strategies to employ. Understanding these four differences between distance education and face-to-face instruction is a critical backdrop for effective instructional design.

When considering distance education as a setting for instructional design, perhaps the most salient fact is the reality that the instructor and learner (as well as the learner and other learners) are separated by space. The success of distance education instructional design depends on the extent to which the educational institution and instructor (aided by the instructional designer) are able to foster meaningful dialogue between instructors and learners, as well as between learners and other learners. Instructional designers use varying combinations of print and electronic communications media to deliver instruction to learners, leading some to suggest that the term *mediated instruction* is a better description for the method than *distance education*.

The mediation of instruction began with correspondence as a way to connect learners and instructors in distance education, but as newer and more efficient technologies developed, the media employed gradually expanded to include audiotapes, videotapes, radios, television broadcasts, and satellite transmission. Each new medium required instructional designers to modify their courses to reflect the medium's strengths and weaknesses. Contemporary distance education course design is being shaped primarily by the use of computers and the Internet (World Wide Web) to bridge the distance between teachers and learners, as well as between learners. The terms *Web-based training (WBT)* and *online learning* are emerging to distinguish distance education that uses the Web as a communication method in contrast to older forms of distance education. Because most instructional designers are not communication or technology specialists, instructional designers working with distance education programs usually function as part of a larger design team. Design teams help foster a collaboration in which academic content specialists combine with instructional designers, media specialists, editors, and others to create viable and effective educational programs.

Web-based distance education programs can take two different forms, asynchronous (programs in which learners and instructors are not online at the same time) and synchronous (programs in which the instructor and learners are online at the same time). Given the difficulties inherent with distance learners being in different time zones, as well as the expense usually required for synchronous technical connections, most contemporary distance education is following an asynchronous form of course design. Some instructional designers follow an asynchronous approach in which self-study materials are posted on the Web and perused by learners at their own pace, an approach that sees the Internet as primarily a distribution medium for learning materials. The majority of quality distance education programs, however, use an interactive asynchronous approach in which "classes" for learners begin on a particular day with a cohort of other learners. The cohort of learners is taught by a faculty member who interacts with individuals or the cohort through group conferencing software. This interactive model is employed because of the close

parallels with quality traditional learning environments (face-to-face). In traditional settings, learners have access to learning materials, a professor, and other students. The interactive, asynchronous approach duplicates these dimensions by giving the learner, through communications media, access to the same three items. With such forms of distance education, the Internet is primarily a communications facilitator between instructor and students, as well as between students and students, and only secondarily a medium for distribution of learning materials.

## DESIGNING INTERACTIVITY INTO DISTANCE EDUCATION PROGRAMS

Although similarities exist between distance education courses and traditional classroom instruction that influence the instructional design process, many important differences exist between these forms of educational programming. For example, traditional learners gather at a fixed time and place for their learning, whereas Web-based learners can choose their own time and place for either totally self-directed study or asynchronous learning. Traditionally, faculty and learners interact in person in face-to-face settings, whereas distance education forces participants to rely on electronic or print interaction. In face-to-face settings, group activities are often limited by group size and instructional time, whereas in distance education settings group learning activities are able to extend beyond the space and time of the classroom, particularly for those using communication tools like e-mail, chat rooms, and bulletin boards.

Instructional designers must make provision for three types of interaction in distance education programs. First, they must ensure that the design permits adequate interaction between the learner and the formal course content. This is done by ensuring that the learner has access in a timely fashion to the formal course content through textbooks, course Web pages, study guides, tapes, CD-ROMs, and so on, and that course assignments encourage the learner to critically reflect on the material. Second, they must ensure that the design permits adequate learner-to-instructor interaction. In addition to providing mechanisms for timely responses to learner questions, courses must be designed to encourage learners to become active participants in the learning environment. Third, instructional designers must ensure that the design permits adequate learner-to-learner interaction. Constructivist learning theory suggests that people learn best when they actively construct their own understanding through interaction with fellow learners, teachers, and previous experiences with the area of knowledge. Well-designed distance education programs can actually increase this possibility by permitting learners the time to develop more reasoned responses in the course "discussions." Learner-to-learner interaction creates a process in which learners interpret and analyze others' writings, reflect on their own knowledge and readings, present their points of view, and provide pointers to information that supports their ideas. Discussion forums enable learners to become active participants in discussing topics presented in class and in bringing to the group additional information sources. Asynchronous participation allows learners time to reflect and carefully construct their points of view. Learning theory also suggests that the ability to contribute to a community creates the potential for learning, and discussion forums develop feelings of comradeship and community and the sense of team sharing. Thus, instructional designers need to keep interaction as a central consideration when designing distance education programs.

## SOME CORE STRATEGIES WHEN DESIGNING DISTANCE EDUCATION PROGRAMS

When designing instruction for distance education programs, designers should begin the process by studying distance education research findings and becoming familiar with the strengths and weaknesses of mediated instruction, as well as the current debates and issues. Designers should analyze the strengths and weaknesses of possible distance delivery approaches in terms of learner needs and course requirements before selecting a mix of instructional technology. Generally, distance education courses follow an integrative strategy, such as supplementing a Web-based course with content narrative placed in a print-based study guide. For certain courses, the development of tapes, videos, interactive CD-ROMs, and other learning resources could supplement the online aspects of the course. Instructional designers in distance education need to be realistic about the costs of technology—with every component added, the overall cost of the program grows and the learning curve for the students increases.

Finally, when designing instruction for distance education programs designers should be sure to provide hands-on training with the technology of delivery to both instructors and learners. Many learners are novices in the delivery format, so training must be designed under the assumption that learners have a limited competency. Designers should not underestimate the time needed to develop distance education courses—the more technologically complex the course becomes, the greater the development timeline.

*—Gary William Kuhne*

***See also*** COMPUTER-BASED TRAINING (CBT); DESIGNING LEARNING ENVIRONMENTS; DISTRIBUTED LEARNING/DISTRIBUTED EDUCATION; TEACHING IN AN ELECTRONIC CLASSROOM; WEB-BASED COURSE MANAGEMENT SYSTEMS (WBCMS)

## Bibliography

Moore, M. G., & Cozine, G. T. (Eds.). (2000). *Web-based communications, the Internet, and distance education.* College Park, PA: The American Center for the Study of Distance Education.

Moore, M. G., & Kearsley, G. (1996). *Distance education: A systems view.* Belmont, CA: Wadsworth.

Palloff, R. M., & Pratt, K. (2001). *Lessons from the cyberspace classroom.* San Francisco: Jossey-Bass.

Rajasingham, L., & Tiffin, J. (1995). *In search of the virtual class: Education in an information society.* London and New York: Routledge.

Rossman, M., & Rossman, M. (Eds.). (1995). *Facilitating distance education.* San Francisco: Jossey-Bass.

Verduin, J. R., Jr., & Clark, T. A. (1991). *Distance education: The foundations of effective practice.* San Francisco: Jossey-Bass.

Willis, B. (Ed.). (1994). *Distance education strategies & tools.* Englewood Cliffs, NJ: Educational Technology.

# INSTRUCTIONAL TECHNIQUES

Instructional techniques are methods or strategies that are used to help support the teaching and learning process. Typically the term refers to methods used by a teacher to help students learn, such as lecture or discussions. However, it also can refer to strategies used by an individual for self-instruction.

Instructional techniques for face-to-face classrooms are well-established, with years of practice, although variations on techniques are developed and techniques may gain or lose popularity based on dominant pedagogical thought at a given time. In distributed learning environments, instructional techniques have been based on traditional ones, with modifications to help accommodate characteristics of the distributed learning system.

## LEARNING THEORIES AND INSTRUCTIONAL TECHNIQUES

Inherent in different instructional techniques are theories of how people learn, with the goal that the technique supports or facilitates the learning process. Techniques that rely heavily on stimulus-response patterns support behaviorist learning principles; in a distributed environment this might include some forms of simulation and self-testing. Techniques that focus on how content is structured and presented are more cognitivist in nature, whereas those that rely heavily on distributed interaction among multiple learners tend to promote a constructivist theory of learning. Web-based communication tools in particular have been hailed as supporting constructivist or social learning practices. Most distributed learning techniques draw on elements of more than one learning theory, however. As with any learning situation, distributed learning techniques should be selected at least in part on the basis of their ability to support necessary components of learning, which may mean the availability of consistent and immediate feedback, flexible organizational and annotation schemes, or means of communicating with others.

## SELECTING TECHNIQUES FOR DISTRIBUTED LEARNING

Determining the appropriate instructional technique for a distributed learning activity requires a context-sensitive approach. Considerations include learning goals and objectives, learner characteristics, subject matter area, and specific medium of instruction. For example, students who have lower literacy skills may not learn well when text-heavy instructional techniques are involved. If an instructor is required to use a particular delivery system, learning activities should be designed to take advantage of the system's strengths and avoid any poor or "buggy"

features. Features that work only on certain computer platforms may prevent some students from participating. If learners are located in many different time zones, it may make sense to move to an asynchronous medium rather than require some learners to participate in the middle of the night.

In terms of learner interactions, some instructional techniques work better when synchronous, or real-time, technologies are used, whereas others are better suited to asynchronous interactions. The difference between the two usually is evident in the pacing and level of reflection achieved by students. Asynchronous technologies, like discussion boards, allow learners to work at their own most comfortable speeds and repeat or review course content as needed, which tends to result in more reflective contributions to the learning environment. Synchronous technologies, such as live chat or Webcasting, more closely simulate a face-to-face classroom environment. They are useful for instances in which a single thread of dialogue—whether it be spoken or written—is intended to be followed by all participants.

Other distributed learning techniques may not rely on human interaction at all. Instead, the learner interacts with a computer. Techniques used in this type of distributed learning may include watching prepared lecture videos or reading lecture notes, playing learning games against the computer, participating in simulations, and taking self-tests. Various instructional techniques and their use in distributed learning situations are discussed in the following sections.

### Lecture

The hallmark characteristic of a lecture is the direct dissemination of information from an instructor to students. It tends not to be terribly interactive, and it follows the prescribed path designed by the instructor. Any interactions that do occur typically take the form of students asking for clarification or repetition.

In a synchronous distributed medium, such as videoconference or Webcast, an instructor can essentially give a speech to students who are listening at remote sites. The lecture can be archived for later review or reuse. Sometimes learners are able to communicate with the instructor during the lecture using the same or less technology-intensive real-time media (such as text chat); often, however, the communication is one-way. In distributed classes that rely on primarily asynchronous media, an instructor might disseminate information by posting lecture notes or messages that serve as "mini-lectures."

## Group Discussion

*Discussion* is a generic term that encompasses many instructional activities. The common element is communication among the various participants, and it can be used to encourage students to become active participants in the learning environment. Discussion is an effective instructional technique when an instructor wants to elicit public student responses or encourage the sharing or exploration of ideas within a group. In order for discussion to be successful, there must be a clear intent or purpose. Failing that, it is likely that the participants either will not participate or will flounder in their efforts to interact productively and in a way that meets the learning objectives. Although extended periods of silence in a face-to-face scenario often prompt participation out of discomfort, the same cannot be said when a distributed medium is used.

Distributed media pose their own special challenges to discussion leaders and participants. In a synchronous medium, some concerns may include speed of participant connections, language abilities of the participants, typing speed of the participants, and turn taking. These concerns focus on issues that are likely to affect an individual's ability to be an active participant in the discussion. In an asynchronous medium, a major challenge can be the creation of true dialogue as opposed to the disjointed posting of thoughts at different times by different participants.

Particular activities that rely on discussion as an instructional technique include debate, role play, and starter-wrapper.

### Debate

Debate via a distributed medium can be done in many ways; the essence remains the same as a face-to-face debate. Participants take different sides of an issue and prepare and present their arguments. When a synchronous medium is used, it works best if individuals debate each other or if groups are co-located. A moderator is useful to help maintain an orderly interaction. When an asynchronous medium is used, individuals and groups may privately prepare their arguments in one discussion space and then meet the other side in a public space. Timing in the form of deadlines is important to ensure that there is responsive dialogue between both sides.

### Starter-Wrapper and Role Play

In the starter-wrapper and role play techniques, learners are assigned specific roles to play in the assigned discussion. These techniques are most likely to be used with asynchronous discussion, and roles may serve both administrative and pedagogical functions within the discussion environment. Both techniques may be used together.

The starter-wrapper technique involves the use of two roles. The starter must begin the discussion, typically involving a summary of the course readings along with extension questions to be addressed by the rest of the discussants. The wrapper ends the discussion, providing a summary of the points made by the various discussants.

In role play, additional roles may be assigned to help ensure that a variety of viewpoints are heard in the discussion. For example, some students may be asked to be optimists, while others are to serve as pessimists on the discussed topic. Other possible roles include journalist, researcher, adventurer, and teacher.

## Delphi Technique, Polling, and Other Survey Methods

One of the strengths of Web-based distributed learning is the ability to poll learners through the use of online survey tools. These tools can be used in a variety of ways. Opinion polling can be used to gauge overall class opinion on a topic. With the results, the instructor might then start the class by presenting the minority point of view, ensuring it is heard. Alternatively, the results can be used to gain student interest by showing them how they compare to a larger population that was polled on the same topic.

Survey tools also can be used to help determine group consensus. The Delphi Technique is one such method, involving iterative rounds of surveys. In the first survey, participants share their personal views on items. In subsequent rounds, they are told the overall group rating and may change or keep their previous rating based on the strength of their opinion. Typically people with weak opinions will move their rating toward the mean, and the result is a sense of items on which there is great consensus and items on which disparate and strong points of view exist. This technique is useful for stimulating discussion of controversial topics.

Finally, survey tools can be used for formative course evaluation. Although this is not quite an instructional technique by itself, it certainly can be used to help gather information that will lead to the improvement of other instructional techniques in the distributed learning medium.

## Problem-Based Learning

Problem-based learning (PBL) is learning that occurs through the process of working through an authentic problem. It is particularly powerful when preparing a learner for an authentic performance in a situation in which information must be gathered and decisions must be made. This technique is commonly used in medical schools and professional schools. When done via a Web-based medium, PBL may involve a number of authentic problem documents shared with learners via the Web, or it may take the form of an interactive simulation. Discussion boards can be used to facilitate collaborative or team-based problem-based learning.

Planning distributed PBL generally is labor-intensive for the instructor, who must devise the problem and either prepare or ensure the existence of adequate resources to help the learners solve the problem. It also typically requires close monitoring of student performance, either by a live human or, in the case of simulation-based PBL, the computer system.

## Simulation

Simulation is a useful instructional technique for engaging learners in experiences that are close to authentic ones. In the more passive sense, a computer-based simulation could be used to conduct a science experiment or see how a particular concept or phenomenon unfolds. This is passive because there is one clear path to success, and it is unlikely that the learner will deviate from this path and make his or her own decisions. Simulation is an excellent technique in these instances because it allows learning to occur in a no-risk, realistic environment in which the phenomenon can be repeatedly explored without using additional resources.

More complex simulated environments, however, encourage learner exploration and decision making. Simulation-based soft-skills training is becoming popular in the corporate education world, allowing employees to learn how to handle real-world situations by interacting with simulated characters while trying to meet particular goals. The simulation provides an authentic yet safe learning environment, because poor decisions will not have a real-life impact.

## Self-Testing

Many Web-based learning systems include robust objective-based testing systems. These systems can be used not only for summative course assessments, but also as a self-assessment tool for individual learners. Students can take self-tests to determine whether they have mastered the required course content, and the computer can provide students with instant scoring and feedback on their performance. Additionally, instructors can use self-test results to determine areas in which students are performing well or poorly.

## CLOSING

Ideally, in a given distributed learning situation, instructional techniques will be selected to take advantage of the medium's strengths and minimize awareness of its weaknesses. The techniques mentioned in this entry, along with variations and other techniques, should be considered tools an instructor may choose to help facilitate distributed learning.

*—Vanessa Dennen*

*See also* Simulations; Telephone Teaching

## Bibliography

Bonk, C. J., & King, K. S. (Eds.). (1998). *Electronic collaborators: Learner-centered technologies for literacy, apprenticeship, and discourse.* Mahwah, NJ: Erlbaum.

Hanna, D. E., Glowacki-Dudka, M., & Conceicao-Runlee, S. (2000). *147 practical tips for teaching online groups: Essentials of Web-based education.* Milwaukee: Atwood.

Stephenson, J. (Ed.). (2001). *Teaching and learning online: New pedagogies for new technologies.* London: Kogan Page.

# INTELLECTUAL PROPERTY

The origin of copyright protection in this country is the Constitution of the United States, which directs the Congress to pass laws "To promote the Progress of

Science and the useful Arts, by securing for limited Times to Authors and Inventors the exclusive Right to their respective Writings and Discoveries." The central purpose of copyright is not to give a monopoly or economic reward to the author, but to promote the betterment of society by encouraging the creation of and the public's access to useful works. This balance of interests is codified by granting several exclusive rights to owners and then limiting those rights in certain circumstances. The current copyright law of the United States is the Copyright Act of 1976, as amended ("the Act").

## ORIGINALITY AND FIXATION

Boiled down to its essence, copyright protection turns on the existence of two essential elements: the *creation of an original expression* that *is fixed in a tangible medium.* Facts, discoveries, and ideas in and of themselves are not subject to copyright protection because they do not exist as a result of an act of authorship. For that reason, the Supreme Court has held that collections of data such as the white pages of a phone directory are not copyrightable because they lack the necessary minimum degree of originality. However, factual compilations can be protected by copyright if there is originality in selection, coordination, or arrangement of the data. In general, therefore, what is subject to copyright protection is *how* authors express facts and ideas in "original works of authorship." Novelty is not required, only some modest degree of originality. The degree of originality sufficient to meet this constitutional element is minimal (requiring only that the work be the independent creation of the author). Nevertheless, originality is absolutely essential. Literary, dramatic, musical, artistic, and certain other intellectual works are subject to copyright protection, whether the work is published or unpublished.

Under the Act, copyright protection adheres immediately with the fixation of the original work of authorship in a tangible medium of expression—on paper, on canvas, on film, or any other medium through which the work can be perceived or communicated, including via the Web. It is not necessary to file a copy of the work with the Copyright Office in Washington or to place a copyright notice on the work, although there are distinct benefits to doing both of these things. The protection is automatic with the "fixation."

## TERM OF COPYRIGHTS AND THE PUBLIC DOMAIN

Copyright protection exists for a prescribed number of years depending on the type of work involved. For works created after December 31, 1978, the effective date of the 1976 Act, the term of copyright protection is the life of the author plus 70 years. For joint works, the term is the life of the last surviving author plus 70 years. For works made for hire, the term is 95 years from the first date of publication or 120 years from creation of the work, whichever is shorter. For pre-1978 works that are still entitled to copyright protection, the total term of the copyright is 95 years. When copyright protection expires, the work enters the public domain and at that point may be used without permission.

## COPYRIGHT NOTICE

The use of a copyright notice has not been required under U.S. law since the United States adhered to the Berne Convention, effective March 1, 1989. However, use of a notice is often beneficial for works created since March 1, 1989, and is still relevant to the copyright status of older works. A copyright notice informs the public that the work is protected by copyright, and it identifies the owner of the copyright and the year of first publication. If a work is infringed, the appearance of a proper notice of copyright on the published copy accessed by the defendant in a copyright infringement suit generally forecloses a defense of innocent infringement in mitigation of actual or statutory damages. Innocent infringement occurs when the infringer did not realize that the work was protected.

## COPYRIGHT OWNERSHIP

Four forms of copyright ownership are recognized under the Act. In general, the owner of a copyright is the *author* of the work. The author frequently is the creator. For example, the artist creating a watercolor painting, the writer of a novel or a textbook, or the individual who snapped the photograph generally is the owner of the copyright.

A *joint work* is a work prepared by two or more authors with the intention at the time of creation that the individual contributions be merged into inseparable or interdependent parts of a single copyrightable work. This is defined in Section 101 of the Act. This is similar in concept to the normal way in which a husband and wife purchase a home. They are deemed tenants by the entireties, meaning that they both own the property. In a similar vein, the authors of a joint work are considered to be co-owners under Section 201(a) of the Act. Each owns the whole and may independently exploit the work, but they must make an accounting to the other.

A *collective work* contains a number of contributions, each of which are separate and independent works, that are assembled into a collective whole; examples are an anthology or an encyclopedia. Under Section 201(c) of the Act, the copyrights in the separate contributions to the collection are distinct from the copyright in the collection itself. In other words, absent a written agreement, the owner of the copyright in the collective work is deemed to have acquired only the rights to reproduce and distribute the contribution as a part of the collective work; each contributor retains the copyright to his or her individual work.

There are two types of *works made for hire*. The first is a work prepared by an employee within the scope of his or her employment. The second is a work that has been specifically ordered or commissioned for use as one of the following, *provided* the parties agree in writing that the work shall be deemed a work made for hire:

- A contribution to a collective work
- Part of a motion picture or other audiovisual work
- A translation
- A supplementary work
- A compilation
- Instructional text
- A test
- Test answer material
- An atlas
- A sound recording

## EXCLUSIVE RIGHTS OF COPYRIGHT OWNERS

The Act gives the owner of a copyright a bundle of exclusive rights to exercise or to authorize others to exercise. The exclusive rights of a copyright owner are the rights to:

- *Reproduce* the copyrighted work
- Prepare *derivative* works or adaptations based on the copyrighted work

- *Distribute* copies of the copyrighted work to the public by sale or other transfer of ownership, or by rental, lease, or lending
- *Perform* the copyrighted work publicly, in the case of literary, musical, dramatic, and choreographic works, pantomimes, and motion pictures and other audiovisual works
- *Display* the copyrighted work publicly, in the case of literary, musical, dramatic, and choreographic works, pantomimes, and pictorial, graphic, or sculptural works, including the individual images of a motion picture or other audiovisual work

## COPYRIGHT INFRINGEMENT

Any exercise of a copyright owner's exclusive rights without the permission of the owner or the authority of one of the Act's limitations on those rights is an infringement. Copyright infringement is a "strict liability offense," and those who help or make it possible for another to infringe a copyright may be liable as contributory infringers. There are three types of copyright infringement: direct, vicarious, and contributory. A *direct* infringer is an individual who violates any of the exclusive rights of the copyright owner, per Section 501(a) of the Act. A *vicarious* infringer is one who has the right to control the infringing activities of another and profits from the infringement, or one who actively operates or supervises the operation of a place where the infringement occurs or controls the content of the infringing program and expects commercial gain or some other direct or indirect benefit from the infringement. A *contributory* infringer is one who has knowledge of the infringing activity and induces, causes, or materially contributes to the infringing conduct of another.

## INFRINGEMENT PENALTIES AND REMEDIES

The Act gives federal courts a variety of sanctions to impose if a person or entity is found to have infringed a copyright. The court may:

- Issue an injunction.
- Impound and destroy infringing articles.
- Award actual damages and lost profits proven by the plaintiff.
- In the case of a registered work, the copyright owner may elect before a final judgment to receive *statutory damages* instead of actual damages of between $750

and $30,000 for the infringement of any one work, and up to $150,000 in the case of a willful infringement.

- In the case of a registered work, award attorneys fees and costs.
- Impose criminal penalties in the case of willful infringement engaged in for the purpose of commercial advantage or private financial gain, as well as order the destruction of all infringing copies and all facilities used to manufacture the infringing copies.

## SPECIAL RULE FOR NONPROFIT INSTITUTIONS

The Act provides an important limitation on remedies in the case of innocent infringement by a nonprofit educational entity. The court can remit damages where an employee of a nonprofit educational institution, library, or archive acting within the scope of employment and believing that use of a copyrighted work was permitted as a fair use infringes the copyright by reproducing the work. In addition, the Act generally permits a court to reduce statutory damages to as little as $200 if it finds that the infringer was unaware and had no reason to believe that use of a copyrighted work constituted an infringement.

## FAIR USE (SECTION 107)

Although the *fair use* doctrine was developed by the courts over many years, it was not until the passage of the Act in 1976 that this doctrine was codified as a statutory provision. Fair use permits the use of a copyrighted work without the permission of the copyright owner for such purposes as teaching, research, scholarship, comment, criticism, or news reporting. A basic underlying principle of fair use is that it assumes good faith and fair dealing. Fair use can include the ability to reproduce copies of portions of a work, including making multiple copies for classroom use. There is no quantitative or other bright line test for determining whether a particular use is a fair use or an infringement. Each determination turns on the unique facts of each case.

The Act specifies four factors that a court must weigh in making a determination of whether a use without permission is an infringement or is permissible under Section 107:

1. The purpose and character of the use, including whether the use was for a commercial or a nonprofit educational purpose

2. The nature of the copyrighted work—the courts accord greater protection to creative works than factual works
3. The amount and substantiality of the amount of the work used in relation to the whole work
4. The effect of the use on the potential market for and value of the work

The courts have tended to give greater weight in their deliberations to factor 3 and, in particular, to factor 4.

## VOLUNTARY FAIR USE GUIDELINES

Because there is no bright line defining when a use is fair and when it is an infringement, there have been efforts over the years to develop voluntary fair use guidelines governing educational use of copyrighted materials. Content owners and educational communities developed classroom copying guidelines in 1976 (see U.S. Copyright Office Circular 21, *Reproduction of Copyrighted Works by Educators and Librarians*). Circular 21 includes guidelines for use by nonprofit educational institutions with regard to reproduction of books and periodicals for classroom distribution and for off-air copying of television programs. The *Guidelines for Classroom Copying in Not-For-Profit Educational Institutions With Respect to Books and Periodicals* require that the amount copied be brief, as defined below, and spontaneous. Spontaneity means that the teacher's inspiration to copy and use the work and the "moment of . . . use" for "maximum teaching effectiveness" are so close that it would be unreasonable to expect a timely reply to a request for permission.

For teachers, the *Books and Periodical Guidelines* allow single-copy reproductions of:

- A chapter of a book
- An article from a periodical or newspaper
- A short story, essay, or short poem
- A chart, graph, diagram, drawing, cartoon, or picture from a book, periodical, or newspaper

For *classroom use,* the *Books and Periodical Guidelines* allow the making of *multiple* copies by or for the teacher for distribution to students of the following works:

- *Poetry*—A complete poem of no more than 250 words, and if not printed no more than two pages, or an excerpt of not more than 250 words of a longer poem

- *Prose*—Either a complete article, story, or essay of less than 2,500 words, or an excerpt from any work of prose if not more than 1,000 words or 10% of the work, whichever is less, but in any event a minimum of 500 words
- *Illustration*—One chart, graph, diagram, drawing, cartoon, or picture per book or periodical
- *Special works*—For a "special" work (a work of poetry or prose that combines language with illustrations), an excerpt of not more than two of the published pages and containing not more than 10% of the text

In addition, the *Books and Periodical Guidelines* prohibit using more than one short poem, article, story, or essay or two excerpts of the same author, and not more than three from the same collective work or periodical during one class term. Moreover, a maximum of nine instances of multiple copying per class per term is permitted. These limits do not apply to current news periodicals and newspapers. Other prohibitions include that multiple copying must not be a substitute for the purchase of books, reprints, or periodicals; must not be directed by a supervisor; and may not be repeated with respect to the same item over multiple terms. The charge to the student may not exceed the actual reproduction cost.

The *Guidelines for Off-Air Recording of Broadcast Programming for Educational Purposes* permit the off-air recording of a broadcast program simultaneously with its broadcast or cable transmission for use by nonprofit educational institutions. The *Off-Air Recording Guidelines* require that:

- The copying must be made by or at the direction of the teacher.
- It must be for use in a classroom "or similar places devoted to instruction."
- The recording need not be used in its entirety, but the tape may not be altered in any way or combined or merged into teaching anthologies or compilations.
- The copy must include the copyright notice broadcast with the program.
- The copy may be retained for a maximum of 45 days and then must be destroyed.
- The copy may be used once in the course of relevant teaching activities, and repeated once for instructional reinforcement if needed within the 45 day window.

- After the first 10 consecutive school days, off-air recording may be used up to the end of the 45 day period only for teacher evaluation purposes and not for exhibition to students.
- Programs may not be regularly recorded in anticipation of need.
- A limited number of copies of the recording may be made to meet "legitimate needs of teachers."
- The educational institution must establish procedures to maintain the integrity of the *Off-Air Recording Guidelines.*

## THE EDUCATIONAL USE EXEMPTION (SECTIONS 110(1) AND (2))

The Act contains a specific exemption that gives nonprofit educational institutions the ability in certain circumstances to use copyrighted works in face-to-face settings, and a more limited right for accredited nonprofit institutions to transmit works without the permission of the copyright owner. The broader face-to-face provision specifies that instructors and students at nonprofit educational institutions can perform or display copyrighted works in a classroom or similar place devoted to instruction in the course of face-to-face teaching activities. Note that it applies only to performance and display rights and does not permit reproduction, distribution, or the making of derivative works. There is a proviso that if a copy of a movie or other audiovisual work is being performed under this exemption, the copy used must have been lawfully made.

In 2002, Congress amended Section 110(2) and Section 112 of the Act with the passage of the Technology, Education and Copyright Harmonization Act (the TEACH Act). This measure became law at the end of 2002.

The TEACH Act's Section 110(2) amendments that *expand* instructor rights include:

- Transmission of the performance via digital networks of an entire nondramatic literary or musical work; and reasonable and limited portions of all other performances, including those incorporated in any type of audio-visual work, such as videotapes and films, and any dramatic musical work
- Transmission of displays of works via digital networks, including still images, in amounts comparable to typical face-to-face displays in a live classroom session

- Transmissions made to students officially enrolled in the class wherever they are located, whether in a classroom, a library, a dorm room, at work, or at home

The counterbalancing *limitations and restrictions* include:

- The transmitting institution must be accredited and nonprofit.
- The transmission of the performance or display must be part of the systematic "mediated instructional activities" of an accredited nonprofit institution or governmental body; "mediated instructional activities" consist of the use of works 1) as an integral part of the class experiences controlled by or under the direct supervision of the instructor; and (2) analogous to a live classroom performance or display directly related and of material assistance to the teaching content; and made solely for and, to the extent technologically feasible, limited to reception by students officially enrolled in the class for which the transmission is made or to officers or employees of governmental bodies. Password access or similar authentication systems are sufficient, as opposed to a general requirement of network security. Works primarily produced or marketed for the digital distance education market, works not lawfully acquired or made, and works such as textbooks and coursepacks typically purchased by students individually are *not* covered under Section 110(2).
- The transmitting institution must employ technological measures that "reasonably prevent" the students receiving the transmissions from retaining the works beyond the "class session" and from redistributing the works to others; this does not constitute an institutional guarantee that the technology selected will be infallible; nor does it require monitoring of recipient conduct.
- The length of an asynchronous "class session" varies from student to student. It generally is the period during which a student is logged onto the institution's server.
- The material may not remain in accessible form on the student's computer, but it may remain on the institution or governmental body's server for use in one or more courses, and may be accessed by a student each time he or she logs on to participate in a particular class session.
- The transmitting institution may not interfere with any technological protection measures incorporated by the copyright owner to defeat retention and distribution. The institution must provide students, faculty, and affected staff with information that describes and promotes compliance with copyright laws, provide notice that the material contained in the course may be copyrighted, and adopt and maintain institutional policies on copyright.

The TEACH Act adds a new Section 112(f) to the Copyright Act. This provision gives eligible transmitting institutions a limited right to make copies of digital works and digitize portions of analog works in order to make the performances and displays authorized by Section 110(2), provided that the copies are retained by the institution and used only for the authorized transmission. The digitizing of the needed portion of the analog work is the result of the fact that either no digital version of the work exists or the existing digital version incorporates technological protection measures that prohibit its use as authorized by Section 110(2).

## OWNERSHIP OF DISTRIBUTED LEARNING COURSEWARE

As more and more colleges and universities incorporate telecommunications-based courseware and delivery methods, faculty and administrators are increasingly asking who owns the electronic course. Faculty members tend to view electronic courseware in the same way they view lecture notes, textbooks, and articles—this is the product of my solitary intellectual endeavors, I am the creator and author of the work; therefore I am the owner, not my employer. This view of copyright ownership of scholarly works is premised on academic freedom and the traditional academic exception. A scholarly work created by an instructor within the scope of employment or at the direction of the dean is, by law, a work made for hire and, therefore, owned by the institution. However, it is common to find that higher education intellectual property policies voluntarily confer ownership of such works on the faculty member.

Notwithstanding the complete rewrite of the Copyright Act in 1976 and the adoption of a definition of works made for hire, the great majority of colleges and universities have continued to honor the teacher exception of excluding traditional works such as textbooks, lecture notes, journal articles, tests, and the like from the institution's works *made-for-hire* policy. However, the trend appears to be moving toward a work *made-for-hire* approach for distributed learning courses, at least where substantial institutional resources are employed in the development and production of the electronic course—essentially, the typical institutional patent model. The use of substantial institutional resources, in the view of many administrators, takes electronic courses out of the realm of the model of a single academic producing a work on his or her own, and justifies institutional ownership.

Two other ownership considerations need to be mentioned. If the electronic work is the result of the work of two or more creators who have contributed copyrightable expression to the finished product and merged their contributions into one inseparable work, the electronic course could be considered to be a joint work. The Act permits joint owners of copyrighted works to individually exploit the work, subject to an accounting to the other joint owners for any profits earned from the work. Thus, a situation could arise where the faculty member, together with a graphic artist who is working within the scope of employment, creates a single, inseparable electronic course. Each has contributed copyrighted expression. In this circumstance, where an institution observes the textbook tradition for faculty and the work *made-for-hire* model for other employees, absent a contract to the contrary, the faculty member and the institution could be deemed to be joint owners.

Finally, an electronic course could be considered to be a collective work under the Act if it consists of the integration of a number of individual copyrighted works into a final product. Such a collective work might be owned by either the institution or the faculty member who assembled the course, depending on the copyright policy in force. Unless the individual contributors expressly transferred their rights to the institution, the owner of the copyright in the collection could only reproduce and distribute the course in its entirety, and would be prohibited from exploiting the individual contributions. Any policy or agreement between an educational institution and its faculty members that specifies faculty member ownership of electronic works should provide the institution with a royalty free, nonexclusive license, at least for a specified period of time, to make adaptations of, and to transmit, distribute, perform, reproduce, or display the electronic coursework to its students regardless of their location. If the institution is the owner of the

work, the policy should give the creating faculty member a royalty free, nonexclusive license, at least for a limited period of time, to use the work at another nonprofit institution in the event of a change of employment. The policy should also deal with the faculty member's right to attribution and the right to update the course.

## ONLINE COPYRIGHT INFRINGEMENT LIABILITY

Enactment of the Digital Millennium Copyright Act (DMCA) in the Fall of 1998 brought to a close a multi-year effort by content owners, copyright users (including libraries, community colleges, and other educational interests), the Clinton Administration, and Congress to clarify the responsibilities of Internet service providers (ISPs) for the copyright infringing activities of their subscribers. Educational institutions that provide Internet and online access to their students, faculty, and staff are considered to be ISPs, just like AOL and other commercial service providers. The DMCA establishes a system of liability safe harbors and also implements the 1996 World Intellectual Property Organization (WIPO) Copyright Treaty. The safe harbors include passive transmission, cached copies, user-stored information, information location tools, indemnification for misrepresentation, and wrongful takedown.

Section 512(e) incorporates a special rule to determine when a nonprofit college or university is deemed to have knowledge of the infringing activities of its faculty members and graduate teaching assistants and, therefore, liability for infringement. It applies only when these employees are "performing a teaching or research function." For the purposes of the passive transmission (e.g., routing) and caching safe harbors, such a faculty member or graduate student will be considered independent of the institution. For the purposes of the user stored information and information location tools safe harbors, their knowledge or awareness of infringing activities will not be attributed to the educational institution if 1) the faculty member or graduate student employee's infringing activities do *not* involve providing online access to instructional materials required or recommended for a course taught at the institution by the employee within the preceding 3 years; 2) the institution has not received more than two nonactionable DMCA notifications over the period in which the employee engaged in infringing activities;

and 3) the institution has provided all users of its network or system with information accurately describing and promoting compliance with copyright laws. On this last item, the legislative history clarifies that an institution will be in compliance with this requirement if it provided access to guidelines or other materials prepared by the Register of Copyrights. Thus, an institution may, but is not required to, develop its own guidance. Moreover, the Register's materials provide a balanced view of copyright, stressing not only the exclusive rights of copyright owners, but also the statutory limitations on those rights, including fair use and the educational use and library exceptions (see Table 1).

## COPYRIGHT RESOURCES

—*Kenneth D. Salomon*
—*Michael B. Goldstein*

*See also* FEDERAL LAWS; LEGAL ISSUES; PLAGIARISM

## Bibliography

### *U.S. Copyright Office Resources*

The Copyright Act of 1976, as amended: http://www.loc.gov/copyright/title17

Copyright Office Forms: http://www.loc.gov/copyright/forms

Copyright Registration Procedures: http://www.copyright.gov/register/index.html

Register of Copyrights. *Report on Copyright and Digital Distance Education:* http://www.loc.gov/copyright/disted.

U.S. Copyright Office Web page: http://lcweb.loc.gov/copyright

U.S. Copyright Office. *Circular 21, Reproduction of Copyrighted Works by Educators and Librarians*: http://lcweb.loc.gov/copyright/circs/circ21.pdf.

U.S. Copyright Office. *Copyright Basics:* http://www.loc.gov/copyright/circs/circ1.html

U.S. Copyright Office. *Summary of the Digital Millennium Copyright Act of 1998:* http://thomas.loc.gov/cgi-bin/query/D?c105:2:./temp/~c105V4JTy6::

World Intellectual Property Organization Treaty: http://www.loc.gov/copyright/wipo/treat1.htm

### *Copyright Guidelines*

CCUMC Fair Use Guidelines for Educational Multimedia: http://www.indiana.edu/~ccumc/copyright/ccguides.html

Educational fair use guidelines for distance learning published in the final report to the commissioner on the

**Table 1**    Term of Copyrights and the Public Domain

| Date Of Work | Protected From | Term |
|---|---|---|
| Created 1-1-78 or after | When work is fixed in tangible medium of expression | Life + 70 years (or if work of corporate authorship, the shorter of 95 years from publication or 120 years from creation) |
| Published before 1923 | In public domain | None |
| Published from 1923–63 | When published with notice | 28 years + could be renewed for 47 years, now extended by 20 years for a total renewal of 67 years. If not so renewed, now in public domain |
| Published from 1964–77 | When published with notice | 28 years for first term; now automatic extension of 67 years for second term |
| Created before 1-1-78 but not published | 1-1-78, the effective date of the 1976 Act that eliminated common law copyright | Life + 70 years or 12-31-2002, whichever is greater |
| Created before 1-1-78 but published between then and 12-31-02 | 1-1-78, the effective date of the 1976 Act that eliminated common law copyright | Life + 70 years or 12-31-2047, whichever is greater. |

Source: Laura N. Gasaway, Director of the Law Library and Professor of Law at the University of North Carolina (see, http://www.unc.edu/~unclng/public-d.htm). Reprinted with permission.

conclusion of the conference on fair use: http://www.uspto.gov/web/offices/dcom/olia/confu/confurep.htm

*Guidelines for classroom copying in not-for-profit educational institutions with respect to books and periodicals* (Copyright Office Circular 21, pp. 9–11)

*Guidelines for off-air recording of broadcast programming for educational purposes* (Copyright Office Circular 21, p. 22)

### Higher Education Copyright Resources

CopyOwn: A Resource on Copyright Ownership for the Higher Education Community: http://www.inform.umd.edu/CompRes/NEThics/copyown

Copyright Management Center, Indiana University-Purdue University-Indianapolis: http://www.iupui.edu/~copyinfo/home.html

Copyright Permission Pages, A Service of the Professional Center Library for Law and Management, Wake Forest University: http://www.law.wfu.edu/library/copyright

Harper, Georgia. (2001). *Crash Course in Copyrights:* http://www.utsystem.edu/ogc/IntellectualProperty/cprtindx.htm#top.

JEFFSelects—Multimedia Copyright Information: http://jeffline.tju.edu/SML/JEFFSelects/copyright.html

*Multimedia Copyright Information, Academic Resources:* http://oac1.oac.tju.edu/~rod/academic.html

### Licensing Resources

For reproduction of text: The Copyright Clearance Center, http://www.copyright.com

For use of books and journals: Copyright Permission Pages, http://www.law.wfu.edu/library/copyright

For use of photographs online: Media Image Resource Alliance, http://www.mira.com

For public performance of home videos and videodiscs: Motion Picture Licensing Corporation, http://www.mplc.com

For performance of musical works: ASCAP, http://www.ascap.com; BMI, http://www.bmi.com; SESAC, http://sesac.com

For reproduction and distribution of musical works in phonorecords and for synchronization rights: The Harry Fox Agency, www.nmpa.org/hfa.html. (Phonorecords are the material objects in which sounds [other than those accompanying a movie or other audiovisual work] are fixed and from which they can be perceived, reproduced, or otherwise communicated. Section 101 of the Act.)

### TEACH Act

Crews, Kenneth D. *New Copyright Law for Distance Education: The Meaning and Importance of the TEACH Act.* http://www.ala.org/washoff/teach.html

Gasaway, Laura N. (November 25, 2002). *TEACH Act Comparison Chart,* University of North Carolina. http://www.unc.edu/%7Eunclng/TEACH.htm

Harper, Georgia. (2002). *The TEACH Act Finally Becomes Law.* http://www.utsystem.edu/ogc/intellectualproperty/teachact.htm

Salomon, Kenneth D. *Technology, Education and Copyright Harmonization Act of 2002.* http://www.dlalaw.com/site/page_1.asp?section=4&subsection=3&seqa=0&seqb=0&seqc=0&PgId=700

The TEACH Toolkit, An Online Resource for Understanding Copyright and Distance Education: http://www.lib.ncsu.edu/scc/legislative/teachkit

Technological Requirements of the TEACH Act: http://www.ala.org/Content/NavigationMenu/Our_Association/Offices/ALA_Washington/Issues2/Copyright1/Distance_Education_and_the_TEACH_Act/teachdrm.pdf

# INTERACTIVE TEXTBOOK

An interactive textbook combines content found in traditional, paper-based textbooks with the active-learning components possible in an electronic environment. With interactive textbooks, it is possible for students to gain immediate feedback on problem-solving exercises and to take advantage of other forms of active learning. Interactive textbooks represent an opportunity to expand, explore, and capitalize on new ways to interact with information.

Six key issues exist regarding interactive textbooks: social, legal, pedagogical, economic, technical, and content.

## SOCIAL

Interactive textbooks constitute a considerable challenge to existing norms of authoring, publication, and use of texts. No innovation is easily adopted as a replacement for a known technology. Some of the social barriers to the adoption of interactive textbooks include:

- *Not used to it*—For example, an instructor might not assign an interactive textbook for a course because (1) he or she has never used it, and therefore (2) he or she cannot expect students to use it.
- *No reward*—Faculty members at universities may be reluctant to author interactive textbooks because of fear that such publications may not count toward promotion.
- *Haves and have-nots*—This issue will also appear in the economic category, but bears mentioning here because widespread adoption of interactive textbook technology will be impacted by who can afford the equipment necessary to take advantage of it.

Some of the social advantages to interactive textbooks include:

- *Distance collaboration*— Students working in small groups might be able to use interactive textbooks in chat rooms for peer learning.
- *Dynamic authorship*—Authors are able to bring in guest lecturers for classes, and are able to change content more easily.
- *Distance education solutions*—Educators looking for innovative ways to deliver off-campus course content that rivals the richness of in-class delivery may find interactive textbooks to be a promising answer.

## LEGAL

Intellectual property remains one of the major stumbling blocks for electronically based information. Libraries currently are grappling with copyright as it pertains to interactive textbooks. Printed materials are sold to libraries under the assumption that they may be used by anyone who enters the building. Electronic licensing, on the other hand, operates under the "per seat" model, and therefore, only "registered" library users may use electronic resources under most agreements. The question remains, then, one of access to interactive textbooks. If we assume that in the long run, interactive textbooks will become more ubiquitous in collections, then access will become a more heated issue than it was with a print-dominated collection.

## PEDAGOGICAL

Course delivery is undergoing substantial changes as distance learning, and even traditional classroom instruction, challenges conventional notions of reading and lecture. In fact, interactive textbooks blur the distinction between reading and lecture. Interactive textbooks can carry video clips of people talking about and demonstrating concepts, for example. Conversely, a teacher in a classroom might use the interactive features in an electronic text to demonstrate a concept. There is clearly a need for research that shows effective ways to employ interactive texts as pedagogical tools.

## ECONOMIC

One of the current barriers to entry into the market of highly interactive textbooks is the high cost of development. In order to author interactive content for interactive textbooks, considerable resources are invested in computer programming, graphic design, and text generation appropriate for interactive content. With upfront costs of this magnitude, publishers must sell more units to make economies of scale. With a simple scanned book, the production costs are much more limited, and therefore sales should recoup initial costs more quickly, albeit by sacrificing content richness.

## TECHNICAL

The technical issues associated with the production of interactive textbooks include the design and programming of interactive modules. In some ways, technical issues are the easiest to deal with. The types of devices on the market today hint at tomorrow's readers. Currently, interactive textbooks may be read on computers or on portable devices such as the Rocket Interactive textbook reader. Future technologies include folding screens with high-resolution displays, as well as wearable displays (e.g., glasses with readers, or even optical implants).

In the past, the main problems with interactive textbooks were the quality of display and the limited portability of the devices used to read them. It is conceivable that these problems will be overcome in the next 2 to 10 years.

## CONTENT

Of the issues discussed so far, content is, by far, the most important. For interactive textbooks, the production of content requires different considerations than those necessary for static textbooks. Among the questions facing authors of interactive textbooks:

- What content features are appropriate for interactive textbooks (e.g., hypertext, hands-on learning, tools for student-to-student and student-to-instructor collaboration)?
- What new types of interaction are possible? (That is, what are the limitations of interaction in an interactive textbook?)
- To what extent can readers contribute to content, such as through annotations?

Currently, content in electronic textbooks ranges from scanned versions of print textbooks (scanned P-books) to electronic textbooks offering some form of interactive content. Scanned P-books are simply electronic copies of print books. One site that hosts a variety of P-books is Project Gutenberg, which houses classic books that have become public domain. These books are stored in simple text format. In contrast, interactive textbooks allow users to "read" actively via activities such as participation in hands-on exercises, contribution to content via annotations, linking to other interactive texts, and the support of collaborative learning.

In short, it is necessary to completely rethink what a "book" is. With interactive textbooks, we are introduced to a different model of reading and learning, and we face many conceptual challenges in content development.

*—David B. Robbins*

*See also* ELECTRONIC JOURNALS AND PUBLICATIONS

## Bibliography

Brusilovsky, P., & Anderson, J. (1998). ACT-R Electronic Bookshelf: An adaptive system to support learning ACT-R on the Web. In *WebNet 98 World Conference of the WWW, Internet, and Intranet Proceedings* (pp. 92–97). Norfolk, VA: Association for the Advancement of Computers in Education (AACE).

Letts, M. (2001). E-textbooks test emerging platform. *The Seybold Report, 1*(1). Retrieved September 19, 2002, from http://www.seyboldreports.com/TSR/free/0101/html/ebooks.html.

Lonsdale, R., & Armstrong, C. (2001). Electronic books: Challenges for academic libraries. *Library Hi-Tech, 19*(4), 332–339.

Rose, M. J. (2000). The future of E-textbooks. *Wired, 8*(8). Retrieved September 19, 2002, from http://www.wired.com/news/culture/0,1284,38061,00.html.

## Web-Based Resources and Examples of Electronic Textbooks

E-books.org: *http://e-books.org* (accessed September 19, 2002).

The e-Learning Centre: http://www.e-learningcentre.co.uk/eclipse/default.htm (accessed September 19, 2002).

MathResources: http://www.mathresources.com (accessed September 19, 2002).

NetLibrary: http://www.netlibrary.com (accessed September 19, 2002).

The Online Books Page: http://onlinebooks.library.upenn.edu (accessed September 19, 2002).

The TeleRead list of E-book–related sites: http://www.teleread.org/bookrelatedsitesonthenet.htm (accessed September 19, 2002).

# INTERNET

Often called the "network of networks," the Internet is a global network that uses wires and a common set of communication rules to link networks of all sizes, allowing them to share information. Characterized technically by an open and decentralized architecture that supports different network designs, the Internet is, to date, free from external regulation or monopolistic control. It is a genuinely shared, universal resource that has revolutionized the communications world, both technically and socially, by providing users with opportunities for new modes of interaction.

## AN EXPONENTIAL DEVELOPMENT

In 1962 the concept of a global planetary network first emerged when Joseph Carl Robnett Licklider of MIT presented the idea of a set of interconnected computers, a "Galactic Network," in a series of memos. Shortly after this he became the first head of the computer research program at ARPA (Advanced Research Projects Agency), part of the United States Department of Defense. Licklider succeeded in convincing his successors of the importance of his concept, and in 1966 Robert Taylor proposed this network as a solution to the problem of the high cost of maintaining the 17 separate mainframes housed in research centers across the country. Indeed, although we often hear that the Internet was created in response to the threat of a potential nuclear attack, it was fundamentally financial and scientific efficiency concerns that motivated ARPA to fund a project to create a network of distant computers. The idea of a communication system resistant to a nuclear attack was, however, at the center of the research conducted by one of the three groups, the RAND Corporation, which at the time was working on an idea that would be essential to the creation of the ARPA network: packet switching. Also developed by Leonard Kleinrock of MIT and Donald Davies of the National Physical Laboratory in Middlesex (England), packet switching divides messages into "packets," which are transmitted independently through any available network and then reassembled at the final destination. Thus, two computers need no direct functional circuit between them to be able to communicate, and no links are essential for the network to operate. This particular technology is the source of the decentralized nature of the Internet.

In 1967, with Licklider's ideas and packet switching in mind, Lawrence Roberts created the first network design of what would become the ARPANET, an ARPA network of four nodes that gave birth to the Internet. It wasn't until December 1969, however, that this basic network was effectively implemented and used, linking four American research centers: the Stanford Research Institute (SRI), the Network Measurement Center at UCLA, the University of California in Santa Barbara, and the University of Utah. Almost a year later, the first ARPANET protocol, the device driver Network Control Protocol (NCP), was introduced by the Network Working Group, finally allowing users to create applications. When ARPANET, then linking 37 nodes, was publicly shown for the first time at the October 1972 inaugural meeting of the International Conference on Computer Communications in Washington, D.C., it was already supporting one truly promising application: e-mail. The first successful e-mail program had been created by Ray Tomlinson of Bolt Beranek and Newman (BBN) in March 1972, and an e-mail utility had been proposed by L. Roberts, in July of the same year. The utility allowed users to list, selectively read, file, forward, and respond to messages. Interestingly, it was already noticeable at this time that e-mail, not

long-distance computing, was the most popular Internet application—a large number of users were already interested enough in e-mail exchange to resist network administrators' efforts to minimize its use.

The next step in the Internet's history was the development of a new protocol supporting an open-architecture network environment. When Robert E. Kahn arrived at ARPA in 1972, he brought with him the idea of an open-architecture network that would allow every network linked to ARPANET to be separately designed and developed following the specific needs of its users. Because the NCP protocol was not able to adapt to this structure, Kahn decided to create a new communication protocol that would act more like a set of communication rules between networks of all sizes and designs. With the help of Vinton Cerf of SRI, Kahn finally defined the TCP/IP protocols suite, the first version of which was distributed in September 1973. The complementary TCP and IP protocols are two distinct layers of the Internet structure. IP is dedicated to the addressing of packets, and TCP provides the transport reliability and forwarding services of the Internet, in that sense working above the IP protocol. NCP was officially replaced by TCP/IP in 1983. The fact that these protocols were public domain strongly encouraged Internet development by creating a common language with which applications could be built.

In addition to the TCP/IP protocol, another important innovation took place in the 1970s: the development of hardwired local area networks (LANs). These networks were developed in 1973 at Xerox's Palo Alto Research Center. Their creation was an offshoot of the invention of Ethernet, a technology that links personal computers with more powerful hosts. This invention profoundly changed the global design of the Internet by encouraging the replacement of very large networks with many PCs and workstations linked to a reduced number of hosts by means of a LAN. Although ARPANET was initially designed on the idea of a few large networks, the astonishing popularization of PCs that took place in the last few decades has drastically changed the structure of the Internet, which now contains more LANs than multi-host national or regional networks.

At the same time that there was a strong increase in the number of networks, a sizable global movement toward the adoption of this computer interconnection technology was taking place. Many U.S. government departments and academic institutions were creating their own networks, the most notable of which were CSNET, implemented for the academic and industrial computer science community; the Unix-based giant bulletin board USENET, born in 1979; and BITNET, the first general-purpose academic network, which went online in 1981. Not intended initially to be linked to ARPANET, these networks saw their role transformed when the general change from NCP to TCP/IP took place and gave them the opportunity to be connected to ARPANET's structure. This sudden growth in the number of networks linked to the ARPANET coincided with its restructuring into two different networks: MILNET was created for American military matters, and the rest of ARPANET became the first backbone, high-speed Internet as we know it today.

Another major change to the Internet's structure occurred in 1983, when Paul Mockapetris invented the Internet's addressing system. This invention solved the problem of memorizing an exponentially growing number of addresses by implementing the Domain Name System (DNS), which resolves hierarchical host names into Internet addresses.

As the Internet continued to expand, another major structural change took place in 1985, when the National Science Foundation (NSF) built a new high speed backbone, the NSFNET, and allowed all academic institutions free access to it in exchange for their agreement to use the TCP/IP protocol and, in 1986, the DNS naming system. The choices made by the NSF—the obligation to comply to a specific suite of protocols and naming system, as well as the exclusion of commercial organizations from the NSFNET backbone—markedly influenced further developments of the Internet. These decisions helped to impose TCP/IP and DNS as Internet standards, while at the same time creating a strong impulse for private companies to build their own backbone networks. In fact, private companies' active participation in infrastructure development was encouraged by the U.S. government, who wanted to be able to withdraw someday from backbone funding. It was in this context that the commercialization of the Internet really began.

The first subscription-based commercial Internet company (UUNET) was founded in 1987; many other companies soon followed. This concentration of private and public funding for the improvement of the Internet led to exponential growth of the network's structure. When the ARPANET backbone was decommissioned on June 1, 1990, it was only so that it could

be replaced by more powerful backbones, able to handle increasing demand, which has grown even more noticeable since the advent of the World Wide Web in 1991. Some early Internet applications included Archie (the first Internet search engine, developed in 1990 at McGill University in Canada) and Gopher (created in 1991 by Mark McCahill to provide administrators with the ability to place information on menus); however, it was the invention of the World Wide Web by CERN researcher Tim Berners-Lee that really started a new phase in the life of the Net. The ease of navigation offered by hypertext has been a key component of the massive adoption of the Internet—the first step toward user-friendly interfaces. This adaptation to human characteristics continued with the release, in February 1993, of Mosaic, a user-friendly graphical user interface created by Marc Andreessen, who one year later offered Netscape (an improved Mosaic) to the public. The exponential increase in the Internet's popularity that followed brought even more private funding, allowing the NSF to stop funding its backbone in 1995.

Some important challenges must be met in the next few years by the Internet industry and the different groups in charge of defining Internet standards—the Internet Society with its Internet Engineering Task Force (IETF), the Internet Architecture Board, and the Web-oriented World Wide Web Consortium (W3C). The unexpected popularity of the network, with approximately 700 million users, is posing a serious threat to the Internet's efficiency. Addressing and routing questions, in particular, now have to be reconsidered because the large number of networks connected to the Internet cause an important memorization problem for routers. These routers are having a hard time remembering all of the possible routes, thus slowing the transport of packets. This problem also reveals an eventual lack of available addresses for the new networks created. Indeed, the TCP/IP protocol was designed at a time when nobody could have predicted the exponential growth of the Internet. At the time, 32-bit addresses seemed to offer enough potential to answer all future needs; however, it's now obvious that there will soon be a shortage in addresses if a new protocol is not created. To solve this problem, a protocol called IP version 6, with addresses containing 128 bits, is presently being created. The Internet2 project, a reincarnation of the initially academic-oriented ARPANET that is being administered by the University Corporation for Advanced Internet

Development (UCAID) in collaboration with some corporations, is also attempting to solve the Internet's speed problems, particularly for multimedia data exchange.

## TECHNICAL STRUCTURE

The Internet's infrastructure is a three-layered hierarchy of interconnected networks, expanding from LANs to regional networks to backbone or national high-speed links. Personal computers are connected to the Internet either through a private LAN, owned by an organization, or through an Internet service provider (ISP). ISPs connect PCs to the host computer, usually through a modem that transforms data into sound and then back into data in order to allow the use of telephone line or fiber-optic cables. Physically linked by this wire system, the multiple hosts (or nodes) forming the Internet exchange information by means of packet switching. The original message is divided into a number of smaller entities that are independently sent, mostly through electrical or optical lines but also by means of satellite or digital radio, between routers. These are powerful computers in charge of reading the packet's destination address before consulting a routing table to choose the best link to the next router.

The mandatory use of IP addressing allows packets to be routed correctly, because the IP header that accompanies the packet contains the origin and destination addresses in a standardized form. The complementary protocol, TCP, then transmits the message from end-to-end by controlling the general flow and recovering any packets lost in transmission. The TCP/IP protocol suite, which contains other protocols such as the File Transfer Protocol (FTP), which uploads and downloads files, and the Simple Mail Transfer Protocol (SMTP) for e-mail, is located between the applications and the physical networks of the Internet. This allows all applications to be adapted to the suite's standards, a flexibility that is a key element of the Internet, making it a general infrastructure that can support many kinds of applications.

The commercialization of the Internet and the fast evolution of the telecommunication field are creating new possibilities in terms of applications and infrastructure development. The improvement of the networks' bandwidth, thanks to innovations such as the Asynchronous Transfer Mode (ATM), framed switched services, and the convergence of many technologies, allows us to consider the advent of Internet telephony and Internet television as a near reality. Nomadic computing, combining portable communication tools with network technology, is also one of the many developments that are now underway.

## THE INTERNET REVOLUTION

Although the Internet used to be a social phenomenon restricted to a relatively small community of academicians and military representatives, it is now undoubtedly profoundly influencing the everyday lives of most people living in Western societies. The integration of the Internet into our working environments and our daily lives seems to mark not only the emergence of a new mode of communication, but also the redefinition of potential forms of collaboration, a decrease in the importance of distance and time limits in our relationships, and great hopes in terms of democracy. Indeed, many people have felt that the anarchic structure of the Internet would allow a revival of active citizenship by providing better access to all kinds of information at a low cost. The Internet was seen by some as a potential alternative to the traditional unidirectional mass media, encouraging real societal debates through a direct dialogue between citizens. It was at the same time seen as a way to increase people's politicization by removing the time and distance limits between individuals, which would facilitate the political mobilization of small interest groups and the creation of virtual communities of all kinds.

Today, with the growing commercialization of the Internet and some pleas for a formal regulation of this technology, many people are more ambivalent about the Internet's potential within an international civil society. Although it is true that some militants do use the Internet as a way to organize their political actions and discuss societal problems, it also is becoming more obvious that few people really can (or want to) take on such a demanding role that requires not just time, but also an understanding of all the information available on the Net.

At the same time, the new information-based society that the Internet has promoted poses important problems at an international level. Indeed, there is a clear indication that a new gap is being created due to the inevitably inequitable access of the world's citizens to new technologies. The poorest countries are falling even further behind in the global economy because they cannot fund the informatization of their society by developing the necessary infrastructure. Those who don't have access to Internet technologies, both in Western societies and around the world, could be less and less able to adapt to working environments that are making greater use of these tools every day.

—*Pierre-Léonard Harvey*
—*Karine Vigneault*

*See also* E-MAIL; INTRANET; INTERNET SERVICE PROVIDER; NETWORKS; WORLD WIDE WEB

### Bibliography

Brown, J. M. (1994). The global computer network: Indications of its use worldwide. [Electronic version]. *The International Information & Library Review, 26,* 51–65.

Castells, M. (2001). *The Internet galaxy: Reflections on the Internet, business, and society.* Oxford, NY: Oxford University Press.

Fisher, H. (2001). *Le choc du numérique: essai.* Montréal, Canada: VLB éditeur.

Huitema, C. (1995). *Le routage dans l'Internet.* Paris, France: Eyrolles.

Kaminow, I. P. (1997). The Internet and society. [Electronic version]. *Optical Fiber Technology, 3,* 279–299.

Leiner, B. M., Cerf, V. G., Clark, D. D., Kahn, R. E., Kleinrock, L., Lynch, D. C., Postel, J., Roberts, L. G., & Wolff, S. (August 2000). *A brief history of the Internet.* Retrieved from http://www.isoc.org/internet/history/brief.shtml#References.

Toutain, L. (1999). *Réseaux locaux et Internet: des protocoles à l'interconnexion.* Paris, France: Hermès.

# INTRANET

An intranet is a technology-mediated model used in distributed learning to display information, to interact, and to communicate within a secure, networked environment. In distributed learning, intranets are used for intense asynchronous and synchronous communication between professors and students via e-mail, digital drop-boxes, threaded discussions, chat rooms, forms, and course content materials (i.e., syllabi, lecture notes, and study guides). An intranet allows the use of videoconferencing, teleconferencing, streaming audio/video, database integration, and relationship management software. An intranet resembles an Internet Web site but is open only to registered participants.

## INTRANET TECHNOLOGY: THE VIRTUAL CLASSROOM AND DISTANCE ADMINISTRATION

Intranet technology includes a browser (either Netscape Navigator or Internet Explorer) to view information, security measures, a networked environment, database integration, and relational management software. The *browser* is used to display information on the PC, allowing computer language (source code) to be viewed as pictures and text. In the virtual classroom, the browser is the actual interface that appears on the students' and instructors' screen. The leading browsers are Netscape Navigator and Microsoft Internet Explorer.

*Security* is essential for an intranet's success, and it is ensured through at least four measures: encryption, firewalls, passwords, and proxy servers.

- Encryption technology encodes and decodes communications across the intranet. Intricate formulas are used for sensitive data, such as a student's name and social security number. Not all data are encrypted, however, because encryption would slow processing time.
- An intranet connected to the Internet employs firewalls to block unwanted information. This is done by inspecting the packets of information coming into and leaving the site.
- Intranet sites employ logins and passwords in order to identify the appropriate users. To gain access, students must identify themselves as members of the class by providing a unique user name and password each time they log into the site.

- A proxy server is a security measure that routes information to and from the Internet. Students often directly contact the Internet from the virtual classroom intranet. By using a proxy server, student and intranet site information are not sent out onto the Internet during the interaction between the intranet and the Internet.

Students and instructors are able to communicate via an intranet through a networked environment. The two main types of networked environments are local area networks (LANs) and wide area networks (WANs). A LAN is a group of interconnected computers with the ability to communicate and interact with each other in one geographical location. In a local environment, the LAN is sufficient to host a virtual classroom. In distributed learning, a WAN is set up, using servers, to connect computers that are geographically dispersed.

The intranet displays information in the virtual classroom via the browser. Information must be delivered quickly and must be easy to navigate. Templates, generated by databases, are used to lay out the information. By integrating a database system with the Web site for the class, students at a distance have the ability to navigate the site at greater speed.

Relationship management software allows students to view class schedules, register for classes, and view other administrative information via a secure intranet. Students can access student account information, allowing for convenient remote administration. This differs from a school's Web site in that security measures (explained earlier) are used to identify matriculated students.

Relationship management software is an integral component of intranets in distributed education. The relationship management software acts as the student's primary interface with the school, where the student may have little or no face-to-face interaction with administration.

## INTRANET COMMUNICATION

The geographically dispersed nature of distributed learning creates a convenient environment for students. Asynchronous communication takes place using threaded discussions, e-mail, the digital drop-box, forms, and course content materials. Synchronous communication is possible through chat and streaming audio/video. The term *asynchronous* means that the student and the instructor are not communicating in real time. *Synchronous* means that they are communicating in real time.

Threaded discussions are the primary communication tool. The instructors post discussion topics and students respond asynchronously. Threaded discussions create intense interaction between the students and the instructor. Each post is viewable by all participants in the virtual class. One-on-one communications take place through e-mail. Sensitive (or private) material is also sent via e-mail.

The digital drop-box is used for document sharing. Participants can upload documents to a secure location on the intranet, and then designate who has access to the material. Drop-boxes are typically used for the course content materials, such as lesson plans, syllabi, and instructor notes. Students usually upload papers and final projects to the digital drop-box.

## EXAMPLES OF INTRANETS IN DISTRIBUTED LEARNING

There are many examples of intranets used in distributed learning. Most employ the elements explained in the previous sections, yet each has a substantially different functionality. FELIX, used by The Fielding Graduate Institute, is an example of an intranet used primarily for administrative purposes. In addition to administrative information, FELIX offers links to directories (faculty, student, and staff); library services; and institutional, research, and event information. FELIX also provides a digital "workspace" where students can navigate between different threaded discussions. FELIX has the capability to host online seminars and courses that are open only to registered participants. Another example of an intranet is Blackboard, a robust, modifiable site that allows for nearly all of the elements mentioned in the previous section. The Blackboard intranet site is used by many academic institutions to teach courses at a distance and also as a supplement to on-campus classes. The site typically contains instructor information, course content information, and communication capabilities. Tests are administered and graded electronically on the site, reducing the need for scheduling of proctored examinations. A third example of an intranet used in distributed learning is the DeVry University Student On-line System (DSOS). Students primarily use DSOS to register for classes, check for academic and financial holds, and build unofficial course schedules.

*—Jason C. Vallee*

***See also*** Browser; Distributed Learning/Distributed Education; Networks; Virtual Classroom

## Bibliography

Blackboard: http://www.blackboard.com.

Complete Intranet Resources: http://intrack.com/intranet/.

DiMattia, S. (2002). Creative intranets. *Library Journal, 127*(12), 40–42.

Fichter, D. (2001). Zooming in: Writing content for intranets. *Online, 25*(25), 80–83.

Hanynes, B. R. (2000). Building an intranet in electronic and electrical engineering. *International Journal of Electrical Engineering Education, 37*(3).

Intranet Journal: http://www.intranetjournal.com.

# INTERNET SERVICE PROVIDER (ISP)

An Internet service provider (ISP) provides the link between a personal computer and the Internet. It also supplies other related services to individuals, organizations, and companies including, but not limited to, e-mail, virtual hosting, and Web site construction. An ISP has the equipment, registrations, and telecommunication access necessary to be a point of presence on the Internet for the geographic area served. Larger ISPs often provide multiple Internet access methods distinguished by speed, cost, and cabling, including dial-up, Digital Subscriber Line (DSL), cable modem, ISDN, T-1, and T-3.

The term *ISP* is sometimes used interchangeably with OSP (online service provider). However, an OSP provides extensive content, a large menu of online services, and often its own browser. AOL (America Online) is an example of an OSP, whereas Verizon and Earthlink are examples of ISPs. An ISP or OSP is an essential link in the Internet-based network of learners, teachers/trainers, and information resources.

Distributed learning organizations usually provide ISP services for their faculty/trainers, students, staff, and alumni by either building the computing infrastructure internally or outsourcing it. Other institutions allow members of their learning communities to contract independently with their ISP of choice in order to access Web-based learning resources. In the mid to late 1990s some higher education institutions started outsourcing remote access services to provide Internet access for faculty and students off-campus and for on-campus users who did not have network connections. As the number of users increased, so did the time they spent on the network.

## PROTOCOLS

A protocol is a standard way of communicating across a network that allows two dissimilar or similar systems to communicate. In a computer network, a protocol is the special set of rules that end points in a telecommunication connection use when they communicate.

The basic communication language of the Internet is called the Transmission Control Protocol/Internet Protocol (TCP/IP), defined at the end of this entry. Many Internet users are familiar with the higher layer application protocols that use TCP/IP to get to the Internet. These include Telnet, which provides logon access to remote computers; File Transfer Protocol (FTP); the World Wide Web's Hypertext Transfer Protocol (HTTP); and the Simple Mail Transfer Protocol (SMTP). These and other protocols are often packaged together with TCP/IP as a suite of applications available as part of an operating system environment, such as Microsoft Windows, or provided by an ISP for Linux or Unix operating systems.

## TELNET

Telnet is a text-only protocol that facilitates logon to a remote computer for use of programs and data that the remote owner has made available. Telnet was the first widespread protocol that university communities used to access remote computers. Telnet provides a command channel connection to support FTP (defined in the next section), which facilitates file transfer directly between a remote computer (host) and a personal computer. Current operating environments, such as Microsoft Windows, Macintosh, and Linux, include or will support a Telnet application to provide access to a remote computer.

Over time, Telnet has become less popular, but it remains in use to access certain types of campus e-mail accounts, by software developers and system administrators working with remote machines, and for anyone who needs applications or data located at a particular remote computer.

Hytelnet was the first online, hypertext directory of Telnet sites on the Internet and included mostly details and links for Telnet access to library catalogs. It was compiled in 1990 but is no longer maintained, and none of the links are active. The closest successor to Hytelnet is LibDex (http://www.libdex.com), which offers access details for Web-based library catalogs. For historical interest, there is a Hytelnet archive that shows the Telnet sites that were active before the World Wide Web at http://www.lights.com/hytelnet/.

## FTP

File Transfer Protocol (FTP) allows the transfer of files between two computers, There are three leading approaches to transferring files using FTP:

1. Through an Internet connection using programs like WS_FTP, Fetch, or Anarchie.
2. With an Internet browser, such as Netscape or Internet Explorer (IE). For example, in the browser address window type "ftp.servername.com" to gain access to the remote FTP computer named "server-name."
3. A simple command interface FTP application that can run from a DOS prompt or from Start/Run in Windows or older shell accounts.

Currently, FTP is commonly used to transfer Web page files from the designer's PC to the computer that acts as their server for everyone on the Internet. It is also used to download programs and other files to a PC computer from other servers. Like the Hypertext Transfer Protocol (HTTP), which transfers displayable Web pages and related files, and the Simple Mail Transfer Protocol (SMTP), which transfers e-mail, FTP is an application protocol that uses the Internet's TCP/IP protocols (see the next section).

After Telnet and FTP, but before the World Wide Web, there was Gopher. The Internet Gopher is a distributed document delivery service that works across computer networks. It follows a client-server model that permits users to browse, search, and retrieve documents residing on server machines. The Gopher information system software was developed at the University of Minnesota.

## TCP/IP

Transmission Control Protocol/Internet Protocol (TCP/IP) is the basic communication language or protocol of the Internet. It can also be used as a communications protocol in a private network (either an intranet or an extranet).

TCP/IP is a two-layer program. The higher layer, Transmission Control Protocol, manages the assembly of a message or file into smaller units of data that are transmitted over the Internet and received by a TCP layer that reassembles the packets into the original message. The lower layer, Internet Protocol, handles the address part of each packet so that it gets to the right destination. Each gateway computer (router) on the network checks this address to see where to forward the message. Even though some data units (packets) from the same message are routed differently than others, they are reassembled at the destination.

TCP/IP uses the client-server model of communication in which a computer user (a client) requests and is provided a service (such as calling forth a Web page into a browser window) by another computer (a server) in the network. TCP/IP communication is primarily point-to-point, meaning each communication is from one point (or host computer) in the network to another point or host computer. TCP/IP and the higher-level applications that use it are collectively said to be "stateless" because each client request is considered a new request unrelated to any previous one (unlike ordinary phone conversations that require a dedicated connection for the call duration). Being stateless frees network paths so that everyone can use them continuously. (Note that the TCP layer itself is not stateless as far as any one message is concerned. Its connection to the remote computer remains in place until all packets in a message have been received.)

—*Virginia A. McFerran*

*See also* BROWSER; INTERNET

### Bibliography

Abbate, Janet. (2000). *Inventing the Internet paperback.* Cambridge: MIT Press.

Devlin, Maureen, Larson, Richard, & Meyerson, Joel. (Eds.). (2000). *The Internet and the university: 2000 forum.* Retrieved from http://www.educause.edu/forum/ffpiu00w.asp.

Further reading on FTP: http://www.cis.ohio-state.edu/cs/Services/rfc/rfc-text/rfc0765.txt

Further reading on Hytelnet: http://www.lights.com/hytelnet/

# IT SECURITY

Security refers to the act of maintaining the integrity of resources under one's control, whether this means installing a deadbolt on a door or ensuring that computer systems are invulnerable. Along with advances in technology come people whose goal is to misuse them.

As society becomes more technology-oriented, increasing numbers of "hackers" and "crackers" try their hand at breaking into newer, faster, bigger systems. As educational institutions develop and implement more sophisticated technology, they must provide increasingly sophisticated levels of security to protect the technology, its users, and the data stored on its network.

Making educational systems secure requires providing security in four major areas:

- The means of accessing technology systems must be kept secure.
- The technology systems, themselves, must be protected from intruders.
- The databases and information resources must be kept free from tampering and corruption.
- Preserving the invulnerability of the physical plant in which the technology systems are housed must be taken as a fundamental step, without which other security measures are useless.

In information technology systems that support distributed education, special security concerns arise. These are discussed later.

## ACCESS SECURITY

To secure access, systems must be in place that ensure the appropriate identification, authentication, authorization, and accountability of the people and the programs that access technology and information assets. Just as equipment and physical plant are assets that belong to an institution, databases and files of information are also critical assets that must be protected. Various processes for maintaining access security exist. Each one, and its role in creating and maintaining security, is described below.

### Identification

Individual users or automated processes must have unique names, or identifiers, to distinguish them from other users or processes. Identifiers are often based on an individual's name (e.g., jsmith). Some contain clues as to the user's organizational affiliation (e.g., payr0111). Some are purely random sets of characters. The more desirable kinds of identifiers provide some type of clue as to the person (or office) to whom they are assigned. Identifiers can be of any length, but most computer systems work best with identifiers composed of eight or fewer characters. Translators called *aliasing systems* can be used to assign longer and more intuitive names (e.g., John.Smith), which are then converted into identifiers that the computer systems will recognize. Process identifiers are almost always associated with a functional business area and functional process of which they are part.

### Authentication

After an identity is established it must be authenticated, or confirmed as genuine, before access can be granted. Authentication verifies that the person or program communicating as an identity is the person or program assigned that identity.

Methods of authentication can generally be grouped into one of three categories: something that one knows, something that one carries, or an attribute—that is, a physical characteristic. Examples of these three methods of authentication include passwords (these are known), "smart cards" and password generator cards (these are carried), and biometrics such as fingerprints or retina patterns (these are attributes). Collectively, these methods are known as *authentication factors*. The combination of identity and required authentication factors is commonly called the user or process *credential*. Credentials are the keys that give users access to systems or resources to which they have been granted permission by the owner of the system, application, or data.

### Passwords

Passwords are by far the most common method of authentication. Well-constructed passwords, stored in secure password databases, are adequate for protecting most common computer systems, databases, and networks. On the other hand, badly chosen passwords are virtually useless in deterring determined intruders. It is the responsibility of the user to construct an effective password, one that cannot be discovered by the various mechanisms for doing so. Ease of discovery makes a password ineffective. Passwords that bear a direct association with users' families, tastes, or preferences are easy to guess. A determined questioner could easily ferret out passwords associated with the users' interests (e.g., basketball, clarinet, birth date).

Various ways exist of cracking passwords. Interacting with users in a way that elicits information about their passwords is known as *social engineering.* Intruders may probe for facts about password owners, such as the names of their children. Scam artists have posed as technicians, warning users of technical problems that threaten dramatic loss or damage to their data. Having aroused users' fears, they then offer to fix the problems, but claim they need the users' passwords to do so.

Another method of password theft is through automated programs called *password crackers.* An intruder gains access to a password file from a computer system and copies it. Such files are almost always encrypted (encryption software uses a random number generator to set up a key that assigns new values to letters and numbers, effectively "scrambling" text), but they are not difficult to find. The intruder then uses the program to walk through a sequence of dictionaries in various languages, representing various interest groups (e.g., Spanish, Estonian, Klingon, and jargon), and encrypt each word using standard encryption software. The program compares the resulting characters with each encrypted password in the password file, hoping to match a character string that cracks the password. Today's powerful computers make the process of comparison quick, even on the largest password files.

The best defense against these brute-force password crackers is for systems administrators to periodically execute the same cracking programs on passwords in their own password databases, and on new passwords as they are chosen. Any passwords this global sweep manages to crack must be changed.

A good password contains several important characteristics. It may combine upper- and lowercase letters, along with some numbers. Special characters (e.g., * & - $ %) may be used if the system supports them. "Grapes" is an ineffective password. But "Gra15pes" is better, because it mixes upper- and lowercase letters and breaks the common dictionary word with numbers. A very effective strategy is to create passwords derived from phrases. The password "MdB15fs" comprises the first letter of each word in the phrase "My dog Bruno fetches sticks," broken up by the dog's age. This password is less crackable than "Gra15pes" because it is not based on a single word found in an English-language dictionary.

### Multi-factor Authentication

One way to dramatically increase access security is to require multiple and varied authentication factors.

This challenges potential intruders to overcome multiple barriers that tend to be progressively more complex. For example, a user may be required to enter a username and password, followed by a second password generated by a token device such as a password generator or smart card.

### Password Generators

A password generator avoids the single memorized (or static) password, and works well in remote authentication. These devices are about the size of ID cards or small calculators and have a small display window. Some display a password that changes every 60 seconds. Others generate a password when the user activates the device. The user copies this password into the session, and the computer being connected compares it with the password it expects to receive. These devices require no special equipment in users' homes.

### Smart Cards

Smart cards have imbedded intelligence. They can provide authentication and act as ID cards, physical access cards, library cards, and debit cards. Some can double as calculators. These cards may require special monitors, magnetic strip readers, or other devices. Depending on features and volume purchased, smart cards can cost between $10 and $150.

## Authorization

After the user's identity is authenticated, the owner's authority to access systems and data is checked, and access is then granted or not granted. Authorization can be tied to a resource, to an individual, or to a profile. If it is associated with a resource, the authorization software looks for the user's identity on a list of authorized users. When authorization is tied to an individual (such as the owner of a resource), the software checks the user's record for a listing of the given resource. The user may also be part of a group that is granted access.

## Accountability

The last step in securing access, accountability, tightly couples the processes of identification, authentication, and authority. This makes it more difficult to electronically intercept or guess the credential, or "hijack" the identity of an authorized user to access systems or data. This process also makes it possible to identify the user to whom the credentials are assigned. A user whose identity can be confirmed within a reasonable doubt can be held accountable.

A variety of means exist for increasing the level of accountability. Among them are unique identifiers, strict password selection rules, password expiration, session timeouts, use of multiple authentication factors, and encrypting the session data (especially passwords) that traverse a data network.

## TECHNOLOGY SECURITY

It is critical to be proactive in protecting technology resources from trespass and tampering. Systems must be scanned continually for vulnerabilities. It doesn't matter how secure users' passwords are if a system administrator has failed to repair a security flaw that then opens the computer to compromise.

Intruders compromise systems for different reasons. They may try to steal data or use systems as a base of operations for intruding into other commercial or government computers. They might hide illegal materials such as bootleg movies or hacking tools on compromised systems.

Software and hardware security "bugs" can be discovered in various ways. Manufacturers, security analysts, or technicians may discover them during testing, analysis, or system maintenance. In such cases, the manufacturer is usually informed, and will often repair the vulnerability by publishing a software patch (a piece of code added to an existing program). By contrast, hackers who routinely scan Internet-connected computers for vulnerabilities do so in order to exploit them for their own purposes.

If a system is compromised, it is possible that a crime has been committed. A decision must be made about whether to attempt to identify and prosecute the intruder, or to clean up the mess and resume operations. In an investigation, the system is turned over to security analysts and law enforcement officials who perform "computer forensics," analyzing the computer for technical evidence that points to the identity and location of the perpetrator. Some of what they look for is analogous to electronic "fingerprints."

During the investigation the system is not available for use. This sometimes means that the decision to track an intruder hinges on whether back-up systems are available to handle the work in the meantime. In either case, the affected system or software must be reinstalled using software that is free of viruses and vulnerabilities.

## INFORMATION SECURITY

Along with the technology used to store and access them, data and information assets must be protected from inappropriate disclosure and modification. Generally, the more secure and well managed are systems and databases, the better protected are the data that reside on them.

Protecting data requires more than effective technology solutions. Human factors also come into play. In many cases, personal or proprietary information is inappropriately disclosed because someone put a computer file in the wrong directory, displayed it on a public-access computer, or incorrectly set access permissions. It is critical that people who handle or have access to sensitive data are trained in how to protect that information.

## SECURITY CHALLENGES IN DISTRIBUTED EDUCATION

Computers that support distributed education (DE) face the same general security threats common to all Internet-connected systems and data. They are targeted by hackers for the same reasons as are other computers on university campuses.

In fact, intruders find university systems especially attractive because they tend to be large and connected by very fast networks. Also, the ability to access and distribute information is fundamental to the business and culture of higher education. However, institutions are now paying much greater attention to security issues on their campuses.

Distributed education offers its own set of security challenges. Two challenges discussed here are authentication mechanisms and copyright issues.

### Authenticating Distributed Education Students

Although assigning online identities to remote students is not a challenge, managing the authentication factors for these students can be difficult. This becomes an issue when students forget passwords. As in any controlled access situation, the campus must first verify students' identities before issuing new passwords. On residential campuses, students visit the appropriate office to validate their identities.

For distributed students, one option is "validating questions." The system works like this: When students establish their association with the university in some way, for example, by registering or paying fees, they answer a series of questions about themselves—questions whose answers they alone are likely to know. When they forget their passwords, they interact with an online application that asks them at least two of these questions. If they provide the right answers, the process allows them to choose new passwords.

This process requires users' cooperation. They must provide the appropriate information in advance. They must understand the importance of taking the time to handle this administrative task at the beginning of the semester. And they must always answer the questions exactly as they initially answered them, including spelling and use of upper- and lowercase, because the process is often automated. But these are minor caveats, and this method of authenticating remote users is straightforward and cost effective.

## Protecting Copyright

Fundamental to the academic content of DE programs are proprietary materials that the institution develops or licenses from copyright owners. Protecting these materials from unauthorized access and use is a major concern for DE system administrators.

Copyright principles and laws are designed to protect the rights of the copyright owner and help the institution fulfill its responsibilities to the copyright owner. They also guard institutionally owned intellectual property against inappropriate use. For these laws to be effective in protecting the interests of the institution, institutions must take prudent steps to protect the works they cover, or the institutions' rights may not be upheld in court. However institutions choose to authorize the use of copyrighted property, such as class materials, those means must be effective in granting access to enrolled students and barring others. Without this marker of intention, institutions are not seen as upholding their obligations under the law, or demonstrating their intent to actively protect their own rights under the same laws.

Finally, although some traditional self-defense methods can be applied to securing computers that support distributed education, these computers cannot be "hidden" from the Internet as can other systems that support only on-campus functions. As the customers of distributed education are almost all, by definition, off-campus, the computers must be fully visible to the Internet. This requires that all components of security—access security, technology security, and information security—receive special, dedicated attention.

—*Michael McRobbie*

*See also* FEDERAL LAWS; INTELLECTUAL PROPERTY; LEGAL ISSUES

## Bibliography

Bosworth, Seymour. (Ed.). (2002). *Computer security handbook.* New York: John Wiley & Sons.

Cheswick, William R., & Bellovin, Steven M. (1994). *Firewalls and Internet security.* Boston, MA: Addison-Wesley.

Kaufman, Charlie, Perlman, Radia, & Speciner, Mike. (2002). *Network security: Private communication in a public world.* Upper Saddle River, NJ: Prentice Hall.

National Institute of Standards and Technology. (1994). *Security in open systems.* Publication 800–7. Retrieved from http://csrc.nist.gov/publications/nistpubs/800-7/main.html.

Russell, Deborah, & Gangemi, G. T. (1991). *Computer security basics.* Sebastopol, CA: O'Reilly.

# KNOWLEDGE BUILDING/KNOWLEDGE WORK

Dozens of software systems are classified as knowledge building environments. "Knowledge building environment" has an attractive, 21st century, knowledge society ring to it, but how is a *knowledge building* environment different from a *learning* environment, and what makes it an *environment* rather than a *tool?* This entry addresses these questions, providing answers that suggest that a fully realized knowledge building environment is substantially different from a learning environment, incorporating different forms of support to accomplish a different level of process, and playing a role in a different kind of education or workplace culture.

## KNOWLEDGE BUILDING: THE FOUNDATION OF KNOWLEDGE BUILDING ENVIRONMENTS (KBEs)

Although the term *knowledge building* now appears in tens of thousands of Web documents, it is almost never defined, the implication being that its meaning is transparent from the juxtaposition of two familiar words. Yet the idea of knowledge as a human construction is a very recent notion in the history of thought, and even today it remains far from universally accepted. When the term *knowledge building* is used in business contexts it is roughly equivalent to *knowledge creation*, and is associated with innovation, intellectual property, intellectual capital, and knowledge work. In educational contexts, however, knowledge building tends to be equated with such familiar approaches as learning by discovery, project-based learning, anchored instruction, and collaborative learning. Thus, it is used as a synonym for *constructivist learning* and offers no evident advantage over this older and more familiar term.

Knowledge building was introduced into the educational literature in the 1980s in order to create a conceptual bridge between knowledge creation as it is handled in the larger "knowledge society," and fundamentally similar work that can be carried on in education. Knowledge building is activity focused on the generation of new knowledge and the improvement of ideas that have a public life and that are of value to others. Stated differently, knowledge builders construct a life for ideas beyond their minds and personal notebooks—they do more than learn. One marker of a knowledge building environment is that it can support idea development in both education and workplace situations. This is in contrast to the common situation in knowledge-based organizations in which one technology (often called "knowledgeware") is used in the creative work of the organization and an entirely separate technology (often called "courseware") is used for learning. Both economically and technologically, e-learning is treated as a separate world from the ongoing creative work of an organization.

Knowledge building environments (KBEs) bring these different worlds of knowledge work together into one coherent framework, while bringing innovation closer to the central work of the organization. Members are inducted into a progressive enterprise in which they are continually contributing to the shared intellectual property of the organization. They advance community resources by contributing their ideas, alongside resources from the world at large. Learning is necessitated by this process, and integral to it. The resultant community knowledge is a growing resource—a form of what has come to be called "intellectual capital"—that other community members can build on. Each advance precipitates further advances, with the result that at both the individual and group levels there is a continual movement beyond current understanding and best practice, toward the ideal of "lifelong innovativeness."

Following from the learning/knowledge-building distinction, a KBE is defined as *any environment (virtual or otherwise) that enhances collaborative efforts to create and continually improve ideas.* That is a minimum requirement. An optimal KBE will exploit the fullest possible potential of ideas to be improved by situating them in worlds beyond the minds of their creators and compounding their value so that collective achievements exceed individual contributions. Among the characteristics of an effective KBE are supports for the formulation of knowledge problems, for preserving ideas and making them accessible as objects of inquiry, for dialogue that is democratic and favorable to idea diversity, for constructive criticism and analysis, for organizing ideas into larger wholes, and for dealing with recognized gaps and shortcomings of ideas. A local KBE gains strength by being embedded in a broader KBE—people beyond the local community pursuing the same knowledge goals. Thus, the ideal KBE is one in which the knowledge building work of a local community both draws upon and affords some level of participation in the larger knowledge building activity of society.

## THE KNOWLEDGE BASE FOR DESIGN OF KBEs

The social, cultural, and cognitive dynamics that inform the design of KBEs are summarized in this section. Knowledge scientists have studied the history of thought and its evolution, as well as the practices of novice and expert knowledge workers—listening in on their conversations, collecting sketches and artifacts produced and revised as problem solving proceeds, analyzing notebooks and other accounts of scientific breakthroughs, recording and analyzing team meetings, and analyzing protocols as problem solvers "think aloud." The following are pertinent

conclusions drawn from this work, from the field of memetics (the evolution of ideas), and from the writings of sociocultural and constructivist theorists.

An innovation dynamic links social and technological advances. In the case of knowledge building, externalized, organizational memory provides a powerful resource for knowledge advancement; advances are realized through collective responsibility for knowledge creation.

Striking parallels exist in the processes of knowledge creation across age and field of inquiry. The knowledge building trajectory starts with the early, natural ability to play with ideas and extends to the not-so-natural and relatively rare intentional processes that serve to continually improve ideas. These knowledge-intensive processes enable deep understanding and provide the essential link between learning and knowledge creation.

Knowledge advancement is fundamentally a sociocultural process, enhanced by cultures of innovation. Bakhtin used the term *intertextuality* to indicate how the voices of others are integrated into what we think, write, and say. "Standing on the shoulders of giants" is a rough approximation. Cultures of innovation provide a broad base, making productive use of diverse contributions and allowing innovation to become the cultural norm.

Ideas are the building blocks of invention. Their improvement starts with their objectification as cultural artifacts and is enhanced by community discourses that maximize their potential. Aristotle's physics made it into our culture, and were superseded by Newton's; Newtonian physics gave way to Einstein's relativity theory; relativity was further advanced by quantum theory. Breakthroughs were not achieved through adherence to fixed beliefs or consensus as a goal, but through efforts to account for all unexplained or "anomalous" facts. Arguments and negotiations surely occurred, but advances were more dependent on identification of weaknesses in current constructions, designs for new proofs and demonstrations, and engaging others in critical review. Improving ideas, not winning arguments, is the essence of knowledge building.

Knowledge builders take charge at the highest levels of the range of sociocognitive activity that characterizes productive research and design teams. This includes goal setting, resource providing, monitoring, and modification of goals and strategies in light of progress or difficulties—the same tasks that are customarily reserved for teachers, curriculum experts, managers, facilitators, standard setters, and evaluators.

Our expanded understanding of knowledge building opens the possibility of knowledgeware that renders its hidden dynamics transparent and embeds them in systems of interaction between people and ideas, leading to dramatically improved and expanded conditions for idea improvement. The ideal KBE would be one that makes this possibility a reality.

## HOW KBEs ARE DIFFERENT FROM CSCL

A number of noteworthy computer supported collaborative learning (CSCL) tools are referred to as KBEs, though without explanation of in what particular way they support knowledge building. If the concept of KBE is to contribute something distinctive, then its models and defining characteristics obviously cannot be shared with all collaborative learning environments. Yet a review of technologies referred to as KBE implies precisely that. For example, Stahl defines a KBE as "a software environment designed to support collaborative learning." He elaborates, "The most common element . . . is the discussion forum [that] allows people to respond to notes posted by one another. Typically there is a thread of responses to posted notes, with a tree of divergent opinions."

A KBE should be distinguishable from CSCL by virtue of its focus on processes of knowledge creation and idea improvement and by virtue of its ability to represent the resulting community knowledge. Accordingly, the inclusion of generic CSCL tools such as electronic whiteboards, discussion forums, chat, shared folders; supports for multimedia, visualization, and annotation and for argumentation, negotiation, weighing evidence, and other discourse forms; and data representation and analysis cannot be taken as definitive. Any or all may play a role, but no combination of them will constitute a KBE. The following are characteristics that distinguish a KBE and that are not common to CSCL:

- Support for self-organization that goes beyond division of labor. New knowledge is always emerging through a self-organizing process. A KBE should support this process and remain faithful to the essential characteristics of knowledge building discussed in the preceding section. At the least, it should not thwart them through strict editorial controls; by turning all of the high-level management work over to

facilitators; or by using fill in the blanks, prompts, fixed sequences, prepackaged activities, and other micro-management strategies.

1. Shared, user-configured design spaces that represent collective knowledge advances built from the contributions of team members. Continually creating something greater than the best of the available contributions becomes a natural part of the day-to-day work of the organization.

2. Support for citing and referencing one another's work so that contributions to the evolution of ideas are evident and can become objects of discourse in their own right, much as is the case in the history of thought.

3. Ways to represent higher-order organizations of ideas and to signal the rising status for improved ideas as contrasted with their nondescript entry in threads, folders, and repositories where they are lost amid information glut.

4. Ways for the same idea to be worked with in varied and multiple contexts and to appear in different higher-order organizations of knowledge. Flexible import-export allows all of the valued ideas and artifacts of an organization (or representations of them) to be incorporated into knowledge building discourse.

5. Systems of feedback to enhance self- and group-monitoring of ongoing processes and to tap idea potential—as distinguished from assessment and management tools used exclusively for filing, organization, and end-of-work or external evaluation.

6. Opportunistic linking of persons and groups—with the possibility of crossing traditional discipline, sector, cultural, and age boundaries—by virtue of contributions and shared knowledge-building goals. Searches are not limited to finding notes and documents; the ideas represented in texts and artifacts also serve a matchmaking function, allowing participants to locate others working on parallel problems, and to identify the cutting edge of their area of inquiry.

7. Ways for different user groups to customize the environment and to explore the within- and between-community corridors that extend and provide continuity to their knowledge work.

CSCL environments designed for collaborative learning and knowledge sharing typically lack these characteristics and accordingly should not be confused with KBEs.

## APPROACHES TO KBE DESIGN

The goal in KBE design is to enhance the capacity of communities to innovate, by capturing their inventiveness and converting it into something of social value. The eight distinguishing characteristics of a KBE outlined in the preceding section represent ideals to work toward in software design rather than prescriptions that can be implemented directly. The most sustained effort to achieve these ideals has been the development of computer supported intentional learning environments (CSILE), which evolved into Knowledge Forum. The CSILE initiative began in 1983, pre-dating the educational availability of the Internet. Accordingly, "early on" it had only a limited ability to link people and groups. In line with the theoretical underpinnings of knowledge building, an Internet-savvy version of Knowledge Forum has not only enabled the extension of knowledge building communities across disciplines, sectors, ages, and cultures worldwide, but has also supported a much fuller range of knowledge building requirements: deep embedding of knowledge objects (notes and views can live within other notes and views); "rise-above" functionality, which enables successively higher-order representations of ideas; and embedded scaffolds, problem statements, and keywords to enrich conceptual linking and searching. Drag-and-drop additionally provides user-friendly means for producing graphical organizers so that multiple, conceptually distinct representations of notes can be created and notes can be organized and reorganized to reflect knowledge advances.

Whereas the client-server version of Knowledge Forum makes direct use of Internet protocols, several recent efforts, including a different version of Knowledge Forum, have attempted to realize knowledge building principles through browser-based software. Current Web technology, however, severely constrains what can be done to allow end users to create and manipulate successively higher-order knowledge objects, which is a fundamental technical requirement for a KBE. Browser-based applications, for example, use some form of threaded discourse, which forces dialogue into a hierarchical framework, making it difficult to link diverse ideas and create higher-order knowledge structures. Various avenues toward overcoming these constraints are being explored. On another front, wireless and mobile technologies and automated assessment techniques are opening up new possibilities for idea-driven, opportunistic, and creative efforts, but not without new challenges to collective efforts and risk-taking with ideas. In all of these explorations it becomes especially important to retain a firm conceptual grip on what makes a KBE.

There has been one short-lived effort to design a KBE "killer app" through agreement on a set of interoperable Web-based tools. A component-oriented approach to software design makes good sense at the programming level, but when applied at the level of functional design it tends to result in what critics call "featuritis"—a proliferation of individually attractive features that cumulatively defeat the basic purpose of the software.

The adequacy of any KBE must ultimately be judged by knowledge advances resulting from its use. Collaboration, discussion, and information sharing may all increase, but if there are no corresponding knowledge advances, we do not have an effective KBE. As the preceding discussion indicates, there is a great deal of interest in knowledge building and in technology to support it in education and knowledge work. An extensive design community (see http://ikit.org) is just being formed explicitly to advance understanding of how new knowledge is created and to develop the technologies and research required to advance that agenda.

—*Marlene Scardamalia*

***See also*** Designing Learning Environments; Knowledge Management; Learning Communities; Sociotechnical Issues

## Bibliography

Aunger, R. (Ed.). (2001). *Darwinizing culture: The status of memetics as a science.* Oxford, UK: Oxford University Press.

Bereiter, Carl. (2002). *Education and mind in the knowledge age.* Mahwah, NJ: Lawrence Erlbaum.

Drucker, P. (1985). *Innovation and entrepreneurship: Practice and principles.* New York: Harper and Row.

Koschmann, T. (1996). *CSCL: Theory and practice of an emerging paradigm.* Hillsdale, NJ: Lawrence Erlbaum.

Lakatos, I. (1970). The methodology of scientific research programmes. In I. Lakatos & A. Musgrave (Eds.),

*Criticism and the growth of knowledge* (pp. 91–195). Cambridge, MA: Cambridge University Press.

Norman, D. A. (1993). *Things that make us smart.* Reading, MA: Addison-Wesley.

Scardamalia, M. (2002). Collective cognitive responsibility for the advancement of knowledge. In B. Smith (Ed.), *Liberal education in a knowledge society* (pp. 67–98). Chicago: Open Court.

Scardamalia, M., & Bereiter, C. (in press). Knowledge building. In *Encyclopedia of education,* 2nd edition. New York: Macmillan Reference.

Scardamalia, M., Bereiter, C., McLean, R. S., Swallow, J., & Woodruff, E. (1989). Computer supported intentional learning environments. *Journal of Educational Computing Research, 5,* 51–68.

Stahl, G. (2000). A model of collaborative knowledge-building. In B. Fishman & S. O'Connor-Divelbiss (Eds.), *Fourth international conference of the learning sciences* (pp. 70–77). Mahwah, NJ: Lawrence Erlbaum.

Stewart, T. A. (1997). *Intellectual capital: The new wealth of nations.* New York: Doubleday.

Wilson, B. (Ed.). (1996). *Constructivist learning environments: Case studies in instructional design.* Englewood Cliffs, NJ: Educational Technology.

# KNOWLEDGE ECONOMY

The knowledge economy is one in which the generation and the exploitation of knowledge has come to play the predominant part in the creation of wealth. It is not simply about pushing back the frontiers of knowledge; it is also about the more effective use and exploitation of all types of knowledge in all manner of economic activity.

—(Houghton & Sheehan, 2000)

To remain relevant in a changing world, educators—whether based in universities, organizations, communities, or homes—need to be cognizant of the unique nature, requirements, and opportunities of today's knowledge economy. Social, organizational, and political changes are inextricably tied to changing economies. Widespread use of Internet-based communication and instant access to dispersed information accelerate change in our interdependent world. The strategic competencies needed in the knowledge economy include creating and sharing knowledge, building effective social learning networks, promoting collaboration and innovation, and understanding how to effectively manage the social and technical aspects of knowledge systems.

The emergence of our knowledge economy is accompanied by new questions about social and cultural divisions, where differences in education and economic conditions are exacerbated by unequal access to knowledge. Fundamental issues arise concerning participation in governance, intellectual property rights, and public policy. The role of knowledge is ambiguous. Knowledge can be a common good that is accessible by all, or a commodity that is privately owned for the benefit of a few. The value of knowledge can increase—and sometimes diminish—as it is shared. Although wealth and power can come from sharing knowledge, there also can be advantages to withholding knowledge.

While debates on these issues continue, leading economists assert that the key to economic development is the capacity to access, generate, and transfer knowledge—and to acquire ways of thinking that accept change, refute the inevitability of poverty, and embrace knowledge, technology, science, and education.

## INTANGIBLE RESOURCES AND TACIT KNOWLEDGE

Although all economic change may be connected to widespread social access to new ideas, the knowledge economy elevates the value of intangible knowledge resources. Traditional economics stress the importance of resources that are easily measured and quantified, such as labor, land, and tangible capital. The knowledge economy values intangible resources such as tacit knowledge, capacities for knowledge sharing, continuous learning, and knowledge generation.

Explicit knowledge is codifiable—it can be converted into discrete codes without losing its meaning. Tacit knowledge, however, is based in experience and is often unconscious, making it difficult to articulate, evaluate, and transfer to others. Intangible resources are embedded within participatory ways of organizing in which collaboration flourishes, norms and policies support continuous learning, and traditions honor the creation and application of innovation. They include the knowledge and learning capacities of individual employees as well as the organization's policies and capacities for collaboration, innovation, and knowledge generation.

Intangible assets refer to those specific attributes of an organization that differentiate it from all others. Because of the difficulty in recognizing and valuing intangible assets, there remain large discrepancies between the value stated in a financial statement and an organization's market value. This gap has increased in the knowledge economy, where the intangible assets are often the basis of sustainability, innovation, and competitive advantage. Although still in the early stages, emerging critical and social accounting methods offer viable strategies to evaluate and report on intellectual, social, and other forms of intangible assets.

## KNOWLEDGE SHARING, BOUNDARIES, ALLIANCES, AND NETWORKS

In a knowledge economy, value and productivity are increased when knowledge is used and shared. Knowledge sharing occurs at multiple levels within an organization. Knowledge can be shared in a person-to-person modality within a single team or department. As a team goes from one project to another or as the team's membership changes, knowledge is dispersed into new contexts. Knowledge dissemination often goes beyond institutional boundaries and extends into other organizations and groups through transfer opportunities such as conferences, associations, publications, and online discussions.

As networking, expertise sharing, and information dispersion grow in importance, the knowledge boundaries of a firm extend beyond its production boundaries. The management of knowledge and the strategies for its communication become as critical for an organization's success as the management of production resources and processes. Individuals and organizations gain competitive advantages by forming networks with effective communication linkages. These interdependencies support affiliations, partnerships, consulting arrangements, and other formalized alliances. In these networking environments, an important competency is the capacity to effectively integrate and synthesize diverse streams of knowledge into cohesive, useful, and reliable resources.

Communities of practice support learning and knowledge sharing through social networks of people who share a commitment to work together and have similar work experiences and responsibilities. These groups are key contributors to building intangible assets and are nurtured by organizational strategies that value knowledge sharing. Online communities of practice use the Internet and electronic communication to support knowledge sharing and collaborative learning when these social networks are geographically dispersed.

Most professional and academic attention focuses on ways corporations and large organizations can thrive in the knowledge economy. However, small businesses, nonprofit organizations, and other institutions with limited resources also need to establish learning environments, develop new competencies for innovation and knowledge generation, and build capacities to succeed in the knowledge economy.

## THE KNOWLEDGE WORKER

Knowledge workers have to develop a repertoire of specialized skills and competencies to meet the needs of the new economy. Although scholars debate whether the knowledge economy represents a dramatic shift from prior economies, they agree that increased attention is being given to the importance of knowledge, interconnectivity, and intangible capital for economic well being.

The generation of new knowledge produces increasingly complex levels of specialization based on factors such as professional field and organization, and on the interactions among these levels. The knowledge worker needs to know how to successfully navigate these complex levels of knowledge. Competencies of the knowledge worker also include the ability to extricate knowledge from a wide variety of contexts and cognitive skills to quickly learn to use new technologies.

These competencies appear to be best developed within nonhierarchical work environments that promote integrity, trust, personal values, and ethics. Effective management acts with integrity while enabling innovation and sustained success within the knowledge economy.

## LEARNING IN THE KNOWLEDGE ECONOMY

Changes in the economic system make some existing skills and competencies obsolete, while increasing the importance of others. The knowledge economy places an emphasis on continuous learning. An ever-widening array of new competencies are needed to effectively use emerging technologies, generate and share knowledge, and support innovation.

Many of the skills and competencies that are needed in the new economy are best developed in collaborative learning environments that often differ from the traditional classroom and curriculum structures. The needs of today's students are different, as people continue to learn throughout their careers and build on their past experiences. Learning occurs in online environments, in the workplace, in evening and weekend classes, and in specialized retreats and conferences. Educational institutions and organizational learning programs are, themselves, part of our complex knowledge economy, and subject to its changing nature.

Learning in an online, distributed environment supports the development of competencies such as collaboration, information sharing, and knowledge generation that are essential for successfully navigating within a changing knowledge economy. Distributed environments offer a unique opportunity for approaches to pedagogy and learning that promote knowledge sharing and collaboration with learners who come from different social, organizational, and cultural backgrounds.

## KNOWLEDGE AND DEVELOPMENT

Public policy analysts are developing approaches to evaluate the performance of regions, states, and countries through a series of indicators for knowledge jobs, workforce education, market globalization, economic dynamism and competition, degree of transformation to a digital economy, and capacity for technological innovation. Statistics that are used to measure these categories come from a variety of sources including the U.S. Department of Labor, the World Economic Forum, and Development Gateway. These studies show that although access to the Internet and other communication is growing, many populations are still outside of the knowledge economy.

Organizations such as the World Bank now view economic development as including learning about knowledge sharing; networked organizations; and support for human dignity, mutual respect, innovation, and change. The dominance of the emerging global economic environment favors those with access to technologies, advanced education, and cultures that embrace the attributes of the knowledge economy. In a knowledge economy, there are "digital divides" between the technological "haves" and "have nots."

There is a pervasive impact when people and countries are excluded from the knowledge economy because of poverty, the lack of access to technologies and education, and other determinants.

Knowledge and information exist within cultural and linguistic systems that have unique values and ways of knowing. Concerns exist about the values that are embedded within the technologies and systems of the knowledge economy and their potential to dominate other cultures. The European Union is addressing issues such as the European identity and political agendas in the knowledge economy. These initiatives are aided by the development of analytic methods with which to evaluate information and improve the ways in which it can benefit developing countries by building on indigenous cultures.

With all of its promises, paradoxes, and challenges, the knowledge economy offers unprecedented new opportunities to improve the ways we learn and work together.

—*Niels Agger-Gupta*
—*Dorothy E. Agger-Gupta*

*See also* CULTURAL ACCESS/DIGITAL DIVIDE; GLOBALIZATION; SOCIOCULTURAL PERSPECTIVES

## Bibliography

Ackerman, M., Pipek, V., & Wulf, V. (Eds.). (2003). *Sharing expertise: Beyond knowledge management.* Cambridge: The MIT Press.

Afele, J. S. (2002). *Digital bridges: Developing countries in the knowledge economy.* Hershey, PA: Idea Group Publishing.

Atkinson, R. D. (2002). *The 2002 state new economy index. The Progressive Policy Institute (PPI).* Retrieved March 8, 2003, from http://www.neweconomyindex.org/states/2002/index.html.

Brusoni, S. (1999). *Innovation in the knowledge economy: A summary of research issues* (Report Deliverable 2A-D2A). Brighton, UK: Science and Technology Policy Research, University of Sussex.

Cross, R., & Israelit, S. (2000). *Strategic learning in a knowledge economy: Individual, collective and organizational learning processes.* Woburn, MA: Butterworth-Heinemann.

Development Gateway. http://www.developmentgateway.org.

Forum, W. E. (2003). *World economic forum.* Retrieved March 8, 2003, from http://www.weforum.org.

Guthrie, J., Petty, R., & Johanson, U. (2001). Sunrise in the knowledge economy: Managing, measuring and reporting intellectual capital. *Accounting, Auditing, and Accountability Journal, 14*(4), 365–382.

Houghton, J., & Sheehan, P. (2000). *A primer on the knowledge economy.* Victoria, Australia: Center for Strategic Economic Studies, Victoria University.

Howitt, P. (1996). *The implications of knowledge-based growth for micro-economic policies.* Calgary, Canada: The University of Calgary Press.

Johannessen, J.-A., Olaisen, J., & Olsen, B. (1999). Managing and organizing innovation in the knowledge economy. *European Journal of Innovation Management, 2*(3), 116–128.

Lesser, E. L., Fontaine, M. A., & Slusher, J. A. (Eds.). (2000). *Knowledge and communities (Resources for the knowledge-based economy).* Woburn, MA: Butterworth-Heinemann.

Loasby, B. J. (1999). *Knowledge, institutions, and evolution in economics.* London: Routledge.

Mokyr, J. (2002). *The gifts of Athena: Historical origins of the knowledge economy.* Princeton, NJ: Princeton University Press.

Paige, H. (2002). An exploration of learning, the knowledge-based economy, and owner-managers of small book-selling businesses. *Journal of Workplace Learning, 14*(6), 233–244.

Rodrigues, M. J. (Ed.). (2002). *New knowledge economy in Europe: A strategy for international competitiveness and social cohesion.* Northampton, MA: Edward Elgar Publishing.

Seetharaman, A., Sooria, H. H. B. Z., & Saravanan, A. S. (2002). Intellectual capital accounting and reporting in the knowledge economy. *Journal of Intellectual Capital, 3*(2), 128–148.

Stiglitz, J. (1999, January 27). *Public policy for a knowledge economy.* Paper presented at the Department for Trade and Industry and Center for Economic Policy Research, London, U.K.

U.S. Department of Labor. (2002). *Occupational Employment Statistics.* Bureau of Labor Statistics. Retrieved March 8, 2003, from http://www.bls.gov/oes/home.htm.

# KNOWLEDGE MANAGEMENT

Organizations need to know a good deal about themselves in order to operate successfully. Knowledge management asks and answers questions an organization has about its knowledge:

- What do we know?
- Where do we keep it?
- How do we get to it?
- How do we use it?
- What does it mean?
- How does it affect the enterprise?

Knowledge management is the natural outgrowth of several older methods of dealing with information. Organizations originally operated under the belief that it was sufficient to store data and information in large repositories (databases) and to access what was needed to create financial reports. In the 1980s database analysts and researchers began to realize the value of what their organizations knew. In the 1990s that realization developed into the understanding that the most successful organizations were capable of learning faster than their competition. The root of learning faster is in knowing how to answer such questions as those listed above. Organizations are using knowledge management (KM) and its components (e.g., business intelligence, data mining, data warehousing) to create and improve their learning environments.

## BASICS

At the very base of KM is the realization that data and information are not knowledge; they are the elements that make up knowledge. Information stored for posterity—but unused—will not create knowledge that an organization can use to learn or to improve itself. Today there are enormous amounts of data impinging on us as individuals and as organizations, information that requires that we organize it into usable knowledge. Organizations need to improve how they use the huge amount of information that they have available to them. The first step in this is to define knowledge and how to obtain and use it. Various definitions of KM have been offered as it has grown culturally and technically. For this entry's purposes, KM is defined as the identification, acquisition, creation, verification, indexing, storage, delivery, and sharing of information, and the application of that knowledge to an organization's planning and development. Even though KM grew out of technology (e.g., databases, spreadsheets, analysis tools), knowledge managers began to realize that technology was not the driving force or even the most important factor in creating and using knowledge. The most important change that KM has undergone in the last 10 years is the realization that managing knowledge is a cultural and social process more than it is a technical process.

## CULTURAL AND SOCIAL CHANGES ABOUT KNOWLEDGE MANAGEMENT

It is a recent realization that knowledge is the most valuable asset an organization possesses. Knowledge management began as an outgrowth of database technology and was an attempt to assemble and control organizational knowledge. It is difficult for those inside an organization to share their knowledge with others if they believe that some person or group has control of the knowledge. All organizations are political, and employees quickly realize that giving up knowledge into a controlled, political system might not be to their advantage. The tendency of the individual is to hold onto knowledge possessed. As organizations began to realize that knowledge is a strategic asset, managing it became more important than just arranging more data.

Actually, KM is a cultural change and growth process. First, knowledge must be shared. Sharing knowledge must be based in trust and in face-to-face interaction. To share knowledge, tacit knowledge—knowledge internal to individuals—must be converted to explicit knowledge and codified. Second, because knowledge arrives in many modes, the users must be multi-literate. It is not sufficient to be "information literate"; today's users must be able to employ many literacies: media literacy, visual literacy, numerical literacy, text literacy, social literacy. Third, KM is a disciplined approach to using knowledge—not a specific technology or product. Any KM that creates value must link knowledge to an organization's strategic goals, to the work processes, and to the cultural, physical, and virtual environments of the organization. Fourth, for an organization to successfully implement KM, the management must be aware of and be the driving force behind the cultural changes that will take place as KM is developed and as employees learn that the more they exchange information, the more the organization becomes a "learning organization." After the social and cultural change process is in place—about 90% of the effort—the technology can be selected and built around the social and cultural framework. It is important to remember that the technology is just a tool to collect, access, and disburse the knowledge.

## APPLYING KNOWLEDGE MANAGEMENT

Even though cultural changes need to be planned and in place before the technology can be used, it is good to have simultaneous awareness of the current and developing technologies that KM utilizes. Most KM begins with capturing physical information by:

- Scanning technology used to enter physical documents into computer storage as pictures. The pictures of the documents are retrievable and viewable, but not searchable or modifiable.
- Character recognition techniques to allow scanned document pictures to be converted to electronic documents. This software can be used to recognize handwritten documents through intelligent character recognition (ICR) and printed documents through optical character recognition (OCR).
- Data entry of information into databases, spreadsheets, or electronic documents to create new information.
- Capturing digital documents to bring various existing electronic documents into a database and to create indices to allow access and retrieval.
- Interviewing employees, ex-employees, and vendors to collect business policies, practices, rules, processes, procedures, lessons learned, and business experience (both general and specific to the organization). The tacit information is collected, indexed, and coded into explicit knowledge. The knowledge is then stored in accessible data warehouses where it can be researched and used by other employees and organizational partners.

After knowledge is collected, codified, and stored, the original information has to be managed so that it can be searched on demand. Among the technology available for managing documents are:

- Computer-output laser disk (COLD) on laser disks, CD-ROM, or DVD media.

- Network storage on storage area networks (SAN) and network attached storage (NAS).
- Microfiche filming of individual physical documents (pictures of documents—viewable, but not searchable).
- Computer output microfiche (COM) outputs microfiche (rather than paper) directly from a computer. Again, these are pictures of reports on film and are viewable but not searchable.
- Databases (e.g., Access, SQL, Oracle), spreadsheets (e.g., Excel), word processing documents (e.g., Word, WordPerfect), HTML-based documents (Hypertext Markup Language), and XML documents (Extensible Markup Language). These types of documents are viewable, searchable, and—best of all—already electronically stored.
- Physical paper reports have been the normal output record for several decades, but are bulky to store and hard to access and to search. However, they are easy to read.

The data, in all their varied formats, are stored in a data warehouse. The warehouse is more than a database because it includes all types of data and a workflow process for users to access them, convert them into knowledge, and share them with other users. Because knowledge needs to be classified, data dictionaries of meta-data are built. The data warehousing process includes capturing the data, collecting information about the data, creating meta-data, cataloging the data, storing on- and offline data, cleaning the data (i.e., making all the data fit the same standards), converting data formats, and navigating the data. Data warehousing also includes protecting the data and knowledge value by managing the physical security of access to the knowledge, electronic security of the knowledge, the backup and recovery processes, and disaster preparedness.

After the data are stored, the organization can begin to use access techniques to convert the raw data in the data warehouse into knowledge that can be used, shared, and reconstructed in many formats. Techniques to convert data into knowledge include statistical analysis, logical analysis, performance analysis, and data mining (extraction of predictive knowledge). Knowledge about the organization and operations may then be used in content management and presentation systems, learning management systems, work flow systems, business rules, group work, and group sharing systems.

## THE PAYOFF FOR DISTRIBUTED EDUCATION

Three basic prerequisites are necessary to successfully use organizational knowledge:

1. Realizing that the organization's knowledge is its most valuable asset
2. Realizing that the data and information an organization holds are not knowledge until converted, verified, and made accessible
3. Realizing that the resulting knowledge needs to be managed

After an organization comes to these conclusions and begins to develop and deploy knowledge management, there will be a dramatic effect on an institution's administrative, academic, and financial users.

Academic users will be able to share knowledge more rapidly and more easily. Online access to grades, the grading process, and transcripts will facilitate the records process for students—it will even allow students and faculty to take care of their own records needs without the help of a physical data clerk. Managing the content of the curriculum, access to coursework—both online and offline—and course information will also allow students and faculty to access more quickly and accurately the information they need. Online course registration will reduce the student's dependence on physical presence and staff resources, allowing the staff to be reassigned to other duties.

Administrative users will have immediate access to records and student information. They will also have faster and more current access to marketing and recruitment information. Access to organizational tacit knowledge (in an explicit and logical fashion) will shorten training cycles and improve service and support for the students and faculty. Financial users will be able to do online bidding and procurement, take online applications (and collect funds immediately), collect financial aid information and disburse funds electronically, and make online payments. Online access to business and financial records will allow business to continue whether users are local, remote, or traveling. Using data mining and business intelligence techniques on the organizational knowledge will allow more informed fiscal decisions to be made.

The Fielding Graduate Institute provides examples of the value of KM in the area of distributed education.

Because Fielding Graduate Institute's users are distributed, the organization has developed online systems to access the knowledge that is available for faculty and students. The faculty have online access to papers written by students. They can review the student's work, make suggestions, collaborate with students and other faculty about the work, and grade the work in an online environment that is an access point to the databases. Students are able to set up coursework and contract with faculty, and the resulting agreements are stored in the database. The knowledge base will also issue certificates of completion for coursework automatically upon course and grading completion. The knowledge base at Fielding Graduate Institute also includes students' access to their own information and their ability to keep their own records up-to-date. All of these types of access save the students and faculty time waiting for papers or grades to arrive. Time saved from automation of these processes equates to money saved for students, faculty, and staff.

Students and faculty also have access to the knowledge and search capabilities of an online library database that provides tools for research into knowledge stored in Fielding Graduate Institute databases and repositories at other institutions of higher education. The library knowledge base includes access to abstracts, reference indices, full-text journal articles, and books.

## CONCLUSION

Ultimately, managing organizational knowledge will improve access to that knowledge, allow users to improve their understanding of the organization and its processes, facilitate sharing the knowledge, and enhance collaboration and improve responsiveness without increasing staff. Using the knowledge base and workflow processes will reduce—not eliminate— the amount of paper necessary and decrease the number of users who need to be involved in each element of daily operations. Data mining and statistical analysis will improve executive reporting, key marketing and recruitment decisions, and strategic planning.

*—Phil Beneker*

*See also* Strategic Planning

## Bibliography

Brown, J. S., and Duguid, P. (2000). *The social life of information.* Cambridge, MA: Harvard Business School Press.

Davenport, Thomas H., & Prusak, Laurence. (2000). *Working knowledge.* Cambridge, MA: Harvard Business School Press.

Dixon, Nancy M. (2000). *Common knowledge: How companies thrive by sharing what they know.* Cambridge, MA: Harvard Business School Press.

Drucker, Peter. (1993). *Post-capitalist society.* New York: Harper Business Press.

Grayson, C. J., & O'Dell, Carla S. (1998). *If only we knew what we know: The transfer of internal knowledge and best practice.* New York: Free Press.

Liebowitz, Jay. (1999). *Knowledge management handbook.* Boca Raton, FL: CRC Press.

Lyman, P., & Varian, H. R. (2002). *How much information?* Retrieved from http://www.sims.berkeley.edu/research/projects/how-much-info/summary.html.

Senge, Peter M. (1990). *The fifth discipline: The art and practice of the learning organization.* New York: Doubleday.

Tiwana, Amrit. (1999). *The knowledge management toolkit: Practical techniques for building a knowledge management system.* Upper Saddle River, NJ: Prentice Hall.

Von Krogh, Georg, Ichijo, Kazuo, & Nonaka, Ikujiro. (2000). *Enabling knowledge creation: How to unlock the mystery of tacit knowledge and release the power of innovation.* Oxford: Oxford University Press.

# LEARNING CIRCLES

*Online learning circles* are teams of learners situated in a small number of schools (5–10) who share a common goal of acquiring a deeper understanding of topics arranged around themes. They exchange ideas on a set of related projects defined by each of the participants. For example, in a "Places and Perspectives" learning circle, students might share views on a current ethnic conflict, describe local heroes, create international timelines, conduct World War II interviews, simulate letter writing during the 1850s, and create cost-of-living place profiles. The norm of reciprocity is critical; the expectation is that each team will contribute in some way to each of the circle projects. The learning circle is a task-based learning community; the task for students is to summarize their learning in a circle booklet, report, or newspaper. Each school team is responsible for collecting and summarizing the circle work on the topic they sponsored. The outcome—a record of the collective circle thinking—is published collaboratively by everyone in the circle.

## CHARACTERISTICS OF A LEARNING CIRCLE

Distinguishing characteristics of online learning circles are diversity, respect, project-based learning, reciprocity, and phase-structured interaction.

*Diversity.* Although learning circles are a form of "community" learning, the goal is to unite people with diverse perspectives, in contrast to a goal of collecting like-minded people. Cross-cultural awareness involves learning how people who look very similar are different and how people who look different are similar. Local communities and neighborhoods offer a limited range of variability. Network learning can extend the range of interactions, helping students from different regions of the world understand how their cultural lenses provide different images and understandings on similar topics.

*Respect.* Discussions take place in the somewhat neutral ground of cyberspace, attempting to create an atmosphere of mutual trust and understanding. In some cases, the distance and the lack of visual markers make it easier to engage people whose different physical appearance, ethnicity, age, gender, linguistic styles, socioeconomic characteristics, or capabilities might impede communication. Instead, the "voice" created in cyberspace creates the impression of the writer. Well-dressed students in a suburban neighborhood school and students with purple spiked hair, tattoos, or torn clothes do not often share the same context; however, learning circles make it somewhat easier to share ideas across these boundaries, increasing student sensitivity to common human conditions.

*Project-Based Learning.* The results of project-based learning are most effective when the learning is well integrated with curricular objectives of a larger unit of study. The teaming of classrooms from around the world brings together teachers who have very different curricular objectives. Because it is not possible for a single project to be connected to the diverse curricula of the participants, learning circles match student teams around themes and use multiple projects. Each classroom team takes the leadership role in sponsoring a project that extends their classroom curriculum. The majority of the whole-class work is directed to designing, collecting, and analyzing the work of their circle partners on their sponsored project. By dividing the class into teams, students respond to the projects sponsored by other schools concurrently.

*Reciprocity.* Each class depends on others in the circle for information. At the same time, they serve as the source of regional knowledge for others. Although there is a circle facilitator, the learning circle is an exercise in participatory management. The participants are the leaders of their project, and the leaders are also participants in the projects of others. The circle facilitator reflects back on and monitors the progress as participants work on the projects. The goal is to have at least one person from each class team participate in each circle project. The circle facilitator often charts the progress so that the degree of reciprocity of work is evident to the group.

*Phase Structure for Interactivity.* Learning circles are highly interactive, participatory settings in which the goal is to discover, share, and express knowledge through a process of open dialogue and deep reflection around issues or problems. Each class team makes a commitment to the circle to help make the projects of the other teams a success. The phase structure begins with the organization of the circle. The classroom teachers read the teachers' guide, and mutual expectations and understandings are established. The circle opens with activities to build trust and cohesion. The circle then frames the projects, students exchange their work, and they organize the publication. This brings the circle to a close.

## THE ORGANIZATIONAL SUPPORT OF LEARNING CIRCLES

Learning circle structure provides a strong sense of "ownership" of the issues, a connection between personal experiences and group perspectives, and strategies for finding common ground. If circle participants engage in active, respectful dialogue there is not a strong need for a leader to orchestrate the interaction. There does, however, need to be a larger structure that supports the organization of the circles. This can be an educational institution, a civic organization, or a service organization. This group sets up the process,

assigns people to circles, organizes the facilitation, establishes the timeline, designs the infrastructure, distributes common resources, and collects and shares the resulting publications. The organization provides the links among the individual learning circles, making it possible for them to work collaboratively both as members of their circle and as members of the community.

Examples of organizations that use this online learning circle model illustrate the way this structure operates within communities. The first online learning circles were supported by the AT&T Learning Network from 1987–1996; in 1997 they moved to the Internet, supported by the International Education and Resource Network. In Mexico, the Secretaría de Educación de Nuevo Leóns supports "Los Círculos de Aprendizaje." Learning circles also connect students from South Africa, Jamaica, Ghana, Zimbabwe, and the Netherlands through a project called "Global Teenagers." Another project that uses some aspects of the learning circle structure and teacher guide is the "Friends and Flags Project" organized in Israel by Karren Eine. At the teacher development level, Bank Street College and Education Development Corporation have incorporated some aspects of learning circles in their design of the "Mathematic Learning Forums." More recently, learning circles are being used as one of the mechanisms of online peer collaboration in the Master of Arts Educational Technology Program at Pepperdine University.

## BRIEF HISTORY OF FACE-TO-FACE LEARNING CIRCLES

The use of a circle as both the layout and a metaphor for a meeting of equals is as old as the use of fire. Circles have been used as a mechanism for organizing and honoring collective wisdom in many indigenous cultures. For example "wisdom circles" brought together early native councils of elders to discuss problems in a spirit of shared community respect while honoring and respecting the voice of each person. The circle is also an integral symbol in the spiritual community of Buddhists.

An early use of learning or "study circles" as an informal vehicle for adult learning and social change was the Chautauqua Assembly in New York, founded in 1870. It used study circles as a means of postsecondary education for those that might not have had access to colleges. The assembly would send out packets of discussion materials, and small groups would form and meet to discuss the ideas in a democratic forum. Instead of material being delivered in a lecture, citizens would learn from the process of collaborative discussions with their peers.

Learning circles have served as an effective strategy and method to help people come to terms with important social and political issues. They have been instrumental in community learning with clear links to social change. Over time and across countries, civic organizations, neighborhood communities, trade unions, churches, and social justice groups have used them to empower their members to make choices and take action.

College educators involved in service learning use learning circles to structure their yearly conference in place of more traditional meeting formats. They do this because the learning circle embodies democratic principles of effective service-learning college/community partnerships—principles of equal participation, of give and take, and of honoring collective wisdom.

The use of community-wide study circles or learning circles fosters new connections among community members, leading to increased participation in community action. They create a structure for connecting citizens and government, both at an institutional level and among community members. Learning Circles Australia and Study Circles in the United States provide extensive examples of how the learning circle model operates in face-to-face settings.

## THE FORMATION OF ONLINE LEARNING CIRCLES

Beginning in the 1980s, researchers began to see the potential of linking computers to emerging online contexts and using them for students to engage in global cross-classroom learning. The Intercultural Learning Network was one early effort that provided the context for thinking about how to structure online learning for large groups of students while maintaining the sense of ownership and connection to classroom learning. At the time there were a number of emerging models, including paired students (computer pals) and paired schools (sister schools), schools grouped around a single project idea or plan, and large discussion forums around an idea or subject area. Learning circles provided for small, participatory, democratic team learning within a larger educational structure.

More recently, learning circles are being used as part of the online structure of courses at Pepperdine University as a form of collaborative support for adults engaged in action research in their workplace. Although each student in the graduate program has his or her own research, they are consultants, advisers, and critical friends on the research of their colleagues in the learning circle.

## LEARNING BENEFITS FOR STUDENTS AND TEACHERS

Computer-mediated communication allows teachers and students to work cooperatively with peers around the world, and gives students purpose and audience for their writing. This process helps students realize the diversity of world views and the role of language in organizing experience. It provides teachers an extensive professional and educational resource.

This multi-project team approach to exploring and solving real-world problems provides a strategy for integrating projects with classroom activities and situating knowledge and skills in a community of learners. The open structure of learning circles encourages teachers to share their best teaching activities with their peers. However, a structure that encourages creativity is subject to projects of uneven quality. Although many teachers demonstrate unusual skill, talent, and creativity in the design of network learning from the beginning, other teachers find it takes time and experimentation. One or more projects may appear superficial to teachers with more experience. Sometimes a specific simulation may interest a majority of the circle, and yet be of little interest to a specific teacher or class. Each learning circle contains a unique set of people who create a specific learning context. Teachers who have participated in dozens of learning circles view them in much the same way they do different years of teaching—different groups of students lead to very different teaching and learning experiences.

Do students who work across classrooms learn any more or any better than students within an enclosed classroom? This is an important question with only partial answers. The learning circle concept evolved from research that suggested that writing for a distant peer audience improved language skills. The use of standardized and controlled tests in the area of writing and language mechanics makes it easier to assess the benefits in this area.

Teachers and students report other benefits that are more difficult to quantify: deeper understandings of issues from multiple perspectives, increased sensitivity to multicultural differences, systemic awareness of social/global issues, and the development of cooperative team skills. For example, teachers report that students spontaneously found and shared stories or information about places to which they were connected and were more interested in events and people in these locations. They would share these reports with their partners and often hear very different perspectives. Sometimes the requests from network partners resulted in students searching for the best ways to describe themselves. For example, Alaskan students invited The Elders to come to their class and help them answer questions about their Eskimo way of life, and thus about themselves. Learning circle discussions often approach controversial issues. Regional and cultural values can lead to very different judgments of what is appropriate for students, and this in itself is a very interesting learning experience. Cross-classroom collaboration often provides rich learning opportunities for exploring and understanding systemic relationships, but the use of these opportunities depends on the skill of the teacher who directs the learning. It is unlikely that these openings will lead to systemic understandings without the skill of experienced teachers using these openers to encourage further research on these topics.

Knowledge constructed through interaction with community leaders, teachers, and classmates is likely to be retained long after information memorized from books is forgotten. The teachers' role shifts because they often walk a very fine line between encouraging student research in their community and ensuring that students are not indoctrinated with a single position on controversial issues.

Qualitative analysis of learning circles suggests that they also contribute to the teacher's knowledge. Teachers collaborate with other educators without leaving their classroom, developing flexible and creative ways to extend learning by using technology. Their exchanges encourage the diffusion of creative ideas, provide support for difficult challenges, and create a vehicle for cooperative plans to renew schools. In survey results, teachers list their own professional development as one of the most significant reasons for continued participation. The degree and intensity of these changes vary, and are often difficult to predict. These areas need more systematic exploration.

More information about learning circles can be found at these Internet locations:

- *IEARN*—Online learning circles, including a link to the Learning Circles Teacher Guide: http://www.iearn.org/circles
- *Educators for Community Engagement*—Use of learning circles to structure a yearly conference: http://www.e4ce.org/ng2002.htm
- *Learning circles for social causes in Australia*—http://www.learningcircles.org.au
- Study circles for political issues in the United States—http://www.studycircles.org

*—Margaret Riel*

*See also* CURRICULUM MODELS; LEARNING COMMUNITIES; ONLINE LEARNING ENVIRONMENTS

## Bibliography

Campbell, S. A. (1998). *A guide for training study circle facilitators*. Retrieved from http://www.studycircles.org/pdf/training.pdf.

Deming, W. E. (1993). *The new economics for industry, government and education.* Cambridge: MIT Center for Advanced Engineering Study.

Garfield, C., Spring, C., & Cahill, S. (1998). *Wisdom circles: A guide to self-discovery and community building in small groups.* Sunnyvale, CA: Hyperion.

Levin, J. A., Riel, M., Rowe, R. D., & Boruta, M. J. (1984). Muktuk meets Jacuzzi: Computer networks and elementary school writers. In S. W. Freedman (Ed.), *The acquisition of written language* (pp. 160–171). Hillsdale, NJ: Ablex.

Levin, J., Riel, M., Miyake, N., & Cohen, M. (1987). Education on the electronic frontier: Tele-apprentices in globally distributed educational contexts. *Contemporary Educational Psychology, 12,* 254–260.

Riel, M. (1985). The computer chronicles newswire: A functional learning environment for acquiring literacy skills. *Journal of Educational Computing Research, 1,* 317–337.

Riel, M. (1987). The intercultural learning network. *The Computing Teacher Journal, 14,* 27–30.

Riel, M. (1989). Four models of educational telecommunications: Connections to the future. *Education & Computing, 5,* 261–274.

Riel, M. (1990). Cooperative learning across classrooms in electronic learning circles. *Instructional Science, 19,* 445–466.

Riel, M., & Harasim, L. (1994). Research perspectives on network learning. *The International Journal of Machine-Mediated Learning, 4*(2 & 3), 91–114.

Riel, M., & Polin, L. (in press). Communities as places of learning. In Barab, S. A., Kling, R., & Gray, J. (Eds.), *Designing for virtual communities in the service of learning.* Cambridge, MA: Cambridge University Press.

# LEARNING COMMUNITIES

A *learning community* is a group of people who share knowledge about a topic, connect with each other, and create common practices. *Communities of practice, learning networks,* and *knowledge networks* are other common terms for learning communities. All organizations contain informal networks of people who share ideas and help each other with everyday work problems. Sometimes these networks congeal around a topic and the network forms spontaneously into a learning community. The topic could be a discipline, such as geology, biochemistry, social work, or civil engineering. Or it could cross several disciplines, such as a type of oil field, people who serve a particular customer, or an emerging technology. These spontaneous learning communities spring from people's natural need to learn from and help each other. They typically have no formal structure, explicit goal, or recognition from the organizations in which they form. Community members typically help each other solve problems, offer their advice, and develop new approaches or tools for their field.

When first forming, the difference between spontaneous learning communities and personal networks is that communities focus on a topic. However, over time members of a learning community can form a strong sense of common identity and shared practice. Learning communities often focus on topics members have spent years studying and feel passionate about, such as a scientific, technical, or professional discipline. As a result, they often develop emotionally strong bonds with other members. Regularly helping each other makes it easier for community members to show their weak spots and learn together in the "public space" of the community. Frequently, one or more members feel a strong enough sense of obligation to the community that they informally take on a leadership role, networking among members, organizing meetings, and identifying good tools, techniques, and approaches.

As community members share ideas and experiences, they develop a shared way of doing things—a set of common practices. Sometimes they formalize these in guidelines and standards, but often they simply remain "what everybody knows" about good practice. In a long-lived community, members' contact with each other can become deep and rich enough that they develop an intimate knowledge of how each person practices their craft. Although participation is purely voluntary, spontaneous learning communities continue because the advice and camaraderie members receive from each other are worth the time it takes to participate.

## INTENTIONAL LEARNING COMMUNITIES

Recognizing the effectiveness of spontaneous learning communities at developing and sharing knowledge, some companies have begun forming intentional communities and using them to help manage the knowledge in their organization, asking the community to connect practitioners of that field of knowledge, organize and maintain the documents and other materials related to it, and develop best practices. Other companies have simply seeded learning communities by providing them with information technology, meeting rooms, tools, and funds to travel for face to face events. This light handed support is often enough to stimulate the networking that is at the heart of learning communities. Still other organizations have built learning communities into their organizational strategy by forming communities around strategic organizational issues, like developing a new organizational capability, sharing expertise that exists in disparate pockets of the organization, bringing new members of a field up to speed, or developing, organizing, and sharing best practices. When forming these more strategically oriented learning communities, companies usually provide them with considerably more resources, such as a full-time leader, time for core members to participate, and funds to hire researchers, support staff, or members to develop best practices. These strategic communities also often ask particular experts to participate, such as thought leaders or representatives from different divisions or geography. In exchange, companies often ask strategic learning communities to provide specific deliverables, such as an agreed-upon approach to a particular work process, a set of documented procedures, or best practices. But even these more formal learning communities remain networks of people who are passionate about a topic, share insights, and develop a common approach to that topic.

## LEARNING COMMUNITIES CROSS BOUNDARIES

Even though people participate in communities for their personal benefit, learning communities are a vehicle for knitting an organization together across boundaries. Learning communities have a fluidity that most other organizational structures lack. Because they are formed around a fairly wide topic, rather than a particular piece of work, they often shift focus as the needs of their members change. Because most members' participation is voluntary, the size and composition of the community shifts as members change their level of participation, new members join, and old members drop out. As a result, learning communities can link people together from different teams, divisions, business units, and geographical areas, crossing organizational boundaries without creating conflicts of organizational structure or placing members in a position of balancing conflicting loyalties. The community is the members' resource for getting help with everyday work. As organizations become more global, many have realized that they have pockets of knowledge in different locations, and learning communities are a fluid and relatively simple method for knitting those pockets together. Community members participate to pursue their personal passion, but in doing so they strengthen the social fabric of the organization.

## FUNCTIONS OF A LEARNING COMMUNITY

Learning communities typically engage in four basic activities: helping each other, developing and sharing best practices, stewarding a body of knowledge, and fostering innovation. Although most communities engage in all of these functions, communities often focus primarily on one.

*Helping.* Most communities have some mechanisms for community members to help each other solve everyday problems and share ideas. To do this communities need both a method to connect with other members and forums for sharing ideas. For example, scientists in an oil technology service firm post requests for help or ideas in a threaded discussion that runs on the community's Web site. Typically, several people respond in the threaded discussion, and then those involved discuss the issue on the telephone or through e-mail. The Web facilitates connections; the help occurs mostly one-on-one. Of course, when getting advice from other community members, the individual must rely on his or her own judgment about the soundness of the advice.

*Best-Practice Sharing.* Some communities focus primarily on developing, validating, and disseminating specific practices. When developing best practices, communities use a specific process to verify the effectiveness and benefit of practices. For example, in a manufacturing company, the best practice replication process begins with a standard form for operators and engineers to describe a new practice and calculate its costs and benefits. Several layers of subject matter experts then assess the practice's applicability in other manufacturing plants. Community leaders from each plant meet occasionally to discuss how the best practice replication process is working in their manufacturing area. In addition, plant managers track the number of practices implemented in each of the company's 150 manufacturing plants throughout the world. In communities that focus on sharing best practices, members are tied together through this process of practice identification, verification, and distribution.

*Stewarding Knowledge.* Communities that focus on stewarding a body of knowledge host forums for members to connect and develop new practices, but their main intent is to organize, upgrade, and distribute the knowledge their members use day-to-day. The community takes responsibility for the overall management of the knowledge of the craft, serving its members' everyday needs for information, insight, and help. An international consulting firm, for example, estimates that it has 1.2 million documents in its general, unfiltered repositories; 875,000 documents in its discussion databases; and 50,000 documents organized into comprehensive packs of materials on specific topics. The primary focus of its 150 communities is to find, organize, and distribute these insights throughout the organization. Communities that focus on stewarding a body of knowledge typically require considerable staff to organize and manage the community's knowledge.

*Innovation.* Of course, all communities innovate by encouraging individuals to develop and contribute practices. But some communities' specific intent is to foster unexpected ideas and innovations by mixing members who have different perspectives. An automobile manufacturer community connects 240 world experts from many different parts of the company and many different disciplines to assess new directions in research. This community is designed to encourage engineers, marketers, and researchers to see ideas from each other's point of view, and from that clash of perspectives develop more innovations as well as ideas on how those innovations could be realized in new or improved products.

## LEARNING COMMUNITIES AND TRADITIONAL LEARNING

Because learning communities are composed of practitioners collaboratively solving everyday problems and developing new practices, they deal with a different kind of knowledge than traditional learning forums, such as training, mentoring, or libraries. Even when stewarding a body of knowledge, learning communities focus primarily on developing, codifying, and sharing emerging knowledge about the *application* of tools and methods.

As a result, learning communities do not replace other organizational learning mechanisms, but complement the codified knowledge in libraries and training. For example, one organization encourages its technical trainers to participate in communities in their domain. Community discussions help them identify emerging training needs. Mentoring or apprenticeships are also complemented by learning communities because mentoring typically focuses on individual learning needs, whereas communities focus on common ones. In some instances, learning communities take responsibility for mentoring. One community, for example, found that many new practitioners were going to a few individuals who had become well known for their mentoring ability. Because these experts had become overwhelmed with requests, the community divided the newer members among other senior members to more evenly distribute mentoring responsibility.

## COMMUNITIES FILL A SOCIAL NEED

It is interesting that learning communities have become increasingly popular as globalization has loosened many people's ties to their geographic neighborhoods. By providing a forum in which members can ask for help, express their ideas and opinions, share insights, and get to know each others' strengths and weaknesses, community members develop a kind of craft intimacy with each other. Perhaps this intimacy, even though it is limited to a technical or professional discipline, helps assuage an eroding sense of human connection many people experience in other areas of their lives.

*—Richard McDermott*

*See also* COLLABORATION; LEARNING CIRCLES; SOCIOTECHNICAL ISSUES; VIRTUAL COMMUNITIES

### Bibliography

Brown, John S., & Duguid, Paul. (2000). *The social life of information.* Boston: Harvard Business School Press.

McDermott, Richard. (1999). How information technology inspired, but cannot deliver knowledge management. *California Management Review, 41,* 4.

Saint-Onge, Hubert, & Wallace, Deb. (2002). *Communities of practice.* Boston: Butterworth-Heinemann.

Wenger, Etienne, McDermott, Richard, & Snyder, William. (2002). *Cultivating communities of practice.* Boston: Harvard University Press.

# LEARNING ENVIRONMENTS

Distributed education learning environments were initially conceptualized as the extension of traditional classrooms and teachers, usually via lecture formats, to new locations. In addition to correspondence study, which involved a single learner studying with a teacher independently at a distance, the most common form of distributed education throughout the decade of the 1980s was the connection of off-campus learners at scheduled times via electronic technologies such as audio conferencing, video conferencing, or computer conferencing. Very often, especially when utilizing video connections, learners traveled to a central location, such as a community site or an educational center, to access the technology and to meet with other learners.

These traditionally structured and institutionally framed definitions of distributed and distance education resulted in pedagogical strategies that originally focused on content presentation, primarily through readings and/or lectures. Learning environments were heavily dependent on teacher-directed instructional goals and activities. This dimension of distributed education is rapidly changing as systems have become more robust in their connective capabilities and technology access in homes and businesses has improved.

## NEW LEARNING ENVIRONMENTS

New learning environments are emerging, in which learners are dynamically connected through the Internet and other advanced technologies with each other, with faculty mentors, and with institutional academic support structures in ways not imagined just a few years ago. Choices regarding pedagogy, technology, culture, and strategy are becoming increasingly complex and blurred. These emerging learning environments have come into prominence in concert with a set of new learning theories, especially constructivist learning theory, that builds on the work of diverse thinkers such as John Dewey and Lev Vygotsky. Both Dewey and Vygotsky argued strongly that learning occurs most effectively when connected to the personal experience and knowledge base of the learner, and when situated in a social context in which the learner leads the "construction" of his or her own knowledge through interaction with others and with guidance from the teacher. Constructivist learning theory suggests a much more active role for the learner in initiating and directing his or her own learning, with the teacher's role being to create and facilitate learning environments that encourage interaction among learners as well as with the teacher.

More specifically, constructivist principles suggest that effective learning environments should: 1) encourage the engagement of the learner with both the content and other learners; 2) create systematic opportunities within and outside of the "classroom" for learners to learn and to demonstrate or model what has been learned; and 3) involve assessment strategies that enable the growth and development of the learner in personally meaningful and measurable ways. In summary, emerging learning environments are changing from being the product of an "industrial process of mass distribution of knowledge," to becoming a process whereby learners' needs for knowledge are addressed through customized and highly personal strategies that are initiated by the learner with assistance from and in consultation with the teacher.

## EFFECTIVE LEARNING ENVIRONMENTS

Art Chickering and Stephen Ehrmann define seven principles of good teaching practice as a framework for organizing new learning environments. Positive learning environments encourage the following:

1. Learner–teacher contact
2. Cooperation among learners
3. Active learning by doing
4. Prompt feedback
5. Task orientation
6. High expectations for learning
7. A safe context where diverse talents and ways of learning are respected

Multiple terms have emerged to describe learning environments that foster these characteristics and that are based on constructivist learning theory. Terms such as *collaborative learning, cooperative learning, problem-based learning, communities of practice,* and *learning communities* have joined the common lexicon of the classroom where lecture, discourse, and debate have been dominant methodologies. Other terms, such as *interactive learning, team learning, discourse communities,* and *case teaching,* are also frequently used to describe emerging learning strategies and environments. Although each of these terms carries with it subtle differences in approach, all imply the purposeful creation of active, engaged learning environments.

## COLLABORATIVE, COOPERATIVE, AND TEAM-BASED LEARNING ENVIRONMENTS

Collaborative, cooperative, and team-based learning share a number of basic constructive assumptions about learning. Learning is active, and shared among learners and teachers. The teacher sets the stage for learning to occur, but does not dominate the environment. Group- and team-based activities are frequently used, and individuals accept responsibility and leadership for their own learning and for contributing to the learning of others. Through hands-on activities, learners have the opportunity to test skills and knowledge acquired and to develop higher order thinking skills. Opportunities for exercising leadership help to develop a range of process skills that contribute to future learning capabilities. Learning with others and the development of community help to increase retention and persistence among learners, and opportunities to interact socially help learners to develop a better appreciation and value of, and respect for, the ideas and diverse backgrounds of others.

To be effective, collaborative learning should incorporate and reflect the personal philosophy of the teacher. Fundamentally, collaborative learning relies heavily on the input, direction, and shaping of content by learners. Collaborative learning also frequently involves the creation of teams. Within the collaborative classroom, group members share authority and responsibility, and all are equally responsible for the group's actions. The role of the teacher is to frame the context of interaction in ways that respect and highlight group members' abilities and contributions. Team-based learning builds on collaborative learning strategies by integrating the development of leadership, facilitation, and problem-solving skills into overall goals for learning.

Like collaborative learning, cooperative learning involves learners working together closely in groups to achieve joint learning, with one subtle but important difference. Within cooperative learning, the teacher provides more structure for, focus on, and design of the learning activities the group pursues, including specifying intended learning outcomes. Cooperative learning emanates from the philosophical writings of John Dewey, stressing the social nature of learning, and the work on group dynamics by Kurt Lewin. Despite these subtle differences, cooperative and collaborative learning provide systematic models for approaching the classroom through the lens of the learner.

## PROBLEM-BASED LEARNING ENVIRONMENTS

Problem-based learning is an even more structured form of cooperative learning in which individual and group learning emerges from learners interacting with problems that are created, organized, and presented by the instructor. Correct and incorrect solutions to problems are often anticipated by the instructor, and feedback and discussion focus on amplifying and understanding why problems can be approached from multiple perspectives, with each perspective being more or less suitable to the problem.

Although problem-based learning involves teamwork, cooperation, and collaboration, its structure always implies a prominent role for the teacher

both in developing the problem and in assessing the performance of the teams or groups addressing the problem. Designing effective problems, creating appropriate and pleasant learning environments, contributing knowledge to help learners address the problem, and stimulating critical evaluation of ideas are all expectations for effective teachers using problem-based learning. The teacher closely monitors, but does not interfere with, learner efforts to address a problem, and is readily available to act as a consultant when assistance is requested.

Defining the problem appropriately and effectively is critical for learning to occur. Problem-based learning is often employed in professional fields such as medicine, business, and law; however, it is increasingly employed in a range of disciplines to help learners think creatively beyond the boundaries of the classroom.

## LEARNING COMMUNITIES AND COMMUNITIES OF PRACTICE

Learning communities are intentionally created environments for learning that bridge courses, programs, academic departments, or living facilities to create a joint quest for learning among members and participants. As Parker Palmer suggests, a major goal of the learning community is to create a safe psychological climate or a space for learning, enabling learners with different backgrounds, ethnicities, religions, and other characteristics to learn from each other intensively and cooperatively. Learning communities are often designed to integrate diverse disciplines and fragmented curricula. Like other forms of collaborative learning, they are also intended to build social and team skills, increase enthusiasm for learning, reduce attrition rates from courses and institutions, and validate the worth of each student as a person and learner.

Communities of practice are learning communities designed especially for professionals who need to keep up with current ideas, knowledge, and applications in a field or discipline. Learning within a community of practice becomes an act of membership in the community, and a way of validating one's own professional perspectives and knowledge within the peer group of the profession. Within a community of practice, the processes of learning and membership are intertwined, and learning becomes an act of membership within the community. The goal of the community of practice as a whole is to anticipate and respond to learner needs. It is this goal that sustains the learner's membership in the community. Knowledge is integrated with practice. Learning within a community of practice involves the interaction between doing and knowing; learning is the result of doing. As the Chinese proverb states, "I hear, and I forget; I see, and I remember; I do, and I understand."

## THE ROLE OF DISTRIBUTED EDUCATION TECHNOLOGIES IN CREATING COLLABORATIVE ENVIRONMENTS

One of the major challenges for the future is whether distributed education technologies can truly compensate for the significant advantages of face-to-face environments for collaboration. Many believe that this face-to-face interaction is necessary to overcome feelings of separation and to build trust—a condition widely recognized as necessary for establishing the environment required for collaborative learning.

Constructivist learning environments are predicated on the assumption that individuals learn best not only through designing their own learning experiences within the context of an organized learning experience, but in situations that involve others in pursuit of a common goal. As noted in other sections, collaborative learning contexts are being created in virtual environments through collaborative team-based activities and team-based learning. Although these goals are common to both physical and virtual environments, collaborative and team-based learning face special and critical challenges in virtual environments, including the following:

- Variations in learner interest and readiness to use technology
- Variations in learner interest and readiness to work in teams
- Creating trust and collegiality in virtual, communication-rich environments
- Building trust and feelings of personal safety among team members

## SUMMARY

A major challenge for teachers and organizations in the knowledge age is to transform distributed education learning environments from being teacher-centered and discipline-based to becoming learner-centered, collaborative, and interdisciplinary, in order for learners to gain the skills necessary to live and work in a rapidly changing economy.

*—Donald E. Hanna*

***See also*** Learning Communities

### Bibliography

Chickering, A., & Ehrmann, S. (October 1996). Implementing the seven principles: Technology as lever. *AAHE Bulletin,* 3–6.

Hanna, D. E. (2000). Approaches to learning in collegiate classrooms. In D. E. Hanna and Associates (Eds.), *Higher education in an era of digital competition: Choices and challenges* (pp. 45–69), Madison, WI: Atwood.

Johnson, D. W., Johnson, R., & Holubec, E. (1993). *Circles of learning: Cooperation in the classroom,* 4th ed. Edina, MN: Interaction.

Lambert, L., et al. (1995). *The constructivist leader.* New York: Teachers College Press.

Parker, P. (1998). *The courage to teach: Exploring the inner landscape of a teacher's life.* San Francisco: Jossey-Bass.

Vygotsky, L. (1962). *Thought and language.* Cambridge: MIT Press.

# LEARNING MANAGEMENT SYSTEMS (LMS)

A *learning management system (LMS)* is a set of integrated software services that organizes and supports online learning, education, and training. These systems usually provide content uploading and distribution, class administration, and discussion facilities (asynchronous threaded discussion and, less commonly, synchronous or "chat" services). Some offer additional functionality such as assessment tools for online quizzing and testing; homework submission tools for managing the collection, grading, and redistribution of homework assignments to students in an online class; and student profiling to track the progress and performance of individual students using the system. LMSs are generally obtained in the form of a comprehensive software package that presents a unified graphical user interface (GUI) and a consistent method of navigation to guide the user through the system, and delivers these services through a browser connected to the World Wide Web (Web).

Learning management systems in corporate settings may include a catalog of course offerings, along with the ability to match training opportunities with particular job requirements or professional development goals.

Alternate definitions for LMS include:

Learning Management System is a broad term that is used for a wide range of systems that organize and provide access to online learning services for students, teachers, and administrators. These services usually include access control, provision of learning content, communication tools, and organizations of user groups. (Paulsen, M. F., 2002)

LMS (learning management system): Software that automates the administration of training events. The LMS registers users, tracks courses in a catalog, and records data from learners; it also provides reports to management. An LMS is typically designed to handle courses by multiple publishers and providers. It usually doesn't include its own authoring capabilities; instead, it focuses on managing courses created by a variety of other sources. (Kaplan-Leiserson, E., 2003)

The term *LMS* is predominantly used in the United States; in the United Kingdom the term *virtual learning environment (VLE)* is roughly comparable.

## BACKGROUND AND RELATED TERMS

The exact meaning of LMS is imprecise. Vendors include a wide range of services that differ from one LMS software package to the next. This inexactness is further complicated by variants on the term, such as learning content management system (LCMS), managed learning environment (MLE), course management system (CMS), and content management system (CMS).

## COURSE MANAGEMENT SYSTEM/ CONTENT MANAGEMENT SYSTEM

Two widely used and, unfortunately, functionally related software systems share the same three-letter acronym. CMS could refer to a course management system or to a content management system. Content management systems typically focus on the content itself rather than the learner. They provide ways of entering, managing, distributing, and tracking the use

of defined pieces of content (documents, images, files, or any other arbitrary collection of bits). They typically concentrate their attention on the workflow associated with the life cycle of digital content from ingestion (entrance into the system), through intellectual property management, revision, access control (selective distribution), and reuse. Content management systems often form the back end to large Web sites that populate multiple Web pages with content elements from the same underlying source (usually a database). The fluidity of the term's meaning demonstrates the uncertainty among the producers of this type of software as to exactly what should be included in software systems that deliver education and training to online students, professionals, and adult learners.

The use of the term *course management system* to represent the automated content management and delivery of learning material over the Web probably predates the emergence of LMS. CMS initially described software written to provide online services to assist teaching for an individual class. As the software began to be applied to larger numbers of courses or training modules, developers paid greater attention to the users' experiences of interacting with multiple online courses. This research expanded the feature set for both the instructor or faculty member using the system to teach and the student taking more than one course delivered by a single system. Today, the phrases *enterprise course management system* and *learning management system* are for all practical purposes synonymous.

## LEARNING CONTENT MANAGEMENT SYSTEM (LCMS)

Learning content management systems are similar to content management systems in all areas where content is focused on the management and distribution of learning materials. Current system design emphasizes the benefits associated with separating presentation, logic, and behavior in learning objects; LCMS design implements this separation with the intention of maximizing the reuse of the material it stores. LCMS also includes content creation or authoring tools that make the content developer, not the learner, the primary beneficiary of this software.

## MANAGED LEARNING ENVIRONMENT (MLE)

The term *managed learning environment (MLE)* is used in the United Kingdom to describe software that would be considered a learning management system or VLE if it were integrated into the enterprise student information system, financial record system, and enterprise resource planning systems found in many universities and colleges. The closest equivalent terminology for MLEs in the United States is probably *enterprise learning management system,* connoting the integration of the LMS into the enterprise systems of a university campus or large corporation.

## CONTENT AUTHORING

Learning management systems, course management systems, and even Web pages require digital content. Creating that content requires authoring tools. A basic text editor can be used to embed HTML tags to display formatted text on the Web. Authoring tools could thus include a simple text editor. However, the Web is fundamentally a multimedia environment, requiring authoring tools that support the creation and distribution of multimedia objects. These tools are often classified by the type of complex multimedia content that they produce (for example, simulation authoring tools or assessment authoring tools).

## COMMERCIAL VENDORS

In the United States, the commercial market for learning management systems has well over 100 vendors. Typical among LMS vendors for higher education are Blackboard (www.blackboard.com) and WebCT (www.webct.com). The corporate training LMS contains more differentiated offerings, with vendors typically aligning with particular vertical segments such as human resource training, work skills training, and the like.

Nearly all Web-enabled distance learning uses some type of learning management system to present students with online course materials. The LMS could be installed and run from the university campus or corporate IT unit, or contracted through services known as application service providers (ASPs).

## SCALABILITY AND INTERCONNECTIVITY

Individual developers or faculty members new to learning management systems often initially used them to create supplementary Web pages containing useful course material. As the scope of their objectives expanded from managing the content and student

interactions within one course to handling these issues in multiple courses, developers had to face increasing numbers of users and system load. How this increase in use is addressed determines the scalability of the LMS solution. LMSs must provide high performance as measured in response time from the perspective of the individual user, efficient use of computing resources from the perspective of the system, and higher reliability as the organizations and corporations depending on it shift to view the LMS as a mission-critical resource. Scalability remains a serious concern for large installations such as large universities, multi-campus systems, or large corporations seeking to support their employees' training needs with an LMS operating at one or a few data centers.

Interconnectivity has multiple dimensions. From the perspective of the organization implementing an LMS, interconnectivity refers to the ability to easily integrate the LMS into existing enterprise software systems on which the organization depends. Early LMS implementations were largely stand-alone packages, replicating critical functions such as authorizing users to access learning materials, authenticating an individual trying to access the system as a valid member of the organization or company, and storing user performance records (e.g., course grades) internal to the LMS. Many colleges and companies have already made investments in software systems to handle these functions, but getting the LMS to communicate and securely exchange data with them has required customized programming.

These difficulties have driven a number of efforts including standards development (see the following section) and defining interfaces to provide ways of interconnecting the LMS with other enterprise systems and services. Several large enterprise software system providers have established proprietary interfaces with LMS to connect student records, human resources, and financial records with the LMS. The other side of this problem is the integration of individual, often function-specific software tools into the LMS to provide extended capabilities such as more advanced assessment; instant messaging; and synchronization of content, calendar information, and announcements with personal digital appliances (PDAs). Blackboard, for example, has developed a set of interface definitions it refers to as "Building Blocks" that open up narrow windows into their learning management system to connect specific applications. The open source movement has pushed for standard application programming interfaces (APIs) to accomplish this kind of enterprise integration and feature extension. These APIs would allow application developers to have a common, uniform set of interfaces for which they can code.

## SPECIFICATIONS, STANDARDS, AND OPEN SOURCE

The development of LMSs has been significantly influenced by the emergence of specifications and standards intended to ease system development by vendors, installation and support by implementers, and portability of content for users. Specifications are guidelines and suggestions for implementing something. They are a tool to help the developer, implementer, or administrator make decisions by creating a shared vocabulary and constructs about a particular topic. Specifications, unlike standards, capture rough consensus and evolve rapidly. Standards, on the other hand, are published documents that set out specifications and procedures designed to ensure that a material, product, method, or service, such as a learning management system, meets its purpose and consistently performs to its intended use.

Specifications relevant to learning management systems are those involving data (e.g., IMS Content Packaging) and those pertaining to behavior, that is, how the components of a learning system are expected to work together. Behavioral specifications for learning management systems are emerging from the open source development work underway by the Open Knowledge Initiative (http://web.mit.edu/oki). Data specifications that support exchange of information from one system to another and behavioral specifications that aim to provide functional interoperability of learning system components, as well as smooth LMS enterprise infrastructure implementation, are both critical to future learning management systems.

### Relevant Specification Bodies

IMS Global Learning Consortium, Inc. (http://www. imsproject.org)

Advanced Distributed Learning/SCORM (http://www. adlnet.org)

Aviation Industry CBT Committee (http://www. aicc.org)

### Standards Bodies

Institute of Electrical and Electronics Engineers—Learning Technology Standards Committee (http://ltsc. ieee.org/ltsc/)

### Open Source LMS Development

Open Knowledge Initiative (http://web.mit.edu/oki/)

CHEF (University of Michigan) (http://www. chefproject.org)

CourseWork (Stanford University) (http://aboutcourse work.stanford.edu)

Open Learning Management System (http://www. psych.utah.edu/learn/olms/)

—*Phillip D. Long*

*See also* VIRTUAL LEARNING TOOLS

### Bibliography

Carmean, C., & Hafner, J. (2003). Mind over matter: Transforming course management systems into effective learning environments. *EDUCAUSE Review, 37*(6), 27–34.

Edu-tools. Retrieved March 7, 2003, from http://www. edutools.info/index.jsp.

Kaplan-Leiserson, E. (2003). *E-learning glossary.* Retrieved March 6, 2003, from http://www.learningcircuits. org/glossary.html

Long, P. D. (2003, January). Learning management systems: Seeking paradigms for collaboration. *Syllabus.* Retrieved from http://www.syllabus.com/article.asp?id= 7096.

Paulsen, M. F. (July 2002). *Online education systems: Discussion and definition of terms.* Retrieved March 6, 2003, from http://www.nettskolen.com/in_english/ webedusite/

Rossette, Allison. (Ed.). (2002). *The ASTD e-learning handbook: Best practices, strategies, and case studies for an emerging field.* New York: McGraw-Hill.

## LEARNING OBJECTS

Learning objects are digital resources, modular in nature, that are used to support learning. They include, but are not limited to, simulations, electronic calculators, animations, tutorials, text entries, Web sites, bibliographies, audio and video clips, quizzes, photographs, illustrations, diagrams, graphs, maps, charts, and assessments. They vary in size, scope, and level of granularity ranging from a small chunk of instruction to a series of resources combined to provide a more complex learning experience.

There is much debate over what constitutes a learning object. Some researchers differentiate between an information or knowledge object and a learning object. In their view, a knowledge or information object contains only content, with no instructional strategies, whereas a learning object contains instructional content complete with instructional strategies such as a stated objective and outcome and possibly a related assignment and assessment. The Learning Technology Standardization Committee of the IEEE (The Institute of Electrical and Electronics Engineers, commonly referred to as the "Eye-Triple-E") uses a much broader definition and considers "any entity, digital or non-digital, that can be used, re-used or referenced during technology-supported learning" as a learning object. Most educational technology experts agree that for their purposes, a learning object can be any digital resource that can be reused to support learning. It can be accessed and used individually or can be combined into learning modules, complete with the instructional strategies required to create self-contained lessons.

Learning objects and learning modules are often compared to LEGOs, small building blocks that can be assembled, disassembled, and reused to create a variety of larger objects. These objects can then be combined with each other and new LEGO blocks to form bigger and different types of objects. A more sophisticated way to look at learning objects is to envision them as atoms. Unlike LEGOs, atoms must be assembled in a specific order based on their individual makeup and, therefore, not every atom is combinable with every other atom. Furthermore, it takes training and expertise to manipulate atoms, whereas anybody can play with LEGOs.

## A HISTORICAL PERSPECTIVE

Object-oriented environments are not an original notion. Computer science has spun off an entire classification of software applications based on object-oriented programming protocols. The use of learning objects to impart knowledge and skill is not an original

notion; business and industry have applied this concept successfully to training since the mid-1990s. In work influenced by instructional designers Ruth Clark (information mapping) and M. David Merrill (component display theory), Cisco's Worldwide Training department introduced the concept of reusable information objects (RIOs) to support the e-learning needs of its employees and customers. A RIO is defined as a concept, fact, process, principle, or procedure that matches a single learning objective to a specific task (otherwise, it's not a very specific definition). Several RIOs can be combined to create a reusable learning object (RLO). The RLO wraps the pedagogy and context required to meet the learning objective around the RIOs. Components can include an introduction, a summary, and assessment instruments. In 1994, strategist Wayne Hodgins was attributed with coining the phrase *learning objects* when he named a Computer Education Management Association (CedMa) working group "Learning Architectures and Learning Objects."

## ATTRIBUTES OF LEARNING OBJECTS

Although they vary in content, scope, and size, learning objects share a common set of attributes. First, learning objects are self-standing, nonproprietary, media independent, application neutral, and accessible over the Internet. That means that the user should not have to download plug-ins or be required to purchase specialized software or proprietary players in order to access and use the object. Objects should be available through a universally accepted Web browser and work on the commonly used hardware platforms.

Second, learning objects can be recombined and grouped together or accessed as separate units. They can be easily integrated into full-blown lessons or they can be embedded into a just-in-time approach to learning. Just-in-time learning allows learners to customize their own learning or training experiences, taking into account their location and time commitment, their level of knowledge and competency, their learning style preference, and their educational and career goals.

Third, learning objects are designed to be sharable and reusable, which means that the same object can be used in multiple contexts, across a multitude of disciplines. For example, a learning object simulating a volcanic eruption could be used in a geology or geography course and at the same time provide meaningful insight to history students studying Pompeii. The simulation itself might be useful to design students studying animation. One instructor might incorporate the learning object in a class lecture or in online course materials, whereas another might assign it as homework or as review. In another scenario, a student might choose to incorporate it into a multimedia presentation.

Finally, learning objects are searchable on a variety of attributes so that members of disparate disciplines can locate, filter, update, and manage the objects and collections of objects specific to their interests and needs. These objects also have to be identified in ways that allow for sharing and interoperability between servers, Web sites, applications, and popular commercial learning management systems. In order to accomplish this, objects must be tagged with a variety of data descriptors. These data, called *metadata tags,* describe the learning objects' data.

For example, if faculty members in the college of dentistry decide to share their individual collections of images depicting teeth, they would have to develop a common vocabulary of metatags to describe each object in each of their respective collections. One faculty member might be interested in the shape of teeth, whereas another might be interested in trauma to the mouth. An anthropology professor who is researching human teeth formation in a variety of ancient cultures and a forensic scientist looking at dental records to identify corpses would require a very different set of descriptors in order to locate objects in the collection relevant to their individual needs. In order to meet the collective needs of diverse sets of users, a broad set of attributes must be identified, agreed upon, and tagged. In addition, the files need to be described as learning objects, complete with ownership information, technical data, access permissions, version dates, and the like. Metatagging schemes can even manage rights and can assign and electronically collect usage fees.

Numerous groups are currently developing technical metatagging specifications that will allow for universal structural rules, document type definitions, and indexing and retrieval protocols. One example is the U.S. government's Advanced Distributed Learning (ADL) Initiative. It recently released the Shareable Content Object Reference Model (SCORM) as a reference guide for building digital libraries and objects. Another organization, the Instructional Management System (IMS) Global Learning Consortium is in the process of developing open specifications for facilitating online distributed learning activities. In addition,

the Dublin Core Metadata Initiative is an open forum working to develop interoperable online metadata standards to support both education and business.

## REPOSITORIES AND REFERATORIES

Learning objects are accessible and searchable through Web-based repositories and "referatories." A repository and a referatory differ in where the learning object is stored. In a repository, objects reside within a database on the same server that hosts the Web-enabled gateway to the collection. The organization that administers the collection is responsible for updating material and most likely holds some intellectual property rights over the content. In this scenario, the object is usually available only from that particular site. In a referatory, objects are housed on remote servers, and they are linked and accessible through the collection's database-driven gateway. In the referatory model, authors or their institutions host and maintain their own objects. The ownership and intellectual property remains with the author or institution. The same object might be submitted to several collections, sometimes even unbeknownst to the author.

There are two main categories of collections— general and discipline-specific. Within these categories there are open, free access collections and fee-based, proprietary collections. Many sites house a combination of free and fee-based objects, modules, and courses. An example of a free, open-access collection is the Multimedia Educational Resource for Learning and Online Teaching (MERLOT) (http://www.merlot.org). Fathom (http://fathom.com) supports both free and fee-based selections, whereas the Lydia Global Repository (http://www.lydialearn.com) is representative of a fee-based collection. Examples of discipline-specific collections include The Harvey Project for Human Physiology (http://harveyproject.org) and the Science, Math, Engineering and Technology Education (SMETE) Digital Library (http://www.smete.org). The objects associated with these two collections are currently free to use.

Many of the collections provide peer and user reviews of the learning objects. Others support diverse user communities of educators and learners who help the collection grow by contributing materials and adding assignments and user comments. Some provide professionally designed, structured curriculum frameworks for sharing lessons. All comply with some subset of metatagging standards and all boast of powerful and flexible database search engines. A few have unique visual interfaces for navigating content and organizing and presenting knowledge. The fee-based models have built-in mechanisms for aggregating and syndicating copyright-cleared learning content while tracking, managing, and financially rewarding the individual or institution's intellectual property rights.

## ADVANTAGES OF USING LEARNING OBJECTS

The reason that there is so much interest in and excitement about learning objects within the educational community is that they represent a major paradigm shift in learning. Whenever a new technology is introduced it tends to emulate what came previously. For example, when motion pictures were first introduced the technology was used primarily to film plays. When technology was initially used to deliver instruction, content was formatted to imitate the book—a primarily text-based, one-dimensional, and linearly organized delivery model. Learning objects provide an innovative way to mix and match a variety of content modalities and build engaging and flexible learning experiences. Learning objects also take advantage of the computer's inherent power and capability to securely store and quickly retrieve information searched on a wide array of descriptors.

One advantage of using learning objects in teaching is that modular approaches to education encourage competency-based learning. A competency refers to the learner's demonstrated knowledge, skills, or abilities performed to a specific standard or outcome. In a competency-based educational environment, learners can customize their learning pathways to meet their specific needs, oftentimes at their own pace and from the comfort of their home or workplace.

Another advantage is that developing learning objects, in the long run, can save development time and money over developing full-fledged courses. Technology-enhanced course development is very labor intensive and costly. However, in learning object creation, the development team works with much smaller components, and if the final product is tagged correctly, it can be easily located and reused by others, within and across disciplines. This eliminates the cost of developing redundant content, because everything does not have to be "created from scratch" each time.

In addition, because the units are self-standing and granular, they take less time to revise and update. Content can be kept current and new material can be easily interjected into an existing course to reflect a late-breaking and newsworthy event, a new scientific finding, or a shift in topic. There also is revenue potential for learning object authors and/or their institutions if there is market demand for their creations. Learning objects are not only the purview of industry and higher education. K–12 educational institutions, government agencies, publishers, libraries, public television and radio stations, and museums are all wrestling with how to translate analog data into accessible and reusable digital content.

Finally, the use of learning objects provides an opportunity for students and others in a community of practice to participate and be co-contributors in the teaching and learning process. This sharing of knowledge and dynamic interaction engages both teachers and learners. That translates into a richer and more productive educational experience.

## DISADVANTAGES OF USING LEARNING OBJECTS

The major disadvantage to introducing learning objects into the traditional curriculum is that it represents a huge educational paradigm shift. Adhering to a curriculum composed of learning objects and modules means that the teacher is no longer the sole expert in the class. Furthermore, the standard lecture, the text-based course notes, and the essay exam are not always conducive to granularity and online delivery. The student would be better served if these traditional instructional strategies were replaced by learning modules composed of interactive simulations, audio/video examples, problem-based case studies, and competency-based portfolios. It also takes time, talent, and an upfront monetary investment to deconstruct and convert course content into this new framework and to develop new material. Faculty members can tackle development on their own, but it would be best to invest in the talents of a professional team made up of the faculty member serving as content specialist, instructional designers and technologists, graphic designers, programmers, editors, and even videographers, photographers, and audio producers.

Another disadvantage is quality control. Many of the collections rely on peer and user review to identify the best contributions. However, in the collections in which anyone can contribute, there is no way to assess if a learning object provides correct and factual information, is pedagogically sound, or is even accessible from one day to the next.

Finally, some educators are fearful that administrators will replace the faculty member's role with courses strung together with learning objects. This fear is unfounded because it is the faculty member who adds the instructional "glue" to the educational experience by planning the design of the course, which is then complemented by learning objects.

## THE FUTURE

Learning objects have great promise in education. The off-the-shelf technology is becoming easier to use so that educators, students, and developers can create higher quality, interactive learning objects. As bandwidth and computing power increase, learning object developers can incorporate audio and video solutions to bring concepts to life. Metatagging standards will ensure that learning objects can be easily identified and retrieved by a broad audience. Research is underway to federate databases and "harvest" metatags across collections so that super-searches can span multitudes of database collections. More and more educational institutions are exploring opportunities to join the learning object movement by providing incentives for faculty to "granularize" their course materials. These institutions are building and supporting their own collections or are partnering with other institutions and corporations in consortial agreements.

—*Susan E. Metros*

*See also* AUTHORING TOOLS; EVOLVING TECHNOLOGIES; INSTRUCTIONAL COURSE DESIGN; VIRTUAL LEARNING TOOLS

### Bibliography

Cisco Systems, Inc. (2000, September 14). *Reusable learning object strategy: Definition, creation process, and guidelines for building.* Retrieved September 14, 2001, from http://www.cisco.com/warp/public/10/wwtraining/elearning/implement/rlo_strategy_v3–1.pdf.

Learning Technology Standardization Committee. (March 12, 2000). *Draft standard for learning object metadata.* Retrieved from http://ltsc.ieee.org/doc/wg12/LOMv4.1.htm.

Longmire, Warren. (2001). *A primer on learning objects.* Retrieved from http://www.learningcircuits.org/mar2000/primer.html.

Merrill, M. David. (1999). Instructional transaction theory (ITT): Instructional design based on knowledge objects. In Charles M. Reigeluth (Ed.), *Instructional design theories and models: A new paradigm of instructional technology.* Mahwah, NJ: Lawrence Erlbaum.

Wiley, David A. (2001). Connecting learning objects to instructional design theory: A definition, a metaphor, and a taxonomy. In David A. Wiley (Ed.), *The instructional use of learning objects.* Bloomington, IN: Association for Educational Communications and Technology.

## LEARNING PLATFORMS

Understanding *learning platforms* begins by understanding the concepts of *learning* and *platform*. The simple definition of learning is "a change in the probability of future behavior as the result of experience." These changes are believed to take place within the neural connections inside the brain of the learner. This point is important because the effects of learning experiences cannot be directly observed, and can only be inferred from the subsequent behavior of the learner. The definition of a platform in the online environment is "a Web desktop from an application service provider." Most commonly, this platform requires the learner to have a Web browser and PC connected to the Internet to be able to use the Web application. Access to the platform is usually further controlled by a security authorization process that requires the learner to use a special username and password to login.

A *learning platform,* then, is a Web application service that is intended to facilitate the achievement of learning goals by the user. The intention of the application service is important because creative educators have found many unconventional ways to use various products and services to facilitate learning. The builders of learning platforms also have taken some unconventional approaches to designing their products that embody different aspects of pedagogy, with the consequence that no single set of features defines the genre of online learning platforms. However, there are shared commonalities underlying these diverse application services.

## CONCEPTUAL CHARACTERISTICS OF LEARNING PLATFORMS

Platforms can be considered learning platforms when they contain two characteristics; many of the existing learning platforms contain three. The first characteristic is preexisting content, ranging from zero content to content analogous to a textbook's worth of learning. At its extreme, preexisting content embodies the traditional pedagogical position that the desired goal is for the learner to understand the thoughts of the author of the content and be able to demonstrate an understanding of that perspective.

The second characteristic is collaborative learning, ranging from no collaboration to highly interactive live audio and video participation. At its extreme, collaborative learning provides interactions that are windows into the minds of others in the course. It is through these mutual interactions that knowledge is created in the constructionist pedagogy view. The learning platform provides the mechanism to enable this more egalitarian type of pedagogy. The desired goal is for the student to participate in creating the knowledge and understanding that arises from the interaction among the students and the instructor/facilitator.

The third characteristic is learner evaluation, ranging from no evaluation to extensive standardized examinations that provide the basis for the certification of successful completion of learning goals. This evaluation provides the bridge between the learning situation and the external processes involved in recognizing learning accomplishment. Evaluation has historically posed significant technical challenges in the online environment due to insecure standards for online evaluation, as compared to face-to-face, proctored evaluations.

Based on this analysis of learning platforms there are four different styles of platforms:

1. *Personal interest course model*—Preexisting content + collaborative learning with no evaluation
2. *Traditional individual learner pedagogy, self study courses*—Preexisting content + evaluation with no interaction
3. *Graduate seminar pedagogy*—Collaborative learning + evaluation with no preexisting content
4. *All pedagogies accommodated by using subsets of the features available*—Preexisting content + collaborative learning + evaluation

## FEATURES OF LEARNING PLATFORMS

These three characteristics of learning platforms can be further understood by considering the specific features that exemplify them.

### Evaluation

The evaluation characteristic is supported in learning platforms with features that facilitate the process of determining grades in credit courses. These features range from simple online grading tools like a gradebook to sophisticated tools that enable authentication, automated testing, student self-assessment, student tracking, course management, and even integration with the institutional student information system.

An example of an evaluation feature is automated testing and scoring. Tools allow instructors to create, administer, and score objective tests. They may also provide support for proctored testing in a suitable computer lab classroom, as an approach to ensuring academic honesty. A fully developed testing tool in a learning platform could be used to enhance the evaluation of student learning.

A learning platform with such a testing tool could create assessments that use the following types of questions: true/false, fill in the blank, matching, multiple choice, ordering, calculated answer, and short answer/essay. Questions could be drawn from existing test banks that could be both built within the learning platform and imported from external files. The Mathematics Markup Language equation editor could enable students to enter and edit mathematical notations. Students could use a rich text editor for writing short answer/essay type questions. Questions and answers could be randomized to provide different forms of the test to different students. The testing tool could support timed test submission, completion, and results recovery. Proctored exams could be facilitated by a test scheduler and could allow a proctor to shut off browser controls during an exam. The automated scoring could score multiple-choice and multiple-answer type questions with optional immediate feedback. The automated scoring of short answers and essays could include the highlighting of words from the answer key, checking for plagiarism, and calculating the similarity between current essay answers and previously graded answers. The automated scoring could also provide the instructor with a gradebook of test results, and statistical analyses of the tests and the individual test items. Instructors could also override the automated scoring and determine how and when results would be communicated to students.

## Preexisting Content

The preexisting content characteristic is supported in learning platforms with features that enable the creation, organization, and navigation of lesson content. The lesson content facilities in some products enable compliance with existing standards for accessibility for persons with disabilities and other instructional standards.

An example of a preexisting content feature is instructional standards compliance, which concerns how well a product conforms to standards for sharing instructional materials with other online learning systems. Instructional standards compliance involves trying to make it possible for applications from different producers to work well together. Several proposed standards exist, but the most prominent are the standards developed by the Sharable Content Object Reference Model (SCORM) Project; there are currently very few compliance certification opportunities. Fully developed compliance with instructional standards in a hypothetical learning platform could enhance preexisting content by facilitating the sharing of existing content between publishers, authors, and institutions.

Such a standards-compliant learning platform could provide ongoing support for open industry standards for data exchange, including Instructional Management Systems (IMS) and SCORM, to enable interoperability, object reusability, and global portability of content. By complying with the instructional standards, the learning platform could incorporate course content received from publishers, content developed with standards-compliant external tools, and content created for different versions of the learning platform. The eduworks.com Web site contains a list with many reference points for instructional standards, and the standards are still developing.

## Collaborative Learning

The collaborative learning characteristic is supported in learning platforms by features that enable mediated student interaction tools such as discussion forums, internal e-mail, real-time chat, whiteboards,

and exchanging files. The important learning content is generated and shared in the process of the mediated student interactions and student–faculty interactions, rather than being located in some course structure as in the case of the preexisting content characteristic.

An example of a collaborative learning feature is discussion forums. Discussion forums are online tools that capture the exchange of messages over time, sometimes over a period of days, weeks, or even months. Threaded discussion forums are organized into categories so that the exchange of messages and responses are grouped together. A fully developed discussion forum in a hypothetical learning platform could be used to enhance collaborative learning.

Using such a discussion forum, students could view discussions by author, by date, and by thread. The instructor could create separate discussions located side by side, organized to display relevant content for small groups of selected students and teaching assistants. The creation of new threads could be disabled, whereas anonymous postings and file attachments could be enabled. Instructors could choose to moderate the discussion forums, and could set up an unlimited number of forums that can be opened for defined time periods. There could also be a discussion management function to summarize all posts in a date range. When replying to a thread, the student could view all of the responses while composing a response. The discussion software could include a rich text editor component for formatting posts; posts could be in plain text, smart text, or HTML. Posts could also allow embedded images or URLs. The discussion tool could enable a student to participate solely through e-mail. The entire discussion could be saved or printed for offline reading.

## General Considerations

Providing services with a learning platform also entails some more general considerations that are common in many different kinds of application services, but may be more specialized for learning platforms. These specialized features revolve around the different roles and requirements of students, instructors, registrars, and technical administrators. A few examples of these features are hosting services, registration, secure transactions, and technical support. The specifics of these features can sometimes play a decisive role in the selection of a learning platform, in addition to the various features described above and, of course, the cost considerations.

Some kinds of single dimension application services, such as conventional user-navigated Web sites, e-book readers, and some forms of online tutors/manuals that lack any evaluation or human interaction, are excluded from this conceptual definition of learning platforms. This definition would also exclude interaction-only application services such as discussion boards, chat rooms, normal e-mail, listserv, person-to-person video, and voice chat. Applications that allow only evaluation, such as online assessments, online surveys, and online performance tests, would also be excluded from the definition. In the past, several of these single-dimension applications services were used to facilitate educational goals, but they were neither intended nor designed for that purpose. The lack of a variety of learning platforms inspired much early ingenuity, but now the market for learning platforms contains hundreds of application services offering diverse sets of features and capabilities.

## CONCLUDING COMMENT

In the near future these platforms will become smarter and adapt more gracefully to individual students. Learning platforms are also beginning to provide accessibility for persons with disabilities. Encouraging the development of learning platforms that intelligently adapt to the varying needs of the learner is the near-term goal of the standardization efforts of Advanced Distributed Learning's SCORM initiative. Although these efforts are focused on the reuse of sharable learning objects, the framework is developing rapidly to provide intelligent sequencing of learning activities for individual learners. A research version of this sequencing development can be seen in John Anderson's Pump Algebra Tutor, which uses artificial intelligence to literally build a model of the learner's understandings and misunderstandings, and then provide learning activities based on that model. As with a human tutor, when the student makes an error the tutor makes an intelligent guess about the reason for the error and then proceeds to correct the student's misunderstanding rather than simply providing the correct answer.

The idea of facilitating learning with specialized services on the Web has given rise to a genre of learning platforms. Paralleling the explosive growth in distributed learning have been advances in the development of a multiplicity of diverse approaches to learning platforms. The one characteristic that they all share is the intention to facilitate the achievement of learning goals by the student. Beyond that intention there is no simple defining set of features for these application services. Mostly, but not all, platforms are browser-based, Web desktop clients linked to remote application servers. Most of the learning facilitation provided by these platforms is via interface and navigation design to help students be productive learners. With increasingly inexpensive computer processing, the door is opening to permit more computer power for better use of the truly scarce resource—the learner's time.

—*Bruce Landon*

*See also* VIRTUAL LEARNING TOOLS

## Bibliography

Khan, Badrul. (Ed.). (1997). *Web-based instruction.* Englewood Cliffs, NJ: Educational Technology.

EduTools. (n.d.) Descriptive reviews of learning platforms intended for higher education. Retrieved from http://www.edutools.info.

French, D., Olrech, N., Johnson, C. L., & Hale, C. (Eds.). (2002). *Online teaching guide: From lecture enhanced to virtual learning.* e-Linkages, Inc. in cooperation with Trafford Publishing.

IMS Global Learning Consortium. http://www.ims-project.org.

Koedinger, Ken, & Anderson, John. (1999). *Pump Algebra Project: AI and high school math.* Retrieved from http://act.psy.cmu.edu/ACT/awpt/awpt-home.html.

Advanced Distributed Learning (ADL). (n.d.). *SCORM Overview.* Retrieved from http://www.adlnet.org/index.cfm?fuseaction=scormabt&cfid=3293&cftoken=83765286.

# LEARNING TECHNOLOGY STANDARDS

The purpose of this entry is to describe the concept of technology-based learning standards and their implementation. Given the enormity and complexity of this topic, this entry will provide only a brief overview and perspective.

## THE VISION

To provide some context for the nature of learning standards, it is important to note the overarching need for personalization This one feature makes learning more effective by being relevant to each individual and his or her circumstances. The ultimate goal is to deliver

- To the right person
- At the right time and place
- In the right amount
- In the right context
- On the right device
- Using the right medium

Standards play an enabling role in the realization of this vision.

## WHY STANDARDS?

Historically, emerging new technologies such as railway track gauges, telephone dial tones, videotape formats, e-mail protocols, and computer platforms often start out by basing the technology on a proprietary set of specifications to make the new product unique. Unfortunately, this often means that these emerging technologies will not work well with other similar or competing products. Because these technologies often do not meet the needs of end users, the market typically drives business, academia, and government leaders to work together to develop common standards, thereby allowing a variety of products to co-exist. This convergence of technologies is very important for consumers. Products that adhere to standards will provide consumers with wider product choices and a better chance that the products in which they invest will avoid quick obsolescence.

In the world of digital learning content, common standards for content meta-data, content packaging, content sequencing, question and test interoperability, learner profiles, run-time interaction, and the like are requisite for the success of the knowledge economy and for the future of learning. Fortunately, the first versions of these standards and specifications are now arriving. The question is, "How can these standards be integrated into future plans as well as into current projects?"

Why should an organization care about the emergence and convergence of learning standards? The answer boils down to the need for organizations to protect and increase their return on investment in the learning technologies they purchase and in the learning content and services they develop. Organizations spend millions of dollars on technologies, content, and services to improve knowledge and skills. If the systems cannot grow and be sustained, maintained, and delivered to the learners, the investment will be wasted, or at least vastly less effective in returning results.

Within the context of the vision for personalized learning and sustained human performance improvement, standards are critical enablers that help to ensure six "abilities":

1. Interoperability
   - Mix and match content from multiple sources and within multiple systems.
   - Multiple systems communicate, exchange, and interact transparently.
2. Reusability
   - Content and code can be assembled, disassembled, and reused quickly and easily.
   - Content objects can be assembled and used in a context other than that for which they were originally designed.
3. Manageability
   - The system can track the appropriate information about the learner and the content.
   - The complex selection and assembly of "just the right" material can be managed.
4. Accessibility
   - A learner can access the appropriate content at the appropriate time on the appropriate device.
5. Durability
   - Buyers are not "trapped" by a particular vendor's proprietary learning technology.
   - No significant additional investment is required for reusability and interoperability, or to replace evolving technology.
6. Affordability
   - The learning technology investments are wise and risk adverse.

## HOW STANDARDS ARE FORMED

In the learning world, long before the term *e-learning* appeared, many organizations around the world began working diligently to create specifications to guide the evolution of learning-related technologies, creating resources and methods such as meta-data, learner profiling, content sequencing, Web-based courseware, and computer-managed instruction. This early work was done by such groups as ARIADNE in Europe, the Dublin Core for libraries, the Institute of Electrical and Electronics Engineers (IEEE), the Aviation Industry's CBT Committee (AICC), and the EDUCAUSE IMS Consortium. At first, these groups focused on different areas of the standards, working simultaneously but not in coordination. The U.S. Department of Defense has taken a leadership role in bringing together the work of these disparate organizations into a common and usable reference model, known as the Sharable Content Object Reference Model (SCORM). SCORM is a unified set of core specifications and standards for e-learning content, technologies, and services. Today, these various specification and standards bodies are working together on SCORM. Even at this early stage, SCORM has proven that the existing specifications and standards are able to deliver on the promises of interoperability and reusability and provide the foundation for how organizations will use learning technologies to sequence, assemble, and operate in the learning environment of the future. Ongoing work in this area promises to convert even more of the potential into reality.

## STANDARDS AND SPECIFICATIONS SIMPLIFIED

Two of the most important points to emphasize are that standards are systemic in nature; and that standards-based learning solutions are an integrated collection of individual specifications, products, and services. As with any complex system, it is not always easy to distinguish the various components and their roles, yet without doing so it is not possible to understand them.

To understand standards, it is important to understand the following key terms that relate to their evolution:

- *Specification*—A specification is a documented description. Some "specs" are certified as a formal standard, which means they are accredited after having progressed through the four stages outlined below.
- *De jure standard*—By right; of right; by law—often opposed to "de facto." The designation/certification of a specification's status by an accredited body.
- *De facto standard*—Existing in fact whether with lawful authority or not. Typically occurs when a critical mass or majority chooses to adopt and use a specification; for example, TCP/IP, HTTP, and VHS are all de facto standards.

The ideal state is when a *de jure* standard is also a *de facto* standard (e.g., HTTP).

Specifications evolve and become standards over time and then go through several phases of development before they are widely adopted, becoming *de facto*. Although there is no absolute process in the creation of *de jure* standards, development tends to follow a highly iterative process model typically composed of the following four stages:

1. *R&D*—Research and development is conducted to identify possible solutions.
2. *Specification development*—When a tentative solution appears to have merit, a detailed written specification must be documented so that it can be implemented and codified. Various consortia or collaborations, such as AICC, IMS, and ARIADNE, dedicate teams of people to focus on documenting the specifications.
3. *Testing/Piloting*—The specifications either are put into use in test situations or are developed as pilot projects to determine what works, what doesn't, what is missing, user reactions, and so on.
4. *Accredited and international standard status*—The tested and roughly complete specifications are reviewed by an accredited standards body and then are made broadly/globally applicable by removing any references to specific industries, originators, and contributors. They are then taken through an open, consensus-based process to produce a working draft that is then officially balloted. If approved, the specification receives official certification by the accredited standards body and is made available to all through this body.

The different organizations and groups do not conflict or compete with each other. Instead, these various organizations have different roles and responsibilities in a very complementary and holistic model. Each of the standards organizations has specific milestones and project schedules for their initiatives.

## STANDARDS GROUPS: COMPETITION OR COOPERATION?

It is neither accurate nor useful for vendors to tell customers that they "conform" to a specific group. Groups like IEEE, ISO, and CEN/ISSS are only umbrella organizations inside of which many individual standards are being developed. The same clarification applies to organizations developing specifications, such as IMS, ADL, AICC, and ARIADNE. The discussion instead should be about *solving specific problems,* and issues such as learning object metadata, content interoperability, student profiling, sequencing, content packaging, or question and test interoperability should be addressed. Conformance or compliance to the individual standard or specification will make the most sense to everyone interested in developing working solutions for real problems.

Those interested in implementing these standards and specifications should review the Advanced Distributed Learning (ADL) initiative, and in particular, the SCORM v1.3 document. The ADL site contains a large collection of documents, tools, XML DTDs, and other valuable resources that have been nicely organized (http://www.adlnet.org/Scorm/downloads.cfm).

SCORM provides a "powerfully neutral" reference model for implementation. SCORM is not a standard itself, but rather a reference model that serves to test the effectiveness and real-life application of a collection of individual specifications and standards. SCORM is, in essence, a *de facto* model because the group was not chartered as a standards-approving body, but rather as a model that governments around the world, as well as the learning industry as a whole, are in the process of voluntarily adopting.

Of course these standards are still far from "finished"; there is a lot of work yet to do both in improving what is now available and in working on additions. However, the SCORM document provides everything, from the long-term ADL strategy underlying the current work, to the conceptual basis, and details regarding the implementation reference model.

## CONCLUSION

To ensure interoperability of Web-based courseware and systems when implementing standards within an organization, it is important to gain support from senior levels of the organization. One needs to decide whether standards need to be adhered to across the organization from the outset or whether areas within an organization should be phased into conformance as the need for interoperability increases. Sometimes it is easier to gain support for standards after some benefits can be shown, rather than trying to enforce standards on all areas at once. This is a

long-term and strategic approach that will evolve and develop over a long period.

*—Wayne H. Hodgins*

*See also* DELIVERY SYSTEMS; KNOWLEDGE ECONOMY; LEARNING MANAGEMENT SYSTEMS (LMS)

## Bibliography

ADL. (n.d.). *Academic ADL co-lab.* Retrieved from http://www.academiccolab.org/Resources/index.html. The ADL Co-Lab serves as an academic partner and ADL link to test, evaluate, and demonstrate ADL-compliant tools and technologies to enhance teaching and learning. It also serves as an academic demonstration site for ADL tools and content, including those developed by the federal government, academia, and industry.

CETIS: The Centre for Educational Technology Interoperability Standards. (n.d.). Retrieved from http://www.cetis.ac.uk. CETIS represents U.K. higher-education and further-education institutions on international learning technology standards initiatives.

Duval, Erik, Hodgin, Wayne, Sutton, Stuart, & Weibel, Stuart L. (April 2002). Metadata principles & practicalities. *D-Lib Magazine.* Retrieved from http://www.dlib.org/dlib/april02/weibel/04weibel.html.

*Fastrak Consulting:* http://www.fastrak-consulting.co.uk/tactix/features/objects/objects.htm.

Greenberg, Jane. (Ed.). (2000). *Metadata and organizing educational resources on the Internet.* Haworth Information Press co-published simultaneously as *Journal of Internet Cataloging, 3*(1 and 2/3).

Hodgins, Wayne. (2000). *Into the future.* Retrieved from http://www.learnativity.com/into_the_future2000.html. This report was commissioned by the National Governors Association (NGA) and the American Society for Training & Development (ASTD) for their recent joint sponsorship of the Commission on Technology and Adult Learning. The paper is written in a very modular form and is all public domain. The full 50-page color document is available for download as a PDF.

*The Instructional Use of Learning Objects:* http://reusability.org/read/.

*Learning Content Management Systems:* http://www.elearningpost.com/elthemes/lcms.asp.

*Learning Circuits: Primer on Learning Objects:* http://www.learningcircuits.org/mar2000/primer.html.

Maisie Center eLearning Consortium. (March 2002). *Making sense of standards and specifications: A decision maker's guide to their adoption.* Retrieved from http://www.masie.com/standards/.

SCORM. *SCORM best practices guide for content developers.* Retrieved from http://www.lsal.cmu.edu/lsal/expertise/projects/developersguide/index.html.

SCORM. (November 2002). *The SCORM implementation guide: A step by step approach.* Retrieved from http://www.adlnet.org/index.cfm?fuseaction=rcdetails&libid=493&cfid=46932&cftoken=99748855. The document focuses on the practical application of the SCORM and serves as a beginning point for instructional designers responsible for SCORM implementation.

*Stephen's Web: Learning Objects:* http://www.atl.ualberta.ca/downes/naweb/Learning_Objects.htm.

# LEGAL ISSUES

Education is a hyper-regulated industry. Because it is so central to national culture, every nation has enacted rules governing not only who can provide education at varying levels, but also in most cases how that education will be provided, who is qualified to teach and who is eligible to learn and be subsidized, where education will take place, and what outcomes are expected. For generations the notion of "sovereignty of place" has made perfect sense: Education was defined by students arrayed in front of an instructor, gathered together within the confines of a classroom.

Distributed learning has altered not only the manner in which learning takes place, but also the fundamental concept of how it should—and can—be regulated. When the teacher is in one location and the learner in another, perhaps separated by hundreds or thousands of miles, at which location is the "institution"? When the only connection between the teacher and learner is the flow of electrons through a telephone cable, what right does the state where the learner is located have to regulate the conduct of the teacher? The legal premises that undergird the regulation of education—in the United States and throughout the world—are fundamentally altered by the interposition of technology between learner and instructor. The old rules do not work. New ones are still evolving.

## WHO REGULATES

In most nations, the regulation of education is a national responsibility, generally housed in an agency known as a Ministry of Education. In a few nations, control of education is devolved to a subnational level. Such is the case in the United States, where since the inception of the nation, control of education has been considered a function of the individual states. It is in that context that the authority to operate a school or college and the right to award an educational credential is uniformly issued by or under the authority of a state government. Indeed, the Tenth Amendment to the Constitution, the so-called "Reserved Powers Clause," has long been cited as the basis for the argument that education is fundamentally a responsibility of the states: "The powers not delegated to the United States by the Constitution, nor prohibited by it to the States, are reserved to the States respectively, or to the people." Federal law has consistently paid obeisance to this concept, and indeed one of the basic education statutes, the General Education Provisions Act, declares:

> No provision of any applicable program shall be construed to authorize any department, agency, officer, or employee of the United States to exercise any direction, supervision, or control over the curriculum, program of instruction, administration, or personnel of any educational institution, school, or school system.

Although the power of the purse strings has allowed rather more federal intervention into the classroom (most notably in the imposition of prescriptive rules under the No Child Left Behind Act), the principle remains embedded in the federal–state compact as it relates to control of education.

## STATE CONTROL

The concept of a state-based regulatory structure, with each state establishing its own statutory framework for the regulation of educational institutions "operating" within its borders, was eminently reasonable when institutions were located in a "place." The term *operating* naturally coincided with *physical presence*: The institution was *physically* within the state, and indeed the term *institution* has historically implied a teaching facility that aggregates students at a particular place, commonly known as a "campus" or "school." State regulatory schemes are dramatically different, ranging from the extremely prescriptive (New York) to minimal (Delaware), and in isolated cases, nonexistent (Montana).

## WHO IS REGULATED

The level of state regulation varies substantially depending on the *level* and *type* of institution. Elementary and secondary education are far more closely regulated than postsecondary and higher education. For reasons arising from a certain mistrust of the commercial marketplace, for-profit (sometimes referred to as "proprietary") institutions are generally more highly regulated than public or nonprofit institutions. Oddly, this is more common at the postsecondary level, whereas at the K–12 level it is the public institutions that are subject to the most intrusive controls. At the postsecondary level, regulation of for-profit institutions is also often separated from regulation of nonprofit and public institutions. It is interesting to note that an out-of-state ("foreign") *public* institution is generally treated for purposes of state law as an independent (or, in some cases, a *proprietary*) institution.

## REGULATING DISTRIBUTED LEARNING

Because state control is based on the concept of physical presence, the advent of distributed learning has enormously complicated the regulation of education. Distributed learning raises questions as to not only *who* (that is, the identity of the institution) is regulated, but also *what conduct* is to be controlled. The interstate delivery of postsecondary education brings the traditional exercise of states' rights under the Reserved Powers Clause into conflict with the protection of interstate commerce under the Commerce Clause. The earliest direct challenge to state regulation of programs originating outside of the state ("foreign programs") was based on control of correspondence study. In the century-old case of *International Text-Book Co. v. Pigg,* 217 U.S. 678 (1910), a correspondence school that employed agents in a state other than its place of business for the purpose of advertising the school's programs—consisting of sending educational materials through the mail—was found to be engaged in "commerce among the states within the meaning of the Constitution of the United States." However, that decision limited the states' role in the regulation of interstate aspects to only the kind of distance education that was provided through correspondence (i.e., lesson plans sent through the mail).

The legal foundations of state regulation of "foreign" institutions arose not in the context of distributed learning, but with distributed *institutions.* The proliferation of "branch campuses" provided the impetus for state laws seeking to limit foreign intrusion. In the key case of *Nova University v. The University of North Carolina,* 287 S.E.2d 872 (N.C. 1982), a state court held that the power of a state to regulate the conferral of degrees did not give the state the power to regulate the content of courses offered at a branch within the state. However, the courts have supported laws that regulate the *authority to operate* rather than *quality* of operations. In *Nova University v. Educational Institution Licensure Commission,* 483 A.2d 1172 (D.C. App. 1984), the District of Columbia Court of Appeals distinguished between teaching, which it confirmed to be constitutionally protected under the First Amendment, and offering of programs leading to a recognized degree, which the court held to require state authorization. The court enunciated a three-pronged state interest test: maintenance of the integrity of the degree-granting process, protection of state residents against fraud and substandard education, and protection of "legitimate institutions and of those holding degrees from them." The case established the jurisprudence that states *may,* with a properly crafted statute, regulate the conduct of out-of-state institutions that *establish a presence* within their borders.

## THE CONCEPT OF PHYSICAL PRESENCE

If states can regulate institutions *physically present* within their borders, how does this concept apply to distributed learning, where the institution's presence may be minimal or nonexistent? By the 1980s, the use of telecommunications technology began to raise a new specter of uncontrollable delivery of educational services by foreign institutions. The emerging mode of delivery was broadcast and cable television, through which a new vehicle, *telecourses,* was delivered. Courses were broadcast (or cable cast) by institutions into adjacent states. The critical question was not whether such activities *should* be regulated, but whether they *could,* raising the still-central distinction between the assertion of jurisdiction and the ability to exercise it.

States (and foreign nations) have taken different approaches to the definition of what constitutes physical presence sufficient to give the state the authority to regulate institutional conduct. One test is the "footprint in the sand": Does the institution have some physical operations within the boundaries of the state? At one extreme is a classroom, a physical extension of the campus. At the other are autonomous students working at computers in the privacy of their homes. Between the two is a line separating the existence of physical presence from its absence. Various regulatory models have emerged. Most common is a standard that looks to some physical manifestation of the institution, such as testing sites or counseling centers—anything that results in the *aggregation* of students. Of 37 states responding to a 1999 survey conducted by the New Hampshire Postsecondary Education Commission, 23 reported that they required "authorization/licensure of out-of-state programs" and of those, all but two indicated that "physical presence" was a "central issue" in asserting regulatory jurisdiction. In the same survey, 13 of the 37 states responding indicated that their regulations "specifically address electronically delivered programs from out-of-state." Some states go further, looking for persons *within the state* who are acting on behalf of the institution in the furtherance of its educational mission. New York, for example, has listed a set of characteristics that would constitute "presence" and therefore trigger state jurisdiction. The state would consider a distributed learning institution to fall under its regulatory control if the institution met any of the following conditions:

- Operates an instructional site (a physical site at which instruction is given by a faculty member to a group of students) in New York State. The fact that the instruction at that site is given through an electronic medium (e.g., satellite delivery, videotape) rather than through an instructor physically present in the room does not change the fact that it is an instructional site.
- Sponsors organized activities within the state that are related to the academic program (e.g., advising, mentoring, study groups, examination administration).
- Has a representative, whether paid or not, acting on its behalf within the state to arrange or conduct instructional or academic support activities. This would include a commercial vendor acting on behalf of the institution or a New York higher education institution providing services to students of the out-of-state institution.

A few states take the concept of "assisting the institution" as far as the telecommunications medium itself. Colorado law, for example, provides that

In addition [to the traditional concepts of physical presence, an] institution has physical presence in Colorado if it delivers, or plans to deliver, instruction in Colorado, and receives assistance from any other organization within the state in delivering the instruction, such as, but not limited to, a cable television company or a television broadcast station that carries instruction sponsored by the institution.

Advertising and promotion also afford a basis for the assertion of jurisdiction without any *instructional* presence within the state. A distinction is often drawn between the presence of advertising (sales) agents within the state and the *act* of advertising, the former being more highly regulated. Likewise, the use of the terms *college* and *university* are regulated in many states; Massachusetts prescribes a fine of $1,000 as well as the prospect of an injunction to prevent the unauthorized use of the proscribed words. States also often draw a distinction between programs that are available to the general public and those that are offered only to a specific cohort, such as employees or military personnel. These "closed sites," typically a business or military base, are considered in some states as exceptions to licensure laws, although often there are tight restrictions on the exception. Other states ignore the distinction entirely. And a very few states take the mighty leap of asserting jurisdiction if the institution is simply *instructing* its citizens. The Georgia education code prohibits institutions from offering "postsecondary instruction leading to a postsecondary degree or certificate to Georgia residents from a location outside this state by correspondence or any telecommunications or electronic media technology unless issued a current [Georgia] certificate of authority."

The problem with a diminished concept of presence lies not in the assertion of jurisdiction but in its enforcement. It is one thing to prohibit an institution from operating a counseling center or contracting for secure testing without state approval; it is quite something else to prohibit an institution with only an ethereal connection with a state (via the Internet) from offering instruction to the residents of that state.

## FEDERAL CONTROL OF DISTRIBUTED LEARNING

In the United States, the federal government ostensibly exercises only a peripheral role in education. It provides funding for programs that are carried out by states, local school districts, and postsecondary institutions. In the case of higher education, the vast majority of funds are funneled to institutions in the form of student financial assistance. The students receive the federal funds, which they then carry to the institutions of their choice. This portability (the exact opposite of the structure in elementary and secondary schools) has resulted in a uniquely pluralistic system of over 6,000 institutions, about half of which are nonprofit and public.

Although the federal government, through the Department of Education, does not directly control institutions, restrictions on the use of funds can sharply skew institutional conduct. For decades the term *distributed learning* was a synonym for correspondence study, and as such was relegated to the far periphery of federal support. The advent of telecommunications and its application to education, first through television and then the Internet, radically altered the legal framework as much as it transformed the pedagogical environment. But the law moves in ponderous fashion, and it was only in 1996 that the foundation federal statute supporting postsecondary education, the Higher Education Act of 1965, was amended to begin to put technology-mediated learning on a footing equal to that of other pedagogies. That process remains incomplete: Students who are enrolled in distributed learning through telecommunications technologies, and the institutions in which they enroll, remain discriminated against in terms of access to funds and in the flexibility to fully make use of the medium.

## MANAGING THE LEGAL BASIS OF DISTRIBUTED LEARNING

The question of how to properly regulate the interstate delivery of distributed learning encouraged a joint effort on the part of the State Higher Education Executive Officers Association (SHEEO) and the Council on Postsecondary Accreditation (COPA) to propose the creation of a national (but not federal) framework for the regulation of distance learning. The abiding premise was that states and accreditors should agree on a common set of standards for the assessment of telecommunicated learning. Each state *into which* an education service is delivered would give "full faith and credit" to the qualitative review performed by the state (and accreditor) of the originating institution's domicile. Unfortunately, the effort failed: States could not agree among themselves on a common regulatory framework.

Since the abortive SHEEO-COPA effort, there have been signs of a resurgence of interest in a common approach to regulating distributed learning. The *Standards of Good Practice* developed by the Western Cooperative for Educational Telecommunications provides a starting point for the adoption of generally accepted standards for technology-based distributed learning. Each of the regional and national accrediting commissions with responsibility for higher and postsecondary education have adopted *Principles of Good Practice for Distance Education* along roughly comparable lines, which augers well for common standards of quality and effectiveness.

Such voluntary efforts do not, however, overcome the inherent power and right of sovereign states to regulate education. To many regulators, distributed learning and its offshoot, technology-mediated learning, represent not an opportunity to expand opportunity and access, but a threat to the ability to properly protect the citizens of their jurisdiction from the predations of those bent on taking advantage of a gullible population. At the same time, there are significant issues of personal rights arising from the regulation of telecommunicated learning. Does discriminating against students or institutions engaged in distributed education through technology-mediated learning challenge the constitutional guarantee of equal protection. Equal protection is not an absolute: The question is whether the discrimination furthers a legitimate governmental interest, and if so does it do so in a rational manner? Likewise, do state laws that protect local institutions raise antitrust issues? Although states are generally exempt from the requirements of the federal antitrust laws, the question remains whether actions by *non*public entities (such as accreditors) in constraining telecommunicated learning pose antitrust issues.

## PRACTICAL CONSEQUENCES OF THE LEGAL THEORIES

The consequences of state assertion of jurisdiction over the interstate delivery of distributed learning are significant. The requirement that the institution submit to the differing regulatory requirements of multiple jurisdictions raises a number of serious issues. There is the possibility of *mutually exclusive* state requirements, as well as the potential impossibility (or impracticality) of adjusting a program that is uniformly distributed (e.g., via the Internet) to meet varying state requirements. The result might be enforced homogeneity (lowest common denominator) of instructional services, substantial delay in implementing a program, and, lurking just below the surface, the refusal of instrumentalities of a state to recognize credentials awarded by the institution. This is a particularly important issue in terms of professional education where subsequent licensure is required; some states simply will not recognize degrees granted by non–state-approved institutions, or, more ominous, those gained through the use of anything other than face-to-face instruction.

All this leaves a set of issues to be addressed. First, does state regulation of technology-mediated postsecondary instruction inherently impose an excessive burden on interstate commerce? If so, should there be federal pre-emption respecting interstate delivery of postsecondary education via the Web? Alternatively, does the historic pre-eminence of the states in the regulation of education *require* state oversight to protect the public and the integrity of academic credentials? Or, is state regulation inherently a way for in-state institutions to protect their territory (and market) from foreign invasion? Subordinate issues include how state tuition policies are to be applied, and from this flows the question of whether there should be interstate compacts so that students can reciprocally benefit from in-state tuition.

## INTERNATIONAL REGULATION OF DISTRIBUTED LEARNING

When it comes to the regulation of education the United States is a microcosm of the world. In controlling education, to a very large extent the states act as though they are sovereign nations, each state education department acting like a Ministry of Education. On the international stage the situation is strikingly similar. Every nation regulates education, and every nation is free to set its own standards. When international education was based on building classrooms and sending students across oceans, that was a plausible structure. But technology-mediated learning ignores national boundaries, and the attempt to control the Internet has proven a fool's errand. International law typically relegates control of education to the domestic agenda, but that is changing, and with it comes the sense that some form of international protocols may be

necessary to provide for the free flow of distributed learning across international borders. International trade agreements, such as the General Agreement on Trade and Services (GATS), which historically have excluded education from their purview, are likely to become vehicles for the structuring of global patterns of comity and competition.

*—Michael B. Goldstein*

*See also* ACCREDITATION; FEDERAL LAWS

### Bibliography

Eaton, J. (2001). *Distance learning: Academic and political challenges for higher education accreditation.* Washington, DC: Council for Postsecondary Accreditation.

Goldstein, M. (1993). *The regulatory and policy environment of telecommunicated learning.* Retrieved from http://www.dlalaw.com.

Lenn, M. P., & Campos, L. B. (Eds.). (1999). *Multinational discourse on professional accreditation, certification, and licensure: Bridges for the globalizing professions.* Washington, DC: National Committee for International Trade in Education.

Lenn, M. P., Deupree, J., & Johnson, M. E. (Eds.). (2002). *Proceedings of the OECD/US forum on trade in educational services.* Washington, DC: National Committee for International Trade in Education.

SHEEO. (1984). *Report on project Alltel (authorization and licensure of learning via telecommunications).* Denver: SHEEO.

National Commission on Web-Based Education. (2001). *The power of the Internet for learning: Moving from promise to practice.* Washington, DC: National Commission on Web-Based Education. Retrieved from http://www.hpcnet.org/webcommission/index.htm.

# LIBRARY SERVICES

In the traditional academic environment, library services have been closely associated with the physical library building(s) on campus, both representatively and as the location where collections of printed materials are maintained, reference assistance and instruction are delivered, and access to electronic resources is provided. In the distributed education environment, it is or must often be assumed that the actual or potential client of library services will rarely or never come to that physical library, if indeed there even is one; yet, as much as possible, the same resources and services must be made available to them. The planning of library services for distributed education differs to some extent from traditional academic institutions, presenting library administrators with different sets of challenges.

## TRADITIONAL, CAMPUS-BASED INSTITUTIONS

Many academic institutions that have delivered traditional, campus-based instruction for a long time recently have begun to be engaged in distributed or distance education. In these environments, libraries are often charged with supporting the "new population" of off-campus students, and perhaps also remotely located faculty members, in addition to the regular clientele of students, faculty, and staff on campus. This new charge to the library may come from top-level administrators of the institution and may not allow sufficient time for planning service and resource delivery, or provide the necessary additional funding. This may be based on the misconception that it is easier for the library to serve clients that don't come to the library, when in fact the opposite tends to be the case. Library managers in traditional, campus-based academic institutions are therefore well advised to not only stay tuned to, but also to seek to influence the planning of new, distributed-learning programs. Staying informed will help ensure that the library will not be caught by surprise with new expectations, but rather can support these new learners with the same degree of attention given to the on-campus population. With regards to providing distributed learners access to the scholarly literature, libraries in these settings can leverage the print collection they have already built, but must develop methods of delivering the works to this new group of users who cannot be expected to come to the library to obtain them.

## NONTRADITIONAL, VIRTUAL, AND/OR GEOGRAPHICALLY DISPERSED INSTITUTIONS

Planners of library services face a different set of opportunities and challenges in institutions that were founded with the intent to provide distance or distributed education, and that are not based on one or more physical campuses. On the one hand, they can develop the required services without a "legacy" user population

to consider; in this context, building a "virtual" library, with no dedicated library building or print collection, can be a practical option. On the other hand, this means having to come as close as possible to the resources and services that can be delivered in a traditional library using largely "virtual means," including being able to deliver scholarly literature (journal articles, dissertations, books, and so on) and reference and instructional services to clients.

## VIRTUAL REFERENCE SERVICES AND INSTRUCTION

Even in a distributed learning model that provides for some form of regular in-person meetings, learners will probably want to use most of the available face-to-face time to interact with faculty. The help of librarians, by contrast, is more often needed in connection with work being due, be it the first paper or the final touches to a dissertation, and that can happen almost any time, any day. The traditional reference desk interaction between librarians and their clients is thus not an option. This issue has made *virtual reference* (VRef) one of the hottest topics in librarianship, not only in distributed education environments, but also in traditional universities and colleges where many students prefer to stay in their dorm rather than making a trip to the library to ask for help. A wide range of activities has come to be understood as VRef—some libraries simply receive and respond to inquiries via electronic mail; others are experimenting with or instituting software solutions that allow for simultaneous "chatting" and searching of online resources. The latter, more advanced form of VRef (also called "live reference") holds promise for a breakthrough in reference services in distributed education, overcoming the potential feeling of disconnectedness and lack of rapport between client and librarian. Both people can simultaneously navigate and search the same online resources and "talk" (be it using voice or typing) about that experience as if they looked at the same computer screen, though they may be thousands of miles apart.

Important considerations for library managers with advanced VRef implementations include: the relative immaturity of the software in this area; determining how many days per week and hours per day such a service can and should be staffed, especially in this age of "24/7" expectations; the psychological adaptation such interactions require of both librarians and clients; and the fact that an already frustrated or "lost" client, searching for that elusive piece of research online, will feel even more lost should an implemented VRef solution hinder, rather than improve, the experience of seeking and receiving help from a "virtual librarian." The planning and delivery of virtual *instruction* involves many of the same considerations, and can to some extent utilize the same software solutions as virtual reference, but in a "one-to-many" mode. Without additional training, many librarians will be no more comfortable with delivering online instruction, be it synchronous or asynchronous, than with providing VRef; and the learners most in need of information competency improvement may be the very same user group that is most uncomfortable with utilizing information technology. The latter problem should also serve to remind institutional and library managers that in distributed learning, computer literacy is a prerequisite to achieving information literacy, but the two are often mistakenly equated.

## ACQUISITION OF ELECTRONIC INFORMATION RESOURCES

Libraries, both inside and outside of academia, have been acquiring and licensing electronic content for decades, from journal indexes on CD-ROMs to full-text articles in online databases. With the World Wide Web's rise, and concomitant flat-fee pricing models, the access to licensed online content shifted from mediated mode—a librarian performing searches for the client, often because pricing was by the usage minute and quite high—to unmediated searches being conducted by the clients themselves. This trend has been strong in traditional, campus-based libraries, where many clients, especially younger students, simply prefer to obtain articles online than from a hardcopy journal, even if the library has it. In virtual libraries, this model of content delivery is absolutely central and vital to their operation.

The distributed learning environment requires, from the learners' perspective, information to be available "just in time" and from wherever the learner is located; from the library operation's perspective, it may not be sensible or feasible to acquire, house, and manage a growing physical collection that the clients will never visit, but from which items needed by the clients must be extracted and delivered (whether by mail, fax, or electronically) on demand. Thus, administrators of libraries serving distributed learning can

plan on spending a good deal of staff time and funds on electronic information resources even before helping and training clients in their use.

Time must be spent on resource selection, which should involve consultations with faculty and students as well as ongoing usage and value assessments; resource acquisition, which can involve surprisingly complex contract negotiations, because there are almost no standards for pricing or delivery and access conditions; remaining alert to new opportunities, such as consolidating access to different databases through fewer online service vendors than before; and addressing and resolving access control matters, discussed in the following section.

Even more recent than the availability of full-text articles online, the growing number of available electronic books should also be considered for content acquisition for library services in distributed learning. Pricing models for electronic books are still quite varied, ranging from payment only for sections copied or printed, with free viewing, to the "one-time purchase, one reader at a time usage" model that emulates the acquisition of printed books. A library can often acquire for-fee online information resources at a substantially lower price by joining a consortium (or several) that can negotiate favorable contracts with a vendor on behalf of several or dozens of member institutions.

Finally, because not all scholarly writing is available in electronic format, electronic information resources will probably need to be supplemented by library services through traditional document delivery services. These services can be outsourced—the outside company obtains articles, book chapters, and such from a physical collection and delivers them to the library, or better yet directly to the library's client, via mail, fax, or electronic delivery methods.

## ISSUES OF AUTHENTICATION AND AUTHORIZATION FOR ONLINE DATABASES

Vendors of for-fee online resources typically offer two methods of access for subscribing libraries and, per contractual agreement, their clientele, which for academic institutions typically means currently enrolled students, faculty, and staff. Both methods have implications for issues of authentication (proving that user A—and only user A—is user A, and not B or C) and authorization (for example, establishing that user A has a certain right, by lieu of being a student, that user B, who is a graduate, does not).

One of these methods is a username/password combination, which is given to the clients of the library. This method presents no strictly technical problems, but has enormous potential user support problems (the larger the user base, the worse) because clients will often enter their usernames and/or passwords incorrectly or try to use outdated ones. Furthermore, the username and/or password will have to be frequently changed for security (authorization control) reasons, exacerbating the aforementioned problem. This method is therefore only feasible for fairly rarely utilized resources in fairly small institutions.

The other method is via recognition of the IP (Internet Protocol) address of every computer from which access to the online resource is attempted; access is granted only to certain IP addresses. The licensing library simply informs the vendor of the range of authorized IP addresses, and then controls access to those IP addresses so only its clientele can use them. This is relatively easy in a traditional physical library environment, where all computers in the library are on a local network and thus have a predictable and limited range of IP addresses. In distributed learning, however, most clients wishing to access an online resource licensed by their school will do so using a computer at their home or work, which could have Internet access through any Internet service provider. This means that the range of IP addresses is usually not known to the subscribing institution (unless it provides a modem dial-in pool and requires its clients to use it, a solution often not feasible or desirable for reasons of telephony costs and connectivity speed), so it cannot provide that information to the vendor.

A way around this problem is to use a proxy server located at the subscribing library's institution, thus providing a known IP address. All of the library's clients who want to access an online resource it subscribes to must do so by "going through" that proxy server, thus appearing to the online resource vendor to come from the proxy server's IP address and receiving access. Some proxy servers fulfill this function by having each library client specify his or her network address in the Web browser. Unfortunately, this can cause new user support issues, especially for a nontechnical clientele and for support delivered over a distance. Others methods, however, verify identity seamlessly, without requiring the user to make any changes to his or her Web browser. However, as Internet service providers increasingly seek to control the environment and methods of their customers'

access to the Internet, and as more and more workplaces and individuals employ firewalls and other network security measures, the proxy server's role in relaying access to a licensed online resource can be undermined. Therefore, regardless of how clients are given access to the online content that should be regarded as vital to their learning and research, planners and administrators of library services, in a distributed learning environment, must be prepared to deal with both problems and solutions that are technically complex, and accordingly require skilled staff for support and implementation.

—*Stefan Kramer*

*See also* COMPUTER LITERACY; INFORMATION LITERACY; LIBRARY TECHNOLOGIES

## Bibliography

Association of College and Research Libraries. (2000). *Guidelines for distance learning library services.* Retrieved May 22, 2002, from http://www.ala.org/Content/NavigationMenu/ACRL/Standards_and_Guidelines/Guidelines_for_Distance_Learning_Library_Services1.htm.

Birch, K., & Young, I. A. (2001). Unmediated document delivery at Leeds University: From project to operational system. *Interlending & Document Supply, 29*(1), 4–10.

Calvert, H. M. (2001). Document delivery options for distance education students and electronic reserve service at Ball State University Libraries. *Journal of Library Administration, 31*(3/4), 109–125.

Linden, J. (2000). The library's Web site is the library: Designing for distance learners. *College & Research Libraries News, 61*(2), 99–101.

Sloan, B. (2002). *Digital reference services bibliography.* Retrieved May 22, 2002, from http://www.lis.uiuc.edu/~b-sloan/digiref.html.

# LIBRARY TECHNOLOGIES

Library technologies include a variety of systems for automating the delivery and maintenance of library resources and services. As in many other areas of information technology, the emergence of the Internet, and the World Wide Web in particular, has revolutionized the ways library resources can be used and managed.

## ONLINE CATALOG

Almost all libraries have moved the information about their collections out of card catalogs and made it available in online public access catalogs (OPACs). Initially, OPAC access required a dedicated terminal attached to a central computer. These terminals were typically available only at the library. Although this configuration provided greatly enhanced search capabilities, it did not help the remote patron searching for research material. Now most OPACs are available on the Web, so the distance education student can begin the research process without actually visiting the library.

The information in OPACs is highly structured, with specific fields for author and title data. All descriptive data (such as keywords and subject headings) are related to authority lists of standard terms. Relational databases excel at storing and indexing these kinds of data, and are used by most catalog systems. Typical catalog systems also contain patron records for each user of the library. These records are needed for automating circulation functions. They also can be used to validate users of the online library services described in the next section. Before accessing the service, it requests the patron's library card number and checks it against the catalog database.

Traditionally, OPACs contain bibliographic information about the library's holdings, but academic institutions with many (and sometimes only) distance education students have begun to use the OPAC technology to maintain large bibliographies of printed material that may be available from other libraries. These databases provide the same bibliographic control and search capabilities as the OPAC, but describe material that is available to the patron at a library in their area, or through inter-library loan.

An even more ambitious trend is to try to catalog significant electronic resources that are available on the Web. These finding aids may make use of an OPAC's database, allowing searches by subject categories, but unlike traditional OPACs or bibliographical' search results, they provide links to the catalogued material on the Web.

## ONLINE SERVICES

A library is more than a warehouse of books. The technical, access, and reference services provided by libraries constitute the real value they contribute to their academic institutions. Libraries are increasingly applying computer technologies to streamline these services and bring them to distance education students and other remote patrons. For example, modern OPAC systems often include online renewal and similar functions. Patrons can log in remotely to the OPAC, see what material they have checked out, renew items that are coming due, and even place holds on items that others have checked out.

Another service increasingly provided through the OPAC is to request material, either from other libraries through inter-library loan or from the local library via electronic document delivery. In this case, the distance education student can request an item, and have it scanned into digital form and delivered to them over the Internet. This is typically done with journal articles; copyright laws and staff resource limitations make scanning entire books impractical. Black-and-white (or "grayscale") scanners are available from a number of vendors for very low cost. These scanners can generate images of article pages in a variety of formats, such as TIFF or JPEG. Software is often used to convert the page images to Portable Document Format (PDF), so multiple pages can be contained in one file. PDF requires a special viewing program (Adobe Acrobat), but the viewer is free and very commonly available.

Similar technology is used to digitize material for course reserves. Instead of coming to the library and checking out reserve material for short-term on-site loan, electronic reserves allow the patron to download the material from the Web for viewing or printing. As with electronic document delivery, copyright laws limit access to the digital material. In particular, to conform to fair-use provisions, access is often restricted to students and instructors of a specific course. The patron records in the OPAC do not typically include course registration information. If those data are not available to the electronic reserves system through a campus directory, then special login names and passwords must be distributed to each class to control access to its reserves.

As institutions begin deploying technology to manage online courses, the trend is to integrate electronic reserves systems with the course management system. This integration means that students can get to course reserves only by logging into the course management system, and they do not have to go to multiple Web sites to get material for one course. This convergence of technologies is seen in a few other areas, as online library services (e.g., online renewal, electronic document delivery) are integrated with campus portal systems. "Web services" technologies provide a convenient means for providing the services through another Web site rather than directly to the patron. The library Web service responds to requests from the campus portal with data encoded in the Extensible Markup Language (XML), which the portal application can understand and format for its HTML pages.

Reference services provide a means for library patrons to get help with their academic research. Technology developed in the business world to help companies interact online with their customers is being applied in the academic library to provide online reference services. Online "chat" provides a mechanism for patrons to ask questions and get immediate responses. Collaboration software allows the reference librarian to share online content such as databases and electronic journals with a remote patron. They can use "co-browsing" to help the patron search for the materials they want and create appropriate citations and bibliographies.

## ELECTRONIC RESOURCES

The print resources traditionally included in a library are increasingly available in electronic formats. This trend started with bibliographic databases such as DIALOG, BRS, and Orbit. Originally offered as a dial-up network service, many of these databases were made available on CD-ROM as that technology became available. Libraries would set up shared CD-ROM towers that could be accessed by public computers in the library. This provided an interface that was much faster, less expensive, and easier to use than the old dial-up terminal sessions, but concurrent use was limited to the number of CD-ROM drives available for loading a database CD.

Now these resources have moved to the Web. Many libraries are replacing their CD-ROM subscriptions with access to Web databases that provide more up-to-date information to patrons both in the library and off-campus. Web technologies for searching and retrieving electronic information have proved so appealing that academic journals and books are now being provided to libraries in this way.

The information in electronic journals and manuscripts is much less structured than that of the online catalogs and bibliographies, and relational databases are not as effective for searching. Information retrieval (IR) technologies are used to provide search results based on relevance rather than exact matches. For example, thesauri, word stemming, and related techniques are used to identify relevant documents that may not share any words with a query. Proximity and other context analysis techniques are used to rank result sets for relevance.

To make use of these resources, libraries need to deploy technology to identify and authenticate patrons and authorize them to use the licensed Web site. The simplest way to do this is by providing a list of valid network IP addresses to the vendor that identifies computers that are on the campus network. However, this does not help the distance education student who cannot get a campus IP address. The most popular solution for off-campus patrons is to set up a proxy server at the library that a remote patron logs into and uses to make requests to the licensed database site. Most Web browsers provide a way to specify a proxy server for particular Web sites, so requests to those sites are automatically directed to the proxy server, which passes the request results back through to the browser.

But this configuration is difficult to set up and maintain on each patron's computer. A pass-through or "rewriting" proxy server simplifies the configuration by reading the HTML pages that are passed through it and rewriting URLs of sites to proxy into addresses that direct the browser back to the proxy server. This means the configuration is all done on the proxy server rather than on each browser. The patron is directed to the proxy server by the links to resources on library Web pages, and subsequent links are redirected by the proxy server's rewriting of URLs.

The latest technology to enhance the electronic resources offered by the library is context-sensitive cross-linking. This allows the placement of links to related resources on resource pages. For example, a citation in a bibliographic database might have a link to the full-text online article if the institution subscribes to that electronic journal. The service must be context-sensitive so the link is displayed only if it is available to a particular patron and, when the cross-linked resource is available from multiple sources, the link is to the most appropriate resource for this patron. The OpenURL technology standard enables context-sensitive linking. OpenURL provides a way to transfer the information about a resource from the resource page to a program that can provide appropriate services in a given context.

## THE DIGITAL LIBRARY

Libraries are also using technology to put their own resources and special collections online. Correspondence, photographs, illustrations, and other types of special material are scanned into digital form and made available in digital libraries. Unlike electronic reserves and document delivery, these materials are for more permanent use or are archival and require higher quality digitization techniques. Typically, 24-bit color rather than grayscale is used. High-resolution master images in TIFF format are created and stored on tape, CD-ROM, or, more recently, DVDs. These masters are often either uncompressed or compressed using a "lossless" mechanism that allows the uncompressed data to be exactly re-created.

A lower-resolution image, suitable for display on common PC monitors, is created from the master for viewing and downloading via the Web. JPEG is a popular format because it includes a compression mechanism that is "lossy," but is still very difficult to visually distinguish from the uncompressed version. The compressed file can be transmitted over the Web more quickly and uncompressed and displayed by most Web browsers without special software. New formats are being defined that use "wavelet" compression technology to provide even higher resolution with small file sizes. Some of these formats, such as LuraDocument and DjVu, take advantage of the increased resolution to provide enhanced interactive functionality, such as panning and zooming, but they require special plug-in software in the browser to use.

Similar technology is used to digitize other media, such as audio and video, which require much larger file sizes to store and transmit. For example, an audio collection can be digitized into uncompressed WAV files for archiving while a lower quality compressed MP3 or RealAudio version can be provided over the Web. These compressed formats can also be streamed, so the user can start listening to the audio (or viewing video) as it is being transmitted rather than having to download the entire file before using it.

Digital libraries must provide ways for users to find the relevant digital objects they contain. Searching based on the contents of a media file is still very experimental technology and is very seldom used. Rather, information about the resources, called "metadata," is entered into a database or XML data format. The metadata are indexed for searching in a relational database or information retrieval (IR) system.

Optical character recognition (OCR) is a technique that can be employed on images of typewritten text to convert it into computer-readable text. This technology analyzes the image and tries to recognize the letters of the words. These are written to a text file that can be displayed and indexed. Depending on the quality of the original and the image, a certain number of errors can be expected in OCR-derived text, and correcting the text can be as labor intensive as metadata creation. Often, the OCR text is used just for indexing, where some level of errors can be tolerated, and the image itself is used for display.

When a text is going to be used extensively for teaching and researching it may be worth the effort to correct all the errors in the OCR text or, if the original is handwritten or very difficult to read, transcribe the text manually. In this case, it becomes even more useful if the text is marked up with tags that describe physical and intellectual aspects of the document. The Text Encoding Initiative (TEI) has defined a set of markup tags for including these kinds of descriptions in electronic documents. The tag set, originally based on SGML, now makes use of XML, so many tools are available for encoding and processing the marked-up text.

The next challenge for the digital library is to improve the integration of disparate collections with each other and with the other services of the library. Two technologies in particular are being used to build virtual digital collections out of multiple local and remote resources.

Federated or distributed searching allows queries to be sent to multiple resources and the results combined and displayed to the patron. The resources can include digital collections, bibliographic databases, and many of the other kinds of resources described earlier. Z39.50 is a query protocol that has long been used by libraries to do federated searches of catalogs. Because most catalog systems support this standard query format, the federated search simply sends the same query to multiple resources and concatenates the results. Many newer electronic resources do not support Z39.50, and federated search systems must be much more sophisticated to translate a patron's search query into multiple formats and process results that are also in a variety of formats.

An alternative to federated searching is harvesting, in which the metadata for the virtual collection are gathered on a periodic basis from multiple resources. Searches can search the local copy of the metadata to find out what specific items are relevant and only go to the remote server to get the digital object. Multiple query protocols do not need to be supported, and performance is typically much faster than with federated searches.

Both federated searching and harvesting require that metadata conform to common standards for interoperability. Even if the query protocol is the same between two resources, they cannot be queried together if there is not some basis for comparing basic fields such as title, author, and subject. The Machine-Readable Cataloging (MARC) format is a solution to this problem, and has been particularly used by libraries for catalog systems for many years. However, as technology has driven new metadata needs, and the schema has been expanded to meet those needs, MARC has become increasingly complicated and difficult to use.

A more recent approach is represented in the Dublin Core metadata initiative. Their philosophy is based on a minimal set of core metadata, enhanced by additional packages of metadata that are controlled and used by specific communities. General-purpose queries can be restricted to the core set, and virtual collections of a particular subject area can make use of their community-specific metadata.

Standards such as MARC and Dublin Core for metadata, XML for text encoding and Web services, and Web and IP protocols for information transmission provide a basis for the convergence of library and other academic services for distance education. These technologies are being deployed to provide access to library resources and services for remote students. And the resources themselves are increasingly not on campus, or in any one place, as virtual collections are being created for specific educational and research purposes from a variety of resources.

—*Don Gourley*

*See also* INFORMATION LITERACY; LIBRARY SERVICES

## Bibliography

Besser, Howard. (2002). The next stage: Moving from isolated digital collections to interoperable digital libraries. *First Monday, 7*(6).

Cooper, Michael. (1996). *Design of library automation systems: File structures, data structures, and tools.* New York: John Wiley & Sons.

Dowler, Lawrence. (Ed.). (1997). *Gateways to knowledge: The role of academic libraries in teaching, learning and research.* Cambridge: The MIT Press.

Goerwitz, Richard. (June 1998). Pass-through proxying as a solution to the off-campus Web-access problem. *D-Lib Magazine.*

Lesk, Michael. (1997). *Practical digital libraries: Books, bytes & bucks.* San Francisco, CA: Morgan Kaufmann Publishers.

Lynch, Clifford. (1997). Building the infrastructure of resource sharing: Union catalogs, distributed search, and cross-database linkage. *Library Trends, 45*(3).

Sloan, Bernard. (1997). Service perspectives for the digital library: Remote reference services. *Library Trends, 47*(2).

Witten, Ian, Moffat, Allister, & Bell, Timothy. (1999). *Managing gigabytes: Compressing and indexing documents and images,* 2nd edition. San Francisco, CA: Morgan Kaufmann Publishers.

# LICENSING

Copyright law gives owners of copyrights certain exclusive rights in their works. The copying, publication, public performance, display, distribution, or the making of an adaptation of a copyrighted work by someone other than the owner of the copyright is an infringement, unless done either with the permission of the copyright owner or under the authority of one of the exemptions to the exclusive rights of owners recognized by the Copyright Act, such as fair use. This entry discusses the basics of licensing copyrighted works for educational use.

## WHY LICENSE?

The fair use doctrine is inherently ambiguous. A determination of whether a particular use of material from a copyrighted work is fair or an infringement turns on the specific facts of each case. Educators reaching students via interactive networks were accorded new freedom in the incorporation of copyrighted works into online courseware when President Bush signed the Technology, Education and Copyright Harmonization (TEACH) Act into law in December 2002. However, a degree of uncertainty remains. That fact, combined with the potential monetary liability for infringement, means that it often may be preferable to obtain permission for a specific use from the copyright owner. This is particularly the case if an instructor intends to use the materials repeatedly for the same class or course over a period of time. All of a copyrighted work, or portions of it, may be licensed for educational use by obtaining from the owner of the work or the owner's designated representative, such as a collective licensing organization, the right to use the work. Licenses can be rigid or flexible, extremely narrow or very broad. Thus, they can be for single or multiple uses, of specific duration or in perpetuity, exclusive or nonexclusive, for a royalty or royalty free, worldwide or geographically bounded, for use in only one distribution medium or any and all media, and so on.

## TYPES OF LICENSES

Different types of licenses are available depending on how the copyrighted work will be used.

- *Site licenses* are employed to secure all uses of a copyrighted work by a specific user or group of users during a specified period of time. They address situations in which there are multiple users, and take into account the number and nature of the users. Site licenses often are specific to a location or defined by some other identifiable criteria. A community college system, for example, might secure 35 site licenses for the use of a telecourse over a 3-year period.
- *Transactional licenses for analog uses* grant permission to make copies on paper of works for distribution to students as supplementary materials. A typical example is a license to include a copyrighted work or portion of the work in a traditional paper course pack. The copyright owner generally receives a negotiated per student license fee.
- *Transactional licenses for digital uses* grant permission to use a specific copyrighted work in a digital form. A transactional digital license may be used to authorize the digitization of analog course materials; incorporation of a work in a digital course pack; or distribution, display, or performance of a work in a digital form. Again, the copyright owner generally will require a fee for the use of the work.

## REQUESTING PERMISSION

A request may be initiated by sending a letter, calling, or, in some cases, as with many collective licensing organizations, via e-mail. The request needs to be specific, identifying

1. The specific material to be used by:
   - Author
   - Book, journal, movie, photograph title (volume, issue, edition)
   - Page/image/table number
2. All of the specific permissions you require, such as:
   - Reprint
   - Photocopy
   - Quote from
   - Transmit
3. What the work will be incorporated into, such as:
   - Multimedia courseware
   - Online course materials
   - A print publication
4. How the material will be distributed or published:
   - Method of distribution
   - Publisher
   - Anticipated distribution or publication date
   - Anticipated length of the work
   - Target market
   - Any technologies that will be employed to protect the work from unauthorized access, copying, and redistribution

If one can identify the author of the work and the publisher, one can contact them directly to secure permission; however, one needs to be sure that the person giving permission through the license has the authority to do so. Care is needed in this regard because the apparent copyright owner is not always the current owner. Note that many copyright registrations can be searched online to determine the current owner. Go to http://www.copyright.gov/records/ and click on the "Search Records" tab on the U.S. Copyright Office's Web page.

Another alternative to securing a license is to work through a collective licensing organization. Different organizations exist for different types of works, including

- The Copyright Clearance Center (http://www.copyright.com) for books and journal articles
- The Media Image Resource Alliance (http://www.mira.com), the American Society of Media Photographers (http://www.asmp.org), and Aurora Photos (http://www.auroraphotos.com), among others, for images
- ASCAP (http://www.ascap.com), BMI (http://www.bmi.com), SESAC (http://www.sesac. com), and the

Harry Fox Agency (http://www.harryfox.com) for various uses of musical works
- The Motion Picture Licensing Corporation (http://www.mplc.com) and Movie Licensing USA (http://www.movlic.com), among others, for public performance of movies
- Individual news organizations for the use of news items
- Samuel French, Inc. (http://www.samuelfrench.com), Baker's Plays (http://bakersplays.com), Dramatists Play Service, Inc. (http://www.dramatists.com), and Music Theater International (http://www.mtishows.com), among others, for the use of plays and musicals.

Even though it is not required by law, no matter whether permission is granted directly by the owner of the copyright or through a collective licensing organization, it is always preferable that the license be *in writing*. It should clearly describe the scope of the license, all terms, and, with specificity, the intended use of the material. If the format of the use is uncertain, the license should include alternatives. If an *oral* license is received, the precise terms of what was requested and granted should subsequently be carefully summarized in a document. It is good practice to send the person granting the oral license a copy of the summary accompanied by a request that he or she initial and return it if it is accurate is good practice. Retaining a copy of the summary in one's records is essential.

## SOME CONCLUDING THOUGHTS

The contemplated method of distribution of the work that will incorporate the licensed material should be specified both in the request for permission and in the actual licenses. From the educator's point of view, however, it is important to include as much flexibility as possible in the license, particularly with regard to media of distribution. New distribution technologies arise frequently and licenses, ideally, should be written in a way that reflects that reality. The broadest form of a distribution license would specify "technologies now in use or subsequently developed." Where electronic distribution is to be used, it is advisable to specify in the license the technologies and techniques that will be employed to protect the integrity of the copyrighted material from access by unauthorized users and from unauthorized reproduction or downstream redistribution.

Finally, use of material under a license should include attribution and applicable citations together with any copyright notice from the original work.

—*Kenneth D. Salomon*

*See also* PLAGIARISM; SITE LICENSES

## LITERATURE SEARCHING

The common desire for many researchers in the traditional academic library setting is to first find and then use resources located in the library, whether online or in the stacks, and then, only if needed, obtain materials from somewhere else. Often this includes interaction with a reference librarian, during which the librarian will often conduct a reference interview, which consists of asking the researcher a set of open-ended questions. These help the librarian determine what the researcher really wants and gauge how to best instruct the researcher on how to find it. But due to the lack of a physical library in the distributed education environment, librarians and researchers must communicate by telephone or "virtually." Searching for scholarly work must be done in online databases or catalogs. This has one great advantage—the ability to search at home or from other remote locations as long as there is a computer with Internet access. One great disadvantage, however, is not being able to simply browse for materials in the library stacks.

In the distributed education setting, unless students have the opportunity to meet reference librarians, they usually have to submit reference questions via telephone or "virtually" by electronic mail or virtual reference software. Regardless of the method of communication, however, the librarian still often has to conduct a reference interview. This can be difficult given that the librarian cannot rely on face-to-face communication, the researcher's body language, or the researcher's tone of voice to help in assessing the reference question. Therefore, the librarian must often do his or her best to conduct the reference interview in such a way as to determine what the researcher really wants while avoiding too many open-ended questions, conducted over the phone or virtually, that might frustrate the researcher to such a point that interest in the transaction is lost.

In the distributed education environment, it is tempting for students to search for scholarly data on the Internet first, but the Internet is not maintained by a set of professional individuals, and no groups catalog it. Sources found on the Internet can be tampered with or be complete hoaxes. This is why librarians emphasize first searching for scholarly work in online catalogs or databases before doing so on the Internet.

Accessing entire books is taken for granted in the traditional library setting, but in the distributed education environment, it can be much harder than retrieving entire journal articles or dissertations. The last two are included in various proprietary databases, some of which include full text that can be printed out in whole. Books, on the other hand, are not indexed in such databases. There are, however, slowly expanding electronic book collections that have been developed by various companies. Electronic books (called e-books) are digitized versions of complete books that are electronically accessible from an e-book company, much in the same way that digitized journal articles are from online databases. The problem with e-books, however, is that they cannot be handled physically, pages cannot be turned, and they cannot be printed out in their entirety due to copyright restrictions. Even further, many scholarly books are not yet digitized and they might never be, for a variety of reasons. If a book is not available electronically, the researcher's options for retrieving it consist of visiting a local library to borrow it, ordering it via inter-library loan, or purchasing it. Some document delivery companies do offer book loans, but the cost can be quite high.

Dissertations are somewhat easier to obtain because of the development of online proprietary databases that index full-text, digitized dissertations that were published from the mid-1990s onward. Dissertations that are not digitized can often still be purchased from database companies or obtained in book format, assuming they have been published. Searching for and downloading journal articles in full text is becoming easier, too. Many online proprietary databases are increasing their collection of indexed full-text articles. In addition, distributed learning institutions can directly subscribe to online journals. This enables researchers to access online journals' contents directly, bypassing the need to search in databases.

In general, however, online searching for subjects should not be limited to just looking in full-text databases and online journals exclusively. Often, one can find highly relevant citations for articles in abstract and citation-only databases. Those kinds of databases often index a much greater number of sources than full-text ones because citations and abstracts take far less time to digitize and far less room to store than full text. Yet even if a researcher has found a relevant article from a journal not available in full text online, it can still be obtained it by other methods. However, the researcher will have go to a library to find the journal, order a copy via interlibrary loan, order a copy from a document delivery service, or order the issue from the publisher.

Many of the online citation and abstract-only databases also index journal articles by means of controlled subject terms that are more specific than those used in full-text databases. Therefore, they are often easier to search for specific subjects than are full-text databases. This is not to say that citation and abstract-only databases are better than full-text ones, but at times, the former can be better suited for specific subject searches. For example, the Educational Resources Information Center (ERIC) database, produced by the U.S. Department of Education, contains only abstracts and citations, but it also provides online access to its thesaurus of subject terms, which allows researchers to browse, even from remote locations, for specific terms that best represent the concept(s) they are searching.

Therefore, in the distributed education environment, researchers should be prepared to allocate enough time to contact reference help when necessary and familiarize themselves with online catalogs and databases. These actions can be frustrating at first, but they are very rewarding once the particular advantages of these resources, and how they work in general, are understood.

*—Alain Dussert*

***See also*** LIBRARY SERVICES; LIBRARY TECHNOLOGIES; VIRTUAL CAMPUS

## Bibliography

Cal Poly State University, San Luis Obispo. (March 1999). *Use technological tools.* Retrieved June 21, 2002, from http://multiweb.lib.calpoly.edu/infocomp/modules/04_ use/index.html.

Ohio State University Libraries. (1997). *netTutor: Specialized databases.* Retrieved June 21, 2002, from http://gateway. lib.ohio-state.edu/tutor/databases/.

Sloan, B. (2002). *Digital reference services bibliography*. Retrieved June 21, 2002, from http://www.lis.uiuc.edu/~b-sloan/digiref.html.

University of Texas at Austin. (October 1999). *Texas information literacy tutorial*. Retrieved June 21, 2002, from http://tilt.lib.utsystem.edu.

# LURKING

Lurking is the practice of reading messages that have been contributed to a discussion area or bulletin board in an online course, but not posting messages oneself. Students who lurk in a discussion will typically read all, or most, messages, but contribute nothing of their own.

Most online delivery software such as Blackboard or WebCT will be able to give the teacher a report of how many discussion messages each individual has read, and how many he or she has posted. This gives a rough idea of what is going on, but it isn't the whole story. Using the software, a very long, considered, and interesting message counts the same as one that just says "I agree with Fred." Just as in a face-to-face situation, the teacher needs to keep up with the discussion in order to get a clear picture of what is going on.

It has been reported that in typical online discussions about 50% of students lurk. This may seem like a high number of people who are not participating, but in postcourse evaluation, these students say consistently that they have benefited from reading what others had to say. Instructors' views of lurking should not be colored by comparison to the one-to-one relationship between teacher and student that exists in face-to-face teaching. Some authors have suggested that peer pressure may force people to contribute in face-to-face classes, even if students don't have anything interesting to say—these students may therefore always have "lurked," or "learned passively," because their contributions have not added either to their understanding or that of others.

The term *lurking* has unpleasant connotations, and several more positive alternatives have been proposed, such as *passive* or *silent participation, witness learning,* or *browsing,* any of which may be more descriptive of what is actually going on. However, lurking can be a problem in a course, particularly if it leads to bad feelings or demotivation among the students. It is often obvious to a group that the same people are making most of the contributions, and this situation can make active contributors very irritated. They may feel that they are providing insights and ideas that help others, but that they are not getting a fair exchange from their peers. Contributors may feel discouraged when their message does not receive any response, or assume that others think their ideas are uninteresting, irrelevant, or stupid. Finally, the reason for discussions in any learning situation is to enable people to develop their ideas by trying them out with other people, considering the responses they get, and then developing their thoughts. People need active feedback and discussion in order to develop their ideas further, and if individuals are not participating, they may be stuck in a situation where they are not forming and articulating their own opinions. Although they think that they are benefiting, they are not being challenged enough to get the most that they can from the discussion. Some active contributors will also feel that it is unfair to read something that may be illuminating or innovative and then not to acknowledge the work that has gone into it by providing a comment.

When considering how to manage lurking, it may be useful for the teacher to make a direct comparison with the face-to-face situation. It is common to find that a minority of group members is making the majority of the contributions, whereas the others tend to listen. It may be that they find it difficult to speak in public, or maybe the active contributors don't leave space for them, or it may be that they have little to add. In the face-to-face situation, we know that the quiet person is listening by seeing nonverbal reactions such as nodding, making eye contact, and changing their facial expressions. In the online environment, the lack of these cues can cause frustration among the group. Face-to-face, from time to time, many teachers will challenge the quiet members of the group personally to encourage their contribution and to make sure that they know there is a place in the discussion for them, "What do you think, Alice?" or "What would you do in that situation, John?" This is also a useful strategy for online courses. Sending a personal e-mail can be a way of reminding the student of the need to take part, without drawing the attention of others to the individual, who may have lacked the confidence to get involved. It is important to lay down ground rules for discussion at the outset, or to get the students to do this as part of the initial discussions. These could include making sure there is a shared understanding at the very beginning of why lurking may be detrimental to the discussion as a whole, making it clear that all contributions should be valued, and that feedback is important when people have made contributions. Teachers need to ensure that they are in a position to contribute actively as well, and not too busy. It may be useful to plan time to send personal e-mails to encourage those who have not yet contributed and to thank those who have.

Lurking will be reduced if discussions are structured and have clear outcomes, with links to the final assessment of the course. A useful way of encouraging good quality discussion may be to allow students to submit, as part of an assignment a portfolio of their contributions, together with a contextual commentary. It may be helpful to divide the discussion area into smaller groups, with limited membership in each, because "quieter" students may feel anxious about having a large readership. One should make sure that disabled students have access to the discussion area, and that they feel that they can maintain the pace. Finally, it's important to keep the discussion area tidy, so that people are not overwhelmed by the volume of messages; old messages can be archived.

*—Rachel Forsyth*

***See also*** CRITICAL DIALOGUES; TEACHING IN AN ELECTRONIC CLASSROOM; WEB-BASED COURSE MANAGEMENT SYSTEMS (WBCMS)

## Bibliography

Bernath, U., & Rubin, E. (2001). Professional development in distance education: a successful experiment. In F. Lockwood & A. Gooley. (Eds.), *Innovation in open and distance learning* (pp. 213–223). London: Kogan Page.

Palloff, R. M., & Pratt, K. (1999). *Building learning communities in cyberspace.* San Francisco: Jossey-Bass.

Salmon, G. (2000). *E-Moderating: The key to teaching and learning online.* London: Kogan Page.

# M

## MARKETS/MARKETING

Distance learning is becoming increasingly market driven. In its early years, distance learning was conceived as a means to reach learners who had little access to education; public institutions served those needs through distributed programs. During the 1990s, private and for-profit institutions, and even many public and nonprofit organizations, began to see distance learning as a revenue-producing initiative. With increasingly more distance learning programs experiencing pressure to operate at break-even levels or even make a profit, the ability to generate and sustain enrollment growth is critical to ensuring a healthy revenue stream. Even in institutions where there is less concern about profitability, consistent enrollment growth is often one of the most important measures used to evaluate success. Marketing is playing an increasingly important role in enrollment growth for distance learning programs.

Marketing has two concurrent thrusts: internal and external. Internal marketing is critical in settings where key decision makers and stakeholders fail to comprehend the importance of distance learning to the overall mission of the institution. Internal marketing efforts are driven toward generating and maintaining interest and enthusiasm about distance learning initiatives. In businesses, schools, and colleges, managers, administrators, finance officers, and faculty require a continuous flow of marketing communications to advance the cause of distance learning. Particularly in corporations, internal marketing to employees is essential to maintain high participation in distance learning programs.

External marketing is directed toward potential customers of the distance learning program, and it is most crucial in a competitive environment where learners have alternate sources of programs. Fundamentally, the application of sound education marketing principles will be effective in reaching potential distance learners. However, marketing to distance learners can be distinctly different from marketing to potential on-campus learners for at least three reasons. First, distance learners can be difficult to reach because they are often located in dispersed geographical areas. Second, depending on the program mix, targeted distance learners may have little in common with each other to justify consolidated marketing efforts. For example, an institution seeking to market a specialized graduate-level engineering program would need to disseminate information about the program differently than it does for undergraduate liberal arts programs aimed at adult students. This challenge is magnified dramatically when combined with the effects of geographic dispersion. Third, the element of distance creates new opportunities and challenges in the selection of the most appropriate communications vehicle for marketing information.

A sound marketing plan is an essential cornerstone of marketing distance learning. Just as distance learning programs seek to be consistent with the overarching mission of the institution, so too should the marketing plan fit into the context of marketing the organization. Therefore, the institution should invest in disciplined and systematic market analysis or needs assessments, building cohesive market strategies, summarizing specific marketing activities and responsibilities, and evaluating the success of marketing programs. Key elements of a marketing plan for distance learning typically include situation analysis; assessment of marketing strengths and weaknesses; analysis of marketing opportunities and threats; marketing goals and objectives; marketing strategies, tactics, and responsibilities; marketing budget; and performance measurement and metrics.

The strategic plan and direction for the distance learning organization are the starting point for the marketing plan and strategy. The strategic plan should provide guidance on target learner populations, institutional strengths and weaknesses, linkage with initiatives in other parts of the institution, and technological direction. In the absence of a strategic plan for distance learning, marketers can use their departmental or institutional strategic plans as a reasonable proxy.

The identification of the key market segments is the foundation for sound distance learning marketing. Market segments are distinct groupings of potential learners who have some key characteristic in common, such as academic interest, geographic location, employment status, or affiliation with the institution. Each segment can be targeted using a different marketing strategy that responds to the unique needs of the group. These market segments may be quite different from the market segments for on-campus students. In defining market segments, it is important to make every attempt to ensure that they are fairly homogeneous in membership, reasonably large, and mutually exclusive.

After segments have been identified, it is important to identify the specific educational and service needs of each segment in order to develop effective marketing strategies. Formal needs assessments and targeted market research studies can be valuable tools in uncovering and prioritizing these needs. Distance learning needs and preferences are most typically summarized into categories such as academic content, technology and access, tuition, and support services.

An analysis of demographic and other trends shaping each market segment is useful in identifying those market segments that offer the greatest potential for the institution in terms of enrollment, strategic positioning, service to the community, or partnerships with other organizations and institutional departments. Key questions to ask in this analysis include: How large is this segment? At what rate is it growing? In what ways would access to distance education impact this segment? Which other institutions are currently providing educational opportunities to this segment? What are the economic drivers of this segment?

Another key marketing consideration in the institution's history with distance learning and its internal capabilities to develop, market, and deliver programming via distance learning. It is important to include an analysis of enrollment trends and the financial performance of both distance learning and classroom-based programs. An inventory of current marketing activities and a qualitative or quantitative assessment of their effectiveness are other valuable tools in analyzing the institution's current marketing capabilities. Available Web site traffic metrics, conversion statistics, and other marketing research efforts can be effective at quantifying marketing effectiveness. Scalability is a critical factor in the success of distance learning initiatives; therefore, the ability of the institution to develop, deliver, and support distance learning programming is a vital consideration.

A comprehensive distance learning marketing strategy incorporates all four elements of the marketing mix: product, price, promotion, and distribution. It is important to develop a positioning strategy for each key learner segment and to vary the elements of the marketing mix in response to specific needs or preferences. Institutional culture or policies may dictate how much control the distance learning director has on curriculum offerings (product) and tuition (pricing). An existing technology platform may be a constraint that needs to be factored into distribution decisions, but there may be considerable flexibility in developing partnerships with businesses or other organizations to attract students.

Within the constraints of the marketing budget, distance learning directors often have the most direct control over the promotional strategy. Experienced distance learning directors and practitioners have discovered that the most effective promotional strategies involve both traditional and electronic media. Examples of distance learning promotional activities using traditional media include printed brochures, radio and television advertising, college and career fairs, and other print-based advertisements. Institutional Web pages, pop-over/under advertisements, e-mail distributions, banner ads, and hotlinks from other Web sites are common marketing tools that use electronic media.

Evaluating the effectiveness of marketing activities is a commonly overlooked element of marketing planning. Distance learning programs are often easy targets for budget reductions and limited marketing investment during challenging economic times. Therefore, it is particularly important for distance learning programs to quantify the return on marketing investment in order to continue to secure the necessary resources for development, operations, and marketing for continued growth. Examples of commonly used metrics include enrollment growth, net profit, the number of program hour enrollments, Web site traffic and conversion rates, aided and unaided awareness rates, and return on marketing investment.

—*Shari Lamkin Treichler*
—*Richard T. Hezel*

*See also* DEMOGRAPHICS; UNBUNDLING OF HIGHER EDUCATION

# MBA ONLINE

Online MBA programs burst onto the scene in the mid 1990s as the vanguard of Internet degree programs. American business schools, public and private, graduate some 100,000 MBA students annually from traditional classroom programs, a number far below the estimated demand for the domestic economy. Capacity limitations of campus-based programs, even with evening and weekend programs, leave a significant underserved population of working adults in need of business training. Many of these people want an MBA degree for advancement, but may not be in a position to leave their current jobs to attend school. Additionally, the world market offers a seemingly bottomless pool of candidates interested in an American-style MBA education, but who don't have the means to attend American business schools.

A variety of online MBA offerings have come forward to fill this market gap—some from traditional education institutions, others from "new schools" created by private for-profit ventures. Enrollment in online MBA programs is growing slowly but steadily as the cost advantage and convenience of these programs outweigh the risks of taking a nontraditional approach to education. Employers are increasingly willing to fund online degrees as in-service training, and a broader acceptance of online degrees seems to be inevitable.

Finding the right online program requires a bit of hard work. Because online students are not bounded by location, they have many programs from which to choose. Outside the traditional business core courses common to all MBA programs, the programs vary greatly in their advanced courses and specializations, as well as in course delivery methods, timetables, schedules, number of credits required, length of time to complete the degree, and costs. Prospective students need to read the fine print regarding these programs and do a lot of comparison shopping. The following categories of online MBA programs cater to a variety of circumstances:

- *Top-ranked business schools at private universities*—Few of these offer online MBAs, and they tend to be highly selective and expensive. Duke University's Fuqua School is probably the best-known example. Some of these schools offer degrees or at least courses through partnership arrangements with for-profit distribution firms. Online Cardean University works with several well-known business schools. They offer "branded" degrees with the widest possible recognition, but at a price.
- *State schools with outreach missions*—Many state university business schools are ranked among the top business schools, and may offer high value, lower cost online MBA programs with highly targeted (often regional) acceptance by employers. Arizona State University and Indiana University offer online MBAs to groups of employees of corporate clients. Other schools such as the University of Maryland have created for-profit subsidiaries for the delivery of online degrees. *Note: Many of these programs such as NYU-Online have been reabsorbed back into the parent institution.*
- *Full-time online institutions*—A growing list of dedicated online colleges and universities are leading the way in filling the demand for online MBA programs for adult learners. These programs are cost-competitive and usually (but not always) carry accreditation, are eligible for federal scholarships, and have financial aid programs. Most recognizable is the University of Phoenix, which probably has the longest running program and the greatest number of students in this field. Others include Jones International, Capella, Keller, National, and Walden universities.

The last category is different in that these schools are entirely focused on providing the best possible online experience. Their business success depends on delivering quality product and student satisfaction. They tend to be well organized and have thought through all of the special needs and considerations required of online students. They are proactive about counseling, are serious about quality control, and have a strong customer service orientation.

An online MBA program is likely to provide a more systematic delivery of instruction; it takes *more* careful organization of course material to teach online than it does for a classroom presentation. A special advantage is that students learn collaboration in virtual workgroups, an invaluable skill in the information age, and will certainly be forced to exercise and sharpen business communication skills. Class participation in discussions is an essential part of taking a course online and, of necessity, students learn to organize their thoughts in writing.

An online MBA is not for everyone. It requires persistence, strong motivation, discipline, organization, and a willingness to dedicate time. There is more opportunity to let things slide in on-campus programs than in a virtual classroom. Surprisingly, there is also less anonymity in an online class than in a classroom. Lost, however, is the personal camaraderie of classmates and the casual contact with faculty. On the other hand, students will not likely have to quit their jobs to get an online MBA, and most employers will contribute to the cost.

A good starting point to learn about business schools, including online programs, is the *Business Week* site, www.businessweek.com/bschools/. Get Educated's Best Distance Learning Graduate Schools: Business & Management, 2002 provides a free, 128-page, downloadable document (www.geteducated. com/bdlgs_bm.htm), which includes listings for 99 accredited distance-learning MBAs. Finally, using any Internet search engine, enter "online MBA" and watch the list grow.

*—Gene Ziegler*

*See also* CORPORATE TRAINING; DEGREES/DEGREE PROGRAMS; GRADUATE STUDY

# MEDIA

At one level, media are at the very heart of the distributed learning process, because the various forms of media enable distributed learners to engage in educational courses or programs. Without media (particularly if print media are included in the definition), no distributed learning would take place. "Conventional" education is bounded by place and by time, usually taking place face-to-face and in an educational institution. Media enable teachers and learners to be spatially separated—they do not have to be co-located for educational processes to occur. Further, some media (such as books, tapes, and disks) enable teachers and learners to be temporally separated—learning can happen whenever it is suitable for the learners. These spatial and temporal qualities describe the delivery functions of media as the means by which learners can interact with teachers and resources. However, media need to be considered at another level when they are used for education—that of the message that is being conveyed. This involves understanding the different forms in which information can be conveyed or communicated for teaching and learning (e.g., didactic presentation, case study, discussion, interactive exercise), and how those messages are intended to serve desired educational goals. In education, what is conveyed by media is more important than how it is conveyed, although the latter can set limits on what it is possible to convey. So, understanding the use of media for distributed learning is not simply a technical issue, but also involves comprehending how media can contribute to the educational process.

## DIFFERENT FORMS OF DISTRIBUTED LEARNING

Distributed learning can occur in institutions whose primary focus is campus-based teaching and learning, or it can take place in organizations that were not established to cater to on-campus education. In institutions of the former type, distributed learning involves the spatial separation of teachers and learners for example, to enable groups of students on two or more campuses to take shared courses, or to reach an "extended classroom" of learners in dispersed locations concurrently with those at the host institution. When face-to-face instruction is not the primary concern, distributed learning can also involve temporal separation. This method is particularly evident in institutions that achieve economies of scale by spreading the high front-end costs of developing high-quality media-based learning materials and resources over large numbers of students and several presentations.

Often learners study such materials independently, rather than in groups at a limited number of locations. Increasingly, however, "conventional" institutions are introducing elements of distributed learning into their courses for on-campus students, often as a means of coping with expanding student numbers or to offer greater flexibility for learners.

## DELIVERY

The delivery function of media has become more complex in recent years due to digitization and the development of a variety of communications networks. Technologies are emerging, developing, and combining to such an extent that the possibilities for conveying information and data are expanding dramatically. However, the availability of media is not ubiquitous; it varies considerably from country to country, between urban and rural areas and between different social groups. Further, the media available in institutions are unlikely to be accessible to the general public.

It is useful to think of all "messages" in terms of the constituent parts: writing, speech and sounds, and pictures (still and/or moving). Each of these elements, and combinations of them, can be delivered by a variety of means, some more familiar and widely available than others. People can receive or retrieve writing (words and symbols) in the form of printed text, from a computer disk, or via a telecommunications network (e.g., fax, e-mail, mobile phone, Web). Similarly, moving pictures can be delivered to a screen by a terrestrial television broadcast, a cable and/or satellite transmission, a telephone network, or a storage device used at the point of reception (e.g., videocassette, DVD, CD-ROM, TiVo box).

Although it might be possible for the same "message" or content to be delivered by a number of different media, each medium has its own set of characteristics such that the method of delivery influences the ways in which learners can attend to and interact with the content being conveyed. For example, a radio program has the potential to reach a very large audience, but must be listened to when broadcast and offers no opportunities for learners to control or interact with the linear structure. If made available on the Internet or delivered on audiocassette or audio CD, it could reach an audience more widely dispersed (although listeners would need to have access to suitable equipment) and learners can exercise some control over when and how they listen. Not only can listeners hear the recording whenever it is most appropriate or convenient, they are also able to use it in an active way—to stop, replay it, or skip sections as they choose. A CD's index can give the user very precise control to locate and play (or replay) particular segments as required. It follows that if learners can relate to the resources in ways that are influenced by the means of delivery, it is possible for teachers to structure materials to take advantage of particular forms of delivery so that they enable and encourage appropriate learning processes.

## THE MESSAGE CONVEYED BY MEDIA

What is conveyed by any medium, the message function, is a variable that renders simple models of media use totally inadequate. Most media are capable of conveying messages in a variety of forms, particularly when they are used for the purpose of education rather than solely for entertainment. For example, a videocassette can carry sequences of varying lengths, from very short vignettes to a full-length feature film or theatrical production. It can contain a narrative story, a real-life case study, a demonstration of a scientific experiment, or a musical performance. It can also present a compilation of newsreel stories relating to a particular topic or era.

Each of these methods not only presents some content (i.e., story, case study, experiment), but also references some form of teaching. In the case of a narrative story, the teacher's voice explicitly provides a starting point; it then develops a particular line of exposition or argument (drawing upon evidence as appropriate) before coming to a conclusion. In contrast, for learners to make sense of a case study, they might be required to analyze or evaluate the material presented using one or more explanatory theories or frameworks. The particular theory or framework to be applied might or might not be explicitly stated in the video presentation, so the "teacher's voice" might or might not be evident. The video compilation of newsreel clips need not contain any explicit teaching per se, but could be used in a variety of settings for learners to examine historical and social issues with the aid of teaching from another source. In much the same way, a set of resources on the World Wide Web might be linked by a simple contents page, a timeline, or a set of "themes" (without apparent teaching), allowing learners to explore at will. They could also be linked by a guiding narrative that provides teaching for specified educational tasks and outcomes.

## SELECTING MEDIA FOR DISTRIBUTED LEARNING

Despite various claims that have been made over many decades, there is no "super medium" for education. In practice, there are very few universal generalizations that can be applied when selecting media for distributed learning. Life would be much simpler if it were possible to say, "If you want to teach $x$, then you should use medium $y$," or "$c$ is the most effective medium if you want learners to achieve outcome $d$." However, there are usually too many variables that need to be considered, not least the economic ones (i.e., what is already available for use or can be afforded as an additional facility). Effective use of media for educational purposes depends on the consideration of (at least) three interacting sets of factors:

- *The context of media use*—Will a medium be used by groups of learners or by individuals? Will teachers and learners be working synchronously (at the same time) or asynchronously (not at the same time)? Will learners be studying at home, at their workplace, in a classroom with fellow students, in a laboratory, or in a library or resource center? Each context will present different possibilities in terms of what media might be accessible and how they can be used by learners to achieve the desired educational goals.

- *The characteristics of the medium*—What form of communication does a particular medium allow (one-way, two-way, multi-way)? Does it enable and support interactive activities? Does the medium facilitate dialogue between human participants in the learning process? What contribution(s) can the medium make to the overall teaching and learning development and does it need to be combined with other media?

- *The educational design*—How will the "message" or content conveyed by the medium be designed to promote teaching and/or learning? Will the "teacher's voice" be implicit or explicit (i.e., integral within the message, or provided in some other way)? What pedagogical approaches can be supported by a particular medium?

## COSTS OF MEDIA FOR DISTRIBUTED LEARNING

Practical expediency and cost often play a crucial role in decisions made about the use of media for distributed learning. Individual teachers might consider what media possibilities are available to them, what enhancements might be feasible, and how they can make the best use of whatever facilities are accessible. Institutions, in contrast, are more likely to be concerned about what media systems and services they can afford to acquire, maintain, and support. It has been suggested that the costs of media-based distributed learning are lower than conventional teaching and training, but it is necessary to take all of the costs into account, not least those relating to the human input required to develop and maintain materials and resources and to support the learning process. The overall costs of media for distributed learning can usefully be categorized as capital or recurrent, or as being fixed or variable.

- *Capital and recurrent costs*—Capital costs are those incurred in acquiring premises, equipment, and the like. Some of these costs might be one-time costs, whereas others will be part of an ongoing schedule of acquisitions and replacements. For distributed learning, there are not only the central capital costs to be considered, but also the local capital costs for providing multiple facilities and/or networks, or for equipping local resource rooms or centers. If learners are dispersed across a wide geographical area, it is possible that the total cost of end-user equipment will be greater than the equipment costs for central development and production. Recurrent costs include the expenses that are incurred as the capital equipment is being utilized (staff and operating costs, the development and production costs of learning materials and resources, and so on). Staff costs constitute a considerable proportion of the total. The development and maintenance of resources by academic staff are very time-consuming, and it is increasingly necessary for technical support staff to maintain and update the hardware, software, and networking facilities, while also provide support to teachers and learners experiencing problems. Recurrent costs can easily exceed the capital costs, and not just for complex materials or computer software resources. Setting up a computer conference might seem to incur relatively low capital costs, but active conferencing requires regular participation by teachers or moderators, so the recurrent costs can be substantial.

- *Fixed and variable costs*—The fixed costs of media development and production are those that are independent of the number of learners for whom resources are created. For example, the cost of developing and maintaining a set of linked Web pages remains more or less constant whether there are 20 or 20,000 learners who view the site. However, if the same set of pages was sent on CD-ROM to individual learners, the copying and distribution costs would vary according to the number of recipients. So, variable costs depend on the number of learners. Both the fixed and the variable cost components for different media vary. Although the fixed and variable costs of audiocassettes and audio CDs are low, both cost components are high for multimedia involving full-motion video sequences.

The number of potential learners is important in determining the cost-effectiveness of any medium. Cost per learner is a key factor to be estimated—when large numbers of learners are involved, high-cost media might be appropriate; for relatively small numbers of learners, however, such media are likely to prove prohibitively expensive.

—*Adrian Kirkwood*

*See also* CURRICULUM MODELS; DELIVERY SYSTEMS; INSTRUCTIONAL COURSE DESIGN

## Bibliography

Bates, A. W. (1995). *Technology, open learning and distance education.* London: Routledge.

Clark, R. E. (Ed.). (2001). *Learning from media.* Greenwich, CT: Information Age Publishing.

Inglis, A., Ling, P., & Joosten, V. (1999). *Delivering digitally: Managing the transition to the knowledge media.* London: Kogan Page.

Laurillard, D. (2001). *Rethinking university teaching,* 2nd Edition. London: Routledge.

Rumble, G. (1997). *The costs and economics of open and distance learning.* London: Kogan Page.

# MEDICAL EDUCATION

Distributed medical education is similar to other forms of education in which distance is involved. It is a simple concept, in which geographical separation (distance) between the teaching expert and students is bridged by means of advanced telecommunications and information technologies that ensure distribution of expert knowledge to a large and widely distributed audience. Although the standard notion of distributed education ensures that "the teacher is brought to the class," it does not provide for the hospital ward to be brought along. Distributed medical education attempts to furnish the solution to this essential issue.

Contrary to many other aspects of distributed education—for example, business, law, engineering, and art—medical training imposes several practical difficulties that must be overcome for such training to become effective. Since its beginning, traced to the legendary Hippocrates, Western medical education was based on mentoring—a process during which a senior and experienced healer imparted expert knowledge to a group of students who, through the development of their own base of experience, passed the cumulative base of medical knowledge to the next generation of physicians. The commonly used aphorism "See one, do one, teach one" retained its validity throughout the centuries, and is still true today. The concept of a "clinical pearl" is another indicator of the essential mentor–student relationship that has been and continues to be the cornerstone of medical practice. The pearl is an elegant but undocumented approach to a medical problem that is passed on to a junior healer by the mentor, whose vast experience allows synthesis of facts into a simple procedure or an unfailing diagnostic pointer.

During its evolution, the *art of healing* slowly transformed into the *science and art of medicine.* Through a series of trials and errors, medicine gradually evolved into a highly complex field requiring increasingly greater mastery of a wide, and incessantly expanding, body of knowledge, techniques, and sheer experience necessary for the art of healing to be practiced efficiently. The most explosive growth of medicine began after World War II, when transfer of many technologies used for predominantly military purposes (such as nuclear physics, computing, and microelectronics) served as probably the most significant factor in changing the face of health care to what it is today.

Rapid and continuing expansion in the understanding of the processes that constitute the basis of both health and disease had a powerful impact on the character of medical education. Prior to the era of "medical revolution," medicine was taught by the rigid lines of knowledge of anatomy, physiology, and pharmacology, followed by demonstration of their roles in the process of disease by exposing the students to patients presenting with progressively more complex problems. Simultaneously, a range of techniques (diagnostic and surgical) was developed so that, at the end of a comparatively grueling period of several years of intense study, the new physician was expected to competently handle a wide range of commonly encountered problems.

Presently, although the basic pattern has not changed, both students and practicing physicians are exposed to the explosive growth of medical knowledge and rapid changes of practice based on new medical discoveries. Hence, the education provided by the institutions of medical learning is largely limited to what is known today. Everything that will happen tomorrow must be gathered through the process of continuous medical education (CME) mandated by the legislatures of an increasing number of countries.

Prior to the introduction of the Internet and the World Wide Web, the problem of CME was daunting. Several issues conspired against the effective postgraduate education of a large number of health care workers at the same level of impeccable quality and standards that govern education at schools of medicine and allied health professions. The sheer size of the professional population that needs continuous postgraduate education—either as refresher training (e.g., training in Advanced Cardiac Life Support) or merely to keep abreast of the latest changes in medical practice—the distance from centers of medical education where such courses are commonly held, interruption of practice caused by participation in training, and (often most importantly) the associated cost were among the principal factors that significantly affected the ability to stay current, particularly among providers working in rural, remote, or economically depressed regions. Moreover, the classical dissemination of new medical facts and discoveries through professional journals was proving inadequate due to the exponential growth of essential information that was published in a vast variety of printed sources such as journals, books, and guidelines. Even more significantly, by the time the data emerged in print, there was a risk they would be obsolete due to discoveries that took place in the interim. Hence, it is not surprising that the rapid growth of Internet access, high-speed connectivity, increasing sophistication of Web-based medical sites, and the dynamic growth in the range and flexibility of electronic medical educational tools are probably among the most significant developments that changed the face of postgraduate medical education by allowing access to the best sources of knowledge and medical expertise without leaving one's office.

Presently, there are a wide variety of CME offerings that utilize the Internet as a carrier medium and provide medical distance education. Although many distance-based medical education programs allow interaction between the expert tutor and the trainees, the degree of that interaction varies. As a result, Internet-based distance medical education resources can be broadly subdivided into passive and active. Web sites such as WebMD (http://www.webmd.com) and its associated Medscape (http://www.medscape.com), E-Medicine (http://www.emedicine.com), and Virtual Hospital (http://www.vh.org) are among the most popular in the passive category. Entering any of these sites, the user can gain access to the latest information on current medical practice, updates on new drugs, information on medical alerts, or current guidelines on treatment of disease. Many of these sites—for example, WebMD or the American Heart Association's Web site (http://www.americanheart.org)—offer quizzes and tests whose completion awards CME credits. In principle, the use of such learning resources does not differ much from reading professional literature; the only difference is that the information is updated often on a daily basis, its acquisition is vastly cheaper (the price of Internet access vs. the price of a journal or a book), it is more convenient (one's own computer terminal vs. a visit to the library), and the information is often much broader (summary papers by recognized experts with references to subject-specific literature and other sources vs. the need to use several journals and books). In short, the passive Internet-based learning resources offer the convenience of accessing expert knowledge, assimilating it, and eventually testing the level of acquisition from essentially any computer on earth.

The principal merit of the technology-based approach to learning medicine is the learner's freedom from physical contact with the centers of medical education and their educational resources without the loss of the quality of the acquired knowledge. It is important to note, however, that although Internet-based medical information tools allow both maintenance of one's knowledge base and its continuous expansion, they do not allow training in the practical implementation of such knowledge.

The development of High Fidelity Patient Simulators (HFPS), also known as Human Patient Simulators (HPS), along with virtual reality (VR) medical training platforms, was the essential step that allowed practical introduction of distance medical learning based on the demand for active participation of the students through real-time interaction with simulation platform(s) that could be located several thousands miles away from the student site. Student access to the remote simulation training unit is provided by a variety of high-speed telecommunication channels (DSL, ATM, satellite, or wireless). The expert mentor interacts in real time with the simulator and the trainees, despite the fact that the mentor's location may be completely separated from the simulation platform, the students, or both. Medical training based on distributed simulation employs many of the principles originally developed by the U.S. Department of Defense and provides learners with a very fast-paced, practical training in a "synthetic" environment whose intensity (including that of stress) is arguably as close to reality as can be attained outside real-life activities. It also allows projection of medical training expertise at very large distances, without the expert having to leave the site of the parent institution.

Distance learning based on HFPS has been developed under the direction of Dag von Lubitz. Presently, HFPSs are routinely used in distance training in both prehospital and hospital-level emergency and trauma medicine by MedSMART, Inc. (Ann Arbor, MI), a non-profit organization devoted solely to such operations on a worldwide scale. Arguably the most advanced surgical distance training system has been created by the group headed by George Graschew at the Charité Hospital in Berlin. The system (OP 2000/GALENOS) is based on immersive virtual reality and allows full interaction and control of the VR-rendered surgical patient by the remote trainee. As with HFPS-based distance training, the location of the teaching expert is entirely independent from the location of either the training platform or the students. OP 2000/GALENOS has been successfully tested and evaluated in Europe, and its fusion with HFPS distance training is under development. Practical worldwide deployment of the combined system will introduce an unprecedented level of sophistication, realism, and interactivity into the realm of distance medical education. As such, it will be of unquestionable significance for medical education and training in rural, remote, and economically underprivileged regions of the globe.

TV broadcasting of HFPS-based training offers another highly alluring and potentially effective form of distributed medical learning. Although the level of interactivity is significantly reduced compared to either the OP 2000 or MedSMART concepts, the combination of HFPS and television permits dissemination of simulation-based training conducted by the leading experts over a very wide area (continental/transcontinental). Most importantly, the only technical requirement imposed upon the learner in this form of distance learning is the possession of a TV set.

—*Dag K. J. E. van Lubitz*

*See also* DEGREES/DEGREE PROGRAMS; GRADUATE STUDY; TELEHEALTH AND TELEMEDICINE

## Bibliography

Adams, L. B., Jr. (Ed.). (1982). *The aphorisms of Hippocrates.* New York: The Classics of Medicine Library.

Graschew, G., Rakowsky, S., Balanou, P., & Schlag, P. M. (2000). Interactive telemedicine in the operating theatre of the future. *J. Telemed. Telecare 6* (Suppl. 2), 820–824.

Graschew, G., Roelofs, T. A., Rakowsky, S., & Schlag, P. M. (2002). Interactive telemedical applications in OP 2000 via satellite. *Biomed. Tech. (Berl.) 47* (Suppl. 1, Pt. 1), 330–333.

Lock, S., Last, J. M., & Dunea, G. (Eds.). (2001). *The Oxford illustrated companion to medicine.* Oxford: Oxford University Press.

Neyland, D. I. (1997). *Virtual combat: A guide to distributed interactive simulation.* Mechanicsburg, PA: Stackpole Books.

Porter, R. (Ed.). (1996). *The Cambridge illustrated history of medicine.* Cambridge: Cambridge University Press.

Treloar, D., Montgomery, J., Russell, W., & The Medical Readiness Trainer Team. (2001). On site and distance education of emergency medicine personnel with a human patient simulator. *J. Mil. Med, 166,* 1003–1006.

von Lubitz, D. K. J. E., Carrasco, B., Gabbrielli, F., Lewine, H., Ludwig, T., & Poirier, C. (2003). Transatlantic medical education: Preliminary data on distance-based high fidelity human patient simulation training. In J. Westwood (Ed.), *Medicine meets virtual reality 2003.* Amsterdam: IOS Press.

Von Lubitz, D. K. J. E., Levine, H., & Wolf, E. (2002). The goose, the gander, or the Strasbourg paté for all: Medical education, world, and the Internet. In W. Chin, F. Poatricelli, & V. Milutinovoc (Eds.), *Electronic business and education: Recent advances in Internet infrastructures* (pp. 189–210). Boston: Kluwer.

# METACOMMUNICATION

*Metacommunication* is a term used to refer to anything that a person takes into account as an aid in interpreting what another person is saying, the nature of a given situation, how to comprehend what is happening, and so on. Metacommunication is generally considered to be a message that is not expressed in words but that accompanies a message that is expressed in words. It is, therefore, any clue or evidence that a person uses in understanding something or someone. It is communication about communication. Communication carries a message, or meaningful content, as well as a command or cue about how to interpret the message. Face-to-face communication allows the receiver of the message to ask questions about the cues being received in order to clarify the message being transmitted. When discussion occurs about what is being said, how listening occurs, and what is being understood, communication improves. In face-to-face communication, metacommunication often refers to nonverbal means of communicating, such as the use of facial expressions or gestures and tone of voice. However, given that auditory and visual cues are missing from the online communication process, metacommunication takes on new meaning in that environment, and generally involves the sometimes difficult interpretation of text-based communication. The cues or commands needed for interpretation of the message often need to be overt, such as the inclusion of symbols or pictures that convey emotion (also known as "emoticons") or through explicit description of emotion or intent. Care needs to be taken in the construction of messages contributed to an online discussion so that metacommunicative cues are included to aid in interpretation of thought and meaning.

Metacommunication can be related to metalearning, which is defined as learning how to learn. In the traditional academic world, metalearning often refers to the learning of processes that can optimize learning (e.g., learning skills to improve memory or reading ability). In the field of online education, however, metalearning refers to learning how to learn through the use of technology. In so doing, people learn more about technology and how it impacts the learning process. Metacommunication and metalearning can also be related to the term *transformative learning,* coined and written about by Jack Mezirow and Patricia Cranton. Transformative learning is an outcome of metacommunication or metalearning. It is a process of using a prior interpretation to revise or create a new interpretation of one's experience as a means of guiding future action. In other words, through feedback and reflection on communication, new approaches to old situations or problems result and a transformation of the learner can occur.

Exploring the communication process in online learning is a phenomenon that occurs through interaction in the online course. It tends to occur whether or not the instructor or facilitator plans for it, but can be incorporated into the course through the request for and provision of feedback, both from instructor to student and from student to student. Teaching students to provide good, substantive feedback to one another as a part of the learning process assists with learning through metacommunication. Substantive feedback goes beyond saying "Good job" or "I agree," and provides evaluative comments that promote reflection and the development of critical thinking skills. Consequently, good feedback entails seeking first to understand or clarify the ideas of the other, and then supporting the ideas presented, beginning a new topic or moving the discussion in a new direction, or somehow adding to the discussion by critically reflecting on what is being discussed.

Providing guidance on online communication skills helps to avoid situations that can interfere with the communication or metacommunication process, such as flaming (responding to another person in anger) or misinterpreting thoughts or ideas. In this regard, providing online students with information about netiquette (the guidelines for professional online communication) and emoticons can support the ability to interpret metacommunication. Netiquette rules dictate, for example, that messages should not be typed in all capital letters, because this conveys anger or force. Likewise, all lowercase should not be used because it symbolizes passivity or submissiveness. Many people, when first communicating online, are unaware of these rules and may make errors. Using symbols such as :) to express happiness, :( to express sadness, or ;) to express teasing helps the reader to know the intent of the message. Students can also be encouraged to "bracket" their emotions in order to express them in the context of an online message. For example, a student might write, "[Picture me standing on a soapbox with a raised fist as I say this] I had great difficulty with this week's reading assignment and found it to be upsetting." In so doing, the writer in this example conveys a sense of dissatisfaction, anger, or unhappiness with minimal risk that the message will be interpreted as a personal attack.

In conclusion, providing communication guidelines at the beginning of an online course and educating students as to what comprises appropriate communication in the online environment, along with tips and tricks to express emotion, can assist students in developing metacommunication skills. They will learn how to deliver and receive messages appropriately and know how to ask for clarification should that be needed.

*—Rena M. Palloff*
*—Keith Pratt*

*See also* CRITICAL DIALOGUES; FEEDBACK; TRANSFORMATIONAL LEARNING

## Bibliography

Bateson, Gregory. (1972). *Steps to an ecology of mind.* New York: Chandler.

Branco, Angela. (July 2000). Metacommunication and the development of the "self." *Proceeds of the Third Conference for Sociocultural Research.* Retrieved from http://www.fae.unicamp.br/br2000/trabs/1980.doc.

Cranton, Patricia. (1994). *Understanding and promoting transformative learning.* San Francisco: Jossey-Bass.

Mezirow, Jack. (1990). *Fostering critical reflection in adulthood: A guide to transformative and emancipatory learning.* San Francisco: Jossey-Bass.

Watzlawick, Paul, Beavin, J. H., & Jackson, D. D. (1967). *Pragmatics of human communication: A study of interactional patterns, pathologies, and paradoxes.* New York: W. W. Norton.

# N

## NETIQUETTE

*Netiquette* is actual or recommended codes of behavior, conduct, and communication for people who interact over the Internet, in cyberspace, or in networked environments. In society, the rules and conventions of face-to-face etiquette that regulate social and professional behavior, and that are enforced by group pressure, have developed over time and in particular contexts. Although there are different social contexts in electronic and online environments, such as e-mail, newsgroups, online courses, and salons, for the user these are largely mediated through a device, such as a computer monitor displaying text, with few reminders of the differences among these environments and of the social and cultural rules that prevail in them. Different conventions also apply in the business, educational, personal, and public domains.

Every communication medium or technology has specific characteristics in two dimensions: within itself and in the way it impacts the surrounding social environment. Specific rules of netiquette are created to socially regulate both of these. When one is writing a letter in the United States, for example, etiquette dictates that the letter begin with "Dear _____" and end with some formalized greeting such as "Yours truly," "Sincerely yours," "Warmly," or the like, depending on the relationship between the writer and the intended recipient. This sort of etiquette is culturally specific. Instead of "Sincerely yours," Germans write "with highest respect," and the French must write an entire sentence requesting recipient to accept the expression of the writer's distinguished consideration.

The introduction of new technologies, for which rules of etiquette have not yet been worked out by society, brings with it changes, ambiguities, and conflicts about appropriate social behavior and meanings. A letter sent by e-mail will not always contain the same greeting and salutation as would a letter sent via postal mail. Until the advent of mobile phones, it was considered impolite in most circles to carry on a phone conversation while seated at a dinner table with others. Now such behavior is common in some circles. In the early 21st century, letters to the editors of newspapers are filled with comments, frustrations, and recommendations about the inappropriate and appropriate use of mobile phones. In the United States, laws have been passed regulating the use of mobile phones while driving a vehicle, and processes are under way to develop explicit social codes and etiquette regulating the use of mobile phones in public places. Social uproars have arisen in response to the inappropriate forwarding to others of e-mail messages intended only for the recipient, and there is controversy about whether e-mail messages written by employees belong to them or to their employers. Technological change, because it is intertwined with social change, often creates the need for new social codes and rules.

Netiquette has arisen for several reasons. First, as a substantial number of people began to interact over computer networks it became clear, partly through misunderstandings, conflicts, or disruptions, that cyberspace is like any other domain of social life in requiring a normative background to function effectively and civilly.

Second, as noted above, in face-to-face interaction, social norms, meanings, and intentions are expressed through visual, nonverbal, and bodily cues, such as facial expression, tone of voice, and gesture, that surround and shape communication. These cues are often unavailable in cyberspace, which creates possibilities for misunderstandings that would not occur in face-to-face interaction, where for example, the meaning of words is usually framed by tone of voice, and the same word can have a different interpersonal meaning or emotional impact based on this framing. The tone of voice is lacking in the text of an e-mail message. This has led to the widespread use of "emoticons," visual symbols such as ;-) that represent emotion and help to communicate the affective intent of a word or sentence.

Third, networked environments frequently bring together individuals from different regions, cultural backgrounds, and social statuses who cannot rely on a common, taken-for-granted normative background.

Fourth, many individuals originally enter cyberspace with a feeling of adventure and exploration that involves a sense of escape or relief from the social norms and cultural values that regulate the rest of their lives. In its early days, observers of cyberspace frequently described it as having a "Wild West," "free-for-all" atmosphere that emphasized individualistic and unconventional behavior and a disregard of social norms. Even now, entering a new online environment can be like travelling to a new country with an alien culture.

Fifth, the electronic communication media themselves have distinctive technical properties that can make communication, especially when undertaken by the inexperienced, impact others in unanticipated, unintended, and occasionally problematic ways. For example, a large file that was easy for the sender to transmit may be difficult for the receiver to receive, or a message may transmit a computer virus, or files may be in incompatible formats. A mailing list may send a message to an individual on vacation in a way that initiates an infinite e-mail loop of "on vacation" messages where list members who do not know how to unsubscribe compound the problem by sending "unsubscribe" messages to the members of the list.

Finally, there appear to be distinctive social and psychological properties of communication and interaction in cyberspace that differ from those in face-to-face interaction. An example is "flaming," in which individuals suddenly erupt in expressions of anger and hostility. Another is a widespread tendency to believe and transmit rumors and misinformation received or encountered in cyberspace.

Individuals used to operating on traditional campuses and participating in classrooms will find that in distributed education they need to attend to features of the digital learning environment and make explicit expectations regarding behavior and communication. They cannot assume common understanding among participants. Administrators need to develop and post policies concerning rights and responsibilities for the use of electronic communication, and learning facilitators need to provide guidelines for participation. Because the usual mechanisms of reinforcement present on campuses and in classrooms by virtue of tradition, architecture, and other visual cues are missing, ways of reiterating norms need to be found and employed, the details of which will vary depending on the electronic medium. For example, a frequently asked questions (FAQ) document can be posted on a Web site and linked to from an online classroom; subscribers to an e-mail list can receive a "welcome" message explaining the purpose of the list and what is deemed appropriate and inappropriate behavior. A similar message can be sent out periodically.

Consider that humans have 50,000 years of experience in the use of speech and gestures and another 5,000 years of writing. Now consider that the telephone is only 100 years old and the World Wide Web close to a decade! Add to that the fact that individuals and organizations worldwide are now linked, and it is not surprising that there is unevenness of behavior and confusion in online communication.

Rules of netiquette for making interaction smoother, more harmonious, more rational, and more civil can be codified in explicit documents. An example is the Internet's "official" netiquette document, RFC 1855 on "Netiquette Guidelines." Because of the status and richness of this document, a number of the points made above are illustrated here with quotes:

> Unless you have your own Internet access through an Internet provider, be sure to check with your employer about ownership of electronic mail. Laws about the ownership of electronic mail vary from place to place.
>
> Unless you are using an encryption device (hardware or software), you should assume that mail on the Internet is not secure. Never put in a mail message anything you would not put on a postcard.

Respect the copyright on material that you reproduce. Almost every country has copyright laws.

If you are forwarding or re-posting a message you've received, do not change the wording. If the message was a personal message to you and you are re-posting to a group, you should ask permission first. You may shorten the message and quote only relevant parts, but be sure you give proper attribution.

A good rule of thumb: Be conservative in what you send and liberal in what you receive. You should not send heated messages (we call these "flames") even if you are provoked. On the other hand, you shouldn't be surprised if you get flamed and it's prudent not to respond to flames.

Be careful when addressing mail. There are addresses which may go to a group but the address looks like it is just one person. Know to whom you are sending.

Remember that people with whom you communicate are located across the globe. If you send a message to which you want an immediate response, the person receiving it might be at home asleep when it arrives. Give them a chance to wake up, come to work, and login before assuming the mail didn't arrive or that they don't care.

Remember that the recipient is a human being whose culture, language, and humor have different points of reference from your own. Remember that date formats, measurements, and idioms may not travel well. Be especially careful with sarcasm.

Use mixed case. UPPER CASE LOOKS AS IF YOU'RE SHOUTING.

Don't send large amounts of unsolicited information to people.

Read both mailing lists and newsgroups for one to two months before you post anything. This helps you to get an understanding of the culture of the group.

Consider that a large audience will see your posts. That may include your present or your next boss. Take care in what you write. Remember too, that mailing lists and newsgroups are frequently archived, and that your words may be stored for a very long time in a place to which many people have access.

If you find a personal message has gone to a list or group, send an apology to the person and to the group.

When sending a message to more than one mailing list, especially if the lists are closely related, apologize for cross-posting.

Do NOT assume that ANY information you find is up-to-date and/or accurate. Remember that new technologies allow just about anyone to be a publisher, but not all people have discovered the responsibilities that accompany publishing.

Since the Internet spans the globe, remember that Information Services might reflect culture and life-style markedly different from your own community. Materials you find offensive may originate in a geography which finds them acceptable. Keep an open mind. (Hambridge, 1995)

There are many good examples of such netiquette codes on the Web; some are listed in the Bibliography section. Inevitably they reflect the time of their writing or a particular electronic communication tool, and these issues must be taken into consideration when considering whether to apply or translate them into a different online environment. The key features of good netiquette are courtesy and common sense, which are not always evident. As educators, how will social norms be communicated? Following is a meta-guideline checklist to be used as a reminder of issues that the distributed educator will want to take into account in developing netiquette for her or his own environment.

## META-GUIDELINE CHECKLIST

A checklist for electronic communications could be divided in a variety of ways, such as the nature of the communication (one-to-one, one-to-many), the particular medium (e-mail, Web conference, chat), or an individual's relationship to it (administrator, user). This meta-guideline checklist uses content and context as category headings.

### Content:

- Legal implications—developing policies and communicating them to users
- Ownership of e-mail and other files
- Intellectual property and copyright
- What material is proper to post or send and what is prohibited (e.g., advertising)
- What material is available and what is not
- Academic freedom and freedom of speech
- Inflammatory or incendiary content

### Context:

- What are the rules for being a responsible citizen on your network?

- Who is the audience; are there multiple audiences that need to be addressed?
- Server side—What software (courseware, groupware, e-mail, etc.) tools are you making available?
- Client side—Is everyone using the same or different browsers, word processors, e-mail clients, etc.?
- One-to-one, one-to-many—same or different guidelines?
- Is there specific information that should always appear, never appear, or is optional in a message or post (full name, e-mail address, geographic location, subject)? Are anonymous postings permitted?
- Privacy issues
- Relationship issues
- How to present oneself
- Sharing material—Should attached files be in particular formats only? Is it appropriate to send an attachment to a mailing list?
- Are particular fonts required or problematic for any reason?
- Who does a user contact for help, and how much and what information does the user need to provide?
- Are there expectations for responses? In a particular time frame? There are both human and technical implications. For example, in an online discussion some time may need to elapse before a posted item will show up on a server.
- Are there system rules or disc storage space, archiving, or other technical administrative issues?

Initially, Internet users hoped that technology would solve many of our social problems. Instead, users need to be educated and re-educated to understand their roles online. At the same time, advanced technology still promises to help create online spaces that are easier for new users to enter and participate in more gracefully.

—*Shelley K. Hughes*
—*Jeremy J. Shapiro*

*See also* E-MAIL; INTELLECTUAL PROPERTY; ONLINE LEARNING ENVIRONMENTS; POLICIES

## Bibliography

Hambridge, S. (1995). *RFC 1855 netiquette guidelines.* Retrieved May 30, 2002, from http://www.dtcc.edu/cs/rfc1855.html.

Hawke, C. S. (2001). *Computer and Internet use on campus: A legal guide to issues of intellectual property, free speech, and privacy.* San Francisco, CA: Jossey-Bass.

Rinaldi, A. H. (1998). *The Net: User guidelines and netiquette.* Retrieved May 30, 2002, from http://www.fau.edu/netiquette/net/.

Shapiro, J. J., & Hughes, S. K. (2002). The case of the inflammatory e-mail: Building culture and community in online academic environments. In K. E. Rudestam & J. Schoenholtz-Read (Eds.), *Handbook of online learning: Innovations in higher education and corporate training* (pp. 91–124). Thousand Oaks, CA: Sage.

Shea, V. (September/October 1994). Core rules of netiquette. *Educom Review*, 58–62.

Shea, V. (December 7, 1997). *Netiquette.* Albion Books. Retrieved June 15, 2002, from http://www.albion.com/netiquette/book/index.html.

# NETWORKS

A network is a system of connection points that are loosely linked to allow the exchange of information or material resources among them. Characterized by their connectivity, that is, their technical capacity to be linked to a network that is itself connective, the points (nodes) are usually complementary and can function alternately as emitters, simple transmitters, or receivers of resources that can be rerouted by many nodes before reaching their final destination. An addressing system adapted to the specific network's nature must be put in place for the nodes to know which is the intended receiving point of a particular flow, a routing process that takes various forms depending on the type of system considered (human, technical, logical). In fact, although the concept of network is a rather old one, already embodied in the Roman aqueduct systems, the last century saw the beginning of networks being integrated into different disciplines, a phenomenon leading to their being frequently used to systemically describe material structures as well as human communities.

Networks are the basis of many of our modern communication systems, from railways and roads to telephones, television, electronics, and computers. Networks are a central characteristic of information and communication technologies. The network configuration of these telecommunication tools introduces new possibilities in terms of interpersonal communication and individual action. New types of social relationships are being created.

The concept of a *network* is also used in other fields of knowledge, such as management, publicity, sociology, and anthropology, to express the idea of informal relationship systems and their economic potential. This extended use of the concept, combined with its importance in the rapid technological developments experienced by the new technologies industry in the last decades, has even led some academicians to describe our society as a "network nation"—a description first made by Hiltz and Turoff in the late 1970s but still defended by many today.

## A TECHNICAL REVOLUTION: COMMUNICATION NETWORKS

Although mail, telegram, and telephone networks were the central means of distance communication for decades, since the 1960s there has been an unprecedented development in the performance of telecommunication networks—a trend toward rapid technical improvements so vigorous that some even describe it as a revolution. Although, despite its limited bandwidth, the telephonic infrastructure is still the central network linking one location to another, its transmission capacities, as well as the range of existing alternatives to it, have greatly increased. Technologies such as fiber-optic cable and satellite transmission now provide promising, high-efficiency transmission options.

A first giant step in the improvement of telephone networks was the early replacement of analog signals with numeric ones, a phenomenon that took place in the 1960s under pressure for better signal quality and cost reduction. This technology allows one line to conduct more than one signal at a time by compressing messages that have previously been transformed from variable analog signals into binary series of numbers by means of quantification and sampling. This advance clearly helped enhance signal quality because the variations in transmission no longer endanger the correct reception of the initial signal. At the same time, the possibility of shared channels for multiple signals helped reduce transmission costs and opened telephone lines to any numeric media.

Parallel to this improvement, the computer networking initiatives of the late 1960s brought packet switching technology, a mode of transmission specifically built to handle variable flows of data. Packet switching is currently a central characteristic of the Internet's structure. Flexible and efficient, packet switching has become a key element of current and future multifunction networks. Indeed, the important convergence of various media toward numeric signals, a phenomenon that led Nicholas Negroponte to talk about a "numeric world," is likely to generate common solutions to many current transmission problems.

The very large size of multimedia messages, compared to voice or textual data, poses particular challenges to network transmission capacities and their convergence. This circulation problem was anticipated years ago, when the demand for the exchange of multimedia data exploded following the unexpected popularization of personal computers and the Internet. Solving this problem is critical.

## NETWORKED LEARNING SOLUTIONS

With the improvement of network performance, current and upcoming applications are opening the way to substantive new modes of interaction and learning. Distance learning has a long history—the first form of distributed learning was personal instruction mediated through traditional postal mail. However, it has undergone fundamental and rapid changes over the last century or so through the progressive development of telecommunication networked technologies.

The telephone, of course, was an early and widespread educational tool, useful to support learners but mainly used as a complement to written instructions, not as a solution on its own. Television was then cast as the new answer for distance learning, leading to the popularization of the idea of university classes offered directly on television to a delocalized group of students. However, this mode of distance learning has not succeeded; nor did the subsequent CD-ROM trend. These tools offered no opportunities for interaction between learners, and often were not dynamic enough to keep learners' attention focused. In addition, they left no room for interpersonal communication, an element that can be particularly motivating and supportive of the learning process. Finally, because these methods need a lot of start-up time and because it was impossible to update their content automatically, they were not well adapted to corporate purposes.

The current accelerated development in telecommunication networks and in user-friendly application creation paved the way for a renewal of off-campus and corporate distributed learning. Indeed, the instantaneity of information delivery and updates offered by networked tools is a key characteristic of e-learning as it is understood today, ensuring the accuracy of the content provided. At the same time, networked learning stations have introduced the possibility of effective synchronous or asynchronous communication among learners, or between them and their instructor. By overcoming the isolation that was an endemic part of previous distance learning processes, a social dimension was thus re-created.

The reintroduction of interpersonal communications (through a virtual community of learners that can be limited to members of a specific organization or open to any individual who registers for a particular class) is one of the principal explanations for the efficiency of today's distributed learning solutions. The integration of interpersonal communications takes into account some crucial principles of the learning process as understood by cognitive science and constructionist pedagogy. The diversification of the modes of knowledge acquisition available to the learner, by means of interactive interfaces and possible participation in a virtual community, facilitates the process by answering the needs of all styles of learning, not just the conceptual or abstract style usually associated with academic training. The development of technical networks connected learners while also leaving them a strong independence in their own learning experience. Once networked technically, learners also become networked socially.

## SOCIAL ORGANIZATION

Georg Simmel's early work on social circles and the sociometric movement of the 1940s marked the beginning of network analysis in the social sciences. This is a formal approach to analyzing the social links present in natural communities or institutionalized groups and their environment. Focusing either on a particular individual or a population as a whole, network analysis attempts to draw a qualitative portrait of the many relationships that constitute an individual's or population's social environments. The first step toward this mapping is discovering the individual's position, understood as a node's position in the global system, and the multiple links connecting them. These links have to be separately characterized in terms of type and strength of the relationship in order for the analyst to reveal the underlying structure of the whole. The presence or absence of structural patterns—for example, the existence of subgroups or cores in the system—is then evaluated at the same time as the whole is defined through the determination of its structural variables. The network's range (size and heterogeneity), density, boundedness, and centrality (that is, the existence or not of prominent nodes in terms of connectivity between individuals) are thus measured in order to complete the analysis. The general system portrait emerging from this analysis suggests likely future developments. A network with a high range, for example, is usually more capable of seeking and finding new resources, because the presence of weak ties in heterogeneous systems ensures a greater openness toward other networks and thus a potential for innovation.

Network analysis refuses to consider a particular group as completely separate from the others and impermeable to outside influence. It views a network as an open system in which linkages between multiple networks and their formal boundaries are not relevant as an *a priori* constraint. In that sense, it is a systemic perspective that differs considerably from other modes of sociological inquiry because it reduces the importance of the traditional social and geographical categories as structural determinants of communities. In one view, although communities have been largely modeled by geographical proximity (neighborhoods) for centuries, the urbanization movement and the rapid pace of technological developments during the last century led to a progressive reorganization in our mode of affiliation, first toward primary social groups at the expense of neighbors and then around delocalized groups of interest. The opportunities offered by asynchronous and relatively inexpensive technologies of communication would erase the community's territorial anchorage, the time and space limits traditionally inherent in interpersonal communication.

There are, however, some opponents to this minimization of the link between territory and community. Some researchers believe that physical proximity is still a very strong determinant in group formation. For example, the contextuality of an interaction, that is, its concrete social and sociotemporal conditions, is seen by certain people as inseparable from its meaning.

## COMMUNITY AND CORPORATE NETWORKING

Network configuration is seen by many as a key characteristic of our societal paradigm, a morphology that answers better than any other to the fast-changing and complex nature of our environment. Preserving a maximum flexibility in the system, while also introducing a structure stable enough for it to be manageable, the network configuration ensures an openness to innovation and, hence, seems particularly appropriate when rapid adaptation to change is fundamental to an organization's survival. Many corporations are thus starting to reconsider their internal structure and their relationships with other organizations in terms of networks. They are creating strategic partnerships to increase their effectiveness and flexibility instead of trying to be largely self-sufficient in their production process. The Japanese *Keiretsus* (working groups) used in the automobile and financial industries, as well as in other fields, constitute excellent examples of long-term inter-organizational collaboration that led to the creation of corporate networks and allowed rapid adaptations to environmental changes—a competitive advantage that appeared quite significant over the years. Fundamentally a risk sharing strategy, this mode of stable corporate networking helps lessen transaction costs for all partners.

In the communitarian field, as well, networking is becoming an increasingly widespread mode of organization, facilitated by the exponential popularization of technologies of communication such as the Internet. At the local as well as at the international level, individuals or small groups are trying to enhance their political weight by creating links with other groups endorsing some of their points of view. Coalitions reacting to the impact of the globalization movement, for example, are built around organizations that are sometimes only loosely linked together. The openness to other networks offered by weak ties within the system is a key element of their power to mobilize. Just as they facilitate distance education by reintroducing interpersonal communication opportunities, telecommunication networks support civil engagement by breaking the isolation of community groups while also providing them with relatively affordable and accessible ways to create links between themselves, thus increasing information circulation and action coordination.

All of these network developments support the emergence of concepts and practices such as learning organizations, lifelong continuing education, autonomous learning in everyday life, networking ecosystems, and sustainable development training.

—*Pierre-Léonard Harvey*
—*Karine Vigneault*

*See also* Computer-Mediated Communication (CMC); Evolving Technologies; Virtual Communities

## Bibliography

Castells, M. (1996). *The rise of the network society.* Cambridge, MA: Blackwell.

Henri, F., & Lundgren-Cayrol, K. (2001). *Apprentissage collaboratif à distance: pour comprendre et concevoir les environnements d'apprentissage virtuels.* Québec, Canada: Presses de l'Université du Québec.

Offner, J.-M., & Pumain, D. (Dir). (1996). *Réseaux et territoires: significations croisées.* Saint-Étienne, France: Éditions de l'Aube

Poulin, D., Montreuil, B., & Gauvin, S. (1994). *L'entreprise réseau: bâtir aujourd'hui l'organisation de demain.* Montréal, Canada: Publi-Relais.

Rolin, P., Martineau, L., Toutain, L., & Lefroy, A. (1997). *Les Réseaux: principes fondamentaux.* Paris, France: Hermès.

Wellman, B. (1997). An electronic group is virtually a social network. In S. Kiesler (Ed.). *Culture of the Internet* (pp. 179–205). Mahwah, NJ: Lawrence Erlbaum.

# NORMS

Generally, group norms can be defined as the unspoken rules or standards that guide a group and define acceptable and unacceptable behavior by group members. They derive from the implicit expectations of members, from the implicit and explicit direction of leaders, and from the influence of members. Norms appear early in the life of a group and are often difficult to change. They soon become accepted as the legitimate procedures of the group and come to regulate group performance. Norms come to delineate what any specific member of a group may or may not do. Not only do norms regulate behavior, however, but they also define how people should feel and even influence how people think. Norms are enforced through sanctions and rewards that are provided by other group members.

In most groups, norms are invisible and taken for granted. Members of groups may pay keen attention to task, to membership, or to the strategies the group chooses, but not to the processes of interaction. Who speaks first? Who is allowed to be late? Who decides and who has influence? Norms are often quite difficult to discuss because they are implicit and unconscious. It has been suggested that norms form along four dimensions: affect, power, status, and achievement. People create norms about the affective dimensions of relationships, that is, how personal will we be with each other, how are feelings to be expressed, and how will we show approval and disapproval to each other? Power or control, decision making, and authority are a domain covered by norms about who decides, how much involvement less powerful members have, and where the boundaries of the group's control end. Groups have norms about status and acceptance: Who can belong to this group, and is membership based on role, status, or personal characteristics? Finally, Parsons argued that norms govern whether members are valued for their achievements and success, professional skills, or other personal qualities.

In some groups, some norms may be made explicit through conscious agreements. There may be a written dress code, for instance, or a statement of standards for certain types of conduct. In the online classroom, it is very productive to create a set of explicit, shared norms at the outset. Training and preparation, particularly time spent face-to-face prior to the initiation of project work, is best spent consciously establishing and clarifying the norms and expectations for online participation.

Leaders or facilitators in the online setting can shape norms by explaining their function and enforcing them during the work. For example, a facilitator may promote vigorous participation by requesting responses from members, by modeling feedback, by reinforcing good responses, or by asking questions. The usual nonverbal cues (such as smiling and nodding) by which leaders often reinforce members are not available in the virtual environment. Leaders and facilitators are also important models for norms. They need to be responsive, to check on the group at regular intervals, to provide good feedback, and to trust the processes of the group. They also may need to address the level of comfort in the group directly.

It is also important for the group to develop the ability to self-monitor its norms. The facilitator might point out conforming and nonconforming behaviors so the group can begin to take responsibility for itself. The facilitator can ask group members to examine and evaluate how the group is doing and whether explicit shared norms are being met. The ability to set, understand, and self-monitor norms in the online environment constitutes a level of meta-learning about the self, the environment, and the group that is, in some ways, a unique event. Members often find it easier to perceive abstract dimensions of social interaction in an unfamiliar medium. Working in a virtual setting, as opposed to face-to-face, can offer an opportunity to reframe interaction in powerful ways.

It might well be argued that if work regarding the setting and enactment of norms was done consciously in any environment, all groups would prove more productive and less conflicted. Certainly, the opportunity to learn about group process and the role of the self in the group exists in the face-to-face setting. However, this work is rarely done because members bring so many previous expectations to the educational setting. Not only is it, perhaps, easier to create sensitivity to norms in the virtual environment, but it is also doubly important because many of the physical and nonverbal cues that promote process discussions will be missing subsequent to training or orientation. Furthermore, behaviors ordinarily expected in the work setting are rather different than those required by the virtual environment, so norms members bring with them can be counterproductive. Although computer-mediated communication (CMC) eliminates some troublesome face-to-face norms (for example, no one needs to keep a straight face or show up at the same time as everyone else), it offers its own unique challenges and benefits. In the asynchronous online environment, instructors might consider the benefits of some of the following norms:

- Minimal frequency of participation—for instance, participants might be expected to log on at regularly scheduled intervals in the process of doing an assignment.

- Requiring that work be composed offline and sent as an attachment from a word-processing program in order to encourage more thoughtful and reflective participation.

- Making deadlines and breaks in the work explicit. An explicit schedule is particularly critical if members of the group are required to collaborate or comment on each other's work.

- Placing a premium on reflective responses, particularly in an asynchronous environment. The scheduling of the work should permit maximal thoughtfulness.

- Encouraging affective disclosure. Unless there is live Webcasting, the online environment does not offer the ordinary cues to social orientation that we take for granted in face-to-face engagement. Team members must explicitly indicate emotional tone, tentativeness/certainty, anxiety, investment, motivation, and the like. For example, a learner who is uncertain about how to express him- or herself on a particular topic might be encouraged to begin by making the following parenthetical remark: "(I'm not sure this is the best way to express this idea, but, here goes . . . )."

- Requiring that all prerequisite documents and postings be read prior to participation, particularly if the work is to be collaborative or if members will comment on the work of others in the group.

- Agreements that support equity should be made prior to beginning the project work. Explicit norms that require all members to respond to all postings or all members to read all documents and postings can support the equity balancing effect of the medium.

- Methods and deadlines for decisions and conclusions should be explicit. Will complete agreement be required for decision making or conclusion? Will members be allowed to block consensus? By what date must members lodge objections?

- Related to the foregoing suggestion, the process for making decisions in the absence of team members should be explicitly articulated and discussed. It might be noted here that proceeding with members in absentia powerfully reinforces the norms of participation and equity balancing.

- Provisions for a safety net should be discussed and articulated at the outset of any inquiry. What happens if the conferencing software system or Web server crashes? What should be done if learners unexpectedly lose access to their ISP? How will the work proceed in the event of a major disruption such as severe weather? Specific plans for the use of fax, phone, and Internet alternatives, such as e-mail or face-to-face meetings, in the event of systemic failures at the individual, team, and system level should be explicit.

*—Judith Stevens-Long*

*See also* GROUP PROCESS; NETIQUETTE

## Bibliography

Napier, R. W., & Gershenfeld, M. K. (1993). *Groups: Theory and experience,* 5th Ed. New York: Houghton Mifflin.

Parsons, T., & Shils, E. A. (1951). *Toward a general theory of action.* Cambridge, MA: Harvard University Press.

Stevens-Long, J., & Crowell, C. (2000). The design and delivery of an interactive on-line education. In K. Rudestam & J. Schoenholtz-Read (Eds.), *Handbook of online learning.* Thousand Oaks, CA: Sage.

Yalom, I. (1995). *The theory and practice of group psychotherapy,* 4th Ed. New York: Basic Books.

# ONLINE LEARNING

Online learning involves the delivery of courses and learning components via the Internet. These courses and course components are delivered from an educational provider to a student. Although online learning is one form of distance learning or e-learning, these terms are often used interchangeably. Generally, online learning is to some degree self-directed and self-paced, and can provide group or individual instruction. An online learning environment also can complement a face-to-face learning environment; in this case, the result is often called *blended learning*. Most of all, online learning environments are fast, fluid, and flexible; they provide for different ways of learning and greater access to learning, and as such, they will increasingly become a part of every learning activity in education, at home, and in the workplace.

Online learning is as multimedia rich as bandwidth, hardware, and software allow, and it can include text and graphics, animation and simulations, audio and video, discussion boards, e-mail, chats, testing, and some form of progress reports. Components called *learning objects* for a course are created and managed within a learning or course management system, generally hosted by the educational provider. The management system acts as a student's primary point of contact with the provider and often includes or is linked to student support services. Increasingly, these management systems include or are linked to tools such as e-folios, with which a student can capture explicit and tacit knowledge.

An increasingly robust body of literature suggests both positive and negative implications of knowledge delivery using the Internet. Benefits of online learning environments include flexibility, participation quality and quantity, communication openness, and later access for reference purposes. In online learning environments, students have access to searchable repositories of online resources including insights from communities of practice; new and richer patterns of interactivity can occur between and among learners, faculty, mentors, and other experts; and deeper learning can result from the ability to have time to reflect on one's level of understanding.

Unfortunately, many online learning environments have merely digitized existing processes and practices, thereby failing to yield greater access to learners, increased cost savings, enhancements in the learner experience, or competitive advantage. When an online learning environment is designed largely to replicate existing face-to-face teaching, designers often force the online environment into a codified structure, thereby missing many of its benefits. The replication of traditional approaches online often results in the assumption that all students are the same and misses taking full advantage of the networked environment.

## FACTS AND PROJECTIONS

The majority of online learners have educational goals similar to those of all students; that is, online learners take courses in pursuit of degrees or to attain specific skills or other knowledge needed in their workplaces or for their professions. To date, quite often most of the participants in online learning have been an institution's own core students rather than new students reached through distance learning.

However, as online learning environments tend to be more customized, they better meet the needs of a growing segment of less "traditional" learners, or those who are unable to attend a traditional place-based institution. The increased access that an online learning environment provides has resulted in a recent projection of 100 million online learners. Merrill Lynch predicts that the online learning market will soon approach $25 billion; the number of 4-year, for-profit institutions that provide online learning environments grew by 266% over the last 10 years; and *U.S. News and World Report* lists more than 150 online graduate degree programs. Obviously, all projections are time bound and future growth depends on factors discussed throughout this entry. However, currently thousands of sites list the myriad of online learning opportunities; one example is World Wide Learn (http://www.worldwidelearn.com/index.html), where potential learners can locate hundreds of online courses, accredited degree programs, certificates, and professional learning resources offered by institutions, companies, and individuals from all over the world.

Despite these facts and projections, current approaches to online learning continue to limit its reach because online course portals are largely passive; that is, although they list courses and programs, they often do not provide learners with direct access to the courses. Learners are still left to navigate between portal and specific educational institutions and their specific admission and registration processes.

Advocates of online learning look to the development of online marketplaces where learners may select, register for, and be delivered courses and course components from a variety of institutions. The current eArmyU.com initiative delivers on this promise. One entity—PricewaterhouseCoopers—acts as a broker between multiple institutions and the learner. For the eArmyU learner, this learning marketplace provides a wide selection of learning possibilities with a single point of contact. The student saves time and is better served. For those institutions partnering in the eArmyU effort, this service extends their reach and allows them to focus on specific course offerings.

Additional examples include the National Coalition for Telecommunications Education and Learning (NACTEL, see http://www.nactel.org), in which a cluster of telecommunications industries identified a specific employee learning need and contracted with the Council for Adult and Experiential Learning (CAEL, see http://www.cael.org) to locate an educational provider and deliver courses customized to their needs. Coalitions, consortia, and corporate universities continue to develop in large part to serve such specific learning needs. The number of corporate universities now well exceeds 2,000, and if the current rate of growth continues, corporate universities will outnumber traditional universities by 2010.

## ISSUES

The majority of innovative online learning initiatives are being spearheaded by industry, as the previous examples illustrate. Established higher education institutions simply have difficulty dealing with online learning. This can be attributed to the nature of the more closed and conservative operations of the institution. The entire structure of higher education is based on a cadre of highly educated faculty who came from the same environment they serve. Much of education is still in the teaching mode versus the learning mode, and there remains great resistance to building a balance between place-based and online environments. Online learning is difficult for mainstream institutions because of the disruptive nature of pursuing what is largely perceived as a "fringe" market—in this case the fringe market being online or lifelong learners. Because the existing structure was established on the remnants of an agrarian model, and given the entrenched industrial model of mass education, it is unlikely that mainstream higher education will meet the new needs of learners, at least not as stand-alone entities. Thus, the transformation to online learning will continue to grow fastest in the private and for-profit sectors where traditional lessons of growth, scale, and consolidation become blended with plans for increasing returns and shrinking costs. The private sector is capturing the for-profit online learning market, and eventually the lessons learned may permeate into public sector education.

The establishment of guidelines and standards for online learning is one area that has permeated the public sector. Emerging standards now exist for vocabularies and metadata associated with learning objects, for modular content packaging and management, learner records, security, integration with enterprise systems, and organizational workflow. As part of ongoing accreditation, note the Higher Learning

Commission's documentation of *Best Practices for Electronically Offered Degree and Certificate Programs,* and its *Statement of Commitment by the Regional Accrediting Commissions for the Evaluation of Electronically Offered Degree and Certificate Programs.* In addition, the Institute for Higher Education Policy has prepared a report titled *Quality on the Line: Benchmarks for Success in Internet-Based Distance Education* (http://www.ihep.com/Pubs/PDF/Quality.pdf). These benchmarks include guidelines for institutional support, course development, teaching and learning, course structure, student support, faculty support, evaluation, and assessment.

These guidelines work to elevate the stature of online learners enrolled in established institutions. Until recently, serving online learners has not been part of the mainstream campus agenda for most institutions due to a lack of both the resources and the flexibility to meet the unique needs of these students. Where service has been provided, it has most frequently come from the units offering distance courses or programs (e.g., the Division of Continuing Education). On many campuses this has resulted in duplicate student support systems, one for off-campus and one for on-campus students.

The most significant concern surrounding online learning continues to be intellectual property issues. The process of digitizing course materials makes it possible to package courses to be delivered by people other than the original author(s). Courses have become "commoditized" and sought as commercial products by online learning companies, for-profit universities, and publishers. Thus, institutions and authors are encountering new, different opportunities and obstacles.

## FUTURE DEVELOPMENTS AND CHALLENGES

Future developments in online learning will include increased branding, partnering, competition, and development of reusable learning components that can be assembled and reassembled into learning environments with ease, similar to a Lego set. Knowledge blogs known as "klogs" will increase exponentially and will become integral to online learning environments. A klog—a personal Web page with notes, comments, ideas, and insights—relating to a specific skill or trade can become a valuable component of an online learning environment.

Access will continue to be an important issue, and computer-savvy students will demand that online learning be a blended part of any personal or professional learning experience. Interest in knowledge management—defining and capturing knowledge in small pieces along with powerful search engines for retrieval when and where a learner needs the information—will spur further development of online learning components. Collaborative learning also will increase as online learning environments are better designed to meet the needs of learners working around the globe; these needs include simulations, providing alternative perspectives, and allowing users to compare approaches with others.

Challenges include integrating online learning in place-based institutions; designing blended learning models; making learning management systems work for learners; creating more compelling content and interactivity; supporting online learning communities of practice; integrating multiple learning systems across an institution or organization; educating faculty, staff, and administrators to the power of this disruptive technology; partnering to design online learning environments; and taking online learning global.

Overall, our attempts at conceptualizing the future of online learning will demand more imagination than insight, more partnering than established processes, and more storytelling than strategic planning.

—*Ann Hill Duin*

*See also* E-LEARNING STRATEGIES; INTELLECTUAL PROPERTY

## Bibliography

Bonk, Curtis. (2002). *Current myths and future trends in online teaching and learning.* Retrieved from http://www.tafefrontiers.com.au/static/curt.pdf.

The Futures Project. (June 2002). *An update on new providers.* Retrieved from http://www.futuresproject.org/publications/new_providers_update.pdf.

Higher Learning Commission. (2000). *Best practices for electronically offered degree and certificate programs.* Retrieved from http://www.ncahigherlearningcommission.org/resources/electronic_degrees/.

Norris, Donald, Mason, Jon, & Lefrere, Paul. (2003). *Transforming e-knowledge: A revolution in the sharing of knowledge.* Ann Arbor, MI: Society for College and University Planning.

Twigg, Carol A. (2001). *Innovations in online learning: Moving beyond no significant difference.* Online monograph published by the Center for Academic Transformation. Retrieved from http://www.center.rpi.edu/PewSym/Mono4.html.

**Table 1**    Institutional Objectives in Online Learning Strategies

## Objectives

*Institutional objectives indicated below are matched in the right-hand columns by strategic areas with which they most closely align.*

| | *Social* | *Research* | *Pedagogy* | *Economic* |
|---|:---:|:---:|:---:|:---:|
| Extend mission outside region, beyond constituency | • | • | • | • |
| Provide flexible teaching and learning locations and schedules | • | • | • | • |
| Give access to students who cannot attend class on campus | • | • | | • |
| Further extend the democratization of the university | • | | | |
| Secure additional revenue | | | | • |
| Supplement in-class lectures | | | • | |
| Perform research on alternative learning and instruction | | • | • | |
| Introduce innovative teaching and learning practices | | • | • | |
| Provide new programs without new classrooms, facilities | | | • | • |
| Give students experience of working with online tools | | • | • | |
| Provide extended opportunities to learn collaboratively | | • | • | |
| Allow interaction with other parts of country, other cultures | • | • | • | |
| Extend the learning space from the classroom to the world | • | • | • | |

# ONLINE LEARNING ENVIRONMENTS

As the online learning train picks up speed across the academic landscape, hundreds of colleges and universities have come on board[1]—some with merely a handful of students, others with tens of thousands. At institutions that have yet to climb on, many wonder whether it is worth creating potential conflicts with faculty, staff, and trustees. Is it worth carrying the burden of a new infrastructure? What are the academic consequences? On what basis is online education justified?

Colleges and universities come on board for many cogent reasons—some having to do with the institution's mission, others for prudent economic motives, and still others for a variety of other aims. Most offer e-learning to achieve intertwined goals. As Table 1 shows, online learning gives schools opportunities to explore various strategic objectives with a number of implications.

## LEARNING EFFECTIVENESS[2]

When most people think of online learning, the image that frequently comes to mind is of an isolated student facing a computer screen, entirely alone.

Although this perception is partly correct—e-learning is performed by an individual stationed at a screen—the fact is that most Web-based learning at colleges and universities in the United States is actually highly interpersonal, instructor-led, and takes place in a "virtual classroom" in which other classmates continuously participate in threaded discussions and in other interactive activities over the Internet. For many, the online experience can be far less alienating than in a conventional classroom.

Over the last decade, numerous scholarly efforts have sought to determine the efficacy of online education. Most of the literature compares traditional classroom delivery with technology-supported education. By now—even though conventional wisdom holds that the campus constitutes the *sine qua non* of an educational experience—accumulated evidence from thousands of studies shows that there is "no significant difference" between the two modes.[3] In one "blind" study, a professor who taught the same class online and in a conventional setting graded exams drawn from both classes unaware of the source of the tests. As expected from earlier research, results showed that, independent of delivery, students in both courses performed equally well.[4]

One of the supporting "pillars" of Sloan-C, a consortium sponsored by the Alfred P. Sloan Foundation composed of institutions and organizations committed to quality online education (http://www.sloan-c.org/index.asp), is the assurance that schools must offer the same quality online as they do in traditional programs. According to this principle, "interaction is the key"—with online courses encouraging interaction of students with their instructors, classmates, and materials almost daily. For Sloan, this style of online learning is known as asynchronous learning networks (ALN).

At institutions currently engaged in—or considering—delivering online courses, schools must collect quantifiable data to establish baseline results. These must then be measured against continuing efforts to improve or extend e-learning. When colleges collect outcomes data from students in conventional classrooms—test scores, grades, and course and program completion rates, among other information—they must gather them equally from distance-learning students. According to Sloan-C guidelines on learning effectiveness, online programs must track instructional methods, student populations, and class size, with each institution aiming to guarantee that the quality of instruction, whether on campus or online, achieves comparable learning outcomes.

This key principle not only ensures high student learning standards, but also is critically important for institutional accreditation. Recent objectives issued by regional higher education accrediting bodies for online as well as on-campus programs depend on institutions securing rich comparative quantitative results that show that both modes offer the same content, with the same or equally qualified faculty, at the same standard.[5]

Most educators agree that the debate over the quality of online learning vs. conventional classroom teaching is no longer as contentious as it was when Web-based education first entered higher education. Research is turning to more complex questions about the value of online learning.

Do certain students—say, for example, foreign born who fear their accents place them at a disadvantage in traditional classrooms—perform better online? Does e-learning offer working professionals the opportunity to complete their degrees more rapidly than in conventional settings? Are women—who now make up a far greater proportion of students online than men—more likely to participate actively than in conventional male-dominated classrooms? What about the effectiveness of online learning for black,

Hispanic, and other underrepresented students? Are there benefits for physically or psychologically challenged students? The next—and far more difficult—phase of quantifying the value of online learning must address determinants other than routine test scores or grades.

## ACCESS

As colleges and universities shift dramatically from housing traditional, full-time residential students to a larger adult and part-time population[6]—students who do not require dormitories or athletic facilities—the demand for remote learning expands in parallel. Eduventures, an educational consulting firm, reports that "non-traditional students—of which working adults compose the vast majority—have been the fastest growing demographic segment" of the higher education student population. "These busy, consumer-savvy students are looking for quality, convenience, and flexibility—qualities that align closely with . . . web-based distance learning."[7] According to the Sloan Foundation, some 3 million students are enrolled in online learning courses nationwide in the 2002–2003 academic year. It is likely that another 3 million or more take online courses abroad.

Institutions that have not taken steps to open their gates to adult and part-time learners may have already begun to see their enrollments decline. Schools offering online educational opportunities openly invite nontraditional students—a population that may be prevented from enrolling in residential colleges or even coming to school at a set time of day or evening because of obligations at work or at home. Because of family or job obligations, students at a considerable distance—either in this country or abroad—may not be able to attend classes at a campus far from their home, making it impossible for them to enroll in programs that may be especially suited for them.

Some may not be able to take courses on campus because of other, even more serious, obstacles. For many, physical, language, social, or psychological barriers turn the classroom into a troubling, rather than a welcoming, environment. Sloan-C, in its guidelines on access, declares, "All learners who wish to learn online have the opportunity and can achieve success."

Marketing and promotion of online courses depends crucially on the audience schools expect to serve. Institutions that plan to deliver online courses

**Table 2**     Online Learning Options

| Option | Instruction | Location | Attendance |
|---|---|---|---|
| Entirely online (ALN) | Instructor-led | Virtual | Not required |
| Hybrid | Instructor-led | Virtual and campus | Partially on campus |
| Supplemental | Instructor-led | Virtual and campus | On campus |
| Self-learning | No instructor* | Virtual | Not required |

*Some self-learning "modules," often used in corporate training, provide mentors who communicate with students by e-mail or by telephone.

essentially to their present population, either to supplement traditional instruction or to shift students from a physical to a virtual classroom, will promote their programs quite differently from those that plan to reach out around the country or around the world.

Local marketing often requires the exploitation of conventional vehicles—print catalogs, posters, flyers, and advertisements in local media. Institutions that seek to go beyond must exploit newer technologies—educational and professional Web sites, portals, search engines, and e-mail messages sent to acquired or shared databases. Of course, schools that aim to appeal to a regional audience must also engage in e-marketing to achieve their ends. After all, prospective students for online programs are more likely to be found on the Web. On the whole, e-marketing is less costly than conventional print promotion.

The most successful schools offer nearly identical programs on campus and online to students with academic profiles much the same as those who attend conventional classes. Students tend to select an institution—whether on campus or online—largely because of its reputation and because its programs match their educational or career objectives. Still, a number of notable universities that entered the online education arena early chose to create programs independent of their faculty, offering courses delivered by instructors from outside the institution. They introduced educational programs with which they had not been identified with historically. By and large, they have not succeeded. The most visible failures are several elite U.S. universities that offered programs that diverged markedly from those for which the schools had been most noted. Strategically, for most schools, it is wiser to follow well-trodden academic paths, staying close to an institution's strengths, pursuing its historical mission, and satisfying its natural audience, whether at a distance or at home.

Digital libraries, online registration, and other services have transformed the campus experience, not only for distance learners, but remarkably for the residential population, too. Various course management systems and other software now make it possible for students and faculty to communicate with one another over long distances as well as providing a convenient supplement to classroom instruction. Many schools that do not offer distance-learning programs nonetheless offer online facilities for faculty to post syllabi, course materials, and other documents on the Web. Exploiting courseware management systems, conventional classroom instructors can communicate with their students after class in online discussion groups and can post grades and other data.

For many schools, online learning provides "supplemental" tools for traditional classroom instruction. For others, it offers the opportunity to free classroom space by migrating one or more on-campus classes to the Web in what is known as "hybrid" courses, with some instruction performed in the classroom and the rest online. Some hybrid programs offer Web-based instruction during most of the semester and provide an on-campus experience on weekends or during the summer (see Table 2).

## COST EFFECTIVENESS

Although a handful of schools have stumbled, the economic health of online education could not be more robust. Calling attention to a number of failures of online enterprises at notable universities—after many millions of dollars of investment—the popular press has fed the fears of those who believe that the road to online education is economically treacherous. For the media, these failures are red flags waved at university administrators and faculty, cautioning them against serious financial dangers facing institutions that enter the online world.

Most schools that offer online programs have shown a dramatic rise in enrollments, with a 20% growth rate in the last 3 years.[8] At Stevens Institute of Technology, for example, online enrollment has been doubling every semester, with parallel growth in tuition revenue. Some universities—notably, State University of New York, University of Maryland University College, and University of Phoenix—claim online student enrollments of more than 50,000, with the University of Maryland serving more than 80,000. These and other schools have found that online learning can generate considerable revenue by extending their current student population, moving students from a physical to a virtual space, licensing Web courses, and increasing enrollments and, consequently, tuition revenue.[9]

By and large, colleges and universities charge the same tuition on campus and online. The practice follows the principal that, if the programs offer the same content, with the same or equally qualified faculty, eventually reporting the same outcomes, there should be no difference in tuition either. Nevertheless, some schools tack on a "technology fee" to recover some of the additional cost that the institution may have invested. But on the whole, schools have concluded that the perception of equivalence can be undermined if the schools introduce a different tuition schedule for the two modes.

The few schools that reported financial failures often ignored sound business practices. In some cases, spending for course development and infrastructure was so great that it would have been impossible to earn back investments for years. Some spent as much as $250,000 on a single course. Many believed that for online courses to be pedagogically sound, it was essential for them to introduce fairly expensive simulations, animations, videos, interactive software, and other high-end multimedia. Others invested several million dollars in course management software.

More prudent schools have wisely chosen to be cautious, investing modestly in course development and information technology. University of Phoenix, one of the more successful for-profit online institutions, claims that it spends no more than $10,000 on any single online course. Most public and private universities invest far less. The Sloan Foundation reports that colleges and universities spend between $2,000 and $8,000 on course development. In the end, just

like any responsible enterprise, sound financial planning and cautious investments in personnel and technology, coupled with modest revenue projections, protect fledgling online ventures from economic failure.

Surprisingly, technology is not the principal ingredient in online learning programs. By now, a handful of quality courseware management systems are available from commercial vendors, often at licensing fees that are not impossible to manage. In selecting one, it is wise to engage faculty and technology staff in the decision, keeping in mind ease of use and compatibility with other campus systems, as well as price.

Most course management systems offer a suite of software options that provide nearly all tools faculty and students need to communicate effectively. The ability to upload and download text documents, slides, and other files; the ability to e-mail collectively to the entire class or to an online "team"; the ability to send e-mail individually to an instructor or to a student; the ability to hold a "threaded discussion"; the ability to access an online bulletin board; and the ability to share files are among the principal components of an acceptable system. Others include online calendars, the ability to generate quizzes and examinations, and a feature that allows instructors to post grades so that students can access them online. Online courses must also be secure, permitting only those authorized to gain access by password identification. More sophisticated options are a "whiteboard" that permits students and faculty to draw online and a mathematical equation editor. At its best, the system selected must integrate seamlessly with other online services—applications, registration, and transcripts among other Web-accessible files.

As the industry matures, vendors compete with one another to achieve an acceptable package, incorporating the latest and most user-friendly tools at a competitive price. If a school selects one of the principal brands, there is a good chance that the software, service, and price will be very close to the others. In today's marketplace, it is unlikely that an institution will make a foolish choice. What's more, even if something does go seriously wrong, most courseware management systems are now nearly interoperable, able to migrate online courses from one to another, even if the one selected fails.

The cost of the software that manages online learning represents a fraction of what institutions spend on information technology more generally. Licensing fees for course software usually occupy only a small portion of other expenses—with faculty compensation being the biggest—that make up the bill for an online education program.

For smaller and mid-sized schools, it may be wise to consider sharing resources with other institutions. Or it may be prudent to allow a more experienced or larger university to handle software and infrastructure necessary to run a smooth operation. Some vendors will provide just the course management system, others will provide hosting, and still others faculty training. Depending on the quality and extent of an institution's resources, it may be best to engage a vendor prepared to perform all tasks necessary.

At the start, it is prudent to introduce the simplest tools, keeping the learning curve as low as possible for faculty and students. Later, as faculty and IT staff gain experience, it may be appropriate to add more exotic features, such as streaming voice and video. In the beginning, and for many in the long run, a text-based online learning model turns out to be the most successful, not only from an economic perspective, but also pedagogically.

Sums required to introduce course management systems, specialized software, and other information technology and training personnel add new lines to an institution's already thin budget. But when these allocations are measured against the vastly more expensive burden of building and maintaining campus dormitories, parking lots, athletic facilities, and other structures and services required to house a campus population, the cost of supporting online students is small. According to Sloan guidelines, cost effectiveness must be attuned to institutional goals while tuition and fees reflect the cost of delivering services.

## FACULTY SATISFACTION

In part because of resistance by some faculty to online instruction—with a few believing that e-learning will corrupt the quality of higher education—most schools do not *require* that faculty teach online. Rather, they encourage those with a desire to teach on the Web to do so voluntarily.

Early adopters often enter immediately, eager for the challenges and to be at the leading edge of pedagogy. Frequently, they emerge as proselytizers, informing the rest of the community about their positive experiences. Curiously, many who teach online after strong resistance often join the ranks of the newly converted and are among the most vocal supporters. In time, those who occupy the middle ground with a "wait-and-see" attitude often drift into the online learning camp as most of us do eventually when new technologies are widely adopted.

Web faculty compensation often parallels what professors are paid on campus. Some institutions provide economic and other incentives to teach online. A number present Web faculty with laptops or give them release time from their normal teaching load to allow them to migrate their face-to-face courses to Web instruction.

Most colleges and universities are careful not to engage special online instructors—large numbers of part-time or adjunct faculty—fearing that senior faculty will dismiss distance learning as a second-class enterprise. In any case, given the standard that the quality of online instruction is equal to what is offered on campus, it is unwise to turn to inexperienced instructors.

Once a faculty member agrees to teach online, in most cases, the university steps in to offer faculty instruction. At some schools, faculty training comes under "information technology." At other schools, it is handled by a separate online learning unit. No matter where the responsibility falls, online training is a major departure from tradition because, historically, most college faculty enter the classroom with little or no pedagogical knowledge.

Although there is now a large library of effective practices that may be used as models for quality online faculty development,[10] one of the most rigorous approaches comes from the State University of New York's SUNY Learning Network[11]—a comprehensive system that offers, among other key elements, a Web site, pedagogy workshops, a handbook, a helpdesk, and an instructional design partner.

Those who agree to teach online at some schools are required to complete training sessions to master e-learning tools. At Stevens Institute of Technology, online instructors sign an agreement with the university that requires them to complete a series of courses in the school's online learning system. Online instructors at Stevens are also required to attend semiannual Web faculty colloquia at which novice instructors receive pedagogical guidance from more experienced online faculty.

Among the thorniest issues facing academic institutions since the introduction of online learning is that of intellectual property. Who owns the rights to

Web-based courses? Should copyright be in the name of the developer or the university? If a school engages faculty to develop online courses, may the institution have someone else teach them? Do Web faculty have portability rights, allowing them to take their e-courses when they leave? Should schools pay course developers separately from their normal compensation as faculty? Should faculty be compensated separately for online instruction?

Although these questions seemed intractable at first, many universities have come to an accommodation with their faculty. A few institutions have concluded that the university owns all the rights, including copyright. Others give copyright to the faculty. Most have decided to share ownership. One solution,[12] widely adopted by colleges and universities, provides for the faculty to retain all rights in the course, apart from online instruction, allowing them freedom to teach face-to-face, publish, consult, or perform any other academic task with the material. In return, course developers voluntarily transfer their rights to the online course to the university. In this way, the faculty retains its traditional academic freedom, while the schools gain the right to commercialize Web-based courses.

Studies of faculty at many institutions show that online instructors are among the most satisfied, giving quite high ratings for their personal experience as well as for the quality of student learning. Research at the State University of New York reveals that many find online instruction satisfies their highest intellectual and pedagogical aims, occasionally emerging as a superior mode when compared with face-to-face teaching.[13] Under Sloan-C guidelines, "Faculty [should] achieve success with teaching online, citing appreciation and happiness."

## STUDENT SATISFACTION

At the conclusion of most college and university courses, students are asked to complete paper-based surveys evaluating their classroom experience, reporting on their perceptions of how well faculty performed as well as whether students accomplished what they set out to achieve, among other perceptions of the value of each course. In order to gauge the effectiveness of online education, students at a distance must perform similar evaluations. In the largest continuing study of student perceptions of their online courses, performed at the SUNY Learning Network, most students reported that their online experience was equal to, or better than, that in traditional classrooms.[14]

To achieve such results, the most successful schools have introduced online student services that provide nearly all the elements that the campus population has come to expect. At Stevens Institute of Technology, for example, online students can accomplish nearly everything on the Web that their peers do routinely on campus—apply and register, get academic advice, buy textbooks, pay tuition, gain access to the school's digital library, and perform course evaluations.

An Eduventures report[15] concludes that e-learning must offer these features to students: interactions and presentations in online classes must be engaging; communication forums, learning materials, and advice must be continuously available; online transactions must be seamless; and questions must be answered and support provided around the clock.

According to Sloan-C, "Students are successful in learning online and typically pleased with their experience." On the whole, the literature supports that claim.[16] Students appear satisfied when there is robust online discussion with their instructors and classmates; when their online learning experience matches their expectations; when university services—advising, registration, and access to materials—is at least as good as those provided on campus; when they are given an effective orientation about how to learn online; and when their educational outcomes are productive for their careers, professional aims, and intellectual development.

Success in online learning depends crucially on thoughtful planning and sound research. Above all, it requires broad academic and administrative participation. Before the first course is delivered online, institutions must come to terms with how it might affect all walks of university life—students, faculty, finance, admissions, information technology, the library, trustees, even the bookstore. Of course, overparticipation and overly cautious planning can lead to academic paralysis. Schools that select a champion who commands respect among faculty and staff can help navigate competing interests to achieve consensus and help move things forward.[17] Perhaps the most significant predictor of success is institutional commitment—financial, technical, and legal—in an atmosphere that supports and encourages online education.

—*Robert Ubell*
—*A. Frank Mayadas*

*See also* DISTRIBUTED LEARNING/DISTRIBUTED EDUCATION

## Notes

1. See Sloan-C Catalog of Online Education Programs at http://sloan-c.org/programs/index.asp.

2. The headings in this article are drawn from the Sloan-C "Five Pillars." See also *Elements of quality: The Sloan-C framework.* (2002). New York: Alfred P. Sloan Foundation.

3. Russell, Thomas L. (1999). *The no significant difference phenomenon,* 4th Edition. Raleigh, NC: North Carolina State University. Web address: http://teleeducation.nb.ca/nosignificantdifference/.

4. Fallah, Hosein, & Ubell, Robert. (December 2000). Blind scores in a graduate test: Conventional compared with Web-based outcomes. *JALN, 4*(2).

5. See, for example, *Characteristics of excellence in higher education: Eligibility requirements and standards for accreditation.* (2002). Philadelphia: Middle States Commission on Higher Education.

6. National Center for Educational Statistics. (October 2002). *Projections for educational statistics to 2012,* 31st Edition. Washington, DC: U.S. Department of Education.

7. Gallagher, Sean. (September 2002). Distance learning at the tipping point. *Eduventures Report.*

8. Sloan Foundation estimate.

9. Kelley, Kimberly B., & Bonner, Kimberly M. (February 2001). Courseware ownership in distance learning: issues and policies. *Sloan Consortium Newsletter.*

10. See Sloan-C, *Effective practices in faculty satisfaction* at http://www.sloan-c.org/effective/SortByFacultySat.asp.

11. See SUNY Learning Network, *Comprehensive faculty support* at http://www.sloan-c.org/effective/details4.asp?FS_ID=15.

12. Ubell, Robert. (2001). Who owns what? Unbundling Web course property rights. *Educause Quarterly, 1.* See also Kelley, Kimberly B., & Bonner, Kimberly M. (February 2001). Courseware ownership in distance learning: Issues and policies. *Sloan Consortium Newsletter.*

13. Fredericksen, Eric, Pickett, Alexandra, Shea, Peter, Pelz, William, & Swan, Karen. (2000). Factors influencing faculty satisfaction with asynchronous teaching and learning in the SUNY learning network. *JALN, 4*(3).

14. Fredericksen, Eric, Pickett, Alexandra, Shea, Peter, & Pelz, William. (2000). Student satisfaction and perceived learning with on-line courses: Principles and examples from the SUNY learning network. *JALN, 4*(2).

15. Gallagher, Sean. (September 2002). Distance learning at the tipping point. *Eduventures Report.*

16. See *Effective practices for student satisfaction* at http://www.sloan-c.org/effective/SortByStudentSat.asp.

17. Hezel, Richard T. (October 2002). How to plan for your institution's distance learning efforts. *Educational Pathways.*

# ONLINE ORIENTATION AND NAVIGATION TOOLS

Online orientations are a good tool for helping students to begin an online course or program. Often, online orientations include an overview of the course management software that will be used to deliver courses as well as tips for becoming a successful student online. Online orientations can be conducted synchronously (meaning in real time) using chat or other software that enables students to engage with each other and a facilitator at a designated time. Online orientations are also conducted asynchronously. Asynchronous orientations are generally interactive and conducted through posting to a moderated or facilitated discussion board using the same software that will be used for courses. Online orientations are also conducted in a computer-based format, meaning that the student interacts only with a computer and a Web site, moving through a series of screens that provide information. Tests and quizzes may or may not be used to assess knowledge acquisition in an online orientation.

Students are often drawn to online learning for the convenience it holds for them, such as an ability to continue working without interruption. However, in order to be successful, students need an orientation to what is generally a new form of learning for them as well as how to navigate the courses that they will be taking. Regardless of what draws students to the online classroom, they are generally unaware of the demands that online learning will place on them as learners. Because they are entering online programs and courses with expectations that may not match the reality of online learning, online orientations become an important entry point to the online classroom, not just from the standpoint of using the hardware and software, but also in terms of the differences in teaching and learning and how to be an effective online student. Some institutions incorporate mandatory face-to-face sessions to provide an orientation to the program and courses. Some deliver orientation programs completely online. Regardless of how it is delivered, the assumption behind a good online orientation is to maximize the educational potential for both the online classroom and the online students who populate it.

Before even beginning an online orientation, prospective students need to determine whether online learning is the preferred method for them. Prediction of potential success is often left to self-assessment. Most self-assessments include a look at skills, goals, attitudes, and abilities and are useful in helping a student who may be "on the fence" to make a decision about whether to proceed with an online class. Although many institutions do not make self-assessments available, there are numerous assessments available on the Internet. A self-assessment should not be the final determining factor in whether a student will be successful, however. It should be used only as an information gathering tool for the prospective student. Many students, after they have experienced a good orientation to online learning, find that they adapt well to this environment. Consequently, assessment through trial and error should not be discouraged.

A comprehensive orientation to online learning, whether conducted online or face-to-face, should contain the following:

- The basics of logging on to the Internet, including the use of a browser, accessing the course site, using course management software, saving and printing material found online, basic Internet searching, and the use of e-mail
- Understanding what is required to become a successful online learner, including time requirements and time management
- The differences between a face-to-face and online course, including the role of the instructor and the roles of students as well as expectations about how students will be evaluated
- Interaction between the instructor and students and among students
- How to give feedback to other students and receive feedback from others
- Appropriate interaction and communication, including the rules of "netiquette," or the proper way to communicate online, and the use of "emoticons," which are text-based symbols that communicate emotion, such as :) as an indication of humor or :( as an indication of unhappiness
- How to get help when it is needed

Help should also be easily available throughout the online orientation, should students need it.

If the institution cannot or does not provide student training about how to learn online, then suggestions for how to be successful in an online course become the responsibility of the faculty who are delivering the courses. Even if an institutional orientation does not

occur, incorporating additional information into the course is a good idea. Ways in which faculty can orient students within an online course include holding a face-to-face, "hands-on" orientation, if possible, to show students the course site and discuss online learning, providing students with a list of frequently asked questions and responses to those questions, including basic information about how to navigate the course site, as well as information about what is expected of them in the learning process and information to assist them in successfully completing the course.

Regardless of how it is delivered, an online orientation to both courses and software is an important tool to ensure the success of online students. The inclusion of online orientation should be considered in the development phase of online courses and programs.

*—Rena M. Palloff*
*—Keith Pratt*

*See also* ADMISSION CRITERIA AND PROCESSES; ORIENTATION; STUDENT PREPARATION

### Bibliography

Gilbert, Sara Dulaney. (2001). *How to be a successful online student.* New York: McGraw-Hill.

Palloff, Rena M., & Pratt, Keith. (2001). *Lessons from the cyberspace classroom.* San Francisco: Jossey-Bass.

Palloff, Rena M., & Pratt, Keith. (2003). *The virtual student: A profile and guide.* San Francisco: Jossey-Bass.

# ONLINE UNIVERSITIES

There is a diverse profile of the online university, which continues to redefine itself in new ways that are quite different from the traditional campus profile. This entry will help establish the specific types of organizations that may be defined as true "online universities," differentiating them from universities that simply have some of their activities and programs online. This entry also provides context for establishing a broad and inclusive working definition of *online universities.*

One definition of online university is that of an institutional structure that may be either for-profit or nonprofit in terms of corporate structure; is specifically designed to offer distributed education, including degrees; and which declares itself to be an "online university." This definition assumes that the way in which courses and programs are offered; the methods of access; residence requirements, including how residence is defined; and the methods of the offerings follow an emerging, identifiable pattern.

Diversity exists among online universities, including subsets by type. Although there are a variety of descriptions, all of them include the use of newer communication technologies in a distributed way, including both wired and wireless online initiatives. In the greater educational community, the vast majority of colleges and universities are increasingly using media in both classroom and nonclassroom environments. Most universities now offer at least some courses online. In addition, virtually everyone in all facets of today's universities is using e-mail, which means that nearly all students and universities are online to some degree. Rapidly developing digital advances are moving this online environment forward apace, continually improving both the technical and virtual elements.

A milestone was achieved in California in 1972, through a project entitled Project Outreach. This project facilitated legislation allowing the use of public funds to pay for nonclassroom-based instruction. Prior to the coordinated instructional systems legislation in California, public funds could only be used for "seat time" classes in traditional classroom settings. The changes that have occurred over the past 30 years are well known, and are beyond the scope of this discussion. Simply, the funding metric has changed, enabling the online educational experience to develop.

There have been successes and failures among the online universities. Reviewing some of these will clarify similarities and differences among them, and provide some reasons for their success or failure.

There are distinctions between for-profit and not-for-profit online universities. Industry analysts report that profit-centered online universities seem to be having significant success. This is likely attributable to several factors including the developed business skills of their top leadership, adequate capitol, mission focus, and sharply defined objectives for success. The Apollo Group's University of Phoenix Online has shown significant student satisfaction and success and is considered by many to have led the way in today's online business. At the time of this writing, Strayer Online University has also had significant market and

financial success among the publicly traded online universities. The University of Phoenix Online and Strayer Online University are two examples of online universities that are tracked by the financial markets. Based on present successes, companies such as Sylvan Learning have declared their intent to expand aggressively into the online higher-education market. Sylvan has invested in a number of universities including Walden University and National Technological University (NTU). Corinthian Colleges are also pursuing online education as a means of achieving earnings and establishing a presence in the online university market. Career Education Corporation, which acquired American InterContinental University, is another example of a for-profit initiative. Recently, AIU Online was included in the U.S. Department of Education's Distance Education Demonstration Project.

Those described to this point are accredited by regional accrediting agencies. There are some unaccredited, profit-making online universities that have achieved reported economic success. One example is Kennedy-Western University, which has a significant history in serving the corporate education market. Some of these unaccredited online universities are an extended version of their campus-based units, an expansion they consider to be an advantage. This is not the case with Kennedy Western, however, which is completely online. Among online universities, "residence" is defined as the relationship between the faculty member and the student, and does not generally require a geographic or face-to-face physical presence.

Nonprofits have had a mixed experience with online education, caused, to a great extent, by factors that include putting the wrong management in charge (i.e., individuals without distributed learning skill sets) and lethargic, politically laden approaches to implementation, including building a number of inappropriate and arcane practices into their infrastructures. One that has not been successful is The Open University of the United States, launched by the British Open University. (In contrast, The British Open University itself has been very successful.) Columbia, eCornell, Vanderbilt University Online, and several others that have pursued the online university initiative have invested substantial sums of money without implementation success. Most claim insufficient funds as a primary reason for their failure. Professionals in the field disagree. The Western Governors University (WGU) is another, unique example of a nonprofit online university; it is still in its early stages, and struggling.

The Fielding Graduate Institute is doing very well and, increasingly, the Fielding Graduate Institute model is being recognized as one of the best and most successful of the distributed independent nonprofit structures. The Fielding collaborative and tutorial model is becoming an object of study because of its success and appeal. Although the Fielding Graduate Institute does not consider itself in the online category, it fits the definition, is distributed based on sound educational practice, and is a good example of success. Jones International University, the first fully accredited, fully Web-based online university is another milestone institution defining the nature of an accredited, fully online university. In the broader arena, community colleges such as Coastline Community College, in California, and Rio Salado Community College, in Arizona, are admired, mature examples of successful community colleges that pioneered distance-learning models. Each of these distributed community colleges is a separate accredited institution, but is nested within multi-college systems. This follows the "university college" model of a separate but integrated configuration that is found in many universities.

Antioch University, Alliant University, Capella University, DeVry University, and Touro International University (a separate but linked online university division of Touro University) provide additional examples of online universities.

A relevant point here is to recognize that the online university of the future will not reflect individuals' current experiences, nor will it be the same as the online universities already in existence. Online universities are being adapted and redefined, creating a series of new and differing models. However, all are distributed, use media and telecommunications technologies, combine sound combinations of psychology and technology, and will primarily evolve from the models described here.

Online-centric universities must address administrative and political challenges, personnel and funding policies, accreditation and standards, and the requirements of state authorizing agencies, all of which were generally developed in the era of the conventional classroom. Online universities, by definition, ignore geographical and political boundaries. They are based on the emerging precept of overcoming distance (i.e., that "distance is dead").

Internationally, the British Open University is the largest university in the United Kingdom, and presently reports more than 250,000 students. Other online universities are located in the Netherlands, Australia, China, and many other countries. What is characteristic of adult learners in online university programs worldwide is that "learning how to learn" is a quality necessary for success, and these programs are not for everyone. Self-motivation and discipline are key characteristics of independent learners. Proactive institutional support systems are also important to student success.

There is no accepted universal definition of distance learning, or of the online university. Only the passage of time and the continuing refinement of the literature will clarify the neologisms, to help to perfect the emerging language of independent leaning and the online university.

Online programs exist along a continuum, from colleges utilizing various technologies and campus-based instruction to those that offer only online learning options. In addition, a newly accepted definition of *residence* is emerging. In the distributed setting, *residence* is defined by many as the connected relationship between the student and the faculty member, rather than physical presence at a specific location.

What seems clear and common with respect to all universities is that the explosive growth of information technology, the wired and wireless World Wide Web, and the development of all aspects of life are changing because of the rapidly emerging PDA, PCTV, and interactive television and computer combination devices. In addition, the new understanding and acceptance of multiple intelligences, multiple literacies, and alternative learning styles portends that all education of the future will be "Net enhanced."

The Internet and Web continue to shrink the world. Increased understanding and respect for different learning styles and transformational learning are growing. The corporate university using media and online learning will continue to increase as a phenomenon. New audio-visual capability is increasing the sensory nature of online learning. Emerging techniques such as tele-collaboration, digital libraries, print on demand, wireless connectivity, declining technology costs, and acceptance of alternative learning styles are increasing. The trend toward transformational learning, "learning how to learn," is growing, as is the percentage of the population going to, and staying in, colleges and universities, earning degrees, changing careers, and simply continuing to pursue education and learning for all manner of reasons.

The distributed, independent, freestanding online university is one of the institutional configurations of our future. This type of program will coexist with the traditional institutions that have served, and will continue to serve, well. The market for online education will experience significant growth throughout the next decade. The airplane did not replace the automobile, or the ships at sea. All represent forms of transportation. Differing educational structures offer choice, options, and diverse access to adult learning. This will be the case with respect to the future of the university. New media and communications technologies are changing the way we live, work, and learn. The freestanding online college and university, both as an outreach of a traditional campus institution—although probably encased in a separate legal structure—and the freestanding online university are now part of the fabric of global higher education.

In perspective, much of what we take for granted today was revolutionary as recently as 10 years ago. The same will be the case 10 years from now. All present initiatives should be considered pioneering efforts at this stage. Studying the current spate of online universities provides information that serves as a guide in the global transformation of online learning.

The online universities of today are profit and nonprofit, capitalize on diversity, use nonclassroom-based asynchronous strategies, are e-centric, and are a defined part of the global adult learning community of institutions. They ignore geography and liberally use telecommunications. Finally, in most cases, in defining themselves, they simply tell you that they belong to the cohort of "online universities."

—*Bernard J. Luskin*

*See also* Distributed Learning/Distributed Education; Virtual Campus

# OPERATIONS AND MANAGEMENT

There is no one correct way to design the operation and management structure to support a distance or distributed learning system. Every unit is a unique entity constructed to respond to a defined set of resource parameters, mission statement, and program design. Identifying staff to address the functional needs of a

project under development and providing adequate support resources are crucial to project success. A thorough understanding and process mapping of current processes can provide insights into potential bottlenecks, delays, or points of communication breakdowns. Creating project management systems that enable individual team members to monitor completion to date as well as plan for their inputs and contributions serves as a vital link in what is often a complicated and occasionally convoluted development cycle. Finally, an administrative structure that enables those closest to the project to access resources, when necessary, and to resolve issues and problems, can serve the mission of the unit and lead to several project outputs.

## PREPARATION OF MATERIALS

The organization and management of instructional and design and development services encompasses a wide range of activities necessary to conceptualize, plan, produce, and publish instructional materials via distance or distributed education. Due to the diversity of tasks required to prepare materials for delivery at a distance, a variety of skills and competencies are needed, ranging from editor to Web developer. The specific operational and management structure of a service unit designed to address these needs is dependent on the delivery model and technologies employed. Print-based/correspondence distance education systems require less technology-supported systems than Internet- or Web-based systems. Many distance or distributed learning systems today represent a mixture of methods and delivery models, challenging the operation and management systems created to support these endeavors. For example, many print-based distance education units are supplementing their print resources with communications networks via online bulletin boards and e-mail lesson submissions. Vital to every service unit, however, is a core of skilled professionals possessing a set of competencies, a project management and tracking system, and a set of defined process and procedure guidelines. In addition, administrative systems are necessary to manage the overall system and ensure a most efficient and effective process.

## SKILLS AND COMPETENCIES

In order to address the design, development, and production of instructional materials for delivery via distance or distributed learning, eight competencies should be considered. Regardless of the eventual delivery model, or the number of staff assigned to the task, these competencies must be addressed if the project is to be completed on time and within budget.

- The foremost skill necessary is *project leadership,* which includes the ability to marshal required resources, manage complex teams, and instill a sense of direction and vision for the completed work.
- Closely related to leadership is *project management.* This is the ability to monitor and manage the costs and timelines of a project.
- The third competency required is that of *instructional design,* referring to the sequencing of educational elements, selection of media, and use of pedagogical strategies within the learning product.
- Another crucial competency is that of *distance education pedagogy,* that is, an ability to design the events of instruction when there is no planned face-to-face interaction. Specifically, this is a "translator" role of converting the teaching methods and strategies successful in a face-to-face environment to methods and strategies that will work at a distance. Of particular importance in this skill set is an ability to represent the needs of the learner in the design of the instruction.
- The fifth competency, *proficiency in instructional technology,* is highly dependent on the delivery model selected. Print-based, correspondence-style programs require significantly less technology-literate staff than course materials designed and delivered via the Web. Increasingly, however, even traditional print-based programs are tapping into the enhanced communications capabilities of the Internet to increase interactions among participants.
- In many institutions, a series of *administrative tasks* may be necessary before the course or learning event can be made publicly available at a distance. Understanding how to successfully implement a course within the institutional setting is a critical skill necessary in the operation.
- Often, *faculty development,* either formal or informal, must be planned and executed in order to prepare the faculty for success online. The task of providing faculty with the skills necessary to author and instruct a course at a distance is the responsibility of the design and development unit. Whether this is accomplished through formal faculty development workshops, online classes, or informal technical training programs, properly preparing faculty to succeed in a distance learning model is a critical step to program success.
- Finally, a range of competencies in *multimedia materials production* must be accounted for within the production cycle. This, of course, is dependent on the technology base of the learning program. In a print-based operation, core services of editors, graphic artists, technical typists, and copyright clearance staff will be required. For Web-based delivery, a wider range of development services may be required including multimedia developers and technical programmers.

## PROJECT MANAGEMENT AND TRACKING SYSTEMS

Critical to the success of any organizational and management scheme for a production unit is a system, or series of systems, that enables staff to plan the use of resources, project that use over time, and track progress toward goals. In particular, projects to develop instructional materials for delivery online require the coordination of multiple inputs, such as faculty and staff, responsible for various components at various stages of product development. From the concept stage of design through materials production, tasks necessary to complete each phase must be monitored and checked as completed or not, and signoff points must be identified that allow the next phase to progress as scheduled. Whether the system is a formalized software solution for project management or an informal checklist of tasks and timelines, a project cannot be completed successfully without a mechanism for charting its course.

In many cases, the resources necessary to complete a project may not reside in a single unit. For example, an outside media service unit may be responsible for generating graphics, streamed video, or audio for an online biology project. The subject matter expert is most likely a faculty member in the science department, and perhaps a graduate student is providing research data to support a particular lesson. The role of the project manager is to orchestrate the production and flow of content, including text from the faculty and images from media services, with the construction of the course pages and their integration into a learning management system. Given a specific project life cycle of 6 to 8 months, all materials and production need to be outlined and their completion scheduled in order for the project to be available for student enrollment on the planned date. A project management system that specifies the tasks in each phase will enable the project manager to schedule necessary resources at appropriate intervals throughout the project. In addition, a tracking system will allow the project participants to communicate and monitor progress on a regular basis in order to plan their contributions to the project. Increasingly, project teams are turning to centrally located tracking software that permit access from Web sites at multiple locations.

Another valuable planning tool for project teams is "contingency planning." This step engages all team members to identify resolutions for problems as they occur throughout the life of the project. Understanding the trigger points and resolution protocol will allow problems to be quickly and successfully addressed with minimal disruption to the process. This is often much easier to do before a critical technical or personnel issue is at hand.

## PROCESS AND PROCEDURE GUIDELINES

In any organization dealing with multiple inputs and handoffs, defined policy and procedures for the operation are vital time and energy savers. Although initially difficult to quantify, they serve the long-term goal of understanding and mapping the procedural flow of the life of a project. Process guidelines define the flow of materials within and between work units. These guidelines are developed after a systems analysis describes the task to be accomplished and the steps necessary to accomplish those tasks. Often, process analysis and definition start with a documentation of how things are done currently and then a statement of the "desired state" of events in the ideal situation. This process analysis should include duration of task, time interval between tasks, and handoff points between units. The analysis of how things are currently done and the desired state should identify gaps that need to be addressed and inefficiencies that add to project costs or time.

Procedural guidelines are developed following the documentation of process workflow. These guidelines define policies for how tasks are to be completed, levels of authority and responsibility, and protocol for problem resolution. In particular, these guidelines are helpful in defining the handoffs between organizational units involved in a project. For a relatively new distance learning organization, the statement of procedural guidelines can serve as an anchor during the transitional phase between course design and development, and course delivery. Keep in mind that flexibility is necessary until the appropriate guidelines have had a chance to solidify. This flexibility calls for creativity, resourcefulness, and a great deal of patience with new and emerging procedures.

In managing the design and development of instructional materials for delivery via distance or distributed learning in a dual mode institution—that is, an institution supporting both a resident-based and distance-based program—precedent may have already been established for how tasks are completed. With the convergence of these two delivery systems, many process and procedural guidelines may need to be revisited and the underlining assumptions challenged. Ultimately, the goal would be to serve all students seamlessly with materials developed once and delivered via a variety of delivery systems.

## ADMINISTRATIVE SYSTEMS

Organizing and managing the resources needed to produce products for delivery via distance or distributed learning models is part art and part science. The challenge lies in allocating resources to a rapidly moving project stream. The speed with which new technologies emerge further stresses the durability of any definition of process and procedures. In order to meet the production needs of the delivery model, and presuming some level of analysis of process mapping, the challenge remains of channeling resources to an ever-shifting list of priorities. Even after the analysis of process and the definition of procedures, the resulting approach will be less than perfect. Unanticipated project barriers appear, staff turnover and attrition occur, and resources need to be controlled where no authority exists.

Creating an administrative structure that enables data to be collected and reacted upon, allows for a degree of flexibility for unexpected and unplanned project adjustments, and managing complex and sometimes politically charged projects can tax even the most well-planned unit. Using a multi-layered management team approach, where spheres of responsibilities can be assigned, is one way to manage this task. Making the roles and rules of the team participants clear is vital to the efficiency and success of the project. Designing a method for accessing necessary resources and a protocol for problem resolution can alleviate tension and stress in the system.

Creating and charging effective project teams allows the individuals closest to the project's needs to bring to bear the skills and competencies necessary for project completion. Typically, the lead designer serves as the project manager and is responsible for orchestrating the necessary resources. Other team members may include the subject matter expert, graphic artists, editors, and multimedia producers. In many situations these individuals may be assigned to multiple projects, making the planning of their inputs and responsibilities a crucial element in overall project success. These teams may also be charged with "contingency planning" in order to anticipate unforeseen project delays. For project teams to be effective, they must have a defined budget, scope of work, and resource allocation list to draw upon. It is their responsibility to manage the necessary elements and use of resources to accomplish the stated project goal.

In order to account for resource use and progress toward timelines, a time-tracking system may be employed. A time-tracking system is a method of capturing time spent on tasks associated with a specific project. The degree of specificity is dependent on the degree of data one wishes to receive from the system. Even a "global" system that enables team participants to assign hours worked on a specific project can provide valuable data for project management as well as information for a more realistic budgeting process for future endeavors. More specific tracking systems, for example tracking time spent per task of a project, will help identify where resources are being consumed rather than relying on hearsay or intuition. An important management feature of any production unit is the budgeting and projection of resource use. A time-tracking system is a valuable tool for accounting for actual time on task to date and degree of completion to goal.

*—Lawrence C. Ragan*

*See also* ADMINISTRATIVE LEADERSHIP; ONLINE LEARNING ENVIRONMENTS

### Bibliography

Barone, Carol A., German Jr., Robert F., Katz, Richard N., Long, Philip E., & Walsh, Barry. (2000). *Information technology, systems, and services in higher education: A primer.* Washington, DC: EDUCAUSE.

Barone, Carole, & Hagner, Paul. (Eds.). (August 2001). Technology-enhanced teaching and learning: Leading and supporting the transformation on your campus. *EDUCAUSE Leadership Strategies Series No. 5.* San Francisco: Jossey-Bass.

Hawkins, Brian L., & Battin, Patricia. (Eds.). (September 1998). *The mirage of continuity: Reconfiguring academic information resources for the 21st century.* Washington, DC: Council on Library and Information Resources.

Oblinger, Diana. (June 1999). Putting students at the center: A planning guide to distributed learning. *The EDUCAUSE Monograph Series, 1.*

*Recruiting and retaining information technology staff in higher education.* (August 2000). An EDUCAUSE Executive Briefing developed in cooperation with the College and University Professional Association for Human Resources (CUPA-HR) and the National Association of College and University Business Officers (NACUBO). Retrieved from http://www.educause.edu/pub/eb/eb1.html.

## ORIENTATION

Orientation is a process in which an individual becomes familiarized with a new environment, a new group of people, and/or a new culture. Orientation provides an opportunity to set expectations for members of the group, reflect on the history of the organization, and review the shared values of those involved. Other topics that are often covered during an orientation program include new member benefits, member services and resources, and a tour of the facilities to assist in overall acclimation to the organization. When a new group of members are inducted into an organization, they are often referred to as a *cohort*.

Throughout this entry, the term *new member* is used to refer to new employees with a business, new members of a club or organization, and/or new students entering an educational setting. For instance, orientation in higher education is commonly thought of as a program to welcome new students and to help them transition to the college environment. (*College* is used here as a generic term for any institution of higher education.) Orientation programs are created for first-year students (i.e., freshmen), transfer students, international students, graduate students, and more recently, for the family members of new students.

Common goals of an orientation program are to:

- Welcome and introduce new members to the organization, resources, services, and staff
- Increase member knowledge, comfort, and familiarity with the new environment
- Set expectations and establish an understanding of organizational traditions, customs, and norms
- Provide an opportunity for new members to connect with other members, staff, and administrators
- Provide the information necessary to enhance a new member's performance with the organization

Among these goals, the overarching mission of an orientation is to assist in the new member's transition to increase his or her satisfaction and retention with the organization.

Often, orientation programs are held for special populations within an organization. These orientation programs are designed to address the special needs and necessary accommodations of these new members as well as to introduce them to each other to create a network of support at an early stage in their experience with the organization. Although specialized orientations are necessary and beneficial, it is also important to have new members participate in other activities where they might meet a more representative part of the whole organization to increase their awareness of their new environment. Overall, it is important to create an opportunity for new members to learn about what they have in common and create a support network, while also helping them recognize and appreciate their differences.

Due to the realization that a successful transition has a significant impact on member satisfaction and retention, organizations are incorporating additional, more extensive orientation activities. One example is pairing new members with mentors who have had more extensive experience with the organization. This mentoring relationship can continue over the first year or throughout both members' involvement with the organization. The mentor's role can include the responsibility to continue informing the new member of the organization's common terminology and language, providing insight about organizational dynamics and relationships with other entities, and serving as a resource for the new member. This type of activity serves as extended orientation and expands on

topics introduced during the initial new member orientation. In the example of higher education, extended orientations are seen in the form of first-year seminars, residence hall–based learning communities, and first-year interest groups. These lengthier activities extending throughout the first semester or quarter may grant academic credit and may be considered to go beyond orientation to acclimation or transition to the new campus. Similarly, in businesses or other environments, initial orientation programs and more protracted efforts are not interchangeable and do not replace each other. However, they do supplement one another, with an initial orientation experience leading into a more in-depth and extensive effort to support new members' transition to the organization.

In higher education, orientation needs to be sensitive to the developmental process that the student and the student's family are experiencing. As such, family programs should emphasize the transition that may occur at home while the student is away at college, the changing relationships between the college student and the family members, and insight into what a college student might experience developmentally during the first year of college. Because of what they learn through orientation programs, family members may be much more satisfied with the institution the student is attending and can be of greater assistance in the adjustment of the student to college. Correspondingly, in businesses and other organizations, similar efforts are emerging that focus on introducing the family members to the new culture and environment.

It is becoming more common and more important for orientation programs to build partnerships with other related agencies in an organization or institution. To serve new members, it is necessary to collaborate with other entities and provide as much information as possible without being repetitive and overlapping efforts. On college campuses, orientation programs frequently work closely with campus activity centers to plan and implement welcome week activities before the beginning of the fall semester. In addition to these common partnerships, the collaborative effort found in any college orientation program extends to academic departments, service offices, and student affairs functional areas (e.g., housing, academic advising, campus activities, health services, and student unions). The relationship between an orientation program and its campus is mutually beneficial in that an orientation program depends on other offices to provide information to new students, while the offices on campus depend on the orientation program to educate new students about their services. Further, through the collaboration of academic and student affairs organizations, orientation programs can "seamlessly" present a variety of services in order to introduce students to their new campus community with emphasis on the social and academic transition.

Another trend within the field of orientation includes technology. Technological advances have added to the abilities of orientation programs to serve new members. Because of the convenience of the World Wide Web and CD-ROM capabilities, orientation programmers can conveniently and efficiently serve their audience using a form of communication to which our society is becoming more accustomed. Interactive Internet or CD-ROM orientations can be completed before a new member even sets foot on the physical property of the organization. For larger companies with new members across the country or around the world, an online orientation can reach a wider audience and send a common message and experience to all new members simultaneously. Whether new members can be effectively oriented entirely online remains to be seen. Nevertheless, this appears to be an increasing trend, and services are available to help organizations create and customize these virtual orientations.

Whether orientation programs range from one day to one week, whether they target a specific population or a general population, orientation will continue to serve as one of the first impressions that an individual has of any organization, business, or educational setting. As a result, orientation programs will need to continuously assess the culture and adjust to changes within the given organization and the needs of the individuals being oriented.

—*Kerry Nakasone*
—*Paul Shang*

*See also* ONLINE ORIENTATION AND NAVIGATION TOOLS

## Bibliography

Howe, N., & Strauss, W. (2000). *Millennials rising: The next great generation.* Vancouver, WA: Vintage Books.

Mullendore, R. H., & Hatch, C. (2000). *Helping your first year college student succeed: A guide for parents.* Columbia, SC: National Resource Center for First Year Experience and Students in Transition.

National Orientation Directors Association (NODA). (May 2002). *NODA mission, values, and strategic priorities.* Retrieved from http://www.nodaweb.org/mission.htm.

Upcraft, M. L., & Mullendore, R. H. (1993). *Designing successful transitions: A guide for orienting students to college.* Columbia, SC: National Resource Center for First Year Experience and Students in Transition.

## OUTCOMES

Outcomes are the result of an activity or process. The unit of analysis—either institutional, programmatic, or student—characterizes higher education outcomes. Outcomes of distributed learning are similar to higher education outcomes, differing in the mode of instructional delivery.

Academic outcomes—what students take away from the learning and teaching process—fall into two general categories. One type is student behavioral outcomes, such as "the student is employed in her field of study." Student behavioral outcomes include traditional measures of retention and graduate rates. Distributed learning environments can result in similar behavioral outcomes, including:

- The number and percentage of students enrolled in a course that re-enroll in the next course in a sequence
- The number and percentage of students returning and enrolling in the next term of study
- The number and percentage of students retained at an institution or within a program from one fall term to the next fall term

Outcome measures that may be more important in a distributed learning environment are the number and percentage of students who enroll *and then complete* a course.

The other type of academic outcome is student learning outcomes. These result from individual students having an educational encounter with a higher education institution. There are four types of student learning outcomes:

1. *Knowledge outcomes* are specific disciplinary facts or procedural steps students learn (for instance, a student knows the elements of the periodic table).
2. *Skills* consist of activities or actions that students perform (for instance, a student constructs a business plan).

3. *Attitudinal outcomes* are students' beliefs or values including ethics, empathy, and respect for others (for instance, a student responds ethically to a morally ambiguous situation).

4. *Abilities* synthesize the previous three types of outcomes—knowledge, skill, and attitude—in complex situations (for instance, a student participates in leadership and followership behavior as warranted during a team project).

The type of student learning outcome resulting from a particular course, curricular activity, or enrollment in a program of study derives from the instructor's outcome specifications for that course, curriculum, or program. With the increase in distributed learning in higher education in which the dimensions of time and physical proximity are no longer standardized in the educational process, instructors are finding that competencies are increasingly useful as expressions of learning outcomes. Competencies are clear statements of what students will know and can do as a result of participating in an educational activity, whether it is a single assignment, a full course, or a program. Student learning outcomes written as competencies differ from teaching objectives in that the subject of the statements is the student not the instructor, and the outcome is a deliberate statement of what learning will occur rather than the teaching technique used to foster learning. (Outcomes often include competencies from along a continuum of simple to complex, as outlined in Bloom's Taxonomy of Educational Objectives.)

Although not all subject matter is amenable to learning and instruction via distributed learning, much of it is. Subject matter delivered in both a conventional and a distributed learning environment would have the same student learning outcomes. What might differ would be the methods used to assess those student learning outcomes; for example, a student's written communication skills may be easier to assess in an online environment than her oral presentation abilities.

Student learning outcomes can be expressed in terms of absolute attainment or in terms of change or growth in attainment. Expressing the absolute level of learning at the completion of the educational encounter is known simply as student learning outcomes (for example, the student reads at the college junior level). The growth or change in level of learning is known as "value-added." This requires measuring both the incoming or entry level and the exit level

of attainment for a specified learning outcome in order to determine the amount of change (for instance, "the student will increase her reading ability three grade levels," requires knowing at what reading level the student entered in addition to her reading level upon completion of the course). Psychometricians, statisticians, and institutional researchers have access to background academic variables (ACT/SAT scores, high school grade point average, etc.) that may also influence these outcome measures. Regression techniques can be used to control for the influence of these variables on the outcome measures to determine how much learning can be attributed to background characteristics or to the learning process itself.

—*Karen Paulson*

***See also*** Assessment of Prior Learning; Assessment of Student Competence

## Bibliography

Bloom, B. S. (1956). (Ed.). *Taxonomy of educational objectives.* 2 vols. New York: David McKay.

Ewell, P. T. (September 2001). *Accreditation and student learning outcomes: A proposed point of departure.* Washington, DC: Council on Higher Education Accreditation.

# OUTSOURCING

Outsourcing is the business or management practice of having an external organization provide a needed function or service through some form of contractual arrangement. If an existing function or service is outsourced, the contractor may hire some or all of the incumbent staff. In some arrangements, the contractor is required to work with incumbent staff—at least for a period of time.

Outsourcing has been practiced by the government and corporate sectors for decades and has evolved through three distinct stages. Michael F. Corbett identifies these stages as tactical, strategic, and transformational.

## STAGE 1: TACTICAL OUTSOURCING

Early outsourcing efforts tend to be tactical in nature, aimed at solving specific organizational problems. These could include a one-time, fixed term need; peak activity loads; a troubled department or division; inadequate funds for capital investments; poor managerial performance; lack of appropriate talent; and to cut or minimize cost or personnel. Many tactical relationships are forged to yield immediate cost savings, relieve staffing pressures, avoid dealing with labor unions, shrink or eliminate the need for future investment, and, sometimes, provide injection of cash from sale of assets.

The primary focus of tactical outsourcing is the development and negotiation of a contract and the accountability of the service provider for the contracted services. Although many tactical relationships have been successful, others failed because of unclear or even impossible expectations, poorly constructed contract documents, or lack of adequate contract oversight. As a result, some organizations, particularly educational institutions, became wary of outsourcing as a solution.

## STAGE 2: STRATEGIC OUTSOURCING

As outsourcing achieved some level of success, executives realized that instead of losing control over the outsourced function they actually achieved broader control over all the functions they were responsible for. They also were able to focus more on the strategic aspects of their work. For example, instead of worrying about staffing clerical positions, the registrar can focus more on developing enhanced services for students. Information technology executives can turn over the day-to-day operations of a data center and begin to focus on serving the needs of the faculty, students, and staff of the institution.

As these shifts occur, they are accompanied by changes in how and where outsourcing is applied. Outsourcing relationships grow in size (in terms of dollar value), the scope of the service provider's involvement expands, and the duration of the relationship lengthens. Management perception shifts from a view of outsourcing as a buyer/provider relationship to more of a business partnership. The purpose of this partnership is no longer simply to fix or avoid a problem. Instead, it is focused on identifying the core business or mission of an organization and on partnering with an external provider for noncore activities, thereby allowing the organization to concentrate on its core competencies.

This approach was particularly prevalent during the 1990s as organizations began to focus and

streamline their activities and operations. Their philosophy was not to be a world leader in all aspects of the enterprise—just in the core business. In distributed learning environments, this would translate into a focus on teaching and learning. Many academic institutions are now entering this strategic phase of outsourcing, moving beyond the sometimes adversarial vendor/supplier relationship into long-term partnerships focused on mutual benefit.

## STAGE 3: TRANSFORMATIONAL OUTSOURCING

Transformational outsourcing recognizes that outsourcing can be instrumental to achieving desired change in an organization. Outside specialists can bring innovative approaches to an organization that would be difficult for those entrenched within the organization to develop. Transformational outsourcing requires the creation of interdependencies among the parties, such that the success of any one party is dependent on the success of all the others. Only when this is achieved can outsourcing relationships become very powerful forces for change. These relationships are rarely defined as outsourcing relationships—they tend to be called partnerships, collaborations, and strategic alliances.

For distributed education, transformational outsourcing could leverage curriculum design and development efforts across institutions and across a much wider audience of students. It could be used to complement and expand on an institution's more traditional offerings and catalyze change throughout the institution. Used as a transformational force, outsourcing could help an organization reach new customers/audiences, and create new products and services. Examples of transformational outsourcing in education include various distance education and virtual university consortia.

The University of Pennsylvania has had a long history of outsourcing, and recently acknowledged that

> [f]or-profit companies are increasingly playing a role in distributed learning. Firms that own videoconferencing facilities and equipment as well as the necessary production and marketing expertise are particularly well positioned in this emerging field. . . . Collaborating with for-profit companies has potential advantages. . . .

Key reasons for pursuing external collaborations are the university's decentralized institutional structure; high initial costs of staffing, infrastructure, and support; uncertainty about which techniques and directions will ultimately succeed; and a desire to test-launch new programs quickly.

## WHAT TO OUTSOURCE

The decade of the 1990s was one of declining student enrollments, state budget cuts, decreased funding for research, and increased pressures to limit tuition growth, which resulted in limited revenue sources. A 1996 survey conducted by American School & University found that colleges and universities had turned increasingly to outsourcing, and that only about 6% produced all services in-house. In 2000, the National Association of College and University Business Officers found that the most common examples of outsourcing in higher education are campus food services and bookstores. Increasingly, academic institutions are outsourcing legal services, financial services, and information technology services. And although they tend to perform much of the teaching and research-related functions in-house, it can be argued that the use of adjunct faculty is an extreme form of outsourcing (outsourcing of course delivery to individual contractors).

In a distributed learning environment, many of the administrative support functions, such as registration, computing services, and financial aid disbursement, are often outsourced to others. Functions close to the academic core of educational institutions, such as library services and student advising, are sometimes outsourced as well.

Just about any function or service that is not considered "core" to an organization is a potential candidate for outsourcing. This includes all infrastructure and centrally managed services, activities for which there is weak management, and newly emerging activities for which there are insufficient human, technological, or infrastructure resources.

## PROBLEMS WITH OUTSOURCING

Opponents of outsourcing express concerns about loss of control, particularly regarding academic course content, admission standards, and distribution.

Intellectual property rights and tax law compliance need careful attention in outsourcing collaborations. Careful monitoring of individual outsourcing contracts is recommended.

Other concerns include dependency on external sources and employee and external community reaction to the letting go of employees. The most vocal critics of outsourcing tend to be those employees in the function or service to be outsourced because they are concerned over lost jobs and potential reductions in salaries or benefits. To minimize the potential negative effect of outsourcing on institutional morale and public relations, Ender and Mooney suggest outsourcing management personnel only, downsizing the staff through attrition, involving employees in selection of the contractor, and frequently rebidding of the contract.

In the final analysis, outsourcing should be considered carefully and solutions crafted to ensure that the service provider is able to deliver and that the outsourcing relationship promotes the vision, mission, and values of the institution.

*—Jose-Marie Griffiths*

*See also* ADMINISTRATIVE PLANNING AND SUPPORT OF INFORMATION TECHNOLOGY; FINANCE

## Bibliography

Eleey, M., & Comegno, M. (January 1999). Using external collaborations to advance distributed learning at the University of Pennsylvania. *T.H.E. Journal ONLINE.* Retrieved from http://www.thejournal.com.

Ender, K. L., & Mooney, K. A. (1994). From outsourcing to alliances: Strategies for sharing leadership and exploiting resources at metropolitan universities. *Metropolitan Universities: An International Forum, 5*(3), 51–60.

Gilmer. S. W. (November 1997). The winds of privatization: A typology for understanding the phenomenon in public higher education. Paper presented at the annual meeting of the Association for the Study of Higher Education, Albuquerque, NM.

Jeffries, C. L. (1996). The privatization debate: Examining the decision to outsource a service. *Business Officer, 29*(7), 26–30.

Michael F. Corbett & Associates, Ltd. (2001). *Ten years of outsourcing practice: Tactical, strategic, and transformational.* Retrieved from http://www.firmbuilder.com/articles/19/50/591.

# P

## PEDAGOGY/ANDRAGOGY

Pedagogy and andragogy are two different orientations to teaching, in which the age and developmental stage of the learners determine the educational methods used. Pedagogy is the art and science of helping children and adolescents learn; andragogy is the art and science of helping adults learn.

The distinction between these two approaches is mostly associated with the work of Malcolm Knowles, who developed a theory of adult education grounded in andragogical practices. (However, earlier references to the term exist in the work of Eduard Lindeman, one of the earliest American writers on adult education.) For Knowles, pedagogy is an approach to teaching in which there is a clear difference between learners' and teachers' levels of expertise; where learners need strong external direction; where the responsibility for setting goals, conducting learning, and evaluating progress clearly rests with the teacher; and where learners bring very little relevant previous experience, knowledge, or skill to the educational situation. Pedagogy is didactic in intent and form and, in Knowles' view, observable in K–12 schooling.

Andragogy, in contrast, is premised on a number of assumptions Knowles makes about adult learners, whom he describes as a "neglected species." Adults are assumed to prefer self-directed approaches to learning. Although adults are temporarily willing to submit to external direction, they are thought always to desire and enact a tendency to self-directedness as they mature. Because adults bring rich experiences to their learning, they are viewed by the andragogical model as able to learn more effectively through experiential, problem-solving, and dialogic methods. Adults are also presumed to be motivated by an internal desire to learn skills and knowledge that will help them deal with immediate, real-life problems. The traditional emphasis of liberal adult education on lifelong learning projects undertaken for their own sake because of the innate fascination they hold for learners has little place in the andragogical model.

The assumptions of andragogy suggest a specific set of practices for working with adult learners. Programs should be established that incorporate the maximum opportunity for adults to exercise control over the design, conduct, and evaluation of their learning. In such programs the educator moves aside and is viewed as a facilitator or resource person, connecting learners to appropriate resources, brokering connections with other learners and other bodies of information, and assisting with reflective analysis. This emphasis on self-direction is taken by many to fit comfortably within the paradigm of online education. An andragogical program also places a strong emphasis on experiential methods of learning. Discussion, problem-solving, simulations, games, brainstorming, and participatory theater are all used to help adults connect their previous experiences to new learning. Knowles also advocates the organization of learning programs around "life application" categories so that adults can see a clear connection between their learning activities and the problems with which they are dealing in their everyday existence.

The andragogical model has a number of implications for distributed learning. It suggests that participants must be able to state their wants, needs, and expectations before the start of a program, and that these should be responded to in some public manner by those in control of the program. For example, in online environments participants can create their own chat rooms or listserv to negotiate common wants, and then post these on a learning community Web site that faculty and counselors have access to. Online environments are also well suited to the facilitator as broker role because links to relevant Web sites can be built into the course design. The reflective analysis emphasized in andragogy is particularly suited to distributed learning formats, given the greater amount of time participants have to frame thoughtful responses. In face-to-face, synchronous learning the pressure to perform, to say something impressive as a topic is being discussed, can prevent reflective analysis. Such pressure is felt much less acutely in distributed learning. It is quite possible to set up online threaded discussions that mirror face-to-face discussions, but that remove the cultural and contextual pressures that stop some learners from contributing.

## CRITICISMS OF THE PEDAGOGY/ANDRAGOGY DIVIDE

A number of criticisms regarding the division between pedagogy and andragogy have been made since the distinction was first popularized in the 1970s. Many feel that the division oversimplifies learning, implying an either/or approach that does not fit most learners or most learning contexts. At times some learners work in ways we could describe as andragogical, but at other times they clearly look for strong external direction. The choice of whether or how far to take control over learning, or the extent to which experiential methods of learning are useful, rests on learners' previous experiences in the area of learning chosen, on their learning styles, on their habits and dispositions, and on their level of developed ability. At different times the same learner will choose to work experientially and self-directedly, or by listening to or watching experts demonstrate their knowledge or skill.

The concept of *andragogy* is also criticized as culture blind, neglecting to acknowledge that people with different racial identities and people who have grown up informed by different cultural traditions will find its practices alienating and demeaning. It fits the individualistic ethos valued in American culture but is less connected to cultures that value collectivity and interdependence. In cultures where reverence for the teacher is strong, it is unrealistic to expect learners to opt for a lack of teacher direction, or to embrace experiential methods. In cultures that value silence and reflection, an emphasis on discussion is often experienced as intimidating (in this case, the aforementioned opportunity for greater reflection in distributed learning is a real strength). In cultures where standing out is a sign of class or racial betrayal, andragogy's emphasis on self-direction is contradictory.

Sequencing learning around developmental tasks or life-application categories will also vary greatly according to class and cultural contexts. Developmental tasks do not exist *sui generis*. They are culturally framed, representing the dominant group's ideas of what kinds of behaviors best fit society's needs. In addition, the focus on organizing educational programs around learning needs that have immediate application to adults' lives neglects those learning efforts that, although they may not seem immediately relevant, in the long term can be defended as being in the learner's best interests. If adults' identities, preferences, and learning choices reflect the dominant ideology, then the learning projects they engage in are likely to support, rather than challenge, the status quo—a situation that threatens the democratic health of society.

Knowles himself recognized that his original formulation was oversimplified. The 1970 subtitle of the first edition of his influential book *The Modern Practice of Adult Education* was "Andragogy versus Pedagogy." By the time the second edition appeared in 1980, this subtitle had changed to "From Pedagogy to Andragogy," with Knowles emphasizing that these two approaches were complementary poles on a continuum, rather than diametrically opposed. He admitted that there were certain situations in which it was both desirable and appropriate for adults to submit to teacher authority, and he came to advocate an important role for educators in assisting adults to make informed choices between these orientations. In the last two decades, many adult educators have criticized the cultural blindness of andragogy and its lack of attention to context, although the concept is still used by many as a badge of identity that signifies what is distinct and different about working with adult learners. Some have reframed the concept with a critical edge to focus on adults' efforts to empower themselves through community action.

## CONCEPTIONS OF THE TEACHER'S ROLE IN PEDAGOGY/ANDRAGOGY

One of the most contentious issues surrounding the debate on pedagogy and andragogy is the role of the teacher. In adult education there is a strong tradition of the teacher being at one with learners. The role of teacher is often claimed to move continuously around learning groups, with all members of the group at some time assuming teaching roles irrespective of their role or status. Andragogy sees the teacher as a resource person in service to adult learners, with the teacher's specific role and contributions being determined by the learners' needs. In this conceptualization, teachers are less directive and more reactive, with such reactiveness being taken as a sign of a democratic, learner-centered responsiveness. When andragogically inclined teachers refuse to move front and center, they often pride themselves on their affirmational stance and the way that their refusal to exercise power honors learners' voices and promotes learners' participation.

However, studies of how adults experience learning point out that in learners' eyes, teachers never give away their power. Even if they profess to work collegially and democratically, and to have no greater power than anyone else in the learning situation, teachers are still accorded great credibility by learners and watched very carefully. Indeed, it seems that the optimal mix of characteristics identified by many adults for their learning is the teacher's possession of credibility as well as the demonstration of authenticity. Authenticity is traditionally valued by adult education. It is seen in the consistency of teachers' words and actions, in teachers' responsiveness to learners' concerns, in their willingness to bring their own personhood into their teaching, and in their demonstrating a respect for each learner's integrity. Credibility is much less valued in the adult educational tradition and plays little part in articulations of andragogy. But to adult learners, a teacher's credibility is all-important. Examples of teacher credibility that are often cited by adults are teachers' demonstrable command of a subject or skill, their experience with teaching in the area concerned, their possession of a clear rationale for practice that can be articulated upon request, and the teacher's exhibiting a concern that learners understand the material because to the teacher it is clear that the material has innate importance.

Teachers committed to working andragogically frequently declare their "at one-ness" with students.

Believing themselves and their students to be moral equals, they like to view their relationship with learners as one where a temporary, almost accidental imbalance exists. However, in learners' eyes, culturally learned habits of reliance on, or hostility toward, authority figures (especially those from the dominant culture) cannot so easily be broken. Like it or not, in the strongly hierarchical culture of higher education, with its power imbalances and its clear demarcation of roles and boundaries, teachers cannot simply wish their influence away. No matter how much they might want it to be otherwise, and no matter how informal, friendly, and sincere toward students they might be in their declarations of "at one-ness," teachers *are* viewed as different, at least initially. Critically aware teachers reject as naive the assumption that by saying they are the students' friend and equal they thereby become so.

Andragogues committed to a vision of themselves as nondirective facilitators of learning, or as resource people there only to serve needs defined by students, often adopt the "fly on the wall" approach to teaching. They will put students into groups, give only minimal instructions about what should happen, and then retreat from the scene to let students work as they wish. However, this retreat is only partial. Teachers rarely leave the room entirely for long periods of time. Instead, they sit at their desk, or off in a corner, observing groups getting started on their projects. For students to pretend as if a teacher is not in the room is almost impossible. Knowing that a teacher is nearby will cause some students to perform as the good, task-oriented members of the group. Others will just clam up for fear of saying or doing something stupid while a teacher is watching.

Students will wonder how the teacher thinks they are doing and will be watching closely for any cues of approval or censure that he or she drops. Students' awareness of the power relationship that exists between themselves and their teachers is such that it pervades nearly all interactions between them.

Those faculty involved in distributed learning may believe, mistakenly, that learners feel themselves to be free from teacher surveillance. In fact, studies have shown that learners are very aware of the teacher's presence (albeit at one stage removed) in distributed formats. For example, in asynchronous online courses students know that teachers are reading their postings, checking the amount of time between postings, making sure that the required minimum number of postings are made by students within the allotted time, and so on. Although the teachers' bodies are not physically present in distributed learning, their mental presence is felt. Michel Foucault's work on surveillance, and his concept of the *Panopticon,* can be applied directly to distributed learning formats, despite their apparent learner-centeredness.

Paulo Freire has made an important distinction between authoritative and authoritarian teaching. Authoritative teaching is teaching where the teacher is respected by students because of the expertise she or he possesses, but where the teacher uses that expertise in a respectful way, depending on the needs and situations of the learners. Authoritarian teachers, on the other hand, use their power to underscore the differences between themselves and learners, and to bolster their own egos. Michel Foucault's work on the interconnections between power and knowledge illuminates how teachers can never assume that because of their andragogical, democratic intentions their learners will feel empowered. Much of Foucault's analysis focuses on how apparently liberatory, andragogical practices (organizing students into participatory discussion circles, using learning contracts) are experienced by adult learners as heightened forms of surveillance.

## REFRAMING PEDAGOGY AS CRITICAL PEDAGOGY

In the years since Paulo Freire published *Pedagogy of the Oppressed,* a number of writers have reframed the concept of pedagogy to include a liberatory, critical edge that stands very much against the authoritarian didactism of Knowles' characterization of pedagogy. This body of work was first named by Peter McLaren as *critical pedagogy.* Central to critical pedagogy is the role of the teacher as penetrator of false consciousness. Critical pedagogy analyzes education as a process through which dominant social and economic groups impose values and beliefs that legitimize their own power and position of control. The teacher's task is to expose and resist these processes by finding and creating spaces (often called *public spheres*) in which students can learn to become aware of how these processes happen and how to fight against them. Education properly conducted is viewed as a dialogue among equals, an endeavor in cooperative learning. Through this dialogue students are helped to name, honor, and understand their own experiences. They do this by using categories of analysis that they have evolved themselves rather than those that have been externally imposed on them by the dominant culture. Action and reflection are seen as being in a state of constant and productive tension, often referred to as *praxis.* The point of education is not just to understand the world, but also to change it, often through collective endeavor.

Analytical concepts central to this tradition are those of class, power, gender, ethnicity, hegemony, and conflict. Terms used to describe the process of critical pedagogy are those of transformation, liberation, emancipation, empowerment, and ideology critique. Critical pedagogy becomes a means by which people are helped to break out of oppressive ways of thinking and acting that seem habitual but that have been imposed by the dominant culture. They are helped to create forms of thinking and living that are more democratic, congenial, and true to their own experiences. Teaching is understood to be political by definition. Teachers have a choice to work either in ways that legitimize and reinforce the status quo or in ways that liberate and transform the possibilities people see in their lives.

The pedagogy/andragogy debate is one in which considerations of the chronological age of learners has given way to discussions of the contextuality of learning, and one where a prescriptive methodological bifurcation ("pedagogy bad, andragogy good") has been replaced by a realization that the surface forms of teaching—whether superficially autocratic lectures or superficially democratic discussions—matter less than the differential ways these forms are experienced by learners. As Freire acknowledged before his death, discussions in which instructors quietly lead the conversation to predetermined conclusions can be exercises in insidious manipulation, whereas listening to critically stimulating lectures that offer a different perspective on the familiar can be a consciousness-raising experience.

Distributed learning formats can be reframed as critical pedagogies. The focus of distributed learning can be on matters of social justice, exclusion, equity, and the ways in which race, class, and gender work to the advantage of some while marginalizing others. In online environments, teachers can post critical reflections on their own chat room contributions and course procedures, and students can post anonymous evaluations on teachers' contributions that have been compiled in student-only chat rooms. The critical theorist

Marcuse's elaboration of rebellious subjectivity suggests that in a learner's detachment from the need to meet with others at a defined place and time lies a potentially revolutionary opening. Without some form of separation from peers and teachers Marcuse suggested that learners would mimic unthinkingly the views and preferences of the majority. Deprived of the usual weekly engagement in the typical face-to-face classroom, the learner is less likely to be enveloped by the tentacles of anonymous authority. The authority of imagined common sense, public opinion, and conventional wisdom is mentally ingrained, it is true, but it is also reinforced each time learners come together in a classroom to find that the authority of "official" knowledge is once again underscored. When learners are stripped of this weekly 2-hour classroom gathering they are more likely to explore, or at least be open to, diverse perspectives that stand against the kind of pseudo-thinking whereby the learner simply paraphrases what he or she feels others are thinking, or want to think.

*—Stephen D. Brookfield*

*See also* ADULT EDUCATION LEARNING MODEL; SELF-DIRECTED LEARNING

## Bibliography

Boshier, R., & Wilson, M. (1998). Panoptic variations: Surveillance and discipline in Web courses. *Proceedings of the Adult Education Research Conference, No. 39.* San Antonio: University of the Incarnate Word, 43–48.

Brookfield, S. D. (1990). *The skillful teacher.* San Francisco: Jossey-Bass.

Brookfield, S. D. (1995). *Becoming a critically reflective teacher.* San Francisco: Jossey-Bass.

Foucault, M. (1980). *Power/Knowledge: Selected interviews and other writings, 1972–1977.* New York: Pantheon.

Freire, P. (1970). *Pedagogy of the oppressed.* New York: Continuum.

Knowles, M. S. (1980). *The modern practice of adult education: From pedagogy to andragogy,* 2nd Edition. New York: Cambridge.

Knowles, M. S. (1984). *Andragogy in action: Applying modern principles of adult learning.* San Francisco: Jossey-Bass.

Marcuse, H. (1964). *One dimensional man.* Boston: Beacon.

McLaren, P. (1997). *Life in schools: An introduction to critical pedagogy in the foundations of education,* 3rd Edition. White Plains, NY: Longman.

# PLAGIARISM

The common definition of *plagiarism* is the unauthorized use of other persons' written or artistic material without attribution, whether this use is intentional or through carelessness. Plagiarism is seen as a form of stealing, where the perpetrator gains credit—whether authorship, an enhanced reputation, or material benefits—from a contribution when the work came from the productivity of others who are not given proper credit. In addition to the main text, plagiarized work could include footnotes and citations—any material from sources that are not made known and for which one is seeking credit.

Although plagiarism has been obvious in education and the arts for millennia, it takes on added interest in the Internet-focused forms of education. Members of the educational institution have the ability to connect to Web sites and academic material in unheard of scope, and that is fragmentary and transitory in nature. This allows individuals to more easily piece together or "patchwork" academically valuable material that is likely to be unknown even by those with a solid knowledge of an area of scholarship and that, without appropriate software, cannot be easily located. To identify plagiarized work, educational institutions are increasingly using Web sites such as EVE? (http://www.canexus.com/eve/index.shtml) and Turnitin.com, which can identify strings of words from the millions of Web sites to which students have access. Distributed learning environments have several characteristics that increase the possibilities of plagiarism: minimal personal interaction among learners, enhanced heterogeneity of participants living in home cultural environments, and learners' engagements that often speak to their creative interests that are reflected through new ways of using existing foundational materials.

## KNOWLEDGE AS INTELLECTUAL PROPERTY

Unlike traditional educational settings where individuals communicate both verbally and through written products, distributed learning environments rely nearly totally on written work and interaction. Students spend less time in peer interaction and devote greater attention to written sources for their scholarship, usually communicating the results of such activities through papers. It is common, and often second nature, for faculty to be able to identify different academic styles within a presentation, in addition to being sensitive to the complexity of the work, and both in relation to what a student likely already knows about a topic. Although faculty may not be aware of the sources of plagiarized work, they usually are sensitive to when a paper's origins do not lie with the writer.

It is common for college Web sites and orientation materials to include substantial information regarding plagiarism, including examples of both appropriate and inappropriate practices for using and citing referenced material. In addition, instructors are encouraged to make assignments less likely to invite plagiarism. For example, asking a student to submit increasingly detailed outlines of an assigned paper or meeting with students to discuss a developing paper reduce the likelihood of the inappropriate use of existing work.

Although colleges typically do not define learners' involvement with institutional writing centers and resulting staff and peer involvement in student papers as plagiarism, carelessness is typically not considered a valid excuse for failing to credit a source. Even when the source is noted in a paper's reference section, failure to use appropriate quotation marks around the copied work will often lead to a person being charged with plagiarism and subsequently receiving a failing grade for a submitted paper, if not expulsion from the academic environment.

There is a philosophical challenge to the common understanding of plagiarism. Some in education complain about what they perceive to be a changing relationship between higher education and society, where postsecondary institutions are now perceived to be more entrepreneurial than in the past. That is, they are seen as seeking organizational gains rather than contributing to the long-term health of society. Critics believe that knowledge should not be considered a possession, but should be developed for its societal value, and they challenge institutional practices where knowledge is considered owned. The challenges to higher education as a capitalistic institution devolve, through the back door, into the issue of plagiarism, where using the stock of knowledge as a common possession is seen as legitimate.

An additional dimension has to do with the national or geographical culture from which scholars produce their work. Many claim that certain societies, as in Asia, are more likely to have different attitudes regarding how existing knowledge is used and the necessary attributions to it. Work in some societies is seen as having no ownership, but has general cultural value and is usable by all members. To claim that a person is plagiarizing by using certain cultural bodies of knowledge without attribution is seen by some as another way in which the Western world maintains its dominance among other national cultures, and which in an increasingly international postsecondary environment is ignored.

## IMITATION AND CONTINUITY

Another aspect of plagiarism focuses on similarity or imitation, which is of particular interest for learners in a distributed environment where students are motivated by the important questions and goals that have brought them to the institution. They may link their work to existing substantive patterns without a full awareness of the contexts with which it is associated. One can ask the question, at what point does the work of foundational thinkers in an area become part of the knowledge landscape and not need to be cited? Are there, or should there be, different expectations for students depending on their substantive involvements and backgrounds?

Students are not alone in linking their ideas to mature work without attribution. Scholars often use grand theories and prominent concepts, taking them from one location and using them in others, or continue with a line of scholarship or thinking begun by another. At some points, it is quite difficult to distinguish where one line of thinking begins and another line has left off. Important ideas become entwined into the everyday conversations of different communities of scholarship. The development of new work grows from the canon, where certain questions, styles, and even affective dimensions are stylized.

Here, for scholars, plagiarism is not stealing, but relates to unwritten codes around the movement or maturation of fields, or an idea. For students in distributed environments, it has to do with the maturation of their ideas and questions, at times with an unawareness of the full setting in which they are located. Both speak to the use of knowledge at an advanced stage, but for one the context is the community of scholars and the other the person's own, more private productivity.

## TEXTUAL COHERENCE

As noted earlier, students in distributed environments, with access to an endless number of Web sites, can engage in "patchwriting," where a writer with limited added value brings together without acknowledgement the works of others in creating a new product. This is plagiarism. It is of particular concern for a distributed educational environment in which students often do not share common readings but explore their own topics through examinations of distributed learning resources. Materials are used from these sources in a way that will allow for a coherence that is the student's and is different than the intentions of the various authors.

Although bringing together Web materials in new ways can be a deliberate attempt to make others' work appear to be one's own, another way to understand this activity is as a creative act, developing a new product out of existing materials, to use them in different combinations and ways. People who do this kind of writing need to be especially vigilant regarding their own products to ensure that they attribute the sources of their unique contributions.

## COMMUNITY

Individuals often write collaboratively; co-authorship is a favored mode of working and is perceived to be necessary in terms of multidisciplinary orientation. As well, many learners have commitments to community and communality and want to produce it through their professional activities. Charges of plagiarism can come from those who want to maintain the strict individual focus of the academy and not move into an alternative production model. This issue is especially relevant in distributed learning environments in which students often find joint work a way to maintain their commitments to the learning environment, allowing for a kind of peer support that is not available in the traditional sector from either classroom peers or faculty.

## CONCLUDING COMMENT

The issue of plagiarism, while appearing simple, is complex. Critics of the traditional academy claim that charges such as "plagiarism" are designed to freeze the consideration of alternative ways of engaging in higher learning. Those who are more traditional see this as a ploy by those with social agendas to realize them by reshaping a fragile institution that requires high attentiveness to maintain its integrity.

—*Robert V. Silverman*

*See also* ETHICS; INTELLECTUAL PROPERTY

## Bibliography

Buranen, Lise, & Roy, Alice M. (1999). *Perspectives on plagiarism and intellectual property in a postmodern world.* Albany, NY: State University of New York Press.

LaFollette, Marcel C. (1992). *Stealing into print: Fraud, plagiarism, and misconduct in scientific publishing.* Berkeley, CA: University of California Press.

Lindey, Alexander. (1952). *Plagiarism and originality.* New York: Harper & Brothers.

St. Onge, K. R. (1988). *The melancholy anatomy of plagiarism.* Lanham, MD: University Press of America.

White, Harold Ogden. (1965). *Plagiarism and imitation during the English renaissance.* New York: Octagon.

## POLICIES

Policies are written guiding principles designed to ensure decision making that is consistent with an entity's mission and philosophy. Policies can be generalized into three arenas—organizational, contractual, and relational—and tend to be broad statements that have the effect of a law in that violation of established policies generally carries a penalty or prescribed consequences.

Policies are established by the highest-level governing body, which may be a board or top management, and serve as the foundation on which procedures are built. A policy establishes what is acceptable to occur, whereas procedures operationalize something by outlining how it is to occur. For example, in the workplace there may be a policy on telecommuting that allows employees to work from home or another remote location via technology. The office or unit responsible for interpreting policy for the organization would establish procedures for day-to-day use to ensure consistency in the application of the policy. Therefore, a manager, having received this policy and the accompanying procedures, would have the flexibility to determine which positions qualify for the telecommuting provision and the criteria by which such an arrangement can be implemented and terminated for employees in that unit. Generally, organizations make their policies available upon request through a policy manual in hard copy or on their Web site.

## CONTRACTUAL POLICIES

The best-known contractual policy is the insurance policy, which is a contract between the person, persons, or entity being insured and the insurance provider(s). The policy provides, in detail, the conditions of coverage, the criteria for coverage, exceptions to the coverage, and conditions by which the coverage may continue or cease. Common insurance policies include medical, life, automobile, home, travel, professional liability, and medical malpractice. Each is a written contract between two or more entities and generally requires the expressed agreement of parties involved to make any changes to it.

Within each type of policy are levels of coverage; for example, a homeowner's policy may include, at a minimum, fire, theft, damage, and medical coverage for persons injured on the insured property. The insured party can select the amount of up-front, out-of-pocket expenses they are willing to incur prior to the insurance provider paying expenses. This is known as the "deductible." Generally, the higher the deductible the insured party is willing to pay, the lower the monthly premium will be. These contractual policies are written in very detailed language. The penalty for violation is generally cessation of coverage.

## RELATIONAL POLICIES

The best-known relational policy is foreign policy. This term indicates an established set of beliefs by which nations frame their international interaction. Foreign policy tends to stipulate the conditions of war, peace, and international negotiations, such as treaties. Some factors that impact foreign policy and define the constraints are geopolitics, military capabilities, and the economy. The penalty for violation can range from economic sanctions to war.

Public policy is the area in which laws are constructed—the guiding principles by which decisions are made that affect the public sector. Interested citizens; local, state, and federal lawmakers; and public interest groups may all significantly impact the formation and subsequent passage of policy. Much of it is constructed in the form of a resolution that contains information about a subject in the format of "whereas," followed by the points that the decision makers need to know about the subject. The resolution generally contains the outcome that is desired by the maker of the resolution.

## ORGANIZATIONAL POLICIES IN DISTRIBUTED LEARNING

Some policies that may be found in a distributed learning community include broad areas such as institutional policy, academic policy, financial policies and information, and student rights and responsibilities. Within each may be a wide range of policies addressing specific issues applicable to the members of that community. Such policies generally include a broad policy statement, standards that are expected, and the penalty for violation of such policy, which may include disciplinary action for students and employees.

### Institutional Policy

Generally the following issues fall under institutional policy, because they apply to all members of the institutional community including students, faculty, administrators, staff, and visitors:

*Academic Honesty and Plagiarism.* This issue is addressed in all academic institutions; this policy establishes that submitting work done by others and representing it to be one's own is a serious violation and can lead to expulsion. Such policy is widely distributed, many times by each professor in all classes, and can be found on an institution's Web site and in student handbooks. Honesty and integrity in one's work on the part of students, faculty, and staff is the expected standard.

*Academic Freedom.* This policy addresses the rights of faculty to teach and freely express thoughts within the academic environment, whether in a classroom or through distance learning, as long as the method of teaching and the thoughts expressed do not cross constitutionally impermissible boundaries.

*Drug and Alcohol Abuse.* This policy generally prohibits the use and/or sale of illicit drugs and alcohol under the auspices of the academic institution, whether on actual property or through the use of the school's equipment and/or technology resources. Most academic institutions have a "zero tolerance" policy, which means that the first offense may result in expulsion of students and termination of employees.

*Research Ethics.* This addresses human subjects in research policy, and may also be known as research ethics policy. It addresses the treatment and interaction with humans in all types of research that may be conducted in the academic programs of that institution, including interviews, focus groups, surveys, and other studies or projects for which individuals are the subjects of study. The intent of such policy is to ensure the fair, equitable, and dignified treatment of human subjects so as not to violate any confidentiality that may have been established and to ensure that humans are aware of and consent to participating in research studies.

*Electronic Network Access and Institutional Technology.* These policies address the use of computers, Web sites, and network access through the academic institution and explicitly stipulate acceptable and unacceptable behavior. These policies tend to carry very direct and strict penalties up to and including termination of employees and expulsion of students for inappropriate and/or egregious acts. Generally forbidden behavior may include unauthorized access to and use of the electronic network; sending and/or posting derogatory and/or profane messages; and plagiarizing work from and/or to the network. Academic institutions tend to have very specific guidelines in order to protect the intellectual property contained on their site, and to protect the authorized users of the site from harmful Web viruses and predators. These policies become particularly critical in a distributed learning environment where the primary source of communication and interaction is online. Such policies serve to establish community norms in an effort to provide a safe, harassment-free, and respectful environment.

Another issue that may be addressed in these policies is online calendaring and notification. Unlike traditional academic institutions, students cannot walk to a faculty office and find the schedule for office hours. In a distributed learning environment the issues of calendaring and notification become a part of the community norm. When faculty and/or students will be away from the online environment for an extended period of time, it is the norm to post such absences prior to leaving the environment. This will allow those who have a need to communicate to know that a response may not be forthcoming due to a prolonged absence. The inability to see and speak to co-learners tends to make the online interaction take on a heightened meaning, and the absence of response may be negatively received as ignoring messages or postings.

The online community requires the articulation of standards, expectations, and values and many of those take the form of policy.

*Sexual Harassment, Equal Opportunity/Affirmative Action, and Americans With Disabilities Act.* Although there are federal, state, and local laws addressing nondiscrimination, the prohibition of sexual harassment, and access for persons with disabilities, organizations tend to establish policies addressing these issues as well in order to communicate their commitment to these issues as a part of their guiding principles. The layering of policies over established federal, state, and local laws serves to strengthen the institution's right to take disciplinary action on a very local level without having to wait for external relief.

Academic policies may address the following: access to student records; student and institutional rights of disclosure of directory information in compliance with the Family Educational Rights and Privacy Act of 1974 (FERPA); degree requirements and exemptions; transfer credit; grades and credit; transcripts; enrollment; academic year; leaves and withdrawals; articulation agreements; concurrent enrollments; and satisfactory academic progress. For doctoral programs, the policies will also include advancement to candidacy, dissertation research, dissertation defense or final oral reviews, licensure (for applicable fields of study), graduation ceremony participation, and doctoral degree completion.

Financial policies include issues such as schedule of fees; tuition payment information, including delinquency and refunds; tuition reduction during candidacy (dissertation process) for doctoral students; credit card payment; tuition waiver for staff and dependents; and student financial aid. Student rights and responsibilities may include policies on student conduct and student grievance procedures.

Policies related to faculty include, at a minimum, the issues of recruitment, promotion and tenure, merit pay, and sabbatical leave. Such policies will address similar issues in all institutions of higher education including those dedicated to distributed learning. For example, a sabbatical leave policy will establish the fact that faculty, after a stipulated number of years, may apply for a one-semester or full academic year leave with pay from the institution, for the purpose of research, working on a special project, or gaining additional learning in a specific field. Such leave must result in some benefit for the institution and the faculty member is generally required to make a presentation to the college or university, and agree to remain with the institution for a specified amount of time following the sabbatical leave.

Personnel policies will establish the foundation for establishing and maintaining the organization's overall human resources/personnel program for employees, including recruitment, hiring, nepotism, pay along with other compensation and benefits, promotion, performance evaluation, conflict of interest, disruptive behavior, discipline, layoff, and termination. Such policies serve to protect the institution from decision making that results in disparate and/or discriminatory treatment of employees. Personnel policies serve as guidelines for managers and supervisors when making decisions about employees. For example, if an institution has a nepotism policy outlining the fact that no employee can hire, supervise, or otherwise make decisions about a relative at the institution, such policy protects the institution from allegations of actual or perceived favoritism among family members.

The policy on grades will generally address how students may challenge a grade if they feel that it was given in an unfair manner. The policy will protect the rights of the student and the faculty, and internal procedures can be outlined to ensure that this occurs. Some institutions have a "grade forgiveness" policy that allows a student who received a grade below a "C" to retake the course; the highest grade received will be assigned for that course and the lower grade will be erased from the record, thereby not negatively impacting the grade point average (GPA).

Visual identity policies are becoming more prevalent as organizations look at "branding," a concept that allows the public to identify a company or product. Visual identity policies establish a consistent "look" or identifying characteristics that are permitted for public display. This establishes the guidelines for letterhead, business cards, Web pages, brochures, and other communication documents representing the organization. In a distributed learning environment, visual identity becomes extremely important for recruitment of students and for marketing the quality of the product. The competition on the Internet demands that institutions establish a brand that is readily identifiable and that customers remember. Therefore, policies are established to protect that identity from being copied, reproduced, and/or misrepresented.

Although policies carry the weight of law within organizations, they are designed to ensure the integrity of the decision-making process and to promote a sense of fairness in organizational, contractual, and relational treatment. They are further designed to protect constituents from predators, both online and in face-to-face interactions.

*—Mary L. O'Neal*

***See also*** FACULTY POLICIES

## Bibliography

Campbell, N. (1998). *Writing effective policies and procedures: A step-by-step resource for clear communication.* New York: AMACOM.

Dolowitz, D. (2003). A policy-maker's guide to policy transfer. *The Political Quarterly, 74*(1), 101–108.

GSC Online. (1997). *Plagarized dot com: The instructors guide to Internet plagiarism.* Retrieved from http://plagiarized.com.

Nagel, S. (2002). Win-win public policy across six policy fields. *International Journal of Organization Theory and Behavior, 5*(1 & 2), 13.

Page, S. (2000). Best Practices in Policies and Procedures. New York: Process Improvement Publishing.

Peabody, L., & Gear, J. (1998). *How to write policies, procedures & task outlines: Sending clear signals in written directions,* 2nd Edition. Ravensdale, WA: Idyll Arbor.

Standler, R. B. (2000). *Plagiarism in colleges in USA.* Retrieved from http://www.rbs2.com/plag.htm.

# PROGRAM EVALUATION

In U.S. colleges and universities, the program, not the course, is what is typically assessed by external agencies. As more and more institutions have gone from offering single distributed learning courses to offering full programs available in a distributed learning format, it became necessary to develop some consistent criteria that both institutions and their accrediting bodies could use to assess quality. In 2000, the Council of Regional Accrediting Commissions (which consists of the chief executive officer and the chair of the board for each of the regional accrediting associations in the United States) asked the staff of the WCET (an international organization headquartered with the Western Interstate Commission for Higher

Education) to develop a set of evaluation criteria that all the commissions could use. Much of the following is drawn from that work, a great deal of which was done by John Witherspoon.

In evaluating distributed learning programs, it helps to separate the components involved in developing, offering, and supporting a program. The divisions in this entry are:

- Institutional context and commitment
- Curriculum and instruction
- Faculty support
- Student support
- Evaluation and assessment

These components are discussed in the following sections. Note that technology is addressed throughout this entry, but the specific technology used is rarely a significant element.

## INSTITUTIONAL CONTEXT AND COMMITMENT

Electronically offered programs both support and extend the roles of educational institutions. Increasingly they are integral to academic organization, with growing implications for institutional infrastructure. In their content, purposes, organization, and enrollment history (if applicable) the programs should be consistent with the institution's role and mission.

A healthy institution's purposes change over time. The institution is aware of accreditation requirements and complies with them. Each accrediting commission has established definitions of what activities constitute a substantive change that will trigger review and approval processes. The appropriate accreditation commission should be notified and consulted as to whether an electronically offered program represents a major change. The offering of distributed programs can affect the institution's educational goals, intended student population, curriculum, modes, or venue of instruction, and can thus have an impact on both the institution and its accreditation status.

The institution also needs to ensure adequacy of technical and physical plant facilities, including appropriate staffing and technical assistance, to support its electronically offered programs.

The internal organizational structure that enables the development, coordination, support, and oversight of electronically offered programs will vary from

institution to institution. Ordinarily, however, it will include the capability to:

- Facilitate the associated instructional and technical support relationships
- Provide (or draw upon) the required information technologies and related support services
- Develop and implement a marketing plan that takes into account the target student population, the technologies available, and the factors required to meet institutional goals
- Provide training and support to participating instructors and students
- Ensure compliance with copyright law
- Contract for products and outsourced services
- Assess and assign priorities to potential future projects
- Ensure that electronically offered programs and courses meet institution-wide standards, both to provide consistent quality and to provide a coherent framework for students who may enroll in both electronically offered and traditional on-campus courses
- Maintain appropriate academic oversight
- Maintain consistency with the institution's academic planning and oversight functions, to ensure congruence with the institution's mission and allocation of required resources
- Ensure the integrity of student work and faculty instruction

In its articulation and transfer policies, the institution must judge its courses and programs on their learning outcomes and the resources brought to bear for their achievement, not on modes of delivery. The institution should strive to ensure a consistent and coherent technical framework for students and faculty. When a change in technologies is necessary, it is introduced in a way that minimizes the impact on students and faculty. Students should receive reasonable technical support for the hardware, software, and delivery system required in the program.

The selection of technologies is based on appropriateness for the students and the curriculum. It is recognized that availability, cost, and other issues are often involved, but program documentation should include specific consideration of the match between technology and program.

Finally, the institution needs to understand the legal and regulatory requirements of the jurisdictions in which it operates (e.g., requirements for service to those with disabilities, copyright law, state and national requirements for institutions offering educational programs, and international restrictions such as export of sensitive information or technologies).

## CURRICULUM AND INSTRUCTION

Methods change, but standards of quality endure. The important issues are not technical but curriculum-driven and pedagogical. Decisions about such matters are made by qualified professionals and must focus on learning outcomes for an increasingly diverse student population.

As with all curriculum development and review, the institution should ensure that each program of study results in collegiate-level learning outcomes appropriate to the rigor and breadth of the degree or certificate awarded by the institution; that the electronically offered degree or certificate program is coherent and complete; and that such programs leading to undergraduate degrees include general education requirements.

Academically qualified persons should participate fully in the decisions concerning program curricula and program oversight. It is recognized that traditional faculty roles may be unbundled and/or supplemented as electronically offered programs are developed and presented, but the substance of the program, including its presentation, management, and assessment, are the responsibility of people with appropriate academic qualifications.

In designing an electronically offered degree or certificate program, the institution needs to provide a coherent plan for the student to access all courses necessary to complete the program, or clearly notify students of requirements not included in the electronic offering. Hybrid programs or courses, mixing electronic and on-campus elements, are designed to ensure that all students have access to appropriate services.

Although important elements of a program may be supplied by consortial partners or outsourced to other organizations, including contractors who may not be accredited, the responsibility for performance remains with the institution awarding the degree or certificate. It is the institution in which the student is enrolled, not its suppliers or partners, that has a contract with the student. Therefore, the criteria for selecting consortial partners and contractors, and the means to monitor and evaluate their work, are important aspects of the program plan. In considering consortial agreements, issues such as ensuring that enhancing service to students is a primary consideration and that incentives do not compromise the integrity of the institution or of the educational program must be addressed. Consideration should also be given to the effect of administrative arrangements and cost-sharing on an institution's decision making regarding curriculum.

Current examples of consortial and contractual relationships include:

- Faculty qualifications and support
- Course material
  - Courses or course elements acquired or licensed from other institutions
  - Courses or course elements provided by partner institutions in a consortium
  - Curricular elements from recognized industry sources (e.g., Microsoft or Novell certification programs)
  - Commercially produced course materials ranging from textbooks to packaged courses or course elements
- Course management and delivery
  - WebCT, Blackboard, eCollege, and the like
- Library-related services
  - Remote access to library services, resources, and policies
  - Provision of library resources and services (e.g., online reference services, document delivery, print resources)
- Bookstore services
- Services providing information to students concerning the institution and its programs and courses
- Technical services
  - Server capacity
  - Technical support services, including help desk services for students and faculty
- Administrative services
  - Registration, student records, and so on
  - Services related to orientation, advising, counseling, or tutoring
  - Online payment arrangements
  - Student privacy considerations

The importance of appropriate interaction (synchronous or asynchronous) between instructor and students and among students is reflected in the design of the program and its courses, and in the technical facilities and services provided.

## FACULTY SUPPORT

As indicated earlier, faculty roles are becoming increasingly diverse and reorganized. For example, the same person may not perform both course development and direct instruction to students. Regardless of who performs which of these tasks, important issues are involved.

In the development of an electronically offered program, the institution and its participating faculty need to consider issues of workload, compensation, ownership of intellectual property resulting from the program, and the implications of program participation for the faculty member's professional evaluation processes. This mutual understanding is based on policies and agreements adopted by both parties.

The institution should provide an ongoing program of appropriate technical, design, and production support for participating faculty members. Those responsible for program development should receive orientation and training to help them become proficient in the uses of the program's technologies, including potential changes in course design and management; those working directly with students should also receive training in the uses of the technologies, including strategies for effective interaction.

## STUDENT SUPPORT

Colleges and universities have learned that the twenty-first century student is different, both demographically and geographically, from students of previous generations. These differences affect everything from admissions policy to library services. Reaching these students, and serving them appropriately, are major challenges to today's institutions.

The institution needs to maintain an administrative, financial, and technical commitment to continue the program for a period sufficient to enable all admitted students to complete a degree or certificate in a publicized time frame.

Prior to admitting a student to the program, the institution should:

- Ascertain by a review of pertinent records and/or personal review that the student is qualified by prior education or equivalent experience to be admitted to that program, including, in the case of international students, English language skills
- Inform the prospective student concerning required access to technologies used in the program
- Inform the prospective student concerning technical competence required of students in the program
- Inform the prospective student concerning estimated or average program costs (including costs of information access) and associated payment and refund policies
- Inform the prospective student concerning curriculum design and the time frame in which courses are offered, and assist the student in understanding the nature of the learning objectives
- Inform the prospective student of library and other learning services available to support learning and the skills necessary to access them
- Inform the prospective student concerning the full array of other support services available from the institution
- Inform the prospective student about arrangements for interaction with the faculty and fellow students
- Assist the prospective student in understanding independent learning expectations as well as the nature and potential challenges of learning in the program's technology-based environment
- Inform the prospective student about the estimated time for program completion

Appropriate services must be available for students of electronically offered programs, based on the assumption that these students will not be physically present on campus. With variations for specific situations and programs, these services, which are possibly coordinated, may include:

- Accurate and timely information about the institution, its programs, courses, costs, and related policies and requirements
- Preregistration advising
- Application for admission
- Placement testing
- Enrollment/registration in programs and courses
- Financial aid, including information about policies and limitations, information about available scholarships, processing of applications, and administration of financial aid and scholarship awards
- Secure payment arrangements
- Academic advising
- Timely intervention regarding student progress
- Tutoring
- Career counseling and placement
- Academic progress information, such as degree completion audits

- Library resources appropriate to the program, including reference and research assistance; remote access to databases, online journals and full-text resources; document delivery services; library user and information literacy instruction; reserve materials; and institutional agreements with local libraries
- Training in information literacy, including research techniques
- Bookstore services, including ordering, secure payment, and prompt delivery of books, course packs, course-related supplies and materials, and institutional memorabilia
- Ongoing technical support, preferably offered during evenings and weekends as well as normal institutional working hours
- Referrals for student learning differences, physical challenges, and personal counseling
- Access to grievance procedures

A sense of community is important to the success of many students, and an ongoing, long-term relationship is beneficial to both student and institution. The design and administration of the program should take this factor into account as appropriate, through such actions as encouraging study groups, providing student directories (with the permission of those listed), including off-campus students in institutional publications and events, including these students in definitions of the academic community through such mechanisms as student government representation, sending invitations to campus events including graduation ceremonies, and similar strategies of inclusion.

## EVALUATION AND ASSESSMENT

Both the assessment of student achievement and the evaluation of the overall program take on added importance as new techniques evolve. For example, in asynchronous programs the element of seat time is essentially removed from the equation. Sustained, evidence-based, and participatory inquiry should be conducted as to whether distance learning programs are achieving institutional objectives. The results of such inquiry can guide curriculum design and delivery, pedagogy, and educational processes, and may affect future policy and budgets, and perhaps have implications for the institution's roles and mission.

As a component of the institution's overall assessment activities, documented assessment of student achievement should be conducted in each course and at the completion of the program, by comparing student performance to the intended learning outcomes.

When examinations are employed (e.g., paper, online, demonstrations of competency), they should take place in circumstances that include firm student identification; other measures should also be taken to ensure the integrity of student work.

Documented procedures ensure that personal information is protected in the conduct of assessments and evaluations and in the dissemination of results.

Overall program effectiveness is determined by such measures as:

- The extent to which student learning matches intended outcomes, including for degree programs both the goals of general education and the objectives of the major
- The extent to which student intent is met
- Student retention rates, including variations over time
- Student satisfaction, as measured by regular surveys
- Faculty satisfaction, as measured by regular surveys and by formal and informal peer review processes
- The extent to which access is provided to students not previously served
- Measures of the extent to which library and learning resources are used appropriately by the program's students
- Measures of student competence in fundamental skills such as communication, comprehension, and analysis
- Cost effectiveness of the program to its students, as compared to campus-based alternatives

Continual institutional self-evaluation directed toward program improvement, targeting more effective uses of technology to improve pedagogy, advances in student achievement of intended outcomes, improved retention rates, effective use of resources, and demonstrated improvements in the institution's service to its internal and external constituencies is vital. The program and its results should be reflected in the institution's ongoing self-evaluation process and be used to inform the plans of the institution and those responsible for its academic programs. This evaluation should take place in the context of the regular evaluation of all academic programs.

These principles of good practice have been adopted by all the U.S. regional accrediting associations and are being reviewed by institutions as they assess what is necessary to develop a good quality distributed learning program.

—*Sally M. Johnstone*

*See also* ACCREDITATION

# PROGRAMMING AND SCRIPTING LANGUAGES

Although they may be portrayed as such in the popular media, computers are not "smart." However, they are very fast at doing what they are told to do. Programming languages are how a user tells the computer what to do. Using programming languages, the user can tell a computer what input data to use, how to process those input data, and how to output the results.

Languages can be divided into two broad categories: operating system (OS) languages and application languages. Operating system languages include Microsoft's Disk Operating System (DOS) and Windows; Apple's Macintosh OS X; and network operating systems (NOS) such as Novell, Unix, Linux, or Windows 2000 Server. Operating systems and network operating systems are written in a mix of high-level languages and assembly language (e.g., the Unix OS was written in the C language) and they form the basis for the user's interaction with a computer's hardware. The focus of this entry is application languages because these are used to interact with a computer's software—they are how the user tells the computer what to compute.

Application languages are divided into four general categories:

- Microcode or machine language
- Assembly language
- High-level languages
- Very high-level languages

Microcode and machine languages are coded for specific processors in binary and look like this: 0110001001111000010101011101110100111000011 0010111101111001110. . . .

Because this is not easily readable by the human eye, assembly languages such as C were developed to make programming an easier task. Assembly languages—although able to process very quickly—still have two basic flaws. These languages are very processor-specific (assembly programs written for one microprocessor do not work on others) and they are cryptic to read. To remedy these problems, higher-level languages were developed. Most users and programmers work with languages in the final two categories because these languages are most similar to human language. High-level programming languages such as FORTRAN and COBOL were developed to be portable between computers and to improve the speed with which developers could write and understand the programs they were creating. The very high-level languages (e.g., Excel, Access, Statistical Program for Social Sciences [SPSS], Mathematica) were developed later to allow even more general users—those without specialty training in programming—to work directly with their computers.

The instructions to a computer still need to be in machine language before they can be executed, so interpreters and compilers were developed to convert high-level user-readable code into machine code. The easiest method of conversion—interpreting—simply takes the program code that the user writes (source code) and translates it into machine code (object code) that the computer can use. The interpreter process is quick and useful for testing, but the user's program has to be re-interpreted every time the program needs to run, making it inefficient over time. The solution to this was to use a compiler to convert the programming language source code into machine-readable object code. Compiling takes the user's source code, converts it to machine-level code, merges it with various libraries of standard machine code, and creates an "object module." The compiler puts one or more object modules together to create executable code (a program or ".exe" file) that can then be processed on demand without any further interpretation.

Programming languages were originally developed as procedural languages that ran one process at a time and completed that process before beginning on the next process. For example, the program that processes accounts receivable runs before accounts payable, and the payables process has to complete before the general ledger programs are processed. In the 1980s, a new type of programming language began to appear—object-oriented programming (OOP) languages. Object-oriented languages allow multiple processes to simultaneously co-exist and wait for user request or input before processing. Object-oriented languages allow processes like Windows icons to be present at the same time and available whenever the user selects them. Both procedural languages (e.g., Cobol, Basic, C) and object-oriented languages (e.g., C++, C#, Java) have a place in today's programming environment and give programmers and users a wide choice of tools to use with their computers.

## TYPES OF LANGUAGES

The microcode languages are very processor-specific and are denoted by the type of processor on which they are executed (e.g., 6502, 68000, × 86, Pentium, Reduced Instruction Set Chip [RISC], Alpha). Assembly languages are similarly linked to the processor or computer on which they run (e.g., IBM, HP, × 86).

The high-level languages have developed in families of languages, usually stemming from one root language. The first programming languages were procedural languages created to run on large computers and include FORTRAN (FORmula TRANslation), Algol (ALGOrithmic Language), and COBOL (COmmon Business Oriented Language). These were used for science, engineering, and business, respectively. The C language family was originally developed to write OS software and includes C, C++, C#, and Visual C++. The BASIC (Beginner's All-purpose Symbolic Instruction Code) language developed from a simple procedural language intended for instruction on computers into several generic BASIC languages (BASICA, GW Basic, QuickBasic) and into the object-oriented Visual Basic. Other languages, such as Pascal (designed to be machine-independent), Lisp (designed to define and apply functions), Smalltalk (designed as a language processor), Logo (a teaching language), and Prolog (designed to state rules and prove theorems) were developed to meet specific needs.

As use of the Internet and the World Wide Web grew, other languages were developed to handle processing at both the user (client) computer and at the server computers. Markup languages (e.g., Hypertext Markup Language [HTML], Dynamic Hypertext Markup Language [DHTML], Extensible Markup Language [XML]) were developed to handle hypertext processing on the client's computer. Scripting languages such as Java, JavaScript, JavaBeans, J++, Java Server Pages (JSP), Active Server Pages (ASP), PHP, Perl, and Common Gateway Interface (CGI)

were developed to process information between the client's computer and server processes. Scripting languages interact with markup languages in the user-input forms seen on Web sites. The programmer uses a markup language (HTML, for example) to place a form on a Web page and serve the form to the user's Web browser. A scripting language (such as ASP, Perl, PHP, or JSP) interacts with the HTML and takes the input from the form on the client's Web browser to the server and places it into a database or text file for storage. Many of these languages have been packaged together in tool sets such as Visual Studio and the ".NET" tools.

As more people began to use computers and needed to interact directly with the data on their computers, very high-level languages were developed to allow them access to their data without needing the skills of a programmer. Very high-level languages are designed to help reduce programming design and development time and cost. These languages include:

- Structured Query Language (SQL), which is built into programs such as Oracle, Microsoft Access, MSQL, and MySQL
- Visual Basic for Applications (VBA) and macro languages (built into Word, Excel, and PowerPoint)
- Mathematics languages (built into MathLab, Mathematica, SPSS, and SAS)
- Computer Aided Software Engineering (CASE) tools

## STEPS IN USING PROGRAMMING LANGUAGES

There are five basic steps in creating a program or a system of programs:

1. Analysis and discovery
2. Define solution algorithm
3. Create the code
4. Test and debug the code
5. Create the program documentation

During the analysis and discovery process, the programmer works with the user to discover and create the information needed for input and the process(es) that are performed, and defines what the user expects as output from the process. The analyst researches the request to ensure that the user's proposal fits within existing systems and procedures. During the analysis, the user and analyst will also determine whether the process itself is repeated often enough to warrant the process of automation. The analysis step creates lists of data, files, information needed, processes needed, and reports desired—all the information necessary for the next step.

Next, a step-by-step process is created to accomplish what the user requested (as modified by the analysis and discovery process). Creating the algorithm includes converting the user's ideas into logical and mathematical statements that will then be broken down further into lines of computer code. Creating flow charts (a visual diagram of the proposed logic) and pseudo-code (a simple English-based code) then moves the algorithm from analysis and theory to paper design.

During the third step, the programmer selects a programming language and writes the code that will perform the user's request. The programming language will be selected based on efficiency and effectiveness in serving the user's needs. The programmer then combines the knowledge created by the analysis, algorithms, logic statements, pseudo-code, and flow chart diagrams together into lines of programming code that tell the processor how to access the input data, control specific functions, and process the information.

The fourth step is a feedback loop to help refine and redesign the analysis, algorithms, and code as needed to fulfill the user's request. Both the programmer and the user test each function to determine that everything works as planned. They review the output reports and files to ensure that they contain the knowledge desired. The programmer debugs the code when there are problems in the code or when the user reports a function not working as expected. All of this information is fed back into the analysis and algorithm process so that improvements to the code can be developed and revised before the program is implemented for an entire organization. After all the features are tested and verified the program is declared final and the code implemented. The testing process has added many terms to the general lexicon: *alpha testing* (a process in which the programmers and a limited number of users test a program); *beta testing* (a widely expanded testing group, including many internal users and potentially some external users); and *going gold* (the program is completed, working as expected, verified by all testers, and being implemented or packaged and sold).

The last step in the process is for the programmer, user, and technical writer to create written, verbal, or multimedia documentation of the programming process. Documentation will be created at various levels and for specific purposes at each level. Documentation at the project management level will include all project plans, lessons learned, analysis, and testing. Documentation at the programming level will include all analysis, algorithms, programming code, inputs, outputs, testing cycles and results, and files used in creating the program. Documentation at the user and trainer levels will include all inputs, outputs, files needed, reports, testing results, and training sessions planned or performed.

The complexity of the project or the program will determine whether all these steps are taken to their extremity or whether they are brief. The number of tasks, complexity of the user request, and number of staff assigned will be determinants in the complexity and length of the project.

## USING PROGRAMMING LANGUAGES IN DISTRIBUTED EDUCATION

Programming languages have many applications in distributed education from the academic to the operational. Programming has a direct academic application, for example, when a course is given online that involves learning one or more programming languages. Operationally, programming is used to create applications that the administrators will use to collect, process, and report on data indicating how the organization is standing financially. Programming has a direct application to both the academic and operational when creating a Web site for an educational organization.

First, in the more traditional vein, programming is used to maintain mainframe and other operational "legacy" applications. Programming languages are used to create and maintain the financial reporting and general ledger, payroll, student information systems (SIS), facilities management, financial aid, and other support services that keep an educational institution running on a daily basis. The languages that support these systems tend to be the traditional procedural languages—Cobol, Basic, and SQL.

Second, newer languages and techniques are being used to support institutional migration from multiple databases to knowledge management. For example, SQL, Access, and Visual Studio tools are used in addition to the more traditional tools to improve access to institutional information and knowledge. Operational and academic developers use these tools to develop workflow and peer-to-peer collaboration tools for students, faculty, and administration. As the Web develops further, programming languages—especially the markup and scripting languages—are being used to move user functions from legacy systems and access methods to a Web-based environment. In this new environment all users will be able to share data, documents, and institutional knowledge anytime and anywhere.

Last, Web-based markup languages, scripting languages, and tools like Visual Studio .NET are used to develop an institution's Web presence. These tools are used to develop the Web pages that display course offerings, student guides, and the active pages and forms that take a prospective student's application or their financial aid information directly from their Web browser (i.e., Netscape Navigator or Microsoft Internet Explorer). These Web-based programming languages are used to build interactive Web pages that display specific institutional information based on the user's individual needs and are also used to develop "Web portals" that select and feed information to users based on their individual input.

—*Phil Beneker*

**See also** KNOWLEDGE MANAGEMENT

## Bibliography

Association for Computing Machinery (ACM) publications and special interest groups (e.g., SIGGRAPH). On the Web at www.acm.org.

Detmer, Richard C. (2001). *Introduction to 80X86 assembly language and computer architecture.* Sudbury, MA: Jones & Bartlett.

Groff, James R., & Weinberg, Paul N. (1999). *SQL: The complete reference.* Emeryville, CA: Osborne McGraw-Hill.

Horton, Ivor. (1998). *Beginning Visual C++ 6.* Chicago: Wrox.

Horton, Ivor. (2002). *Beginning Java 2 SDK 1.4 edition.* Chicago: Wrox.

Irwin, Michael R., Prague, Cary N., & Reardon, Jennifer. (2001). *Microsoft Access 2002 Bible gold edition.* Hoboken, NJ: John Wiley & Sons.

Lemay, Laura, & Cadenhead, Rogers. (2001). *Sams teach yourself Java 2 in 21 days, professional reference edition,* 2nd Edition. Indianapolis: Sams.

Lomax, Paul, & Petrusha, Ron. (Eds). (1998). *VB and VBA in a nutshell: The languages.* Sebastopol, CA: O'Reilly.

Ray, Deborah S., & Ray, Eric J. (1999). *Mastering HTML 4 premium edition.* Alameda, CA: Sybex.

Schwartz, Randal L., & Phoenix, Tom. (2001). *Learning Perl,* 3rd Edition. Sebastopol, CA: O'Reilly.

Welling, Luke, & Thomson, Laura. (2001). *PHP and MySQL Web development.* Indianapolis: Sams.

Wright, Peter. (1998). *Beginning Visual Basic 6.* Chicago: Wrox.

# PUBLIC TELEVISION

Public television in the United States is a multifaceted, noncommercial media enterprise that provides a broad range of informational, cultural, and educational programming and services to the American people through local public television stations. It began as educational television and continues to pioneer the use of new technologies to improve the accessibility and quality of lifelong learning.

## UNDERSTANDING PUBLIC TELEVISION

American public television is a unique phenomenon. Not only is it different from commercial broadcasting, but it is also very unlike public service or government-supported television elsewhere in the world. It is a complicated, multi-layered institution that does not lend itself to facile analyses or simple comparisons.

Public television is composed of over 350 independent local public television stations as well as national and regional organizations that provide funding, programming, and other services. It consists of signature national television series and local broadcast schedules and services determined by individual stations in response to community needs. It also consists of national and local education service, delivered by stations in a wide variety of permutations. And it also is the strong national brand of PBS and the cherished local identity and affiliation of stations.

It is no wonder that each of public television's many constituencies tends to see it quite differently, as a local institution, an instructional service to schools, a college of the air, a media buy, a national network, a source of production funding, a safe haven from media violence, an impenetrable bureaucracy, a government-supported agency, or a public interest medium.

Some analysts describe the Byzantine structure of public television as its Achilles heel; others argue that the pluralism of public television is the reason it continues to enjoy the support of the American public despite the proliferation of new media options.

## THE GENESIS OF PUBLIC TELEVISION

Television in the United States began as a commercial enterprise in the mid-1930s. It was not until 1952 that the Federal Communications Commission (FCC) reserved educational television (ETV) channels throughout the nation. The "reserved channels" became the foundation of what later would become known as public television.

ETV stations emerged one at a time at the grass roots level. There was not any national ETV network, and almost no national funding to support ETV. Individual states, localities, community groups, universities, and school boards applied to the FCC to secure the licenses for the reserved noncommercial channels, and these entities provided the funds, usually very limited, to operate the stations. The first ETV station, KUHT, licensed to the University of Houston, began broadcasting in 1953. During the next decade over 100 ETV stations went on the air in communities throughout the country.

In 1967 The Carnegie Commission on Educational Television issued its landmark report that laid out an ambitious blueprint for the future of noncommercial television, and proposed a new name to reflect a new and broader public service mission: "public television." Later that same year, many of the commission's recommendations were incorporated into the Public Broadcasting Act of 1967, which was signed into law by President Lyndon B. Johnson as part of his "Great Society" program.

The Public Broadcasting Act established the basic principles and framework of public television as we know it today. It recognized the importance of an independent public television system and affirmed the centrality of local stations in serving the public interest through education, culture, and information. To ensure the viability and vitality of public television, the act provided federal funds to supplement local sources of funding and to support station operations, program production, and a new interconnection among the stations. It also created and earmarked funding for the Corporation for Public Broadcasting (CPB), a private, nonprofit organization charged with distributing the federal funding to noncommercial television and radio stations and to support program production. CPB was given the additional responsibilities of ensuring objectivity and balance in public television programming and shielding the enterprise from government interference. At the same time, the act established a 15-member CPB Board, to be appointed by the President of the United States and confirmed by the Senate, of which not more than 8 members may be from the same political party. Over the years CPB has been at the center of controversies relating to political interference and program content, which have stemmed, at least in part, from the compromises about its structure and role that were required to get the Public Broadcasting Act enacted into law.

To avoid concentrating too much power and control in one national organization, the Public Broadcasting Act specifically prohibited CPB from operating the new interconnection system that would distribute programming to stations. PBS was established in 1969 as a private, nonprofit membership corporation of public television stations, with responsibility for managing the interconnection. Both PBS and CPB are prohibited from producing programs; independent producers, stations, and other organizations create the programs seen on U.S. public television. Over time PBS's role has expanded to include program funding, acquisition, distribution, and promotion; education services; new media ventures; fundraising support; engineering and technology development; and video marketing.

The geometry of public television might best be described in terms of a triangle: the national organizations, CPB and PBS, are at two corners and the 350+ community-based stations are at the third. Which of the vertices is at the top was and is a matter of considerable debate.

Whichever way the triangle is oriented, one cannot assume that public television stations are a monolith. They range from large sophisticated media organizations to small "mom and pop" operations. There are subgroups according to licensee type (such as the state networks, the university licensees, the school board stations, and community), primary mission (education, community service, or general audience programs), and by market size. In addition, there are numerous issues around which stations form coalitions and alliances (i.e., local values and culture), some of lasting duration and others quite ephemeral. It is not surprising that achieving consensus in public television has proved to be an elusive goal.

Public television stations continue to be financed from a combination of sources. All stations receive federal funding through CPB, based on a matching formula that takes into account such factors as the size of the community being served and the amount of funds the station is able to raise from other sources, including membership, local underwriting of programs, and grants. Stations that are licensees of states, local governments, school districts, or universities typically receive an annual appropriation of funding, which in some cases makes up a relatively small portion of the station's overall budget. "Community licensees," that is, those stations that are licensed to nonprofit community organizations, are even more dependent on fundraising. One source of revenue that is *not* available to public television stations is the sale of advertising: The Public Broadcasting Act prohibits commercial advertising, although "noncommercial underwriting" is permitted. To this day, most public television stations wage a continuing battle to raise sufficient funds to cover basic operations, including programming and outreach services, even as competition for viewers from better financed competitors, like cable and new digital media, has accelerated.

## PUBLIC TELEVISION AND DISTRIBUTED LEARNING

Public television was a pioneer and continues to be a leader in applying technologies for public service and education. The first educational television stations broadcast instructional programming, and many stations continue to do so today. Closed captioning and descriptive video are used to improve accessibility for the visually and hearing impaired and for language instruction. The satellite technology used by PBS to distribute programming to its member stations also delivers telecourses to colleges, training to business, and classes to schools. As new technologies have emerged, public television has expanded beyond broadcast and satellite to develop more accessible interactive learning through the Internet, digital video devices (DVDs), and personal digital assistants (PDAs).

Today, public television is ubiquitous: It is available to 99% of American homes with televisions and to an increasing number of digital multimedia households and institutions, and it serves nearly 100 million people each week.

A wide range of educational services, of all types, at all levels, and using a variety of technologies are made available through the separate and combined efforts of PBS, CPB, local stations, and other public television organizations.

PBS's educational services cover the spectrum of lifelong learning, from school readiness and parent education to teacher professional development and classroom resources, adult education and literacy, and college courses leading to undergraduate and graduate degrees. The Corporation for Public Broadcasting helps to make available the educational and teacher training resources of the Annenberg/CPB service (described below).

Each local public television station works in partnership with schools, colleges, libraries, museums, and other community organizations to adapt national PBS and CPB initiatives to meet local needs and to develop its own distinctive learning services. The scope of public television's educational services is extensive. The following illustrate some of the different kinds of distributed learning offered through public television:

- PBS TeacherLine addresses the need for quality classroom instruction. It offers educators online professional development in the areas of mathematics and technology integration. TeacherLine provides self-paced and facilitated learning opportunities, state and local certificate programs, and access to quality classroom resources. Online learning modules are media-rich mini-courses that emphasize learning by doing and are led by trained facilitators. The modules use streaming video, slides, animations, simulations, and applets and include activities, assessments, and assignments. An online Community Center provides teachers with a forum to share ideas with each other, have live chats with experts, and access links to other resources. More than 30 public television stations use their local education agencies to deliver TeacherLine in their communities.

- Created through a partnership between the Annenberg Foundation and the Corporation for Public Broadcasting, the Annenberg Channel is a free satellite educational channel for educators and other adult learners. Available to public television stations, schools, colleges, libraries, and public access cable channels, it is available 24 hours a day, 7 days a week. The channel is also streamed on the Web in a free broadband simulcast. Programs are coordinated with Web and print materials.

- Workplace Essential Skills and GED Connection, part of the PBS LiteracyLink Project managed by Kentucky Educational Television, target adults who want to improve basic job skills and earn a high school diploma equivalency. Workplace Essential Skills combines video programs with print and Web-based lessons that cover basic reading, writing, and math skills applied in realistic work scenarios. It is offered through public television stations, on the Web, and through career centers in local communities. GED Connection is a multimedia instructional series that enables adults to earn a high school equivalency diploma from home. It includes 39 half-hour video programs with workbooks, online lessons, and practice tests. An earlier GED series helped more than 2 million people pass the test for the equivalency diploma.

- The PBS Adult Learning Service (ALS) was launched over 20 years ago to expand access to higher education by leveraging public television's satellite distribution capability. ALS offers telecourses consisting of video, text, and other components through local partnerships of public television stations and colleges. Colleges adapt the courses as needed, assign instructors, determine assignments and assessments, enroll students, and award grades and credit. Students watch the video component of the courses on public television, videocassette, or direct broadcast satellite. Since 1981 more than 5 million students have enrolled in these courses. The Web is now playing an important role as a component of many ALS telecourses and as the platform for complete courses.

## THE FUTURE

Public television is in the process of transitioning from analog to digital technology. This change is expected to open extraordinary new opportunities to offer educational services that are more accessible, interactive, and personalized.

The implications for distributed learning could be very significant. However, it would be premature to jump to the future before understanding the origins and structure of public television and the scope and nature of its current educational services. They will shape, for better or worse, how public television's new digital capacity and capabilities will be used and whether public television will be a leader in providing a new generation of digital learning.

—*Jinny Goldstein*

*See also* TELECOURSES

### Bibliography

Carnegie Commission on Educational Television. (1967). *Public television: A program for action.* New York: Harper and Row.

Carnegie Commission on the Future of Public Broadcasting. (1979). *A public trust. The report of the Carnegie Commission on the future of public broadcasting.* New York: Bantam.

Current Publishing Committee and the National Public Broadcasting Archives. (March 12, 2003). *Public Broadcasting PolicyBase.* Retrieved from http://www.current.org/pbpb/index.html.

Grossman, Larry, & Minow, Newton. (June 2002). *A digital gift to the nation.* Digital Promise Project. Retrieved from http://www.digitalpromise.org/report/0front.pdf.

Twentieth Century Fund. Task Force on Public Television. (1993). *Quality time? The report of the Twentieth Century Fund task force on public television.* New York: Twentieth Century Fund Press.

Witherspoon, John, & Kovitz, Roselle. (2000). *A history of public broadcasting.* Washington, DC: Current Publishing Committee.

# R

## RELATIONSHIPS

Relationships in distance learning tend to be less hierarchical than in the traditional academy. The concept of learning at a distance is rooted historically in attempts to break down barriers to education and make it available in spite of age, circumstance, and location. Currently most distance learners are adults with a high degree of motivation. Furthermore, the increasingly available technologies through which distance learning occurs demand and encourage a degree of negotiation between students and teachers.

## DISTANCE TECHNOLOGIES

The nature of the medium matters. Distance learning commonly incorporates intermittent face-to-face meetings and telephone conversations. Video conferencing is a less common but potentially significant mode of communication. E-mail has transformed communication across distances, particularly between individuals. Currently, however, the dominant forum is the virtual classroom. Computer technology has a particular impact on distance learning, allowing a dispersed group to maintain regular contact in a way that approximates the traditional classroom or seminar. But the virtual classroom differs from the physical one in significant ways.

Conducted at a physical remove, without cues of body language or tone of voice, online relationships are particularly vulnerable to misunderstanding or attenuation. Critical feedback or expressions of disagreement need to be more consciously balanced with affirmations of good will. Presence must be actively and regularly confirmed. Without relationships that are consciously established and maintained, the online learner can quickly come to feel isolated. The attentiveness that results from this need to build contact has its own rewards, contributing to the intimacy and high level of interpersonal focus—counterintuitive to many—that, in practice, characterizes the skillfully conducted distance learning relationship.

## FACE-TO-FACE LEARNING AND RELATIONSHIPS

In a face-to-face learning community, a range of nonverbal interactions can help to shape the learning experience. The teacher and student peers can encourage an individual's contribution to discussion with attitudes of attention and positive response. For the teacher, even the silent presence of a student in the classroom might offer significant evidence as to whether a learning relationship is developing appropriately. A range of interactions, equivalent to such encounters as the unscheduled chat between students in the corridor or the formal appointment in the professor's office, can be replicated online. What cannot be replicated are the visual indicators that help the participants to understand what is expected and what the boundaries are, or to fine-tune a message in spontaneous response to the recipient's reactions.

In a well-constructed online environment, this drawback can be turned to advantage in two ways. The fact that more of what would normally go unsaid has to be verbalized—the unspoken rules, the subtle shades of response, the conventions of thought not otherwise articulated and therefore not scrutinized—has an obvious benefit in the context of a shared intellectual exploration. There is also an element of liberation. The silent language of posture and facial expression can intimidate as easily as it can encourage. Whether intentionally or not, a frown can silence a speaker as effectively as a smile can draw the speaker out. For the teacher or student who anticipates a disappointed or hostile response, sensitivity can become self-censorship.

The challenge and the opportunity of distance learning springs from its focus on thoughtful verbal interaction, unassisted and uncluttered by physical presence. The partial anonymity that makes the online participant no more or less than the words she or he offers is inherently democratizing. But whatever the primary medium of communication, everyone involved in a distance learning community—students, faculty, and institutional staff—shares responsibility for forging and maintaining appropriate, dignified, and meaningful connections.

## TYPES OF RELATIONSHIPS IN DISTANCE LEARNING COMMUNITIES

At the heart of any community is a mesh of relationships. In a distance learning community, relationships exist between students and faculty, between the institution and its students, between the institution and its faculty members, and among students, whether actively fostered by the institution or growing spontaneously from shared experience. There is also the relationship the student develops with him- or herself through the process of learning.

## TECHNIQUES FOR FORMING AND MAINTAINING RELATIONSHIPS

Clear expectations are critical in all dealings between students and faculty. It is advisable to agree on learning contracts and to establish clear deadlines. It is helpful to reach an explicit understanding on the number of contacts that will occur, on the form of a particular contact (on a Web site, by e-mail, by phone, or face-to-face), and on its extent. Both parties need to be clear about the agenda of a particular meeting or exchange, and to avoid ambiguity over its outcome. For students not used to self-directed learning, the lack of constant contact with faculty may seem disorienting. For faculty not used to distance mentoring, the need to give individual attention to

students, exchanging the coherence of the lecture for the improvisations of dialogue, will demand a new approach to time management. When the relationship works, however, the student can benefit from one-on-one mentoring and progress more rapidly through ownership of the learning process. For the teacher, a relationship built, at least in part, on student initiative, while demanding flexibility and a willingness to relinquish control, can offer a refreshing degree of partnership.

Navigating one's way through the administrative requirements of an academic institution can present challenges at the best of times. When the institution is physically inaccessible and misunderstandings cannot be straightened out face-to-face, the challenge is that much greater. Deadlines and requirements—what the student should expect from the institution as well as what the institution should expect from the student—should be clearly established, and published in unambiguous form. Access by phone or e-mail to administrators able to answer questions and offer practical advice is essential. Teachers also will appreciate clarity and accessibility. Opportunities should be established to interact with faculty colleagues and to share information on the content of academic courses and on issues relating to the progress and welfare of individual students.

## GEOGRAPHICALLY–BASED SUPPORT GROUPS

Distance learning communities need to rely on various means of communication among students, for student support and friendship. Some institutions, such as the Fielding Graduate Institute, encourage the formation of geographically-based cluster groups to foster relationships among students. Learners located in a given area can meet regularly to support one another academically, to learn together, and to sustain friendships. Students engaged in Web-based learning, who encounter each other regularly online in the structured environment of the virtual classroom and in informal lounges or chat rooms, often form enriching relationships through the struggle and excitement of the shared learning experience. Although forging relationships at a distance can be difficult, there are the rewards of widening horizons, both personal and professional, and learning from other students of diverse culture and circumstance.

## RELATIONSHIP CHALLENGES AND OPPORTUNITIES

Distance learning can be a lonely experience. Learning while in the midst of work, managing one's personal life, or raising children requires depths of self-discipline. The rhythms of classroom attendance and the structure of support from teachers and peers encountered in real time and in real space are not available. The distance learner is under more pressure to take responsibility for his or her own learning and, in many cases, to define its path. The pressing demands of ordinary life always threaten to push academic commitment aside. At its least, learning at a distance is the only option when circumstances of geography and life commitments render attendance at an institution inconvenient or impossible. At its best, it can allow an integration of learning with other aspects of life, and encourage the internalizing of knowledge that characterizes education at its most vital.

—*Leni Wildflower*

*See also* COLLABORATION; SYNCHRONOUS FORMATS

### Bibliography

Anderson, W. A. (1977). *The future of the self: Inventing the postmodern person.* New York: Jeremy P. Tarcher/ Putnum.

Horizon. (2000). *Challenges in implementing distance learning programs.* Retrieved from http://www.horizon. unc.edu/projects/resources/44items.asp

Rudestam, K., & Schoenholtz-Read, J. (Eds.). (2002). *Handbook of online learning.* Thousand Oaks, CA: Sage.

# RESIDENCE HALLS

On many residential campuses, the largest network of computers is found in the residence halls. With as many as 20,000 students living on some college campuses, each with his or her own Internet connection, the computer services demanded by these students dwarfs that of the combined faculty and staff network on campus.

Developing network computing for residence halls presented some unique challenges. Many college residence halls were built in the 1960s to accommodate a surge in enrollments. The federal government provided low-interest loans for housing construction, and large numbers of residence halls were constructed under these federal programs. The first response to address the demand for residence-hall computing was to install computer labs in residence halls. This approach was less costly than wiring an entire building for computer access, and most students did not own their own computers. For a short time, this approach was adequate. As demand increased and more students had their own computers, however, another approach was needed. Most universities had installed coaxial cable in residence halls for cable television and had upgraded telephone systems in residence halls throughout the late 1970s and early 1980s. At some universities, this wiring could be adapted for Internet use. However, in most residence halls, new wiring had to be installed with separate computer ports for each student in a building. Rewiring old residence halls for Internet access in what came to be known as a "port for every pillow" was costly. Wireless communication was used in a few residence halls to overcome the expense of running separate connections to every room, but wireless access lagged at least 10 years behind the demand curve for computer access in every residence hall room. Where standard wireless connections were not possible, either an Etherloop or DSL type of connection using telephone lines was established. Installing the wiring, routers, and computer relay equipment was expensive and became part of the cost of residence hall operations. Residence halls currently being constructed are usually prewired with computer access to every room, and many also include computer lab facilities in the residence halls.

Because of the demand for residence hall computing, housing organizations have hired what are commonly referred to as "ResNet" administrators who are responsible for the administration, maintenance, and technical expertise for the servers, routers, and other equipment necessary to operate the extensive residence hall computer network. A unique feature of residence halls is that they operate 24 hours a day, 7 days a week. Unlike most college campuses, where the demands for computing are greatest during the day and early evening, demand for residence hall computing increases in the evening and on weekends. Although this may appear at first to be a satisfactory solution to access and computing resources, the overlapping periods when there is a high demand from residence hall users and campus-based users conducting research can produce significant delays.

Unlike the demands placed on a university's computing network for research, class instruction, and administration, much of the demand placed on the computer network—particularly the Internet—comes from social and recreational use by students during the evening hours. MP3 file transfers, video files, Internet gaming, e-mail traffic, video editing, and Web surfing consume a large amount of bandwidth and can slow Internet access to a crawl in the evening hours. Administrators have attempted to address these problems by restricting the speed at which students can transmit data over the Internet, so that a student's computer does not become a download site for others; by using firewalls; and by constructing an elaborate set of policies that regulate campus computing usage. The residence hall computing policies usually include regulations restricting the operating of a commercial Web site using the institution's computing network, file transfers between students and nonstudents, pirating of unauthorized software, hacking into protected computer sites, and operating pornographic Web sites. Many of these policies are difficult to monitor, difficult to enforce, and can present complicated legal issues, particularly at state universities.

Computer privacy is a matter of concern among students, and access to information stored on institutional servers can become an issue. Residence hall living has some unique privacy issues, such as the right of one student to use an activated Webcam in his or her room and how this decision affects the privacy rights of another student sharing that room.

Although universities customarily provide specifications necessary for people to connect their computers to the residence hall computer network, on most campuses, students bring with them a variety of computer hardware. Some of this equipment meets institutional specifications and can be easily connected; other equipment can require elaborate modifications to get a satisfactory connection to the residence hall computing network. To accommodate these student needs, most residence hall operations employ full-time technicians and student technicians to assist students in connecting to the residence hall computer network. Sometimes these technical support assistants repair and help students modify their equipment and provide student computer assistance throughout the academic year.

Increasingly, students are finding that online distance education courses offer a more flexible schedule for them and that they can live on campus in a residence hall, take several classes on campus, and enroll for a distance-learning course through their own university and meet the academic requirements for their program. In this way, residence halls serve not only the social, recreational, and educational support role on a college campus, but also in many cases serve as the student's classroom.

## FUTURE ISSUES

It is difficult to speculate on where technology will lead. There appears to be an increasing demand for wireless connections, greatly expanded bandwidth, and storage capacity. Older residence halls often do not operate very well with wireless communications; the steel and concrete structure of residence halls tends to make wireless connections more difficult. Increasing bandwidth is a technology issue, generally beyond the scope of residence hall administrators. However, as the ability to increase bandwidth emerges, students will demand that residence hall administrators install the necessary equipment to get the fastest access available.

The costs associated with these continuing upgrades, generally passed on to students in the form of rent, can be considerable. For residence hall administrators, bandwidth is an economic issue. Most institutions purchase their own bandwidth and additional fiber optic lines to make the necessary connections; but bandwidth is an operating cost similar to heating and electricity, and there is a reluctance to incur this additional expense unless it provides a significant advantage to the operation of the residence halls or to the quality of education students are receiving.

Of increasing concern is the amount of time students spend on the Internet in various cyber-communications in ways that have limited their social interaction with other students in the residence halls. Although some research has suggested that this is a current problem, the research is not conclusive and requires greater study.

—*Gregory S. Blimling*

*See also* STUDENT SERVICES

# RETENTION

College student retention continues to be a concern to colleges and universities. When students leave college prematurely, they can lose self-esteem and confidence in their abilities. They may not realize the real reasons for their departure and see it as a life failure. Students need to be able to complete programs that they are interested in pursuing. Students who are recruited and admitted to a college should have a reasonable expectation that programs and services will provide them with an opportunity for success.

With the publication in 1975 of his article "Dropouts from Higher Education: A Theoretical Synthesis of the Recent Literature" in *A Review of Educational Research,* Tinto enumerated a theoretical framework to explain student leaving behavior from higher education. No blame was apportioned to either colleges or the student. Rather, Tinto looked at previous studies and presented a theoretical model of attrition.

The Tinto model took a sociological approach to looking at the issue and posited that it was the interaction between the student and the academic and social systems of college that influenced staying and/or leaving behavior. Since its initial publication, the Tinto model has become the most widely accepted theoretical model for student retention/attrition from higher education. The Tinto model posits that individual pre-entry college attributes (family background, skill and ability, prior schooling) form individual goals and commitments. The individual's goals and commitments interact over time with institutional experiences (the formal and informal academic and social systems of an institution). The extent to which the individual becomes academically and socially integrated into the formal and informal academic and social systems of an institution determines the individual's departure decision.

The Tinto model expanded on Spady's model, which stated that personal attributes interact with environmental influences. The interaction of personal attributes and environmental influences gives the student opportunities for successful assimilation into the social and academic systems of an institution. A student's decision to either remain or withdraw is influenced by the rewards found within these systems.

The notion of "student involvement," as expressed by Astin, also supports this idea. Student involvement refers to the amount of physical and psychological energy that a student devotes to the academic experience. Astin believes that the highly involved student who devotes considerable energy to studying, participates in student organizations, and interacts frequently with faculty members is more committed to the institution. The more committed to the institution,

the higher the likelihood of success. Therefore, anything that is done to enhance a student's commitment to a goal and to the institution should further enhance his or her social and academic integration, and therefore promote retention.

Distributed learning takes many forms, from the electronic classroom to video conferencing, the World Wide Web, e-mail, distribution lists, and chat rooms, so the student's ability to become integrated into the formal and informal academic and social systems of a college may be limited. In addition, the learning can take place in a traditional semester (15 weeks) format or shorter or longer periods of time.

There is a paucity of data about the effects of distributed learning courses or programs on student retention. However, because in many cases the student will not be in a formal campus environment, how does a student in a distributed learning course or program become integrated into the formal and informal academic and social systems of a college?

This can occur and be facilitated by the course/program instructor and campus offices (public relations, student affairs, academic affairs). The course/program instructor can set up discussion groups, e-mail contact, video conferencing, and course/program e-mail and paper newsletters. Other campus offices can keep the student informed of academic information through the same media, and student affairs can do the same, as well as provide career and job search criteria on the Web for easy searching. Students can be encouraged to stop in for a visit if traveling to the area where the main college campus is located. Continuing contact with the student will help ensure that he or she feels a part of a greater whole while meeting academic requirements.

A student is retained in a distributed learning course and/or program if he or she is making satisfactory progress toward a personal and/or educational objective consistent with the college's mission.

*—Alan Seidman*

*See also* FINANCIAL AID; STUDENTS

## Bibliography

Astin, A. W. (July/August 1985). Involvement: The cornerstone of excellence. *Change,* 35–39.

Astin, A. W. (1993). *What matters in college: Four critical years revisited.* San Francisco: Jossey-Bass.

Bers, T. H., & Nyden, G. (2000). The disappearing student: Students who leave before the census date. *Journal of*

*College Student Retention: Research, Theory & Practice, 2*(3), 205–218.

Braxton, J. M. (Ed.). (2000). *Reworking the student departure puzzle.* Nashville, TN: Vanderbilt University Press.

Seidman, A. (1996, Spring). Retention revisited: R = E, Id + E & In, Iv. *College and University, 71*(4), 18–20.

Spady, W. (1971). Dropouts from higher education: Towards an empirical model. *Interchange, 2,* 38–62.

Tinto, V. (1975). Dropouts from higher education: A theoretical synthesis of the recent literature. *A Review of Educational Research, 45,* 89–125.

Tinto, V. (1993). *Leaving college: Rethinking the causes and cures of student attrition,* 2nd Edition. Chicago: The University of Chicago Press.

# S

## SCHOLAR PRACTITIONER MODEL

The term *scholar practitioner* expresses an ideal of professional excellence grounded in theory and research, informed by experiential knowledge, and motivated by personal values, political commitments, and ethical conduct. Scholar practitioners are committed to the well-being of clients and colleagues, to learning new ways of being effective, and to conceptualizing their work in relation to broader organizational, community, political, and cultural contexts. Scholar practitioners explicitly reflect on and assess the impact of their work. Their professional activities and the knowledge they develop are based on collaborative and relational learning through active exchange within communities of practice and scholarship.

The scholar practitioner ideal has been analyzed from various perspectives as to the nature of skilled and principled action ranging from adult development and higher education to epistemology and social systems. Professional fields such as education, medicine, clinical psychology, social work, program evaluation, management, engineering, architecture, and law all have addressed this role. Each of these areas has a distinct practice track—as teacher, scholar, health care professional, psychotherapist, social worker, evaluator, manager, business consultant, engineer, architect, and lawyer. Experts in these fields possess a deep understanding of subject matter and practice knowledge and, compared to novices, demonstrate effective, efficient, and creative problem solving.

Debate across professional fields has not settled on a single specification for what a scholar practitioner should be able to do at a practical level. Areas of competence are diverse and include depth in a discipline and its methods for creating knowledge, educational expertise (whether as a teacher, change agent, or leader), capacity for teamwork across fields and public and private sectors, and skilled commitment to ethical conduct, diversity, and a global perspective. The variety of perspectives on the topic is reflected in several related terms and emphases such as reflective practitioner, scientist practitioner, citizen scholar, public intellectual, and practitioner scholar. Four cross-cutting perspectives help illuminate the ideal of the scholar practitioner and the varied issues that influence its evolution.

## EDUCATING THE SCHOLAR PRACTITIONER

Accredited schooling and formal licensing or codes of conduct are hallmarks of a profession and guide educational practices for the scholar practitioner. Currently there is a resurgent interest in reforming and broadening the practice of graduate and professional education, both within disciplines and across types such as doctoral, medical, legal, and other helping professions. One of the forces driving this examination is the emergence of distributed forms of education and lifelong learning that allow flexibility of time, place, format, individual definition of goals, and social grouping. Virtual learning environments increase the possibilities for collaborative educational relationships that are especially suitable for adult and mid-career students whose commitments and ways of learning may not be compatible with traditional settings.

Notwithstanding these developments and the fact that effective practitioners require an experiential knowledge base, their formal education is composed largely of didactic learning, whether in the physical or virtual classroom, grounded in theory and in research that presumably "underlies" practice expertise. Even professionally oriented programs, such as those in business, nursing, and social work, typically employ didactic methods to present basic concepts and analytic techniques prior to field-based learning of practitioner skills.

This Platonic ideal, which emphasizes underlying theory and analytic technique, exists for several reasons. It affirms a norm of humility in Western science that knowledge evolves and requires conceptual and empirical challenge in a continual analysis of truth. This premise reinforces the idea that practitioner work, whether as healer, teacher, or leader, should be based on more than personal prejudice, power, or the influence of authority figures and fads. The ability to interpret client and societal needs based on the most reliable knowledge is critically important to being a competent and ethically responsible practitioner, especially in high-stakes helping professions such as medicine.

The emphasis on theory and research has a political rationale as well. Within the broad context of modernity and the rise of science and technology, establishing theoretical and empirical knowledge is essential to achieving status as a profession. The more determinate and prominent the knowledge base—as in the physical and life sciences—the greater the prestige and power of the field. For example, Ph.D. clinical psychologists vie for privilege against M.D. practitioners within a health care system that distributes enormous resources. The caliber of research training in Ph.D. programs becomes one lever in that contest. Practitioner degrees such as the Psy.D. and Ed.D. in psychology and education emphasize empirical inquiry that is more closely tied to practice settings than to theoretical questions. These and similar programs are aimed more at the practitioner scholar than at the scholar practitioner, thereby highlighting the status and resource competition issues.

Finally, educating for interpersonal nuances and situational uncertainties of practitioner work, as well as related ideas about ethics and values, is generally done through experiential methods such as case teaching, mentoring, practicums, and field internships. These are more expensive forms of education than a sequenced classroom curriculum. Practice knowledge often is tacit and therefore difficult to codify for educational purposes in comparison to theory and research methods. Hence, experiential learning often conflicts with mass-production institutional imperatives for most educational organizations. The resulting bias toward didactically taught content knowledge becomes self-perpetuating because the majority of teachers who educate scholar practitioners were themselves trained through the same method. The lack of attention to and expertise in experiential learning leads to wide variation in the degree to which it is used systematically to enhance and assess the acquisition of practice knowledge. For John Dewey, whose work provides a foundational rationale for experiential learning, it is not just the experience but the quality of and reflection on experience that lead to important learning.

Given that practitioners work on human affairs, it can be argued that postbaccalaureate professional training for the scholar practitioner should be grounded in a broad liberal arts undergraduate education as a means of strengthening general analytic capacities as well as historical, aesthetic, and spiritual ways of knowing. Cost notwithstanding, the same argument applies to professional graduate education where knowledge of the humanities offers balance to the more technocratic scholarly approaches of the social and natural sciences.

## KNOWLEDGE FORMS AND METHODS

Knowledge takes many forms—personal, practical, artistic, scholarly, political, and spiritual—each of which plays a role in the work of the scholar practitioner, who often contends with uncertainty about problem definition and intervention impact. This uncertainty, in turn, exists within the normal context of practitioner work in which novel patterns of information, situational constraint, and value conflict are common. Professional education programs, however, emphasize only a few forms of knowledge and historically have embodied a hierarchical relationship in which scholarly knowledge derived from theory and research is passed on for practical application in particular situations. The terms *theory* and *research,* which are used somewhat interchangeably here, encompass a wide range of epistemological and methodological approaches. Constructivist epistemology, experiential pedagogy, and many applied research strategies including action and evaluation research attempt to equalize this relationship. However, they often eschew general theory for an emphasis on situational knowledge, thereby substituting one hierarchy for another.

Methods for creating and testing new knowledge are also circumscribed. In the social sciences, these scholarship skills typically include using research designs and methods of sampling to make comparisons and render judgments of cause and effect, employing empirical methods for gathering data, measuring and making representations of reality, and using statistical, simulation, and qualitative methods for analyzing data and substantiating interpretations or conclusions. Postmodern understanding from the humanities has widened the methodological choices in the social sciences in which subjective voice, situational nuance, and societal perspective highlight how knowledge is socially and psychologically constructed and used. Qualitative and expressive/artistic methods are added to the traditional tools of experiments and surveys. Criteria for sound evidence have evolved from the traditional reliability and validity standards to include considerations such as authenticity, trustworthiness, utility, and praxis.

These developments help foster a more integrated basis for the dual facets of the scholar practitioner role. They strengthen the status of tacit knowledge in comparison to formal knowledge and create opportunities to explore how practitioner knowledge derived from experience can strengthen research-based findings and inquiry. For example, traditional research methods attempt to control or isolate what are considered confounding factors, such as the background characteristics of clients who seek treatment, from the pure effects of the treatment. This research design practice is used so that one can judge the efficacy of a treatment in order to make important decisions about investing in it for the general good of others. The practitioner, however, must accommodate, not control, a wide variety of background characteristics in working with clients. Reliable research results that indicate increased risks for hormone therapy for menopause symptoms, for example, do not dictate the choices that might be made in the context of an individual's life situation. Understanding this choice process can identify additional outcomes as well as illuminate the ever-present interaction of generic treatments with individual and social factors. Thus, control and accommodation as well as research and practice knowledge together provide a more complete understanding and basis for action.

Also, practitioner work occurs within institutional settings that provide continual economic, societal, and ethical challenges that research knowledge can guide only at a very general level. For instance, the research findings on school choice and learning outcomes must be interpreted by educational practitioners within the historical context of racial and economic segregation, democratic ideals, and the needs of particular communities and their constituents.

An important value of scholarly skills is that they have a significant degree of cross-disciplinary application, whereas practice skills are more linked to particular professions. It is possible for scholars from diverse disciplines to have reasoned exchange about research evidence and criteria for judging its merit. The social invention of scholarly content and methods thus makes possible disciplinary and social boundary crossing for the benefit of all. On the other hand, the historical emphasis on theoretical knowledge and research skills results in neglect of practice capacities such as teaching, consulting, colleagueship in a workplace, and the moral dimensions of one's work, as well as the forms and sources of knowledge that are associated with these skills.

One approach to equalizing the treatment of theory and practice knowledge forms is to identify practitioner *principles* that occupy a middle ground between general theoretical orientations and profession-specific techniques. Practice principles of this kind, whether aimed at individuals, groups, organizations, or communities, would have in common such concerns as establishing trusting and respectful relationships, effective communications, diagnostics, and facility with negotiation, motivation, and change dynamics. Along with research methods (i.e., design, measurement, analysis) these practice principles constitute an epistemology of scholarly practice that illuminate how professionals can think and act reflectively and strategically.

## THE SCHOLAR PRACTITIONER AS AN ADULT LEARNER

As an adult learner with professional practice, personal growth, and intellectual development goals, the ideal scholar practitioner interrelates concepts, understandings, and methods from varied theoretical and practice perspectives. In addition, scholar practitioners employ research and practice principles in complementary ways such as using their experiential knowledge to enrich theoretical concepts and using structured empirical inquiry to examine the effectiveness of professional interventions. They draw upon knowledge from multiple sources including theory-based propositions, case-based best practices, and values-based maxims and morals. These varied forms of knowledge are continuously acquired through didactic, experiential, and cultural means. Scholar practitioners seek continuing education that adds to their skills and offers new insight into knowledge previously acquired. The ideal of the scholar practitioner defines this effort in terms of lifelong learning that expands the individual's capacity for insight, reflection, and effective action.

The term *andragogy* represents an approach to adult learning based on both formal and tacit knowledge, as well as the personal and professional values that individuals bring to their learning. Andragogy emphasizes an active and defining role for individuals in what and how they learn and may include goals of personal and professional transformation. Transformational andragogy, as applied to the scholar practitioner, seeks to nurture flexible interpretive and emotional capacities in the learner that support examination of tacit assumptions, exploration of cultural diversity, integration of varied intellectual perspectives, and incorporation of unifying aspirations for humanity.

## ATTRIBUTES OF THE SCHOLAR PRACTITIONER

The ideal of the scholar practitioner also can be examined in relation to an individual's cognitive, personal, and behavioral attributes in the context of adult development. Theory and research on individuals who excel in their professions as innovators and problem-solvers identify several intellectual capacities. For example, comparisons of novices and experts show the latter as having well-defined hierarchical knowledge structures with many lateral connections among concepts that allow them to abstractly, efficiently, and creatively interpret information from their everyday work. Experts are able to frame situations from multiple perspectives, pose competing hypotheses, and identify evidence that would test alternative explanations.

In addition to these cognitive attributes, the fully developed adult professional shows the capacity for emotional intelligence and use of self that is both unified and differentiated across settings and roles.

Tolerance of difference and ambiguity is linked with compassion for life and a commitment to improving the human condition. Development of these affective and behavioral dimensions is a challenging but critical aspect of the scholar practitioner as an agent of change for individuals, organizations, and communities.

The concept of *wisdom* captures the essence of much of the foregoing discussion, in that it represents an integration of cognitive, affective, and behavioral dimensions. The work of wisdom for a scholar practitioner requires alternating between the abstract and the observable, questioning what is taken for granted and overlooked, complicating with unexpected findings, and simplifying with new interpretations. These intellectual and social skills require multiple forms of intelligence and are manifested through principled and ethical action. Nurturing the capacity for wisdom is the goal of education and lies at the heart of the scholar practitioner ideal.

—*Charles McClintock*

*See also* ADULT EDUCATION LEARNING MODEL; EXPERIENTIAL LEARNING; GRADUATE STUDY

## Bibliography

Boyer, Ernest L. (1990). *Scholarship reconsidered: Priorities of the professoriate.* Princeton, NJ: Carnegie Foundation for the Advancement of Teaching.

Curry, Lawrence, Wergin, Jon, & Associates. (1993). *Educating professionals: Responding to new expectations for competence and accountability.* San Francisco: Jossey-Bass.

Kitchener, Karen, & King, Patricia. (1991). A reflective judgment model: Transforming assumptions about knowing. In Jack Mezirow (Ed.), *Fostering critical reflection in adulthood.* San Francisco: Jossey-Bass.

Knowles, Malcolm S., Holton III, Elwood F., & Swanson, Richard A. (1998). *The adult learner.* 5th Edition. Woburn, MA: Butterworth-Heinemann.

Nyquist, Jody D. (2002). The Ph.D.: A tapestry of change for the 21st century. *Change, 34*(6), 12–20.

Schön, Donald A. (1983). *The reflective practitioner: How professionals think in action.* New York: Basic Books.

Shulman, Lee S. (1987). Knowledge and teaching: Foundations of the new reform. *Harvard Educational Review, 57,* 1–22.

Sternberg, Robert J., & Horvath James A. (Eds.). (1999). *Tacit knowledge in professional practice.* Mahwah, NJ: Lawrence Erlbaum.

# SELF-DIRECTED LEARNING

Self-directed learning is learning in which the design, conduct, and evaluation of a learning effort are directed by the learner. Such learning was said to represent the submerged part of the adult learning iceberg in an influential series of studies undertaken by the Canadian researcher Allen Tough in the 1960s and 1970s. Tough speculated that self-directed learning efforts accounted for more than 80% of all adult learning. Self-directed learning efforts are not to be thought of as occurring in isolation, however, because a consistent theme of research in this area is the way in which learners move in and out of learning networks and consult a range of peers and experts. The key point is that decisions about what and how to learn, and which resources to consult, rest with the learner.

Tough's work triggered a host of replicatory studies conducted across the English-speaking world and influenced Malcolm Knowles' concept of *andragogy*, regarded by many as the conceptual cornerstone of adult education. Self-directed learning has become so popular that an annual international conference is now held on the topic, a widely used self-directed learning readiness scale has been developed, and various models of self-directed growth and development have been proposed. The emergence of online learning formats and asynchronous modes of instruction has provided a boost to the idea given that such approaches place more control over decisions regarding the pace (though often not the direction) of learning in the learner's hands.

Several explanations have been proposed to account for the popularity of the idea of self-directed learning. One is that in an era of cost-cutting and reductions in public spending, purse holders are eager to seize on any idea that suggests that adults are quite capable of conducting and managing their own learning without the assistance of professional adult educators. If the empirical accuracy of Tough's work is accepted, then it potentially provides a rationale for channeling limited educational funds away from adult education (because adults, as self-directed learners, are teaching themselves anyway) and toward K–12 schooling. Another line of argument suggests that the ideology of self-direction, of adults individually pulling themselves up by their bootstraps and moving ahead with their own learning efforts, fits congenially with the American ethos of libertarian individualism.

It is noticeable that self-directed learning has been met with much less fanfare in cultures that prize the collective over the individual, and in which individual and group identity are fused. There is also the argument that proposing self-directed learning as a distinctively adult mode of learning, seen much less often in children and adolescents, solves for adult educators the thorny question of how they are to describe themselves. If self-direction is an adult-specific learning modality then at a stroke adult educators can claim a distinctive identity for themselves as facilitators of self-directed learning.

## THE SELF IN SELF-DIRECTED LEARNING

Since Tough's initial research there have been three decades of critical analysis of its contentions and presuppositions, much of it centering on the nature of the "self" in a self-directed learning project. It is important to recognize that the self that is involved in conducting learning is culturally formed and bound. Who we are and how we decide what it is important for us to be able to know or do are questions of culture. The self in a self-directed learning project is not an autonomous, innocent self, contentedly floating free from cultural influences. It has not sprung fully formed out of a political vacuum. It is, rather, an embedded self, a self whose instincts, values, needs, and beliefs have been shaped by the surrounding culture. As such, it is a self that reflects the constraints and contradictions, as well as the liberatory possibilities, of that culture. The most critically sophisticated and reflective adults cannot escape their own autobiographies. Only with a great deal of effort and a lot of assistance from others can we become aware of how what we think are our own wholly altruistic impulses, free from any bias of race, gender, or class, actually end up reinforcing repressive structures. Hence, an important aspect of a fully adult self-directed learning project should be a reflective awareness of how one's desires and needs have been culturally formed and of how cultural factors can convince one to pursue learning projects that are against one's own best interests.

Philip Candy is one of the few scholars who has consistently argued for this kind of constructivist interpretation of self-directed learning. He argues that learning in its fullest context is a social activity, and the attainment of full personal autonomy must recognize this. Candy warns us to remember that adults are powerfully affected by aspects of their backgrounds in ways that limit and constrain their ability to be self-directing in certain learning situations. Other researchers have pointed out the macro-cultural construction of self-direction. In certain cultures a decision to learn on one's own, and to be the ultimate arbiter of one's decisions regarding learning, would result in the learner committing cultural suicide. Furthermore, those with a learned propensity for self-direction may have acquired this habit in childhood because of their membership in a social class that values individual initiative and provides the financial resources for children to conduct their own learning projects.

## SELF-DIRECTED LEARNING AND THE POLITICS OF LEARNER CONTROL

At the intellectual heart of self-direction is the issue of control, particularly control over what are conceived as acceptable and appropriate learning activities and processes. Exercising self-direction requires that certain conditions be in place regarding access to resources, conditions that are essentially political in nature. An understanding of self-direction that focuses on the learner's control over learning, and on the importance of full access to information in self-directed learning, implies an important political dimension to the idea.

The one consistent element in the majority of definitions of self-directed learning is the importance of the learner's exercising control over all educational decisions. What should be the goals of a learning effort, what resources should be used, what methods will work best for the learner, and by what criteria the success of any learning effort should be judged are all decisions that are said to rest in the learner's hands. This emphasis on control—on who decides what is right and good and how these things should be pursued—is also central to notions of emancipatory adult education.

Self-direction as an organizing concept for adult education therefore contains some powerful implications for practice that are political in nature. It implies a democratic commitment to shifting to learners as much control as possible for conceptualizing, designing, conducting, and evaluating their learning and for deciding how resources are to be used to further these processes. Honoring people's self-direction is not the same as abandoning one's convictions and purposes as an educator in a mistaken act of pedagogic abnegation. Thought of politically, self-direction can more

accurately be seen as part of a populist democratic tradition that holds that people's definitions of what is important to them should frame and instruct governments' actions, and not the other way round. This is why the idea of self-direction is viewed with suspicion by advocates of a core or national curriculum, and why it is opposed so vehemently by those who see education as a process of induction into cultural literacy. Emphasizing people's right to self-direction also invests a certain trust in their wisdom, in their capacity to make wise choices and take wise actions. Advocating that people should be in control of their own learning is based on the belief that if people had a chance to give voice to what most moves and hurts them, they would soon show that they were only too well aware of the real nature of their problems and of ways to deal with these.

If the self-conscious, self-aware exertion of control over learning is placed at the heart of what it means to be self-directed, it raises a host of questions about how control can be exercised authentically in a culture that is itself highly controlling. For example, it is easy to imagine an inauthentic form of control in which adults feel that they are framing and taking key decisions about their learning, all the while being unaware that this is happening within a framework that excludes certain ideas or activities as subversive, unpatriotic, or immoral. "Controlled self-direction" is, from a political perspective, a contradiction in terms, a self-negating concept as erroneous as the concept of limited empowerment. On the surface learners may be said to be controlling their learning when they make decisions about pacing, resources, and evaluative criteria. But if the range of acceptable content has been preordained so that they deliberately or unwittingly steer clear of things that they sense are deviant or controversial, then they are controlled rather than in control. They are victims, in effect, of self-censorship, willing partners in hegemony and successful exercisers of disciplinary power.

*Hegemony* describes the process whereby ideas, structures, and actions come to be seen by people as both natural and axiomatic—as so obvious as to be beyond question or challenge—when in fact they are constructed and transmitted by powerful minority interests to protect the status quo that serves these interests so well. A fully developed self-directed learning project would have at its center an alertness to the possibility of hegemony. Those engaged in this fully realized form of self-directed learning would understand how easily external control can unwittingly be internalized in the form of an automatic self-censorship—an instinctive reaction that "I can't learn this because it's out of bounds" (that is, unpatriotic, deviant, or subversive). A fully adult form of self-direction exists only when learners examine their definitions of what they think it is important for them to learn for the extent to which these end up serving repressive interests.

Being in control of learning means that learners make informed choices. Making informed choices means, in turn, that they act reflectively in ways that further their interests. But informed choices can be made only with as full a knowledge as possible about the different options open to learners and the consequences of each of these. Control that is exercised on the basis of limited information and unexamined alternatives is a distorted, mindless, and illusory form of control. It may lead people to devote enormous amounts of energy to making individual incremental adjustments to their daily existence without realizing that these tinker with symptoms while leaving unaddressed the structural changes necessary if their efforts are to have anything other than fleeting significance. With regard to the importance of having full access to all relevant information and of being aware of how learning projects have been culturally framed, it is important to acknowledge that these are tentative ideals. Learners will never be in a position of total omniscience where they have constant access to every piece of relevant information about all the problems that face them, and where they possess such a pure and undistorted insight into their own motivations and impulses that it enables them to distinguish between real and artificial needs, and between constraining short-term and empowering long-term interests. However, it is just as important that educators act as if these ideals could be realized. For control to mean anything it is crucial that learners have access to significant information. What a learner defines as significant information, however, may be regarded by someone else as privileged or confidential. Consequently, taking control of their learning is likely to bring adults into direct conflict with powerful entrenched interests.

An inauthentic, limited form of self-direction is evident when learners' efforts to develop themselves as learners remain at the level of philosophical preferences because the resources needed for action are unavailable or denied to them. Exercising control over learning is meaningless if control comprises only an intellectual analysis of one's problems and solutions. Learners may believe they have an accurate reading of their condition, and they may secure all kinds of promises from those in power to do something about it when resources are more plentiful, but if this is the extent of their control then they are doing little more than playing an intellectual game. So as well as the resources of adequate time and energy needed to make reflectively informed decisions, self-directed learning also implies that learners have access to the resources needed to act on these decisions. Being self-directed can therefore be inherently politicizing as learners come to a critical awareness of the differential distribution of resources necessary to conduct their self-directed learning efforts.

Self-directed learning will likely exercise an influence for many more years. Its ideological congeniality in a culture of individualism ensures its continuing popularity, while the liberatory possibilities it contains appeal to the democratic, activist strain in much adult educational work.

*—Stephen D. Brookfield*

***See also*** ADULT EDUCATION LEARNING MODEL; PEDAGOGY/ANDRAGOGY

## Bibliography

Brookfield, S. D. (1985). *Self-directed learning: From theory to practice.* San Francisco: Jossey-Bass.

Candy, P. C. (1991). *Self direction for lifelong learning.* San Francisco: Jossey-Bass.

Hammond, M., & Collins, R. (1991). *Self-directed learning: Critical practice.* New York: Nichols.

Tough, A. M. (1979). *The adult's learning projects: A fresh approach to theory and practice in adult learning.* Toronto: Ontario Institute for Studies in Education.

# SIMULATIONS

Simulations are based on a simple, but effective, learning strategy—practice makes perfect. Not just any practice will do. The practice needs to take place in context. Simulations are used to teach a specific process (the practice) within a specific environment (the context). This is the goal of simulation, and many argue that simulation is not a luxury but a necessity for certain types of learning to take place.

Some of the primary benefits of simulations are:

- The closer the simulation resembles a learner's actual environment, the greater the retention.
- Simulations provide a safe environment in which to make mistakes. Some of the best learning comes from assessing one's own mistakes.
- Simulations allow learning to take place without pulling expensive equipment offline (e.g., simulation-based training for F-15 aircraft—it's very expensive to pull a $40 million aircraft out of service for training purposes).
- Creating the simulation can help to streamline the processes that are being taught (i.e., improvements in process are often made when creating simulations).
- Well-designed simulations often significantly reduce learning time.
- Simulations allow practice for hazardous procedures, such as shutting down a nuclear reactor.

Although simulations aren't the answer for every situation or type of content, the use of simulations in blended learning often yields impressive results. The following sections describe some of the more common simulations.

## SOFTWARE (IT/APPLICATION) SIMULATIONS

This is probably the most common type of simulation. Almost 60% of commercial e-learning courses available today deal with software application or IT topics. They are generally straightforward, and the better ones allow the user to try out all of the features of the software that is being taught.

## BUSINESS SIMULATIONS

This kind of simulation is generally used to help people understand the dynamics behind the choices people make when running a business. Some of these can be very life-like and complex; others can be as simple as a tutorial that uses simple math to teach basic business skills (e.g., how to perform an inventory). The better ones use complex algorithms and include virtual characters with life-like back-and-forth conversation that challenge learners to understand

how decisions can affect a large organization's success or failure.

## SITUATIONAL SIMULATIONS

These include role-playing simulations and case-based scenarios. Situational simulations are typically developed to assist learners in problem solving. These programs allow learners to react to hypothetical cases. Learners are typically members of the environment in these simulations, rather than being some external force that manipulates variables at will. They typically incorporate situations in which participants react to many decision alternatives and feature a best—or optimal—sequence of right or wrong decisions. Others focus on making the best compromise possible, rather than finding the optimal sequence of best decisions. Situational simulations are most commonly used in soft skill simulations, or what some call "people skills."

## TECHNICAL SIMULATIONS

This category includes process simulators and time-based scenarios. A good example of a time-based scenario can be observed at many mortgage company Web sites, where you choose a 15- or 30-year mortgage rate, set other variables, and then observe a graph showing how those decisions change your payment schedule over the life of the loan. It is much easier to teach the principle of interest using this type of simulation versus explaining the concept of interest using simple examples in a paper-based exercise.

## PROCEDURAL SIMULATIONS

Having learners sequence a list of steps in a process most often does not work, although many e-learning courses use this approach. The proactive approach is to have learners perform the steps in a simulated environment. For example, consider the start-up procedure in an airplane. Instead of sequencing a list of tasks, the pilot-trainee can perform the actual steps (looking at gauges in the proper sequence, etc.). Retention and learner satisfaction are much higher when using this approach. Procedural simulations are sometimes called "task simulators." For step-by-step processes, it is hard to beat a simple procedural simulation to make the learning fast, easy, and effective.

## VIRTUAL WORLDS

These are usually extremely complex 3-D visualizations that allow learners a wide latitude of action and movement and aim to create a landscape that can be explored, as opposed to a test that has right and wrong answers. A good example of a virtual world application is a spatial representation of several different types of 747 commercial aircraft created for Air Force base fire fighters. These fire fighters are required to be familiar enough with commercial aircraft that they can find and rescue the crew of a commercial 747 in the event of an emergency landing. This kind of simulation allows them to become acutely familiar with the smallest of details. They are very expensive to build, and thus tend to be for very specialized purposes.

## THE FUTURE OF SIMULATIONS

Given the impressive results that can be obtained by the use of simulations, the corporate world has particularly embraced them, and the majority of simulations being created today lean toward teaching processes, procedures, and soft skills in a corporate training environment. However, the use of simulations in online learning is sure to be expanded beyond the corporate sphere, most notably in the use of virtual "characters" as teachers and guides. The phenomenal growth of computer gaming lends further evidence to the idea that people prefer to be thoroughly engaged and taught at the same time (computer gaming is, at root, simulation). Simulations have already proven themselves as the most user-friendly and engaging way for people to learn, and they will surely be a key component in the future of online learning, perhaps for the simple reason that they are the next best thing to being there.

*—Brandon Hall*

*See also* EXPERIENTIAL LEARNING; INSTRUCTIONAL TECHNIQUES; VIRTUAL LEARNING TOOLS

### Bibliography

Beckschi, Peter, Hall, Brandon, & Piskurich, George M. (1999). *The ASTD handbook of training design and delivery.* New York: McGraw-Hill.

Kelton, W. David, & Law, Averill M. (1999). *Simulation modeling and analysis.* New York: McGraw-Hill.

## SITE LICENSES

A site license is an agreement between a software company and an institution or individual that spells out how many individuals can have access to a particular software program. Site licenses for online programs specify the number of users that can have access to an online service via a server or the Web. Site licenses for programs on CD-ROM or disks specify onto how many computers a program can be loaded. Site licenses also spell out the appropriate and inappropriate uses of the program. The latter is designed to provide protection from lawsuits involving the use of the program for illegal or otherwise unsavory purposes, or to try to ensure that users pay an additional amount if they use the program for business rather than educational or personal use.

A site license is a little like booking a group bus tour for a particular number of people. If fewer than the target number of people decide to go on the tour, the price is still the same. If a larger number of people decide to go on the tour, they need to be accommodated, and another bus will have to be hired. Similarly, if a site license specifies that the program can be loaded onto no more than 10 computers at a time, it can be loaded onto from 0 to 10 computers. To legally run it on 12 computers, however, one might need to pay the additional price for a site license that specifies 25 computers as the maximum.

Other conditions listed in the site license contract include such things as details on rules regarding the intended purpose, copying, ownership, upgrades, and uses of the program, as well as related legal definitions. It may also specify the degree to which free updates will be made available, and for how long a period of time.

*—Lynn H. Collins*

*See also* LICENSING

## SKILL DEVELOPMENT

Professionals who want to collaborate at a distance in virtual environments must recognize and develop specific communication and collaboration skills for effective computer-mediated relationships. *Virtual* is defined here to mean not in actual fact (e.g., like professional teams that meet in a specific place at prearranged times), but in essence. The essence of virtual teams is the quality of relationships among their members versus the time and location of their work.

Professional collaboration in teams can take place synchronously, as in face-to-face meetings, by using desktop and real-time data conferencing, electronic meeting systems, and video and audio conferencing. Virtual teams can also conduct their work asynchronously with e-mail, bulletin boards, interactive Web sites, and non–real-time database sharing and conferencing. The main advantages of asynchronous collaboration are: 1) Work/contributions can be completed at any time desired and from any place with Internet access; and 2) Asynchronous media are conducive to substantive, thoughtful collaboration/writing that is focal for professional teams working at a distance. The main issue is the quality of the collaboration, not the frequency of communication. Virtual professional teams may also incorporate both synchronous and asynchronous work mediums in a mixed format. For example, a team that meets initially face-to-face may complete most of its work via bulletin boards and threaded conversations asynchronously, and use periodic conference calls (synchronous) to review overall progress and general sharing. Virtual teams add complexity to the professional collaborative process.

Effective virtual teams, working in interactive Web sites (i.e., Web sites that provide space for storing, changing, and retrieving information, documents, and attachments), must build relationships and trust, create an identity, and maintain agreement on purpose, goals, objectives, deliverables, tracking decisions, and team collaborative processes. Professional online collaboration requires attention to the team's ongoing development, always building a greater sense of community through the use of succinct, content-rich communication in which everyone's input is seen as valuable. Helpful suggestions include:

- Support everyone's unique contributions and efforts for goal-attainment, especially in the early stages of online work.
- Build appropriate team norms regarding sharing, conversational tones, brevity, timeliness of work, and individual responsibility for maintaining a professional collaborative culture.
- Develop a personal presence in online interactions, stay present, and let team members know about predictable absences.

- Provide sufficient structure for when, where, and what is expected of each team member in terms of participation, processes, and deliverables.
- For online work conducted through threaded conversations (e.g., bulletin boards), maintain clear boundaries around topics, work products, chat areas, information posting, discussions, and other necessary or desired interactions.
- Encourage a high level of information sharing, including ideas, writing, and other work products; knowledge resources; references; URLs; and other areas of intellectual property. Trust, professional integrity, and ethical conduct are paramount for effective virtual collaboration.
- Note all relevant milestones, and support individual autonomy and responsibility.

Professional collaboration often entails handling diverse perspectives, personalities, cultural differences, and conflicts that naturally arise in the collaborative process. The added dimension of working virtually, at a distance, means that there are often no visual clues to help facilitate interpersonal interaction. Therefore, misunderstandings and miscommunications can take place more easily. As part of the team's online culture, it is important that each member encourage engagement around diverse opinions, novel perspectives, and creative decisions, using and supporting the team's resources. Team members should discuss early on the possibilities for misunderstanding, confusion, and frustration with both the collaborative process online and the technology that supports it. Teams should articulate how these communication problems should be resolved (e.g., provide a specific discussion section on the team's computer-mediated workspace for questions and requests for clarification). Team members should be encouraged to avoid direct confrontations when working online. These problems are best handled synchronously, in person or over the phone when necessary, with the parties involved. In general, creating a climate of "agree to disagree" allows virtual and face-to-face collaboration to continue.

## EXAMPLES OF ONLINE COLLABORATION

The following two examples of computer-mediated professional collaboration help to illustrate the contributions of working virtually and at a distance.

The first scenario involved post-graduate training of mental health professionals in group psychotherapy.

The group psychotherapy program applied Web-based technology to complement face-to-face training. The group met face-to-face, at 6-week intervals, for theory presentations and experiential leadership training. In between these meetings, the group interacted asynchronously in threaded conversations as they addressed case presentations and responded to applied theory questions. Each trainee participated in presenting case material from his or her professional work as well as addressing and supporting the work of others. In turn, these rich interactions carried over into the overall collaboration of the group at face-to-face meetings.

The second scenario involved a cardiac rehabilitation team (cardiologist, physical and exercise therapist, psychologist, nutritionist, yoga and meditation trainer, and an administrative person) that developed a virtual patient record accessed via an interactive Web site. All of the professionals worked within a 10-mile radius; however, face-to-face team meetings seemed impossible to schedule. Asynchronously, the team was able to work closely, at a distance, adding data and reviewing each patient record at their own pace and location. Ongoing case discussions and consultations, via Web forums, were integrated into the ongoing treatment planning. Although all of the actual rehabilitation services were provided directly to patients, collaboration among the professional staff increasingly took place online. Face-to-face meetings were used for discussing difficult cases, best practices, and socializing to maintain the desired level of interpersonal and team connection. Again, the professionals' experience of working virtually as well as face-to-face was that the two relational mediums/formats complemented each other well.

Among the chief obstacles to working effectively in computer-mediated environments are the need for proper hardware, effective software, technical support, and the knowledge and skills for working collaboratively in virtual professional teams.

—*Dean S. Janoff*

*See also* COLLABORATION; COMPUTER-BASED TRAINING (CBT); WORK-BASED DISTRIBUTED LEARNING

### Bibliography

Janoff, D. S. (2002). Healthcare meets technology: Web-based professional training, consultation, and collaboration. In K. Rudestam & J. Schoenholtz-Read (Eds.), *Handbook of online learning: Innovations in higher education and corporate training.* Thousand Oaks, CA: Sage.

Janoff, D. S., & Schoenholtz-Read, J. (1999). Group supervision meets technology: A model for computer-mediated group training at a distance. *International Journal of Group Therapy, 49,* 255–272.

# SOCIAL CONSTRUCTIONISM

Social constructionism cannot be reduced to a fixed set of principles, but is a continuously unfolding conversation about the nature of knowledge, truth, objectivity, and our understanding of the world. However, several themes are characteristic of writings that identify themselves as constructionist:

- It is typically assumed that our accounts of the world—scientific and otherwise—are not dictated or determined in any principled way by what there is. Rather, the terms in which the world is understood are generally held to be social artifacts, products of historically situated interchanges among people. Knowledge, truth, objectivity, and rationality are thus achieved within communities for their particular purposes. This line of reasoning does not at all detract from the significance of these communal constructions, whether scientific and otherwise. People's constructions of the world and self are essential constituents of the broader practices of their culture—justifying, sustaining, and transforming various patterns of action. Also, different communities of meaning making may contribute differentially to the resources available to humankind, whether they be scientific, moral, theological, aesthetic, or otherwise.

- Constructionism challenges the warrant of any group—science included—to proclaim truth, knowledge, objectivity, or rationality beyond its perimeters. What is true, real, and good within one tradition may not be within another, and there are no criteria for judging among traditions that are themselves free of traditions, their values, goals, and way of life. Challenging imperialistic or universal claims is as essential as honoring the variety of constructed worlds found throughout the world.

- For constructionists, spoken and written language typically are viewed as the major media of construction.

Language, for the constructionist, does not function as a mirror or map of the world as it is, but as a means of enabling a community to coordinate itself around various actions. In this sense language is a pragmatic device functioning, for example, to organize action, justify and correct behavior, and generate intelligibility.

- The individual is no longer viewed as the basic atom or building block of society. Rather, individual rationality, motivation, conscience, and the like are viewed as relational achievements. The forms and processes of relationship hold the keys to future well-being.

## SOCIAL CONSTRUCTIONISM AND SOCIAL SCIENCE

The social constructionist views favored by this composite of developments offer an alternative to traditional empiricist accounts of science and human understanding. As the constructionist alternative has developed, one may discriminate between two phases, *deconstructive* and *reconstructive.* In the former phase, pivotal assumptions of scientific rationality, along with bodies of empirically justified knowledge claims, are placed in question. Thus, an extensive body of literature has emerged, questioning the warrant and the ideological implications of claims to truth, empirical hypothesis testing, universal rationality, laws of human functioning, and so on.

Immersion in the literature alone might lead some to the conclusion that social constructionism is nihilistic in its aims. However, as many believe, the deconstructive process is only a necessary prolegomenon to reconstructive undertakings. With traditions denaturalized, the way is opened for considering more adequate futures. Within the reconstructive phase, the chief focus is on ways in which scientific inquiry, informed by constructionist views, can more effectively serve the society of which it is a part. From this emerging sensibility, several developments are noteworthy. First, constructionist ideas place a strong emphasis on theoretical creativity; rather than "mapping the world as it is," the invitation is to create intelligibilities that may help us to build new futures. Theories of collaborative cognition, distributed learning, the relational self, and actor-networks are illustrative. Second, constructionism has stimulated much work in cultural study, the critical and illuminating

examination of everyday life practices and artifacts. Third, constructionist ideas have lent themselves to a variety of new research methodologies. Such methods differ from the traditional empiricist orientations in stressing multiple perspectives, political consequences, collaborative knowledge making, and non-elitist forms of representation. Finally, constructionist ideas have helped to generate a range of new practices in therapy, organizational change, and education in particular. Many scholars also find that in challenging disciplinary boundaries to knowledge, constructionist ideas invite broad-ranging dialogue. Thus, new areas of interest have been spawned, linking, for example, theology and constructionism, literary theory and social movements, and personality study and ethical theory.

## THE CONTEXT OF DISTANCE LEARNING

Distance learning uses a wide range of information technologies that provide learning opportunities outside the boundaries of the traditional classroom. New technologies—the Internet, digital TV, CD-ROMs, e-mail, video teleconferencing, newsgroups, chat rooms, instructional software, interactive virtual classrooms, and streaming videos—are making educational resources available to a broader public. In particular, the world is witnessing a rapid growth of asynchronous distance education. Asynchronous learning is a "pull" mode in which students work at their own pace, with unlimited availability of learning resources, any time of the day or night. Students can learn within the comfort of their own homes, the workplace, the library, or virtually anyplace they may have access to the relevant technology. Such flexible scheduling is more congenial than traditional education to career and family needs; it is also creating a new population of adult learners. In many cases, students log in when it is convenient for them; they can review prerecorded lectures if they miss them when they were delivered in "real time."

Web-based courses extend the reach and capacities of universities. Universities now boast that they are "global campuses," accessible to anyone on the Internet. A resident of Alabama can receive a degree from an institution in New York without ever visiting that state. The University of Phoenix online education program is so successful that it has created new online doctoral programs, and is the fastest growing university in the world. One can enter the Web and experience an interactive tutorial on an array of topics, from

Basic Accounting to Kinship and Social Organization. In the parlance of distributed learning, there is a pervasive tendency to think of learning in terms of the individual agent. Learning is geared to individual work schedules, individual skill levels, and individual motivation. It is the individual who benefits from education and learning opportunities; the individual observes, reflects, enters data, writes, speaks, builds skills and competencies, and finally demonstrates successful learning through skill assessment and testing.

## THE INDIVIDUALIST ORIENTATION TO DISTRIBUTED LEARNING

Much of our thinking about learning and education are products of an Enlightenment tradition that posits individual minds capable of acquiring knowledge about the external world. Following this Cartesian tradition, the most important skill necessary for developing knowledge is rational thought. Knowledge is the outcome of careful reasoning and observation: Individuals accumulate objective knowledge when they have access to "facts" and rigorously reason about their observable effects in the external world. In the Enlightenment tradition, barriers to objectivity, such as desire, bias, and motivation, are to be eliminated. Education is seen as liberating; individuals learn, grow, and develop as they accumulate objective knowledge about the world.

The traditional model of education, not surprisingly, resonates with the Enlightenment view of knowledge and posits learners as self-contained, detached, unbiased, unemotional individual agents. Paulo Freire refers to the "banking concept" of education. In this view, learning occurs when the riches of knowledge are deposited into the empty vault of the learner's mind. Here, teachers see students as blank slates and students see teachers as unquestionable authority. Often, this view lends itself to a mode of memorization of information that the teacher provides, while the student accepts that what the teacher presents is true, context-free fact. Following the banking metaphor, the student receives, files, and stores the deposits. Teachers make information available in various currencies, such as lectures, books, and blackboard outlines; or perhaps CD-ROMS, streaming videos, and self-paced software packages. A successful learning experience under this concept is one in which students are expectant receptacles who leave the classroom or the computer terminal enriched with the teacher's knowledge.

There is some indication that the educational community continues to frame distributed learning in banking terms. Online learning and computerized training are depicted as transferring preselected, ready-made knowledge that has already been approved by some distant, invisible authority. E-learning has been depicted in metaphors of commerce and capitalist exchange. Education is a commodity that is "delivered"; skills, like products, are "acquired." We hear of new e-superlearners, "whiz kids," and "hyper learners" and are witnessing new levels of professional certification, including software engineers and network engineers. Learning is paced by the student's ability, initiative, and "capacity to acquire material." Various evaluation models propose measuring inputs, processes, and outcomes; accreditation bodies closely attend to questions regarding quality of student learning and offer a variety of assessment techniques, including proposals to measure knowledge and skills, attitudes, values, beliefs, and cognitive outcomes. Administrators diligently measure and compare variable costs and fixed costs. Distributed learning manuals encourage administrators and teachers to weigh the best media choice for transferring a curriculum.

## TOWARD A SOCIAL CONSTRUCTIONIST ALTERNATIVE

As can be seen, a constructionist orientation to knowledge and the individual differs substantially from most existing practices of distance learning. First, constructionism claims that it is in the context of relational exchanges that individual utterances and skills acquire meaning. Thus, distance learning practices that simply make materials available to students, and test them on their level of mastery, are but rudimentary in their ultimate efficacy. Without the kinds of dialogue that enable students to participate in the process of co-construction, the ultimate significance of the learning experience may be minimal. By the same token, the banking concept of education is viewed as problematic. For the constructionist, knowledge gains its significance through its use value within contexts of application. When it is used only for purposes of passing an examination, its potentials are minimized. Further, the common practice of presenting knowledge as authoritative, virtually unassailable, and value neutral is placed in jeopardy. For the constructionist, all knowledge is generated within communities for their own specific purposes, and these purposes are typically wedded to visions of the good. To teach bodies of material without encouraging discussion of their broader sociopolitical implications is virtually a form of proselytization.

There are many developments in the field of education that have either been spawned by constructionist educators or are congenial with constructionist ideas. In the constructionist view, current distance learning practices could be vitally enriched by exploring these developments and experimenting with their pedagogical implications. Specifically, from a constructionist standpoint, current practices might be significantly enhanced by 1) placing greater emphasis on dialogue, both with educators and with fellow participants; 2) broadening the domain of accepted discourse, so that students from varying traditions are given voice; 3) developing contexts for applying the materials presented through existing technologies; and 4) encouraging reflexive dialogue on the broader social and political implications of various bodies of knowledge. Ultimately there are gains to be made by moving from evaluations based on examinations of "the minds of individual students," to dialogue on the multiple, varied, and emerging outcomes of the educational experience.

*—Kenneth V. Gergen*
*—Frank Barrett*

*See also* GRADUATE STUDY; KNOWLEDGE BUILDING/
KNOWLEDGE WORK

## Bibliography

Bruffee, K. A. (1993). *Collaborative learning.* Baltimore: Johns Hopkins University Press.

Bruner, J. (1996). *The culture of education.* Cambridge, MA: Harvard University Press.

Denzin, N., & Lincoln, Y. (Eds.). (2001). *Handbook of qualitative methods.* Thousand Oaks, CA: Sage.

Friere, P. (1985). *The politics of education.* South Hadley, MA: Bergin and Garvey.

Gergen, K. J. (1994). *Realities and relationships.* Cambridge: Harvard University Press.

Gergen, K. J. (1999). *An invitation to social construction.* London: Sage.

Kuhn, T. S. (1970). *The structure of scientific revolutions.* Chicago: University of Chicago Press.

Latour, B. (1987). *Science in action.* Cambridge: Harvard University Press.

Middleton, D., & Edwards, D. (Eds.). (1990). *Collective remembering.* London: Sage.

Sarbin, T., & Kitsuse, J. (Eds.). (1994). *Constructing the social.* London: Sage.

Simons, H. (Ed.). (1990). *Case studies in the rhetoric of the human sciences.* Chicago: University of Chicago Press.

# SOCIAL ISSUES

From the earliest days of the Internet, people have gone online to interact with others in ways encompassing almost all imaginable social relationships and human activities:

People in *virtual communities* use words on screens to exchange pleasantries and argue, engage in intellectual discourse, conduct commerce, exchange knowledge, share emotional support, make plans, brainstorm, gossip, feud, fall in love, find friends and lose them, play games, flirt, create a little high art and a lot of idle talk. (Rheingold, 1993, p. 3)

Internet technologies have spawned the development of online communities that extend beyond geographic boundaries to create global societies of like-minded individuals in virtual space, connected by particular social issues of interest. In short, nearly all aspects of human activity take place online among people who may never meet face-to-face.

## UNDERSTANDING SOCIAL CHANGE: MULTIPLE FACETS AND UNDERSTANDINGS

Historically, technology, culture, and social change are intricately intertwined. The development of the printing press in the 15th century allowed the easy spread of vernacular languages and ideas, expanded the ability and influence of dissident groups to promote their causes, and directly led to the development of the modern "nation-state."

Theories of social change reflect differing understandings about the nature of reality. To some, learning and social change are synonymous. In this view, change is about shifts in ways of understanding the nature of the world. Social change, therefore, is about facilitating individual learning. Social systems then change through the interaction of the newly aware individuals.

Change may be about altering existing social structures or it may be about maintaining and regulating social values. For some, change is objective, measurable, and potentially predictable (also called *positivism*); for others change is an immeasurable, subjective experience for participants in learning activities (also called *post-positivism*). Others see conflict and change, with recurring patterns of dominance, oppression, and emancipation, as the basic characteristic of all social organization. Social constructionists believe every society develops a consensus through its stories and conversations about the nature of "reality." Changing the stories that are told and passed on about reality therefore changes the consensus and leads to social change.

## SOCIAL ISSUES ONLINE

Individuals who engage in online learning have the world as their "virtual" community, even while they continue to live in, and influence, their local communities. The online, distributed environment changes the lives of individuals, communities, and societies in paradoxical ways: It is empowering yet colonizing, liberating yet controlling and even addictive, global yet intensely personal. Social issues may concern social justice, reforming existing social values, or extending social values to those who had been excluded from them. They may promote a particular political, governmental, or corporate action. They may try to preserve the status quo; strengthen resistance against new, democratic, socialist, totalitarian, or "immoral" values; or seek to return social values to an earlier "golden era."

Prior to the introduction of e-mail (1971), the Internet (1980), the World Wide Web (1992), and hypertext graphic browsers (Mosaic, 1993), groups promoting social change agendas were predominantly local organizations. These groups are now online, where they organize and develop strategies for promoting their issues on local, state, national, and international levels through online communication. Some online communities remain out of the public eye in order to engage more freely in their interests or to instigate subversive radical change or resistance.

## DISTRIBUTED LEARNING AND LOCAL COMMUNITY CHANGE

Extending education beyond a privileged few and increasing access to community-based education has always promoted social change. Paulo Freire's successful literacy campaign with peasants in Brazil in the 1960s involved a rediscovery of the principle that adults can successfully learn—provided there is a clear motivating purpose for learning. The need for decent housing, employment, clean water, sanitation, and health care provided the critical motivation for learning how to write protest letters to the Brazilian government. Freire's participatory learning process became a model for adult learning emulated by educators on a global scale, including the development of online communities of learners.

With access to the Internet and online education rapidly expanding within developed and developing countries, we are just beginning to see its social impact. The nature of this influence is associated with social issues such as government accessibility and accountability, equality, and freedom from oppression, censorship, and constraints. People who engage in online learning communities continue to reside and work in their local community yet share ideas and learning with others living almost anywhere, often in other countries, and with different cultures, values, and first languages. The exchange of ideas in online communities may fuel social change in ways unanticipated by those who introduce distributed learning, as participants become contributors as well as the recipients of ideas. Even in remote and economically poor communities, people are linking their local communities with global online learning communities and sharing ideas, information, and values. Many examples exist of Internet-based learning activities in global and multicultural education, among many school and community-based learning topics, through direct interactions with other learners across the globe.

Social change is constrained when the content and format of online learning is controlled by network policies, censorship, and other restrictions. However, attempts to limit online learning may serve to increase change as technical restrictions are often bypassed through the use of private Web sites and e-mail communication that is beyond formal control.

## PARTICIPATORY DEVELOPMENT AND THE DIGITAL DIVIDE

There is concern about "electronic colonization" in which a global pop culture and dominant languages, such as English, overwhelm local languages and cultures. Participation in online dialogue requires both literate participants and adequate technology.

The online world excludes languages with no written form and people without Internet access.

Participatory development of communication resources became established in the late 1970s through UNESCO initiatives that emphasized access, participation, and self-management in economic, social, cultural, and political activities. A number of foundations, notably the Markle Foundation (http://www.markle.org), fund technology and grassroots policy solutions in developing countries to promote universal participation in the Internet and address the international "digital divide" between individuals with technological resources and the vast majority of the world without such access.

The advent of the World Wide Web and the loosening of commercial restrictions on the Internet (1992) led to the expansion of *freenets,* noncommercial local Internet service providers (ISPs), across the United States and Canada dedicated to removing economic barriers to online participation and creating venues for online communities. Some of these freenets began as e-mail bulletin board systems. A well-known example is the Whole Earth 'Lectronic Link (WELL) (http://www.well.org), in the San Francisco Bay area, co-founded in 1985 by Stewart Brand and Larry Brilliant to spark dialogue about the diverse topics in Brand's Whole Earth Catalog.

Initial efforts to increase online access in underserved communities have focused on increasing the number of computers and building the communications infrastructure. For example, Apple computers made a strategic decision in the 1980s to give Apple computers to schools, even though few software programs were initially available. Less attention has been given to the design of culturally appropriate pedagogies and software content among those whose language and/or culture differs from those who supply the technologies.

Differences such as age, gender, ethnicity, language, nationality, abilities, socioeconomics, and education influence the ways in which people learn. The online learning environment erases some of the visible potential obstacles in face-to-face learning programs, such as gender, race, age, or disability, and also increases participation from individuals who prefer having time to compose their thoughts in the online environment rather than interacting face-to-face.

As in local communities, in online meeting places there are different ways of engaging, with some people participating in most of the conversation, while others read the messages but remain silent.

## ONLINE SOCIAL CHANGE MOVEMENTS

Social change movements emerge from within online communities. Whether the social change movement is focused on achieving a specific end goal or is a sustained virtual meeting of people with common professional or social interests, the online environment is a powerful meeting place for generating collective action. People who have never met in person—and who may differ in age, language, ethnicity, or socioeconomic situations—use the online environment to support each other and promote shared interests. Through Web sites, newsgroups, and e-mail listservs, the Internet helps groups shape a coherent advocacy voice for public accessibility policy issues with regard to these differences in language, race, disability, culture, age, gender, socioeconomic status, and in other areas such as health care, law, and education.

Web sites may be fully open to the public, with no registration required, or may restrict access to members only. Some online communities are designed to remain hidden from view by nonmembers. Groups as diverse as pro-life and pro-choice advocates, advocates for the homeless, and independent news broadcasters all use online communication as a political tool to share information with each other—and to protect themselves from uninvited outsiders.

## HOME ON THE WEB

Online communities are "home" to people who consider virtual affiliations to be as important as in-person relationships. Virtual communities based on nationality keep people connected with others from their homeland, even as they immigrate to other countries. Through online connections via Web-based forums, news sites, e-mail, and other forms of communication, there is a continuous flow of ideas and information between people who remain in the homeland and those who immigrate to other countries. With this sustained and frequent communication, social change is inevitable among both those who have left and those who remain at home.

Other forms of virtual communities are created by people who share religious, ethnic, language, or other unique bonds and commitments. People may worship together, with online celebrations of rituals and ceremonies.

## ONLINE LEARNING AND DISSIDENT ACTIVISM

The Internet has raised the capacity of dissidents to extend their messages, unhampered by geographic and economic barriers. Through e-mail messages and newsletters, linked to their Web sites, community activists and other resistance groups try to increase the numbers of people who hear their messages. Some activist virtual communities sponsor online petitions and surveys in support of social change. E-mail petitions and surveys are easy to create and distribute, but often have low response rates. The casual construction of many of these instruments leads to unreliable and potentially invalid results that cannot be generalized beyond the individuals who responded. Web-based petitions are harder to create, but there is reliable control over who can electronically sign a petition, ensuring all targeted responders have access to the program. Online letter sign-on petitions are sent to a specific person in the government or another institution, but often have limited effectiveness. Typically, institutions and government assign a lower weight to e-mail "sign-on" letters when compared to individually composed e-mail letters, which, in turn, are given less value than handwritten letters sent via post.

Activist coalitions flourish within educational communities, with or without the consent and support of the academic administration. With the advent of the Internet, students and faculty alike use Web sites and e-mail to distribute information and join with others who share their goals. Independence movements in Burma, Tibet, and Malawi are led by students sharing technology, helping fellow expatriates go online, and building support for democratic resistance movements. Independent news services are created and maintained by people with university or community college connections. These news services, built and managed by volunteers, are linked together globally, creating an international network of independent news sources that publish their own perspectives on local and global issues—promoting social change through alternative online learning.

Distributed online learning will continue to impact social issues as millions of people, previously excluded because of social, physical, economic, language, geography, and other barriers, become part of the global exchange of ideas and information on social issues. As e-mail and Web access continue to expand in all areas of the globe, whether sponsored by corporate interests, public foundations, or personal initiatives, these massive increases in accessibility to the world's knowledge are creating far-reaching social change.

—*Niels Agger-Gupta*

*See also* Cultural Access/Digital Divide; Demographics; Globalization

### Bibliography

De Vaney, A., Gance, S., & Ma, Y. (Eds.). (2000). *Technology and resistance: Digital communications and new coalitions around the world* (Vol. 59). New York: Peter Lang.

Engel, C., & Keller, K. H. (Eds.). (2000). *Understanding the impact of global networks on local social, political and cultural values* (Vol. 42). Baden-Baden, Germany: Nomos.

Harasim, L. (Ed.). (1993). *Global networks: Computers and international communication.* Cambridge: The MIT Press.

Hill, K. A., & Hughs, J. E. (1998). *Cyberpolitics: Citizen activism in the age of the Internet.* New York: Rowman & Littlefield.

Hobart, M. E., & Schiffman, Z. S. (1998). *Information ages: Literacy, numeracy and the computer revolution.* Baltimore, MD: The Johns Hopkins University Press.

Horton, M., & Freire, P. (1990). *We make the road by walking: Conversations on education and social change.* Philadelphia: Temple University Press.

Kling, R. (Ed.). (1991). *Computerization and controversy: Value conflicts and social choices* (2nd ed.). San Diego: Academic.

Rheingold, H. (1993, 1994). *The virtual community: Homesteading on the electronic frontier.* New York: Harper Perennial (originally published by Addison-Wesley).

U.S. Department of Commerce—Economics and Statistics Administration. (2002). *A nation online: How Americans are expanding their use of the Internet.* Retrieved from http://www.esa.doc.gov/nationonline.cfm.

## SOCIOCULTURAL PERSPECTIVES

Social and cultural perspectives on learning suggest that all learning (and the knowledge that results from it) is distributed—not only across space and time, but also across artifacts, bodies, and social groups. In this regard, such a perspective contrasts strongly with more conventional learning perspectives. The latter, in keeping with psychological assumptions, focus primarily on the minds of individuals. Thus, conventional perspectives allow for learning to be distributed across space and time but subordinate or simply reject other forms of distribution. So where social and cultural perspectives focus on groups, social practice, and human activity, conventional perspectives view learning primarily in terms of individual minds. Context—social or material—becomes at best a useful prop, but for the most part, a distraction. Although the pragmatic philosopher and educational pioneer John Dewey clearly saw learning as situated in social and material contexts, and although the work of Russian psychologists such as Vygotsky and Lyontev has seeped into cognitive science, in general, modern Western education has held closely to the psychological-individualist viewpoint. This viewpoint is clearly reflected in the history of testing, which has primarily sought to assess individuals in isolation. Social and cultural approaches to learning would suggest that what is primarily tested in such circumstances is the ability to take tests. Thus, from one perspective the issue of "transfer" (from the setting of education and testing to the setting of practice) is a major puzzle; from the other it is simply an inevitable outcome of the way learning is approached. Given the contrast between these perspectives, there is inevitably significant tension between the sociocultural and the psychological-individualist camps—a tension that increases around discussions of appropriate technologies for distributing learning.

By the end of the twentieth century, the hold that the psychological point of view had over learning (and consequently over the design of learning environments) faced serious challenges, both pragmatic and theoretical. Pragmatically, it had become increasingly clear that the attempt to prepare and test people individually and in isolation for a world in which they are expected to work collaboratively and in context is self-evidently problematic. (A noteworthy survey revealed that graduates of the most celebrated business schools—Harvard, Wharton, and Stanford, among them—were held in surprisingly low esteem by business recruiters. These graduates, the recruiters argued, were so fiercely individualistic and competitive that it was hard to integrate them into a workplace.)

Increasingly, educators have sought to devise collaborative forms of education, particularly in vocational and professional schools. Such attempts nonetheless remained handicapped by, on the one hand, highly individualizing technologies, and on the other, the stubborn belief that the learning that goes on in such environments can be traced to and assessed in the individual participants. Consequently, learners in collaborative environments often find themselves nonetheless addressed (by technologies), assessed, and rewarded individually.

Pragmatic doubts about the individualist and mentalist approach reflect underlying theoretical claims of sociocultural theorists that learning is situated. We all learn in context. Our ability to use what we learn reflects both the content of learning and the context of use. Context here includes the bodies, the artifacts, the people, and the institutions involved. Learning is not, then, merely the acquisition of facts or routines. Nor is performance their reiteration. Rather, learning involves developing the ability to participate in social practices. As the philosopher Gilbert Ryle suggested, there is a critical distinction between "know that," the knowledge of facts, and "know how," the ability to put those facts to use in socially recognized ways. Learning the rules of chess, to use Ryle's example, is not the same as learning how to play chess in ways that other chess players accept. Learning to be a psychologist requires more than the acquisition of the facts of psychology. And, Ryle notes, "we learn how through practice." By practice, Ryle emphatically does not mean by rote exercise. He uses the term in the way it is used when we talk of medical or legal practice, reflecting appropriate engagement in complex social behavior.

So a sociocultural view of learning suggests that learning is not reflected in the content of an isolated mind. Rather, learning reflects and is reflected in engagement with and participation in social practices—in the communities and the institutions that help constitute that practice. In learning, people are implicitly or explicitly developing a social identity—learning how to be a practitioner and to be recognized by other practitioners. (Thus one thing that schoolchildren learn with consummate skill is the practice of being a school child.) And this is achieved by working with practitioners and using the tools they use in authentic practice. Of course, not all learning is so clearly oriented toward a particular practice. Equally, it is not simply a process of building storehouses of information in the mind.

Nonetheless, what people learn is inevitably assimilated to the identity they are in the process of developing. Learning is then very much closer to the concept of *Bildung* than of building, to notions of formation than of information. Although most practices require a significant portion of "know that," this generally proves unserviceable without participation in the requisite "know how." And know how resides in and is distributed across social communities into which, as a process of learning in practice, learners become members.

As learning is distributed across artifacts as well as across practice and practitioners, changes in the types of artifacts used can have significant effects on learning processes. Learning a practice, after all, includes learning to use the tools of that practice appropriately. Plato presumably recognized this link between learning and tools. His instinctive distaste for books appears to reflect a fear that these new tools would effect a fundamentally different kind of distribution (which they did). It is not surprising, then, that new discussions of distributed learning arise in the context of the (relatively) newly available digital tools and that arguments about new tools (and thus, implicitly if not explicitly, new distributions) can be fierce. (Some arguments seem to assume that new distributions will inevitably be more egalitarian; others deny the inevitability of such outcomes.)

Yet the availability of new artifacts has produced a curious paradox. For although their very significance suggests that learning is not simply situated in individual minds but is distributed across artifacts and the social groups that use them, in education many new technologies initially heightened the focus on individuals and information in isolation. And it deepened, in many cases, the antipathy of some learning technologists to sociocultural theories (and vice versa). So although new communications artifacts offer intriguing new ways to help bring people into communities of practice, some technology design seems more fit for maintaining and perfecting isolation. The prime advantage of distributed learning, from this viewpoint, is in allowing people to supersede not only time and space, but also the campus, the classroom, the worksite, and other repositories of social context. (Indeed, although the book and the chalkboard are readily taken to be learning technologies, the campus, classroom, and worksite rarely are.) If learning is taken as little more than a quest for information, motivated by individual need, then, as some have suggested, this quest may best be served by software agents that can recognize this need and find the best available means in a digital network to provide it. From this perspective, one can become a psychologist without ever having to deal with a human subject, a fellow learner, or a practitioner. The critical question, of course, is whether learning can be redefined in this way.

That some new distributed learning technologies seem inherently to answer "yes" reflects the deep roots that modern educational technologies still have in artificial intelligence (AI). Computers and minds, AI assumed, work in similar ways. (The idea that the mind may not be a Turing machine is rarely discussed.) Both can be depicted as primarily information processors. And both are highly individual. As computing itself has become more distributed and less easily isolated to particular machines, so this view of learning (and AI) has become less plausible even to those who still equate minds and computers. Nonetheless, much learning technology still targets individuals in isolation from peers, practitioners, and practices. The way the campus and the classroom demanded that people come together and that the book's stable form helped enact communities of readers thus appear simply as defects of these older technologies. Seeking to rise above these defects, some distributive technologies seek to make learning independent of time, place, and social demands. Consequently, the idea of distance education has received a lot of attention, although the temporality of asynchronous learning has started to gain almost as much importance as the spatiality of distance learning.

The demands of time and space can indeed be extremely constraining. But, and this is easily overlooked, they can also be extremely resourceful. And the ability to transcend time and space makes it easy to overlook other important issues. Britain's Open University (OU), for example, is often held up as the cynosure of distance education. Yet the OU didn't actually face unprecedented demands of physical distance. Britain, after all, is a remarkably small island with a disproportionately large population and a significant number of institutions of higher education. The distance that the OU bridged was principally a matter of social distance. When the OU was developed, social background cut large numbers of people off from higher education. The OU skillfully addressed that problem. Yet discussions of new distance technologies for learning rarely give social distance as much consideration as geographical distance.

The technologies of the OU in its early days— letters, books, radio, television, and videotape, and, significantly, summer schools and weekend workshops—did not simply provide individuals with access to information. They also gave access to communities of learners and scholars, helping to bind isolated people into the world of higher education and scholarship. The modern technological imperative often seeks the reverse, to free people from the need to be bound together. As such, it still favors a psychological-individual view of learning and rejects sociocultural arguments. Yet there is nothing inherent in the technology (its roots in AI and psychology aside) that demands this. It is quite plausible to consider the task of design as one of freeing people from restrictions of space and time while nonetheless helping to bind them into learning communities, connecting them to practitioners and practices in new and powerful ways. But these two paradigms are quite distinct, one focused on individuals and information, the other on communities and the communication of social practice. Hence the two perspectives of distributed learning lead to quite different views of what distribution is and how it can be supported.

*—Paul Duguid*

*See also* CAFÉ; DEMOGRAPHICS; LEARNING COMMUNITIES; SCHOLAR PRACTITIONER MODEL

## Bibliography

Engestrom, Yrjo, & Middleton, David. (Eds.). (1996). *Cognition and communication at work.* New York: Cambridge University Press.

Lave, Jean, & Wenger, Etienne. (1991). *Situated learning: Legitimate peripheral participation.* New York: Cambridge University Press.

Ryle, Gilbert. (1949). *The concept of mind.* London: Hutchinson.

Twigg, Carol. (2000). Distance education: An oxymoron? *Ubiquity: An ACM IT Magazine and Forum.* Retrieved from http://www.acm.org/ubiquity/views/c_twigg_1.html.

Wenger, Etienne. (1987). *Artificial intelligence and tutoring systems: Computational and cognitive approaches to the communication of knowledge.* Los Altos, CA: Morgan Kaufmann.

# SOCIOTECHNICAL ISSUES

The current framework for sociotechnical systems (STS) can be traced to the groundbreaking action-science studies carried out by Fred Emery and Eric Trist. Their revolutionary experiments first took place in Great Britain in 1949 in a South Yorkshire coal mine. Coal being then the primary source of energy, organizational researchers continually monitored and evaluated such factors as operational efficiency, work group productivity, morale, and job satisfaction. At the South Yorkshire mine, Trist observed the emergence of a novel work group phenomenon consisting of highly collaborative and self-regulating work teams. Although the current *Ortgeist* (spirit of the place) had become progressively more mechanized, conversely these autonomous work groups demonstrated cooperation and commitment, outperforming traditionally managed bureaucratic operations set forth as one-man–one-task roles. Thanks to the studies of Emery and Trist, organizational managers began to consider the relations between both social and technical systems.

It was Trist who coined the phrase *sociotechnical system*—the interaction of people (a social system) with tools and techniques (a technical system). Sociotechnical studies approached the organization as a social system focusing wholly on group relations in depth on three levels—*primary work systems, whole organization systems,* and *macrosocial systems.* Primary work systems consist of one or more face-to-face work units each collaborating jointly on set tasks, usually with support from specialist personnel and representatives of management plus the relevant equipment and other resources. Whole organization systems involve an enterprise-wide effort. "At one limit to these would be plants or equivalent self-standing workplaces. At the other they would be entire corporations or public agencies" (Trist, 1981, p. 11). Finally, macrosocial systems include systems in communities and entire business sectors as well as societal institutions.

The sociotechnical process emphasized group relations, empowering autonomous internal regulation. Trist recognized the emergence of this concept as a new organizational paradigm. This novel "organismic" model enabled autonomous work groups to assume responsibility for the entire work cycle. The sociotechnical approach challenged the current mechanistic management paradigm where coordination and control had been externally located at the top of the organizational ladder in a hierarchical management archetype, where the flow of information was situated one-way, top-down. Operational decisions were firmly dictated by the organization's supervisors. Sociotechnical systems, on the other hand, focused on the relationship between perception and action, thereby creating enabling constructs for shared values and collaborative decision making. Sociotechnical tools and techniques commonly combined comparative and longitudinal evaluation with action learning. An action research process also known as *praxis* directed system members toward action opportunities, providing feedback at all levels regarding the changes being implemented within dynamic and living organizations, institutions, and entire communities.

Today, organizational managers who advocate sociotechnical systems seek to create enabling constructs using information systems (IS), for instance, to accelerate communication, learning, and knowledge sharing. STSs represent an interpretive process made possible by optimizing the "goodness of fit" between technology and human systems. Indeed, multi-factor analysis suggests that by maximizing the degree of self-regulation, work group productivity and job satisfaction will be consistently higher. Thus, sociotechnical systems create the organizational context for knowledge sharing, learning, and innovation, enabling work groups to think and learn collaboratively. This allows them to develop original work patterns, maintain flexibility, and achieve competitive advantage.

## KEY INFLUENCES

The sociotechnical approach was developed as a radical alternative to Frederick Taylor's concept of scientific management, which attempted to improve productivity through psychosocial means. Taylor's ideas appeared to work and so his "stick-and-carrot" psychology had enormous influence among management at that time, and still does. It is believed that Taylor's scientific management influenced Emery and Trist in the conceptual reframing of work organizations as sociotechnical systems. In addition, sociotechnical systems evolved along with the *open systems* notion of self-regulation and what biologist Ludwig von Bertalanffy referred to as *equifinality,* meaning different paths leading to the same place;

that is, systems somehow link up and influence one another. This postmodern principle shaped both research methodology and project design, drawing attention to the self-regulating properties of an organization continuously evolving, adapting to changes in its environment from the inside out and outside in.

Perhaps the most significant influences came from London's Tavistock Institute of Human Relations, of which Eric Trist was a founding member, as well as from Kurt Lewin's action research in the United States. Both Lewin in the United States and the Tavistock Institute in the United Kingdom approach initiating significant changes in organizations by applying theory to practice, utilizing participatory action research. Trist also collaborated closely with Wilfred Bion, a psychiatrist who devised the leaderless group method. Bion conducted studies in parallel with Lewin's action research. In 1957, the Tavistock Institute pioneered a new form of participatory action learning based on Bion's "T-groups"—a learning system in which the control is shifted to the organization's members.

The general aim of Tavistock was, and still is, to promote social innovation in both private and public institutions, building on the capacity to envision options other than repetition and reproduction of past behavior. Although sociotechnical thinking dominated action research worldwide, it was the Tavistock exposition of the relationship between participatory research and its implications for action opportunities that provided credence to the sociotechnical process for organizational development and change.

## PRINCIPAL WORK DESIGN

The STS work design is based on the premise that outcomes such as work group productivity and job satisfaction can be manipulated by jointly optimizing both the social and technical factors of the workplace. Further, STS embraces the strategic choice model. From this perspective, organizational members within work groups have some agency of choice—adjusting, interpreting, and monitoring the technology and not the other way around. Although the research idiom is action science, the reporting protocol is the case study.

The sociotechnical experience may be carried out at any one of three broad levels, from micro to macro. It is an integral and multidimensional process in that each level eclipses and transcends the prior level; that is, each level is interrelated and interconnected. As mentioned earlier, *primary work systems* are the small work units or subsystems ensconced throughout the whole organization, such as a line department or service unit; *whole organization systems* are larger enterprise-wide systems consisting of several work units; and *macrosocial systems* embody community-wide systems and institutions operating within an industry sector.

These three stages of development involve within group and between group experiences, but it is the conscious and unconscious encounters between individuals that most influence the group's patterns of interaction. It is an emotional as well as cognitive experience in that STS empowers organizational members to ask questions and challenge assumptions. This shifts the locus of responsibility from outside the group to inside, and it is this shift in consciousness that creates opportunities for original learning and knowledge discourse. It also creates a space of uncertainty because the STS learning process requires that its participants acknowledge when something does not work. Trist observed that changes in technology bring about changes in values, cognitive structures, lifestyles, habitats, and communications. Sociotechnical phenomena are both contextual and organizational. Being both enabled and constrained by technological structures often results in regressive patterns of interaction. This paradox also accounts for the STS phenomena of "interpretive flexibility" and breakthrough learning.

## DEVELOPMENTS IN SOCIOTECHNICAL SYSTEMS

The Internet and information systems (IS) hold the potential to link information technology (IT), such as search engines, message boards, e-zines, and knowledge management (KM), for instance, together with "tacit" experiences that connect people with technology. In every aspect this has the appearance of a sociotechnical experience. Today, many organizations are developing KM systems that are intended to increase the flow of knowledge at multiple levels: in the workplace, at home, and in the broader community. With the advent of the Internet, work experiences continue to transform from production-oriented to knowledge-centered, from competitive to collaborative, and from mechanistic to organismic. IT and KM provide the technical framework for knowledge sharing while allowing supervisors to manage the boundary conditions of the workplace environment.

As such, autonomous work groups have once again emerged, freeing their members to flexibly manage their own activities.

It is this continued redirection away from one person/one task micromanagement and toward information exchange and the advancement of knowledge technology that is fueling the re-emergence of sociotechnical systems at the primary group and organizational level. The innovations of many entrepreneurs and the combined knowledge derived from "think tanks," "skunk-works," and rogue subgroups within organizations are contributing to the advancements that continue to connect us socially and technically. Indeed, producing and sharing knowledge is a key characteristic of sociotechnical systems. Current IT and KM systems attempt to shrink the epistemic gap by creating a virtual space for collaborative learning. In this view, autonomous work groups enact common values, social cooperation, and self-control. After all, the Internet is fundamentally based on the cybernetic concept of self-regulation. Trist always believed that a catalyst for change was new technology—more complex primary work systems would emerge as computer-aided technology advanced. This appears to be so.

On the surface, IT, KM, and e-learning have the appearance of a true sociotechnical system. But not all efforts to connect people with technology are sociotechnical systems. Emery distinguished between *operative* and *regulative* institutions. Sociotechnical systems are exclusively operative. The vast majority of Internet-based learning processes are regulative in that management is primarily concerned with instilling the "interest group's" (those in power positions) values, norms, and goals upon their subordinates. A technocratic approach has the appearance of fitting people with technology; however, such regulative models fail to spark innovation and change.

The Internet exemplifies many of the sociotechnical features first set forth by Emery and Trist. Many organizations are enabling the fit between technology and human systems by applying STS at the primary group and organizational levels. On the Web, virtual learning community members participate in structured and nonstructured learning experiences made possible by open systems or e-learning technology. Another area where STS has once again emerged is online learning or e-learning. Both traditional and nontraditional universities now offer online classes. As it is currently practiced and applied, computer-mediated learning or e-learning connects people with technology. In addition, the open systems nature of e-learning enables collaborative decision making, self-regulation, and work group autonomy. This interface again has the appearance of a sociotechnical system.

A few distance learning programs have emerged with an intentional sociotechnical design. Individuals participating in virtual work groups undergo a transformation through which they establish the validity for new ways of learning and knowing. This type of learning is often an emotional as well as an intellectual experience undertaken in terms of the concept of a learning society. In this example, learning and knowing take place at three levels—the individual level, the group level, and the macrosocial level, where participants are encouraged to apply theory to practice. This is the basis for the researcher/practitioner model. However, the vast majority of distance-learning institutions are much more *regulative,* and are not a genuine STS effort.

Trist often referred to these types of efforts as *technocratic bureaucracies,* overemphasizing the technologies that drive the system from a strictly IT or scientific view that science and technology are the only legitimate and useful modes of knowledge. Trist believed that an overemphasis on an IT solution—a system for change belonging to engineering disciplines far removed from sociotechnical considerations—minimizes the role of the individual and the significance of social interaction. In other words, IT-developed e-learning frameworks often remove responsibility from the individual by placing it instead on the technology. In this view, engineers following the "technological macrosocial imperative" simply design whatever organization the technology seems to require. Proceeding in this way creates barriers that are presumed to be offset by improving socioeconomic conditions. For instance, regulative e-learning resembles that of an online classroom where learning is hierarchical and highly transactional. Information has a price.

## CONCLUDING REMARKS

It is people and not technology that are changing the way organizations share, transfer, and leverage knowledge, presenting sociotechnical concepts to a wider field of possibilities. A new generation of sociotechnical systems is igniting the e-learning revolution. To a great extent, it is the distance learner who is driving these innovations. Over the past few years, an individual's

ability to use technology effectively has begun to catch up with technological developments. Traditional and nontraditional educational institutions, for instance, have searched for new ways to prepare students to become knowledge workers. The result is that technology is now struggling to keep up with user demands. The e-learning revolution is revitalizing STS technologies.

In the 21st century, the technical and societal climates appear positive for sociotechnical systems. The Internet brings together the computer, media, and the distributed intelligence of the family and the community. This constitutes a new basis for the effectiveness of sociotechnical organizations. However, management opposition persists because STS by nature enables collaborative decision making and shared leadership. Management has been reluctant to give up the power and authority they have worked so hard to establish. Indeed, STS challenges the traditional management taboos of sharing information and knowledge with subordinates on a need to know basis only. The central tenet of a technocratic bureaucracy is that decision making is top-down and implementation is bottom up. Amazingly, many postmodern organizational leaders still believe information is best kept in the minds of senior management who have been trained how to use it, make decisions, and implement policy. In this mechanistic model, managers pretend to know and employees pretend to cooperate.

STS continues to struggle within organizations. Under the best of conditions, STS and all change interventions tend to suffer from "fade-out" when the inside champion departs and there is no one to take over the leadership. When this occurs, the organization simply regresses to conventional patterns of interaction. Sociotechnical systems take the shape of organismic self-regulating formations, which enable the emergence of a new leadership paradigm, the integral leader. Effective sociotechnical systems are increasingly more evident and unmistakably integrate both social and technical systems, providing an operative model for integral leadership. Examples are everywhere and include hospital emergency rooms, trauma units, air traffic control centers, and research labs, to name a few. STS exists anywhere self-regulating and autonomous work groups collaborate, share knowledge, and remain agile under turbulent conditions. STS provides the framework for organizational members to lead with confidence in times of uncertainty.

*—John W. Aldridge*

*See also* CORPORATE TRAINING

## Bibliography

Trist, E. L. (1981). The evolution of socio-technical systems: A conceptual framework and an action research program. *Ontario Quality of Working Life Center, Occasional Paper no. 2.*

Weisbord, M. R. (1987). *Productive workplaces: Organizing and managing for dignity, meaning, and community.* San Francisco: Jossey-Bass.

---

# SPECIAL NEEDS POPULATION

When discussing distributed learning, the special needs population consists of persons with disabilities who need special hardware and/or software to permit them to use standard computers easily and efficiently. Actually, some people that are usually included in the special needs population have no problems with computers. Someone who has no use of his or her legs, for example, will have no problems in using a computer. For the most part, the population in question is largely made up of people that were previously considered "print impaired." Someone who is blind cannot read a computer monitor. Someone with low or poor vision will have difficulty seeing the display. Anyone with motor impairments that limit hand functioning will have some degree of difficulty using the keyboard and mouse depending on the degree of that impairment.

Much of the power of digitized information is that it can be input into the computer and output from the computer with a variety of tools. Information is normally input into the computer from the keyboard, but it is also common to do it by scanning information on an optical scanner. The output is commonly output to the monitor and also to a printer. This flexibility of the computer is expanded further by the ability of each individual to tailor many features of the computer's interface to suit personal preferences. The appearance and size of the font on the monitor can be altered to personal taste. The icons can be made larger or smaller and the foreground and background colors can be modified. Larger and brighter fonts on the display can assist someone who is aging. This means that the standard computer can be personalized in limited ways to assist some features of a disability.

It is important to recognize that the world is not actually divided into two categories: able and disabled.

Instead, there is a graduated continuum with fully able at one end and totally disabled at the other end. The special hardware and software used by this so-called special needs population is nothing more than an extension of the modifications to the interface utilized by everyone. If the designers had wished, the features of this special adaptive computer hardware and software could be built into every computer. Adaptive computer technology empowers persons with disabilities like nothing before in history. It opens the world of information and enables people with disabilities to participate more fully in society.

## ALTERNATIVE OUTPUT DEVICES

### Screen Readers

The screen reader is software that takes what is displayed on the monitor and speaks it with synthetic speech. This permits someone who is blind to be a skilled computer user. Not only does it "read" what is being displayed, it enables the user to hear what is being input and allows him or her to catch mistakes. The screen reader can only read text, however. Icons and other graphics need to have a verbal label associated with them so the reader can identify them verbally. Users who are blind cannot, at present, make use of the mouse. Navigating the desktop and programs is done with keystroke alternatives. In most cases this involves the Tab key, the arrows, and the Enter key. The screen reader is an output device, but by speaking keyboard strokes it simultaneously assists the user's input.

### Refreshable Braille Displays

Refreshable Braille displays are a combination of software and hardware. The device is a strip that has a number of movable pins. The strip is attached to the computer and placed below the keyboard. The pins are raised or lowered to represent a line of text in Braille. Depending on the size and cost of a device, it will represent all or part of one line from the computer monitor. In effect, it is a small Braille window into the monitor. It has buttons that enable the user to display different parts of the monitor. The user can also use it to proof what has been input from the keyboard.

### Braille Embosser

This is the equivalent of a printer. Instead of a jet or laser printer, the Braille embosser outputs hard copy Braille for a person who is a Braille reader.

## Screen Magnifiers

Screen magnification software enlarges what is being displayed from 2 to as much as 16 times in size. This enables people with low or limited vision to see what is being displayed. It also permits changing font types and colors. When the material being displayed is enlarged several times, most of it is pushed beyond the edges of the display. The user has to scroll up, down, left, and right with the mouse to get the entire picture. The enlarged letters on the screen also make it simple for the user to check his or her keyboard input and make corrections.

## Show Sounds

For the most part, persons who are deaf have little trouble with computer use. However, it is common for a computer to signal a situation, such as an error message or a notice that new mail has arrived, with a sound. Showing sounds will substitute the computer-generated sound with a visual signal.

## ALTERNATIVE INPUT DEVICES

### Alternative Keyboards

Users with motor impairments that limit their hand movements may use one of several alternative keyboards. There is a one-handed keyboard, where the user depresses combinations of keys instead of a single key to simulate the standard keyboard. There is also an on-screen keyboard, which is software that places a picture of a keyboard at the bottom of the display. The cursor moves left to right across the top row, and when the user signals with a single switch, it stops and begins moving down the column until it receives another signal and then inputs that key into the application being used. So long as the user can manipulate one muscle and trigger a switch, he or she can use the computer. Another device has the user sipping and puffing on a straw switch that sends Morse codes signals to the computer. The code sends letters and the computer inputs that letter as if the equivalent key had been pressed.

### Voice Recognition

Voice recognition software lets a user talk into a microphone, and the computer breaks that input into digitized sound patterns. Very complex software scans those patterns and matches them with letters and phrases. Finally, it outputs to the monitor the text equivalent of the spoken input. The spoken word is transformed into text that can be manipulated in a word processor or output to a printer. Someone who cannot use his or her hands can become an efficient computer user by using this software. Voice recognition software is also useful for people who have carpal tunnel syndrome or repetitive stress injury.

Voice recognition was originally designed for persons with disabilities, but it has come to have general, widespread use. People who never learned to type or keyboard find traditional input tedious and error-prone. Many professionals use this instead of more old-fashioned dictating devices.

## Optical Character Recognition (OCR)

Optical character recognition (OCR) software works in conjunction with a scanner to first make a picture of a page of hard copy print, and then analyze the picture to recognize the text. Finally, the software creates a text file that can be used by a word processor or other text processing software. Technically, this is an input device. However, persons with disabilities are primarily interested in the final output from the text document. People who cannot read the original print page can now use adaptive software to enable them to read the final product from the computer. It indirectly provides access to print materials for the formerly print impaired.

## ADAPTIVE COMPUTER TECHNOLOGY RESOURCES

For more information on adaptive technologies for people with disabilities, look up any of these tools in any search engine. EASI (Equal Access to Software and Information) has a Web page devoted to adaptive hardware and software resources at http://www.rit.edu/~easi/resource.htm.

## THE INTERNET

People who were unable to read print books, papers, and magazines had been starved for information, but the adapted computer has opened the information age to them, enabling them to have independent access to innumerable books, papers, magazines, and much more. They have gone from being the information hungry to experiencing the modern stresses of information overload. In many respects, the Web is more exciting and important to the special needs population than it is for the general public.

Because of the nature of digitized information, the Web has become a dissemination engine for text, graphics, data, audio, and video. Depending on the exact format selected to store and display information, people with disabilities either share in its use or may be excluded from accessing it.

In 2001, the Federal Access Board's Section 508 standards for accessibility took effect. These standards are mandated for all federal Web sites, and they are becoming a model for many other sectors of society. Section 508 requires that all graphics and images have a text label associated with them that can be read by screen reader software and which will identify that graphic or image. Multimedia presentations will provide synchronized captions for users who are deaf, and, when necessary, they will also have an accompanying audio track describing action in videos for users who are blind.

## DISTRIBUTED LEARNING AND USERS WITH DISABILITIES

During the late 1990s, distance learning spread across schools and universities like wildfire. By the early twenty-first century, these same technologies were integrated into the on-campus courses as well, enhancing the role of distributed computing in education. Although this development held the promise of providing a more level playing field for students with disabilities, designers frequently neglected their special needs in creating courseware interfaces.

In the early 1980s a professor at the Rochester Institute of Technology who is blind reported an e-mail interchange with a student who is deaf where she confessed that this was the first time she had "talked" to a teacher without someone in between. The professor was able to grade papers submitted electronically without having someone read them to him, which encouraged his involvement in distance education in the early 1980s (http://www.rit.edu/~nrcgsh/arts/open.htm).

With the coming of the Web, distributed learning systems became highly graphical. Although this created barriers for users who are blind, it was helpful to many students with learning disabilities. The World Wide Web Consortium became concerned with developing design standards that would make the Web universally accessible to users with different software, hardware, and physical disabilities. In 1997 it created the Web Accessibility Initiative (WAI) to create Web guidelines that would make all the features of the Web accessible to users with disabilities using specialized software. These guidelines are available at http://w3.org/wai. In 2001, the U.S. government published mandated standards for federal Web sites; these Section 508 standards are available at http://access-board.gov.

Although there are 14 WAI guidelines and 16 Section 508 standards, there are only a few issues that cause the vast majority of problems. Screen reading software for the blind cannot "read" images. However, if the designer associates a text tag with the image, the software can speak that to the user. With the more recent multiplication of multimedia on the Web, students who are deaf also are shut out of important content. Web designers can now use Synchronized Multimedia Integration Language (SMIL) to stream a text transcription with the audio, providing online captions for these users.

Courseware management system vendors are now going back and building such accessibility features into their systems. Schools and universities are now making faculty and other content providers aware of the need to post content in accessible formats. Educational institutions should be aware that it is the school that is required to provide equal access to learning and not the courseware management system vendor, and schools need to investigate the accessibility of a product before selecting it. EASI has created the National Center for Accessible E-learning (http://www.rit.edu/~easi/index.htm) to be a clearinghouse for information on how to have online learning include students and faculty with disabilities.

The primary advantage of online course content for students with disabilities is that it is in electronic format, making it accessible to them with the use of specialized software on a computer. It transcends the limitations caused by any print impairment that they have. When the course format is asynchronous, students can take as long as they need to read and reply to material. Although online learning also removes the burden of travel to class for students with disabilities, many fear that it will only serve to increase social isolation. However, although it may limit face-to-face isolation, it may actually increase social interaction through online relationships.

*—Norman Coombs*

*See also* ADAPTIVE TECHNOLOGY; DISABILITY LAW; VOICE
ACTIVATION PROGRAMS

## Bibliography

Federal Access Board (Section 508 standards): http://www.
access-board.gov

National Center for Accessible E-learning: http://www.rit.
edu/~easi/index.htm

National Center for Accessible Media: http://ncam.wgbh.
org

Online courses on accessible Web design and other adaptive technology information: http://easi-courses.org

Web Accessibility Initiative: http://www.w3.org/wai/

WebAIM—excellent self-instruction resources: http://www.
webaim.org

# STAFFING

The creation and delivery of Web-based distance learning modules or courses require a team with skills and expertise that vary regarding subject matter, instructional technology, educational psychology, multimedia development, network and Web administration, communication, marketing, help-desk, administration, and training. The needs of the organization, combined with its goals and budget, dictate the combination of these skills required. However, most development and delivery environments must have representation from each area to be effective and successful. This entry describes the skills for each area of expertise and how they impact the design and delivery process. It also describes combinations of expertise required at different stages of development in Web-based learning environments.

## SUBJECT MATTER EXPERTISE

The traditional description of a subject matter expert (SME) is a person with a theoretical and practical knowledge of the content. So the ideal SME for architecture would be a person with an advanced degree, like a Ph.D., in the subject and who has worked as an architect. This type of individual is hard to find, so the SME is often a person who has either one or the other qualification. The SME in many universities may be someone who has earned a terminal degree in the field, but has not necessarily worked outside academia. The experts who have worked outside academia may lack the advanced degrees. If the organization would like both aspects covered in its staff it may be necessary to bring together a team of SMEs consisting of those who have advanced degrees and those who have worked outside academia in their field of expertise.

## INSTRUCTIONAL TECHNOLOGIST

Instructional designers or instructional technologists require expertise in many areas of designing learning environments, including

- Knowledge of instructional design models and theories (such as Dick & Carie's ADDIE, Jonassen's Well-Structured & Ill-Structured Problem Solving, Merrill's Component Display Theory CDT, and motivational models like Keller's Attention, Relevance, Confidence, Satisfaction [ARCS]). The knowledge should extend to understanding the power of multimedia learning environments and applications, including Spiro's Cognitive Flexibility Theory, Mayer's Multimedia Learning, and Salomon & Pea's Computers as Cognitive Tools.
- Learning objectives (such as Bloom's hierarchy— recall, analysis, and synthesis). This also requires an understanding of task analysis of activities (observations, surveys, and interviews to collect data on what steps are necessary to perform a task).
- Instructional strategies (such as advanced organizers, examples, rehearsal, and sequencing).
- Learning styles and individual differences (such as prior knowledge, field independence/dependence, and personality traits).
- Assessment strategies to measure what was learned, how much was learned, and any feedback to the students.
- Evaluation strategies (formative and summative) to evaluate the effectiveness of the learning modules during the development phase as well as at the time of delivery.

## EDUCATIONAL PSYCHOLOGIST

Educational psychology is the basis for most of the research supporting instructional technology. Understanding learners and their needs, as well as understanding how to assess learning, requires people with educational psychology skills. Many areas of research in educational psychology have contributed to the development of collaborative learning, multimedia learning, learner control, adaptive testing, reliability and validity of examinations and other assessments, hypertext interactions, and theories of intelligence and information processing. The educational psychologist on the team should be familiar with these lines of research and be able to apply them to distance learning environments.

## MULTIMEDIA DEVELOPMENT SPECIALIST

Knowing the theoretical basis and research findings of multimedia environments on learning does not translate directly to being able to create such environments. Multimedia specialists are people with expertise in using computer applications to build the necessary interfaces and apply the research findings within the courses. Examples include:

- *Web-page design*—Macromedia Dreamweaver, Microsoft FrontPage
- *Graphics tools*—Adobe Photoshop
- *Animation and video processing*—Macromedia Flash, ColdFusion, Adobe Premiere
- *Interfacing*—PERL or CGI scripts that will connect special tools like databases or spreadsheets to Web-based environments
- *Course management systems*—ANGEL, Blackboard, eCollege, and WebCT

This person's skills must extend to understanding the software and how each piece of software interacts with the variety of Internet browsers on the market (such as Netscape Navigator and Internet Explorer).

## NETWORK AND WEB ADMINISTRATOR

Depending on the organization's level of computer support, the team may need one or more people with skills in purchasing, setting up, and maintaining network servers and hubs and installing software. This role may or may not be combined with Web administration, and requires the skills to create and maintain the Web presence of the organization. The Web administrator must have expertise in both the hardware and software of maintaining Web-based distance learning courses, but also must serve as the leader to maintain consistency and editorial review of the content and uniformity of the organization's image. This role can be critical to an organization that is focused

on projecting a uniform image in all its courses, but less important in an organization that follows a decentralized approach to course design and delivery.

This role is also dependent on the course management system that may be used by the organization. For example, eCollege offers a complete hosting service with support 24 hours a day, 7 days a week, so the organization can concentrate on the course design and delivery and not concentrate on the hardware, maintenance, and support. However, there are costs associated with this method that may not be within the budgets of many organizations.

## COMMUNICATION SPECIALIST

The communication specialist in a Web-based distance learning environment performs many tasks, including reviewing interactions and course content, being the spokesperson for the organization's distance learning opportunities, and coordinating the marketing and help-desk support for all the users (including designers, professors, SMEs, and students).

## MARKETING SPECIALIST

Marketing distance learning programs requires expertise in understanding the organizational direction, reaching a diverse audience, being able to compete in a crowded marketplace, and providing creative originality to advertising. The marketing specialist must have good oral and written communication skills, while also being artistic, understanding the business environment as well as the educational environments, and working in the fast-paced Web-based environment.

## HELP DESK SUPPORT SPECIALIST

Any technology-rich environment usually requires support for all its users in the form of a help desk. This help desk utility is necessary for the designers (who need information about the particular technologies used in their design, operating systems like Windows or UNIX, etc.), professors (e.g., my Web page looks different on different browsers), and students (e.g., How do I log into the course? How do I get Media Player to view the video?).

## TRAINERS

Trainers may or may not be part of the help desk team. They play similar roles in conducting formal training for use of the technologies as well as the delivery of the courses. They are also usually charged with creating written materials that may be sent to users and students on how to download software, how to prepare for the course, how to take a test, and how to view a video. Having trainers assigned to the task makes sure that the instructional designers are not overloaded with both designing and training. It also shows how important the support tasks are to having a smooth effort to design and deliver Web-based courses.

## ADMINISTRATORS/MANAGERS

Hiring people with a variety of skills is not always the final solution. The team needs unifying leadership that sets the goals, interfaces with senior administrators and decision makers, and secures funding. Hiring the team members, setting goals, managing their efforts, communicating with all stakeholders, and planning are also part of the role of manager(s). Web-based learning environments cannot rely on the efforts of professors and designers alone, but must be a priority of the larger organization and must be reflected in the budget. A good manager must be able to see the larger picture and lead the teams as well as work with other decision makers to achieve buy-in from the academic community.

## CONCLUSION

The personnel described in this document have a variety of skills, but they all contribute to a well-designed Web-based distance learning environment. Depending on the course management software chosen by the organization and its needs (small development, with 1 to 5 courses vs. large scale development with full degree programs and 30–50 courses from a variety of departments), this team may vary in numbers and specialties.

*Kay Wijekumar*

**See also** ADMINISTRATIVE LEADERSHIP; OUTSOURCING

# STRATEGIC PLANNING

Strategic planning is the formulation of plans to achieve an organization's long- and short-range goals.

This activity is framed by the decisions and actions that lead to and support the strategic plan and the evaluation and feedback that allow for adjustment to the plan going forward. These preliminary actions include the formulation or clarification of an organization's mission, philosophy, and goals; the evaluation and matching of internal conditions and capabilities with an assessment of the external environment; and the choice of the most desirable options to support the organization's mission.

The actual plan includes long-term objectives and strategies to achieve the most desirable options and the incremental short-term objectives and strategies (usually annual) that support those long-range plans. The plan is supported by details that include information about budget allocations, tasks, people, structures, technologies, and reward systems.

Many people confuse strategy with operational effectiveness. For a business plan to be strategic it will usually focus on the strengths of an organization and its uniqueness in the marketplace. Operational effectiveness or continuous improvement does not necessarily address this uniqueness and may actually serve to dilute it.

The goal of a strategic plan should be to make sure that all activities involved in achieving the final goal are coordinated and support the uniqueness of the organization. The choices about what *not* to include are as important as the choices to be included in the plan. This is especially true of the delivery of the educational offerings that fall under the umbrella of distributed learning. A look at the turbulent history of the distributed learning landscape will suggest some of the dangers of not keeping a tight rein on strategic planning for distributed learning.

## HISTORY OF STRATEGIC PLANNING FOR DISTRIBUTED LEARNING

Distributed learning first emerged as a solution in the private sector in the late 1980s. As companies shifted their operations to international and then global strategies, they needed a way to address the training of widely dispersed populations of employees and customers without incurring excessive expense. Companies began to experiment with a variety of methods to create a "virtual classroom," including

- *Teleconferencing*—Connecting groups of people via telephone

- *Satellite broadcasts and video conferencing*— Connecting groups of people via video, which allowed them to see one another and the instructor and to share their work
- *Computer-based training (CBT)*—A continuum ranging from text and graphics-based presentations to fully interactive multimedia classes
- Training offered via the Internet or a company's extranet

The promise and appeal of a multimedia interactive learning environment seemed as if it would be relatively simple to attain. This did not prove to be the case. The technology was very expensive, averaging $100,000 for one hour of produced instruction. The greatest expense became the cost of keeping the content refreshed and accurate. This issue led to the first attempts at strategic planning within the distributed learning environment. It emerged in two ways. Organizations, in discovering that this effort was not trivial, often either chose to move the technology and planning internally into a more robust "corporate university" setting or chose to outsource the entire effort. Many small distributed learning production companies emerged in response to this growing trend. These companies began to help larger companies focus their distributed learning planning efforts in the following areas: quality content that addressed the goals of the organization; developing infrastructure (delivery and logistics); and developing an overall education strategy that made sense for the business.

Toward the end of the 1990s, the same distributed learning companies began to partner with universities who were starting to target the education dollars of these corporate customers. At first, this partnership worked well because educational institutions could utilize the expertise and technology of the distributed learning company and the distributed learning company could capitalize on the university's ability to offer a full degree program.

By 1999, the trend was moving toward the offering of a degree to individuals from a variety of universities funded by the corporation. By 2000, distance learning companies were participating in the strategic planning of the corporation and offering degrees from universities that met the corporation's specific goals. During this period, the first of three shakeouts occurred. In an effort to ensure content quality and keep the course material accurate, the cost of production per course rose to between $300,000 and $1 million annually. Distance learning companies hoped to be able to broker these courses to a number of universities to recoup their expenses, but this did not prove to be the case. Universities pride themselves on their own courses, and the failure of that strategy proved the undoing of several distributed learning firms.

In 2001, the distributed learning companies who had survived this painful lesson and the market downturn primarily adopted the strategy of developing customized programs for corporations with specific universities. A second shakeout occurred when many distributed learning companies proved unable to manage their university partnerships within the cost constraints dictated by the marketplace.

The most recent shakeout occurred in 2002 as corporations struggled to build strategic "managed" education plans in a bear market economy in collaboration with their distributed learning partners. As money grew tighter, these partners found that they could not fit their educational offerings to the constraints of the diminished corporate infrastructure. They were also faced with educational institutions that had taken the production in-house and were going to market as competitors, often hiring key people from the defunct distributed learning companies. This "managed education" approach, however, continues to be the dominant trend for the distributed learning production companies. It is called business process outsourcing (BPO).

Typically, when universities go to market, they usually take a business-to-consumer approach (B to C). With BPO, the distributed learning vendors are trying to compete by using a business-to-business (B to B) strategy, tying themselves directly to the corporation's strategic missions and developing customized services and solutions. It remains to be seen how well this strategy will work as they are entering a new market relationship with new competitors. They are competing against consulting companies who tend to provide analysis but no solutions (a potential partnering arrangement) and distributed learning software companies who offer diagnostics and their own specific software solutions.

## STRATEGIC PLANNING FOR DISTRIBUTED LEARNING

In the case of distributed learning, the term *strategic planning* is defined as the overarching plan to implement a distance learning methodology as a strategy within the organization. This plan for distributed learning in a private enterprise needs to be grounded in the educational philosophy of the organization. Does the organization want to invest in the intellectual capital of its workforce? Is it expecting a measurable increase in productivity? Is education a well-deserved reward or a reluctantly given benefit? This philosophy will dictate several factors:

- *Program definition*—University portfolio or company-specific customized program
- *Resources*—Course design and course management by internal staff, outsourced services, or automated software system
- *Policies and processes*—Who can participate and when, intellectual property rights, privacy
- *Financial terms*—Full or partial company contribution for university offerings, payment processing, and financing instruments
- *Metrics and reports*—Program performance, participant lifecycle, audits, and benchmarks

These factors along with the organization's infrastructure (or its willingness to commit budget to its infrastructure) will determine reasonable strategies for implementing a distributed learning offering.

In the case of an educational institution either engaged in or looking to enter the distributed learning marketplace, the strategy becomes a little more complicated. In addition to all of the above factors, the institution must calculate the cost of marketing its offerings in a very competitive environment. This is another reason for the proliferation of university/distributed learning provider alliances. Another common strategy to mitigate the competitive risk is the emerging "higher education consortia," in which several universities band together to share the infrastructure, delivery system, and marketing costs. This strategy allows the participating universities to arrive at price parity as they enter the marketplace.

Educational institutions must also coordinate supporting processes such as their application process, registration, student academic counseling, library access, and articulation (transferability of courses) and placement services. These are key to the student interface and can be exceedingly challenging in an online environment. Another set of issues centers on the faculty. The key issue is faculty workload. Other issues include the following: What defines an online course? How many students can participate? How long will the course last? What are the expectations of online faculty availability? The answers to these questions will determine how disparate the institution's online courses are from its traditional courses. A greater difference between these types of courses makes the issue of faculty workload more complex. Universities that differentiate between these two types of courses—for instance, by allowing online courses to move away from the normal semester structure—often struggle with issues of workload equity and what is a reasonable number of courses for a faculty member to teach. Issues can also arise concerning the preparation and training of faculty for the online environment, the conversion and/or development of online courses and whether or not the faculty member will be compensated for that work, and finally, whether the developing faculty member or the institution owns the intellectual property, in this case the developed course. All of these policies and issues need to be thought out in the institutional strategic plan, ensuring that the plan for distributed learning fits with the university's institutional, academic, and financial model.

Whether private organization or educational institution, the variety of factors that must be considered in the delivery of distributed learning make strategic planning critical. Stories of poor transition and failed attempts to deliver on the early promise and potential of this technology, as well as the instances where a clearly defined strategy has provided a viable offering in the marketplace, make a clear case for a careful strategic planning effort.

*—Linda F. Crafts*

*See also* ADMINISTRATIVE LEADERSHIP; ALLIANCES; FINANCE; LEGAL ISSUES

## Bibliography

Brown, Stephen. (2001). Strategic planning for distributed learning. Online Seminar. Retrieved November 15, 2002, from http://distlearn.man.ac.uk?distance/strategic-Planning/IDL-StrategicPlanning.htm.

Graves, William. (2000). The law of the virtual campus. Paper presented at NLII meeting. Retrieved November 15, 2002, from http://www.educause.edu/asp/doclib/abstract.asp?ID=NLI0013.

Hawkins, Brian L. ( July-August 1999). Distributed learning and institutional restructuring. *Educom Review*,

*34*(4). Retrieved November 15, 2002, from http://www. educause.edu/ir/library/html/erm9943.html.

Hawkins, Brian L., & Oblinger, Diana. (2000). Distributed learning. Paper presented at EDUCAUSE. Retrieved November 15, 2002, from http://www.educause.edu/asp/doclib/abstract.asp?ID=EDU0039.

Porter, Michael E. (November-December 1996). What is strategy? *Harvard Business Review,* 61–78.

Virginia Tech Strategic Planning: Distance Learning. (2001). Retrieved November 15, 2002, from http://www.iddl.vt.edu/about/plan.php.

# STREAMING MEDIA

*Streaming media* is a way to deliver digital information via the World Wide Web. Text, audio, graphics, animations, still images, and video data can be distributed from archived files or Webcast live (in real time) to a learner's desktop computer. A hyperlink on a Web page initiates the request for a media file from a streaming media server (computer). Large media files are compressed or encoded into small packets of data in order to be transmitted to the learner's desktop. These packets are sent in continuous streams over network connections from the streaming media server to the user's desktop computer in real time (synchronously). The desktop computer launches a media player (formats include Windows, Real, and QuickTime) that decodes the incoming data and stores them temporarily in a buffer. The media player will begin to show the file when there is a sufficient amount of data in the buffer. New packets of data from the server continuously fill the buffer as the media player uses data, hence the term *real time.* Prior to the development of streaming technology, the user would have to wait for the entire file to download to the hard drive in order to view the media. Streaming media offers student flexibility in the delivery method of instruction (any time, any place) and flexibility in access to a variety of media.

## TECHNICAL CONSIDERATIONS

The amount of data in the buffer and the speed at which the file is delivered and played depends on the network conditions, such as bandwidth rate and traffic demand on the network. Bandwidth is like the "pipeline" for data flow. It refers to the amount of data able to be passed in kilobits per second (Kbps).

Broadband network connections allow data to be sent more quickly to the user's computer, thus allowing more data to be delivered per second. The advantage of streaming packets of information is that the end user can begin to view the media file as soon as enough data is received so that the file appears as a steady stream of audio and video. Additionally, multiple users can have access to the same streams simultaneously.

Because streaming media data are transmitted via networks, the rate of bandwidth available to the network is critical. Broadband network connections (high-speed connections of 200Kbps or higher such as DSL or cable modem) will allow more data to be sent faster. A narrowband (i.e., dial-up modem using a phone line) will limit the speed at which packets of data are delivered to the user. Packets can get lost and out of order depending on bandwidth and network constraints.

The streaming format has unique production concerns due to compression ratios. Depending on available bandwidth, visual information can be lost or picture sizes can be small. Tips for video production are to use optimum lighting, simple backgrounds, and close-up shots, and to limit camera movement. There are a wide range of production values for streaming video depending on the purpose for which it is being used. Examples span from high-end, professionally produced media to student or faculty-produced media. What instructional developers need to keep in mind is that learners' access can be limited by servers, bandwidth, and Internet access. Some of the instructional applications of streaming media have been to use preproduced media, live streams or Webcasts, and live-to-archived files for later viewing.

To distribute and support streaming media involves coordination of institutional resources. Information technology, instructional support, and design personnel need to leverage resources for infrastructural and instructional needs. One of the many considerations is the impact of using streaming media on servers and networks. Another consideration is technical training and support of the instructors and learners.

## INSTRUCTIONAL APPLICATIONS

The instructional use of streaming media should reflect what are known to be effective teaching and learning practices, regardless of the delivery method of instruction. Streaming media delivers highly graphic and visual information and can be a valuable teaching tool. Selection of media should be based on instructional goals and the competencies that learners are to have after instruction.

Because watching a video or listening to audio is inherently passive and not interactive, streaming media best facilitates student learning when used with active instructional strategies. For example, a student could assess his or her own learning by answering a computer-based quiz that checks comprehension of the learning objectives associated with the media clip. Streaming media should support those essential activities in which the student must engage to achieve learning outcomes. To be fully integrated into the instructional design of a course, the learning outcomes expected from the use of streaming media should be measured or assessed. The unique characteristics of streaming media will add value to the instructional process if it is integrated into the overall design of the learning experience.

Streaming media add value if information is provided that is otherwise unavailable to the student. Additionally, media add value if the learner has opportunities to practice new skills and knowledge and to engage in construction of knowledge. For example, students in nursing programs can view demonstrations and procedures multiple times, if necessary, prior to hands-on practice. Conceptual knowledge, such as modeling of physics principles, can be demonstrated by multimedia.

One example of using streaming media to foster peer interaction is to deliver professionally produced case studies so learners can discuss or offer solutions via electronic forums or threaded discussion. At the other end of the spectrum, students could actually create streaming media themselves as a learning activity, depending on the identified instructional outcomes.

A learner can also select the media that match the preferred personal learning style: text, graphics, audio, or visual. Animated models, charts, and graphs, which learners can manipulate, will appeal to kinesthetic learners. Examples exist of graphical or animated programs for demonstrating physics and chemistry that calculate different outputs depending on the values entered by the learner. Some of the laboratory simulations developed for Web delivery are very interactive.

## CONCLUDING COMMENTS

Streaming media offers student flexibility in the delivery method of instruction (any time, any place) and flexibility in access to a variety of media. When used to address specific learning objectives, combined with active learning strategies (such as collaborations and threaded discussions) and fully integrated into the instructional design, streaming media add value to the learning environment.

To successfully distribute streaming media, the demands on institutional infrastructure and support services can be great. Media servers and high speed networks with adequate bandwidth are required. With coordination and planning to meet the needs of the end users, some of the issues can be ameliorated.

—*Martha Meacham*

***See also*** HYPERMEDIA; INFORMATION RETRIEVAL; MEDIA

## Bibliography

Berge, Z. (1996). Where interaction intersects time. *MC Journal: The Journal of Academic Media Librarianship*, *4*, 1. Retrieved from http://wings.buffalo.edu/publications/mcjrnl/v4n1/berge.html.

Brey, R., Carter, W., & Meacham, M. (2002). *Effective use of streaming media for e-learning and its impact on it planning and operations*. EduCause regional conference, EduTex, Austin, TX. Retrieved from http://irt.austin.cc.tx.us/presentations/reports2002/.

Collis, B., & Peters, O. (2000). Educational applications of WWW-based asynchronous video. In N. Corric, T. Chambel, & G. Davenport (Eds.), *Multimedia '99* (pp. 177–186). Vienna: Springer-Verlag.

RealNetworks. (2002). *Streaming media FAQ*. Retrieved from http://www.realnetworks.com/resources/startingout/get_started_faq.html?UK=X.

University of Wisconsin-Madison. (2002). *Streaming media*. Retrieved from http://streaming.doit.wisc.edu/showcase/index.htm.

# STUDENT PREPARATION

Student preparation for distance education coursework is similar to preparation for traditional postsecondary education coursework. Students in distance education do face additional challenges and have some additional needs that must be met. On the other hand, students often take advantage of unique aspects of distance education formats that alleviate challenges in traditional formats. As a result of the similarities in preparation, students in distance education programs and coursework exhibit many of the same outcomes as those in traditional classrooms: academic success as well as academic struggle and failure. Student preparation will be examined in this entry in three aspects: going to college (prior to enrollment); preparing for class (ongoing issues and tasks); and preparing for program completion (considering next steps).

## GOING TO COLLEGE

Although admission to most distance education programs requires preparation and review of previous academic credentials, similar to traditional programs, in the case of programs that are exclusively online, student self-selection is a primary factor. Students in the enrollment planning process will consider program credibility and reputation, expected program outcomes, cost of attendance, and employer confidence. The most critical factor, however, is access. Increased participation nationally in distance education programs reflects growing confidence in the medium. Access and opportunity to continue or complete educational goals is a large factor driving student enrollment decisions.

Once an enrollment decision is made, a student must navigate initial orientation and advising, course registration, and access to textbooks and other key resources, as well as review a checklist of key technologies. Similar to programs for adult and returning students, participants in distance education programs face some personal barriers. Management of time and regaining confidence in academic performance are primary; however, students are also required to navigate complex technologies, often with minimal guidance. Online, published, or asynchronous orientation tools are often supplemented by professional staff advising and coaching.

Assessing the credibility and reputation of distance education programs remains a challenge for most consumers. More than a dozen independent regional and national associations have issued criteria and standards for quality in distance education programs (many of which emphasize very different components: student–instructor engagement, uses of technology, comparability with traditional classes, and so forth). Furthermore, increased marketing and presentation of distance education programs, varying endorsements, and an abundance of regional and national accreditations contribute to uncertainty in the

decision-making process. Increasing participation by traditional education providers, corporate and for-profit collaborations with traditional partners, and several hundred commercial agencies makes the available options for distance education nearly endless. State and federal agency involvement in monitoring these options remains limited; consumer protection and advocacy are also limited.

Distance education programs and courses primarily serve students at the undergraduate level. Online and distance programs for both undergraduate and graduate students are available in a wide range of majors; however, business, management, computer information, education, and social sciences predominate. As with any college selection process, prospective students are provided literature (print and Web-based) and often engage a counselor or marketing (sales) representative as part of the decision process. A key variable for student selection—and part of the preparation process—involves an assessment of perceived service quality.

Student cost of attendance for distance education programs varies greatly among different education providers. An important factor is the federal government's regulations regarding distance learning, which have been undergoing revision and review for some time. State-assisted community colleges and universities offering distance programs are negotiating with governing boards to determine whether these programs warrant subsidies. Private and independent institutions apply complex discounting and leveraging awards to student charges that can substantially alter the final cost for enrollment. Employer and corporate reimbursement programs provide another key variable in student cost of attendance. Often, this relates to employer assessment of quality and outcomes from the distance education program.

After a student has made the decision to matriculate, the distance education program generally offers some form of orientation and assistance to learn key expectations and policies. This may be as simple as a distributed handbook or referral to a Web site, engaged and personal telephone and online counseling sessions, or physical meetings at a campus or designated site. Goals for orientation to a distance education program are often quite pragmatic: a review of core technologies, expectations, key timelines, and contacts. Although orientation may be individual or group oriented, the content is directed to meet the basic functional needs of the individual learner. By contrast, orientations for traditional campus-based programs tend to incorporate substantial community development and interactive activity. These are significant and reflect differences in intended outcomes as well as very real differences in the expectations of student participants.

Many distance learning programs require broader student competency and experience with computer skills. Increased familiarity with Internet and Web navigation, knowledge of basic terminology, access to computer hardware and software, and a connection to the Internet enhance student performance in these programs. Several distance learning and online programs establish minimum requirements for computer systems (computer memory, speed, and operating systems). Other programs conduct a "basic skills" assessment as a condition for class participation. The need or expectation for student computer competency to be successful in distance learning and online programs is further complemented by a degree of self-discipline on the part of the learner. Many distance learning programs are more self-directed or self-paced, with less structure than traditional classrooms. As a result, students who are comfortable as independent learners may make a more successful start in distance learning programs.

Academic advising and course registration are, increasingly, becoming similar between traditional and distance education programs. Uses of technology to facilitate course registration are comparable for all students. Student preparation for course registration varies by program—much as with traditional programs. Varying with institutional resources and philosophy, students register for class with or without the oversight of an academic adviser. Registration itself is often self-managed via automated, electronic enrollment management information systems.

There remain slight limitations on the range and type of courses available to students through distance education, particularly through online coursework. Many institutions have partnered with broader multi-institution consortia, affording students access to hundreds or thousands of fully transferable online courses.

Information about and access to core tools for classroom success are primarily available through electronic services. Increasingly critical is access to the course portal or the institutional e-mail address that allows access to the course. Several institutions now utilize software that automates generation and assignment of student e-mail and password upon admission to the program. Students are able to confirm their admission, secure an e-mail address and password, complete an online orientation, review course requirements and section availability, register for classes, and pay the charges—all from the comfort of any Internet-connected location in the world, from any time zone at any time, and without the need to interact with an institutional staff member.

## PREPARING FOR CLASS

Once admitted, enrolled, and registered, students continue preparation on a course-by-course basis. Preparation practices for distance education students are similar to those of students in traditional courses: review assigned readings, prepare for exams, and access faculty and tutorial assistance. In distance education programs, however, these resources may be gained through electronic presentations.

In contrast to traditional classroom study, enrollment in distance education programs requires the student to gather resources from many locations. Textbooks for the course may be sold and delivered through a campus bookstore or may be purchased from any of several online bookstores. Time for ordering and shipping varies greatly and can have an influence on student preparedness for class. Additional course readings—packets of articles often sold through the bookstore or available at the library—are either provided via electronic library access or sold and distributed through the bookstore. Again, time and technology are critical agents influencing student preparation.

Many institutions have enhanced library resources with access to full-text holdings through the Internet. Syllabi for classes—and the class portals—are often available on the Internet. Several institutions have enabled students to review specific assignments—even complete projects and quizzes—without regard for timing or sequence. Other institutions have "protected" the sequence of the course material and require students to maintain a predetermined pace (this keeps students working as a group and enables the instructor to broadcast responses to questions, assuming that students are dealing with shared issues).

Students enrolled in distance education programs often face similar "home study" challenges as do commuting students, including finding appropriate time and space to focus on coursework. For online classes, this may also require focused and dedicated use of a home computer that may also be shared with family members. At the same time, students also benefit from greater interaction with family. Distance education programs often allow working adults with children access to continuing and higher education.

Traditional resources commonly provided to campus-based students must be sought in different ways. Academic support services, counseling, tutoring, career planning, and other student affairs functions are often made available for distance education students, but not to the same extent or breadth as for campus-based students. As a result, these types of services may be underutilized. This does affect student preparation for continuing enrollment. One consequence may be a more varied enrollment pattern—more frequent "stop out" and higher attrition (as is generally the case for adult students in higher education).

## PREPARING FOR PROGRAM COMPLETION

Students in college each make unique preparations for completing their program of study. This often includes participating in graduation ceremonies, engaging in alumni activities, and conducting a search for career or graduate school.

Student career and professional commitments serve as primary influences in decision making and preparation at program completion. Plans for continuing study, relocation, and career change each reflects core choices of access, time, and need. Distance education programs focus substantially on program selection and course presentation. As such, student preparation for entry to such programs and class work in support of these programs is moderately supported. Student preparation for program completion and departure remains more personal. Access to traditional placement or career planning services is limited. Although online resume and position search services abound, advice and assistance with interview preparation and campus-based field interviews by employers remain difficult to provide in distance formats.

—*Don Rosenblum*

*See also* ADMISSION CRITERIA AND PROCESSES; ASSESSMENT OF PRIOR LEARNING; ASSESSMENT OF STUDENT COMPETENCE

## Bibliography

Aslanian, Carol. (2001). *Adult students today.* College Board. New York.

Grill, Jennifer. (1999). *Access to learning: Rethinking the promise of distance education.* Arlington: Adult Learning.

Porras-Hernandez, Laura Helena. (2000). *Student variables in the evaluation of mediated learning environments.* Melbourne: Distance Education.

Schulman, A. H., & Sims, R. L. (1999). Learning in an online format versus an in-class format: An experimental study. *T.H.E. Journal, 26*(11), 54.

Young, Suzanne, Cantrell, Pamela P., & Shaw, Dale G. (Winter 2001). Online instruction: new roles for teachers and students. *Academic Exchange Quarterly, 5*(4), 11.

# STUDENT SERVICES

## REGISTRATION

Distance learning presented new challenges for student affairs organizations with traditional roots in developing strong interpersonal ties with students. First attempts at working with students through an electronic medium came as a result of the need to find more efficient ways of registering students for courses. Early in the 1960s, various forms of IBM-style punch cards were used at large universities to register students for courses. This cumbersome system of sorting computer cards migrated into stand-alone terminals where operators used computerized systems to register students for classes.

The problem with both of these processes was that they were inefficient and forced students to stand in lines to register for courses. Paper records were still maintained, and the system still had data-entry problems. To eliminate the lines, many institutions purchased commercially available telephone course registration systems. Telephone registration systems using digital telephones allowed students to connect to a pool of computer modems and enter the course numbers they needed on a voice-prompted telephone interactive system. This system worked relatively well on smaller campuses but was not efficient on larger campuses. Telephone lines got blocked, students waited on hold for long periods of time, and they were forced to continually call back until they could get the courses they wanted.

The most efficient system has been online registration using the Internet. A user-friendly Web page that allows students to point and click on courses and build their course schedules in real time has gained the greatest student and institutional support. The same system also has worked well for students in remote locations who enroll in distance learning courses, and for first-year students who can register for courses without traveling to campus. Although there were some initial problems with these systems due in part to concerns about Internet security, virus protection, privacy, and secure financial transactions, most of these problems were overcome with advances made on commercial sites that were later adapted to the needs of universities.

Online registration and student information systems, which had been developed earlier to maintain student records, presented universities with other opportunities to serve the information needs of students. Secure, encrypted Internet access and students receiving Web-based e-mail addresses at the time they enrolled made it possible for universities to send electronic grade reports to students, allowed students to drop and add courses online, gave students access and download capability to unofficial academic transcripts, and allowed students to request official transcripts online.

## ADMISSIONS

With registration accessible online at many institutions, it was a logical transition to online admissions applications. Building secure and interactive Web sites and having this information communicate efficiently with student information systems, financial aid, and registration presented the biggest problems. Large institutions frequently had proprietary software systems developed independently, and communication among administrative offices using various software programs was difficult. It was not unusual to find a financial aid office using one software system, the cashier's office using another software system, and registration using a completely different software system. The challenge was to have these systems communicate accurately so that data entry did not need to be duplicated and the accuracy and security of records could be maintained. Social security numbers were the most common method for identifying students

among these systems. This worked well until federal law began regulating the use of social security numbers and identity theft became an increasing concern. Student numbers and student passwords have become substitutes for the use of student social security numbers.

Most institutions have some version of online admission that permits students to either download the admissions application, complete it, and send it to the institution through traditional mail or to enter the required information and submit the application online. Admissions software can track students who make initial inquiries about the institution, allowing the institution to personalize its responses to students and keep a record of what information a student has received, what information the institution has received from the student, and what information is needed to complete the admissions process.

A large part of admissions work is marketing the institution. Most university admissions Web sites are designed to be the window onto the campus and to advance the institution in the most favorable way possible. Flash technology, Web-based movies, interactive campus tours, voice testimonials from students, and visually interesting photographs and graphics that portray campus life and its academic reputation inhabit these Web sites. They require constant monitoring and updating, as well as the services of Internet architects to put the best view of the institution forward to prospective students.

The admissions office is the portal for students interested in learning about the campus and what it has to offer. Students can often access course schedules, faculty resumes, public relations information, a list of alumni in their area of academic program interest, information about the athletic programs, student life information, and a host of other information about the institution. Technology allows students to complete applications online, attach essays or portfolios, connect to sites where they can have SAT or ACT scores sent to institutions, estimate the amount of financial aid they may be eligible to receive, and, in some cases, connect to other institutions where they can request that a high school academic transcript or a college transcript be submitted. Although most of this can be done electronically, and electronic signatures are legal, not all institutions permit electronic signatures; and many still require written verification for certain types of information. Admissions application fees can be paid by credit card, and students can often track where their application is in the admissions process.

## ACADEMIC ADVISING

Anchored strongly in a philosophy of personal contact with students, it was difficult for many academic advisers to conceptualize academic advising using the medium of computerized distance learning. The potential and advantages of distance education forced academic advisers to consider how to use the new technology. Like many of the technology advances in higher education, electronic forms of academic advising happened because of student demand and competition from other institutions.

Academic advising through distance learning presented unique challenges. Institutional curricula usually required course prerequisites for enrollment to advanced courses, sequencing requirements in other courses, and a set of core courses for students that varied by college, by program of study, and by various accreditation standards for professional practice in a field. Add to this the need to retain concurrent sets of graduation requirements to reflect the program of study under which students had matriculated, and the complexity of the problems begins to emerge. One set of requirements did not work for all students. Most institutions started by developing proprietary systems to audit academic requirements for various programs of study. Commercial programs were developed, but the idiosyncrasies of institutional curricula and the niche specialties of programs made adoption of commercial programs difficult. Institutions reverted to many methods to work with academic advising of students. The telephone still provides a very direct and easy way for students to get information and have specific questions answered by academic advisers. This is supplemented by e-mail exchanges with academic advisers, information provided on Web sites, and a complex system of holds, authorizations, verifications, and other checks that advising software programs allow academic advisers to use to guide students through the process of completing graduation requirements.

What these systems do not do well is provide advice and guidance to students about what various academic programs have to offer. They are designed more for students who have made a decision about entering a particular field and are generally not well designed to address students who are undecided or uncertain about a career direction. Preprofessional programs with a fairly lock-step set curriculum are well suited for academic advising programs using electronic media. Also, programs that are designed simply to add information to a student's background, such as a degree in liberal studies, work reasonably well. Academic programs that offer multiple paths and options are not as well suited for electronic forms of academic advising and degree audits.

## ISSUES AND CONCERNS

Security is one of the continuing concerns of administrators responsible for the increasing technical sophistication of Web-based registration, admission, and academic advising. The Family Educational Rights and Privacy Act requires that student records be confidential. Unfortunately, some individuals have vigorously pursued ways of hacking into university computer systems to gain unauthorized access to institutional records. Virtually all universities that have developed sophisticated registration, admissions, and academic advising systems also employ sophisticated security systems, firewalls, and various forms of encryption to protect student records and to deter unauthorized access. Despite these efforts, security is sometimes breached and presents a continuing concern.

Institutions have become so dependent on the computerized systems of records, admission, and academic advising that when there is a security breach, a computer failure, or a computer virus that infects institutional records, the institution can cease to function. Not only do such occurrences disrupt the ability of the institution to provide education to students, but they also present a financial threat to institutions when institutions cannot register students for classes or admit students using these computerized methods. The security threat also requires institutions to maintain a staff of trained professionals in information technology capable of responding quickly to breaches and to constantly upgrade software and computers to protect the institution against these threats. Additional costs associated with upgrading computers for greater access by more students at quicker speeds and the need to adapt to evolving technologies so that institutional sites can handle the newest programs being produced commercially also present service, maintenance, and staffing demands on institutions that are an increasing financial drain on institutional resources.

Integrated commercial programs for registration, student financial aid, cashier, housing, admissions, and similar services are available from many vendors. The costs associated with these programs include not only an annual lease payment and service support contract, but also the expense and time necessary to train student affairs practitioners about the systems and to keep people up-to-date with the constant changes, upgrades, and modifications to these complex integrated software programs.

Mergers and acquisitions among vendors that provide integrated student services software programs also cost institutions money. When one company is purchased by another, the customers of the company that was purchased are usually transitioned to the software program of the new company. Not only is this transition usually time consuming, but it also can cost institutions large sums of money to convert to the product of the new vendors, and leaves institutions vulnerable to decisions made for commercial incentives outside the institution's control.

*—Gregory S. Blimling*

*See also* ACADEMIC ADVISING; ADMINISTRATIVE LEADERSHIP; CAREER PLANNING AND DEVELOPMENT; ORIENTATION; RESIDENCE HALLS; SPECIAL NEEDS POPULATION

# STUDENTS

Students pursuing higher education away from a primary/main campus often deal with unique challenges, but may also benefit from familiar surroundings, access to critical resources, and opportunities to remain involved with family and work commitments. Possible challenges for students when studying away from a main campus include concern for adequacy of academic resources, interaction with faculty outside of class time, and minimal engagement with traditional aspects of campus community. Potential opportunities include the ability to maintain commitments to family and work, reduced costs and expenses for college attendance, and—often—greater flexibility in personal scheduling.

## HOME AND AWAY FROM CAMPUS

Distance education can include remote site-based, online, or hybrid forms of instruction. Distinguishing characteristics may include cohort-based enrollments, smaller section sizes, increased use of adjunct instructors, and asynchronous online engagement. Each of the characteristics may alter the relationship between student and instruction and affects the quality of the higher education experience.

Much of the research and study of students who commute to college (as opposed to living "in residence" on a college campus) are relevant to a discussion of the experience of students at home involved in distance education. Common and shared campus life is a greater challenge, as are informal contacts and interactions between student and instructor and between student and student affairs professional. In the case of a "commuting" student, the primary focus of the day often revolves around basic living concerns: employment, basic maintenance (housing, meals, transportation, shopping), and core personal relationships. In contrast, a traditional student's experience living "in residence" on a college campus includes a greater engagement and immersion in a wider range of campus life: lectures and movies, campus clubs and leadership, intramurals and dining halls, casual conversations with instructors, and late night study groups with classmates.

The analogy between commuter student and distance education student is not complete, however. Although both populations share demographic qualities (often older, usually employed more hours), the issue of access to and distance from a main campus has a substantial impact on the student–college relationship. Commuting students may be limited by time and competing demands restricting access to and use of campus-based resources, services, faculty, and facilities. For a student engaged in distance education, access to campus is often mediated through other vehicles. Web-based student services, a field-based campus representative, telephone and fax interaction, and printed catalogs and mailings often replace more personal interaction traditionally provided within the college setting.

## STUDENT CHARACTERISTICS

Distance education programs are among the fastest growing segments of enrollment strategies in higher education. More than one-third of all postsecondary institutions in the United States offer distance education programs; another one-fifth plan to add such programs within 3 years. Distance education programs are more likely to be offered by public institutions, and more often by large or medium institutions.

Students in distance education programs are enrolled primarily at the undergraduate level. Institutions appear most likely to offer courses in the humanities, social and behavioral sciences, and business or management. Delivery format varies extensively, and includes both video (two-way and one-way) and Web- and Internet-assisted instruction (both synchronous and asynchronous). Synchronous instruction refers to "live" presentation (both teacher and learner are present simultaneously, although not necessarily in the same location). Asynchronous instruction is neither time nor location dependent (instruction is accessed at times and places selected by the learner).

Students enrolled in such programs are often older, and balance family, home, work, and school responsibilities. Students choose to enroll in distance education courses for several reasons, most often based on access and convenience.

## CRITICAL ISSUES IN DISTANCE EDUCATION

Several defining contexts may help frame the experience for students enrolled in distance education programs and their relationship with college. These critical issues include identification, relationship, access to resources, managing time, communicating expectations, academic outcomes, and student development.

### Identification

Students enrolled in distance programs, particularly those offered via online or Web-based media, may not ever personally meet primary faculty or academic leadership. As a result, the identity of the student-learner may be an issue of concern. Verification of student identity is a basic requirement to ensure that work submitted and evaluated reflects the performance of the enrolled student. Institutions are developing and using creative tools to verify student identity—each with some limitations. Many institutions use a primary entrance essay as a basis to evaluate other written work, seeking concordance in style and voice. For online distance education, some institutions have required students to complete examinations in a proctored setting (such as a local library or community college). Other institutions have required periodic

"institutes" where participating students congregate for an annual face-to-face interaction with classmates and faculty. (However, this can be quite costly and burdensome for students and institution alike.) Instructors also have tested the use of computer-based cameras to visually verify the identity of the student. (However, this often requires synchronous interaction, which is complicated as online instruction becomes more global.)

For all students (distance and traditional), identification of authorship is a primary concern in higher education. Student access to and use of external assistance (peers and co-workers, term paper services, and uncited passages from digital sources) demands high vigilance on the part of the instructor, and often influences strategies for coursework and evaluation.

Site-based distance education programs often have greater reliance on the use of adjunct instructors to provide delivery of the curriculum. Although these instructors are well qualified to present material— often serving as professionals in the specific field or discipline—the adjunct is sometimes at a disadvantage regarding familiarity with student work. Adjunct instructors are less likely to interact with other adjunct (or full-time) instructors regarding the performance and style of individual students.

As institutions develop and expand distance education programs, issues of identification continue to be addressed. Creative uses of technology enhance interaction and support confirmation of identity in student–institutional interactions. Many of these technologies have translated to services for traditional students, as well (for example, Web-based course registration, electronic paper submissions, online examinations and automated test scoring, and electronic grade books).

### Relationships

One hallmark of higher education is the intellectual relationship that emerges among students and between student and instructor. The traditional classroom setting invites not only presentation of material and assessment of learning, but also interaction through office hours, conversations, discussion, and questions. Interactive video and other synchronous forms of distance education often mimic traditional classroom instruction. Other forms of distance education, however, have developed alternative tools to support instruction. This is especially evident in asynchronous online classes, where students and instructors review materials through chat rooms, directed and shared writings with class members, and short video broadcasts incorporating demonstrations and lectures. Students can access course material from published texts, Web sites recommended by the instructor, and expanded course syllabi serving as study guides—often, thorough texts on their own.

## Access to Resources

Distance education programs are attractive to students primarily for the convenience of access and flexibility of schedule. A trade-off for this convenience is often a limit in access to core resources. Study on a traditional campus comes with access to modern research libraries and library staff. Faculty members, in addition to teaching class sessions, maintain office hours for individual discussion and mentoring. Teams of student affairs professionals are available to assist with personal and professional development: assisting with selection and affirmation of major, reflection and decision making with regard to career choice, and counseling on a range of personal matters. For many students, the campus also becomes a center for recreational, social, and cultural interaction. Distance education programs may minimize these services.

Creative uses of technology have significantly expanded access to academic and administrative resources: online writing labs, electronic libraries (digital full text access to thousands of journals as well as interlibrary loan delivery worldwide), personalized publishing and electronic textbooks, expanded service hours, Web-based and toll-free phone access, and so forth. However, students in distance programs are clearly making choices regarding access needs for various resources to support their continuing education.

Students studying from home must have access to certain basic technology, which allows connection to services and resources (as well as instruction). Online and Web-based classes often specify minimum computer and connectivity requirements, and may request specific operating platforms and software. As tools to deliver online education become more powerful, so, too, have requirements for students' computing resources increased.

## Managing Time and Obligations

Distance education programs afford students greater flexibility. Web- and Internet-based courses are often asynchronous, and allow students complete latitude to engage material when convenient. This tends to require greater self-discipline than most traditional classes. Site-based, synchronous, and two-way video distance education classes often require fewer "contact" hours than traditional classes. As a result, students must review course content through readings. Interaction with classmates and with the instructor is available for clarifying concepts and testing comprehension.

Student "attendance" in online classes is related more to engagement and access to material on site than to physical presence in a classroom. Asynchronous classes (online classes that do not require specific times for interaction between student and instructor) can be completed before or after work, at lunchtime, or after a household has settled for the night. Not surprisingly, adult women comprise the largest population of students enrolling in online classes.

## Communicating Expectations

Students enrolled in distance education classes often require greater self-discipline. Clear communication of class expectations can serve as a critical resource to this end. Many distance education classes break the course into smaller units, often corresponding to a single week for the class. This can serve as a vehicle to help instructors monitor student progress and performance and review feedback, which occurs more frequently through class discussion and interaction.

## Assessment of Academic Outcomes

Evaluation of student learning traditionally has included grading quizzes and examinations, reviewing written papers, and assessing classroom participation, presentations, labs, and so forth. Distance education classes often require additional tools for evaluation. Often, evaluation tools are combined as a "portfolio," seeking to determine whether a student has accomplished—and can demonstrate—mastery of a predetermined set of intended learning outcomes. The student in this class has the responsibility of demonstrating mastery of these outcomes. In turn, this has the potential to create a much greater role for and collaboration between student and instructor as partners in a "learning community."

## Student Growth and Development

The literature regarding traditional higher education environments addresses student personal and professional growth and development. Often, this is considered the "curriculum" of student affairs professionals, using residence halls, athletics, campus clubs and organizations, and co-op and internship experiences as the classroom. For many reasons, students enrolled in distance education may not have the same access to this curriculum. Nonetheless, developmental and growth issues continue to occur—just not in the context of the college campus.

## STUDENTS AT HOME

Distance education programs appear to respond to a gap in postsecondary education access, providing opportunities for degree programs and course completion at times and locations not previously available. Further, Internet and online distance education allow students to "unbundle" traditional educational packages that have been location and time bound. Earlier limitations of correspondence coursework appear to be resolved through the use of increasingly sophisticated technologies. Nonetheless, current models for distance education appear attractive to specific student populations and require personal discipline and commitment—from both student and instructor—to replicate aspects of the traditional college environment.

—*Don Rosenblum*

*See also* ALUMNI; DEMOGRAPHICS; SPECIAL NEEDS POPULATION

## Bibliography

AAUP. (1999). *Statement on distance education.* Retrieved from http://www.aaup.org/statements/Redbook/StDistEd.HTM.

Kirkwood, Adrian. (2000). *Learning at home with information and communication technologies.* Melbourne: Distance Education.

Lewis, L., Snow, K., Farris, E., Levin, D., & Greene, B. (1999). *Distance education at postsecondary education institutions: 1997–1998.* U.S. Department of Education: Office of Educational Research and Development.

National Center for Education Statistics: http://nces.ed.gov.

Nobel, David. (1998). Digital diploma mills: The automation of higher education. Retrieved from http://firstmonday.dk/issues/issue3_1/noble/.

Noble, D. F. (1998). Digital diploma mills, part II: The coming battle over online instruction. Retrieved from http://communication.ucsd.edu/dl/ddm2.html.

Noble, D. F. (1998). Digital diploma mills, part III: The bloom is off the rose. Retrieved from http://communication.ucsd.edu/dl/ddm3.html.

Noble, David. (2002). Technology and the commodification of higher education. *Monthly Review, 53*(10), 26.

# STUDY GUIDES

Study guides serve as maps to assist the learner in organizing, focusing on, and exploring the wide range of subject matter available in the pursuit of knowledge. There are various types and styles of study guides; some are in hard copy, and increasingly more are found online via the Internet.

There are study guides designed to assist high school guidance counselors, students, and parents in selecting colleges and universities. Those guides may be organized geographically, categorically (public, private, 2- or 4-year), by level (undergraduate or graduate), or by discipline to be studied. Such guides may provide information about colleges and universities including whether the institution is accredited, the number of students enrolled, the number and types of majors offered, the cost of tuition and fees, and admission criteria. Some study guides geared toward compiling information about colleges and universities are designed in a cross-referenced format that allow the reader to search by location, areas of study, size, cost, level of education (2-year, 4-year, undergraduate, or graduate), and funding status (public or private).

A study guide for undergraduate students may contain tips for developing effective study skills, because it is recognized that many students may not be prepared for the transition from the more rigid structure of high school to the liberal self-directed structure of higher education. The development of effective study skills may be outlined to address study habits, time management, stress management, self-discipline, and the essentials of planning and organizing within the process of studying.

A study guide for graduate education may include a higher level of study skills such as how to plan and conduct research, how to write for publications, as well as tips on time management and stress management. Such study guides will often refer the reader to other sources for further reading and/or to Internet links.

Other types of study guides include those designed to assist learners in a particular field or program of study. Those study guides are generally prepared by the faculty who facilitate and/or assess the learning in that course or knowledge area. Such study guides may contain a historical overview of the subject; an outline of the theorists, theories, and/or guiding principles the learner should be familiar with; an annotated bibliography; and other suggested readings. Some guides contain a recommended order of study that closely resembles a course syllabus. Others may contain samples of successful theses, papers, and/or journal articles prepared by prior learners. These samples may assist the learner in gaining a perspective on how the course or knowledge area can successfully be approached.

Study guides designed to address particular fields of study, such as humanities, business management, or natural sciences, may offer the reader an overview of constraints that a learner may face, while indicating the preferred prerequisites. For example, if the area of study in the humanities focuses on British literature of the 1600s, the study guide may indicate that the learner would be expected to have completed prior courses in world literature or world history in order to more fully appreciate and understand the literature. Another example may be the prerequisite of proficiency in a foreign language if a course requires reading or translating a foreign language, or if the course includes travel to that country for an extended period of time.

Study guides are designed to assist the learner in giving direction to the thinking process by presenting a number of avenues that might be taken to reach the "learning goal" for that course or knowledge area. Each avenue offers a different view of the terrain that can be explored and the pedagogical needs that can be met through the course or knowledge area. For example, it is important for the learner to understand the delivery system by which he or she will obtain the knowledge. Classroom instruction is very different from distance/distributed or online course delivery, where Web pages may be used for distribution of lecture notes, articles, homework assignments, and examinations. One avenue may lead the learner to develop and use skills in the area of face-to-face interaction and involvement that the classroom offers, whereas the online or distance/distributed learning model may require the learner to be more self-directed, self-motivated, engaged in his or her studies, and proficient in technology. The study guide can allow the reader to compare delivery systems and weigh the assets and liabilities of various components against personal and/or professional needs.

Study guides can assist the learner in establishing learning goals and in identifying what the gain will be from completing the course or knowledge area. The learner may also gain insight as to how the acquisition of knowledge can be applied to practice. For example, a study guide in business management may provide the reader with examples of how former students applied the gained knowledge to practice by establishing a business in their local area, or, if a degree was earned in that field, how the students advanced within their companies or organizations.

Typically study guides provide order to the learning process, while often indicating levels of competency and rigor expected by the assessing faculty, thereby enabling the learner to determine an appropriate time frame for planning and completing the work. For example, the study guide may provide a suggested order of study resulting in an overview of the course matter, followed by an in-depth study and analysis of the subject or specific area of study within the course matter, and finally an analysis of how the learning can be or was applied within the learner's lived experience(s). This can also serve as a reflexive tool to allow the learner to gauge progression in the iterative process of acquiring new knowledge.

*—Mary L. O'Neal*

***See also*** Asynchronous Formats; Curriculum Models; Designing Learning Environments; Plagiarism; Social Constructionism

## Bibliography

Brockett, R. G. (1985). Methodological and substantive issues in the measurement of self-directed learning readiness. *Adult Education Quarterly, 36,* 15–24.

Bruner, J. (1996). *The culture of education.* Cambridge, MA: Harvard University Press.

Garrison, D. R. (1987). Self-directed and distance learning: Facilitating self-directed learning beyond the institutional setting. *International Journal of Lifelong Education, 6,* 309–318.

Hawley, W., & Valli, L. (2000). Learner-centered professional development. *Research Bulletin, Phi Delta Kappa International, 27,* 7–10.

Starnes, B., & Paris, C. (2000). Choosing to learn. *Phi Delta Kappa, 81*(5), 392–397.

# SYNCHRONOUS FORMATS

The Internet allows tens of millions of Americans to participate in a thriving social world where they can engage in serious and satisfying contact with online communities and educational institutions. A recent survey reported that 84% of Internet users have contacted some form of an online group or educational chat group that is either synchronous, meaning occurring in real time, or asynchronous, referring to not interacting at the same time. That fact means that more Americans have used the Internet to contact a chat group than have received news online, searched for health information, or even purchased something on the Internet.

Online synchronous chats can be distant geographically and allow users to connect easily with others around the world. Survey research indicates that a large number of those who participate in online groups said the Internet had helped them get to know people they would not otherwise have met. Most interesting is the fact that many of those who participate in online groups indicated that the Internet has helped them connect with people from different racial, ethnic, or economic backgrounds than their own.

## TYPES OF SYNCHRONOUS CHATS

A synchronous chat happens in real time. Anyone who has visited a chat room has experienced a synchronous chat. This can be a powerful tool for an instructor or facilitator to use in Web-based training. This tool also can be used as a form of lecture. It offers a chance for two-way communication between the instructor and the learner, and in some cases between peers.

The synchronous lecture can use audio and video as well as chalkboard programs, also known as whiteboards. Some instructors also use slide shows in the form of PowerPoint presentations. The student communication takes place via the telephone or Internet, in the latter case using Voice Over Internet Protocol (VOIP) or text.

Synchronous chat is a very effective tool for a lecture session. The instructor and students are present at the same time in a chat room, usually some material is reviewed prior to class (for example, reading the textbook, notes, or articles), and the time is used for discussion and clarification. Following are definitions of the various types of synchronous chats.

## Text-Based Chat

The most simple communication tools on the Web are the text-based chats. Their birth started with Internet Relay Chat (IRC). Participants can navigate together and talk to each other by typing or cutting and pasting text. Many universities use this type of synchronous chat solely because it involves less faculty and student technical training and can cross many platforms (e.g., Macintosh and Unix systems). Instant messenger (IM) software, such as Yahoo! Messenger, MSN Messenger, America Online (AOL) Instant Messenger, and Paltalk offer simple text chat, but some of these programs have upgraded to audio and video functions.

## Graphics-Based Chat

Some text chat applications make use of the graphical capabilities of the Internet, featuring animated graphical figures called avatars, which can interact with other avatars much like videogame characters. Avatars are able to walk, fly, and look around the virtual world. They are also able to build and manipulate three-dimensional objects, perform virtual actions, and chat with other connected users.

## Audio/Video-Based Chats

These are interactive text chats that can also use audio and/or video for communication enhancement. They do require the downloading of some plug-ins or some special software. Yahoo! Messenger has both audio and multiple video interaction possibilities. Microsoft's MSN Messenger has audio and a video component with the operating system Windows XP. America Online's Instant Messenger has audio. These three offer platforms for both PCs and Macs. Other systems such as Paltalk and CUseeMe provide audio and multiple video possibilities. These IMs provide instant communication by voice and video, and if the receiver has the same software and plug-ins, both parties can see and hear each other. These audio and visual functions require a Webcam or a digital camcorder, a microphone, and speakers. Some newer personal digital assistants (PDAs) also have the capability of transmitting sound and video. Video in these IMs is usually produced by a Webcam attached to a Universal Serial Bus (USB) port, or a digital camcorder attached to a USB port or using FireWire or IEEE 1394 technology.

Within the audiovisual chat domain there are free and proprietary systems that also allow sharing of desktop documents and applications, in order to teach an individual how to use a software program, or even allow control of another's desktop. The prominent free program is Microsoft's NetMeeting, which has text chat and audio and video chat between two persons, as well as application sharing. A multipoint server, often purchased by corporations, allows for more than two people to use the audio and visual capabilities. Most corporations use a telephone conferencing service instead of Internet audio (Voice Over IP) because no participant learning is required and Internet voice is often not as reliable with dial-up computers or in the case of a congested Internet. Webex and Raindance, amid a long list of other companies, offer audio, video, application sharing, and telephone conferencing services for live meetings.

## Shared Whiteboards

Simple whiteboards are found in NetMeeting and Webex, and within educational-based systems such as WebCT, Blackboard, and eCollege. Everyone can draw on the whiteboard and all will see the same image on their computer.

## Shared Web Navigation

Shared Web navigation is similar to application sharing—individuals browse the Web together or students navigate based on the lecture or presentation material. This can happen in several ways. First, some chat programs allow users to enter a Web site address and will control the browsers of all users in order to load that specific page. Second, a Web site address

can be entered into the text window of a chat. The recipient can then click the hyperlinked site, which will open another browser window and take the person to that address.

## EDUCATIONAL OUTCOMES OF SYNCHRONOUS CHATS

Within the process of synchronous chats, faculty are primarily process facilitators and coaches, and encourage students to initiate discussions, collaborate with each other, and effect critical analyses of course content in its process.

The initial student response from a synchronous chat is passive, but students quickly become proactive initiators. If collaboration occurs quickly, students can be empowered through self-directed work teams and can meet together on their own time without the instructor to discuss questions, concepts, and papers. Another outcome is that structure is less authoritarian and less hierarchical than in traditional classrooms, and there may be more personal self-disclosure of individual students that allows for a more relaxed pace.

An instructor's interpersonal skills usually ensure quality interaction, and a skilled facilitator is necessary in the synchronous chat room. For those chat rooms that have only text as the means of communication, nuances of the written word replace nonverbal behavior.

There are several synchronous chat drawbacks:

- *The Dominating Chatter*—Have this student hold responses until asked.
- *The Detached Chatter*—Prompt this student to perform with a specific task.
- *The Aggressive Chatter*—Set specific behavioral guidelines, either privately or in a group format.
- *Chaotic Chatters*—Multiple conversations going on at once: Post an agenda in advance or intervene with a focus on a different task, or in the case of text-only chats, type using uppercase and SHOUT FOR ORDER.

## USING SYNCHRONOUS FORMATS

Once connected to the Internet, a wide variety of information sources are available for use as an educational medium. Collaboration with colleagues, research groups, discussion lists, or newsgroups can be valuable. Telemedicine makes use of the Internet to enable doctors to diagnose and treat patients far from their offices or hospitals. Psychotherapy may become an Internet reality in a few years, and educators have already used the Internet to educate all ages of students. The use of instant messengers in medicine, business, and psychology can be considered a sped-up version of e-mail, with immediate real-time response. Speeding along the Internet, especially if messages are encrypted against hacking, instant messaging lets professionals consult on tough cases, speed up test results, and even chat with their patients or clients.

## Pedagogic Uses of Chat

Interactive chats help provide a very effective type of student engagement. The chat allows an instructor to observe in real time what students are thinking and how they are progressing. The interactive chat helps distance students not to feel so isolated and invisible and creates community interaction.

## Oral Quizzes

Students can meet with the instructor online and be quizzed on course content. The instructor can assess how well the student knows the material in just a few minutes of questions and answers. This supports a very student-centered approach to teaching.

## Transcripts Used as Study Tools

After each chat session, posting the chat transcripts to a Web page can provide a record of the conversations that took place during the chat. If audio or telephone chat was used, several programs are available that will record this content, but this process is not as easily saved as the text chat. Document sharing programs can create copies of documents that were posted during a live chat as well. This offers students an opportunity to review the complete discussion that transpired and gives those who were not present a chance to know what took place.

## Brainstorming and Small Group Sessions

Students can brainstorm as a warm-up activity for writing assignments. This can function as a prewriting phase for the rough draft of a group paper. If a class is broken into small groups of two to five students, they can schedule their own live chat sessions to work together on a project.

## Guest Speakers

Inviting a guest to a course chat session (an outside expert, another instructor, etc.) can provide students with information about real world experiences concerning the course subject matter.

## Virtual Office Hours

Setting weekly times when the instructor is available online so students can contact the faculty member about the class can be a valuable tool.

## Starting and Ending Times

Chat sessions can be set up well in advance so students have time to arrange their schedules to be able to attend. This will also give participants time to prepare for the discussion. Ending a chat when the time is up is extremely important because chatting is a high-intensity activity, and it is difficult for many participants to stay focused for long periods.

## Topic of Conversation

The chat session should be limited to one specific topic. Students must come prepared to discuss one topic only. This lends structure to the discussion and helps the chat session stay focused.

## Late Participants

If students join the chat session after it has started, taking a moment to orient them to the discussion by summarizing the current thread of conversation gives everyone a break and allows late students to catch up.

## Chat Etiquette

A list of protocols for students to follow should be published at the beginning of the course. This will help maintain order and clear communication in the discussion.

## SUMMARY

A characteristic of the Internet that distinguishes it from other media is its ability to unite a community of people who want to exchange information and ideas. Periodicals and newspapers try to do this by publishing letters to the editor. Television and radio programs often accept viewer calls and e-mail. But only the Internet can offer the level of interactivity that truly assists the development of community. That creation of connection is what makes synchronous chat an integral element of the online learning environment.

*—Lynne Saba*

*See also* ASYNCHRONOUS FORMATS; GRAPHICS; MEDIA; STREAMING MEDIA

## Bibliography

Chambers, J. A. (Ed.). (2001). *Selected papers from the 12th International Conference on College Teaching and Learning.* Jacksonville, FL: Florida Community College at Jacksonville.

Chou, C. C. (2001). Formative evaluation of synchronous CMC systems for a learner-centered online course. *Journal of Interactive Learning Research, 12*(2–3), 173–192.

Ellis, T. J., & Cohen, M. S. (2001). Enhancing distance learning with multimedia: Λ win win? In J. Λ. Chambers (Ed.), *Selected papers from the 12th International Conference on College Teaching and Learning* (pp. 59–66). Jacksonville, FL: Florida Community College at Jacksonville.

Hodges, P., & Saba, L. (2002). Teaching statistics online. In K. E. Rudestam and J. Schoenholtz-Read (Eds.), *Handbook of online learning: Innovations in higher education and corporate training.* Thousand Oaks, CA: Sage.

Kazmer, M. M., & Haythornthwaite, C. (2001). Juggling multiple social worlds: Distance students online and offline. *American Behavioral Scientist, 45*(3), 510–529.

Menduno, M. (1998). Prognosis: Wired. Why Internet technology is the next medical breakthrough. *Hosp Health Netw, 72*(21), 28–30, 32–35.

Pew Internet & American Life Project. Retrieved August 5, 2002, from http://www.pewtrusts.com/news/index.cfm?image=img4&page=nr1&name=Press%20Releases

Rainie, L., Horrigan, John, & Beck, Barbara. (October 31, 2001). *Surveys: 90 million have participated in online groups.* News Release. Grantee Press Releases.

Talamo, A., & Ligorio, B. (2001). Strategic identities in cyberspace. *Cyberpsychol Behav, 4*(1), 109–112.

# T

## TEACHING IN AN ELECTRONIC CLASSROOM

In early versions of distance learning (DL), experts worried about students' commitment to active participation, impersonal computer interfaces, and lack of face-to-face contact. Today, however, a larger portion of DL students are adults voluntarily returning to education for career development or the intrinsic satisfactions of learning, bringing with them more disciplined study habits and more life experience for grounding the subject matter. Younger learners, too, are now fully at ease with computers, using them for socializing as well as academics. Also, the cumbersome log-in protocols of earlier decades have given way to connections that are "always on." Leading-edge instruction formats have also changed dramatically, moving away from the 1960s "correspondence courses" for students working in isolation toward more collaborative forms of learning in groups. Computers once focused on "programmed instruction," using narrowly constrained paths to correct answers, now function as portals to webs of conversational inquiry, offering continually refreshed knowledge resources open to anyone. Whereas early DL emphasized knowledge "push" through traditional pedagogy, newer approaches respond to information "pull" by students as they perceive the need for it. In all these ways, DL interfaces are becoming more engaging and attractive. The Web-based interface has also become a medium for teachers to share evolving instructional practices.

Nevertheless, DL often stays rooted in traditional pedagogy. Virtual lectures and restricted reading lists tend to persist unless students are given more explicit responsibility for self-directed study, taking advantage of group learning and the growing wealth of Internet resources. With this in mind, an early pioneer of DL, Charles Wedemeyer, noted that Americans have a much stronger cultural orientation to self-directed study than Europeans, despite Europe having provided many of the early models for DL.

Effective teaching methods vary from the initial days of a course to later stages, and still other methods apply to re-energizing students when participation flags.

### INITIATING THE COURSE

Several principles help students get on track in a new course: psychological safety, clear expectations, establishment of community, and manageable challenges.

### Psychological Safety

*Psychological safety* calls for a virtual "space" where students feel they belong and that has an overview of the course structure, assignments, key learning resources, and places for informal conversation. A good portal (home page) for the course provides a map for clear orientation, but also evokes a sense of challenge and engagement, such as might come from a campfire, a cathedral, or a mythical country. A "café" space allows students a sense of community beyond formal assignments, and café discussions can provide faculty with insight into student concerns and personal interests that can be drawn on to design assignments or provide feedback. Even in face-to-face classrooms, educators often emphasize the importance of bringing the full "self" into play, beyond fulfillment of others' expectations; this aspect of psychological safety is especially important for DL.

## Clear Expectations

*Clear expectations* include expected frequency of check-in; length of assignments; scope and depth of comments students make on each other's work; and resources for use beyond assigned readings, such as phone conferences, e-mail, external Web sites, and chat rooms. Not all expectations need to be made explicit. Some can be modeled by the instructor, and some can be provided on a need-to-know or just-in-time basis—such as reminders about netiquette and rigorous adherence to standards for citing other authors' work. Anticipated difficulties should be pointed out and treated as positive but challenging learning opportunities. Subtler reinforcements, too, can be brought to bear, along the lines of the Pygmalian effect (students doing better because they glimpse the instructor's confidence in them) or the Hawthorne effect (improved performance due to the instructor's responsiveness in making small adjustments as the course evolves). Another important expectation is for students to develop a habitual rhythm of participation, which is encouraged by posing many small assignments and collaborative tasks, with less emphasis on independent work in isolation.

## Establishment of Community

*Establishment of community* needs special attention in the absence of face-to-face interactions. Many find that DL can create a powerful sense of group intimacy, especially where asynchronous communication allows each voice to be as clear and loud as any other, where shy students can adopt a more extroverted "online persona," and where conversations center around the group rather than the teacher. Team size can affect the sense of team belonging, with a size of about seven students usually working best, but larger teams can handle tasks if they are broken down into subteams.

DL classes often start with self-introductions—brief biographies or a short self-description emphasizing things that wouldn't be known from a student's resume, yearbook, or photograph. A sense of belonging often develops in the context of collaborative problem-solving, so it can help to begin a course with this kind of assignment. Some instructors ask teams to be conscious about developing a "transactive memory"—group knowledge about who knows what, and how to use it—a skill that helps the group achieve not only problem-solving skills, but also social skills and cohesiveness, and a stronger sense of efficacy for each of its members.

## Manageable Challenges

*Manageable challenges* are part of any good instruction, but DL shifts the context for making them work. Games and simulated problem-solving have been part of computer-mediated learning and programmed instruction since the 1960s, as evidenced by the extensive collection of commercial software now using games for educational purposes. In DL, the absence of a face-to-face presence is an advantage for games that involve groups, bringing the imagination into play, removing inhibitions, and making the playing arena seem more safely contained.

Games can include treasure hunts for Internet-based information, providing practice in the use of search engines and access to electronic libraries, as well as developing students' critical judgment about the validity of information retrieved from unpublished sources. For a course in English, some "lead" students might do a book report on a core reading, with the other students then commenting on those book reports in the voice of assigned personas—Shakespeare, perhaps, or a contemporary historian, or a modern politician, or one of the book's own characters. A class in sociology might assign students to take on the "voice" of different personality types. Other courses might set up a debate to compare and contrast ideas and methods: In what ways is a particular metaphor suitable or misleading in a particular application? How many people in the world speak English—and why do various sources estimate those numbers so differently? Of two films currently available for rent, which gives the best lessons for mobilizing a group to action?

Games can impart substantive knowledge, but they also develop collaboration and resourcefulness skills. This involves not just learning, but learning how to learn—a meta-skill that will serve students in other classes, as well as in career development. Collaborative resourcefulness in DL has a parallel in John Dewey's view of education as a process that needs to be embedded in the larger context of community knowledge and learning outside the school, as well as in Jean Piaget's view of learning as a largely unconscious development of social skills while engaged in specific tasks. Seymour Papert's work in computer- and Internet-based learning similarly emphasizes the value of going beyond "dissociate learning" (using knowledge divorced from everyday experience) in favor of "syntonic learning," which brings into play exploration and invention (as children learn to talk and ride bikes without formal training), motivated by discovery in the context of things familiar from personal experience.

## MAINTAINING COURSE MOMENTUM

Keeping up active dialogue involves attention to pace, student roles, interim evaluations, positive tone, faculty responsiveness, and instructional "scrapbooks."

### Pace

*Pace* is best when it is varied, as in a good novel, speech, or musical composition. Strong elements of predictability in early stages can allow for a richer mix of drama and surprise as things progress. Periods of active participation can be alternated with time out for reflection; well-defined assignments can be interspersed with student-designed tasks; formal presentations can be mixed with playful game exercises; and focused problem-solving algorithms can alternate with exploratory heuristics that challenge students to get out of the box.

### Student Roles

*Student roles* in DL can be extended well beyond conventional pedagogy. A virtual classroom can allow multiple activities to proceed simultaneously, allowing for individual differences. In this sense, DL functions much like a one-room schoolhouse, where several kinds of learning are happening in parallel and where students are given strong orientation and extra responsibilities for self-directed study. In this context, the DL teacher may encourage buddy systems for students to give or receive help when needed, and even to take on coaching-assistant roles, building on individual strengths such as expertise in search engines, particular knowledge areas, or troubleshooting computer problems (which students can often handle better than their elder teachers).

### Interim Evaluations

In the absence of face-to-face cues about satisfactory performance, *interim evaluations* may be especially important for DL. Mid-course student evaluations can be brief, noting strengths and areas for improvement in a couple of sentences. Student self-evaluations are also used sometimes, asking each student to assess progress using criteria such as participation rate, constructive contributions, resourcefulness in using the Internet, and originality of postings. Each student might also be asked to create personalized self-evaluation criteria, to reflect his or her own personal strengths and interests. Other evaluation questions can serve both as feedback to the instructor and as reinforcement to the student; for example, "What is the most important thing you have learned in this course so far?"

### Positive Tone

*Positive tone* is more important in DL than in a classroom, because words have a more indelible impact when they are posted to a group bulletin board than when they are spoken in person, and postings include no gestures or intonation to moderate words. Tone is partly a matter of netiquette, but it also involves deliberate emphasis. Good teachers have always known that wrong answers are a good springboard for new learning, and early versions of programmed instruction took pains to handle incorrect answers with positive emphasis on next steps to the right answer, instead of simply responding, "Wrong, try again." Positive tone can also be developed by using a conversational voice, addressing people by name, calling attention to things people do well, providing positive feedback for people taking creative risks, or using games like collaborative writing where each person adds a new sentence to the work of others.

### Faculty Responsiveness

*Faculty responsiveness* has two facets—timing and depth. Instructors need to check in frequently, leaving tracks of their presence, however faint, so that students know their voices are being heard. If a question or comment is directed at a particular person— either instructor or student—that person's name should be prominent as an alert in the subject heading. At times the instructor (or student) may want to post a reply to the effect, "Hmmm, I hear you, but let me think about this a bit." Delay allows time to draft a more thoughtful reply offline, put it aside, and come to the question later with a fresh mind, to reconsider how one's own reply might be misread or carry an unintended subtext, especially if emotional issues are involved. Extra time also allows the final response to weave in concrete examples, orientation to upcoming assignments, or relevant references from literature or Web sites.

DL instructors often report that students' response to feedback is rather unpredictable: An immediate but well-crafted piece of faculty feedback may fall on deaf ears, or even provoke a kind of anxiety that seems to say, "Your answer came so quickly, it seems you didn't take much time to think about it." Other times, a teacher's short spontaneous remark is recalled by a student months later as "making all the difference for me in that course."

When new to DL (or new to teaching) faculty often fall into traditional classroom roles of lecturing, perhaps in an unconscious effort to demonstrate personal expertise and keep the focus on a safe, predictable track. But in DL, each student already has access to virtually unlimited information on any given subject, so the function of an instructor shifts considerably, from knowledge provider to knowledge enabler. This calls for extra attention in helping students become critical consumers of information gleaned from sources outside traditional reading lists and lectures. Another knowledge-enabling function of DL faculty is to help students integrate theory with personal experience, an important step in knowledge validation that Internet access alone cannot provide, but that the instructor can model through example.

### Instructional Scrapbooks

*Instructional "scrapbooks"* are the DL learning equivalent of traditional lectures, but comprise collections of shorter materials posted as needed in response to specific issues that arise unscheduled in any particular course. Much like resources used for just-in-time manufacturing, the elements of a scrapbook represent knowledge on demand, "pulled" by real-time student questions, rather than "pushed" through lectures and textbooks. Scrapbook elements might include brief story-based illustrations of theories, references to additional literature and Web sites, or copies of inspired postings from other classes. By including

gems culled from student work, the instructor can show the value placed on the students' own capacity to make important contributions to learning, through original thinking, resourcefulness, or personal experience.

In most cases, postings from the scrapbook will need to be personalized and edited for adaptation to particular questions or issues raised. Some scrapbook elements may be more self-contained and formalized as part of a resource toolkit, including skill-building guides for speed reading, note-taking, use of correct citations, and effective writing. The key feature of a scrapbook is its timely use in the appropriate moment. Different from regular assignments, postings from a scrapbook element need to resonate with the issues that arise at unpredictable times, while also reflecting each instructor's personal teaching style and the mood of a particular dialogue. This just-in-time quality of learning is one of the hallmarks of DL, given its immediate electronic access to highly diverse forms of information, and its departure from single-text, single-teacher, limited-dialogue forms of instruction.

## RE-ENERGIZING

Almost every course finds some students falling behind, especially in dialogue-based DL where discussion threads can proliferate in several unpredictable directions at once. Instructors can also feel left behind, disoriented, and out of control in the unpredictable creativity of a DL classroom. At times, this leads to widespread feelings of frustration, guilt, inability to catch up, and paralysis, where almost everyone feels they are being left behind by everyone else, yet few are willing to express their sense of vulnerability. Often it is the most diligent students who feel this sense of information overload and progressive alienation most acutely, a process sometimes described as the "jungle syndrome."

One solution is to alert students to the problem and reduce the personal sense of burden. Creation of "watertight" compartments between phases of the course can help cut off loose threads of discussion to start new topics afresh. "Time-out" interludes can be inserted for reflection and minimal posting, or to shift assignments toward independent rather than collaborative work. Group cohesion and confidence can also be boosted by refocusing work on challenging but manageable collaborative tasks, falling back on techniques used at the initiation of the course.

The jungle syndrome can also be headed off by encouraging students to use concrete, graphic language, with metaphors and scenarios and specific examples that can be mentally visualized, giving a sense of "place" to each discussion. New ideas can often be grasped most easily in the form of graphic pictures or verbal imagery. Concretely named metaphors and images ("the green halo" or the "Abilene paradox") help memory retention and provide specific, memorable "tags" for retrieving information from earlier dialogues or the Web, using "Find" commands or search engines.

It helps students and faculty alike to acknowledge that nobody needs to have all the answers. The resources now available on the Internet far exceed anyone's grasp, so the teacher's role is no longer to provide an expert response to every question, but sometimes to say, "I don't know the answer, let's see how we can find it."

*—Barclay Hudson*

*See also* E-Learning Strategies; Experiential Learning; Facilitation; Instructional Techniques

## Bibliography

Hudson, B. (2000). Edge of chaos: The sweet spot for Internet-rich pedagogy. In J. Chambers (Ed.), *Selected papers from the 11th international conference on college teaching and learning* (pp. 99–109). Jacksonville, FL: Center for the Advancement of Teaching and Learning.

Hudson, B. (2002). The jungle syndrome: Some perils and pleasures of learning without walls. In K. E. Rudestam & J. Schoenholtz-Read (Eds.), *Handbook of online learning. Innovations in higher education and corporate training* (pp. 185–220). Thousand Oaks, CA: Sage.

Lumsdaine, E., & Lumsdaine, M. (1993). *Creative problem solving. Thinking skills for a changing world.* 2nd Ed. New York: McGraw-Hill.

Palmer, P. (1998). *The courage to teach. Teaching from within.* San Francisco: Jossey-Bass.

Papert, S. (1993). *Mindstorms: Children, computers, and powerful ideas.* 2nd Ed. New York: Basic Books.

Taylor, R. (1980). *The computer in the school. Tutor, tool, tutee.* New York: Teachers College Press.

Wedemeyer, C. (1971). Independent study. In L. C. Deighton (Ed.), *The encyclopedia of education, 4.* New York: Macmillan.

Wlodkowski, R. I. (1985). *Enhancing adult motivation to learn.* San Francisco: Jossey-Bass.

# TEAM TEACHING

Team teaching is an approach to creating and facilitating a learning environment and process that is shared by two or more educators. Although the major responsibilities are similar to those for courses being taught by a single educator (e.g., planning, course design, development of syllabi, creation of lesson plans or content, presentation, interaction with learners, evaluation, etc.), sharing these functions offers benefits to learners and educators while also posing additional responsibilities and challenges.

Team teaching in a distributed learning environment sits at the intersection of two sets of concepts and methods: the attributes and processes of successful teams and those of effective distributed learning situations in which most of the interaction occurs using online tools.

There are two key elements of a successful team teaching relationship: sharing and collaborating on the work of leading the class and managing the relationship between or among the members. This way of working is characterized by interdependence and joint responsibility and accountability for achieving desired outcomes; therefore, a collaborative process is required. The educators must determine how they will work together, including dividing or sharing various responsibilities, interacting and communicating with each other, assessing and evaluating the progress of the class individually and collectively, identifying and resolving issues or problems with the class and each other, and making decisions or changes. The teaching team will be confronted with the same issues and opportunities as any team that is jointly creating a product or outcome. In the case of teaching, the learning needs of participants are a critical component, and there are also other stakeholders (e.g., the sponsoring institution, administration, other faculty, academic requirements) whose interests must also be considered in the team's overall design and approach to learning.

Team teaching in a distributed learning environment poses particular challenges beyond those typically faced by either teams or learners who are co-located. These issues and potential obstacles to distributed leaning are central to its success, and team teaching in these conditions adds an additional variable—the need to manage the relationship(s) and issues within the team. The team must deal with these issues on multiple levels. If the teaching team itself is geographically distributed, their own process will be further complicated, and they will likely experience the same distance-imposed challenges as the learners. They will also need to plan for and manage the dispersed learning community. In the event that the design of the course also requires learners to collaborate, these issues add an additional level of complexity that must be designed for and managed.

Some of these challenges include:

- *Loss of visual and nonverbal cues*—Effective communication is the result of both verbal and nonverbal interactions. All geographically dispersed work groups are hindered by the loss of the nonverbal component. The team must develop heightened awareness of how and when learners (as well as they themselves) experience and manifest the effects of diminished visual, nonverbal, and social cues as well as a process for how best to compensate for them, quickly and directly addressing problems as they arise.

- *Distortion of time*—When team and/or class members are located in different time zones, another common grounding and orienting mechanism—the assumption that time is linear and sequential—is lost. There are frequently long lags between inputs and responses among members, while in the meantime, the interaction and work of the group continues. This interrupts the normal flow of communication and frequently creates a very disjointed process. The team must establish methods, agreements, and processes for minimizing and managing these disruptions and their effects.

- *Fear of being misunderstood*—A common effect of working in a distributed and time-distorted environment that lacks opportunities for face-to-face interaction and informal communication is members worrying about and experiencing themselves as being misunderstood. Sorting this out, especially when the opportunities for direct, verbal communication are limited and the parties may not have met in person or developed sufficient trust, is so complex as to discourage risk taking and personal disclosure. Both are required for effective interaction, learning, and collaboration.

- *Need for exaggerated structure and processes*—The antidote for these challenges is recognizing that they occur in all distributed work and learning environments and carefully planning how the teaching team will work together to manage and resolve them. This requires the team to create their own agreements and plans as well as to communicate thoroughly and frequently to class members about the content, the processes, and the meta-process of the learning group.

- *Radio silence*—All of these challenges, along with the normal interruptions of daily life, often contribute to lapses of participation in the distributed, online community. When the principal means of communication is computer-based, this is called "radio silence." These absences also exacerbate the problems already identified, and the result can be gridlock within the learning group. The teaching team must be clear about how it will manage absences and be proactive in anticipating the dynamics that result from nonparticipation of one or more members.

In addition to the issues of geographic dispersion, the teaching team may also face other challenges. Competition among members and failure to meet commitments are problems often encountered by teams. They are best addressed by the team's attention to and awareness of its own process and experience and a commitment to deal promptly and thoroughly with such issues.

Working interdependently is harder. Simply put, the work of coordinating and collaborating takes additional time and energy. Each time another member is added to the teaching team, this work becomes more complex and is further complicated by the growing number of interfaces and interdependencies that must be managed.

Team teaching also offers added benefits to both learners and teachers.

- *Synergy*—The members of the teaching team need to identify and plan what each person uniquely can contribute—and then must determine how the contributions can be woven together to create a seamless and synergistic experience.

- *Multiple points of view*—Each member of the team brings a different perspective to both the topic of the course and the group dynamics of the class. It is important that all members of the teaching team participate actively in class forums or discussions. This variety enriches the experience and learning of all.

- *Opportunity for behavior modeling*—The online learning experience is enhanced by interactivity and careful attention to the behavioral dynamics of the medium. Members will learn about these aspects of the experience when the teaching team consciously models effective, facilitative behaviors.

- *Shared workload*—The multiple responsibilities of designing and facilitating learning experiences, especially the administrative ones, can be divided. Primary responsibility for various aspects of course content preparation and presentation may be assigned to individual or subgroups. When a member of the team is unavailable, others can provide backup and coverage for him or her, thus providing more flexibility for the faculty.

These benefits, however, will be realized only if the teaching team is willing to make the investment in being a team, with all that implies, rather than simply dividing up the various responsibilities for managing the class and delivering the content. They must anticipate and thoughtfully design the learning experience—both content and process—that effectively manages the benefits and constraints of distributed environments.

—*Tracy C. Gibbons*

*See also* COLLABORATION; FACILITATION

## Bibliography

Duarte, D. L., & Snyder, N. T. (1999). *Mastering virtual teams: Strategies, tools, and techniques that succeed.* San Francisco: Jossey-Bass.

Gibbons, T. C., & Brenowitz, R. S. (1998, 2000). *Developing virtual and geographically dispersed teams in cyberspace.* CoastWise Consulting, Inc. Retrieved from www.coastwiseconsulting.com/article_virtual_teams.htm.

Hiltz, S. R., & Turoff, M. (1993). *The network nation: Human communication via computer.* Cambridge: The MIT Press.

Larson, C. E., & LaFasto, F. M. J. (1989). *TeamWork: What must go right/what can go wrong.* Newbury Park, CA: Sage.

Larson, C. E., & LaFasto, F. M. J. (2001). *When teams work best: 6000 team members and leaders tell what it takes to succeed.* Thousand Oaks, CA: Sage.

Lipnack, J., & Stamps, J. (1997). *Virtual teams: Reaching across space, time, and organizations with technology.* New York: John Wiley.

Rudestam, K. E., & Schoenholtz-Read, J. (Eds.). (2002). *Handbook of online learning: Innovations in higher education and corporate training.* Thousand Oaks, CA: Sage.

# TELECOMMUTING/TELEWORKING

Teleworking is one form of *remote work.* Remote work is work that is performed away from the principal office or work site, one or more days per week. Information and communications technologies, such as telephones, personal computers, and fax machines, are used to stay connected to the workplace and to communicate with co-workers.

*Telecommuting* is a related term that is sometimes used. Jack Nilles, a researcher at the University of Southern California, coined the word *telecommuting* during the oil crisis of the early 1970s. He believed that information technology (IT) could substitute for physical travel to and from work by car, thus conserving fuel.

The term *telework* is used more frequently in Europe, and *telecommuting* is used more frequently in the United States. Because "tele" means distance, telework refers to work done at a distance. *Telework* is a preferable term because it more aptly describes the fact that workers work at a distance from the location of their employer. That is, the work is moved to the worker, rather than asking the worker to move to the work. In this manner, work need not be restricted to the office or to a conventional office schedule. Rather, work can be performed anytime, anywhere.

Today's teleworking and telecommuting options go beyond energy conservation; they represent strategic management initiatives that can have a substantial impact on productivity, job satisfaction, organizational commitment, and work/family balance, and can enhance competitive advantage for firms that use them properly.

## FORMS OF TELEWORK

Telework can assume one of the following four forms: home-based, satellite offices, neighborhood telework centers, and mobile telework. Home-based telework refers to employees that work at home on a regular basis. This is the most common telework location.

Satellite offices consist of regional branches of a single organization located near residential locations of its employees. This closer location reduces commuting time. Any employee that lives near the IT-equipped satellite office may work there, regardless of his or her job duties.

Neighborhood telework centers are shared office facilities where employees from different organizations conduct their work close to their respective residences. Several companies may jointly lease and share office space. Workspace may be divided into separate areas for employees of each company.

Finally, mobile telework comprises work conducted away from any single location while using tools such as laptop computers and cellular phones to communicate with clients, coworkers, and other members of the organization. Mobile telework includes work conducted while in transit, such as in cars or on planes, as well as in temporary settings such as hotel rooms.

## TELEWORKING POPULATION

Telework has become an increasingly popular work option. The Telework America 2001 study sponsored by the International Telework Association and Council and funded by AT&T estimates the current number of teleworkers in the United States to be about 28.8 million, approximately one in every five workers. The population of teleworkers worldwide is estimated to reach 100 million by 2007.

Work has been revolutionized, and in its wake, so have social and cultural norms regarding the work domain. Boundaries between work and family have blurred; laptop computers, personal digital assistants (PDAs), and cellular phones have become standard office issue; and the 8-hour workday has become an anachronism. Debate over the social and political consequences of telework is continuing to mount as the teleworking population grows rapidly. The potential benefits of telework have made it an alluring alternative for both employees and employers.

## ADVANTAGES OF TELEWORK

Employees cite numerous advantages associated with telework. The primary benefit that most teleworkers report is increased efficiency. Teleworking often indicates greater employee focus and dedication than is typically found in the traditional on-site

setting. Specifically, most teleworkers are able to complete the same amount of work while off-site in approximately half the amount of time spent on site. This increased productivity typically results from elimination of distractions often found at work, such as unscheduled interruptions, hallway chat, and so forth. Other benefits include enhanced scheduling flexibility, increased autonomy, reduced commute-related stress, improved productivity, increased organizational commitment, and greater job satisfaction.

Employers likewise benefit from teleworking programs. Productivity gains, improved service delivery, increased job satisfaction, and reduced turnover reported by teleworkers increase profits and customer satisfaction. Additionally, telework initiatives present cost-saving opportunities to companies in the form of reduced absenteeism, fewer worker compensation claims, and lower overhead costs.

In an era marked by hypercompetition, turbulent financial markets, global expansion, and pressure for rapid product development, teleworking initiatives offer organizations access to a wider talent pool for recruitment, selection, and retention purposes. By allowing firms to focus on core business processes, teleworking initiatives may reduce costs associated with labor by outsourcing nonessential jobs or by converting salaried workers to hourly or piece-rate payment schedules. Moreover, the ability to schedule work so that it bridges the boundaries of time and space allows organizations to maintain a competitive edge by responding swiftly, adaptively, and precisely to market pressures that emerge unpredictably outside traditional working hours and locations.

## CHALLENGES OF TELEWORK

The benefits of telework are counterbalanced by challenges it presents to both employees and organizations. Interestingly, some telework advantages, such as creating a work/family balance, maintaining a satisfying home environment, and increased work focus, are also included in the list of challenges cited by teleworking employees. One of the biggest difficulties in telework is employee self-management. Lack of self-management makes it particularly difficult for teleworkers to work from home. These difficulties can be attributed to household distractions that are nonexistent at on-site work places. Although the ability to combine nonwork tasks with work responsibilities is considered to be one benefit of telework, these distractions can make completion of assigned work responsibilities difficult for some teleworkers. Moreover, the opportunity to work at home can tempt many to work too many hours.

Similarly, the opportunity to increase the amount of time spent with one's family is a benefit with potentially negative consequences. Although many employees are able to increase the amount of time spent with their families by working at home, some employees are compelled to use their time to work intensely for longer periods of time. The tendency to increase work time can be attributed to the availability of work-related tools and the autonomy with which to use them. This overwork can lead to workaholism, an addiction to work that can not only impair employee performance through stress-related illness, burnout, and lowered productivity, but also harm familial relations. Often, "more time with family" can connote both reduced work–family conflict and increased stress at home.

Even if teleworkers are able to separate their personal time from their work time, they may have difficulty with the isolation associated with working off-site. Lack of social interaction with one's colleagues and supervisors is a common complaint voiced by teleworkers, particularly those engaged in full-time telework. The isolated nature inherent in the remote work environment may reduce opportunities for networking, socialization, and career advancement.

As a result of diminished visibility in the office, others within the organization may assume that these teleworking individuals are less serious about their careers. This decreased visibility often causes teleworkers to be passed over for promotions. In addition, changes in communication processes associated with teleworking can alter the perceptions of organizational associates. More than traditional on-site workers, teleworkers must communicate clearly and assertively with others in order to avoid misunderstandings that would ordinarily be evident in face-to-face interactions. Teleworkers need to be especially aware of the intent of their messages and be precise in the communication of such messages to both other organization-based employees and fellow teleworkers.

Among the challenges of telework at the organizational level are performance monitoring, managerial controls, and schedule maintenance. Within any telework initiative, management faces the difficult task of monitoring work that is performed remotely. The lack of direct observation and clear communication provided by face-to-face contact with employees can reduce performance. The telework setting challenges traditional concepts of leadership and requires organizations to seek alternatives. External control is difficult for a distributed workforce. Managers whose reports cannot be directly observed may be judged less effective.

Additionally, charges of inequity with regard to telework opportunities have recently come under scrutiny. Professional employees, many of whom enjoy a high degree of autonomy in their jobs, are typically granted the option to telework more often than nonprofessional employees. Moreover, inequitable treatment of professional and nonprofessional employees may generate resentment among work groups, effectively creating a fragmented workforce within the organization that separates into different employee castes. However, increased formalization of supervision may carry the additional risk of reducing job satisfaction among those who telework. The implications of this last point arguably present the greatest challenges to the telework initiative as a whole.

Finally, the novel character of telework challenges basic assumptions about work in general. Irregular working hours and casual dress may convey an unprofessional image. Physical artifacts or symbols, which serve to sustain organizational culture by strengthening employee identification with the organization, are also absent. Work is also constrained by the opportunities afforded by IT.

## FUTURE DIRECTIONS

Recent advances in IT offer workers unprecedented opportunities for flexibility and autonomy. In the future, IT will make it easier to move work to the best workers, wherever they may be located around the world. This trend will make labor markets global in nature. Firms will gain competitive advantage to the extent that they can tap into global labor markets and effectively manage remote workers. Workers will identify less with a physical place and will instead attach themselves to their employing organization by aligning personal needs with organization culture and values. This will require managers to forsake traditional emphasis on command and control and instead use trust and collaboration to enforce the psychological contract with their employees. This trend toward decentralization will have a powerful impact on how we define work and where we live.

*—Donald D. Davis*
*—Janet Bryant*
*—Michael Mihalescz*
*—Rebecca Say*

*See also* OPERATIONS AND MANAGEMENT; STAFFING

## Bibliography

Davis, D. D., & Polonko, K. A. (2001). *Telework in the United States: Telework America Survey 2001.* Washington, DC: International Telework Association and Council.

Froggatt, C. C. (2001). *Work naked: Eight essential principles for peak performance in the virtual workplace.* San Francisco: Jossey-Bass.

International Telework Association and Council. (Ed.). (2000). *E-work guide: How to make telework work for your organization.* Washington, DC: International Telework Association and Council.

Langhoff, J. (1996). *The telecommuter's advisor: Working in the fast lane.* Newport: Aegis.

Lipnack, J., & Stamps, J. (2000). *Virtual teams: People working across boundaries with technology.* 2nd Ed. New York: John Wiley.

Nilles, J. M. (1998). *Managing telework: Strategies for managing the virtual workforce.* New York: John Wiley.

# TELECOURSES

Telecourses are entire courses of for-credit or not-for-credit study that may be distributed through telecommunications or by videotape; include the range of standards-based course requirements, assignments, quizzes, and tests associated with traditional face-to-face courses; integrate ongoing teacher–student communication; and are supported by print-based and electronic materials.

Historically, the roots of telecourses reside in correspondence courses. The technologies of broadcasting and the VCR, however, gave rise to telecourses, which later were delivered via satellite. Most telecourse instruction made the transition to the Internet, which provided e-mail interaction between student and instructor and the distribution of ancillary materials. Some telecourses use the Internet for the distribution of substantial, on-demand, video portions of the telecourse.

The Open University in the United Kingdom was among the first institutions to produce and distribute telecourses systematically. In the United States, telecourses originated in live broadcast productions, usually broadcast by educational (public) television stations. Later, courses were delivered via cable and instructional television fixed service (ITFS). At some colleges with production facilities, closed-circuit college courses were offered live or stored on videotape for later broadcast or for retrieval by individual students.

Few of the telecourses before the 1980s were especially well produced. Uninspired delivery, "talking heads," and a lack of authentic and timely contact between student and instructor all undercut the confidence in telecourses that had been initially voiced by supporters. The failure of the first generation of telecourses to demonstrate economic feasibility also cast doubt on this form of distance learning. In 1981, however, with $150 million, Walter H. Annenberg established at the Corporation for Public Broadcasting (CPB) the Annenberg/CPB Project, whose goal was to improve the access to and quality of higher education. Over 10 years, the project created numerous, visually attractive telecourses—in fact, enough telecourses to enable a student to complete the general requirements for an associate degree in arts and sciences. Also in the United States, a consortium of colleges and producers, who called themselves the Telecourse People and included the Dallas County Community College District, Miami-Dade Community College, and Coastline Community College, produced many other telecourses for use by colleges and broadcast stations. The TeleLearning People, as they later became known, along with PBS, were the major distributors of telecourses. Until 1999, when the Internet gained dominance, telecourses constituted the primary means by which distance learners received their course instruction.

The majority of telecourses have targeted and continue to target adult audiences, either college-going populations of learners, nontraditional adult learners, or those adults engaged in workforce training. Although many pedagogical experts believe that younger students learn best in traditional school settings, high school students in rural or underserved schools without access to advanced courses sometimes participate in telecourses.

The huge start-up costs associated with these virtual degree programs, institutions, and courses, as well as the limited time that was spent on planning these initiatives, meant financial difficulty was a given. The inability to produce a profit or even secure enough revenue to support their operations caused many institutions to significantly retreat from online education by 2000. Online programs were reformatted so that campus-based courses, not just distance learning courses, were also supported. Some virtual institutions entirely disappeared. By this time, advances in technology meant that it was becoming easier to incorporate video and audio into online courses.

Today, "telecourses" usually include a combination of online content and discussion, video (through either video streaming, videotape, or CD-ROM), print materials, and even face-to-face meetings. It is anyone's guess what telecourses will look like in another 10 years, but odds are that they will continue to be offered by institutions of higher education and other providers intent on making instruction available to busy, motivated adults.

—*Richard T. Hezel*
—*Paula Szulc Dominguez*

**See also** COMPUTER-BASED TRAINING (CBT); DELIVERY SYSTEMS; DISTRIBUTED LEARNING/DISTRIBUTED EDUCATION; ONLINE LEARNING

# TELEHEALTH AND TELEMEDICINE

The terms *telehealth* and *telemedicine* frequently are used interchangeably; however, telemedicine generally refers to the use of telecommunications to provide clinical care at a distance, whereas telehealth is much broader in scope and more inclusive. According to the U.S. Office for the Advancement of Telehealth (http://telehealth.hrsa.gov), telehealth is the use of electronic information and telecommunications technologies to support long-distance clinical health care, patient and professional health-related education, and public health and health administration.

Telehealth dates to the late 1800s when rural physicians used the newly invented telephone to provide support to their patients. The first real surge of interest in telehealth, however, came in the late 1970s with the introduction of personal computers. This interest continued through the 1980s as technological improvements gave rise to telehealth programs, and peaked in the late 1990s as technology costs decreased. Future directions likely will include continued integration of technology, communications, and caregiving, particularly with digitizing information, expanding wireless applications, migrating technology to providers' desktops and patients' homes, and the globalization of health care.

Health care applications of technology generally reflect two kinds of activities: store-and-forward technologies (asynchronous) and real-time interactions (synchronous). Store-and-forward allows one user to manipulate information and forward it to a second party for them to manipulate. Sending an e-mail with an attachment is an example of store-and-forward telehealth. The second type of activity, synchronous interaction, takes place in "real time" with two (or more) parties interacting concurrently. A videoconference is a typical synchronous activity.

Telehealth and telemedicine include a variety of health-related activities, including using the Internet to obtain or view health information (more typical of individual use) or using store-and-forward applications (most common among two or more parties). Videoconferences between patients and health professionals are the stereotypical telehealth or telemedicine activity, but actually account for only a modest portion of all telehealth activity.

## CLINICAL AND TRAINING APPLICATIONS

Telehealth has been implemented rapidly in rural and underserved areas because it is seen as a tool to reduce health disparities and to improve access, particularly when barriers exist—be they social, economic, climatological, or geographic. Although there are many studies reporting on user satisfaction with telehealth, there are few clinical trials or good economic analyses, although studies are underway. Telehealth has successfully been implemented in closed settings like prisons, in poor communities without full-time providers, in climate-challenged areas where evacuation is difficult, and in geographically isolated areas where the distances to care are great. Telehealth also has proven useful for training, including supervision and distance delivery of health care education for professionals and patients.

## DIGITAL DIVIDE

The digital divide is the separation of those with high-technology access from those without. Because telehealth is seen as a tool to reduce health disparities, the digital divide is a major barrier to the success of telehealth and telemedicine. Population, income, and race are predictors of access, with higher density areas, wealthier people, and whites more likely to have access than others.

## TECHNOLOGY

Giant strides have been made in the recent past regarding the adaptation of existing technology and the creation of new types of technology for the support of health care. Some technology, for example, filmless radiology, is so pervasive that is has become the standard of practice; other technologies are making headway, but have not become a standard of practice. An example of emerging but not standard technology is the use of digital non-mydriatic retinal cameras in diabetic retinopathy, macular degeneration, and glaucoma screening.

Another set of devices uses low-bandwidth "plain old telephone service" (POTS) videoconferencing technology. Although these devices have many uses, they are particularly good for monitoring. The units can be moved from place to place easily because they are small—about the size of a deli sandwich—and they require no special wiring. For training and supervision, rather than locate the unit in a particular facility, the student carries the unit as he or she rotates from site to site. These same units also can be used for home health monitoring, transmitting vital signs, medication use, weight, and the like. Global positioning systems, common in cars, have been adapted to watches worn by Alzheimer's patients, allowing caregivers to locate electronically a patient who may have wandered away and gotten lost. There are an increasing number of wireless systems, even though there are still problems with signal "bleed" among some medical devices. Wireless laptops and handheld units are increasingly functional; some training programs require students to purchase them as part of their standard supplies. Lessons are automatically downloaded through a wireless system and can even be distributed across multiple training facilities so that all students in a class receive the same lesson in multiple facilities.

Experimentation with remote surgery is also underway. When extremely fine handwork is necessary, having the surgeon control a robotic device may improve the outcome because the robotic devices can be smaller and steadier than a surgeon's hands.

## FINANCING AND REIMBURSEMENT

The Balanced Budget Act of 1997 (P.L.105–33, BBA) was the first federal legislation allowing for reimbursement of services provided via telehealth. This legislation, which went into effect January 1, 1999, reimbursed select services for patients located in federally defined rural Health Professional Shortage Areas (HPSAs). Although groundbreaking, this legislation was controversial because 1) it reimbursed in HPSAs, 2) required fee-sharing, 3) limited eligible presenters, and 4) had no payment for telephone line charges or facility fees. The Balanced Budget Refinement Act of 1999 (P.L. 106–113, BBRA) amended these provisions. Requirements for fee splitting and telepresenters were removed. Additional types of consultations and originating sites were included and a facility fee was added. Although the BBRA addressed a number of difficult reimbursement issues, it still only recognized real-time videoconferencing as acceptable telemedicine, with the exception of demonstration sites in Alaska and Hawaii. Recently proposed legislation has sought to remedy this problem, but to date it has not been enacted into public law.

## LEGAL ISSUES

Prior to telehealth, the patient and provider were physically at the same location, thus the state with jurisdiction was clear. Telehealth raises new issues. If a consumer located in state A sues a practitioner located in state B for advice given via telehealth, wherein lies the jurisdictional authority in this case? Is the jurisdiction the same for a Web site as it is for a two-way teleconferencing unit? Is there any recourse if the health care originates outside of the United States? Does a health professional's malpractice insurance include coverage for care provided at a distance? As yet, there is no clear legal or regulatory guidance on these issues, although some cases are making their way through the courts. Prudent professionals understand the limits of their insurance; they usually are licensed in the states in which they live as well as the states to which they "telecommute" to provide care.

Privacy is different in distributed systems compared to paper systems. In a paper system, only those who could physically touch the paper could access data; and unless copies were made, viewing was limited to one location at a time. In distributed systems, a viewer can be located at a distance from the data, and multiple people can view the data simultaneously. In response to concerns about the privacy of data, the United States passed the Health Insurance Portability and Accountability Act of 1996 (HIPAA). The U.S. Department of Health and Human Services (HHS) issued the regulations and the U.S. Office for Civil Rights (OCR) is responsible for implementing and enforcing the privacy regulation. The first final rule was published in the *Federal Register* (65 FR 82462) on December 28, 2000, with a compliance date of April 14, 2003. Final modifications, published on August 14, 2002, substantially reduced the original protections.

Because systems are distributed and can be accessed from multiple points without the person being seen, authentication is a key issue: Is the person who he or she claims to be, and does this person have authorization to view these data? Authentication can be accomplished through passwords as well as through biometric devices such as retinal scans or thumbprints. Most systems rely on a combination of methods. Although there are no completely secure systems, the surveillance possible on most electronic systems exceeds that common in paper systems. Moreover, should unauthorized access occur, electronic traces are generally easier to follow than the clues available in the physical paper world.

The Federal Communications Commission (FCC, http://www.fcc.gov) is responsible for the regulation of telecommunications, including telecommunications used in health care. One example of the FCC's regulatory authority is the implementation of digital television (DTV). Some types of medical telemetry devices use vacant TV channels. The FCC, at the direction of Congress, has apportioned currently unused channels to TV stations to be used for DTV, requiring device users to adjust so that they operate on vacant channels. The FCC alerted the manufacturers, installers, and users of medical devices through information published in the *Federal Register* (62 FR 58656, October 30, 1997) that they may need to take action to avoid interference to their operations during the transition to DTV service.

Another activity of the FCC is the Universal Service Plan, which is designed to encourage the growth of telehealth in rural areas by making telecommunications rates for public and nonprofit rural health care providers comparable to those paid in urban areas. Although the Universal Service Plan has been fraught with bureaucratic difficulties, those who have been able to take advantage of its support have benefited greatly. Section 254(h)(1)(A) of the Communications Act of 1934, which was implemented by the FCC on May 8, 1997, requires that public and nonprofit rural health care providers receive the telecommunications services necessary for the provision of health care services at rates comparable to those in urban areas.

*—B. Hudnall Stamm*

***See also*** ASYNCHRONOUS FORMATS; CULTURAL ACCESS/DIGITAL DIVIDE; INFORMATICS; INTERNET; LEGAL ISSUES; MEDICAL EDUCATION

## Bibliography

Center for Telemedicine Law: http://www.ctl.org

Darkins, A. W., & Carey, M. A. (2000). *Telemedicine and telehealth: Principles, policies, performance, and pitfalls.* New York: Springer.

Jerome, L. W., DeLeon, P. H., James, L. C., Folen, R., Earles, J., & Gedney, J. J. (2000). The coming age of telecommunications in psychological research and practice. *American Psychologist, 55,* 407–421.

National Telecommunications and Information Administration. (1999). Falling through the Net: Defining the digital divide. Retrieved March 11, 2001, from http://www.ntia.doc.gov/ntiahome/fttn99/contents.html.

Office for the Advancement of Telehealth: http://telehealth.hrsa.gov.

Shortliffe, E. H., Wiederhold, G., Perreault, L.E., & Fagan, L. M. (Eds.). (2000). *Medical informatics: Computer applications in health care and biomedicine.* Heidelberg, Germany: Springer Verlag.

Stamm, B. H., & Perednia, D. (2000). Evaluating psychosocial aspects of telemedicine & telehealth systems. *Professional Psychology Research and Practice, 31,* 184–189.

Telemedicine Information Exchange: http://tie.telemed.org.

# TELEPHONE TEACHING

The idea of using telephone equipment to distribute and gather information is not new; it has been around for as long as the telephone itself. However, telephone teaching, relatively new to the scene, can now be found throughout the world. In its simplest form telephone teaching (or teleteaching) is merely the process of conducting classes over the telephone rather than in person, typically with the teacher on one end of the telephone line connected in real-time to students scattered elsewhere. The single most significant, and obvious, feature of this teaching and learning method is that it negates the necessity of teachers and students being in the same geographic location at the same time.

More broadly, the term *teleteaching* can also apply to almost any online system that uses telephonic equipment to transmit content or otherwise enhance the learning environment without in-person encounters. These systems include voice mail messages, e-mail communications, facsimile transmissions, Web cameras, Internet chat rooms, online bulletin board postings, and Web sites.

## EARLY DEVELOPMENT

An example of early teleteaching technology is a movie information line or the IRS tax tips line; they are methods of organized and purposeful learning—that is, using telephone equipment to gather information whereby the process of listening to recorded messages is used. However, as we know, effective teaching requires more interaction in terms of how teachers and students engage one other.

First instances of teleteaching included a group of students gathered in the same room around a telephone that was set up to a speaker while connected to the teacher located elsewhere. This early use of remote teaching can be viewed as making the best of an adverse situation when local teachers were nonexistent or temporarily unavailable. As technology developed and equipment costs became more affordable, telephone teaching continued to evolve and expand to include more applications reaching more people, even when it was not fueled by necessity.

## METHODOLOGY

Commonly, teacher and students connect by telephone at a pre-arranged day and time for their class by connecting to a telephone link—rented from the phone company and referred to as a *bridge*—that is capable of handling multiple users simultaneously. The teacher either calls all the students or the students place the call, with long-distance charges billed to the calling parties. With long-distance telephone rates available for just pennies per minute, it has become a viable alternative to commuting to school for both teachers and students when considering alternative expenses (such as transportation availability, gasoline prices, and parking fees) even if distance is not necessarily a factor. Perhaps even more significant is the convenience and time savings of being able to call in to participate in classroom activities without having to leave the safety and comfort of home or office at varying times throughout the day or days of the week.

In addition to educational classes, businesses can conduct training courses when hands-on access to equipment or machinery is not necessary. Employees located worldwide can connect by telephone more expeditiously and economically than they could assemble for in-person training sessions. Additionally, individuals can sign up to learn a wide array of "how-to" topics over the telephone; Internet searches will yield seemingly endless possibilities.

## ADVANTAGES

The benefits of telephone teaching are far-reaching and can be measured from both teacher and student perspectives. More students can be reached across greater distances, and more diversity creates richer learning environments. Student-to-student interaction is often increased, and students are more likely to ask questions because of the conversational atmosphere that talking on the telephone creates. Even introverted students will often participate when too shy to do so in person. Telephone teaching can more easily incorporate the use of guest lecturers when they are otherwise unavailable due to cost or time or distance restraints. It can also help alleviate student overcrowding that may exist in traditional educational settings—especially for the more popular subjects.

## DISADVANTAGES

Problems encountered can also be measured from both teacher and student perspectives. Problems faced by teachers while telephone teaching include the inability to read facial expressions and body language of their students—unless a student literally speaks up, he or she might never get the help needed. Because their face-to-face contact is lacking, with the teacher and students never meeting, they remain anonymous—which isn't necessarily problematic unless one tries to act as an impostor or use a hidden identity for other deceptive purposes.

Students can be distracted by home or office activities and noises that would not be present in a traditional classroom. Also, telephone and other support equipment may be unavailable, unreliable, or too cost prohibitive. Class content involving a lot of graphics may suffer unless support of other electronic apparatus is equally available to all students.

## FUTURE USE

Despite the advantages to telephone teaching, some believe in the continued need for traditional classroom settings. However, telephone teaching—along with all the supporting technology—clearly has a place in the future of educational systems. Telephone teaching may not ever be able to fully replace traditional classroom settings—nor was it ever intended to. It is, however, proving to be a useful alternative that can replace traditional classroom settings, especially for rural and remote students where teachers are unavailable.

## CONCLUDING COMMENT

Technological advancements continue to develop and keep stride with this method of teaching. Students can now pursue their educational goals regardless of where they live—as long as they have the necessary equipment available. Access to the Internet—whether at home or at work—enhances the learning experience even more. The proliferation of cellular telephone systems, the capacity and speed of fiber optic communication lines, the movement toward mainstream use of satellite communications, and the increase in interactive television programming are but a few examples of how advancing technology will better serve future telephone teaching.

—*Janice Safian Bock*

*See also* EVOLVING TECHNOLOGIES; TEACHING IN AN ELECTRONIC CLASSROOM; TELECOURSES

### Bibliography

The American Journal of Distance Education: http://www.ajde.com

The Distance Educator Web site: http://www.distance-educator. om

# TEXTUAL COMPUTING

Textual computing broadly refers to the use of information and communication technologies (ICT) for the analysis, encoding, presentation, or interchange of textual materials, in particular in the areas of scholarship and teaching. The use of computers for the analysis of textual materials goes back to the late 1940s, the earliest days of stored program computing. The pioneer of textual computing is generally acknowledged to be Father Roberto Busa, who worked with IBM on the development of programs for producing lemmatized concordances, laboriously entering texts on punched cards and constructing huge lexical and morphological databases. Early textual computing was largely mechanistic and concerned more with scientific analysis than with imaginative reading. Linguistic applications reliant upon the analysis of large quantities of data were the most popular application. Stylostatistics, which offers analyses of textual corpora for authorship attribution or dating, was a common technique, but one that was not taken up by mainstream textual scholars or literary critics. Easier forms of input via keyboard and better screens first encouraged word processing, and then electronic mail. These, more than any other development, encouraged textual scholars to begin speculating on the nature of text and textuality in the new fluid media, and allowed discussions on these matters across space and time on electronic discussion lists.

The development of hypertext and multimedia has received attention from a broad range of scholars, both for their abilities to map complex textual spaces and integrate nontextual materials and for the theoretical illuminations possible when conceptualizing textual theories. Computing techniques have also proven invaluable in textual editing, where the management of networks of complex variant readings has always stretched the presentation capabilities of the printed page and the cognitive capacity of the human brain and memory. In linguistics, the availability of very large corpora of written and spoken text, both contemporary and historical, has transformed language study. The sharable qualities of electronic text have generated the growth of text archives and electronic text centers, which are now developing into full-scale digital libraries. There also has been an explosion in the availability of texts of varying quality, from both public domain sources and commercial and academic publishers. In particular, there is a huge amount of electronic text available on the Internet from all discipline areas.

The two key problems posed by the rapid development of electronic text from a myriad of sources over the past 50 years have been the consistency and cohesiveness in the encoding of textual features and the vexing issue of special and non-Roman character sets.

## AVAILABILITY OF ELECTRONIC TEXT

Text archives and electronic text centers offer free access to many thousands of texts for analysis and reuse. The Oxford Text Archive (http://ota.ahds. ac.uk), for example, has more than 2,000 texts available in many languages and from all periods. The Electronic Text Center at the University of Virginia Library (http://etext.lib.virginia.edu) has around 70,000 texts in languages as diverse as Latin, Apache, Japanese, and Chinese. Texts from reliable centers such as these are generally of good quality, consistently encoded, and contain full bibliographic information; they are also free. Other free sources of text are more variable in quality, so users need to be aware of the status of the materials provided. Yet other suppliers have good quality texts for which the users are required to pay.

Modern linguistics and lexicography rely heavily on large electronic corpora to give accurate information about language usage at different periods of time. Corpus work began in the 1960s with collections such as the *Brown Corpus* (of American English) and the *Lancaster-Oslo-Bergen Corpus* (of British English), both of which contain around 1 million words of English. These sound extensive, and indeed were of enormous value in the early days, but corpora of this size are not adequate for accurate linguistic research, particularly for rare words or constructions; more recent corpora are orders of magnitude larger than these. The *British National Corpus (BNC)* contains some 100 million words of written and spoken English, and the COBUILD *Bank of English* has 330 million words of modern English. With historical materials, it is possible to build corpora that encompass the totality of the extant writings in a language or of a particular period. For example, the *Toronto Corpus of Old English* holds the complete texts of literary materials written in English between 450 and 1100, and the *Thesaurus Linguae Graecae* contains all literary materials written in ancient Greek between the fifth century BCE and the eighth century CE. These two resources have been invaluable for the study of texts from these periods, because they allow comparisons and precise citations as never before.

Other textual resources that have been made increasingly available are the complete corpora of particular works, authors, or genres. There are many versions of the Bible and Bible commentaries, and almost as many complete Shakespeare collections (though perhaps one might pick out the *Arden Shakespeare* as a particularly valuable collection). *Literature Online,* produced by Chadwyck-Healey, is a rich collection of literary and linguistic texts in many languages and from many periods that has been widely used by researchers and students for a number of years.

## TEXTUAL ANALYSIS AND HYPERTEXT

The proliferation of electronic textual resources offers diverse opportunities for new kinds of study, interpretation, and analysis of written works, and analytic tools have been available for many years to assist in this. The nature of early programs such as OCP (the Oxford Concordance Program), which allowed rapid and easy manipulation of alphanumeric symbols, sometimes tended toward a somewhat mechanistic approach, concerned more with scientific analysis than with imaginative reading, though many excellent studies have been produced that have illuminated the critical appreciation of literary works. Of note here is the work of John Burrows on Jane Austen's novels, and numerous analytic articles on the dating and authorship of literary, philosophical, religious, and historical works by critics such as David Holmes and Thomas Merriam, many of which are published in the journals *Literary and Linguistic Computing* and *Computers and the Humanities.* Linguistic applications reliant upon the analysis of large quantities of data have been popular, and stylometry, which offers analyses of textual corpora for authorship attribution or dating, was and remains useful, but has largely not been taken up by mainstream textual scholars or literary critics. More popular recently is the work of such major literary and textual critics as Kathryn Sutherland and Jerome McGann, who have used hypertext theories and methods to situate literary works in their cultural contexts, and have encouraged students to engage with new debates and new readings.

## TEXTUAL EDITING

For the textual editor and textual critic, the new possibilities offered by textual computing have enabled large-scale projects that can break free of the restrictions of the printed page in trying to represent all the variant stages of a work, or body of work, and its transmission. Computerized methods as applied to textual criticism were initially used to assist the scholar in the production of the conventional end product: a printed critical edition of the text with the base text printed in full and the variants from other texts at the foot of the page or at the end of the work. Now developments in textual presentation software using structural markup and hypertext linking mechanisms mean that critical editions also can be published in electronic form. Many large, collaborative editing projects have been embarked upon that would not have been possible or that would have taken entire scholarly lifetimes of several individuals without computer assistance. The *Electronic Beowulf Project,* the *Canterbury Tales Project,* the *Wittgenstein Archive,* the *Women Writers Project,* and various editions of Yeats and Joyce would all have been much more difficult, if not impossible, without electronic tools and techniques.

## TEXT ENCODING

The most important single development in textual computing is probably the advent of the variant forms of Standard Generalized Markup Language (SGML), which allow the interchange of electronic texts without loss of complex features that are recorded in the originals. Five hundred years of printing history mean that we take for granted the meaning added to texts by the use of special characters and punctuation, stylistic features, fonts, type sizes, and marginalia, which are often represented differently when the texts are converted to electronic formats. Scholarly initiatives such as the Text Encoding Initiative (TEI), the Making of America Project (MoA), and the Metadata Encoding and Transmission Standard (METS) have produced

sets of guidelines for the consistent encoding of these complex features. The TEI guidelines, for instance, offer sets of recommendations for the encoding and representation of the features for the preparation of electronic texts of many different kinds. These guidelines are used by many projects, text centers, individual scholars, and publishers to ensure that consistency is maintained and reusability and exchange are facilitated. The advent of the Unicode standards of character set encoding means that special characters are no longer the acute problem they were, although some rarer languages are less well-covered than most.

*—Marilyn Deegan*

*See also* DOCUMENT MANAGEMENT SYSTEMS; HYPERTEXT; LIBRARY TECHNOLOGIES

### Bibliography

Condron, F., Fraser, M., & Sutherland, S. (2001). *Digital resources for the humanities.* Morgantown, VA: West Virginia University Press.
Hockey, S. (2000). *Electronic texts in the humanities: Principles and practice.* Oxford: Oxford University Press.
Sutherland, K. (1997). *Electronic text: Investigations in method and theory.* Oxford: Clarendon Press.

## TIME MANAGEMENT

Time management in a distributed learning environment is the skill of effectively allocating available time such that the goals associated with learning are completed. Whether from the perspective of a student or a teacher, concerns about the effective use of time take on new meaning. Managing time in the context of an online environment requires one to incorporate the well-tested basics of traditional time management principles along with those techniques that are unique to effectively accomplishing tasks and priorities in a distributed learning situation. Factors unique to this environment include asynchronous access, with class in session effectively 24 hours a day, 7 days a week; multiple time zones; and factors such as course design and participation norms unique to distance learning.

The following are considerations for students:

- Check in on a regular basis. Set specific times of the day and week to check in rather than continuously feel as if there is always something waiting to be read and you are late if you haven't read it the same day as posted. This will help to avoid feelings of information overload.

- Set one time daily, or every other day, to accomplish specific course-related tasks. Develop a habit based on what allows you to be most productive (e.g., a set time for administrative tasks such as logging on and downloading material separate from time to read and study the material).

- Print messages and uploaded papers to read when offline. For example, you might want to read while waiting at the doctor's office. Jot notes in the margin about your response while reading the message. This makes it easier to post a response if you have had time to think about the material before responding.

- Establish clear priorities. This will facilitate the completion of major tasks on a timely schedule. Time management experts generally agree that this is an essential step to remain focused on accomplishing one's goals.

- Allocate blocks of time to accomplish course requirements. For example, set a specific time for reading assignments and preparing for online discussion, reading other students' postings, writing your responses, participating in team assignments such as preparing an online poster session, and writing and posting longer papers.

- Be prompt when it is your turn to post a paper or a response. Collaborative learning in an asynchronous learning environment requires timely participation and meeting established norms such as deadlines.

The following are considerations for teachers:

- Create a hospitable space for students to get to know one another and to share their ideas and new learning effectively.

- Establish guidelines for participation such as time limits for commenting on given sections of material. The amount of discussion expected or required (e.g., two postings per week) should be clear to all participants.

- Control class size. The number of students enrolled in a class will affect participation levels and workload, so be careful not to let classes get too large. Research shows that more time is needed than in face-to-face instruction, thereby underscoring the importance of allowing adequate time to respond to students' posts and supporting a sense of learning community.

- Consider course design options. It is important to have a manageable amount of material both for the entire course and for each week's discussions. The workload can be managed with the following approaches: use of teams to study and present specific subtopics, staggered deadlines for different groups of students, and different types of assignments for various types of learning (e.g., present case studies, create poster sessions).

- Establish office hours either by telephone or online. For example, commit to being online for certain blocks of time, establish a chat area at a certain time, or establish a space for responding to students' questions in real time.

The following are general tips for both students and teachers:

- Build the necessary time for the course into your schedule. Estimate time needed for each task the course requires, and schedule time throughout each week of the course to do this work. It is ideal if the days and times of day are routine so you can more easily build these tasks (particularly the priority ones) into your daily/weekly schedule.

- Remember that habits are the key to good time management and that good results come from good habits. The opportunity lies in managing your life priorities such that you identify and develop habits designed to support your success.

- Determine what information would be useful to have in hard copy to help manage what you keep in soft copy. For example, it may be of value to have a hard-copy calendar posted in your study area with due dates for assignments in easy-to-read-at-a-glance format.

- Set time limits. Decide how many hours a week you are going to dedicate to the course, and section this time according to time required to complete the course requirements throughout the duration of the course. These are your priorities and should be scheduled on your calendar. This will help you identify deadlines (and start times) for each assignment or task, thereby staying focused on the goals and objectives of the course and/or program.

- Overcome procrastination. Consider marking both the day you will start and the day you will complete a course assignment on your hard-copy calendar so as to better plan time to complete the essential components of each assignment. If you struggle with getting started with a complex or larger assignment, divide it into more manageable subtasks and plan start and end dates for the subtasks. After you complete the first subtask, the momentum of getting part of the task done will more likely carry you through its completion. Time management experts generally agree that doing the toughest jobs first helps get the larger task done by giving you a sense of accomplishment when finished.

- Schedule time to plan, organize, and take care of administrative tasks. For example, before logging off each day, list the things that need to get done next time you log on, or the next day. Also, make time to organize your files (hard- and soft-copy ones) to keep your information organized as you go. It is a good idea to do these types of tasks at times of the day when your energy is lower, perhaps either as a warm-up task when you first get ready to work, or as an end of the work period task when you are tired.

- Identify tasks and manage to a task list with priorities clearly marked. Have priority tasks integrated into your daily schedule so that they get done efficiently. For example, if reading postings and responding to them twice each week is a priority, make sure your schedule on the days you plan to do this lists this task first. Have a realistic plan for how you will spend your time on the days you work on the course. It is also important to allow for some flexibility in your schedule so that if and when interruptions occur, they don't necessarily cause you to be late in completing an important task. It is also a good idea to set aside time to master plan, or analyze your time use and identify any modifications that would help you improve your ability to complete your priorities.

- Organize your electronic files so that you can easily find the information you need. For example, you may want to have a folder for the online class with subfolders for each component of the class. Additionally, you may find it useful to create a set of subject files for information that you use across courses.

- Create efficient office space by organizing your desk to hold only what you need to do your current work. Consider this prime real estate and allow it to hold only what you are currently working on. This will help focus your attention on the current task and

reduce potential distractions. Have the resources you need to complete course assignments close at hand, ideally in the same room where you are working.

*—Nancy C. Willis*

***See also*** SKILL DEVELOPMENT

## Bibliography

Covey, S. R., Merrill, A. R., & Merrill, R. R. (1994). *First things first.* New York: Simon & Schuster.

Ellis, David. (1994). *Becoming a master student*, 7th ed. Boston, MA: Houghton Mifflin.

Mayer, Jeffrey J. (1999). *Time management for dummies.* New York: John Wiley.

Palloff, R. M., & Pratt, K. (1999). *Building learning communities in cyberspace.* San Francisco, CA: Jossey-Bass Inc.

Rudestam, K. E., & Schoenholtz-Read, J. (Eds.). (2002). *Handbook of online learning: Innovations in higher education and corporate training.* Thousand Oaks, CA: Sage.

# TRANSCRIPTS

The academic transcript is a subset of the student's total academic record at the institution. It is essentially a neutral document, recording the basic identifying information about the person whose record it is, the history of his or her enrollment status at the institution, courses attempted and completed, grades received, and any degrees earned. The total academic record may contain many other pieces of information about the student, but the transcript is a succinct document, usually no more than two to three pages, and does not usually contain narrative text, but rather a chronological listing of academic work. Narrative transcripts, in contrast, will have a page or more written by the instructor and dedicated to a detailed description of the student's performance in the course.

The transcript is used as a conduit of information, and is sent to a person or agency by the institution, but only at the request of the student or former student. That person or agency, in turn, uses the transcript to review the academic performance of the student. A common use for the transcript is for a potential employer to review it to verify the student's educational accomplishments as a precursor to making a job offer. Transcripts also are used as part of the admissions criteria to other schools; for example, a student applying to a graduate degree program would need to supply transcripts from his or her undergraduate school(s). Transcripts are also an essential document in the acceptance of transfer credit from one school to the next.

The transcript is considered a legal document and supercedes the diploma, which in the United States is considered largely ceremonial. In this modern computer era, transcripts are generally produced as printed reports from the student information system or database maintained by the institution. However, prior to computerized student information systems, a document known as the Permanent Record Card was used to maintain the transcript record of a student. Even now, many older institutions do not have their earlier student transcript records computerized, so these transcripts may be issued as a photocopy of the permanent record card.

An official transcript is usually produced on security paper with a watermark or some other identifier to avoid fraud, and must contain the signature of the certifying official (usually the registrar), the institutional seal, and the date of issue. A key or legend should accompany each paper transcript issued so that the elements of the transcript, such as grades, can be clearly understood by the reviewer of the document. Transcripts not received directly from the issuing institution should not be considered official.

## DISTRIBUTED EDUCATION OFFERINGS

A course is not considered a distance education offering if less than 50% of the content is delivered online. In that case, the online instruction would be considered only supplemental to the main mode of instructional delivery, which is typically face-to-face. Some colleges and universities distinguish courses that are entirely Internet- or Web-based by using an "I" or "W" on the transcript after the course number. The transcript key, if one exists, would explain this designation. Other modes of distributed learning delivery, such as independent study, are not usually identified on the transcript. If a degree program is made up entirely of distributed learning coursework, the transcript is not likely to include this designation.

Ongoing debate exists regarding this designation practice, specifically with regard to individual courses. Some constituencies, such as employment agencies or licensing boards, believe that the quality of courses not delivered face-to-face must be lower than those that are, and thus want to see displayed the delivery methods of the various courses. However, those opposed to such a transcript display argue that many factors affect the instructional quality for any given course, and that non–face-to-face delivery should not be prejudged. This side of the issue maintains that the transcript aims to be a neutral, historical, and legal document, and that variables that are subjective and opinion should not be based on it.

## INTERNATIONAL TRANSCRIPTS

Transcripts also are available from international schools; however, in many foreign countries, the diploma, which displays the title of the degree earned, and not the transcript is considered the essential document. Due to the popularity of American higher education, international applications for admission are on the rise, and may make up a significant portion of an institution's applicant pool. Translating services are available that will translate international transcripts into the language needed for review. In addition, the translation may even include an interpretation of the educational record to provide a basis for determination of degree equivalency.

—*Bridget Lee Brady*

*See also* COURSE CREDIT/CREDIT TRANSFER; ENROLLMENT STATUS

### Bibliography

Aucoin, Paul, Bolli, Gerhard J., Bradely, Elva E., Brown, William O., Mack, Greta S., Posey, Columbus H., Robertson, Michael N., & Stewart, John T. (1996). *AACRAO academic record and transcript guide*. Washington, DC: American Association of Collegiate Registrars and Admissions Officers.

# TRANSFORMATIONAL LEARNING

In many circles, adult learning means getting trained for a new job or career. No one would argue that learning assists career development, but transformational learning is much more than "training," and it affects more than "career" issues. The most important characteristics of transformational learning for adults, throughout their lives, include repurposing, ongoing individual development, and continuous preparation for the future.

## REPURPOSING

Adult learning, at its best, is an inside-out process, developing in relation to one's deepest stirrings and dreams, which foster plans and decisions around a personal sense of life purpose. Purpose is a profound commitment to a compelling expectation, an expression of ultimate concerns and basic values. One's sense of purpose is not static. It changes and evolves throughout the adult lifecycle. There is a continuous process of "repurposing," which may result in a continuation of life as it has been, or a very different life design. Repurposing is a self-conscious process that is never-ending. It is a self-directed process, affecting everything one does. Effective repurposing requires one to engage in learning and unlearning.

## ADULT DEVELOPMENT

Like repurposing, adult development occurs throughout the lifecycle. The conscious and aware person does not develop according to some cultural blueprint, but from inner values and strategic choices. It is driven by intentionality and continuous learning. Such learning is "holistic," combining cognitive growth, emotional development, and decision making. Learning is "transformational" when adults—through choice or circumstance—shift gears in some major way to seek new possibilities in their lives, such as pursuing unfulfilled dreams or pursuing new directions in their careers, relationships, social responsibilities, or financial situation. Because there is so much change in the postmodern world, an increasing number of turning points and critical events in human lives require re-evaluation. These are the primary places where transformational learning takes place.

Transformational learning involves a fundamental re-evaluation of some or all of one's roles, priorities, vision, and goals, and results in new understandings of self and new commitments to future life possibilities. The center of this ongoing learning is the individual person. Each person must learn how to pick and choose ways to gain the skills necessary for successful maturation. This might be retooling for a new career, stepping into a new level of leadership, or retreating from the routines of the work world and into the art of living.

Human development, across the adult years, is the personal context of transformational learning, because the focus of learning shifts throughout the lifecycle. There is a developmental flow with many variations throughout the adult years. Although this development is not age-specific, the general flow is as follows:

- In one's twenties, a central transformational learning task is the shift from "adolescent" and "dependent" modalities to "adult," "independent," and "interdependent" ways of being. One typically wants to "launch" successfully into adult life, through dreams, educational training, peer and mentoring relationships, traveling, experimenting with work and relationship roles, and practicing the management of money. Fortunately, a 20-year-old is used to being a learner, but the shift from "student" to "independent worker" often requires transformational learning that spans several years. Life transitions require more time than one normally anticipates, because they involve emotional issues that usually adapt more slowly than conceptual ones.
- In one's thirties, there is typically a desire to "settle down," deal with marriage or its alternatives, perhaps begin a family, progress significantly in career and financial areas, deepen friendships, and deal with "life/work balance." One wants and expects "learning" to help facilitate these outcomes, and often that learning will be "transformative."
- In one's forties, a profound evaluation of the life course often occurs. The result usually falls into these categories: repurpose in some major way; consider major changes in the areas of careers, geographic location, and intimate relationships; find new dreams and make peace with "mid-life"; and assume leadership responsibility in selected social roles (schools, clubs, politics, and such). Perhaps the most remarkable learning at this point in life is the discovery of an inner self—a dialogue between inner and outer life that functions as a reliable guide to the future, a gyroscope for both inner and outer life. Just as the twenties were a major departure from the teens, the forties are often a creative bridge into the midlife years, which may extend through the fifties and beyond. These shifts all require major learning and adaptation, and often that learning is transformative, opening up new directions and deepening life's journey.

- In one's fifties, entrepreneurial roles are often attractive, as a way to take charge of one's work life. Other developments that may take place include simplifying one's life, investing more time in travel, developing retirement plans, serving on boards of agencies, putting children through college, and assuming a variety of mentoring and leadership roles. Learning serves the goals of independence and interdependence, and often that learning will be transformative.

- In one's sixties, seventies, and beyond, there often is a shift from a "work-oriented" to a "service-oriented" life. Generativity and legacy are strong motivators for this cohort for moving beyond full-time work roles into mentoring and consultative roles, particularly in the nonprofit and social service areas. One-on-one mentoring is an attractive function for many, whereas others prefer becoming mentors to the culture. Transformational learning is often required to accomplish this transition to a life of considerable freedom and opportunities.

A demographic trend in all the industrialized nations of the world at this time is the shift from populations that are predominantly "young" to populations that are predominantly "old." By the year 2030, the median age of Americans will be 57. It is very possible that 30 years from now, if not sooner, "transformational learning" will be taught and modeled by "seniors" or "elders," who will have experienced the benefits and necessity of continuous learning, including deep learning that fosters renewal and new beginnings.

## PREPARATION FOR THE FUTURE

The context, in our era, for these profound personal developments is rapid and continuous social change. At some point in the 20th century we shifted from a culture of predominantly stability and structure to a culture of predominantly change and transitions. The ability to manage significant amounts of ongoing change is demanded of both individual adults and social institutions as never before. Yet few of us are prepared or trained to manage the complex levels of change that affect our lives and culture. In order for adults to continue to grow and develop effectively in a world of complex and unpredictable change, they need to be continuously engaged in a self-directed learning process. This is a major challenge for transformational learning.

Many of today's leaders will simply ignore the complex dimensions and learning demands of what lies ahead, and maintain the status quo. Others will be more prophetic, and introduce transformational learning as a form of fostering a consciousness capable of imaginatively finding new possibilities within the chaos of our times. Transformational learning leads to looking "outside the box," while searching for new possibilities for enriching human life, not only in our culture, but throughout our global village.

During the last 60 years, "adult learning" has been managed largely by evening courses of secondary schools and extension courses of colleges and universities. Typical courses led by professors are seldom transformational in dimension. They are more likely to be about the transfer of knowledge by presenting ideas and a discussion of the past and present. As essential as that is, transformational learning requires "dialogue" and "debate" throughout a learning community. This movement toward holistic, self-directed learning in short-term learning sessions coupled with high-tech learning contacts is one format capable of fostering "transformational learning."

*—Pamela D. McLean*
*—Frederic M. Hudson*

*See also* Adult Education Learning Model; Self-Directed Learning

## Bibliography

Hudson, F. M. (1999). *The adult years: Mastering the art of self renewal.* San Francisco: Jossey-Bass.

Hudson, F. M., & McLean, P. (1996). *LifeLaunch: A passionate guide to the rest of your life.* Santa Barbara, CA: Hudson Institute Press.

Knowles, M. S., & Associates. (1982). *Andragogy in action.* San Francisco: Jossey-Bass.

Senge, P. (1990). *The fifth discipline: The art and practice of the learning organization.* New York: Doubleday.

Vaill, Peter B. (1996). *Learning as a way of being: Strategies for survival in a world of permanent white water.* San Francisco: Jossey-Bass.

# U

## UNBUNDLING OF HIGHER EDUCATION

Unbundling is the disaggregation of complex activities into component parts. Distributed learning provides the opportunity to use unbundling more widely within colleges and universities. In higher education, unbundling is primarily applied to the faculty role. Conventionally, the faculty role contains three functions: research, teaching, and service (institutional, professional, and public service). Although tradition envisions all three functions being discharged by each individual faculty member, in practice academic institutions have met many needs by hiring individuals to carry out only one function or allowing multiple individuals to collectively fulfill functions. Unbundling formalizes the differentiation process by identifying activities within each function and allocating individuals and resources to meet functional requirements in the aggregate.

Unbundling goes beyond designating generic functions. It requires specification of activities *within* each function. Under most conditions, an individual faculty member may carry out five distinct activities when teaching or delivering instruction:

- Designing the course or curriculum
- Developing the course or curriculum by selecting appropriate instructional methods and course materials, or creating those course materials
- Delivering the subject matter previously selected either in person (such as through lectures) or through the use of various forms of media

- Mediating (also called tutoring) the learning process, which helps students understand materials in ways tailored to their individual learning styles and levels of understanding
- Assessing individual student learning through appropriate methods and assignments designed to certify the attainment of a given level of competence

Academic advising could be included as yet another activity.

First- and second-year lecture courses at many large institutions provide an example of how the five unbundled instructional activities are enacted. Subject matter is determined by a departmental committee (the *design* activity) and defined largely by required course sequencing. Either the committee or a designated faculty member selects textbooks and readings to link with materials used in other courses. These readings, which shape the content of daily lectures and assignments, comprise a large portion of course *development*. A senior faculty member lectures to large groups of students twice a week based on specified texts the students presumably will have studied (the *delivery* activity). Graduate teaching assistants (TAs) lead smaller discussion sections throughout the week (the *mediating* activity). TAs also frequently grade quizzes, term papers, and examinations (the *assessing* activity), often suggesting final grades that faculty members of record rarely change. In this familiar scenario, senior faculty members perform only a few of the five unbundled instructional activities alone. Committees, other nonfaculty staff, and print/media material accomplish the rest.

Distributed learning permits accomplishing some of these activities through the judicious use of technology, especially in the "delivery of content" arena (creating capital for labor substitutions). Other approaches might involve a finer or more deliberate division of labor among the faculty, creating new kinds of instructional staff, or deploying non–tenure track instructional staff (such as adjunct faculty, graduate teaching assistants, or undergraduate assistants) in new ways (creating labor for labor substitutions). Other arrangements might rely on resources from outside the institution to discharge an activity (a form of outsourcing); for example, relying on external vendors or publishers to develop course materials.

Traditional colleges and universities rarely have a single pattern for providing instruction. Most academic institutions offer a combination of laboratory, seminar, and lecture classes, each with a distinct instructional pattern. Upper division and graduate classes employ different instructional techniques than lower division classes. Instructional approaches vary by academic discipline. Some students today enroll at multiple institutions simultaneously, experiencing several instructional patterns in any given time period. New instructional technologies also add to the instructional patterns enacted by institutions. For example, face-to-face, video, asynchronous online, and synchronous computer chat rooms result in new instructional patterns.

"Nontraditional" institutions can enact quite different instructional patterns, and instructional patterns can vary within traditional academic institutions. Instructional agents can be redirected to different activities to better achieve student learning and institutional effectiveness goals. Dissecting instructional activities in this manner permits academic leaders to achieve institutional missions and goals by differentiating activities best accomplished by full-time tenure track faculty members from those best provided by other instructional agents.

As processes, unbundling and distributed learning provide an occasion for faculty and administrators to rethink conventional procedures. As a practical tool, unbundling allows deans, department chairs, and their faculties to compare costs of instruction under different scenarios, and to distribute workloads to increase effectiveness and efficiency. Particularly important is the potential of unbundling as part of a larger strategic process to re-evaluate instructional delivery.

Another way for traditional institutions to unbundle the faculty role is to better utilize teaching professionals in instruction. Applying technology to achieve economies of scale in instructional delivery that enhance student learning productivity highlights the need for faculty members to improve the mediating activity; that is, providing the critical individual intellectual interaction and links that students use as they learn the material being presented. The mediating activity lies at the heart of good teaching. It is the instructional activity least amenable to mechanical solutions. Even the best software cannot anticipate all of the wrong turns human learners can take, all of the ways they can misconstrue sentences, or all of the questions they can ask. As the lecture course example illustrates, much of this mediating activity has been and is still being performed by graduate assistants or by part-time adjunct faculty. Some tenure-track faculty members do not want to perform this role and are not trained to do it. Many faculty members may not be comfortable with the level of interpersonal interaction required for successful mediation. In other cases, faculty members are rewarded for other activities such as research and student contact hour production. In the future, full-time teaching professionals who are neither apprentices nor adjuncts may perform this activity more frequently, although they are not the disciplinary experts typically thought of as "the faculty."

Unbundling permits administrators and their faculties to focus faculty attention on the material they must know intimately to be good teachers. Programmers, instructional developers, and videographers (among others) can translate the subject matter—learned from the faculty member—into instructional materials to take full advantage of pedagogically sound uses of modern technology. Unbundling can also be useful in comparing the costs associated with different forms of instruction. Because many current cost and workload studies include only the time spent by full-time tenure-track faculty members, the work done by graduate assistants and adjunct faculty is not incorporated. When teaching professionals' time is included and accounted for—as well as the costs of any associated technology—institutions can obtain more accurate estimates of instructional costs.

Research on the costs of distance education versus traditional courses is scarce and gives mixed results. Some researchers find teaching in a distance format is less overall work than on-campus instruction; others find that distance-delivered courses take significantly more work. Several problems complicate this assessment. There are no historical time and cost data for instructional activities in traditional courses. In addition, comparing instructional activity, time, and cost data for courses at different points in the development process (for instance, comparing never-before-offered courses with mature courses) is problematic. Also, instructional activity data that are gathered are often not comparable. The problem of incomparability in cost studies is partially addressed by the use of unbundling. By identifying and defining specific instructional activities—and standardizing these definitions—decisions can be made regarding whether an activity explicitly occurred, who or what accomplished that activity (instructional agent), how much time was spent by which agent on the activity, and how much money was used on that activity. Although unbundled activities provide a more solid basis for determining instructional costs per student than is possible with the broad categories of teaching, research, and service, without some alignment or standardization of the activities, little meaningful comparison is possible.

Most academic institutions have not systematically examined the unbundling of faculty roles. In particular, traditional colleges and universities have not paid sufficient attention to the growing need to acquire and nurture a new kind of "paraprofessional" staff to support ongoing instructional development. These paraprofessionals are technologically skilled, schooled in a variety of pedagogical approaches, and sufficiently anchored in the disciplines to be credible with mainline faculty. The role of teaching professionals and paraprofessionals must be explicitly included when conducting institutional workload and instructional cost studies or planning future forms of instructional delivery.

Academic leaders can use unbundling and distributed learning to enhance student learning productivity by improving access and fostering learning by better deploying instructors and other professionals within the academy to best advantage.

*Source:* Adapted from "Reconfiguring Faculty Roles for Virtual Settings." *Journal of Higher Education (Special Issue: The Faculty in the New Millennium), 23*(1), 123–140, 2002.

—*Karen Paulson*

*See also* ADJUNCT FACULTY; FACULTY POLICIES

## Bibliography

Finkelstein, M. J., Frances, C., Jewett, F. I., & Scholz, B. W. (Eds.). (2000). *Dollars, distance, and online education: The new economics of college teaching and learning.* Phoenix: The American Council on Education and Oryx Press.

Jewett, F. I. (2000). A framework for the comparative analysis of the costs of classroom instruction vis-à-vis distributed instruction. In M. J. Finkelstein, C. Frances, F. I. Jewett, & B. W. Scholz (Eds.). *Dollars, distance, and online education: The new economics of college teaching and learning* (pp. 85–122). Phoenix: The American Council on Education and Oryx Press.

Jones, D. (2001). *Technology costing methodology handbook—version 1.0.* Boulder, CO: Western Interstate Commission for Higher Education, Western Cooperative for Educational Telecommunications.

Jones, D. P., & Jewett, F. I. (2000). Procedures for calculating the costs of alternative modes of instructional delivery. In M. J. Finkelstein, C. Frances, F. I. Jewett, & B. W. Scholz (Eds.). *Dollars, distance, and online education: The new economics of college teaching and learning* (pp. 213–238). Phoenix: The American Council on Education and Oryx Press.

Paulson, Karen. (2002). Reconfiguring faculty roles for virtual settings. *Journal of Higher Education (Special Issue: The Faculty in the New Millennium), 23*(1), 123–140.

# VIRTUAL CAMPUS

A virtual campus is a:

- Virtual location in cyberspace
- Web-based community of learning
- Web-based distance education (e learning) metaphor modeled on a genuine campus and thus mirroring the organization and the services normally expected in a campus context

A virtual campus provides traditional campus services such as:

- Consulting the policies, rules, and regulations
- Browsing the course catalog
- Browsing the syllabus of a specific course
- Registering for one or more courses
- Attending distance education courses
- Accessing the library's card catalogs
- Sharing the community's resources
- Participating in public events and discussions (forums and the like)
- Interacting with associations and groups with shared interests
- Communicating with one's peers

These are implemented with software solutions like these:

- Web site
- Secured access to registrar, library, and one's personal space

- Anonymous or secured access to an FTP server for resource distribution and sharing
- E-mail for each campus member
- Mailing lists and newsgroups aimed at specific needs/groups
- Forums for informing the community and for debating issues
- Chat rooms for faculty ("teachers' lounge")
- Chat rooms for students ("students' lounge")
- Tracking and notification of presence and disposition of peers
- E-groups and other groupware technologies
- Web-based courses and/or CBT

## VARIOUS VIRTUAL CAMPUSES

The interface of the virtual campus does not necessarily have to be a 3-D model or an image map of an actual or imagined campus. In some cases, it is not represented visually at all, as with a text-based virtual campus. Real-time interaction is frequently featured in virtual campuses, text-based and otherwise. Virtual campuses provide access to learning materials and use the metaphor of a physical campus, but in many cases it is difficult to distinguish a virtual campus from an ordinary educational Web site hosted by a university. To add to the confusion, the definition of *virtual campus* of the Office de la Langue Française (OLF) includes traditional means of communication like television and the telephone.

According to Forum Telecom, a virtual campus is a Web site that provides pedagogical resources for a community of learners, and various means of communication and collaboration that allow its participants to interact with their teacher and with each other. It is roughly equivalent to the notion of a "portal," a well-focused, user-friendly thematic interface between the learners and the instruction being offered.

A model of the virtual campus was explored and presented in 1992 by the Télé-Université and its LICEF research center (Province of Quebec, Canada). This model is based on the networking of diversified actors and resources. Its aim is to provide synchronous and asynchronous access to a variety of learning resources: trainers and tutors, content experts, managers, and designers. These different actors have access to servers offering multimedia, courseware, integrated tools for task achievement and training, individual/group messages, projects, and activities.

The Swiss Virtual Campus, when released, will provide students with a virtual mobility that will allow them to play an active role in the learning process by participating in courses via the Web. The objectives of the Swiss Virtual Campus are: 1) to develop easily accessible Web-based teaching modules for basic and specialized studies, particularly for courses that attract large numbers of students; 2) to improve the quality of learning and strengthen interactive teaching by adding Web-based courses to traditional classroom teaching; 3) to strengthen the collaboration between universities and federal institutes of technology and universities of applied sciences; and 4) to develop high-quality teaching materials and methods.

## DFAIT VIRTUAL CAMPUS

The Department of Foreign Affairs and International Trade (DFAIT) is a Canadian organization with thousands of employees working in 158 locations worldwide. In 1996 DFAIT conducted a study of the various means of delivering distance learning services. It evaluated technologies ranging from e-mail to teleconferencing. In 1997, DFAIT hosted a few correspondence courses, developed an orientation video, and tested a number of CBT solutions. Since then, the exponential growth in the use of the Web for personal, educational, or business reasons has increased the acceptance of computer-mediated learning, and many corporations are now using information technologies and their corporate intranets to deliver training. Consistent with this trend, DFAIT determined that a Web-based application would be the most cost-effective way to build distance learning services. A prototype was developed and tested in 1997, and a first version of its virtual campus was available for pilot implementation in 1998. DFAIT was the first ministry of foreign affairs in the world to develop and launch a virtual campus using Web-based technology. Its virtual campus gained international recognition in 1998 at the International Conference of the Deans of Diplomatic Academies in Seoul, and it was featured in April 1999 in Washington, D.C., at a conference entitled "Designing a Virtual Corporate University."

DFAIT's virtual campus is a tool designed to manage distance learning services that can be delivered digitally, including courses, reference materials, and job aids. It also provides pedagogical, technical, and operational expertise to help training managers deliver intranet-based learning. Its primary goals are to extend learning opportunities to employees abroad and to support major departmental training initiatives. Although it contains material relevant to current training projects, the virtual campus is not merely a repository of past training material. It is used as a timely, cost-effective method of delivering prerequisite classes or to complement classroom training. The virtual campus improves a company's ability to respond quickly to departmental training initiatives, improves employees' ability to learn in the language of their choice, helps subject matter experts facilitate a course, and provides employees distance learning opportunities.

Specifically, the virtual campus is an intranet application designed to provide and manage distance learning services for the employees of DFAIT and for other government departments who have access to DFAIT's system. The virtual campus will continue to evolve within this environment. Other than some generic courses open to all employees at all times, this site contains only the courses that are currently being delivered to participants who are preregistered for that course. Access to most courses is controlled because they are supported by an instructor who helps learners throughout the course. The center is entered through the Registrar's Office, which contains information on courses and registration. Once registered, the student is taken to the Study Room, where he or she has access to the course instructions and materials. From the Study Room, the student may, depending on the particular needs of each course, have access to a Resource Centre, where he or she can find additional resources to help with the course; to a BBS, where the instructor and the learners can leave and respond to questions; and to a Conference Room, which can hold electronic meetings. Finally, once a course is completed, the student is invited to proceed to the Evaluation Hall to fill out an evaluation form and, in some cases, to complete a knowledge and skills test.

The goals of the virtual campus are to diversify the way training is delivered, to encourage continuous learning in the workplace, to extend learning opportunities to employees abroad (in accordance with the distance learning component of DFAIT's training strategy), to reduce the time spent in classrooms, to contain training costs, and to take advantage of existing infrastructure to deliver training and other learning services from the desktop. The virtual campus offers learners an opportunity to train on a flexible schedule during working hours at the office. It gives them the flexibility to schedule their own course times and the freedom to meet their overall training goals. It also enables departmental subject matter experts to facilitate a course without any time or location restrictions. Despite this convenience, virtual campus courses require as much time and energy as classroom training and an even greater individual commitment.

## TECFA VIRTUAL CAMPUS

The TECFA virtual campus goes beyond traditional hypertexts and e-mails by providing truly interactive educational activities and resources that allow students to participate in online exercises, get direct immediate feedback, and exchange their experiences with others. The campus is organized as a set of independent zones, each corresponding to a different course. Within a zone, students will find different buildings in which the students play predefined pedagogical scenarios. They perform successive activities in particular rooms, eliciting knowledge and interactions. There are also rooms for traditional support that contain various online resources related to educational technology, such as reviewed papers, summarized articles, and student works. TECFA's virtual campus provides three interfaces that allow students to explore the content of the campus and engage in activities: 1) the classic Hypertext Markup Language (HTML) format, 2) a 3-D Virtual Reality Modeling Language (VRML) scene requiring a plug-in, and 3) a Mud Object Oriented (MOO)-based interface.

The TECFA Workflow Management Tool is an online tool that increases the quality of exchanges between students and teaching staff. Everything students and teachers need to know is displayed by the system. The feedback that teachers provide is permanently available to all concerned parties, a form of collective memory that alleviates the burden of tracking e-mails and verbal communications. This workflow management tool also provides specific tools for students. At any given moment, they can find their current state of progress, the available resources for their project, and so forth. This workflow management tool is also a very useful instrument for the teachers. With it, they can inspect the composition of groups, their progress, and the documents that they requested, as well as annotate their students' work, make comments, and suggest resources.

Most Web sites in education keep the learner in a passive role—reading texts, watching video sequences, or listening to audio files—which contradicts current theories of learning. Starting from the facts that passive absorption of content is not learning and that the Internet is not interactive per se, the TECFA virtual campus attempts to solve these limitations. Specifically, TECFA is designing and proposing student activities that use a constructivist approach where learners activate certain cognitive processes to learn an unknown concept without knowing its definition.

## THE POLITICS OF THE VIRTUAL CAMPUS CONCEPT

What is the future of the virtual campus in terms of learning? Will it individualize education further? Or will it depersonalize it? Will the communication and collaboration tools that groupware and community-ware are designed to provide radically change the face of education by allowing promising new pedagogies to take hold (socioconstructivism, for example) and/or new communitarian approaches to teaching and learning in the form of communities of interest, communities of practice, and communities of learning? In fact, virtual communities will be far more interactive and collaborative than learners are accustomed to, providing benefits as well as difficulties for practitioners as well as for researchers of this field.

As globalization of the markets takes place on a worldwide scale, education is necessarily affected. Universities and colleges are increasingly appearing online, in addition to having brick-and-mortar campuses, so many of them are projecting that an increasing number of their new clients will be distance learners from around the world. Learners are no longer as tied to their local campuses, and a brisk worldwide competition is under way among all of these institutions to attract learners away from each other. Many believe that this tug-of-war for learners and the concomitant commercialization pressures of globalization are deteriorating an already fragile situation. This competition is being felt most keenly by underfunded campuses that are not competing effectively.

Many are also concerned about the impact that virtual campuses will have on the human resources employed in the brick-and-mortar campuses. Some researchers believe there is no need for real infrastructures when the same learning can be achieved from the comfort of home. But this argument does not take into account many of the tangible and intangible benefits of face-to-face meetings with flesh-and-blood learners and teachers. Many subjects—performance skills, for example—cannot be adequately taught through a computer interface, and some skills, aptitudes, and attitudes may not lend themselves to a computer-mediated approach. As always, it is not the technologies that determine what we will do, but rather our values and goals that will determine what uses will be made of the technologies at our disposal.

*—Pierre-Léonard Harvey*
*—Alain Farmer*

*See also* FACULTY POLICIES

### Bibliography

Foulke-Ffeinberg, F. (1998). *The virtual campus.* Allen, TX: Pan-Tech International.

Van Dusen, D.G. (1997). The virtual campus: Technology and reform in higher education. *Ashe-Eric Higher Education Report, 25*(5). New York: John Wiley & Sons.

Verdejo, M. F., & Davies, G. (Eds.). (1999). *The virtual campus—trends for higher education and training.* Dordrecht, The Netherlands: Kluver Academic.

# VIRTUAL CLASSROOM

Virtual Classroom was the name of software developed at New Jersey Institute of Technology in the 1980s: a computer-mediated communication system enhanced to create an asynchronous teaching and learning environment on computer networks. It was designed to enhance and support collaborative learning activities among the members of a distributed class. Studies of this original system, as well as of many subsequent implementations of asynchronous learning networks on many campuses, indicate that if a learning community is built that supports student–student communication and collaboration, as well as frequent and extensive interaction between students and the instructor, then the virtual classroom type of learning environment not only increases access to learning opportunities, but also is as effective as or more effective than traditional classrooms.

## SOFTWARE TO CREATE A VIRTUAL CLASSROOM

Rather than being built of the bricks and whiteboards that create the spaces and tools for learning in a traditional classroom, a classroom is "virtual" if the "spaces," structures, and tools are constructed in software. Some of these communication structures resemble facilities or procedures used in traditional classrooms, such as software to support the examination process. Other methods of supporting interaction would be difficult or impossible in the "face-to-face" environment, such as the use of anonymity or pen names. Virtual classrooms are accessed not by traveling to a university, but by connecting through the Internet. Although students may occasionally participate at the same time (synchronously), participation is generally asynchronous, that is, the virtual classroom participants log in any time around the clock, and from any location in the world where the equipment and Internet access are available. A more generic term for this type of system is *asynchronous learning network (ALN),* or just *learning network.*

The basic conferencing system for the Virtual Classroom program (called EIES, Electronic Information Exchange System) included threaded discussions, e-mail, the ability to sort communications into new messages and those already read, and many other features that have become common for a computer-mediated communication system. Later, the ability to attach an "activity," which was a program to support specific structures and functions for communication, was added. Following an architectural analogy, some of the major features in the Virtual Classroom program are shown in Table 1, as they correspond to or contrast with the traditional classroom.

The most unique and widely used of the special "activities" is the response activity. It can be tailored

**Table 1**    Some Communication Structures in the Virtual and Traditional Classrooms

| Virtual Classroom Software Feature | Function | Traditional Classroom Equivalent |
|---|---|---|
| Conferences | Class discussion and lectures | Classroom |
| Messages | "Private" student–student & student–teacher discussions | Office hours<br>"Hallway" conversations |
| Notebooks | Individual and working groups composition and storage of documents | Paper & ring-binders<br>Word processor & diskette |
| Exam Activity | Timed student–teacher feedback with no other communication permitted during test taking | Exam |
| Gradebook Activity | Teacher may record and change grades and averages; student may access only his or her grades | Gradebook (paper) |
| Response Activity | Force independent thinking and active participation | |

by the instructor who sets it up; for instance, the instructor can decide whether anonymous replies will be permitted. The most common format is that each student is required to individually answer the question posed; he or she can see the answers of others and join a general discussion about the question. This is very useful for making sure that each student can independently think through and enter his or her own ideas, without being influenced by responses made by others, while also benefiting from seeing and discussing the ideas of the other students. It is a process of forced active participation that is not available in the traditional classroom, where as soon as one student answers, everybody else hears the answer, and usually only a minority of students participate in discussion at all.

Although online discussion and collaborative activities are key aspects of a successful virtual classroom type of environment, other media that emphasize individual learning are also used for most courses. For example, just as in a traditional course, there will be textbooks and readings. Most courses will have lectures, but rather than being delivered "live," the material is recorded; initially, videotapes were popular, but more recently, multimedia digital lectures have become more common.

Many different software platforms have emerged that support a virtual classroom type of experience; they all enhance the classroom-like interaction among students as well as between instructor and students. New Jersey Institute of Technology's Virtual Classroom software was in continuous development and use from about 1985 until 2000, after which various commercially available ALN systems have been used.

## TEACHING AND LEARNING EFFECTIVENESS IN THE VIRTUAL CLASSROOM

Both students and teachers need to learn new techniques in order to maximize satisfaction and enjoyment in the virtual classroom environment. Because few nonverbal cues are available, written text needs to be explicit. For example, the student cannot see the smiles and nods of the instructor to perceive that an answer is "correct"; the instructor has to explicitly acknowledge the communication and comment upon it. The instructor cannot see puzzled frowns or hands waving in the air to indicate that the students are confused about something. In order to make sure that students are working steadily and comprehending the materials, regular checks need to be built in, such as online quizzes or weekly required postings of the "main ideas" from readings or recorded lectures.

The beginning of the course is especially important; the virtual professor should require students to introduce themselves and begin interacting from "day one." Techniques such as inviting students to post their photos or a digitized audio presentation, or having one or more synchronous "chat" sessions at the beginning of the course, can help in quickly building the feeling of a "real class" in the virtual environment.

In the NJIT studies, one of the consistently strongest correlates of students' overall evaluation of an online course is whether they felt that they had better communication with their professor than in traditional courses. To achieve improved communication, faculty not only need to be online daily or more, but they also need to learn how to build a learning community in this new environment. The instructor must rethink and reshape his or her role as a teacher. Managing the course and keeping it organized takes a great deal of planning and effort. The effective virtual professor creates a set of materials and assignments and reward structures that encourage students to look upon their interactions with their peers as the most valuable aspect of the course, rather than to focus on memorizing lecture-type material presented by the instructor. Among the types of assignments that might be used to accomplish this are debates, team projects, and student presentations.

Extensive evaluation studies have been conducted regarding the virtual classroom (VC) at NJIT, using a variety of research methods, including student questionnaires, interviews of faculty and students, comparison of grades in roughly "matched" sections of courses, and analysis of course transcripts. Some disadvantages have been reported; for example, a higher percentage (52%) of the students reported that they were more likely to stop "attending class" when busy with other things, as compared to cutting a face-to-face class. In large classes in particular, information overload is a problem, with thousands of comments being contributed during the course. However, most students felt that the advantages outweighed the disadvantages. VCs are "more convenient" overall than on-campus courses. Only 15% of students did not "feel more involved in taking active part" in their courses. VC students reported higher subjective satisfaction with the VC than the traditional classroom on a number of dimensions, including improved access to their professor and overall quality of the educational experience. Students tend to perceive the experience as "group learning" rather than individual learning, and the more they perceive this, the more likely they are to judge the outcomes of the VC to be superior.

A collection and analysis of the results of all empirical studies of the effectiveness of ALNs is being constructed as part of a "WebCenter Learning Networks Effectiveness Research" (see http://www.alnResearch.org). From an initial set of 19 empirical studies that compare ALNs and traditional courses on the same campus, the evidence is overwhelming that well-designed ALNs are as effective as, or more effective

than, traditional courses. By 2002, there were over a million students enrolled in courses involving online learning. Faculty are learning how to be effective "virtual professors" in this environment, students are learning how to work with their peers to build and share knowledge, and the software commercially available to support such processes is improving. However, challenges remain, particularly in terms of software that adequately supports discussions and collaborative learning activities for relatively large classes.

*—Starr Roxanne Hiltz*

***See also*** Asynchronous Formats; Collaboration; Learning Communities; Teaching in an Electronic Classroom

## Bibliography

Coppola, N. W., Hiltz, S. R., & Rotter, N. (2002). Becoming a virtual professor: Pedagogical roles and asynchronous learning networks. *JMIS, 18*(4), 169–190.

Harasim, L., Hiltz, S. R., Teles, L., & Turoff, M. (1995). *Learning networks: A field guide to teaching and learning online.* Cambridge: MIT Press.

Hiltz, S. R. (1994). *The virtual classroom: Learning without limits via computer networks.* Norwood, NJ: Ablex (Human-Computer Interaction Series).

Hiltz, S. R., Benbunan-Fich, R., Coppola, N., Rotter, N., & Turoff, M. (2000). Measuring the importance of collaborative learning for the effectiveness of ALN: A multi-measure, multi-method approach. *JALN 4,* 2.

Hiltz, S. R., & Turoff, M. (2002). What makes learning networks effective? *Communications of the ACM, 45* (2), 56–59.

Turoff, M., & Hiltz, S. R. (1995). Software design and the future of the virtual classroom. *Journal of Information Technology for Teacher Education, 4*(2), 197-215.

# VIRTUAL COMMUNITIES

A community is made up of people communicating and sharing a common interest. A virtual community is simply a community in which people communicate and share a common interest, without meeting physically. They are freed from the constraints of location and time with the help of computer networks and technology. They are also known as cyber-communities, online communities, electronic communities, and e-groups.

There are several types of virtual communities, including communities of practice or professional communities, learning communities, communities of hobby or interest, and communities of friends. Members of communities usually use groupware or communityware (software that facilitates group sharing, communication, and coordination) and the Internet to share information and ideas with other like-minded individuals.

## ORIGINS OF THE WORD

The term *virtual community* first appeared around 1968 in diverse articles. It was popularized in 1993 by Howard Rheingold in his book *Virtual Communities—Homesteading on the Electronic Frontier Reality*. The term *virtual community* was first used to describe cyberspace, but as people began differentiating the Internet (the interconnected networks of computers), the World Wide Web (hypertext, graphical interfaces, and standard protocols), cyberspace (a mental representation of digital interactions), and the different tools and applications of the digital world, virtual community took on the meaning it now has.

## HISTORY OF VIRTUAL COMMUNITIES

The first virtual communities appeared in the late 1960s on ARPANET, the network used by American military researchers to share computer data. In the 1970s virtual communities began to contain more communication tools, like electronic mail, enhancing the usability of the network and facilitating interaction. As new computers and new networks linked, ARPANET developed into the Internet as we know it today.

After publication in 1978 of the Nora-Minc report on the social appropriation of technology and computerization of France—a report that suggested connecting business and homes to central computers—the ambitious Minitel project made its appearance in France. It was a mini-computer linked to a national network managed by the national public phone company. At first, it was merely a basic news and phone directory, but it soon exploded into a popular electronic mail medium. The managers of the network were taken aback by the unanticipated importance of e-mail, and were powerless to stem the tide of messages, many of which were erotic in nature. The

volume of mail was so brisk that the system eventually crashed in 1985. Despite this, the Minitel system played a major role in the early development of telematics, and the crash is paradoxically a good illustration of the social importance of virtual communications. The point is that the system was designed for a specific purpose—a news and phone directory—but became an important communication tool when users began using it in their own idiosyncratic ways. Powerless, the French authorities let it evolve to respond to the needs of the users, even if its effective uses were far different than those that had been foreseen by the designers of the system.

In 1980 the first multi-user dungeons (MUDs) were introduced in England. MUDs are interactive online games and forums, allowing multi-person interactions in cyberspace. Later in the 1980s, in North America, Freenets (free networks) and fee-based bulletin board systems (BBSs) were popular cyber-activities, hosted by computer servers accessible by modems and phone lines, that offered basic communication services like forums and bulletin boards. The arrival of personal computers heralded the first tools that allowed almost anyone to create virtual communities.

An important organization in the domain of virtual communities, the WELL (The Whole Earth'Lectronic Link), came online in 1985. It was a pioneering forum service that brought together independent cyberspace thinkers; it has evolved into one of the major virtual communities.

In the early 1990s, the arrival of the World Wide Web set the stage for the rapid proliferation of virtual communities. The Web is a standard protocol to help communication among the growing quantities of computers on networks of which the Internet is made. It was the common standard needed to democratize the networks, allowing almost anyone to use the Internet without any deep knowledge of computers, and using relatively inexpensive hardware (a phone line and a modem). As more and more people accessed the Internet, more virtual communities were developed, the propensity to share digital resources became more widespread, and, as a consequence of this sharing, more and more open-source tools became available to users and their communities of interest.

## THE TECHNICAL LEVEL

Virtual communities do not have to be very elaborate. At the technical level, a virtual community can be created with only access to the Internet and a mailing list that sends a group's messages to all of its members at once. Many tools are available with which to create and manage a virtual community. In recent years, increasingly sophisticated groupwares and intranets allow real-time and integrated communication for communities, but most communities still use middle range groupware solutions that remain relatively simple to undertake. Online services like YahooGroups or MSN Communities have mailing list services, document distribution, voting, polls, databases, forums, and so on. However, it is not the technology that makes a community what it is—it is the way the technology is used to communicate and share.

## RETURNING TO THE ORIGINAL IDEOLOGY

The early ancestors of the World Wide Web were created by scientists to share common interests virtually, thus creating virtual communities of research scientists. Virtual communities are midway between mass communication and one-to-one communication. But in the first years of the World Wide Web, in the mid-1990s, the Internet was believed to be a mass medium that could reach everyone with the same message. This misunderstanding led to several problems, and partially explains events like the financial crash of March 2000 and the growing lack of confidence in the Internet as a profitable business medium. Some very important concepts were forgotten: The first is the modern consumerist attitude, where each individual wants to be treated as unique and served as he or she pleases, because people are starting to understand how important they are in the business process. Second is the concept that technologies are not merely for automating or computerizing tasks otherwise performed by humans. The focus must be on the basic psychosocial needs of the humans that are using them to achieve their human goals. The business community is starting to realize what sociologists have been trying to explain for a decade: Don't expect people to adapt to the technology that can be produced. Instead, develop technology that focuses on satisfying their genuine needs. The features and the appearance of the tools are not the most important factors. The technology must satisfy a need; the manner in which the technology satisfies the need is a close second in importance. Ownership of and free access to the sources of these technologies are also major factors. That is why

the Internet is going back to the original ideology with virtual communities: by the people and for the people.

## PSYCHOSOCIOLOGICAL ASPECTS

Many families are collapsing. Social values are migrating. People are less and less part of social networks based on a shared lineage (family), a shared location (neighborhood), mutual socioeconomic support (groups), or other traditional community-building criteria. Virtual communities, on the other hand, are potentially an excellent antidote to the fragmentation of our social, political, and economic solidarities, allowing us to reach out to like-minded people wherever they may be found in our "global village."

Humans are social animals. Socialization is an important need, not very far behind basic needs such as food, rest, and shelter. Virtual communities are now evolving in a manner akin to the evolution of the telephone, which has been a very important socialization process for decades. Virtual communities have their rules and practices, exactly like traditional communities do, and when cyberspace cannot provide a concrete action found in real life, metaphors are used. An example of this is the ASCII symbols that denote emotions, known as smileys or as emoticons (a contraction of "emotion" and "icon").

So, even though expressing emotion in cyberspace is less concrete, community bonds and friendships are nonetheless possible in cyberspace. And the fact that people participate in virtual communities doesn't necessarily mean that they don't have opportunities for traditional face-to-face contact. As a matter of fact, the stereotype of the overenthusiastic networking geek with underdeveloped social skills is practically nonexistent.

Are virtual communities genuine communities in a sociological sense? One of the first to define community scientifically was Ferdinand Tönnies, in 1887. He defined it as an ideal type of a collective will governing social relationships among humans. Even if there is no consensus on the definition of the concept, in 1955, a researcher named George Hillery found three common denominators among nearly 100 different scientific definitions of community: 1) a community includes people who are involved in social interaction; 2) a community involves a shared space; and 3) a community includes members who have some common ties. Possible common ties include shared lifestyles, norms, values, psychological identification, and the use of shared institutions. Almost all of the sociological definitions of community include these three elements.

So is a virtual community a genuine community in the sociological sense? It depends on the interpretation of community. Are interactions in computer networks real sociological interactions? Are virtual shared common ties real ones? Can a mental representation of digital interactions be viewed as a genuine form of space? Some sociologists, like Barry Wellman and Barry Leighton, believe in emancipated communities, but they are not arguing that genuine social communication is necessarily tied to any spatial location or any spatial preconditions. In other words, spatial proximity is not a make-or-break criterion for the concept of sociopolitical community, especially when one takes into account the democratization of information technologies and the new unprecedented opportunities they provide for discourse and debate about our shared interests with respect to sociopolitical issues.

## DESIGNING VIRTUAL COMMUNITIES

The ultimate goal that one should endeavor to attain when developing a virtual community is to make the information and experience sharing as valuable for the individual as it is for the community. If the object of the communication is more valuable for the individual, then it will not be shared for very long, because individuals will keep it for themselves. Consequently, if the object is more valuable for the community than for the individuals, the individuals will not make an effort to get the result of the communication.

There is not a unique way to create a virtual community, but experienced professionals use basic multimedia project management outlines, focusing on the needs of the community and the feedback given by the community. Acknowledgment of the needs and engagement, and not technological tools, are most important: One can always adapt the tools, but individuals will resist a system that doesn't fit their normal social network behaviors.

## E-LEARNING AND VIRTUAL COMMUNITIES

Virtual communities of learning have considerable pedagogical potential. Imagine study groups, sharing with classmates to assist and motivate students as they progress through their studies in traditional schools. Communities, virtual or otherwise, are the same—the learners get support from other agents (teachers and peers) and provide help to their peers whenever they can reciprocate. The early computer-based training and e-learning systems did not take communities in account, because most were developed with too much focus on technology. But, as transdisciplinary socioconstructivist teaching strategies catch on and virtual communities of learning become more widespread, the learning community itself will increasingly adapt these virtual forms of community (groupware and communityware) to satisfy their genuine needs, including the need to be a social agent participating in the co-construction of their collective knowledge and identity.

*—Pierre-Leonard Harvey*
*—Nicolas Bertrand*

***See also*** Groupware; Internet; Learning Communities; World Wide Web

## Bibliography

Barlow, J. P. (1996). *A declaration of the independence of cyberspace.* Davos, Switzerland. Retrieved from http://www.eff.org/~barlow/.

Cartier, M. (2000). *Les Portails de 2ème génération.* Retrieved from http://www.ledevoir.com.

Coon, D. A. (1996). *An investigation of the #FRIENDS Internet relay chat as a community.* Master Thesis. Southeastern Louisiana University. Retrieved from http://www.davidcoon.com.

Harvey, P. L. (1995). *Cyberespace et communautique: Appropriation-Réseaux-groupes virtuels.* Québec, Canada: Les Presse de l'Université Laval.

Harvey, P. L., & Lemire, G. (2001). *La nouvelle éducation: NTIC, transdisciplinarité et communautique.* Québec, Canada: Les Presse de l'Université Laval.

Nora, S., & Minc, A. (1978). *L'informatisation de la société—Rapport au Président de la République Française.* Paris, France: La documentation française.

Offner, J. M. (1996). *Réseaux et territoires-significations croisées.* St-Étienne, France: Éditions de l'aube.

Rheingold, H. (1993). *Virtual communities—Homesteading on the electronic frontier reality.* Canada: Addison-Wesley.

# VIRTUAL LEARNING TOOLS

The concept of virtual learning tools is complex and relies on the background of the reader for interpretation. Applications ranging from spreadsheets, databases, concept mapping tools, and collaboration tools to course management systems have been used as learning tools in virtual learning environments. This entry identifies the purpose of virtual learning tools and presents examples of where these tools can be used.

The purpose of virtual learning tools is to facilitate learning in a distributed environment where the learners and the teachers do not have to be in the same location or even meet at the same time. The learning objectives are, however, the same whether the learners are in a distributed or location-bound environment. For example, if a course is designed to teach learners how to build a bridge, the goal is for the learner to learn all the basic requirements of bridge building and apply the requirements to create a design. This requirement does not change whether the learner is in a classroom with a teacher or online, learning at his or her own pace. What is different is the tools available in the environment and how the tools are used.

The tools of the virtual environment should facilitate communication, information transmission, practice, assessment, feedback, and problem solving.

## COMMUNICATION TOOLS

The communication tools in distributed environments include e-mail, discussion/bulletin boards, and chat rooms. The use of these tools requires careful planning and incorporation into the learning environment. For example, e-mail can be overwhelming to the instructor and students. Students and instructors must be given guidelines on how to create a meaningful subject heading and construct an e-mail that is concise and informative. Similarly, discussion boards are useful only when the learning activity guides the students on how to communicate effectively. Research has shown that students conducting a debate or argument on a topic create postings of substance and refrain from paraphrasing each other.

Enhancement tools are also now available that allow learners to tag their postings in constructing arguments, grade discussion board postings, and manage/mediate chat room postings. The chat room management tools allow the instructor to disallow postings that are not in the thread. Similar tools on discussion boards allow the instructor to organize the postings and for students to search and follow different threads than those included in the initial postings. Scardamalia and Bereiter's Knowledge Integration Environment is also an example of effective use of discussion boards that are designed to focus on knowledge creation and learning.

## INFORMATION TRANSMISSION

Information transmission tools are mostly hypertext-based with audio, video, and simulations. Mayer's multimedia learning principles are critical to this area. They focus on the overuse of unnecessary graphics called *seductive details* and using narration with graphics instead of text description. Another concern is the use of hyperlinks to allow students to gather more information. When students follow the links they must have a purpose, and students should be able to easily navigate back to the learning environment.

## PRACTICE

Practicing the skills that are the goal of the learning environment requires the real tools that a professional will use. For example, if students are required to learn Java programming online they must have the necessary editors and deployment tools to create and test their programs. If students are learning how to take a patient's blood pressure, they must have access to the procedure as well as a blood pressure gauge and stethoscope. This complicates the learning environment design, but every effort must be made to allow the learner to use the real tools.

## ASSESSMENT

Assessment is an important part of any learning environment, and the tools necessary to support this function may be built into the learning modules or created separately. For example, an interactive system can be built allowing the student to solve problems and receive feedback immediately. These activities can also be logged for grading purposes.

Many courses, however, use the easier approach of creating assessment using multiple choice, true/false, or essay tests. There are many tools available within course management systems that allow the easy creation of these types of assessments.

## FEEDBACK

Feedback is a critical part of any learning environment, and even more important in a distributed environment where the learners do not have face-to-face interactions with the instructor. The nonverbal interactions in the classroom environment cannot be easily constructed online, so special care should be given to creating appropriate feedback for the student to proceed without feeling isolated and lost.

The use of all the communication tools listed here is helpful. Additional interactions on problem solving can also be created using simple CGI scripts or simulation environments where students can make a move and get an immediate response as to whether they are on the correct path.

Other distributed learning tools should be included as needed to support the learning objectives. These may include the following:

- Concept mapping tools like Inspiration that allow learners to organize and present their knowledge.
- Graphical design tools like Visio that allow the construction of specialized design documents.
- Spreadsheets like Lotus 1–2–3 or Excel to enter and analyze data. They also can serve as tools that foster higher order skills like hypothesis testing instead of concentrating on simple calculations like multiplication and division. For example, students studying weather forecasting can see if high pressure causes the temperature to drop and skies to clear if given a spreadsheet with data collected from many locations.
- Databases like FileMaker Pro, Access, or Oracle can be used to organize information, analyze information, and make connections.
- Argumentation tools like Questmap allow users to construct arguments in an organized manner. These tools force learners to focus on supporting or disputing statements and provide support for their positions.
- Expert systems and decision support tools allow students to experience problem-solving patterns and learn how ideal solutions are created. An expert system directs students to think about the options at each step of the problem-solving process and make the best choices.

The learning tools chosen for the learning environment depend on the learning objective and preferences of the instructors and designers.

—*Kay J. Wijekumar*

*See also* Document Management Systems; E-mail; Feedback; Learning Management Systems (LMS)

# VIRUSES

A computer virus is a malicious software program that runs against the wishes of the computer owner after being loaded without that owner's knowledge. Depending on how the software code that runs the virus program was written, the virus can also duplicate itself many times over. Even if simply duplicating itself is all a virus does, the virus can cause problems because it will quickly use up the host computer's memory and, thus, slow that computer to a crawl or freeze it completely. Other types of viruses are more complicated and are able to move across networks, even if there are security systems in place. Sophisticated viruses can cause serious damage to a computer by altering files and/or deleting the contents of a computer's hard drive(s).

In order for any virus to start working, the recipient must take some sort of action to activate the virus. This is why viruses are usually transmitted via applications, which are programs that must be executed in order to run. A common way of sending a virus to a computer is to send the virus as an attachment to an e-mail message. When the unsuspecting recipient double-clicks on the attachment, this executes the application, which runs the virus. A common myth is that opening an e-mail message starts a virus when, in actuality, it is the opening of the attachment within the e-mail message that usually starts the virus. Some viruses cause damage immediately whereas others are designed to cause damage later or at a prescribed date and time.

## TYPES OF VIRUSES

Viruses are often lumped together in the same category as worms and Trojan horses. A *worm* is a computer virus that can duplicate itself, but cannot attach itself to another program as a usual virus can.

A *Trojan horse* is an actual program, but it cannot duplicate itself. Like a virus, a Trojan horse can cause considerable damage to a computer because it disguises itself as a harmless program. Thus, the unsuspecting recipient executes the malicious software code when launching the Trojan horse program. A common Trojan horse is a program that advertises itself as ridding a computer of viruses when, in fact, the program introduces viruses to the computer. This is why it is important to use anti-virus programs from trusted sources.

In a more inclusive definition of viruses, unsolicited e-mail, also known as spam, and chain letter e-mail messages could be considered viruses. This is because spam and chain letter e-mail messages get sent to millions of computer users who are often are on the same networks. If the e-mail systems on these networks have not been protected properly, the spam and chain letter e-mail messages will clog the e-mail systems and, thus, bring the computer servers and network to a grinding halt. A common virus of this type is for a cracker/hacker to send out an e-mail message warning users of a virus that does not exist. The recipients of this false e-mail message forward that message to their e-mail administrator and their friends thinking they are being helpful when, in fact, they are flooding the e-mail systems with duplicate copies of the same message. This flooding can create a minor problem by locking up the e-mail administrator's e-mail program, or it can create a more serious problem of slowing down the entire network by using up the network's bandwidth.

## VIRUS PROTECTION

There are various ways to protect against a computer virus. The most basic is to install an anti-virus program on the computer. Any computer that is connected to the Internet or that opens floppy disks, CD-ROMs, or other external media that were created by someone other than the computer owner should be running an installed anti-virus program. Anti-virus programs can be configured in many ways, but their basic purpose is to check the computer for the most commonly known viruses. In order to do so, these anti-virus programs work off a list of viruses, often called a *virus definition list.* Because computer hackers/crackers are constantly writing new viruses, the better anti-virus programs automatically download new

virus definition lists to the computer on a regular basis.

Another basic way to protect against computer viruses is to be certain to be connected to an e-mail system that is properly managed with e-mail quotas and system-level anti-virus and spam protections in place. More complicated protections include the use of firewalls on networks and personal firewalls to protect home and home office computers. Firewalls can be in the form of hardware or software that examines each piece of data that passes through the firewall. The examination is based on a set of rules that the firewall administrator configures based on appropriate security criteria. There are several ways to examine the data, and many firewalls use more than one methodology.

Virtual private networks (VPNs) create secure, private networks that run on top of the Internet through the use of specific encryption and other security methodologies that allow communication between point A and point B only. VPNs can be helpful in preventing viruses from entering a network because only authorized users can send information on the private network. However, this does not stop an authorized person from accidentally or maliciously introducing a virus to the VPN.

In a distributed learning environment, every possible method should be considered to prevent viruses. This includes educating the community of users in the distributed learning environment so that they understand what is—and what is not—a virus. It also involves suggesting that users of the distributed learning environment should have trusted and up-to-date anti-virus software installed on their computers in order to prevent the spread of viruses throughout the user community. It involves educating the user community on the download and upload policies of the distributed learning environment, as well as what e-mail messages should never be forwarded throughout the community. It can involve educating the user community on the proper use and installation of personal firewalls and reminding the user community to properly back up their computers in order to be able to rebuild a computer that might become infected and damaged by a virus.

On the network end, preventing viruses in a distributed learning environment involves having competent computer system and network administrators managing the environment's network so that e-mail systems are configured properly, the network is protected with appropriate security and firewalls, antivirus software is installed on all computer servers to stop any viruses from being transferred across the enterprise from user to user, and proper monitoring occurs to understand normal usage patterns in order to watch for hackers/crackers that might try to introduce viruses to the network. Professional system and network administrators will constantly be educating themselves on trends and changes in the virus protection area of computing. They will also keep proper usage and performance logs, online and offline documentation of the network, and secure backups of the key data in order to keep the networks safe from viruses. These steps may seem like a lot of work, but these are standard services considered part of the daily job duties of professional computer network and system administrators.

## CONCLUDING COMMENT

Like all infectious viruses, computer viruses are a part of daily life. With proper preventative practices, human beings are much more likely to protect a computer from viruses than to protect our own bodies from viruses. Virus protection in the distributed learning environment involves an educational partnership between the user community and the computer professionals managing the learning environment. Fortunately, this is a partnership that is primarily successful and is inexpensive and easy to implement.

*—Debra J. DeWeese*

*See also* E-MAIL; IT SECURITY

## Bibliography

Bagnall, Brian, & Stranger, James. (2000). *E-mail virus protection handbook: Protect your e-mail from viruses, Trojan horses, and mobile code attacks.* Rockland, MA: Syngress.

Gordon, Sarah, Paquette, Jeremy, & Smith, George. (2003). *Maximum virus security: A hacker's guide to protecting your network and computing resources from virus attacks.* Indianapolis, IN: Sams.

Ford Jr., Jerry Lee. (2001). *Absolute beginner's guide to personal firewalls.* Indianapolis, IN: Que.

Grimes, Roger A. (2001). *Malicious mobile code: Virus protection for Windows.* Sebastopol, CA: O'Reilly.

# VOICE ACTIVATION PROGRAMS

Voice activation technology has begun to enjoy wide popularity, and has been deployed in diverse applications ranging from telephone dialing and telephonic response systems to managing assistive programs or as a device for people with mobility impairment. Voice activation programs (VAPs) are a subset of the more powerful voice recognition speech engines utilized to replace hardware devices in more complete computing systems.

VAP systems can "learn" differing sounds in varying dialects from different people. Most personal applications require some training for optimum results, but a few, such as automated answering and selection systems deployed by banks and other institutions, are sufficiently simple when utilized by speakers with minimal accents.

The complexities of the English language, where many spoken words may have from two to five meanings apiece, have forced the technology to go beyond the development of mere databases storing a series of independent words. Current systems employ complex algorithms for context-sensitive determination of which "word" is in actual use. These algorithms will, in milliseconds, review the two words previously spoken with the two words following to give a best determination of the intended message or direction. Dictionaries in the databases build from word definitions. In this way, the databases "build knowledge" in an apparently human fashion: one word at a time, yet with context and usage applied over time.

It is important to note that lexicons (language databases) have been developed for a wide variety of languages. Each is independent and must be incorporated into an application to work successfully. Multi-language applications utilize selection criteria for each lexicon to access the appropriate selected, voice-activated application. Because much of this technology has been developed through the efforts of American companies, English is the predominant language within the VAP markets to date. In such areas as education, proper phonetic use is imperative because the database modules can be easily confused by accents and pronunciations that are not mainstream "American."

Language research labs have used computer programs to "line up" words next to each other to try to determine how many times specific words usually "go together" in natural human speech in conjunction with the large database definitions for each word.

Both approaches, the characteristics list approach and the "line-up" approach, have proved unwieldy. Often the number of times words pair up does not provide significant insight into which characteristics of different definitions for the same word would apply to which usage.

Most commercial systems require specific voice commands or work by recognizing particular words that act as commands. Commands essentially limit the field of words a system has to recognize, thereby helping to increase the rate at which computers can accurately understand speech.

Many of today's speech recognition software can reach up to 90% accuracy in speech-to-text applications; the percentage is even higher with individual "training," often a time consuming task. But strong accents, high-pitched voices, and speech impediments can throw accuracy rates off.

VAPs utilize much smaller databases aimed at specific applications and, therefore, accuracy rates approach 99% in many cases. These application-specific programs overcome one of the inherent shortcomings of the more complex speech-recognition systems: extremely large storage requirements and the use of large amounts of computer memory. VAPs often can be limited to only 200–500 KB (kilobytes) of storage and may require about 256 KB of RAM, depending on the number of command sets deployed in each application. Voice tags (the stored voice WAV files attached to a contact or command) likewise may require only a few KB per command. Simplifying each instruction set has allowed for significant cost reductions from earlier models.

Background noise can also confuse voice-activation systems. Unlike people, computers cannot focus on a particular speaker and drown out the rest of the background noise. Noise reduction technologies employed within current telephones and the use of a quiet setting help to reduce this obvious interference. Although noise reduction microphone/headsets are the state-of-the-art currently, significant progress is being made in the development of fixed, controlled user microphones that will automatically mask out intrusive background noise to focus on a single user.

## USER SECURITY ISSUES AND OTHER TECHNOLOGY APPLICATIONS

In addition to the more common applications of voice activation programming, two other applications of similar technologies fall into this general category: security applications and voice-embedded computer applications. The latter are currently being employed successfully within the education marketplace on an increasing basis. Each area uses a different technology.

In order to prevent unauthorized use of a computer system, whether standalone or in a networked environment, "voice security" has become a method of choice, often rivaling password protection or other digital "fingerprinting" methods. In this model, voice prints (almost as unique as traditional fingerprinting) are taken from the authorized user. A computer will compare the voiceprint on record to the requested user to ensure authenticity. Levels can be set to a low level (quick identification with some measure of error) or to a very high level, which is currently used by government agencies for classified entry.

Of greater significance and use within the distance learning market is a voice activation program segment that uses voice compression to make annotations and comments within documents such as term papers, theses, and other traditional text documents authored in Microsoft Word, WordPerfect, or another word-processing program. In this application, a user (professor or teacher) has the option of inserting one or multiple "voice comments" directly into a submitted document, rather than typing or editing the document via traditional text.

The advantages are obvious: speed of entry and the use of intonation and inflection to make a necessary point or observation. Earlier technologies made such advances awkward and difficult, if for no other reason than mere file size. Voice files are, by their very nature, large in size and therefore difficult to transmit electronically via Internet or intranet applications. New developments in compression technology now allow compression levels to reach 20X to 120X, which overcomes previous transmission obstacles and file size issues. Such applications of voice compression technologies, along with convenient embedment routines, are becoming increasingly popular within both secondary education and the university environment.

*—Rolf C. Rudestam*

*See also* ADAPTIVE TECHNOLOGY; EVOLVING TECHNOLOGIES; IT SECURITY; STREAMING MEDIA

## Bibliography

ABLEDATA, a Source for Information on Assistive Technology. Sponsored by the National Institute on Disability and Rehabilitation Research, U.S. Department of Education: http://www.abledata.com.

VoiceCommands.net is a division of Voice Technology Services, based in Sacramento, California: http://www.voicecommands.net/aboutus.html. This site provides a series of VoiceCommand learning guides.

# WEB-BASED COURSE MANAGEMENT SYSTEMS (WBCMS)

Web-based course management systems (WBCMS) are hypertext-related software tools designed to aid in the development and delivery of Web-based courses or Web supplements to traditional classroom-based courses. These courses or supplements are used in K–12 classrooms, universities, corporations, military training, and learning environments. Current examples of WBCMS include ANGEL, Blackboard, eCollege, Prometheus, and WebCT. This entry includes a summary of functions of WBCMS, including infrastructure, applications, issues, and enhancements.

## FUNCTIONALITY OF WBCMS

The functionality of WBCMSs includes course management tools (such as a course overview, navigation bars, menus, calendars, grade processing, help, customizable Web pages, and maintenance of course enrollee lists), content presentation tools (such as notes with hypertext and multimedia, syllabi, and tests [multiple choice, true/false, and essay]), and communication tools (such as e-mail, bulletin boards, chat rooms, white boards, and some streamed video). Course designers and facilitators can choose to customize and use all of these tools and incorporate them into the course.

A commonly used WBCMS lists the following tools for designers.

*File Management Utilities.* Upload File, Create, Edit, Copy, Move, Rename, Delete, Zip, Unzip, and Download. These tools allow users to manage course syllabi, course notes, and other materials in the form of Word, WordPerfect, or other types of files. For example, the user may create a PowerPoint presentation for the course and use the WBCMS commands to select the file and upload it into the course. Larger groups of files may be condensed using the Zip utilities, which compress the files into manageable smaller sizes. After the files are uploaded into the WBCMS they are unzipped to provide the original files.

*Course Management.* Manage Students, Track Students, Manage Presentation Groups, Manage Teaching Assistants, Track Pages, Backup Course, Reset Course, and Share Access. Users of WBCMS can add students to the class roster (which is available in a format similar to a spreadsheet). As assignments are graded, the grades appear automatically in the student's view of the grade sheet. Access to update this information can be limited to the instructor and teaching assistants. Information on how often students have visited the course pages and how many assignments have been completed can be viewed here as well. Students can also be assigned to groups using this tool and work within the groups for some or all activities (using an e-mail group or a discussion board for communication). Finally, the course can easily be copied for long-term storage or to be modified for future use with the *Backup Course* command.

*Course Settings.* Instructor Name, Language, Design View, Student View, Welcome Page, Course Menu, Course Appearance, Page Colors, Background, Image, Icon Style, Replace Icon, Hide Left Navigation Bar, Show Left Navigation Bar, Hit Counter. As the initial course is set up on the WBCMS, the system requires that an instructor's name be entered as well as options to choose what types of colors, background images, icons, and navigation menu buttons will be used. The designer also has the option of creating a welcome page using the tools or to upload another file that was created using an HTML editor. A hit counter keeps track of how many times the pages/courses have been visited.

*Tools to Be Used by the Students.* Pages/URLs, Organizer Page, Single Page, URL. Students can also use the WBCMS tools to identify the types of information they would like to link to, like e-mail and other Web pages. They also can add entries to the calendar to remind them of course-related deadlines (like group project submissions and meetings). For example, an organizer page may contain links to frequently viewed Web pages and/or grade review pages.

*Contents and Related Tools.* Content Module, Syllabus, Glossary, Index, Calendar, Image Database, CD-ROM, Compile, Search, Resume Course. Course information like the syllabus, notes, deadlines, calendar, and any supporting materials like images and CD-ROM–based textbooks can be uploaded using the WBCMS tools or created within the environment. For example, if the professor has a glossary of frequently used terms already created in a Word file, the file may be uploaded using the commands in the WBCMS. If such a file does not exist, then the glossary can be typed into the WBCMS in the same way in which it would be typed using word processing software. Commands like *Compile* are used to pull together all the materials related to the course, verify that the hyperlinks are active, and view how the final product would appear to the student.

*Communication Tools.* Discussions, Mail, Chat, Whiteboard. Communication between the instructor and the students as well as among the students in the course is usually handled using discussion boards (sometimes referred to as bulletin boards), e-mail, chat rooms, and whiteboards. The discussion board is an asynchronous method of communication that

students can enter at any time to create a message or reply to an existing message (which can be threaded, so that it will follow the initial message with the same subject heading). The message is accessible to all members of the course or group, as designated by the instructor. The messages can be read as often as needed. The instructor has the choice of creating public (all participants in the course) or private (a subset of people chosen by the instructor) groups within the discussion board. Different types of discussion threads can also be created by the instructor to lead a conversation. For example, discussion boards can be created to allow students to discuss a reading, to conduct a debate, or to get help from colleagues on course-related problems.

*Evaluation Tools.* Quiz, Self Test, My Grades, Assignments. Course assessments can be created using the quiz utilities. The tools allow the instructor to enter questions and create multiple choices, and then select the correct answer. After the questions are all entered the instructor sets when the quiz should be active and how much time should be allocated for the quiz, as well as the number of times students may take the quiz. Options for these types of assessments include self-test items (for students to check their understanding without grade penalties), true/false, and essay exams. After the student completes the quizzes and examinations, the grading may be done automatically, giving the student his or her grade immediately, or the instructor can choose to perform the grading at a later time. When the grades are posted students can see how they have performed on the course using the My Grade utility, which will give them their scores. Other utilities include exam statistics for student and instructor, which provide the mean and median for the scores.

*Study Tools.* My Progress, Language, Student Homepages, Student Presentations, Student Tips. Students also can view their progress using the grade sheet and view their access history on the calendars. They also have the option of introducing themselves to their colleagues in the course by creating a Web page within the WBCMS or by uploading HTML files with information about themselves and/or pictures. They can also upload project files for submission as well as other course information like PowerPoint presentations. They may also get help at any time by using the tips created by the instructor or by using the

WBCMS tutorials. For example, the tutorial allows the student to take a sample quiz, get help in creating a Web page, or learn how to post to a discussion board.

## USING A WBCMS

The tools just listed can be used to upload notes and syllabi, create a course calendar, generate quizzes, and provide updates to students on their status. Uploading notes and syllabi can be done in a few steps (usually by supplying a file name and the location, followed by the type of file and where the file should be linked to). Quizzes can also be uploaded or can be entered directly by typing the questions followed by the multiple choices as well as the correct answer. Grading and student notification can be automated, giving students updates on their performance as soon as they complete the test. These are some basic elements of the course content.

Communications in these Web-based or Web-enhanced courses can be asynchronous or synchronous. Discussion forums (also known as bulletin boards) are asynchronous tools with which students can post their thoughts or conduct discussions. Students may also communicate using e-mail or chat rooms. Whiteboards or display screens are also used in conjunction with chat rooms in synchronous modes to diagram or describe any part of the discussion. Some advanced systems also provide streaming audio and video with the chat rooms. These advanced features are constrained by the bandwidth and transmission and reception speeds of Internet connections.

Creating the course framework and communications are major components of the WBCMS utilities, but they are only one major component of the WBCMS. The larger framework of hosting the system is very important as well.

## WBCMS INFRASTRUCTURE

The WBCMS infrastructure can vary from software that is purchased or licensed by a university with course development and support in-house to software with licenses that are issued based on the number of students in the course and that provide hosting through an external company with or without support for course development. The software usually resides on a networked server and supports Web access for hundreds or thousands of users (including students,

designers, and instructors). Most are compatible with current Web browsers like Netscape Navigator and Microsoft Internet Explorer. However, some of the tools are hardware and software (including operating system) dependent, requiring Java-enabled systems for support of functions like chat applets. Students and other users must have Internet access to use these systems.

This infrastructure can support a wide range of courses and course support needs, but blending the team necessary to support effective course development requires instructional technologists, subject matter experts, computer technologists, graphic designers, and help-desk support for faculty, students, and designers. The availability (24 hours a day, 7 days a week) of the support services affects the quality of the course and students' reception of the course.

Many of the current evaluations of WBCMS evaluate the availability of support, costs, number of tools available, and quality of the available tools. This does not begin to cover the issues that are at the heart of any learning environment, which depends on broader areas of research like educational psychology, instructional technology, and instructional design.

## INSTRUCTIONAL DESIGN AND WBCMS

Creating Web-based or Web-enhanced courses requires a strong instructional design (ID) model, knowledge of the course content and objectives, profile of the learners, and available tools (not limited to the WBCMS). A variety of process-oriented ID models like Dick & Carey's ADDIE; theory-oriented models like Keller's ARCS; collaborative learning; and constructivist learning environments can be used to design instruction. There are also some instructional methods that have been designed specifically for the World Wide Web, such as WebQuests, that may be used as a WBCMS. Mayer's Multimedia Learning Theory and research are also very important factors that are useful for Web-based course design.

Courses designed within WBCMS frameworks have included notes, PowerPoint presentations, readings/references, links to other sites, bulletin board postings, discussions, syllabi, calendars, tests, and grading. Courses designed around active learning principles and/or constructivist philosophies have used blended techniques where the WBCMS is used for some parts of the course requiring bulletin boards, chat rooms, and syllabi, which are enhanced with activities using tools like concept maps, databases, simulations, and spreadsheets.

## ISSUES REGARDING WBCMS

Issues related to these applications include a heavy reliance on collaborative activities (not all learning occurs through collaboration), a lack of support for laboratory-type domains like chemistry, a need for scientific notation (such as the summation sign), a lack of research-based development of models and/or techniques for creating learning environments for the Web, and a lack of instructional design theory and tools to support the course design.

Conducting a biology or chemistry experiment is complicated in real life, but is almost impossible to mimic in an online environment. Some tools are available that provide simulations, but these are not advanced enough to provide real-life experiences. Regarding scientific notation, most of the WBCMS support standard hypertext documents, but require the designers to use graphics files (e.g., GIF, JPEG, LaTEX) to create scientific equations. After the text has been created in a Word, WordPerfect, or PowerPoint file, the designer must create the equations in another equation editor and paste the images into the document. This becomes very cumbersome for creation and modification of notes. A lack of instructional design theory and tools is also a major drawback in these WBCMS. The training in and use of these tools leads one to believe that uploading and downloading, notes and PowerPoint, quizzes and discussion constitute a good course and a good learning environment.

The extensive research on multimedia learning should provide guidance and influence the design of the WBCMS itself, as well as designers creating courses or supplements in WBCMS. Finally, the cognitive impact of using the WBCMS methods of presentations (hyperlinked notes, chat rooms, bulletin boards) has not been researched.

In conclusion, the WBCMS are tools just like Word, WordPerfect, or PowerPoint, with a general set of functions available for users. How the tool is used to create a learning environment or to enhance learning depends on the designers and their skills in combining the objectives of the course with the background of the learners to facilitate the learning process.

—*Kay Wijekumar*

*See also* HYPERTEXT; INSTRUCTIONAL COURSE DESIGN; SITE LICENSES; STUDY GUIDES; VIRTUAL LEARNING TOOLS

## Bibliography

Abbey, B. (Ed.). (2001). *Instructional and cognitive impacts of Web-based education.* Hershey, PA: Idea Group Publishing.

Jonassen, D. H. (1999). Designing constructivist learning environments. In C. M. Reigeluth (Ed.), *Instructional-design theories and models: A new paradigm of instructional theory* (pp. 215–240). Mahwah, NJ: Lawrence Erlbaum.

Keller, J. M. (1983). Motivational design of instruction. In C. M. Reigeluth (Ed.), *Instructional-design theories and models: An overview of their current status* (pp. 383– 434). Hillsdale, NJ: Lawrence Erlbaum.

Keller, J. M. (1987). Developing and use of the ARCS model of instructional design. *Journal of Instructional Development, 10*(3), 2–10.

Mayer, R. E. (2001). *Multimedia learning.* Cambridge: Cambridge University Press.

Nelson, L. M. (1999). Collaborative problem solving. In C. M. Reigeluth (Ed.), *Instructional-design theories and models: A new paradigm of instructional theory* (pp. 241–267). Mahwah, NJ: Lawrence Erlbaum.

Passerini, K., & Granger, M. J. (2000). A developmental model for distance learning using the Internet. *Computers and Education, 34,* 1–15.

Reigeluth, C. M. (Ed.). (1999). *Instructional-design theories and models: A new paradigm of instructional theory.* Mahwah, NJ: Lawrence Erlbaum.

# WEB PORTALS

Web portals were introduced in 1998 as a means of tailoring information and services on the Web to the tastes, proclivities, and needs of the individuals consuming them. Portals are often misunderstood and have been described by many as the most abused term in IT. Providers of Web-based information technology applications occasionally cloud the issues related to portals by referring to their nonportal products. In essence, portals are Web sites that have been tailored to specific audiences and communities for the purposes of: 1) facilitating access to information, 2) providing personalized access to online services, and 3) fostering community among audiences that share needs or purposes. Within 4 years of their introduction, Web portals were implemented—at the institutional level—at more than 20% of U.S. colleges and universities. More than one-half of the respondents in one recent higher education survey indicated their intention to implement an institutional Web portal within 12 months.

## THE WEB PORTAL IN HISTORICAL CONTEXT

Two important historical trends influenced the development and ongoing evolution of Web portals: the evolution of the World Wide Web as a "place" for conducting business, gathering information, and exchanging ideas and tasks; and the shift from mass production to mass customization as a product and service delivery strategy.

The broad introduction of the World Wide Web in the mid-1990s has revolutionized how people use computers and networks to work, learn, and recreate. Colleges and universities were among the first to seize the opportunities presented by this technology, and in less than a decade have built Web sites consisting of millions of pages of text, sound, and image-based information. The Web is a frontier and the underlying authoring technologies made it easy for organizations throughout the academy to establish an outpost on the Internet. As a result, college and university Web sites evolved as a patchwork quilt of uncoordinated pages, each bearing the official marks and *imprimaturs* of the institution. As projects were completed and grants expended, Web links were broken and Web sites disused. The institutional Web site—from the user's standpoint—appeared disorganized, fragmented, and unmaintained, often containing conflicting information, if indeed information could be found within the metaphorical haystacks of the Web.

During this same period, considerable progress was made in shifting the dominant manufacturing and distribution paradigm of U.S. business from one characterized by scale economies and the mass production and inventory of goods to one characterized by just-in-time, mass customized goods and services.

Within this context, IT vendors developed the portal concept to make the Web an effective environment in which individuals and communities could work, learn, and socialize. The dominant promises of Web portals were to: 1) provide a single and coordinated gateway or portal into the holdings and services of the institution; and 2) provide views of the institution's holdings and services that are tailored or personalized to the needs of subcommunities such as students, faculty, staff, or patients.

## THE EARLY EXPERIENCE OF WEB PORTALS IN HIGHER EDUCATION

From the outset, Web portals were a misunderstood artifact of the dot-com era. Within months of their introduction, a confusing taxonomy began to evolve. *Horizontal* or *megaportals* such as Yahoo! and America Online described the large commercial portals that appeared to serve the entire Internet. *Vertical portals* described portals that were smaller and narrower in scope. These portals served specific communities of interest or markets. *Enterprise portals* refer to portals that have been deployed to integrate the information and services developed by organizations to service their major internal and external stakeholders. These portals can be either horizontal—spanning the breadth of the enterprise's services and information—or vertical, designed to address specific functions (e.g., employee benefits lookups) or processes (e.g., hiring).

When introduced, portals were most often provided at no cost to clients—including higher education institutions—providing clients were willing to give the portal providers the right to sell advertising on the campus portal. This practice hastened the initial diffusion of portal technology within higher education, created a significant amount of controversy over the merchandizing of the institution's Web presence, and was eventually replaced by more traditional licensing arrangements in the wake of the dot-com era's demise.

## uPORTAL AND THE COMING OF AGE OF WEB PORTALS IN HIGHER EDUCATION

In addition to the early portal vision being anchored in an advertising model of cost recovery, the portal was heralded as a technology touchstone, encompassing functionality to include aesthetics, Web navigation, user authentication, Internet security, and more. It was, in the language of 1998–2000, a "thick portal." This notion of Web portal as the solution to many of IT's most vexing problems was both alluring and ultimately infeasible.

In 1999, a talented group of higher education information technologists reconceptualized the portal vision in higher education and developed uPortal, a

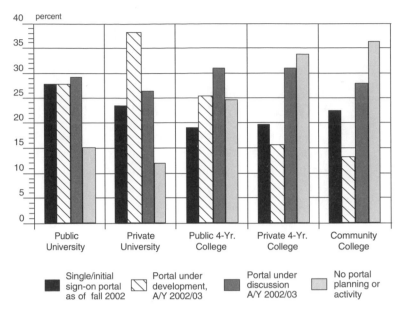

**Figure 1**

Source: Kenneth C. Green, Campus Computing Survey, 2002.

free, sharable portal under development by institutions of higher education. uPortal is an open-standard effort using Java, Extensible Markup Language (XML), Java Server Pages (JSP), and Java 2 Enterprise Edition (J2EE). Its developers envision an institutional portal as an abridged and customized version of the institutional Web presence—a "pocket-sized" version of the campus Web. The uPortal technology adds "community" to the campus Web presence, while customization allows each user to define a unique and personal view of the campus Web. Community tools, such as chat, forums, and surveys, are able to plug into this reconceptualized and much "thinner" portal. Importantly, nearly 40 colleges and universities have adopted this portal, and SCT—a major commercial portal supplier—has incorporated the uPortal code set into its Luminis product to support user management, content management, and data integration. Additionally, important application vendors of enterprise resource planning (ERP) and course management system (CMS) technologies have also announced support for uPortal's framework.

A concurrent trend in Web portal's second generation—partially stimulated by the designers of uPortal—was the emergence of the portal as a service gateway for Web-based services offered or organized by the institution or enterprise. In their first incarnation, Web portals were conceived of as information

portals and were designed to facilitate the needed discovery of information resources scattered about the Web frontier. These early portals focused on content aggregation. The success of early portals in pursuit of this objective made it natural for those thinking about Web portals' second generation to focus on the portal as the organizing principle and technology for rationalizing the frontier of electronic services that have proliferated in the past 5 years.

The maturation of this technology and its shift of focus toward personalization and integration has made it possible for Web portals to assume a place of importance in higher education's information technology environment. According to the Campus Computing Survey, over 60% of private, 4-year universities have either implemented an institutional portal or planned to do so in the 2002–2003 academic year (see Figure 1).

## WEB PORTALS IN THE FUTURE OF HIGHER EDUCATION

Very few enterprises, educational or not, have implemented fully deployed portals. As a result, the full benefits of this technology have yet to be classified and captured in any systematic way. At the same time, early leading adopters have uncovered flaws. Among these are stranded investments in "thin" architectures that will not scale; high total cost of ownership for those who invested in prebuilt components (channels or portlets); and continued governance challenges. In particular, the early emergence of numerous institutional portals and IT applications with portal-like functions in the absence of standards for interoperability risks the emergence of a new kind of frontier. IT industry experts describe the evolution of a third generation of Web portals in which Web services will become the *de facto* standard for channels being developed for delivery through the portal. If true, application developers and commercial vendors will wrap their application components in standards-based wrappers, greatly enhancing the potential of the Web portal to achieve its original vision of Web integration. Some describe the emerging focus of Web portals as being about unification, in which the portal provides the mechanism for integration between legacy applications and data at the component level. If successful, this incarnation of Web portals will make them the chief tool for developing and deploying applications in the academy.

## PORTAL ISSUES AND CONCERNS

A number of prominent information technologists in higher education identify the portal as a genuine instrument of institutional change. If indeed the promise of the portal is institutional unification and if, further, colleges and universities are very loosely coupled organizations, portal technologies are both promising and daunting. Their socialization within higher education will not be easy. Common issues and concerns raised include:

- *Financial performance*—Portals are an element of an overall IT architecture and service delivery strategy. To the extent that this architecture and strategy are not understood, portal investments may be at risk.
- *Lack of ownership*—Portals are boundary spanning activities by definition. The promise of unification cannot or should not be the promise of the IT organization, which is not organizationally placed at most institutions to affect unifying activities in a credible fashion. If the institution's IT organization is the tool maker, the provost, or some other senior campus leader, must wield the tool.
- *Lack of clarity and priority over the portals' primary beneficiaries*—In the early days of portals, their focus was on students in the belief that students are customers and that their satisfaction with the virtual campus experience would drive loyalty and a host of other good things. Many current portal developers are focusing on other campus stakeholders such as staff and faculty in the belief that the payoffs to the institution, accruing from these stakeholders, may be higher. Although priority decisions must be made, it is nevertheless important for the portal "owner" to situate priorities within an inclusive vision that makes the benefits of the portal architecture accessible to many.
- *Lack of clarity about expected benefits*—The term *portal* has been misused and miscommunicated, creating unclear and conflicting expectations regarding its benefits. Institutions that define the success of these projects before implementing them are likely to experience greater relative success.
- *An incomplete architecture*—As portals have come to be viewed as being somewhat thinner from a capabilities and architecture point of view, the success of the portal increasingly depends on other elements of the institutional IT architecture, such as directory services, transaction processing, user authentication, and single sign-on. Imbalances among these elements of an overall IT architecture lead to suboptimal performance of the portal and misperceptions about the portal's worth and performance capabilities.
- *A portal framework that no one uses*—The success of any new technology depends on user engagement and user education. Unless the portal performs in ways that are agreeable to the institution's end users, it will fail to achieve its promise. Similarly, in a very busy world, few people use portals unless the information and services that can be accessed through the portal are of great value. Although deploying the portal is ambitious, equal or greater attention must be spent on developing and maintaining the suite of services and the information resources that are enabled by the portal.

*—Richard Katz*

*See also* INFORMATION TECHNOLOGY (IT); WEB SITES

### Bibliography
Charp, Sylvia. (September 2002). Administrative and instructional portals. *T.H.E. Journal,* 12–14.

Katz, Richard N. (2002). *Web portals in higher education.* San Francisco: Jossey-Bass.

Phifer, Gene. (December 12, 2001). Portals in 2002: A year of major change. *Gartner Research Note. Strategic Planning,* SPA-15–0306, 1–3.

Phifer, G., & Berg, T. (September 25, 2000). "Portal": The most abused term in IT. *Gartner Research Note. Tutorials,* TU–12–0464, 1–2.

Roth, Craig. (May 24, 2002). *Top 10 portal pitfalls—and how to avoid them.* Retrieved from www.zdnet.com.

Strauss, Howard. Web portals: A home page doth not a portal make. *The Edutech Report, 15*(11), 1–3.

Zastrocky, Michael, & Phifer, Gene. (August 10, 2000). Best practices in deploying institution-wide portals. *Gartner Research Note. Commentary,* COM-11–7295.

## WEB SITES

A Web site is a system of interconnected Web pages designed to deliver information to and store information for users. A specific location within the World Wide Web, a Web site most commonly consists of an initial "home" page that users see when they come to the site. Along with the home page, a site typically includes many additional pages, as well as other tools and resources that are housed within its location. A site is owned and managed by an individual or an organization.

In an academic environment, particularly a distributed learning setting, there are often multiple content owners, managers, and contributors working within a centralized system. Because a distributed learning environment spans multiple areas, a Web site often becomes a central point for gathering, storing, sharing, and processing information to facilitate the learning process and build a sense of community among its users.

## WEB SITE USE

The information delivered via and stored within a site comes in many forms. It is common to find text; graphical elements; files; documents; audio/video components; online tools for communication, coursework, and transactional use; access to research-oriented tools; and other resources. In a distributed learning environment, users often rely heavily on Web sites to gather and share information, communicate with colleagues, distribute written work, access Web-based course tools, perform research via online databases, and transact with their college, university, or institution.

A distributed learning setting contains systems of records and an institution with which the learner must interact. Much of this interaction takes place via a Web site that has integrated transactional capabilities. Examples of transactional elements include online forms that capture and transmit personal and other information, course registrations, payments, and other commerce-oriented links.

Communication that takes place via a Web site can be synchronous or asynchronous. Although the Web itself is an asynchronous environment, synchronous communication can be channeled via a Web site. Synchronous communication takes place in real time, which requires users to be at their computers at a specific time for a live conversation via instant messaging tools, class lecture, or other interaction that uses the Web as a delivery vehicle. Asynchronous communication can be performed any time and can take place via

e-mail, collaborative Web-based communication tools, and other forms of information transfer.

Learning and community building are facilitated and enabled by each of these modes of communication, along with the other tasks and activities users can perform via a distributed learning environment's Web site. This is why the Web has become an indispensable resource for most learning environments, particularly distributed ones. The things that users do on a Web site, how they interact with it, along with its overall visual and functional design, comprise the entire user experience.

## WEB SITE DEVELOPMENT AND DESIGN—A PRIMER

A successful Web site is designed purposefully around the needs of its users. Several fundamental elements comprise the total experience the user will have on the site. Two critical concepts, embedded within these elements, are *simplicity* and *usability*. By definition, usability refers to the creation of easy-to-use products or systems that match as closely as possible with users' needs. Simplicity is inherent in this. To apply these concepts to Web development and design means that all the elements of a site's design work together with the goal of providing a high-quality, user-centered experience.

Designing Web sites for distributed learning differs from designing sites for other purposes in that the needs of users in a distributed learning environment are unique. To be user-centered in this environment is to be student- or learner-centered—carefully considering the Web-based needs of that particular learning community.

For these reasons, it is very important to plan prudently around several essential areas. These include:

- General planning, audience definition, and development of guiding principles, requirements, and standards
- Information architecture and navigation design
- Graphic design and page layout
- Content creation and writing
- Searchability, information retrieval, and integration of other tools and resources
- Usability testing
- Management and standards

These areas are discussed in the following sections.

## GENERAL PLANNING

This step in the development and design of a distributed learning Web site is extremely important. If site planners have not been assigned at the outset, this is the time to charge the appropriate individuals with the task. Site planners will think about who the users will be and what they should be able to accomplish using the site. Asking many high-level questions will facilitate the development of the vision for the site.

The right questions and answers will assist in defining developmental and operational standards so that the site can be well managed and maintained over time. The process also helps in developing guiding principles and requirements that will be the foundation upon which the site will be built. Users need to be able to trust the Web site in the same way they trust the organization that governs it. Careful planning with this need in mind is a means to creating a successful Web environment for users in a distributed learning setting.

## INFORMATION ARCHITECTURE AND NAVIGATION DESIGN

The practice of information architecture has traditionally been applied in areas such as library science and information retrieval, human computer interaction (HCI) development, interface and interaction design, and other areas where managing information in a systematic way has been of great importance. The ability for the user to find information efficiently on a Web site is critical. How well the information is designed, organized, categorized, and labeled—elements of the information architecture—along with the effectiveness of the navigation scheme have a direct impact on the usability of the site.

It is important to develop these schemes before any actual programming or building of the Web site occurs. Site planners need to consider the content to be delivered via the Web site and how users think about that content. Gathering user input early in the process is one of many ways to design an effective scheme.

User feedback about content organization, categorization, and labeling can be gathered by representative audience members by using techniques such as card sorting exercises, site maps, and wireframe reviews. These techniques help in building a well-organized site that will fulfill users' needs. Site maps display the general categories of the site and the hierarchical relationships among them. They often resemble hierarchical organizational charts, and are developed on paper. A wireframe is another visual representation of the future Web site. It contains no design or graphical elements to distract the process. Much like a blueprint to a house, a wireframe provides a printed, visual map of site elements and can assist tremendously in refining site-wide features. These methods of gathering representative audience feedback reduce rework in later stages and almost always have positive effects on the final site.

Navigation design needs to be created so that it provides users with context about where they are within the whole Web site. People should be able to move freely from section to section within the site by using a navigational system that promotes easy access to content, tools, and resources. If users are confused about where they are in relation to different areas of the site, the navigation design is likely faulty and users will spend—and potentially waste—a great deal of time looking for information and will become frustrated. When users get frustrated, there are many potential impacts. Learners may lose trust in the organization or ultimately even decide to leave the institution and seek out other learning opportunities.

A good user experience is one where people have easy access to the things they need and have clear understanding of where they are within the site at all times. Solid information architecture and good navigation design are critical components in achieving this end.

## GRAPHIC DESIGN AND PAGE LAYOUT

The old adage "form follows function" is good, solid practice in Web design. The graphic design and page layout should be consistent and complementary to the functionality of the site. The site should not contain gratuitous graphical elements that can slow down page load times and detract from functionality. Visual cues such as icons and color should be applied in order to assist users in understanding where they are in the context of the whole site, thus complementing the navigation design. Both page layout and graphic design should ensure that the content of interest to the user is the most prevalent element on the page. Pages should be easy to scan visually because users do not read Web content on-screen in the same way that they read printed material.

Design should accommodate multiple computer platforms, versions, and types of Web browsers. Particularly in a distributed learning environment, an organization cannot easily enforce standard computer configurations, which means the Web pages must be flexibly designed. Pages should load quickly via a standard 56Kbps dial-up connection so that users have quick access to the content they need.

## CONTENT CREATION AND WRITING

Writing for the Web is not the same as writing for print. Screens are not built for reading, which means users scan for relevant information and will print lengthy content to read offline. Concise, clear, jargon-free, noncolloquial writing is most beneficial and should be broken up into pieces or "chunks." The best Web content has a clear "voice" or tone and commits to and applies standards for elements such as case usage, punctuation, grammar, and visual display including items like headers, fonts, and style types.

Lengthy content should be broken up across multiple pages or be supplemented by navigation aids such as "back-to-top-of-page links." Printability is important and content should be available in Portable Document Format (PDF) or via other printer-friendly methods.

Key content phrases and words, overall taxonomies, and page titling also need to be applied to the content within a site. This is for the reader of the content on the page as well as to ensure searchability. For search mechanisms to be functional these elements need to be applied to individual pages so that keyword- and phrase-based searches yield relevant results.

## SEARCHABILITY, INFORMATION RETRIEVAL, AND INTEGRATION

In a distributed learning setting, searching for and retrieving information is very important. Having an integrated search function that is coordinated with the content within the site is one-half of the equation. The other half is returning relevant and usable results to users. The display of the results should provide users a relevant rank order and highlight the original search terms. Results should be linked to the appropriate pages and, ideally, results should suggest other potentially relevant pages to the user.

The search mechanism, along with other tools and resources, should be well-integrated within the site. Even if the tools are provided by different departments within the organization or external vendors, the user should experience as seamless a presentation as possible. This means careful consideration needs to be given to the application of the design, layout, navigation, and access methods for all tools and resources available on the site.

## USABILITY TESTING

During the development of a Web site, site planners and designers should apply usability testing techniques to gather feedback about the site before it is released. Testing will disclose whether users can do the things they need to and find information easily on the site.

Usability testing is likely to reveal issues to site owners before the site is made widely available, providing an opportunity for improvement and fine tuning. Acquiring this feedback directly from representative users is much more beneficial than relying on developers, or those more familiar with the Web overall, because they come to a site with a fresh perspective. Objective testing of the site, and appropriate application of the feedback, can ultimately improve the final product.

## MANAGEMENT AND STANDARDS

Users expect Web sites to be, among other things, accurate and up-to-date. In order for this to be accomplished, a site needs to be well-managed, which includes having clear publishing guidelines and standards. It should be apparent to users who governs the site and how to communicate with site owners. Ideally, content will be time-stamped so users know how up-to-date the content is or simply when it was last updated.

Highly evolved Web sites will employ some type of content management system (CMS) that allows content contributors and managers to make changes and/or additions to their content without having to use programming languages or other complex Web publishing techniques. Within a well-structured CMS, content owners will adjust only their content, allowing site owners to focus on maintaining defined site-wide standards. A blend of centralized and decentralized management for diverse, complex Web sites leverages the very nature of a distributed learning environment.

## BEYOND THE BASICS

The previous pages provide a generalized overview of Web sites, their use, development, and design. In the context of distributed learning settings, institutions will continue to rely heavily on the Web as a critical instrument for learning, growth, and change. Given that change is a constant, the answer to providing users with a Web experience they can trust, that facilitates learning and that inspires a community sentiment, is to maintain focus on usability, simplicity, and constant consideration for the end user.

*—Larissa Schwartz*

*See also* GRAPHICS; WORLD WIDE WEB

### Bibliography

Argus Center for Information Architecture: http://argus-acia.com.

Good Experience: http://www.goodexperience.com.

IAwiki: http://www.iawiki.net/IAwiki.

Jakob Nielsen: http://www.useit.com.

Jesse Garret: http://www.jjg.net.

Koman, R., & Niederst, J. (1998). *Web design in a nutshell: A desktop quick reference.* Sebastopol, CA: O'Reilly.

Krug, S. (2000). *Don't make me think.* Indianapolis, IN: Que.

Louis Rosenfeld: http://louisrosenfeld.com/home/

McGovern, G. (2001). *The Web content style guide.* Englewood Cliffs, NJ: Prentice Hall.

Morville, P., & Rosenfeld, L. (1998). *Information architecture for the World Wide Web.* Sebastopol, CA: O'Reilly.

Nielsen, J. (2000). *Designing Web usability, the practice of simplicity.* Indianapolis, IN: New Riders Publishing.

Peter Morville: http://semanticstudios.com/about/morville.html.

Usability Net: http://www.usabilitynet.org.

World Wide Web Consortium: http://www.w3.org.

# WORK-BASED DISTRIBUTED LEARNING

Work-based distributed learning is the use of information and communication technologies for providing networked training and educational opportunities to employees anytime, anywhere. It is being used to enhance employee performance and personal growth, help product or service development, promote stronger linkages with suppliers or clients, and provide access to educational opportunities for lifelong learning.

The major players in the field include corporations that have been using distributed learning to train staff, universities that are providing access to higher education programs such as undergraduate degrees and MBAs, companies that are opening their online training facilities to clients and suppliers, labor unions that are training their members in subjects such as collective bargaining, companies that are providing training certificates, and courseware-writing companies and other software producers.

The technologies enabling work-based distributed learning include personal computers, educational computer conferencing systems, CD-ROMs, video conferencing, satellite transmission, television, videotapes, radio, and film, plus software such as course authoring tools and learning management systems (LMS). A basic dividing line between the technologies is how they adapt to time—whether they are "synchronous" or "asynchronous." A synchronous technology, such as video conferencing or television broadcasting, demands that people communicate, or be available for communications, at the same time. An asynchronous technology, such as e-mail or computer conferencing, allows people to communicate at times they choose. Another consideration is whether the technologies are designed for personal use (such as a training CD-ROM) or group interactivity (such as a computer conferencing system or "virtual" classroom).

The use of technology to provide occupational distance education has a long history, including the use of computer-based training (CBT), which began in the 1960s. A dramatic increase in activity related to distributed occupational learning came with the introduction of the personal computer in the 1980s and the World Wide Web in the 1990s. These new technologies opened a vast range of possibilities that enabled employees to participate in educational activities either on the job or in their own time. People began to study via distributed learning technologies in order to upgrade their skills for improving their productivity, securing promotions, changing employment, or finding work. For others, distributed learning allowed them to pursue educational credentials such as certificates from IT companies or degrees from public or private universities.

A crucial difference between traditional distance education programs organized prior to the 1990s and distributed education programs today is online (via computer communications) networking. Distributed training and education programs may utilize personal-use technologies such as CD-ROMs, but what makes them different from the rote-learning methods of early CBT programs or the self-study mode of correspondence courses is the capability of people to engage in activities such as group discussion and work via computer communications.

The software being used to enable distributed learning includes course authoring tools, computer conferencing facilities, and learning management systems (LMS). Course authoring tools are computer programs aimed at helping instructional designers create distributed learning or computer-based self-study courses. In the jargon of the industry they help subject matter experts (SMEs) with instructional systems design (ISD). Some authoring tools consist of "plug-ins" (accessory programs) for word processing or Web page creation software. Others are self-contained programs for creating complete courses. Most authoring tools allow for the creation of text and graphic tutorials; training simulations with audio, video, and animation shows; multiple choice questionnaires; remedial responses; and quizzes. The more full-featured tools contain text outliners, script-writing functions, and story-boarding capabilities. The second generation of authoring tools developed in the late 1990s began using an "object-oriented" approach to course development. "Learning objects" are reusable units (such as a company description) that can be assembled into multiple configurations in order to develop new courses.

A computer conferencing system organizes the asynchronous messages of learners into shared message groupings. These groupings, commonly called *conferences* or *virtual classrooms,* promote group cohesiveness and collaborative learning because the participants can easily see all the messages related to a specific topic or produced by a particular group. E-mail could be used for distributing the messages, but it is less effective than computer conferencing because the messages are interspersed with the person's other e-mails, thereby reducing the sense of group cohesiveness that is essential for successful educational activities. Most computer conferencing

systems aimed at the educational market also include calendar tools, student tracking capabilities, and other course-management functions.

Learning management systems (LMS) are computer programs that deal with the logistics of managing a community of learners: the registration of participants, educational activity tracking, the employment history and specialities of instructors, classroom allocation, and other related matters. Most allow managers to track the learning achievements of individuals in order to record acquired competencies and skills. Employees also can use the systems to help plan their long-term training and educational needs. Many human resource management programs are building LMS capabilities into their systems.

Like any other application of technology, distributed learning has its advantages and disadvantages. The advantages include providing access to training when and where employees need it (for example, while developing a new service or product); shortening time spent in expensive classroom-based training; training staff scattered over vast geographical areas or in remote locations while retaining local flexibility; increasing access to training or education; saving on travel and classroom costs; amortizing training development expenses and instructor costs over larger audiences; and making specialized instructors accessible to more people. Perhaps the most important advantage is that distributed learning provides the opportunities to build a more technologically adept workforce that not only knows how to find training when it needs it, but also can apply its learning to the creation of new knowledge, products, or services. The disadvantages include a potential lessening in face-to-face educational activity (still the ultimate educational experience), money wasted on poorly designed or executed courses, alienation of employees who are less technologically comfortable than others, and courses that do not respond to the needs of the learners.

A successful implementation of distributed learning is most probably a "blended" solution that brings into play many different training elements. For example, an employee could work with a CD-ROM, attend a face-to-face class, access just-in-time training modules via the Web, participate in an online course, and work via e-mail or computer conferencing with an online mentor. The key to success may be to use these different elements to reinforce each other. Employees could be asked to use a training CD-ROM or attend an online course before a face-to-face classroom activity.

As well, they could be asked to participate in an online course after a classroom-based session so they can keep in touch with the facilitator and other participants as they apply the general concepts they learned in the class to their specific situations.

Of course, simply ensuring that employees have access to technologies such as CD-ROMs or learning opportunities such as online courses is no guarantee of success. Equal attention must be paid to the pedagogies—the learning theories and practices that are applied. CBT, which was introduced in the 1960s to great enthusiasm, failed largely because its rote-learning strategy was found to be boring. Traditional correspondence courses in which learners work on their own with printed or electronic material and have access to a tutor over the phone or even e-mail have large dropout rates. But distributed learning programs that blend personal-use technologies with group interactivity can keep learners interested and engaged on a long-term basis if effective online learning strategies are applied.

This has raised interest in applying the lessons of online collaborative learning (OCL), first studied in school and university contexts, to the world of work. Collaborative learning techniques emphasize learner participation in a networked environment. They include group work assignments, role-playing, conference moderating by learners, and other exercises that promote peer-to-peer teaching and learning. Participants—including the instructor or facilitator—become equal partners in the process.

The effectiveness of OCL techniques in training and education has encouraged their application in product or service development. Teams trying to create, produce, and market new products or services in a rapid development cycle can maximize their creative potential and productivity by working within a collaborative learning environment. The use of OCL technologies for developing new services and products either locally or globally may even eclipse the use of distributed learning in the more formal educational or training arenas.

The ability of teams to work and learn globally could prove to be the most significant effect of the introduction of computer communications. Production teams can work on a project 24 hours a day by passing work on to partners based in other time zones. Programmers can be based far away from design or production centers without any loss in time or productivity and still participate in global team learning. All

of which can be advantageous. At the same time, however, multinational corporations can take advantage of the technologies to distance themselves (literally) from the working conditions imposed by their contractors thousands of miles away.

The advent of global learning/working networks could also prove to be momentous for developing countries. Their workforces could gain access to training opportunities formerly denied them because of cost or distance. Brain drain caused by learners staying in the countries where they have studied would be lessened, and new avenues for increased global commercial activity could be made available. However, in order to take advantage of the opportunities being produced by computer communications, developing countries need help to improve their technological, legislative, and commercial infrastructures. This can be done by encouraging more investment in developing countries, promoting debt relief linked to technological advancement, and designing technologies that take into account Third World conditions.

However, despite the potentials, and the vast sums being spent on it, distributed learning was far from being widely adopted as the new millennium began. Predicting its future based on relatively few projects conducted by early adopters is problematic—especially given the history of the introduction of technologies. Many technologies, such as records, film, radio, TV, and CBT, were heralded by predictions of "revolutions" in education. But, despite some isolated successes such as *Sesame Street,* their predicted potentials were not realized. Partly this is because the introduction of a new technology always emphasizes its positives as a way of getting the technology accepted—and greater educational opportunity is always seen as a positive. The negative effects of a new technology are not usually known until the technology is more widely used. Unknown negative effects caused by distributed learning may yet hinder its widespread acceptance. For example, when it was being introduced, some critics pointed to the proliferation of unaccredited and even accredited organizations providing online learning certificates based on unsubstantial programs of study—so-called "diploma mills." This could not only dilute the attraction of online credentials, but also debase the quality of education in society. Also, LMSs could build employee resistance to distributed learning if they are badly managed but still used to track learning achievements for promotions or even disciplinary action. A combination of these and other potentially negative effects could seriously retard or block the acceptance of distributed learning in the workplace.

Still, there are indications that the effects of distributed learning may be more substantial than previous educational "revolutions," which were based more on hope, enthusiasm, and an unconscious bowing to technological determinism than reality. Employees are adopting computer communications at home and at work. The increased speed of technological change is demanding constant updating of skills. New generations of users, who have been taught computer skills from an early age, are coming into the work world. Lifelong learning is being accepted as being as necessary as high-school or university education. And technology is making access to training or educational opportunities convenient—anytime, anywhere. Given all this, distributed learning may produce a revolution comparable to the introduction of compulsory primary education in the 19th century. In the end, it may be that no distinction is made between employees and learners, that everybody goes through life, as Marshall McLuhan put it, "learning a living."

*—Marc Bélanger*

*See also* Corporate Training; Distributed Learning/Distributed Education

## Bibliography

Bélanger, M. (2001). Technology organizing and unions. In *e-commerce vs. e-commons: Communications in the public interest.* Ottawa: Canadian Centre for Public Alternatives.

Feenberg, A. (2002). The factory or the city: Which model for online education? In A. Feenberg (Ed.), *Transforming technology: A critical theory re-visited.* New York: Oxford University Press.

Harasim, L., Hiltz, S. R., Teles, L., & Turoff, M. (1995). *Learning networks: A field guide to teaching and learning online.* Cambridge: The MIT Press.

Hiltz, S. R., & Turoff, M. (1993). *The network nation: Human communication via computer.* Rev. ed. Cambridge: MIT Press.

McLuhan, M. (1964). *Understanding media: The extensions of man.* New York: McGraw-Hill.

Noble, D. F. (1997). *Digital diploma mills: The automation of higher education.* New York: Monthly Review Press.

Rosenberg, M. J. (2001). *E-learning: Strategies for delivering knowledge in the digital age.* New York: McGraw-Hill.

Rossett, A. (Ed.). (2002). *The ASTD e-learning handbook: Best practices, strategies and case studies for an emerging field.* New York: McGraw-Hill.

# WORLD WIDE WEB

The World Wide Web has been described by Tim Berners-Lee, its founder, as "the universe of network-accessible information, an embodiment of human knowledge." More technically, it can be thought of as being all the resources, including Internet servers and users on the Internet, that use the Hypertext Transfer Protocol (HTTP) and that are formatted in Hypertext Markup Language (HTML). HTML supports links that permit users to hop from one document or Internet site to another by clicking on highlighted text or graphics known as "hot spots" using Web browsers such as Microsoft Internet Explorer or Netscape Navigator. The Web is not the same as the Internet. It is an information-sharing protocol that makes use of the Internet.

Because it consists of a vast network of storehouses of knowledge, the Web can be viewed as the ultimate learning tool. Computer-based training and the dynamic aspect of the Internet make nontraditional online learning (or e-learning) a very attractive prospect. The World Wide Web is opening up opportunities for learning, opportunities for research, and opportunities for "browsing" through enormous amounts of information. Through the Web, many educators and institutions are discovering e-learning and are building course material for learners who want to further their education without having to physically attend classes and disrupt a regular work schedule.

Employers today are increasingly demanding that their workers possess not so much the ability to memorize facts, but the ability to learn new methods, new programs, and new skills. The new kind of self-learning fostered on the Web can enable learners with the necessary skills, while supporting and supplementing their ability to learn.

In the past, learners relied on print-based correspondence courses (with maybe a video- or audiocassette thrown in). Telephone tutors were available at restricted hours, and many times if the tutors had a large number of students assigned, they were difficult to reach. There was little synchronous contact or immediacy.

In contrast, learning on the Web can be immediate. The Web can be used either as a teaching tool on its own or as a supplement to other forms of instruction. Learners can study from their own homes or their institutions. Alternatively, they can visit publicly accessible computer labs or work from a classroom with a teacher up front.

What makes the Web an outstanding learning environment? It possesses several key characteristics that together lend themselves to an environment that is conducive to education. The Web is:

- Open
- Distributed
- Dynamic
- Globally accessible
- Filtered
- Interactive
- Archival

## THE WEB IS OPEN

No one owns the Web. Based on commonly accepted protocols and technical standards, it is open to anyone who has the tools to use it. Early in its existence, the Web was supported on only a few operating systems or platforms. Today, virtually all operating systems and computer platforms are Web-compatible, and some of the newer and most exciting developments, such as peer-to-peer file sharing and the development of learning objects, have been born out of the sharing, multi-user environment that the Web fosters.

With this global acceptance and adherence to common standards, it is easy for the educator to write material and Web pages, which can be accessed throughout the world on all kinds of computers with similar results. The Web is also flexible and open to integration with other media. Video and audio clips are available on the Web, though the time it takes to download some of these images has, until recently, been a hindrance to their widespread use. As bandwidth becomes wider (i.e., as faster connections can be made more easily and from more locations) and connections become faster the speed of download is improving.

However, the very openness of the Web itself can be intimidating. Which lesson or course do you choose? There are more than 70,000 fully online lessons and courses currently available (see http://telecampus.edu), and many hundreds of thousands more that are a combination of online, correspondence, and classroom-based training. With the Web as unregulated as it is at present, it can be difficult to gauge the quality of an online course or online school.

## THE WEB IS DISTRIBUTED

No single computer could possibly hold all of the material now available on the Web. The *Web* in World Wide Web suggests a widespread, dispersed, or *distributed* system, distributed physically and geographically. Graphics, text files, video clips, sound bites, articles, archives, and documents are spread over network servers throughout the planet. This is what distributed means—no central point of control. Data is regularly duplicated on servers and networks in different regions and continents to allow local users faster access to popular software, news articles, and the like.

The open architecture of the Web lends itself to learning, in that collaboration can take place among learners who suffer from geographical separation. On the Web, it doesn't matter where you are, you have access to the same information that anyone else has (unless a political or other entity filters your content). So, although thousands of kilometers, culture, and homeland can separate learners, they can still collaborate on a project together by communicating electronically and accessing the plethora of online information sources. From two geographically distant positions, using different hardware, with separate operating systems, users can work together on shared projects.

To some, the absence of centralized control means that the Web may seem out of control. Some people react negatively to an environment they can't control. Learners accustomed to the dominant role of a teacher will also have to adjust their thinking, taking a more active part in their own learning.

## THE WEB IS DYNAMIC

The Web is changing all the time. It is the most fluid medium in the history of recorded information. Thousands of new Web sites come online daily; at the same time, other Web sites move locations, change Internet addresses, and change their "look and feel." News reports, weather, and sports are updated to the second. The Web is in a constant state of change.

However, with the fluidity of the Web comes issues of concern. A site you discovered yesterday, for example, might not be there today. To educators who want to begin to put their work online, the implications are clear: The constant desire or necessity to change and update sites can erode much of the time dedicated for ongoing development of new ideas and resources. Classroom instruction preparation can interfere with the design, maintenance, or facilitation of an online course. A system of checks and balances is necessary to not only foster further development, but also update and maintain what has been created.

How can learners keep on top of new information? Many Web sites offer e-mail bulletins of new stories, articles, products, and services. These simple newsletters take much of the work out of tracking updates to favorite sites. Free online services are also available to users who wish to track changes and updates to one or a number of Web sites.

## THE WEB IS GLOBALLY ACCESSIBLE

A few years ago, the Web was accessible only by power users at home and folks lucky enough to have a network at their school or office. Those who could access the Internet had to contend with clunky graphics and roughly formatted text. The first HTML pages in the infancy of the Web were not pretty. Furthermore, access to the Internet did not necessarily automatically grant access to the World Wide Web. Some regions and countries simply did not have the infrastructure or cabling networks to support and sustain the kind of increased traffic (additional strain on existing phone lines and data transmissions) that the explosion of the Web caused in most of North America and Western Europe. Moreover, many schools and businesses installed firewalls to block certain kinds of data from being received on computers in their networks.

However, these issues for most users are a part of the past. Entrepreneurs and governments in countries and regions of all sizes are coming to the same conclusions about the power and effectiveness of the Web to teach. As a global medium, the Internet and Web are now available virtually everywhere from a cyber-pub in a small town in Ireland to cyber-cafes in the Philippines. Access is now available in hospital waiting rooms and in homes and classrooms.

Today, you don't have to turn villages into towns—or towns into big cities—in order to be part of the high-tech age. You can continue to enjoy the quality of

rural life in isolated regions, and yet still have the world—literally—at your fingertips. Thanks to technology, people in rural areas can also share in the wonderful resources to be found in urban centers.

## THE WEB IS FILTERED

Studying, communication, and interaction of all kinds over the Web are filtered by the medium. Socioeconomic, gender, and geographical barriers do not pass through this filter—anonymous, direct communication and data does. Online learners are hidden behind electronic "screens" and can remain somewhat anonymous. Learners are judged solely by their submitted work and their participation in online discussion forums, not by how they look, what they wear, or which god they pray to.

This "anonymity filter" has proven to have a positive effect on shyer learners, who are more likely to respond in class discussions and debates when they have the time to think beforehand. Also, learners whose first language is not the language of the class have the time to compose answers they feel good about. The filter is especially beneficial for rural learners and for the disabled.

People are social creatures, however, and for some this type of learning experience can be difficult. Something is definitely missing when written communication is the only communication one has. Much of how we know people is by the subtle nuances of body language, vocal inflection, and expression. Sometimes this incomplete communication can lead to *flaming*—an angry retort to something that a user considered offensive. It is quite easy to interpret online messages the wrong way and become confused, misled, or offended. Usually no offense is meant—a conclusion that would be evident if bodily expressions and verbal clues existed. Many people insert *smileys* in the text to alleviate some of the ambiguity of text-only communications. Smileys, or *emoticons*, are combinations of ASCII characters that represent a facial expression (e.g., :-) indicates a happy thought or joke, :-( is often used to portray displeasure or sadness, and :-o could indicate surprise or shock). Individuals have also created a language of acronyms to aid in speeding up electronic communications by reducing the amount of typing necessary to convey a point; for example IMHO (in my humble opinion) and LOL (laughing out loud).

## THE WEB IS INTERACTIVE

The hypermedia environment of the World Wide Web also supports interactivity. Navigating through the screens of an interesting, colorful Web site maintains learners' interest and can keep their brains active. Constructive learning environments can be created in which the learners actively collaborate with the teacher and other learners in the building of Web pages and shaping of their online environment. Learners can see other learners' work and profit from their inspiration and understanding. Using computer conferencing, e-mail, and other Internet features, learners can also comment on each other's creations and discuss variations and other possibilities. They can also participate in group discussions and have ongoing conversations with the teacher and individual learners.

Software tools are available that allow teachers to scribble, point, annotate, and make brief notes on learner compositions (as in an essay marked on paper), that would otherwise require long, wordy explanations for each point. These tools are being incorporated into audio and video conferencing software, and are now becoming commonplace. Interactive, constructive criticism *in context* is a valuable tool in overcoming distance delivery issues.

## THE WEB IS ARCHIVAL

The World Wide Web is a giant library of facts and knowledge. Every day, it gets larger as more data is recorded, stored, and archived for future use. The media used to store data electronically makes the Web both cost- and time-effective. Permanent records of Web course materials and online interactive sessions are stored and then made available for scholarly research or for online use in future classes. Program evaluators can use these records to show the extent of learner participation. Learner discussion records, groups and project work, and commentaries can be used to add to the content of the course.

With the increasing number of computer users "going online" and the obvious increase in storage and archival capacity associated with these new additions, information and stored data that might not otherwise have been made available to users is now as easy to retrieve as any other document.

Mailing list archives, online conference notes, lecture summaries, qualitative and quantitative study analyses, and research on innumerable topics are being saved for the world to use. This trend will undoubtedly continue and grow in scope as the cost of large storage devices and handy consumer devices such as recordable CD-ROM, rewritable CD-ROM, and recordable DVD drives increase in popularity.

With the development of international standards for interoperability such as the IEEE LTSC (Institute of Electrical and Electronics Engineers and the Learning Technology Standards Committee), intelligent agents are now being built that support the use of Web-based learning objects among different learning managing systems. Repositories of these learning objects, such as MERLOT (Multimedia Educational Resource for Learning and Online Teaching) and CAREO (Campus Alberta Repository of Educational Objects), are appearing on the Web, making it possible for both learners and teachers to access high-quality lessons on a wide variety of subjects. This is opening up a wide range of opportunities for learners, from just-in-time snippets of learning to fully developed courses and programs. Learning on the World Wide Web has arrived.

—*Rory McGreal*

*See also* Cyberspace; Internet; Web Sites

## Bibliography

Adelsberger, H. H., Collis, B., & Pawlowski, J. M. (2002). *Handbook of information technologies for education and training* (International Handbooks on Information Systems). Heidelberg, Germany: Springer-Verlag.

Burniske, R. W., Monke, L., & Soltis, J. F. (2001). *Breaking down the digital walls: Learning to teach in a post-modern world.* New York: SUNY.

CAREO: http://www.careo.org.

Haughey, M., & Anderson, T. (1998). *The pedagogy of the Internet.* Toronto: Cheneliere/McGraw-Hill.

Horton, William K. (2001). *Designing Web-based training: How to teach anyone anything anywhere anytime.* Hoboken, NJ: John Wiley & Sons.

MERLOT: http://www.merlot.org.

Rosenberg, M. J. (2000). *E-Learning: Strategies for delivering knowledge in the digital age.* New York: McGraw-Hill.

Rudestam, K. E., & Schoenholtz-Read, J. (Eds.). (2002). *Handbook of online learning: Innovations in higher education and corporate training.* Thousand Oaks, CA: Sage.

Schank, R. C. (2001). *Designing world-class e-learning: How IBM, GE, Harvard Business School, and Columbia University are succeeding at e-learning.* New York: McGraw-Hill.

Teaching and Learning on the Web: http://www.mcli.dist. maricopa.edu/tl/.

TeleCampus: http://telecampus.edu.

World Wide Web Consortium: http://www.w3.org.

# Appendix A:
# Prominent Distributed Learning Programs

Argosy University
Argosy Online
20 S. Clark, 3rd Floor
Chicago, IL 60603
Fax: 312-201-1907
http://www.argosyu.edu

*Overview:* The American Schools of Professional Psychology, the Medical Institute of Minnesota, and the University of Sarasota merged in 2001 to create Argosy University. The merger was an effort to expand program offerings, offer more resources to students, and enrich the learning environment at each campus. The Higher Learning Commission of the North Central Association of Colleges and Schools accredits AU. Argosy University Online offers courses in the areas of psychology, business, education, and general education. Most courses are taught by faculty who also teach at one of the campuses. Faculty are said to be "experienced teachers and practitioners in their fields of expertise." Although the courses do not make it possible to complete an entire degree online, they are designed to allow working professionals more options for obtaining a degree. It is possible to complete up to 50% of a degree program via online courses, once accepted by the program. One may enroll in online courses prior to acceptance into a program. Many of the in-residence courses are also offered in flexible course formats that allow degree completion without disrupting one's current personal schedule.

California State University Monterey Bay
100 Campus Center
Seaside, CA 93955-8001
Phone: 831-582-4500
http://extendeded.csumb.edu

*Overview:* California State University Monterey Bay's (CSUMB) Office of Distributed Learning & Extended Education offers an online Liberal Studies Distributed Degree Completion program. Various courses are open to everyone on a fee per course basis. Registration dates are posted per term. Open University courses are regular CSUMB courses that are available to the general public for Fall and Spring semesters only, on a space-available basis with instructor approval.

Capella University
222 South 9th Street, 20th Floor
Minneapolis, MN 55402
Phone: 888-CAPELLA
http://www.capella.edu/gateway.aspx

*Overview:* Capella University (CU), founded in 1993, offers more than 500 online courses, as well as undergraduate and graduate degree programs in 40 areas of specialization. Master's degrees, bachelor's degrees, and certificates are available in the School of Technology. Ph.D.s, master's degrees, and graduate certificates are available in the School of Psychology,

School of Human Services, and School of Education. Ph.D.s, master's degrees, graduate certificates, bachelor's degrees, and M.B.A.s are available in the School of Business. CU courses are asynchronous, which means one can participate at any time from any Internet connection anywhere in the world. CU is accredited by The Higher Learning Commission, and is a member of the North Central Association of Colleges and Schools. CU prides itself as having redefined adult education by removing "old school" barriers. Their mission "is to deliver the highest quality bachelor's, master's and doctoral programs through innovative forms of distance learning."

⸻⬥⸻

Cardean University
Phone: 866-948-1289
http://www.cardean.edu

*Overview:* Created by Andrew Rosenfield, an economist, educator, and lawyer, and Gary Becker, a professor of economics at the University of Chicago, Cardean "blends Internet technology and progressive ideas in education, using content from five universities," into its M.B.A. program. Cardean has formed an academic consortium with five institutions: Columbia Business School, Stanford University, University of Chicago Graduate School of Business, Carnegie Mellon, and the London School of Economics and Political Science. In 2000, Cardean gained accreditation from the Accrediting Commission of the Distance Education and Training Council. The Cardean M.B.A. "is built on the concept of active learning," meaning that it provides both individual and corporate learning. Professional development courses are available in accounting, business communications, business law and policy, e-commerce, finance, management and organizational behavior, marketing, quantitative methods, and strategy. The M.B.A. stresses corporate finance, business communications, financial accounting, managing organizations, and principles of marketing. M.B.A. studies can lead to a concentration in leadership, finance, accounting and information systems, marketing, strategy and economics, or e-commerce.

⸻⬥⸻

Central Michigan University
Mount Pleasant, MI 48859
Phone: 989-774-4000
http://www.ddl.cmich.edu

*Overview:* Founded more than a century ago as a teacher's college, Central Michigan University (CMU) is now a doctoral and research public university. Although CMU's main campus is located in Mount Pleasant, the College of Extended Learning delivers undergraduate and graduate programs to more than 8,000 students in more than 60 locations throughout the United States, Canada, and Mexico. Undergraduate programs are Bachelor of Science with Major in Administration, Bachelor of Applied Arts with Major in Administration, and Bachelor of Science with an option in Community Development. Graduate programs are Master of Science in Administration, Master of Science in Nutrition and Dietetics, and Doctorate in Audiology. CMU stresses that they offer "undergraduate and graduate degree programs through a variety of delivery methods" and that they "strive to provide convenient, timesaving services, without sacrificing high academic standards."

⸻⬥⸻

City University
11900 N.E. First Street
Bellevue, WA 98005
Phone: 888-42CITYU
http://www.cityu.edu

*Overview:* City University (CU) offers distance education utilizing Internet courses and traditional correspondence-based courses. Faculty and students in online courses communicate and collaborate using threaded discussions, real-time chats, course e-mail, and online file exchanges. CU offers most of its degree programs through distance learning. This option allows students to earn degrees and certificates entirely by independent study. Students follow the lessons and assignments outlined in the study guide. As the term proceeds, students and instructors remain in contact via mail, phone, or e-mail. CU offers more than 50 programs at the undergraduate and graduate levels. These programs cover a variety of academic fields ranging from business management and technology to counseling and teacher preparation. In addition, CU offers specialized programs, such as the Intensive English Program (IEP) and a language-assisted M.B.A. program, for international students in the Seattle, Washington/Vancouver, British Columbia, area. CU's mission is "to provide educational opportunities world wide, primarily to segments of the population not being fully served." It is based on three philosophical principles: "education is a lifelong process and must be relevant to students' aspirations; education should be affordable and offered, as much as possible, at the student's convenience; and the opportunity to learn should be open to anyone with the desire to achieve." CU is fully accredited by the Commission on Colleges & Universities of the Northwest Association of Schools and Colleges, and the International Assembly for Collegiate Business Education.

◆

Colorado State University
Division of Educational Outreach
Fort Collins, CO 80523
Phone: 970-491-5288
http://www.learn.colostate.edu/csun/

*Overview:* Since 1967, Colorado State University has delivered instructional programs to students who are unable to attend classes on campus. Colorado State is accredited by The Higher Learning Commission and is a member of the North Central Association. Part of the Division of Educational Outreach's mission is: "We welcome the opportunity to share with you the University's research and educational resources in distance and traditional formats throughout your career and your lifetime." The distance degrees and online learning programs offer bachelor of science, bachelor of arts, and master's degrees. The Independent Learning program offers academic credit courses in numerous subjects. Students do not need to be admitted to Colorado State University to register for courses in the Independent Learning program or in certificate programs. Independent Learning programs take place in Northern Colorado, in Denver, or at business sites, and they offer degrees and courses via distance education using online, videotape, and correspondence methods.

◆

Connecticut Distance Learning Consortium
55 Paul Manafort Dr.
New Britain, CT 06053
Phone: 860-832-3888
http://www.ctdlc.org

*Overview:* The Connecticut Distance Learning Consortium (CTDLC) is a Connecticut agency that provides services to Connecticut's colleges and universities that make it easier for them to offer online courses and degree programs. The CTDLC was created in October 1996 when over 30 public and independent collegiate institutions met and agreed that Connecticut needed to systematically mount distance deliverable education. Institutional members are "committed to providing the delivery of high quality online courses cost effectively and assuring that Connecticut is a national leader in distance education." CTDLC members are accredited by the State of Connecticut and the New England Association of Schools and Colleges Commission on Institutions of Higher Education. Salient parts of the CTDLC mission are: "(1) provide a single point of presence for Distance Learning offered by Connecticut public and independent education institutions; (2) provide a high quality infrastructure by maintaining a state of the art web-based delivery system that is available to all members; and (3) market CTDLC member courses and programs in Connecticut, nationally, and internationally."

◆

DePaul University
School for New Learning
25 E. Jackson
Chicago, IL 60604
Phone: 312-362-8001
http://snl.depaul.edu

*Overview:* The School for New Learning (SNL) was established in 1972 as one of the nine colleges and schools of DePaul University. SNL classes are offered in over 130 academic majors in undergraduate, graduate, professional, and doctoral programs at various DePaul campuses in and around Chicago. Students can also take SNL courses over the Internet, by being monitored on a project conducted in the workplace, by phone and e-mail correspondence, by taking courses at a local college, by internship, or by working with an instructor on an independent research project. There are also online Bachelor of Arts degrees that can be designed with one's own focus area or concentration. DePaul University, the School for New Learning, and the online degree are fully accredited by the North Central Association. Overall, DePaul aims to build "strong relationships with students to assist them in developing their skills and abilities to advance their careers, lifelong learning skills and general knowledge."

◆

Duke University
Fuqua School of Business
Box 90120
Durham, NC 27708-0120
Phone: 919-660-7700
http://www.fuqua.duke.edu/index_40.html

*Overview:* Fuqua, founded in 1970 with 12 students, now has an annual enrollment in its degree programs of approximately 1,000. Programs include an M.B.A. (daytime) program, the M.B.A.—Global Executive program, the M.B.A.—Weekend Executive program, the M.B.A.—Cross Continent program, and a Ph.D. program. The Cross Continent program maximizes flexibility by combining week-long residencies in either Durham, North Carolina, or Frankfurt, Germany, with Internet-enabled distance learning from anywhere in the world. The Global Executive program is designed for executives with an average of 14 years' experience and global responsibilities; it combines traditional teaching with Internet-enabled distance learning. It includes in-classroom residencies in Asia, South America, Europe, and the United States to enhance understanding of global business. Part of the overall Fuqua mission is "to provide the highest quality education for business and academic leaders, and promote the advancement of the understanding and practice of management through research."

◆

Excelsior College
7 Columbia Circle
Albany, NY 12203-5159
Phone: 888-647-2388
http://www.regents.edu

*Overview:* Thirty years ago Regents College was founded to make college degrees more accessible to busy, working adults. Recently, it was renamed Excelsior College. Excelsior offers 30 different degree programs at the associate and baccalaureate level in business, liberal arts, nursing, and technology; two master's-level degree programs in liberal studies and nursing; and one certificate program in nursing. There is also a Master of Arts degree in Liberal Studies and a Master of Science in Nursing with a major in Clinical Systems Management. Excelsior is accredited by the Commission on Higher Education of the Middle States Association of Colleges and Schools. Associate and bachelor's degree programs in nursing are accredited by the National League for Nursing Accrediting Commission (NLNAC). Bachelor's degrees in electronics engineering technology and nuclear engineering technology are accredited by the Technology Accreditation Commission. Overall, Excelsior emphasizes "as a world leader in distance education, we do not insist that learning can take place only in the classroom. Instead, we know there are many avenues for earning college credit. We give our students access to more avenues than most traditional colleges and universities because we know it's not realistic to expect busy, active adults with family and career commitments to drop out of life to earn a degree."

◆

Fielding Graduate Institute
2112 Santa Barbara Street
Santa Barbara, CA 93105
Phone: 800-340-1099
http://www.fielding.edu

*Overview:* The Fielding Graduate Institute (FGI) was founded in 1974 by former higher education administrators and educators who "envisioned a nationally recognized graduate school, which would serve mid-career professionals who wanted to pursue an advanced degree but whose educational and professional objectives could not be met by traditional institutions of higher education." FGI offers doctoral and master's degree programs in psychology, organizational studies, educational leadership and change, and the applied behavioral and social sciences. These programs are offered within three schools: Psychology, Human and Organization Development, and Educational Leadership and Change. The Ph.D. Program in Clinical Psychology is the only distributed learning program currently accredited by the American Psychological Association. Overall, FGI stresses a flexible education model designed to meet the needs of adult learners who have responsibilities beyond those of traditional students: study, work, family, and community. FGI is accredited by the Western Association of Schools and Colleges.

———————◆———————

Franklin University Community College Alliance
201 S. Grant Avenue
Columbus, OH 43215
Phone: 888-341-6237
http://alliance.franklin.edu

*Overview:* The Community College Alliance (CCA) offers an online Bachelor of Science degree through an educational alliance with more than 180 community and technical colleges in the United States and Canada. A degree can be in one of seven major areas: Applied Management, Business Administration, Computer Science, Digital Communication, Health Care Management, Management Information Sciences, and Public Safety Management. CCA, which gives students at 2-year colleges the opportunity to complete their bachelor's degree online without leaving their community, began offering classes through a limited number of alliances in September 1998, after the Franklin University Board of Trustees committed $4.45 million for curriculum design meant to capitalize on the online learning approach, and established a technology center, among other things. The Franklin mission is to provide "student-centered lifelong higher education in

a global context, in partnership with the community, accomplished through excellence in teaching appropriate technology and measurably effective learning." Franklin University is accredited by The Higher Learning Commission of the North Central Association of Colleges and Schools.

———————◆———————

George Washington University
Distance Learning Opportunities
2121 Eye Street
Washington, DC 20052
Phone: 202-994-4949
http://www.gwu.edu/~distance/index.html

*Overview:* George Washington University uses a variety of distance learning techniques to reach students outside the traditional classroom. Students progress through courses on their own. Undergraduate degrees are Bachelor of Science in Health Sciences and the Navy College Program for Afloat College Education. Graduate degrees are Accelerated Master's Degree in Tourism Administration, Master's in Project Management, and a Master's in Health Sciences. Certificate programs are E-Learning and Distance Education, Event Management, International Public Health, and Clinical Research Administration. In addition, there is the Educational Technology Leadership Program, delivered entirely at a distance. Instruction is delivered using a number of technologies, depending on what is most appropriate for the subject and students interested in it. Audio technologies such as telephone conference calls or radio allow synchronous delivery of instruction to all students. Video technologies such as videotape, compressed digital video, cable, or satellite-delivered programming are used for more flexibility with instruction. Computer-based learning technologies such as CD-ROM, the Internet, and desktop videoconferencing are used to tailor individual instruction. Support technologies such as e-mail, fax, phone, and the Internet are used to facilitate interactivity. Combinations of these methods of instruction are also used. In addition, partnerships with other universities and organizations are designed to "facilitate tailoring degree and certification coursework to suit specialized audiences."

◆

Georgia Institute of Technology
Center for Distance Learning
Atlanta, GA 30332
Phone: 404-894-8572
http://www.conted.gatech.edu/distance/

*Overview:* Center for Distance Learning (CDL) professional development programs are available via traditional classrooms at its Atlanta campus, or via videotape, satellite, interactive compressed video, or desktop technologies. The CDL's distance learning programs are available internationally and deliver graduate-level courses in the following fields: electrical and computer engineering, environmental engineering, health physics/radiological engineering, industrial engineering, and mechanical engineering. Video cameras record instructor presentations and student/instructor interactions during regular Georgia Tech graduate classes. The videotape and supporting materials are sent to off-campus students, who participate in classroom activities by watching the taped classes at their chosen location. Courses in mechanical engineering, electrical engineering, and environmental engineering are also offered over the Internet and via CD-ROM. Founded in 1885, "Georgia Tech has always focused its efforts on preparing students to use their innovative skills and strong work ethic to solve real-world problems and improve the lives of people around the globe."

◆

Indiana Wesleyan University
4301 South Washington St.
Marion, IN 46953
Phone: 800-895-0036
http://onlinemba.net

*Overview:* Founded in 1920, Indiana Wesleyan University (IWU) is an evangelical Christian university with a vision "to prepare each student to become a world changer." Over 8,300 students are enrolled in 70 remote locations and in online programs leading to undergraduate and graduate degrees. Numerous distance learning degrees include: Bachelor of Science in

Business Information Systems, Bachelor of Science in Management, Master's in Business Administration (M.B.A.), Master of Science in Management, and Master's in Education. Other areas of study include: Business Administration Management, Business Information Systems, Education, Biblical Literature, English, and Music. A wide variety of credit courses are available only via IWU Online, which offers students a "virtual classroom" forum to interact with faculty and fellow working professionals on a broad range of issues. It combines Web page discussion forums, live chats, collaborative software, and e-mail to facilitate interaction. Other options for instruction include joining a "learning team" by taking one course at a time with other students. This includes interaction online with fellow classmates as well as professors for group learning.

◆

Jones International University
30 North LaSalle Street, Suite 2400
Chicago, IL 60602-2504
Phone: 800-621-7440
http://www.jonesinternational.edu

*Overview:* Founded in 1993 by Glenn R. Jones and launched in 1995, Jones International University (JIU) has United States regional accreditation. Faculty are from institutions in over 25 countries. JIU is a fully online school that develops and offers courses, executive and professional education programs, and degree programs to adult learners worldwide. Faculty, staff, and students interact via asynchronous online technologies such as e-mail and online forums. JIU does not have a traditional campus or satellite campus requirements. JIU offers bachelor's and master's degrees in more than 55 executive and professional education programs ranging from e-commerce and information technology to marketing and project management. To better serve its expanded global student base, JIU also offers its M.B.A. and M.Ed. degree programs in Spanish. Its mission statement stresses that it will "employ in instruction and student services new technologies, including computer-based instruction, the Internet, videotapes, and the World Wide Web, as well as long-established teaching techniques as appropriate for students and subject matter."

◆

Michigan State University
Virtual University
East Lansing, MI 48824
Phone: 517-355-2345
http://vu.msu.edu

*Overview:* Michigan State's Virtual University (VU) refers to courses and instructional programs offered via the Internet and other technologically enhanced media. In addition to offering courses within regular fields of study, VU also hosts a number of degree and certificate programs for students not seeking to become regular degree candidates. Such programs include Justice, the College of Education Teaching Series, Human Environment and Design Facility Management, Molecular Laboratory Diagnostics, and Packaging. Some VU courses are also offered through Michigan State's Evening College. The Evening College is a program of the MSU Alumni Association and offers numerous evening and weekend university-quality, noncredit courses with "no tests, no grades, no exams, no-stress-learning for personal enrichment."

——————◆——————

Naval Postgraduate School
589 Dyer Road, Room 103C
Monterey, CA 93943-5100
Phone: 831-656-3093
http://www.dlrc.nps.navy.mil

*Overview:* In 1909, the Postgraduate Department of the U.S. Naval Academy was established at Annapolis. In 1919, it was renamed the United States Naval Postgraduate School (NPS). The school was officially established in California in December 1951. Currently, the student body includes officers of all five U.S. services, approximately 25 allied services, and civilians. NPS provides graduate degrees, continuous learning opportunities, and refresher and transition education programs. These programs are under the auspices of the four graduate schools: Graduate School of Business & Public Policy, Graduate School of Engineering & Applied Sciences, School of International Graduate Studies, and Graduate School of Operational & Information Sciences. All the schools place emphasis on education and research programs that are relevant to the Navy, defense, and national and international security interests. Graduate-level courses are faculty-led, interactive, and asynchronous, and

require a bachelor's degree. Overall, NPS stresses an "intent is to make courses more accessible to the Naval Forces, via emerging technologies" meaning that programs can be completed "with minimal time away from your professional/operational pursuits."

——————◆——————

New Jersey Institute of Technology
University Heights
Newark, NJ 07102
Phone: 800-624-9850
http://cpe.njit.edu/DL/

*Overview:* New Jersey Institute of Technology (NJIT) is a public research university with over 8,000 undergraduate and doctoral students in 80 degree programs with another 10,000 professionals in continuing education programs. NJIT prides itself on providing "learning alternatives" such as courses taught at extension sites, or courses, certificates, and degrees offered via their online eLearning program. The eLearning program offers bachelor's degrees, master's degrees, or Ph.D.s in subject areas such as computer science, environmental science, information science, management, or transportation. There are also professional development short courses, certificates, and license reviews, along with continuing educational units, professional development hours, and certifications. Graduate certificates are also available in information technology. Of note is the eLearning program's motto, that it is "America's Perennially Most Wired University."

——————◆——————

New School University
New School Online University
68 Fifth Avenue
New York, NY 10011
Phone: 212-229-5880
http://www.dialnsa.edu

*Overview:* The New School for Social Research was founded in 1919 as a center for "discussion, instruction and counseling for mature men and women." In 1997, it was officially renamed New School University. In 1994, The New School launched its distance-learning program that became the New School Online University (NSOU), a completely asynchronous and interactive online learning environment. NSOU is an entirely separate online university for The New School, with its own courses, public events, programs, library, student services, and social venues for extracurricular discussions. Currently, more than 3,000 students from all 50 states and more than 60 foreign countries participate in more than 300 courses each year. Courses are offered for degree credit, general credit, and noncredit. They are offered in many areas including the social sciences, humanities, physical sciences, foreign languages, English language studies, fine arts, communication, business, computer applications, and culinary arts. All NSOU faculty teach in traditional classrooms, frequently alternating between online and campus environments each semester. NSOU is fully accredited by the Commission on Higher Education of the Middle States Association of Colleges and Schools. A privately supported institution, NSOU is chartered as a university by the Regents of the State of New York.

New York Institute of Technology
Manhattan Campus
1855 Broadway
New York, NY 10023-7692
Phone: 631-348-3058
http://www.nyit.edu

*Overview:* The New York Institute of Technology (NYIT) was founded in 1955 as "a private, independent, nonsectarian, coeducational institution" and is accredited by the Commission on Higher Education of the Middle States Association of Colleges and Schools. As part of its mission "to offer access to opportunity to all qualified students," NYIT has created several offsite programs for students outside the New York metropolitan area at cooperating institutions. Those provide facilities and management services, but NYIT faculty teach courses, and degrees are granted according to NYIT's academic policies. Cooperating institutions are in Florida, China, Egypt, Jordan, Taiwan, Canada, and in four Teachers Centers in New York State. NYIT's Online Campus, however, offers degrees and courses completely over the Internet, as well as Web-enhanced courses, where courses are taught in a traditional classroom setting, but include supplemental materials accessible online. The Online Campus offers Bachelor of Science

degrees in Behavioral Sciences and in Business Administration. Bachelor of Arts degrees are offered in Professional Services in Hospitality and Management and in Interdisciplinary Studies. A Master of Science in Energy Management is also offered. And, in addition to entire degree programs, the Online Campus offers dozens of individual courses applicable toward an on-campus degree.

New York University
School of Continuing and Professional Studies
145 4th Avenue, Room 201
New York, NY 10003
Phone: 212-998-7200
http://www.scps.nyu.edu/online/index.jsp

*Overview:* Founded in 1831, New York University (NYU) includes 14 schools and colleges in 6 major centers in Manhattan. Since 1934, nearly 2 million people have studied in the School of Continuing and Professional Studies (SCPS), which operates an online campus called The Virtual College, provided via the Internet through a Web portal. Asynchronous lectures, synchronous lectures, readings, assignments, communication, collaboration, and other services are all available via the portal. Programs in The Virtual College include master's degrees in the following centers of study: Foreign Languages and Translation Studies; Hospitality, Tourism, and Sports Management; Instructional Design and Online Education; and Marketing and Management, which also includes a Graduate Certificate in Information Technology. Stressed is that at "the SCPS Virtual College, students from all over the U.S.—and all over the world—can come together to share their ideas and experiences while tapping into the wealth of knowledge and wisdom of our university."

Northern Arizona University
College of Health Professions
NAU Box 15015
Flagstaff, AZ 86011-5015
Phone: 928-523-4331
http://www.nau.edu/hp/distributed/

*Overview:* Northern Arizona University's (NAU) College of Health Professions offers distributed learning programs delivered via the Internet and television. Programs include: Bachelor of Science Completion Program in Dental Hygiene; Bachelor of Science or Bachelor of Applied Science in Health Promotion, RN; Bachelor of Science in a Nursing Completion Program; and a Post-Professional Clinical Doctorate in Physical Therapy. NAU has been offering on-campus degree programs in health promotion– related areas for over 50 years. The College of Health Professions began offering the distributed learning degree in Health Promotion in 2000. By 2002, more than 80 students were enrolled in the program from 9 states and 11 different allied health areas. Overall, the College of Health Professions continues to place strong emphasis on its distributed learning programs; part of its mission statement is "to be recognized regionally and nationally as a leader in the use of distance learning and information technologies to provide training in health and human service professions to the rural and diverse populations of Arizona."

◆

Nova Southeastern University
Distance Education
3301 College Avenue
Ft. Lauderdale, FL 33314
Phone: 800-541-6682
http://www.nova.edu/cwis/disted/

*Overview:* Nova Southeastern University (NSU) is a nonprofit institution founded in 1964 as Nova University of Advanced Technology. In 1974, the Board of Trustees changed the university's name to Nova University. In 1994, Nova University merged with Southeastern University of the Health Sciences to form Nova Southeastern University. Now, NSU's programs are administered through academic centers that offer courses at Fort Lauderdale campuses. Distance education refers to courses taught at locations outside the Fort Lauderdale area, including selected international sites in the Caribbean, Canada, China, Dominican Republic, France, Greece, Panama, Puerto Rico, and Venezuela. Many of NSU's distance education courses use the traditional classroom setting. Others use telecommunication technologies exclusively, or in combination with a classroom setting. Bachelor's, master's, and doctoral degrees are available in numerous schools, including Allied Health, Business, Computer & Information Sciences,

Criminal Justice, Education, Law, Optometry, Oceanography, Psychology, Humanities, and Social Sciences. Graduate degrees are also offered in Pharmacy. NSU is accredited by the Commission on Colleges of the Southern Association of Colleges and Schools, and emphasizes that its mission is to offer "academic programs at times convenient to students, employing innovative delivery systems and rich learning resources on campus and at distant sites."

◆

Ohio University
Lifelong Learning Programs
Haning Hall, Ohio University
Athens, OH 45701
Phone: 877-OULEARN
http://www.ohiou.edu/lifelong/

*Overview:* Established in 1804, Ohio University is the oldest public institution of higher learning in the state of Ohio. Its mission is "to extend learning opportunities beyond its classrooms." The programs and services of the Division of Lifelong Learning thus offer several kinds of courses, including term-based and self-paced online courses. In both, lesson content is presented via the Internet and all course communication is by e-mail, including lesson submission and instructors' responses. Colleges and majors include Arts & Sciences, Business, Communication, Education, Engineering, Fine Arts, Health & Human Services, Honors Tutorial, and Osteopathic Medicine. An M.B.A. is also offered. Ohio University is fully accredited by the North Central Association of Colleges and Schools, as well as by a number of professional accrediting agencies.

◆

OnlineLearning.net
12975 Coral Tree Place
Los Angeles, CA 90066
Phone: 800-784-8436
http://www.onlinelearning.net

*Overview:* OnlineLearning.net is part of the Online Higher Education division of Sylvan Learning Systems, Inc., and has accepted more than 20,000 enrollments in 1,700 online courses since 1996. Accredited, graduate-level extension and graduate-credit courses are offered in teacher education. "By combining technological innovation with extraordinary customer service, the company is committed to bringing the best in educational resources to adult learners around the world—anytime, anywhere, at any stage in life." Programs they offer are: Certificate in Character Education, Certificate in College Counseling, Cross-Cultural Language and Academic Development Program, Online Teaching Program, Teaching English as a Foreign Language Program, and Teaching English to Speakers of Other Languages Program. OnlineLearning.net has also teamed with the University of San Diego and UCLA Extension to offer even more courses. In addition, the National Education Association has "selected OnlineLearning.net as its partner in online education for teachers."

---------◆---------

The Open University
Walton Hall
Milton Keynes
MK7 6AA, UK
Phone: + 44 (0) 1908 274066
http://www.open.ac.uk

*Overview:* The Open University (OU), founded in 1969, has over 200,000 students worldwide. Courses are available throughout Europe, and, by means of partnership agreements with other institutions, in other parts of the world as well. Two-thirds of students are between 25 and 44 years old, but students can enter starting at the age of 18. Undergraduate courses are available to anyone, regardless of qualifications. OU offers over 360 undergraduate and graduate courses in the arts, modern languages, social sciences, health and social welfare, mathematics, computing, business management, education, and law. Instruction is delivered online via a variety of methods such as electronic discussion groups, e-mail, and computer-mediated conferencing. Other instructional media include CD-ROMS, DVDs, textbooks, TV, and audio and videotapes. More than 150,000 OU students study via online methods, however. Personal instruction and support come from distributed tutors and a network of regional study centers and annual residential schools. Overall, OU stresses that it "continues to develop its e-learning activities" and that it "strongly believes the new media offer a more advanced and interactive form of learning than can be gained by using traditional audio-visual products or conventional teaching methods alone." But OU also states that it "does not strive to become an online university" and that "the

best outcomes for learning are usually achieved by striking a balance between using traditional and new media, individually selecting and developing the products that are best suited for each purpose."

---------◆---------

Penn State World Campus
World Campus Student Services
The Pennsylvania State University
207 Mitchell Building
University Park, PA 16802-3601
Phone: 800-252-3592
http://www.worldcampus.psu.edu/pub/index.shtml

*Overview:* In 1892, Penn State began its correspondence study "to meet the agricultural education needs of isolated farmers." Today, its World Campus has students in all 50 U.S. states, the District of Columbia, 2 territories, and 20 countries including Argentina, Austria, Canada, Chile, China, Costa Rica, Japan, and Malaysia. The overall mission of Penn State's World Campus is "to provide learners worldwide with access to Penn State academic programs and resources in a sustainable, technology-based learning environment." It offers more than 30 bachelor's and master's degrees, post-baccalaureate certificates, and noncredit professional development programs. Courses are offered in timeframes that are comparable to traditional semester schedules, meaning that they have fixed start and end dates. Contents and activities for most courses are available in electronic format, so access to the Internet is required. But instruction via a combination of methods, including the Internet, CD-ROM, e-mail, and printed materials, is given as well. Penn State is accredited by the Middle States Association of Colleges and Schools and the National Council for Accreditation of Teacher Education.

---------◆---------

Portland State University
School of Extended Studies
Post Office Box 751
Portland, OR 97207
Phone: 503-725-3000
http://extended.pdx.edu/homepages/distance_n_onlin e/index.shtml

*Overview:* Portland State University (PSU) was established as the Vanport Extension Center in 1946, and in

1952 moved to downtown Portland. In 1955, the Vanport Extension Center became Portland State College, a 4-year institution. Graduate studies were added in 1961, doctoral programs began in 1968, and the college was granted university status in 1969. Now, however, PSU's School of Extended Studies stresses, "distance delivery modes are customized to fit the specific needs of the faculty and students." As a result, a wide variety of distance courses and programs are delivered, and correspondence accomplished, via a range of audio, video, and Web-based technologies. In addition, the School of Extended Studies offers degree programs in a number of disciplines at various locations in Oregon, including PSU's main campus.

◆

San Diego State University
5500 Campanile Drive
San Diego, CA 92182
Phone: 619-594-5200
http://www-rohan.sdsu.edu/~dl/index.html

*Overview:* San Diego State University's (SDSU's) distributed learning program relies on highly interactive online courses distributed through the Internet. It also offers compressed video (two-way video/audio) courses and televised courses on San Diego's local cable channels. Degree programs include Master of Science in Rehabilitation Counseling, Master of Science in Regulatory Affairs, and Master in Education Leadership. A certificate program is also available in Instructional Technology. SDSU also offers numerous for-credit courses via the Internet, compressed video, or television, all of which meet or exceed the Western Association of Schools and Colleges' guidelines for distance education.

◆

Thomas Edison State College
Distance and Independent Adult Learning
101 W. State St.
Trenton, NJ 08608-1176
Phone: 609-292-4000
http://www.tesc.edu

*Overview:* Thomas Edison State College (TESC) was created by the State of New Jersey to develop high-quality, accessible educational opportunities for adults. It originated from "the idea that mature adults needed high quality educational opportunities designed especially for their needs." Students earn degrees through distance education by completing independent study courses or online courses. Each independent study course is designed for independent, distance learning and is structured around weekly readings, video, and/or audiotapes and written assignments. Interaction between students and faculty is via telephone, mail, or e-mail. Online courses are delivered via the Internet using the Blackboard platform. Students in these courses communicate with faculty, mentors, and fellow students using e-mail and submit assignments to faculty through the Web. TESC offers associate, bachelor's, and master's degrees in over 100 areas of study. These degrees can be earned through distance education methods by students in every state in the United States and 86 countries around the world. TESC is also accredited by the Middle States Association of Colleges and Schools.

◆

Union Institute & University
National Headquarters
440 E. McMillan Street
Cincinnati, OH 45206-1925
Phone: 800-486-3116
http://www.tui.edu

*Overview:* Union Institute & University was founded in 1964 as a consortium that included 10 liberal arts colleges such as Hofstra, Bard College, Antioch College, and Sarah Lawrence College. These institutions collaborated with "the goal of providing innovative higher education alternatives to working adults." The consortium dissolved in 1982 but an independent, not-for-profit university offering baccalaureate and doctoral programs remained, now called Union Institute & University, accredited by the North Central Association. Union's mission is "to offer personalized bachelor's, master's, and doctoral degree programs designed for the lifelong learner." Hence, the university offers undergraduate degrees in a learner's concentration of choice, and an array of master's and doctoral degrees in which one can concentrate on a variety of specialization areas. These can be earned via online distance learning methods or in a classroom setting from nearby academic centers.

◆

University Alliance
9417 Princess Palm Ave.
Tampa, FL 33619
Phone: 800-404-7355
http://www.universityalliance.com

*Overview:* University Alliance (UA) works with regionally accredited partner universities to provide, via the Internet, associate's, bachelor's, and master's degrees and continuing education certificate programs that require no classroom attendance. Partner universities are Jacksonville University, Regis University, Saint Leo University, University of South Florida, and Villanova University. Each university is solely responsible for all academic areas including admissions, academic advisement, program coordination, educational content, faculty, grades, transcripts, and the granting of degrees. UA is responsible for program delivery, technical development and support, student enrollment, and registration. Degrees offered are bachelor of arts, bachelor of science, master's degrees, associate of arts, project management certificate programs, and health care certificate programs in such areas as business, computer information systems, health care management, project management, and nursing. UA stresses that in its service to students, it "strives to provide each student with personal attention and service that begins before you apply and continues throughout your coursework."

———————◆———————

University of California, Berkeley
Extension Online
2000 Center Street, Suite 400
Berkeley, CA 94704
Phone: 510-642-4124
http://learn.berkeley.edu

*Overview:* The University of California (UC) Extension program was established in 1913 "to expand the resources of the University throughout the community, the state, and the nation." UC Berkeley Extension, however, is part of the Continuing Education department of UC Berkeley, with more than 3,000 courses offered annually to the public at locations around the San Francisco Bay area and through distance learning in the Extension Online program. Extension Online distance learning courses either are asynchronous,

meaning one can enroll anytime and finish within 6 months or a year, depending on the type of course, or have fixed start and finish dates. Extension Online offers online courses that are accessed remotely over the Internet, and independent learning courses that use printed course materials. Interaction with instructors in either type of course includes regular mail, fax, or e-mail. Catalog listings include courses in Arts & Humanities, Business & Management, Computer Science & Engineering, Education, Health Sciences, High School Courses, E-Commerce, Mathematics & Statistics, Natural Sciences, and Social Sciences. UC Extension and Extension Online courses are open to the general public. Unless otherwise indicated, any interested adult may enroll.

———————◆———————

University of Central Florida
UCF Virtual Campus–The Center for Distributed
   Learning
Orlando, FL 32851
Phone: 407-823-2000
http://distrib.ucf.edu

*Overview:* The University of Central Florida (UCF) was founded in 1963. Its Virtual Campus defines distributed learning as including "traditional delivery technologies such as video tape, interactive television and web-based instruction to provide services to students at a distance. However, Distributed Learning at UCF also encompasses the use of computer resources to extend and enhance traditional classroom instruction." Part of its distributed learning program is the online program, Online@UCF, which consists of upper-division and graduate-level courses and programs offered via the Web. Undergraduate degrees in Online@UCF are: Bachelor of Science in Vocational Education and Industry Training, RN, Bachelor of Science in Nursing, Bachelor of Science in Health Services Administration, and Bachelor of Arts or Science in Liberal Studies. Graduate programs include: Educational Media Master's Degree, Master of Science in Forensic Science, Master of Arts or Education in Vocational Education and Industry Training, Master of Arts in Instructional/Educational Technology, Master of Science in Criminal Justice, and Master of Science in Nursing. Graduate certificate programs are offered as well. Overall, the distributed learning program at UCF strives, "through the use of technology to enhance and deliver programs, courses, and learning environments for all UCF students."

◆

University of Colorado
Online and Distance Education Programs
35 SYS, 914 Broadway
Boulder, CO 80309-0035
Phone: 303-492-6201
http://www.cu.edu/explore/online.html

*Overview:* Founded in 1876 with a campus in Boulder, the University of Colorado (CU) now includes 4 campuses and offers 18 distance education degree programs and a large, growing number of certificate programs. Some programs are available completely online; others are available through a mix of different media. CU Online also offers a hybrid course, which "uses technology-delivered instruction (web, CD-ROM, etc.) as a substitute for a portion of the instruction that a student would otherwise receive in a campus classroom or lab." In hybrid courses, students meet for approximately 50% of their normal classroom hours on campus, but they do the remainder of their work online. Distance learning is available from campuses in Boulder, Denver, and Colorado Springs. In addition, CU at Interlocken offers graduate, professional development certificate programs, and courses in classrooms located at the Interlocken Business Park in Broomfield, Colorado.

◆

University of Florida
Distance Learning
2209 NW 13th St., Suite D
Gainesville, FL 32609
Phone: 352-392-2137
http://www.fcd.ufl.edu

*Overview:* The University of Florida offers undergraduate and graduate degrees via online distance learning and credit via self-directed correspondence courses. These degree programs require formal admission. Most courses are Web-based, but some are delivered by other technologies. Online bachelor's degrees are offered in two schools, Business Administration

and Fire and Emergency Services. Online master's degrees are offered in nine schools: Agriculture, Business Administration, Health Science in Occupational Therapy, International Construction Management, Engineering, Industrial & Systems Engineering, Pharmacy and Pharmaceutical Sciences, Soil and Water Science, and Veterinary Medical Sciences. Doctorate degrees are offered in two schools, Audiology and Pharmacy. Professional certificates in other areas that do not necessarily require formal admission are also offered. The Division of Continuing Education (DOCE), which distance learning is a part of, states that part of its overall mission is "to develop and offer continuing education programs designed to meet a wide range of personal and professional educational and learning needs."

◆

University of Idaho
Engineering Outreach
Moscow, ID 83843
Phone: 888-884-3246
http://www.uidaho.edu/eo/index.html

*Overview:* The University of Idaho (UI) College of Engineering's Engineering Outreach (EO) Program was founded in 1975. It uses a variety of media resources, including videotape, e-mail, the Internet, CD-ROM, DVD, and print materials, to deliver courses to more than 350 students worldwide each semester. EO offers more than 90 continually updated courses in 9 graduate programs for graduate degrees, certificates, and professional advancement. EO courses are semester-based, and all are professionally recorded in a studio classroom at UI. EO prepares DVD, CD-ROM, or VCR copies of lessons and printed course materials (if any), and ships them weekly to students. Graduate degree programs are available in Biological & Agricultural Engineering, Civil Engineering, Computer Engineering, Computer Science, Electrical Engineering, Engineering Management, Mechanical Engineering, Teaching Mathematics, and Psychology. Certificates are available after completing a series of courses predetermined by the academic department in a specific emphasis area.

◆

University of Maryland University College
3501 University Blvd. East
Adelphi, MD 20783
Phone: 800-888-UMUC
http://www.umuc.edu/gen/virtuniv.html

*Overview:* University of Maryland University College (UMUC) offers online distance education programs. UMUC's decision to develop a virtual university for online programs "was driven by the needs of part-time, adult students who juggle many responsibilities and require the flexibility and convenience that online education provides." Undergraduates can choose from 17 majors and 20 minors online or from 20 certificate programs available online. Graduate students can choose from a large number of online certificate programs and master's degrees. Some programs include proctored exams given at remote test sites. Online programs also use UMUC's own online delivery software that allows students to interact directly with instructors and each other. UMUC is accredited by the Commission on Higher Education of the Middle States Association of Colleges and Schools.

———————◆———————

University of Nebraska-Lincoln
Department of Educational Administration
Lincoln, NE 68588
Phone: 402-472-7211
http://edadone.unl.edu/welcome.htm

*Overview:* The University of Nebraska-Lincoln, Department of Educational Administration offers online doctoral degrees, master's degrees, and nondegree graduate studies. The department stresses that it offers degrees of "benefit to many practitioners working in community colleges, technical institutes, four year colleges and universities throughout the United States and the world." The following programs are offered: a Ph.D. or Ed.D. in Administration, Curriculum and Instruction; an M.A. or M.Ed. in Educational Administration; and nondegree studies in areas relating to higher education and leadership. Almost all coursework required for degrees is provided online, with Lotus Notes being the dominant delivery system. Instruction is based on a "collaborative learning-reflection on practice" approach "conducted through interactive computer-based communications and journalizing methodologies." Distributed learning and collaboration take place

through "virtual groups" whose members are widely distributed geographically.

———————◆———————

University of New England
Distance Education
11 Hills Beach Road
Biddeford, ME 04005
Phone: 207-283-0171
http://distance.une.edu

*Overview:* University of New England (UNE) is an independent, coeducational university with two distinctive campuses in Maine—the University Campus and Westbrook College Campus. UNE offers a four-course sequence in Educational Law that is offered with collaboration of faculty from regional law schools. Distance education programs include a Certificate of Advanced Graduate Study in Educational Leadership and a master's degree in education. Both were designed for "providing knowledge, skills, and practice for future educational leaders of the world." In the certificate program, students who wish to obtain basic administrative certification can take courses in School Law, School Finance, Organizational Theory & Strategic Planning, or Supervision & Evaluation of School Personnel. Students in the certificate program must complete a one-week residential integrating seminar, titled Professional Planning, Ethics, and Responsibilities, that brings together all students in the program for an intensive session each summer.

———————◆———————

University of North Texas
Distributed Learning @ UNT
P.O. Box 311277
Denton, TX 76203
Phone: 940-565-2000
http://web2.unt.edu/courses/home/home.cfm

*Overview:* University of North Texas (UNT) was established in 1890 as a teacher education facility. UNT's distributed learning program emphasizes that its "distributed (or distance) learning is a type of education where students complete courses and programs at home or work, communicating with faculty and other students via e-mail, electronic forums, videoconferences and other forms of computer-based communication." UNT offers accredited certificate, endorsement, and master's degree programs within six schools: School of Library and Information Sciences, School of Merchandising and Hospitality Management, College of Education, School of Community Service, Applied Gerontology, and Behavior Analysis. Overall, UNT emphasizes that its vision is to "be one of the state's top-tier universities—a premier educational, intellectual, research and cultural resource." UNT also stresses that in order to achieve its vision, it will "lead in offering learners access to education through satellite locations, the Internet and other electronic resources, and partnerships with other institutions."

◆

University of Phoenix
Phone: 800-MY-SUCCESS
http://www.phoenix.edu/index.asp

*Overview:* Bachelor's, master's, or doctoral degrees can be earned on campus, online, or using a combination of both, in certain subjects. Founded in 1976, "University of Phoenix was among the first accredited universities to provide college degree programs via the Internet, starting in 1989." Currently, the university's degree programs are in business, management, technology, education, and nursing. Although 100% of its curriculum can be completed via the Internet, the university does have over 125,000 students taking in-person courses at more than 116 campuses and learning centers in 23 states, as well as Puerto Rico and Vancouver, British Columbia. Overall, the university stresses that it is "a private, for-profit higher education institution whose mission is to provide high quality education to working adult students" and that it has a "commitment to educational excellence and unsurpassed student service."

◆

University of Southern Colorado
Division of Continuing Education
2200 Bonforte Blvd.
Pueblo, CO 81001-4901
Phone: 719-549-2316
http://coned.uscolo.edu

*Overview:* University of Southern Colorado (USC) is a member of the Colorado State University System, accredited at the bachelor and master level by the Commission on Institutions of Higher Education of the North Central Association of Colleges and Schools. External degree completion programs, such as a

Bachelor of Science in Social Science, Sociology, or Sociology/Criminology, are offered via independent study or at USC extension sites. Independent study courses are available to those who are unable to attend classes on campus or who prefer this method. Working professionals in the field of education can obtain recertification credits through CD-ROM–based specialized education courses. Noncredit, online courses are offered for professional development or personal growth in a variety of topics, including computers, the Internet, personal enrichment, entrepreneur/business, business administration/management, writing, and Spanish.

◆

University of Southern Mississippi
Department of Continuing Education and Distributed
    Learning
Box 5136
Hattiesburg, MS 39406-5136
Phone: 601-266-4186
http://www.cice.usm.edu/cc/

*Overview:* Founded in 1913, the University of Southern Mississippi's Department of Continuing Education and Distance Learning (CEDL) has sought "to link individuals of all ages and stages of life to the resources of the University." The CEDL currently provides conferences, seminars, training programs, workshops, and intensive weekend and extension courses for academic credit. Independent, self-paced high school and college courses are available via traditional correspondence or the Internet. Online semester-based college credit courses, in a large number of academic subjects, are also offered. CEDL also has a professional development program that consists of in-person seminars, workshops, and classes, and professional development courses that are entirely Web-based. CEDL also offers continuing education units garnered via traditional methods.

◆

University of Tennessee
Distance Education & Independent Study
1534 White Avenue
Knoxville, TN 37996-1525
Phone: 800-670-8657
http://www.anywhere.tennessee.edu

*Overview:* The University of Tennessee's Distance Education and Independent Study Department offers a range of M.B.A. offerings, and master of science degrees in Civil Engineering, Environmental Engineering, General Environmental Engineering, Information Sciences, Engineering Management, and Nuclear Engineering. Graduate certificates are available in Nuclear Criticality Safety, Maintenance and Reliability Engineering, and Applied Statistics. A Bachelor of University Studies is also available, as are professional certificates in information technology, and college courses in a variety of subjects. Instruction is delivered via the Internet (with some interaction via e-mail or a desktop delivery system), videotape, video-conference, correspondence, or enhanced courses, which have some online presence but also require substantial on-campus attendance and in-person participation. Overall, the Distance Education & Independent Study department emphasizes that "learning virtually anywhere is what UT's Distance Education and Independent Study programs and courses are all about."

◆

University of Washington
Distance Learning
4311 11th Avenue Northeast
Seattle, WA 98105
Phone: 206-543-2320
http://www.extension.washington.edu/dl/

*Overview:* Founded in 1861, the University of Washington (UW) is composed of the Seattle, Bothell, and Tacoma campuses, all with the primary mission of "the preservation, advancement, and dissemination of knowledge." UW Distance Learning currently offers 10 degrees, 27 certificates, and more than 300 courses via distance learning. Most programs rely on the Internet and e-mail for construction and communication with instructors and fellow students. Some courses start and finish at set times whereas others are self-directed independent study. Some degree programs can be taken entirely via distance learning, whereas others feature both distance learning and classroom meetings. Programs include master's degrees in Engineering, Health Sciences, Information Science, and Social Work. There are also certificate programs in Business and Management, Computing and Technology, Education, Health and Medical, Architectural and Environmental, and Arts and Humanities, as well as a graduate program in Construction Engineering. Overall, UW stresses that its distance learning courses "are more than just regular classes converted into a Web site" and that

they "are academically rigorous, suitable for a distance format, and convenient."

◆

University of Wisconsin Extension
UW-Extension headquarters
432 N. Lake Street
Madison, WI 53706
Phone: 608-262-3980
http://www1.uwex.edu

*Overview:* Founded in 1907, the University of Wisconsin (UW) Extension Division was created "to extend the resources of the University to serve the needs of Wisconsin people" and "to address the relevant social, economic, environmental and cultural issues of its citizens." Today, UW's Extension Division has collaborative relationships with 26 UW universities and colleges, 72 Wisconsin counties, and local, state, and federal agencies and groups. Students can participate in extension programs through a variety of delivery methods, such as workshops, one-on-one counseling, interactive networks, or correspondence study. Numerous associate's, bachelor's, and master's degree programs, along with certificate programs, are available via these instruction methods or through distance education, which includes instruction via audio conferencing, interactive video conferencing, the Internet, telecourses, Web conferencing, and the Wisconsin Regional Videoconference Networks. Overall, UW Extension stresses that its mission is "to provide, jointly with the UW institutions and the Wisconsin counties, an extension program designed to apply University research, knowledge, and resources to meet the educational needs of Wisconsin people, wherever they live and work."

◆

Virginia Polytechnic Institute and State University
Institute for Distance & Distributed Learning
Blacksburg, VA 24061
Phone: 540-231-6000
http://www.iddl.vt.edu

*Overview:* The Institute for Distance & Distributed Learning (IDDL) was developed in 1997 to provide "a one-stop-shop for distance learning at the university" and to provide "leadership, management, coordination and support to Virginia Tech's eLearning activities and initiatives." There are 24 degree, certificate, and licensure programs offered at a distance in the following areas: Business Administration, Career & Technical Education, Engineering, Health Promotion, Information Technology, Instructional Technology, Ocean Engineering, and Political Science. IDDL takes a holistic approach to distance learning because "all aspects of a student's educational experience are considered," and because it "works hand-in-hand with faculty and other members of the university community to achieve an optimal experience for distance learners."

◆

Walden University
155 Fifth Avenue South
Minneapolis, MN 55401
Phone: 800-WALDEN-U
http://www.waldenu.edu

*Overview:* Founded in 1970, Walden University's mission is to provide "adult learners broad access to the highest quality post-secondary education through a distance learning environment. Walden's learner centered programs prepare its graduates to achieve professional excellence and to effect positive social change." Modes of instruction include Knowledge Area Modules, residencies, and online courses. The modules combine online activities and face-to-face meetings at Walden's Summer Session or other designated residencies. Academic residencies and face-to-face sessions are held throughout each year at locations around the United States. Generally, however, students pursue degrees through asynchronous courses via Walden's online classroom environment. Master's and Ph.D. degrees are available in the School of Education, School of Health & Human Services, and in the Dual Degrees program. Bachelor's, master's, and Ph.D. degrees are available in the School of Management and in the School of Psychology. Walden is accredited by the Higher Learning Commission of the North Central Association.

◆

Washington State University
Office of Distance Degree Programs
Van Doren Hall 202/204
PO Box 645220
Pullman, WA 99164-5220
Phone: 509-335-3557
http://www.distance.wsu.edu

*Overview:* Washington State University's (WSU's) distance instruction is provided via the Internet or video, with in-person instruction on campus or at learning centers distributed throughout Washington. WSU's Office of Distance Degree Programs stresses "with the power of technology and the will to expand higher education, WSU now offers high quality, accredited programs to individuals no matter where they live." Some degrees can be completed with no site-based participation, whereas others require participation delivered at specific locations and times. Bachelor of arts degrees requiring no site-based participation are in the schools of Social Sciences, Business Administration, Criminal Justice, Human Development, and Humanities. The Bachelor of Science in Agriculture also requires no site-based participation. The Bachelor of Arts in Education does require site-based participation. Graduate and professional degrees offered are: Bachelor of Science in Nursing (BSN) for Registered Nurses, Master of Science in Agriculture, Master of Engineering Management, and External Doctor of Pharmacy. WSU is accredited by the Commission on Colleges of the Northwest Association of Schools and Colleges.

◆

Western Governors University
2040 E. Murray Holladay Rd., Suite 106
Salt Lake City, UT 84117
Phone: 801-274-3280
http://www.wgu.edu/wgu/index.html

*Overview:* Western Governors University (WGU) was founded at a meeting of the Western Governors' Association in June 1995, when the governors appointed a team to create a western virtual university. WGU now offers distance-learning courses from approximately 50 education providers throughout the United States. Instruction is given in a myriad of ways, from the Internet to satellite to the Postal Service. WGU grants associate's degrees, bachelor's degrees, teaching endorsements, and master's degrees in Business, Information Technology, and Education. Degrees are awarded on completion of competencies, which include demonstrating skills and knowledge on a series of assessments carefully selected to measure students' knowledge of a field of study. Programs are not based on required courses. The vision of WGU overall "is to serve the needs of today's Information Age citizens. WGU does that through the use of technology to overcome barriers of time and distance." WGU's accreditation has been approved by the

Commission on Colleges and Universities of the Northwest Association of Schools and of Colleges and Universities, the Higher Learning Commission of the North Central Association of Colleges and Schools, the Accrediting Commission for Community and Junior Colleges of the Western Association of Schools and Colleges, and the Accrediting Commission for Senior Colleges and Universities of the Western Association of Schools and Colleges.

*—Alain Dussert*

# Appendix B:
# Select Print and Nonprint Resources on Distributed Learning

## Periodicals and Web Sites

American Journal of Distance Education: http://www.ajde.com

Chronicle of Higher Education: http://chronicle.com

Distance Education Clearinghouse: http://www.uwex.edu/disted/

Distance Education Report: http://www.magnapubs.com/archive/der/

Journal of Continuing Higher Education: http://www.acheinc.org/publicat.html#journal

Journals in Distance Education: http://www-icdl.open.ac.uk/lit2k/journals.ihtml

Online Journal of Distance Learning Administration: http://www.westga.edu/~distance/ jmain11.html

The Technology Source: http://ts.mivu.org

United States Distance Learning Association Journal: http://www.usdla.org/html/membership/publications. htm

World Wide Learn: http://www.worldwidelearn.com

## Books

Berge, Z. L. (Ed.). (2000). *Sustaining distance training: Integrating learning technologies into the fabric of the enterprise.* Hoboken, NJ: John Wiley & Sons.

Discenza, R., Howard, C., & Schenk, K. (Eds.). (2003). *Design and management of effective distance learning programs.* Hershey, PA: IRM Press.

Gilbert, S. D. (2000). *How to be a successful online student.* New York: McGraw-Hill.

Harry, K. (1999). *Higher education through open and distance learning.* New York: Routledge.

Luskin, B. J. (2002). *Casting the net over global learning: New developments in workforce and online psychologies.* Irvine, CA: Griffin Publishing Group.

Maddux, C. D., Ewing-Taylor, J., & Johnson, D. L. (Eds.). (2002). *Distance education: Issues and concerns.* Binghamton, NY: Haworth Press.

Mehrotra, C., Hollister, C. D., & McGahey, L. (2001). *Distance learning: Principles for effective design, delivery, & evaluation.* Thousand Oaks, CA: Sage.

Melton, R. F. (2002). *Planning and developing open and distance learning: A framework for quality.* New York: Routledge.

Moore, M. G., & Cozine, G. T. (Eds.). (2000). *Web-based communications, the Internet and distance education.* University Park, PA: American Center for the Study of Distance Education.

Moore, M. G., & Shin, N. (Eds.). (2000). *Speaking personally about distance education: Foundations of contemporary practice.* University Park, PA: American Center for the Study of Distance Education.

Oblinger, D. G., Barone, C. A., & Hawkins, B. L. (2001). *Distributed education and its challenges: An overview.* Washington, DC: American Council on Education.

Palloff, R. M., & Pratt, K. (1999). *Building learning communities in cyberspace: Effective strategies for the online classroom.* Hoboken, NJ: John Wiley & Sons.

Perraton, H. D. (2000). *Open and distance learning in developing countries.* New York: Routledge.

Peters, O. (1999). *Learning and teaching in distance education: Analyses and interpretations from an international perspective.* London: Kogan Page.

Simonson, M. R. (2002). *Teaching and learning at a distance: Foundations of distance education.* Upper Saddle River, NJ: Prentice Hall.

Simpson, O. (2002). *Supporting students in open and distance learning*, 2nd Edition. London: Kogan Page.

Von Phummer, C. (2000). *Women and distance education: Challenges and opportunities.* New York: Routledge.

Vrasidas, C., & Glass, G. V. (Eds.). (2002). *Distance education and distributed learning.* Greenwich, CT: Information Age Publishing.

Williams, M. L., Paprock, K., & Covington, B. (1999). *Distance learning: The essential guide.* Thousand Oaks, CA: Sage.

## Guides, Bibliographies, and Handbooks

Baker, J. D. (2000). *Baker's guide to Christian distance education: Online learning for all ages.* Ada, MI: Baker Books.

Bear, J., & Bear, M. P. (2003). *Bears' guide to earning degrees by distance learning,* 15th ed. Toronto, ON: Ten Speed Press.

Bear, J., & Bear, M. P. (2001). *Bears' Guide to the Best Computer Degrees by Distance Learning.* Toronto, ON: Ten Speed Press.

Bear, J., Bear, M. P., Head, T., & Nixon, T. C. (2001). *Bears' guide to the best education degrees by distance learning.* Toronto, ON: Ten Speed Press.

Bellows, E. A. (2003). *Education via long distance learning: Index and analysis of new information with guide book for consumers, reference and research.* Annandale, VA: ABBE Publishers Association of Washington, D.C.

Chute, A., Thompson, M., & Hancock, B. (1998). *The McGraw-Hill handbook of distance learning.* New York: McGraw-Hill Professional.

Criscito, P. (2002). *Barron's guide to distance learning: Degrees, certificates, courses.* Hauppauge, NY: Barron's Educational Series, Inc.

Fusco, M., & Ketcham, S. E. (2002). *Distance learning for higher education: An annotated bibliography.* Englewood, CO: Libraries Unlimited.

*Game plan for distance learning: Complete introduction to the world of distance learning.* (2001). Princeton, NJ: Peterson's.

*Guide to distance learning programs 2003.* (2003). Princeton, NJ: Peterson's.

*Guide to distance learning programs in the U.S.A. 2001.* (2001). Victoria, BC: EI Education International, Ltd.

*Guide to distance learning programs in Canada 2001.* (2000). Victoria, BC: EI Education International, Ltd.

Harrison, N. (1998). *How to design self-directed and distance learning programs: A guide for creators of Web-based training, computer-based training and self-study materials.* New York: McGraw-Hill Trade.

Meyer, R. A. (2001). *IDECC distance education standards and resource guide: Principles for designing and delivering quality distance education courses.* Montgomery, AL: ARELLO.

Mills, D. Q. (2001). *Internet university, graduate studies: Your guide to online college courses.* Anaheim, CA: Cyber Classics, Inc.

Mood, T. A. (1995). *Distance education: An annotated bibliography.* Englewood, CO: Libraries Unlimited, Inc.

Moore, G., Winograd, K., & Lange, D. (2001). *You can teach online!: Guide to building creative learning environments.* Burr Ridge, IL: McGraw-Hill/Irwin.

Moore, M. G., & Anderson, W. (Eds.). (2003). *Handbook of distance education.* Mahwah, NJ: Lawrence Erlbaum.

Omoregie, M., & Farish-Jackson, J. (2003). *A guide to distance education.* Lanham, MD: University Press of America.

Rudestam, K. E., & Schoenholtz-Read, J. (Eds.). (2002). *Handbook of online learning: Innovations in higher education and corporate training.* Thousand Oaks, CA: Sage.

Safko, J. L. (2001). *Astronomy study guide and exercises for distance education.* Dubuque, IA: Kendall/Hunt.

Slade, A. L., & Kascus, M. A. (1996). *Library services for off-campus and distance education: The second annotated bibliography.* Englewood, CO: Libraries Unlimited, Inc.

Slade, A. L., & Kascus, M. A. (2000). *Library services for open and distance learning: The third annotated bibliography.* Englewood, CO: Libraries Unlimited, Inc.

Thorson, M. K. (2000). *Campus-free college degrees: Thorson's guide to accredited college degrees through distance learning.* Tulsa, OK: Thorson Guides.

Wall, M. (2001). *The Sunday Times guide to education online.* North Pomfret, VT: Trafalgar Square.

Walston, R. L. (1999). *Walston's guide to Christian distance learning: Earning degrees nontraditionally.* Longview, WA: Persuasion Press.

Williams, M. L., Paprock, K., & Covington-Jones, B. (1998). *Distance learning: The essential guide.* Thousand Oaks, CA: Sage.

Yates, J. M. (2003). *Interactive distance learning in preK-12 settings: A handbook of possibilities.* Englewood, CO: Libraries Unlimited, Inc.

## Articles

Anderson, T. (2001). The hidden curriculum in distance education. *Change, 33*(6), 28–35.

Annison, J. (2002). Action research: Reviewing the implementation of a distance-learning degree programme utilizing communication and information technologies. *Innovations in Education and Teaching International, 39*(2), 95–106.

Arnone, M. (2002). Ford and GM establish distance-education programs for employees. *Chronicle of Higher Education, 48*(34), A33.

Arnone, M. (2002). Historically black colleges grapple with online education. *Chronicle of Higher Education, 48*(30), A27-A28.

Arnone, M. (2002). Many students' favorite professors shun distance education. *Chronicle of Higher Education, 48*(35), A39-A40.

Baron, J. D. (2001). Designing and delivering an online course for K-12 educators. *T.H.E. Journal, 28*(9), 68.

Barron, B. B. (2002). Distant and distributed learners are two sides of the same coin. *Computers in Libraries, 22*(1), 24–28.

Beard, L. A., & Harper, C. (2002). Student perceptions of online versus on campus instruction. *Education, 122*(4), 658–663.

Beaudoin, M. F. (2002). Distance education leadership: An essential role for the new century. *Journal of Leadership Studies, 8*(3), 131–144.

Beck, J. (2001). Casino workers ripe for distance education: Atlantic Cape Community College targets the swing-shift population. *Hispanic Outlook in Higher Education, 11*(18), 28.

Bennett, J. F., & Bennett, L. B. (2002). Assessing the quality of distance education programs: The faculty's perspective. *Journal of Computing in Higher Education, 13*(2), 71–86.

Berge, Z. L. (2002). Obstacles to distance training and education in corporate organizations. *Journal of Workplace Learning, 14*(5), 182–189.

Berge, Z. L., & Mrozowski, S. (2001). Review of research in distance education, 1990 to 1999. *American Journal of Distance Education, 15*(3), 5–19.

Bollag, B. (2001). Developing countries turn to distance education. *Chronicle of Higher Education, 47*(40), A29-A30.

Brotherton, P. (2002). eArmyU improves educational access for soldiers. *Black Issues in Higher Education, 19*(1), 32–34.

Carnevale, D. (2001). Should distance students pay for campus-based services? *Chronicle of Higher Education, 48*(3), A35.

Carnevale, D. (2002). 12-hour rule, viewed as limiting distance education, expires. *Chronicle of Higher Education, 49*(12), A36.

Carnevale, D. (2002). Distance education attracts older women who have families and jobs, study finds. *Chronicle of Higher Education, 49*(11), A33.

Carrell, L. J., & Menzel, K. E. (2001). Variations in learning, motivation, and perceived immediacy between live and distance education classrooms. *Communication Education, 50*(3), 230–240.

Cohen, D. (2002). Course-management software: Where's the library? *EDUCAUSE Review, 37*(3), 12–13.

Cooke, J., & Veach, I. (1997). Enhancing the learning outcome of university distance education: An Australian perspective. *International Journal of Educational Management, 11*(5), 203–208.

Coombs, S. J., & Rodd, J. (2001). Using the Internet to deliver higher education: A cautionary tale about achieving good practice. *Computers in the Schools, 17*(3–4), 67–90.

DeBry, D. P. (2001). Globalizing instructional materials: Guidelines for higher education. *TechTrends, 45*(6), 41–45.

Distance education is harder on women than on men, study finds. (2001). *Chronicle of Higher Education, 48*(5), A48.

Distance education teachers work more, report says. (2002). *Academe, 88*(3), 20.

Eastman, J. K. (2001). New horizons in distance education: The online learner-centered marketing class. *Journal of Marketing Education, 23*(1), 25.

Ereaux, J. (1999). A literature guide: Forward into the past; Blending Native wisdom with technology for distance education. *Tribal College Journal of American Indian Higher Education, 10*(3), 40.

Forinash, K., & Wisman, R. (2001). The viability of distance education science laboratories. *T.H.E. Journal, 29*(2), 38–45.

Forman, D., Nyatanga, L., & Rich, T. (2002). E-learning and educational diversity. *Nurse Education Today, 22*(1), 76–84.

Foster, A. (2002). Colleges, fighting U.S. trade proposal, say it favors for-profit distance education. *Chronicle of Higher Education, 48*(19), A33-A35.

Furst-Bowe, J., & Dittmann, W. (2001). Identifying the needs of adult women in distance learning programs. *International Journal of Instructional Media, 28*(4), 405–413.

FYI: Distance education: On-line music education. (2001). *Teaching Music, 9*(1), 59–61.

Gal-Ezer, J., & Lupo, D. (2002). Integrating Internet tools into traditional CS distance education students' attitudes. *Computers & Education, 38*(4), 319–329.

Garifo, C. (1999). Learning across the miles: Distance education an increasingly prevalent choice for Jewish studies. *Jewish News of Greater Phoenix, 52*(10), 10.

Geelan, D. R., & Taylor, P. C. (2001). Embodying our values in our teaching practices: Building open and critical discourse through computer mediated communication. *Journal of Interactive Learning Research, 12*(4), 375–401.

Graf, N. M., & Stebnicki, M. A. (2002). Using e-mail for clinical supervision in practicum: A qualitative analysis. *Journal of Rehabilitation, 68*(3), 41–49.

Group uses distance education to acclimate American students to study abroad. (2001). *Chronicle of Higher Education, 48*(2), A43.

Hartman, J., Lewis, J. S., & Sterkel Powell, K. (2002). Inbox shock: A study of electronic message volume in a distance managerial communication course. *Business Communication Quarterly, 65*(3), 9–28.

Heerema, D. L., & Rogers, R. L. (2001). Avoiding the quality/quantity trade-off in distance education. *T.H.E. Journal, 29*(5), 14–21.

Hirschbuhl, J., Zachariah, S., & Bishop, D. (2002). Using knowledge management to deliver distance learning. *British Journal of Educational Technology, 33*(1), 89–93.

Hodgkinson, M., & Holland, J. (2002). Collaborating on the development of technology enabled distance learning: A case study. *Innovations in Education and Teaching International, 39*(2), 89–94.

Issing, L. J., & Schaumburg, H. (2001). Educational technology as a key to educational innovation: State of the art report from Germany. *TechTrends, 45*(6), 23–28.

Kim-Rupnow, W. S., Dowrick, P. W., & Burke, L. S. (2001). Implications for improving access and outcomes for individuals with disabilities in postsecondary distance education. *American Journal of Distance Education, 15*(1), 25–40.

Kurtz, M. J., & Holden, B. E. (2001). Analysis of a distance-education program in organic chemistry. *Journal of Chemical Education, 78*(8), 1122–1125.

Latanich, G., Nonis, S. A., & Hudson, G. I. (2001). A profile of today's distance learners: An investigation of demographic and individual difference variables of distance and non-distance learners. *Journal of Marketing for Higher Education, 11*(3), 1–16.

Lee, J. (2002). Faculty and administrator perceptions of instructional support for distance education. *International Journal of Instructional Media, 29*(1), 27–45.

Lefoe, G., Gunn, C., & Hedberg, J. (2002). Recommendations for teaching in a distributed learning environment: The students' perspective. *Australian Journal of Educational Technology, 18*(1), 40–56.

Locatis, C., & Weisberg, M. (1997). Distributed learning and the Internet. *Contemporary Education, 68*(2), 100–103.

Mangan, P. (2001). What is distance learning? *Management Quarterly, 42*(3), 30–35.

Moore, M. G., Lockee, B., & Burton, J. (2002). Measuring success: Evaluation strategies for distance education. *Educause Quarterly, 25*(1), 20–26.

Nebraska researchers measure the extent of "link rot" in distance education. (2002). *Chronicle of Higher Education, 48*(34), A31.

Noble, D. F. (2002). Technology and the commodification of higher education. *Monthly Review, 53*(10), 26–40.

Northrup, P. T., & Rasmussen, K. (2001). Considerations for designing Web-based programs. *Computers in the Schools, 17*(3–4), 33–46.

Novak, R. J. (2002). Benchmarking distance education. *New Directions for Higher Education, 118*, 79–92.

Olsen, F. (2002). Chinese institutions look toward distance education. *Chronicle of Higher Education, 49*(8), A38.

Osborn, V. (2001). Identifying at-risk students in videoconferencing and Web-based distance education. *American Journal of Distance Education, 15*(1), 41–54.

Passig, D. (2001). Future online teachers' scaffolding: What kind of advanced technological innovations would teachers like to see in future distance training projects? *Journal of Technology and Teacher Education, 9*(4), 599–605.

Petrides, L. A. (2002). Web-based technologies for distributed (or distance) learning: Creating learning-centered educational experiences in the higher education classroom. *International Journal of Instructional Media, 29*(1), 69–77.

Ramirez, A. Y. (2002). A little change does me good: Incorporating Web-enhanced technology within multicultural education. *Multicultural Education, 10*(2), 38–39.

Richardson, J. T. E., & Woodley, A. (2001). Perceptions of academic quality among students with a hearing loss in distance education. *Journal of Educational Psychology, 93*(3), 563–570.

Roach, R. (2001). Maryland community colleges push computer literacy among South African teachers. *Black Issues in Higher Education, 18*(14), 50.

Rosenbaum, D. B. (2001). E-learning beckons busy professionals; Electronic education offers anywhere, anytime flexibility . . . but not without problems. *ENR, 246*(21), 38–42.

Ross, K. R., Batzer, L., & Bennington, E. (2002). Quality assurance for distance education: A faculty peer review process. *TechTrends, 46*(5), 48.

Saba, F. (2000). Distributed education, expertise, and cognition. *Distance Education Report, 4*(2), 1.

Scagnoli, N. I. (2001). Student orientations for online programs. *Journal of Research on Technology in Education, 34*(1), 19–27.

Serwatka, J. A. (2002). Improving student performance in distance learning courses. *T.H.E. Journal, 29*(9), 46–51.

Shea, T., Motiwalla, L., & Lewis, D. (2001). Internet-based distance education—the administrator's perspective. *Journal of Education for Business, 77*(2), 112–117.

Sjogren, J. & Fay, J. (2002). Cost issues in online learning: Using "co-opetition" to advantage. *Change, 34*(3), 52–57.

Slick, J. F. (2001). Measuring corporate readiness to implement distance education. *Performance Improvement, 40*(10), 39–42.

Stallings, D. (2002). Measuring success in the virtual university. *Journal of Academic Librarianship, 28*(1–2), 47–53.

Thompson, H. (2002). The library's role in distance education. *College & Research Libraries News, 63*(5), 338–340.

Tiene, D. (2002). Digital multimedia & distance education: Can they effectively be combined? *T.H.E. Journal, 29*(9), 18–22.

Treloar, D. (2001). On-site and distance education of emergency medicine personnel with a human patient simulator. *Military Medicine, 166*(11), 1003.

Vincent, A., & Ross, D. (2002). Monitoring quality of distance learning: How will accrediting agencies and universities cope? *International Journal of Management, 19*(3), 464–471.

Wetsit, D. (1999). Emphasizing the human being in distance education. *Tribal College Journal of American Indian Higher Education, 10*(3), 14.

Wright, V. H., Marsh, G. E., & Miller, M. T. (2000). A critical comparison of graduate student satisfaction in asynchronous and synchronous course instruction. *Planning and Changing, 31*(1–2), 107–118.

Young, J. R. (2002). The 24-hour professor: Online teaching redefines faculty members' schedules, duties, and relationships with students. *Chronicle of Higher Education, 48*(38), A31–A33.

*—Stefan Kramer*

# Appendix C:
# Conferences on
# Distributed Learning

## Entry Format

- Conference name
- Web site about conference series (or latest in series)
- *Organizer(s)/Sponsor(s)*
- Description

### Annual Conference on Distance Teaching and Learning

http://www.uwex.edu/disted/conference/
*University of Wisconsin-Madison*
This "event attracts more than 1000 distance educators, trainers, and executives from over 550 organizations nation wide and around the world."

### Annual Distance Education Conference

http://www.cdlr.tamu.edu
*Center for Distance Learning Research*
This conference is held in Austin, Texas. "Presentations model and emphasize the use of communication technologies and exemplary teaching practices currently used in the field of Distance Education."

### Cambridge International Conference on Open and Distance Education

http://www2.open.ac.uk/r06/conference/conference.htm
*The Open University in the East of England*
This conference series, which began in 1983, "takes as its theme the future of open and distance teaching and learning." Attendance is limited to ensure interactivity for the participants.

### Computer Support for Collaborative Learning (CSCL)

http://www.intermedia.uib.no/cscl/
*InterMedia, University of Bergen* and *InterMedia, University of Oslo, Norway*
"CSCL is a genuinely interdisciplinary field which strives to create a better understanding of collaborative learning that is mediated by a diverse set of computational technologies."

### Computers and Advanced Technology in Education (CATE), including the IASTED International Symposium on Web-Based Education (WBE)

http://www.iasted.com/conference.htm (lists numerous IASTED conferences)
*International Association of Science and Technology for Development (IASTED)*
CATE-2003 and WBE-2003 provide "an excellent opportunity for faculty, scholars, administrators, and practitioners to meet well-known experts from all over the world and to discuss innovative ideas, research results, and best practices on various topics of technology-enhanced education, online education and training, new Web-based teaching and learning technologies, testing and assessment issues of online education . . . and many other related issues."

### DETC Distance Education Workshop
### DETC Annual Conference

http://www.detc.org/content/meetingsReports.html
*Distance Education and Training Council (DETC)*
The DETC offers a Distance Education Workshop every fall. Every spring, the DETC holds its Annual

Conference. Full reports of both events are available on the Web site.

### EDEN Annual Conference

http://www.eden.bme.hu/contents/conferences/annual/annual.html

*European Distance Education Network (EDEN)*

"The annual conferences of EDEN are held in different regions of Europe, supporting . . . in this way the collaboration of professional communities, enlargement of contacts of experts [among] the Northern, Central, or Southern part of the continent, and [helping] to enhance East/West cooperation."

### ED-MEDIA World Conference on Educational Multimedia, Hypermedia & Telecommunications

http://www.aace.org/conf/edmedia/

*Association for the Advancement of Computing in Education*

"This annual conference serves as a multi-disciplinary forum for the discussion and exchange of information on the research, development, and applications on all topics related to multimedia, hypermedia and telecommunications/distance education."

### E-Learn World Conference on E-Learning in Corporate, Government, Healthcare, and Higher Education

http://www.aace.org/conf/eLearn/

*Association for the Advancement of Computing in Education*

"The E-Learn conference series is an international forum designed to facilitate the exchange of information and ideas on the research, issues, developments, and applications of a broad range of topics related to e-Learning. E-Learn is a . . . collaboration between the top public and private academic researchers, developers, education and business professionals, and end users from the Corporate, Healthcare, Government, and Higher Education sectors."

### Information Technology and Distance Education

http://www.utpb.edu/reach/itde/

*University of Texas System*

"This annual conference serves as a multidisciplinary forum for the discussion and exchange of information on research and applications related to information technology and distance education in higher education."

Institute for Managing and Developing e-Learning (MDE)

http://www.wcet.info/Events/mde/

*Western Cooperative for Educational Telecommunications (WCET)*

Intended for participants (limit: 60 for 2003) whose "job is concerned with managing distance learning or integrating technologies into instruction."

### International Conference on Advanced Learning Technologies (ICALT)

http://lttf.ieee.org/events.htm

*IEEE Computer Society Learning Technology Task Force (LTTF)*

This conference "intends to bring together academics, researchers and industry practitioners who are involved or interested in the design and development of advanced and emerging learning technologies with ultimate aim to empower individuals and organisations in building competencies for exploiting the opportunities of the knowledge society."

### International Conference on New Educational Environments (ICNEE)

http://www.icnee.ch/default.htm

*Swiss Information and Communications Technologies Network and University of Applied Sciences of Central Switzerland*

"The 5th International Conference on New Educational Environments (5. ICNEE) focuses on results and experiences of international research in methodology and technology related to blended learning, teaching and distance collaboration. Further emphasis lies on the implementation, application and impacts of these learning concepts in educational institutions and on the identification of their future potential. International researchers, teachers and students present their experiences based on best practice and lessons learned." Recent conference locations have included Lucerne, Lugano, and Fribourg in Switzerland.

### LEARNTEC

http://www.learntec.de

*Karlsruher Messe- und Kongress-GmbH*

This is an annual European conference and specialist trade fair for educational and information technology, held in Karlsruhe, Germany, every winter.

## Libraries Without Walls

http://www.cerlim.ac.uk/main/conferevents.html

*Centre for Research in Library & Information Management (CERLIM), Department of Information and Communications, Manchester Metropolitan University*

This biannual conference series brings "together international perspectives on the delivery of library and information services to users who are not in the physical library."

## NAWeb: Annual Conference on Web-based Teaching and Learning

http://naweb.unb.ca

*University of New Brunswick, Canada*

The focus of this conference is "How do you make Web-based education even better than 'traditional' educational venues? How do you foster the sense of campus community online, with students and educators who may never meet face-to-face? How do you make Web technology work to support learning—and not the other way around?"

## ODLAA Forum

http://www.odlaa.org/forum.html

*Open and Distance Learning Association of Australia (ODLAA)*

"Every two years ODLAA arranges a Forum in a different Australian city. . . . [ODLAA] encourage people from all parts of the educational spectrum to be involved whether they be teachers, trainers, designers, managers or policy makers from the first years of school to post graduate; government, private or military; recreational, vocational, or lifelong learning."

## Off-Campus Library Services Conference

http://ocls.cmich.edu/conference.htm

*Central Michigan University Libraries and College of Extended Learning*

Attendees of these conferences, which are held every other year, "are dedicated to providing library services and instructional support to adult learners located at a distance from their main campuses, corporate or institutional headquarters, or primary training sites."

Online Educa Berlin
Online Educa Barcelona
http://www.online-educa.com
http://www.online-educa-barcelona.com

*ICWE (International Conferences, Workshops and Exhibitions) GmbH*

These two independent conferences on e-learning are aimed at participants from education, government, and industry. Online Educa Berlin claims to be "the world's largest international e-learning conference." Forty percent of the Online Educa Barcelona 2002 participants came from Latin America.

## Sightings 20/20: CADE-ACED 2003 Conference

http://www.cade-aced2003.ca

*Canadian Association for Distance Education (CADE/ACED)*

The conference goal is "to examine and discuss issues and accomplishments in: ongoing research, new content for new technology, learner services, global reach, workplace learning."

## Sloan-C International Conference on Asynchronous Learning Networks

http://www.aln.org/conference/

*Sloan Consortium*

This conference on online learning is co-sponsored by academic institutions such as New York University, the University of Maryland, and Pennsylvania State University, and the Alfred P. Sloan Foundation–funded Sloan Consortium (Sloan-C), whose goal is "to make education a part of everyday life, accessible and affordable for anyone, anywhere, at any time, in a wide variety of disciplines."

## Society for Information Technology & Teacher Education International Conference (SITE)

http://www.aace.org/conf/site/

*Association for the Advancement of Computing in Education*

"This annual conference offers opportunities to share ideas and expertise on all topics related to the use of information technology in teacher education and instruction about information technology for all disciplines in preservice, inservice, and graduate teacher education as well as faculty and staff development."

## Virtual Educa

http://www.educoas.org/virtualeduca/

*Inter-American Agency for Cooperation and Development (OAS), European Commission, Inter-American Development Bank (INDES), Distance University of Spain (UNED), and others*

This is an international conference on education, training and new technologies with a "Latin American/Hispanic Focus, Global Perspective."

## World Conferences on Open and Distance Education

http://www.icde.org

*International Council for Open and Distance Education (ICDE)*

The ICDE organizes the World Conferences on Open and Distance Education every other year.

World Education Market

http://www.wemex.com

*Reed Midem, a division of Reed Exhibitions*

"WEM is the . . . international marketplace that brings buyers, government decision-makers and leading institutions together with . . . suppliers of . . . content, technology and expertise. . . . WEM puts . . . in touch with potential buyers, suppliers, producers, publishers, distributors or partners for sales, marketing and distribution, for product development, for technical support, localisation and successful market entry into new territories."

*—Stefan Kramer*

# Index